ISBN: 9781290971140

Published by:
HardPress Publishing
8345 NW 66TH ST #2561
MIAMI FL 33166-2626

Email: info@hardpress.net
Web: http://www.hardpress.net

Cornell Law School Library

THE LAW

OF

SURETYSHIP AND GUARANTY

AS

ADMINISTERED BY COURTS OF COUNTRIES WHERE
THE COMMON LAW PREVAILS.

BY

GEORGE W. BRANDT,

OF THE CHICAGO BAR.

SECOND EDITION.

VOL. I.

CHICAGO:
CALLAGHAN AND COMPANY.
1891.

STATE JOURNAL PRINTING COMPANY,
PRINTERS AND STEREOTYPERS,
MADISON, WIS.

PREFACE.

The object sought in this work is to present a comprehensive view of the law of Suretyship and Guaranty, as administered by courts of countries where the common law prevails. To that end all the reports have been examined by the author, and the points decided in such cases as related to sureties and guarantors have been carefully noted.

The following pages, it is believed, contain references to substantially all the reported cases bearing on the subject treated of herein.

It is hoped that the great difficulty of arranging into a convenient form for reference the mass of material, covering, as it does, almost every phase of the transactions of men with each other, has been in a measure overcome.

GEORGE W. BRANDT.

Chicago, July, 1878.

In preparing the second edition of this work the same course has been pursued as in the construction of the original volume, the examination of the authorities having been continued to this date.

GEORGE W. BRANDT.

Chicago, September, 1891.

LIST OF CHAPTERS.

CHAPTER I.

Page

Of the Contract 1

CHAPTER II.

Of the Statute of Frauds 70

CHAPTER III.

Of the Liability of the Surety or Guarantor Generally . 131

CHAPTER IV.

Of the Liability of the Surety when the Principal is Discharged, or Not Originally Bound 214

CHAPTER V.

Of Continuing Guaranties 228

CHAPTER VI.

Of Cases where the Surety on a General Obligation is Liable Only for Limited Time or Act or Amount 243

CHAPTER VII.

Of the Liability of Accommodation Parties to Negotiable Instruments, and of the Blank Indorser of Another's Obligation 260

CHAPTER VIII.

Of the Notice and Demand Necessary to Charge a Guarantor 277

CHAPTER IX.

Of the Rights of the Surety or Guarantor Against the Principal 312

CHAPTER X.

Of the Rights of the Surety or Guarantor Against the Creditor and Third Persons 350

CHAPTER XI.

Of the Rights of Sureties and Guarantors Between Each Other — Contribution 382

CHAPTER XII.

Page

Of Subrogation 433

CHAPTER XIII.

Of the Discharge of the Surety or Guarantor by Payment . 480

CHAPTER XIV.

Of the Discharge of the Surety or Guarantor by the Giving of Time 496

CHAPTER XV.

Of the Discharge of the Surety or Guarantor by Alteration of the Contract 551

CHAPTER XVI.

Of the Discharge of the Surety or Guarantor by Misrepresentation, Concealment, Fraud, or Non-compliance with the Terms upon which he Became Bound 584

CHAPTER XVII.

Of the Discharge of the Surety or Guarantor by the Creditor Relinquishing Security for the Debt 623

CHAPTER XVIII.

Of the Discharge of the Surety or Guarantor by the Creditor Negligently Losing Security for the Debt 647

CHAPTER XIX.

Of Sureties on Obligations Given in the Course of the Administration of Justice 662

CHAPTER XX.

Of Bail 705

CHAPTER XXI.

Of Sureties on Official Bonds 738

CHAPTER XXII.

Of Statutes Relating to Sureties and Guarantors 864

CHAPTER XXIII.

Of Evidence 881

TABLE OF CASES.

[THE LETTER *v* FOLLOWS THE NAME OF THE PLAINTIFF.]

Aaron *v.* Mendel, 78 Ky. 427. §§ 339, 576.
Stillwell *v.*, 69 Mo. 539. §§ 342, 353, 356, 357.
Abat, Kuhn *v.*, 14 Martin (La.), 2 N. S. 168. § 120.
Abbey *v.* Van Campen, 1 Freem. Ch. (Miss.) 273. § 227.
Abbott, Bancroft *v.*, 3 Allen, 524. § 225.
v. Brown, 30 Ill. App. 376. § 1.
v. Brown, 131 Ill. 108. §§ 111, 137.
Brown *v.*, 110 Ill. 162. § 426.
Durfee *v.*, 61 Mich. 471. § 365.
Fewlass *v.*, 28 Mich. 270. § 128.
Mariners' Bank *v.*, 28 Me. 280. §§ 29, 352.
Probate Judge *v.*, 50 Mich. 479. § 586.
Shamburg *v.*, 112 Pa. St. 6. § 36.
Town of Barnett *v.*, 53 Vt. 120. §§ 517, 596, 644.
Abeel *v.* Radcliff, 13 Johns. 297. § 80.
Abel *v.* Alexander, 45 Ind. 523. §§ 344, 354.
Abercrombie, Hellams *v.*, 15 S. C. 110. § 224.
v. Knox, 3 Ala. 728. § 97.
Able, Payne *v.*, 7 Bush (Ky.), 344. § 472.
Abrahams *v.* Jones, 20 Bradw. (Ill. App.) 83. § 23.
People *v.*, 6 Daly (N. Y. Com. Pl.). 120. § 511.
Abrams *v.* Pomeroy, 13 Ill. 133. § 127.
Acers *v.* Curtis, 68 Tex. 423. §§ 283, 288.
Ackley, Gerber *v.*, 37 Wis. 43. § 566.
Adams *v.* Bean, 12 Mass. 139. § 87.
Brown *v.*, 1 Stew. (Ala.) 51. § 61.
Commonwealth *v.*, 3 Bush (Ky.), 41. § 526.
v. Dansey, 6 Bing. 506. § 60.
Deberry *v.*, 9 Yerg. (Tenn.) 52. § 30.
v. Flanagan, 36 Vt. 400. §§ 261. 265.
Fullam *v.*, 37 Vt. 391. §§ 64, 69.
Hewitt's Adm'r *v.*, 1 Patton, Jr. & Heath (Va.), 34. § 439.
v. Hodgepeth, 5 Jones' Law (N. C.), 327. § 515.
Holyoke *v.*, 1 Hun (N. Y.), 223. § 472.
v. Hyams (Cir. Ct. D. Conn.), 8 Fed. Rep. 417. §§ 128, 593.
Irvine *v.*, 48 Wis. 468. §§ 29, 357.
v. Jones, 68 Ala. 117. § 588.
v. Jones, 12 Pet. 207. §§ 81, 186, 187.
Jordan, Adm'r, *v.*, 7 Ark. (2 Eng.) 348. § 212.
v. Kellogg, 63 Mich. 105. § 152.
Kennedy *v.*, 5 Har. (Del.) 160. § 498.
Langley *v.*, 40 Me. 125. § 505.
v. Logan, 25 Gratt. (Va.) 201. §§ 366, 431, 436.
Lovett *v.*, 8 Wend. 380. § 403.
Lowry *v.*, 22 Vt. 160. §§ 116, 203, 204.

Adams v. McMillan, 7 Port. (Ala.) 73. §§ 80, 90.
Munson v., 89 Ill. 450. § 14.
v. Olive, 57 Ala. 249. § 469.
v. People, 12 Bradw. (Ill. App.) 380. § 503.
Rix v., 9 Vt. 233. § 247.
v. Roane, 7 Ark. (2 Eng.) 360. § 606.
Roberts v., 6 Port. (Ala.) 361. § 290.
v. Tator, 57 Hun (N. Y.), *332. § 247.
Thompson v., 1 Freeman's Ch. (Miss.) 225. §§ 268, 439.
United States v. (Cir. Ct. D. Oreg.), 24 Fed. Rep. 348. § 558.
Ware v., 24 Me. 177. § 17.
Adams & Alexander v. Gleaves, 10 Lea (Tenn.), 367. § 319.
Adams & French Harvesting Co. v. Tomlinson Bros., 58 Iowa, 129. § 102.
Adams Bank v. Anthony, 18 Pick. 238. § 242.
Adamson, Jackson v., 7 Blackf. (Ind.) 597. § 226.
Adcock v. Fleming, 2 Dev. & Batt. Law (N. C.), 225. § 67.
Adderton, Ellis, Adm'r, v., 88 N. C. 482. § 45.
Addyman, Beckett v., Law Rep. (9 Q. B. Div.) 783. § 284.
Adee v. Adee, 16 Hun (N. Y.), 46. § 519.
Toles v., 84 N. Y. 222. § 493.
Toles v., 91 N. Y. 562. §§ 99, 519.
Adger, Bank v., 2 Hill, Eq. (S. C.) 262. § 309.
Adington, Allen v., 7 Wend. 9. § 73.
Adkinson v. Barfield, 1 McCord (S. C.), 575. § 64.
Adler v. State, 35 Ark. 517. § 500.
Adler & Levy, Friedman v., 36 La. Ann. 384. § 480.
Admire, Magruder v., 4 Mo. App. 133. §§ 288, 295.
People v., 39 Ill. 251. § 579.
Adm'r of Evans, Ex'r of McCall v., 2 Brev. (S. C.) 3. § 243.
Adm'r of Wilson v. Green, 25 Vt. 450. §§ 234, 626.
Adm'rs of Pond v. Warner, 2 Vt. 532. §§ 221, 222.
Adock v. Fleming, 2 Dev. & Bat. Law (N. C.), 225. § 197.
Ætna Ins. Co., Byrne v., 56 Ill. 321. § 97.
Hough v., 57 Ill. 318. §§ 97, 298.
v. Mabbett, 18 Wis. 667. § 422.
Affeld v. People, 12 Bradw. (Ill. App.) 502. § 27.
Agawam Bank v. Sears, 4 Gray, 95. § 381.
v. Strever, 16 Barb. (N. Y.) 82. § 171.
Agawam Woolen Co., Jordan v., 106 Mass. 571. § 450.
Agee v. Steele, 8 Ala. 948. § 362.
Agricultural Bank v. Bishop, 6 Gray, 317. § 352.
Agnew v. Bell, 4 Watts (Pa.), 31. §§ 254, 268.
v. Merritt, 10 Minn. 308. §§ 35, 375.
Ah Jim, Bing Gee, Adm'r, v., 7 Fed. Rep. 811. § 473.
Ahrend v. Odiorne, 125 Mass. 50. § 45.
Aiken v. Cheeseborough, 1 Hill, Law (S. C.), 172. § 67.
v. Duren, 2 Nott & McCord (S. C.), 370. § 68.
Marshall v., 25 Vt. 249. § 40.
Mathews v., 1 N. Y. 595. § 298.
v. Peay, 5 Strob. Law (S. C.), 15. § 284.
Sapp v., 68 Iowa, 699. § 211.
Aikenhead, People v., 5 Cal. 106. § 543.
Ainsworth v. Territory, 3 Wash. Terr. 270. §§ 509, 519.
Airns v. Marks, 3 Lea (Tenn.), 568. § 603.
Akeley, Bosman v., 39 Mich. 710. § 98.
Alabama Gold Life Ins. Co. v. Anderson, 67 Ala. 425. § 324.
Albany City Fire Ins. Co. v. Devendorf, 43 Barb. (N. Y.) 444. § 364.

Albany Dutch Church *v.* Vedder, 14 Wend. 165. § 425.
Albee *v.* People, 22 Ill. 533. § 43.
Soule *v.*, 31 Vt. 142. § 72.
Alber *v.* Forelicht, 39 Ohio St. 245. § 449.
Jones *v.*, 70 Ill. 34. § 182.
Albert, Eisenberg *v.*, 40 Ohio St. 631. § 35.
Albertson, Harbaugh *v.*, 102 Ind. 69. § 43.
v. McGee, 7 Yerg. (Tenn.) 106. § 452.
v. State, 9 Neb. 429. § 628.
Albright *v.* Mills, 86 Ala. 324. § 566.
Alcock *v.* Hill, 4 Leigh (Va.), 622. § 344.
Watson *v.*, 4 De Gex, Macn. & Gor. 242. § 444.
Alcorn, Byers *v.*, 6 Bradw. (Ill. App.) 39. § 276.
v. Commonwealth, 66 Pa. St. 172. § 240.
v. State, 57 Miss. 273. § 531.
Alcott, Bishop *v.*, 86 N. Y. 503. § 50.
Alden, State *v.*, 12 Ohio, 59. § 339.
Aldine Publishing Co., Simon *v.*, 14 Daly (N. Y. Com. Pl.), 279. § 461.
Aldrich *v.* Aldrich, 56 Vt. 324. §§ 293, 296.
v. Ames, 9 Gray, 76. §§ 60, 72.
v. Blake, 134 Mass. 582. § 332.
v. Chubb, 35 Mich. 350. §§ 100, 101.
Miller *v.*, 31 Mich. 408. § 252.
Aldricks *v.* Higgins, 16 Serg. & Rawle, 212. § 163.
Aldridge *v.* Harper, 10 Bing. 118. § 482.
v. Turner, 1 Gill & Johns. (Md.) 427. §§ 13, 82.
Alexander, Abel *v.*, 45 Ind. 523. §§ 344, 354.
v. Bank of Commonwealth, 7 J. J. Marsh. (Ky.) 580. § 434.
v. Bates, 33 Ga. 125. § 504.
v. Bouton, 55 Cal. 15. § 35.
v. Bryan, 110 U. S. 414. § 578.
Alexander, Cotton *v.*, 32 Kan. 339. §§ [illegible], 460.
Fowler *v.*, 1 Heisk. (Tenn.) 425. § 30.
Hamar *v.*, 5 Bos. & Pul. 241. § 73.
v. Mercer, 7 Ga. 549. § 544.
Morning *v.*, 10 Heisk. (Tenn.) 606. § 487.
Parker *v.*, 2 La. Ann. 188. § 447.
Sidner *v.*, 31 Ohio St. 378. § 571.
Torrence *v.*, 85 N. C. 143. § 33.
Alford, Board of Supervisors *v.*, 65 Miss. 63. § 544.
v. Irwin, 34 Ga. 25. § 499.
Algar, Jarmain *v.*, 2 Car. & P. 249. § 70.
Alger *v.* Scoville, 1 Gray, 391. §§ 64, 72.
Allaire *v.* Ouland, 2 Johns. Cas. 52. § 60.
Allan *v.* Kenning, 9 Bing. 618. § 158.
Allegheny City, Moore *v.*, 18 Pa. St. 55. § 523.
Allen *v.* Adington, 7 Wend. 9. § 73.
v. Ayers, 3 Pick. 298. § 115.
v. Bennett, 3 Taunt. 169. §§ 80, 89.
v. Breslauer, 8 Cal. 552. § 507.
Brooks *v.*, 62 Ind. 401. § 341.
Bull *v.*, 19 Conn. 101. § 29.
Bushee *v.*, 31 Vt. 631. § 76.
v. Central Savings Bank, 4 Mo. App. 66. § 92.
v. Coffil, 42 Ill. 293. § 183.
Corielle *v.*, 13 Iowa, 289. §§ 29, 356.
Costley *v.*, 56 Ala. 198. § 638.
v. Culver, 3 Denio, 284. §§ 48, 330.
v. Eighmie, 14 Hun (N. Y.), 559. § 62.
Fresno Enterprise Co. *v.*, 67 Cal. 505. § 167.
Gifford *v.*, 3 Met. (Mass.) 253. § 348.
v. Hubert, 49 Pa. St. 259. § 1.
v. Jones, 8 Minn. 202. § 330.
Kay *v.*, 9 Pa. St. 320. § 188.
v. Marney, 65 Ind. 398. § 411.

Allen, McCombs v., 18 Hun (N. Y.), 190. § 150.
v. Morgan, 5 Humph. (Tenn.) 624. §§ 18, 251.
Nichols v., 22 Minn. 283. §§ 67, 101.
v. O'Donald, 23 Fed. Rep. 573. § 426.
v. O'Donald, 28 Fed. Rep. (Cir. Ct. D. Oreg.) 346. § 34.
People v., 86 Ill. 166. § 585. *
v. Pike, 3 Cush. 238. §§ 186, 188.
Powell v., 11 Bradw. (Ill. App.) 129. §§ 308, 311.
v. Pryor, 3 A. K. Marsh. (Ky.) 305. §§ 53, 67.
v. Ramey, 4 Strob. Law (S. C.), 30. § 533.
v. Rundle, 50 Conn. 9. §§ 100, 644.
v. Sanders, 34 N. J. Eq. 203. § 587.
Sanford v., 1 Cush. 473. § 98.
v. Scarff, 1 Hilton (N. Y.), 209. § 76.
Schoonover v., 40 Ark. 132. § 306.
Smith v., Saxton (N. J.), 43. § 141.
Snell v., 1 Swan (Tenn.), 208. § 627.
State v., 2 Humph. (Tenn.) 258. § 500.
v. State, 61 Ind. 268. § 542.
v. Thompson, 10 N. H. 32. § 65.
Wadsworth v., 8 Gratt. (Va.) 174. §§ 117, 194, 203.
Whitney v., 21 Cal. 233. § 459.
v. Wood, 3 Ired. Eq. (N. C.) 386. § 290.
v. Woodard, 125 Mass. 400. § 237.
Alley, Egerton v., 6 Ired. Eq. (N. C.) 188. § 237.
Allis, Northwestern Mut. Life Ins. Co. v., 23 Minn. 337. § 97.
v. Ware, 28 Minn. 166. § 559.
Allison v. Farmers' Bank, 6 Rand. (Va.) 204. § 561.
Allison v. Rutledge, 5 Yerg. (Tenn.) 193. § 117.
Shaver v., 11 Grant's Ch. 355. § 397.
v. State, 8 Heisk. (Tenn.) 312. § 173.
v. Sutherlin, 50 Mo. 274. § 306.
v. Thomas, 29 La. Ann. 732. §§ 40, 342, 371.
Allman, Stevens v., 19 Ohio St. 485. § 540.
Allnutt v. Ashenden, 5 Man. & Gr. 392. §§ 85, 86, 165.
Allsburg, United States v., 4 Wall. 186. § 127.
Allshouse v. Ramsay, 6 Whart. (Pa.) 311. § 62.
Almoney, Spencer v., 56 Md. 551, 562. § 236.
Alpaugh, Attenstein v., 9 Neb. 237. § 529.
Alsop v. Price, 1 Doug. (Eng.) 160. § 150.
Alsup, State v., 91 Mo. 172. § 545.
Amana Lodge, Johnston v., 92 Ind. 150. § 311.
Ambler v. Leach, 15 W. Va. 677. § 438.
Ambrose, United States v., 2 Fed. Rep. 552. § 519.
United States v., 7 Fed. Rep. 554. § 510.
Ament, Perkins v., 2 Head (Tenn.), 110. § 114.
American Bank v. Baker, 4 Met. (Mass.) 164. §§ 397, 426.
American Land Co. v. Grady, 33 Ark. 550. § 316.
Ames, Aldrich v., 9 Gray, 76. §§ 60, 72.
Josselyn v., 3 Mass. 274. § 182.
v. Maclay, 14 Iowa, 281. § 149.
Maggs v., 4 Bing. 470. § 62.
Amherst Bank v. Root, 2 Met. (Mass.) 522. §§ 172, 425, 555, 560, 625.
Amicable Mutual Life Ins. Co. v. Sedgwick, 110 Mass. 163. §§ 392, 396.
Amis, Armour v., 4 La. Ann. 192. § 426.

Ammidown, Towne *v.*, 20 Pick. 535. § 139.
Ammons *v.* People, 11 Ill. 6. § 511.
v. Whitehead, 31 Miss. 99. § 456.
Amonett, McKee *v.*, 6 La. Ann. 207. § 312.
Ancion *v.* Guillot, 10 La. Ann. 124. § 22.
Anderson, Alabama Gold Life Ins. Co. *v.*, 67 Ala. 425. § 324.
v. Bellenger & Ralls, 87 Ala. 334. §§ 378, 416.
v. Blakely, 2 Watts & Serg. (Pa.) 237. § 164.
Carrington *v.*, 5 Munf. (Va.) 32. § 90.
v. Chick, Bailey, Eq. (S. C.) 118. § 90.
Decker *v.*, 39 Barb. (N. Y.) 346. § 486.
v. Harold, 10 Ohio, 399. § 89.
v. Hayman, 1 H. Black. 120. §§ 76, 78.
Hodgson *v.*, 5 Dow. & Ry. 735. §§ 66, 67.
Knapp *v.*, 7 Hun (N. Y.), 295. § 472.
Livingston *v.*, 80 Ga. 175. § 320.
v. Longden, 1 Wheat. 85. § 538.
Low *v.*, 41 Iowa, 476. § 7.
v. Mannon, 7 B. Mon. 217. § 356.
v. May, 10 Heisk. (Tenn.) 84. § 116.
Nelson *v.*, 2 Call (Va.), 286. § 458.
v. Norvill, 10 Bradw. (Ill. App.) 240. § 88.
v. Pearson, 2 Bailey, Law (S. C.), 107. § 261.
v. Sloan, 1 Col. 484. § 464.
Smith's Ex'rs *v.*, 18 Md. 520. § 262.
v. Spence, 72 Ind. 315. § 57.
State *v.*, 16 Lea (Tenn.), 321. § 642.
Tankersley *v.*, 4 Des. Eq. (S. C.) 44. § 221.
v. Walton, 35 Ga. 202. § 224.
Anderson Bros. Mfg. & R'y Co., Monroe *v.*, 65 Iowa, 692. § 401.
Andes, Burson *v.*, 83 Va. 445. § 93.
Andre *v.* Bodman, 13 Md. 241. § 62.
v. Fitzhugh, 18 Mich. 93. § 470.
Andrews, Baskin *v.*, 53 Hun (N. Y.), 95. § 140.
Crane *v.*, 10 Col. 265. § 463.
George *v.*, 60 Md. 26. § 37.
v. Jones, 10 Ala. 400. § 52.
Keirn *v.*, 59 Miss. 39. § 353.
v. Marrett, 58 Me. 539. § 363.
v. Smith, Tyrwh. & Gr. 173. § 63.
Spaulding *v.*, 48 Pa. St. 411. § 67.
v. Varrell, 46 N. H. 17. § 236.
Waterbury *v.*, 67 Mich. 281. § 234.
Wright *v.*, 70 Me. 86. § 247.
Andrus *v.* Bealls, 9 Cowen, 693. § 572.
v. Chretien, 7 La. O. S. (4 Curry), 318. § 50.
Mercien *v.*, 10 Wend. 461. § 64.
Anglim, Pacific Guano Co. *v.*, 82 Ala. 492. § 237.
Anguey, Cole County *v.*, 12 Mo. 132. § 125.
Anonymous, Brookes' New Cas. 172. § 397.
Annable, Russell *v.*, 109 Mass. 72. § 151.
Annett *v.* Terry, 35 N. Y. 256. § 638.
Anniss, Brickwood *v.*, 5 Taunt. 614. § 493.
Ansley, Carlos *v.*, 8 Ala. 900. § 226.
Anspach, Webb *v.*, 3 Ohio St. 522. § 536.
Anstey *v.* Marden, 1 Bos. & Pul. N. R. 124. § 65.
Anthony, Adams Bank *v.*, 18 Pick. 238. § 242.
v. Capel, 53 Miss. 350. § 146.
v. Kasey, 83 Va. 338. § 640.
v. Percifull, 8 Ark. (3 Eng.) 494. §§ 274, 286.
Smith *v.*, 5 Mo. 504. § 191.
State *v.*, 30 Mo. App. 638. § 528.
Antrim, Hatch *v.*, 57 Ill. 106. § 103.
Antrobus *v.* Davidson, 3 Merivale, 569. §§ 223, 238.
Apgar's Adm'rs *v.* Hiler, 4 Zabr. (N. J.) 812. §§ 60, 208, 217, 229.

Appeal of Guenther, 40 Wis. 115. § 138.
Apperson v. Cross, 5 Heisk. (Tenn.) 481. § 342.
v. Gogin, 3 Bradw. (Ill. App.) 48. § 45.
v. Wilbourn, 58 Miss. 439. § 287.
Appleby v. State, 45 N. J. Law, 161. § 531.
Applegate, Uhler v., 26 Pa. St. 140. §§ 353, 355.
Appleton v. Bascom, 3 Met. (Mass.) 169. § 209.
v. Parker, 15 Gray, 173. § 364.
Arbogast v. Hays, 98 Ind. 26. §§ 230, 307.
Archer, Buckner v., 1 McMullan, Law (S. C.), 85. § 638.
Gosbell v., 2 Adol. & Ell. 500. §§ 89, 90.
v. Hale, 4 Bing. 464. § 482.
v. Hudson, 7 Beav. 551. § 397.
Archer's Ex'r, United States v., 1 Wall. Jr. 173. § 139.
Archibald, Sievewright v., 17 Ad. & Ell. (N. S.) 103. § 80.
Ardern v. Rowney, 5 Esp. 254. § 67.
Ardery's Adm'r, Henderson's Adm'r v., 36 Pa. St. 449. § 342.
Arents v. Commonwealth, 18 Gratt. (Va.) 750. §§ 48, 102.
Armington v. State, 45 Ind. 10. § 530.
Armistead v. Ward, 2 P. & H. (Va.) 504. §§ 356, 364.
Armitage v. Pulver, 37 N. Y. 494. § 288.
Armor v. Amis, 4 La. Ann. 192. § 426.
Craddock v., 10 Watts (Pa.), 258. § 137.
Arms v. Ashley, 4 Pick. 71. § 86.
Armstead v. Thomas, 9 Ala. 586. § 350.
Armstrong, Baere v., 26 Hun (N. Y.), 19. § 473.
Bond v., 88 Ind. 65. § 330.
v. Cook, 30 Ind. 22. § 401.
v. Corporation of Huron, 27 Up. Can. (Q. B.) 533. § 402.
v. Foster, 6 Ont. (Can.) 129. § 593.
Armstrong, Harshman v., 43 Ind. 126. § 261.
v. Harshman, 61 Ind. 52. § 260.
Hawes v., 1 Bing. N. C. 761. §§ 82, 84, 85.
Hodges v., 3 Dev. Law (N. C.), 253. § 225.
Hudelson v., 70 Ind. 99. § 140.
Lewis v., 80 Ga. 402. §§ 426, 451.
Newbury v., 6 Bing. 201. § 84.
Perry v., 39 N. H. 583. §§ 114, 360.
v. State, 7 Blackf. (Ind.) 81. § 541.
v. United States, Peters' Cir. Ct. R. 46. § 519.
Armstrong's Appeal, 5 Watts & Serg. (Pa.) 352. § 308.
Arnold, Cummings v., 3 Met. (Mass.) 486. § 81.
v. Hicks, 3 Ired. Eq. (N. C.) 17. § 237.
Miller v., 65 Ind. 488. §§ 242, 344.
Quillen v., 12 Nev. 234. § 470.
Smith v., 5 Mason (C. C.), 414. § 90.
v. Stedman, 45 Pa. St. 186. § 64.
Arnot v. Erie R. R. Co., 67 N. Y. 315. § 107.
v. Erie R. R. Co., 5 Hun, 608. § 5.
Arrington, Choate v., 116 Mass. 552. § 526.
v. Porter, 47 Ala. 714. § 630.
Artcher v. Douglass, 5 Denio, 509. § 151.
Ashby's Adm'x v. Smith's Ex'r, 9 Leigh (Va.), 164. § 437.
Ashby v. Johnson, 23 Ark. 163. § 448.
v. Sharp, 1 Litt. (Ky.) 156. § 450.
v. Tureman, 3 Litt. (Ky.) 6. § 475.
Ashdown, West v., 1 Bing. 464. § 493.
Ashenden, Allnutt v., 5 Man. & Gr. 392. §§ 85, 86, 165.
Ashford, Jones v., 79 N. C. 172. §§ 97, 101, 106.
v. Robinson, 8 Ired. Law (N. C.), 114. §§ 67, 82, 100, 142.
Ashley, Arms v., 4 Pick. 71. § 86.
Killian v., 24 Ark. 511. §§ 47, 176, 192.

Ashton v. Bayard, 71 Pa. St. 139. §§ 17, 102.
Stout v., 5 T. B. Mon. (Ky.) 251. § 242.
Ashurst v. Ashurst, 13 Ala. 781. § 624.
Askins v. Commonwealth, 1 Duvall (Ky.), 275. § 501.
Aspinwall, Ogden v., 7 Dow. & Ryland, 637. § 123.
Association of Baltimore, Meredith v., 60 Cal. 617. § 462.
Assurance Co., Benham v., 7 Wels., Hurl. & Gor. 744. § 404.
Astling, Philips v., 2 Taunt. 206. §§ 201, 397.
Aston, Sanderson v., Law Rep. 8 Exch. 73. §§ 399, 423.
At, Deer Lodge Co. v., 3 Mont. 168. § 508.
Atchison, Col. & Pac. R. R. Co., Van Allen v., 3 Fed. Rep. 545 (Cir. Ct. D. Kan.). § 10.
Atchison, Topeka & Santa Fe R. R. Co. v. Fletcher, 35 Kan. 236. § 6.
Atherton, State v., 40 Mo. 209. §§ 422, 425.
Athol Machine Co. v. Fuller, 107 Mass. 437. § 7.
Atkins v. Baily, 9 Yerg. (Tenn.) 111. § 636.
McDonald v., 13 Neb. 568. § 531.
State v., 53 Ark. 303. § 577.
Atkinson, Company of Proprietors of Liverpool Water Works v., 6 East, 507. § 166.
v. Fox, 53 Miss. 733. § 487.
v. Foxworth, 53 Miss. 741. § 471.
Grayson v., 2 Ves. Sr. 454. § 89.
Semple v., 64 Mo. 504. § 364.
v. Stewart, 2 B. Mon. (Ky.) 348. § 291.
Atlanta National Bank v. Douglass, 51 Ga. 205. § 388.
Atlantic & N. C. R. R. Co. v. Cowles, 69 N. C. 59. § 558.
Atlantic & Pacific Telegraph Co. v. Barnes, 64 N. Y. 385. § 423.
Atlas Bank v. Brownell, 9 R. I. 168. §§ 420, 423, 625.
Atlee, Heitz v., 67 Iowa, 483. § 341.
Voorhies v., 29 Iowa, 49. § 101.
Attenstein v. Alpaugh, 9 Neb. 237. § 529.
Attix, Wilds v., 4 Del. Ch. 253. § 242.
Atwell's Adm'r v. Towles, 1 Munf. (Va.) 175. § 137.
Atwood v. Cobb, 16 Pick. 227. § 81.
Danker v., 119 Mass. 146. § 26.
Aubert, Castling v., 2 East, 325. §§ 54, 65, 70.
Auburn, First National Bank of, Crandall v., 61 Ind. 349. § 380.
Auchampaugh v. Schmidt, 77 Iowa, 13, 17. §§ 3, 245.
Auchampaugh, Adm'r, v. Schmidt, 70 Iowa, 642. § 148.
Aud v. Magruder, 10 Cal. 282. §§ 29, 177.
Auditor, Bennett v., 2 W. Va. 441. § 371.
Augero v. Keen, 1 Mees. & Wels. 390. § 172.
Augusta Savings Bank, Twigg v., 26 S. C. 612. § 437.
Ault, White v., 19 Ga. 551. § 34.
Aultman v. Hefner, 67 Tex. 54. § 236.
Aultman & Co., Emerson v., 69 Md. 125. §§ 82, 91.
Austen v. Baker, 12 Modern, 250. § 77.
Austin v. Belknap, 54 Vt. 495. § 426.
v. Curtis, 31 Vt. 64. § 366.
v. Dorwin, 21 Vt. 38. §§ 348, 353, 356.
v. Gibson, 28 Up. Can. (C. P.) 554. § 376.
Mellendy v., 69 Ill. 15. § 335.
Merwin v., 58 Conn. 22. § 227.
v. Raiford, 67 Ga. 201. § 586.
v. Richardson, 1 Gratt. (Va.) 310. § 26.
Spaulding v., 2 Vt. 555. § 215.
State v., 35 Minn. 51. § 151.
Wright v., 56 Barb. (N. Y.) 13. § 336.
Auth, German American Bank v., 87 Pa. St. 419. §§ 555, 558.

Averett, Council *v.*, 90 N. C. 168. § 465.
Avery, Keim & Co. *v.*, 7 Neb. 54. § 235.
v. Rowell, 59 Wis. 82. § 19.
Aycock *v.* Leitner, 29 Ga. 197. § 507.
Ayer, Brown *v.*, 24 Ga. 288. §§ 40, 146.
v. Getty, 46 Hun (N. Y.), 287. § 624.
Ayers, Allen *v.*, 3 Pick. 298. § 115.
v. Burns' Adm'r, 87 Ind. 245. § 227.
Clinton Bank *v.*, 16 Ohio, 283. § 115.
v. Dixon, 78 N. Y. 318. § 37.
Robbins *v.*, 10 Mo. 538. § 66.
Aylesworth, Enos *v.*, 8 Ohio St. 322. § 507.
Ayres *v.* Milory, 53 Mo. 516. § 407.
Babbet, Conger *v.*, 67 Iowa, 13. § 235.
Babbitt *v.* Shryer, 70 Ind. 513, 517. § 407.
Babcock *v.* Blanchard, 86 Ill. 165. § 329.
v. Bryant, 12 Pick. 133. § 192.
v. Hubbard, 2 Conn. 536. § 208.
Baby *v.* Baby, 8 Up. Can. (Q. B.) 76. §§ 97, 552.
Bachelder *v.* Fiske, 17 Mass. 464. §§ 274, 284, 289.
Backhouse *v.* Hall, 6 Best & Smith, 507. § 118.
Backus *v.* Coyne, 45 Mich. 584. §§ 254, 283.
Irwin *v.*, 25 Cal. 214. § 638.
People *v.*, 117 N. Y. 196. §§ 396, 549.
v. Shipherd, 11 Wend. 629. § 101.
Bacon *v.* Chesney, 1 Starkie, 192. § 415.
Goodyear Dental Vulcanite Co. *v.*, 151 Mass. 460. § 151.
Harvey *v.*, 9 Yerg. (Tenn.) 308. § 604.
Miles *v.*, 4 J. J. Marsh. (Ky.) 457. § 212.
Williams *v.*, 2 Gray, 387. §§ 80, 90.
Bacot, Doughty *v.*, 2 Desaus. Eq. (S. C.) 546. § 33.
Badger *v.* Barnabee, 17 N. H. 120. § 17.
v. Daniel, 79 N. C. 372. § 639.
Baere *v.* Armstrong, 26 Hun (N. Y.), 19. § 473.
Bagg, Palmer *v.*, 56 N. Y. 523. § 120.
Bagley *v.* Blark, 7 Bosw. (N. Y.) 94. § 392.
Bagot *v.* State, 33 Ind. 262. § 628.
Bagott *v.* Mullen, 32 Ind. 332. § 264.
Bagwell, Held *v.*, 58 Iowa, 139. §§ 518, 526.
Miller *v.*, 3 McCord, Law (S. C.), 429. § 46.
Bailey *v.* Boyd, 75 Ind. 125. § 385.
Clason *v.*, 14 Johns. 484. §§ 80, 89.
Clore *v.*, 6 Bush (Ky.), 77. § 559.
Coleman *v.*, 4 Bibb (Ky.), 297. § 90.
Commonwealth *v.*, 129 Pa. St. 480. § 558.
v. Croft, 4 Taunt. 611. § 15.
Dinkins *v.*, 23 Miss. 284. § 312.
v. Edwards, 4 Best & Smith, 761. § 375.
Faulkner *v.*, 123 Mass. 588. § 333.
v. Freeman, 11 Johns. 221. § 87.
v. Freeman, 4 Johns. 280. § 13.
v. Griffith, 40 Up. Can. (Q. B. Div.) 418. §§ 362, 378.
Hicks *v.*, 16 Tex. 229. § 212.
Higdon *v.*, 26 Ga. 426. §§ 29, 431.
v. Larehar, 5 R. I. 530. § 92.
Munden *v.*, 70 Ala. 63. § 268.
v. New, 29 Ga. 214. §§ 609, 610.
v. Ogden, 3 Johns. 399. §§ 81, 89.
Rapelye *v.*, 3 Conn. 438. § 190.
Rapelye *v.*, 5 Conn. 149. § 161.
v. Rogers, 1 Greenl. (Me.) 186. § 574.
v. Rosenthal, 56 Mo. 385. § 456.
Scott *v.*, 23 Mo. 140. § 30.
v. Seals, 1 Har. (Del.) 367. § 498.
Bailie, Walsh *v.*, 10 Johns. 180. § 117.

Baily, Atkins *v.*, 9 Yerg. (Tenn.) 111. § 636.
Bainbridge, Smith *v.*, 6 Blackf. (Ind.) 12. § 198.
v. Wade, 16 Adol. & Ell. (N. S.) 89. §§ 82, 84, 86.
Baines *v.* Barns, 64 Ala. 375. § 587.
Bainton, Mayberry *v.*, 2 Harr. (Del.) 24. §§ 18, 198.
Baird, Cowan *v.*, 77 N. C. 201. § 402.
Kinard *v.*, 20 S. C. 377. § 310.
v. Rice, 1 Call (Va.), 18. § 434.
v. Trustees of Schools, 106 Ill. 657. § 597.
Webb *v.*, 27 Ind. 368. § 408.
Baker's Adm'r, Gilmer's Adm'r *v.*, 24 W. Va. 72. § 648.
Baker, American Bank *v.*, 4 Met. (Mass.) 164. §§ 397, 426.
Austen *v.*, 12 Modern, 250. § 77.
Board of Trustees *v.*, 34 Ill. App. 620. § 596.
Brewster *v.*, 97 Ind. 260. § 14.
v. Briggs, 8 Pick. 122. §§ 62, 180, 182, 243, 245, 425.
Brooks *v.*, 9 Daly (N. Y. Com. Pl.), 398. § 95.
Campbell *v.*, 46 Pa. St. 264. § 343.
Chaplin *v.*, 124 Ind. 385. § 39.
v. Cornwall, 4 Cal. 15. § 82.
Currier *v.*, 51 N. H. 613. § 281.
v. Dering, 8 Adol. & Ell. 94. § 89.
v. Frellsen, 32 La. Ann. 822. § 478.
Hammock *v.*, 3 Bush (Ky.), 208. § 488.
Ingersoll *v.*, 41 Mich. 48. § 3.
v. Kellogg, 29 Ohio St. 663. § 605.
v. Kennett, 54 Mo. 82. § 153.
Kerr *v.*, Walker (Miss.), 140. § 29.
King *v.*, 7 La. Ann. 570. § 525.
v. Merriam, 97 Ind. 539. § 486.
Moore *v.* (Cir. Ct. E. D. Wis.), 34 Fed. Rep. 1. § 297.
v. Morrison, 4 La. Ann. 372. §§ 22, 465.
Osborne & Co. *v.*, 34 Minn. 307. § 84.
Baker, Palmer *v.*, 23 Up. Can. (C. P.) 302. § 81.
v. Preston, 1 Gil. (Va.) 235. § 628.
v. Rand, 13 Barb. (N. Y.) 152. § 164.
Riddle *v.*, 13 Cal. 295. § 110.
Sawyers *v.*, 72 Ala. 49. § 329.
State *v.*, 64 Mo. 167. § 412.
Strong *v.*, 25 Minn. 442. § 628.
Balcombe, Kingsley *v.*, 4 Barb. (N. Y.) 131. §§ 61, 69.
Baldridge, Knode *v.*, 73 Ind. 54. § 622.
Baldwin, Derry Bank *v.*, 41 N. H. 434. § 41.
v. Dow, 130 Mass. 416. § 47.
v. Fleming, 90 Ind. 177. § 265.
Frelinghuysen *v.* (Dist. Ct. D. N. J.), 16 Fed. Rep. 452. §§ 425, 561.
v. Gordon, 12 Mart. (La.) O. S. 378. §§ 145, 239.
v. Heirs, 73 Ga. 739. §§ 56, 76, 77.
King *v.*, 2 Johns. Ch. 554. §§ 238, 239.
Lartigue *v.*, 5 Mart. (La.) O. S. 193. §§ 22, 630.
Lee *v.*, 10 Ga. 208. § 440.
Metzner *v.*, 11 Minn. 150. § 30.
Payne *v.*, 14 Barb. (N. Y.) 570. § 77.
Preble *v.*, 6 Cush. 549. § 72.
University of Cambridge *v.*, 5 Mees. & Wels. 580. § 119.
v. Western Reserve Bank, 5 Ohio, 273. § 345.
Bales *v.* State, 15 Ind. 321. § 545.
Ball *v.* Chancellor, 47 N. J. Law, 125. § 592.
v. Gilson, 7 Up. Can. (C. P.) 531. § 29.
Stamford, etc. Banking Co. *v.*, 4 De Gex, F. & J. 310. § 35.
Wild Cat Branch *v.*, 45 Ind. 213. § 411.
Ballard *v.* Brummitt, 4 Strob. Eq. (S. C.) 171. § 576.
Cole's Adm'r *v.*, 78 Va. 139. § 100.

Ballard, Cross *v.*, 46 Vt. 415. § 137.
Daniel *v.*, 2 Dana (Ky.), 296. §§ 264, 290.
Russell *v.*, 16 B. Mon. (Ky.) 201. § 115.
Ballew *v.* Roler, 124 Ind. 557. § 316.
Ballou, Cutler *v.*, 136 Mass. 337. § 162.
Balser *v.* Wood, 69 Ind. 122. § 226.
Baltimore First National Bank *v.* Gerke, 68 Md. 449. § 394.
Baltimore & Ohio R. R. Co. *v.* Bitner, 15 W. Va. 455. § 236.
Strawbridge *v.*, 14 Md. 360. § 395.
Baltis, Kendall *v.*, 26 Mo. App. 411. § 247.
Baltz, Emery *v.*, 94 N. Y. 408. § 134.
Emery *v.*, 22 Hun (N. Y.), 434. § 236.
Bamford *v.* Iles, 3 Wels., Hurl. & Gor. 380. § 170.
Bampton *v.* Paulin, 4 Bing. 264. §§ 63, 66, 68.
Bancroft *v.* Abbott, 3 Allen, 524. § 225.
v. Pearce, 27 Vt. 668. § 228.
Bane, Roberts *v.*, 32 Tex. 385. § 375.
Bangs *v.* Bangs, 41 Hun (N. Y.), 41. § 409.
Jones *v.*, 40 Ohio St. 139. § 379.
v. Mosher, 23 Barb. (N. Y.) 478. § 364.
v. Strong, 10 Paige, Ch. 11. § 345.
v. Strong, 4 N. Y. 315. § 40.
v. Strong, 7 Hill (N. Y.), 250. §§ 40, 360.
Bank *v.* Adger, 2 Hill, Eq. (S. C.) 262. § 309.
v. Barnes, 7 Ont. (Can.) 309, 320. § 133.
v. Douglas, 4 Watts (Pa.), 95. § 325.
v. Duncan, 52 Miss. 740. § 615.
v. Fleshman, 22 W. Va. 317. § 480.
v. Fordyce, 9 Pa. St. 275. §§ 48, 434.
v. Hammond, 1 Rich. Law (S. C.), 281. § 199.
v. Haskell, 51 N. H. 116. §§ 245, 414.
Bank *v.* Klingensmith, 7 Watts (Pa.), 523. § 239.
v. Knotts, 10 Rich. Law (S. C.), 543. §§ 143, 202.
McDowell *v.*, 1 Harr. (Del.) 369. §§ 40, 432.
v. Munford, 6 Ga. 44. §§ 29, 606.
v. Simpson, 90 N. C. 467. § 150.
South Carolina Mfg. Co. *v.*, 6 Rich. Eq. (S. C.) 227. § 251.
Spalding *v.*, 9 Pa. St. 28. § 248.
v. Springer, 7 Ont. (Can.), 309. § 555.
Bank of Albion *v.* Burns, 46 N. Y. 170. §§ 35, 342.
Bank of Alabama *v.* McDade, 4 Port. (Ala.) 252. § 218.
Bank of America, Kirkman *v.*, 2 Cold. (Tenn.) 397. § 248.
Bank of Brighton *v.* Smith, 5 Allen, 413. § 24.
v. Smith, 12 Allen, 243. §§ 559, 627.
Bank of British North America *v.* Cuvillier, 14 Moore's Privy Council Cas. 187. § 174.
Bank of Burlington *v.* Beach, 1 Aiken (Vt.), 62. § 114.
Bank of California *v.* Webb, 94 N. Y. 467. § 330.
Bank of Commerce *v.* McChord, 4 Dana (Ky.), 191. § 379.
Bank of Commonwealth, Alexander *v.*, 7 J. J. Marsh. (Ky.) 580. § 434.
Bank of Cumberland, Hopewell *v.*, 10 Leigh (Va.), 206. § 328.
Bank of Decatur *v.* Johnson, 9 Ala. 621. § 447.
Bank of Gettysburg *v.* Thompson, 3 Grant's Cases (Pa.), 114. § 442.
Bank of Hopkinsville *v.* Rudy, 2 Bush (Ky.), 326. § 308.
Bank of Illinois *v.* Sloo, 16 La. (Curry), 539. §§ 186, 189.
Bank of Kentucky, Pendleton *v.*, 17 B. Mon. (Ky.) 171. §§ 366, 560, 627.

Bank of Kingston, Chester *v.*, 16 N. Y. 336. §§ 337, 428.
Bank of Lansingburg, Ives *v.*, 12 Mich. 361. § 426.
Bank of Lansingburgh, Nevins *v.*, 10 Mich. 547. § 81.
Bank of Lexington, F. & M., *v.* Crosby, 4 J. J. Marsh. (Ky.) 366. § 375.
Bank of Limestone *v.* Penick, 2 T. B. Mon. (Ky.) 98. § 380.
Bank of Middlebury *v.* Bingham, 33 Vt. 621. §§ 114, 351.
Bank of Missouri, Furnold *v.*, 44 Mo. 336. § 323.
v. Matson, 24 Mo. 333. § 437.
v. Matson, 26 Mo. 243. § 32.
Bank of Mobile, Curry *v.*, 8 Port. (Ala.) 360. § 381.
Hetherington *v.*, 14 Ala. 68. § 438.
Ige *v.*, 8 Port. (Ala.) 108. § 360.
v. Mobile & Ohio R. R. Co.. 69 Ala. 305. § 329.
Bank of Monroe *v.* Gifford, 72 Iowa, 750. § 401.
Bank of Montpelier *v.* Joyner, 33 Vt. 481. § 114.
Bank of Montreal, Cumming *v.*, 15 Grant's Ch. 686. § 359.
v. McFaul, 17 Grant's Ch. 234. § 147.
v. Munster Bank, 11 Irish Law Rep. 417. § 104.
Bank of Mount Pleasant, Sprigg *v.*, 10 Pet. (U. S.) 257. § 41.
Bank of New South Wales, Taylor *v.*, Law Rep. (11 App. Cases), 596. § 431.
Bank of Newbury *v.* Richards, 35 Vt. 281. § 114.
v. Sinclair, 60 N. H. 100. § 200.
Bank of New York *v.* Livingston, 2 Johns. Cas. 409. § 102.
Bank of Northern Liberties *v.* Cresson, 12 Serg. & Rawle (Pa.), 306. § 520.
Bank of Old Dominion, McVeigh *v.*, 26 Gratt. (Va.) 785. § 437.
Bank of Orleans *v.* Barry, 1 Denio, 116. § 184.
Boughton *v.*, 2 Barb. Ch. 458. § 280.
Wilson *v.*, 9 Ala. 847. § 350.
Bank of Pennsylvania, Manufacturers' & Mechanics' Bank *v.*, 7 Watts & Serg. 335. § 40.
v. Potius, 10 Watts (Pa.), 148. §§ 306, 367, 568.
Bank of Penn Township, McMullin *v.*, 2 Pa. St. 343. § 220.
Bank of Rutland, West *v.*, 19 Vt. 403. § 208.
Bank of Scotland, Smith *v.*, 1 Dow. 272. § 422.
Bank of St. Albans *v.* Smith, 30 Vt. 148. §§ 29, 107.
Bank of Steubenville *v.* Leavitt, 5 Ohio, 208. § 372.
Bank of Toronto *v.* Hunter, 4 Bosw. (N. Y.) 646. § 302.
v. Wilmot, 19 Up. Can. (Q. B.) 73. § 392.
Bank of United States, Conway *v.*, 6 J. J. Marsh. (Ky.) 128. § 115.
v. Magill, 1 Paine, 661. § 396.
McGill *v.*, 12 Wheat. 511. § 396.
v. Stewart, 4 Dana (Ky.), 27. § 325.
Bank of Upper Canada *v.* Covert, 5 Up. Can. K. B. (O. S.) 541. § 393.
v. Thomas, 11 Up. Can. (C. P.) 515. § 32.
Bank of Vincennes, Sterne *v.*, 79 Ind. 549. § 438.
Bank of Virginia *v.* Boisseau, 12 Leigh (Va.), 387. § 328.
Bank of Washington, Barrington *v.*, 14 Serg. & Rawle (Pa.), 405. § 561.
v. Barrington, 2 Pen. & Watts (Pa.), 27. § 396.
v. Creditors, 86 N. C. 323. § 592.
Bank of Wilmington & Brandywine, McDowell *v.*, 2 Del. Ch. 1. § 342.
Bank of Wheeling, M. & M., *v.* Evans, 9 W. Va. 373. § 342.

Bank of Whitehaven, Dawson *v.*, 4 Ch. Div. 639. § 35.
Bank of Wooster *v.* Stevens, 6 Ohio St. 262. § 235.
Banks *v.* Brown, 4 Yerg. (Tenn.) 198. § 452.
Davis *v.*, 45 Ga. 138. § 17.
Stovall *v.*, 10 Wall. 583. § 580.
White *v.*, 21 Ala. 705. § 269.
Bank's Ex'rs, Mountjoy *v.*, 6 Munf. (Va.) 387. § 229.
Bankstone, Goff *v.*, 35 Miss. 518. § 402.
Banning, Wolf *v.*, 3 Minn. 202. § 35.
Barbee, Smyth *v.*, 9 Lea (Tenn.), 173. § 487.
Barber *v.* Bucklin, 2 Denio, 45. §§ 69, 72.
v. Burrows, 51 Cal. 404. § 370.
Continental Life Ins. Co. *v.*, 50 Conn. 567. § 342.
v. Gillson, 18 Nev. 89. § 36.
v. Morton, 45 Up. Can. (Q. B.) 386. § 387.
Starrett *v.*, 20 Me. 457. § 114.
Swain *v.*, 29 Vt. 292. § 276.
Barbour, Phares *v.*, 49 Ill. 370. § 428.
Barclay *v.* Lucas, 1 Durn. & East, 291. § 121.
v. Miers, 70 Ind. 346. § 648.
Bardwell *v.* Lydall, 7 Bing. 489. § 330.
Barefoot, State *v.*, 104 N. C. 224. § 566.
Barefoot's Ex'rs, Simmons *v.*, 2 Haywood (N. C.), 606. § 12.
Barfield, Adkinson *v.*, 1 McCord (S. C.), 575. § 64.
Barger, Blandford's Adm'r *v.*, 9 Dana (Ky.), 22. § 438.
Barickman *v.* Kuykendall, 6 Blackf. (Ind.) 21. § 80.
Barker, Bill *v.*, 16 Gray, 62. § 118.
v. Bucklin, 2 Denio, 45. § 66.
v. Buel, 5 Cush. 519. § 247.
Driscoll *v.*, 2 P. & B. (N. B.) 407. § 378.
Frye *v.*, 4 Pick. 382. §§ 143, 242.
Lanusse *v.*, 3 Wheat. 101. § 134.
Barker *v.* McClure, 2 Blackf. (Ind.) 14. §§ 368, 372.
Merriman *v.*, 121 Ind. 74. § 363.
v. Parker, 1 Durn. & East, 287. § 119.
Price *v.*, 4 Ellis & Black. 760. § 376.
v. Scudder, 56 Mo. 272. §§ 67, 98.
Smith *v.*, 6 Watts (Pa.), 508. § 500.
Warren *v.*, 2 Duvall (Ky.), 155. § 73.
Barklie, Bixby *v.*, 26 Hun (N. Y.), 275. § 426.
Barksdale *v.* Butler, 6 Lea (Tenn.), 450. § 631.
Barman *v.* Carhartt, 10 Mich. 338. § 98.
Barnabee, Badger *v.*, 17 N. H. 120. § 17.
Barnard, Dalton *v.*, 150 Mass. 473. § 470.
v. Darling, 11 Wend. 28. § 572.
v. Heydrick, 49 Barb. (N. Y.) 62. § 89.
Lyde *v.*, Tyrwh. & Gr. 250. § 73.
Sampson *v.*, 98 Mass. 359. § 386.
Barnbill, Peters *v.*, 1 Hill, Law (S. C.), 234, 237. §§ 211, 214.
Barnes, Atlantic & Pacific Telegraph Co. *v.*, 64 N. Y. 385. § 423.
Bank *v.*, 7 Ont. (Can.) 309, 320. § 133.
Citizens' Bank *v.*, 70 Iowa, 412. § 416.
Hansen *v.*, 3 Gill & Johns. (Md.) 359. § 80.
Hotchkiss *v.*, 34 Conn. 27. §§ 156, 157.
v. Mott, 64 N. Y. 397. §§ 34, 451.
Vinyard *v.*, 124 Ill. 346. § 93.
v. Whitaker, 45 Wis. 204. § 563.
Barnet *v.* Abbott, 53 Vt. 120. § 517.
Barnett *v.* Smith, 17 Ill. 565. § 119.
Barney *v.* Clark, 46 N. H. 514. §§ 246, 437.
Daniels *v.*, 22 Ind. 207. § 21.
v. Forbes, 118 N. Y. 580. §§ 13, 14.
Foster *v.*, 3 Vt. 60. §§ 98, 101.

Barney, Gaston v., 11 Ohio St. 506. § 330.
v. Grover, 28 Vt. 391. § 207.
v. Patterson, 6 Harr. & Johns. (Md.) 182. § 80.
Peck v., 13 Vt. 93. §§ 187, 199, 204.
Barnitz, Ege v., 8 Pa. St. 304. § 100.
Barns, Baines v., 64 Ala. 375. § 587.
v. Barrow, 61 N. Y. 39. § 117.
Barnsback v. Renier, 8 Minn. 59. § 230.
Barnum, Childs v., 11 Barb. (N. Y.) 14. § 84.
Baron, Adm'r, Raney v., 1 Fla. 327. § 464.
Barrell v. Trussell, 4 Taunt. 117–20. §§ 13, 65, 82.
Barrett, Clark v., 19 Mo. 39. § 604.
Duff v., 15 Grant's Ch. 632. § 371.
Lapham v., 1 Vt. 247. § 84.
Perry v., 18 Mo. 140. §§ 607, 613.
Sisson v., 2 N. Y. 406. § 31.
State v., 121 Ind. 92. § 581.
Barringer v. Warden, 12 Cal. 311. § 66.
Barrington, Bank of Washington v., 2 Pen. & Watts (Pa.), 27. § 396.
v. Bank of Washington, 14 Serg. & Rawle (Pa.), 405. § 561.
Rees v., 2 Vesey, Jr. 540. § 364.
Barrow, Barns v., 61 N. Y. 39. § 117.
v. Lane, 5 Vt. 161. § 182.
Rhinelander v., 17 Johns. 538. § 339.
v. Shields, 13 La. Ann. 57. § 426.
Stewart v., 55 Ga. 664. § 233.
Welsh v., 9 Rob. (La.) 535. § 519.
Barry, Bank of Orleans v., 1 Denio, 116. § 184.
v. Frayser, 10 Heisk. (Tenn.) 206. §§ 466, 481.
v. Larabie, 7 Mont. 179. § 599.
v. Law, 1 Cranch (C. C.), 77. § 89.
v. Ransom, 12 N. Y. 462. §§ 60, 261.
Rice v., 2 Cranch (C. C.), 447. § 68.
v. Screwmen's Benevolent Ass'n, 67 Tex. 250. §§ 526, 628.
Barstow v. Gay, 3 Greenl. (Me.) 409. § 89.
Perkins v., 6 R. I. 505. § 143.
Wood v., 10 Pick. 368. § 97.
Barth, Studley v., 54 Mich. 6. § 76.
Bartholomew v. Seaman, 25 Hun (N. Y.), 619. § 199.
Bartlett, Appellant, 82 Me. 210. § 517.
Bartlett, Chicago, B. & Q. R. R. v., 20 Bradw. (Ill. App.) 96. § 558.
v. Cunningham, 85 Ill. 22. § 606.
McKim v., 129 Mass. 226. § 526.
State v., 30 Miss. 624. § 520.
v. Willis, 3 Mass. 86. § 22.
Wright v., 43 N. H. 548. §§ 352, 376.
Bartley v. Yates, 2 Hen. & Mun. (Va.) 398. § 26.
Bartlow v. Bonde, 3 Dana (Ky.), 591. § 436.
Bartol, Freeport v., 3 Greenl. (Me.) 340. § 80.
Barton v. Croydon, 63 N. H. 417. § 324.
v. Speis, 5 Hun, 60. § 137.
Bascom, Appleton v., 3 Met. (Mass.) 169. § 209.
Basham v. Commonwealth, 13 Bush (Ky.), 36. § 571.
Bashford v. Shaw, 4 Ohio St. 264. §§ 101, 202.
Baskin v. Andrews, 53 Hun (N. Y.), 95. § 140.
v. Godbe, 1 Utah, 28. § 342.
Bass, Hobson v., Law Rep., 6 Ch. App. Cas. 792. § 253.
Bassett v. Crafts, 129 Mass. 513. §§ 42, 521.
Furber v., 2 Duvall (Ky.), 433. § 345.
Bastow v. Bennett, 3 Camp. 220. § 161.
Batchelor, Broom v., 1 Hurl. & Nor. 255. § 84.
Batdorf, Harner v., 35 Ohio St. 113. § 334.
Bate, Hunt v., Dyer, 272a. § 17.
Bateman, Mallet v., Law Rep. 1 C. P. 163. §§ 74, 75.

Bateman v. Phillips, 15 East, 272. § 81.
Phillips v., 16 East, 356. § 82.
Bates, Alexander v., 33 Ga. 125. § 504.
Beach v., 12 Vt. 68. §§ 101, 441.
v. Branch Bank Mobile, 2 Ala. 689. § 604.
Darst v., 51 Ill. 439. §§ 221, 324, 329.
Greene v., 74 N. Y. 333. § 363.
Pickett v., 3 La. Ann. 627. §§ 207, 212.
Puckett v., 4 Ala. 390. § 75.
v. Starr, 6 Ala. 697. § 77.
State v., 36 Vt. 387. §§ 521, 557.
v. State, 75 Ind. 463. § 520.
v. State Bank, 7 Ark. (2 Eng.) 394. § 605.
Stearns v., 46 Conn. 306. § 324.
Supervisors of Rensselaer v., 17 N. Y. 242. § 522.
Treasurers v., 2 Bailey, Law (S. C.), 362. §§ 519, 624.
v. Wiggin, 37 Kan. 44. § 231.
Bates, Adm'r, Cain v., 35 Mo. 427. § 448.
Bateson v. Gosling, Law Rep. 7 Com. Pl. 9. § 147.
Battle v. Blake, 1 Dev. Law (N. C.), 381. § 101.
v. Hart, 2 Dev. Eq. (N. C.) 31. § 253.
Batturs v. Sellers, 5 Harr. & Johns. (Md.) 117. § 90.
Bauer v. Gray, Adm'r, 18 Mo. App. 164. §§ 230, 329.
Baugh, Himrod v., 85 Ill. 435. § 236.
Baugher's Ex'rs v. Duphorn, 9 Gill (Md.), 314. § 335.
Baum, Dawson v., 3 Wash. Terr. 464. § 490.
Meggett v., 57 Miss. 22. § 342.
Baumann v. James, Law Rep. 3 Ch. App. 508. § 81.
Baxter, Downer v., 30 Vt. 467. § 217.
v. Marsh, 1 Yerg. (Tenn.) 460. § 516.
Bay v. Tallmadge, 5 Johns. Ch. 305. § 40.
Bayard, Ashton v., 71 Pa. St. 139. §§ 17, 102.
Bay City, McCormick v., 23 Mich. 457. § 410.
Stevenson v., 26 Mich. 44. § 530.
Bays v. Conner, 105 Ind. 415. § 36.
Beabout, Watson v., 18 Ind. 281. § 137.
Beach, Bank of Burlington v., 1 Aiken (Vt.), 62. § 114.
v. Bates, 12 Vt. 68. §§ 101, 441.
v. Boynton, 26 Vt. 725. § 604.
v. Elliott, 44 Conn. 237. § 515.
Wood v., 7 Vt. 522. § 86.
v. Zimmerman, 106 Ind. 495. § 344.
Beadle Co. Nat. Bank v. Hyman, 33 Ill. App. 618. § 104.
Beal v. Brown, 13 Allen, 114. § 227.
Beale, Crofts v., 11 Com. B. 172. § 16.
Beall v. Cochran, 18 Ga. 38. § 149.
v. Territory, 1 New Mex. 507. § 578.
Bealls, Andrus v., 9 Cow. 693. § 572.
Beals & Hammer, Van Patton & Marks v., 46 Iowa, 62. § 4.
Beaman v. Blanchard, 4 Wend. 432. § 258.
Bean, Adams v., 12 Mass. 139. § 87.
v. Chapman, 62 Ala. 58. § 145.
Coleman v., 1 Abb. Rep. Om. Cas. (N. Y.) 394. §§ 42, 406.
Conger v., 58 Iowa, 321. § 416.
v. Parker, 17 Mass. 591. § 151.
Sanders v., Busb. Law (N. C.), 318. § 570.
v. Valle, 2 Mo. 103. § 82.
Beard, Ford v., 31 Mo. 459. § 342.
Nixon v., 111 Ind. 137. § 293.
v. Roth (Cir. Ct. E. D. Ark.), 35 Fed. Rep. 397. § 587.
State v., 11 Rob. (La.) 243. § 370.
v. Union & Am. Pub. Co., 71 Ala. 69. § 236.
Bearden, Hazen v., 4 Sneed (Tenn.), 48. § 77.
Beardslee, Buckley v., 2 South. 572. § 82.

Beardsley, Castle *v.*, 10 Hun (N. Y.), 343. § 82.
Hammel *v.*, 31 Minn. 314. § 1.
Warner *v.*, 8 Wend. 194. § 239.
Bearsh, Sears *v.*, 7 La. Ann. 539. § 464.
Beasley *v.* State, 53 Ark. 67. § 502.
Beatie *v.* Calhoun, 73 Ga. 269. § 7.
Beattie *v.* Browne, 64 Ill. 360. § 182.
McConnell *v.*, 34 Ark. 113. § 306.
Beatty, Union Bank *v.*, 10 La. Ann. 378. § 413.
Beaubien *v.* Stoney, Speer's Eq. (S. C.) 508. § 430.
Beavan, Bushuell *v.*, 1 Bing. N. C. 103. §§ 64, 74, 85.
Beavans, Wilson *v.*, 58 Ill. 232. § 67.
Beaver *v.* Beaver, 23 Pa. St. 167. § 226.
Fleming *v.*, 2 Rawle (Pa.), 128. § 310.
v. Slanker, Adm'r, 94 Ill. 175. §§ 298, 315.
Bechtel, Hoffman *v.*, 52 Pa. St. 190. § 101.
Beck, Taylor *v.*, 13 Ill. 376. § 242.
Becket, Chater *v.*, 7 Term R. 201. §§ 52, 64.
v. Tarrant, 61 Tex. 402. § 295.
Beckett *v.* Addyman, Law Rep. (9 Q. B. Div.) 783. § 284.
Pitts *v.*, 13 Mees. & Wels. 743. §§ 80, 89.
Becker *v.* Northway, 44 Minn. 61. § 236.
Beckham *v.* Pride, 6 Rich. Eq. (S. C.) 78. § 280.
Beckley *v.* Eckert, 3 Pa. St. 292. § 50.
v. Munson, 22 Conn. 299. § 217.
Beckman, Thomas *v.*, 1 B. Mon. (Ky.) 29. §§ 214, 631.
Beckwith, Lowe *v.*, 14 B. Mon. (Ky.) 150. §§ 157, 192, 197.
Neuman *v.*, 5 Lans. (N. Y.) 80. § 570.
Bedell, Sharp *v.*, 5 Gil. 88. § 449.
Bedford, Kenningham *v.*, 1 B. Mon. 325. § 356.
Bedwell *v.* Gephart, 67 Iowa, 44. §§ 426.
Bee, Neely *v.*, 32 W. Va. 519. § 274.
Beebe *v.* Dudley, 26 N. H. 249. §§ 188, 202.
Musick *v.*, 17 Kan. 47. § 580.
Beech, Union Bank *v.*, 3 Hurl. & Colt. 672. §§ 147.
Beehervaise *v.* Lewis, Law Rep. 7 Com. Pleas, 372. § 236.
Beeker *v.* Saunders, 6 Ired. Law (N. C.), 380. § 101.
Beekman *v.* Hale, 17 Johns. 134. § 190.
Remsen *v.*, 25 N. Y. 552. § 239.
Beers *v.* Shannon, 73 N. Y. 292. § 112.
Beesley *v.* Hamilton, 50 Ill. 88. § 402.
Beeson *v.* Beeson's Adm'r, 1 Har. (Del.) 466. § 498.
Beezeley, Welford *v.*, 1 Ves. Sr. 6. § 89.
Begole *v.* Stimson, 39 Mich. 288. § 494.
Behm, Stewart *v.*, 2 Watts (Pa.), 356. § 151.
Bein *v.* Heath, 12 How. 168. § 476.
Belanger, Verret *v.*, 6 La. Ann. 109. § 638.
Belcher *v.* Branch, 11 R. I. 226. § 577.
v. Smith, 7 Cush. 482. § 183.
Belches, West *v.*, 5 Munf. (Va.) 187. § 267.
Belding *v.* State, 25 Ark. 315. § 500.
Belfast Banking Co. *v.* Hamilton, 12 Law Rep. (Irish), 105. § 155.
v. Stanley, Irish, 1 Com. Law, 693. § 342.
Belfield Union *v.* Pattison, 2 Hurl. & Gor. 623. § 554.
Belknap, Austin *v.*, 54 Vt. 495. § 426.
Bell, Agnew *v.*, 4 Watts (Pa.), 31. §§ 254, 268.
v. Boyd, 76 Tex. 133. § 286.
Boyd *v.*, 69 Tex. 735. § 139.
v. Bruen, 1 How. 169. § 92.
Clark *v.*, 8 Humph. (Tenn.) 26. § 225.
Clarke *v.*, 2 Litt. (Ky.) 164. § 486.
Crathern *v.*, 45 Up. Can. (Q. B.) 473. § 161.

Bell, Dickason v., 13 La. Ann. 249. § 149.
Evans v., 45 Tex. 553. § 100.
Gates v., 3 La. Ann. 62. § 20.
Inhabitants of Colerain v., 9 Met. (Mass.) 499. § 547.
v. Jasper, 2 Ired. Eq. (N. C.) 597. § 288.
Macdonald v., 3 Moore's Priv. Co. Cas. 315. § 448.
v. Mahin, 69 Iowa, 408. §§ 382, 384.
v. Manning, 11 Grant's Ch. 142. § 147.
v. McConkey, 82 Va. 176. § 237.
McNairy v., 5 Rob. (La.) 418. § 634.
v. Moffat, 4 P. & B. (N. B.) 121. § 179.
v. Norwood, 7 La. (4 Curry), 95. § 118.
v. People, 94 Ill. 230. § 585.
v. Rawson, 30 Ga. 712. § 500.
Rayner v., 15 Mass. 377. § 516.
v. Welch, 9 Man., Gr. & Scott, 154. § 85.
Bell's Adm'r v. Jasper, 2 Ired. Eq. (N. C.) 597. § 256.
Bellenger & Ralls, Anderson v., 87 Ala. 334. §§ 378, 416.
Belleville Savings Bank v. Bornman, 124 Ill. 200. §§ 402, 405.
Belloni v. Freeborn, 63 N. Y. 383. §§ 92, 220.
Bellows v. Lovell, 5 Pick. 307. § 437.
Bellume v. Wallace, 2 Rich. Law (S. C.), 80. § 247.
Belt, McCune v., 45 Mo. 174. §§ 260, 268.
Benedict v. Miner, 58 Ill. 19. § 384.
v. Olson, 37 Minn. 431. § 242.
v. Rea, 35 Hun (N. Y.), 34. § 439.
v. Sherill, Lalor's Sup. to Hill & Denio, 219. § 116.
Stamford Bank v., 15 Conn. 437. §§ 305, 330.
Thrall v., 13 Vt. 248. § 114.
Wheeler v., 36 Hun (N. Y.), 478. § 237.
Benefield, Eaton v., 2 Blackf. (Ind.) 52. § 578.
Benfield, People v., 80 Mich. 265. § 596.
Bengal v. Radakissenmitter, 4 Moore's Privy Council Cases, 140. § 330.
Bengal Government, Lalla Bunseedhur v., 14 Moore's Indian Appeal, 86. § 542.
Benham v. Assurance Co., 7 Wels., Hurl. & Gor. 744. § 404.
Benne v. Schnecko, 100 Mo. 250. §§ 310, 311.
Benneson v. Savage, 130 Ill. 352. § 367.
Bennett, Allen v., 3 Taunt. 169. §§ 80, 89.
v. Auditor, 2 W. Va. 441. § 371.
Bastow v., 3 Camp. 220. § 161.
v. Buchanan, 3 Ind. 47. § 211.
v. Dowling, 22 Tex. 660. § 217.
Eastman v., 6 Wis. 232. § 84.
v. Graham, 71 Ga. 211. §§ 586, 638.
Lord Haberton v. Beatty, 386. §§ 34, 429.
Singer Mfg. Co. v., 28 W. Va. 16. §§ 45, 259.
v. State, 58 Miss. 556. § 521.
Bensinger v. Wren, 100 Pa. St. 500. § 396.
Benson, Rooker v., 83 Ind. 250. § 298.
Wood v., 2 Cr. & Jer. 94. §§ 17, 52.
Bent v. Cobb, 9 Gray, 397. § 90.
v. Hartshorn, 1 Met. (Mass.) 24. § 160.
Bentham v. Cooper, 5 Mees. & Wels. 621. § 85.
Bentley v. Harris' Adm'r, 2 Gratt. (Va.) 358. §§ 256, 480.
Weed v., 6 Hill (N. Y.), 56. § 234.
Bently v. Gregory, 7 T. B. Mon. (Ky.) 368. § 229.
Benton, Bigelow v., 14 Barb. (N. Y.) 123. § 132.
Bird v., 2 Dev. Law (N. C.), 179. § 221.

Benton *v.* Fletcher, 31 Vt. 418. §§ 100, 183.
v. Gibson, 1 Hill, Law (S. C.), 56. §§ 100, 201.
v. Pratt, 2 Wend. 385. § 73.
State *v.*, 48 N. H. 551. § 516.
Benzion, State *v.*, 79 Iowa. 467. § 509.
Berand, Chase *v.*, 29 Cal. 138. § 456.
Berg *v.* Radcliff, 6 Johns. Ch. 302. § 141.
Bergstroem *v.* State, 58 Tex. 92. § 139.
Berkey *v.* Judd, 34 Minn. 393. § 409.
Miller *v.*, 27 Pa. St. 317. § 444.
Morrison *v.*, 7 Serg. & Rawle (Pa.), 238. § 211.
Berkowitz, Hendrie *v.*, 37 Cal. 113. § 643.
Bermes, Town of Union *v.*, 44 N. J. Law, 269. § 628.
Bernero, Schaeffer *v.*, 11 Mo. App. 562. § 588.
Bernhard *v.* City of Wyandotte, 33 Kan. 465. §§ 546, 644.
Bernheim, Teller *v.*, 3 Phila. (Pa.) 299. § 100.
Berning, State *v.*, 6 Mo. App. 105. § 540.
Berrien County Treasurer *v.* Bunburg, 45 Mich. 79. § 597.
Berrington, Rees *v.*, 2 Ves. Jr. 540. § 238.
Berry, Bryan *v.*, 6 Cal. 394. §§ 20, 177.
Paul *v.*, 78 Ill. 158. § 33.
v. Pullen, 69 Me. 101. § 342.
Ruggles *v.*, 76 Me. 262. § 505.
Searing *v.*, 58 Iowa, 20. §§ 311, 645.
State *v.*, 34 Ga. 546. § 498.
Withers *v.*, 25 Kan. 373. §§ 176, 202.
Berryman *v.* Mauker, 56 Iowa, 150. § 380.
Robinson *v.*, 22 Mo. App. 509. § 382.
Berthold, Adm'x, *v.* Berthold, 46 Mo. 557. § 298.
Besore *v.* Potter, 12 Serg. & Rawle (Pa.), 154. § 141.
Bessinger *v.* Dickerson, 20 Iowa, 260. § 563.
Besshears *v.* Rowe, 46 Mo. 501. § 17.
Best *v.* Johnson, 78 Cal. 217. § 593.
v. Stow, 2 Sandf. Ch. 298. § 405.
Bethune *v.* Dozier, 10 Ga. 235. §§ 388, 605.
Bevans, Wilson *v.*, 58 Ill. 232. § 63.
Beveridge *v.* Chetlain, 1 Bradw. (Ill. App.) 231. § 519.
Bewley *v.* Whiteford, Hayes (Irish Rep.), 356. § 85.
Beyerle *v.* Hain, 61 Pa. St. 226. § 546.
Bibb, Ellis *v.*, 2 Stew. (Ala.) 63. §§ 342, 347.
v. Martin, 14 Smedes & Mar. (Miss.) 87. § 326.
Bick *v.* Reese, 52 Hun, 125. § 9.
Bickerton, Bruce *v.*, 18 W. Va. 342. § 292.
Bickford, Blodgett *v.*, 30 Vt. 731. § 246.
Bicknell, Evans *v.*, 6 Vesey, Jr. 174. § 73.
Gill *v.*, 2 Cush. 355. § 90.
Bicksford *v.* Gibbs, 8 Cush. 154. §§ 15, 204.
Bidwell, Parker *v.*, 3 Conn. 84. § 496.
Bigelow *v.* Benton, 14 Barb. (N. Y.) 123. § 132.
v. Bridge, 8 Mass. 275. § 168.
Cahill *v.*, 18 Pick. 369. §§ 75, 76.
v. Comegys, 5 Ohio St. 256. § 486.
Dewitt *v.*, 11 Ala. 480. § 342.
Dorman *v.*, 1 Fla. 281. §§ 87, 88.
Bill *v.* Barker, 16 Gray, 62. § 118.
Billings, Manufacturers' Bank *v.*, 17 Pick. 87. § 339.
Billingsby, Day *v.*, 3 Bush (Ky.), 157. § 617.
Billington *v.* Waggoner, 33 N. Y. 31. § 356.
Bine, Saline Co. *v.*, 65 Mo. 63. § 428.
Bing, Smith *v.*, 3 Ohio, 33. § 278.
v. Tyler, 79 Ill. 248. § 126.
Bing Gee, Adm'r, *v.* Ah Jim, 7 Fed. Rep. 811. § 473.
Bingham, Bank of Middlebury *v.*, 33 Vt. 621. §§ 114, 351.

Bingham, Blydenburgh *v.*, 38 N. Y. 371. § 431.
County of Wapello *v.*, 10 Iowa, 39. § 543.
Lamoille Co. Nat. Bank *v.*, 50 Vt. 105. § 235.
Binkard, Shaw *v.*, 10 Ind. 227. § 357.
Binsse *v.* Wood, 37 N. Y. 526. § 110.
Birchim, State *v.*, 9 Nev. 95. § 512.
Birckhead *v.* Brown, 5 Hill (N. Y.), 634. §§ 81, 116.
Bird *v.* Benton, 2 Dev. Law (N. C.), 179. § 221.
v. Blossee, 2 Vent. 36. § 80.
v. Boulter, 4 Barn. & Adol. 443. § 90.
v. Gammon, 5 Scott, 213. § 64.
v. Gammon, 3 Bing. N. C. 883. § 62.
Sacramento Co. *v.*, 31 Cal. 66. § 553.
State *v.*, 2 Rich. Law (S. C.), 99. § 538.
Birdsall *v.* Heacock, 32 Ohio St. 177. § 165.
Birge, Claiborne *v.*, 42 Tex. 98. § 361.
Birkett *v.* McGuire, 31 Up. Can. (C. P.) 430. § 36.
Birkey, Butler *v.*, 13 Ohio St. 514. § 266.
Birkholm, Chandler *v.*, 44 N. J. Eq. 554. § 577.
Birkmyr *v.* Darnell, 2 Lord Raymond, 1085. § 54.
v. Darnell, 1 Salk. 27. §§ 56, 77.
Birlye, Clarke *v.*, Law Rep. (41 Ch. Div.) 422. § 439.
Bishop, Agricultural Bank *v.*, 6 Gray, 317. § 352.
v. Alcott, 86 N. Y. 503. § 50.
v. Day, 13 Vt. 81. § 223.
v. Freeman, 42 Mich. 533. § 93.
Hidden *v.* 5 R. I. 29. § 335.
Hudson *v.*, (Cir. Ct. N. D. Ia., E. D.). 32 Fed. Rep. 519. §§ 551, 588.
Krug *v.*, 44 Ohio St. 221. §§ 476, 480.
Pidcock *v.*, 3 Barn. & Cress. 605. § 420.
Bishop, Rush *v.*, 60 Tex. 177. § 296.
Tousey *v.*, 22 Iowa, 178. § 362.
Bissel, Butler *v.*, 1 Root (Conn.), 102. § 506.
Felton *v.*, 25 Minn. 15. § 298.
Bissell *v.* Saxton, 77 N. Y. 191. § 526.
v. Saxton, 66 N. Y. 55. §§ 545, 628.
Bitner, Baltimore & Ohio R. R. Co. *v.*, 15 W. Va. 455. § 236.
Bittick *v.* Wilkins, 7 Heisk. (Tenn.) 307. § 317.
Bitting *v.* Moore, 53 Iowa, 593. § 590.
Bivins *v.* Helsey, 4 Met. (Ky.) 78. § 402.
Willis *v.*, 76 Ga. 745. § 492.
Bixby *v.* Barklie, 26 Hun (N. Y.), 275. § 426.
Bizzell *v.* Smith, 2 Dev. Eq. (N. C.) 27. § 242.
Blache, Mayer *v.*, 3 La. (Curry), 500. §§ 425, 557.
Black, Carter *v.*, 4 Dev. & Bat. Law (N. C.), 425. § 210.
v. Doherty, 22 New Brunswick Rep. 215. § 77.
Doggett *v.*, 40 Fed. Rep. 439. § 466.
Furst & Bradley Mfg. Co. *v.*, 111 Ind. 308. §§ 191, 193, 197, 199, 203.
Irick *v.*, 2 C. E. Green (N. J.), 189. §§ 223, 237, 434, 435.
v. Oblender, 135 Pa. St. 526. § 538.
v. Ottoman Bank, 15 Moore's Priv. Coun. Cas. 472. § 423.
Sherman *v.*, 49 Vt. 198. § 265.
Waldrip *v.*, 74 Cal. 409. §§ 212, 310, 645.
Wheeling *v.*, 25 W. Va. 266. §§ 534, 538.
Black River Bank *v.* Page, 44 N. Y. 453. § 446.
Blackburne *v.* Boker, 1 Pa. Law Jour. Rep. 15. § 102.
Blackener *v.* Davis, 128 Mass. 538. § 26.
Blackford, People *v.*, 16 Ill. 166. § 548.
Blackiston, Morgan *v.*, 5 Harr. & Johns. (Md.) 61. § 474.

Blackman v. Joiner, 81 Ala. 344. § 311.
Blackmore, King v., 72 Pa. St. 347. § 332.
State v., 7 Heisk. (Tenn.) 638. § 112.
Blackney, Dauber v., 38 Barb. (N. Y.) 432. § 67.
Black's Ex'rs, Martin v., 20 Ala. 309. § 61.
Blackstone Bank v. Hill, 10 Pick. 129. § 352.
Blackwell, Davis v., 5 Bradw. (Ill. App.) 32. § 19.
v. Wilson, 2 Rich. Law, 322. § 497.
Blagden v. Bradbear, 12 Ves. 466. § 90.
Blaine v. Hubbard, 4 Pa. St. 183. § 373.
Blair, Broyles v., 7 Yerg. (Tenn.) 279. § 484.
Curtis v., 26 Miss. 309. § 90.
v. Perpetual Ins. Co., 10 Mo. 559. §§ 395, 627.
Planters' & Merchants' Bank v., 4 Ala. 613. § 114.
v. Snodgrass, 1 Sneed (Tenn.), 1. § 80.
State v., 32 Ind. 313. § 385.
Blake, Aldrich v., 134 Mass. 582. § 332.
Battle v., 1 Dev. Law (N. C.), 381. § 101.
Bridge's Adm'r v., 106 Ind. 332. § 148.
v. Cole, 22 Pick. 97. § 60.
v. Downey, 51 Mo. 437. § 205.
Driscoll v., 9 Irish Ch. Rep. 356. § 42.
McKim v., 132 Mass. 343. § 526.
McKim v., 139 Mass. 593. § 627.
Penn. Coal Co. v., 85 N. Y. 226. § 7.
State v., 2 Ohio St. 147. § 148.
Thomas v., 136 Mass. 568. § 527.
Thomas v., 126 Mass. 320. § 526.
v. White, 1 Younge & Coll. (Exch.) 420. § 352.
White v., 22 Wend. 612. § 498.
Blakey v. Johnson, 13 Bush (Ky.), 197. § 378.
Blakely, Anderson v., 2 Watts & Serg. (Pa.) 237. § 164.
Newcomb v., 1 Mo. App. 289. § 366.
Blalack v. State, 3 Tex. App. 376. § 497.
v. Peake, 3 Jones' Eq. (N. C.) 323. § 317.
Blanchard, Babcock v., 86 Ill. 165. § 329.
Beaman v., 4 Wend. 432. § 258.
Dexter v., 11 Allen, 365. § 58.
Gay & Co. v., 32 La. Ann. 497. § 1.
Gibbs v., 15 Mich. 292. § 76.
Mann v., 2 Allen, 386. § 73.
Bland, Smith v., 7 B. Mon. (Ky.) 21. § 583.
Blandford's Adm'r v. Barger, 9 Dana (Ky.), 22. § 438.
Blandin, Tucker v., 48 Hun (N. Y.), 439. § 116.
Blanton, Jones v., 6 Ired. Eq. (N. C.) 115. §§ 267, 288, 292, 540.
Blark, Bagley v., 7 Bosw. (N. Y.) 94. § 392.
Blatchford v. Milliken, 35 Ill. 434. § 177.
Blatner, Starr v., 76 Iowa, 356. § 383.
Blauser v. Diebl, 90 Pa. St. 350. § 583.
Blazer v. Bundy, 15 Ohio St. 57. §§ 40, 354.
Bleakley v. Smith, 11 Simons, 150. § 89.
Bledsoe v. Nixon, 68 N. C. 521. § 313.
Blest v. Brown, 3 Giffard, 450. § 401.
Bliss, Bull v., 30 Vt. 127. §§ 100, 197.
Sedgwick v., 23 Neb. 617. § 106.
Block v. Estes, 92 Mo. 318. § 572.
Kock v., 29 Ohio St. 565. § 215.
Blodgett v. Bickford, 30 Vt. 731. § 246.
Gannett v., 39 N. H. 150. § 306.
Blood, Firman v., 2 Kan. 496. § 176.
v. Hardy, 15 Me. 61. § 90.

Bloom & Co. *v.* Kern, 30 La. Ann. 1263. § 165.
v. Warder, 13 Neb. 476. § 199.
Blore *v.* Sutton, 3 Meriv. 237. § 89.
Blossee, Bird *v.*, 2 Vent. 36. § 80.
Blount, Noole *v.*, 77 Mo. 235. § 225.
Blow *v.* Maynard, 2 Leigh (Va.), 29. § 212.
Bluck, Chapman *v.*, 5 Scott, 515. § 80.
Blum, McIlhenny Co. *v.*, 68 Tex. 197. § 154.
Blunt, Green *v.*, 59 Iowa, 79. § 434.
Simpson *v.*, 42 Mo. 542. § 609.
Wright *v.*, 74 Me. 92. § 505.
Blutcher *v.* Stewart, 11 Mees. & Wels. 857. § 86.
Blydenburgh *v.* Bingham, 38 N. Y. 371. § 431.
Ogden *v.*, 1 Hilton (N. Y.), 182. § 28.
Blythe, Hagood *v.* (Cir. Ct. D. S. C.), 37 Fed. Rep. 249. § 595.
Boaler *v.* Mayor, 19 J. Scott (N. R.), 76. § 376.
Board Commissioners, Davis *v.*, 72 N. C. 441. § 225.
Driskill *v.*, 53 Ind. 532. § 606.
v. Jameson, 86 Ind. 154. §§ 227, 238.
Lewis *v.*, 70 Ga. 486. § 408.
Board of Education *v.* Cain, 28 W. Va. 758. § 591.
v. Fonda, 77 N. Y. 350. § 545.
v. Jewell, 44 Minn. 427. § 558.
v. Quick, 99 N. Y. 138. § 554.
Reed *v.*, 39 Ohio St. 635. § 597.
v. Thompson, 33 Ohio St. 321. §§ 3, 14.
Board Police Clark Co. *v.* Covington, 26 Miss. 470. §§ 344, 370.
Board School Directors *v.* Brown, 33 La. Ann. 383. §§ 11, 555.
Eastin & Breaux *v.*, 40 La. Ann. 705. § 590.
Board of Supervisors *v.* Alford, 65 Miss. 63. § 544.
v. Bristol, 15 Hun (N. Y.), 116. §§ 624, 628.
Board of Supervisors *v.* Clark, 92 N. Y. 391. § 548.
v. Ehlers, 45 Wis. 281. § 542.
v. Hall, 47 Wis. 208. § 597.
v. Jones, 19 Wis. 51. § 557.
v. Otis, 62 N. Y. 88. § 555.
v. Pabst, 70 Wis. 352. § 542.
Board of Trustees *v.* Boker, 34 Ill. App. 620. § 596.
Cassady *v.*, 93 Ill. 394. § 257.
Ladd *v.*, 80 Ill. 233. § 406.
Neil *v.*, 31 Ohio St. 15, 41. §§ 137, 644.
Potter *v.*, 11 Bradw. (Ill. App.) 280. § 543.
Boardman, Gillighan *v.*, 29 Me. 79. §§ 15, 82, 202.
v. Larrabee, 51 Conn. 39. § 342.
v. Spooner, 13 Allen, 353. §§ 80, 90.
Boatmen's Savings Bank *v.* Johnson, 24 Mo. App. 316. § 147.
Boatt *v.* Brown, 13 Ohio St. 364. § 379.
Boaz, Elliott *v.*, 13 Ala. 535. § 415.
Bobb & Alexander, State *v.*, 39 Mo. App. 543. § 503.
Bobbitt *v.* Shryer, 70 Ind. 513, 516. §§ 258, 261, 265.
Bobo *v.* Vaiden, 20 S. C. 271. § 581.
Bocard *v.* State, 79 Ind. 270. § 624.
Bochmer *v.* County of Schuylkill, 46 Pa. St. 452. § 522.
Bockenstedt *v.* Perkins, 73 Iowa, 23. § 546.
Bockholt *v.* Kraft, 78 Iowa, 661. § 35.
Boddam, East India Company *v.*, 9 Ves., 464. § 141.
Bodey, Holt *v.*, 18 Pa. St. 207. § 434.
Bodman, Andre *v.*, 13 Md. 241. § 62.
Bodman & Co., Fishback *v.*, 14 Bush (Ky.), 117. §§ 305, 308.
Boeckeler, Tolle, Ex'x, *v.*, 12 Mo. App. 54. §§ 268, 324.
Boeckner, United States *v.*, 21 Wall. 652. § 396.
Boehm *v.* Campbell, 3 Moore, 15. § 84.
v. Campbell, 8 Taunt. 679. § 84.

Boehme *v.* Murphy, 46 Mo. 57. § 158.
Bogarth *v.* Breedlove, 39 Tex. 561. § 381.
Boggs *v.* State, 46 Tex. 10. §§ 558, 611.
Bogue *v.* Melick, 25 Ill. 91. § 178.
Bohannon *v.* Combs, 12 B. Mon. (Ky.) 563. § 262.
Bohlens, Muller *v.*, 2 Wash. C. C. 378. § 71.
Boice *v.* Main, 4 Denio, 55. § 570.
Boisseau, Bank of Virginia *v.*, 12 Leigh (Va.), 387. § 328.
Boker, Blackburne *v.*, 1 Pa. Law Jour. Rep. 15. § 102.
Bold, London Assurance Co. *v.*, 6 Adol. & Ell. (N. S.) 514. § 118.
Boling *v.* Young, 38 Ohio St. 135. § 342.
Bolling *v.* Doneghy, 1 Duvall (Ky.), 220. § 290.
Lyon *v.*, 9 Ala. 463. § 310.
Bollman *v.* Pasewalk, 22 Neb. 761. § 152.
Boltz's Estate, 133 Pa. St. 77. §§ 318, 320.
Bomar *v.* Wilson, 1 Bailey, Law (S. C.), 461. § 519.
Bond *v.* Armstrong, 88 Ind. 65. § 330.
Horton *v.*, 28 Gratt. (Va.) 815. § 237.
Pipkin *v.*, 5 Ired. Eq. (N. C.) 91. § 342.
v. Ray, 5 Humph. (Tenn.) 492. § 576.
State *v.*, 121 Ind. 187. § 529.
Thompson *v.*, 1 Camp. 4. § 73.
Bonde, Bartlow *v.*, 3 Dana (Ky.), 591. § 436.
Bondie *v.* Bourassa, 46 Mich. 321. § 616.
Bone *v.* Torrey, 16 Ark. 83. §§ 211, 633.
Bonham *v.* Galloway, 13 Ill. 68. § 322.
Bonine *v.* Denniston, 41 Mich. 292. § 3.
Bonner, Tatum *v.*, 27 Miss. 760. § 105.
v. Young, 68 Ala. 35. § 588.
Bonney *v.* Bonney, 29 Iowa, 448. § 426.
v. Seely, 2 Wend. 481. §§ 211, 212.
Bonsal *v.* Harker, 2 Har. (Del.) 327. § 506.
Bonser *v.* Cox, 4 Beav. 379. § 403.
v. Cox, 6 Beav. 110. § 123.
Bonta *v.* Curry, 3 Bush (Ky.), 678. § 441.
v. Mercer County Court, 7 Bush (Ky.), 576. § 555.
Bonvillam, Verret *v.*, 32 La. Ann. 29. § 480.
Boody *v.* United States, 1 Woodb. & M. 150. § 548.
Boomer, Braley *v.*, 116 Mass. 527. § 472.
Boon, State *v.*, 44 Mo. 254. § 118.
Boone Co. *v.* Jones, 54 Iowa, 699. §§ 22, 413, 517, 555, 628, 642.
v. Jones, 58 Iowa, 373. § 257.
Boorman, Oakley *v.*, 21 Wend. 588. §§ 88, 96.
Booth, Comegys *v.*, 3 Stew. 14. § 373.
v. Radford, 57 Mich. 357. § 616.
v. Storrs, 75 Ill. 438. § 407.
v. Wiley, 102 Ill. 84. § 237.
Boothby, Morley *v.*, 3 Bing. 107. §§ 82, 85.
Boothly, Morley *v.*, 10 Moore, 395. §§ 15, 17.
Borchenius, Klepper *v.* 13 Bradw. (Ill. App.) 318. § 261.
Borden *v.* Gilbert, 13 Wis. 670. § 138.
v. Houston, 2 Tex. 594. §§ 42, 550.
Bordelon, Gaillard *v.*, 35 La. Ann. 390. § 578.
v. Weymouth, 14 La. Ann. 93. § 364.
Border Grange Bank, Stovall *v.*, 78 Va. 188. §§ 227, 260.
Bordley, Buchanan *v.*, 4 Harr. & McH. (Md.) 41. § 342.
Boring, Dewitt *v.*, 123 Ind. 4. § 648.

Borland v. Curry, Irish Law Rep. (4 Q. B., C. P. & Ex.) 273. § 217.
Bornman, Belleville Savings Bank v., 124 Ill. 280. §§ 402, 405.
Borough of Elizabeth, Seiple v., 3 Dutcher (N. J.), 407. § 42.
Borst, Herrick v., 4 Hill (N. Y.), 650. § 239.
Bosman v. Akeley, 39 Mich. 710. § 98.
Bossard, Phillips v., 35 Fed. Rep. (Dist. Ct. D. S. C.) 99. § 425.
Bosson, Williams v., 11 Ohio, 62. § 185.
Bostick, Hill v., 10 Yerg. (Tenn.) 410. § 366.
Kyle v., 10 Ala. 589. § 356.
Bostock, Wardens of St. Saviors Southwark v., 5 Bos. & Pul. 175. § 168.
Boston Hat Manufactory v. Messinger, 2 Pick. 223. § 393.
Boston & Sandwich Glass Co. v. Moore, 119 Mass. 435. §§ 156, 162.
Bostwick, Camp v., 20 Ohio St. 337. § 295.
Nelson v., 5 Hill, 37. § 197.
v. Van Voorhis, 91 N. Y. 353, 363, 364. §§ 136, 422.
Boswell v. Colquitt, 73 Ga. 63. § 503.
v. Lainhart, 2 La. (Miller), 397. § 519.
Bothrill, Nothingham Hide Co. v., L. R. 8 Com. Pl. 694. § 158.
Bothwell v. Sheffield, 8 Ga. 569. § 569.
Bauar v. Macdonald, 3 H. of L. Cases, 226. § 393.
Boughton v. Bank of Orleans, 2 Barb. Ch. 458. § 280.
Bouldin, Holland v., 4 T. B. Mon. (Ky.) 147. § 507.
Boult v. Brown, 13 Ohio St. 364. § 384.
Boultbee v. Stubbs, 18 Vesey, 20. § 376.
Boulter, Bird v., 4 Barn. & Adol. 443. § 90.
Cameron v., 9 Up. Can. (C. P.) 537. § 280.
Boulware v. Hartsook's Adm'r, 83 Va. 679. §§ 31, 259.
v. Robinson, 8 Tex. 327. § 211.
Bourassa, Bondie v., 46 Mich. 321. § 616.
Bourcier & Pond, Hill & Co. v., 29 La. Ann. 841. §§ 237, 440, 447.
Bourn, English v., 7 Bush (Ky.), 138. § 609.
Bourne, Dowbiggen v., 2 Younge & Collyer (Exch.), 462. § 310.
v. Mount Holly Nat. Bank, 45 N. J. Law, 360. § 422.
v. Todd, 63 Me. 427. § 580.
Bouton, Alexander v., 55 Cal. 15. § 35.
Boutte v. Martin, 16 La. (Curry), 133. § 242.
Bovard, Simpson's Ex'rs v., 74 Pa. St. 351. §§ 381, 411.
Bovill v. Turner, 2 Chitty, 205. § 165.
Bowditch v. Green, 3 Met. (Mass.) 360. § 271.
Bowdoinham National V. B., Jenkins v., 58 Me. 275. § 441.
Bowen, Carpenter v., 42 Miss. 28. § 324.
Durand v., 73 Iowa, 573. § 101.
v. Evans, 1 Lea (Tenn.), 107. § 543.
v. Hoskins, 45 Miss. 183. § 275.
Bower v. Comm'rs of Wash., 25 Pa. St. 69. § 557.
Bowers v. Cobb, Ex'r (Cir. Ct. D. Mass.), 31 Fed. Rep. 678. §§ 45, 599.
Bowers, Adm'r, v. Fleming, 67 Ind. 541. § 531.
Bowes, Woodworth v., 5 Ind. (3 Port.) 276. § 256.
Bowker v. Bull, 1 Simons (N. S.), 29. §§ 34, 315.
Bowland, Loughridge v., 52 Miss. 546. § 207.
Bowler, Connecticut Mut. Life Ins. Co. v., 1 Holmes, 263. § 397.
Bowles, Fond du Lac Harrow Co. v., 54 Wis. 425. § 394.

Bowling *v.* Flood, 1 Lea (Tenn.), 678. § 367.
Bowls, Gray *v.*, 1 Dev. & Batt. (N. C.) 437. § 468.
Bowmaker *v.* Moore, 3 Price, 214. § 482.
Bowman *v.* Ex'rs of Herr, 1 Pen. & Watts (Pa.), 282. § 574.
Governor *v.*, 44 Ill. 499. § 371.
Riddle *v.*, 27 N. H. 236. § 208.
State *v.*, 10 Ohio, 445. § 151.
Woodbury *v.*, 14 Me. 154. § 221.
Bowne, Thompson *v.*, 39 N. J. Law (10 Vroom), 2. §§ 242, 342.
Bowser *v.* Rendell, 31 Ind. 128. §§ 266, 380.
Box, Lemmon *v.*, 20 Tex. 329. § 70.
Boyce *v.* Murphy, 94 Ind. 1. § 76.
Pride *v.*, Rice's Eq. (S. C.) 275. § 141.
Boycot, Manley *v.* § 29.
Boyd, Bailey *v.*, 75 Ind. 125. § 385.
Bell *v.*, 76 Tex. 133. § 286.
v. Bell, 69 Tex. 735. § 139.
Briggs *v.*, 37 Vt. 534. §§ 115, 260, 283.
v. Brooks, 34 Beav. 7. § 227.
v. Caldwell, 4 Rich. Law (S. C.), 117. § 580.
Collins *v.*, 14 Ala. 505. § 210.
v. Gault, 3 Bush (Ky.), 644. § 575.
Mayhew *v.*, 5 Md. 102. § 397.
McMillan *v.*, 40 Ohio St. 35. § 571.
v. Moyle, 2 Com. B. 644. § 17.
v. Myers, 12 Lea (Tenn.), 175. § 318.
Pickett *v.*, 11 Lea (Tenn.), 498. § 480.
Rathbone *v.*, 30 Kan. 485. § 487.
v. Snyder, 49 Md. 325. §§ 81, 193, 194.
Steele *v.*, 6 Leigh (Va.), 547. § 359.
v. Swing, 38 Miss. 182. § 521.
v. Titzer, 6 Cold. (Tenn.) 568. § 606.
United States *v.*, 5 How. 29. § 628.
Boyd, United States *v.*, 15 Pet. 187. § 526.
Williams *v.*, 75 Ind. 286. §§ 36, 347.
Boyd's Adm'r, Hailey *v.*, 64 Ala. 399. §§ 574, 577.
Boydell *v.* Drummond, 11 East, 142. § 80.
Boyden *v.* United States, 13 Wall. 17. § 558.
Boyer, Burr *v.*, 2 Neb. 265. § 445.
Johnson *v.*, 3 Watts (Pa.), 376. § 493.
Morgan *v.*, 39 Ohio St. 324. § 165.
Boykin *v.* Dohlonde, 1 Sel. Cas. Ala. 502. § 76.
Boyle *v.* Bradley, 26 Up. Can. (C. P.) 373. § 171.
Corprew *v.*, 24 Gratt. (Va.) 284. § 542.
v. St. John, 28 Hun (N. Y.), 454. § 573.
Boyles, Jackson *v.*, 64 Iowa, 428. § 383.
Boynton, Beach *v.*, 26 Vt. 725. § 604.
Nelson *v.*, 3 Met. (Mass.) 396. §§ 64, 68.
v. Phelps, 52 Ill. 210. § 477.
v. Pierce, 79 Ill. 145. §§ 176, 182.
v. Robb, 22 Ill. 525. § 477.
Turrill *v.*, 23 Vt. 142. §§ 356, 359.
Brachman, Rutherford *v.*, 40 Ohio St. 604. §§ 346, 377.
Bracken Co. Com'rs *v.* Daum, 80 Ky. 388. § 518.
Brackenridge, Lewis *v.*, 1 Blackf. (Ind.) 112. § 504.
Brackett, Hall *v.*, 62 N. H. 509. §§ 172, 396, 642.
v. Rich, 23 Minn. 485. §§ 98, 198.
Bradbear, Blagden *v.*, 12 Ves. 466. § 90.
Bradbury *v.* Morgan, 1 Hurl. & Colt. 249. § 133.
Bradford *v.* Consaulus, 3 Cow. 128. § 500.
v. Frederick, 101 Pa. St. 445. § 481.

Bradford, Hawley v., 9 Paige, 200. § 35.
Jones v., 25 Ind. 305. § 286.
Sawyer v., 6 Ala. 572. § 438.
Scott v., 5 Port. (Ala.) 443. § 607.
Bradford, Adm'r, v. Marvin, 2 Fla. 463. § 316.
Bradley, Boyle v., 26 Up. Can. (C. P.) 373. § 171.
v. Burwell, 3 Denio, 61. § 284.
v. Cary, 8 Greenl. (Me.) 234. § 189.
Churchill v., 58 Vt. 403. § 14.
Derossett v., 63 N. C. 17. § 281.
v. Kesee, 5 Cold. (Tenn.) 223. § 414.
Lewis v., 2 Ired. Law (N. C.), 303. § 189.
McKnight v., 10 Rich. Eq. (S. C.) 557. § 224.
Parker v., 2 Hill (N. Y.), 584. §§ 17, 151.
v. Richardson, 23 Vt. 720. § 71.
Ryan v., Taylor, Law & Eq. (N. C.) 77. § 505.
Seaver v., 6 Greenl. (Me.) 60. § 203.
Bradner v. Garrett, 19 La. (Curry), 455. § 29.
Bradshaw v. Combs, 102 Ill. 428. § 360.
McDonald v., 2 Kelly (Ga.), 248. § 537.
Bradwell v. Spencer, 16 Ga. 578. § 639.
Brady, Morrow v., 12 R. I. 130. § 109.
v. Peiper, 1 Hilton (N. Y.), 61. § 405.
v. Reynolds, 13 Cal. 31. §§ 177, 391.
v. Sackrider, 1 Sandf. (N. Y.) 514. § 76.
Bragg v. Patterson, 85 Ala. 233. §§ 254, 311.
v. Shain, 49 Cal. 131. § 397.
Braiden v. Mercer, 44 Ohio St. 339. § 632.
Brainard v. Jones, 18 N. Y. 35. § 112.
v. Reynolds, 36 Vt. 614. § 98.
Braley v. Boomer, 116 Mass. 527. § 472.
Braman v. Howk, 1 Blackf. 392. § 356.
Bramble, Hall v., 2 Dak. 189. § 578.
v. Ward, 40 Ohio St. 267. § 347.
Bramblett, Rodenburger v., 78 Ind. 213. § 329.
Bramhall, Hoy v., 4 C. E. Green (N. Y.), 563. § 34.
Bramlett, Koenig v., 20 Mo. App. 636. § 199.
Bramley v. Wilds, 9 Lea (Tenn.), 674. § 532.
Bramwell v. Farmer, 1 Taunton, 427. § 512.
Branch, Belcher v., 11 R. I. 226. § 577.
Commonwealth v., 1 Bush (Ky.), 59. §§ 501, 502.
v. Commonwealth, 2 Call (Va.), 510. § 528.
v. Macon & Brunswick R. R. Co., 2 Woods, 385. § 324.
Warren v., 15 W. Va. 21, 26. § 419.
Branch Bank, Houston v., 25 Ala. 250. § 316.
Mauldin v., 2 Ala. 502. § 18.
Branch Bank of Mobile, Bates v., 2 Ala. 689. § 604.
Cullum v., 23 Ala. 797. § 324.
Hooks v., 8 Ala. 580. § 448.
v. James, 9 Ala. 949. §§ 29, 342.
Winter v., 23 Ala. 762. § 448.
Brand v. Whelan, 18 Bradw. (Ill. App.) 186. § 59.
Brandenburg v. Flynn's Ex'r, 12 B. Mon. (Ky.) 397. § 262.
Brandon v. Medley, 1 Jones' Eq. (N. C.) 313. 271.
Kerr v., 84 N. C. 128. § 531.
Brand's Adm'r, Warfield v., 13 Bush (Ky.), 77. § 586.
Brandt, Sharman v., 40 Law Jour. (N. S.) 312. § 90.
Brant v. Green, 6 Leigh (Va.), 16. § 90.
Brash & Son, Eckman & Vetsburg v., 20 Fla. 763. § 104.

Brassfield, Commonwealth *v.*, 7 B. Mon. (Ky.) 447. § 624.
Brather *v.* Gammon, 25 Kan. 397. § 357.
Braught *v.* Griffith, 16 Iowa, 26. § 304.
Brawer, Chamberlain *v.*, 3 Bush (Ky.), 561. § 412.
Bray, Horn *v.*, 51 Ind. 555. § 60.
v. Marsh, 75 Me. 452. §§ 49, 184, 204.
Moore *v.*, 10 Pa. St. 519. § 309.
Brayton *v.* Towns, 12 Iowa, 346. § 570.
Breckenridge *v.* Taylor, 5 Dana (Ky.), 110. §§ 255, 283, 288, 635.
Breden, County of Fontenac *v.*, 17 Grant's Ch. 645. §§ 526, 555.
Breed *v.* Hillhouse, 7 Conn. 523. §§ 16, 193, 204.
Breedlove, Bogarth *v.*, 39 Tex. 561. § 381.
Breese *v.* Schuler, 48 Ill. 329. § 236.
First Nat. Bank of Fort Dodge *v.*, 39 Iowa, 329. § 236.
Bremridge, Evans *v.*, 2 Kay & Johns. 174. § 402.
Brengle *v.* Bushey, 40 Md. 141. § 367.
Creager *v.*, 5 Harr. & Johns. (Md.) 234. § 323.
Brennan, Stinson *v.*, Cheves' Law (S. C.), 15. § 214.
Brenner, Ray *v.*, 12 Kan. 105. § 448.
Brent *v.* Green, 6 Leigh (Va.), 16. § 90.
Heidenheimer Bros. *v.*, 59 Tex. 533. § 571.
Breslauer, Allen *v.*, 8 Cal., 552. § 507.
Bresler *v.* Pendell, 12 Mich. 224. § 76.
Brett, Wood *v.*, 9 Grant's Ch. 452. § 147.
Brettel *v.* Williams, 4 Wels., Hurl. & G. 623. §§ 18, 80, 87.
Brevard, Lang *v.*, 3 Strob. Eq. (S. C.) 59. § 445.
Mushat *v.*, 4 Dev. (N. C.) 73. § 52.
v. Wylie, 1 Rich. Law (S. C.), 38. § 632.
Brewer *v.* Franklin Mills, 42 N. H. 292. § 304.
Ladd *v.*, 17 Kan. 204. § 483.
v. Knapp, 1 Pick. 332. § 108.
Mobile & Montgomery R'y Co. *v.*, 76 Ala. 135. §§ 342, 359.
Brewster *v.* Baker, 97 Ind. 260. § 14.
v. Cowen, 55 Conn. 152. § 516.
Lewis *v.*, 2 McLean, 121. §§ 201, 203.
v. Silence, 8 N. Y. 207. §§ 84, 88.
Worthan *v.*, 30 Ga. 112. § 355.
Breyfogle, People *v.*, 17 Cal. 504. § 151.
Briant, Claflin *v.*, 58 Ga. 414. § 186.
Brick *v.* Freehold National Banking Co., 8 Vroom (N. J.), 307. §§ 440, 441.
Brickett, Commonwealth *v.*, 8 Pick. 138. § 496.
Brickhead *v.* Brown, 5 Hill (N. Y.), 634. § 397.
v. Brown, 2 Denio, 375. § 397.
Brickinden, Tolhurst *v.*, Cro. Jac. 250. § 16.
Brickwood *v.* Anniss, 5 Taunt. 614. § 493.
Bridgam, Hunt *v.*, 2 Pick. 581. § 143.
Bridge, Bigelow *v.*, 8 Mass. 275. § 168.
Bridge's Adm'r *v.* Blake, 106 Ind. 332. § 148.
Bridges *v.* Phillips, 17 Tex. 128. § 154.
Bridgham, Hunt *v.*, 2 Pick. 581. § 342.
Brien *v.* Smith, 9 Watts & Serg. (Pa.) 78. § 315.
Briggs, Baker *v.*, 8 Pick. 122. §§ 62, 180, 182, 243, 245, 425.
v. Boyd, 37 Vt. 534. §§ 115, 260, 283.
v. Evans, 1 E. D. Smith (N. Y.), 192. § 77.
Gleason *v.*, 28 Vt. 135. § 62.
v. Hinton, 14 Lea (Tenn.), 233. §§ 267, 463, 571, 572.
Lamb *v.*, 22 Neb. 138. § 14.
v. Latham, 36 Kan. 205. § 13.

Briggs *v.* Law, 4 Johns. Ch. 22. § 405.
Lee *v.*, 39 Mich. 592. § 204.
v. Norris, 67 Mich. 325. §§ 99, 346.
Whipple *v.*, 28 Vt. 65. § 209.
Whipple *v.*, 30 Vt. 111. § 228.
Brigham *v.* Wentworth, 11 Cush. 123. § 398.
Bright *v.* Lennon, 83 N. C. 183. §§ 254, 257, 267, 283.
v. McKnight, 1 Sneed (Tenn.), 158. § 194.
State *v.*, 14 S. C. 7. §§ 508, 510.
Briley *v.* Sugg, 1 Dev. & Bat. Eq. (N. C.) 366. § 312.
Brillhart, McConnell *v.*, 17 Ill. 354. §§ 89, 90.
Brinagar's Adm'r *v.* Phillips, 1 B. Mon. (Ky.) 283. § 342.
Brink *v.* Reid, 122 Ind. 257. § 377.
Sears *v.*, 3 Johns. 210. § 82.
Brinker, Woolworth *v.*, 11 Ohio St. 593. §§ 361, 372.
Brinkerhoff, Parks *v.*, 2 Hill (N. Y.), 663. § 26.
Brinsley, Prescott *v.*, 6 Cush. 233. § 115.
Brinson *v.* Thomas, 2 Jones' Eq. (N. C.) 414. § 317.
Brinton *v.* Gerry, 7 Bradw. (Ill. App.) 238. 434.
Brisbin, County Com. of Ramsey Co. *v.*, 17 Minn. 451. § 521.
Haight *v.*, 100 N. Y. 219. § 578.
Briscoe, Givens *v.*, 3 J. J. Marsh. (Ky.) 529. §§ 252, 358.
Huddleston *v.*, 11 Vesey, 583. §§ 80, 89.
Brisendine *v.* Martin, 1 Ired. Law (N. C.), 286. § 286.
Brison, West *v.*, 99 Mo. 684. §§ 40, 245, 370.
Bristol, Board Supervisors *v.*, 15 Hun (N. Y.), 116. §§ 624, 628.
Bristow *v.* Brown, 13 Irish Com. Law Rep. 201. § 250.
British American Assurance Co. *v.* Neil, 76 Iowa, 645. § 602.
Britt, Prince *v.*, 8 Heisk. (Tenn.) 290. § 524.
Britton *v.* Dierker, 46 Mo. 591. § 379.
Ellett *v.*, 10 Tex. 208. § 82.
State *v.*, 102 Ind. 214. § 113.
v. State, 115 Ind. 55. § 113.
Broad *v.* City of Paris, 66 Tex. 119. §§ 542, 628.
Broadbent, Liversidge *v.*, 4 Hurl. & Nor. 603. § 66.
Broadhead, United States *v.*, 127 U. S. 212. § 112.
Brobst *v.* Skillen, 16 Ohio St. 382. § 537.
Brock, Kinyon *v.*, 72 N. C. 554. § 101.
Parham Sew. Mach. Co. *v.*, 113 Mass. 194. §§ 114, 118.
Selser *v.*, 3 Ohio St. 302. §§ 379, 412.
Turnbull *v.*, 31 Ohio St. 649. § 353.
Brockett *v.* Martin, 11 Kan. 378. § 563.
Brodie *v.* St. Paul, 1 Vesey, Jr., 326. § 80.
Brokam *v.* Field, 33 Ill. App. 138. § 34.
Bronaugh *v.* Neal, 1 Rob. (La.) 23. § 236.
Brooke, Brooks *v.*, 12 Gill & Johns. (Md.) 306. § 141.
Wynn *v.*, 5 Rawle (Pa.), 106. § 217.
Brooking *v.* Farmers' Bank, 83 Ky. 431. § 245.
Brookins *v.* Shumway, 18 Wis. 98. § 359.
Brooks *v.* Allen, 62 Ind. 401. § 344.
v. Baker, 9 Daly (N. Y. Com. Pl.), 398. § 95.
Boyd *v.*, 34 Beav. 7. § 227.
v. Brooke, 12 Gill & Johns. (Md.) 306. § 141.
v. Carter, 36 Ala. 682. § 239.
Chase *v.*, 5 Cush. 43. § 343.
Chilton *v.* (Md. 1890), 20 Atl. Rep. 125. § 37.
Coburn *v.*, 78 Cal. 443. §§ 199, 589.
Fowler *v.*, 13 N. H. 240. §§ 347, 354.

Brooks *v.* Governor, 17 Ala. 806. § 535.
Haigh *v.*, 10 Adol. & Ell. 309. § 86.
Harris *v.*, 21 Pick. 195. §§ 29, 60, 245.
v. Hope, 139 Mass. 351. § 582.
v. Miller, 29 W. Va. 499. § 573.
v. People, 15 Bradw. (Ill. App.) 570. § 632.
v. Shepherd, 4 Bibb (Ky.), 572. § 488.
v. Whitmore, 139 Mass. 356. § 540.
v. Whitmore, 142 Mass. 399. § 585.
v. Wright, 13 Allen, 72. § 351.
York Co. M. F. Ins. Co. *v.*, 51 Me. 506. §§ 408, 412.
Brooksheir, Police Jury Vermillion Parish *v.*, 31 La. Ann. 736. §§ 175, 523.
Brookshire, Landrum *v.*, 1 Stew. (Ala.) 252. § 211.
Broom *v.* Batchelor, 1 Hurl. & Nor. 255. § 84.
Oldham *v.*, 28 Ohio St. 41. § 265.
Broome *v.* United States, 15 How. 143. § 527.
Broughton *v.* Robinson, 11 Ala. 922. § 295.
v. Wimberly, 65 Ala. 549. § 290.
Broune *v.* Carr, 2 Russ. 600. § 150.
Broussard, Moore *v.*, 20 Mart. (La.), 8 N. S. 277. § 342.
Browder, Thomas *v.*, 33 Tex. 783. § 565.
Brower, Salem Manuf. Co. *v.*, 4 Jones' Law (N. C.), 429. § 202.
Brown, Abbott *v.*, 30 Ill. App. 376. § 1.
v. Abbott, 110 Ill. 162. § 426.
Abbott *v.*, 131 Ill. 108. §§ 111, 137.
v. Adams, 1 Stew. (Ala.) 51. § 61.
v. Ayer, 24 Ga. 288. §§ 40, 146.
Banks *v.*, 4 Yerg. (Tenn.) 198. § 452.
Beal *v.*, 13 Allen, 114. § 227.
Birckhead *v.*, 5 Hill (N. Y.), 634. §§ 81, 116, 397.
Blest *v.*, 3 Giff. 450. § 401.
Brown, Boatt *v.*, 13 Ohio St. 364. §§ 379, 384.
Board School Directors *v.*, 33 La. Ann. 383. §§ 11, 555.
Brickhead *v.*, 2 Denio, 375. § 397.
Bristow *v.*, 13 Irish Com. Law Rep. 201. § 250.
v. Brown, 47 Mo. 130. § 17.
v. Brown, 17 Ind. 475. § 614.
v. Burrows, 2 Blatch. 340. § 112.
Canal & Banking Co. *v.*, 4 La. Ann. 545. §§ 408, 638.
v. Chambers, 63 Tex. 131. § 438.
Christner *v.*, 16 Iowa, 130. §§ 34, 352.
Church *v.*, 21 N. Y. 315. § 84.
Church *v.*, 29 Barb. (N. Y.) 486. § 85.
v. Colquitt, 73 Ga. 59. § 516.
v. Commonwealth, 114 Pa. St. 335. §§ 603, 623.
Corporation of Welland *v.*, 4 Ont. (Can.) 217. § 629.
Cox *v.*, 6 Jones' Law (N. C.), 100. § 197.
Crapo *v.*, 40 Iowa, 487. § 131.
v. Curtis, 2 N. Y. 225. §§ 67, 102.
Curtis *v.*, 5 Cush. (Mass.) 488. §§ 62, 64.
v. Davenport, 76 Ga. 799. § 414.
v. Dillahunty, 4 Sm. & Mar. (Miss.) 713. § 498.
Dunbar *v.*, 4 McLean, 166. § 197.
Ellis *v.*, 6 Barb. 282. § 179.
v. Ex'rs of Riggins, 3 Kelly (Ga.), 405. §§ 40, 434, 438.
Foote *v.*, 2 McLean, 396. § 197.
v. Gibbons, 37 Iowa, 654. § 428.
Gossin *v.*, 11 Pa. St. 527. § 315.
Gray *v.*, 1 Rich. Law (S. C.), 351. § 576.
Gray's Ex'rs *v.*, 22 Ala. 262. §§ 235, 345.
v. Grover, 6 Bush (Ky.), 1. § 642.
Haden *v.*, 18 Ala. 641. §§ 239, 342.
v. Haggerty, 26 Ill. 469. §§ 29, 337.
Halstead *v.*, 17 Ind. 202. §§ 242, 355.

Brown, Hunt *v.*, 5 Hill, 145. § 88.
Hurley *v.*, 98 Mass. 545. § 81.
Jaffray *v.*, 74 N. Y. 393. § 17.
v. Jessup, 19 Oreg. 288. § 10.
Johnson *v.*, 51 Ga. 498. § 117.
Jones *v.*, 11 Ohio St. 601. § 362.
Kennedy *v.*, 21 Kan., 171. § 481.
v. Kidd, 34 Miss. 291. § 225.
Kinloch *v.*, 1 Rich. (S. C.) 223. § 78.
Kinloch *v.*, 2 Spear's Law (S. C.), 284. § 75.
v. Kirk, 20 Mo. App. 524. §§ 37, 315, 342.
Krutsinger *v.*, 72 Ind. 466. § 648.
v. Lang, 4 Ala. 50. § 318.
Latham *v.*, 16 Iowa, 118. § 563.
v. Lattimore, 17 Cal. 93. § 539.
Lee *v.*, 21 Kan. 458. § 628.
Leroux *v.*, 12 Com. B. 801. § 52.
Lonsdale *v.*, 4 Wash. 148. § 16.
Mann *v.*, 71 Tex. 241. § 356.
Melton *v.*, 25 Fla. 461. § 180.
Merrimack County Bank *v.*, 12 N. H. 320. §§ 330, 345, 347.
v. McDonald, 8 Yerg. (Tenn.) 158. § 280.
People *v.*, 2 Doug. (Mich.) 9. § 385.
v. People, 24 Ill. App. 72. § 509.
v. Phipps, 6 Sm. & Mar. (Miss.) 51. § 533.
Pike *v.*, 7 Cush. 133. §§ 53, 72.
v. Probate Judge, 42 Mich. 501. § 410.
v. Prophit, 53 Miss. 649. §§ 356, 397.
v. Ray, 18 N. H. 102. § 268.
v. Reasner, 5 Bradw. (Ill. App.) 45. § 176.
Riggins *v.*, 12 Ga. 271. § 345.
Risley *v.*, 67 N. Y. 160. § 139.
v. Roberts, 9 La. Ann. 256. § 359.
Russell *v.*, 21 Mo. App. 51. §§ 351, 376.
Seeley *v.*, 14 Pick. 177. § 505.
Shepherd *v.*, 30 W. Va. 13. § 569.
v. Sneed, 77 Tex. 471. §§ 548, 555.
v. State, 6 Tex. App. 188. § 510.
Brown *v.* State, 18 Tex. App. 326. §§ 408, 493.
State *v.*, 11 Ired. Law (N. C.), 141. § 566.
v. State, 23 Kan. 235. §§ 540, 546.
State *v.*, 16 Iowa, 314. §§ 502, 505.
State *v.*, 80 Ind. 425. § 585.
v. Strait, 19 Ill. 88. § 66.
v. Taber, 5 Wend. 566. § 115.
Ten Eyck *v.*, 3 Pinney (Wis.), 452. §§ 49, 138, 199.
Water Power Co. *v.*, 23 Kan. 676. § 205.
v. Weatherby, 71 Mo. 152. § 385.
Wheeler & Wilson Mfg. Co. *v.*, 65 Wis. 99. § 394.
v. Will, 103 Ind. 71. § 7.
Wilson *v.*, 2 Beasley (N. J.), 277. § 298.
Woolsey *v.*, 74 N. Y. 82. § 7.
v. Wright, 7 T. B. Mon. (Ky.) 396. § 234.
Yancey *v.*, 3 Sneed (Tenn.), 89. § 196.
Young *v.*, 53 Wis. 333. §§ 84, 159.
Brown's Adm'r, Giles *v.*, 60 Ga. 658. § 579.
Brown & Co. *v.* Rathburn, 10 Oreg. 158. § 427.
Browne, Beattie *v.*, 64 Ill. 360. § 182.
v. Carr, 7 Bing. 508. § 430.
Wolfe *v.*, 5 Ohio St. 304. § 202.
Brownell, Atlas Bank *v.*, 9 R. I. 168. §§ 420, 423, 625.
Brownelow *v.* Forbes, 2 Johns. 101. § 494.
Browning *v.* Fountain, 1 Duvall (Ky.), 13. § 114.
v. Merritt, 61 Ind. 425. § 182.
Broyles *v.* Blair, 7 Yerg. (Tenn.) 279. § 484.
Brubaker *v.* Okeson, 36 Pa. St. 519. § 246.
Bruce *v.* Bickerton, 18 W. Va. 342. § 292.
v. Edwards, 1 Stew. (Ala.) 11. §§ 29, 239.
Napier *v.*, 8 Clark & Fin. 470. § 166.

Bruce *v.* United States, 17 How. 437. §§ 43, 546.
Bruen, Bell *v.*, 1 How. 169. § 92.
Bruff, Wooddell *v.*, 25 W. Va. 465. § 537.
Brugniere, Dussol *v.*, 50 Cal. 456. § 291.
Brumble *v.* Ward, 40 Ohio St. 267. § 377.
Brummitt, Ballard *v.*, 4 Strob. Eq. (S. C.) 171. § 576.
Brune, Enders *v.*, 4 Rand. (Va.) 438. § 298.
Brunel, Gallagher *v.*, 6 Cowen, 347. §§ 73, 74.
Bruner, Moore *v.*, 31 Ill. App. 400. § 288.
Brunskill, Holme *v.*, Law Rep. (3 Q. B. Div.) 495. §§ 108, 389.
Brunton *v.* Dullens, 1 Foster & Fin. 450. § 76.
Brush *v.* Carpenter, 6 Ind. 78. § 60.
v. Raney, 34 Ind. 416. § 405.
Brutton, Lake *v.*, 8 De Gex, Macn. & Gor. 440. § 307.
Bry, McGuire *v.*, 3 Rob. (La.) 190. §§ 361, 523, 554.
Bryan, Alexander *v.*, 110 U. S. 414. § 578.
v. Berry, 6 Cal. 394. §§ 20, 177.
Heart *v.*, 2 Dev. Eq. (N. C.) 147. § 298.
v. Henderson, 88 Tenn. (4 Pickle), 23. § 36.
v. Hunt, 4 Sneed, 543. § 81.
v. Kelly, 85 Ala. 569. § 624.
v. McDowell, 15 Lea (Tenn.), 581. § 287.
Sebastian *v.*, 21 Ark. 447. § 574.
Bryant, Babcock *v.*, 12 Pick. 133. § 192.
Hamilton *v.*, 114 Mass. 543. § 472.
Hancock *v.*, 2 Yerg. (Tenn.) 476. § 239.
Laythoarp *v.*, 2 Bing. N. C. 755. § 89.
v. Owen, 1 Kelly (Ga.), 355. §§ 546, 639.
Whitman *v.*, 49 Vt. 512. § 75.
Bryant, Guardian, *v.* Owen, 1 Kelly (Ga.), 355. § 639.
Bryce, Clark *v.*, 64 Ga. 486. § 408.
Osborne *v.* (Cir. Ct. E. D. Wis.), 23 Fed. Rep. 171. § 236.
Buchanan, Bennett *v.*, 3 Ind. 47. § 211.
v. Bordley, 4 Harr. & McH. (Md.) 41. § 342.
v. Clark, 10 Gratt. (Va.) 164. § 302.
Moale *v.*, 11 Gill & Johns. (Md.) 314. § 80.
Buchanan Bank, Lowen *v.*, 78 Mo. 67. § 434.
Buchard *v.* Cavins, 77 Tex. 365. § 19.
Buchtel, Lumber Co. *v.*, 101 U. S. 633. § 414.
Rowe *v.*, 13 Ind. 381. § 607.
Buck, Henrie *v.*, 39 Kan. 381. § 93.
v. Sanders, 1 Dana (Ky.), 187. § 237.
v. Smiley, 64 Ind. 431. § 377.
Buckalew *v.* Smith, 44 Ala. 638. § 239.
Buckhannon, Thompson *v.*, 2 J. J. Marsh. (Ky.) 416. §§ 12, 22.
Buckland, United States *v.* (Cir. Ct. D. S. C.), 33 Fed. Rep. 156. § 502.
Bucklen *v.* Huff, 53 Ind. 474. § 344.
Bucklin, Barber *v.*, 2 Denio, 45. §§ 66, 69, 72.
Buckles, Davis Sewing Machine Co. *v.*, 89 Ill. 237. § 406.
Buckley *v.* Beardslee, 2 South. 572. § 82.
Lawson *v.*, 49 Hun (N. Y.), 329. § 241.
Buckley's Distributees, Seawell, Adm'r, *v.*, 54 Ala. 592. § 580.
Buckman, Goodwin *v.*, 11 Iowa, 308. § 100.
Buckmaster *v.* Harrop, 7 Vesey, 341. § 90.
Bucknell, Maule *v.*, 50 Pa. St. 39. § 69.
Buckner *v.* Archer, 1 McMullan, Law (S. C.), 85. § 638.

Buckner v. Clark's Ex'r, 6 Bush, 168. § 13.
v. Morris, 2 J. J. Marsh. (Ky.) 121. § 313.
Buckner's Adm'r v. Stewart, 34 Ala. 529. § 290.
Budd, People v., 57 Cal. 349. § 515.
Shinn v., 1 McC. (N. J.) 234. § 298.
Buehler, Coe v., 110 Pa. St. 366. § 191.
Buel, Barker v., 5 Cush. 519. § 247.
v. Gordon, 6 Johns. 126. § 220.
Buffalo Co., Van Sickel v., 13 Neb. 103. §§ 546, 547, 628.
Buffington v. Smith, 58 Ga. 341. § 514.
Buford v. Cox, 3 Lea (Tenn.), 518. § 603.
v. Francisco, 3 Dana (Ky.), 68. § 226.
Bugg, State v., 6 Rob. 63. § 145.
Buie v. Wooten, 7 Jones' Law (N. C.), 441. § 491.
Building Association v. Cummings, 45 Ohio St. 664. § 27.
Bulkley, Graves v., 25 Kan. 246. §§ 636, 637.
v. Lord, 2 Stark. 406. § 127.
Bull v. Allen, 19 Conn. 101. § 29.
v. Bliss, 30 Vt. 127. §§ 100, 197.
v. Bowker, 1 Sim. (N. S.) 29. §§ 34, 315.
v. Coe, 77 Cal. 54. §§ 35, 448.
Hill v., 1 Gilm. (Va.) 149. § 342.
Pledge v., Johns. (Eng. Ch.) 663. § 461.
Bull's Head Bank, McMillan v., 32 Ind. 11. §§ 1, 195.
Bullard v. Gilette, 1 Mont. Terr. 509. § 455.
v. Ledbetter, 59 Ga. 109. § 245.
Buller, Mortlock v., 10 Vesey, 292. § 90.
Bullitt's Ex'rs v. Winstons, 1 Munf. (Va.) 269. § 373.
Bullock v. Campbell, 9 Gill (Md.), 182. §§ 207, 230.
Grubb v., 44 Ga. 379. § 506.
Bullock, Joues v., 3 Bibb (Ky.), 467. § 434.
v. Lloyd, 2 Car. & P. 119. § 60.
v. Taylor, 39 Mich. 137. § 383.
Bumpass, Heise v., 40 Ark. 545. § 181.
Bunburg, Berrien County Treasurer v., 45 Mich. 79. § 597.
Bunbury, Weiner v., 30 Mich. 201. § 615.
Bunce v. Bunce, Kirby (Conn.), 137. § 208.
Bundy, Blazer v., 15 Ohio St. 57. §§ 40, 354.
Bunker v. Ireland, 81 Me. 519. § 106.
v. Tufts, 55 Me. 180. § 209.
Bunn v. Jetmore, 70 Mo. 228. § 151.
Bunting, Draughan v., 9 Ired. Law (N. C.), 10. §§ 61, 281.
v. Ricks, 2 Dev. & Bat. Eq. (N. C.) 130. § 237.
Syme v., 91 N. C. 48. § 531.
Bunzl, Goodwin v., 102 N. Y. 224. § 449.
Burch, Cordle v., 10 Gratt. (Va.) 480. § 42.
v. Watts, 37 Tex. 135. § 473.
Burchard, Ferry v., 21 Conn. 597. § 145.
Burdett, Clark v., 2 Hall (N. Y.), 217. § 196.
v. Lowe, 22 Hun (N. Y.), 588. § 452.
Burford, Goode v., 14 La. Ann. 102. § 581.
Burfoot, Wilson v., 2 Gratt. (Va.) 134. § 523.
Burgess v. Dewey, 33 Vt. 618. § 356.
v. Eve, 13 Eq. 450. § 161.
Taylor v., 5 Hurl. & Nor. 1. § 342.
Burgett v. Paxton, 15 Bradw. (Ill. App.) 379. § 93.
v. Paxton, 99 Ill. 288. § 329.
Burghart, Lane v., 1 Adol. & Ell. (N. S.) 933. § 62.
Burk v. Chrisman, 3 B. Mon. (Ky.) 50. § 316.
May v., 80 Mo. 675. § 329.
Burkard, Delaware, L. & W. R. R. Co. v., 114 N. Y. 197. § 95.

Burke *v.* Cruger, 8 Tex. 66. §§ 30, 367.
v. Glover, 21 Up. Can. (Q. B.) 294. § 482.
v. Pinnell, 93 Ind. 540. § 645.
Turton *v.*, 4 Wis. 119. § 77.
Whiting *v.*, Law Rep. 6 Ch. App. Cas. 342. § 256.
Burkhalter, Starret *v.*, 86 Ind. 439. § 352.
Burkhard, Delaware, Lack. & W. R. R. Co. *v.*, 36 Hun (N. Y.), 57. §§ 161, 343.
Burkhart, People *v.*, 76 Cal. 607. §§ 588, 589.
Burkholder, Stickler *v.*, 47 Pa. St. 476. § 240.
Burks *v.* Wonterline, 6 Bush (Ky.), 20. § 417.
Burlingame, Crist *v.*, 62 Barb. (N. Y.) 351. §§ 92, 160.
Hartman *v.*, 9 Cal. 557. §§ 29, 242.
Talmage *v.*, 9 Pa. St. 21. § 358.
Burlington Ins. Co. *v.* Johnson, 120 Ill. 622. § 93.
v. Johnston, 24 Ill. App. 565. § 602.
Burnap *v.* Nat. Bank of Potsdam, 96 N. Y. 125. § 34.
v. Robertson, 75 Ga. 689. § 416.
Burnell, Gwynne *v.*, 7 Clark & Finnelly, 572. § 547.
Burnet *v.* Courts, 5 Harr. & Johns. (Md.) 78. § 336.
Burnett *v.* Henderson, 21 Tex. 588. § 521.
v. Millsaps, 59 Miss. 333. §§ 257, 264.
Burney, Wilson *v.*, 8 Neb. 39. § 329.
Burnham *v.* Choat, 5 Up. Can. K. B. (O. S.) 736. § 291.
v. Gallentine, 11 Ind. 295. § 102.
State *v.*, 44 Me. 278. § 500.
Burns, Bank of Albion *v.*, 46 N. Y. 170. §§ 35, 342.
Cave *v.*, 6 Ala. 780. § 282.
v. Huntington Bank, 1 Pen. & Watts (Pa.), 395. § 310.
Ketchell *v.*, 24 Wend. 456. § 47.
Burns *v.* Parish, 3 B. Mon. (Ky.) 8. §§ 211, 216.
v. Parks, 53 Ga. 61. § 233.
Savage *v.*, 3 Mont. 527. § 601.
v. Semmes, 4 Cranch (Cir. Ct.), 702. § 186.
Burns' Adm'r, Ayers *v.*, 87 Ind. 245. § 227.
Burr *v.* Boyer, 2 Neb. 265. § 445.
Burroughs *v.* Lott, 19 Cal. 125. § 288.
v. United States, 2 Paine, 569. § 324.
Burrows, Barber *v.*, 51 Cal. 404. § 370.
Brown *v.*, 2 Blatch. 340. § 112.
v. McWhann, 1 Des. Eq. (S. C.) 409. § 309.
Burrus, Thomas *v.*, 23 Miss. 550. § 46.
Burson *v.* Andes, 83 Va. 445. § 93.
v. Kincaid, 3 Pen. & Watts (Pa.), 57. § 154.
Burt *v.* McFadden, 58 Ill. 479. § 399.
v. Horner, 5 Barb. (N. Y.) 501. §§ 98, 101.
Burtis, Adm'r, *v.* Wait, 33 Kan. 478. § 150.
Burton *v.* Hansford, 10 W. Va. 470. §§ 181, 182.
Hunt *v.*, 18 Ark. 188. § 480.
Mason *v.*, 54 Ill. 349. § 182.
v. Mill, 78 Va. 468. § 298.
Mitchell *v.*, 2 Head (Tenn.), 613. §§ 385, 439.
Parish of St. Helena *v.*, 35 La. Ann. 521. § 521.
Ross *v.*, 4 Up. Can. (Q. B.) 357. § 157.
v. Rutherford, Adm'r, 49 Mo. 255. § 230.
Tunnell *v.*, 4 Del. Ch. 382. § 580.
Weeks *v.*, 7 Vt. 67. § 73.
Burwell, Bradley *v.*, 3 Denio, 61. § 284.
Bush, Clark *v.*, 3 Cow. 151. § 112.
v. Critchfield, 5 Ohio, 109. § 132.
Dempsey *v.*, 18 Ohio St. 376. § 310.
Donley *v.*, 44 Tex. 1. § 184.

Bush, Greer *v.*, 57 Miss. 575. § 121.
v. Stamps, 26 Miss. 463. § 326.
Van Slyck *v.*, 123 N. Y. 47. § 593.
Bushee *v.* Allen, 31 Vt. 631. § 76.
Bushell, Beavan *v.*, 1 Bing. N. C. 103. §§ 64, 74, 85.
Bushey, Brengle *v.*, 40 Md. 141. § 367.
Bushnell *v.* Church, 15 Conn. 406. §§ 193, 195, 626.
Bushong *v.* Taylor, 82 Mo. 660. §§ 212, 230, 329.
Buss, Pledge *v.*, Johnson (Eng. Ch.), 663. § 426.
Bussell, Page *v.*, 2 Maule & Sel. 551. § 220.
Bussier *v.* Chew, 5 Phil. (Pa.) 70. §§ 117, 162.
Buster, People *v.*, 11 Cal. 215. § 540.
Butcher, Fernan *v.*, 113 Pa. St. 292. § 469.
v. Stewart, 11 Mees. & Wels. 857. § 62.
Butler, Barksdale *v.*, 6 Lea (Tenn.), 450. § 631.
v. Birkey, 13 Ohio St. 514. § 266.
v. Bissel, 1 Root (Conn.), 102. § 506.
v. Butler's Adm'r, 8 W. Va. 674. § 212.
Capel *v.*, 2 Sim. & Stu. 457. § 445.
Grimes *v.*, 1 Bibb (Ky.), 192. § 519.
Guild *v.*, 127 Mass. 386. §§ 426, 431.
v. Hamilton, 2 Des. Eq. (S. C.) 226. § 342.
Hoffman *v.*, 105 Ind. 371. § 302.
Knotts *v.*, 10 Rich. Eq. (S. C.) 143. §§ 133, 295.
People *v.*, 74 Mich. 643. §§ 569, 594.
v. Rawson, 1 Denio, 105. § 138.
Sheldon *v.*, 24 Minn. 513. § 67.
v. State, 20 Ind. 169. § 537.
v. Sugarloaf, 6 Pa. St. 262. § 131.
v. United States, 21 Wall. 274. § 408.
Buttles, Starling *v.*, 2 Ohio, 303. § 607.
Buzzell, Farmington Savings Bank *v.*, 61 N. H. 612. § 20.
Byers *v.* Alcorn, 6 Bradw. (Ill. App.) 39. § 276.
v. Harris, 67 Iowa, 685. § 342.
v. Hussey, 4 Col. 515. § 342.
v. McClanahan, 6 Gill & Johns. (Md.) 250. §§ 60, 264, 292.
Byrne *v.* Ætna Ins. Co., 56 Ill. 321. § 97.
v. Muzio, Law Rep. Irish (8 Q. B., C. P. & Ex.), 396. § 423.
Byron, People *v.*, 3 Johns. Cas. 531, 574. § 573.
Caballero *v.* Slater, 14 Com. B. (5 J. Scott), 300. § 84.
Cabot, Hayden *v.*, 17 Mass. 169. § 213.
Cabot Bank *v.* Morton, 4 Gray, 156. § 28.
Cadwell *v.* Randall, 36 Mich. 251. § 492.
Cady *v.* Sheldon, 38 Barb. (N. Y.) 103. § 98.
Cage *v.* Foster, 5 Yerg. (Tenn.) 261. § 293.
Cahill *v.* Bigelow, 18 Pick. 369. §§ 75, 76.
Cahill's Appeal, 48 Mich. 616. § 152.
Cahn, Heintz *v.*, 29 Ill. 308. § 176.
Cailleux *v.* Hall, 1 E. D. Smith (N. Y.), 5. § 66.
Cain *v.* Bates, Adm'r, 35 Mo. 427. § 448.
Board of Education *v.*, 28 W. Va. 758. § 591.
v. Williams, 16 Nev. 426. § 439.
Cairnes' Adm'r, Mendel *v.*, 84 Ind. 141. § 618.
Cake *v.* Lewis, 8 Pa. St. 493. § 220.
Caldwell, Boyd *v.*, 4 Rich. Law (S. C.), 117. § 580.
v. Gaus, 1 Mont. 570. § 485.
v. Heitshu, 9 Watts & Serg. (Pa.) 51. §§ 16, 415.
Kenner *v.*, Bailey Eq. Cas. (S. C.) 149. § 243.
v. Roberts, 1 Dana (Ky.), 355. § 290.

Caldwell, Root & Sons Music Co. *v.*, 54 Iowa, 432. § 647.
v. Sigourney, 19 Conn. 37. § 143.
Caldwell's Ex'r *v.* McVickar, 9 Ark. (4 Eng.) 418. § 342.
Calef, McDougal *v.*, 34 N. H. 534. § 130.
Calhoun, Beatie *v.*, 73 Pa. 269. § 7.
Ewins *v.*, 7 Vt. 79. § 73.
Wheatley's Heirs *v.*, 12 Leigh (Va.), 264. § 302.
Calkin, Scott *v.*, 139 Mass. 529. § 182.
Calkins, Canada Life Assurance Company *v.*, 24 N. B. 276. § 392.
Fuller *v.*, 22 Iowa, 301. §§ 530, 559.
Callahan *v.* Saleski, 29 Ark. 216. § 454.
Callaway County Savings Bank *v.* Terry, 13 Mo. App. 99. §§ 97, 329.
Callen, Rizer *v.*, 27 Kan. 339. § 211.
Callihan *v.* Tanner, 3 Rob. (La.) 299. §§ 342, 371.
Calloway, Pannill's Adm'r *v.*, 78 Va. 387. § 43.
Calloway County Court, Craig *v.*, 12 Mo. 94. § 143.
Nolly *v.*, 11 Mo. 447. §§ 528, 628, 641.
Calvert *v.* Good, 95 Pa. St. 65. § 356.
v. Gordon, 3 Man. & Ryl. 124. § 133.
Hill *v.*, 1 Rich. Eq. (S. C.) 56. § 385.
v. London Dock Co., 2 Keen, 638. § 397.
v. Peebles, 82 N. C. 334. §§ 303, 329.
Warre *v.*, 2 Nev. & Per. 126. § 122.
Calvin *v.* Wiggam, 27 Ind. 489. § 356.
Calvo *v.* Davies, 8 Hun (N. Y.), 222. § 37.
Cambridge Savings Bank *v.* Hyde, 131 Mass. 77. § 378.
Camden *v.* McKoy, 3 Scam. (Ill.) 437. § 176.
Cameron *v.* Boulton, 9 Up. Can. (C. P.) 537. § 280.
v. Clark, 11 Ala. 259. § 63.
v. Justices, 1 Kelly (Ga.), 136. § 578.
Kerr *v.*, 19 Up. Can. (Q. B.) 366. § 347.
Cameron's Adm'r, Pugh *v.*, 11 W. Va. 523. § 235.
Cammack, Norton *v.*, 10 La. Ann. 10. § 467.
Cammeyer, Rucker *v.*, 1 Esp. 105. § 90.
Camp *v.* Bostwick, 20 Ohio St. 337. § 295.
v. Howell, 37 Ga. 312. § 356.
v. Simmons, 62 Ga. 73. §§ 176, 261.
Campbell, Boehm *v.*, 8 Taunt. 679. § 84.
Boehm *v.*, 3 Moore, 15. § 84.
v. Baker, 46 Pa. St. 243. § 343.
Bullock *v.*, 9 Gill (Md.), 182. §§ 207, 230.
Chaffin *v.*, 4 Sneed (Tenn.), 184. § 262.
Cupp *v.*, 103 Ind. 213. § 7.
v. Findley, 3 Humph. 330. § 82.
Gambill *v.*, 12 Heisk. (Tenn.) 737. §§ 580, 584.
v. Gates, 17 Ind. 126. § 405.
v. Goodall, 8 Bradw. (Ill. App.) 266. § 329.
Keaton's Distributees *v.*, 2 Humph. (Tenn.) 224. § 586.
v. Lacock, 40 Pa. St. 448. § 48.
v. Macomb, 4 Johns. Ch. 534. § 223.
McDaniel *v.*, 78 Ga. 188. § 510.
McKee *v.*, 27 Mich. 497. §§ 217, 264.
Moore *v.*, 36 Vt. 361. § 304.
v. Moulton, 30 Vt. 667. § 114.
Newman *v.*, Mar. & Yerg. (Tenn.) 63. § 616.
Pelzer *v.*, 15 S. C. 581. § 7.
v. Robinson, 27 Grant's Ch. (Can.) 634. § 37.
Stevens *v.*, 6 Iowa (Clarke), 538. § 605.

Campbell *v.* Tate, 7 Lans. (N. Y.) 370. § 29.
Underwood *v.*, 14 N. H. 393. § 82.
Waller *v.*, 25 Ala. 544. § 282.
Warner *v.*, 20 Ill. 283. § 352.
Wilcox *v.*, 106 N. Y. 325. § 37.
Wilson *v.*, 1 Scam. (Ill.) 493. § 97.
Campbell & Jones *v.* Murray, 62 Ga. 86. § 3.
Campau *v.* Seeley, 30 Mich. 57. § 493.
Campion *v.* Whitney, 30 Minn. 177. § 34.
Canada Agricultural Ins. Co. *v.* Watt, 30 Up. Can. (C. P.) 350. § 392.
Canada Life Assurance Company *v.* Calkins, 24 N. B. 276. § 392.
Canada West Ins. Co. *v.* Merritt, 20 Up. Can. (Q. B.) 444. § 131.
Canadian Bank *v.* Northwood, 14 Ont. (Can.) 207. § 376.
Canadian Bank of Commerce *v.* Green, 45 Up. Can. (Q. B.) 81. § 245.
Canal & Banking Co. *v.* Brown, 4 La. Ann. 545. §§ 408, 638.
Canan, Comm'rs *v.*, 2 Watts (Pa.), 107. § 391.
Canby *v.* Griffin, 3 Har. (Del.) 333. § 500.
Candee, Castle *v.*, 16 Conn. 223. § 177.
Cannell *v.* Crawford Co., 59 Pa. St. 196. § 536.
Cannon *v.* Connaway, 5 Del. Ch. 559. § 268.
Gary *v.*, 3 Ired. Eq. (N. C.) 64. § 237.
Gibbs *v.*, 9 Serg. & Rawle (Pa.), 198. §§ 202, 203, 205.
Capel, Anthony *v.*, 53 Miss. 350. § 146.
v. Butler, 2 Sim. & Stu. 457. § 445.
Capen, Gridley *v.*, 72 Ill. 11. § 111.
Melendy *v.*, 120 Mass. 222. § 158.
Caperton *v.* Gray, 4 Yerg. (Tenn.) 563. § 75.
Capital Bank, Hall *v.*, 71 Ga. 715. § 342.
Caraway, Cook *v.*, 29 Kan. 41. § 8.
Card, Carr *v.*, 34 Mo. 513. § 97.
Cardell *v.* McNeil, 21 N. Y. 336. § 67.
Carder, Smith *v.*, 33 Ark. 709. § 410.
Cardwell, Wayne Agricultural Co. *v.*, 73 Ind. 555. § 412.
Carey, People *v.*, 5 Daly (N. Y. Com. Pl.), 533. § 511.
v. State, 34 Ind. 105. § 581.
Carhart *v.* Ryder, 11 Daly (N. Y. Com. Pl.), 101. § 109.
Carhartt, Barman *v.*, 10 Mich. 338. § 98.
Carker *v.* State, 43 Ark. 132. § 495.
Carkin *v.* Savory, 14 Gray, 528. §§ 122, 359.
Carleton, Rollstone Nat. Bank *v.*, 136 Mass. 226. § 394.
Savage's Adm'r *v.*, 33 Ala. 443. § 605.
State *v.*, 1 Gill (Md.), 249. § 371.
Carlile, Ordinary *v.*, 1 McMullan, Law (S. C.), 100. § 638.
Carlisle, Harris *v.*, 12 Ohio, 169. § 275.
v. Wilkins' Adm'r, 51 Ala. 371. § 325.
Carlon *v.* Dixon, 12 Oreg. 144. § 32.
v. Dixon, 14 Oreg. 293. § 492.
Carlos *v.* Ansley, 8 Ala. 900. § 226.
Carlton, White *v.*, 52 Ind. 371. §§ 272, 286.
Carman *v.* Elledge, 40 Iowa, 490. § 193.
v. Noble, 9 Pa. St. 366. §§ 221, 247.
Carmody *v.* State, 105 Ind. 546. § 504.
Carnegie *v.* Morrison, 2 Met. (Mass.) 381. § 81.
Carney *v.* Walden, 16 B. Mon. (Ky.) 388. § 131.
Carpenter *v.* Bowen, 42 Miss. 28. § 324.
Brush *v.*, 6 Ind. 78. § 60.
v. Devon, 6 Ala. 718. § 40.
v. Doody, 1 Hilt. (N. Y.) 465. §§ 567, 570.
Dubuque First National Bank *v.*, 41 Iowa, 518. § 203.

Carpenter, Hubbell *v.*, 5 N. Y. 171. § 147.
v. Kelly, 9 Ohio, 106. §§ 271, 293.
Kennedy *v.*, 2 Whart. (Pa.) 344. §§ 139, 281.
v. King, 9 Met. (Mass.) 511. §§ 29, 40, 245.
v. McLaughlin, 12 R. I. 270. § 180.
v. Minter, 72 Tex. 370. § 212.
People *v.*, 7 Cal. 402. § 512.
v. Turrell, 100 Mass. 450. § 472.
Van Wart *v.*, 21 Up. Can. (Q. B.) 320. §§ 116, 117.
v. Wall, 4 Dev. & Batt. (N. C.) 144. § 67.
Carr, Browne *v.*, 2 Russ. 600. § 150.
Browne *v.*, 7 Bing. 508. § 430.
v. Card, 34 Mo. 513. § 97.
v. Howard, 8 Blackf. (Ind.) 190. §§ 242, 374.
Lusby *v.*, 60 Md. 192. § 281.
Sutherland *v.*, 85 N. Y. 105. § 524.
Veazie *v.*, 3 Allen, 14. § 359.
Carraway *v.* Odeneal, 56 Miss. 223. § 372.
Carrigan, Tipton *v.*, 10 Bradw. (Ill. App.) 318. § 448.
Carrington *v.* Anderson, 5 Munf. (Va.) 32. § 90.
v. Carson, Conf. Rep. (N. C.) 216. § 289.
Carroll, Corbitt *v.*, 50 Ala. 315. §§ 154, 521.
Holliman *v.*, 27 Tex. 23. § 566.
v. Nixon, 4 Watts & Serg. (Pa.) 517. § 247.
Waters *v.*, 9 Yerg. (Tenn.) 102. § 531.
v. Weld, 13 Ill. 682. §§ 176, 182.
Carroll & Co. *v.* Hamilton, 30 La. Ann. 520. §§ 465, 466.
v. Ruggles, 69 Iowa, 269. § 408.
Carsan *v.* Maxwell, 39 Minn. 391, 393. § 1.
Carson, Carrington *v.*, Conf. Rep. (N. C.) 216. § 289.
Crawford *v.*, 35 Ark. 565. § 524.
Carson, Ferguson *v.*, 13 Mo. App. 29. § 463.
Globe Mutual Ins. Co. *v.*, 31 Mo. 218. § 366.
v. Hill, 1 McMullan, Law (S. C.), 76. § 410.
Territory *v.*, 7 Mont. 417. § 548.
Carson Opera House Ass'n *v.* Miller, 16 Nev. 327. § 397.
Carson's Adm'r, Ferguson's Adm'r *v.*, 86 Mo. 673. §§ 208, 310, 463.
Carstairs *v.* Rolleston, 1 Marsh. 207. § 148.
Cartenel *v.* Newton, 79 Ind. 1. § 346.
Carter *v.* Black, 4 Dev. & Bat. Law (N. C.), 425. § 210.
Brooks *v.*, 36 Ala. 682. § 239.
Dorriss *v.*, 67 Mo. 544. § 476.
v. Duggan, 144 Mass. 32. § 571.
v. Duncan, 84 N. C. 676. § 364.
Halliburton *v.*, 55 Mo. 435. § 220.
v. Hampton's Adm'x, 77 Va. 631. § 133.
v. Mulreim, 82 Cal. 167. § 476.
O'Neill *v.*, 9 Up. Can. (Q. B.) 470. § 399.
Rice *v.*, 11 Ired. (N. C.) 298. § 66.
Shultz *v.*, Spear's Eq. (S. C.) 533. § 313.
Spencer *v.*, 4 Jones' Law (N. C.), 287. § 204.
Stewart *v.*, 4 Neb. 564. § 27.
v. White, L. R. 25 Ch. D. 666. § 201.
Woodburn *v.*, 50 Ind. 376. § 352.
Carter Bros. *v.* Young & Co., 9 Lea (Tenn.), 210. § 586.
Carter's Ex'rs, Catlett *v.*, 2 Munf. (Va.) 24. § 578.
Cartsaphan, Purvis *v.*, 73 N. C. 575. § 35.
Caruthers *v.* Dean, 11 Smedes & Mar. (Miss.) 178. § 438.
Carville *v.* Crane, 5 Hill, 483. §§ 59, 74.
Cary, Bradley *v.*, 8 Greenl. (Me.) 234. § 189.
Cary & Masters, People *v.*, 6 Daly (N. Y. Com. Pl.), 406. § 511.

Case *v.* Howard, 41 Iowa, 479. §§ 194, 365.
v. Luse, 28 Iowa, 527. § 103.
v. O'Brien, 66 Mich. 289. §§ 37, 362.
White *v.*, 13 Wend. 543. §§ 98, 101.
Casey *v.* Peebles, 13 Neb. 7. § 517.
Cash *v.* People, 32 Ill. App. 250. § 571.
Cashin *v.* Perth, 7 Grant's Ch. & App. Rep. 340. § 422.
Caskey, Dixon *v.*, 18 Ala. 97. § 537.
Casky *v.* Haviland, 13 Ala. 314. § 627.
Cason, State *v.*, 11 S. C. 392. §§ 569, 636.
Casoni *v.* Jerome, 58 N. Y. 315. § 406.
Casper *v.* People, 6 Bradw. (Ill. App.) 28. § 566.
Cassady *v.* Trustees of Schools, 105 Ill. 560. §§ 112, 589, 597, 628.
v. Board of Trustees, 93 Ill. 394. § 257.
Cassidy, Coe *v.*, 72 N. Y. 133. § 109.
Cassilly, Clements *v.*, 4 La. Ann. 380. § 402.
Cassitys *v.* Robinson, 8 B. Mon. (Ky.) 279. § 624.
Castle *v.* Beardsley, 10 Hun (N. Y.), 343. § 82.
v. Candee, 16 Conn. 223. § 177.
v. Rickly, 44 Ohio St. 490. § 176.
Castling *v.* Aubert, 2 East, 325. §§ 54, 65, 70.
Caston *v.* Dunlap, Rich. Eq. Cas. (S. C.) 77. § 242.
Cates *v.* Kittrell, 7 Heisk. (Tenn.) 606. § 100.
Simmons *v.*, 56 Ga. 609. § 330.
v. Thayer, 93 Ind. 156. § 344.
Cathcart *v.* Gibson, 1 Rich. Law (S. C.), 10. § 260.
v. Robinson, 5 Pet. 264. § 405.
Catlett *v.* Carter's Ex'rs, 2 Munf. (Va.) 24. § 578.
Catlin, Perkins *v.*, 11 Conn. 213. §§ 177, 182.
Caton, Redhead *v.*, 1 Starkie, 12. § 57.
v. Shaw, 2 Harris & Gill (Md.), 13. § 194.
Catton *v.* Simpson, 8 Adol. & Ell. 136. § 229.
Caulfield, Delacour *v.*, 1 Irish Com. Law, 669. § 538.
Cave *v.* Burns, 6 Ala. 780. § 282.
Patterson *v.*, 61 Mo. 439. § 153.
Cavender *v.* Ward, 28 S. C. 470. § 23.
Cavins, Buchard *v.*, 77 Tex. 365. § 19.
Cawley *v.* People, 95 Ill. 249. §§ 410, 422, 517, 546, 603, 628.
Cayce, State *v.*, 85 Mo. 456. § 571.
Cecil, Dills *v.*, 4 Bush (Ky.), 579. § 438.
v. Early, 10 Gratt. (Va.) 198. §§ 42, 520.
Center *v.* Finch, 22 Hun (N. Y.), 146. § 574.
Central Mills Co. *v.* Stewart, 133 Mass. 461. § 517.
Central Savings Bank, Allen *v.*, 4 Mo. App. 66. § 92.
v. Shine, 48 Mo. 456. § 189.
Shine's Adm'r *v.*, 70 Mo. 524. § 93.
Chace, Hawkins *v.*, 19 Pick. 502. §§ 89, 90.
Chadley, Cuxon *v.*, 3 Barn. & Cress. 591. § 66.
Chadwick, State *v.*, 10 Oreg. 465. § 560.
v. United States (Cir. Ct. D. Mass.), 3 Fed. Rep. 750. §§ 548, 595.
Chaffe *v.* Taliaferro, 58 Miss. 544. § 95.
Chaffee *v.* Hooper, 54 Vt. 513. § 572.
v. Jones, 19 Pick. 260. §§ 180, 258, 288, 293.
v. Memphis, C. & N. W. R. R. Co., 64 Mo. 193. § 180.
Chaffin *v.* Campbell, 4 Sneed (Tenn.), 184. § 262.
Chafoin *v.* Rich, 77 Cal. 476. §§ 177, 589.
Chairman of Schools *v.* Daniel, 6 Jones' Law (N. C.), 444. § 174.
Chalaron *v.* McFarlane, 5 La. (Curry), 227. § 410.
Chalker, Watrous *v.*, 7 Conn. 224. § 52.

Chalmers, People *v.*, 60 N. Y. 154. §§ 93, 128.
Chamberlain *v.* Braner, 3 Bush (Ky.), 561. § 412.
v. Godfrey, 36 Vt. 380. § 630.
Hammond *v.*, 26 Vt. 406. § 100.
v. Hopps, 8 Vt. 94. § 25.
Lucas *v.*, 8 B. Mon. (Ky.) 276. § 60.
Chambers, Brown *v.*, 63 Tex. 131. § 438.
v. Cochran, 18 Iowa, 159. §§ 40, 250.
Cooper *v.*, 4 Dev. (N. C.) 461. § 62.
Haddens *v.*, 2 Dall. (Pa.) 236. § 220.
Kerns *v.*, 3 Ired. Eq. (N. C.) 576. § 274.
M'Dowell *v.*, 1 Strobh. Eq. (S. C.) 347. § 80.
v. Robbins, 28 Conn. 544. § 68.
v. Waters, 7 Cal. 390. § 486.
Weed *v.*, 40 Up. Can. (Q. B.) 1. § 95.
Chambliss, Hunt *v.*, 7 Smedes & Mar. (Miss.) 532. §§ 258, 261.
Champion *v.* Griffith, 13 Ohio, 228. §§ 176, 177.
v. Plummer, 1 Bos. & Pul. (N. R.) 252. § 81.
Champlain, Sluby *v.*, 4 Johns. 461. § 228.
Champomier *v.* Washington, 2 La. Ann. 1013. § 464.
Chancellor, Ball *v.*, 47 N. J. Law, 125. § 592.
Chandler *v.* Birkholm, 44 N. J. Eq. 554. § 577.
v. Higgins, 109 Ill. 602. §§ 36, 312.
v. State, 1 Lea (Tenn.), 296. §§ 523, 524.
State *v.*, 79 Me. 172. §§ 493, 509.
Menaugh *v.*, 89 Ind. 94. § 41.
v. Westfall, 30 Tex. 475. §§ 176, 182.
Chapeze *v.* Young, 87 Ky. 476. §§ 29, 259.
Chapin *v.* Lapham, 20 Pick. 467. §§ 55, 58.
Chapin *v.* Merrill, 4 Wend. 657. § 60.
Chaplin *v.* Baker, 124 Ind. 385. § 39.
Roche *v.*, 1 Bailey (S. C.), 419. § 58.
Chapman, Bean *v.*, 62 Ala. 58. § 145.
v. Bluck, 5 Scott, 515. § 80.
Chilton *v.*, 13 Mo. 470. § 272.
v. Commonwealth, 25 Gratt. (Va.) 721. § 338.
Johnston *v.*, 3 Pen. & Watts (Pa.), 128. §§ 100, 101.
v. McGrew, 20 Ill. 101. § 386.
Peabody *v.*, 20 N. H. 418. § 209.
v. Ross, 12 Leigh (Va.), 565. § 60.
v. Sutton, 2 Com. B. 634. § 17.
v. Todd, 60 Me. 282. § 439.
Chappee *v.* Thomas, 5 Mich. 53. § 615.
Chaquette, Adm'r, *v.* Ortet, 60 Cal. 594. §§ 578, 580.
Chard *v.* Hamilton, 56 Hun (N. Y.), 259. § 139.
Charles, Foster *v.*, 6 Bing. 396. § 73.
v. Haskins, 12 Iowa, 329. §§ 566, 569.
Charter, Knight *v.*, 22 W. Va. 422. § 438.
Chase *v.* Berand, 29 Cal. 138. § 456.
v. Brooks, 5 Cush. 43. § 343.
v. Day, 17 Johns. 114. §§ 76, 77.
Goodman *v.*, 1 Barn. & Ald. 297. §§ 62, 82.
v. Hathorn, 61 Me. 505. §§ 115, 151.
Herford *v.*, 1 Rob. (La.) 212. § 427.
v. Lowell, 7 Gray, 33. § 80.
v. McDonald, 7 H. & J. (Md.) 160. § 93.
v. Welty, 57 Iowa, 230. § 262.
Chasten, West *v.*, 12 Fla. 315. §§ 36, 223.
Chater *v.* Becket, 7 Term R. 201. §§ 52, 64.
Chatterton, Nickerson *v.*, 7 Cal. 568. § 486.
Cheek *v.* Glass, 3 Ind. 286. § 352.
Shortrede *v.*, 1 Adol. & Ell. 57. §§ 84, 86.
Cheeney *v.* Cook, 23 N. Y. 495. § 84.

Cheeseborough, Aiken *v.*, 1 Hill, Law (S. C.), 172. § 67.
Cheeseman, United States *v.*, 3 Sawyer, 424. § 170.
Chelmsford Company *v.* Demarest, 7 Gray, 1. §§ 168, 624.
Cheltenham Fire Brick Co. *v.* Cook, 44 Mo. 29. § 624.
Chenault, Ragan *v.*, 78 Ky. 545. § 90.
Cheney, Williams *v.*, 3 Gray, 215. § 222.
Cherry *v.* Heming, 4 Wels., Hurl. & Gor. 631. § 89.
v. Miller, 7 Lea (Tenn.), 305. §§ 344, 426.
v. Monro, 2 Barb. Ch. 618. § 37.
v. Wilson, 78 N. C. 164, 166. § 257.
Cheshire, Leary *v.*, 3 Jones' Eq. (N. C.) 170. § 268.
Chesney, Bacon *v.*, 1 Starkie, 192. § 415.
Chester *v.* Bank of Kingston, 16 N. Y. 336. §§ 337, 428.
Chetlain, Beveridge *v.*, 1 Bradw. (Ill. App.) 231. § 519.
Chew, Bussier *v.*, 5 Phil. (Pa.) 170. §§ 117, 162.
v. Ellingwood, 86 Mo. 260. §§ 422, 425, 561.
Chicago & A. R. R. Co. *v.* Higgins, 58 Ill. 128. § 122.
Chicago & N. W. R. R. Co., Smith *v.*, 18 Wis. 17. § 126.
Chicago, B. & Q. R. R. *v.* Bartlett, 20 Bradw. (Ill. App.) 96. § 558.
Chicago Carpet Co., Powell *v.*, 22 Ill. App. 409. § 204.
Chichester *v.* Mason, 7 Leigh (Va.), 244. § 444.
Chick, Anderson *v.*, Bailey, Eq. (S. C.) 118. § 90.
Rochester Savings Bank *v.*, 64 N. H. 410. §§ 346, 347.
Rolston *v.*, 1 Stew. (Ala.) 526. § 18.
Snyder *v.*, 112 Ind. 293. § 45.
Chickasaw County *v.* Pitcher, 36 Iowa, 593. § 363.
Chickering, Dedham Bank *v.*, 3 Pick. 335. § 173.
Dedham Bank *v.*, 4 Pick. 314. § 560.
Child, Glidden *v.*, 122 Mass. 433. § 76.
v. Powder Works, 44 N. H. 354. § 222.
Childers *v.* State, 25 Tex. App. 658. § 515.
Childress, Ferguson *v.*, 9 Humph. (Tenn.) 382. § 372.
Macey *v.*, 2 Tenn. Ch. (Cooper), 438. §§ 61, 91.
Miller *v.*, 2 Humph. (Tenn.) 320. § 612.
Ruddell *v.*, 31 Ark. 511. § 605.
Childs *v.* Barnum, 11 Barb. (N. Y.) 14. § 84.
Jones *v.*, 8 Nev. 121. § 221.
Rankin *v.*, 9 Mo. 665. §§ 186, 188, 204.
Chilton *v.* Brooks (Md. 1890), 20 Atl. Rep. 125. § 37.
v. Chapman, 13 Mo. 470. § 272.
v. Robbins, 4 Ala. 223. § 349.
Chipman *v.* Iambro, 16 Ark. 291. § 633.
Chisholm, Lowndes *v.*, 2 McCord, Eq. (S. C.) 455. § 303.
People *v.*, 8 Cal. 29. § 434.
Chisolm, Pittman *v.*, 43 Ga. 442. § 100.
Chittenden, Nurre *v.*, 56 Ind. 462. § 260.
Choat, Burnham *v.*, 5 Up. Can. K. B. (O. S.) 736. § 291.
Choate *v.* Arrington, 116 Mass. 552. § 526.
v. Quinichett, 12 Heisk. (Tenn.) 427. § 150.
v. Thorndike, 138 Mass. 371. § 586.
Chollan *v.* Temple, 39 Ark. 238. § 289.
Choppin *v.* Gobbold, 13 La. Ann. 238. § 62.
Chorlton, Newton *v.*, 2 Drewry, 333. § 426.
Choteau *v.* Jones, 11 Ill. 300. § 207.
Chouteau *v.* Thompson, 3 Ohio St. 424. § 218.

Chretien, Andrus *v.*, 7 La. O. S. (4 Curry), 318. § 50.
Chrisfield *v.* Murdock, 55 Hun (N. Y.), 143. § 558.
Chrisman, Burke *v.*, 3 B. Mon. (Ky.) 50. § 316.
v. Jones, 34 Ark. 73. §§ 262, 292.
v. Perrin, 67 Ind. 586. § 377.
v. Tuttle, 59 Ind. 155. §§ 241, 354, 609.
Chrisman's Adm'x *v.* Harman, 29 Gratt. (Va.) 494. § 480.
Christal *v.* Kelly, 24 Hun (N. Y.), 155. § 465.
Christian *v.* Clark, 10 Lea (Tenn.), 630. § 577.
v. Keen, 80 Va. 369. §§ 35, 388.
Christie *v.* Simpson, 1 Rich. Law (S. C.), 401. § 90.
Valentine *v.*, 1 Rob. (La.) 298. § 26.
Christiner *v.* Brown, 16 Iowa, 130. § 34.
Christman, Mathews *v.*, 12 Smedes & Mar. (Miss.) 595. §§ 193, 194.
Christmas, Thornhill *v.*, 10 Rob. (La.) 543. § 504.
Christner *v.* Brown, 16 Iowa, 130. § 352.
Christopher, Hayden *v.*, 1 J. J. Marsh. (Ky.) 382. § 66.
Christy's Adm'r *v.* Horne, 24 Mo. 242. § 605.
Chubb, Aldrich *v.*, 35 Mich. 350. §§ 100, 101.
Church *v.* Brown, 29 Barb. (N. Y.) 486. § 85.
v. Brown, 21 N. Y. 315. § 84.
Bushnell *v.*, 15 Conn. 406. §§ 193, 195, 626.
v. Howard, 17 Hun (N. Y.), 5. § 381.
v. Howard, 79 N. Y. 415. § 619.
v. Simmons, 83 N. Y. 261. § 452.
Churchill *v.* Bradley, 58 Vt. 403. § 14.
Ide *v.*, 14 Ohio St. 372. §§ 280, 342.
Manisty *v.*, Law Rep. (39 Ch. Div.) 174. § 320.
Churchill, State *v.*, 48 Ark. 426. §§ 93, 378, 385, 408, 411, 426.
Churn, Ward *v.*, 18 Gratt. (Va.) 801. § 411.
Chute *v.* Pattee, 37 Me. 102. § 354.
Citizens' Bank *v.* Barnes, 70 Iowa, 412. § 416.
Citizens' Bank of Bowling Green *v.* Moorman, 38 Mo. App. 484. § 351.
Citizens' B'ld'g & Loan Ass'n, Gass *v.*, 95 Pa. St. 101. § 648.
Citizens' Ins. Co. *v.* Cluxton, 13 Ont. (Can.) 382. § 395.
Corporation of City of London *v.*, 13 Ont. (Can.) 713. § 257.
Citizens' Ins. Co. of St. Louis, Hecox *v.* (Cir. Ct. N. D. Ill.), 2 Fed. Rep. 535. § 547.
Citizens' Nat. Bank, Fitch *v.*, 97 Ind. 211. § 199.
Citizens' Savings Bank *v.* Ole, 47 Iowa, 492. § 638.
City of Atchison, Manley *v.*, 9 Kan. 358. § 557.
City of Butte *v.* Cohen, 9 Mont. 435. §§ 175, 597.
City of Chicago, Foss *v.*, 34 Ill. 488. § 426.
v. Gage, 95 Ill. 593. §§ 385, 386, 410, 517, 534, 546, 559, 628.
City of Evansville *v.* Morris, 87 Ind. 269. § 25.
Ohning *v.*, 66 Ind. 59. § 628.
City of Fall R. *v.* Riley, 140 Mass. 488. § 521.
City of Fond du Lac *v.* Moore, 58 Wis. 170. § 8.
City of Harrisonville *v.* Porter, 76 Mo. 358. § 591.
City of Hartford *v.* Franey, 47 Conn. 76. §§ 545, 546.
City of Indianapolis *v.* Skeen, 17 Ind. 628. § 124.
City of Keokuk *v.* Love, 31 Iowa, 119. §§ 301, 306, 318.
City of Lafayette *v.* James, 92 Ind. 240. § 549.

City of Litchfield, Linch *v.*, 16 Bradw. (Ill. App.) 612. § 529.
City of Lowell *v.* Parker, 10 Met. (Mass.) 309. §§ 566, 636.
City of Maquoketa *v.* Willey, 35 Iowa, 323. § 437.
City of New Orleans *v.* Gauthreaux, 36 La. Ann. 109. §§ 541, 571.
Schmidt *v.*, 33 La. Ann. 17. § 571.
v. Waggaman, 31 La. Ann. 299. § 175.
City of Newton *v.* Devlin, 134 Mass. 490. § 601.
City of Paducah *v.* Cully, 9 Bush (Ky.), 323. § 42.
City of Paris, Broad *v.*, 66 Tex. 119. §§ 542, 628.
City of Pittsburgh, Hostetter *v.*, 107 Pa. St. 419. § 632.
City of San Jose *v.* Welch, 65 Cal. 358. § 529.
City of St. Louis *v.* Sickles, 52 Mo. 122. § 565.
City of Wilmington *v.* Nutt, 78 N. C. 177. § 532.
City of Wyandotte, Bernhard *v.*, 33 Kan. 465. § 546.
City Bank, Stetson *v.*, 2 Ohio St. 167. § 627.
v. Young, 43 N. H. 457. § 442.
City Bank of N. O., Stetson *v.*, 12 Ohio St. 577. § 175.
City Council *v.* Paterson, 2 Bailey, Law (S. C.), 165. § 555.
City Council of Montgomery *v.* Hughes, 65 Ala. 201, 204. §§ 93, 539.
City National Bank *v.* Dudgeon, 65 Ill. 11. § 315.
v. Phelps, 86 N. Y. 484. §§ 160, 396.
City Savings Bauk *v.* Hopson, 53 Conn. 453. § 193.
Claflin *v.* Briant, 58 Ga. 414. § 186.
v. Cogan, 48 N. H. 411. § 150.
v. Ostrom, 54 N. Y. 581. § 48.
Claget *v.* Salmon, 5 Gill & Johns. (Md.) 314. §§ 376, 387.
Clagett, Salmon *v.*, 3 Bland's Ch. (Md.) 125. § 376.
Claggett, Rockingham Bank *v.*, 29 N. H. 292. § 313.
Claiborne *v.* Birge, 42 Tex. 98. § 361.
Clancy *v.* Piggott, 4 Nev. & Man. 496. §§ 77, 82.
Clanin *v.* Esterly Harvesting Machine Co., 118 Ind. 372. § 104.
Clanton *v.* Coward, 67 Cal. 373. § 210.
Clap, Harris *v.*, 1 Mass. 308. § 112.
Clapp *v.* Rice, 13 Gray, 403. § 261.
v. Rice, 15 Gray (Mass.), 557. §§ 277, 291.
v. Seibrecht, 11 La. Ann. 528. § 467.
Shippen's Adm'r *v.*, 36 Pa. St. 89. § 440.
Clardy, Hendry *v.*, 8 Fla. 77. § 574.
Clare, Traders' National Bank *v.*, 76 Tex. 47. § 38.
Claremont Bank *v.* Wood, 10 Vt. 582. § 41.
Clark, Barney *v.*, 46 N. H. 514. §§ 246, 437.
v. Barrett, 19 Mo. 39. § 604.
v. Bell, 8 Humph. (Tenn.) 26. § 225.
Board of Supervisors *v.*, 92 N. Y. 391. § 548.
v. Bryce, 64 Ga. 486. § 408.
Buchanan *v.*, 10 Gratt. (Va.) 164. § 302.
v. Burdett, 2 Hall (N. Y.), 217. § 196.
v. Bush, 3 Cow. 151. § 112.
Cameron *v.*, 11 Ala. 259. § 63.
Christian *v.*, 10 Lea (Tenn.), 630. § 577.
v. Clark, 86 Mo. 114. § 431.
Farnsworth *v.*, 44 Barb. 601. § 17.
v. Fredenburg, 43 Mich. 263. § 585.
Geiger *v.*, 13 Cal. 579. § 186.
v. Gordon, 82 Ga. 613. § 494.
v. Gordon, 121 Mass. 330. § 108.
Howard *v.*, 36 Iowa, 114. § 358.
Hunter *v.*, 28 Tex. 159. § 438.

Clark *v.* Hyman, 55 Iowa, 14. § 161.
Kellum *v.*, 97 N. Y. 390. §§ 545, 624.
Keer *v.*, 11 Humph. (Tenn.) 77. § 276.
Kingston Mut. Ins. Co. *v.*, 33 Barb. (N. Y.) 196. § 167.
v. Lamb, 76 Ala. 406. § 570.
Lee *v.*, 1 Hill (N. Y.), 56. §§ 42, 126, 630.
McAllister *v.*, 86 Ill. 236. § 640.
Menifee *v.*, 35 Ind. 304. § 344.
v. Merriam, 25 Conn. 576. §§ 176, 177, 182, 199.
v. Morgan, 13 Bradw. (Ill. App.) 597. §§ 1, 137.
Nolan *v.*, 10 B. Mon. (Ky.) 239. § 440.
v. Oman, 15 Gray, 521. § 222.
v. Patton, 4 J. J. Marsh. (Ky.) 33. § 358.
Pike's Adm'r *v.*, 3 B. Mon. 262. § 356.
v. Potter County, 1 Pa. St. 159. § 556.
Prince *v.*, 127 Mass. 599. § 469.
v. Remington, 11 Met. (Mass.) 361. § 192.
v. Ritchie, 11 Grant's Ch. 499. § 403.
v. Roberts, 26 Mich. 506. § 28.
Russell *v.*, 7 Cranch, 69. §§ 73, 92.
v. Sickler, 64 N. Y. 231. § 339.
v. Sigourney, 17 Conn. 511. § 143.
v. Small, 6 Yerg. (Tenn.) 418. §§ 13, 82.
St. Louis Building & Savings Ass'n *v.*, 36 Mo. 601. § 323.
Struthers *v.*, 30 Pa. St. 210. § 130.
Waterman *v.*, 76 Ill. 428. § 236.
Weed *v.*, 4 Sandf. (N. Y. Sup. Ct.) 31. § 85.
Whiting *v.*, 17 Cal. 407. § 342.
v. Wilkinson, 59 Wis. 543. §§ 112, 546.
Young *v.*, 2 Ala. 264. § 288.
Clark's Ex'r, Buckner *v.*, 6 Bush, 168. § 13.
Clarke *v.* Bell, 2 Littell (Ky.), 164. § 486.
v. Birlye, Law Rep. (41 Ch. Div.) 422. § 439.
De Castro *v.*, 29 Cal. 11. § 459.
Emery *v.*, 2 J. Scott (N. S.), 582. § 220.
v. Henty, 3 Younge & Coll. (Exch.) 187. § 364.
Pond *v.*, 14 Conn. 334. § 218.
Clarkson *v.* Commonwealth, 2 J. J. Marsh. (Ky.) 19. § 578.
Gardner *v.*, 13 Ill. 347. § 344.
Jenkins *v.*, 7 Ohio, 72. §§ 242, 344, 353.
Clary & Whaley *v.* Haines, 61 Ga. 520. § 465.
Clason *v.* Bailey, 14 Johns. 484. §§ 80, 89.
Merritt *v.*, 12 Johns. 102. §§ 89, 90.
Sanders *v.*, 13 Minn. 379. § 66.
Clay, Commonwealth *v.*, 9 Phila. (Pa.) 121. § 506.
v. Edgerton, 19 Ohio St. 549. § 199.
Goodloe *v.*, 6 B. Mon. (Ky.) 236. §§ 272, 444.
v. Schmitzell, 5 Phila. (Pa.) 441. § 262.
v. Severance, 55 Vt. 300. § 208.
Wagnon *v.*, 1 A. K. Marsh. (Ky.) 257. § 68.
v. Walton, 9 Cal. 328. § 70.
Clay County *v.* Simonsen, 1 Dak. 403. § 591.
Clearwater, Fowler *v.*, 35 Barb. (N. Y.) 143. § 67.
Cleasby, Morris *v.*, 4 Maule & Sel. 566. § 71.
Cleaves *v.* Foss, 4 Greenl. (Me.) 1. § 90.
Clegg *v.* Darragh, 63 Tex. 357. § 492.
Clegge, Woodward *v.*, 8 Ala. 317. § 427.
Clements *v.* Cassilly, 4 La. Ann. 380. § 402.
v. Langley, 2 Nev. & Man. 269. § 276.

Clementson, Coulthart *v.*, Law Rep. (5 Q. B. Div.) 42. § 135.
Clendaniel, Hastings *v.*, 2 Del. Ch. 165. § 381.
Clendenin, Johnson *v.*, 5 Gill & Johns. (Md.) 463. § 500.
Shaeffer *v.*, 100 Pa. St. 565. § 270.
Cleveland, Mobile Mut. Ins. Co. *v.*, 76 Ala. 321. § 11.
v. Skinner, 56 Ill. 500. § 516.
Thomas' Ex'r *v.*, 33 Mo. 126. § 436.
Cleveland R. R. Co., Connecticut, etc. Ins. Co. *v.*, 41 Barb. (N. Y.) 9. § 84.
Clevenger, Proudfoot *v.*, 33 W. Va. 267. § 129.
Click *v.* McAfee, 7 Port. (Ala.) 62. § 62.
Snyder *v.*, 112 Ind. 293. §§ 3, 193, 203.
Clifford *v.* Marsdon, 14 Oreg. 426. § 509.
Clinan *v.* Cook, 1 Schoales & Lef. 22. §§ 80, 90.
Clinton *v.* Nelson, 2 Utah Terr. 284. § 595.
Western N. Y. Life Ins. Co. *v.*, 66 N. Y. 326. § 406.
Clinton Bank *v.* Ayers, 16 Ohio, 283. § 115.
Clippinger *v.* Creps, 2 Watts (Pa.), 45. § 372.
Cloclough, McLure *v.*, 17 Ala. 89. § 417.
Clompton's Ex'rs *v.* Hall, 51 Miss. 482. § 17.
Clopton *v.* Spratt, 52 Miss. 251. § 444.
Smith *v.*, 48 Miss. 66. §§ 30, 243, 364, 609.
Clore *v.* Bailey, 6 Bush (Ky.), 77. § 559.
Ross *v.*, 3 Dana (Ky.), 189. § 233.
Closen, Hays *v.*, 20 Kan. 120. § 93.
Clossey, Union Bank *v.*, 10 Johns. 271. § 560.
Cloud, Price *v.*, 6 Ala. 248. §§ 616, 628.
Clough, Ford *v.*, 8 Greenl. (Me.) 334. § 521.
Clouser, Hart *v.*, 30 Ind. 210. § 379.
Clow *v.* Derby Coal Co., 98 Pa. St. 432. § 426.
Cluff *v.* Day, 23 J. & S. (N. Y. Super. Ct.) 460. § 586.
Clune *v.* Ford & Eagan, 55 Hun, 479. § 17.
Cluxton, Citizens' Ins. Co. *v.*, 13 Ont. (Can.) 382. § 395.
Clymer *v.* De Young, 54 Pa. St. 118. §§ 63, 66.
Coates *v.* Coates, 33 Beavan, 249. §§ 125, 431.
Coats, Equitable Life Assurance Co. *v.*, 44 Mich. 260. § 602.
v. McKee, 26 Ind. 223. §§ 35, 397.
v. Swindle, 55 Mo. 31. §§ 29, 618.
Cobb, Atwood *v.*, 16 Pick. 227. § 81.
Bent *v.*, 9 Gray, 397. § 90.
v. Curts, 4 Littell (Ky.), 235. § 24.
v. Haynes, 8 B. Mon. (Ky.) 137. §§ 256, 635.
Howell *v.*, 2 Cold. (Tenn.) 104. § 223.
v. Little, 2 Greenl. (Me.) 261. § 102.
Lombart *v.*, 14 Me. 222. § 291.
v. Page, 17 Pa. St. 469. § 13.
Parham *v.*, 9 La. Ann. 423. § 475.
State *v.*, 71 Me. 198. § 508.
Webster *v.*, 17 Ill. 459. §§ 47, 176.
Cobb, Ex'r, Bowers *v.* (Cir. Ct. D. Mass.), 31 Fed. Rep. 678. §§ 45, 599.
Coble, Governor *v.*, 2 Dev. Law (N. C.), 489. § 539.
Cobleigh, Northumberland *v.*, 59 N. H. 250. § 628.
Coburn *v.* Brooks, 78 Cal. 443. §§ 199, 589.
Conn *v.*, 7 N. H. 368. § 227.
v. Wheelock, 34 N. Y. 440. § 288.
Cochran, Beall *v.*, 18 Ga. 38. § 149.
Chambers *v.*, 18 Iowa, 159. §§ 40, 250.
v. Dawson, 1 Miles (Pa.), 276. § 102.
Deal *v.*, 66 N. C. 269. § 342.

Cochran *v.* Kennedy, 10 Daly (N. Y. Com. Pl.), 347. § 161.
Sample *v.*, 82 Ind. 260. § 426.
United States *v.*, 2 Brock. 274. § 337.
v. Walker's Ex'rs, 82 Ky. 220. § 277.
Cochrane *v.* Cushing, 124 Mass. 219. § 150.
Eastern Union Railway Co. *v.*, 9 Wels., Hurl. & Gor. 197. § 121.
Cocke *v.* Hoffman, 5 B. J. Lea (Tenn.), 105. § 267.
State *v.*, 37 Tex. 155. § 512.
Cockrill *v.* Dye, 33 Mo. 365. § 614.
Cockrum, Mays *v.*, 57 Tex. 352. § 139.
Codwise, Dickinson *v.*, 1 Sandf. Ch. 214. § 35.
Cody, Studebaker *v.*, 54 Ind. 586. §§ 47, 193.
Coe *v.* Buehler, 110 Pa. St. 366. § 191.
Bull *v.*, 77 Cal. 54. §§ 35, 448.
v. Cassidy, 72 N. Y. 133. § 109.
v. Duffield, 7 Moore, 252. § 87.
v. New Jersey Midland R. R. Co., 27 N. J. Eq. 110. § 298.
Coffelt *v.* Wise, 62 Ind. 451. § 12.
Coffenbury, Supervisors of St. Joseph *v.*, 1 Manning (Mich.), 355. § 22.
Coffil, Allen *v.*, 42 Ill. 293. § 183.
Coffin *v.* McLean, 80 N. Y. 560. § 236.
v. Trustees, 92 Ind. 337. § 16.
Coffman, Morgan *v.*, 8 La. Ann. 56. § 447.
Thompson *v.*, 15 Oreg. 631. § 29.
v. Wilson, 2 Met. (Ky.) 542. § 402.
Cogan, Claflin *v.*, 48 N. H. 411. § 150.
Coger's Ex'rs *v.* McGee, 2 Bibb (Ky.), 321. § 405.
Coggeshall *v.* Ruggles, 62 Ill. 401. §§ 129, 212.
Cogswell *v.* State, 65 Ind. 1. § 577.
Cohea *v.* Commissioners, 7 Sm. & Mar. (Miss.) 437. § 448.
Cohen, City of Butte *v.*, 9 Mont. 435. §§ 175, 597.
Doran *v.*, 147 Mass. 342. § 469.
Cohen *v.* Golding, 27 La. Ann. 77. § 588.
Strohecker *v.*, 1 Spear (S. C.), 349. § 67.
Cohn, Seawell *v.*, 2 Nev. 308. § 370.
v. Wright, 66 Ga. 119. § 524.
Coit, Erie Co. Savings Bank *v.*, 104 N. Y. 532. § 14.
Coker, Robertson *v.*, 11 Ala. 466. § 417.
Colbert, Curan *v.*, 3 Kelly (Ga.), 239. §§ 40, 434.
Colbourn *v.* Dawson, 10 Com. B. (1 J. Scott), 765. § 87.
Colburn, Loehr *v.*, 92 Ind. 24. § 324.
Colcord, New Hampshire Savings Bank *v.*, 15 N. H. 119. §§ 347, 426.
Coldham *v.* Showler, 3 Man., Gr. & Scott, 312. § 87.
Cole, Blake *v.*, 22 Pick. 97. § 60.
v. Crawford, 69 Tex. 124. § 571.
v. Dyer, 1 Cro. & Jer. 461. §§ 82, 85.
v. Fox, 83 N. C. 463. § 30.
Huff *v.*, 45 Ind. 300. §§ 355, 379.
v. Justice, 8 Ala. 793. § 236.
Kearsley *v.*, 16 Mees. & Wels. 128. § 376.
Manufacturers' Bank *v.*, 39 Me. 188. § 115.
v. Merchants' Bank, 60 Ind. 350. §§ 47, 106.
State *v.*, 13 Lea (Tenn.), 67. § 532.
Thomas *v.*, 10 Heisk. (Tenn.) 411. § 449.
Cole County *v.* Anguey, 12 Mo. 132. § 125.
Coleen, Whitehurst *v.*, 53 Ill. 247. § 615.
Colegate, Lynch *v.*, 2 H. & J. (Md.) 34. § 403.
Coleman *v.* Bailey, 4 Bibb (Ky.), 297. § 90.
v. Bean, 1 Abb. Rep. Om. Cas. (N. Y.) 394. §§ 42, 406.
Commonwealth *v.*, 2 Met. (Ky.) 382. § 501.

Coleman, Edwards v., 6 T. B. Mon. (Ky.) 567. §§ 342, 345.
v. Forbes, 22 Pa. St. 156. § 143.
v. Fuller, 105 N. C. 328. § 617.
v. Stockton, 39 Ind. 106. § 235.
v. Waller, 3 Younge & Jer. 212. § 416.
Colemard v. Lamb, 15 Wend. 329. § 398.
Coles, Hulme v., 2 Simons, 12. § 368.
v. Pack, 5 Com. Pl. 65. § 161.
v. Trecothick, 9 Vesey, 234. §§ 80, 89, 90.
Coles' Adm'r v. Ballard, 78 Va. 139. § 100.
Coley, McCrary v., Ga. Dec. 104. § 40.
Colgin v. Henley, 6 Leigh, 85. §§ 17, 82, 105.
Colgrove v. Tallman, 2 Lans. (N. Y.) 97. § 32.
v. Tallman, 67 N. Y. 95. §§ 36, 239.
Collier v. Leonard, 59 Ga. 497. § 587.
Sherwood v., 3 Dev. Law (N. C.), 380. § 310.
Wheeler v., Moo. & Mal. 123. § 81.
Collinge v. Heywood, 9 Adol. & Ell. 633. § 230.
Collins v. Boyd, 14 Ala. 505. § 210.
Corkins v., 16 Mich. 478. § 64.
Crawford v., 45 Barb. (N. Y.) 269. § 486.
v. Everett, 4 Ga. 266. § 176.
v. Gwynne, 2 Moore & Scott, 640. § 555.
v. Mitchell, 5 Fla. 364. §§ 43, 471.
v. Paris, 57 Ind. 151. § 468.
Penn v., 5 Rob. (La.) 213. § 389.
v. Prosser, 1 Barn. & Cress. 682. § 439.
Rankin v., 50 Ind. 158. § 290.
Smith v., 42 Kan. 259. § 509.
Collum v. Emanuel, 1 Ala. 23. § 301.
Colman v. Eyles, 2 Stark. 62. § 76.
Colorado Springs Co., Winne v., 3 Col. 155, 159, 160. §§ 340. 344, 377.
Colquitt, Boswell v., 73 Ga. 63. § 503.
Brown v., 73 Ga. 59. § 516.
Hartley v., 72 Ga. 351. § 500.
Renfroe v., 74 Ga. 618. § 534.
v. Simpson, 72 Ga. 501. § 412.
v. Smith, 65 Ga. 341. § 502.
v. Smith, 76 Ga. 709. § 598.
Watts v., 66 Ga. 492. § 637.
Weldon v., 62 Ga. 449. § 510.
West v., 71 Ga. 559. § 500.
Colt v. Root, 17 Mass. 229. § 72.
Columbia Sewer Pipe Co. v. Gauser, 58 Mich. 385. § 156.
Colvin, Roberts v., 3 Gratt. (Va.) 358. § 342.
Coman, People v., 5 Daly (N. Y. Com. Pl.) 527. § 511.
v. The State, 4 Blackf. (Ind.) 241. § 371.
Combe v. Woolf, 8 Bing. 156. §§ 342, 344.
Combs, Bohannon v., 12 B. Mon. (Ky.) 563. § 262.
Bradshaw v., 102 Ill. 428. § 360.
v. People, 39 Ill. 183. § 151.
Comegys, Bigelow v., 5 Ohio St. 256. § 486.
v. Booth, 3 Stew. 14. § 373.
v. Cox, 1 Stew. (Ala.) 262. § 373.
v. State Bank, 6 Ind. 357. § 271.
Comfort v. Eisenbeis, 11 Pa. St. 13. § 220.
Comins v. Pottle, 22 Hun (N. Y.), 287. § 139.
Commercial Bank, Hardcastle v., 1 Har. (Del.) 374. § 323.
v. Western Reserve Bank, 11 Ohio, 444. §§ 40, 436.
Commercial Nat. Bank v. Gorham, 11 R. I. 162. § 175.
Wayne v., 52 Pa. St. 343. §§ 124, 422.
Commissioner v. Ex'r of Robinson, 1 Bailey, Law (S. C.), 151. § 413.
Commissioners v. Canan, 2 Watts (Pa.), 107. § 391.
Cohea v., 7 Sm. & Mar. (Miss.) 437. § 448.

Commissioners *v.* Mayrant, 2 Brev. (S. C.) 228. § 570.
Comm'rs Berks Co. *v.* Ross, 3 Binney (Pa.). 520. § 433.
Comm'rs of Charities *v.* O'Rourk, 34 Hun (N. Y.), 349. § 45.
Comm'rs Jefferson Co. *v.* Lineberger, 3 Mont. 231. §§ 22, 23.
Comm'rs Missoula Co. *v.* McCormick, 4 Mont. 115. § 546.
Comm'rs Ripley Co., Dickerson *v.*, 6 Ind. 128. §§ 30, 243, 348, 374.
Comm'rs Roads and Revenues, Lewis *v.*, 70 Ga. 486. § 597.
Comm'rs Stokes Co., Davis *v.*, 74 N. C. 374. § 225.
Comm'rs of Wake *v.* Magnin, 78 N. C. 186. § 597.
Comm'rs of Wash., Bower *v.*, 25 Pa. St. 69. § 557.
Commonwealth *v.* Adams, 3 Bush (Ky.), 41. § 526.
Alcorn *v.*, 66 Pa. St. 172. § 240.
Arents *v.*, 18 Gratt. (Va.) 750. §§ 48, 102.
Askins *v.*, 1 Duvall (Ky.), 275. § 501.
v. Baily, 129 Pa. St. 480. § 558.
Basham *v.*, 13 Bush (Ky.), 36. § 571.
Branch *v.*, 2 Call (Va.), 510. § 528.
v. Branch, 1 Bush (Ky.), 59. §§ 501, 502.
v. Brassfield, 7 B. Mon. (Ky.) 447. § 624.
v. Brickett, 8 Pick. 138. § 496.
Brown *v.*, 114 Pa. St. 335. §§ 603, 623.
Chapman *v.*, 25 Gratt. (Va.) 721. § 338.
Clarkson *v.*, 2 J. J. Marsh. (Ky.) 19. § 578.
v. Clay, 9 Phila. (Pa.) 121. § 506.
v. Coleman, 2 Met. (Ky.) 382. § 501.
Cooper *v.*, 13 Bush (Ky.), 654. § 515.
v. Cox's Adm'r, 36 Pa. St. 442. § 540.
Commonwealth, Crawn *v.*, 84 Va. 282. § 555.
Crutcher *v.*, 6 Wharton (Pa.), 340. § 493.
Daly *v.*, 75 Pa. St. 33. § 172.
Ditmars *v.*, 47 Pa. St. 335. § 563.
v. Douglas, 11 Bush (Ky.), 607. § 502.
Evans *v.*, 8 Watts (Pa.), 398. § 636.
v. Fairfax, 4 Hen. & Munf. (Va.) 208. § 167.
Finney's Adm'rs *v.*, 1 Pen. & Watts (Pa.), 240. § 426.
v. Ford, 29 Gratt. (Va.) 683. § 524.
v. Gabbert's Adm'r, 5 Bush (Ky.), 438. § 548.
Garber *v.*, 7 Pa. St. 265. § 638.
v. Gilson, 8 Watts (Pa.), 214. § 583.
v. Gould, 118 Mass. 300. § 630.
Greenwell *v.*, 78 Ky. 320. § 571.
Hale *v.*, 8 Pa. St. 415. § 563.
v. Hilgert, 55 Pa. St. 236. § 583.
Holandsworth *v.*, 11 Bush, 617. § 8.
v. Holmes, 25 Gratt. (Va.) 771. §§ 371, 548.
v. House, 13 Bush (Ky.), 680. § 499.
v. Hughes, 13 Bush (Ky.), 349. § 493.
Johnson *v.*, 2 Duvall (Ky.), 410. § 8.
v. Johnson. 3 Cush. 454. § 496.
v. Jackson's Ex'r, 1 Leigh (Va.), 485. § 522.
v. Kendig, 2 Pa. St. 448. §§ 25, 563.
v. Lentz, 106 Pa. St. 643. § 569.
Little *v.*, 48 Pa. St. 337. § 128.
McClure *v.*, 80 Pa. St. 167. § 576.
McMicken *v.*, 58 Pa. St. 213. § 517.
Mears *v.*, 8 Watts (Pa.), 223. § 517.
Medlin *v.*, 11 Bush (Ky.), 605. § 500.

Commonwealth, Miller *v.*, 8 Pa. St. 444. § 527.
Miller *v.*, 127 Pa. St. 122. § 495.
v. Miller's Adm'rs, 8 Serg. & Rawle (Pa.), 452. §§ 40, 434.
Mitchell *v.*, 12 Bush (Ky.), 247. § 494.
Monteith *v.*, 15 Gratt. (Va.) 172. § 42.
Offutt *v.*, 10 Bush (Ky.), 212. § 539.
v. Overby, 80 Ky. 208. § 499.
v. Pray, 125 Pa. St. 542. § 583.
v. Preston, 5 T. B. Mon. (Ky.) 584. § 555.
v. Proctor, 98 Ill. 558. § 432.
Ramey *v.*, 83 Ky. 534. § 502.
v. Ramsay, 2 Duvall (Ky.), 386. § 8.
v. Ray, 3 Gray, 441. § 89.
Richards *v.*, 40 Pa. St. 146. § 448.
v. Risdon, 8 Phila. (Pa.) 23. § 540.
v. Rogers, 53 Pa. St. 470. § 585.
Runner *v.*, 78 Ky. 556. § 502.
Small *v.*, 8 Pa. St. 101. § 586.
Smith *v.*, 59 Pa. St. 320. § 569.
Smith *v.*, 25 Gratt. (Va.) 780. § 371.
v. Sommers, 3 Bush (Ky.), 555. § 565.
Stanton *v.*, 2 Dana (Ky.), 397. § 568.
v. Stub, 11 Pa. St. 150. § 578.
v. Swope, 45 Pa. St. 535. § 533.
v. Teevens, 143 Mass. 210. § 505.
v. Toms, 45 Pa. St. 408. § 170.
Walker & Hubbard *v.*, 79 Ky. 292. § 505.
v. Webster, 1 Bush (Ky.), 616. § 499.
Weddington *v.*, 79 Ky. 582. § 514.
v. Wenrick, 8 Watts (Pa.), 159. § 579.
White's Ex'rs *v.*, 39 Pa. St. 167. § 138.
Willes *v.*, 85 Ky. 68. § 515.
Wintersoll *v.*, 1 Duvall (Ky.), 177. § 502.
v. Wolbert, 6 Binney (Pa.), 292. § 555.
Commonwealth, Xander *v.*, 102 Pa. St. 434. §§ 406, 574.
Company of Proprietors of Liverpool Water Works *v.* Atkinson, 6 East, 507. § 166.
Compher *v.* People, 12 Ill. 290. § 548.
Compton, Freeland *v.*, 30 Miss. 424. § 344.
Henry *v.*, 2 Head (Tenn.), 549. § 237.
Smith *v.*, 6 Cal. 24. § 415.
Stone *v.*, 5 Bing. N. C. 142. § 419.
Comstock *v.* Creon, 1 Rob. (La.) 528. § 434.
v. Gage, 91 Ill. 328. §§ 419, 534, 597.
Kimball *v.*, 14 Gray, 508. § 73.
Conant, Dana *v.*, 30 Vt. 246. §§ 98, 100.
v. Patterson, 7 Vt. 163. § 515.
Skinner *v.*, 2 Vt. 453. § 77.
Concord *v.* Pillsbury, 36 N. H. 310. § 236.
Condon, Finney *v.*, 86 Ill. 78. § 429.
Cone, State *v.*, 32 Ga. 663. § 497.
Congdon, Pitts *v.*, 2 N. Y. 352. § 67.
v. Read, 7 R. I. 406. § 163.
Conger *v.* Babbet, 67 Iowa, 13. § 235.
v. Bean, 58 Iowa, 321. § 416.
Conkey *v.* Hopkins, 17 Johns. 113. § 60.
Conklin *v.* Conklin, 54 Ind. 289. § 607.
De Vries *v.*, 22 Mich. 255. § 7.
Conkling, National Mech. Bkg. Ass'n *v.*, 90 N. Y. 116. § 394.
Conn *v.* Coburn, 7 N. H. 368. § 227.
Connaway, Cannon *v.*, 5 Del. Ch. 559. § 268.
Connecticut Mut. Life Ins. Co. *v.* Bowler, 1 Holmes, 263. § 397.
Connecticut, etc. Ins. Co. *v.* Cleveland R. R. Co., 41 Barb. (N. Y.) 9. § 84.
Connecticut Mut. Life Ins. Co. *v.* Scott, 81 Ky. 540. §§ 118, 422, 423.
Connelly, Sharpe, Adm'r, *v.*, 105 N. C. 87. § 603.

Connelly, Thomas *v.*, 104 N. C. 342. §§ 531, 566..
v. Weatherly, 33 Ark. 658. § 574.
Conner, Bays *v.*, 105 Ind. 415. § 36.
v. Howe, 35 Minn. 518. § 329.
v. Keese, 32 Hun (N. Y.), 98. § 572.
v. Reeves, 103 N. Y. 527. §§ 110, 630, 637.
Schermerhorn *v.*, 41 Mich. 374. §§ 98, 100.
Connerat *v.* Goldsmith, 6 Ga. 14. § 58.
Connor, Maxwell *v.*, 1 Hill, Eq. (S. C.) 14. § 243.
v. Williams, 2 Rob. (N. Y.) 46. § 66.
Conolly *v.* Kettlewell, 1 Gill (Md.), 260. §§ 76, 78.
Conover *v.* Hill, 76 Ill. 342. § 284.
v. Inhabitants of Middletown, 42 N. J. Law, 382. § 524.
State *v.*, 4 Dutcher (N. J.), 224. § 566.
Conover's Case, 35 N. J. Eq. 108. § 540.
Conrad *v.* Foy, 68 Pa. St. 381. § 240.
Smith *v.*, 15 La. Ann. 579. § 268.
Consaulus, Bradford *v.*, 3 Cowen, 128. § 500.
Considine *v.* Considine, 9 Irish Law Rep. 400. § 230.
Consolidation Bank, Marsh *v.*, 48 Pa. St. 510. §§ 29, 66.
Consolidated Presbyterian Society *v.* Staples, 23 Conn. 544. § 63.
Constable, Coykendall *v.*, 48 Hun (N. Y.), 360. § 606.
Walker *v.*, 1 Bos. & Pul. 306. § 90.
Constant, Hall *v.*, 2 Hall (N. Y.), 205. § 353.
v. Matteson, 22 Ill. 546. § 328.
Continental Life Ins. Co. *v.* Barber, 50 Conn. 567. § 342.
Converse *v.* Cook, 25 Hun (N. Y.), 44. § 239.
Davis *v.*, 35 Vt. 503. § 417.
Convery *v.* Langdon, 66 Ind. 311. § 226.
Conway *v.* Bank of United States, 6 J. J. Marsh. (Ky.) 128. § 115.
v. Cunningham, 6 Rich. (S. C.) 351. § 161.
Hempstead *v.*, 6 Ark. (1 Eng.) 317. § 243.
Conwell *v.* McCowan, 53 Ill. 363. § 315.
Cook, Armstrong *v.*, 30 Ind. 22. § 401.
v. Caraway, 29 Kan. 41. § 8.
Cheeney *v.*, 23 N. Y. 495. § 84.
Cheltenham Fire Brick Co. *v.*, 44 Mo. 29. § 624.
Converse *v.*, 25 Hun (N. Y.), 44. § 239.
v. Freudenthal, 80 N. Y. 202. § 519.
Hargroves *v.*, 15 Ga. 321. §§ 17, 82.
v. King, 7 Bradw. (Ill. App.) 549. § 460.
v. Orne, 37 Ill. 186. §§ 186, 193.
Rice *v.*, 71 Me. 559. § 31.
v. Southwick, 9 Tex. 615. §§ 176, 182.
State *v.*, 31 Mo. App. 57. § 463.
Thomas *v.*, 8 Barn. & Cress. 728. §§ 60, 72.
Wood *v.*, 31 Ill. 271. § 572.
Cooke *v.* ———. Freeman's Ch. 97. § 265.
Clinan *v.*, 1 Schoales & Lefroy, 22. §§ 80, 90.
v. Crawford, 1 Tex. 9. § 464.
v. Nathan, 16 Barb. (N. Y.) 342. §§ 98, 401.
Northern Bank of Kentucky *v.*, 13 Bush (Ky.), 340. § 334.
Simson *v.*, 8 Moore, 588. § 118.
Cooksey, McNeilly *v.*, 2 Lea (Tenn.), 39. § 438.
Coolbaugh, Ramsey *v.*, 13 Iowa, 164. § 473.
Cooley, Ordinary *v.*, 1 Vroom (N. J.), 179. § 22.
Coombs *v.* Parker, 17 Ohio, 289. § 446.
Coons, Norton *v.*, 3 Denio, 130. § 258.

Coons, Norton *v.*, 6 N. Y. 33. § 261.
v. People, 76 Ill. 383. § 545.
Coope *v.* Twynam, 1 Turner & Russ. 426. § 259.
Wade *v.*, 2 Simons, 155. § 321.
Cooper, Bentham *v.*, 5 Mees. & Wels. 621. § 85.
v. Chambers, 4 Dev. (N. C.) 461. § 62.
v. Commonwealth, 13 Bush (Ky.), 654. § 515.
v. Dedrick, 22 Barb. (N. Y.) 516. §§ 47, 84, 643.
Duffield *v.*, 87 Pa. St. 443. § 309.
v. Evans, Law Rep. 4 Eq. Cas. 45. §§ 244, 403.
v. Fisher, 7 J. J. Marsh. (Ky.) 396. § 365.
Franklin Bank *v.*, 36 Me. 179. §§ 22, 25, 419, 420, 422.
Harbord *v.*, 43 Minn. 466. § 47.
Hayes *v.*, 14 Bradw. (Ill. App.) 490. § 236.
v. Jenkins, 32 Beav. 337. § 307.
v. Joel, 1 De Gex, Fish. & J. 240. § 127.
Jones *v.*, 1 Cowp. 227. § 75.
Joyner *v.*, 2 Bailey, Law (S. C.) 199. §§ 26, 530.
v. Martin, 1 Dana (Ky.), 23. § 268.
v. Middleton, 94 N. C. 86. §§ 324, 577.
v. Page, 24 Me. 73. §§ 96, 199.
v. People, 85 Ill. 417. § 591.
Peppin *v.*, 2 Barn. & Ald. 431. § 168.
Phillips *v.*, 59 Miss. 17. § 486.
v. Rhodes, 30 La. Ann. 533. § 460.
v. Shaver, 101 Pa. St. 547. § 99.
v. State, 5 Tex. App. 215. § 500.
State *v.*, 53 Miss. 615. §§ 520, 521, 642.
v. Wilcox, 2 Dev. & Bat. Eq. (N. C.) 90. § 434.
Coots, Farnsworth *v.*, 46 Mich. 117. § 378.
v. Farnsworth, 61 Mich. 497. §§ 29, 599.
Koch *v.*, 43 Mich. 30. § 494.
Coover, Henderson *v.*, 4 Nev. 129. § 555.
Coovert, Mercer County *v.*, 6 Watts & Serg. (Pa.) 70. § 122.
Cope *v.* Smith, Ex'r, 8 Serg. & Rawle (Pa.), 110. §§ 239, 342.
Copeland, Davis *v.*, 67 N. Y. 127. § 126.
Copis *v.* Middleton, 1 Turner & Russ. 224. §§ 313, 315.
Coppock, Orrell *v.*, 26 Law Jour. Ch. 269. § 67.
State *v.*, 79 Iowa, 482. § 509.
Corbet *v.* Evans, 25 Pa. St. 310. § 130.
Corbett, Ordinary *v.*, Bay (S. C.), 328. § 586.
Corbin *v.* McChesney, 26 Ill. 231. § 63.
Thurber *v.*, 51 Barb. (N. Y.) 215. § 36.
Corbitt, Carroll *v.*, 57 Ala. 579. § 154.
v. Carroll, 50 Ala. 315. § 521.
Corcoran, Wood *v.*, 1 Allen (Mass.), 405. § 62.
Cordaman *v.* Malone, 63 Ala. 556. § 487.
Cordevoille, Merchants' Bank *v.*, 4 Rob. (La.) 506. § 442.
Cordier *v.* Thompson, 8 Daly (N. Y. Com. Pl.) 172. § 200.
Cordle *v.* Burch, 10 Gratt. (Va.) 480. § 42.
Cordray *v.* State, 55 Tex. 140. § 175.
Corduan, Dane *v.*, 24 Cal. 157. § 242.
Corielle *v.* Allen, 13 Iowa, 289. §§ 29, 356.
Corkins *v.* Collins, 16 Mich. 478. § 64.
Cornell *v.* Eagan, 13 Daly (N. Y. Com. Pl.), 505. § 388.
v. Prescott, 2 Barb. (N. Y.) 16. § 37.
Cornes *v.* Wilkin, 14 Hun (N. Y.), 428. § 284.
Cornwall, Baker *v.*, 4 Cal. 15. § 82.
Cornwell *v.* Holly, 5 Rich. Law (S. C.), 47. § 357.
Cornwell's Appeal, 7 Watts & Serg. (Pa.) 305. § 307.

Corporation of Adjala *v.* McElroy, 9 Ont. (Can.) 580. §§ 172, 423.
Corporation of Chatham *v.* McCrea, 12 Up. Can. (C. P.) 352. § 100.
Corporation of City of London *v.* Citizens' Ins. Co., 13 Ont. (Can.) 713. § 257.
Corporation of Houghton *v.* Freeland, 26 Grant's Ch. (Can.) 500. § 558.
Corporation of Huron *v.* Armstrong, 27 Up. Can. (Q. B.) 533. § 402.
Corporation of Ontario *v.* Paxton, 27 Up. Can. (C. P.) 104. § 553.
Corporation of Oxford *v.* Gair, 15 Ont. (Can.) 362. § 597.
Corporation of Welland *v.* Brown, 4 Ont. (Can.) 217. § 629.
Corporation Village Ganandque *v.* Stunden, 1 Ont. (Can.) 1. § 419.
Corprew *v.* Boyle, 24 Gratt. (Va.) 284. § 542.
Cortesy, Kane *v.*, 100 N. Y. 132. §§ 367, 632.
Corwin, Fithian *v.*, 17 Ohio St. 118. § 342.
Corwin, Adm'r, Nelson, Adm'r, *v.*, 59 Ind. 489. § 589.
Corwine, United States *v.*, 1 Bond, 339. § 399.
Cory *v.* Leonard, 56 N. Y. 494. § 323.
Cosgrave Brewing & Malting Co. *v.* Starrs, 5 Ont. (Can.) 189. §§ 118, 161.
Coshow, Howard *v.*, 33 Mo. 118. § 72.
Cost, Hosefield *v.*, Addison (Pa.), 152. § 226.
Coste, State *v.*, 36 Mo. 437. § 638.
Coster *v.* Mesner, 58 Mo. 549. § 362.
Coster's Ex'r, Union Bank *v.*, 3 N. Y. 203. §§ 81, 87, 196.
Costley *v.* Allen, 56 Ala. 198. § 638.
Cotten, Ex'r, Mitchell *v.*, 2 Fla. 136. § 334.
Mitchell *v.*, 3 Fla. 134. § 417.
Cotton *v.* Alexander, 32 Kan. 339. §§ 205, 460.
Cotton *v.* State, 64 Ind. 573. § 576.
Cotton's Guardian *v.* Wolf, 14 Bush (Ky.), 238. §§ 22, 576.
Cotulla *v.* Goggan & Bros., 77 Tex. 32. § 460.
Couch *v.* Terry, 12 Ala. 225. § 289.
v. Waring, 9 Conn. 261. § 148.
Coulter, Schmidt *v.*, 6 Minn. 492. § 272.
Coulthart *v.* Clementson, Law Rep. (5 Q. B. Div.) 42. § 135.
Council *v.* Averett, 90 N. C. 168. § 465.
Council of Middlesex *v.* Peters, 9 Up. Can. (C. P.) 205. § 404.
Council Bluffs Bank, Jones *v.*, 34 Ill. 313. § 67.
Countryman, Dunham *v.*, 66 Barb. (N. Y.) 268. § 360.
County of Fontenac *v.* Breden, 17 Grant's Ch. 645. §§ 526, 555.
County of Galveston, Kempner *v.*, 73 Tex. 216. § 597.
County of Jackson, Simon *v.*, 63 Tex. 428. § 597.
County of Macoupin, Miller *v.*, 2 Gilman (Ill.), 50. § 542.
County of Pine *v.* Willard, 39 Minn. 125. §§ 518, 546, 547.
County of Redwood *v.* Tower, 28 Minn. 45. §§ 542, 589.
County of Schuylkill, Bochmer *v.*, 46 Pa. St. 452. § 522.
County of Scott *v.* Ring, 29 Minn. 398, 401. §§ 537, 542, 543, 551.
County of Wapello *v.* Bingham, 10 Iowa, 39. § 543.
County of Waseca *v.* Sheehan, 42 Minn. 57. § 555.
County Comm'rs of Ramsey Co. *v.* Brisbin, 17 Minn. 451. § 521.
County Court, Leonard *v.*, 25 W. Va. 45. § 601.
Coupland, Wilson *v.*, 5 Barn. & Ald. 228. § 66.
Courtis *v.* Dennis, 7 Met. (Mass.) 510. § 192.
Courtney, Franklin Life Ins. Co. *v.*, 60 Ind. 134. § 379.

Courts, Burnet *v.*, 5 Harr. & Johns. (Md.) 78. § 336.
Couturier *v.* Hastie, 8 Wels., Hurl. & Gor. 40. § 71.
Hastie *v.*, 9 Wels., Hurl. & Gor. 102. § 71.
Covert, Bank of Upper Canada *v.*, 5 Up. Can. K. B. (O. S.) 541. § 393.
Covey *v.* Neff, 63 Ind. 391. § 205.
Covilland, Williams *v.*, 10 Cal. 419. § 365.
Covington, Board Police Clark Co. *v.*, 26 Miss. 470. §§ 344, 370.
Haynes *v.*, 9 Sm. & Mar. (Miss.) 470. § 342.
Leak *v.*, 99 N. C. 559. §§ 290, 295, 648.
Wall *v.*, 83 N. C. 144. § 590.
Cowan *v.* Baird, 77 N. C. 201. § 402.
v. Duncan, Meigs (Tenn.), 470. § 262.
Morrell *v.*, Law Rep. (7 Ch. Div.) 151. §§ 17, 95.
Coward, Clanton *v.*, 67 Cal. 373. § 210.
Cowell *v.* Edwards, 2 Bos. & Pul. 268. § 288.
Cowen, Brewster *v.*, 55 Conn. 152. § 516.
v. State, 3 Tex. App. 380. § 509.
Cowgill, Gowing *v.*, 12 Iowa, 495. § 562.
v. Linville, 20 Mo. App. 138. § 318.
Cowles, Atlantic & N. C. R. R. Co. *v.*, 69 N. C. 59. § 558.
v. Peck, 55 Conn. 251. §§ 97, 100.
Cowles, Ex'r, *v.* Peck, 55 Conn. 251. § 13.
Cowper *v.* Smith, 4 Mees. & Wels. 519. § 150.
Cox, Bonser *v.*, 4 Beav. 379. 403.
Bonser *v.*, 6 Beav. 110. § 123.
v. Brown, 6 Jones' Law (N. C.), 100. § 197.
Buford *v.*, 3 Lea (Tenn.), 518. § 603.
Cox, Comegys *v.*, 1 Stew. (Ala.) 262. § 373.
High *v.*, 55 Ga. 662. § 245.
Keaton *v.*, 26 Ga. 162. § 97.
Lansdale *v.*, 7 T. B. Mon. (Ky.) 401. § 254.
Maples *v.*, 74 Ga. 701. § 215.
v. Mobile & Girard R. R. Co., 44 Ala. 611. §§ 344, 356.
Newton *v.*, 76 Mo. 352. § 517.
North *v.*, 89 N. C. 44. § 491.
Phillips *v.*, 61 Ind. 345. § 183.
Reid *v.*, 5 Blackf. (Ind.) 312. § 612.
Roper *v.*, Law Rep. Irish (10 Q. B., C. P. & Ex. Div.), 200. § 421.
Scales *v.*, 106 Ind. 261. § 605.
v. Thomas' Adm'x, 9 Gratt. (Va.) 312. §§ 38, 42.
v. Weed Sewing Machine Co., 57 Miss. 350. § 195.
Worth *v.*, 89 N. C. 44. § 371.
Cox's Adm'r, Commonwealth *v.*, 36 Pa. St. 442. § 540.
Cox & Spurgin *v.* Hill, 5 Lea (Tenn.), 146. § 524.
Coykendall *v.* Constable, 48 Hun (N. Y.), 360. § 606.
Coyne, Backus *v.*, 45 Mich. 584. §§ 254, 283.
Cozard, Lyttle *v.*, 21 W. Va. 183. § 408.
Cozens, Jemison *v.*, 3 Ala. 636. § 467.
Crabtree *v.* Graham, 81 Ga. 290. § 580.
McHaney *v.*, 6 T. B. Mon. (Ky.) 104. § 434.
Craddock *v.* Armor, 10 Watts (Pa.), 258. § 137.
Craft *v.* Dodd, 15 Ind. 380. § 608.
v. Isham, 13 Conn. 28. §§ 190, 203, 204.
Moss *v.*, 10 Mo. 720. § 436.
Crafts, Bassett *v.*, 129 Mass. 513. §§ 42, 521.
Crosby *v.*, 5 Hun (N. Y.), 327. § 325.
v. Mott, 4 N. Y. 604. § 38.

Craig *v.* Craig, 5 Rawle (Pa.), 91. § 205.
v. Calloway County Court, 12 Mo. 94. § 143.
Durham *v.*, 79 Ind. 117. § 324.
Force *v.*, 2 Hals. (N. J.) 272. § 342.
v. Herring & Turner, 80 Ga. 709. §§ 45, 487.
v. Hobbs, 44 Ind. 363. § 407.
v. Miller, 34 Ill. App. 325. § 648.
v. Milne, 25 Grant's Ch. (Can.) 259. § 593.
v. Parkis, 40 N. Y. 181. §§ 48, 50, 98, 101.
v. Phipps, 23 Miss. 240. § 100.
State *v.*, 58 Iowa, 238. § 381.
v. Vanpelt, 3 J. J. Marsh. (Ky.) 489. § 52.
Crain, Riggan *v.*, 86 Ky. 249. § 90.
Cramb, Reed *v.*, 22 Ill. App. 34. § 34.
Cramer, Greene *v.*, 2 Connor & Law. 54. § 90.
v. Tittle, 72 Cal. 12. § 9.
Cranim, Simeon *v.*, 121 Mass. 492. § 470.
Crandall *v.* First National Bank of Auburn, 61 Ind. 349. § 380.
Crane *v.* Andrews, 10 Col. 265. § 463.
Carville *v.*, 5 Hill, 483. §§ 59, 74.
v. Gough, 4 Md. 316. § 52.
Hayden *v.*, 1 Lans. (N. Y.) 181. § 163.
Humphreys *v.*, 5 Cal. 173. § 342.
Jaffray *v.*, 50 Wis. 349. § 342.
Jewett *v.*, 35 Barb. (N. Y.) 208. § 250.
v. Newell, 2 Pick. 612. § 423.
Crane Bros. Manuf. Co., Penny *v.*, 80 Ill. 244. § 97.
Cranmer *v.* McSwords, 26 W. Va. 412. § 217.
Cranor *v.* Reardon, 39 Mo. App. 306. § 449.
Cranston, United States *v.*, 3 Cranch, 289. § 565.
Crapo *v.* Brown, 40 Iowa, 487. § 131.
Crathern *v.* Bell, 45 Up. Can. (Q. B.) 473. § 161.
Craven *v.* Freeman, 82 N. C. 361. §§ 267, 276.
Crawford *v.* Carson, 35 Ark. 565. § 524.
Cole *v.*, 69 Tex. 124. § 571.
v. Collins, 45 Barb. (N. Y.) 269. § 486.
Cooke *v.*, 1 Tex. 9. § 464.
v. Foster, 6 Ga. 202. §§ 402, 642.
v. Gaulden, 33 Ga. 173. §§ 40, 353.
Hellen *v.*, 44 Pa. St. 105. § 240.
Hikes *v.*, 4 Bush (Ky.), 19. § 216.
v. Howard, 9 Ga. 314. § 570.
v. King, 54 Ind. 6. § 63.
v. Kirksey, 55 Ala. 282. § 462.
Marcy *v.*, 16 Conn. 549. § 60.
v. Penn, 1 Swan (Tenn.), 388. § 575.
v. Richeson, 101 Ill. 351. §§ 301, 320, 329.
Tiffany *v.*, 1 McCarter (N. J.), 278. § 405.
v. Turk, 24 Gratt. (Va.) 176. § 637.
v. Sterling, 4 Esp. 207. § 18.
Wilson *v.*, 47 Iowa, 469. § 205.
v. Wood, 7 Ga. 445. §§ 566, 567, 637.
Crawford Co., Cannell *v.*, 59 Pa. St. 196. § 536.
Crawford's Adm'r, Muldoon *v.*, 14 Bush (Ky.), 125. § 318.
Crawley, Hanson *v.*, 41 Ga. 303. § 381.
Crawn *v.* Commonwealth, 84 Va. 282. § 555.
Craythorne *v.* Swinburne, 14 Ves. 160. §§ 261, 265.
Creager *v.* Brengle, 5 Harr. & Johns. (Md.) 234. § 323.
Creagh, Waters *v.*, 4 Stew. & Port. (Ala.) 410. § 245.
Crears *v.* Huuter, Law Rep. (19 Q. B. Div.) 341. § 16.
Crease's Ex'r, Smith *v.*, 2 Cranch, C. C. 481. §§ 243, 364.
Creasor, Sloan *v.*, 22 Up. Can. (Q. B.) 127. § 391.
Creasy, Haycraft *v.*, 2 East, 92. § 73.

Creath's Adm'r *v.* Sims, 5 How. 192. § 342.
Creditors, Bank of Washington *v.*, 86 N. C. 323. § 592.
Morgan *v.*, 1 La. (Miller), 527. § 363.
Creigh *v.* Hedrick, 5 W. Va. 140. § 30.
Creighton *v.* Rankin, 7 Clark & Finnelly, 325. § 555.
Cremer *v.* Higginson, 1 Mason, 323. §§ 118, 163, 192.
Creon, Comstock *v.*, 1 Rob. (La.) 528. § 434.
Creps, Clippinger *v.*, 2 Watts (Pa.), 45. § 372.
Crescent City M. & T. Co., Malone *v.*, 77 Cal. 38. § 165.
Cresson, Bank of Northern Liberties *v.*, 12 Serg. & Rawle (Pa.), 306. § 520.
Cressy *v.* Gierman, 7 Minn. 398. § 563.
Creswell, Hall's Adm'r *v.*, 12 Gill & Johns. (Md.) 36. § 212.
Green *v.*, 2 Perry & Dav. 430. § 61.
Green *v.*, 10 Adol. & Ell. 453. § 60.
Creusbauer, State *v.*, 68 Mo. 254. §§ 22, 632.
Creyon, Leland *v.*, 1 McCord (S. C.), 100. §§ 75, 78.
Crickett, Mayhew *v.*, 2 Swanst. 185. §§ 434, 436.
Mayhew *v.*, 2 Swanst. 193. § 255.
Crim *v.* Fitch, 53 Ind. 214. § 72.
v. Fleming, 101 Ind. 154. §§ 147, 440.
Cripps *v.* Hartnoll, 4 Best & Smith, 414. §§ 59, 60.
Crisfield *v.* State, 55 Md. 192. § 208.
Crist *v.* Burlingame, 62 Barb. (N. Y.) 351. §§ 92, 160.
Critchett *v.* Hall, 56 N. H. 324. § 574.
Critchfield, Bush *v.*, 5 Ohio, 109. § 132.
Crittenden *v.* Fiske, 46 Mich. 70. §§ 160, 204.
Crittenden, Hank *v.*, 2 McLean, 557. § 201.
Crocker *v.* Gilbert, 9 Cush. 131. § 107.
Crockett, Green *v.*, 2 Dev. & Bat. Eq. 390. § 237.
Rodes *v.*, 2 Yerg. (Tenn.) 346. § 247.
Trotter *v.*, 2 Port. (Ala.) 401. § 440.
Crockford, Knight *v.*, 1 Esp. 190. § 89.
Crockwell, Victor Sew. Mach. Co. *v.*, 2 Utah Terr. 557. §§ 92, 602.
Croft, Bailey *v.*, 4 Taunt. 611. § 15.
v. Johnson, 5 Taunt. 319. § 493.
v. Moore, 9 Watts (Pa.), 451. § 309.
Thomas *v.*, 2 Rich. Law (S. C.), 113. § 16.
Crofts *v.* Beale, 11 Com. B. 172. § 16.
v. Johnson, 1 Marsh. 59. § 342.
Crom *v.* Murphy, 12 B. Mon. (Ky.) 444. § 309.
Cromach, Patchin *v.*, 13 Vt. 330. § 4.
Cromer *v.* Cromer's Adm'r, 29 Gratt. (Va.) 280. § 220.
Crommelin, Wittrum *v.*, 72 Cal. 89. § 461.
Cromwell, McClurkey *v.*, 11 N. Y. 593. § 601.
Crook *v.* Hudson, 4 Lea (Tenn.), 448. § 577.
McDowell *v.*, 10 La. Ann. 31. § 222.
Crooker, Smith *v.*, 5 Mass. 538. § 386.
Crosby *v.* Crafts, 5 Hun (N. Y.), 327. § 325.
F. & M. Bank of Lexington *v.*, 4 J. J. Marsh. (Ky.) 366. § 375.
v. Middleton, Finch's Precedents, 309. § 141.
v. Wyatt, 26 Me. 156. § 261.
v. Wyatt, 10 N. H. 318, and 23 Me. 156. §§ 295, 345.
Cross, Apperson *v.*, 5 Heisk. (Tenn.) 481. § 342.
Ballard *v.*, 46 Vt. 415. § 137.
Firemen's Ins. Co. *v.*, 4 Rob. (La.) 508. § 7.

Cross v. Richardson, 30 Vt. 641, 647. §§ 64, 69.
v. Rowe, 22 N. H. 77. § 114.
Skiff v., 21 Iowa, 459. § 317.
v. Sprigg, 2 Macn. & Gor. 113. § 369.
v. Wood, 30 Ind. 378. § 356.
Crosson, Long v., 119 Ind. 3. § 45.
Crosthwaite, Jones v., 17 Iowa, 393. § 153.
Crothwaite, Penrice v., 11 Martin (La.), O. S. 537. § 515.
Crouch v. Edwards, 52 Ark. 499. § 586.
Croughton v. Duval, 3 Call (Va.), 69. § 242.
Crouse v. Paddock, 8 Hun (N. Y.), 630. § 516.
Crow, Thalheimer v., 13 Col. 397. §§ 236, 464.
Crowdus v. Shelby, 6 J. J. Marsh. (Ky.) 61. § 208.
Crowley, Tessier v., 17 Neb. 207. §§ 8, 19.
Croydon, Barton v., 63 N. H. 417. § 324.
Croydon Gas Co. v. Dickinson, Law Rep. 2 Com. Pl. Div. 46. § 369.
Crozier v. Grayson, 4 J. J. Marsh. (Ky.), 514. § 212.
Cruger, Burke v., 8 Tex. 66. §§ 30, 367.
Gosman v., 7 Hun, 60. § 7.
Crum v. Wilson, 61 Miss. 233. §§ 43, 145, 521.
Crump, Ennis v., 6 Tex. 85. §§ 604, 611.
v. McMurty, 8 Mo. 408. § 305.
Cruse v. Foster & Estes, 76 Ga. 723. §§ 56, 76, 77.
Crutcher v. Commonwealth, 6 Wharton (Pa.), 340. §§ 235, 493.
v. Trabue, 5 Dana (Ky.), 80. § 347.
Whitaker v., 5 Bush (Ky.), 621. § 408.
Winham v., 2 Tenn. Ch. (Cooper), 535. § 97.
Cuddeback, Knowles v., 19 Hun (N. Y.), 590. § 30.
Culbertson v. Stillinger, Taney's Decisions (Camp.), 75. § 226.
v. Smith, 52 Md. 628. § 82.
Cullom v. Dolloff, 94 Ill. 330. § 532.
v. Gaines, 1 Ala. 23. § 97.
Cullum v. Branch Bank at Mobile, 23 Ala. 797. § 324.
Cully, City of Paducah v., 9 Bush (Ky.), 323. § 42.
Culver, Allen v., 3 Denio, 284. §§ 48, 330.
v. Reno Real Estate Co., 91 Pa. St. 367. § 18.
v. Wilbern, 48 Iowa, 26. § 235.
Culvert, Gordon v., 2 Sim. 253. § 133.
Cumming v. Bank of Montreal, 15 Grant's Ch. 686. § 359.
Cummings v. Arnold, 3 Met. (Mass.) 486. § 81.
Building Association v., 45 Ohio St. 664. § 27.
v. Little, 45 Me. 183. §§ 29, 33, 137.
v. Mugge, 94 Ill. 186. § 476.
Richter v., 60 Pa. St. 441. § 310.
Cummins v. Garretson, 15 Ark. 132. § 606.
Kimble v., 3 Met. (Ky.) 327. § 214.
Cumpston v. McNair, 1 Wend. 457. § 98.
Cunningham, Bartlett v., 85 Ill. 22. § 606.
Conway v., 6 Rich. (S. C.) 351. § 161.
Mowbray v., Hilary Term, 1773. § 75.
Osborn v., 4 Dev. & Bat. Law (N. C.), 423. § 278.
State v., 10 La. Ann. 393. §§ 496, 505.
v. State, 116 Ind. 433. § 510.
v. Wrenn, 23 Ill. 64. § 403.
Cupp v. Campbell, 103 Ind. 213. § 7.
Curan v. Colbert, 3 Kelly (Ga.), 239. §§ 40, 434.
Curd, Landis v., 63 Mo. 104. § 252.

Cureton, Earl *v.*, 13 S. C. 19. § 615.
Curiac *v.* Packard, 29 Cal. 194. § 339.
Curl, Thwaits *v.*, 6 B. Mon. (Ky.) 472. § 77.
Currie *v.* Hodgins, 42 Up. Can. (Q. B.) 601. § 376.
Small *v.*, 5 De G., M. & G. 141. § 397.
Small *v.*, 2 Drewry, 102. §§ 12, 419.
Currier *v.* Baker, 51 N. H. 613. § 281.
v. Fellows, 27 N. H. 366. § 274.
Klein *v.*, 14 Ill. 237. §§ 176, 178.
Curry *v.* Bank of Mobile, 8 Port. (Ala.) 360. § 381.
Bonta *v.*, 3 Bush (Ky.), 678. § 441.
Borland *v.*, Irish Law Rep. (4 Q. B., C. P. & Ex.) 273. § 217.
v. Hale, 15 W. Va. 867. § 37.
Knighton *v.*, 62 Ala. 404. §§ 298, 301, 320, 426, 430.
People *v.*, 59 Ill. 35. § 540.
v. Wright, 86 Tenn. 636. § 571.
Curry's Ex'rs, Lucas *v.*, 2 Bailey, Law (S. C.), 403. § 580.
Curtan *v.* David, 18 Nev. 310. § 7.
Curtis, Acers *v.*, 68 Tex. 423. §§ 283, 288.
Austin *v.*, 31 Vt. 64. § 366.
v. Blair, 26 Miss. 309. § 90.
v. Brown, 5 Cush. (Mass.) 488. §§ 62, 64.
v. Dennis, 7 Metc. 510. § 1.
v. Hubbard, 6 Met. (Mass.) 186. § 387.
v. Moss, 2 Rob. (La.) 367. § 151.
v. National Bank, 39 Ohio St. 579. § 586.
v. Parks, 55 Cal. 106. § 293.
Ryde *v.*, 8 Dow. & Ry. 62. § 84.
v. Tyler, 9 Paige's Ch. 432. § 324.
United States *v.*, 100 U. S. 119. § 112.
Curtiss, Brown *v.*, 2 N. Y. 225. §§ 67. 102.
Curts, Cobb *v.*, 4 Littell (Ky.), 235. § 24.
Cushing, Cochrane *v.*, 124 Mass. 219. § 150.
Cushing, McCollum *v.*, 22 Ark. 540. §§ 186, 187, 198.
National Bank *v.*, 53 Vt. 321. § 315.
People *v.*, 36 Hun (N. Y.), 483. § 598.
Cushman *v.* Dement, 3 Scam. (Ill.) 497. § 176.
Hall *v.*, 16 N. H. 462. § 268.
United States *v.*, 2 Sumn. 426. § 139.
Cussen, Provincial Bank *v.*, Law Rep. Irish (18 Q. B., C. P. & Ex. Div.), 382. § 431.
Cust. Hope *v.*, 1 East, 53. § 18.
Cuthbert *v.* Huggins, 21 Ala. 349. § 537.
Cutler *v.* Ballou, 136 Mass. 337. § 162.
v. Emery, 37 N. H. 567. §§ 60, 264.
v. Evans, 115 Mass. 27. § 471.
Field *v.*, 4 Lans. (N. Y.) 195. § 239.
Fisher *v.*, 20 Mo. 206. § 122.
v. Hinton, 6 Rand. (Va.) 509. § 78.
Jenness *v.*, 12 Kan. 500. §§ 35, 357.
v. Roberts, 7 Neb. 4. §§ 408, 411, 517.
Singley *v.*, 7 Conn. 291. § 86.
United States *v.*, 2 Curtis, 617. §§ 556, 627.
Cutter, Irish *v.*, 31 Me. 536. §§ 49, 184.
v. Richardson, 125 Mass. 72. § 469.
Cutts, Read *v.*, 7 Greenl. (Me.) 186. §§ 1, 201.
Cuvillier, Bank of British North America *v.*, 14 Moore's Privy Council Cas. 187. § 173.
Cuxon *v.* Chadley, 3 Barn. & Cress. 591. § 66.
Cuyler *v.* Ensworth, 6 Paige's Ch. 32. § 279.
White *v.*, 1 Esp. 200. § 58.
White *v.*, 6 Durn. & East, 176. § 249.
Dabney, Thornton *v.*, 23 Miss. 559. § 344.

Dacker *v.* Rapp, 67 N. Y. 464. § 369.
Dailey, Pearson *v.*, 7 Lea (Tenn.), 674. § 586.
State *v.*, 4 Mo. App. 172. §§ 539, 588.
Dair *v.* United States, 16 Wall. 1. § 408.
Dahlman *v.* Hammel, 45 Wis. 466. §§ 16, 84.
Dale, Follmer *v.*, 9 Pa. St. 83. § 343.
Robinson *v.*, 38 Wis. 330. § 365.
Daley, Henry *v.*, 17 Hun (N. Y.), 210. §§ 236, 416.
Dalton *v.* Barnard, 150 Mass. 473. § 470.
Daly *v.* Commonwealth, 75 Pa. St. 33. § 172.
Dana *v.* Conant, 30 Vt. 246. §§ 98, 100.
Downer *v.*, 17 Vt. 518. § 236.
McMillan *v.*, 18 Cal. 339. § 471.
Whittier *v.*, 10 Allen, 326. § 81.
Dance *v.* Girdler, 4 Bos. & Pul. 34. § 396.
Dandridge, Dibrell *v.*, 51 Miss. 55. § 616.
Spottswood *v.*, 4 Munf. (Va.) 289. § 579.
Dane *v.* Corduan, 24 Cal. 157. § 242.
v. McArthur, 57 Ala. 448. § 571
Danforth *v.* Semple, 7 Leg. News, 205. § 356.
Daniel, Badger *v.*, 79 N. C. 372. § 638.
v. Ballard, 2 Dana (Ky.), 296. §§ 264, 290.
Chairman Schools *v.*, 6 Jones' Law (N. C.), 444. § 173.
v. Daniel, 39 Ark. 266. § 480.
v. Hunt, 77 Ala. 567. § 324.
Isaac *v.*, 8 Adol. & Ell. (N. S.) 500. § 342.
v. Joyner, 3 Ired. Eq. (N. C.) 513. § 221.
v. McRae, 2 Hawks (N. C.), 590. § 260.
Morrill *v.*, 47 Ark. 316. § 486.
Daniels *v.* Barney, 22 Ind. 207. § 21.
v. Gower, 54 Iowa, 319. § 407.
v. Larendon, 49 Tex. 216. § 480.
Daniels, Thayer *v.*, 110 Mass. 345. § 230.
Danker *v.* Atwood, 119 Mass. 146. § 26.
Dann, Smith *v.*, 6 Hill (N. Y.), 543. § 123.
Dannah, Wright *v.*, 2 Camp. 203. § 90.
Danner, Hartman *v.*, 74 Pa. St. 36. § 356.
Dansey, Adams *v.*, 6 Bing. 506. § 60.
Darby, State *v.*, 11 Mo. App. 528. § 617.
Dare *v.* Hull, 70 Ind. 545. § 355.
Darling, Barnard *v.*, 11 Wend. 28. § 572.
v. McLean, 20 Up. Can. (Q. B.) 372. § 363.
Darlington *v.* McCunn, 2 E. D. Smith (N. Y.), 411. § 76.
Darnell, Birkmyr *v.*, 1 Salk. 27. §§ 56, 77.
Birkmyr *v.*, 2 Lord Raymond, 1085. § 54.
v. Tratt, 2 Car. & P. 82. § 58.
Darragh, Clegg *v.*, 63 Tex. 357. § 492.
Sale *v.*, 2 Hilton (N. Y.), 184. § 81.
Tenth National Bank *v.*, 1 Hun (N. Y.), 111. § 624.
Darst *v.* Bates, 51 Ill. 439. §§ 221, 324, 329.
Dart *v.* Sherwood, 7 Wis. 523. §§ 31, 137.
Darter *v.* State, 5 Blackf. (Ind.) 61. § 625.
Dartmouth *v.* Silly, 7 Ell. & Black. 97. § 552.
Darwin, Gillespie *v.*, 6 Heisk. (Tenn.) 21. § 443.
Dashiel, United States *v.*, 4 Wall. 182. § 558.
Dauber *v.* Blackney, 38 Barb. (N. Y.) 432. § 67.
Dauchy, French *v.*, 57 Hun (N. Y.), 100. § 592.
Daughtry, Evans *v.*, 84 Ala. 68. § 402.

Daum, Bracken Co. Comm'rs *v.*, 80 Ky. 388. § 518.
Davenport, Brown *v.*, 76 Ga. 799. § 414.
v. King, 63 Ind. 64. § 377.
Davey *v.* Prendergrass, 5 Barn. & Ald. 187. § 374.
David, Curtan *v.*, 18 Nev. 310. § 7.
v. Malone, 48 Ala. 428. § 342.
Davids, Jones *v.*, 4 Russ. 277. § 313.
Davidson, Antrobus *v.*, 3 Merivale, 569. §§ 223, 238.
v. Farrell, 8 Minn. 258. § 615.
Menard *v.*, 3 La. Ann. 480. § 392.
Pope *v.*, 5 J. J. Marsh. (Ky.) 400, § 222.
Victoria Mutual Fire Ins. Co. *v.*, 3 Ont. (Can.) 378. § 629.
Davies, Calvo *v.*, 8 Hun (N. Y.), 222. § 37.
v. Funston, 45 Up. Can. (Q. B.) 369. § 16.
v. Humphreys, 6 Mees. & Wels. 153. §§ 207, 208, 230, 287, 295.
v. London & Provincial Ins. Co., Law Rep. 8 Ch. Div. 469. § 419.
Mutual Life Ins. Co. *v.*, 12 J. & S. (N. Y. Super. Ct.) 172. §§ 37, 606.
Offord *v.*, 12 J. Scott (N. S.), 748. § 134.
Royal Ins. Co. *v.*, 40 Iowa, 469. § 133.
v. Stainbank, 6 De G., M. & G. 679. § 359.
Turner *v.*, 2 Esp. 478. § 264.
Daviess Co. Sav. Ass'n *v.* Sailor, 63 Mo. 24. § 252.
Davis *v.* Banks, 45 Ga. 138. § 17.
Blackener *v.*, 128 Mass. 538. § 26.
v. Blackwell, 5 Bradw. (Ill. App.) 32. § 19.
v. Board of Comm'rs, 72 N. C. 441. § 225.
v. Comm'rs Stokes Co., 74 N. C. 374. § 225.
v. Copeland, 67 N. Y. 127. § 126.
Davis *v.* Converse, 35 Vt. 503. § 417.
v. Emerson, 17 Me. 64. § 283.
Fellers *v.*, 22 S. C. 425. § 648.
Fuller *v.*, 1 Gray, 612. § 500.
Gross *v.*, 87 Tenn. (3 Pick.) 226. §§ 287, 288.
Hathaway *v.*, 33 Cal. 161. § 448.
Hayes *v.*, 18 N. H. 600. § 268.
Hollister *v.*, 54 Pa. St. 508. §§ 236, 331.
v. Hoopes, 33 Miss. 175. § 143.
v. Huggins, 3 N. H. 231. § 242.
v. Kingsley, 13 Conn. 285. § 625.
v. Lane, 10 N. H. 156. § 354.
v. Mikell, 1 Freem. Ch. (Miss.) 548. §§ 29, 40, 434.
v. McCurdy, 50 Wis. 569. § 577.
v. Old Colony R. R. Co., 131 Mass. 258. § 6.
Partridge *v.*, 20 Vt. 499. §§ 47, 183.
v. People, 1 Gilm. (Ill.) 409. § 371.
Pintard *v*, 1 Spencer (N. J.), 205. §§ 30, 242.
Preston *v.*, 8 Ark. (3 Eng.) 167. § 137.
Protection Ins. Co. *v.*, 5 Allen, 54. §§ 195, 202.
Rader *v.*, 5 Lea (Tenn.), 436. §§ 152, 565.
Sample *v.*, 4 Greene (Iowa), 117. § 565.
v. Shields, 24 Wend. 322. § 89.
v. Shields, 26 Wend. 34. § 89.
v. Smith, 5 Ga. 274. § 313.
v. Stainbank, 6 De Gex, M. & G. 679. §§ 244, 369.
State *v.*, 12 S. C. 528. § 503.
State *v.*, 88 Mo. 585. § 571.
State *v.*, 96 Ind. 539. § 594.
v. State, 5 Tex. App. 48. § 385.
v. Statts, 43 Ind. 103. § 153.
Taylor *v.*, 38 Miss. 493. § 609.
Thomas *v.*, 14 Pick. 353. §§ 190, 192.
v. Toulmin, 77 N. Y. 280. §§ 236, 281.
Tucker *v.*, 15 Ga. 573. § 504.

Davis, Tyler *v.*, 63 Miss. 345. § 487.
v. Van Buren, 6 Daly (N. Y. Com. Pl.), 391. § 139.
v. Van Buren, 72 N. Y. 587. § 139.
v. Wells, 104 U. S. 159. §§ 13, 186, 204.
Wells, Fargo & Co. *v.*, 2 Utah Terr. 411. §§ 193, 203.
Willis *v.*, 3 Minn. 17. § 426.
Davis' Adm'r, Gross *v.*, 87 Tenn. (3 Pickle), 226. § 283.
v. Sneed, 33 Gratt. (Va.) 705. § 592.
Davis' Ex'r, Stewart *v.*, 18 Ind. 74. § 405.
Davis Sewing Machine Co. *v.* Buckles, 89 Ill. 237. § 406.
v. McGinnis, 45 Iowa, 538. § 119.
v. Mills, 55 Iowa, 543. § 202.
v. Jones, 61 Mo. 409. § 193.
v. Richards, 115 U. S. 524. § 186.
Davy, Dry *v.*, 2 Perry & Dav. 249. § 118.
Dawley, Fernald *v.*, 26 Me. 470. § 261.
Dawson *v.* Bank of Whitehaven, 4 Ch. Div. 639. § 35.
v. Baum, 3 Wash. Terr. 464. § 490.
Cochran *v.*, 1 Miles (Pa.), 276. § 102.
Colbourn *v.*, 10 Com. B. (1 J. Scott), 765. § 87.
v. Holt, 12 Lea (Tenn.), 27. § 452.
v. Lee, 83 Ky. 49. § 214.
v. Pettway, 4 Dev. & Bat. Law (N. C.), 396. § 260.
v. State, 38 Ohio St. 1. § 551.
Toomer *v.*, Cheves (S. C.), 68. § 80.
Wilson *v.*, 52 Ind. 513. § 432.
Day *v.* Billingsby, 3 Bush (Ky.), 157. § 617.
Bishop *v.*, 13 Vt. 81. § 223.
Chase *v.*, 17 Johns. 114. §§ 76, 77.
Cluff *v.*, 23 J. & S. (N. Y. Super. Ct.) 460. § 586
v. Elmore, 4 Wis. 190. §§ 84, 97, 100.
Flint *v.*, 9 Vt. 345. § 180.
Day, Holmes *v.*, 108 Mass. 563. § 278.
James *v.*, 37 Iowa, 164. § 37.
Marsh *v.*, 18 Pick. 321. § 126.
Pickering *v.*, 3 Houst. (Del.) 474. §§ 338, 423, 536.
Pickering *v.*, 2 Del. Ch. 333. § 559.
v. Rumey & Co., 40 Ohio St. 446. § 434.
v. Swann, 13 Me. 165. § 209.
D'Wolf, Quintard *v.*, 34 Barb. (N. Y.) 97. § 62.
v. Rabaud, 1 Pet. 476. §§ 60, 74, 86.
De Beil *v.* Thomson, 3 Beav. 469. § 80.
De Castro *v.* Clarke, 29 Cal. 11. § 459.
De Cottes *v.* Jeffers, 7 Fla. 284. § 224.
De Graw, Oshiel *v.*, 6 Cow. 63. § 112.
De Greiff *v.* Wilson, 30 N. J. Eq. 435. § 630.
De Jarnette, Tyus *v.*, 26 Ala. 280. §§ 269, 301.
De Pelanconi, People *v.*, 63 Cal. 409. § 509.
De Peyster, Wheelwright *v.*, 4 Edwards' Ch. 232. § 35.
De Vries *v.* Conklin, 22 Mich. 255. § 7.
De Witt, Mitchell *v.*, 25 Tex. (Supplement), 180. § 262.
De Wolf, Graeter *v.*, 112 Ind. 1. § 112.
De Young, Clymer *v.*, 54 Pa. St. 118. §§ 63, 66.
Deacon, Pearl *v.*, 24 Beav. 186. § 335.
Deadman, Ellis *v.*, 4 Bibb (Ky.), 466. § 80.
Deakin *v.* Stanton, 3 Fed. Rep. 435. § 476.
Deal *v.* Cochran, 66 N. C. 269. § 342.
Dean, Caruthers *v.*, 11 Smedes & Mar. (Miss.) 178. § 438.
Labadie *v.*, 47 Tex. 90. § 480.
Morton *v.*, 13 Met. (Mass.) 385. §§ 80, 90.
Richardson School Fund *v.*, 130 Mass. 242. § 165.
Wilson & Co. *v.*, 21 S. C. 327. § 104.
Dearborn *v.* Parks, 5 Greenl. (Me.) 81. § 66.

Dearborn v. Sawyer, 59 N. H. 95. § 202.
Deardorff v. Foreman, 24 Ind. 481. § 407.
Deatherage, Robertson v., 82 Ind. 511. § 259.
Deberry v. Adams, 9 Yerg. (Tenn.) 52. § 30.
Deblois v. Earle, 7 R. I. 26. § 108.
Dechaums, Reynolds v., 24 Tex. 174. § 8.
Decker v. Anderson, 39 Barb. (N. Y.) 346. § 486.
v. Gaylord, 8 Hun (N. Y.), 110. § 108.
v. Judson, 16 N. Y. 439. § 42.
Dederer, Yale v., 18 N. Y. 265. § 7.
Dedham Bank v. Chickering, 3 Pick. 335. § 173.
v. Chickering, 4 Pick. 314. § 560.
Dedrick, Cooper v., 22 Barb. (N. Y.) 516. §§ 47, 84, 643.
Deer Lodge Co. v. At, 3 Mont. 168. § 508.
Deere, Mansur & Co., Hardware Co. v., 53 Ark. 140. § 206.
Deering v. Earl of Winchelsea, 2 Bos. & Pul. 270. § 255.
Deery, People v., 6 Daly (N. Y. Com. Pl.), 493. § 511.
Deforest, Drakeley v., 3 Conn. 272. § 63.
Degge, Jones v., 84 Va. 685. § 140.
Deifendorf, Elwood v., 5 Barb. (N. Y.) 398. § 211.
Deitzler v. Mishler, 37 Pa. St. 82. § 38.
Delacour v. Caulfield, 1 Irish Com. Law, 669. § 538.
Delaney v. Tipton, 3 Hayw. (Tenn.) 14. § 223.
Delaplaine v. Hitchcock, 4 Edwards' Ch. 321. § 40.
Delaware, L. & W. R. R. Co. v. Burkhard, 114 N. Y. 197. § 95.
v. Burkhard, 36 Hun (N. Y.), 57. §§ 161, 343.
v. Oxford Iron Co., 38 N. J. Eq. 151. §§ 212, 223.
Demarest, Chelmsford Company v., 7 Gray, 1. §§ 168, 624.
Demass, Reusch v., 34 Mich. 95. § 484.
Dement, Cushman v., 3 Scam. (Ill.) 497. § 176.
Dempsey v. Bush, 18 Ohio St. 376. § 310.
Denick v. Hubbard, 27 Hun (N. Y.), 347. §§ 240, 357.
Denil v. Martel, 10 La. Ann. 643. § 347.
Dening, Taylor v., 3 Nev. & Per. 228. § 89.
Denio v. State, 60 Miss. 949. § 548.
Denison v. Gibson, 24 Mich. 187. §§ 34, 35, 124, 234.
Denmire, German-American Bank v., 58 Iowa, 137. § 614.
Dennard v. State, 2 Kelly (Ga.), 137. § 501.
Dennett, Haines v., 11 N. H. 180. § 381.
Ingalls v., 6 Greenl. (Me.) 79. § 205.
McCann v., 13 N. H. 528. § 339.
Dennie, Harrington v., 13 Mass. 93. § 499.
v. Smith, 129 Mass. 143. § 636.
Dennis, Courtis v., 7 Met. (Mass.) 510. §§ 1, 192.
v. Gillespie, 24 Miss. 581. § 263.
Mayor of Cambridge v., Ell., Black. & Ell. 660. § 169.
v. Piper, 21 Ill. App. 169. § 353.
Dennison v. Soper, 33 Iowa, 183. § 205.
Stone v., 13 Pick. 1. § 52.
Denniston, Bonine v., 41 Mich. 292. § 3.
Denson v. Miller, 33 Ga. 275. § 605.
Denton, Fairlie v., 2 Man. & Ry., 353. § 66.
v. Woods' Adm'r, 11 Lea (Tenn.), 505. § 452.
Deobold v. Oppermann, 111 N. Y. 531. §§ 3, 14, 587.
Depriest, Franklin's Adm'r v., 13 Gratt. (Va.) 257. § 43.
Deputy, Redman v., 26 Ind. 338. § 356.

Derby Coal Co., Clow *v.*, 98 Pa. 432. § 426.
Dering, Baker *v.*, 8 Adol. & Ell. 94. § 89.
Derossett *v.* Bradley, 63 N. C. 17. § 281.
Derrickson, Dickerson *v.*, 39 Ill., 574. § 200.
Waples *v.*, 1 Harr. (Del.) 134. § 505.
Derry Bank *v.* Baldwin, 41 N. H. 434. § 41.
Heath *v.*, 44 N. H. 174. §§ 111, 243.
Desmarais, Romero *v.*, 4 N. M. 367. § 209.
Dessar, Reisnner *v.*, 80 Ind. 307. § 486.
Detroit *v.* Houghton, 42 Mich. 459. § 590.
v. Weber, 26 Mich. 284. §§ 547, 555, 557.
Detroit Savings Bank *v.* Ziegler, 49 Mich. 157. § 561.
Devendorf, Albany City Fire Ins. Co. *v.*, 43 Barb. (N. Y.) 444. § 364.
Devers *v.* Ross, 10 Gratt. (Va.) 252. § 374.
Devinney *v.* Lay, 19 Mo. 646. § 604.
Devlin, City of Newton *v.*, 134 Mass. 490. § 601.
Ring *v.*, 68 Wis. 384. § 14.
v. Woodgate, 34 Barb. (N. Y.) 252. § 67.
Devon, Carpenter *v.*, 6 Ala. 718. § 40.
Devore *v.* Mundy, 4 Strob. Law (S. C.), 15. § 362.
Dewees, Scott *v.*, 2 Tex. 153. § 611.
Dewey, Burgess *v.*, 33 Vt. 618. § 356.
v. Reed, 40 Barb. (N. Y.) 16. § 379.
Dewitt *v.* Bigelow, 11 Ala. 480. § 342.
v. Boring, 123 Ind. 4. § 648.
Dewitt Co. Nat. Bank *v.* Nixon, 125 Ill. 615. § 176.
Dexter *v.* Blanchard, 11 Allen, 365. § 58.
Dey *v.* Martin, 78 Va. 1. § 388.
Diamond *v.* Petit, 3 La. Ann. 37. § 464.
Dibrell *v.* Dandridge, 51 Miss. 55. § 616.
Dick, Lee *v.*, 10 Pet. 482. §§ 186, 188.
v. Stoker, 1 Dev. Law (N. C.), 91. § 494.
Dickason *v.* Bell, 13 La. Ann. 249. § 149.
Dickeman, People *v.*, 3 Abb. Rep. Om. Cas. 520. § 569.
Dickerson, Bessinger *v.*, 20 Iowa, 260. § 563.
v. Comm'rs Ripley Co., 6 Ind. 128. §§ 30, 243, 348, 374.
v. Derrickson, 39 Ill. 574. § 200.
v. Herman, 9 Daly (N. Y. Com. Pl.), 298. § 477.
Manufacturers' Bank *v.*, 41 N. J. Law, 448. 548.
Mayor of Newark *v.*, 45 N. J. Law, 38. § 597.
Placer County *v.*, 45 Cal. 12. §§ 538, 627.
v. State, 20 Neb. 72. §§ 43, 504.
Thompson *v.*, 22 Iowa, 360. § 541.
Toomer *v.*, 37 Ga. 428. § 445.
v. Turner, 15 Ind. 4. § 185.
Dickey *v.* Rogers, 19 Martin (La.), 7 N. S. 588. §§ 208, 229.
Dickinson *v.* Codwise, 1 Sandf. Ch. 214. § 35.
Croydon Gas Co. *v.*, Law Rep. 2 Com. Pl. Div. 46. § 369.
Hunter *v.*, 10 Humph. (Tenn.) 37. § 199.
Hyner *v.*, 32 Ark. 776. §§ 7, 11.
Inhabitants of Phipsburg *v.*, 78 Me. 457. § 546.
Morley *v.*, 12 Cal. 561. § 434.
Smith *v.*, 6 Humph. (Tenn.) 261. § 49.
Dicks, Walker *v.*, 80 N. C. 263. § 227.
Dickson *v.* McPherson, 3 Grant's Ch. App. 185. § 415.
Dickson, Adm'r, Scott *v.*, 108 Pa. St. 6. § 603.
Diefendorf, Second Nat. Bank of Peoria *v.*, 90 Ill. 396. §§ 93, 117.
Diehl, Blauser *v.*, 90 Pa. St. 350. § 583.

Dierker, Britton v., 46 Mo. 591. § 379.
Diers, Newton Wagon Co. v., 10 Neb. 284. §§ 14, 197.
Dietrich v. Mitchell, 43 Ill. 41. § 178.
Diffenderfer, Winder v., 2 Bland's Ch. (Md.) 166. § 298.
Dignan v. Shields, 51 Tex. 322. §§ 22, 648.
Dill v. Lawrence, 109 Ind. 564. § 113.
Root v., 38 Ind. 169. § 608.
Dillahunty, Brown v., 4 Sm. & Mar. (Miss.) 713. § 498.
Dillenbeck v. Dygert, 97 N. Y. 303. § 260.
Dillingham v. Jenkins, 7 Sm. & Mar. (Miss.) 479. § 413.
Montgomery v., 3 Sm. & Mar. (Miss.) 647. §§ 342, 625.
Dillon v. Holmes, 5 Neb. 484. § 242.
v. Russell, 5 Neb. 484. § 342.
v. Schofield, 11 Neb. 419. § 487.
v. Smith, 10 Heisk. 595. § 103.
St. Albans Bank v., 30 Vt. 122. § 153.
Dills v. Cecil, 4 Bush (Ky.), 579. § 438.
Dilts v. Parke, 1 South. (N. J.) 219. § 63.
Stout v., 1 Southard (N. J.), 218. § 317.
Dime Savings Bank, Price v., 124 Ill. 317. §§ 34, 342.
Dineen v. Williams, 138 Mass. 367. § 502.
Dinkins v. Bailey, 23 Miss. 284. § 312.
Dinsmore, Hilton v., 21 Me. 410. § 63.
v. Tidball, 34 Ohio St. 411. § 424.
Dipple, Harner v., 31 Ohio St. 72. § 4.
District Township of Fox v. McCord, 54 Iowa, 346. § 546.
District Township Union v. Smith, 39 Iowa, 9. §§ 558, 559.
Ditmars v. Commonwealth, 47 Pa. St. 335. § 563.
Ditson, White v., 140 Mass. 351. §§ 629, 645.
Dix v. Morris, 66 Mo. 514. §§ 583, 632.
Dixon, Ayers v., 78 N. Y. 318. § 37.
Carlon v., 12 Oreg. 144. § 22.
Carlon v., 14 Oreg. 293. § 492.
v. Caskey, 18 Ala. 97. § 537.
v. Dixon, 31 Vt. 450. § 407.
v. Ewing's Adm'r, 3 Ohio, 280. § 434.
v. Frazee, 1 E. D. Smith (N. Y.), 32. §§ 76, 78.
v. Hatfield, 2 Biug. 439. § 77.
Marshall v., 82 Ga. 435. § 351.
Montpelier Bank v., 4 Vt. 587. § 437.
v. Spencer, McKay & Co., 59 Md. 246. §§ 363, 364.
Steel v., Law Rep. (17 Ch. Div.) 825. § 268.
Sykes v., 9 Adol. & Ell. 693. § 85.
v. Vanderberg, 35 N. J. Eq. 47. § 139.
Doak, Smith v., 3 Tex. 215. §§ 30, 402.
Doane, State v., 30 La. Ann. 1194. § 505.
v. Telegraph Co., 11 La. Ann. 504. § 128.
Dobbins, Jordan v., 122 Mass. 168. § 134.
Dobbs v. Justices, 17 Ga. 624. §§ 559, 567, 627.
Dobell v. The Ontario Bank, 3 Ont. (Can.) 299. § 6.
Dobschuetz, Mueller v., 89 Ill. 176. § 376.
Dobson v. Prather, 6 Ired. Eq. (N. C.) 31. § 435.
Dobyns v. McGovern, 15 Mo. 662. § 582.
Dock v. Hart, 7 Watts & Serg. 172. § 52.
Dodd, Craft v., 15 Ind. 380. § 608.
v. Dreyfus, 17 Hun (N. Y.), 600. § 36.
Governor v., 81 Ill. 162. § 531.
v. Wilson, 4 Del. Ch. 399. § 329.
v. Winn, 27 Mo. 501. § 439.
Dodds v. Duncan, 12 Lea (Tenn.), 731. § 487.
Dodge, Johnson v., 17 Ill. 433. § 90.
v. Kinzy, 101 Ind. 102. § 7.

Dodge *v.* Lean, 13 Johns. 508. § 81.
Mackey *v.*, 5 Ala. 388. § 119.
Reilly *v.*, 42 Hun (N. Y.), 646. §§ 25, 526, 527.
v. St. John, 96 N. Y. 260. § 576.
Thomas *v.*, 8 Mich. 51. §§ 81, 98.
v. Van Lear, 5 Cranch, C. C. 278. § 80.
Dodgson *v.* Henderson, 113 Ill. 360. § 93.
Henderson *v.*, 9 Bradw. (Ill. App.) 80. § 342.
Johnson *v.*, 2 Mees. & Wels. 653. §§ 80, 89.
Doepner *v.* State, 36 Ind. 111. § 562.
Doggett *v.* Black, 40 Fed. Rep. 439. § 466.
Doherty, Black *v.*, 22 New Brunswick Rep. 215. § 77.
Dohlonde, Boykin *v.*, 1 Sel. Cas. Ala. 502. § 76.
Doidge, Melville *v.*, 6 Man., Gr. & Scott, 450. § 560.
Dolby *v.* Jones, 2 Dev. Law (N. C.), 109. § 450.
Dole *v.* Young, 24 Pick. 250. § 204.
Doles, Jones *v.*, 3 La. Ann. 588. § 630.
Dolloff, Cullom *v.*, 94 Ill. 330. § 532.
Doman, Rindskopf *v.*, 28 Ohio St. 516. §§ 142, 347.
Domestic Sewing Machine Co. *v.* Jackson, 15 Lea (Tenn.), 418. §§ 421, 422.
v. Webster, 47 Iowa, 357. §§ 392, 644.
Donaldson, Yates *v.*, 5 Md. 389. § 29.
Donally *v.* Wilson, 5 Leigh (Va.), 329. § 335.
Donegan, State *v.*, 12 Mo. App. 190. § 580.
State *v.*, 83 Mo. 374. § 632.
Donegby, Bolling *v.*, 1 Duvall (Ky.), 220. § 290.
Donley *v.* Bush, 44 Tex. 1. § 184.
v. Wiggins, 52 Tex. 301. § 569.
Donnelly *v.* Elser, 69 Tex. 287. § 19.
Donner, Frickee *v.*, 35 Mich. 151. § 366.
Donohue *v.* Roberts (Cir. Ct. E. D. Mo.), 1 Fed. Rep. 449. § 587.
Donovan, Friberg *v.*, 23 Ill. App. 58. § 262.
Roberts *v.*, 70 Cal. 108. §§ 399, 423.
Doody, Carpenter *v.*, 1 Hilt. (N. Y.) 465. §§ 567, 570.
Doolan, Lawrence *v.*, 68 Cal. 309. § 524.
Doolittle *v.* Naylor, 2 Bosw. (N. Y.) 206. § 65.
v. Dwight, 2 Met. (Mass.) 561. §§ 211, 273.
Doran *v.* Cohen, 147 Mass. 342. § 469.
Dorman *v.* Bigelow, 1 Fla. 281. §§ 87, 88.
v. Executor of Richard, 1 Fla. 281. § 82.
Dorr, Supervisors Albany *v.*, 7 Hill (N. Y.), 583. § 558.
Dorrington *v.* Minnick, 15 Neb. 397. § 221.
Dorriss *v.* Carter, 67 Mo. 544. § 476.
Dorsey, Neptune Ins. Co. *v.*, 3 Md. Ch. 334. § 306.
v. Wayman, 6 Gill (Md.), 59. § 448.
Dorwin, Austin *v.*, 21 Vt. 38. §§ 348, 353, 356.
Dorwin, Estate of, Peake *v.*, 25 Vt. 28. § 358.
Doster, Pool *v.*, 59 Miss. 258, 263. § 326.
Doty *v.* Ellsbee, 11 Kan. 209. § 530.
Wincherl *v.*, 15 Hun (N. Y.), 1. § 107.
Doud *v.* Waller, 48 Iowa, 634. § 175.
Dougherty, Houston *v.*, 4 Humph. (Tenn.) 505. § 616.
McDougald *v.*, 14 Ga. 674. § 311.
v. Peters, 2 Rob. (La.) 534. § 570.
v. Richardson, 20 Ind. 412. § 40.
Doughty *v.* Bacot, 2 Desaus. Eq. (S. C.) 546. § 33.
v. Savage, 28 Conn. 146. §§ 403, 420.
Douglas, Bank *v.*, 4 Watts (Pa.), 95. § 325.

Douglas, Commonwealth *v.*, 11 Bush (Ky.), 607. § 502.
v. Howland, 24 Wend. 35. §§ 82, 84, 200, 630.
Israel *v.*, 1 H. Black. 239. § 66.
v. Spears, 2 Nott & McC. (S. C.) 207. § 89.
Douglass, Artcher *v.*, 5 Denio, 509. § 151.
Atlanta National Bank *v.*, 51 Ga. 205. § 388.
Glazier *v.*, 32 Conn. 393. § 430.
Municipal Corp. East Lora *v.*, 17 Grant's Ch. 462. §§ 419, 555.
Petty *v.*, 76 Mo. 70. §§ 241, 353.
v. Rathbone, 5 Hill, 143. § 197.
v. Reynolds, 7 Pet. 113. §§ 92, 94, 161, 186, 192, 201, 202, 204, 440.
v. State, 44 Ind. 67. § 352.
State *v.*, 69 Ind. 544. § 509.
Dousay, Mason *v.*, 35 Ill. 424. § 67.
Dover Stamping Co. *v.* Noyes, 151 Mass. 342. § 161.
Dow, Baldwin *v.*, 130 Mass. 416. § 47.
Greely *v.*, 2 Met. (Mass.) 176. §§ 348, 353.
Hetfield *v.*, 3 Dutch. (N. J.) 440. §§ 76, 77.
Jones *v.*, 142 Mass. 130. § 47.
Joslyn *v.*, 19 Hun (N. Y.), 494. § 5.
Thomas *v.*, 33 Me. 390. § 342.
Woodford *v.*, 34 Ill. 424. § 354.
Dowbiggin *v.* Bourne, 2 Younge & Collyer (Exch.), 462. § 310.
Dowden & Co. *v.* Lewis, Irish, 14 Q. B. (C. P. & Ex.) 307. § 369.
Dowell, Silvey *v.*, 53 Ill. 260. § 269.
Dowling, Bennett *v.*, 22 Tex. 660. 217.
Down, Muller *v.*, 94 U. S. 444. § 226.
Downer *v.* Baxter, 30 Vt. 467. § 217.
v. Dana, 17 Vt. 518. § 236.
Dunham *v.*, 31 Vt. 249. §§ 40, 244.
Sylvester *v.*, 18 Vt. 32. §§ 131, 198.
Downer, Sylvester *v.*, 20 Vt. 355. § 182.
Woodstock Bank *v.*, 27 Vt. 539. §§ 126, 199, 204.
Downey, Blake *v.*, 51 Mo. 437. § 205.
v. Hinchman, 25 Ind. 453. § 58.
McClellan *v.*, 63 Cal. 520. § 580.
Downing, Rice *v.*, 12 B. Mon. (Ky.) 44. § 238.
Downs, Erwin *v.*, 15 N. Y. 575. § 28.
Dox *v.* Postmaster-General, 1 Pet. 318. § 555.
Doyal, State *v.*, 12 La. Ann. 653. § 494.
Doyle *v.* White, 26 Me. 341. § 76.
Dozier, Bethune *v.*, 10 Ga. 235. §§ 388, 605.
Lea *v.*, 10 Humph. (Tenn.) 447. § 364.
v. Lewis, 27 Miss. 679. § 301.
v. Lee, 7 Humph. (Tenn.) 520. § 30.
Drabek *v.* Grand Lodge, 24 Ill. App. 82. § 422.
Drake, Edmondston *v.*, 5 Pet. 624. §§ 186, 398.
v. Flewellen, 33 Ala. 106. § 58.
Seaman *v.*, 1 Caines' Rep. 9. § 150.
v. Smythe, 44 Iowa, 410. § 372.
State *v.*, 52 Ark. 350. § 587.
Taylor *v.*, 4 Strobh. (S. C.) 431. §§ 74, 75.
Drakeley, Monson *v.*, 40 Conn. 552. § 258.
Drakely, Gist *v.*, 2 Gill (Md.), 330. §§ 176, 180.
Draper *v.* Pottani, 2 Spear (S. C.), 292. §§ 80, 89.
Richardson *v.*, 87 N. Y. 337. §§ 94, 140.
v. Romeyn, 18 Barb. 166. § 342.
v. Snow, 20 N. Y. 331. § 87.
v. Weld, 13 Gray, 580. § 350.
Wilcox *v.*, 12 Neb. 138. § 193.
Draughan *v.* Bunting, 9 Ired. Law (N. C.), 10. §§ 61, 281.
Drennan, Porter *v.*, 11 Bradw. (Ill. App.) 362. § 91.

Dresler, Fitzgerald *v.*, 7 Com. B. (U. S.) 374. §§ 65, 68.
Dresser, Highland *v.*, 35 Minn. 345. § 87.
Drew *v.* Lockett, 32 Beav. 499. § 316.
Walker *v.*, 20 Fla. 908. § 603.
Dreyfus, Dodd *v.*, 17 Hun (N. Y.), 600. § 36.
Drinker, Stern *v.*, 2 E. D. Smith (N. Y.), 401. § 64.
Driscoll *v.* Barker, 2 P. & B. (N. B.) 407. § 378.
v. Blake, 9 Irish Ch. Rep. 356. § 42.
Driskell *v.* Mateer, 31 Mo. 325. § 246.
Driskill *v.* Board Commissioners, 53 Ind. 532. § 606.
Druett's Adm'r, Peck *v.*, 9 Dana (Ky.), 486. § 420.
Druly, State *v.*, 3 Ind. 431. § 566.
Drummond, Boydell *v.*, 11 East, 142. § 80.
v. Prestman, 12 Wheaton, 515. §§ 116, 117, 626.
Singer Mfg. Co. *v.*, 40 Hun (N. Y.), 260. § 408.
v. Yager, 10 Bradw. (Ill. App.) 380. §§ 254, 260.
Drury *v.* Fay, 14 Pick. 326. §§ 247, 642.
Paine *v.*, 19 Pick. 400. § 129.
State *v.*, 36 Mo. 281. § 540.
Dry *v.* Davy, 2 Perry & Dav. 249. § 118.
Dryden, Gray *v.*, 79 Mo. 106. § 462.
Dubois, Grove *v.*, 1 Term R. 112. § 71.
Dubuisson *v.* Folkes, 30 Miss. 432. §§ 351, 352.
Dubuque First Nat. Bank *v.* Carpenter, 41 Iowa, 518. § 203.
Dubuque County Bank, Heard *v.*, 8 Neb. 10. § 50.
Ducker *v.* Rapp, 67 N. Y. 464. §§ 351, 355.
v. Rapp, 9 Jones & Spencer (N. Y.), 235. § 201.
Dudgeon, City National Bank *v.*, 65 Ill. 11. § 315.
Dudley, Beebe *v.*, 26 N. H. 249. §§ 188, 202.
Schwessler *v.*, 80 Ala. 547. § 320.
Duer *v.* Morrill, 20 Bradw. (Ill. App.) 355. § 351.
Dufau *v.* Wright, 25 Wend. 636. § 108.
Duff *v.* Barrett, 15 Grant's Ch. 632. § 371.
Duffee, Henderson *v.*, 5 N. H. 38. § 288.
Duffield, Coe *v.*, 7 Moore, 252. § 87.
v. Cooper, 87 Pa. St. 443. § 309.
Dugan *v.* Sprague, 2 Ind. 600. § 366.
Duggan, Carter *v.*, 144 Mass. 32. § 571.
White *v.*, 140 Mass. 18. § 410.
Dugger *v.* Wright, 51 Ark. 232. § 586.
Duhamp *v.* Nicholson, 14 Martin (La.), 2 N. S. 672. § 42.
Duke of Marlborough, Kirby *v.*, 2 Maule & Sel. 18. §§ 162, 165.
Dullens, Brunton *v.*, 1 Foster & Fin. 450. § 76.
Dumont *v.* Fry, (Cir. Ct. S. D. N. Y.), 14 Fed. Rep. 293. § 253.
Harbert *v.*, 3 Ind. 346. §§ 348, 356.
v. United States, 98 U. S. 142. § 623.
v. Williamson, 18 Ohio St. 515. § 28.
Dunbar *v.* Brown, 4 McLean, 166. § 197.
Duncan, Bank *v.*, 52 Miss. 740. § 615.
Carter *v.*, 84 N. C. 676. § 364.
Cowan *v.*, Meigs (Tenn.), 470. § 262.
Dodds *v.*, 12 Lea (Tenn.), 731. § 487.
Evans *v.*, 1 Tyrw. 283. § 52.
v. Heller, 13 S. C. 94. § 191.
v. Keiffer, 3 Bin. (Pa.) 126. § 225.
v. Lowndes, 3 Camp. 478. § 18.
Mitchell *v.*, 7 Fla. 13. § 22.
v. Owens, 47 Ark. 388. § 487.
v. State, 7 La. Ann. 377. § 555.

Duncan, Tinkum *v.*, 1 Grant's Cas. (Pa.) 228. § 100.
Wharton *v.*, 83 Pa. St. 40. § 426.
Duncan, Fox & Co. *v.* North & South Wales Bank, Law Rep. (6 H. of L. App. Cases), 1. § 329.
Dunckel, Marsh *v.*, 25 Hun (N. Y.), 167. § 239.
Duncombe, Galbraith *v.*, 28 Grant's Ch. (Can.) 27. § 528.
v. Tickridge, Aleyn, 94. § 58.
Dundas *v.* Sterling, 4 Pa. St. 73. § 415.
Dunham *v.* Countryman, 66 Barb. (N. Y.) 268. § 360.
v. Downer, 31 Vt. 249. §§ 40, 244.
Dunham's Ex'rs, Stothoff *v.*, 4 Harr. (N. J.) 181. §§ 284, 288.
Dunklee, Hamilton *v.*, 1 N. H. 172. § 497.
Dunlap, Caston *v.*, Rich. Eq. Cas. (S. C.) 77. § 242.
Fear *v.*, 1 Greene (Iowa), 331. §§ 176, 202.
v. Foster, 7 Ala. 734. § 468.
v. McNeil, 35 Ind. 316. § 137.
People *v.*, 13 Johns. 437. § 586.
v. Thorne, 1 Rich. (S. C.) 213. § 64.
Dunlop *v.* Gordon, 10 La. Ann. 243. § 122.
Dunn, Kellogg *v.*, 2 Met. (Ky.) 215. § 182.
Leeds *v.*, 10 N. Y. 469. § 123.
Maclean *v.*, 4 Bing. 722. § 90.
v. Parsons, 40 Hun (N. Y.), 77. §§ 415, 434.
v. Slee, 1 Moore, 2. § 280.
v. Sparks, 1 Ind. 397. § 276.
v. Sparks, 7 Ind. 490. § 260.
Spooner *v.*, 7 Ind. 81. § 64.
Smith *v.*, 6 Hill, 543. § 196.
v. Smith, 12 Sm. & Mar. (Miss.) 602. § 402.
State *v.*, 11 La. Ann. 549. §§ 386, 422.
Supervisors of Washington Co. *v.*, 27 Gratt. (Va.) 608. §§ 520, 628.
Dunn *v.* Wade, 23 Mo. 207. § 260.
v. West, 5 B. Mon. (Ky.) 376. § 60.
Dunning *v.* Roberts, 35 Barb. (N. Y.) 463. § 89.
Dunphy *v.* Gorman, 29 Ill. App. 132. § 298.
v. Whipple, 25 Mich. 10. § 537.
Dunsford, Eyre *v.*, 1 East, 318. § 73.
Duphorn, Baugher's Ex'rs *v.*, 9 Gill (Md.), 314. § 335.
Durand *v.* Bowen, 73 Iowa, 573. § 101.
Durein *v.* State, 38 Kan. 485. § 508.
Duren, Aiken *v.*, 2 Nott & McCord (S. C.), 370. § 68.
Durfee *v.* Abbott, 61 Mich. 471. §§ 360, 365.
Woodin *v.*, 46 Mich. 424. § 411.
Durham *v.* Craig, 79 Ind. 117. § 324.
v. Manrow, 2 N. Y. 533. § 67.
Manrow *v.*, 3 Hill, 584. § 88.
McClatchie *v.*, 44 Mich. 435. § 295.
Van Orden *v.*, 35 Cal. 136. § 326.
Durham & Co. *v.* Lisso & Scheen, 32 La. Ann. 415. § 10.
Durkee, Titus *v.*, 12 Up. Can. (C. P.) 367. § 399.
Whitridge *v.*, 2 Md. Ch. 442. § 238.
Durrive, Ledoux *v.*, 10 La. Ann. 7. § 267.
Dussol *v.* Brugniere, 50 Cal. 456. § 291.
Dustin, Oak *v.*, 79 Me. 23. § 504.
Dutchman *v.* Tooth, 5 Bing. N. C. 211. § 84.
Duval, Croughton *v.*, 3 Call (Va.), 69. § 242.
v. Trask, 12 Mass. 154. § 81.
Dwarris, Wood *v.*, 11 Exch. 493. § 405.
Dwight, Doolittle *v.*, 2 Met. (Mass.) 561. §§ 211, 276.
Lewis *v.*, 10 Conn. 95. §§ 112, 158.
v. Linton, 3 Rob. (La.) 57. §§ 182, 405.
v. Pomeroy, 17 Mass. 308. § 405.
v. Williams, 4 McLean, 581. § 100.

Dwinnell, Keith v., 38 Vt. 286. § 161.
Dwyer, English v., Law Rep. Irish (12 Q. B., C. P. & Ex. Div.), 92. § 519.
Dye, Cockrill v., 33 Mo. 365. § 614.
v. Dye, 21 Ohio St. 86. § 448.
v. Mann, 10 Mich. 291. § 209.
Dyer, Poole v., 123 Mass. 363. §§ 470, 516.
Cole v., 1 Cromp. & Jer. 461. §§ 82, 85.
v. Gibson, 16 Wis. 508. § 67.
v. Graves, 37 Vt. 369. § 52.
Miller v., 1 Duvall (Ky.), 263. §§ 435, 438.
Wright v., 48 Mo. 525. § 201.
Dygert, Dillenbeck v., 97 N. Y. 303. § 260.
Dykers v. Townsend, 24 N. Y. 57. § 90.
Dykes, Pilgrim v., 24 Tex. 383. § 371.
Eagan, Cornell v., 13 Daly (N. Y. Com. Pl.), 505. § 388.
Eagle M. & R. Machine Co. v. Shattuck, 53 Wis. 455. § 67.
Eagles v. Kern, 5 Whart. (Pa.) 144. § 636.
Eales v. Fraser, 6 Man. & Gr. 755. § 40.
Earl, Levi v., 30 Ohio St. 147. § 7.
Earl of Winchester, Deering v., 2 Bos. & Pul. 270. § 255.
Earle v. Earle, 17 J. & S. (N. Y. Super. Ct.) 57. § 9.
Evans v., 1 Hurl. & Gor. 1. § 174.
v. Cureton, 13 S. C. 19. § 615.
Deblois v., 7 R. I. 26. § 108.
Early, Cecil v., 10 Gratt. (Va.) 198. §§ 112, 520.
Easter v. White, 12 Ohio St. 213. § 61.
Eastern Township Bank v. St. Johnsbury & L. C. R. Co. (Cir. Ct. D. Vt.), 40 Fed. Rep. 423. §§ 6, 50.
Eastern Union Railway Co. v. Cochrane, 9 Wels., Hurl. & Gor. 197. § 121.
East India Company v. Boddam, 9 Ves. 464. § 141.
East India Company, Law v., 4 Vesey, 824. §§ 93, 427.
Eastin & Breaux v. Board School Directors, 40 La. Ann. 705. § 590.
Eastman v. Bennett, 6 Wis. 232. § 84.
v. Foster, 8 Met. (Mass.) 19. § 324.
Joslyn v., 46 Vt. 258. § 339.
Norton v., 4 Greenl. (Me.) 521. §§ 192, 366.
v. Plumer, 32 N. H. 238. § 333.
East River Bank v. Rogers, 7 Bosw. (N. Y.) 493. § 199.
East Saginaw, White v., 43 Mich. 567. § 548.
Eastwood v. Kenyon, 3 Perry & Dav. 276. § 91.
v. Kenyon, 11 Ad. & Ell. 438. §§ 17, 72.
Eason v. Petway, 1 Dev. & Bat. Law (N. C.), 44. § 97.
Eatman v. Eatman, 82 Ala. 223. § 588.
Eaton v. Benefield, 2 Blackf. (Ind.) 52. § 578.
v. Hasty, 6 Neb. 419. § 298.
v. Lambert, 1 Neb. 339. § 212.
v. Mayo, 118 Mass. 141. § 103.
Eberhardt v. Wood, 2 Tenn. Ch. (Cooper), 488. §§ 267, 276.
Eberhart v. Page, 89 Ill. 550. § 176.
Ecker v. McAllister, 45 Md. 290. § 91.
Eckert, Beckley v., 3 Pa. St. 292. § 50.
v. Louis, 84 Ind. 99. § 382.
v. Myers, 45 Ohio St. 525. § 573.
Eckford's Ex'rs, Mann v., 15 Wend. 502. § 199.
United States v., 1 How. 250. § 338.
Eckman & Vetsburg v. Brash & Son, 20 Fla. 763. § 104.
Eddy v. Heath's Garnishees, 31 Mo. 141. § 559.
v. Roberts, 17 Ill. 505. § 62.
v. Stantons, 21 Wend. 255. § 100.
v. Sturgeon, 15 Mo. 198. § 337.
v. Traver, 6 Paige's Ch. 521. §§ 302, 310.
Edelen v. Gough, 5 Gill, 103. § 82.

Eder, Heynemann *v.*, 17 Cal. 433. § 470.
Edes *v.* Gary & Lanahan, 46 Md. 24. § 141.
Edge *v.* Frost, 4 Dow. & Ry. 243. § 77.
Edgerly *v.* Emerson, 23 N. H. 555. § 304.
Edgerton, Clay *v.*, 19 Ohio St. 549. § 199.
Yale *v.*, 14 Minn. 194. § 17.
Edmiston, Fay *v.*, 25 Kan. 439. §§ 636, 637.
Edmonds *v.* Edmonds, 73 Iowa, 427. § 577.
Goring *v.*, 6 Bing. 94. § 200.
v. Sheahan, 47 Tex. 443. § 212.
Edmonston *v.* Drake, 5 Pet. 624. §§ 186, 389.
Edmunds, Price *v.*, 10 Barn. & Cress. 578. § 368.
Edney, Reynolds *v.*, 8 Jones' Law (N. C.), 406. § 202.
Edson, Fletcher *v.*, 8 Vt. 294. § 222.
Edwards, Bailey *v.*, 4 Best & Smith, 761. § 375.
Bruce *v.*, 1 Stew. (Ala.) 11. §§ 29, 239.
v. Coleman, 6 T. B. Mon. (Ky.) 567. §§ 342, 345.
Cowell *v.*, 2 Bos. & Pul. 268. § 288.
Crouch *v.*, 52 Ark. 499. § 586.
v. Ellis, 27 Kan. 344. § 93.
Frank *v.*, 8 Wels., Hurl. & Gor. 214. § 392.
v. Gunn, 3 Conn. 316. § 494.
v. Jevons, 8 Man., Gr. & Scott, 436. §§ 84, 86.
v. Kelly, 6 Maule & S. 204. §§ 63, 66.
Little *v.*, 69 Md. 499. §§ 88, 91.
Mansfield *v.*, 136 Mass. 15. §§ 261, 289.
Missoula County *v.*, 3 Mont. 60. §§ 22, 546.
People *v.*, 9 Cal. 286. § 517.
Ramskill *v.*, Law Rep. (31 Ch. Div.) 100. § 284.
Skip *v.*, 9 Mod. 438. § 398.
Edwards, State Bank *v.*, 20 Ala. 512. § 434.
Wilson *v.*, 6 Lans. (N. Y.) 134. § 122.
Edwards' Adm'x, Sanders *v.*, 29 La. Ann. 696. § 587.
Egan *v.* Lynch, 17 J. & S. (N. Y. Super. Ct.) 454. § 10.
Egbert, Harriman *v.*, 36 Iowa, 270. § 605.
State *v.*, 123 Ind. 448. § 600.
Ege *v.* Barnitz, 8 Pa. St. 304. § 100.
Egerton *v.* Alley, 6 Ired. Eq. (N. C.) 188. § 237.
Eggleston, Paw Paw *v.*, 25 Mich. 36. § 547.
Ehlers, Board of Supervisors *v.*, 45 Wis. 281. § 542.
Eichelberger *v.* Gross, 42 Ohio St. 549. §§ 540, 577.
Markell *v.*, 12 Md. 78. §§ 218, 224.
v. Morris, 6 Watts (Pa.), 42. § 148.
Eidson *v.* Huff, 29 Gratt. (Va.) 338. § 329.
Eighmie, Allen *v.*, 14 Hun (N. Y.), 559. § 62.
Eilbert *v.* Finkbeiner, 68 Pa. St. 243. § 178.
Einstein, Fisse *v.*, 5 Mo. App. 78. §§ 93, 150, 472.
Eisenbeis, Comfort *v.*, 11 Pa. St. 13. § 220.
Eisenberg *v.* Albert, 40 Ohio St. 631. § 35.
Eisner, Tuska *v.*, 21 J. & S. (N. Y. Super. Ct.) 442. § 377.
Ekel, Snevily *v.*, 1 W. & S. 203. § 183.
Ela, New Hampshire Savings Bank *v.*, 11 N. H. 335. §§ 345, 352.
Webster *v.*, 5 N. H. 540. § 81.
Elam *v.* Heirs of Barr, 14 La. Ann. 682. § 24.
v. Rawson, 21 Ga. 139. § 312.
Elbert *v.* Jacoby, 8 Bush (Ky.), 542. § 542.

Elden *v.* Commonwealth, 55 Pa. St. 485. § 318.
Hubbard *v.*, 43 Ohio St. 380. § 571.
Elder *v.* Warfield, 7 Harr. & Johns. (Md.) 391. §§ 76, 77.
Eldredge, Ralph *v.*, 58 Hun (N. Y.), 203. § 98.
United States *v.*, 5 Utah, 161. §§ 508, 510, 516.
Eldridge, Trentman *v.*, 98 Ind. 525. § 35.
Elevator Company *v.* Memphis & C. R. R. Co., 85 Tenn. (1 Pickle), 703. § 6.
Elfe *v.* Gadsden, 2 Rich. (S. C.) 373. § 80.
Elgutter, Tootle *v.*, 14 Neb. 158. § 160.
Eliff, Garratt *v.*, 4 Humph. (Tenn.) 323. § 616.
Elkin *v.* People, 3 Scam. (Ill.) 207. § 537.
Elkins, Hatch *v.*, 65 N. Y. 489. § 624.
v. Heart, Fitzg. 202. § 70.
Ellair, Michie *v.*, 60 Mich. 73. § 452.
Elledge, Carman *v.*, 40 Iowa, 490. § 193.
Ellenwood *v.* Fults, 63 Barb. 321. § 17.
Ellett *v.* Britton, 10 Tex. 208. § 82.
Ellerbe's Adm'r, Martin *v.*, 70 Ala. 326. §§ 205, 207, 341, 579.
Ellery, Gould *v.*, 39 Barb. (N. Y.) 163. § 47.
Ellicott *v.* Levy Court, 1 Harr. & Johns. (Md.) 359. § 523.
Ellingwood, Chew *v.*, 86 Mo. 260. §§ 422, 425.
Elliot *v.* Hayes, 8 Gray, 164. § 130.
Elliott, Beach *v.*, 44 Conn. 237. § 515.
v. Boaz, 13 Ala. 535. § 415.
v. Giese, 7 Harr. & Johns. 457. § 82.
v. Gray, 4 Stew. & Port. (Ala.) 168. § 467.
v. Harris, 9 Bush (Ky.), 237. § 247.
Perkins *v.*, 8 C. E. Green (N. J.), 526. § 7.
Ellis *v.* Bibb, 2 Stew. (Ala.) 63. §§ 342, 347.
v. Brown, 6 Barb. 282. § 179.
v. Deadman, 4 Bibb (Ky.), 466. § 80.
Embree *v.*, 2 Johns. 119. § 216.
Edwards *v.*, 27 Kan. 344. § 93.
v. Emmanuel, Law Rep. (1 Ex. Div.) 157. § 253.
Fordyce *v.*, 29 Cal. 96. § 372.
v. Hull, 23 Cal. 160. § 464.
Manhattan Ins. Co. *v.*, 32 Ohio St. 388. § 425.
v. McCormick, 1 Hilton (N. Y.), 313. § 389.
v. Witty, 63 Miss. 117. § 10.
Ellis' Adm'r *v.* Adderton, 88 N. C. 482. § 45.
Ellison *v.* Jackson, 12 Cal. 542. § 82.
Pool *v.*, 56 Hun (N. Y.), 108. § 250.
Wiltmer *v.*, 72 Ill. 301. §§ 356, 374.
Ells, Pierson *v.*, 46 Hun (N. Y.), 336. § 480.
Ellsbree, Doty *v.*, 11 Kan. 209. § 530.
Ellsworth *v.* Harmon, 101 Ill. 274. § 47.
Virden *v.*, 15 Ind. 144. §§ 137, 201.
Elmendorph *v.* Tappen, 5 Johns. 176. § 129.
Elmore, Day *v.*, 4 Wis. 190. §§ 84, 97, 100.
Sailly *v.*, 2 Paige Ch. 497. §§ 243, 342.
Elmwood, Rochester City Bank *v.*, 21 N. Y. 88. § 561.
Elser, Donnelly *v.*, 69 Tex. 287. § 19.
Elting *v.* Vanderlyn, 4 Johns. 237. § 16.
Elwood *v.* Deifendorf, 5 Barb. (N. Y.) 398. § 211.
Ely, Harlun *v.*, 55 Cal. 340. § 129.
Manhattan Gas Light Co. *v.*, 39 Barb. (N. Y.) 174. § 118.
Thrasher *v.*, 2 Smedes & Marsh. (Miss.) 139. § 199.
Ward *v.*, 1 Dev. Law (N. C.), 372. § 105.

Emanuel, Collum *v.*, 1 Ala. 23. § 301.
Embree *v.* Ellis, 2 Johns. 119. § 216.
Emerson *v.* Aultman & Co., 69 Md. 125. §§ 82, 91.
Davis *v.*, 17 Me. 64. § 283.
Edgerly *v.*, 23 N. H. 555. § 304.
v. Slater, 22 How. 28. §§ 60, 70.
Emery *v.* Baltz, 22 Hun (N. Y.), 434. § 236.
v. Baltz, 94 N. Y. 408. § 134.
v. Clarke, 2 J. Scott (N. S.), 582. § 220.
Cutter *v.*, 37 N. H. 567. §§ 60, 264.
Jenkins *v.*, 2 Wyom. 58. § 518.
v. Richardson, 61 Me. 99. § 350.
Emicks *v.* Powell, 2 Strob. Eq. (S. C.) 196. § 586.
Emmanuel, Ellis *v.*, Law Rep. (1 Ex. Div.) 157. § 253.
Emmerson *v.* Heelis, 2 Taunt. 38. § 90.
Locknane *v.*, 11 Bush (Ky.), 69. § 379.
Emmons *v.* Meeker, 55 Ind. 321. § 381.
Emmott *v.* Kearns, 5 Bing. N. C. 559. §§ 84, 87.
Enders *v.* Brune, 4 Rand. (Va.) 438. § 298.
Endicott *v.* Penny, 14 Sm. & Mar. (Miss.) 144. § 90.
Eneas *v.* Hooker, 10 Jones & Spen. (N. Y. Sup. Ct.) 517. §§ 199, 378.
Enfaula Nat. Bank, Watts *v.*, 76 Ala. 474. §§ 298, 299, 301.
Engelke, State *v.*, 6 Mo. App. 356. § 639.
England, Martin *v.*, 5 Yerg. (Tenn.) 313. § 74.
v. McKinney, 4 Sneed (Tenn.), 75. § 606.
Engler *v.* People's Fire Ins. Co., 46 Md. 322. § 560.
English *v.* Bourn, 7 Bush (Ky.), 138. § 609.
v. Dwyer, Law Rep. Irish (12 Q. B., C. P. & Ex. Div.), 92. § 519.
English, Vance *v.*, 78 Ind. 80. §§ 442, 445, 446.
Enicks *v.* Powell, 2 Strobh. Eq. (S. C.) 196. § 541.
Ennis *v.* Crump, 6 Tex. 85. §§ 604, 611.
Justices *v.*, 5 Ga. 569. § 517.
v. Waller, 3 Blackf. (Ind.) 472. § 90.
Enos *v.* Aylesworth, 8 Ohio St. 322. § 507.
v. Leach, 18 Hun (N. Y.), 139. § 209.
Enright *v.* Falvey, Law Rep. Irish (4 Q. B., C. P. & Ex. Div.), 397. § 423.
Ensworth, Cuyler *v.*, 6 Paige's Ch. 32. § 279.
Epperson, Taul *v.*, 38 Tex. 492. § 208.
Epping, Robinson *v.*, 24 Fla. 237. § 93.
Equitable Life Assurance Co. *v.* Coats, 44 Mich. 260. § 602.
Erie R. R. Co., Arnot *v.*, 5 Hun, 608. § 5.
Arnot *v.*, 67 N. Y. 315. § 107.
Erie Bank *v.* Gibson, 1 Watts (Pa.). 143. § 240.
Erie Co. Savings Bank *v.* Coit, 104 N. Y. 532. § 14.
Erwin *v.* Downs, 15 N. Y. 575. § 28.
v. Greene, 5 Rob. (La.) 70. § 125.
Esche, Metropolitan Loan Ass'n *v.*, 75 Cal. 513. § 171.
Escoffe, New Orleans C. & B. Co. *v.*, 2 La. Ann. 830. §§ 97, 447.
Esselman, Gilliam *v.*, 5 Sneed (Tenn.), 86. § 301.
Essex Freeholders *v.* Lindsley, 41 N. J. Eq. 189. § 219.
Estate of Desilver, 9 Phila. (Pa.) 302. § 134.
Estate of Leavenworth, Michigan State Bank *v.*, 28 Vt. 209. §§ 134, 366.
Estate of Rapp *v.* Phœnix Ins. Co., 113 Ill. 390. §§ 133, 424.
Esterly Harvesting Machine Co., Clanin *v.*, 118 Ind. 372. § 104.

Estes, Block *v.*, 92 Mo. 318. § 572.
State *v.*, 101 N. C. 541. § 112.
Estudillo. Mulford *v.*, 23 Cal. 94. § 434.
Etcherson, Sanders *v.*, 36 Ga. 404. § 194.
Evans *v.* Bell, 45 Tex. 553. § 100.
v. Bicknell, 6 Vesey, Jr. 174. § 73.
Bowen *v.*, 1 Lea (Tenn.), 107. § 543.
v. Bremridge, 2 Kay & Johns. 174. § 402.
Briggs *v.*, 1 E. D. Smith (N. Y.), 192. § 77.
v. Commonwealth, 8 Watts (Pa.), 398. § 636.
Cooper *v.*, Law Rep. 4 Eq. Cas. 45. §§ 244, 403.
Corbet *v.*, 25 Pa. St. 310. § 130.
Cutter *v.*, 115 Mass. 27. § 471.
v. Daughtry, 84 Ala. 68. § 402.
v. Duncan, 1 Tyrw. 283. § 52.
v. Earle, 1 Hurl. & Gor. 1. § 174.
v. Evans, 16 Ala. 465. § 267.
Farmers' & Mechanics' Bank *v.*, 4 Barb. (N. Y.) 487. § 123.
v. Harris, 15 J. & S. (N. Y. Super. Ct.) 366. § 8.
v. Keeland, 9 Ala. 42. § 234.
Kennedy *v.*, 31 Ill. 258. §§ 29, 356.
v. Lawton, 34 Fed. Rep. 233. § 382.
Leadley *v.*, 9 Moore, 102. § 168.
Merchants' & M. Bank *v.*, 9 W. Va. 393. §§ 342, 381.
Norris *v.*, 2 B. Mon. (Ky.) 84. § 311.
People *v.*, 29 Cal. 429. § 540.
Reed *v.*, 17 Ohio, 128. § 82.
Smith *v.*, 1 Wils. 313. § 89.
State Bank *v.*, 3 J. S. Green (N. J. Law), 155. § 411.
United States *v.*, 2 Fed. Rep. 147. § 509.
Vaughan *v.*, 1 Hill's Eq. (S. C.) 414. § 546.
Whitfield *v.*, 56 Miss. 488. § 579.
v. Whyle, 5 Bing. 485. § 122.
Wilkinson *v.*, 1 C. P. 407. § 80.
Evansville Nat. Bank *v.* Kaufman, 93 N. Y. 273. § 117.
Evarts *v.* Steger, 6 Oreg. 55. § 586.
Eve, Burgess *v.*, 13 Eq. 450. § 161.
Everly *v.* Rice, 20 Pa. St. 297. § 428.
Evers *v.* Sayer, 28 Mich. 47. § 453.
Everson *v.* Gere, 40 Hun (N. Y.), 248. § 47.
Everett, Collins *v.*, 4 Ga. 266. § 176.
Eyre *v.*, 2 Russell, 381. § 333.
Polak *v.*, Law Rep. 1 Q. B. Div. 669. §§ 426, 429.
Townsend *v.*, 4 Ala. 607. §§ 545, 628.
Everts, Mann *v.*, 64 Wis. 372. § 583.
Evoy *v.* Tewksbury, 5 Cal. 285. § 82.
Ewbank, Rowlett *v.*, 1 Bush (Ky.), 477. § 16.
Ewing, Williams *v.*, 31 Ark. 229. § 284.
Ewing's Adm'r, Dixon *v.*, 3 Ohio, 280. § 434.
Ewins *v.* Calhoun, 7 Vt. 79. § 73.
Ex parte Badgley, 7 Cowen, 472. § 515.
Boaker, Law Rep. (14 Ch. Div.) 317. § 6.
Burrell, Law Rep. (1 Ch. Div.) 537. § 252.
Gardom, 15 Vesey, 286. § 18.
Gifford, 6 Vesey, 805. § 439.
Gordon, 15 Vesey, 286. § 82.
Harding, Law Rep. (12 Ch. Div.) 557. § 19.
Lafonta, 2 Rob. (La.) 495. § 496.
Lane, 1 De Gex, 300. § 62.
Miller, 1 Yerg. (Tenn.) 435. § 454.
Minet, 14 Vesey, 189. § 82.
Mure, 2 Cox, 63. § 444.
Pettillo, 80 N. C. 50. § 237.
Rushforth, 10 Vesey, 409. §§ 238, 305, 306.
Snowdon, Law Rep. (17 Ch. Div.) 44. § 287.
Ware, 5 Rich. Eq. (S. C.) 473. § 313.
Williams, 4 Yerg. (Tenn.) 579. § 75, 76.
Young, *In re* Kitchen, Law R. (17 Ch. Div.) 668. § 630.

Exall *v.* Partridge, 8 Durn. & East, 308. § 208.
Exchange Bank *v.* Silliman, 65 N. Y. 475. § 315.
v. Springer, 29 Grant's Ch. (Can.) 270. § 137.
Executor of Heriot, Taylor *v.*, 4 Dev. Eq. (S. C.) 227. § 226.
Executor of McCall *v.* Adm'r of Evans, 2 Brev. (S. C.) 3. § 243.
Executor of Richard, Dorman *v.*, 1 Fla. 281. § 82.
Executor of Robinson, Commissioner *v.*, 1 Bailey, Law (S. C.), 151. § 413.
Executors of Baker *v.* Marshall, 16 Vt. 522. § 437.
Executors of Dennis *v.* Rider, 2 McLean, 451. § 242.
Executors of Riggins, Brown *v.*, 3 Kelly (Ga.), 405. §§ 40, 434, 438.
Executors of White *v.* White, 30 Vt. 338. § 210.
Exeter Bank *v.* Rogers, 7 N. H. 21. § 396.
Eyer, Northumberland Bank *v.*, 58 Pa. St. 97. § 47.
Eyles, Colman *v.*, 2 Stark. 62. § 76.
Eyre *v.* Dunsford, 1 East, 318. § 73.
v. Everett, 2 Russell, 381. § 233.
v. Hollier, Lloyd & Gould (Temp. Plunket), 250. §§ 38, 388.
Silk *v.*, Irish Rep. 9 Eq. 393. § 322.
Faber *v.* Steele, 37 Mo. 71. § 271.
Fackney, Jacques *v.*, 64 Ill. 87. § 315.
Fagan *v.* Jacobs, 4 Dev. Law (N. C.), 263. § 268.
Latham *v.*, 6 Jones' Law (N. C.), 62. § 538.
Sharp *v.*, 3 Sneed (Tenn.), 541. § 353.
Fagin *v.* Goggin, 12 R. I. 398. § 227.
Failor, Russell *v.*, 1 Ohio St. 327. § 267.
Fair *v.* Pengelly, 34 Up. Can. (Q. B.) 611. § 342.
Fairbanks *v.* Lambert, 137 Mass. 373. § 472.
Fairchild, Titus *v.*, 17 J. & S. (N. Y. Super. Ct.) 211. § 592.
Fairfax, Commonwealth *v.*, 4 Hen. & Munf. (Va.) 208. § 167.
Fairhaven Bank, Wilcox *v.*, 7 Allen, 270. § 306.
Fairlie *v.* Denton, 2 Man. & Ry. 353. § 66.
v. Lawson, 5 Cow. 424. § 112.
Falconer, Smith *v.*, 11 Hun (N. Y.), 481. § 464.
Falvey, Enright *v.*, Law Rep. Irish (4 Q. B., C. P. & Ex. Div.), 397. § 423.
Fambro, Chipman *v.*, 16 Ark. 291. § 633.
Farebrother *v.* Simmons, 5 Barn. & Ald. 333. § 90.
Faria, Peckham *v.*, 3 Doug. 13. § 75.
Farmer, Bramwell *v.*, 1 Taunt. 427. § 512.
Hall *v.*, 5 Denio, 484. § 88.
Shelton *v.*, 9 Bush (Ky.), 314. § 277.
State *v.*, 21 Mo. 160. § 566.
v. Stewart, 2 N. H. 97. § 248.
Farmers' Bank, Allison *v.*, 6 Rand. (Va.) 204. § 561.
Brooking *v.*, 83 Ky. 431. § 245.
v. Horsey, 1 Harr. (Del.) 514. § 371.
Sparks *v.*, 3 Del. Ch. 274. §§ 167, 555.
v. Teeters, 31 Ohio St. 36. § 270.
Farmers' Bank of Canton *v.* Raynolds, 13 Ohio, 85. § 446.
Farmers' Bank of Kentucky, Taylor *v.*, 87 Ky. 398. § 327.
Farmers' & Drovers' Bank *v.* Sherley, 12 Bush (Ky.), 304. § 305.
Farmers' & Mechanics' Bank *v.* Evans, 4 Barb. (N. Y.) 487. § 123.
v. Hathaway, 36 Vt. 539. § 416.
Hickok *v.*, 35 Vt. 476. §§ 239, 242, 405.
v. Humphrey, 36 Vt. 554. § 115.
v. Kerchival, 2 Mich. 504. §§ 161, 360, 398.

Farmers' & Mechanics' Bank, Kramer *v.*, 15 Ohio, 253. § 224.
v. Polk, 1 Del. Ch. 167. § 520.
Farmers' National Bank, Uhler *v.*, 64 Pa. St. 406. § 17.
v. Van Slyke, 49 Hun (N. Y.), 7. § 419.
Farmers' & Traders' Bank *v.* Harrison, 57 Mo. 503. § 357.
v. Lucas, 26 Ohio St. 385. §§ 342, 407.
Farmington Savings Bank *v.* Buzzell, 61 N. H. 612. § 20.
Farnsworth *v.* Clark, 44 Barb. 601. § 17.
v. Coots, 46 Mich. 117. § 378.
Coots *v.*, 61 Mich. 497. §§ 29, 599.
Farrar *v.* Kramer, 5 Mo. App. 167. § 390.
Price *v.*, 5 Bradw. (Ill. App.) 536. § 564.
State *v.*, 77 Mo. 175. § 486.
Towns *v.*, 2 Hawks (N. C.), 163. § 104.
v. United States, 5 Pet. 373. § 526.
Farrell, Davidson *v.*, 8 Minn. 258. § 615.
McKensie *v.*, 4 Bosw. (N. Y.) 192. § 82.
Farrington *v.* Gallaway, 10 Ohio, 543. § 29.
Howe Machine Co. *v.*, 82 N. Y. 121. §§ 245, 421, 422, 446.
Farris, Linn County *v.*, 52 Mo. 75. § 412.
v. Martin, 10 Humph. (Tenn.) 495. § 89.
Farrow *v.* Respess, 11 Ired. Law (N. C.), 170. § 100.
Farwell, Hopkins *v.*, 32 N. H. 425. § 333.
v. Lowther, 18 Ill. 252. § 81.
v. Meyer, 35 Ill. 40. § 379.
Father Matthew Society *v.* Fitzwilliams, 84 Mo. 406. §§ 45, 627.
Faulkner *v.* Bailey, 123 Mass. 588. § 333.
People *v.*, 31 Hun (N. Y.), 317. § 558.
Faulkner, People *v.*, 107 N. Y. 477. § 558.
Faurote *v.* State, 110 Ind. 463. § 601.
Faut's Trustee, Warren *v.*, 79 Ky. 1. §§ 347, 382.
Fawcett *v.* Freshwater, 31 Ohio St. 637. § 354.
Harriss *v.*, Law Rep. 8 Ch. App. Cas. 866. § 134.
Fawcetts *v.* Kimmey, 33 Ala. 261. § 315.
Faxon, Marion *v.*, 20 Conn. 486. § 74.
Fay, Drury *v.*, 14 Pick. 326. §§ 247, 642.
v. Edmiston, 25 Kan. 439. §§ 636, 637.
Queen *v.*, Irish Law (4 Q. B., C. P. & Ex.), 606. § 555.
v. Tower, 58 Wis. 286. §§ 347, 349, 356.
Feamster *v.* Withrow, 12 W. Va. 611. §§ 212, 217.
Fear *v.* Dunlap, 1 Greene (Iowa), 331. §§ 176, 202.
Fearn *v.* Ward, 80 Ala. 344. § 311.
Fearnley *v.* London G. & A. Ins. Co., Irish Law Rep. (6 Q. B., C. P. & Ex. Div.) 219. § 423.
Featherstone, Scott *v.*, 5 La. Ann. 306. § 301.
Fee *v.* State, 74 Ind. 66. § 577.
Fegley *v.* McDonald, 89 Pa. St. 128. § 101.
Feigert *v.* State, 31 Ohio St. 432. § 597.
Felch *v.* Lee, 15 Wis. 265. § 336.
Fellers *v.* Davis, 22 S. C. 425. § 648.
Fellows, Currier *v.*, 27 N. H. 366. §§ 268, 274.
v. Prentiss, 3 Denio, 512. §§ 162, 190, 363.
Felton *v.* Bissel, 25 Minn. 15. § 298.
v. Smith, 84 Ind. 485. § 316.
State *v.*, 59 Miss. 402. § 542.
Fenelon Falls Union School, Keith *v.*, 3 Ont. (Can.) 194. §§ 166, 529.
Fenn *v.* Harrington, 54 Miss. 733. § 487.

Fennell *v.* McGuire, 21 Up. Can. (C. P.) 134. §§ 133, 157.
Fensler *v.* Prather, 43 Ind. 119. § 605.
Fentum *v.* Pocock, 5 Taunt. 192. § 185.
Fenwick, Winston *v.*, 4 Stew. & Port. (Ala.) 269. § 911.
Ferguson *v.* Carson, 13 Mo. App. 29. § 463.
v. Childress, 9 Humph. (Tenn.) 382. § 372.
Ghiselin *v.*, 4 Harr. & Johns. (Md.) 522. § 316.
Harris *v.*, 2 Bailey, Law (S. C.), 397. § 256.
v. Hirsch, 54 Ind. 337. § 570.
Laughlin *v.*, 6 Dana (Ky.), 111. § 467.
Leake *v.*, 2 Gratt. (Va.) 419. § 308.
v. State Bank, 8 Ark. (3 Eng.) 416. § 342.
v. Turner. 7 Mo. 497. § 438.
Ferguson, Adm'r, Jeffries *v.*, 87 Mo. 244. § 254.
Ferguson's Adm'r *v.* Carson's Adm'r, 86 Mo. 673. §§ 208, 310, 463.
Fergusson, Haslock *v.*, 7 Ad. & Ell. 86. § 73.
Fernald *v.* Dawley, 26 Me. 470. § 261.
Sawyer *v.*, 59 Me. 500. § 17.
Fernan *v.* Butcher, 113 Pa. St. 292. § 469.
Fernandez, Machardo *v.*, 74 Cal. 362. § 293.
Ferrell *v.* Hunter, 21 Mo. 436. § 407.
v. Maxwell, 28 Ohio St. 383. § 60.
Ferrie, Greene's Ex'rs *v.*, 1 Des. (S. C.) 164. § 322.
Ferris, Ross *v.*, 18 Hun (N. Y.), 210. § 372.
Ferry *v.* Burchard, 21 Conn. 597. § 145.
Miller *v.*, 50 Hun (N. Y.), 256. § 473.
Fessenden *v.* Musey, 11 Cush., 127. § 89.
v. Summers, 62 Cal. 485. § 176.
Feth, Zollickoffer *v.*, 44 Md. 359. § 207.
Fett, McDonald *v.*, 49 Cal. 354. §§ 473, 490.
Fetrow *v.* Wiseman, 40 Ind. 148. §§ 4, 448.
Feusier, Lammon *v.*, 111 U. S. 17. §§ 566, 595.
Few, Kelly *v.*, 18 Ohio, 441. § 182.
Fewlass *v.* Abbott, 28 Mich. 270. § 128.
Fidler *v.* Hershey, 90 Pa. St. 363. § 240.
Fiedler, Imming *v.*, 8 Bradw. (Ill. App.) 256. § 605.
Field, Brokam *v.*, 33 Ill. App. 138. § 34.
v. Cutter, 4 Lans. (N. Y.) 195. § 239.
Harrison *v.*, 2 Wash. (Va.) 136. §§ 94, 139.
Hutson *v.*, 6 Wis. 407. § 87.
v. Rawlings, 1 Gilm. (Ill.) 581. § 131.
Thorner *v.*, 1 Bulstr. 120. § 17.
Wilson *v.*, 27 Hun (N. Y.), 46. § 150.
Fielden *v.* Lohens, 6 Blatchf. 524. § 550.
Fielding *v.* Waterhouse, 8 Jones & Spencer (N. Y.), 424. §§ 271, 298, 426.
Fields, People *v.*, 6 Daly (N. Y. Com. Pl.), 410. § 511.
Filene, Rice *v.*, 6 Allen, 230. § 123.
Files *v.* McLeod, 14 Ala. 611. § 68.
Finch, Center *v.*, 22 Hun (N. Y.), 146. § 574.
Neussam *v.*, 25 Barb. (N. Y.) 175. § 353.
Smith *v.*, 2 Scam. (Ill.) 321. §§ 17, 67, 182.
v. State, 71 Tex. 52. § 524.
Finks, Wolf *v.*, 1 Pa. St. 436. § 345.
Finden, Kemp *v.*, 12 Mees. & Wels. 421. § 283.
Findlay *v.* Trigg's Adm'r, 83 Va. 539. § 583.
Findlay's Ex'rs *v.* United States, 2 McLean, 44. § 40.

Findley, Campbell v., 3 Humph. 330. § 82.
v. Hill, 8 Oreg. 247. §§ 242, 344.
Phenix Insurance Co. v., 59 Iowa, 591. §§ 42, 420.
Robertson v., 31 Mo. 384. § 15.
State v., 10 Ohio, 51. §§ 519, 521.
State v., 101 Mo. 368. §§ 8, 385.
v. State Bank, 6 Ala. 244. § 407.
Fink v. Mahaffy, 8 Watts (Pa.), 384. § 307.
Finkheiner, Eilbert v., 68 Pa. St. 243. § 178.
Finley v. King, 1 Head (Tenn.), 123. § 434.
v. Miller, 26 Mich. 249. § 381.
Finn, State v., 98 Mo. 532. § 526.
State v., 23 Mo. App. 290. § 588.
v. Stratton, 5 J. J. Marsh. (Ky.) 364. § 438.
Finney v. Condon, 86 Ill. 78. § 429.
Ford v., 35 Ga. 258. § 66.
Pickens v., 12 Sm. & Mar. (Miss.) 468. § 444.
Finney's Adm'rs v. Commonwealth, 1 Pen. & Watts (Pa.), 240. § 426.
Finnigan, Hill v., 54 Cal. 311. § 461.
Firemen's Ins. Co. v. Cross, 4 Rob. (La.) 508. § 7.
v. McMillan, 29 Ala. 147. §§ 391, 630.
Perrine v., 22 Ala. 575. § 430.
v. Wilkinson, 35 N. J. Eq. 160. §§ 366, 367.
Firman v. Blood, 2 Kan. 496. § 176.
First Associated Reformed Presbyterian Church, Shaw v., 39 Pa. St. 226. § 363.
First Congregational Society v. Snow, 1 Cush. 510. § 324.
First National Bank, Hartford & N.Y. Transportation Co. v., 46 Conn. 569. § 324.
v. Gerke, 68 Md. 449. § 92.
Lamson v., 82 Ind. 21. § 375.
v. Leavitt, 65 Mo. 562. §§ 351, 363.
v. Lineberger, 83 N. C. 454. §§ 342, 376.
First National Bank, Lovinger v., 81 Ind. 354. § 412.
Marks v., 79 Ala. 550. § 409.
v. Morgan, 73 N. Y. 593. § 139.
Myers v., 78 Ill. 257. § 356.
v. Pierce, 99 Ill. 272. § 342.
v. Smith, 25 Iowa, 210. § 614.
Union Nat. Bank v., 45 Ohio St. 236. § 106.
Zahn v., 103 Pa. St. 576. §§ 100, 644.
First Nat. Bank of Chicago, Nelson v., 48 Ill. 36. § 67.
First Nat. Bank of Fort Dodge v. Breese, 39 Iowa, 640. § 111.
First Nat. Bank of Marshalltown, Middleton v., 40 Iowa, 29. § 488.
First Nat. Bank of Tama City, Melick v., 52 Iowa, 94. § 46.
Firth, Manford v., 68 Ind. 83. § 313.
Fish v. Hayward, 28 Hun (N. Y.), 456. § 37.
Reed v., 59 Me. 358. § 164.
v. Thomas, 5 Gray, 45. § 64.
Fishback v. Bodman & Co., 14 Bush (Ky.), 117. §§ 305, 308.
v. Weaver, 34 Ark. 569. § 319.
Fishburn v. Jones, 37 Ind. 119. § 401.
Cooper v., 7 J. J. Marsh. (Ky.) 396. § 365.
Fisher v. Cutter, 20 Mo. 206. § 122.
Johnson v., 4 Col. 242. § 95.
Keane v., 10 La. Ann. 261. § 110.
v. Stockebrand, 26 Kan. 565. § 339.
Fisk, Wood v., 63 N. Y. 245. § 135.
Fiske, Bachelder v., 17 Mass. 464. §§ 274, 284, 289.
Crittenden v., 46 Mich. 70. §§ 160, 204.
v. McGregory, 34 N. H. 414. § 72.
Fisse v. Einstein, 5 Mo. App. 78. §§ 93, 150, 472.
Fitch v. Citizens' Nat. Bank, 97 Ind. 211. § 199.
Crim v., 53 Ind. 214. § 72.
v. Gardenier, 2 Abbott's Rep. Omitted Cas. 153. § 74.

Fitch, Sewall *v.*, 8 Cowen, 215. § 90.
Fithian *v.* Corwin, 17 Ohio St. 118. § 342.
Fitz, Jones *v.*, 5 N. H. 444. § 266.
Fitzgerald *v.* Dressler, 7 Com. B. (J. Scott). N. S. 374. §§ 65, 68.
Fitzhugh, Andre *v.*, 18 Mich. 93. § 470.
Fitzmaurice, Western B'ld'g Ass'n *v.*, 7 Mo. App. 283. §§ 383, 394, 601.
Fitzwilliams, Father Matthew Society *v.*, 84 Mo. 406. §§ 45, 627.
Flagler, Sanborn *v.*, 9 Allen, 474. § 89.
Flanagan, Adams *v.*, 36 Vt. 400. §§ 261, 265.
v. Post, 45 Vt. 246. § 419.
Fleece *v.* State, 25 Ind. 384. § 512.
Fleenor, Madgett *v.*, 90 Ind. 517. § 226.
v. State, 58 Ind. 166. § 514.
v. Taggart, 116 Ind. 189. § 570.
Fleming, Adock *v.*, 2 Dev. & Bat. Law (N. C.), 225. §§ 67, 197.
Baldwin *v.*, 90 Ind. 117. § 265.
v. Beaver, 2 Rawle (Pa.), 128. § 310.
Bowers, Adm'r, *v.*, 67 Ind. 541. § 531.
Crim *v.*, 101 Ind. 154. §§ 147, 440.
Inhabitants of Wendell *v.*, 8 Gray, 613. § 521.
Jones *v.*, 15 La. Ann. 522. § 29.
v. Odum, 59 Ga. 362. § 434.
State *v.*, 46 Ind. 206. § 575.
State *v.*, 124 Ind. 97. § 532.
Fleshman, Bank *v.*, 22 W. Va. 317. § 480.
Fletcher, Atchison, T. & S. F. R. R. Co. *v.*, 35 Kan. 236. § 6.
Benton *v.*, 31 Vt. 418. §§ 100, 183.
v. Edson, 8 Vt. 294. § 222.
v. Gamble, 3 Ala. 335. §§ 368, 372.
v. Grover, 11 N. H. 368. § 287.
Howard *v.*, 59 N. H. 151. § 144.
v. Jackson, 23 Vt. 581. §§ 281, 282, 283.
Fletcher *v.* Leight, 4 Bush (Ky.), 303. § 411.
v. Menken, 37 Ark. 206. § 465.
Skillett *v.*, Law Rep. 1 Com. Pl. 217. § 398.
Trentman *v.*, 100 Ind. 105. § 405.
Flewellen, Drake *v.*, 33 Ala. 106. § 58.
Flickinger *v.* Saum, 40 Ohio St. 591. § 583.
Flinn, Wright *v.*, 33 Iowa, 159. § 114.
Flint *v.* Day, 9 Vt. 345. § 180.
Johnson *v.*, 34 Ala. 673. § 456.
Municipality of Whitby *v.*, 9 Up. Can. (C. P.) 449. §§ 521, 523, 553.
Trustees of Free Schools *v.*, 13 Met. (Mass.) 539. § 68.
Flippen, Reid *v.*, 47 Ga. 273. §§ 230, 342.
Flood, Bowling *v.*, 1 Lea (Tenn.), 678. § 367.
Florat *v.* Handy, 35 La. Ann. 816. § 175.
Florence *v.* Richardson, 2 La. Ann. 663. § 539.
Flores *v.* Howth, 5 Tex. 329. § 169.
Florida R. R. Co., Vose *v.*, 50 N. Y. 369. § 415.
Flory, Meriden Silver Plate Co. *v.*, 44 Ohio St. 430. §§ 605, 608, 612.
Floyd *v.* Harrison, 4 Bibb (Ky.), 76. § 69.
Hollingsworth *v.*, 2 Har. & Gill (Md.), 87. § 306.
Fluck *v.* Hager, 51 Pa. St. 459. § 332.
Fluker *v.* Henry's Adm'r, 27 Ala. 403. § 39.
Flynn *v.* Mudd, 27 Ill. 323. §§ 29, 352.
v. State, 42 Ark. 315. § 510.
Flynn's Ex'r, Brandenburg *v.*, 12 B. Mon. (Ky.) 397. § 262.
Fogarty, Lockenmeyer *v.*, 112 Ill. 572. § 329.
v. Ream, 100 Ill. 366. §§ 320, 526, 632.
Fogleman, Shoffner *v.*, Winston's Law & Eq. (N. C.) 12. § 316.

Foglesong, Knoblauch *v.*, 37 Minn. 320. § 329.
Foley, Haven *v.*, 18 Mo. 136. § 324.
Folger *v.* Palmer, 35 La. Ann. 814. § 622.
Foljambe, Ogilvie *v.*, 3 Meriv. 53. § 89.
Folkes, Dubuisson *v.*, 30 Miss. 432. §§ 351, 352.
Follett, Manfs. & Merchants' Bank *v.*, 11 R. I. 92. § 383.
Follmer *v.* Dale, 9 Pa. St. 83. § 343.
Folsom, Moore *v.*, 14 Minn. 340. § 178.
Fond du Lac Harrow Co. *v.* Bowles, 54 Wis. 425. § 394.
v. Haskins, 51 Wis. 135. § 137.
Fonda, Board of Education *v.*, 77 N. Y. 350. § 545.
Fontaine, Lee *v.*, 10 Ala. 755. § 63.
Fooks, Strange *v.*, 4 Giff. 408. § 442.
Foot, Wilson *v.*, 11 Met. 285. §§ 29, 33.
Foote *v.* Brown, 2 McLean, 396. § 197.
Jackson *v.* (Cir. Ct. N. D. Ill.), 12 Fed. Rep. 37. § 45.
Forbes, Barney *v.*, 118 N. Y. 580. §§ 13, 14.
Brownelow *v.*, 2 Johns. 101. § 494.
Coleman *v.*, 22 Pa. St. 156. § 143.
v. Jackson, Law Rep. (19 Ch. Div.) 615. § 315.
v. Sheppard, 98 N. C. 111. §§ 30, 376.
Forbis, Hale *v.*, 3 Mont. 395. § 354.
Force *v.* Craig, 2 Hals. (N. J.) 272. § 342.
Ford *v.* Beard, 31 Mo. 459. § 342.
v. Clough, 8 Greenl. (Me.) 334. § 521.
Commonwealth *v.*, 29 Gratt. (Va.) 683. § 524.
v. Finney, 35 Ga. 258. § 66.
Guion *v.*, 12 Rob. (La.) 123. § 515.
Hays *v.*, 55 Ind. 52. § 276.
v. Keith, 1 Mass. 139. §§ 208, 215.
Ford *v.* Stobridge, Nels. 24. § 205.
Stonebraker *v.*, 81 Mo. 532. § 219.
Ford & Eagan, Clune *v.*, 55 Hun, 479. § 17.
Fordyce, Bank *v.*, 9 Pa. St. 275. §§ 48, 434.
v. Ellis, 29 Cal. 96. § 372.
Fore *v.* Hitson, 70 Tex. 517. § 18.
Forelicht, Alber *v.*, 39 Ohio St. 245. § 449.
Foreman, Deardorff *v.*, 24 Ind. 481. § 407.
Forest *v.* Shores, 11 La. (Curry), 416. § 205.
v. Stewart, 14 Ohio St. 246. §§ 101, 199.
Forney, Kendrick *v.*, 22 Gratt. (Va.) 748. §§ 212, 313.
Swope *v.*, 17 Ind. 385. §§ 43, 403.
Forrester *v.* State, 46 Md. 154. § 587.
Stirling *v.*, 3 Bligh, 575. § 439.
v. Vason, 71 Ga. 50. § 574.
Forrest's Ex'rs *v.* Luddington, 68 Ala. 1. § 326.
Forstall, Union Bank *v.*, 6 La. (Curry), 211. § 423.
Forsyth, Singer Mfg. Co. *v.*, 108 Ind. 334. § 86.
Fort, House *v.*, 4 Blackf. (Ind.) 293. § 564.
Fortinberry, State *v.*, 54 Miss. 316. § 148.
Forward *v.* Marsh, 18 Ala. 645. § 565.
Foss *v.* City of Chicago, 34 Ill. 488. § 426.
Cleaves *v.*, 4 Greenl. (Me.) 1. § 90.
Foster, Armstrong *v.*, 6 Ont. (Can.) 129. § 593.
v. Barney, 3 Vt. 60. §§ 98, 101.
Cage *v.*, 5 Yerg. (Tenn.) 261. § 293.
v. Charles, 6 Bing. 396. § 73.
Crawford *v.*, 6 Ga. 202. §§ 402, 642.
Dunlap *v.*, 7 Ala. 734. § 468.
Eastman *v.*, 8 Met. (Mass.) 19. § 324.
v. Hale, 3 Vesey, Jr. 696. § 80.

Foster, Strong *v.*, 17 C. B. (8 J. Scott), 201. §§ 336, 342.
v. Tolleson, 13 Rich. Law & Eq. (S. C.) 31. § 201.
v. Trustees of Athenæum, 3 Ala. 320. § 313.
Vail *v.*, 4 N. Y. 312. § 324.
v. Wise, 46 Ohio St. 20. §§ 581, 585.
Foster & Estes, Cruse *v.*, 76 Ga. 723. §§ 56, 76, 77.
Fouch, Nevin *v.*, 77 Ga. 47. § 45.
Foudry, Havens *v.*, 4 Met. (Ky.) 247. § 328.
Fountain, Browning *v.*, 1 Duvall (Ky.), 13. § 114.
Fourth Nat. Bank *v.* Spinney, 120 N. Y. 560. § 561.
Fowle *v.* Freeman, 9 Vesey, 351. § 89.
Fowler *v.* Alexander, 1 Heisk. (Tenn.) 425. § 30.
v. Brooks, 13 N. H. 240. §§ 347, 354.
v. Clearwater, 35 Barb. (N. Y.) 143. § 67.
Hall *v.*, 6 Hill, 630. § 472.
Mayor of Durham *v.*, Law Rep. (22 Q. B. Div.) 394. § 555.
Newell *v.*, 23 Barb. (N. Y.) 628. § 98.
Teague *v.*, 56 Ind. 569. § 63.
Fowlkes, Moss *v.*, 14 Lea (Tenn.), 382. § 585.
Fox, Atkinson *v.*, 53 Miss. 733. § 487.
Cole *v.*, 83 N. C. 463. § 30.
Hess *v.*, 10 Wend. 436. § 52.
Knight *v.*, Morris (Iowa), 305. § 133.
v. Meacham, 6 Neb. 530. § 562.
v. Parker, 44 Barb. (N. Y.) 541. § 365.
Savage *v.*, 60 N. H. 17. §§ 15, 235.
Foxall, Phillips *v.*, Law Rep. 7 Q. B. 666. § 423.
Foxcroft *v.* Nevins, 4 Greenl. (Me.) 72. § 523.
Foxworth, Atkinson *v.*, 53 Miss. 741. § 471.
Foy, Conrad *v.*, 68 Pa. St. 381. § 240.
Fralick, Millard *v.*, 31 Mich. 431. § 616.
France, Munster & Leinster Bank *v.*, Law Rep. Irish (24 Q. B. & Ex. Div.), 82. § 367.
Francis, Godwin *v.*, 5 Com. P. 295. § 89.
Shane *v.*, 30 Ind. 92. § 570.
Francisco, Buford *v.*, 3 Dana (Ky.), 68. § 226.
Franey, City of Hartford *v.*, 47 Conn. 76. §§ 545, 546.
Frank *v.* Edwards, 8 Wels., Hurl. & Gor. 214. § 392.
Harris *v.*, 29 Kan. 200. § 311.
Harris *v.*, 81 Cal. 280. § 105.
Franklin *v.* Franklin, 71 Ind. 573. § 605.
v. Hammond, 45 Pa. St. 507. § 522.
Tallman *v.*, 14 N. Y. 584. § 80.
Franklin's Adm'r *v.* Depriest, 13 Gratt. (Va.) 257. § 43.
Franklin Bank *v.* Cooper, 36 Me. 179. §§ 22, 25, 419, 420, 422.
v. Stevens, 39 Me. 532. §§ 412, 519.
Franklin Life Ins. Co. *v.* Courtney, 60 Ind. 134. § 379.
Franklin Mills, Brewer *v.*, 42 N. H. 292. § 304.
Franklin Savings Inst. *v.* Reed, 125 Mass. 365. § 403.
Frantz, Martin *v.*, 127 Pa. St. 389. § 295.
Warfel *v.*, 76 Pa. St. 88. § 411.
Fraser, Eales *v.*, 6 Man. & Gr. 755. § 40.
v. Little, 13 Mich. 195. § 112.
v. McConnell, 23 Ga. 368. §§ 29, 38.
Fratenburgh, Oswald *v.*, 36 Minn. 270. § 48.
Frayser, Barry *v.*, 10 Heisk. (Tenn.) 206. §§ 466, 481.
Frazee, Dixon *v.*, 1 E. D. Smith (N. Y.), 32. §§ 76, 78.
Frazier, Keeshug *v.*, 119 Ind. 185. § 60.

Freauer *v.* Yingling, 37 Md. 491. § 442.
Fredenburg, Clark *v.*, 43 Mich. 263. § 585.
Frederick, Bradford *v.*, 101 Pa. St. 445. § 481.
v. Moore, 13 B. Mon. (Ky.) 470. § 439.
Rhoades *v.*, 8 Watts (Pa.), 448. § 386.
Fredericks, State *v.*, 8 Iowa, 553. § 24.
Freeborn, Belloni *v.*, 63 N. Y. 383. §§ 92, 220.
Freehold National Banking Co., Brick *v.*, 8 Vroom (N. J.), 307. §§ 440, 441.
Freeholders of Warren *v.* Wilson, 1 Harr. (N. J.) 110. § 545.
Freeland *v.* Compton, 30 Miss. 424. § 344.
Corporation of Houghton *v.*, 26 Grant's Ch. (Can.) 500. § 558.
Freeman, Bailey *v.*, 4 Johns. 280. § 13.
Bailey *v.*, 11 Johns. 221. § 87.
Bishop *v.*, 42 Mich. 533. § 93.
Craven *v.*, 82 N. C. 361. §§ 267, 276.
Fowle *v.*, 9 Vesey, 351. § 89.
v. Freeman, 2 Bulst. 269. § 15.
v. Mebane, 2 Jones' Eq. (N. C.) 44. § 322.
Neal *v.*, 85 N. C. 441. § 101.
Pasley *v.*, 3 Term R. 51. § 73.
v. Showles, 81 Mo. 540. § 112.
Stedman *v.*, 15 Ind. 86. § 301.
Freeman's Bank *v.* Rollins, 13 Me. 202. § 352.
Freeport *v.* Bartol, 3 Greenl. (Me.) 340. § 80.
Frelinghuysen *v.* Baldwin (Dist. Ct. D. N. J.), 16 Fed. Rep. 452. §§ 425, 561.
Frellsen, Baker *v.*, 32 La. Ann. 822. § 478.
French *v.* Dauchy, 57 Hun (N. Y.), 100. § 592.
v. French, 2 Man. & Gr. 644. §§ 13, 17.
v. Marsh, 29 Wis. 649. § 98.
French, Pigon *v.*, 1 Wash. (U. S.) 278. § 205.
v. State, 53 Miss. 651. § 617.
Sweetser *v.*, 2 Cush. 309. §§ 18, 407.
v. Thompson, 6 Vt. 54. § 65.
Tuckerman *v.*, 7 Greenl. (Me.) 115. § 186.
Freshwater, Fawcett *v.*, 31 Ohio St. 637. § 354.
Fresno Enterprise Co. *v.* Allen, 67 Cal. 505. § 167.
Fretz, Myers *v.*, 4 Pa. St. 344. § 578.
Freudenstein *v.* McNier, 81 Ill. 208. § 570.
Freudenthal, Cook *v.*, 80 N. Y. 202. § 519.
Frevert *v.* Henry, 14 Nev. 191. § 208.
Frey *v.* Hebenstreit, 1 Rob. (La.) 561. § 498.
Freyer, Leffingwell *v.*, 21 Wis. 398. §§ 34, 139.
Friberg *v.* Donovan, 23 Ill. App. 58. § 262.
Frickee *v.* Donner, 35 Mich. 151. § 366.
Fridge *v.* The State, 3 Gill & Johns. (Md.) 103. § 42.
Friedenwald, Moore *v.*, 77 Va. 57. § 237.
Friedline *v.* State, 93 Ind. 366. § 509.
Friedman *v.* Adler & Levy, 36 La. Ann. 384. § 480.
Friend, Woodburn *v.*, 10 La. (Curry), 496. § 438.
Frierson *v.* Williams, 57 Miss. 451. § 144.
Frinden, Kemp *v.*, 12 Mees. & Wels. 421. §§ 288, 289.
Frink *v.* Peabody, 26 Ill. App. 390. § 271.
Peck *v.*, 10 Iowa, 193. §§ 98, 199.
v. Southern Express Co., 82 Ga. 33. § 112.
Frisch *v.* Miller, 5 Pa. St. 310. § 401.
Frith, State *v.*, 14 La. (Curry), 191. §§ 500, 505.
Fritz, German American Savings Bank *v.*, 68 Wis. 390. § 329.

Frost, Edge *v.*, 4 Dow. & Ry. 243. § 77.
v. Mixsell, 38 N. J. Eq. 586. §§ 331, 522, 524.
v. Rucker, 4 Humph. (Tenn.) 57. § 616.
Frost & Co. *v.* Weathersbee, 23 S. C. 354. § 165.
Frow, Jacobs & Co.'s Estate *v.*, 73 Pa. St. 459. § 302.
Frownfelter *v.* State, 66 Md. 80. §§ 422, 547, 642.
Fry, Dumont *v.* (Cir. Ct. S. D. N. Y.), 14 Fed. Rep. 293. § 253.
Meyers *v.*, 18 Bradw. (Ill. App.) 74. § 644.
Neilson *v.*, 16 Ohio St. 552. § 310.
Frye *v.* Barker, 4 Pick. 382. §§ 143, 242.
Fryer, McClurg *v.*, 15 Pa. St. 293. § 100.
Fugate, Adm'x, Pitts *v.*, 41 Mo. 405. § 633.
Fullam *v.* Adams, 37 Vt. 391. §§ 64, 69.
v. Valentine, 11 Pick. 156. § 493.
Fuller, Athol Machine Co. *v.*, 107 Mass. 437. § 7.
v. Calkins, 22 Iowa, 301. §§ 530, 559.
Coleman *v.*, 105 N. C. 328. § 617.
v. Davis, 1 Gray, 612. § 500.
Goodspeed *v.*, 46 Me. 141. § 60.
Gould *v.*, 18 Me. 364. § 273.
Kaighn *v.*, 1 McCarter (N. J.), 419. § 375.
v. Loring, 42 Me. 481. § 332.
v. Milford, 2 McLean, 74. § 342.
v. Scott, 8 Kan. 25. §§ 16, 18, 88, 176, 202.
Stark *v.*, 42 Pa. St. 320. § 250.
v. Tomlinson Bros., 58 Iowa, 111. § 446.
v. Wright, 59 Ind. 333. § 486.
Fullerton, Galbraith *v.*, 53 Ill. 126. § 356.
Fugate, Nash *v.*, 24 Gratt. (Va.) 202. § 408.
Fullerton *v.* Sturges, 4 Ohio St. 529. § 410.
Fulmer *v.* Seitz, 68 Pa. St. 237 § 379.
Fulton *v.* Matthews, 15 Johns. 433. § 342.
v. State, 14 Tex. App. 32. § 175.
Fults, Ellenwood *v.*, 63 Barb. 321. § 17.
Funston, Davies *v.*, 45 Up. Can. (Q. B.) 369. § 16.
Fuqua, Tennessee Hospital *v.*, 1 Lea (Tenn.), 608. § 577.
Fuquay, Johnson *v.*, 1 Dana (Ky.), 514. § 585.
Furber *v.* Bassett, 2 Duvall (Ky.), 433. § 345.
Furbor, Warrington *v.*, 8 East, 242. §§ 208, 210.
Furgerson, McLewis *v.*, 5 The Reporter, 330. § 268.
Furlong *v.* State, 58 Miss. 717. § 570.
Furman *v.* Timberlake, 93 N. C. 66. § 589.
Furness *v.* Read, 63 Md. 1. § 470.
Furnold *v.* Bank of Missouri, 44 Mo. 336. § 323.
Furst & Bradley Mfg. Co. *v.* Black, 111 Ind. 308. §§ 191, 193, 197, 199, 203.
Fusz & Blackner *v.* Trayer & Noble, 39 La. Ann. 292. § 471.
Gabbert's Adm'r, Commonwealth *v.*, 5 Bush (Ky.), 438. § 548.
Gaddie, Whitman *v.*, 7 B. Mon. (Ky.) 591. § 259.
Gadsden, Elfe *v.*, 2 Rich. (S. C.) 373. § 80.
Gadsen *v.* Quackenbush, 9 Rich. Law (S. C.), 222. § 108.
Gaff *v.* Sims, 45 Ind. 262. §§ 1, 197.
Gage, City of Chicago *v.*, 95 Ill. 595. §§ 385, 386, 410, 517, 534, 546, 559, 628.
Comstock *v.*, 91 Ill. 328. §§ 419, 534, 597.
v. Lewis, 68 Ill. 604. §§ 126, 200, 404.
v. Mechanics' Nat. Bank of Chicago, 79 Ill. 62. §§ 199, 242.
v. Sharp, 24 Iowa, 15. § 407.

Gahn *v.* Niemcewicz, 11 Wend. 312. § 35.
Niemcewicz *v.*, 3 Paige, 614. §§ 35, 237.
Gaillard *v.* Bordelon, 35 La. Ann. 390. § 578.
Gaines, Cullom *v.*, 1 Ala. 23. § 97.
Gair, Corporation of Oxford *v.*, 15 Ont. (Can.) 362. § 597.
Gaither, Ijames *v.*, 93 N. C. 358. § 324.
Galbraith *v.* Duncombe, 28 Grant's Ch. (Can.) 27. § 528.
v. Fullerton, 53 Ill. 126. § 356.
Shupe *v.*, 32 Pa. St. 10. § 16.
Gale *v.* Nixon, 6 Cow. (N. Y.) 445. § 80.
Pence *v.*, 20 Minn. 257. § 426.
Gallagher *v.* Brunel, 6 Cowen, 347. §§ 73, 74.
v. White, 31 Barb. (N. Y.) 92. §§ 101, 132.
Wylie *v.*, 46 Pa. St. 205. § 522.
Gallant, Polk *v.*, 2 Dev. & Bat. Eq. (N. C.) 395. § 237.
Gallatin Co., Jones *v.*, 78 Ky. 491. § 642.
Gallaway, Farrington *v.*, 10 Ohio, 543. § 29.
Gallentine, Burnham *v.*, 11 Ind. 295. § 102.
Galloway, Bonham *v.*, 13 Ill. 68. § 322.
Gamage *v.* Hutchins, 23 Me. 565. §§ 142, 197.
Gambill *v.* Campbell, 12 Heisk. (Tenn.) 737. §§ 580, 584.
Gamble, Fletcher *v.*, 3 Ala. 335. §§ 368, 372.
Hooker *v.*, 12 Up. Can. (C. P.) 512. § 364.
Hooker *v.*, 9 Up. Can. (C. P.) 434. § 364.
Gambs, Lewis *v.*, 6 Mo. App. 138. § 585.
Gamewell, Hommell *v.*, 5 Blackf. (Ind.) 5. § 211.
Gammell *v.* Parramore, 58 Ga. 576. § 199.
Gammon, Bird *v.*, 3 Bing. N. C. 883. § 62.
Bird *v.*, 5 Scott, 213. § 64.
Brather *v.*, 25 Kan. 397. § 357.
v. Stone, 1 Vesey, Sr. 339. § 303.
Gannett *v.* Blodgett, 39 N. H. 150. § 306.
Gano *v.* Heath, 36 Mich. 441. § 380.
Gans, Caldwell *v.*, 1 Mont. 570. § 485.
Gansen *v.* Tomlinson, 8 C. E. Green (N. J.), 405. § 125.
Ganser, Columbia Sewer Pipe Co. *v.*, 58 Mich. 385. § 156.
Gantt, Ricks *v.*, 35 La. Ann. 920. § 101.
Gaoler of Philadelphia, Respublica *v.*, 2 Yeates (Pa.), 263. § 496.
Garber *v.* Commonwealth, 7 Pa. St. 265. § 638.
Gard *v.* Stevens, 12 Mich. 292. § 164.
Gardenier, Fitch *v.*, 2 Abbott's Rep. Omitted Cas. 153. § 74.
Gardiner *v.* Hopkins, 5 Wend. 23. § 65.
Praed *v.*, 2 Cox, 86. § 321.
Gardner *v.* Clarkson, 13 Ill. 347. § 344.
v. Gardner, 23 S. C. 588. § 352.
v. Harback, 21 Ill. 129. § 384.
v. King, 2 Ired. Law (N. C.), 297. §§ 17, 132.
v. Lloyd, 110 Pa. St. 278. § 191.
Miller *v.*, 49 Iowa, 234. § 142.
People *v.*, 55 Cal. 304. § 591.
Valloton *v.*, R. M. Charlt. (Ga.) 86. § 190.
v. Van Nostrand, 13 Wis. 543. § 368.
v. Walsh, 5 Ellis & Black. 83. § 380.
Gardner, Adm'r, *v.* Watson, 76 Tex. 25. §§ 156, 159.
Garey *v.* Hignutt, 32 Md. 552. § 97.
Garey & Lanahan, Edes *v.*, 46 Md. 24. § 141.
Gargan *v.* School Dist. No. 15, 4 Col. 53. § 119.
Garland, Prentiss *v.*, 64 Me. 155. § 102.
Garlinghouse, Wright *v.*, 26 N. Y. 539. § 185.

Garnett *v.* Roper, 10 Ala. 842. § 150.
Garr *v.* Martin, 20 N. Y. 306. § 251.
Garratt *v.* Eliff, 4 Humph. (Tenn.) 323. § 616.
Garrels, Suppinger *v.*, 20 Bradw. (Ill. App.) 625. § 298.
Garretson, Cummins *v.*, 15 Ark. 132. § 606.
Garrett, Bradner *v.*, 19 La. (Curry), 455. § 29.
v. Handley, 4 Barn. & Cress. 664. §§ 116, 117.
Overacre *v.*, 5 Lans. (N. Y.) 156. § 539.
Garrison, Gladwin *v.*, 13 Cal. 330. § 218.
Garrott *v.* Ratliff & Williams, 83 Ky. 384. § 90.
Garrow, Phelps *v.*, 8 Paige, Ch. 322. § 76.
Garth, Robinson *v.*, 6 Ala. 204. § 90.
Garton, State *v.*, 32 Ind. 1. § 408.
v. Union City Bank, 34 Mich. 279. § 351.
Garver *v.* Tisinger, 46 Ohio St. 56. § 593.
Garvin *v.* Mobley, 1 Bush (Ky.), 48. § 402.
v. Walsh, 54 Vt. 367. § 495.
Gary *v.* Cannon, 3 Ired. Eq. (N. C.) 64. § 237.
v. State, 11 Tex. App. 527. § 410.
Gary, Wadlington *v.*, 7 Sm. & Mar. (Miss.) 522. §§ 342, 355.
Gaskill, Scofield *v.*, 60 Ga. 277. § 259.
Gaskins, Miller *v.*, 1 Smedes & Mar. Ch. (Miss.) 524. § 149.
Gasquet *v.* Oakey, 19 La. (Curry), 76. § 228.
v. Thorn, 14 La. (Curry), 506. § 201.
Gass *v.* Citizens' Bldg. & Loan Ass'n, 95 Pa. St. 101. § 648.
v. Stinson, 2 Sumner, 453. § 393.
Gaston *v.* Barney, 11 Ohio St. 506. § 330.
Miller *v.*, 2 Hill, 188. § 179.
Gates *v.* Bell, 3 La. Ann. 62. § 20.
Campbell *v.*, 17 Ind. 126. § 405.
Gates *v.* Hughes, 44 Wis. 332. § 36.
v. McKee, 13 N. Y. 232. § 160.
v. Renfroe, 7 La. Ann. 569. § 228.
Schindel *v.*, 46 Md. 604. § 333.
Gatewood *v.* Gatewood, 75 Va. 407. § 311.
v. Leak, 99 N. C. 357. § 648.
Gaulden, Crawford *v.*, 33 Ga. 173. §§ 40, 353.
Gault, Boyd *v.*, 3 Bush (Ky.), 644. § 575.
Gaussen, Ex'r, United States *v.*, 2 Woods, 92. § 548.
Gauthreaux, City of New Orleans *v.*, 36 La. Ann. 109. §§ 541, 571.
Gay, Barstow *v.*, 3 Greenl. (Me.) 409. § 89.
v. Hults, 56 Mich. 153. §§ 113, 175.
v. Mott, 43 Ga. 252. § 15.
National Exchange Bank *v.*, 57 Conn. 224. § 396.
Talbot *v.*, 18 Pick. 534. § 197.
Gay & Co. *v.* Blanchard, 32 La. Ann. 497. § 1.
Gayle, Pearson *v.*, 11 Ala. 278. § 448.
Gaylord, Decker *v.*, 8 Hun (N. Y.), 110. § 108.
Second Nat. Bank *v.*, 34 Iowa, 246. § 202.
Gear, Ripley *v.*, 58 Iowa, 460. § 468.
Geary *v.* Gore Bank, 5 Grant's Ch. 536. § 251.
Gunn *v.*, 44 Mich. 615. § 93.
v. Physic, 5 Barn. & Cres. 234. § 80.
Geddis *v.* Hawk, 1 Watts (Pa.), 280. § 97.
Hawk *v.*, 16 Serg. & Rawle, 23, 33. §§ 97, 240.
Gedye *v.* Matson, 25 Beav. 310. § 306.
Gee, Robinson *v.*, 1 Vesey, Sr. 251. §§ 34, 125.
Gegg, Lucking's Adm'r *v.*, 12 Bush (Ky.), 298. § 215.
Geiger *v.* Clark, 13 Cal. 579. § 186.
Geiger's Adm'r, Harnsberger's Ex'r *v.*, 3 Gratt. (Va.) 144. § 370.

Gell, Tomlinson *v.*, 6 Adol. & Ell. 564. §§ 17, 64.
General Steam Navigation Co. *v.* Rolt, 6 J. Scott (N. R.), 550. § 397.
Generous, Kleinhaus *v.*, 25 Ohio St. 667. § 349.
Genge, Whitnash *v.*, 3 Man. & Ryl. 42. § 629.
Gerber *v.* Ackley, 37 Wis. 43. § 566.
v. Shark, 72 Ind. 553. §§ 314, 329.
Gere, Everson *v.*, 40 Hun (N. Y.), 248. § 47.
Gerke, Nat. Bank of Baltimore *v.*, 68 Md. 449. §§ 92, 93, 394.
German, Harrisburg Bank *v.*, 3 Pa. St. 300. §§ 301, 323.
German-American Bank *v.* Auth, 87 Pa. St. 419. §§ 555, 558.
v. Denmire, 58 Iowa, 137. § 614.
Voss *v.*, 83 Ill. 599. § 432.
German-American Savings Bank *v.* Fritz, 68 Wis. 390. § 329.
German Evan. Luth. St. Matt. Cong., Wehr *v.*, 47 Md. 177. §§ 394, 601.
German Ins. & Savings Inst. *v.* Vahle, 28 Ill. App. 557. § 367.
German Nat. Bank Memphis, White *v.*, 9 Heisk. (Tenn.) 475. § 624.
German Savings Ass'n *v.* Helmrick, 57 Mo. 100. § 353.
Geoghehan, Post *v.*, 5 Daly (N. Y. Com. Pleas), 216. § 77.
George *v.* Andrews, 60 Md. 26. § 37.
McKenna *v.*, 2 Rich. Eq. (S. C.) 15. §§ 275, 283, 288.
Pinard *v.*, 30 La. Ann. 384. § 460.
Spring *v.*, 50 Hun (N. Y.), 227. § 437.
Whitnash *v.*, 8 Barn. & Cress. 556. § 629.
Gephard, Bedwell *v.*, 67 Iowa, 44. § 426.
Gerould *v.* Wilson, 81 N. Y. 573. §§ 580, 585.
Gerrish, Riley *v.*, 9 Cush. 104. § 182.
Gerry, Binton *v.*, 7 Bradw. (Ill. App.) 238. § 434.
Gerson *v.* Hamilton, 30 La. Ann. 737. § 165.
Getty, Ayer *v.*, 46 Hun (N. Y.), 287. § 624.
Gewin, Hodges *v.*, 6 Ala. 478. § 368.
McGehee *v.*, 25 Ala. 176. §§ 565, 570, 572.
Ghiselin *v.* Ferguson, 4 Harr. & Johns. (Md.) 522. § 316.
Gibb, Pibus *v.*, 6 Ell. & Black. 902. § 548.
Gibbons, Brown *v.*, 37 Iowa, 654. § 428.
v. McCasland, 1 Barn. & Ald. 690. § 79.
Gibbs, Bicksford *v.*, 8 Cush. 154. § 15.
v. Blanchard, 15 Mich. 292. § 76.
v. Cannon, 9 Serg. & Rawle (Pa.), 198. §§ 202, 203.
v. Johnson, 63 Mich. 671. § 410.
v. Mennard, 6 Paige, Ch. 258. § 225.
Gibson, Austin *v.*, 28 Up. Can. (C. P.) 554. § 376.
Benton *v.*, 1 Hill, Law (S. C.), 56. §§ 100, 201.
Cathcart *v.*, 1 Rich. Law (S. C.), 10. § 260.
Denison *v.*, 24 Mich. 187. §§ 34, 35, 124, 234.
Dyer *v.*, 16 Wis. 508. § 67.
Erie Bank *v.*, 1 Watts (Pa.), 143. § 240.
Goss *v.*, 8 Humph. (Tenn.) 197. § 276.
Jones *v.*, 82 Ky. 561. § 317.
v. Martin, 7 Humph. (Tenn.) 127. § 616.
Murray *v.*, 28 Grant's Ch. (Can.) 12. §§ 257, 629.
Patterson *v.*, 81 Ga. 802. § 12.
Gibson's Ex'r, Rhea *v.*, 10 Gratt. (Va.) 215. § 385.
Giddens *v.* Williamson, 65 Ala. 439. § 311.
Gierman, Cressy *v.*, 7 Minn. 398. § 563.

Giese, Elliott *v.*, 7 Harr. & Johns. 457. § 82.
Gieseke, Adm'r, *v.* Johnson, 115 Ind. 308. § 212.
Gifford *v.* Allen, 3 Met. (Mass.) 255. § 348.
Bank of Monroe *v.*, 72 Iowa, 750. § 401.
Gilbert, Borden *v.*, 13 Wis. 670. § 138.
Crocker *v.*, 9 Cush. 131. § 107.
Goodwin *v.*, 9 Mass. 510. § 53.
v. Henck, 30 Pa. St. 205. §§ 100, 102.
v. Isham, 16 Conn. 525. § 530.
Johnson *v.*, 4 Hill, 178. § 67.
Moline Plow Co. *v.*, 3 Dak. 239. § 400.
v. Neely, Adm'r, 35 Ark. 24. § 319.
v. Vachon, 69 Ind. 372. § 25.
Gilchrist, Williams *v.*, 11 N. H. 535. § 334.
Gilder *v.* Jeter, 11 Ala. 256. § 356.
Giles *v.* Brown's Adm'r, 60 Ga. 658. § 579.
Ricketson *v.*, 91 Ill. 154. § 210.
Giles' Ex'rs, Lining *v.*, 3 Brev. (S. C.) 530. § 578.
Gilette, Bullard *v.*, 1 Mont. Terr. 509. § 455.
Gilkeson, Johnson County *v.*, 70 Mo. 645. § 614.
Gill *v.* Bicknell, 2 Cush. 357. § 90.
v. Herrick, 111 Mass. 501. § 76.
New Hampshire Savings Bank *v.*, 16 N. H. 578. § 352.
Tomlinson *v.*, Amb. 330. § 57.
Gillam, Smith *v.*, 80 Ala. 296. §§ 150, 324, 326.
Gilleland, Miller *v.*, 19 Pa. St. 119. § 379.
Gillespie *v.* Darwin, 6 Heisk. (Tenn.) 21. § 443.
Dennis *v.*, 24 Miss. 581. § 263.
Kelly *v.*, 12 Iowa, 55. §§ 29, 356.
v. Lake, 85 Cal. 402. § 595.
Miller *v.*, 59 Mo. 320. § 276.
v. Torrance, 25 N. Y. 306. § 236.
Gillett, Mallory *v.*, 21 N. Y. 412. § 59.
Gillett, Mallory *v.*, 23 Barb. (N. Y.) 610. § 64.
v. Rachal, 9 Rob. (La.) 276. §§ 359, 397.
v. Whitmarsh, 8 Adol. & Ell. (N. S.) 966. § 415.
v. Wiley, 126 Ill. 310. § 577.
Gilliam *v.* Esselman, 5 Sneed (Tenn.), 86. § 301.
Gillighan *v.* Boardman, 29 Me. 79. §§ 15, 82, 202.
Gillilan *v.* Ludington, 6 W. Va. 128. §§ 606, 609.
Gillman, People *v.*, 58 Hun (N. Y.), 368. § 508.
Gillson, Barber *v.*, 18 Nev. 89. § 36.
Gilman *v.* Kibler, 5 Humph. 19. § 82.
v. Lewis, 15 Me. 452. § 107.
Taylor *v.*, 25 Vt. 411. § 405.
Gilmer, Pickett *v.*, 32 La. Ann. 991. § 578.
Gilmer's Adm'r *v.* Baker's Adm'r, 24 W. Va. 72. § 648.
Gilmore, Spies *v.*, 1 N. Y. 321. § 179.
State *v.*, 81 Me. 405. § 508.
Warren *v.*, 11 Cush. 15. § 500.
Gilmore's Adm'r, Hammond *v.*, 14 Conn. 479. § 195.
Gilson, Ball *v.*, 7 Up. Can. (C. P.) 531. § 29.
Commonwealth *v.*, 8 Watts (Pa.), 214. § 583.
Giltinan, Strong *v.*, 7 Phila. (Pa.) 176. § 631.
Gingrich *v.* People, 34 Ill. 448. § 499.
Gipson *v.* Ogden, 100 Ind. 20. §§ 29, 355, 371, 375.
Girdler, Dance *v.*, 4 Bos. & Pul. 34. § 396.
Girdlestone, Molson's Bank *v.*, 44 Up. Can. (Q. B.) 54. § 442.
Girling, Wells *v.*, 1 Brod. & Bing. 447. § 21.
Wells *v.*, 8 Taunt. 737. § 138.
Girvin *v.* Hickman, 21 Hun (N. Y.), 316. § 574.
Gist *v.* Drakely, 2 Gill (Md.), 330. §§ 176, 180.
Givan, State *v.*, 45 Ind. 267. § 531.

Givens *v.* Briscoe, 3 J. J. Marsh. (Ky.) 529. §§ 252, 358.
v. Nelson, 10 Leigh (Va.), 382. § 269.
Givens' Case, 34 N. J. Eq. 191. § 583.
Gladwin *v.* Garrison, 13 Cal. 330. § 218.
Glascock *v.* Hamilton, 62 Tex. 143. §§ 139, 263, 270, 290, 439.
Glasgow, Musgrave *v.*, 3 Ind. 31. §§ 62, 339.
v. State, 41 Kan. 333. § 503.
Glass, Cheek *v.*, 3 Ind. 286. § 352.
v. Howell, 2 Lea (Tenn.), 50. § 585.
v. Thompson, 9 B. Mon. (Ky.) 235. § 436.
Wathen *v.*, 54 Miss. 382. § 526.
Glazier *v.* Douglass, 32 Conn. 393. § 430.
Gleason *v.* Briggs, 28 Vt. 135. § 62.
Morse *v.*, 64 N. Y. 204. § 36.
Gleaves, Adams & Alexander *v.*, 10 Lea (Tenn.), 367. § 319.
Gleed, Gregory *v.*, 33 Vt. 405. §§ 13, 82.
Glencove Mut. Ins. Co. *v.* Harrold, 20 Barb. (N. Y.) 298. § 88.
Glenn, Knepper *v.*, 73 Iowa, 730. § 526.
v. Morgan, 23 W. Va. 467. §§ 356, 374.
State *v.*, 40 Ark. 332. § 514.
v. Statler, 42 Iowa, 107. § 127.
Stewart *v.*, 5 Wis. 14. § 138.
v. Wallace, 4 Strob. Eq. (S. C.) 149. § 542.
Williams *v.*, 92 N. C. 253. § 261.
Glidden *v.* Child, 122 Mass. 433. § 76.
Glissman, Rouse *v.*, 29 Ill. App. 321. §§ 3, 14.
Globe Bank *v.* Small, 25 Me. 366. § 197.
Globe Mutual Ins. Co. *v.* Carson, 31 Mo. 218. § 366.
Glover, Burke *v.*, 21 Up. Can. (Q. B.) 294. § 482.
v. Robbins, 49 Ala. 219. § 379.
Wilson *v.*, 3 Pa. St. 404. § 557.
Glyn *v.* Hertel, 8 Taunt. 208. § 122.
Gobbold, Choppin *v.*, 13 La. Ann. 238. § 62.
Godbe, Baskin *v.*, 1 Utah, 28. § 342.
Goddard *v.* Mockbee, 5 Cranch (C. C.), 666. § 63.
Salmon Falls Man. Co. *v.*, 14 How. 447. §§ 80, 89, 90.
v. Whyte, 2 Giff. 449. § 303.
Godfrey, Chamberlain *v.*, 36 Vt. 380. § 630.
Godman *v.* Chase, 1 Barn. & Ald. 297. § 82.
Godwin *v.* Francis, 5 Com. Pl. 295. § 89.
Merriken *v.*, 2 Del. Ch. 236. § 39.
Goff *v.* Bankstone, 35 Miss. 518. § 402.
Goff's Adm'r, Triplett *v.*, 83 Va. 784. § 644.
Goggan & Bros., Cotulla *v.*, 77 Tex. 32. § 460.
Goggin, Fagin *v.*, 12 R. I. 398. § 227.
Gogin, Apperson *v.*, 3 Bradw. (Ill. App.) 48. § 45.
Gokey, Staples *v.*, 34 Hun (N. Y.), 289. § 277.
Gold *v.* Marshall, 76 Va. 668. § 524.
v. Phillips, 10 Johns. 412. § 67.
Golden, Williams *v.*, 10 Neb. 432. § 571.
Golding, Cohen *v.*, 27 La. Ann. 77. § 588.
Goldsberry, Pierce *v.*, 35 Ind. 317. §§ 354, 625.
Goldshede *v.* Swan, 1 Wels., Hurl. & Gor. 154. §§ 77, 86.
Goldsmith, Connerat *v.*, 6 Ga. 14. § 58.
Walker *v.*, 7 Oreg. 161. §§ 34, 415.
Goldstein's Sureties, United States *v.*, 1 Dillon, 413. § 508.
Goles' Adm'r *v.* Van Arman, 18 Ohio, 336. § 137.
Gomez *v.* Lazarus, 1 Dev. Eq. (N. C.) 205. § 322.
Good, Calvert *v.*, 95 Pa. St. 65. § 356.
v. Martin, 17 Am. Law Reg. 111. § 182.

Good *v.* Martin, 95 U. S. 90. §§ 180, 181.
Goodall, Campbell *v.*, 8 Bradw. (Ill. App.) 266. § 329.
v. Wentworth, 20 Me. 322. § 266.
Goode *v.* Burford, 14 La. Ann. 102. § 581.
v. Jones, 9 Mo. 866. § 184.
Goodenow, Stowell *v.*, 31 Me. 538. § 359.
Goodhue *v.* Palmer, 13 Ind. 457. § 357.
Gooding, Hooker *v.*, 86 Ill. 60. § 102.
Goodloe *v.* Clay, 6 B. Mon. (Ky.) 236. §§ 272, 444.
Tudor *v.*, 1 B. Mon. 322. § 356.
Goodman *v.* Chase, 1 Barn. & Ald. 297. § 62.
v. Griffin, 3 Stew. (Ala.) 160. § 239.
v. Litaker, 84 N. C. 8. § 33.
Perkins *v.*, 21 Barb. (N. Y.) 218. § 26.
Rosenbaum *v.*, 78 Va. 121. § 255.
Goodrich, Penfield *v.*, 10 Hun (N. Y.), 41. § 37.
Simmons *v.*, 67 Ga. 750. § 341.
Goodspeed *v.* Fuller, 46 Me. 141. § 60.
Goodwin *v.* Buckman, 11 Iowa, 308. § 100.
v. Bunzl, 102 N. Y. 224. § 449.
v. Gilbert, 9 Mass. 510. § 53.
Jones *v.*, 39 Cal. 493. § 177.
Keith *v.*, 31 Vt. 268. §§ 60, 114, 258, 380.
Railway Co. *v.*, 3 Wels., Hurl. & Gor. 320. § 395.
Sherrell *v.*, 3 Humph. (Tenn.) 419. § 545.
v. Stark, 15 N. H. 218. § 516.
v. State, 18 Ohio, 6. § 536.
Tracy *v.*, 5 Allen, 409. § 636.
Goodwine *v.* State, 81 Ind. 109. § 596.
Goodwyn *v.* Hightower, 30 Ga. 249. § 342.
Goodyear *v.* Watson, 14 Barb. (N. Y.) 481. § 311.
Goodyear Dental Vulcanite Co. *v.* Bacon, 151 Mass. 460. § 151.
Gookin *v.* Sanborn, 3 N. H. 491. § 580.
Goold, Wallace *v.*, 91 Ill. 15. § 176.
Gordon, Baldwin *v.*, 12 Martin (La.), O. S. 378. §§ 145, 239.
Buel *v.*, 6 Johns. 126. § 220.
Calvert *v.*, 3 Man. & Ryl. 124. § 133.
Clark *v.*, 82 Ga. 613. § 494.
Clark *v.*, 121 Mass. 330. § 108.
v. Culvert, 2 Simons, 253. § 133.
Dunlop *v.*, 10 La. Ann. 243. § 122.
Hughes *v.*, 7 Mo. 297. § 607.
Jones *v.*, 82 Ga. 570. § 504.
Kelly *v.*, 3 Head (Tenn.), 683. § 479.
v. Martin, Fitzgibbon, 302. § 77.
v. McCarty, 3 Wharton (Pa.), 407. § 250.
v. Moore, 44 Ark. 349. § 439.
Neal *v.*, 60 Ga. 112. § 487.
v. Sims, 2 McCord, Ch. (S. C.) 151. § 90.
v. Succession of Diggs, 9 La. Ann. 422. § 467.
Gore Bank, Geary *v.*, 5 Grant's Ch. 536. § 251.
Gorham, Commercial Nat. Bank *v.*, 11 R. I. 162. § 175.
Goring *v.* Edmonds, 6 Bing. 94. § 200.
Gorman, Dunphy *v.*, 29 Ill. App. 132. § 298.
Gorrie *v.* Woodley, 17 Irish Com. Law R. 221. §§ 84, 89.
Gorton, Smith *v.*, 10 La. (Curry), 374. § 178.
Gosbell *v.* Archer, 2 Adol. & Ell. 500. §§ 89, 90.
Gosling, Bateman *v.*, Law Rep. 7 Com. Pl. 9. § 147.
Gosman *v.* Cruger, 7 Hun, 60. § 7.
Goss *v.* Davis' Adm'r, 87 Tenn. (3 Pickle), 226. § 283.
v. Gibson, 8 Humph. (Tenn.) 197. § 276.
Kennedy *v.*, 38 N. Y. 330. § 350.
Passumpsic Bank *v.*, 31 Vt. 315. § 407.

Goss *v.* Watlington, 6 Moore, 355. § 629.
Gosserand *v.* Lacour, 8 La. Ann. 75. § 350.
Gossin *v.* Brown, 11 Pa. St. 527. § 315.
Goswiler, Poorman *v.*, 2 Watts (Pa.), 69. § 236.
Goswiller's Estate, 3 Penr. & Watts, 200. § 41.
Gott *v.* State, 44 Md. 319. § 374.
Gottsberger *v.* Radway, 2 Hilton (N. Y.), 342. § 84.
Gough, Crane *v.*, 4 Md. 316. § 52.
Edelen *v.*, 5 Gill, 103. § 82.
Gould, Commonwealth *v.*, 118 Mass. 300. § 630.
v. Ellery, 39 Barb. (N. Y.) 163. § 47.
v. Fuller, 18 Me. 364. § 273.
v. Gould, 8 Cow. 168. § 209.
Manning *v.*, 90 N. Y. 476. § 486.
Middlefield *v.*, 10 Up. Can. (C. P.) 9. § 629.
Mills *v.*, 14 Ind. 278. § 366.
Preston *v.*, 64 Iowa, 44. § 295.
Gourdin *v.* Read, 8 Rich. Law (S. C.) 230. § 410.
v. Trenholm, 25 S. C. 362. §§ 254, 259.
Govan *v.* Moore, 30 Ark. 667. § 129.
Union Bank *v.*, 10 Sm. & Mar. (Miss.) 333. §§ 34, 370, 434.
Governor *v.* Bowman, 44 Ill. 499. § 371.
Brooks *v.*, 17 Ala. 806. § 535.
v. Coble, 2 Dev. Law (N. C.), 489. § 539.
v. Dodd, 81 Ill. 162. § 531.
v. Hancock, 2 Ala. 728. § 565.
Jennison *v.*, 47 Ala. 390. § 439.
v. Lagow, 43 Ill. 134. §§ 371, 386.
Lucas *v.*, 6 Ala. 826. § 636.
M'Broom *v.*, 4 Port. (Ala.) 90. § 631.
McBroom *v.*, 6 Port. (Ala.) 32. § 448.
McGrew *v.*, 19 Ala. 89. § 562.
McNeale *v.*, 3 Gratt. (Va.) 299. § 625.
Governor, Modisett *v.*, 2 Blackf. (Ind.) 135. § 628.
v. Perkins, 2 Bibb (Ky.), 395. § 569.
Rany *v.*, 4 Blackf. (Ind.) 2. § 169.
v. Ridgway, 12 Ill. 14. § 548.
v. Robbins, 7 Ala. 79. § 541.
v. Shelby, 2 Blackf. (Ind.) 557. §§ 624, 636, 638.
Smith *v.*, 2 Rob. (Va.) 229. § 625.
v. Stonum, 11 Ala. 679. § 143.
Gowdy, Wakeman *v.*, 10 Bosw. (N. Y.) 208. § 440.
Gower, Daniels *v.*, 54 Iowa, 319. § 407.
v. Shelton, 16 Lea (Tenn.), 652. § 587.
Gowing *v.* Cowgill, 12 Iowa, 495. § 562.
Grabfelder *v.* Willis, 10 Bradw. (Ill. App.) 330. § 342.
Grace, Hoad *v.*, 7 Hurl. & Nor. 494. §§ 84, 161.
Lipscomb *v.*, 26 Ark. 231. § 220.
Gradle *v.* Hoffman, 105 Ill. 147. § 572.
Grady, American Land Co. *v.*, 33 Ark. 550. § 316.
v. Hughes, 80 Mich. 184. § 578.
Maybury *v.*, 67 Ala. 147. § 463.
Graeter *v.* De Wolf, 112 Ind. 1. § 112.
Graff *v.* Kahn, 18 Bradw. (Ill. App.) 485. § 236.
Grafton Bank *v.* Kent, 4 N. H. 221. § 29.
v. Woodward, 5 N. H. 99. §§ 356, 359.
Graham, Bennett *v.*, 71 Ga. 211. §§ 586, 638.
Crabtree *v.*, 81 Ga. 290. § 580.
Horsey *v.*, Law Rep. 5 Com. P. 9. § 81.
Houck *v.*, 106 Ind. 195. §§ 260, 267, 645.
Houck *v.*, 123 Ind. 277. § 175.
Malling Union *v.*, Law Rep. 5 Com. Pl. 201. § 395.
Miner *v.*, 24 Pa. St. 491. § 133.
Murray *v.*, 29 Iowa, 520. § 29.

Graham v. Musson, 7 Scott, 769. § 90.
Ogle v., 2 Pen. & Watts (Pa.), 132. § 381.
v. Rings, 67 Mo. 324. § 137.
v. Roberson, 79 Ga. 72, 73. § 2.
v. Rush, 73 Iowa, 451. § 380.
v. State, 66 Ind. 386. § 519.
Grahame v. Grahame, Law Rep. Irish (19 Ch. Div.), 249. §§ 156, 161.
Grand Lodge, Drabek v., 24 Ill. App. 82. § 422.
Grand Rapids Savings Bank v. Warren, 52 Mich. 557. § 39.
Grandstaff v. Hampton & Co., 30 Gratt. (Va.) 1. § 537.
Grane, Toplic v., 5 Bing. N. C. 636. § 60.
Granger, Noyes v., 51 Iowa, 227. § 93.
v. Parker, 142 Mass. 186. § 460.
Williams v., 4 Day (Conn.), 444. § 199.
Grant, Hare v., 77 N. C. 203. § 214.
v. Hotchkiss, 26 Barb. (N. Y.) §§ 84, 97.
v. Ridsdale, 2 Harr. & Johns. (Md.) 186. § 158.
Rupert v., 6 Sm. & Mar. (Miss.) 433. § 344.
v. Shaw, 16 Mass. 341. § 67.
Simonson v., 36 Minn. 439. § 397.
v. Smith, 46 N. Y. 93. § 118.
Wells v., 4 Yerg. (Tenn.) 491. § 536.
v. Wolf, 34 Minn. 32. § 77.
Graves v. Bulkley, 25 Kan. 249. §§ 636, 637.
Dyer v., 37 Vt. 369. § 52.
v. Lebanon Nat. Bank, 10 Bush (Ky.), 23. § 422.
Ratcliffe v., 1 Vern. 196. § 139.
Remsen v., 41 N. Y. 471. §§ 44, 366.
Steele v., 68 Ala. 21. §§ 150, 581, 586.
v. Tucker, 10 Sm. & Mar. (Miss.) 9. §§ 406, 408.
Gravett v. Malone, 54 Ala. 19. §§ 630, 640.
Gray, Bauer v., 18 Mo. App. 164. § 329.
v. Bowls, 1 Dev. & Batt. (N. C.) 437. § 468.
v. Brown, 1 Rich. Law (S. C.), 351. § 576.
Caperton v., 4 Yerg. (Tenn.) 563. § 75.
v. Dryden, 79 Mo. 106. § 462.
Elliott v., 4 Stew. & Port. (Ala.) 168. § 467.
Hatton v., 2 Ch. Cas. 164. § 89.
v. Holland, 9 Oreg. 512. § 35.
v. Jenkins, 24 Ala. 516. § 580.
Jernegan v., 14 Lea (Tenn.), 536. § 596.
Kirkpatrick v., 43 Kan. 434. § 617.
Langdon v., 22 Hun (N. Y.), 511. § 475.
v. MacLean, 17 Ill. 404. § 467.
v. McDonald, 19 Wis. 213. § 266.
v. Merrill, 11 Bush (Ky.), 633. § 488.
Miller v., 31 Ill. App. 453. § 608.
Moore v., 26 Ohio St. 525. § 448.
Parrish v., 1 Humph. (Tenn.) 88. § 605.
v. Robinson, 90 Ind. 527. § 141.
Seligman v., 66 Mich. 341. § 439.
v. State, 78 Ind. 68. § 43.
Wyman v., 7 Harr. & Johns. (Md.) 409. § 68.
Gray, Adm'r, Bauer v., 18 Mo. App. 164. § 230.
Gray's Ex'rs v. Brown, 22 Ala. 262. §§ 235, 345.
Grayson v. Atkinson, 2 Ves. Sr. 454. § 89.
Crozier v., 4 J. J. Marsh. (Ky.) 514. § 212.
Grayson's Appeal, 108 Pa. St. 581. § 356.
Greathouse v. Hord, 1 Dana (Ky.), 105. § 252.
Snider v., 16 Ark. 72. §§ 209, 633.
Greely v. Dow, 2 Met. (Mass.) 176. §§ 348, 353.

Green, Adm'r of Wilson *v.*, 25 Vt. 450. §§ 234, 626.
v. Blunt, 59 Iowa, 79. § 434.
Bowditch *v.*, 3 Met. (Mass.) 360. § 271.
Brant *v.*, 6 Leigh (Va.), 16. § 90.
Canadian Bank of Commerce *v.*, 45 Up. Can. (Q. B.) 81. § 245.
v. Cresswell, 2 Perry & Dav. 430. § 61.
v. Creswell, 10 Adol. & Ell. 453. § 60.
v. Crockett, 2 Dev. & Bat. Eq. 390. § 237.
v. Greenboro Female College, 83 N. C. 449. § 333.
Guardians of Litchfield Union *v.*, 1 Hurl. & Nor. 884. § 333.
Head *v.*, 5 Bissell, 311. § 96.
Jimmerson *v.*, 7 Neb. 26. § 231.
v. Kindy, 43 Mich. 279. §§ 481, 486.
v. Locke, 31 La. Ann. 656. § 602.
Mellish *v.*, 5 Grant's Ch. 655. § 434.
Milner *v.*, 2 Johns. Cas. 283. § 500.
Neylan *v.*, 82 Cal. 128. § 109.
Parham *v.*, 64 N. C. 436. § 293.
v. People, 14 Bradw. (Ill. App.) 364. §§ 526, 564.
Platter *v.*, 26 Kan. 252. §§ 160, 161.
Roberts *v.*, 31 Ga. 421. § 494.
Voiles *v.*, 43 Ind. 374. § 380.
Wade *v.*, 3 Humph. (Tenn.) 547. § 215.
v. Wardwell, 17 Ill. 278. § 521.
v. Wynn, Law Rep. 4 Ch. App. Cas. 204. § 147.
v. Yonng, 8 Greenl. (Me.) 14. § 133.
Greenawalt *v.* Kreider, 3 Pa. St. 264. § 240.
Green Bay & Minn. R. R. Co. *v.* Union Steamboat Co., 107 U. S. 98. § 6.
Greenboro Female College, Green *v.*, 83 N. C. 449. § 333.
Greene *v.* Bates, 74 N. Y. 333. § 363.
v. Cramer, 2 Connor & Law. 54. § 90.
Erwin *v.*, 5 Rob. (La.) 70. § 125.
People *v.*, 5 Hill (N. Y.), 647. § 502.
v. Starnes, 1 Heisk. (Tenn.) 582. § 223.
Greene's Ex'rs *v.* Ferrie, 1 Des. (S. C.) 164. § 322.
Greenfield *v.* Yeates, 2 Rawle (Pa.), 158. § 121.
Greenhood, Wakefield *v.*, 29 Cal. 597. § 74.
Greening *v.* Patten, 51 Wis. 146. § 332.
Greenlaw, Jones *v.*, 6 Cold. (Tenn.) 342. § 98.
v. Logan, 2 Lea (Tenn.), 185. § 481.
Greenleaf, Odlin *v.*, 3 N. H. 270. § 230.
Greenlee *v.* Lowing, 35 Mich. 63. § 486.
Greenly, Olmstead *v.*, 18 Johns. 12. § 65.
Greenough *v.* McClelland, 2 Ellis & Ellis, 424. §§ 29, 375.
Greenwell *v.* Commonwealth, 78 Ky. 320. § 571.
Greenwood School Dist., Todd *v.*, 40 Mich. 294. § 342.
Greer *v.* Bush, 57 Miss. 575. § 121.
v. Howard, 41 Ohio St. 591. § 484.
Williams *v.*, 4 Haywood (Tenn.), 235. § 214.
v. Wintersmith, 85 Ky. 516. § 226.
Gregg, Riley *v.*, 16 Wis. 666. §§ 29, 356.
v. Wilson, 50 Ind. 490. § 97.
Gregory, Bently *v.*, 7 T. B. Mon. (Ky.) 368. § 229.
v. Gleed, 33 Vt. 405. §§ 13, 82.
v. Logan, 7 Blackf. (Ind.) 112. § 82.
v. Morisey, 79 N. C. 559. § 532.
v. Murrell, 2 Ired. Eq. (N. C.) 233. § 268.
Rawson *v.*, 59 Ga. 733. § 434.
State *v.*, 88 Ind. 110. § 581.

Gregory, State *v.*, 119 Ind. 503. § 402.
v. Williams, 3 Meriv. 582. § 72.
Gresham *v.* Ware, 79 Ala. 192. § 237.
Greve, Ham *v.*, 34 Ind. 18. §§ 401, 419.
Railsback *v.*, 58 Ind. 72. § 460.
Grice *v.* Ricks, 3 Dev. Law (N. C.), 62. § 197.
Grider *v.* Payne, 9 Dana (Ky.), 188. § 313.
Gridley *v.* Capen, 72 Ill. 11. § 111.
Grieff *v.* Kirk, 17 La. Ann. 25. § 449.
Grier *v.* Wallace, 7 Rich. (S. C.) 182. § 45.
Grieve *v.* Smith, 23 Up. Can. (Q. B.) 23. § 397.
Griff *v.* Steamboat Stacy, 12 La. Ann. 8. § 446.
Griffin, Canby *v.*, 3 Har. (Del.) 333. § 500.
Goodman *v.*, 3 Stew. (Ala.) 160. § 239.
v. Hampton, 21 Ga. 198. § 304.
Lanier *v.*, 11 S. C. 565. § 576.
Lee *v.*, 31 Miss. 632. § 315.
Marsh *v.*, 42 Iowa, 403. § 379.
McKee *v.*, 66 Ala. 211. §§ 529, 591.
v. Moore, 2 Kelly (Ga.), 331. §§ 494, 497.
v. Orman, 9 Fla. 22. § 298.
v. Rembert, 2 Rich. N. S. (S. C.) 410. §§ 116, 204.
Sauer *v.*, 67 Mo. 654. § 460.
v. Wallace, 66 Ind. 410. § 27.
Griffith, Bailey *v.*, 40 Up. Can. (Q. B. Div.) 418. §§ 362, 378.
Braught *v.*, 16 Iowa, 26. § 304.
Champion *v.*, 13 Ohio, 228. §§ 176, 177.
v. Reynolds, 4 Gratt. (Va.) 46. § 406.
State *v.*, 63 Mo. 545. § 571.
v. Turner, 4 Gill (Md.), 111. § 626.
Wooldridge *v.*, 59 Tex. 290. § 462.
Wright *v.*, 121 Ind. 478. §§ 156, 159, 193, 196.
Griggs, Longley *v.*, 10 Pick. 121. § 260.
Grigsby, Hart *v.*, 14 Bush (Ky.), 542. § 7.
v. Shwarz, 82 Cal. 278. § 14.
Yerby *v.*, 9 Leigh (Va.), 387. §§ 89, 90.
Grim *v.* School Directors, 51 Pa. St. 219. § 411.
Grimes *v.* Butler, 1 Bibb (Ky.), 192. § 519.
v. Nolen, 3 Humph. (Tenn.) 412. § 372.
Perigo, G. M. & T. Co. *v.*, 2 Col. 651. § 482.
v. Sherman, 25 Neb. 843. § 219.
Grimmenstein, Redwood City *v.*, 68 Cal. 512. § 591.
Gring's Appeal, 89 Pa. St. 336. § 300.
Grinnell Live Stock Co., Wibaux *v.*, 9 Mont. 154. § 137.
Grisard *v.* Hinson, 50 Ark. 229. § 446.
Mennet *v.*, 79 Ind. 222. § 646.
Griswold, Hazard *v.* (Cir. Ct. D. R. I.), 21 Fed. Rep. 178. §§ 12, 244.
v. Hazard, 28 Fed. Rep. 597. § 244.
Jackson *v.*, 4 Hill (N. Y.), 522. § 630.
Roberts *v.*, 35 Vt. 496. §§ 17, 120.
Grocers' Bank *v.* Kingman, 16 Gray, 473. §§ 22, 395.
Gronbeck, Potter *v.*, 117 Ill. 404. §§ 48, 50, 109, 135.
Groot, Whitney *v.*, 24 Wend. 82. §§ 164, 196.
Gross *v.* Davis, 87 Tenn. (3 Pick.) 226. §§ 283, 287, 288.
Eichelberger *v.*, 42 Ohio St. 549. §§ 540, 677.
v. Parrott, 16 Cal. 143. § 360.
Grout, Hutchins *v.*, 40 Hun (N. Y.), 207. § 449.
Grove *v.* Dubois, 1 Term R. 112. § 71.
v. Johnston, Law Rep. (Irish, 24 Q. B. & Ex. Div.) 352. § 155.
Grover, Barney *v.*, 28 Vt. 391. § 207.
Brown *v.*, 6 Bush (Ky.), 1. § 642.
Fletcher *v.*, 11 N. H. 368. § 287.
v. Hoppock, 2 Dutcher (N. J.), 191. §§ 248, 355.

Grover, Towne v., 9 Pick. 306. § 74.
Grover & Baker Sewing Mach. Co., Hyatt v., 41 Mich. 225. § 526.
Wright v., 82 Pa. St. 88. § 309.
Groves, Kay v., 6 Bing. 276. § 162.
Meguiar v., 1 Fed. Rep. 279. § 367.
Grubb v. Bullock, 44 Ga. 379. § 506.
v. Wysors, 32 Gratt. (Va.) 127. § 321.
Grudle v. Kern, 109 Ill. 557. § 487.
Gruenewald v. Schaales, 17 Mo. App. 324. § 462.
Grundy v. Meighan, 7 Irish Law Rep. 519. § 146.
Gryle v. Gryle, 2 Atkyns, 177. § 89.
Guardian F. & L. Ass. Co. v. Thompson, 68 Cal. 208. § 422.
Guardians of Litchfield Union v. Green, 1 Hurl. & Nor. 884. § 333.
Guardians of Mansfield Union v. Wright, 8 Heisk. (Tenn.) 22. § 524.
Guild v. Butler, 127 Mass. 386. §§ 426, 431.
Haseltine v., 11 N. H. 390. § 218.
v. McDaniels, 43 Kan. 548. § 307.
v. Thomas, 54 Ala. 414. §§ 402, 408, 642.
Guillot, Ancion v., 10 La. Ann. 124. § 22.
Guilmartin, Jackson v., 61 Ga. 544. § 510.
Guion v. Ford, 12 Rob. (La.) 123. § 515.
Guise, Simmons v., 46 Ga. 473. § 363.
Gull v. Lindsay, 4 Wels., Hurl. & Gor. 45. § 62.
Gulseth, Torp v., 37 Minn. 135. § 329.
Gum v. Swearinger, 69 Mo. 553. § 526.
Gunn, Edwards v., 3 Conn. 316. § 494.
v. Geary, 44 Mich. 615. § 93.
v. Madigan, 28 Wis. 158. § 107.
Pawle v., 4 Bing. N. C. 445. § 52.
Gunter, Rosenbaum v., 2 E. D. Smith (N. Y.), 415. § 82.
Gurney, Hubbart v., 64 N. Y. 457. §§ 29, 363.
Patten v., 17 Mass. 182. § 73.
Gustine v. Union Bank, 10 Rob. (La.) 412. §§ 372, 376.
Guthrie v. Morrison, 1 Har. (Del.) 368. § 506.
Steadman v., 4 Met. (Ky.) 147. § 187.
Guy, Lucas v., 2 Bailey, Law (S. C.), 403. § 293.
Guyer v. Spotts, 85 Pa. St. 51. § 452.
Gwathney, Johnston v., 2 Bibb (Ky.), 186. § 519.
Gwyn v. Patterson, 72 N. C. 189. § 408.
Gwynn v. Gwynn, 31 S. C. 482. § 7.
Gwynne v. Burnell, 7 Clark & Finnelly, 572. § 547.
Collins v., 2 Moore & Scott, 640. § 555.
Habersham v. Sears, 11 Oreg. 431. § 569.
Habich, Hyland v., 150 Mass. 112. § 135.
Hacker, Johnson v., 8 Heisk. (Tenn.) 388. § 371.
Hackett, Ward v., 30 Minn. 150. §§ 380, 407.
Hackleman v. Miller, 4 Blackf. (Ind.) 322. § 67.
Haddens v. Chambers, 2 Dall. (Pa.) 236. § 220.
Haddock v. Perham, 70 Ga. 572. § 640.
Haddon v. Hemingway, 39 Mich. 619. § 480.
Haden v. Brown, 18 Ala. 641. §§ 239, 342.
Hadley, Hall v., 4 Neville & Man. 515. § 403.
Hagadorn, Pinckney v., 1 Duer (N. Y.), 89. § 90.
Hagar v. Mounts, 3 Blackf. (Ind.) 57. § 416.
Hager, Fluck v., 51 Pa. St. 459. § 332.
Hagerman, Wolcott v., 50 N. J. Law, 289. § 270.
Hagey v. Hill, 75 Pa. St. 108. § 376.

Haggerty, Brown *v.*, 26 Ill. 469. §§ 29, 337.
People *v.*, 5 Daly (N. Y. Com. Pl.), 532. § 511.
Hagler, Jones *v.*, 6 Jones' Law (N. C.), 542. § 150.
Vancil *v.*, 27 Kan. 407. § 605.
Hagood *v.* Blythe (Cir. Ct. D. S. C.), 37 Fed. Rep. 249. § 595.
Haigh *v.* Brooks, 10 Adol. & Ell. 309. § 86.
Haight *v.* Brisbin, 100 N. Y. 219. § 578.
Mains *v.*, 14 Barb. (N. Y.) 76. §§ 98, 101.
Redfield *v.*, 27 Conn. 31. §§ 43, 97.
Haile *v.* Oliver, 52 Tex. 443. § 616.
Hailey *v.* Boyd's Adm'r, 64 Ala. 399. §§ 574, 577.
Hain, Beyerle *v.*, 61 Pa. St. 226. § 546.
Haines, Clary & Whaley *v.*, 61 Ga. 520. § 465.
v. Dennett, 11 N. H. 180. § 381.
Hairston *v.* Hughes, 3 Munf. (Va.) 568. § 578.
Hake, Wright *v.*, 38 Mich. 525. § 481.
Halderman *v.* Woodward, 22 Kan. 734. §§ 353. 448.
Hale, Archer *v.*, 4 Bing. 464. § 482.
Beekman *v.*, 17 Johns. 134. § 190.
v. Commonwealth, 8 Pa. St. 415. § 563.
Curry *v.*, 15 W. Va. 867. § 37.
v. Forbis, 3 Mont. 395. § 354.
Foster *v.*, 3 Vesey, Jr. 696. § 80.
Harmon *v.*, 1 Wash. Terr. (N. S.) 422. §§ 29, 245.
Inhabitants of Norridgenock *v.*, 89 Me. 362. § 168.
Newcomb *v.*, 90 N. Y. 326. § 239.
v. Russ, 1 Greenl. (Me.) 334. § 516.
Salisbury *v.*, 12 Pick. 416. § 202.
Haley *v.* Petty, 42 Ark. 392. § 526.
Skofield *v.*, 22 Me. 164. § 202.
Hall, Backhouse *v.*, 6 Best & Smith, 507. § 118.
Hall, Board of Supervisors *v.*, 47 Wis. 208. § 597.
v. Brackett, 62 N. H. 509. §§ 172, 396, 642.
v. Bramble, 2 Dak. 189. § 578.
Cailleux *v.*, 1 E. D. Smith (N. Y.), 5. § 66.
v. Capital Bank, 71 Ga. 715. § 342.
Clompton's Ex'rs *v.*, 51 Miss. 482. § 17.
v. Constant, 2 Hall (N. Y.), 205. § 353.
Critchett *v.*, 56 N. H. 324. § 574.
v. Cushman, 16 N. H. 462. § 268.
v. Farmer, 5 Denio, 484. § 88.
v. Fowler, 6 Hill, 630. § 472.
v. Hall, 10 Humph. (Tenn.) 352. § 207.
v. Hall, 34 Ind. 314. § 38.
Hickman *v.*, 5 Littell (Ky.), 338. § 244.
Hodges *v.*, 29 Vt. 209. § 60.
v. Hoxsey, 84 Ill. 616. §§ 302, 428.
v. Hutchons, 3 Mylne & Keen, 426. § 147.
v. McHenry, 19 Iowa, 521. §§ 380, 381.
Merchants' Nat. Bank *v.*, 18 Hun (N. Y.), 176. § 159.
v. Newcomb, 3 Hill, 233. § 179.
v. Newcomb, 7 Hill (N. Y.), 416. § 182.
v. Parker, 37 Mich. 590. § 411.
v. Parker, 39 Mich. 287. § 152.
Queen *v.*, 1 Up. Can. (C. P.) 406. § 170.
v. Rand, 8 Conn. 560. §§ 163, 643.
v. Robinson, 8 Ired. Law (N. C.), 56. § 268.
v. Rodgers, 7 Humph. (Tenn.) 536. § 67.
Rutter *v.*, 31 Ill. App. 647. §§ 580, 586.
Scott *v.*, 6 B. Mon. 285. § 356.
v. Sherwood, 59 Mo. 172. § 279.
v. Smith, 14 Bush (Ky.), 604. §§ 408, 411, 412.

Hall *v.* Smith, 5 How. 96. § 210.
v. Soule, 11 Mich. 494. § 81.
Sparks *v.*, 4 J. J. Marsh. (Ky.) 35. § 342.
Stearns *v.*, 9 Cush. 31. § 81.
v. Thompson, 9 Up. Can. (C. P.) 257. § 147.
Thompson *v.*, 16 Ala. 204. § 82.
Thompson *v.*, 45 Barb. (N. Y.) 214. § 405.
Treasurers of Pickaway *v.*, 3 Ohio, 225. § 578.
v. Weaver (Cir. Ct. D. Oreg.), 34 Fed. Rep. 104. § 383.
v. White, 27 Conn. 488. §§ 515, 631.
v. Williamson's Adm'r, 9 Ohio St. 17. § 474.
Hall, Adm'r, Kayser *v.*, 85 Ill. 511. § 178.
Hall's Adm'r *v.* Creswell, 12 Gill & Johns. (Md.) 36. § 212.
Mathews *v.*, 21 W. Va. 510. § 212.
Halliburton *v.* Carter, 55 Mo. 435. § 220.
Halliday *v.* Hart, 30 N. Y. 474. §§ 353, 643.
Halsa *v.* Halsa, 8 Mo. 303. § 82.
Halsey, Lafarge *v.*, 1 Bosw. (N. Y.) 171. § 236.
Halstead *v.* Brown, 17 Ind. 202. §§ 242, 355.
Ham *v.* Greve, 34 Ind. 18. §§ 401, 419.
Norris *v.*, R. M. Charlt. (Ga.) 267. § 311.
Haman *v.* Howe, 27 Gratt. (Va.) 676. § 403.
Hamar *v.* Alexander, 5 Bos. & Pul. 241. § 73.
Hamblin *v.* McCallister, 4 Bush (Ky.), 418. § 609.
Hamer, Newell *v.*, 4 How. (Miss.) 684. §§ 40, 239.
Hamilton, Beesley *v.*, 50 Ill. 88. § 402.
Belfast Banking Co. *v.*, 12 Law Rep. (Irish), 105. § 155.
v. Bryant, 114 Mass. 543. § 472.
Hamilton, Butler *v.*, 2 Des. Eq. (S. C.) 226. § 342.
Carroll Co. *v.*, 30 La. Ann. 520. §§ 465, 466.
Chard *v.*, 56 Hun (N. Y.), 259. § 139.
v. Dunklee, 1 N. H. 172. § 497.
Gerson *v.*, 30 La. Ann. 737. § 165.
Glascock *v.*, 62 Tex. 143. §§ 139, 263, 270, 290, 439.
v. Johnston, 82 Ill. 39. §§ 176, 210.
McKee *v.*, 33 Ohio St. 7. § 216.
Montgomery *v.*, 43 Ind. 451. § 347.
v. Prouty, 50 Wis. 592. §§ 344, 357.
Ritter *v.*, 4 Tex. 325. § 604.
v. Van Rensselaer, 43 Barb. (N. Y.) 117. § 111.
v. Van Rensselaer, 43 N. Y. 244. § 130.
v. Watson, 12 Cl. & Finn. 109. § 419.
v. Winterrowd, 43 Ind. 393. § 352.
Hamlin, Hatch *v.*, 12 Daly (N. Y. Com. Pl.), 272. § 251.
v. Kinney, 2 Oreg. 91. § 578.
McQuewans *v.*, 35 Pa. St. 517. § 18.
Hammel *v.* Beardsley, 31 Minn. 314. § 1.
Dahlman *v.*, 45 Wis. 466. § 16.
Hammell, Stone *v.*, 83 Cal. 547. § 211.
Hammock *v.* Baker, 3 Bush (Ky.), 208. § 488.
Hammond, Bank *v.*, 1 Rich. Law (S. C.), 281. § 199.
v. Chamberlain, 26 Vt. 406. § 100.
Franklin *v.*, 45 Pa. St. 507. § 522.
v. Gilmore's Adm'r, 14 Conn. 479. § 195.
Newton *v.*, 38 Ohio St. 430. §§ 238, 242, 574.
State *v.*, 6 Gill & Johns. (Md.) 157. § 372.

Hammond, United States *v.*, 4 Biss. 283. § 402.
Woodbury *v.*, 54 Me. 332. § 577.
Hamner *v.* Mason, 24 Ala. 480. § 575.
Hampton, Griffin *v.*, 21 Ga. 198. § 304.
v. Levy, 1 McCord, Eq. (S. C.) 107. § 445.
Levy *v.*, 1 McCord, Law (S. C.), 145. § 30.
v. Phipps, 108 U. S. 260. § 327.
Shehan *v.*, 8 Ala. 942. §§ 605, 618.
State *v.*, 14 La. Ann. 736. §§ 175, 517, 530.
Hampton's Adm'x, Carter *v.*, 77 Va. 631. § 133.
Hampton & Co., Grandstaff *v.*, 30 Gratt. (Va.) 1. § 567.
Hams, State *v.*, 89 Ind. 363. § 597.
Hanaford, Moynahan *v.*, 42 Mich. 329. § 181.
Hancock *v.* Bryant, 2 Yerg. (Tenn.) 476. § 239.
Governor *v.*, 2 Ala. 728. § 565.
Insurance Co. *v.*, 83 Mo. 21. § 342.
Lynch *v.*, 14 S. C. 66. §§ 211, 226, 329.
Parnell *v.*, 48 Cal. 452. § 455.
v. Wilson, 46 Iowa, 352. § 638.
Handley, Garrett *v.*, 4 Barn. & Cress. 664. §§ 116, 117.
Spencer *v.*, 5 Scott (N. R.), 546. § 406.
Handy, Florat *v.*, 35 La. Ann. 816. § 175.
Haney *v.* People, 12 Col. 345. §§ 504, 508.
Hanford *v.* Higgins, 1 Bosw. (N. Y.) 441. § 76.
Quin *v.*, 1 Hill, 82. §§ 63, 74.
v. Rogers, 11 Barb. (N. Y.) 18. § 87.
Union Mutual Life Ins. Co. *v.*, 27 Fed. Rep. 588. § 37.
Hank *v.* Crittenden, 2 McLean, 557. § 201.
Hanna *v.* International Petroleum Co., 23 Ohio St. 622. § 484.
Hannah, King *v.*, 6 Bradw. (Ill. App.) 495. § 210.
Hannibal & St. Joseph R. R. Co., Hurd *v.*, 33 Hun, 109. § 9.
Hansberger's Adm'r *v.* Kinney, 13 Gratt. (Va.) 511. § 352.
Hansen *v.* Barnes, 3 Gill & Johns. (Md.) 359. § 80.
v. Martin, 63 Cal. 282. § 462.
Hanson *v.* Crawley, 41 Ga. 303. § 381.
Whitehouse *v.*, 42 N. H. 9. §§ 60, 258.
Hansford, Burton *v.*, 10 W. Va. 470. §§ 181, 182.
Happe *v.* Stout, 2 Cal. 460. § 84.
Harback, Gardner *v.*, 21 Ill. 129. § 384.
Harbaugh *v.* Albertson, 102 Ind. 69. § 43.
Harbert *v.* Dumont, 3 Ind. 346. §§ 348, 356.
Harbin, Lewis *v.*, 5 B. Mon. (Ky.) 564. § 342.
Harbord *v.* Cooper, 43 Minn. 466. § 47.
Harbridge, State *v.*, 43 Mo. App. 16. §§ 554, 583.
Hard, Quinn *v.*, 43 Vt. 375. § 406.
Hardcastle *v.* Commercial Bank, 1 Har. (Del.) 374. 323.
Hardesty, Jones *v.*, 10 Gill & Johns. 404. § 72.
Harding, Neel *v.*, 2 Met. (Ky.) 247. § 29.
Singstack *v.*, 4 Harr. & Johns. 186. § 90.
v. Tifft, 75 N. Y. 461. § 330.
Hardman, Walker *v.*, 4 Clark & Fin. 258. § 127.
Hardware Co. *v.* Deere, Mansur & Co., 53 Ark. 140. § 206.
Hardwick *v.* Wright, 35 Beavan, 133. § 431.
Hardy, Blood *v.*, 15 Me. 61. § 90.
Nelson *v.*, 7 Ind. 364. § 63.
Ohio & Mississippi R'y Co. *v.*, 64 Ind. 454. § 8.
Hare *v.* Grant, 77 N. C. 203. § 214.

Hare, Jennings v., 104 Pa. St. 489. § 486.
v. Marsh, 61 Wis. 435. § 453.
Harger v. McCullough, 2 Denio, 119. § 39.
Hargett, Sefton v., 113 Ind. 592. § 29.
Hargreave v. Smee, 6 Bing. 244. §§ 92, 158.
Hargreaves v. Parsons, 13 Mees. & Wels. 561. § 72.
Hargroves v. Cooke, 15 Ga. 321. §§ 17, 82.
Harker, Bonsal v., 2 Har. (Del.) 327. § 506.
Harlan v. Wingate, 2 J. J. Marsh. (Ky.) 138. § 243.
v. Sweeney, 1 Lea (Tenn.), 682. § 301.
Harley, Trent Navigation Co. v., 10 East, 34. § 447.
Harman, Chrisman's Adm'x v., 29 Gratt. (Va.) 494. § 480.
v. Howe, 27 Gratt. (Va.) 676. § 480.
Harman's Heirs, King v., 6 La. (Curry), 607. § 325.
Harmon, Pitzer v., 8 Blackf. (Ind.) 112. § 211.
Ellsworth v., 101 Ill. 274. § 47.
v. Hule, 1 Wash. Terr. (N. S.) 422. §§ 29, 245.
v. State, 82 Ind. 197. § 571.
Harner v. Batdorf, 35 Ohio St. 113. § 334.
v. Dipple, 31 Ohio St. 72. § 4.
Harney, State v., 57 Miss. 863. §§ 12, 383, 384, 520.
Harnsberger v. Yancey, 33 Gratt. (Va.) 527. §§ 152, 206, 298.
Harnsberger's Ex'r v. Geiger's Adm'r, 3 Gratt. (Va.) 144. § 370.
Harold, Anderson v., 10 Ohio, 399. § 89.
Harp v. Osgood, 2 Hill (N. Y.) 216. §§ 494, 516.
Harper, Aldridge v., 10 Bing. 118. § 482.
Harper, Lloyds v., Law Rep. (16 Ch. Div.) 290. § 133.
People v., 91 Ill. 357. §§ 578, 603.
State v., 6 Ohio St. 607. § 558.
Harper's Adm'r v. McVeigh's Adm'r, 82 Va. 751. §§ 205, 206, 645.
Harradine, Pooley v., 7 Ell. & Bl. 431. §§ 29, 32, 375.
Harrah v. Jacobs, 75 Iowa, 72. § 230.
Harral, Reynolds v., 2 Strobh. Law (S. C.), 87. § 513.
Harriman v. Egbert, 36 Iowa, 270. § 605.
Harrington v. Dennie, 13 Mass. 93. § 499.
Fenn v., 54 Miss. 733. § 487.
Newlan v., 24 Ill. 206. § 381.
Harris v. Brooks, 21 Pick. 195. §§ 29, 60, 245.
Byers v., 67 Iowa, 685. § 342.
v. Carlisle, 12 Ohio, 169. § 275.
v. Clap, 1 Mass. 308. § 112.
Elliott v., 9 Bush (Ky.), 237. § 247.
Evans v., 15 J. & S. (N. Y. Super. Ct.) 366. § 8.
v. Ferguson, 2 Bailey, Law (S. C.), 397. § 256.
v. Frank, 29 Kan. 200. § 311.
v. Frank, 81 Cal. 280. § 105.
v. Hunthach, 1 Burrows, 373. § 58.
Johnson v., 69 Ind. 305. § 622.
v. McCaslan, 31 S. C. 420. § 7.
v. Newell, 42 Wis. 687. §§ 1, 242.
v. Pierce, 6 Ind. 162. § 182.
Sabin v., 12 Iowa, 87. § 201.
Scott v., 76 N. C. 205. § 356.
v. Simpson, 4 Litt. (Ky.) 165. § 504.
v. State, 54 Ind. 2. § 510.
v. State, 55 Miss. 50. § 521.
Tiddy v., 101 N. C. 589. § 312.
Varnum v., 1 Hun (N. Y.), 451. § 36.
v. Venables, Law Rep. 7 Exch. 235. § 16.
Voltz v., 40 Ill. 155. §§ 201, 202.

Harris *v.* Warner, 13 Wend. 400. § 259.
Wright *v.*, 31 Iowa, 272. §§ 563, 385.
v. Young, 40 Ga. 65. § 17.
Harris' Adm'r, Bentley *v.*, 2 Gratt. (Va.) 358. §§ 256, 480.
Harrisburg Bank *v.* German, 3 Pa. St. 300. §§ 301, 323.
Harrison, Farmers' & Traders' Bank *v.*, 57 Mo. 503. § 357.
v. Field, 2 Wash. (Va.) 136. §§ 94, 139.
Floyd *v.*, 4 Bibb (Ky.), 76. § 69.
Hoboken *v.*, 1 Vroom (N. J.), 73. §§ 22, 44.
Johns *v.*, 20 Ind. 317. § 381.
Lafargue *v.*, 70 Cal. 380. § 81.
v. Lane, 5 Leigh (Va.), 414. § 542.
v. Lumbermen & Mechanics' Ins. Co., 8 Mo. App. 37. §§ 421, 555.
v. McKim, 18 Iowa, 485. § 182.
v. Phillips, 46 Mo. 520. § 273.
v. Sawtet, 10 Johns. 242. § 60.
v. Seymour, Law Rep. 1 Com. Pl. 518. § 398.
Smith *v.*, 33 Ala. 706. § 298.
State *v.*, Harper, Law (S. C.), 88. § 535.
v. Turbeville, 2 Humph. (Tenn.) 242. § 386.
v. Union Pacific R'y Co. (Cir. Ct. E. D. Mo.) 13 Fed. Rep. 522. § 18.
Wardlaw *v.*, 11 Rich. Law (S. C.), 626. § 188.
Waldron *v.*, 2 Oreg. 87. § 502.
Whitby *v.*, 18 Up. Can. (Q. B.) 606. § 521.
Williams *v.*, 11 S. C. 412. § 4.
Harrison's Ex'rs *v.* Price's Ex'rs, 25 Gratt. (Va.) 553. §§ 608, 614.
Harris *v.* Fawcett, Law Rep. 8 Ch. App. Cas. 866. § 134.
Harrold, Glencove Mut. Ins. Co. *v.*, 20 Barb. (N. Y.) 298. § 88.
Harrop, Buckmaster *v.*, 7 Vesey, 341. § 90.
Harsh *v.* Klepper, 28 Ohio St. 200. § 379.
Harshman *v.* Armstrong, 43 Ind. 126. § 261.
Armstrong *v.*, 61 Ind. 52. § 260.
Hart, Battle *v.*, 2 Dev. Eq. (N. C.) 31. § 253.
v. Clouser, 30 Ind. 210. § 379.
Dock *v.*, 7 Watts & Serg. 172. § 52.
v. Grigsby, 14 Bush (Ky.), 542. § 7.
Halliday *v.*, 30 N. Y. 474. §§ 353, 643.
Hubbard *v.*, 71 Iowa, 668. § 363.
v. Hudson, 6 Duer (N. Y.), 294. § 363.
Kountz *v.*, 17 Ind. 329. § 379.
Rhodes *v.*, 51 Ga. 320. § 381.
v. Stribling, 25 Fla. 435. § 576.
v. Tallmadge, 2 Day (Conn.), 381. § 73.
v. United States, 95 U. S. 316. §§ 555, 556.
Wilson *v.*, 7 Taunt. 295. § 90.
v. Woods, 7 Blackf. (Ind.) 568. § 90.
Harter *v.* Moore, 5 Blackf. (Ind.) 367. § 416.
Hartford & N. Y. Transportation Co. *v.* First National Bank, 46 Conn. 569. § 324.
Hartland, Nash *v.*, 2 Irish Law Rep. 190. §§ 84, 123.
Hartley *v.* Colquitt, 72 Ga. 351. § 500.
Jefferson *v.*, 81 Ga. 716. § 566.
People *v.*, 21 Cal. 585. § 151.
Hartman *v.* Burlingame, 9 Cal. 557. §§ 29, 242.
v. Danner, 74 Pa. St. 36. § 356.
Meyer *v.*, 72 Ill. 442. §§ 63, 66.
Morrison *v.*, 14 Pa. St. 55. § 438.
v. Redman, 21 Mo. App. 124. §§ 91, 376.
Hartnoll, Cripps *v.*, 4 Best & Smith, 414. §§ 59, 60.
Hartsell *v.* State, 45 Ark. 59. § 505.

Hartshorn, Bent v., 1 Met. (Mass.) 24. § 160.
Penniman v., 13 Mass. 87. § 89.
Hartsook's Adm'r, Boulware v., 83 Va. 679. §§ 31, 259.
Hartwell v. Smith, 15 Ohio St. 200. § 265.
v. Whitman, 36 Ala. 712. § 268.
Hartwell, Adm'r, Nofsinger v., 84 Mo. 549. § 457.
Harvey v. Bacon, 9 Yerg. (Tenn.) 308. § 604.
Huntington v., 4 Conn. 124. § 75.
Johnson v., 84 N. Y. 363. §§ 276, 284.
Peabody v., 4 Conn. 119. § 75.
Ricketts v., 78 Ind. 152. § 648.
v. State, 94 Ind. 159. § 646.
Harvey's Ex'r, Steptoe's Adm'r v., 7 Leigh (Va.), 501. § 374.
Harwood v. Kiersted, 20 Ill. 367. § 17.
Haseltine v. Guild, 11 N. H. 390. § 218.
Otis v., 27 Cal. 80. § 87.
Hasey, Myrick v., 27 Me. 9. § 50.
Haskell, Bank v., 51 N. H. 116. §§ 245, 414.
Haskins, Charles v., 11 Iowa, 329. §§ 566, 569.
Fond du Lac Harrow Co. v., 51 Wis. 135. § 137.
Hasleham v. Young, 5 Ad. & Ell. (N. S.) 833. § 18.
Haslock v. Ferguson, 7 Ad. & Ell. 86. § 73.
Hassell v. Long, 2 Maule & Sel. 363. § 167.
Hassey v. Wilke, 55 Cal. 528. § 35.
Hastie, Couturier v., 8 Wels., Hurl. & Gor. 40. § 71.
v. Couturier, 9 Wels., Hurl. & Gor. 102. § 71.
Hastings v. Clendaniel, 2 Del. Ch. 165. § 381.
Lee v., 13 Neb. 508. § 93.
Hasty, Eaton v., 6 Neb. 419. § 298.
Hatch v. Antrim, 51 Ill. 106. § 103.
v. Elkins, 65 N. Y. 489. § 624.
Hatch v. Hamlin, 12 Daly (N. Y. Com. Pl.), 272. § 251.
v. Hobbs, 12 Gray, 447. § 161.
v. Morris, 36 Me. 419. § 38.
Hatfield, Dixon v., 2 Bing. 439. § 77.
v. Merod, 82 Ill. 113. § 207.
Hathaway v. Davis, 33 Cal. 161. § 448.
Farmers' & Mechanics' Bank v., 36 Vt. 539. § 416.
McElroy v., 44 Mich. 399. § 223.
Hathorn, Chase v., 61 Me. 505. §§ 115, 151.
State v., 36 Miss. 491. § 554.
Hatton v. Gray, 2 Ch. Cas. 164. § 89.
Hatz's Ex'rs, Kramph's Ex'r v., 52 Pa. St. 525. § 1.
Hauck, Kruttschnitt v., 6 Nev. 163. § 543.
Merchants' Ins. Co. v., 83 Mo., 21. § 352.
St. Joseph F. & M. Ins. Co. v., 71 Mo. 465. § 352.
Haven v. Foley, 18 Mo. 136. § 324.
Havens v. Fondry, 4 Met. (Ky.) 247. § 328.
v. Willis, 100 N. Y. 482. § 316.
Haviland, Casky v., 13 Ala. 314. § 627.
Haw, Police Jury v., 1 La. (Miller), 41. §§ 402, 642.
Tieman v., 49 Iowa, 312. §§ 566, 591.
Hawes v. Armstrong, 1 Bing. N. C. 761. §§ 82, 84, 85.
v. Marchant, 1 Curtis, 136. § 12.
Hawk, Geddis v., 1 Watts (Pa.), 280. § 97.
v. Geddis, 16 Serg. & Rawle, 23. §§ 97, 240.
Hawkes, Sadler v., 1 Roll. Abr. 27, pl. 49. § 16.
Hawkins v. Chase, 19 Pick. 502. §§ 89, 90.
v. Holmes, 1 P. Wms. 770. § 89.
v. Humble, 5 Cold. (Tenn.) 531. § 415.
Jones v., 60 Ga. 52. § 150.
v. May, 12 Ala. 673. § 218.

Hawkins v. Miners' Adm'r, 36 Ark. 145. § 592.
v. New Orleans Print. & Pub. Co., 29 La. Ann. 134. § 118.
v. Rideuhour, 13 Mo. 125. § 249.
Roberts v., 70 Mich. 566. § 102.
Smith v., 6 Conn. 444. § 345.
v. Thornton, 1 Yerg. (Tenn.) 146. § 452.
Hawley v. Bradford, 9 Paige, 200. § 35.
Haycraft v. Creasy, 2 East, 92. § 73.
Wilde v., 2 Duvall (Ky.), 309. § 162.
Hayden v. Cabot, 17 Mass. 169. § 213.
v. Crane, 1 Lans. (N. Y.) 181. § 163.
v. Hill, 52 Vt. 259. § 119.
Melville v., 3 Barn. & Ald. 593. § 164.
v. Rice, 18 Vt. 353. § 261.
v. Thrasher, 18 Fla. 795. §§ 264, 275.
v. Welden, 43 N. J. Law, 128. § 49.
Haydenville Savings Bank v. Parsons, 138 Mass. 53. § 352.
Haydon v. Christopher, 1 J. J. Marsh. (Ky.) 382. § 66.
Hayes v. Cooper, 14 Bradw. (Ill. App.) 490. § 236.
v. Davis, 18 N. H. 600. § 268.
Elliott v., 8 Gray, 164. § 130.
v. Josephi, 26 Cal. 535. § 339.
v. Knox, 41 Mich. 529. § 446.
v. Little, 52 Ga. 555. § 444.
v. Nash, 129 Mass. 62. § 472.
Ranelaugh v., 1 Vernon, 189. § 97.
v. Seaver, 7 Greenl. (Me.) 237. § 580.
State v., 7 La. Ann. 118. § 536.
v. Ward, 4 Johns. Ch. 123. §§ 97, 237, 238.
v. Wells, 34 Md. 512. §§ 344, 360.
West v., 117 Ind. 290. § 219.
Haylen, State Nat. Bank v., 14 Neb. 480. § 50.
Hayman, Anderson v., 1 H. Black. 120. § 76.
Haynes, Cobb v., 8 B. Mon. (Ky.) 137. §§ 256, 635.
v. Covington, 9 Sm. & Mar. (Miss.) 470. § 342.
King v., 35 Ark. 463. §§ 241, 344.
Maxwell v., 41 Me. 559. § 66.
Oxford Bank v., 8 Pick. 423. §§ 183, 197.
Hays, Arbogast v., 98 Ind. 26. §§ 230, 307.
v. Closen, 20 Kan. 120. § 93.
v. Ford, 55 Ind. 52. § 276.
Ranelaugh v., 1 Vernon, 189. § 238.
Hayward, Hord v., 48 Hun (N. Y.), 330. § 439.
Fish v., 28 Hun (N. Y.), 456. § 37.
Hazard v. Griswold, 21 Fed. Rep. 178. §§ 12, 244.
Griswold v., 28 Fed. Rep. 597. § 244.
Mechanics' Bank v., 13 Johns. 353. § 311.
Hazard Powder Co., Martin v., 2 Col. 596. § 84.
Hazen v. Bearden, 4 Sneed (Tenn.), 48. § 77.
Hazlerigg, Newman v., 1 Bush (Ky.), 412. § 334.
Hazzard, Inhabitants of Hancock v., 12 Cush. (Mass.) 112. § 558.
Heacock, Birdsall v., 32 Ohio St. 177. § 165.
Head v. Green, 5 Biss. 311. § 96.
Smyley v., 2 Rich. Law (S. C.), 590. § 153.
Headington v. Neff, 7 Ohio, 229. § 618.
Headlee, Adm'r, v. Jones, 43 Mo. 235. § 364.
Healey v. Scofield, 60 Ga. 450. § 259.
Healy, Higgins v., 15 J. & S. (N. Y. Sup. Ct.) 207. § 42.
Heard v. Dubuque County Bank, 8 Neb. 10. § 50.
v. Lodge, 20 Pick. 53. § 638.
Hearn, Way v., 11 J. Scott (N. S.), 774. § 350.

Heart *v.* Bryan, 2 Dev. Eq. (N. C.) 147. § 298.
Elkins *v.*, Fitzg. 202. § 70.
Zent's Ex'rs *v.*, 8 Pa. St. 337. § 143.
Heath, Bein *v.*, 12 How. 168. § 476.
v. Derry Bank, 44 N. H. 174. §§ 41, 243.
Gano *v.*, 36 Mich. 441. § 380.
Horsey *v.*, 5 Ohio, 353. § 292.
v. Key, 1 Younge & Jer. 434. § 342.
v. Shrempp, 22 La. Ann. 167. § 570.
v. State, 14 Tex. App. 213. § 385.
Heath's Garnishees, Eddy *v.*, 31 Mo. 141. § 559.
Heaton *v.* Hurlburt, 3 Scam. (Ill.) 489. §§ 47, 50, 102.
Joseph *v.*, 5 Grant's Ch. 636. §§ 34, 316.
Hebenstreit, Frey *v.*, 1 Rob. (La.) 561. § 498.
Hebert *v.* Hebert, 22 La. Ann. 308. § 584.
Hecht *v.* Skaggs, 53 Ark. 291. § 586.
v. Weaver (Cir. Ct. D. Oreg.), 34 Fed. R. 111. § 133.
Hecker, Mitchell *v.*, 59 Cal. 558. § 587.
Hecox *v.* Citizens' Ins. Co. of St. Louis (Cir. Ct. N. D. Ill.), 2 Fed. Rep. 535. § 547.
Hedden, Pratt *v.*, 121 Mass. 116. § 17.
Hedgepeth, Adams *v.*, 5 Jones' Law (N. C.), 327. § 515.
Hedges *v.* Strong, 3 Oreg. 18. § 62.
Hedrick, Creigh *v.*, 5 W. Va. 140. § 30.
Heelis, Emmerson *v.*, 2 Taunt. 38. § 90.
Heeter *v.* Jewell, 6 Bush (Ky.), 510. § 570.
Heffernan, Mauri *v.*, 13 Johns. 58. § 205.
Heffield *v.* Meadows, 4 Com. Pleas, 595. §§ 156, 161.
Hefner, Aultman *v.*, 67 Tex. 54. § 236.
Heidenheimer *v.* Mayer, 10 Jones & Spen. (N. Y.) 506. § 127.
Heidenheimer Bros. *v.* Brent, 59 Tex. 533. § 571.
Heintz *v.* Cahn, 29 Ill. 308. § 176.
Heirs of Barr, Elam *v.*, 14 La. Ann. 682. § 24.
Heise *v.* Bumpass, 40 Ark. 545. § 181.
Heishow, Ordinary *v.*, 42 N. J. Law, 15. § 517.
Heitshu, Caldwell *v.*, 9 Watts & Serg. (Pa.) 151. §§ 16, 415.
Heitz *v.* Atlee, 67 Iowa, 483. § 341.
Held *v.* Bagwell, 58 Iowa, 139. §§ 518, 526.
Helgenberg, Irwin *v.*, 21 Ind. 106. § 614.
Hellams *v.* Abercrombie, 15 S. C. 110. § 224.
Hellen *v.* Crawford, 44 Pa. St. 105. § 240.
Heller, Duncan *v.*, 13 S. C. 94. § 191.
Hellman, McCullough *v.*, 8 Oreg. 191. § 391.
Helme, Williams *v.*, 1 Dev. Eq. (N. C.) 151. § 227.
Helmrick, German Savings Ass'n *v.*, 57 Mo. 100. § 353.
Helms *v.* The Wayne Agr'l Co., 73 Ind. 325. § 412.
Helms' Adm'r *v.* Young, 9 B. Mon. (Ky.) 394. § 325.
Helsey, Bivins *v.*, 4 Met. (Ky.) 78. § 402.
Helt *v.* Whittier, 31 Ohio St. 475. § 449.
Heming, Cherry *v.*, 4 Wels., Hurl. & Gor. 631. § 89.
Hemingway, Haddon *v.*, 39 Mich. 619. § 480.
Hemphill, Tremper *v.*, 8 Leigh (Va.), 623. § 417.
Hempstead *v.* Conway, 6 Ark. (1 Eng.) 317. § 243.
v. Watkins, 6 Ark. (1 Eng.) 317. § 239.
Henarie, Weiler *v.*, 15 Oreg. 28. § 92.
Henck, Gilbert *v.*, 30 Pa. St. 205. §§ 100, 102.
Henderson, Bryan *v.*, 88 Tenn. (4 Pickle), 23. § 36.

Henderson, Burnett *v.*, 21 Tex. 588. § 521.
v. Coover, 4 Nev. 129. § 555.
v. Dodgson, 9 Bradw. (Ill. App.) 80. § 342.
Dodgson *v.*, 113 Ill. 360. §§ 93, 342.
v. Duffee, 5 N. H. 38. § 288.
v. Johnson, 6 Ga. 390. § 82.
Kelly *v.*, 1 Pa. St. 495. § 498.
v. Marvin, 31 Barb. (N. Y.) 297. § 123.
v. Rice, 1 Cold. (Tenn.) 223. § 15.
Henderson's Adm'r *v.* Ardery's Adm'r, 36 Pa. St. 449. § 342.
v. Huey, 45 Ala. 275. § 428.
Hendrick *v.* Whittemore, 105 Mass. 23. § 60.
Hendricks, Polkinghorne *v.*, 61 Miss. 366. § 356.
v. Robinson, 56 Miss. 694. § 94.
Stanly *v.*, 13 Ired. (N. C.) 86. § 63.
v. Whittemore, 105 Mass. 23. § 264.
Hendrickson *v.* Hutchinson, 5 Dutch. (N. J.) 180. § 29.
Hendrie *v.* Berkowitz, 37 Cal. 113. § 643.
Hendry *v.* Clardy, 8 Fla. 77. § 574.
Henesmau, Smith *v.*, 30 Ohio St. 662. § 449.
Heney, Mowry *v.*, 86 Cal. 471. § 462.
Henley, Colgin *v.*, 6 Leigh (Va.), 85. §§ 17, 82, 105.
v. Stemmons, 4 B. Mon. (Ky.) 131. §§ 305, 316.
Henniker *v.* Wyman, 58 N. H. 528. § 596.
Henning, Preston *v.*, 6 Bush (Ky.), 556. § 352.
Henrie *v.* Buck, 39 Kan. 381. § 93.
Henry *v.* Compton, 2 Head (Tenn.), 549. § 237.
v. Daley, 17 Hun (N. Y.), 210. §§ 236, 416.
Frevert *v.*, 14 Nev, 191. § 208.
v. Quackenbush, 48 Mich. 415. § 466.
Henry *v.* Sneed, 99 Mo. 407. §§ 46, 234.
Ward *v.*, 5 Conn. 595. § 210.
Henry's Adm'r, Fluker *v.*, 27 Ala. 403. § 39.
Hentges, Wilson *v.*, 29 Minn. 102. § 67.
Henty, Clarke *v.*, 3 Younge & Coll. (Exch.) 187. § 364.
Heppe *v.* Johnson, 73 Cal. 265. §§ 546, 590, 617.
Heralson *v.* Mason, 53 Mo. 211. § 100.
Herford *v.* Chase, 1 Rob. (La.) 212. § 427.
Herman, Dickerson *v.*, 9 Daly (N. Y. Com. Pl.), 298. § 477.
v. Jeuchner, Law Rep. (15 Q. B. Div.) 561. § 219.
Owen *v.*, 13 Beav. 196. § 376.
Hernandez *v.* Stilwell, 7 Daly (N. Y. Com. Pl.), 360. § 197.
Herr, People *v.*, 81 Ill. 125. § 562.
Herr, Ex'rs of, Bowman *v.*, 1 Pen. & Watts (Pa.), 282. § 574.
Herrick *v.* Borst, 4 Hill (N. Y.), 650. § 239.
Gill *v.*, 111 Mass. 501. § 76.
Hogaboom *v.*, 4 Vt. 131. §§ 238, 239, 242, 245.
Kelly *v.*, 131 Mass. 373. § 577.
v. Orange Co. Bank, 27 Vt. 584. § 447.
Herring, Craig *v.*, 80 Ga. 709. § 487.
v. Hoppock, 15 N. Y. 409. § 490.
Herring & Turner, Craig *v.*, 80 Ga. 709. § 45.
Herrington, Packard *v.*, 41 Kan. 469. § 93.
Hersey, Knowlton *v.*, 76 Me. 345. § 165.
Hershey, Fidler *v.*, 90 Pa. St. 363. § 240.
Hershfield, Pinney *v.*, 1 Mont. 367. § 473.
Hershler *v.* Reynolds, 22 Iowa, 152. § 372.
Hertel, Glyn *v.*, 8 Taunt. 208. § 122.
Herter, La Farge *v.*, 3 Denio, 157. § 40.

Herter, La Farge v., 11 Barb. (N. Y.) 159. § 40.
Hess v. Fox, 10 Wend. 436. § 52.
Hess' Estate, 69 Pa. St. 272. § 309.
Hessell v. Johnson, 63 Mich. 623. §§ 402, 410, 411.
Hester, Singer Manuf. Co. v., 71 Mo. 91. § 199.
Singer Manuf. Co. v. (Cir. Ct. W. D. Mo., W. D.), 6 Fed. Rep. 804. § 602.
Hetfield v. Dow, 3 Dutch. (N. Y.) 440. §§ 76, 77.
Hetherington v. Bank at Mobile, 14 Ala. 68. § 438.
v. Hixon, 46 Ala. 297. § 13.
Hewett, Langan v., 3 Smedes & Marsh. 122. § 18.
Hewitt, Lilley v., 11 Price, 494. § 91.
State v., 72 Mo. 603. § 412.
Webb v., 3 Kay & Johns. 438. §§ 147, 376.
Hewitt's Adm'r v. Adams, 1 Patton, Jr. & Heath (Va.), 34. § 439.
Hewlett v. Nutt, 79 N. C. 263. § 531.
v. Schenck, Jr., 82 N. C. 234. § 588.
Heydock, Judge of Probate v., 8 N. H. 491. § 112.
Heydrick, Barnard v., 49 Barb. (N. Y.) 62. § 89.
Heynemann v. Eder, 17 Cal. 433. § 470.
Heywood, Collinge v., 9 Adol. & Ell. 633. § 230.
Hibbs, Kelsey v., 13 Ohio St. 340. § 69.
v. Rue, 4 Pa. St. 348. § 129.
Singer Manufacturing Co. v., 21 Mo. App. 574. § 394.
Hickman, Girvin v., 21 Hun (N. Y.), 316. § 574.
v. Hall, 5 Littell (Ky.), 338. § 244.
v. Hollingsworth, 17 Mo. 475. § 611.
v. McCurdy, 7 J. J. Mar. (Ky.) 555. § 286.
Hickok v. Farmers' & Mechanics' Bank, 35 Vt. 476. §§ 239, 242, 405.
Hicks, Arnold v., 3 Ired. Eq. (N. C.) 17. § 237.
v. Baily, 16 Tex. 229. § 212.
Sawyers v., 6 Watts (Pa.), 76. §§ 373, 550.
State v., 2 Blackf. (Ind.) 336. § 525.
Hidden v. Bishop, 5 R. I. 29. § 335.
Hiers, Baldwin v., 73 Ga. 739. §§ 56, 76, 77.
Higdon v. Bailey, 26 Ga. 426. §§ 29, 431.
v. Vaughn, 58 Miss. 572. §§ 467, 632.
Higgins, Aldricks v., 16 Serg. & Rawle, 212. § 163.
C. & A. R. R. Co. v., 58 Ill. 128. § 122.
Chandler v., 109 Ill. 602. §§ 36, 312.
Hanford v., 1 Bosw. (N. Y.) 441. § 76.
v. Healy, 15 J. & S. (N. Y. Sup. Ct.) 207. § 42.
v. Morrison's Ex'r, 4 Dana (Ky.), 100. § 271.
Ogier v., 2 McCord, Law (S. C.), 8. § 507.
Peirce v., 101 Ind. 178. § 329.
v. State, 87 Ind. 282. §§ 577, 589.
Higginson, Cremer v., 1 Mason, 323. §§ 118, 163, 192.
High v. Cox, 55 Ga. 662. § 245.
Highland v. Dresser, 35 Minn. 345. § 87.
Highland Bank, Lee v., 2 Sandf. Ch. 311. § 415.
Hight, Wiley v., 39 Mo. 130. § 357.
Hightower, Goodwyn v., 30 Ga. 249. § 342.
v. Moore, 46 Ala. 387. § 133.
Wylie v., 74 Tex. 306. § 378.
Hightshue, Shimer v., 7 Blackf. (Ind.) 238. § 449.
Hignutt, Garey v., 32 Md. 552. § 97.
Hikes v. Crawford, 4 Bush (Ky.), 19. § 216.
Hilary v. Rose, 9 Phila. (Pa.) 139. § 100.

Hiler, Apgar's Adm'r *v.*, 4 Zab. (N. J.) 812. §§ 60, 208, 217, 229.
Hilgert, Commonwealth *v.*, 55 Pa. St. 236. § 583.
Hill, Alcock *v.*, 4 Leigh (Va.), 622. § 344.
Blackstone Bank *v.*, 10 Pick. 129. § 352.
v. Bostick, 10 Yerg. (Tenn.) 410. § 366.
v. Bull, 1 Gilm. (Va.) 149. § 342.
v. Calvert, 1 Rich. Eq. (S. C.) 56. § 385.
Carson *v.*, McMullan, Law (S. C.), 76. § 410.
Conover *v.*, 76 Ill. 342. § 284.
Cox & Spurgin *v.*, 5 Lea (Tenn.), 146. § 524.
Findley *v.*, 8 Oreg. 247. §§ 242, 344.
v. Finnigan, 54 Cal. 311. § 461.
Hayden *v.*, 52 Vt. 259. § 119.
Hagey *v.*, 75 Pa. St. 108. § 376.
Jacobs *v.*, 2 Leigh (Va.), 393. §§ 173, 631.
v. Johnston, 3 Ired. Eq. (N. C.) 432. § 89.
v. Kelly, Ridgeway, Lapp & Schoales (Irish), 265. § 303.
v. Kemble, 9 Cal. 71. §§ 565, 570.
Lee *v.*, 83 Ky. 49. § 214.
Leech *v.*, 4 Watts (Pa.), 448. §§ 176, 182, 202.
Loehner *v.*, 17 Mo. App. 32. §§ 475, 480.
v. Manser, 11 Gratt. (Va.) 522. § 310.
v. Morse, 61 Me. 541. § 277.
Munro *v.*, 25 S. C. 476. § 201.
v. Raymond, 3 Allen, 540. § 76.
Second National Bank Lafayette *v.*, 76 Ind. 223. § 432.
v. Sewell, 27 Ark. 15. §§ 444, 568.
v. Sherman, 15 Iowa, 365. § 605.
Stadt *v.*, 9 East, 348. § 84.
v. Sweetser, 5 N. H. 168. § 402.
State *v.*, 17 W. Va. 452. § 554.
v. Witmer, 2 Phila. (Pa.) 72. § 34.
Worcester Savings Bank *v.*, 113 Mass. 25. §§ 16, 418.
Hill *v.* Wright, 23 Ark. 530. § 210.
Hill & Co. *v.* Bourcier, 29 La. Ann. 841. §§ 237, 440, 447.
Hillegas *v.* Stephenson, 75 Mo. 118. § 260.
Hiller *v.* Howell, 74 Ga. 174. § 340.
Hillhouse, Breed *v.*, 7 Conn. 523. §§ 16, 193.
Hilliard, Treasurers *v.*, 8 Rich. Law (S. C.), 412. §§ 535, 567.
Hillyer, Taylor *v.*, 3 Blackf. (Ind.) 433. § 68.
Hilton *v.* Dinsmore, 21 Me. 410. § 63.
People *v.*, 36 Fed. Rep. 172 (Cir. Ct. E. D. Mich.). §§ 529, 565.
Hiltz *v.* Scully, 1 Cinc. 554. § 77.
Himes, Noble *v.*, 12 Neb. 193. §§ 566, 571.
Mortland *v.*, 8 Pa. St. 265. § 154.
Himrod *v.* Baugh, 85 Ill. 435. § 236.
Hinchman, Downey *v.*, 25 Ind. 453. § 58.
Hinckley *v.* Kreitz, 58 N. Y. 583. § 452.
Hinde *v.* Whitehouse, 7 East, 558. § 90.
Hindman *v.* Langford, 3 Strobh. (S. C.) 207. § 65.
Hinds *v.* Ingham, 31 Ill. 400. § 142.
Hine, Stoudt *v.*, 45 Pa. St. 30. §§ 63, 64.
Hinely *v.* Margaritz, 3 Pa. St. 428. § 4.
Hines, White Sewing Machine Co. *v.*, 61 Mich. 423. § 118.
Hinkle, McMullen *v.*, 39 Miss. 142. § 428.
Stewart *v.*, 1 Bond, 506. §§ 17, 62.
Hinkley, McCollum *v.*, 9 Vt. 143. § 239.
Thomas *v.*, 19 Neb. 324. §§ 23, 517.
Hinsdale-Doyle Granite Co., State *v.*, 117 Ind. 476. § 601.
Hinsdill *v.* Murray, 6 Vt. 136. § 268.
Hinson, Grisard *v.*, 50 Ark. 229. § 446.

Hinton, Briggs *v.*, 14 Lea (Tenn.), 233. §§ 267, 463, 571, 572.
Cutler *v.*, 6 Rand. (Va.) 509. § 78.
Hirsch, Ferguson *v.*, 54 Ind. 337. § 570.
Hirst, Pease *v.*, 10 Barn. & Cress. 122. §§ 121, 143.
Hise, Kater *v.*, 79 Ind. 301. § 352.
Hitchcock, Delaplaine *v.*, 4 Edwards' Ch. 321. § 40.
v. Humfrey, 5 Man. & Gr. 559. §§ 161, 201.
v. Lukens, 8 Port. (Ala.) 333. § 63.
Pritchard *v.*, 6 Man. & Gr. 151. § 334.
Hitson, Fore *v.*, 70 Tex. 517. § 18.
Hitt, Humphrey *v.*, 6 Gratt. (Va.) 509. § 438.
Hixon, Hetherington *v.*, 46 Ala. 297. § 13.
Lafayette Co. *v.*, 69 Mo. 581. § 428.
Hoad *v.* Grace, 7 Hurl. & Nor. 494. §§ 84, 161.
Hoag, Viele *v.*, 24 Vt. 46. §§ 243, 244.
Hobart, Sampson *v.*, 28 Vt. 697. §§ 64, 69.
Hobbs, Craig *v.*, 44 Ind. 363. § 407.
Hatch *v.*, 12 Gray, 447. § 161.
Herbert *v.*, 3 Stew. (Ala.) 9. §§ 239, 243.
v. Middleton, 1 J. J. Marsh. (Ky.) 176. §§ 578, 580, 638.
v. Rue, 4 Pa. St. 348. § 378.
Hoblitzell, Lewis *v.*, 6 Gill & Johns. (Md.) 259. § 100.
Hoboken *v.* Harrison, 1 Vroom (N. J.), 73. §§ 22, 44.
Hobson *v.* Bass, Law Rep. 6 Ch. App. Cas. 792. § 253.
v. Hobson's Ex'r, 8 Bush (Ky.), 665. § 617.
Johnson *v.*, 1 Litt. (Ky.) 314. § 125.
Jones *v.*, 2 Rand. (Va.) 483. § 583.
Hoch, Weiler *v.*, 25 Pa. St. 525. § 239.
Hocker *v.* Wood's Ex'r, 33 Pa. St. 466. § 148.
Hodenpuyl, Porter *v.*, 9 Mich. 11. § 347.
Hodge, Robinson *v.*, 117 Mass. 222. § 580.
Turley *v.*, 3 Humph. (Tenn.) 73. §§ 49, 183.
Hodges *v.* Armstrong, 3 Dev. Law (N. C.), 253. § 225.
v. Gewin, 6 Ala. 478. § 368.
v. Hall, 29 Vt. 209. § 60.
Stokes *v.*, 11 Rich. Eq. (S. C.) 135. § 38.
Whitfield *v.*, 1 Mees. & Wels. 679. § 493.
Hodgins, Currie *v.*, 42 Up. Can. (Q. B.) 601. § 376.
Hodgkin *v.* Holland, 34 Ark. 203. §§ 10, 27.
Hodgson *v.* Anderson, 5 Dow. & Ry. 735. §§ 66, 67.
v. Hodgson, 2 Keen, 704. §§ 35, 439.
v. Shaw, 3 Mylne & Keen, 183. §§ 313, 321.
Hodshire, Wasson *v.*, 108 Ind. 26. § 426.
Hodson, Morse *v.*, 5 Mass. 314. § 22.
Smith *v.*, 50 Wis. 279. § 276.
Hoe, Steele *v.*, 14 Adol. & Ell. (N. S.) 431. § 86.
Hoe's Case, 5 Coke, 70 *b*. § 516.
Hoesback, McGovern *v.*, 53 Pa. St. 176. § 128.
Hoey *v.* Jarman, 39 N. J. Law (10 Vroom), 523. §§ 92, 97.
Hoffman *v.* Bechtel, 52 Pa. St. 190. § 101.
v. Butler, 105 Ind. 371. § 302.
Cocke *v.*, 5 B. J. Lea (Tenn.), 105. § 265.
Gradle *v.*, 105 Ill. 147. § 572.
McFillen *v.*, 35 N. J. Eq. 364. § 35.
v. Moore, 82 N. C. 313. § 181.
v. Schwaebe, 33 Barb. (N. Y.) 194. § 251.
v. Smith, 34 Hun (N. Y.), 485. § 486.
v. Steinan, 34 Hun (N. Y.), 239. § 250.

Hoffman & Co., Serra 'E Hijo *v.*, 30 La. Ann. 67. § 150.
Hofheimer *v.* Losen, 24 Mo. App. 652. § 199.
Tischler *v.*, 83 Va. 35. § 161.
Hogaboom *v.* Herrick, 4 Vt. 131. §§ 238, 239, 242, 245.
Hoge, Isett *v.*, 2 Watts (Pa.), 128. § 100.
Hoggatt *v.* Thomas, 35 La. Ann. 298. § 60.
Hogshead *v.* Williams, 55 Ind. 145. §§ 242, 434.
Hohenthal, Turnure *v.*, 4 Jones & Spencer (N. Y.), 79. § 201.
Holandsworth *v.* Commonwealth, 11 Bush, 617. § 8.
Holbrook, Howard *v.*, 9 Bosw. (N. Y.) 237. § 84.
Holbrow *v.* Wilkins, 1 Barn. & Cress. 10. § 201.
Holcomb, Reed *v.*, 31 Conn. 360. § 67.
Holden *v.* Tanners, 6 La. Ann. 74. § 26.
Ruggles *v.*, 3 Wend. 216. § 239.
Holl *v.* Hadley, 4 Neville & Man. 515. § 403.
Holland *v.* Bouldin, 4 T. B. Mon. (Ky.) 147. § 507.
Gray *v.*, 9 Oreg. 512. § 35.
Hodgkin *v.*, 34 Ark. 203. §§ 10, 27.
v. Hoyt, 14 Mich. 238. § 90.
v. Johnson, 51 Ind. 346. § 426.
Scroggin *v.*, 16 Mo. 419. § 413.
v. Teed, 7 Hare, 50. § 118.
Holliday *v.* Poole, 77 Ga. 159. § 416.
Tatum *v.*, 59 Mo. 422. § 571.
Hollier, Eyre *v.*, Lloyd & Gould (Temp. Plunket), 250. §§ 38, 388.
Holliman *v.* Carroll, 27 Tex. 23. § 566.
v. Rogers, 6 Tex. 1. § 208.
Hollingsworth *v.* Floyd, 2 Har. & Gill (Md.), 87. § 306.
Hickman *v.*, 17 Mo. 475. § 611.
Hughes *v.*, 1 Murphy (N. C.), 146. § 515.
Hollingsworth *v.* Tanner, 44 Ga. 11. § 430.
Hollinsbee *v.* Ritchey, 49 Ind. 261. § 225.
Hollister *v.* Davis, 54 Pa. St. 508. §§ 236, 331.
Holloman *v.* Langdon, 7 Jones' Law (N. C.), 49. § 539.
Holloway, Phœnix Mut. Life Ins. Co. *v.*, 51 Conn. 310. § 419.
Holly, Cornwell *v.*, 5 Rich. Law (S. C.), 47. § 357.
Wallace *v.*, 13 Ga. 389. § 572.
Holme *v.* Brunskill, Law Rep. (3 Q. B. Div.) 495. §§ 108, 389.
Holmes, Commonwealth *v.*, 25 Gratt. (Va.) 771. §§ 371, 548.
v. Day, 108 Mass. 563. § 278.
Dillon *v.*, 5 Neb. 484. § 242.
Hawkins *v.*, 1 P. Wms. 770. § 89.
Kinchelse *v.*, 7 B. Mon. (Ky.) 5. §§ 186, 187.
v. Knights, 10 N. H. 175. § 60.
v. Mackrell, 3 Com. B. (N. S.) 789. § 89.
v. Mitchell, 7 J. Scott (N. S.), 361. § 81.
Sidney Road Co. *v.*, 16 Up. Can. (Q. B.) 268. § 411.
v. State, 17 Neb. 73. §§ 27, 517.
v. Steamer Belle Air, 5 La. Ann. 523. § 464.
Ten Eyck *v.*, 3 Sandf. Ch. 428. § 325.
v. Weed, 24 Barb. (N. Y.) 546. § 217.
Holt *v.* Bodey, 18 Pa. St. 207. § 434.
Dawson *v.*, 12 Lea (Tenn.), 27. § 452.
v. McLean, 75 N. C. 347. § 170.
Moore *v.*, 10 Gratt. (Va.) 284. § 105.
Rockville National Bank *v.*, 58 Conn. 526. §§ 347, 376.
Holway, Home Insurance Co. *v.*, 55 Iowa, 571. §§ 420, 422.
Holyoke *v.* Adams, 1 Hun (N. Y.), 223. § 472.
Holzer, Pierce *v.*, 65 Mich. 263. § 318.

Homan, Owen *v.*, 3 Macn. & Gor. 378. § 233.
Home Insurance Co. *v.* Holway, 55 Iowa, 571. §§ 420, 422.
Home National Bank *v.* Waterman, 30 Ill. App. 535. §§ 34, 135.
Home Savings Bank *v.* Traube, 75 Mo. App. 199. §§ 174, 394, 421.
Homer, Lee *v.*, 37 Hun (N. Y.), 634. § 473.
v. Savings Bank, 7 Conn. 478. § 326.
Hommell *v.* Gamewell, 5 Blackf. (Ind.) 5. § 211.
Hood *v.* Hayward, 48 Hun (N. Y.), 330. § 439.
v. Hood, 85 N. Y. 561. §§ 578, 583.
v. Jones, 5 Del. Ch. 77. § 35.
Preston *v.*, 64 Cal. 405. § 468.
State *v.*, 7 Blackf. (Ind.) 127. § 541.
Hook, Payne *v.*, 7 Wall. 425. § 587.
v. Richeson, 115 Ill. 431. §§ 299, 320.
Hooker *v.* Gamble, 9 Up. Can. (C. P.) 434. § 364.
v. Gamble, 12 Up. Can. (C. P.) 512. § 364.
v. Gooding, 86 Ill. 60. § 102.
Hooks *v.* Branch Bank at Mobile, 8 Ala. 580. § 448.
Hooper, Chaffee *v.*, 54 Vt. 513. § 572.
Davis *v.*, 33 Miss. 173. § 143.
v. Hooper's Ex'r, 29 W. Va. 276. §§ 573, 583.
Hoops, Eneas *v.*, 10 Jones & Spen. (N. Y. Sup. Ct.) 517. §§ 199, 378.
Hoover *v.* Morris, 3 Ohio, 56. § 68.
People *v.*, 92 Ill. 575. § 591.
Hope, Brooks *v.*, 139 Mass. 351. § 582.
v. Cust, 1 East, 53. § 18.
Hopewell *v.* Bank of Cumberland, 10 Leigh (Va.), 206. § 328.
Hopkins, Conkey *v.*, 17 Johns. 113. § 60.
v. Farwell, 32 N. H. 425. § 333.
Gardiner *v.*, 5 Wend. 23. § 65.
Hopkins *v.* Orr, 124 U. S. 510. § 464.
v. Spurlock, 2 Heisk. (Tenn.) 152. § 239.
Hopkirk *v.* McConico, 1 Brock. 220. §§ 360, 362.
Hoppock, Grover *v.*, 2 Dutcher (N. J.), 191. §§ 248, 355.
Herring *v.*, 15 N. Y. 409. § 490.
Hopps, Chamberlain *v.*, 8 Vt. 94. § 25.
Hopson, City Savings Bank *v.*, 53 Conn. 453. § 193.
Hord, Greathouse *v.*, 1 Dana (Ky.), 105. § 252.
Horn *v.* Bray, 51 Ind. 555. § 60.
Mayor of Wilmington *v.*, 2 Har. (Del.) 190. § 167.
v. Perry, 14 Hun (N. Y.), 409. § 624.
Perry *v.*, 22 W. Va. 381. § 112.
State *v.*, 70 Mo. 466. § 500.
State *v.*, 94 Mo. 162. § 571.
Horne, Christy's Adm'r *v.*, 24 Mo. 242. § 605.
Horner, Burt *v.*, 5 Barb. (N. Y.) 501. §§ 98, 101.
v. Lyman, 4 Keyes (N. Y.), 237. § 453.
Lyon *v.*, 32 W. Va. 432. § 571.
Neff *v.*, 63 Pa. St. 327. § 379.
Hornsberger *v.* Yancy, 33 Gratt. (Va.) 527. § 268.
Horsey, Farmers' Bank *v.*, 1 Harr. (Del.) 514. § 371.
v. Graham, Law Rep. 5 Com. P. 9. § 81.
v. Heath, 5 Ohio, 353. § 292.
Littler *v.*, 2 Ohio, 209. § 616.
Horton *v.* Bond, 28 Gratt. (Va.) 815. § 237.
v. Manning, 37 Tex. 475. § 176.
Hortop, Taylor *v.*, 22 Up. Can. (C. P.) 542. § 389.
Hortsell *v.* State, 45 Ark. 59. § 510.
Hosea *v.* Rowley, 57 Mo. 357. § 352.
Hosefield *v.* Cost, Addison (Pa.), 152. § 226.
Hoshaw, State *v.*, 86 Mo. 193. § 632.
Hoskins, Bowen *v.*, 45 Miss. 183. § 275.

Hossack, Underwood *v.*, 38 Ill. 208. §§ 15, 16, 176.
Hostetter *v.* City of Pittsburgh, 107 Pa. St. 419. § 632.
Hotchkiss *v.* Barnes, 34 Conn. 27. §§ 156, 157.
Grant *v.*, 26 Barb. (N. Y.) 63. §§ 84, 97.
v. Lyon, 2 Blackf. (Ind.) 222. § 624.
Mosher *v.*, 2 Keyes (N. Y.), 589. § 98.
Mosher *v.*, 3 Abb. Rep. Omitted Cas. (N. Y.) 326. § 84.
Perrine *v.*, 58 Barb. (N. Y.) 77. § 213.
Houck *v.* Graham, 123 Ind. 277. § 175.
v. Graham, 106 Ind. 195. §§ 260, 267, 645.
Hough *v.* Ætna Life Ins. Co., 57 Ill. 318. §§ 97, 298.
Roe *v.*, 3 Salk. 14. § 66.
United States *v.*, 103 U. S. 71. § 595.
Houghton, Detroit *v.*, 42 Mich. 459. § 590.
v. Matthews, 3 Bos. & Pul. 485. § 71.
Spencer *v.*, 68 Cal. 81. § 540.
Strader *v.*, 9 Port. (Ala.) 334. 239.
Houlditch *v.* Milne, 3 Esp. 86. §§ 64, 65, 68.
House *v.* Fort, 4 Blackf. (Ind.) 293. § 564.
Commonwealth *v.*, 13 Bush (Ky.), 680. § 499.
v. Trustees of Schools, 83 Ill. 368. § 448.
Houser, Twitty *v.*, 7 Rich. (S. C.) 153. § 585.
Twitty *v.*, 17 S. C. 1. § 558.
Houston, Borden *v.*, 2 Tex. 594. §§ 42, 550.
v. Branch Bank, 25 Ala. 250. § 316.
v. Dougherty, 4 Humph. (Tenn.) 505. § 616.
Houston *v.* Hurley, 2 Del. Ch. 247. § 434.
Spiers *v.*, 4 Bligh (N. R.), 515. § 118.
How *v.* Kemball, 2 McLean, 103. § 49.
Stillwell *v.*, 46 Mo. 589. § 260.
Howard, Carr *v.*, 8 Blackf. (Ind.) 190. §§ 242, 374.
Case *v.*, 41 Iowa, 479. §§ 194, 365.
Church *v.*, 17 Hun (N. Y.), 5. § 381.
Church *v.*, 79 N. Y. 415. § 619.
v. Clark, 36 Iowa, 114. § 358.
v. Coshow, 33 Mo. 118. § 72.
Crawford *v.*, 9 Ga. 314. § 570.
v. Fletcher, 59 N. H. 151. § 144.
Greer *v.*, 41 Ohio St. 591. § 484.
v. Holbrook, 9 Bosw. (N. Y.) 237. § 84.
Railroad Company *v.*, 7 Wall. 392. § 5.
Staley *v.*, 7 Mo. App. 377. § 460.
Howard Banking Company *v.* Welchman, 6 Bosw. (N. Y.) 280. § 148.
Howarth, Samuell *v.*, 3 Meriv. 272. §§ 243, 343.
State *v.*, 48 Conn. 207. §§ 587, 628.
Howe, Conner *v.*, 35 Minn. 518. § 329.
Haman *v.*, 27 Gratt. (Va.) 676. §§ 403, 480.
v. Mason, 12 Iowa, 202. § 562.
v. Nickels, 22 Me. 175. §§ 186, 192, 203.
Wild *v.*, 74 Mo. 551. § 357.
Howe Machine Co. *v.* Farrington, 82 N. Y. 121. §§ 245, 421, 422, 446.
Howe Sewing Machine Co. *v.* Layman, 88 Ill. 39. § 394.
Howell, Camp *v.*, 37 Ga. 312. § 356.
v. Cobb, 2 Cold. (Tenn.) 104. § 223.
Glass *v.*, 2 Lea (Tenn.), 50. § 585.
Hiller *v.*, 74 Ga. 174. § 340.

Howell *v.* Jones, 1 Cromp., Mees. & Ross. 97. § 364.
Lane *v.*, 1 Lea (Tenn.), 275. § 371.
v. Lawreuceville Mfg. Co., 31 Ga. 663. § 375.
v. Reams, 73 N. C. 391. § 309.
v. Sevier, 1 B. J. Lea, 360. § 356.
Shurts *v.*, 30 N. J. Eq. 418. § 376.
United States *v.*, 4 Wash. 620. § 360.
Williamston *v.*, 4 Ala. 693. § 638.
Howes *v.* Martin, 1 Esp. 162. §§ 60, 68.
Howie, Royston *v.*, 15 Ala. 309. § 438.
Howk, Braman *v.*, 1 Blackf. 392. § 356.
Kirkpatrick *v.*, 80 Ill. 122. §§ 426, 626.
Howland, Douglass *v.*, 24 Wend. 35. §§ 82, 84, 200, 630.
Moore *v.*, 4 Denio, 264. § 96.
Howlett, Staats *v.*, 4 Denio, 559. § 84.
Howley, State *v.*, 73 Me. 552. § 508.
Howry, Miller *v.*, 3 Pen. & Watts (Pa.), 374. § 247.
Howth, Flores *v.*, 5 Tex., 329. § 169.
Hoxsey, Hall *v.*, 84 Ill. 616. §§ 302, 428.
Hoy *v.* Bramhall, 4 C. E. Green (N. J.), 563. § 34.
Stevenson *v.*, 43 Pa. St. 191. § 20.
Hoyt, Holland *v.*, 14 Mich. 238. § 90.
v. Mead, 13 Hun (N. Y.), 327. § 31.
v. Tuthill, 33 Hun (N. Y.), 196. § 439.
Hozier, Peck *v.*, 14 Johns. 346. § 500.
Hubbard, Babcock *v.*, 2 Conn. 536. § 208.
Blaine *v.*, 4 Pa. St. 183. § 373.
Curtis *v.*, 6 Met. (Mass.) 186. § 387.
Denick *v.*, 27 Hun (N. Y.), 347. §§ 240, 357.
v. Elden, 43 Ohio St. 380. § 571.
v. Gurney, 64 N. Y. 457. §§ 29, 363.
v. Hart, 71 Iowa, 668. § 363.
v. Ogden, 22 Kan. 363. §§ 35, 352.
Hubbard *v.* Pace, 34 Ark. 80. § 440.
Hubbell *v.* Carpenter, 5 N. Y. 171. § 147.
McCormick *v.*, 4 Mont. 87. §§ 419, 460.
Thomas *v.*, 15 N. Y. 405. § 630.
Turner *v.*, 2 Day (Conn.), 457. § 54.
Hubble, Murphy *v.*, 2 Duvall (Ky.), 247. § 402.
Huber *v.* Steiner, 2 Scott, 304. § 52.
Hubert, Allen *v.*, 49 Pa. St. 259. § 1.
v. Moreau, 12 Moore, 216. § 89.
v. Turner, 4 Scott (N. R.), 486. § 89.
v. Wendheim, 64 Cal. 213. § 572.
Huddleston *v.* Briscoe, 11 Vesey, 583. §§ 80, 89.
Hudelson *v.* Armstrong, 70 Ind. 99. § 140.
Hudson, Archer *v.*, 7 Beav. 551. § 397.
v. Bishop (Cir. Ct. N. D. Iowa, E. D.), 32 Fed. Rep. 519. §§ 551, 588.
Crook *v.*, 4 Lea (Tenn.), 448. § 577.
Hart *v.*, 6 Duer (N. Y.), 294. § 363.
v. Inhabitants of Winslow, 6 Vroom (N. J.), 437. § 46.
v. Modawell, 64 Ala. 481. § 586.
Penniman *v.*, 14 Barb. (N. Y.) 579. § 101.
Wallace *v.*, 37 Tex. 456. § 35.
Hudspeth, Sprathin *v.*, Dudley (Ga.), 155. § 110.
Huey, Henderson, Adm'r, *v.*, 45 Ala. 275. § 428.
v. Pinney, 5 Minn. 310. §§ 238, 242, 405.
Huff, Bucklen *v.*, 53 Ind. 474. § 344.
v. Cole, 45 Ind. 300. §§ 355, 379.
Eidson *v.*, 29 Gratt (Va.), 338. § 329.
v. Slife, 25 Neb. 448. §§ 102, 242.
Huffman *v.* Hulbert, 13 Wend. 377. §§ 239, 342.
v. Koppelkom, 8 Neb. 344. §§ 23, 566.
Koppelkom *v.*, 12 Neb. 95. § 23.

Hugely, Sullivan *v.*, 48 Ga. 486. § 342.
Huggett, McGurk *v.*, 56 Mich. 187. § 260.
Huggins, Cuthbert *v.*, 21 Ala. 349. § 537.
Davis *v.*, 3 N. H. 231. § 242.
v. People, 39 Ill. 241. §§ 499, 504.
Hughart *v.* Spratt, 78 Ky. 313. § 577.
Hughes, City Council of Montgomery *v.*, 65 Ala. 201, 204. §§ 93, 539.
Commonwealth *v.*, 13 Bush (Ky.), 349. § 493.
Gates *v.*, 44 Wis. 332. § 36.
v. Gordon, 7 Mo. 297. § 607.
Grady *v.*, 80 Mich. 184. § 578.
Hairston *v.*, 3 Munf. (Va.) 568. § 578.
v. Hollingsworth, 1 Murphy (N. C.), 146. § 515.
Knight *v.*, Moody & Mal. 247. § 283.
v. Lawson, 31 Ark. 613. § 63.
v. Littlefield, 18 Me. 400. § 127.
Looney *v.*, 26 N. Y. 514. § 555.
Rothermal *v.*, 134 Pa. St. 510. § 406.
v. State, 28 Tex. App. 499. § 495.
Hulbert, Heaton *v.*, 3 Scam. 489. § 102.
Huffman *v.*, 13 Wend. 377. § 239.
Hulce, Ives *v.*, 17 Bradw. (Ill. App.) 35. § 449.
Hulett, Paris *v.*, 26 Vt. 308. § 324.
v. Soullard, 26 Vt. 295. §§ 208, 217.
Hull, Dare *v.*, 70 Ind. 545. § 355.
Ellis *v.*, 23 Cal. 160. § 464.
v. Jones, 10 Lea (Tenn.), 100. § 577.
State *v.*, 53 Miss. 626, 645. §§ 540, 541, 580.
Hulme *v.* Coles, 2 Simons, 12. § 368.
Hults, Gay *v.*, 56 Mich. 153. §§ 113, 175.
Humbird, State *v.*, 54 Md. 327. § 517.
Humble, Hawkins *v.*, 5 Cold. (Tenn.) 531. § 415.
Humblen *v.* Knight, 60 Tex. 36. § 400.
Humboldt Savings & Loan Society *v.* Wennerhold, 81 Cal. 528. §§ 174, 425, 561.
Hume *v.* Mazelin, 84 Ind. 574. §§ 353, 355.
Humphrey, Farmers' and Mechanics' Bank *v.*, 36 Vt. 554. § 115.
Hitchcock *v.*, 5 Man. & Gr. 559. §§ 161, 201.
v. Hitt, 6 Gratt. (Va.) 509. § 438.
v. Humphrey, 79 N. C. 396. § 577.
Humphreys *v.* Crane, 5 Cal. 173. § 342.
Davies *v.*, 6 Mees. & Wels. 153. §§ 208, 230, 287, 295.
Pratt *v.*, 22 Conn. 317. § 72.
Leggett *v.*, 21 How. 66. § 112.
Noyes *v.*, 11 Gratt. (Va.) 636. §§ 69, 75, 78.
v. St. Louis, I. M. & S. R'y Co. (Cir. Ct. S. D. N. Y.), 37 Fed. Rep. 307. § 104.
State *v.*, 7 Ohio, 224. § 574.
Hungerford *v.* O'Brien, 37 Minn. 306. § 102.
Seabury *v.*, 2 Hill, 80. § 179.
Hunt *v.* Bate, 3 Dyer, 272 (*a*). § 17.
v. Bridgham, 2 Pick. 581. §§ 143, 352.
v. Brown, 5 Hill, 145. § 88.
Bryan *v.*, 4 Sneed, 543. § 81.
v. Burton, 18 Ark. 188. § 480.
v. Chambliss, 7 Smedes & Mar. (Miss.) 532. §§ 258, 261.
Daniel *v.*, 77 Ala. 567. § 324.
v. Knox, 34 Miss. 655. §§ 355, 376.
v. McConnell, 1 T. B. Mon. (Ky.) 219. § 125.
National Eagle Bank *v.*, 16 R. I. 148. § 133.
v. Postlewait, 28 Iowa, 427. § 356.
v. Purdy, 82 N. Y. 486. § 241.
v. Roberts, 45 N. Y. 691. § 134.
Savings Bank *v.*, 72 Mo. 597. § 168.
v. Smith, 17 Wend. 179. § 343.
v. State, 53 Ind. 321. § 408.

Hunt *v.* State, 124 Ind. 306. § 534.
v. United States, 1 Gallison, 32. §§ 433, 555.
v. White, 1 Ind. (Carter), 105. § 574.
Hunt's Ex'r, Taylor *v.*, 34 Mo. 205. § 580.
Huntbach, Harris *v.*, 1 Burrows, 373. § 58.
Hunter *v.* Clark, 28 Tex. 159. § 438.
Crears *v.*, Law Rep. (19 Q. B. Div.) 341. § 16.
v. Dickinson, 10 Humph. (Tenn.) 37. § 199.
Ferrell *v.*, 21 Mo. 436. § 407.
v. Richardson, 1 Duvall (Ky.), 247. § 315.
Truesdell *v.*, 28 Ill. App. 292. § 355.
v. United States, 5 Pet. 173. § 433.
Hunter's Adm'r *v.* Jett, 4 Rand. (Va.) 104. §§ 342, 345.
Huntington *v.* Harvey, 4 Conn. 124. § 75.
Morse *v.*, 40 Vt. 488. §§ 367, 376.
Preston *v.*, 67 Mich. 139. § 390.
v. Wellington, 12 Mich. 10. §§ 67, 73.
Huntington Bank, Burns *v.*, 1 Pen. & Watts (Pa.), 395. § 310.
Huntress *v.* Patten, 20 Me. 28. §§ 100, 235.
Inhabitants of South Berwick *v.*, 53 Me. 89. § 410.
Hurd *v.* Hannibal & St. Joseph R. R. Co., 33 Hun, 109. § 9.
v. Marple, 2 Bradw. (Ill. App.) 402. §§ 342, 343.
Shelton *v.*, 7 R. I. 403. §§ 40, 243.
v. Spencer, 40 Vt. 581. § 426.
Hurlbert, Hoffman *v.*, 13 Wend. 375. § 342.
Hurlburt, Heaton *v.*, 3 Scam. (Ill.) 489. §§ 47, 50.
Newell *v.*, 2 Vt. 351. § 222.
Stevens *v.*, 25 Ill. App. 124. § 226.
Hurlburt, Thayer *v.*, 5 Iowa (Clarke), 521. § 491.
Hurley *v.* Brown, 98 Mass. 545. § 81.
Houston *v.*, 2 Del. Ch. 247. § 434.
v. Stapleton's Adm'r, 24 Mo. 248. § 215.
Hurltin, Smith *v.*, 124 Ind. 434. § 329.
Hurlun *v.* Ely, 55 Cal. 340. § 129.
Hurst, McIntosh *v.*, 6 Mont. 287. § 152.
Hurt, Watson *v.*, 6 Gratt. (Va.) 633. § 176.
Husby, Libby *v.*, 28 Minn. 40. § 615.
Huson, People *v.*, 78 Cal. 154. §§ 43, 518, 627.
Hussey, Byers *v.*, 4 Col. 515. § 342.
Hustis, Schofield *v.*, 9 Hun (N. Y.), 157. § 581.
Huston's Appeal, 69 Pa. St. 483. § 323.
Hutchcraft *v.* Shrout, 1 T. B. Mon. (Ky.) 206. §§ 540, 574.
Hutchings *v.* State, 24 Tex. App. 242. § 509.
Hutchins, Gamage *v.*, 23 Me. 565. §§ 142, 197.
v. McCauley, 2 Dev. & Bat. Eq. (N. C.) 399. § 286.
Hutchinson *v.* Grout, 40 Hun (N. Y.), 207. § 449.
Hendrickson *v.*, 5 Dutcher (N. J.), 180. § 29.
Mayo *v.*, 57 Me. 546. § 7.
McLaren *v.*, 22 Cal. 187. §§ 63, 66.
Springer *v.*, 19 Me. 359. § 49.
v. Woodwell, 107 Pa. St. 509. §§ 93, 429, 645.
v. Wright, 61 N. H. 108. § 345.
Hutchons, Hall *v.*, 3 Mylne & Keen, 426. § 147.
Hutson *v.* Field, 6 Wis. 407. § 87.
Hutte, Wilbur & Son *v.*, 25 S. C. 246. § 578.
Hutton *v.* Padgett, 26 Md. 228. §§ 82, 84.
v. Williams, 35 Ala. 503. § 90.
Hutz' Ex'rs, Kramph's Ex'rs *v.*, 52 Pa. St. 525. § 635.

Huxley, Norton *v.*, 13 Gray, 285. § 73.
Huzzard *v.* Nagle, 40 Pa. St. 178. § 637.
Hyams, Adams *v.*, 8 Fed. Rep. 417. § 593.
Hyatt, Jarvis *v.*, 43 Ind. 163. § 352.
v. Grover & Baker Sewing Mach. Co., 41 Mich. 225. § 526.
Hyde, Cambridge Savings Bank *v.*, 131 Mass. 77. § 378.
Pleeker *v.*, 3 McLean, 279. § 117.
v. Rogers, 59 Wis. 154. § 434.
Smith *v.*, 19 Vt. 54. §§ 77, 138.
Smith *v.*, 36 Vt. 303. § 356.
Hyland *v.* Habich, 150 Mass. 112. § 135.
Hyman, Adams *v.* (Cir. Ct. D. Conn.), 8 Fed. Rep. 417. § 128.
Anderson *v.*, 1 H. Black. 120. § 78.
Beadle Co. Nat. Bank *v.*, 33 Ill. App. 618. § 104.
Clark *v.*, 55 Iowa, 14. § 161.
Hymen, Schwartz *v.*, 107 N. Y. 562. § 165.
Hyner *v.* Dickinson, 32 Ark. 776. §§ 7, 11.
Ide *v.* Churchill, 14 Ohio St. 372. §§ 280, 342.
Smith *v.*, 3 Vt. 290. §§ 82, 86.
v. Stanton, 15 Vt. 685. § 80.
Ige *v.* Bank of Mobile, 8 Port. (Ala.) 108. § 360.
Iglehart *v.* State, 2 Gill & Johns. (Md.) 235. § 638.
Ijames *v.* Gaither, 93 N. C. 358. § 324.
Iles, Bamford *v.*, 3 Wels., Hurl. & Gor. 380. § 170.
Iliff *v.* Weymouth, 40 Ohio St. 101. § 241.
Ilsley *v.* Jones, 12 Gray, 260. § 201.
Imlay, Pearl Street Congregational Society *v.*, 23 Conn. 10. § 430.
Imming *v.* Fiedler, 8 Bradw. (Ill. App.) 256. § 605.
In re Albrecht, 17 Bankr. Reg. 287. § 472.
Babcock, 3 Story, 393. § 238.
In re Blumer & Co. (Dist. Ct. E. D. Pa.), 13 Fed. Rep. 622. §§ 19, 284.
Caton, Ex'r of Berry, 14 Lea (Tenn.), 408. § 426.
Dill, 32 Kan. 668. § 493.
Dryer, 10 Daly (N. Y. Com. Pl.), 8. § 593.
Estate of Connolly, 73 Cal. 423. § 587.
Estate of Hill, 67 Cal. 238. §§ 205, 213.
Fickett, 72 Me. 266. § 324.
Finks, 41 Fed. Rep. (Dist. Ct. W. Div. Va.) 383. § 531.
Gaston, Trustee, 35 N. J. Eq. 60. § 587.
Graves, 1 Cromp. & Jer. 374. § 52.
Groencke, 10 Daly (N. Y. Com. Pl.), 17. § 593.
Hewitt, 10 C. E. Green (N. J.), 210. § 303.
James, 18 Fed. Rep. 853 (Cir. Ct. W. D. Mo.). § 514.
Keily, 9 Irish Ch. 87. § 259.
Kirkwood's Estate, Irish Law Rep. (1 Ch. Div.) 108. § 315.
Kitchen (*Ex parte* Young), Law R. (17 Ch. Div.) 668. § 630.
Lewenthal, 10 Daly (N. Y. Com. Pl.), 14. § 593.
MacDonaghs, Irish (10 Eq.), 269. § 288.
Merwin, 10 Daly (N. Y. Com. Pl.), 13. § 593.
Morrill, 2 Saw. 356. § 332.
Richter's Estate, 4 Bankr. Reg. 222. § 472.
Robinson, Law Rep. 1 Ch. Div. 537. § 252.
West of England Bank, Law Rep. (14 Ch. Div.) 317. § 6.
Yeager, 10 Daly (N. Y. Com. Pl.), 7. § 593.
Independent Dist. *v.* Reichard, 50 Iowa, 98. § 93.
Independent School District Montezuma *v.* McDonald, 39 Iowa, 564. § 545.

Indianapolis M. & C. U., McClosky *v.*, 67 Ind. 86. § 377.
Ingalls *v.* Dennett, 6 Greenl. (Me.), 79. § 205.
Ingels *v.* Sutliff, 36 Kan. 444. §§ 242, 353.
Ingersoll *v.* Baker, 41 Mich. 48. § 3.
  Nicholls *v.*, 7 Johns. 146. § 496.
  v. Roe, 65 Barb. (N. Y.) 346. § 12.
Ingham, Hinds *v.*, 31 Ill. 400. § 142.
Ingham's Adm'rs *v.* McCombs, 17 Mo. 558. 537.
Ingles, Stults *v.*, 84 Va. 844. § 572.
Inglis *v.* Macdougal, 1 Moore, 196. § 150.
  Morley *v.*, 4 Bing. N. C. 58. § 236.
Ingraham, Kane *v.*, 2 Johns. Cas. 403. § 150.
  v. Marine Bank, 13 Mass. 208. § 547.
  Newell *v.*, 15 Vt. 422. § 75.
Inhabitants of Alna *v.* Plummer, 4 Greenl. (Me.) 258. § 90.
Inhabitants of Colerain *v.* Bell, 9 Met. (Mass.) 499. § 547.
Inhabitants Cumberland Co. *v.* Pennell, 69 Me. 357. § 558.
Inhabitants of Farmington *v.* Stanley, 60 Me. 472. §§ 555, 557.
Inhabitants of Hancock *v.* Hazzard, 12 Cush. (Mass.) 112. § 558.
Inhabitants of Middletown, Conover *v.*, 42 N. J. Law. 382. § 524.
Inhabitants New Providence *v.* McEachron, 4 Vroom (N. J.), 339. § 558.
Inhabitants of Norridgewock *v.* Hale, 80 Me. 362. § 168.
Inhabitants of Orono *v.* Wedgewood, 44 Me. 49. § 523.
Inhabitants of Phipsburg *v.* Dickinson, 78 Me. 457. § 546.
Inhabitants of South Berwick *v.* Huntress, 53 Me. 89. § 410.
Inhabitants of Township of Freehold, Patterson *ads.*, 38 N. J. Law, 255. § 547.
Inhabitants of Wendell *v.* Fleming, 8 Gray, 613. § 521.
Inhabitants of Winslow, Hudson *v.*, 6 Vroom (N. J.), 437. § 46.
Inkster *v.* First Nat'l Bank of Marshall, 30 Mich. 143. § 242.
Insurance Co. *v.* Hancock, 83 Mo. 21. § 342.
  v. Kiger, 103 U. S. 352. § 50.
International Bank, Kassing *v.*, 74 Ill. 16. § 219.
International Petroleum Co., Hanna *v.*, 23 Ohio St. 622. § 484.
Irby *v.* Livingston, 81 Ga. 281. § 320.
Ireland, Bunker *v.*, 81 Me. 519. § 106.
Irick *v.* Black, 2 C. E. Green (N. J.), 189. §§ 223, 237, 434, 435.
Irish *v.* Cutter, 31 Me. 536. §§ 49, 184.
Irvine *v.* Adams, 48 Wis. 468. §§ 29, 357.
  Miller *v.*, 1 Dev. & Bat. 103. § 82.
  Pierse *v.*, 1 Minn. 369. § 182.
Irwin, Alford *v.*, 34 Ga. 25. § 499.
  v. Backus, 25 Cal. 214. § 638.
  v. Helgenberg, 21 Ind. 106. § 614.
  v. Kilburn, 104 Ind. 113. § 93.
  McCormick's Adm'r *v.*, 35 Pa. St. 111. § 298.
  Pike *v.*, 1 Sand. (N. Y.) 14. §§ 67, 74.
  v. Sanders, 5 Yerg. (Tenn.) 287. § 453.
  v. State, 10 Neb. 325. §§ 152, 508.
  Stearns *v.*, 62 Ind. 558. § 205.
  Thomas *v.*, 90 Ind. 557. § 486.
Irwine, Sutton *v.*, 12 Serg. & Rawle, 13. § 18.
Isaac *v.* Daniel, 8 Adol. & Ell. (N. S.) 500. § 342.
  Mayer *v.*, 6 Mees. & Wels. 605. §§ 92, 161.
Isett *v.* Hoge, 2 Watts (Pa.), 128. § 100.
Isham, Craft *v.*, 13 Conn. 28. §§ 190, 203, 204.
  Gilbert *v.*, 16 Conn. 525. 530.
Isley, Moore *v.*, 2 Dev. & Batt. Eq. (N. C.) 372. § 281.

Israel v. Douglas, 1 H. Black. 239. § 66.
Ives v. Bank of Lansingburg, 12 Mich. 361. § 426.
v. Hulce, 17 Bradw. (Ill. App.) 35. § 449.
McHard v., 5 Bradw. (Ill. App.) 400. § 346.
v. McHart, 103 Ill. 97. § 176.
Payne v., 3 Dow. & Ryl. 664. § 191.
Willis v., 1 Sm. & Mar. (Miss.) 307. § 30.
Iveson, Other v., 3 Drew. 177. § 139.
Ivey, Johnson v., 4 Cold. (Tenn.) 608. § 339.
Jack v. Morrison, 48 Pa. St. 113. § 325.
v. People, 19 Ill. 57. § 8.
Jackson v. Adamson, 7 Blackf. (Ind.) 597. § 226.
v. Boyles, 64 Iowa, 428. § 383.
Domestic Sewing Machine Co. v., 15 Lea (Tenn.), 418. §§ 421, 422.
Ellison v., 12 Cal. 542. § 82.
Fletcher v., 23 Vt. 581. §§ 281, 282, 283.
v. Foote (Cir. Ct. N. D. Ill.), 12 Fed. Rep. 37. § 45.
Forbes v., Law Rep. (19 Ch. Div.) 615. § 315.
v. Griswold, 4 Hill (N. Y.), 522. § 630.
v. Guilmartin, 61 Ga. 544. § 510.
v. Jackson, 7 Ala. 791. § 17.
v. Jackson, 51 Vt. 253. § 215.
v. Johnson, 67 Ga. 167. § 384.
v. Lowe, 1 Bing. 9. § 80.
v. Maultsby, 78 N. C. 174. § 565.
McKenzie v., 4 Ala. 230. § 63.
v. Michie, 33 La. Ann. 723. § 370.
Mississippi County v., 51 Mo. 23. § 523.
v. Murray, 77 Tex. 644. § 290.
Otto v., 35 Ill. 349. § 44.
v. Patrick, 10 Rich. (S. C.) 197. § 481.
v. Rayner, 12 Johns. 291. §§ 63, 66.
Jackson, Reid v., 1 Ala. 207. § 569.
Saunderson v., 3 Esp. 180. §§ 80, 89.
Saunderson v., 2 Bos. & Pul. 238. §§ 80, 89.
v. State, 30 Kan. 88. § 503.
v. Van Dusen, 5 Johns. 144. § 89.
Jackson's Adm'r v. Jackson, 7 Ala. 791. § 13.
Jackson's Ex'r, Commonwealth v., 1 Leigh (Va.), 485. § 522.
Jacob v. Hill, 2 Leigh (Va.), 393. §§ 173, 631.
v. Kirk, 2 Moody & Rob. 221. §§ 80, 81, 89.
Jacobs, Harrah v., 75 Iowa, 72. § 230.
Watson v., 29 Vt. 169. § 62.
Jacoby, Elbert v., 8 Bush (Ky.), 542. § 542.
Jacocks, Fagan v., 4 Dev. Law (N. C.), 263. § 268.
Jacques, Fackney v., 64 Ill. 87. § 315.
James v., 26 Tex. 320. § 237.
Jaffray v. Brown, 74 N. Y. 393. § 17.
v. Crane, 50 Wis. 349. § 342.
James, Baumann v., Law Rep. 3 Ch. App. 508. § 81.
Branch Bank at Mobile v., 9 Ala. 949. §§ 29, 342.
City of Lafayette v., 92 Ind. 240. § 549.
v. Day, 37 Iowa, 164. § 37.
v. Jacques, 26 Tex. 320. § 237.
v. Kennedy, 10 Heisk. (Tenn.) 607. § 468.
Lee v., 150 Mass. 475. § 471.
v. Long, 68 N. C. 218. § 148.
Odd Fellows Mutual Aid Ass'n v., 63 Cal. 598. § 558.
v. Patten, 8 Barb. (N. Y.) 344. § 89.
v. Scott, 59 Pa. St. 178. § 97.
Smith v., 1 Miles (Pa.), 162. § 221.
v. State, 55 Miss. 57. § 521.
State v., 82 Mo. 509. § 632.
Thurston v., 6 R. I. 103. § 367.
v. Williams, 3 Nev. & Man. 126. §§ 82, 85.
v. Williams, 5 Barn. & Adol. 1109. § 85.

Jameson, Board of Comm'rs *v.*, 86 Ind. 154. §§ 227, 238.
v. Kelly, 1 Bibb (Ky.), 479. § 519.
United States *v.* (Cir. Ct. D. Neb.), 16 Fed. Rep. 331. § 595.
Jansen, People *v.*, 7 Johns. 332. §§ 243, 555.
Janson *v.* Paxton, 22 Up. Can. (C. P.) 505. § 260.
Janvrin, Zollar *v.*, 49 N. H. 114. § 472.
Jarmain *v.* Algar, 2 Car. & P. 249. § 70.
Jarman, Hoey *v.*, 39 N. J. Law (10 Vroom), 523. §§ 92, 97.
v. Wiswall, 9 C. E. Green (N. J.), 267. § 138.
Jarrett *v.* Martin, 70 N. C. 459. § 145.
Jarvis *v.* Hyatt, 43 Ind. 163. § 352.
v. Wilkins, 7 Mees. & Wels. 410. § 84.
Jasper, Bell's Adm'r *v.*. 2 Ired. Eq. (N. C.) 597. §§ 256, 288.
Jasper Co. *v.* Shanks, 61 Mo. 332. § 614.
Jay, Wulff *v.*, Law Rep. 7 Q. B. 756. §§ 442, 445.
Jean Defesse & C. Benoit, State *v.*, 18 La. Ann. 104. § 494.
Jeffers, De Cottes *v.*, 7 Fla. 284. § 224.
v. Johnson, 1 Zab. (N. J.) 73. § 222.
Jefferson *v.* Hartley, 81 Ga. 716. § 566.
v. M'Carthy, 44 Minn. 26. § 45.
Tennell *v.*, 5 Harr. (Del.) 206. § 247.
Jefferson Co., McWatty *v.*, 76 Ga. 352. § 35.
v. Slagee, 66 Pa. St. 202. § 77.
Jeffree, Adm'r, *v.* Walsh, 14 Nev. 143. § 585.
Jeffries *v.* Fergusen, Adm'r, 87 Mo. 244. § 254.
Sweet, Adm'r, *v.*, 48 Mo. 279. § 317.
Jemison *v.* Cozens, 3 Ala. 636. § 467.
v. Governor, 47 Ala. 390. § 439.
Jendervine *v.* Rose, 36 Mich. 54. § 134.
Jenkins *v.* Clarkson, 7 Ohio, 72. §§ 242, 344, 353.
Cooper *v.*, 32 Beav. 337. § 307.
Dillingham *v.*, 7 Sm. & Mar. (Miss.) 479. § 413.
v. Emery, 2 Wyom. 58. § 518.
Gray *v.*, 24 Ala. 516. § 580.
Kelty *v.*, 1 Hilton (N. Y.), 73. § 363.
v. Lockard's Adm'r, 66 Ala. 377. §§ 293, 294.
v. McNeese, 34 Tex. 189. § 434.
v. Nat. V. B. of Bowdoinham, 58 Me. 275. § 441.
People *v.*, 17 Cal. 500. § 42.
v. Reynolds, 3 Brod. & Bing. 14. § 85.
v. Reynolds, 6 Moore, 86. § 82.
v. Robertson, 3 Drewry, 351. § 40.
v. Skillern, 5 Yerg. (Tenn.) 288. § 464.
Wilde *v.*, 4 Paige, 481. § 36.
Jennery *v.* Olmstead, 90 N. Y. 363. § 539.
Jenness *v.* Cutler, 12 Kan. 500. §§ 35, 357.
v. True, 30 Me. 438. § 138.
Jennings *v.* Hare, 104 Pa. St. 489. § 486.
v. Sledge, 3 Kelly (Ga.), 128. § 507.
State *v.*, 14 Ohio St. 73. § 631.
Thomas *v.*, 5 S. & M. (Miss.) 627. § 176.
Woolley *v.*, 5 Barn. & Cres. 165. § 161.
Jennison *v.* Parker, 7 Mich. 355. § 440.
Jensen, Williams *v.*, 75 Mo. 681. § 342.
Jenyns, Thornton *v.*, 1 Man. & Gr. 166. § 86.
Jephson *v.* Maunsell, 10 Irish Eq. 38. § 445.
Jerauld *v.* Trippet, 62 Ind. 122. §§ 242, 434.
Jernegan *v.* Gray, 14 Lea (Tenn.), 536. § 596.

Jerome, Casoni *v.*, 58 N. Y. 315. § 406.
v. McCarter, 21 Wall. 17. § 461.
Jessup, Brown *v.*, 19 Oreg. 288. § 10.
Jester *v.* Sterling, 25 Hun (N. Y.), 344. § 37.
Jeter, Gilder *v.*, 11 Ala. 256. § 356.
Taylor *v.*, 23 Mo. 244. § 427.
Jetmore, Bunn *v.*, 70 Mo. 228. § 151.
Jett, Hunter's Adm'rs *v.*, 4 Rand. (Va.) 104. §§ 342, 345.
Jeuchner, Herman *v.*, Law Rep. (15 Q. B. Div.) 561. § 219.
Jevons, Edwards *v.*, 8 Man., Gr. & Scott, 436. §§ 84, 86.
Jewell, Board Education *v.*, 44 Minn. 427. § 558.
Heeter *v.*, 6 Bush (Ky.), 510. § 570.
Wallace *v.*, 21 Ohio St. 163. § 380.
Jewett *v.* Crane, 35 Barb. (N. Y.) 208. § 250.
Rowley *v.*, 56 Iowa, 492. §§ 245, 383.
Jimmerson *v.* Green, 7 Neb. 26. § 231.
Jjader, Van Doren *v.*, 1 Nev. 380. § 176.
Joel, Cooper *v.*, 1 De Gex, Fish. & Jo. 240. § 127.
John *v.* Jones, 16 Ala. 454. §§ 262, 263, 283.
John Hancock Mut. Life Ins. Co. *v.* Lowenberg, 120 N. Y. 44. § 602.
Johns *v.* Harrison, 20 Ind. 317. § 381.
Nolan, Adm'r, *v.*, 27 Mo. App. 502. § 476.
v. Reardon, 11 Md. 465. §§ 35, 229.
Woodson *v.*, 3 Munf. (Va.) 230. 475.
Johnson, Ashby *v.*, 23 Ark. 163. § 448.
Bank at Decatur *v.*, 9 Ala. 621. § 447.
Best *v.*, 78 Cal. 217. § 593.
Blakey *v.*, 13 Bush (Ky.), 197. § 378.
Johnson, Boatmen's Savings Bank *v.*, 24 Mo. App. 316. § 147.
v. Boyer, 3 Watts (Pa.), 376. § 493.
v. Brown, 51 Ga. 498. § 117.
Burlington Ins. Co. *v.*, 120 Ill. 622. § 93.
v. Clendenin, 5 Gill & Johns. (Md.) 463. § 500.
v. Commonwealth, 2 Duvall (Ky.), 410. § 8.
Commonwealth *v.*, 3 Cush. 454. § 496.
Croft *v.*, 5 Taunt. 319. § 493.
Crofts *v.*, 1 Marsh. 59. § 342.
v. Dodge, 17 Ill. 433. § 90.
v. Dodgson, 2 Mees. & Wels. 653. §§ 80, 89.
v. Fisher, 4 Col. 242. § 95.
v. Flint, 34 Ala. 673. § 456.
v. Fuquay, 1 Dana (Ky.), 514. § 585.
Gibbs *v.*, 63 Mich. 671. § 410.
Gieseke, Adm'r, *v.*, 115 Ind. 308. § 212.
v. Gilbert, 4 Hill, 178. § 67.
v. Hacker, 8 Heisk. (Tenn.) 388. § 371.
v. Harris, 69 Ind. 305. § 622.
v. Harvey, 84 N. Y. 363. §§ 276, 284.
Henderson *v.*, 6 Ga. 390. § 82.
Heppe *v.*, 73 Cal. 265. §§ 546, 590, 617.
Hessell *v.*, 63 Mich. 623. §§ 402, 410, 411.
v. Hobson, 1 Litt. (Ky.) 314. § 125.
Holland *v.*, 51 Ind. 346. § 426.
v. Ivey, 4 Cold. (Tenn.) 608. § 339.
Jackson *v.*, 67 Ga. 167. § 384.
Jeffers *v.*, 1 Zab. (N. J.) 73. § 222.
v. Johnson, 31 Ohio St. 131. § 152.
v. Lawson, 29 Ill. App. 146. § 401.
McCord *v.*, 4 Bibb (Ky.), 531. § 615.
v. McGruder, 15 Mo. 365. § 90.
v. McMillan, 13 Col. 423. § 112.
v. Mills, 10 Cush. 503. § 339.

Johnson, Nichols v., 10 Conn. 192. §§ 80, 81.
Phelan v., 80 Iowa, 727. § 462.
v. Planters' Bank, 4 Sm. & Mar. (Miss.) 165. § 448.
Prather v., 3 Harr. & Johns. (Md.) 487. § 209.
Reinhart v., 62 Iowa, 155. § 268.
Riley v., 8 Ohio, 526. § 406.
v. Searcy, 4 Yerg. (Tenn.) 182. § 342.
Sebastian v., 2 Duvall (Ky.), 101. § 24.
v. Shepard, 35 Mich. 115. § 98.
Somers v., 57 Vt. 274. § 268.
South Carolina Society v., 1 McCord, Law (S. C.), 41. § 167.
Stansfield v., 1 Esp. 101. § 90.
Starry v., 32 Ind. 438. § 439.
Statlings v., 27 Ga. 564. § 354.
Studebaker v., 41 Kan. 326. § 545.
Taylor v., 17 Ga. 521. §§ 415, 567, 637.
Treasurers v., 4 McCord, Law (S. C.), 458. § 433.
Van Winkle v., 11 Oreg. 469. §§ 254, 283.
Ward v., 6 Munf. (Va.) 6. § 372.
v. Weathernax, 9 Kan. 75. §§ 411, 467, 468.
v. Wilmarth, 13 Met. (Mass.) 416. § 202.
v. Witchcott, 1 Roll. Abr. 24, pl. 33. § 16.
Wright v., 8 Wend. 512. § 397.
v. Young, 20 W. Va. 614. § 36.
v. Zink, 51 N. Y. 333. § 37.
Johnson's Adm'rs v. Vaughn, 65 Ill. 425. § 274.
Johnson County v. Gilkeson, 70 Mo. 645. § 614.
Johnston v. Amana Lodge, 92 Ind. 150. § 311.
Burlington Ins. Co. v., 24 Ill. App. 565. § 602.
v. Chapman, 3 Pen. & Watts (Pa.), 18. § 101.
v. Chapman, 3 Pen. & Watts (Pa.), 128. § 100.
Johnston, Grove v., Law Rep. (Irish, 24 Q. B. & Ex. Div.) 352. § 155.
v. Gwathney, 2 Bibb (Ky.), 186. § 519.
Hamilton v., 82 Ill. 39. §§ 176, § 210.
Hill v., 3 Ired. Eq. (N. C.) 432. § 89.
v. Kimball Township, 39 Mich. 187. § 151.
v. May, 76 Ind. 293. §§ 379, 397.
v. Mill, 25 Tex. 704. § 100.
v. Nicholls, Man., Gr. & Scott, 251. § 84.
v. Patterson, 114 Pa. St. 398. §§ 45, 624.
v. Smith, 25 Hun (N. Y.), 171. §§ 43, 580.
Snevily v., 1 Watts & Serg. 307. § 15.
v. Thompson, 4 Watts (Pa.), 446. § 353.
Joice, Stayner v., 82 Ind. 35. § 379.
Joiner, Blackman v., 81 Ala. 344. § 311.
Jones, Abrahams v., 20 Bradw. (Ill. App.) 83. § 22.
Adams v., 12 Pet. 207. §§ 81, 186, 187.
Adams v., 68 Ala. 117. § 588.
v. Albee, 70 Ill. 34. § 182.
Allen v., 8 Minn. 202. § 330.
Andrews v., 10 Ala. 400. § 52.
v. Ashford, 79 N. C. 172. §§ 97, 101, 106.
v. Bangs, 40 Ohio St. 139. § 379.
v. Blanton, 6 Ired. Eq. (N. C.) 115. §§ 267, 288, 292, 540.
Board Supervisors Jefferson Co. v., 19 Wis. 51. § 557.
Boone County v., 54 Iowa, 699. §§ 22, 413, 517, 555, 628, 642.
Boone Co. v., 58 Iowa, 373. § 257.
v. Bradford, 25 Ind. 305. § 286.
Brainard v., 18 N. Y. 35. § 112.
v. Brown, 18 Ohio St. 601. § 362.
v. Bullock, 3 Bibb (Ky.), 467. § 434.

Jones, Chaffee *v.*, 19 Pick. 260. §§ 180, 258, 288, 293.
v. Childs, 8 Nev. 121. § 221.
Choteau *v.*, 11 Ill. 300. § 207.
Chrisman *v.*, 34 Ark. 73. §§ 262, 292.
v. Cooper, 1 Cowp. 227. §§ 75, 77.
v. Council Bluffs Bank, 34 Ill. 313. § 67.
v. Crosthwaite, 17 Iowa, 393. § 153.
v. Davids, 4 Russ. 277. § 313.
Davis Sewing Machine Co. *v.*, 61 Mo. 409. § 193.
v. Degge, 84 Va. 685. § 140.
Dolby *v.*, 2 Dev. Law (N. C.), 109. § 450.
v. Doles, 3 La. Ann. 588. § 630.
v. Dow, 142 Mass. 130. § 47.
Fishburn *v.*, 37 Ind. 119. § 401.
v. Fitz, 5 N. H. 444. § 266.
v. Fleming, 15 La. Ann. 522. § 29.
v. Gallatin Co., 78 Ky. 491. § 642.
v. Gibson, 82 Ky. 561. § 317.
Goode *v.*, 9 Mo. 866. § 184.
v. Goodwin, 39 Cal. 493. § 177.
v. Gordon, 82 Ga. 570. § 504.
v. Greenlaw, 6 Cold. (Tenn.) 342. § 98.
v. Hagler, 6 Jones' Law (N. C.), 542. § 150.
v. Hardesty, 10 Gill & Johns. 404. § 72.
v. Hawkins, 60 Ga. 52. § 150.
Headlee, Adm'r, *v.*, 43 Mo. 235. § 364.
v. Hobson, 2 Rand. (Va.) 483. § 583.
Hood *v.*, 5 Del. Ch. 77. § 35.
Howell *v.*, 1 Cromp., Mees. & Ross. 97. § 364.
Hull *v.*, 10 Lea (Tenn.), 100. § 577.
Ilsley *v.*, 12 Gray, 260. § 201.
John *v.*, 16 Ala. 454. §§ 262, 263, 283.
v. Joyner. 8 Ga. 562. § 215.
v. Keer, 30 Ga. 93. § 403.
v. Knox, 46 Ala. 53. § 150.
v. Kuhn, 34 Kan. 414. § 176.
Jones, Lee *v.*, 14 J. Scott (N. S.), 386. § 422.
v. Letcher, 13 B. Mon. (Ky.) 363. § 264.
Lewis *v.*, 4 B. & C. 506. § 146.
Matheson *v.*, 30 Ga. 306. §§ 29, 405.
Mobile & G. R. R. Co. *v.*, 57 Ga. 198. § 67.
New York Nat. Exch. Bank *v.*, 9 Daly (N. Y. Com. Pl.), 248. § 445.
Paine *v.*, 76 N. Y. 274. § 37.
v. Palmer, 1 Doug. (Mich.) 379. §§ 67, 82.
Partridge *v.*, 38 Ohio St. 375. § 27.
Paul *v.*, 1 Durn. & East, 599. § 220.
v. Post, 6 Cal. 102. §§ 80, 87.
Purefoy *v.*, Freeman's Ch. 44. § 431.
v. Quinnipaick, 29 Conn. 25. § 324.
v. Read, 1 Humph. (Tenn.) 335. § 616.
Redd *v.*, 30 Gratt. (Va.) 123. § 577.
v. Ritter's Adm'r, 56 Ala. 270. §§ 540, 638.
Ross *v.*, 22 Wall. 576. § 604.
v. Ryde, 5 Taunt. 488. § 28.
v. Sarchett, 61 Iowa, 520. §§ 365, 376.
v. Scanland, 6 Humph. (Tenn.) 195. § 521.
v. Scott, 58 Pa. St. 178. § 100.
Sellers *v.*, 22 Pa. St. 423. § 440.
Shimer *v.*, 47 Pa. St. 268. § 240.
v. Shorter, 1 Kelley (Ga.), 294. § 60.
Smith *v.*, 5 Leigh (Va.), 165. § 90.
State *v.*, 82 Mo. 509. § 587.
State *v.*, 3 La. Ann. 9. § 504.
v. State, 11 Tex. App. 412. § 505.
State *v.*, 89 Mo. 470. § 526.
Stein *v.*, 18 Bradw. (Ill. App.) 543. § 390.
v. Swift, 94 Ind. 516. § 406.
v. Thayer, 12 Gray, 443. § 145.

Jones *v.* Tincher, 15 Ind. 308. § 97.
Townsend National Bank *v.*, 151 Mass. 454. § 465.
v. Turner, 5 Litt. (Ky.) 147. § 145.
United States *v.*, 8 Pet. 399. § 416.
United States *v.* (Cir. Ct. W. D. La.), 36 Fed. Rep. 759. § 558.
Vilas *v.*, 10 Paige's Ch. 76. § 356.
Vilas *v.*, 1 N. Y. 274. §§ 243, 357.
v. Ward, 71 Wis. 152. § 349.
v. Whitehead, 4 Ga. 397. §§ 1, 613.
v. Yeargain, 1 Dev. Law (N. C.), 420. § 28.
Jones & Bro. *v.* Kuhn, 34 Kan. 414. § 88.
Jordan *v.* Agawam Woolen Co., 106 Mass. 571. § 450.
v. Dobbins, 122 Mass. 168. § 134.
v. La Vine, 15 Oreg. 329. § 492.
v. Trumbo, 6 Gill & Johns, (Md.) 103. § 342.
v. Volkenning, 72 N. Y. 300. § 476.
Jordan, Adm'r, *v.* Adams, 7 Ark. (2 Eng.) 348. § 212.
Jordin *v.* Loftin, 13 Ala. 547. § 402.
Jorst, Muncey *v.*, 74 Ind. 409. § 619.
Joseph *v.* Heaton, 5 Grant's Ch. 636. §§ 34, 316.
Josephi, Hayes *v.*, 26 Cal. 535. § 339.
Josyln *v.* Dow, 19 Hun (N. Y.), 494. § 5.
v. Eastman, 46 Vt. 258. § 339.
v. Smith, 13 Vt. 353. §§ 143, 342.
Josselyn *v.* Ames, 3 Mass. 274. § 182.
Smith *v.*, 40 Ohio St. 409. § 424.
Joyce *v.* Joyce, 1 Bush (Ky.), 474. § 307.
Matthews *v.*, 85 N. C. 258. § 324.
Joyner, Bank of Montpelier *v.*, 33 Vt. 481. § 114.
v. Cooper, 2 Bailey, Law (S. C.), 199. §§ 26, 530.
Daniel *v.*, 3 Ired. Eq. (N. C.) 513. § 221.
Jones *v.*, 8 Ga. 562. § 215.
Poyne *v.*, 6 Ark. (1 Eng.) 241. § 220.
Judah *v.* Mieure, 5 Blackf. (Ind.) 171. §§ 290, 293.
Murray *v.*, 6 Cow. 484. § 362.
Zimmerman *v.*, 13 Ind. 286. § 399.
v. Zimmerman, 22 Ind. 388. § 399.
Judd, Berkey *v.*, 34 Minn. 393. § 409.
Judice, School Directors *v.*, 39 La. Ann. 896. §§ 517, 521, 642.
Judge, State *v.*, 28 La. Ann. 884. § 10.
State *v.*, 35 La. Ann. 737. § 462.
Judge of Probate *v.* Heydock, 8 N. H. 491. § 112.
Judson, Decker *v.*, 16 N. Y. 439. § 42.
Rindge *v.*, 24 N. Y. 64. § 160.
Juggins, Rainbow *v.*, Law Rep. (5 Q. B. Div.) 422. § 447.
Julian, Kiton *v.*, 4 Ellis & Black. 854. § 169.
Julius, Pecke *v.*, 2 Browne (Pa.), 31. §§ 94, 139.
Jung, Meiswinkle *v.*, 30 Wis. 67. § 357.
Justice, Cole *v.*, 8 Ala. 793. § 236.
Justices, Cameron *v.*, 1 Kelly (Ga.), 36. § 578.
Dobbs *v.*, 17 Ga. 624. §§ 559, 567, 627.
v. Ennis, 5 Ga. 569. § 517.
v. Selman, 6 Ga. 432. §§ 450, 576.
v. Sloan, 7 Ga. 31. § 578.
v. Woods, 1 Kelly (Ga.), 84. §§ 546, 575.
Kagy *v.* Trustees, etc., 68 Ill. 75. § 546.
Kahn, Graff *v.*, 18 Bradw. (Ill. App.) 485. § 236.
Kaighn *v.* Fuller, 1 McCarter (N. J.), 419. § 375.
Paulin *v.*, 3 Dutcher (N. J.), 503. §§ 261, 271.
Kaime, Supervisors Com'rs *v.*, 39 Wis. 468. § 558.
Kaler *v.* Hise, 79 Ind. 301. § 352.
Kamena, Mayor of Hoboken *v.*, 41 N. J. Law, 435. § 597.
Kammer, Sweazy *v.*, 51 Iowa, 642. § 7.

Kane *v.* Cortesy, 100 N. Y. 132. §§ 367, 632.
v. Ingraham, 2 Johns. Cas. 403. § 150.
Van Reimsdyck *v.*, 1 Gall. C. C. 633. § 67.
Kannon *v.* Neely, 10 Humph. (Tenn.) 288. § 197.
Karing, O'Blenis *v.*, 57 N. Y. 649. § 281.
Kasey, Anthony *v.*, 83 Va. 338. § 640.
Lane *v.*, 1 Met. (Ky.) 410. § 24.
Richmond & Petersburg R. R. Co. *v.*, 30 Gratt. (Va.) 218. §§ 424, 425.
Kassing *v.* International Bank, 74 Ill. 16. § 219.
Kastner *v.* Winstanley, 20 Up. Can. 101. §§ 92, 191.
Katz *v.* Moessinger, 110 Ill. 372. § 311.
Kaufman, Evansville Nat. Bank *v.*, 93 N. Y. 273. § 117.
v. Wilson, 29 Ind. 504. § 605.
v. Wolf, 77 Tex. 250. § 579.
Kavanagh, Wells *v.*, 70 Iowa, 519. § 647.
Kay *v.* Allen, 9 Pa. St. 320. § 188.
v. Groves, 6 Bing. 276. § 162.
Kayser *v.* Hall, Adm'r, 85 Ill. 511. § 178.
Kean, North British Mercautile Ins. Co. *v.*, 16 Ont. (Can.) 117. § 602.
Peer *v.*, 14 Mich. 354. § 332.
Keane *v.* Fisher, 10 La. Ann. 261. § 110.
Keirns, Emmott *v.*, 5 Bing. N. C. 559. §§ 84, 87.
Knox *v.*, 73 Iowa, 286. § 577.
v. Montgomery, 4 W. Va. 29. §§ 1, 176.
Kearsley *v.* Cole, 16 Mees. & Wels. 128. § 376.
Keate *v.* Temple, 1 Bos. & Pul. 158. § 78.
Keating, Simmons *v.*, 2 Starkie, 375. § 15.
Keaton *v.* Cox, 26 Ga. 162. § 97.
Keaton's Distributees *v.* Campbell, 2 Humph. (Tenn.) 224. § 586.
Keegan, Whelan *v.*, 7 Irish Com. Law, 544. § 160.
Keehler, United States *v.*, 9 Wall. 83. § 538.
Keel *v.* Levy, 19 Oreg. 450. § 237.
Keeland, Evans *v.*, 9 Ala. 42. § 234.
Keen, Augero *v.*, 1 Mees. & Wels. 390. § 172.
Christian & Gunn *v.*, 80 Va. 369. §§ 35, 388.
Keyser *v.*, 17 Pa. St. 327. § 411.
Keer *v.* Clark, 11 Humph. (Tenn.) 77. § 276.
Jones *v.*, 30 Ga. 93. § 403.
Keese, Conner *v.*, 32 Hun (N. Y.), 98. § 572.
Keeshug *v.* Frazier, 119 Ind. 185. § 60.
Keiffer, Duncan *v.*, 3 Bin. (Pa.) 126. § 225.
Keim & Co. *v.* Avery, 7 Neb. 54. § 235.
Keirn *v.* Andrews, 59 Miss. 39. § 353.
Keith *v.* Dwinnell, 38 Vt. 286. § 161.
v. Fenelon Falls Union School, 3 Ont. (Can.) 194. §§ 166, 529.
Ford *v.*, 1 Mass. 139. §§ 208, 215.
v. Goodwin, 31 Vt. 268. §§ 60, 114, 258, 380.
Kellar *v.* Williams, 10 Bush (Ky.), 216. §§ 262, 451.
Keller *v.* Rhoads, 39 Pa. St. 513. § 230.
State *v.*, 11 Lea (Tenn.), 399. § 600.
Kelley *v.* Gillespie, 12 Iowa, 55. § 29.
Kellogg, Adams *v.*, 63 Mich. 105. § 152.
Baker *v.*, 29 Ohio St. 663. § 605.
v. Dunn, 2 Met. (Ky.) 215. § 182.
v. Kimball, 142 Mass. 124. § 469.
Montgomery *v.*, 43 Miss. 486. §§ 192, 203.
v. Stockton, 29 Pa. St. 460. §§ 131, 186, 187.
Kellum *v.* Clark, 97 N. Y. 390. §§ 545, 624.

Kelly, Bryan *v.*, 85 Ala. 569. § 624.
Carpenter *v.*, 9 Ohio, 106. §§ 271, 293.
Christal *v.*, 24 Hun (N. Y.), 155. § 465.
Edwards *v.*, 6 Maule & S. 204. §§ 63, 66.
v. Few, 18 Ohio, 441. § 182.
v. Gillespie, 12 Iowa, 55. § 356.
v. Gordon, 3 Head (Tenn.), 683. § 479.
v. Henderson, 1 Pa. St. 495. § 498.
v. Herrick, 131 Mass. 373. § 577.
Hill *v.*, Ridgeway, Lapp & Schoales (Irish), 265. § 303.
Jameson *v.*, 1 Bibb (Ky.), 479. § 519.
v. Matthews, 5 Ark. (Pike), 223. § 606.
May *v.*, 61 Ala. 489. §§ 581, 583.
Mayor, etc. of City of N. Y. *v.*, 98 N. Y. 467. § 549.
Ring *v.*, 10 Mo. App. 411. § 601.
v. State, 25 Ohio St. 567. §§ 521, 546.
State *v.*, 32 Ohio St. 421. § 597.
Kelly, Adm'r, May, Adm'r, *v.*, 61 Ala. 489. § 578.
Kelsey *v.* Hibbs, 13 Ohio St. 340. § 69.
Kelty *v.* Jenkins, 1 Hilton (N. Y.), 73. § 363.
Kemball, How *v.*, 2 McLean, 103. § 49.
Kemble, Hill *v.*, 9 Cal. 71. §§ 565, 570.
Kemmerer *v.* Wilson, 31 Pa. St. 110. § 440.
Kemmerer's Appeal, 102 Pa. St. 558. § 332.
Kemp *v.* Frinden, 12 Mees. & Wels. 421. §§ 283, 288, 289.
Rittenhouse *v.*, 37 Ind. 258. § 349.
Kempner *v.* County of Galveston, 73 Tex. 216. § 597.
Kendall *v.* Baltis, 26 Mo. App. 411. § 247.
Wheat *v.*, 6 N. H. 504. §§ 32, 354.
Kendig, Commonwealth *v.*, 2 Pa. St. 448. §§ 25, 563.
Kendrick *v.* Forney, 22 Gratt. (Va.) 748. §§ 212, 313.
Kennaway *v.* Treleavan, 5 Mees. & Wels. 498. § 84.
Kennebec Bank *v.* Tuckerman, 5 Greenl. (Me.) 130. §§ 342, 352.
v. Turner, 2 Greenl. (Me.) 42. § 30.
Kennedy *v.* Adams, 5 Har. (Del.) 160. § 498.
v. Brown, 21 Kan. 171. § 481.
v. Carpenter, 2 Whart. (Pa.) 344. §§ 139, 281.
Cochran *v.*, 10 Daly (N. Y. Com. Pl.), 347. § 161.
v. Evans, 31 Ill. 258. §§ 29, 356.
v. Goss, 38 N. Y. 330. § 350.
James *v.*, 10 Heisk. (Tenn.) 607. § 468.
v. Nims, 52 Mich. 153. § 452.
People *v.*, 58 Mich. 372. § 503.
v. Pickens, 3 Ired. Eq. (N. C.) 147. § 318.
Pierce *v.*, 5 Cal. 138. § 177.
Price *v.*, 16 La. Ann. 78. § 642.
Shropshire *v.*, 84 Ind. 111. §§ 414, 416.
Zane *v.*, 73 Pa. St. 182. § 342.
Kenner *v.* Caldwell, Bailey, Eq. Cas. (S. C.) 149. § 243.
Kennett, Baker *v.*, 54 Mo. 82. § 153.
Kenney *v.* Maseman, 14 Daly (N. Y. Com. Pl.), 379. § 199.
Kenning, Allan *v.*, 9 Bing. 618. § 158.
Kenningham *v.* Bedford, 1 B. Mon. 325. § 356.
Kent, Grafton Bank *v.*, 4 N. H. 221. § 29.
v. Matthews, 12 Leigh (Va.), 573. § 238.
Mayor *v.*, 25 J. & S. (N. Y. Sup. Ct.) 109. §§ 151, 152.
v. Mercer, 12 Up. Can. (C. P.) 30. § 537.
Kenworthy *v.* Schofield, 2 Barn. & Cress. 949. § 90.
Kenyon, Eastwood *v.*, 3 Perry & Dav. 276. §§ 17, 72, 91.

Kenyon's Adm'r, Wernecke *v.*, 66 Mo. 275. § 318.
Keowne, Love *v.*, 58 Tex. 191. § 544.
Kephart, Whitcomb *v.*, 50 Pa. St. 85. § 57.
Kepley *v.* People, 123 Ill. 367. §§ 509, 510.
Kepner, Moore *v.*, 7 Neb. 291. § 481.
Ker, Slawson *v.*, 29 La. Ann. 295. §§ 520, 570.
Kerchival, Farmers' & Mechanics' Bank *v.*, 2 Mich. 504. §§ 161, 202, 398.
Kern, Bloom & Co. *v.*, 30 La. Ann. 1263. § 165.
Eagles *v.*, 5 Wharton (Pa.), 144. § 636.
Grudle *v.*, 109 Ill. 557. § 487.
Kerney's Adm'r *v.* Kerney's Heirs, 6 Leigh (Va.), 478. § 141.
Kerney's Heirs, Kerney's Adm'r *v.*, 6 Leigh (Va.), 478. § 141.
Kernochan *v.* Murray, 111 N. Y. 306. § 135.
Kerns *v.* Chambers, 3 Ired. Eq. (N. C.) 576. § 274.
Kerns, Adm'r, *v.* Ryan, 26 Ill. App. 177. § 355.
Kerr *v.* Baker, Walker (Miss.), 140. § 29.
v. Brandon, 84 N. C. 128. § 531.
v. Cameron, 19 Up. Can. (Q. B.) 366. § 347.
v. Shaw, 13 Johns. 236. § 82.
Kershaw, Ordinary *v.*, 1 McCart. (N. J.) 527. § 580.
Perkins *v.*, 1 Hill, Eq. (S. C.) 344. § 310.
Kershner, United States *v.*, 1 Bond, 432. § 338.
Kesee, Bradley *v.*, 5 Cold. (Tenn.) 223. § 414.
Ketchell *v.* Burns, 24 Wend. 456. § 47.
Ketchum, Williams *v.*, 19 Wis. 231. § 84.
v. Zeilsdorff, 26 Wis. 514. § 486.
Ketter *v.* Thompson, 13 Bush (Ky.), 287. § 256.
Kettle, Powell *v.*, 1 Gilm. (Ill.) 491. § 141.
Kettlewell, Conolly *v.*, 1 Gill (Md.), 260. §§ 76, 78.
Key, Heath *v.*, 1 Younge & Jer. 434. § 342.
Keyes, Mead *v.*, 4 E. D. Smith (N. Y.), 510. § 62.
Keyser *v.* Keen, 17 Pa. St. 327. § 411.
Kezertee, Remington Sewing Machine Co. *v.*, 49 Wis. 409. §§ 421, 647.
Kibler, Gilman *v.*, 5 Humph. 19. § 82.
Kibourn, Martin *v.*, 1 Cent. Law Jour. 94. § 472.
Kidd, Brown *v.*, 34 Miss. 291. § 225.
Kidder *v.* Page, 48 N. H. 380. § 251.
Kiernan, Williams *v.*, 25 Hun (N. Y.), 355. § 583.
Kiersted, Harwood *v.*, 20 Ill. 367. § 17.
Kiger, Insurance Co. *v.*, 103 U. S. 352. § 50.
Kiggin *v.* Sharkey, 3 Lea (Tenn.), 707. § 565.
Kilbourn, Martin *v.*, 12 Heisk. (Tenn.) 331. § 472.
Kilburn, Irwin *v.*, 104 Ind. 113. § 93.
Killian *v.* Ashley, 24 Ark. 511. §§ 47, 176, 192.
Turner, Frazer & Co. *v.*, 12 Neb. 580. § 566.
Kimball *v.* Comstock, 14 Gray, 508. § 73.
Kellogg *v.*, 142 Mass. 124. § 469.
v. Newell, 7 Hill, 116. §§ 58, 153.
v. Roye, 9 Rich. 295. § 103.
Stoddard *v.*, 4 Cush. 604. § 407.
Kimball Township, Johnston *v.*, 39 Mich. 187. § 151.
Kimble *v.* Cummins, 3 Met. (Ky.) 327. § 214.
Kimmel *v.* Lowe, 28 Minn. 265. § 205.
Markland Min'g & M'f'g Co. *v.*, 87 Ind. 560. §§ 1, 93, 411.
Kimmey, Fawcetts *v.*, 33 Ala. 261. § 315.
Kinard *v.* Baird, 20 S. C. 377. § 310.

Kincaid, Burson *v.*, 3 Pen. & Watts (Pa.), 57. § 154.
v. Yates, 63 Mo. 45. § 381.
Kinchelse *v.* Holmes, 7 B. Mon. (Ky.) 5. §§ 186, 187.
Kindy, Green *v.*, 43 Mich. 279. §§ 481, 486.
Kindt's Appeal, 102 Pa. St. 441. § 447.
King *v.* Baker, 7 La. Ann. 570. § 525.
v. Baldwin, 2 Johns. Ch. 554. §§ 238, 239.
v. Blackmore, 72 Pa. St. 347. § 332.
Carpenter *v.*, 9 Met. 511. §§ 29, 40, 245.
Cook *v.*, 7 Bradw. (Ill. App.) 549. § 460.
Crawford *v.*, 54 Ind. 6. § 63.
Davenport *v.*, 63 Ind. 64. § 377.
Finley *v.*, 1 Head (Tenn.), 123. § 334.
Gardner *v.*, 2 Ired. Law (N. C.), 297. §§ 17, 132.
v. Hannah, 6 Bradw. (Ill. App.) 495. § 210.
v. Harman's Heirs, 6 La. (Curry), 607. § 325.
v. Haynes, 35 Ark. 463. § 344.
v. Nichols, 16 Ohio St. 80. §§ 537, 550.
Oldershaw *v.*, 2 Hurl. & Nor. 517. § 84.
Sayre *v.*, 17 W. Va. 562. §§ 364, 374.
Smalling *v.*, 5 Lea (Tenn.), 585. § 532.
v. Smith, 2 Leigh (Va.), 157. § 402.
v. State, 18 Neb. 375. §§ 500, 509.
v. State, 81 Ala. 92. § 402.
v. State Bank, 9 Ark. (4 Eng.) 185. § 342.
v. Summitt, 73 Ind. 312. §§ 91, 227.
Taylor Co. *v.*, 73 Iowa, 153. § 408.
Thayer *v.*, 31 Hun (N. Y.), 437. §§ 240, 355.
v. United States, 99 U. S. 229. § 595.
Yoakley *v.*, 10 Lea (Tenn.), 67. § 389.
Kingham, Reader *v.*, 13 Com. B. (J. Scott), N. S. 344. § 72.
Kingman, Grocers' Bank *v.*, 16 Gray, 473. §§ 22, 395.
Kingsbury *v.* Westfall, 61 N. Y. 356. §§ 93, 108, 389.
v. Williams, 53 Barb. (N. Y.) 142. § 389.
Kingsland, Pfeiffer *v.*, 25 Mo. 66. § 13.
Kingsley *v.* Balcome, 4 Barb. (N. Y.) 131. §§ 61, 69.
Davis *v.*, 13 Conn. 285. § 625.
Kingston Mut. Ins. Co. *v.* Clark, 33 Barb. (N. Y.) 196. § 167.
Kinloch *v.* Brown, 1 Rich. (S. C.) 223. § 78.
v. Brown, 2 Spear's Law (S. C.), 284. § 75.
Kinnaird *v.* Webster, Law Rep. 10 Ch. Div. 139. § 335.
Kinney, Hamlin *v.*, 2 Oreg. 91. § 578.
Hansberger's Adm'r *v.*, 13 Gratt. (Va.) 511. § 352.
Smith *v.*, 6 Neb. 447. § 220.
Kinsey *v.* McDearmon, 5 Cold. (Tenn.) 392. § 324.
Kinyon *v.* Brock, 72 N. C. 554. § 101.
Kinzy, Dodge *v.*, 101 Ind. 102. § 7.
Kipp, Willett *v.*, 12 Hun (N. Y.), 474. § 572.
Kirby *v.* Duke of Marlborough, 2 Maule & Sel. 18. §§ 162, 165.
v. Studebaker, 15 Ind. 45. §§ 195, 399.
Tinsley *v.*, 17 S. C. 1. §§ 21, 22, 42, 46.
v. Turner, Hopkins' Ch. 309. §§ 147, 573.
v. Turner, 6 Johns. Ch. 242. § 147.
Wayne *v.*, 2 Bailey, Law (S. C.), 551. §§ 243, 372.
Whitaker *v.*, 54 Ga. 277. § 245.
Kircher, Knoebel *v.*, 33 Ill. 308. § 384.
Kirk, Brown *v.*, 20 Mo. App. 524. §§ 37, 315, 342.

Kirk, Grieff v., 17 La. Ann. 25. § 449.
Jacob v., 2 Moody & Rob. 221. §§ 80, 81, 89.
O'Howell v., 41 Mo. App. 523. § 29.
Sacramento v., 7 Cal. 419. § 386.
v. Sportsman, 48 Mo. 383. § 588.
Kirkham v. Marter, 2 Barn. & Ald. 613. § 54.
Kirkland, Smith v., 81 Ala. 345. § 402.
Kirkman v. Bank of America, 2 Cold. (Tenn.) 397. § 248.
Rice v., 3 Humph. (Tenn.) 415. § 616.
Kirkpatrick v. Gray, 43 Kan. 434. § 617.
v. Howk, 80 Ill. 122. §§ 426, 626.
Scully v., 79 Pa. St. 324. § 497.
United States v., 9 Wheat. 720. § 555.
Van Rensselaer v., 46 Barb. 194. § 355.
Kirksey, Crawford v., 55 Ala. 282. § 462.
Kiser v. State, 13 Tex. App. 201. § 495.
Kiser & Ullman v. State, 13 Tex. App. 201. § 509.
Kiso, Prior v., 51 Mo. 241. § 390.
Kitchens, Smith v., 51 Ga. 158. § 501.
Kiton v. Julian, 4 Ellis & Black. 854. § 169.
Kittredge, Ulen v., 7 Mass. 233. § 90.
Kittrell, Cates v., 7 Heisk. (Tenn.) 606. § 100.
Kittridge, McComb v., 14 Ohio, 348. § 354.
Kivett v. Young, 106 N. C. 568. § 594.
Klapp, Kleckner v., 2 Watts & Serg. (Pa.) 44. § 137.
Kleckner v. Klapp, 2 Watts & Serg. (Pa.) 44. § 137.
Klein v. Currier, 14 Ill. 237. §§ 176, 178.
v. Mather, 2 Gilman (Ill.), 317. § 288.
Kleinhaus v. Generous, 25 Ohio St. 667. § 349.
Kleinhoffer, Lafayette B'ld'g Ass'n v., 40 Mo. App. 388. §§ 601, 631.
Kleiser v. Scott, 6 Dana (Ky.), 137. § 322.
Klepper v. Borchsenius, 13 Bradw. (Ill. App.) 318. § 261.
Harsh v., 28 Ohio St. 200. § 379.
Kline v. Raymond, 70 Ind. 271. § 383.
Klingensmith, Bank v., 7 Watts (Pa.), 523. § 239.
v. Klingensmith's Ex'r, 31 Pa. St. 460. § 439.
Klink, Russell & Co. v., 53 Mich. 161. § 50.
Klose, Snyder v., 19 Pa. St. 235. § 405.
Klosterman v. Olcott, 25 Neb. 382. § 193.
Knapp v. Anderson, 7 Hun (N. Y.), 295. § 472.
Brewer v., 1 Pick. 332. § 108.
Pfeiffer v., 17 Fla. 144. §§ 342, 574.
v. Swaney, 56 Mich. 345. § 601.
Kneeland, People v., 31 Cal. 288. § 385.
Knepper v. Glenn, 73 Iowa, 730. § 526.
Kniffin, Morris v., 37 Barb. (N. Y.) 336. § 89.
Knight v. Charter, 22 W. Va. 422. § 438.
v. Crockford, 1 Esp. 190. § 89.
v. Fox, Morris (Iowa), 305. § 133.
v. Hughes, Moody & Mal. 247. § 283.
Humblen v., 60 Tex. 36. § 400.
v. Knight, 16 N. H. 107. § 184.
Mayor of Nashville v., 12 Lea (Tenn.), 700. §§ 371, 425, 524.
Phila. & R. R. Co. v., 124 Pa. St. 58. §§ 18, 99.
v. Whitehead, 26 Miss. 245. § 35.
Knighton v. Curry, 62 Ala. 404. §§ 298, 301, 320, 426, 430.
Knights, Holmes v., 10 N. H. 175. § 60.
Knipfer, Supervisors Kewaunee v., 37 Wis. 496. § 557.
Knoblauch v. Foglesong, 37 Minn. 320. § 329.

Knobloch v. Zschwetzke, 21 J. & S. (N. Y. Sup. Ct.) 391. § 37.
Knode v. Baldridge, 73 Ind. 54. § 622.
Knoebel v. Kircher, 33 Ill. 308. § 384.
Knopf v. Morel, 111 Ind. 570. §§ 29, 645.
Knotts, Bank v., 10 Rich. Law (S. C.), 543. §§ 143, 202.
v. Butler, 10 Rich. Eq. (S. C.) 143. §§ 133, 295.
Knowles v. Cuddeback, 19 Hun (N. Y.), 590. § 30.
Knowlton v. Hersey, 76 Me. 345. § 165.
Knox, Abercombie v., 3 Ala. 728. § 97.
Hayes v., 41 Mich. 529. § 446.
Hunt v., 34 Miss. 655. §§ 355, 376.
Jones v., 46 Ala. 53. § 150.
v. Kearns, 73 Iowa, 286. § 577.
Melick v., 44 N. Y. 676. § 130.
Shewell v., 1 Dev. Law (N. C.), 404. § 186.
v. Vallandingham, 13 Smedes & Mar. (Miss.) 526. § 265.
Knox Co. Bank v. Loyd's Adm'r, 18 Ohio St. 353. § 115.
Koch v. Coots, 43 Mich. 30. § 494.
v. Melh urn, 25 Pa. St. 89. § 102.
Kock v. Block, 29 Ohio St. 565. § 215.
Koenig v. Bramlett, 20 Mo. App. 636. § 199.
Koening v. Steckel, 58 N. Y. 475. § 332.
Kohn Bros. v. Washer, 69 Tex. 67. § 8.
Konitzky v. Meyer, 49 N. Y. 571. § 214.
Koontz, Nabb v., 17 Md. 283. §§ 88, 153.
Koppel, Wolff v., 2 Denio, 368. § 71.
Koppelkom, Huffman v., 8 Neb. 344. § 566.
v. Huffman, 12 Neb. 95. § 23.
Kountz v. Hart, 17 Ind. 329. § 379.
Kountze v. Omaha Hotel Co., 107 U. S. 378. § 452.
Kraft, Bockhoit v., 78 Iowa, 661. § 35.
Walters v., 23 S. C. 578. § 143.
Krall v. Libbey, 53 Wis. 292. § 460.
Kramer v. Farmers' & Mechanics' Bank, 15 Ohio, 253. § 224.
Farrar v., 5 Mo. App. 167. § 390.
Kramer & Rahm's Appeal, 37 Pa. St. 71. § 324.
Kramph's Ex'x v. Hutz's Ex'rs, 25 Pa. St. 525. §§ 1, 635.
Kreher v. Mason, 25 Mo. App. 291. § 599.
Kreheval, Farmers' & Mechanics' Bank v., 2 Mich. 504. § 360.
Kreider, Greenawalt v., 3 Pa. St. 264. § 240.
Kreitz, Hinckley v., 58 N. Y. 583. § 452.
Krieger, Lionberger v., 13 Mo. App. 313. § 168.
Lionberger v., 88 Mo. 160. §§ 395, 521, 537, 561, 642.
Kritzer v. Mills, 9 Cal. 21. § 29.
Krohne, Feiss & Co., Zurcher v., 63 Tex. 118. § 45.
Krug v. Bishop, 44 Ohio St. 221. §§ 476, 480.
Krutsinger v. Brown, 72 Ind. 466. § 648.
Kruttschnitt v. Hauck, 6 Nev. 163. § 543.
Kuhn v. Abat, 14 Martin (La.), 2 N. S. 168. § 120.
Jones v., 34 Kan. 414. §§ 88, 176.
Kuns' Ex'r v. Young, 34 Pa. St. 60. § 153.
Kupfer v. Spinhorst, 1 Kan. 75. § 618.
Kurtz v. Stewart, 54 Ind. 178. § 82.
Kurtzeborn, State v., 78 Mo. 98. §§ 168, 537.
Kusterer, Wetherbee v., 41 Mich. 359. § 98.
Kuykendall, Barickman v., 6 Blackf. (Ind.) 21. § 80.
Kyle v. Bostick, 10 Ala. 589. § 356.
v. Proctor, 7 Bush (Ky.), 493. § 389.
Kyner v. Kyner, 6 Watts (Pa.), 221. § 306.
La Farge v. Herter, 3 Denio, 157. § 40.

La Fargo *v.* Herter, 11 Barb. (N. Y.) 159. § 40.
La Roque, Russell *v.*, 11 Ala. 352. §§ 143, 222.
Russell *v.*, 13 Ala. 149. § 328.
La Rose *v.* Logansport National Bank, 102 Ind. 332. §§ 1, 106, 136, 420, 572.
La Vine, Jordan *v.*, 15 Oreg. 329. § 492.
Labadie *v.* Dean, 47 Tex. 90. § 480.
Labouchere, Wythes *v.*, 3 De Gex & Jones, 593. §§ 32, 419.
Lackey *v.* Steere, 121 Ill. 598. § 150.
Lacock, Campbell *v.*, 40 Pa. St. 448. § 48.
Laccste *v.* Splivalo, 64 Cal. 35. § 541.
Lacoume, Stewart *v.*, 30 La. Ann. 157. § 468.
Lacour, Gosseraud *v.*, 8 La. Ann. 75. § 350.
Lacy *v.* Lofton, 26 Ind. 324. § 182.
v. McNeile, 4 Dow. & Ry. 7. § 66.
v. Rollins, 74 Tex. 556. § 270.
Ladd *v.* Brewer, 17 Kan. 204. § 483.
v. Board of Trustees, 80 Ill. 233. § 406.
v. Parnell, 57 Cal. 232. § 615.
Lafarge *v.* Halsey, 1 Bosw. (N. Y.) 171. § 236.
Lafargue *v.* Harrison, 70 Cal. 380. § 81.
Lafayette Bank, Lonsdale *v.*, 18 Ohio, 126. §§ 116, 196.
Lafayette B'ld'g Ass'n *v.* Kleinhoffer, 40 Mo. App. 388. §§ 601, 631.
Lafayette Co. *v.* Hixon, 69 Mo. 581. § 428.
Lafayette Fire Ins. Co. *v.* Remmers, 30 La. Ann. 1347. § 460.
Lagow, Governor *v.*, 43 Ill. 134. §§ 371, 386.
Lahens, Fielden *v.*, 6 Blatchf. 524. § 550.
Pickersgill *v.*, 15 Wall. 140. §§ 94, 139.
Laing *v.* Lee, Spencer, 337. §§ 63, 82.
Tucker *v.*, 2 Kay & Johns. 745. §§ 246, 342.
Lainhart, Boswell *v.*, 2 La. (Miller), 297. § 519.
Lake *v.* Brutton, 8 De Gex, Macn. & Gor. 440. § 307.
Gillespie *v.*, 85 Cal. 402. § 595.
Town of Ashkum *v.*, 12 Bradw. (Ill. App.) 25. §§ 409, 517.
Williams *v.*, 2 Ell. & Ell. 349. § 81.
Lakeman, Mountstephen *v.*, 7 Q. B. 196. §§ 54, 56, 77, 78.
Lakin *v.* State, 89 Ind. 68. § 571.
Lalla Bunseedhur *v.* Bengal Government, 14 Moore's Indian Appeals, 86. § 542.
Lamar, Love *v.*, 78 Ga. 323. § 648.
Lamb *v.* Briggs, 22 Neb. 138. § 14.
Clark *v.*, 76 Ala. 406. § 570.
Colemard *v.*, 15 Wend. 327. § 398.
Rolfe *v.*, 16 Vt. 514. § 130.
Lambert, Eaton *v.*, 1 Neb. 339. § 212.
Fairbanks *v.*, 137 Mass. 373. § 472.
v. Shetler, 71 Iowa, 463. § 345.
v. Shilter, 62 Iowa, 72. § 351.
Lamberton *v.* Windom, 18 Minn. 506. § 440.
Lamkin, Planters' Bank *v.*, R. M. Charlton (Ga.), 29. § 423.
Lammon *v.* Fensier, 111 U. S. 17. §§ 566, 595.
Lamoille Co. Nat. Bank *v.* Bingham, 50 Vt. 105. § 235.
Lamonte *v.* Ward, 36 Wis. 558. § 491.
Lamp *v.* Smith, 56 Ga. 589. § 506.
Lampson *v.* Hobart, 28 Vt. 700. § 67.
Lamson *v.* First National Bank, 82 Ind. 21. § 375.
Lanahan *v.* Porter, 148 Mass. 596. § 469.
Lancaster, Stuart *v.*, 84 Va. 772. § 363.
Vance *v.*, 3 Haywood (Tenn.), 130. § 213.
Land, Pickett *v.*, 2 Bailey, Law (S. C.), 608. § 242.
Landers, McAlester *v.*, 70 Cal. 79. § 109.

Landis v. Curd, 63 Mo. 104. § 252.
York v., 65 N. C. 535. § 226.
Landrum v. Brookshire, 1 Stew. (Ala.) 252. § 211.
Lane, Barrows v., 5 Vt. 161. § 182.
Lane v. Burghart, 1 Adol. & Ell. (N. S.) 933. § 62.
Davis v., 10 N. H. 156. § 354.
Harrison v., 5 Leigh (Va.), 414. § 542.
v. Howell, 1 Lea (Tenn.), 275. § 371.
v. Kasey, 1 Met. (Ky.) 410. § 24.
v. Levillian, 4 Ark. (Pike), 76. § 201.
Portage Co. Branch Bank v., 8 Ohio St. 405. § 381.
Reed v., 61 Vt. 481. § 4.
Robinson v., 14 Sm. & Mar. (Miss.) 161. § 62.
v. Sleeper, 18 N. H. 209. § 218.
v. State, 27 Ind. 108. §§ 540, 626, 628.
v. Westmoreland, 79 Ala. 372. § 205.
Lane's Appeal, 112 Pa. St. 499. § 600.
Lane & Saylor v. Scott & Culver, 57 Tex. 367. § 378.
Lanfrom, Maher v., 86 Ill. 513. §§ 352, 355.
Lang v. Brevard, 3 Strob. Eq. (S. C.) 59. § 445.
Brown v., 4 Ala. 50. § 318.
v. Pike, 27 Ohio St. 498. §§ 93, 449.
Wright v., 66 Ala. 389. §§ 588, 642.
Langan v. Hewett, 3 Smedes & Marsh. 122. § 18.
Langdon, Convery v., 66 Ind. 311. § 226.
v. Gray, 22 Hun (N. Y.), 511. § 475.
Holloman v., 7 Jones' Law (N. C.), 49. § 539.
v. Markle, 48 Mo. 357. § 242.
Langford, Hindman v., 3 Strobh. (S. C.) 207. § 65.
Wilson v., 5 Humph. 320. § 356.
Langford's Ex'r v. Perrin, 5 Leigh (Va.), 552. § 263.
Langley v. Adams, 40 Me. 125. § 505.
Clements v., 2 Nev. & Man. 269. § 276.
Langpre v. White, 6 La. (Curry), 388. § 586.
Lanier v. Griffin, 11 S. C. 565. § 576.
Lank, Treasurers v., 2 Bailey, Law (S. C.), 430. § 172.
Lansdale v. Cox, 7 T. B. Mon. (Ky.) 401. § 254.
Lansing v. Wood, 57 Mich. 201. § 597.
Lanusse v. Barker, 3 Wheat. 101. § 134.
Lapham v. Barrett, 1 Vt. 247. § 84.
Chapin v., 20 Pick. 467. §§ 55, 58.
Laqueer, Prosser v., 4 Hill (N. Y.), 420. § 137.
Larabee, Robinson v., 58 Vt. 652. § 94.
Larabie, Barry v., 7 Mont. 179. § 599.
Laraway, West v., 28 Mich. 464. § 7.
Larehar, Bailey v., 5 R. I. 530. § 72.
Larendon, Daniels v., 49 Tex. 216. § 480.
Large v. Steer, 121 Pa. St. 30, 33, 34. § 477.
Lark, Wallace v., 12 S. C. 576. § 176.
Larrabee, Boardman v., 51 Conn. 39. § 343.
Larson v. Wyman, 14 Wend. 246. §§ 76, 78.
Lartigue v. Baldwin, 5 Martin (La.), O. S. 193. §§ 22, 630.
Lasher v. Williamson, 55 N. Y. 619. § 236.
Lassiter, Moore v., 16 Lea (Tenn.), 630. § 451.
Latham, Briggs v., 36 Kan. 205. § 13.
v. Brown, 16 Iowa, 118. § 563.
v. Fagan, 6 Jones' Law (N. C.), 62. § 538.
Lathrop v. Masterson, 44 Tex. 527. § 413.
Meyer v., 10 Hun (N. Y.), 66. § 37.

Lathrop, Walker *v.*, 6 Iowa (Clarke), 516. § 230.
Latouche *v.* Pallas, Hayes (Irish), 450. § 304.
Lattimore, Brown *v.*, 17 Cal. 93. § 539.
Laub *v.* Rudd, 37 Iowa, 617. § 114.
Laughlin *v.* Ferguson, 6 Dana (Ky.), 111. § 467.
Laughton, State *v.*, 19 Nev. 202. § 603.
Lauman *v.* Nichols, 15 Iowa, 161. § 32.
Laurason *v.* Mason, 3 Cranch, 492. § 81.
Laurens, Street *v.*, 5 Rich. Eq. (S. C.) 227. § 543.
Laurenson *v.* State, 7 Harr. & Johns. (Md.) 339. § 521.
Laval *v.* Rowley, 17 Ind. 36. § 312.
Lavell, Morrison *v.*, 81 Va. 519. § 587.
Law, Barry *v.*, 1 Cranch (C. C.), 77. § 89.
Briggs *v.*, 4 Johns. Ch. 22. § 405.
v. East India Company, 4 Vesey, 824. §§ 93, 427.
Lawrence, Dill *v.*, 109 Ind. 564. § 113.
v. Doolan, 68 Cal. 309. § 524.
v. McCalmont, 2 How. 426. §§ 13, 92.
Middlesex Mfg. Co. *v.*, 1 Allen, 339. § 171.
v. Taylor, 5 Hill, 107. § 90.
v. Walmsley, 12 J. Scott (N. R.), 799. §§ 362, 403.
Lawrenceville Mfg. Co., Howell *v.*, 31 Ga. 663. § 375.
Lawrie *v.* Scholefield, 4 Com. Pl. 622. § 160.
Lawson *v.* Buckley, 49 Hun (N. Y.), 329. § 241.
Fairlie *v.*, 5 Cow. 424. § 112.
Hughes *v.*, 31 Ark. 613. § 63.
Johnson *v.*, 29 Ill. App. 146. § 401.
Osborne *v.*, 26 Mo. App. 549. §§ 88, 199, 549.
v. Wright, 1 Cox, 275. § 290.
Lawson & Bro., Ordeman *v.*, 49 Md. 135. §§ 82, 85.
Lawton, Evans *v.*, 34 Fed. Rep. 233. § 382.
v. Maner, 9 Rich. Law (S. C.), 335. §§ 186, 204.
v. Maner, 10 Rich. Law (S. C.), 323. §§ 161, 362.
Lay, Deminey *v.*, 19 Mo. 646. § 604.
Lyman, Howe Sewing Machine Co. *v.*, 88 Ill. 39. § 394.
Laythoarp *v.* Bryant, 2 Bing. N. C. 755. § 89.
Lazarus, Gomez *v.*, 1 Dev. Eq. (N. C.) 205. § 322.
Lazear *v.* Nat'l Union Bank of Md., 52 Md. 78, 121. § 127.
Le Baron, United States *v.*, 19 How. 73. § 527.
Le Cerf, State *v.*, 1 Bailey Law (S. C.) 410. § 494.
Lea *v.* Dozier, 10 Humph. (Tenn.) 447. § 364.
v. McLennan, 7 Neb. 143. § 332.
Leach, Ambler *v.*, 15 W. Va. 677. § 438.
Enos *v.*, 18 Hun (N. Y.), 139. § 209.
Leadley *v.* Evans, 9 Moore, 102. § 168.
Leahey, Lewis *v.*, 14 Mo. App. 564. § 475.
Leak *v.* Covington, 99 N. C. 559. §§ 290, 295, 648.
Gatewood *v.*, 99 N. C. 357. § 648.
Leake *v.* Ferguson, 2 Gratt. (Va.) 419. § 308.
Lean, Dodge *v.*, 13 Johns. 508. § 81.
Learnan *v.* Sample, 91 Ind. 236. § 297.
Learned *v.* Wannemacher, 9 Allen, 412. § 80.
Leary *v.* Cheshire, 3 Jones' Eq. (N. C.) 170. § 268.
Leavitt, Bank of Steubenville *v.*, 5 Ohio, 208. § 372.
First National Bank *v.*, 65 Mo. 562. §§ 351, 363.
Lyon *v.*, 3 Ala. 430. § 417.
v. Savage, 16 Me. 72. § 374.
Lebanon Nat. Bank, Graves *v.*, 10 Bush (Ky.), 23. § 422.

Lecat v. Tavel, 3 McCord (S. C.), 158. §§ 82, 87.
Leckie v. Scott, 10 La. (5 Curry), 412. § 21.
Ledbetter, Bullard v., 59 Ga. 109. § 245.
v. Torney, 11 Ired. Law (N. C.), 294. § 208.
Ledoux v. Durrive, 10 La. Ann. 7. § 267.
Louisiana State Bank v., 3 La. Ann. 674. §§ 174, 242, 425.
Ledyard, Ohio Life Ins. Co. v., 8 Ala. 866. § 325.
Saint v., 14 Ala. 244. § 317.
Lee v. Baldwin, 10 Ga. 208. § 440.
v. Briggs, 39 Mich. 592. § 204.
v. Brown, 21 Kan. 458. § 628.
v. Clark, 1 Hill (N. Y.), 56. §§ 42, 126, 630.
Dawson v., 83 Ky. 49. § 214.
v. Dick, 10 Pet. 482. §§ 186, 188.
Dozier v., 7 Humph. (Tenn.) 520. § 30.
Felch v., 15 Wis. 265. § 336.
v. Fontaine, 10 Ala. 755. § 63.
v. Griffin, 31 Miss. 632. § 315.
v. Hastings, 13 Neb. 508. § 93.
v. Highland Bank, 2 Sandf. Ch. 311. § 415.
v. Hill, 83 Ky. 49. § 214.
v. Homer, 37 Hun (N. Y.), 634. § 473.
v. James, 150 Mass. 475. § 471.
v. Jones, 14 J. Scott (N. S.), 386. § 422.
Laing v., Spencer, 337. §§ 63, 82.
McDaniel v., 37 Mo. 204. § 279.
New London Bank v., 11 Conn. 112. §§ 252, 324.
People v., 104 N. Y. 441. § 159.
v. Rook, Moseley, 318. § 238.
v. Sewall, 2 La. Ann. 940. § 364.
v. State, 25 Tex. App. 331. §§ 495, 510.
v. State, 51 Miss. 665. § 501.
Sweet v., 3 Man. & Gr. 452. §§ 82, 89.
Tapp v., 3 Bos. & Pul. 367. § 73.
Lee v. Wisner, 38 Mich. 82. §§ 16, 205, 646.
v. Yandell, 69 Tex. 34. § 153.
Lee & Co., Lewis v., 73 Ala. 148. § 624.
v. Stowe, 57 Tex. 441. § 227.
v. Welsing, 70 Iowa, 198. § 385.
Leech v. Hill, 4 Watts (Pa.), 448. §§ 176, 182, 202.
v. Perry, 77 Ind. 422. § 487.
Leeds v. Dunn, 10 N. Y. 469. 123.
Leek, Parker v., 1 Stew. (Ala.) 523. § 209.
Leeman, O'Donnell v., 43 Me. 158. § 80.
Leeming v. Smith, 25 Grant's Ch. (Can.) 256. § 37.
Lees v. Whitcomb, 5 Bing. 34. § 85.
Leffingwell v. Freyer, 21 Wis. 392. §§ 34, 139.
Legette, Magee v., 48 Miss. 139. § 306.
Leggett v. Humphreys, 21 How. 66. § 112.
v. McClelland, 39 Ohio St. 624. § 270.
Leiberman, Pickering v. (Dist. Ct. Dist. Del.), 41 Fed. Rep. 376. § 307.
Leibshultz, Scheid v., 51 Ind. 38. § 26.
Leichner, Vogel v., 102 Ind. 55. §§ 29, 35.
Leigh v. Taylor, 7 Barn. & Cress. 491. § 528.
Leight, Fletcher v., 4 Bush (Ky.), 303. § 411.
Leitner, Aycock v., 29 Ga. 197. § 507.
Leland v. Creyon, 1 McCord (S. C.), 100. §§ 75, 78.
Neponset Bank v., 5 Met. (Mass.) 259. § 432.
Wood v., 1 Met. (Mass.) 387. § 295.
Lemayne v. Stanley, 3 Levinz, 1. § 89.
Lembe v. Routon, 33 La. Ann. 1005. § 468.
Lemmon v. Box, 20 Tex. 329. § 70.

Lemmon v. Strong, 59 Conn. 448. § 48.
v. Strong, 55 Conn. 443. §§ 98, 100, 101.
v. Whitman, 75 Ind. 318. § 356.
Lennon, Bright v., 83 N. C. 183. §§ 254, 257, 267, 283.
Lenox v. Prout, 3 Wheaton, 520. § 438.
Lentz, Commonwealth v., 106 Pa. St. 643. § 569.
Lenwell, Mendenhall v., 5 Blackf. (Ind.) 125. § 366.
Leonard, Cory v., 56 N. Y. 494. § 323.
v. County Court, 25 W. Va. 45. § 601.
Lumsden v., 55 Ga. 374. §§ 434, 447.
v. Mason, 1 Wend. 522. § 67.
Pryor v., 57 Ga. 136. § 129.
v. Speidel, 104 Mass. 356. § 470.
v. Sweetzer, 16 Ohio, 1. § 137.
v. Village of Gibson, 6 Bradw. (Ill. App.) 503. § 373.
v. Vredenburgh, 8 Johns. 29. §§ 13, 15, 17, 69, 82.
Leper, Williams v., 2 Wils. 308. §§ 63, 64, 66, 68.
Lerned v. Wannemacher, 9 Allen, 412. §§ 80, 89.
Leroux v. Brown, 12 Com. B. 801. § 52.
Lesher, Palethorpe v., 2 Rawle (Pa.), 272. § 493.
Leslie, Sill v., 16 Ind. 236. §§ 178, 182.
Letcher, Jones v., 13 B. Mon. (Ky.) 363. § 264.
Letcher's Adm'r v. Yantis, 3 Dana (Ky.), 160. § 613.
Leunig, Ratcliff v., 30 Ind. 289. § 143.
Levering, Rittenhouse v., 6 Watts & Serg. (Pa.) 190. §§ 307, 316.
Levi v. Earl, 30 Ohio St. 147. § 7.
v. Mendell, 1 Duvall (Ky.), 77. §§ 49, 176, 188, 199.
Shuttleworth v., 13 Bush (Ky.), 195. §§ 22, 508.
Levillian, Lane v., 4 Ark. (Pike), 76. § 201.
Levis, Dowden & Co. v., Irish, 14 Q. B. (C. P. & Ex.) 307. § 369.
Levy, Hampton v., 1 McCord, Eq. (S. C.) 107. §§ 30, 445.
Keel v., 19 Oreg. 450. § 237.
v. Merrill, 4 Greenl. 180. § 82.
v. Taylor, 24 Md. 282. § 480.
v. Wise, 15 La. Ann. 38. §§ 21, 642.
Levy Court, Ellicott v., 1 Harr. & Johns. (Md.) 359. § 523.
Lewellyn, Smeidel v., 3 Phila. 70. § 102.
Lewis v. Armstrong, 47 Ga. 289. §§ 426, 451.
v. Armstrong, 80 Ga. 402. § 426.
Beehervaise v., Law Rep. 7 Com. Pleas, 372. § 236.
v. Brackenridge, 1 Blackf. (Ind.) 112. § 504.
v. Bradley, 2 Ired Law (N. C.), 303. § 189.
v. Brewster, 2 McLean, 21. §§ 201, 203.
v. Board Comm'rs, 70 Ga. 486. §§ 408, 597.
Cake v., 8 Pa. St. 493. § 220.
Dozier v., 27 Miss. 679. § 301.
v. Dwight, 10 Conn. 95. §§ 112, 158.
Gage v., 68 Ill. 604. §§ 126, 200, 404.
v. Gambs, 6 Mo. App. 138. § 585.
Gilman v., 15 Me. 452. § 107.
v. Harbin, 5 B. Mon. (Ky.) 564. § 342.
v. Hoblitzell, 6 Gill & Johns. (Md.) 259. § 100.
v. Jones, 4 B. & C. 506. § 146.
v. Leahey, 14 Mo. App. 564. § 475.
v. Lee Co., 73 Ala. 148. § 624.
v. Lewis, 92 Ill. 237. § 225.
Manigay v., Irish Rep. 3 Com. Law, 495. §§ 362, 363.
Mersereau v., 25 Wend. 243. § 72.
Oxford Bank v., 8 Pick. 458. § 352.
v. Palmer, 28 N. Y. 271. § 315.
Ramsey v., 30 Barb. (N. Y.) 403. § 271.

Lewis v. Riggs, 9 Tex. 164. § 604.
v. State, 41 Miss. 686. § 498.
State v., 73 N. C. 138. §§ 42, 559.
Way v., 115 Mass. 26. § 632.
Wheeler v., 11 Vt. 265. §§ 100, 101.
Libbey, Krall v., 53 Wis. 292. § 460.
Libby v. Husby, 28 Minn. 40. § 615.
Libenguth, Moser v., 2 Rawle (Pa.), 428. § 141.
Lichten v. Mott, 10 Ga. 138. § 507.
Lichtenthaler v. Thompson, 13 Serg. & Rawle (Pa.), 157. § 239.
Lichtenwalner, Nat. Loan & B'ld'g Society v., 100 Pa. St. 100. §§ 101, 183.
Liddard, Stead v., 1 Bing. 196. §§ 84, 87.
Liddell v. Wiswell, 59 Vt. 365. §§ 276, 288.
Lidderdale v. Robinson, 2 Brock. 159. § 309.
Lidwell, State v., 11 Mo. App. 567. §§ 537, 546, 588.
Liebbrandt v. Myron Lodge, 61 Ill. 81. § 339.
Lieberman, Pickering v., 41 Fed. Rep. 376 (Dist. Ct. D. Del.). § 4.
Liebke, Thomas v., 81 Mo. 675. § 206.
Life Association v. Neville, 72 Ala. 517. §§ 339, 340.
Life Ass'n of America, Taylor v. (Cir. Ct. W. D. Tenn.), 3 Fed. Rep. 465. §§ 11, 592.
White's Adm'r v., 63 Ala. 419, 426. §§ 1, 339, 340, 342, 425.
Lightbound v. Warnock, 4 Ont. (Can.) 187. § 81.
Lightbown v. McMyn, Law Rep. 33 Ch. Div. 575. § 310.
Likens, McIntosh v., 25 Iowa, 555. § 111.
Lilley v. Hewitt, 11 Price, 494. § 91.
Lilly, Olcott v., 4 Johns. 407. § 497.
v. Roberts, 58 Ga. 363. §§ 431, 436.
Lime Rock Bank v. Mallett, 34 Me. 547. §§ 345, 351, 359.
v. Mallett, 42 Me. 349. §§ 29, 142.
Linch v. City of Litchfield, 16 Bradw. (Ill. App.) 612. § 529.
Lincoln, Merritt v., 21 Barb. 249. § 239.
Lindeman v. Rosenfield, 67 Ind. 246. §§ 342, 354.
Lindell Glass Co., Peckham v., 9 Mo. App. 459. § 599.
Lindley v. State, 17 Tex. App. 120. § 500.
Lindsay, Gull v., 4 Wels., Hurl. & Gor. 45. § 62.
v. Parkinson, 5 Irish Law Rep. 124. § 387.
Lindsey v. Reid, 101 Pa. St. 438. § 632.
Lindsley, Essex Freeholders v., 41 N. J. Eq. 189. § 219.
Lineberger, Comm'rs Jefferson Co. v., 3 Mont. 231. § 23.
First National Bank v., 83 N. C. 454. §§ 342, 376.
Linenschmidt, Peters v., 58 Mo. 464. § 608.
Ling, Wilmington, C. & A. R. R. Co. v., 18 S. C. 116. § 422.
Lining v. Giles' Ex'rs, 3 Brev. (S. C.) 530. § 578.
Lininger v. Raymond, 9 Neb. 40. § 481.
Linn v. McClelland, 4 Dev. & Batt. Law (N. C.), 458. § 293.
United States v., 2 McLean, 501. § 338.
Linn County v. Farris, 52 Mo. 75. § 412.
Linnell, Miles v., 97 Mass. 298. § 13.
Linnenfelser, Stagg v., 59 Mo. 336. § 176.
Linthorne, Rayner v., 2 Car. & P. 124. § 90.
Linton, Dwight v., 3 Rob. (La.) 57. §§ 182, 405.
Yongue v., 6 Rich. Law (S. C.), 275. § 253.
Linscott, Thompson v., 2 Greenl. (Me.) 186. § 229.
Linville, Cowgill v., 20 Mo. App. 138. § 318.

Lionberger *v.* Krieger, 13 Mo. App. 313. § 168.
v. Krieger, 88 Mo. 160. §§ 395, 521, 537, 561, 642.
Lipscomb *v.* Grace, 26 Ark. 231. § 220.
v. Postell, 38 Miss. 476. § 580.
Liquidators Oriental Financial Corporation, Liquidators Overend, Gurney & Co. *v.*, 7 Eng. & Irish App. Cas. 348. § 32.
Lisk *v.* Rosenberger, 82 Mo. 46. § 608.
Lisso & Scheen, Durham & Co. *v.*, 32 La. Ann. 415. § 10.
Litaker, Goodman *v.*, 84 N. C. 8. § 33.
Little, Cobb *v.*, 2 Greenl. (Me.) 261. § 102.
v. Commonwealth, 48 Pa. St. 337. § 128.
Cummings *v.*, 45 Me. 183. §§ 29, 33, 137.
v. Edwards, 69 Md. 499. §§ 88, 91.
Fraser *v.*, 13 Mich. 195. § 112.
Hayes *v.*, 52 Ga. 555. § 444.
v. Little, 13 Pick. 426. § 222.
v. Nabb, 10 Mo. 3. § 82.
Phila. & R. R. R. Co. *v.*, 41 N. J. Eq. 519. §§ 223, 435.
Vicksburg Bank *v.*, 67 Miss. 159. § 599.
Littlefield, Hughes *v.*, 18 Me. 400. § 127.
State *v.*, 4 Blackf. (Ind.) 129. § 562.
Littler *v.* Horsey, 2 Ohio, 209. § 616.
Singer Mfg. Co. *v.*, 56 Iowa, 601. §§ 106, 202.
Littleton *v.* State, 46 Ark. 413. §§ 504, 509.
Liversidge *v.* Broadbent, 4 Hurl. & Nor. 603. § 66.
Livingston *v.* Anderson, 80 Ga. 175. § 320.
Bank of N. Y. *v.*, 2 Johns. Cas. 409. § 102.
Livingstone *v.* Van Rensselaer, 6 Wend. 63. § 268.
Lloyd, Bullock *v.*, 2 Car. & P. 119. § 60.
Lloyd, Gardner *v.*, 110 Pa. St. 278. § 191.
Montefiore *v.*, 15 J. Scott (N. S.), 203. § 118.
North British Ins. Co. *v.*, 10 Wels., Hurl. & Gor. 523. § 419.
Wilson *v.*, Law Rep. 16 Eq. Cas. 60. §§ 36, 376.
Lloyds *v.* Harper, Law Rep. (16 Ch. Div.) 290. § 133.
Lobaugh *v.* Thompson, 74 Mo. 600. § 153.
Lobb *v.* Stanley, 5 Q. B. 574. § 89.
Lochenmeyer *v.* Fogarty, 112 Ill. 572. § 329.
Lock *v.* Reid, 6 Up. Can. Q. B. (O. S.) 295. § 88.
Lockard's Adm'r, Jenkins *v.*, 66 Ala. 377. §§ 293, 294.
Locke, Green *v.*, 31 La. Ann. 656. § 602.
v. McVean, 33 Mich. 473. §§ 92, 123.
Trefethen *v.*, 16 La. Ann. 19. § 204.
Lockett, Drew *v.*, 32 Beav. 499. § 316.
Lockhart, State *v.*, 24 Ga. 420. § 509.
Locknane *v.* Emmerson, 11 Bush (Ky.), 69. § 379.
Lochrane *v.* Solomon, 38 Ga. 286. § 441.
Lockridge *v.* Upton, 24 Mo. 184. § 605.
Lockwood, McCoy *v.*, 71 Ind. 319. § 608.
Thompson *v.*, 15 Johns. 256. § 504.
Lodge, Heard *v.*, 20 Pick. 53. § 638.
Loehner *v.* Hill, 17 Mo. App. 32. §§ 475, 480.
Loehr *v.* Colburn, 92 Ind. 24. § 324.
Loew *v.* Stocker, 68 Pa. St. 226. § 151.
Loftin, Jordin *v.*, 13 Ala. 547. § 402.
Lofton, Lacy *v.*, 26 Ind. 324. § 182.
Logan, Adams *v.*, 27 Gratt. (Va.) 201. §§ 366, 431, 436.
Gregory *v.*, 7 Blackf. (Ind.) 112. § 82.

Logan, Greeulaw v., 2 Lea (Tenn.), 185. § 481.
v. Mitchell, 67 Mo. 524. § 329.
Logansport Nat. Bank, La Rose v., 102 Ind. 332. §§ 1, 106, 136, 420, 572.
Loh v. Judge of Wayne Circuit, 26 Mich. 186. § 615.
Lohman, Taylor v., 74 Ind. 418. §§ 245, 332, 419.
Lombard v. Cobb, 14 Me. 222. § 291.
v. Mayberry, 24 Neb. 674. § 412.
Lomne v. Sweeney, 1 Mont. 584. § 486.
London Assurance Co. v. Bold, 6 Adol. & Ell. (N. S.) 514. § 118.
London & County Banking Co. v. Terry, Law Rep. (25 Ch. Div.) 692. § 118.
London Dock Co., Calvert v., 2 Keen, 638. § 397.
London G. & A. Ins. Co., Fearnley v., Irish Law Rep. (6 Q. B., C. P. & Ex. Div.) 219. § 423.
London & Provincial Ins. Co., Davies v., Law Rep. 8 Ch. Div. 469. § 419.
Louey, Perley v., 17 Up. Can. (Q. B.) 279. § 29.
Long v. Crosson, 119 Ind. 3. § 45.
James v., 68 N. C. 218. § 148.
Hassell v., 2 Maule & Sel. 363. § 167.
v. Miller, 93 N. C. 227. §§ 324, 333.
Morgan v., 29 Iowa, 434. § 531.
Owen v., 112 Mass. 403. § 4.
Reherd v., 77 Va. 839. § 583.
v. Seay, 72 Mo. 648. §§ 168, 537.
State v., 8 Ired. Law (N. C.), 415. § 565.
v. Templeman, 24 La. Ann. 564. § 144.
v. United States Bank, 1 Freeman's Ch. 375. § 467.
Longan v. Taylor, 130 Ill. 412. § 628.
Longden, Anderson v., 1 Wheat. 85. § 538.
Longley v. Griggs, 10 Pick. 121. § 260.
Lonsdale v. Brown, 4 Wash. 148. § 16.
v. Lafayette Bank, 18 Ohio, 126. §§ 116, 196.
Loomer v. Wheelwright, 3 Sandf. Ch. 135. § 35.
Loomis v. Newhall, 15 Pick. 159. §§ 57, 63.
Rice v., 139 Mass. 302. § 108.
Looney v. Hughes, 26 N. Y. 514. § 555.
Loop v. Summers, 3 Rand. (Va.) 511. § 426.
Looper, Turman v., 42 Ark. 500. § 215.
Loosemore v. Radford, 9 Mees. & Wels. 657. § 221.
Lord, Bulkeley v., 2 Stark. 406. § 127.
v. Staples, 23 N. H. 448. § 211.
Warren v., 131 Mass. 560. § 469.
Lord Arlington v. Merricke, 2 Saund. 403. § 166.
Lord Bolton v. Tomlin, 5 Adol. & Ell. 856. § 52.
Lord Haberton v. Bennett, Beatty, 386. §§ 34, 429.
Lord Talbot, Minnitt v., Law Rep. Irish (1 Ch. Div.), 143. § 232.
Loring, Fuller v., 42 Me. 48. § 332.
Moore v., 106 Mass. 455. § 473.
Sohier v., 6 Cush. 537. § 376.
Los Angeles v. Mellus, 59 Cal. 444. §§ 385, 603.
Losen, Hofheimer v., 24 Mo. App. 652. § 199.
Losey, Post, Adm'r, v., 111 Ind. 74. §§ 35, 150.
Lossee v. Williams, 6 Lans. 228. § 17.
Lothrop v. Southworth, 5 Mich. 436. § 640.
Lott, Burroughs v., 19 Cal. 125. § 288.
Loucks, Saltenberry v., 8 La. Ann. 95. § 528.
Loud, Shaw v., 12 Mass. 447. § 214.
Lougee, National Pemberton Bank v., 108 Mass. 371. § 178.
Loughridge v. Bowland, 52 Miss. 546. § 207.

Louis, Eckert *v.* 84 Ind. 99. § 382.
Louisiana State Bank *v.* Ledoux, 3 La. Ann. 674. §§ 174, 242, 425.
v. Orleans Navigation Company, 3 La. Ann. 294. § 5.
Louisville Banking Co., Wooley *v.*, 81 Ky. 527. §§ 401, 440.
Louisville, C. & L. R. R. Co., Pollard *v.*, 7 Bush (Ky.), 597. § 624.
Louisville Mfg. Co. *v.* Welch, 10 How. 461. §§ 123, 202, 203.
Louisville & Nashville R. Co., Phenix Ins. Co. *v.* (Cir. Ct. E. D. N. Y.), 8 Fed. Rep. 142. § 106.
Love, City of Keokuk *v.*, 31 Iowa, 119. §§ 301, 306, 318.
v. Keowne, 58 Tex. 191. § 544.
v. Lamar, 78 Ga. 323. § 648.
Rollins *v.*, 97 N. C. 210. § 460.
Ruffner *v.*, 9 Rich. Law (S. C.), 335. § 204.
Lovejoy, Shriver *v.*, 32 Cal. 574. § 29.
Loveland *v.* Shepard, 2 Hill (N. Y.), 139. § 100.
Lovell, Bellows *v.*, 5 Pick. 307. § 437.
Smith *v.*, 2 Mont. 332. § 562.
Loveman *v.* Taylor, 85 Tenn. (Pickle), 1. §§ 586, 642.
Love's Case, 1 Salk. 28. §§ 64, 65, 72.
Lovett *v.* Adams, 3 Wend. 380. § 403.
Lovinger *v.* First National Bank, 81 Ind. 354. § 412.
Low *v.* Anderson, 41 Iowa, 476. § 7.
Marsh *v.*, 55 Ind. 271. § 185.
Osborn *v.*, 40 Ohio St. 347. §§ 351, 356.
v. Smart, 5 N. H. 353. § 268.
Stafford *v.*, 16 Johns. 67. § 191.
Stafford *v.*, 20 Ill. 152. § 504.
Lowe *v.* Beckwith, 14 B. Mon. (Ky.) 150. §§ 157, 192, 197.
Burdett *v.*, 22 Hun (N. Y.), 588. § 452.
Jackson *v.*, 1 Bing. 9. § 80.
Kimmel *v.*, 28 Minn. 265. § 205.
Lowell, Chase *v.*, 7 Gray, 33. § 80.
Lowen *v.* Buchanan Bank, 78 Mo. 67. § 434.
Lowenberg, Jno. Hancock Mut. Life Ins. Co. *v.*, 120 N. Y. 44. § 602.
Lowing, Greenlee *v.*, 35 Mich. 63. § 486.
Lowndes *v.* Chisholm, 2 McCord, Eq. (S. C.) 455. § 303.
Duncan *v.*, 3 Camp. 478. § 18.
v. Pinckney, 1 Rich. Eq. (S. C.) 155. § 267.
v. Pinckney, 2 Strob. Eq. (S. C.) 44. § 249.
Reade *v.*, 23 Beav. 361. § 39.
Lowry *v.* Adams, 22 Vt. 160. §§ 116, 203, 204.
v. Lumbermen's Bank, 2 Watts & Serg. (Pa.) 210. § 208.
v. McKinney, 68 Pa. St. 294. § 34.
v. Smith, 97 Ind. 466. § 594.
v. State, 64 Ind. 421. § 526.
Lowther, Farwell *v.*, 18 Ill. 252. § 81.
Loyd *v.* McTeer, 33 Ga. 37. § 504.
Loyd's Adm'r, Knox Co. Bank *v.*, 18 Ohio St. 353. § 115.
Lucas, Barclay *v.*, 1 Durn. & East, 291. § 121.
v. Chamberlain, 8 B. Mon. (Ky.) 276. § 60.
v. Curry's Ex'rs, 2 Bailey, Law (S. C.), 403. § 580.
Farmers' & Traders' Bank *v.*, 26 Ohio St. 385. §§ 342, 407.
v. Governor, 6 Ala. 826. § 636.
v. Guy, 2 Bailey, Law (S. C.), 403. § 293.
v. Owens, 113 Ind. 521. § 406.
v. Payne, 7 Cal. 92. § 63.
People *v.*, 93 N. Y. 585. § 566.
v. White Line Transfer Co., 70 Iowa, 541. §§ 44, 259.
Lucas Co. *v.* Roberts, 49 Iowa, 159. § 426.
Luck, Thompson *v.*, 3 Man., Gr. & Scott, 540. § 439.
Lucking's Adm'r *v.* Gegg, 12 Bush (Ky.), 298. § 215.

Lucy, Routon's Adm'r *v.*, 17 Mo. 399. §§ 605, 613.
v. Wilkins, 33 Minn. 21. § 1.
Luddington, Forrest's Ex'rs *v.*, 68 Ala. 1. § 326.
Ludewig, Warfield *v.*, 9 Rob. (La.) 240. § 342.
Ludington, Gillilan *v.*, 6 W. Va. 128. §§ 606, 609.
Ludlow *v.* Simond, 2 Caines' Cases in Error, 1. §§ 93, 397.
Ludwick *v.* Watson, 3 Oreg. 256. § 17.
Lukens, Hitchcock *v.*, 8 Port. (Ala.) 333. § 63.
Lumber Co. *v.* Buchtel, 101 U. S. 633. § 414.
Lumbermen's Bank, Lowry *v.*, 2 Watts & Serg. (Pa.) 210. § 208.
Lumbermen & Mechanics' Ins. Co., Harrison *v.*, 8 Mo. App. 37. §§ 421, 555.
Lumgston, Irby *v.*, 81 Ga. 281. § 320.
Lumpkin *v.* Mills, 4 Ga. 343. § 313.
Lumsden *v.* Leonard, 55 Ga. 374. §§ 434, 447.
Luna, Murray *v.*, 86 Tenn. (2 Pick.) 326. § 585.
Luqueer *v.* Prosser, 1 Hill, 256. § 179.
Lusby *v.* Carr, Ex'r, 60 Md. 192. § 281.
Luse, Case *v.*, 28 Iowa, 527. § 103.
Lutch, Wybrants *v.*, 24 Tex. 309. § 369.
Lutt *v.* Sterrett, 26 Kan. 561. § 449.
Lydall, Bardwell *v.*, 7 Bing. 489. § 330.
Lyde *v.* Barnard, Tyrwh. & Gr. 250. § 73.
Lyle, Robinson *v.*, 10 Barb. (N. Y.) 512. § 261.
Lyman, Horner *v.*, 4 Keyes (N. Y.), 237. § 453.
Mallory *v.*, 3 Pinney (Wis.), 443. § 199.
v. Sherwood, 20 Vt. 42. § 114.
Lynch *v.* Colegate, 2 H. & J. (Md.) 34. § 403.
Lynch, Egan *v.*, 17 J. & S. (N. Y. Super. Ct.) 454. § 10.
v. Hancock, 14 S. C. 66. §§ 211, 226, 329.
Lyndon *v.* Miller, 36 Vt. 329. § 521.
Lyon *v.* Bolling, 9 Ala. 463. § 310.
v. Horner, 32 W. Va. 432. § 571.
Hotchkiss *v.*, 2 Blackf. (Ind.) 222. § 624.
v. Leavitt, 3 Ala. 430. § 417.
v. Osgood, 58 Vt. 707. § 586.
Strong *v.*, 63 N. Y. 172. § 397.
Wadsworth *v.*, 93 N. Y. 201. § 34.
v. Wilder, 24 J. & S. (N. Y. Super. Ct.) 67. § 10.
Lyons *v.* Miller, 6 Gratt. (Va.) 427. § 28.
Young *v.*, 8 Gill (Md.), 162. §§ 288, 291, 292.
Lysaght *v.* Walker, 5 Bligh (N. R.), 1. §§ 84, 86, 331, 627.
Lytle's Ex'rs *v.* Pope's Adm'r, 11 B. Mon. (Ky.) 297. § 287.
Lyttle *v.* Cozard, 21 W. Va. 183. § 408.
Mabbett, Ætna Life Ins. Co. *v.*, 18 Wis. 667. § 422.
Macdonald *v.* Bell, 3 Moore's Priv. Co. Cas. 315. § 448.
Donar *v.*, 3 H. of L. Cases, 226. § 393.
Macdougal, Inglis *v.*, 1 Moore, 196. § 150.
Mace *v.* Wells, 7 How. 272. § 220.
Macey *v.* Childress, 2 Tenn. Ch. (Cooper), 438. §§ 61, 91.
Macgregor, Thomson *v.*, 81 N. Y. 592. § 526.
Machardo *v.* Fernandez, 74 Cal. 362. § 293.
Mack *v.* Sloteman (Cir. Ct. E. D. Wis.), 21 Fed. Rep. 109. § 601.
Mackenzie *v.* Scott, 6 Bro. Parl. Cas. 280. § 71.
Mackey *v.* Dodge, 5 Ala. 388. § 119.
Macklin *v.* Northern Bank of Kentucky, 83 Ky. 314. § 327.
Mackrell, Holmes *v.*, 3 Com. B. (N. S.) 789. § 89.

Maclay, Ames *v.*, 14 Iowa, 281. § 149.
Maclean *v.* Dunn, 4 Bing. 722. § 90.
Maclure, Yorkshire Railway Wagon Co. *v.*, Law Rep. (19 Ch. Div.) 478. § 6.
Macomb, Campbell *v.*, 4 Johns. Ch. 534. § 223.
Macon & Brunswick R. R. Co., Branch *v.*, 2 Woods, 385. § 324.
Macon Savings Bank, Moore *v.*, 22 Mo. App. 684. § 378.
Macready & Burke *v.* Schenck, 41 La. Ann. 456. § 631.
Macrory *v.* Scott, 5 Wels., Hurl. & Gor. 907. §§ 68, 70.
Madden, McGlothlin *v.*, 16 Kan. 466. § 231.
 Rose *v.*, 1 Kan. 445. §§ 31, 618.
 v. State, 35 Kan. 146. §§ 516, 644.
Maddox, McDougald *v.*, 32 Ga. 63. § 544.
 v. Rader, 9 Mont. 126. §§ 112, 571.
Madesker, Parker *v.*, 80 Ind. 155. § 526.
Madgett *v.* Fleenor, 90 Ind. 517. § 226.
Madigan, Gunn *v.*, 28 Wis. 158. § 107.
Magee *v.* Legette, 48 Miss. 139. § 306.
 v. Manhattan Life Ins. Co., 92 U. S. 93, 98. §§ 93, 561.
 v. McManus, 70 Cal. 553. § 329.
Maggs *v.* Ames, 4 Bing. 470. § 62.
Magill, Bank of United States *v.*, 1 Paine, 661. § 396.
Magness, Reynolds *v.*, 2 Ired. Law (N. C.), 26. § 513.
Magnin, Commissioners of Wake *v.*, 78 N. C. 186. § 597.
Magruder *v.* Admire, 4 Mo. App. 133. §§ 288, 295.
 Aud *v.*, 10 Cal. 282. §§ 29, 177.
Mahaska County *v.* Ruan, 45 Iowa, 328. § 559.
Maher *v.* Lanfrom, 86 Ill. 513. §§ 352, 355.
Mahin, Bell *v.*, 69 Iowa, 408. §§ 382, 384.
Mahon, State *v.*, 3 Harr. (Del.) 568. § 496.
Mahurin *v.* Pearson, 8 N. H. 539. § 245.
Main, Boice *v.*, 4 Denio, 55. § 570.
Maingay *v.* Lewis, Irish Rep. 3 Com. Law, 495. §§ 362, 363.
Mains *v.* Haight, 14 Barb. (N. Y.) 76. §§ 98, 101.
Mallet *v.* Bateman, Law Rep. 1 C. P. 163. §§ 74, 75.
Mallett, Lime Rock Bank *v.*, 34 Me. 547. §§ 29, 345, 351, 359.
 Lime Rock Bank *v.*, 42 Me. 349. § 142.
Malling Union *v.* Graham, Law Rep. 5 Com. Pl. 201. § 395.
Mallory *v.* Gillett, 21 N. Y. 412. §§ 59, 64.
 v. Lyman, 3 Pinney (Wis.), 443. § 199.
Malone, Cordaman *v.*, 63 Ala. 556. § 487.
 v. Crescent City M. & T. Co., 77 Cal. 38. § 165.
 David *v.*, 48 Ala. 428. § 342.
 Gravett *v.*, 54 Ala. 19. §§ 630, 640.
 Stewart *v.*, 5 Phila. 440. § 67.
Manchester Iron Manuf. Co. *v.* Sweeting, 10 Wend. 163. § 239.
Mandigo *v.* Mandigo, 26 Mich. 349. § 218.
 Pashby *v.*, 42 Mich. 172. § 226.
Mandel, Rosendorf *v.*, 18 Nev. 129. § 589.
Mandlee, Tricket *v.*, Sid. 45. § 16.
Maner, Lawton *v.*, 10 Rich. Law (S. C.), 323. §§ 161, 186, 362.
Manford *v.* Firth, 68 Ind. 83. § 313.
Manhattan Co., Magee *v.*, 92 U. S. 93. § 561.
Manhattan Ins. Co. *v.* Ellis, 32 Ohio St. 388. § 425.
Manhattan Gas Light Co. *v.* Ely, 39 Barb. (N. Y.) 174. § 118.
Manhattan Life Ins. Co., Magee *v.*, 92 U. S. 93, 98. § 93.

Manisty *v.* Churchill, Law Rep. (39 Ch. Div.) 174. § 320.
Manker, Berryman *v.*, 56 Iowa, 150. § 380.
Manley *v.* Boycot. § 29.
v. City of Atchison, 9 Kan. 358. § 557.
Simpson *v.*, 2 Cromp. & Jer. 12. § 418.
Mann *v.* Blanchard, 2 Allen, 386. § 73.
v. Brown, 71 Tex. 241. § 356.
Dye *v.*, 10 Mich. 291. § 209.
v. Eckford's Ex'rs, 15 Wend. 502. § 199.
v. Everts, 64 Wis. 372. § 583.
Massie *v.*, 17 Iowa, 131. § 303.
State *v.*, 21 Wis. 684. § 566.
Thomas *v.*, 28 Pa. St. 520. § 240.
Wells *v.*, 45 N. Y. 327. § 17.
Witherby *v.*, 11 Johns. 518. § 511.
Wood *v.*, 125 Mass. 319. § 469.
v. Yazoo City, 31 Miss. 574. § 628.
Manning, Bell *v.*, 11 Grant's Ch. 142. § 147.
v. Gould, 90 N. Y. 476. § 486.
Horton *v.*, 37 Tex. 23. § 176.
v. Mills, 12 Up. Can. (Q. B.) 515. § 116.
Mannon, Anderson *v.*, 7 B. Mon. 217. § 356.
Manrow, Durham *v.*, 2 N. Y. 533. § 67.
v. Durham, 3 Hill, 584. § 88.
Mansfield *v.* Edwards, 136 Mass. 15. §§ 261, 289.
Phipps *v.*, 62 Ga. 209. § 219.
Manser, Hill *v.*, 11 Gratt. (Va.) 522. § 310.
Manufacturers' Bank *v.* Billings, 17 Pick. 87. § 339.
v. Cole, 39 Me. 188. § 115.
v. Dickerson, 41 N. J. Law, 448. § 548.
Manufacturers' & Mechanics' Bank *v.* Bank of Pennsylvania, 7 Watts & Serg. 335. § 40.
v. Follett, 11 R. I. 92. § 383.
Manufacturing Co. *v.* Worster, 45 N. H. 110. § 632.
Maples *v.* Cox, 74 Ga. 701. § 215.
v. Sidney, Cro. Jac. 683. § 16.
v. Wightman, 4 Conn. 376. § 4.
Marberger *v.* Pott, 16 Pa. St. 9. § 183.
Marbourg, National Bank *v.*, 22 Kan. 535. § 98.
Marbury, Somerville *v.*, 7 Gill & Johns. (Md.) 275. § 437.
March *v.* Putney, 56 N. H. 34. §§ 199, 202.
Marchant, Hawes *v.*, 1 Curtis, 136. § 12.
Marchman *v.* Robertson, 77 Ga. 41. § 401.
Marcy *v.* Crawford, 16 Conn. 549. § 60.
v. Praeger, 34 La. Ann. 54. § 175.
Marden, Anstey *v.*, 1 Bos. & Pul. N. R. 124. § 65.
Thornburgh *v.*, 33 Iowa, 380. § 245.
Margaritz, Hinely *v.*, 3 Pa. St. 428. § 4.
Marine Bank, Ingraham *v.*, 13 Mass. 208. § 547.
Mariner's Bank *v.* Abbott, 28 Me. 280. §§ 29, 352.
Marion *v.* Faxon, 20 Conn. 486. § 74.
Markell *v.* Eichelberger, 12 Md. 78. § 218.
Markland Mining & Mfg. Co. *v.* Kimmel, 87 Ind. 560, 566. §§ 1, 93, 411.
Markle, Langdon *v.*, 48 Mo. 357. § 242.
Pardee *v.*, 111 Pa. St. 548. § 331.
Marks, Airns *v.*, 3 Lea (Tenn.), 568. § 603.
v. First National Bank, 79 Ala. 550. § 409.
Sterns *v.*, 35 Barb. (N. Y.) 565. § 118.
Marks' Sureties, United States *v.*, 3 Wall. Jr. 358. § 617.
Marlar *v.* State, 62 Miss. 77. § 555.
Marney, Allen *v.*, 65 Ind. 398. § 411.
Marple, Hurd *v.*, 2 Bradw. (Ill. App.) 402. §§ 342, 343.
Marrett, Andrews *v.*, 58 Me. 539. § 363.

Marsdon, Clifford *v.*, 14 Oreg. 426. § 509.
Marsh, Baxter *v.*, 1 Yerg. (Tenn.) 460. § 516.
Bray *v.*, 75 Me. 452. §§ 49, 184.
v. Consolidation Bank, 48 Pa. St. 510. §§ 29, 60.
v. Day, 18 Pick. 321. § 126.
v. Dunckel, 25 Hun (N. Y.), 167. § 239.
Forward *v.*, 18 Ala. 645. § 565.
French *v.*, 29 Wis. 649. § 98.
v. Griffin, 42 Iowa, 403. § 379.
Hare *v.*, 61 Wis. 435. § 453.
v. Low, 55 Ind. 271. § 185.
Pace *v.*, 1 Bing. 216. § 84.
v. Pike, 1 Sandf. Ch. 210. § 37.
v. Pike, 10 Paige's Ch. 595. § 302.
Sandilands *v.*, 2 Barn. & Ald. 673. § 18.
v. Thompson National Bank, 2 Bradw. (Ill. App.) 217. § 19.
Marshall *v.* Aiken, 25 Vt. 249. § 40.
v. Dixon, 82 Ga. 435. § 351.
Executors of Baker *v.*, 16 Vt. 522. § 437.
Gold *v.*, 76 Va. 668. § 524.
Martin *v.*, 60 Vt. 321. § 182.
McNairy *v.*, 7 Humph. (Tenn.) 229. § 557.
Murray *v.*, 94 N. Y. 611. § 37.
Williams *v.*, 42 Barb. (N. Y.) 524. §§ 17, 151.
Wilson *v.*, 15 Irish Com. Law Rep. 466. § 79.
Marshall, First Nat. Bank of, Inkster *v.*, 30 Mich. 143. § 242.
Marston, Richmond *v.*, 15 Ind. 134. § 298.
v. Sweet, 66 N. Y. 207. § 91.
Martel, Denil *v.*, 10 La. Ann. 643. § 347.
State *v.*, 3 Rob. (La.) 22. § 501.
Marter, Kirkham *v.*, 2 Barn. & Ald. 613. § 54.
Martien, Morgan *v.*, 32 Mo. 438. § 367.
Martin, Bibb *v.*, 14 Sm. & Mar. (Miss.) 87. § 326.
v. Black's Ex'rs, 20 Ala. 309. § 61.
Martin, Boutte *v.*, 16 La. (Curry), 133. § 242.
v. Boyd, 11 N. H. 385. § 180.
Bresendine *v.*, 1 Ired. Law (N. C.), 286. § 286.
Brockett *v.*, 11 Kan. 378. § 563.
Cooper *v.*, 1 Dana (Ky.), 23. § 268.
Dey *v.*, 78 Va. 1. § 388.
v. Ellerbee's Adm'r, 70 Ala. 326. §§ 205, 207, 341, 579.
v. England, 5 Yerg. (Tenn.) 313. § 74.
Farris *v.*, 10 Humph. (Tenn.) 495. § 89.
v. Frantz, 127 Pa. St. 389. § 295.
Garr *v.*, 20 N. Y. 306. § 251.
Gibson *v.*, 7 Humph. (Tenn.) 127. § 616.
Good *v.*, 17 Am. Law Reg. 111. § 182.
Good *v.*, 95 U. S. 90. §§ 180, 181.
Gordon *v.*, Fitzgibbon, 302. § 77.
Hausen *v.*, 63 Cal. 282. § 462.
v. Hazard Powder Co., 2 Col. 596. § 84.
Howes *v.*, 1 Esp. 162. §§ 60, 68.
Jarrett *v.*, 70 N. C. 459. § 145.
v. Kibourn, 1 Cent. Law Jour. 94. § 472.
v. Kilbourn, 12 Heisk. (Tenn.) 331. § 472.
McArthur *v.*, 23 Minn. 74. § 298.
v. Marshall, 60 Vt. 321. § 182.
v. Mechanics' Bank, 6 Harr. & Johns. (Md.) 235. § 432.
v. Mitchell, 2 Jacob & Walk. 413. § 89.
Nowland *v.*, 1 Ired. Law (N. C.), 307. § 286.
Overturf *v.*, 2 Ind. (2 Carter), 507. §§ 606, 612.
Patterson *v.*, 7 Ohio, 225. § 218.
v. Pope, 6 Ala. 532. § 330.
Sample *v.*, 46 Ind. 226. § 183.
v. Seeley, 15 Neb. 136. § 570.
v. Shekan, 2 Col. 614. § 239.
Smith *v.*, 4 Des. Eq. (S. C.) 148. § 139.
v. Tally, 72 Ala. 23. §§ 588, 632.

Martin, Tapley v., 116 Mass. 275. § 422.
v. Taylor, 8 Bush (Ky.), 384. § 434.
v. Thomas, 24 How. 315. § 385.
v. Walker, 12 Hun (N. Y.), 46. §§ 226, 322.
Williams v., 2 Duvall (Ky.), 491. § 365.
Wilson v., 74 Pa. St. 159. § 88.
v. Wright, 6 Adol. & Ell. (N. S.) 917. § 157.
Martinnant, Toussaint v., 2 Durn. & East, 100. § 205.
Martz, Morin v., 13 Minn. 191. §§ 72, 89.
Marvil, Redmau v., 73 Ind. 593. § 140.
Marvin, Bradford, Adm'r, v., 2 Fla. 463. § 316.
Henderson v., 31 Barb. (N. Y.) 297. § 123.
Morrison v., 6 Ala. 797. § 312.
Marx v. State, 61 Miss. 478. § 509.
Maryatts v. White, 2 Starkie, 101. § 331.
Mascall, Walton v., 13 Mees. & Wels. 452. §§ 199, 201.
Maseman, Kenney v., 14 Daly (N. Y. Com. Pl.), 379. § 199.
Maskell v. Eichelberger, 12 Md. 78. § 224.
Mason v. Burton, 54 Ill. 349. § 182.
Chichester v., 7 Leigh (Va.), 244. § 444.
v. Dousay, 35 Ill. 424. § 67.
Hamner v., 24 Ala. 480. § 575.
Heralson v., 53 Mo. 211. § 100.
Howe v., 12 Iowa, 202. § 562.
Kreher v., 25 Mo. App. 291. § 599.
Laurason v., 3 Cranch, 492. § 81.
Leonard v., 1 Wend. 522. § 67.
McWilliams v., 31 N. Y. 294. § 115.
v. Nichols, 22 Wis. 576. § 145.
v. Pierron, 69 Wis. 585. §§ 226, 293, 297.
v. Pritchard, 12 East, 227. §§ 92, 160.
v. Richards, 12 Iowa, 73. § 483.
Mason, United States v., 2 Bond, 183. § 520.
Masser v. Strickland, 17 Serg. & Rawle (Pa.), 354. § 636.
Massie v. Mann, 17 Iowa, 131. § 305.
Thompson v., 41 Ohio St. 307. § 378.
Mast & Co., Mowery v., 9 Neb. 445. §§ 137, 179.
Masterson, Lathrop v., 44 Tex. 527. § 413.
Mateer, Driskell v., 31 Mo. 325. § 246.
Mathena v. State, 15 Tex. App. 460. § 175.
Mather, Klein v., 2 Gilman (Ill.), 317. § 288.
Rand v., 11 Cush. 1. § 52.
Matheson v. Jones, 30 Ga. 306. §§ 29, 405.
Mathews v. Aikin, 1 N. Y. 595. § 298.
v. Christman, 12 Smedes & Mar. (Miss.) 595. §§ 193, 194.
v. Hall's Adm'r, 21 W. Va. 510. § 212.
Partee v., 53 Miss. 140. § 295.
v. Phelps, 61 Mich. 327. §§ 156, 161.
Railton v., 10 Cl. & Finn. 934. § 419.
Ritenour v., 42 Ind. 7. § 225.
v. Switzler, 46 Mo. 301. § 330.
Mathewson v. Strafford Bank, 45 N. H. 104. § 353.
Mathis v. Morgan, 72 Ga. 517. § 412, 598.
Matson, Bank of Missouri v., 24 Mo. 333. § 437.
Bank of Missouri v., 26 Mo. 243. § 32.
Gedye v., 25 Beav. 310. § 306.
v. Wharam, 2 Term R. 80. §§ 75, 76, 77, 78.
Matson, Adm'r, State v., 44 Mo. 305. § 439.
Matteson, Constant v., 22 Ill. 546. § 328.
Matthews, Fulton v., 15 Johns. 433. § 342.

Matthews, Houghton v., 3 Bos. & Pul. 485. § 71.
v. Joyce, 85 N. C. 258. § 324.
Kelly v., 5 Ark. (Pike), 223. § 606.
Kent v., 12 Leigh (Va.), 573. § 238.
v. Millsaps, 58 Miss. 564. § 258.
Pratt v., 24 Hun (N. Y.), 386. §§ 161, 387.
State v., 57 Miss. 1. § 591.
Matthis, Powell v., 4 Ired. Law (N. C.), 83. §§ 288, 291.
Mattingly v. Paul, 88 Ind. 95. § 219.
v. Sutton, 19 W. Va. 19. § 227.
Mauer, Lawton v., 9 Rich. Law (S. C.), 335. § 204.
Mauldin v. Branch Bank, 2 Ala. 502. § 18.
Maule v. Bucknell, 50 Pa. St. 39. § 69.
Mauley, Simpson v., 2 Cro. & Jer. 12. § 161.
Maultsby, Jackson v., 78 N. C. 174. § 565.
Maunsell, Jephson v., 10 Irish Eq. 38. § 445.
Mauri v. Heffernan, 13 Johns. 38. § 205.
Maurice, United States v., 2 Brock. 96. § 521.
Maxcey, Robertson v., 6 Dana (Ky.), 101. § 286.
Maxwell, Carsan v., 39 Minn. 391, 393. § 1.
v. Connor, 1 Hill, Eq. (S. C.) 14. § 243.
Ferrell v., 28 Ohio St. 383. § 60.
v. Haynes, 41 Me. 559. § 66.
v. Salts, 4 Cold. (Tenn.) 233. § 489.
Weed Sewing Machine Co. v., 63 Mo. 486. § 153.
May, Anderson v., 10 Heisk. (Tenn.) 84. § 116.
v. Burk, 80 Mo. 675. § 329.
Hawkins v., 12 Ala. 673. § 218.
Johnston v., 76 Ind. 293. §§ 379, 397.
v. Kelly, 61 Ala. 489. §§ 578, 581, 583.
May v. May, 19 Fla. 373. §§ 42, 217.
v. Reed, 125 Ind. 199. § 242.
v. Robertson, 13 Ala. 86. § 417.
Shepherd v., 115 U. S. 505. § 37.
v. Vann, 15 Fla. 553. § 295.
Mayberry v. Bainton, 2 Harr. (Del.) 24. §§ 18, 198.
Lombard v., 24 Neb. 674. § 412.
Maybury v. Grady, 67 Ala. 147. § 463.
Mayer, Heidenheimer v., 10 Jones & Spen. (N. Y.) 506. § 127.
v. Isaac, 6 M. & W. 605. §§ 92, 161.
Patillo v., 70 Ga. 715. § 181.
Mayers, Quine v., 2 Rob. (La.) 510. § 471.
Mayes, State v., 54 Miss. 417. § 542.
Mayfield, Perkins v., 5 Port. (Ala.) 182. § 218.
Wheeler v., 31 Tex. 395. § 116.
v. Wheeler, 37 Tex. 256. §§ 186, 190.
Mayhew v. Boyd, 5 Md. 102. § 397.
v. Crickett, 2 Swanst. 185, 193. §§ 255, 434, 436.
Maynard, Blow v., 2 Leigh (Va.), 29. § 212.
Winneshiek Co. v., 44 Iowa, 15. § 559.
Mayo, Eaton v., 118 Mass. 141. § 103.
v. Hutchinson, 57 Me. 546. § 7.
v. Renfroe & Wilson, 66 Ga. 408. § 517.
Mayo & Pasco v. May, 19 Fla. 373. §§ 574, 577, 639.
Mayor v. Blache, 3 La. (Curry), 500. §§ 425, 557.
Boaler v., 19 J. Scott (N. R.), 76. § 376.
v. Kent, 25 J. & S. (N. Y. Sup. Ct.) 109. §§ 151, 152.
v. Knight, 12 Lea (Tenn.), 700. §§ 425, 524.
v. Ryan, 9 Daly (N. Y. Com. Pl.), 316. §§ 113, 175.
Mayor of Berwick v. Oswald, 1 Ell. & Black. 295. § 552.
Oswald v., 5 H. of L. Cas. 856. § 172.

Mayor of Birmingham *v.* Wright, 16 Ad. & Ell. (N. S.) 623. § 173.
Mayor of Cambridge *v.* Dannis, Ell. Black. & Ell. 360. § 169.
Mayor of Durham *v.* Fowler, Law Rep. (22 Q. B. Div.) 394. § 555.
Mayor of Hoboken *v.* Kamena, 41 N. J. Law, 435. § 597.
Mayor of Nashville *v.* Knight, 12 Lea (Tenn.), 700. § 371.
Mayor of Newark *v.* Dickerson, 45 N. J. Law, 38. § 597.
Mayor of New York *v.* Sibberns, 3 Abb. Rep. Om. Cas. 266. § 548.
v. Kelly, 98 N. Y. 467. § 549.
Mayor of Wilmington *v.* Horn, 2 Har. (Del.) 190. § 167.
Mayor and City Council of Natchitoches *v.* Redmond, 28 La. Ann. 274. §§ 112, 555.
Mayor and Selectmen of Homer *v.* Merritt, 27 La. Ann. 568. §§ 521, 555.
Mayrant, Commissioners *v.*, 2 Prev. (S. C.) 228. § 570.
Mays *v.* Cockrum, 57 Tex. 352. § 139.
Mazelin, Hume *v.*, 84 Ind. 574. §§ 353, 355.
Mazio, Byrne *v.*, Law Rep. Irish (8 Q. B., C. P. & Ex.), 396. § 423.
McAfee, Click *v.*, 7 Port. (Ala.) 62. § 62.
McAliley, Rosborough *v.*, 10 Rich. (S. C.) 235. § 429.
McAlester *v.* Landers, 70 Cal. 79. § 109.
McAllister *v.* Clark, 86 Ill. 236. § 640.
Ecker *v.*, 45 Md. 290. § 91.
Sibley *v.*, 8 N. H. 389. § 448.
Titcomb *v.*, 77 Me. 353. § 274.
McArdle *v.* McDaniel, 75 Ga. 270. § 511.
McArthur, Dane *v.*, 57 Ala. 448. § 571.
v. Martin, 23 Minn. 74. § 298.
McAulay, Verratt *v.*, 50 Ont. (Can.) 313. § 572.
McBroom *v.* Governor, 4 Port. (Ala.) 90. § 631.
v. Governor, 6 Port. (Ala.) 32. § 448.
v. Somerville, 2 Stew. (Ala.) 515. § 480.
McCabe *v.* Raney, 32 Ind. 309. § 413.
v. Sutton, 7 Lea (Tenn.), 248. § 479.
McCaffil *v.* Radcliff, 3 Rob. (N. Y.) 445. § 77.
McCall, Perryman *v.*, 66 Ala. 402. § 165.
McCallister, Hamblin *v.*, 4 Bush (Ky.), 418. § 609.
McCalmont, Lawrence *v.*, 2 How. 426. §§ 13, 92.
McCan, Miller *v.*, 7 Paige Ch. 451. § 342.
McCann *v.* Dennett, 13 N. H. 528. § 339.
McCarter, Jerome *v.*, 21 Wall. 17. § 461.
v. Turner, 49 Ga. 309. §§ 29, 608.
McCarthy, Jefferson *v.*, 44 Minn. 26. § 45.
McCarty, Gordon *v.*, 3 Wharton (Pa.), 407. § 250.
v. Roots, 21 How. 432. § 260.
McCaslan, Harris *v.*, 31 S. C. 420. § 7.
McCasland, Gibbons *v.*, 1 Barn. & Ald. 690. § 79.
McCauley, Hutchins *v.*, 2 Dev. & Bat. Eq. (N. C.) 399. § 286.
v. Offutt, 12 B. Mon. (Ky.) 386. § 488.
Tinker *v.*, 3 Mich. 188. § 49.
McChesney, Corbin *v.*, 26 Ill. 231. § 63.
McChord, Bank of Commerce *v.*, 4 Dana (Ky.), 191. § 379.
McClanahan, Byers *v.*, 6 Gill & Johns. (Md.) 250. §§ 60, 264, 292.
McClatchie *v.* Durham, 44 Mich. 435. § 295.
McClaughry, McNaught *v.*, 42 N. Y. 22. § 15.
McCleary, Mitchell *v.*, 42 Md. 374. § 193.

McClellan *v.* Downey, 63 Cal. 520. § 580.
McClelland, Greenough *v.*, 2 Ell. & Bl. 424. §§ 29, 375.
Leggett *v.*, 39 Ohio St. 624. § 270.
Linn *v.*, 4 Dev. & Batt. Law (N. C.), 458. § 293.
McCloskey *v.* Wingfield, 32 La. Ann. 38. §§ 466, 471.
McClosky *v.* Indianapolis Manuf's & Carpenters' Union, 67 Ind. 86. § 377.
McClosky, Bigley & Co. *v.* Wingfield & Bridges, 29 La. Ann. 141. § 118.
McCluer's Adm'r, Rodgers *v.*, 4 Gratt. (Va.) 81. § 308.
McClure, Barker *v.*, 2 Blackf. (Ind.) 14. §§ 368, 372.
v. Commonwealth, 80 Pa. St. 167. § 576.
v. People, 19 Bradw. (Ill. App.) 105. § 638.
v. Smith, 56 Ga. 439. § 512.
McClung, Union Bank *v.*, 9 Humph. (Tenn.) 98. §§ 351, 352.
McClung's Ex'r, Taylor *v.*, 2 Houston (Del.), 24. §§ 117, 186.
McClurg *v.* Fryer, 15 Pa. St. 293. § 100.
McClurkey *v.* Cromwell, 11 N. Y. 593. § 601.
McColl, Postmaster-General *v.*, 31 U. C. (C. P.) 364. § 595.
McCollum *v.* Cushing, 22 Ark. 540. §§ 186, 187, 198.
v. Hinkley, 9 Vt. 143. § 239.
McComb *v.* Kittridge, 14 Ohio, 348. § 354.
v. Wright, 4 Johns. Ch. 659. § 90.
McCombs *v.* Allen, 18 Hun (N. Y.), 190. § 150.
Ingham's Adm'rs *v.*, 17 Mo. 558. § 537.
McConico, Hopkirk *v.*, 1 Brock. 220. §§ 360, 362.
McConkey, Bell *v.*, 82 Va. 176. § 237.
McConnell *v.* Beattie, 34 Ark. 113. § 306.
McConnell *v.* Brillhart, 17 Ill. 354. §§ 89, 90.
Fraser *v.*, 23 Ga. 368. §§ 29, 38.
Hunt *v.*, 1 T. B. Mon. (Ky.) 219. § 125.
v. Scott, 15 Ohio, 401. § 237.
Wardell *v.*, 23 Neb. 152. § 623.
McCord, District Township of Fox *v.*, 54 Iowa, 346. § 546.
v. Johnson, 4 Bibb (Ky.), 531. § 615.
McCormack, State *v.*, 50 Mo. 568. § 543.
McCormack's Adm'r *v.* Obannon's Ex'r, 3 Munf. (Va.) 484. § 290.
McCormick *v.* Bay City, 23 Mich. 457. § 410.
Comm'rs Missoula Co. *v.*, 4 Mont. 115. § 546.
Ellis *v.*, 1 Hilton (N. Y.), 313. § 389.
v. Hubbell, 4 Mont. 87. §§ 419, 460.
v. Moss, 41 Ill. 352. § 537.
v. Thompson, 10 Neb. 484. § 563.
McCormick's Adm'r *v.* Irwin, 35 Pa. St. 111. § 298.
McCoun *v.* Sperb, 53 Hun (N. Y.), 165. §§ 226, 582.
McCowan, Conwell *v.*, 53 Ill. 363. § 315.
McCoy *v.* Lockwood, 71 Ind. 319. § 608.
v. Payne, 68 Ind. 327. § 140.
Percival *v.* (Cir. Ct. D. Iowa, W. D.), 13 Fed. Rep. 375. § 141.
McCracken *v.* Todd, 1 Kan. 148. §§ 517, 520.
McCrary *v.* Coley, Ga. Dec. 104. § 40.
McCrea, Corporation of Chatham *v.*, 12 Up. Can. (C. P.) 352. § 100.
v. Purmont, 16 Wend. 460. § 89.
McCreary *v.* Van Hook, 35 Tex. 631. § 17.
McCrumer *v.* Thompson, 21 Iowa, 244. § 381.
McCue *v.* Smith, 9 Minn. 252. § 52.
McCullen, Miller & Thompson *v.*, 69 Iowa, 681. § 363.

McCullough, Harger *v.*, 2 Denio, 119. § 39.
v. Hellman, 8 Oreg. 191. § 391.
Moss *v.*, 7 Barb. (N. Y.) 279. § 39.
Moss *v.*, 5 Hill (N. Y.), 131. § 630.
McCune *v.* Belt, 45 Mo. 174. §§ 260, 268.
McCunn, Darlington *v.*, 2 E. D. Smith (N. Y.), 411. § 76.
McCurdy, Davis 5., 50 Wis. 569. § 577.
Hickman *v.*, 7 J. J. Mar. (Ky.) 555. § 286.
McCutcheon *v.* Weston, 65 Cal. 37. § 468.
M'Dade, Bank of Alabama *v.*, 4 Port. (Ala.) 252. § 218.
McDaniel *v.* Campbell, 78 Ga. 188. § 510.
v. Lee, 37 Mo. 204. § 279.
McArdle *v.*, 75 Ga. 270. § 511.
Sasser *v.*, 73 Ga. 547. § 509.
Williams *v.*. 77 Ga. 4. § 503.
McDaniels, Guild *v.*, 43 Kan. 548. § 307.
McDearmon, Kinsey *v.*, 5 Cold. (Tenn.) 392. § 324.
M'Doal *v.* Yeomans, 8 Watts (Pa.), 361. § 98.
McDonald *v.* Atkins, 13 Neb. 568. § 531.
v. Bradshaw, 2 Kelly (Ga.), 248. § 537.
Brown *v.*, 8 Yerg. (Tenn.) 158. § 280.
Chase *v.*, 7 H. & J. (Md.) 160. § 93.
Fegley *v.*, 89 Pa. St. 128. § 101.
v. Fett, 49 Cal. 354. §§ 473, 490.
Independent School District Montezuma *v.*, 39 Iowa, 564. § 545.
Gray *v.*, 19 Wis. 213. § 266.
v. State, 77 Ind. 26. § 577.
McDonough, State *v.*, 9 Mo. App. 63. § 566.
McDougal *v.* Calef, 34 N. H. 534. § 130.
McDougald *v.* Dougherty, 14 Ga. 674. § 311.
v. Maddox, 32 Ga. 63. § 544.
McDowell *v.* Bank, 1 Harr. (Del.) 369. §§ 40, 432.
v. Bank of Wilmington & Brandywine, 2 Del. Ch. 1. § 342.
Bryan *v.*, 15 Lea (Tenn.), 381. § 287.
v. Chambers, 1 Strobh. Éq. (S. C.) 347. § 80.
v. Crook, 10 La. Ann. 31. § 222.
Meade *v.*, 5 Binney (Pa.), 195. §§ 143, 626.
Mims *v.*, 4 Ga. 182. §§ 211, 215.
Nichols *v.*, 14 B. Mon. (Ky.) 5. § 242.
McEachron, Inhabitants New Providence *v.*, 4 Vroom (N. J.), 339. § 558.
McElhaney, State *v.*, 20 Mo. App. 584. § 509.
McElroy, Corporation of Adjala *v.*, 9 Ont. (Can.) 580. §§ 172, 423.
v. Hatheway, 44 Mich. 399. § 223.
McElvain, Treasurers Franklin Co. *v.*, 5 Ohio, 200. § 578.
McEwen, Philbrooks *v.*, 29 Ind. 347. § 445.
McFadden, Burt *v.*, 58 Ill. 479. § 399.
McFarland, People *v.*, 9 Bradw. (Ill. App.) 275. §§ 495, 509.
McFarlane, Chalaron *v.*, 5 La. (Curry), 227. § 410.
Shaw *v.*, 1 Ired. Law (N. C.), 216. § 426.
McFaul, Bank of Montreal *v.*, 17 Grant's Ch. 234. § 147.
McFillen *v.* Hoffman, 35 N. J. Eq. 364. § 35.
McGarry *v.* State, 37 Kan. 9. § 503.
McGee, Albertson *v.*, 7 Yerg. (Tenn.) 106. § 452.
Coger's Ex'rs *v.*, 2 Bibb (Ky.), 321. § 405.
v. Metcalf, 12 Sm. & Mar. (Miss.) 535. §§ 344, 444.

McGehee v. Gewin, 25 Ala. 176. §§ 565, 570, 572.
v. McGehee, 12 Ala. 83. § 263.
v. Owen, 61 Ala. 440. §§ 211, 254, 268, 294.
v. Scott, 15 Ga. 74. § 575.
McGill v. Bank of United States, 12 Wheat. 511. § 396.
McGinnis, Davis Sewing Machine Co. v., 45 Iowa, 538. § 119.
McGlothlin v. Madden, 16 Kan. 466. § 231.
v. Wyatt, 1 Lea (Tenn.), 717. § 575.
McGonigle, State v., 101 Mo. 353. § 385.
McGorney v. The State, 20 Ohio, 93. § 132.
McGovern, Dobyns v., 15 Mo. 662. § 582.
v. Hoesback, 53 Pa. St. 176. § 128.
McLaughlin v., 34 Barb. (N. Y.) 208. § 151.
McGregor, Nading v., 121 Ind. 465. § 193.
McGregory, Fiske v., 34 N. H. 414. § 72.
McGrew, Chapman v., 20 Ill. 101. § 386.
v. Governor, 19 Ala. 89. § 562.
v. Tombeckbee Bank, 5 Port. (Ala.) 547. § 243.
McGruder, Johnson v., 15 Mo. 365. § 90.
McGuire, Birkett v., 31 Up. Can. (C. P.) 430. § 36.
v. Bry, 3 Rob. (La.) 196. §§ 361, 523, 554.
Fennell v., 21 Up. Can. (C. P.) 134. §§ 133, 157.
v. Wooldridge, 6 Rob. (La.) 47. §§ 342, 359.
McGurk v. Huggett, 56 Mich. 187. § 260.
McHaney v. Crabtree, 6 T. B. Mon. (Ky.) 104. § 434.
McHard v. Ives, 5 Bradw. (Ill. App.) 400. § 346.
McHart, Ives v., 103 Ill. 97. § 176.
McHatton, People v., 2 Gilm. (Ill.) 638. §§ 371, 548.
McHenry, Hall v., 19 Iowa, 521. §§ 380, 381.
McHugh, Pharr v., 32 La. Ann. 1280. §§ 45, 238.
McIlhenny Co. v. Blum, 68 Tex. 197. § 154.
McIntosh v. Hurst, 6 Mont. 287. § 152.
v. Likens, 25 Iowa, 555. § 111.
McIntyre v. Trustees of Schools, 3 Bradw. (Ill. App.) 77. § 526.
McIvain, Place v., 38 N. Y. 76. § 364.
McIver v. Richardson, 1 Maule & Sel. 557. § 191.
McKay, Walker v., 2 Met. (Ky.) 294. § 226.
McKee v. Amonett, 6 La. Ann. 207. § 312.
v. Campbell, 27 Mich. 497. §§ 217, 264.
Coats v., 26 Ind. 223. §§ 35, 397.
Gates v., 13 N. Y. 232. § 160.
v. Griffin, 66 Ala. 211. §§ 529, 591.
v. Hamilton, 33 Ohio St. 7. § 216.
State v., 98 N. C. 500. § 628.
McKecknie v. Ward, 58 N. Y. 541. § 369.
McKenna v. George, 2 Rich. Eq. (S. C.) 15. §§ 275, 283, 288.
McKenny's Ex'rs v. Waller, 1 Leigh (Va.), 434. § 438.
McKensie v. Farrell, 4 Bosw. (N. Y.) 192. § 82.
v. Mo. Pac. R'y Co., 24 Mo. App. 392. § 514.
McKenzie v. Jackson, 4 Ala. 230. § 63.
Stroop v., 38 Tex. 132. § 29.
v. Wiley, 27 W. Va. 658. § 373.
McKim v. Blake, 132 Mass. 343. § 526.
v. Bartlett, 129 Mass. 226. § 526.
v. Blake, 139 Mass. 593. § 627.
Harrison v., 18 Iowa, 485. § 182.
v. Morse, 130 Mass. 439. § 577.
v. Williams, 134 Mass. 136. § 576.
McKinnell, Wakefield v., 9 La. (Curry), 449. § 497.

McKinney, England v., 4 Sneed (Tenn.), 75. § 606.
Lowry v., 68 Pa. St. 294. § 34.
Sterne v., 79 Ind. 578. § 438.
Sublett v., 19 Tex. 438. § 230.
v. Whitney, 8 Allen, 207. § 73.
v. Willis, 64 Miss. 82. § 481.
McKinnon v. McKinnon, 81 N. C. 201. § 576.
McKnight v. Bradley, 10 Rich. Eq. (S. C.) 557. § 224.
Bright v., 1 Sneed (Tenn.), 158. § 194.
McKoy, Camden v., 3 Scam. (Ill.) 437. § 176.
McLain v. People, 85 Ill. 205. § 543.
v. Simington, 37 Ohio St. 484. § 27.
Smith v., 11 W. Va. 654. § 243.
McLane v. Ragsdale, 31 Miss. 701. § 230.
McLaren v. Hutchinson, 22 Cal. 187. §§ 63, 66.
v. Watson's Ex'rs, 26 Wend. 425. § 47.
McLaughlin, Carpenter v., 12 R. I. 270. § 180.
v. McGovern, 34 Barb. (N. Y.) 208. § 151.
McLean, Coffin v., 80 N. Y. 560. § 236.
Darling v., 20 Up. Can. (Q. B.) 372. § 363.
Gray v., 17 Ill. 404. § 467.
Holt v., 75 N. C. 347. § 170.
v. McLean, 88 N. C. 394. § 586.
Stevenson v., 11 Up. Can. (C. P.) 208. § 117.
v. State, 8 Heisk. (Tenn.) 22, 253. §§ 523, 524, 548, 628.
v. Towle, 3 Sandf. Ch. 117. § 315.
McLemore v. Powell, 12 Wheat. 554. § 342.
Read v., 34 Miss. 110. § 402.
McLendon, Newsom v., 6 Ga. 392. § 322.
McLennan, Lea v., 7 Neb. 143. § 332.
McLeod, Files v., 14 Ala. 611. § 68.
Smith v., 3 Ired. Eq. (N. C.) 390. § 301.
McLewis v. Furgerson, 5 The Reporter, 330. § 268.
McLosk, Rives v., 5 Stew. & Port. (Ala.) 330. § 248.
McLott v. Savery, 11 Iowa, 323. § 137.
McLure v. Cloclough, 17 Ala. 89. § 417.
McMahan, McWhorter v., 10 Paige, 386. § 90.
McManus, Magee v., 70 Cal. 553. § 329.
McMaster, Smarr v., 35 Mo. 349. § 370.
McMeekin, Wickens v., 15 Ont. (Can.) 408. § 169.
McMicken v. Commonwealth, 58 Pa. St. 213. § 512.
McMillan, Adams v., 7 Port. (Ala.) 73. §§ 80, 90.
v. Boyd, 40 Ohio St. 35. § 571.
v. Bull's Head Bank, 32 Ind. 11. §§ 1, 195.
v. Dana, 18 Cal. 339. § 471.
Fireman's Ins. Co. v., 29 Ala. 147. §§ 391, 630.
Johnson v., 13 Col. 423. § 112.
v. Parkell, 64 Mo. 286. § 41.
McMullen v. Hinkle, 39 Miss. 142. § 428.
v. Neal's Adm'r, 60 Ala. 552. § 324.
v. Riley, 6 Gray, 500. § 52.
McMullin v. Bank of Penn Township, 2 Pa. St. 343. § 220.
Shannon v., 25 Gratt. (Va.) 211. § 434.
McMurray v. Noyes, 72 N. Y. 523. §§ 97, 99, 101.
v. Spicer, Law Rep. 5 Eq. 527. § 81.
McMurty, Crump v., 8 Mo. 408. § 305.
McMyn, Lightbown v., Law Rep. 33 Ch. Div. 575. § 310.
McNair, Cumpston v., 1 Wend. 457. § 98.
Williams v., 98 N. C. 332. § 574.
McNairy v. Bell, 5 Rob. (La.) 418. § 634.
v. Marshall, 7 Humph. (Tenn.) 229. § 557.

McNaught v. McClaughry, 42 N. Y. 22. § 15.
McNeale v. Governor, 3 Gratt. (Va.) 299. § 625.
v. Reed, 7 Irish Ch. Rep. 251. § 315.
McNeese, Jenkins v., 34 Tex. 189. § 434.
McNeil, Cardell v., 21 N. Y. 336. § 67.
Dunlap v., 35 Ind. 316. § 137.
v. Sanford, 3 B. Mon. (Ky.) 11. § 258.
McNeile, Lacy v., 4 Dow. & Ry. 7. § 66.
McNeilly v. Cooksey, 2 Lea (Tenn.), 39. § 438.
McNier, Freudenstein v., 81 Ill. 208. § 570.
McNutt v. Wilcox, 1 Freeman's Ch. (Miss.) 116. § 40.
v. Wilcox, 3 How. (Miss.) 417. § 468.
McPhail, Simpson v., 17 Bradw. (Ill. App.) 499. § 307.
McPherson, Dickson v., 3 Grant's Ch. App. 185. § 415.
v. Meek, 30 Mo. 345. § 210.
v. Talbott, 10 Gill & Johns. (Md.) 499. § 266.
McQuesten v. Noyes, 6 N. H. 19. §§ 38, 339.
McQuewans v. Hamlin, 35 Pa. St. 517. § 18.
McRae, Daniel v., 2 Hawks (N. C.), 590. § 260.
McRea v. McWilliams, 58 Tex. 328. § 595.
McSpedon, Therasson v., 2 Hilton (N. Y.), 1. § 65.
McSwords, Cranmer v., 26 W. Va. 412. § 217.
McTeer, Loyd v., 33 Ga. 37. § 504.
McVean, Locke v., 33 Mich. 473. §§ 92, 123.
McVeigh v. Bank of Old Dominion, 26 Gratt. (Va.) 785. § 437.
Harper v., 82 Va. 751. §§ 205, 206, 297, 645.
McVey, Wilson v., 83 Ind. 108. § 339.
McVicar v. Royce, 17 Up. Can. (Q. B.) 529. § 211.
McVickar, Caldwell, Ex'r, v., 9 Ark. (4 Eng.) 418. § 342.
McWatty v. Jefferson Co., 76 Ga. 352. § 35.
McWhann, Burrows v., 1 Des. Eq. (S. C.) 409. § 309.
McWhorter v. McMahan, 10 Paige, 386. § 90.
v. Wright, 5 Ga. 555. § 247.
McWilliams v. Mason, 31 N. Y. 294. § 115.
v. Norfleet, 60 Miss. 987. §§ 24, 520, 541.
McRea v., 58 Tex. 328. § 595.
Meacham, Fox v., 6 Neb. 530. § 562.
Mead, Hoyt v., 13 Hun (N.Y.), 327. § 31.
v. Keyes, 4 E. D. Smith (N. Y.), 510. § 62.
v. Merrill, 30 N. H. 472. § 234.
v. Parker, 111 N. Y. 259. § 99.
Meade v. McDowell, 5 Binney (Pa.), 195. §§ 143, 626.
Meadows, Heffield v., 4 Com. Pleas, 595. §§ 156, 161.
v. State, 114 Ind. 537. § 112.
Mealing, Steele v., 24 Ala. 285. §§ 268, 269, 272, 444.
Means, Taylors v., 73 Ala. 468. § 287.
Mears v. Commonwealth, 8 Watts (Pa.), 223. § 517.
Whiton v., 11 Met. (Mass.) 563. §§ 177, 197.
Mease v. Wagner, 1 McCord (S. C.), 395. § 58.
Mebane, Freeman v., 2 Jones' Eq. (N. C.) 44. § 322.
Mechanics' Bank v. Hazard, 13 Johns. 353. § 311.
Martin v., 6 Harr. & Johns. (Md.) 235. § 432.
v. Wright, 53 Mo. 153. § 29.
Mechanics' Fire Ins. Co. v. Ogden, 1 Wend. 137. § 198.
Mechanics' Nat. Bank of Chicago, Gage v., 79 Ill. 62. §§ 199, 242.

Mecorney v. Stanley, 8 Cush. (Mass.) 85. § 16.
Medley, Brandon v., 1 Jones' Eq. (N. C.) 313. § 271.
v. Tandy, 85 Ky. 566. § 606.
Medlin v. Commonwealth, 11 Bush (Ky.), 605. § 500.
Meehan, People v., 14 Daly (N. Y. Com. Pl.), 333. § 511.
Meek, McPherson v., 30 Mo. 345. § 210.
Stephens v., 6 Lea (Tenn.), 226. § 284.
Meeker, Emmons v., 55 Ind. 321. § 381.
Meggett v. Baum, 57 Miss. 22. § 342.
Meguiar v. Groves, 1 Fed. Rep. 279. § 367.
Meighan, Grundy v., 7 Irish Law Rep. 519. § 146.
Meinhardt Bros. & Co. v. Mode, 22 Fla. 279. § 104.
Meigs, Waterman v., 4 Cush. 497. § 81.
Meiswinkle v. Jung, 30 Wis. 67. § 357.
Melendy v. Capen, 120 Mass. 222. § 158.
Melhourn, Koch v., 25 Pa. St. 89. § 102.
Melick, Bogue v., 25 Ill. 91. § 178.
v. First Nat. Bank of Tama City, 52 Iowa, 94. § 46.
v. Knox, 44 N. Y. 676. § 130.
Mellen v. Nickerson, 12 Gray, 445. § 418.
Mellendy v. Austin, 69 Ill. 15. § 335.
Mellish v. Green, 5 Grant's Ch. 655. § 434.
Mellus, Los Angeles v., 59 Cal. 444. §§ 385, 603.
Melton v. Brown, 25 Fla. 461. § 180.
Middleton v., 10 Barn. & Cress. 317. § 629.
Melville v. Doidge, 6 Man., Gr. & Scott, 450. § 560.
v. Hayden, 3 Barn. & Ald. 593. § 164.
Memphis & C. R. R. Co., Elevator Co. v., 85 Tenn. 703. § 6.
Chaffee v., 64 Mo. 193. § 180.
Menard v. Davidson, 3 La. Ann. 480. § 392.
v. Scudder, 7 La. Ann. 385. §§ 133, 159, 186, 187, 204.
Menaugh v. Chandler, 89 Ind. 94. § 41.
Mendel, Aaron v., 78 Ky. 427. §§ 339, 576.
v. Cairnes' Adm'r, 84 Ind. 141. § 618.
Mendell, Levi v., 1 Duvall (Ky.), 77. §§ 49, 176, 182, 199.
Mendelsou v. Stout, 5 J. & S. (N. Y. Super. Ct.) 408. § 401.
Mendenhall v. Lenwell, 5 Blackf. (Ind.) 125. § 366.
Menefee, Ross v., 125 Ind. 432. § 205.
Mengy, Sollee v., 1 Bailey, Law (S. C.), 620. §§ 117, 143, 163, 186.
Menifee v. Clark, 35 Ind. 304. § 344.
Menken, Fletcher v., 37 Ark. 206. § 465.
Mennard, Gibbs v., 6 Paige, Ch. 258. § 225.
Mennet v. Grisard, 79 Ind. 222. § 646.
Menzies, Morgan v., 60 Cal. 341. § 462.
Morgan v., 65 Cal. 243. § 462.
Mercer, Alexander v., 7 Ga. 549. § 544.
Braiden v., 44 Ohio St. 339. § 632.
Kent v., 12 Up. Can. (C. P.) 30. § 537.
Mercer County v. Coovert, 6 Watts & Serg. (Pa.) 70. § 122.
Mercer County Court, Bonta v., 7 Bush (Ky.), 576. § 555.
Merchants' Bank, Cole v., 60 Ind. 350. §§ 47, 106.
v. Cordevoille, 4 Rob. (La.) 506. § 442.
v. Rudolf, 5 Neb. 527. § 252.
Merchants' & Mechanics' Bank v. Evans, 9 W. Va. 373. § 381.

Merchants' Ins. Co. *v.* Hauck, 83 Mo. 21. § 352.
Merchants' Nat. Bank *v.* Hall, 18 Hun (N. Y.), 176. § 159.
Tabor *v.*, 48 Ark. 454. § 409.
Mercien *v.* Andrus, 10 Wend. 461. § 64.
Meredith *v.* Ass'n of Baltimore, 60 Cal. 617. § 462.
Meriden Silver Plate Co. *v.* Flory. 44 Ohio St. 430. §§ 605, 608, 612.
Merle *v.* Wells, 2 Camp. 413. § 161.
Merod, Hatfield *v.*, 82 Ill. 113. § 207.
Merriam, Baker *v.*, 97 Ind. 539. § 486.
Clark *v.*, 25 Conn. 576. §§ 176, 177, 182, 199.
v. Rockwood, 44 N. H. 81. § 407.
Merricke, Lord Arlington *v.*, 2 Saund. 403. § 166.
Merrihew, State *v.*, 47 Iowa, 112. §§ 500, 502.
Merriken *v.* Godwin, 2 Del. Ch. 236. § 39.
Merrill, Chapin *v.*, 4 Wend. 657. § 60.
Gray *v.*, 11 Bush (Ky.), 633. § 488.
Levy *v.*, 4 Greenl. 180. § 82.
Mead *v.*, 30 N. H. 472. § 234.
v. Merrill, 53 Vt. 74. § 324.
Skillin *v.*, 16 Mass. 40. § 278.
Merrimack County Bank *v.* Brown, 12 N. H. 320. §§ 330, 345, 347.
Merriman *v.* Barker, 121 Ind. 74. § 363.
Merritt, Agnew *v.*, 10 Minn. 308. §§ 35, 375.
Browning *v.*, 61 Ind. 425. § 182.
Canada West Ins. Co. *v.*, 20 Up. Can. (Q. B.) 444. § 131.
v. Clason, 12 Johns. 102. §§ 89, 90.
v. Lincoln, 21 Barb. 249. § 239.
Mayor and Selectmen of Homer *v.*, 27 La. Ann. 568. §§ 521, 555.
Merryman *v.* The State, 5 Harr. & Johns. (Md.) 423. § 310.
Mersereau *v.* Lewis, 25 Wend. 243. § 72.
Mersman *v.* Werges, 112 U. S. 139. §§ 229, 380.
Merwin *v.* Austin, 58 Conn. 22. § 227.
Mesner, Coster *v.*, 58 Mo. 549. § 352.
Messer *v.* Swan, 4 N. H. 481. § 273.
Messinger, Boston Hat Manufactory *v.*, 2 Pick. 223. § 393.
Metcalf, McGee *v.*, 12 Sm. & Mar. (Miss.) 535. §§ 344, 444.
Metcalfe Co. Ct., Newman *v.*, 4 Bush (Ky.), 67. § 545.
Metropolitan Loan Ass'n *v.* Esche, 75 Cal. 513. § 171.
Mettler, State Bank at New Brunswick *v.*, 2 Bosw. (N. Y.) 392. § 63.
Metzner *v.* Baldwin, 11 Minn. 150. § 30.
Mexican Construction Co. *v.* Renseus, 118 U. S. 49. § 461.
Meyer, Farwell *v.*, 35 Ill. 40. § 370.
v. Hartman, 72 Ill. 442. §§ 63, 66.
Konitzky *v.*, 49 N. Y. 571. § 214.
v. Lathrop, 10 Hun (N. Y.), 66. § 37.
Meyers *v.* Fry, 18 Bradw. (Ill. App.) 74. § 644.
Michell, Holmes *v.*, 7 J. Scott (N. S.), 361. § 81.
Michie *v.* Ellair, 60 Mich. 73. § 452.
Jackson *v.*, 33 La. Ann. 723. § 370.
Michigan State Bank *v.* Estate of Leavenworth, 28 Va. 299. §§ 134, 366.
v. Peck, 28 Vt. 200. §§ 94, 117.
Michigan State Ins. Co. *v.* Soule, 51 Mich. 312. §§ 245, 246.
Mickey, Seymour *v.*, 15 Ohio St. 515. §§ 176, 182.
Micklewait *v.* Noel, 69 Iowa, 344. § 408.
Middlefield *v.* Gould, 10 Up. Can. (C. P.) 9. § 629.
Middleton, Cooper *v.*, 94 N. C. 86. §§ 324, 577.

Middleton, Copis *v.*, 1 Turner & Russ. 224. §§ 313, 315.
Crosby *v.*, Finch's Precedents, 309. § 141.
v. First Nat. Bank of Marshalltown, 40 Iowa, 29. § 488.
Hobbs *v.*, 1 J. J. Marsh. (Ky.) 176. §§ 578, 580, 638.
v. Melton, 10 Barn. & Cress. 317. § 629.
Shields *v.*, 2 Cranch, C. C. 205. § 67.
v. State, 120 Ind. 166. § 44.
Walter *v.*, 68 N. Y. 605. § 572.
Middleton's Sureties, State *v.*, 57 Tex. 185. § 338.
Middlesex Mfg. Co. *v.* Lawrence, 1 Allen, 339. § 171.
Miers, Barclay *v.*, 70 Ind. 346. § 648.
Mieure, Judah *v.*, 5 Blackf. (Ind.) 171. §§ 290, 293.
Mikell, Davis *v.*, 1 Freeman's Ch. (Miss.) 548. §§ 29, 40, 434.
Milam, Ragland *v.*, 10 Ala. 618. § 266.
Miles *v.* Bacon, 4 J. J. Marsh. (Ky.) 457. § 212.
v. Linnell, 97 Mass. 298. § 13.
New Haven Bank *v.*, 5 Conn. 587. § 505.
Pierse *v.*, 5 Mont. 549. § 152.
Roberts *v.*, 12 Mich. 297. § 245.
Standley *v.*, 36 Miss. 434. § 15.
Milford, Fuller *v.*, 2 McLean, 74. § 342.
Milk *v.* Rich, 15 Hun (N. Y.), 178. § 67.
Mill, Burton *v.*, 78 Va. 468. § 298.
Johnston *v.*, 25 Tex. 704. § 100.
Miller *v.* Aldrich, 31 Mich. 408. § 252.
v. Arnold, 65 Ind. 488. §§ 242, 314.
v. Bagwell, 3 McCord, Law (S. C.), 429. § 46.
v. Berkey, 27 Pa. St. 317. § 444.
Brooks *v.*, 29 W. Va. 499. § 573.
Carson Opera House Ass'n *v.*, 16 Nev. 327. § 397.
Cherry *v.*, 7 Lea (Tenn.), 305. §§ 344, 426.
Miller *v.* Childress, 2 Humph. (Tenn.) 320. § 612.
v. Commonwealth, 8 Pa. St. 444. § 527.
v. Commonwealth, 127 Pa. St. 122. § 495.
v. County of Macoupin, 2 Gilman (Ill.), 50. § 542.
Craig *v.*, 34 Ill. App. 325. § 648.
Denson *v.*, 33 Ga. 275. § 605.
v. Dyer, 1 Duvall (Ky.), 263. 435, 438.
v. Ferry, 50 Hun (N. Y.), 256. § 473.
v. Finley, 26 Mich. 249. § 380.
Frisch *v.*, 5 Pa. St. 310. § 401.
v. Gardner, 49 Iowa, 234. § 142.
v. Gaskins, 1 Smedes & Mar. Ch. (Miss.) 524. § 149.
v. Gaston, 2 Hill, 188. § 179.
v. Gilleland, 19 Pa. St. 119. § 379.
v. Gillespie, 59 Mo. 220. § 276.
v. Gray, 31 Ill. App. 453. § 608.
Hackleman *v.*, 4 Blackf. (Ind.) 322. § 67.
v. Howry, 3 Pen. & Watts (Pa.), 374. § 247.
v. Irvine, 1 Dev. & Bat. 103. § 82.
Long *v.*, 93 N. C. 227. §§ 324, 333.
Lyndon *v.*, 36 Vt. 329. § 521.
Lyons *v.*, 6 Gratt. (Va.) 427. § 28.
v. McCan, 7 Paige, Ch. 451. § 342.
v. Miller, Phillips' Eq. (N. C.) 85. § 316.
v. Montgomery, 78 N. Y. 282. § 619.
v. Moore, 3 Humph. (Tenn.) 189. §§ 523, 545.
Neff *v.*, 8 Pa. St. 347. §§ 301, 325.
Norton *v.*, 25 Ark. 108. §§ 43, 325.
v. Ord, 2 Binney (Pa.), 382. § 252.
Osgood *v.*, 67 Me. 174. §§ 147, 345.
Owens *v.*, 29 Md. 144. § 324.
v. Pendleton, 4 Hen. & Munf. (Va.) 436. § 315.
Pickens *v.*, 83 N. C. 543. § 256.

Miller *v.* Porter, 5 Humph. (Tenn.) 294. § 372.
Regina *v.*, 20 Up. Can. (Q. B.) 485. § 172.
v. Ridgely (Cir. Ct. W. D. Tenn.), 22 Fed. Rep. 889. § 181.
v. Rinehart, 119 N. Y. 368. § 105.
Robinson *v.*, 2 Bush (Ky.), 129. § 354.
Roth *v.*, 15 Serg. & Rawle, 100. § 62.
v. Sawyer, 30 Vt. 412. § 268.
Sharp *v.*, 57 Cal. 415. § 339.
v. Shields, 124 Ind. 166. § 7.
Shock *v.*, 10 Pa. St. 401. § 439.
v. Spain, 41 Ohio St. 773. § 346.
v. Speed, 9 Heisk. (Tenn.) 196. § 223.
State *v.*, 5 Blackf. (Ind.) 381. § 312.
v. State, 63 Ind. 219. § 590.
v. Stein, 12 Pa. St. 383. § 402.
v. Stein, 2 Pa. St. 286. § 344.
v. Stewart, 4 Wash. (C. C.) 26. § 393.
v. Stewart, 9 Wheat. 680. §§ 93, 393.
v. Stout, 5 Del. Ch. 259. §§ 207, 223, 298.
Taylor *v.*, Phillips' Eq. (N. C.) 365. § 223.
Trustees Section Sixteen *v.*, 3 Ohio, 261. § 250.
v. Tunis, 10 Up. Can. (C. P.) 423. § 151.
Turner *v.*, 28 Kan. 44. § 618.
Wells *v.*, 66 N. Y. 255. § 263.
Whitcomb *v.*, 90 Ind. 384. § 407.
White *v.*, 47 Ind. 385. §§ 205, 411.
Wire *v.*, 45 Ohio St. 388. § 193.
Miller's Adm'rs, Commonwealth *v.*, 8 Serg. & Rawle (Pa.), 452. §§ 40, 434.
Miller & Thompson *v.* McCullen, 69 Iowa, 681. § 363.
Millett *v.* Parker, 2 Met. (Ky.) 608. § 408.
Millham, People *v.*, 29 Hun (N. Y.), 151. § 502.
Milliken, Blatchford *v.*, 35 Ill. 434. § 177.
v. Pratt, 125 Mass. 374. § 144.
Millikin, Stoner *v.*, 85 Ill. 218. § 412.
Mills, Albright *v.*, 86 Ala. 324. § 566.
Davis Sewing Machine Co. *v.*, 55 Iowa, 543. § 202.
v. Gould, 14 Ind. 278. § 366.
Johnson *v.*, 10 Cush. 503. § 339.
Johnston *v.*, 25 Tex. 704. § 100.
Kritzer *v.*, 9 Cal. 21. § 29.
Lumpkin *v.*, 4 Ga. 343. § 313.
Manning *v.*, 12 Up. Can. (Q. B.) 515. § 116.
State *v.*, 82 Ind. 126. § 42.
Stillwell *v.*, 10 Johns. 304. § 574.
Taylor *v.*, Cowper, 525. § 220.
Trask *v.*, 7 Cush. 552. § 131.
Vankoughnet *v.*, 5 Grant's Ch. 653. § 371.
v. Watson, 1 Sweeney (N. Y.), 374. § 37.
Winckworth *v.*, 2 Esp. 484. § 60.
v. Williams, 16 S. C. 593. § 410.
Milne, Craig *v.*, 25 Grant's Ch. (Can.) 259. § 593.
Houlditch *v.*, 3 Esp. 86. §§ 64, 65, 68.
Milner *v.* Green, 2 Johns. Cas. 283. § 500.
Milory, Ayres *v.*, 53 Mo. 516. § 407.
Milroy *v.* Quinn, 69 Ind. 406. §§ 1, 186, 193.
Millsaps, Burnett *v.*, 59 Miss. 333. §§ 257, 264.
Matthews *v.*, 58 Miss. 564. § 258.
State *v.*, 69 Mo. 359. § 505.
Miner, Benedict *v.*, 58 Ill. 19. § 384.
v. Graham, 24 Pa. St. 491. § 133.
Mines *v.* Sculthorpe, 2 Camp. 215. § 91.
Minis *v.* McDowell, 4 Ga. 182. § 211.
Minis' Adm'r, Hawkins *v.*, 36 Ark. 145. § 592.
Minnick, Dorrington *v.*, 15 Neb. 397. § 221.
Minnitt *v.* Lord Talbot, Law Rep. Irish (1 Ch. Div.), 143. § 232.

Minter v. Branch Bank at Mobile, 23 Ala. 762. § 448.
Carpenter v., 72 Tex. 370. § 212.
Minturn v. United States, 106 U. S. 437. § 555.
Mishler, Dutzler v., 37 Pa. St. 82. § 38.
Missig, People v., 7 Daly (N. Y. Com. Pl.), 23. § 511.
Mississippi County v. Jackson, 51 Mo. 23. § 523.
Missoula County v. Edwards, 3 Mont. 60. §§ 22, 546.
Missouri Pac. R'y Co., McKensie v., 24 Mo. App. 392. § 514.
Mitchell v. Burton, 2 Head (Tenn.), 613. §§ 385, 439.
Collins v., 5 Fla., 364. §§ 43, 471.
v. Commonwealth, 12 Bush (Ky.), 247. § 494.
v. Cotten, Ex'r, 2 Fla. 134, 136. §§ 334, 417.
v. De Witt, 25 Tex. (Supplement), 180. § 262.
Dietrich v., 43 Ill. 40. § 178.
v. Duncan, 7 Fla. 13. § 22.
v. Hecker, 59 Cal. 558. § 587.
Logan v., 67 Mo. 524. § 329.
Martin v., 2 Jacob & Walk. 413. § 89.
v. McCleary, 42 Md. 374. § 193.
Montague v., 28 Ill. 481. § 356.
v. Stewart, 10 Heisk. 18. § 103.
Stubbins v., 82 Ky. 535. § 291.
v. Turner, 37 Ala. 660. § 281.
New Haven Co. Bank v., 15 Conn. 206. §§ 118, 195.
Union Society v., 26 Mo. App. 206. §§ 168, 537.
v. Williamson, 6 Md. 210. §§ 97, 448.
Mitchum v. Richardson, 3 Strob. Law (S. C.), 254. § 413.
Mix v. Singleton, 86 Ill. 194. § 93.
v. Vail, 86 Ill. 40. § 476.
Mixsell, Frost v., 38 N. J. Eq. 586. §§ 331, 522, 524.
Mixter, Pacific National Bank v., 124 U. S. 721. § 469.
Mizner v. Spier, 96 Pa. St. 533. § 106.
Moakley v. Riggs, 19 Johns. 69. § 100.
Moale v. Buchanan, 11 Gill & Johns. (Md.) 314. § 80.
Moberly, Moore v., 7 B. Mon. (Ky.) 299. § 268.
Smith v., 10 B. Mon. (Ky.) 266. §§ 114, 407.
Mobile & Girard R. R. Co., Cox v., 44 Ala. 611. §§ 344, 356.
v. Jones, 57 Ga. 198. § 67.
Mobile & Ohio R. R. Co., Bank of Mobile v., 69 Ala. 305. § 329.
Mobile & Montgomery R'y Co. v. Brewer, 76 Ala. 135. §§ 342, 359.
Mobile Life Ins. Co. v. Randall, 71 Ala. 220. §§ 360, 366.
Mobile Mut. Ins. Co. v. Cleveland, 76 Ala. 321. § 11.
Mobley, Garvin v., 1 Bush (Ky.), 48. § 402.
Mockbee, Goddard v., 5 Cranch (C. C.), 666. § 63.
Modawell, Hudson v., 64 Ala. 481. § 586.
Mode, Meinhardt Bros. & Co. v., 22 Fla. 279. § 104.
Modisett v. Governor, 2 Blackf. (Ind.) 135. § 628.
Modrel, State v., 69 Mo. 152. § 585.
Moessinger, Katz v., 110 Ill. 372. § 311.
Moffat, Bell v., 4 P. & B. (N. B.) 121. § 179.
Moffit v. Roche, 77 Ind. 48. §§ 35, 97.
Mohler, Stickney v., 19 Md. 490. § 39.
Moline Plow Co. v. Gilbert, 3 Dak. 239. § 400.
Molson's Bank v. Girdlestone, 44 Up. Can. (Q. B.) 54. § 442.
v. Turley, 8 Ont. (Can.) 293. §§ 249, 401.
Monmouth First National Bank v. Whitman, 66 Ill. 331. §§ 347, 405.
Monongahela Nat. Bank, Stephens v., 88 Pa. St. 157, 163. § 2.

Monro, Cherry *v.*, 2 Barb. Ch. 618. § 37.
Monroe *v.* Anderson Bros. Mfg. & R'y Co., 65 Iowa, 692. § 401.
Monson *v.* Drakeley, 40 Conn. 552. § 258.
Montague *v.* Mitchell, 28 Ill. 481. § 356.
Syme *v.*, 4 Hen. & Munf. (Va.) 180. § 467.
Montefiore *v.* Lloyd, 15 J. Scott (N. S.), 203. § 118.
Monteith *v.* Commonwealth, 15 Gratt. (Va.) 172. § 42.
Montgomery *v.* Dillingham, 3 Sm. & M. (Miss.) 647. §§ 342, 625.
v. Hamilton, 43 Ind. 451. § 347.
Kearnes *v.*, 4 W. Va. 29. §§ 1, 176.
v. Kellogg, 43 Miss. 486. §§ 192, 203.
Miller *v.*, 78 N. Y. 282. § 619.
v. Russell, 10 La. (Curry), 330. § 214.
Smith *v.*, 3 Tex. 199. § 117.
Stringer *v.*, 111 Ind. 489. § 7.
Montgomery Branch Bank *v.* Perdue, 3 Ala. 409. § 239.
Montpelier Bank *v.* Dixon, 4 Vt. 587. § 437.
Moodie *v.* Penman, 3 Dessaus. Eq. (S. C.) 482. § 129.
Moody, Naylor *v.*, 3 Black. (Ind.) 92. § 438.
v. State, 84 Ind. 433. §§ 541, 581.
Woodson *v.*, 4 Humph. (Tenn.) 303. § 202.
Moon, People *v.*, 3 Scam. (Ill.) 123. § 554.
Moor *v.* Roberts, 3 J. Scott (N. S.), 830. § 132.
Moore *v.* Allegheny City, 18 Pa. St. 55. § 523.
v. Baker (Cir. Ct. E. D. Wis.), 34 Fed. Rep. 1. § 297.
Bitting *v.*, 53 Iowa, 593. § 590.
Boston & Sandwich Glass Co. *v.*, 119 Mass. 435. §§ 156, 162.
Bowmaker *v.*, 3 Price, 214. § 482.
Moore *v.* Bray, 10 Pa. St. 519. § 309.
v. Broussard, 20 Mart. (La.) 8 N. S. 277. § 342.
v. Bruner, 31 Ill. App. 400. § 288.
v. Campbell, 36 Vt. 361. § 304.
City of Fond du Lac *v.*, 58 Wis. 170. § 8.
Croft *v.*, 9 Watts (Pa.), 451. § 309.
v. Folsom, 14 Minn. 340. § 178.
Frederick *v.*, 13 B. Mon. (Ky.) 470. § 439.
v. Friedenwald, 77 Va. 57. § 237.
Gordon *v.*, 44 Ark. 349. § 439.
Govan *v.*, 30 Ark. 667. § 129.
v. Gray, 26 Ohio St. 525. § 448.
Griffin *v.*, 2 Kelly (Ga.), 331. §§ 494, 497.
Harter *v.*, 5 Blackf. (Ind.) 367. § 416.
Hightower *v.*, 46 Ala. 387. § 133.
Hoffman *v.*, 82 N. C. 313. § 181.
v. Holt, 10 Gratt (Va.) 284. § 105.
v. Howland, 4 Denio, 264. § 96.
v. Isley, 2 Dev. & Bat. Eq. (N. C.) 372. § 281.
v. Kepner, 7 Neb. 291. § 481.
v. Lassiter, 16 Lea (Tenn.), 630. § 451.
v. Loring, 106 Mass. 455. § 473.
v. Macon Savings Bank, 22 Mo. App. 684. § 378.
Miller *v.*, 3 Humph. (Tenn.) 189. §§ 523, 545.
v. Moberly, 7 B. Mon. (Ky.) 299. § 268.
v. Paine, 12 Wend. 123. § 147.
v. Peterson, 64 Iowa, 423. § 605.
v. Potter, 9 Bush (Ky.), 357. § 540.
v. State, 28 Ark. 480. § 126.
v. State, 49 Ind. 558. § 573.
State *v.*, 74 Mo. 413. § 558.
Tanner *v.*, 9 Q. B. 1. § 161.
v. Topliff, 107 Ill. 241. §§ 36, 223, 329.
v. Wallers' Heirs, 1 A. K. Marsh. (Ky.) 488. § 150.
Wells *v.*, 3 Rob. (La.) 156. § 128.

Moore, Wesley Church *v.*, 10 Pa. St. 273. §§ 205, 230.
Westbrook *v.*, 59 Ga. 204. § 175.
Wheelright *v.*, 2 Hall (N. Y.), 162. § 15.
White *v.*, 23 S. C. 456. § 94.
Woodward *v.*, 13 Ohio St. 136. § 632.
v. Worsham, 5 Ala. 645. § 337.
Mooring, Woodman *v.*, 3 Dev. Law (N. C.), 237. § 333.
Moorman, Citizens' Bank of Bowling Green *v.*, 38 Mo. App. 484. § 351.
Moreau, Hubert *v.*, 12 Moore, 216. § 89.
Morehead *v.* State, 38 Kan. 489. §§ 501, 509.
Morel, Knopf *v.*, 111 Ind. 570. §§ 29, 645.
Morgan, Allen *v.*, 5 Humph. (Tenn.) 624. §§ 18, 251.
v. Blackiston, 5 Harr. & Johns. (Md.) 61. § 474.
v. Boyer, 39 Ohio St. 324. § 165.
Bradbury *v.*, 1 Hurl. & Colt. 249. § 133.
Clark *v.*, 13 Bradw. (Ill. App.) 597. §§ 1, 137.
v. Coffman, 8 La. Ann. 56. § 447.
v. Creditors, 1 La. (Miller), 527. § 363.
First Nat. Bank *v.*, 73 N. Y. 593. § 139.
Glenn *v.*, 23 W. Va. 467. §§ 356, 374.
v. Long, 29 Iowa, 434. § 531.
v. Martien, 32 Mo. 438. § 367.
Mathis *v.*, 72 Ga. 517. §§ 412, 598.
v. Menzies, 60 Cal. 341. § 462.
v. Menzies, 65 Cal. 243. § 462.
Neil *v.*, 28 Ill. 524. § 26.
Seacord *v.*, 3 Keyes (N. Y.), 636. § 449.
v. Seymour, 1 Reports in Chancery, 120. § 303.
v. Smith, 7 Hun (N. Y.), 244. § 419.
Morgan *v.* Smith Am. Organ Co., 73 Ind. 179. § 599.
State *v.*, 59 Miss. 349. § 521.
v. Thompson, 60 Iowa, 280. § 344.
Thurman *v.*, 79 Va. 367. § 592.
United States *v.*, 11 How. 154. § 558.
United States *v.* (Dist. Ct. E. D. N. Y.), 28 Fed. Rep. 48. § 529.
Wood *v.*, 5 Sneed (Tenn.), 79. § 440.
Morin *v.* Martz, 13 Minn. 191. §§ 72, 89.
Morisey, Gregory *v.*, 79 N. C. 559. § 532.
Morley *v.* Boothly, 3 Bing. 107. §§ 82, 85.
v. Boothly, 10 Moore, 395. §§ 15, 17.
v. Dickinson, 12 Cal. 561. § 434.
v. Inglis, 4 Bing. N. C. 58. § 236.
v. Town of Metamora, 78 Ill. 394. §§ 546, 628.
Wright *v.*, 11 Ves. 12. § 322.
Morning *v.* Alexander, 10 Heisk. (Tenn.) 606. § 487.
Morphew *v.* Tatem, 89 N. C. 183. § 10.
Morrell *v.* Cowan, Law Rep. (7 Ch. Div.) 151. §§ 17, 95.
Morrice *v.* Redwyn, 2 Barnardiston, 26. § 208.
Morrill *v.* Daniel, 47 Ark. 316. § 486.
Duer *v.*, 20 Bradw. (Ill. App.) 355. § 351.
Smith *v.*, 54 Me. 48. § 261.
Morris, Buckner *v.*, 2 J. J. Marsh. (Ky.) 121. § 313.
City of Evansville *v.*, 87 Ind. 269. § 25.
v. Cleasby, 4 Maule & Sel. 566. § 71.
Dix *v.*, 66 Mo. 514. §§ 383, 632.
Eichelberger *v.*, 6 Watts (Pa.), 42. § 148.
Hatch *v.*, 36 Me. 419. § 38.
Hoover *v.*, 3 Ohio, 56. § 68.

Morris v. Kniffin, 37 Barb. (N. Y.) 336. § 89.
v. Morris, 9 Heisk. (Tenn.) 814. § 581.
Rice v., 82 Ind. 204. § 329.
Schneider v., 2 Maule & Sel. 286. § 89.
v. Wadsworth, 17 Wend. 103. § 198.
Morris' Canal & Banking Co. v. Van Vorst's Adm'x, 1 Zab. (N. J.) 100. §§ 395, 425, 560.
Morrison, Baker v., 4 La. Ann. 372. §§ 22, 465.
v. Berkey, 7 Serg. & Rawle (Pa.), 238. § 211.
Carnegie v., 2 Met. (Mass.) 381. § 81.
Guthrie v., 1 Har. (Del.) 368. § 506.
v. Hartman, 14 Pa. St. 55. § 438.
Jack v., 48 Pa. St. 113. § 325.
v. Lovell, 81 Va. 519. § 587.
v. Marvin, 6 Ala. 797. § 312.
Odd Fellows v., 42 Mich. 521. § 113.
v. Page, 9 Dana (Ky.), 428. § 230.
People v., 75 Mich. 30. § 502.
v. Poyntz, 7 Dana (Ky.), 307. §§ 288, 290.
v. Taylor, 21 Ala. 779. § 274.
Taylor v., 26 Ala. 728. § 271.
Tighee v., 116 N. Y. 263. § 60.
v. Turnour, 18 Vesey, 175. § 89.
Warner v., 3 Allen, 566. §§ 258, 267.
v. Yancey, 23 Mo. App. 670. § 487.
Morrison's Ex'r, Higgins v., 4 Dana (Ky.), 100. § 271.
Morrow v. Brady, 12 R. I. 130. § 109.
v. Morrow, 2 Tenn. Ch. (Cooper), 549. § 207.
v. Wood, 56 Ala. 1. § 548.
Slevin v., 4 Ind. (2 Port.) 425. § 440.
Morrow's Adm'r v. Peyton's Adm'r, 8 Leigh (Va.), 54. § 38.
Morse, Hill v., 61 Me. 541. § 277.
Morse v. Hodson, 5 Mass. 314. § 22.
v. Huntington, 40 Vt. 488. §§ 367, 376.
Slingerland v., 7 Johns. 463. § 64.
Morss v. Gleason, 64 N. Y. 204. § 36.
Mortland v. Himes, 8 Pa. St. 265. § 154.
Mortlock v. Buller, 10 Vesey, 292. § 90.
Morton, Barber v., 45 Up. Can. (Q. B.) 386. § 387.
Cabot Bank v., 4 Gray, 156. § 28.
v. Dean, 13 Met. (Mass.) 385. §§ 80, 90.
Rice v., 19 Mo. 263. §§ 40, 439.
v. Roberts, 4 T. B. Mon. (Ky.) 491. § 363.
Ryan v., 65 Tex. 258. §§ 122, 397, 427.
Moseley, Russell v., 3 Brod. & Bing. 211. §§ 17, 84.
Mosely v. Taylor, 4 Dana (Ky.), 542. § 62.
Moser v. Libenguth, 2 Rawle (Pa.), 428. § 141.
Moses, State v., 18 S. C. 366. § 541.
State v., 20 S. C. 465. § 540.
Mosher, Bangs v., 23 Barb. (N. Y.) 478. § 364.
v. Hotchkiss, 2 Keyes (N. Y.), 589. § 98.
v. Hotchkiss, 3 Abb. Rep. Om. Cas. (N. Y.) 326. § 84.
Mosier v. Waful, 56 Barb. (N. Y.) 80. § 100.
Moss v. Craft, 10 Mo. 720. § 436.
Curtis v., 2 Rob. (La.) 367. § 151.
v. Fowlkes, 14 Lea (Tenn.), 382. § 585.
McCormick v., 41 Ill. 352. § 537.
v. McCullough, 5 Hill (N. Y.), 131. § 630.
v. McCullough, 7 Barb. (N. Y.) 279. § 39.
v. Pettengill, 3 Minn. 217. §§ 40. 434, 436.
v. Riddle, 5 Cranch, 351. § 402.
v. State, 10 Mo. 338. § 169.

Most *v.* Nacogdoches Co., 71 Tex. 380. § 524.
Moulton, Campbell *v.*, 30 Vt. 667. § 114.
v. Posten, 52 Wis. 169. § 344.
Westphal *v.*, 45 Iowa, 163. § 105.
Mount Holly Nat. Bank, Bourne *v.*, 45 N. J. Law, 360. § 422.
Mount Olivet Cemetery Co. *v.* Sherbert, 2 Head (Tenn.), 116. § 66.
Mountjoy *v.* Bank's Ex'rs, 6 Munf. (Va.) 387. § 229.
Mountstephen *v.* Lakeman, 7 Q. B. 196. §§ 54, 56, 77, 78.
Mounts, Hagar *v.*, 3 Blackf. (Ind.) 57. § 416.
Mouton *v.* Noble, 1 La. Ann. 192. § 363.
Motivos, Simon *v.*, 1 W. Black. 599. § 90.
Mott, Barnes *v.*, 64 N. Y. 397. §§ 34, 451.
Crafts *v.*, 4 N. Y. 604. § 38.
Gay *v.*, 43 Ga. 252. § 15.
Lichten *v.*, 10 Ga. 138. § 507.
Mowatt, Phœnix Fire Ins. Co. *v.*, 6 Conn. 599. § 500.
Mowbray *v.* State, 88 Ind. 324. §§ 517, 590.
Mowery *v.* Mast & Co., 9 Neb. 445. §§ 137, 197.
Mowry *v.* Heney, 86 Cal. 471. § 462.
Moyle, Boyd *v.*, 2 Man., Gr. & S. 644. § 17.
Moynahan *v.* Hanaford, 42 Mich. 329. § 181.
Mozley *v.* Tinkler, 1 Cromp., Mees. & Ros. 692. § 189.
Mudd, Flynn *v.*, 27 Ill. 323. §§ 29, 352.
Mueller *v.* Dobschuetz, 89 Ill. 176. § 376.
Mugge, Cummings *v.*, 94 Ill. 186. § 476.
Muir, State *v.*, 20 Mo. 303. § 537.
Muldoon *v.* Crawford's Adm'r, 14 Bush (Ky.), 125. § 318.
Nash *v.*, 16 Nev. 404. § 565.
Mulford *v.* Estudillo, 23 Cal. 94. § 434.
Mullen, Bagott *v.*, 32 Ind. 332. § 264.
v. Scott, 9 La. Ann. 173. § 636.
Mullendore *v.* Wertz, 75 Ind. 431. § 38.
Muller *v.* Bohlens, 2 Wash. C. C. 378. § 71.
v. Down, 94 U. S. 444. § 226.
v. Wadlington, 5 Rich. N. S. (S. C.) 342. § 431.
Mullindore *v.* Wertz, 75 Ind. 431. § 645.
Mullins, White Sewing Machine Co. *v.*, 41 Mich. 339. § 394.
Mulreim, Carter *v.*, 82 Cal. 167. § 476.
Mumford, Bank *v.*, 6 Ga. 44. §§ 29, 606.
v. Railroad, 2 Lea (Tenn.), 393. § 394.
Muncey *v.* Joest, 74 Ind. 409. § 619.
Munch, Nelson *v.*, 28 Minn. 314. § 301.
Munden *v.* Bailey, 70 Ala. 63. § 268.
Mundorff *v.* Singer, 5 Watts (Pa.), 172. § 447.
v. Wangler, 12 J. & S. (N. Y. Super. Ct.) 495. § 140.
Mundy, Devore *v.*, 4 Strob. Law (S. C.), 15. § 362.
Odell *v.*, 59 Ga. 641. § 463.
Munford *v.* Rice, 6 Munf. (Va.) 81. § 169.
Munger, Postmaster-General *v.*, 2 Paine, 189. §§ 542, 548.
Municipal Corp. East Zora *v.* Douglas, 17 Grant's Ch. 462. §§ 419, 555.
Municipal Council of Middlesex *v.* Peters, 9 Up. Can. (C. P.) 205. § 401.
Municipality of Whitby *v.* Flint, 9 Up. Can. (C. P.) 449. §§ 521, 523, 553.
Munn, Worrall *v.*, 5 N. Y. 229. § 89.
Munro *v.* Hill, 25 S. C. 476. § 201.
Munson *v.* Adams, 89 Ill. 450. § 14.
Beckley *v.*, 22 Conn. 299. § 217.
Munster Bank, Bank of Montreal *v.*, 11 Irish Law Rep. 417. § 104.

Munster & Leinster Bank *v.* France, Law Rep. Irish (24 Q. B. & Ex. Div.), 82. § 367.
Murdock, Chrisfield *v.*, 55 Hun (N. Y.), 143. § 558.
Murphy, Boehme *v.*, 46 Mo. 57. § 158.
Boyce *v.*, 94 Ind. 1. § 76.
Crom *v.*, 12 B. Mon. (Ky.) 444. § 309.
Hubble *v.*, 1 Duvall (Ky.), 278. § 402.
v. Hubble, 2 Duvall (Ky.), 247. § 402.
Palsgrave *v.*, 14 Up. Can. (C. P.) 153. § 85.
Sullivan *v.*, 23 Minn. 6. § 63.
v. Victor Sewing Machine Co., 112 U. S. 688. § 204.
Murray, Campbell & Jones *v.*, 62 Ga. 86. § 3.
v. Gibson, 28 Grant's Ch. (Can.) 12. §§ 257, 629.
v. Graham, 29 Iowa, 520. § 29.
Hinsdill *v.*, 6 Vt. 136. § 268.
Jackson *v.*, 77 Tex. 644. § 290.
v. Judah, 6 Cow. 484. § 362.
Kernochan *v.*, 111 N. Y. 306. § 135.
v. Luna, 86 Tenn. (2 Pick.) 326. § 585.
v. Marshall, 94 N. Y. 611. § 37.
Murrell, Gregory *v.*, 2 Ired. Eq. (N. C.) 233. § 268.
Railroad *v.*, 11 Heisk. (Tenn.) 715. §§ 167, 600.
Musey, Fessenden *v.*, 11 Cush. 127. § 89.
Musgrave *v.* Glasgow, 3 Ind. 31. §§ 62, 339.
Perfect *v.*, 6 Price, 111. § 342.
Mushat *v.* Brevard, 4 Dev. (N. C.) 73. § 52.
Musick *v.* Beebe, 17 Kan. 47. § 580.
Musket *v.* Rogers, 5 Bing. N. C. 728. § 239.
Mussey *v.* Rayner, 22 Pick. 223. §§ 157, 186, 203.
Musson, Graham *v.*, 7 Scott, 769. § 90.
Mussulman *v.* People, 15 Ill. 51. § 516.
Mutual Life Ins. Co. *v.* Davies, 12 J. & S. (N. Y. Super. Ct.) 172. §§ 37, 606.
Mutual Loan & Bldg. Ass'n *v.* Price, 19 Fla. 127. §§ 168, 626, 555.
Myers, Boye *v.*, 12 Lea (Tenn.), 175. § 318.
Eckert *v.*, 45 Ohio St. 525. § 573.
v. First Nat. Bank, 78 Ill. 257. § 356.
v. Fretz, 4 Pa. St. 344. § 578.
v. United States, 1 McLean, 493. §§ 338, 526.
v. Welles, 5 Hill (N. Y.), 463. 364.
Myles, White's Bank *v.*, 73 N. Y. 335. §§ 156, 159.
Mynatt. Owens *v.*, 1 Heisk. (Tenn.) 675. § 12.
Mynderse, United States *v.*, 11 Blatchford, 1. § 519.
Myres *v.* Parker, 6 Ohio St. 501. § 449.
Myrick *v.* Hasey, 27 Me. 9. § 50.
Wyche *v.*, 14 Ga. 584. § 627.
Myron Lodge, Liebbrandt *v.*, 61 Ill. 81. § 339.
Nabb *v.* Koontz, 17 Md. 283. §§ 88, 153.
Little *v.*, 10 Mo. 3. § 82.
Nacogdoches Co., Most *v.*, 71 Tex. 380. § 524.
Nading *v.* McGregor, 121 Ind. 465. § 193.
Nagle, Huzzard *v.*, 40 Pa. St. 178. § 637.
Nall *v.* Springfield, 9 Bush (Ky.), 673. § 361.
Nance, Simpson *v.*, 1 Spear (S. C.), 4. §§ 61, 63.
Nanz *v.* Oakley, 120 N. Y. 84. §§ 38, 573.
Napier *v.* Bruce, 8 Clark & Fin. 470. § 166.
Nash *v.* Fugate, 24 Gratt. (Va.) 202. § 408.
v. Hartland, 2 Irish Law Rep. 190. §§ 84, 123.

Nash, Hayes *v.*, 129 Mass. 62. § 472.
v. Muldoon, 16 Nev. 404. § 565.
Neal *v.*, 23 Ohio St. 483. § 311.
Reed *v.*, 1 Wils. 305. §§ 54, 57.
Nason *v.* Poor Directors, 126 Pa. St. 445. § 558.
Nathan, Cooke *v.*, 16 Barb. (N. Y.) 342. §§ 98, 401.
Nathans, Pott *v.*, 1 Watts & Serg. (Pa.) 155. § 262.
National Bank *v.* Cushing, 53 Vt. 321. § 315.
Curtis *v.*, 39 Ohio St. 579. § 586.
v. Marhourg, 22 Kan. 535. § 98.
People's Bank *v.*, 101 U. S. 181. § 6.
v. Phelps, 97 N. Y. 44. § 396.
v. Place, 15 Hun, 564. § 356.
Trust Co. *v.*, 101 U. S. 68. § 179.
National Bank of Baltimore *v.* Gerke, 68 Md. 449. § 93.
National Bank of Gloversville *v.* Wells, 79 N. Y. 498. § 6.
National Bank of Potsdam, Burnap *v.*, 96 N. Y. 125. § 34.
National Eagle Bank *v.* Hunt, 16 R. I. 148. § 133.
National Exchange Bank *v.* Gay, 57 Conn. 224. § 396.
v. Silliman, 65 N. Y. 475. § 323.
Thornton *v.*, 71 Mo. 221. § 324.
National Guardian Assurance Society, Towle *v.*, 3 Giff. 42. § 404.
National Loan & B'ld'g Society *v.* Lichtenwalner, 100 Pa. St. 100. §§ 101, 183.
National Mech. B'k'g Ass'n *v.* Conkling, 90 N. Y. 116. § 394.
National Pemberton Bank *v.* Lougee, 118 Mass. 371. § 178.
National Union Bank of Md., Lazear *v.*, 52 Md. 78, 121. § 127.
Nations, Parker *v.*, 33 Tex. 210. § 434.
Naugle *v.* State, 101 Ind. 284. § 543.
Naylor, Doolittle *v.*, 2 Bosw. (N. Y.) 206. § 65.
v. Moody, 3 Blackf. (Ind.) 92. § 438.
Neal, Bronaugh *v.*, 1 Rob. (La.) 23. § 236.
v. Freeman, 85 N. C. 441. § 101.
v. Gordon, 60 Ga. 112. § 487.
v. Nash, 23 Ohio St. 483. § 311.
Pike *v.*, 73 Me. 513. § 508.
Neal's Adm'r, McMullen *v.*, 60 Ala. 552. § 324.
Neberroth *v.* Riegel, 71 Pa. St. 280. § 77.
Needhams *v.* Page, 3 B. Mon. (Ky.) 465. § 176.
Neel *v.* Harding, 2 Met. (Ky.) 247. § 29.
Neelson *v.* Sanborn, 2 N. H. 413. § 82.
Neely *v.* Bee, 32 W. Va. 519. § 274.
Kannon *v.*, 10 Humph. (Tenn.) 288. § 197.
Neely, Adm'r, Gilbert *v.*, 35 Ark. 24. § 319.
Neff, Covey *v.*, 63 Ind. 391. § 205.
Headington *v.*, 7 Ohio, 229. § 618.
v. Horner, 63 Pa. St. 327. § 379.
v. Miller, 8 Pa. St. 347. §§ 301, 325.
Neff's Appeal, 9 Watts & Serg. (Pa.) 36. §§ 97, 431.
Neil *v.* Board of Trustees, 31 Ohio St. 15. §§ 137, 199, 644.
British Am. Assurance Co. *v.*, 76 Iowa, 645. § 602.
v. Morgan, 28 Ill. 524. § 26.
Neilson *v.* Fry, 16 Ohio St. 552. § 310.
v. Williams, 42 N. J. Eq. 291. § 577.
Neimcewicz *v.* Gahn, 3 Paige, Ch. 614. § 237.
Nelson *v.* Anderson, 2 Call (Va.), 286. § 458.
v. Bostwick, 5 Hill, 37. § 197.
Clinton *v.*, 2 Utah Terr. 284. § 595.
v. First Nat. Bank of Chicago, 48 Ill. 36. § 67.
Givens *v.*, 10 Leigh (Va.), 382. § 269.
v. Hardy, 7 Ind. 364. § 63.
v. Munch, 28 Minn. 314. § 301.

Nelson *v.* Richardson, 4 Sneed, 307. § 185.
v. Williams, 2 Dev. & Bat. Eq. (N. C.) 118. § 435.
Neison, Adm'r, *v.* Corwin, Adm'r, 59 Ind. 489. § 589.
Neponset Bank *v.* Leland, 5 Met. (Mass.) 259. § 432.
Neptune Ins. Co. *v.* Dorsey, 3 Md. Ch. 334. § 306.
Nesmith, Swan *v.*, 7 Pick. 220. § 71.
Nettleton, Tilleston *v.*, 6 Pick. 509. §§ 75, 78.
Neussam *v.* Finch, 25 Barb. (N. Y.) 175. § 353.
Neville, Life Association *v.*, 72 Ala. 517. §§ 339, 340.
Nevin *v.* Fouch, 77 Ga. 47. § 45.
State *v.*, 19 Nev. 162. § 558.
Nevins *v.* Bank of Lansingburgh, 10 Mich. 547. § 81.
Foxcroft *v.*, 4 Greenl. (Me.) 72. § 523.
New, Bailey *v.*, 29 Ga. 214. §§ 609, 610.
New Hampshire Savings Bank *v.* Colcord, 15 N. H. 119. §§ 347, 352, 426.
v. Ela, 11 N. H. 335. § 345.
v. Gill, 16 N. H. 578. § 352.
New Haven Bank *v.* Miles, 5 Conn. 587. § 505.
New Haven Co. Bank *v.* Mitchell, 15 Conn. 206. §§ 118, 195.
New Jersey Midland R. R. Co., Coe *v.*, 27 N. J. Eq. 110. § 298.
New London Bank *v.* Lee, 12 Conn. 112. §§ 252, 324.
New Orleans C. & B. Co. *v.* Escoffe, 2 La. Ann. 830. §§ 97, 447.
New Orleans Print. & Pub. Co., Hawkins *v.*, 29 La. Ann. 134. § 118.
New York Nat. Exch. Bank *v.* Jones, 9 Daly (N. Y. Com. Pl.), 248. § 445.
Newbury *v.* Armstrong, 6 Bing. 201. § 84.
Newcomb *v.* Blakely, 1 Mo. App. 289. § 366.
v. Hale, 90 N. Y. 326. § 239.
Hall *v.*, 3 Hill, 233. § 179.
Hall *v.*, 7 Hill (N. Y.), 416. § 182.
Newcomer, Piper *v.*, 25 Iowa, 221. § 29.
v. State, 77 Tex. 286. § 524.
Newell, Crane *v.*, 2 Pick. 612. § 423.
v. Fowler, 23 Barb. (N. Y.) 628. § 98.
v. Hamer, 4 How. (Miss.) 684. §§ 40, 239.
Harris *v.*, 42 Wis. 687. §§ 1, 242.
v. Hurlburt, 2 Vt. 351. § 222.
v. Ingraham, 15 Vt. 422. § 75.
Kimball *v.*, 7 Hill, 116. §§ 58, 153.
v. Norton, 3 Wall. 257. § 470.
Orvis *v.*, 17 Conn. 97. §§ 29, 305.
Prescott *v.*, 39 Vt. 82. § 291.
Newhall, Loomis *v.*, 15 Pick. 159. §§ 57, 63.
Newkirk, Ringgold *v.*, 3 Ark. (Pike), 96. § 197.
Wood *v.*, 15 Ohio St. 245. § 354.
Newlan *v.* Harrington, 24 Ill. 206. § 381.
Newman *v.* Beckwith, 5 Lans. (N. Y.) 80. § 570.
v. Campbell, Mar. & Yerg. (Tenn.) 63. § 616.
v. Hazlerigg, 1 Bush (Ky.), 412. § 334.
v. Metcalfe Co. Ct., 4 Bush (Ky.), 67. § 545.
Streator Coal Co., 19 Bradw. (Ill. App.) 594. § 191.
Newsom *v.* McLendon, 6 Ga. 392. § 322.
Newton, Cartenel *v.*, 79 Ind. 1. § 346.
v. Charlton, 2 Drewry, 333. § 426.
v. Cox, 76 Mo. 352. § 517.
v. Hammond, 38 Ohio St. 430. §§ 238, 242, 574.
State *v.*, 33 Ark. 276. § 627.
Wheeler *v.*, 2 Eq. Cas. 44, ch. 5. § 89.
Newton Wagon Co. *v.* Diers, 10 Neb. 284. §§ 14, 197.

Ney *v.* Orr, 2 Mont. 559. § 459.
Neylan *v.* Green, 82 Cal. 128. § 109.
Niemcewicz *v.* Gahn, 3 Paige, 614. § 35.
Gahn *v.*, 11 Wend. 312. § 35.
Nichol *v.* Ridley, 5 Yerg. (Tenn.) 63. § 80.
United States *v.*, 12 Wheat. 505. § 556.
Nicholls *v.* Ingersoll, 7 Johns. 146. § 496.
Johnston *v.*, Man., Gr. & Scott, 251. § 84.
Nichols *v.* Allen, 22 Minn. 283. §§ 67, 101.
v. Johnson, 10 Conn. 192. §§ 80, 81.
King *v.*, 16 Ohio St. 80. §§ 537, 550.
Lauman *v.*, 15 Iowa, 161. § 32.
Mason *v.*, 22 Wis. 376. § 145.
v. McDowell, 14 B. Mon. (Ky.) 5. § 242.
Noyes *v.*, 28 Vt. 159. §§ 200, 204.
v. Palmer, 48 Wis. 110. § 390.
v. Parsons, 6 N. H. 30. §§ 33, 375.
Scott *v.*, 27 Miss. 94. § 230.
Weld *v.*, 17 Pick. 538. §§ 60, 72.
Nichols, Adm'r, *v.* State, 65 Ind. 512. § 628.
Nicholson, Duhamp *v.*, 14 Martin (La.), 2 N. S. 672. § 42.
v. Paget, 1 Cromp. & Mees. 48. §§ 92, 162.
Nickels, Howe *v.*, 22 Me. 175. §§ 186, 192, 203.
Nicol, State *v.*, 30 La. Ann. 628. §§ 508, 509, 510.
Nickerson *v.* Chatterton, 7 Cal. 568. § 486.
Mellen *v.*, 12 Gray, 445. § 418.
Nims, Kennedy *v.*, 52 Mich. 153. § 452.
Nisbet *v.* Smith, 2 Brown's Ch. Ca. 579. §§ 238, 373.
Nixdorf, Lunstead *v.*, 80 Cal. 647. § 599.
Nixon *v.* Beard, 111 Ind. 137. § 293.
Bledsoe *v.*, 68 N. C. 521. § 313.
Nixon, Carroll *v.*, 4 Watts & Serg. (Pa.) 517. § 247.
Dewitt Co. Nat. Bank *v.*, 125 Ill. 615. § 176.
Gale *v.*, 6 Cow. (N. Y.) 445. § 80.
v. Whitely, 102 Ind. 360. § 7.
Noble, Carman *v.*, 9 Pa. St. 366. §§ 221, 247.
v. Himes, 12 Neb. 193. §§ 566, 571.
Monton *v.*, 1 La. Ann. 192. § 363.
Osborn *v.*, 46 Miss. 449. § 326.
Noel, Micklewait *v.*, 69 Iowa, 344. § 408.
Nofsinger *v.* Hartnett, Adm'r, 84 Mo. 549, 559. § 457.
Nolan *v.* Clark, 10 B. Mon. (Ky.) 239. § 440.
State *v.*, 99 Mo. 569. § 587.
Nolan, Adm'r, *v.* Johns, 27 Mo. App. 502. § 476.
Nolen, Grimes *v.*, 3 Humph. (Tenn.) 412. § 372.
Noll *v.* Oberhellmann, 20 Mo. App. 336. §§ 181, 366.
Nolly *v.* Calloway Co. Ct., 11 Mo. 447. §§ 528, 628, 641.
Noole *v.* Blount, 77 Mo. 235. § 225.
Norfleet, McWilliams *v.*, 60 Miss. 987. §§ 24, 520, 541.
Norman, Ruble *v.*, 7 Bush (Ky.), 582. § 333.
Norment, State *v.*, 12 La. (Curry), 511. § 501.
Norris, Briggs *v.*, 67 Mich. 325. §§ 99, 346.
v. Evans, 2 B. Mon. (Ky.) 84. § 311.
v. Ham, R. M. Charlt. (Ga.) 267. § 311.
v. Pollard, 75 Ga. 358. § 145.
Reed *v.*, 2 Mylne & Craig, 361. § 212.
Schneider *v.*, 2 Maule & Sel. 286. §§ 80, 89.
Woldridge *v.*, Law Rep. 6 Eq. Cas. 410. § 223.
North *v.* Cox, 89 N. C. 44. § 491.
Prairie *v.*, 78 N. C. 169. § 591.

North v. Robinson, 1 Duvall (Ky.), 71. § 72.
Weber v., 51 Iowa, 375. § 580.
North & South Wales Bank, Duncan, Fox & Co. v., Law Rep. (6 H. of L. App. Cas.) 1. § 329.
North British Ins. Co. v. Lloyd, 10 Wels., Hurl. & Gor. 523. § 419.
North British Mercantile Ins. Co. v. Kean, 16 Ont. (Can.) 117. § 602.
North Side Planing Co., Schnell v., 89 Ill. 581. § 178.
North Western R. R. Co. v. Whinray, 1 Hurl. & Gor. (10 Ex. Ch.) 77. § 392.
Northampton Nat. Bank v. Wylie, 52 Hun (N. Y.), 146. § 473.
Northern Bank of Kentucky v. Cooke, 13 Bush. (Ky.), 340. § 334.
Macklin v., 83 Ky. 314. § 327.
Ward v., 14 B. Mon. (Ky.) 283. § 114.
Northern Ins. Co. v. Wright, 76 N. Y. 445. § 101.
Northrop, Tuttle v., 44 Ohio St. 178. § 577.
Northrup, Reed v., 50 Mich. 442. § 616.
Stillman v., 109 N. Y. 473. §§ 48, 50.
Northumberland v. Cobleigh, 59 N. H. 250. § 628.
Northumberland Bank v. Eyer, 58 Pa. St. 97. § 47.
Northway, Becker v., 44 Minn. 61. § 236.
Northwestern Mut. Life Ins. Co. v. Allis, 23 Minn. 337. § 97.
Northwood, Canadian Bank v., 14 Ont. (Can.) 207. § 376.
Norton v. Cammack, 10 La. Ann. 10. § 467.
v. Coons, 3 Denio, 130. § 258.
v. Coons, 6 N. Y. 33. § 261.
v. Eastman, 4 Greenl. (Me.) 521. §§ 192, 366.
Norton v. Huxley, 13 Gray, 285. § 73.
v. Miller, 25 Ark. 108. §§ 43, 325.
Newell v., 3 Wall. 257. § 470.
People v., 9 N. Y. 176. § 521.
v. Reid, 11 S. C. 593. § 238.
Sanford v., 14 Vt. 228. §§ 180, 182.
v. Soule, 2 Greenl. (Me.) 341. § 315.
Vary v., 6 Fed. Rep. (Cir. Ct. W. D. Mich. S. D.) 808. §§ 29, 344, 356.
Norvill, Anderson v., 10 Bradw. (Ill. App.) 240. § 88.
Norwood, Bell v., 7 La. (4 Curry), 95. § 118.
Norwood, Adm'r, Soule v., 30 La. Ann. 486. § 588.
Nothingham Hide Co. v. Bottrill, L. R. 8 Com. Pl. 694. § 158.
Nowland v. Martin, 1 Ired. Law (N. C.), 307. § 286.
Noyes, Dover Stamping Co. v., 151 Mass. 342. § 161.
v. Granger, 51 Iowa, 227. § 93.
v. Humphreys, 11 Gratt. (Va.) 636. §§ 69, 75, 78.
McMurray v., 72 N. Y. 523. §§ 37, 99, 101.
McQuesten v., 6 N. H. 19. §§ 38, 339.
v. Nichols, 28 Vt. 159. §§ 200, 204.
Nugent v. Wolfe, 111 Pa. St. 471. § 61.
Nurre v. Chittenden, 56 Ind. 462. § 260.
Nutt, City of Wilmington v., 78 N. C. 177. § 532.
Hewlett v., 79 N. C. 263. § 531.
Nutzenholster v. State, 37 Ind. 457. § 525.
O'Bannon v. Saunders, 24 Gratt. (Va.) 138. § 567.
O'Blenis v. Karnig, 57 N. Y. 649. § 281.
O'Brien, Case v., 66 Mich. 289. §§ 37, 362.
Hungerford v., 37 Minn. 306. § 102.

O'Callaghan, Queen v., 1 Irish Eq. 439. § 303.
O'Donald, Allen v., 23 Fed. Rep. 573. § 426.
Allen v., 28 Fed. Rep. (Cir. Ct. D. Oreg.) 346. § 34.
O'Donnell v. Leeman, 43 Me. 158. § 80.
v. Smith, 2 E. D. Smith (N. Y.), 124. § 67.
O'Donohue v. Simmons, 31 Hun (N. Y.), 267. § 599.
O'Gorman, State v., 75 Mo. 370. § 517.
O'Howell v. Kirk, 41 Mo. App. 523. § 29.
O'Neill v. Carter, 9 Up. Can. (Q. B.) 470. § 399.
United States v., 19 Fed. Rep. 567. § 385.
O'Rourk, Comm'rs of Charities v., 34 Hun (N. Y.), 349. § 45.
Oak v. Dustin, 79 Me. 23. § 504.
Oakeley v. Pasheller, 10 Bligh (N. S.), 548. § 36.
Oakes, Pemberton v., 4 Russ. 154. §§ 118, 330, 331.
Oakey, Gasquet v., 19 La. (Curry), 76. § 228.
Oakley v. Boorman, 21 Wend. 588. §§ 88, 96.
Nanz v., 120 N. Y. 84. §§ 38, 573.
v. Van Nopper, 100 N. C. 287. § 462.
Oaks v. Scheifferly, 74 Cal. 478. § 599.
Stevens v., 58 Mich. 343. §§ 29, 375.
v. Weller, 13 Vt. 106. §§ 187, 203, 204.
Obannon's Ex'r, McCormack's Adm'r v., 3 Munf. (Va.) 484. § 290.
Obear, Whittemore v., 58 Mo. 280. § 403.
Oberhellmann, 20 Mo. App. 336. §§ 181, 366.
Oberndorff v. Union Bank, 31 Md. 126. § 332.
Oberne, Wieland v., 20 Bradw. (Ill. App.) 118. § 236.
Oberreich, Weed Sewing Machine Co. v., 38 Wis. 325. § 364.
Oblender, Black v., 135 Pa. St. 526. § 538.
Ocheltree, Strunk v., 11 Iowa, 158. § 566.
Odd Fellows v. Morrison, 42 Mich. 521. § 113.
Odd Fellows Mutual Aid Ass'n v. James, 63 Cal. 598. § 558.
Odell v. Mundy, 59 Ga. 641. § 463.
Schaacht v., 52 Cal. 449. § 461.
v. Wooten, 38 Ga. 224. § 472.
Odeneal, Carraway v., 56 Miss. 223. § 372.
Odiorne, Ahrend v., 125 Mass. 50. § 45.
Odlin v. Greenleaf, 3 N. H. 270. § 230.
Odom, Rogers v., 86 N. C. 432. § 531.
State v., 1 Spear's Law (S. C.), 245. § 523.
Odum, Fleming v., 59 Ga. 362. § 434.
Oertling, Stockmeyer v., 35 La. Ann. 467. §§ 254, 267.
Offnutt, Robinson v., 7 T. B. Mon. (Ky.) 540. §§ 142, 363.
Offord v. Davies, 12 J. Scott (N. S.), 748. § 134.
Offutt v. Commonwealth, 10 Bush (Ky.), 212. § 539.
McCauley v., 12 B. Mon. (Ky.) 386. § 488.
Ogburn v. Wilson, 93 N. C. 115. § 319.
Ogden v. Aspinwall, 7 Dow. & Ryland, 637. § 123.
Bailey v., 3 Johns. 399. §§ 81, 89.
v. Blydenburgh, 1 Hilton (N. Y.), 182. § 28.
Gipson v., 100 Ind. 20. §§ 20, 355, 371, 375.
Hubbard v., 22 Kan. 363. §§ 35, 352.
People v., 10 Bradw. (Ill. App.) 226. § 503.
v. Rowe, 3 E. D. Smith (N. Y.), 312. § 389.
Shepard v., 2 Scam. (Ill.) 257. § 230.

Ogier v. Higgins, 2 McCord, Law (S. C.), 8. § 509.
Ogilvie v. Foljambe, 3 Meriv. 53. § 89.
Ogle v. Graham, 2 Pen. & Watts (Pa.), 132. § 381.
Oglesby's Sureties v. State, 73 Tex. 658. § 590.
Ohio, Peabody v., 4 Ohio St. 387. § 564.
Ohio Life Ins. Co. v. Ledyard, 8 Ala. 866. § 325.
Ohio Life Ins. & Trust Co. v. Reeder, 18 Ohio, 35. § 326.
Ohio & Mississippi R'y Co. v. Hardy, 64 Ind. 454. § 8.
Ohning v. City of Evansville, 66 Ind. 59. § 628.
Okeson, Brubaker v., 36 Pa. St. 519. § 246.
Okie v. Spencer, 1 Miles (Pa.), 299. § 364.
Olcott, Klosterman v., 25 Neb. 382. § 193.
v. Lilly, 4 Johns. 407. § 497.
Old Colony R. R. Co., Davis v., 131 Mass. 258. § 6.
Old Town Bank, Street v., 67 Md. 421. § 39.
Oldershaw v. King, 2 Hurl. & Nor. 520. §§ 16, 84.
Oldham v. Brown, 28 Ohio St. 41. § 265.
Olds, Stage v., 12 Ohio, 158. § 137.
Ole, Citizens' Savings Bank v., 47 Iowa, 492. § 638.
Olive, Adams v., 57 Ala. 249. § 469.
Oliver, Haile v., 52 Tex. 443. § 616.
v. Oliver, 4 Rawle (Pa.), 141. § 405.
Oliver's Adm'r, Tinsley v., 5 Munf. (Va.) 419. § 313.
Olmstead v. Greenly, 18 Johns. 12. § 65.
Jenuery v., 90 N. Y. 363. § 539.
Olmsted v. Olmsted, 38 Conn. 309. § 141.
Olson, Benedict v., 37 Minn. 431. § 242.
Omaha Hotel Co., Kountze v., 107 U. S. 378. § 452.
Oman, Clark v., 15 Gray, 521. § 222.
Ontario Bank, Dobell v., 3 Ont. (Can.) 299. § 6.
v. Walker, 1 Hill (N. Y.), 652. § 312.
Oppermann, Deobold v., 111 N. Y. 531. §§ 3, 14, 587.
Orange Co. Bank, Herrick v., 27 Vt. 584. § 447.
Ord, Miller v., 2 Binney (Pa.), 382. § 252.
Ordeman v. Lawson & Bro., 49 Md. 135. §§ 82, 85.
Ordinary v. Carlile, 1 McMullan, Law (S. C.), 100. § 638.
v. Cooley, 1 Vroom (N. J.), 179. § 22.
v. Corbett, Bay (S. C.), 328. § 586.
v. Heishow, 42 N. J. Law, 15. § 517.
v. Kershaw, 1 McCart. (N. J.) 527. § 580.
v. Thatcher, 41 N. J. Law, 403. § 409.
v. Wallace, 2 Rich. Law (S. C.), 460. § 638.
Orford, Wood v., 56 Cal. 157. § 464.
Organ, People v., 27 Ill. 27. § 385.
Oriental Financial Corporation v. Overend, 7 Ch. App. Cas. 142. § 32.
Orleans Navigation Company, Louisiana State Bank v., 3 La. Ann. 294. § 5.
Orman, Griffin v., 9 Fla. 22. § 298.
v. Pueblo, 8 Col. 292. § 590.
Orne, Cook v., 37 Ill. 186. §§ 186, 193.
Orr, Hopkins v., 124 U. S. 510. § 464.
Ney v., 2 Mont. 559. § 459.
State v., 12 Lea (Tenn.), 725. § 543.
Tennant v., 15 Irish Com. Law, 397. § 126.
Orrell v. Coppock, 26 Law Jour. Ch. 269. § 67.
Orsler, State v., 48 Iowa, 343. § 501.

Ortet, Chaquette, Adm'r, *v.*, 60 Cal. 594. §§ 578, 580.
Orvis *v.* Newell, 17 Conn. 97. §§ 29, 305.
Osborn *v.* Cunningham, 4 Dev. & Bat. Law (N. C.), 423. § 278.
v. Low, 40 Ohio St. 347. §§ 351, 356.
v. Noble, 46 Miss. 449. § 326.
Osborne *v.* Bryce (Cir. Ct. E. D. Wis.), 23 Fed. Rep. 171. § 236.
v. Lawson, 26 Mo. App. 549. §§ 88, 199.
v. Smith (Cir. Ct. D. Minn.), 18 Fed. Rep. 126. §§ 101, 106, § 329.
Smith *v.*, 31 Hun (N. Y.), 390. § 140.
v. Stone, 30 Minn. 25. § 18.
v. Thompson, 35 Minn. 229. § 18.
v. United States, 19 Wall. 577. § 556.
v. Van Houten, 45 Mich. 444. § 399.
Osborne & Co. *v.* Baker, 34 Minn. 307. § 84.
Osgood, Harp *v.*, 2 Hill (N. Y.), 216. §§ 494, 516.
Lyon *v.*, 58 Vt. 707. § 586.
v. Miller, 67 Me. 174. §§ 147, 345.
v. Osgood, 39 N. H. 209. § 222.
Vielie *v.*, 8 Barb. (N. Y.) 130. §§ 80, 89.
Oshiel *v.* De Graw, 6 Cow. 63. § 112.
Ostrom, Claflin *v.*, 54 N. Y. 581. § 48.
Oswald *v.* Fratenburgh, 36 Minn. 270. § 48.
Mayor of Berwick *v.*, 1 Ell. & Black. 295. § 552.
v. Mayor of Berwick, 5 H. of L. Cas. 856. § 172.
Other *v.* Iveson, 3 Drew. 177. § 139.
Otis, Board of Supervisors *v.*, 62 N. Y. 88. § 555.
v. Haseltine, 27 Cal. 80. § 87.
Trustees of Schools *v.*, 85 Ill. 179. § 141.
Vivian *v.*, 24 Wis. 518. § 545.
v. Von Storch, 15 R. I. 41. § 29.
Otto *v.* Jackson, 35 Ill. 349. § 44.
People *v.*, 77 Cal. 45. § 617.
Ottoman Bank, Black *v.*, 15 Moore's Priv. Coun. Cas. 472. § 423.
Ouland, Allaire *v.*, 2 Johns. Cas. 52. § 60.
Outlaw *v.* Reddick, 11 Ga. 669. § 224.
Over, Rupp *v.*, 3 Brewster (Pa.), 133. § 233.
Overacre *v.* Garrett, 5 Lans. (N. Y.) 156. § 539.
Overby, Commonwealth *v.*, 80 Ky. 208. § 499.
Overend, Oriental Financial Corporation *v.*, 7 Ch. App. Cas. 142. § 32.
Overton *v.* Tracey, 14 Serg. & Rawle (Pa.), 311. § 202.
v. Woodson, 17 Mo. 453. § 582.
Overturf *v.* Martin, 2 Ind. (2 Carter), 507. §§ 606, 612.
Ovington *v.* Smith, 78 Ill. 250. § 479.
Owen, Bryant *v.*, 1 Kelly (Ga.), 355. §§ 546, 639.
v. Herman, 13 Beav. 196. § 376.
v. Homan, 3 Macn. & Gor. 378. § 233.
v. Long, 112 Mass. 403. § 4.
McGehee *v.*, 61 Ala. 440. §§ 211, 254, 268, 294.
v. State, 25 Ind. 371. § 581.
Third National Bank *v.*, 101 Mo. 558. § 422.
v. Thomas, 3 Myl. & Keen, 353. § 80.
Williams *v.*, 13 Simons, 597. § 315.
Owens, Duncan *v.*, 47 Ark. 388. § 487.
Lucas *v.*, 113 Ind. 521. § 406.
v. Miller, 29 Md. 144. § 324.
v. Mynatt, 1 Heisk. (Tenn.) 675. § 12.
Oxford, Peers *v.*, 17 Grant's Ch. 472. § 419.
Oxford & Worcester R. R. Co., Woodcock *v.*, 1 Drewry, 521. § 384.
Oxford Bank *v.* Haynes, 8 Pick. 423. §§ 183, 197.
v. Lewis, 8 Pick. 458. § 352.

Oxford Iron Co., Delaware, Lackawanna & Western R. R. Co. v., 38 N. J. Eq. 151. §§ 212, 223.
Oxley v. Stover, 54 Ill. 159. § 367.
v. Young, 2 H. Black. 613. § 246.
Pabst, Board of Supervisors v., 70 Wis. 352. § 542.
Pace, Hubbard v., 34 Ark. 80. § 440.
v. Marsh, 1 Bing. 216. § 84.
v. Pace, 19 Fla. 438. §§ 574, 584.
Pacific Guano Co. v. Anglim, 82 Ala. 492. § 237.
Pacific National Bank v. Mixter, 124 U. S. 721. § 469.
Pack, Coles v., 5 Com. Pl. 65. § 161.
Packard, Curiac v., 29 Cal. 194. § 339.
v. Herrington, 41 Kan. 469. § 93.
Pain v., 13 Johns. 174. § 239.
v. Richardson, 17 Mass. 122. § 82.
Paddleford v. State, 57 Miss. 118. § 276.
Paddock, Crouse v., 8 Hun (N. Y.), 630. § 516.
Padgett, Hutton v., 26 Md. 228. §§ 82, 84.
Page, Black River Bank v., 44 N. Y. 453. § 446.
v. Bussell, 2 Maule & Sel. 551. § 220.
Cobb v., 17 Pa. St. 469. § 13.
Cooper v., 24 Me. 73. §§ 96, 199.
Eberhart v., 89 Ill. 550. § 176.
Kidder v., 48 N. H. 380. § 251.
Morrison v., 9 Dana (Ky.), 428. § 230.
Needhams v., 3 B. Mon. (Ky.) 465. § 176.
Prindle v., 21 Vt. 94. § 281.
State v., 63 Ind. 209. § 575.
Paget, Nicholson v., 1 Cromp. & Mees. 48. §§ 92, 162.
Pahlman v. Taylor, 75 Ill. 629. §§ 176, 381.
Paige v. Parker, 8 Gray, 211. §§ 197, 202.
Pain v. Packard, 13 Johns. 174. § 239.
Paine v. Drury, 19 Pick. 400. § 129.
v. Jones, 76 N. Y. 274. § 37.
Paine, Moore v., 12 Wend. 123. § 147.
v. Voorhees, 26 Wis. 522. § 365.
Palethorpe v. Lesher, 2 Rawle (Pa.), 272. § 493.
Pallas, Latouche v., Hays (Irish), 450. § 304.
Palmer v. Bagg, 56 N. Y. 523. § 120.
v. Baker, 23 Up. Can. (C. P.) 302. § 81.
Folger v., 35 La. Ann. 814. § 622.
Goodhue v., 13 Ind. 457. § 357.
Jones v., 1 Doug. (Mich.) 379. §§ 67, 82.
Lewis v., 28 N. Y. 271. § 315.
Nichols v., 48 Wis. 110. § 390.
v. Purdy, 83 N. Y. 144. § 36.
v. Stephens, 1 Denio, 471. § 89.
Stevenson v., 14 Col. 565. § 466.
Thomson v., 3 Rich. Eq. (S. C.) 139. § 311.
Underhill v., 10 Daly (N. Y. Com. Pl.), 478. § 426.
Villars v., 67 Ill. 204. § 448.
v. Woods, 75 Iowa, 402. § 596.
Palsgrave v. Murphy, 14 Up. Can. (C. P.) 153. § 85.
Paunill's Adm'r v. Calloway, 78 Va. 387. § 43.
Pape v. People, 19 Bradw. (Ill. App.) 24. § 546.
Pardee v. Markle, 111 Pa. St. 548. § 331.
Parham v. Cobb, 9 La. Ann. 423. § 475.
v. Green, 64 N. C. 436. § 293.
Parham's Ex'r, Tyree v., 66 Ala. 424. § 226.
Parham Sewing Machine Co. v. Brock, 113 Mass. 194. §§ 114, 118.
Paris, Collins v., 57 Ind. 151. § 468.
v. Hulett, 26 Vt. 308. § 324.
Parish, Burns v., 3 B. Mon. (Ky.) 8. §§ 211, 216.
Parish of St. Helena v. Burton, 35 La. Ann. 521. § 521.
Park v. State, 4 Ga. 329. §§ 504, 515.
v. State, 7 Mo. 194. § 448.
Parke, Dilts v., 1 South. (N. J.) 219. § 63.

Parkell, McMillan *v.*, 64 Mo. 286. § 41.
Parker *v.* Alexander, 2 La. Ann. 188. § 447.
Appleton *v.*, 15 Gray, 173. § 364.
Barker *v.*, 1 Durn. & East, 287. § 119.
Bean *v.*, 17 Mass. 591. § 151.
v. Bidwell, 3 Conn. 84. § 496.
v. Bradley, 2 Hill (N. Y.), 584. §§ 17, 151.
City of Lowell *v.*, 10 Met. (Mass.) 309. §§ 566, 636.
Coombs *v.*, 17 Ohio, 289. § 446.
Fox *v.*, 44 Barb. (N. Y.) 541. § 365.
Granger *v.*, 142 Mass. 186. § 460.
Hall *v.*, 37 Mich. 590. § 411.
Hall *v.*, 39 Mich. 287. § 152.
Jennison *v.*, 7 Mich. 355. § 440.
v. Leek, 1 Stew. (Ala.) 523. § 209.
v. Madesker, 80 Ind. 155. § 526.
Mead *v.*, 111 N. Y. 259. § 99.
Millett *v.*, 2 Met. (Ky.) 608. § 408.
Myres *v.*, 6 Ohio St. 501. § 449.
v. Nations, 33 Tex. 210. § 434.
Paige *v.*, 8 Gray, 211. §§ 197, 202.
Pearson *v.*, 3 N. H. 366. §§ 209, 211.
v. Pitts, 73 Ind. 597. § 25.
Propert *v.*, 1 Russ. & My. 625. § 89.
v. Riddle, 11 Ohio, 102. § 176.
Sherraden *v.*, 24 Iowa, 28. § 442.
State *v.*, 72 Ala. 181. § 146.
v. State, 8 Blackf. (Ind.) 292. § 627.
v. Sterling, 10 Ohio, 357. § 498.
Stewart *v.*, 55 Ga. 656. §§ 29, 345.
Taylor *v.*, 43 Wis. 78. § 563.
Tharp *v.*, 86 Ind. 102. § 375.
v. Wise, 6 Maule & Sel. 239. § 123.
Parkhurst *v.* Van Cortland, 14 Johns. 15. § 80.
Parkinson, Lindsay *v.*, 5 Irish Law Rep. 124. § 387.
Parkis, Craig *v.*, 40 N. Y. 181. §§ 48, 50, 98, 101.
Parks *v.* Brinkerhoff, 2 Hill (N. Y.), 663. § 26.
Burns *v.*, 53 Ga. 61. § 233.
Curtis *v.*, 55 Cal. 106. § 293.
Dearborn *v.*, 5 Greenl. (Me.) 81. § 66.
Parmerlee *v.* Williams, 71 Mo. 410. § 137.
Parnell *v.* Hancock. 48 Cal. 452. § 455.
Ladd *v.*, 57 Cal. 232. § 615.
v. Price, 3 Rich. Law (S. C.), 121. § 344.
Parr, Rawstone *v.*, 3 Russ. 539. § 139.
Parr & Cockey *v.* State, 71 Md. 220. §§ 577, 631.
Parramore, Gammell *v.*, 58 Ga. 576. § 199.
Parrish *v.* Gray, 1 Humph. (Tenn.) 88. § 605.
Parrott, Gross *v.*, 16 Cal. 143. § 360.
Parry *v.* Spikes, 49 Wis. 384. § 82.
Parsons, Dunn *v.*, 40 Hun (N. Y.), 77. §§ 415, 434.
Hargreaves *v.*, 13 Mees. & Wels. 561. § 72.
Haydenville Savings Bank *v.*, 138 Mass. 53. § 352.
Nichols *v.*, 6 N. H. 30. §§ 33, 375.
State *v.*, 89 N. C. 230. § 27.
v. Williams, 9 Conn. 236. § 489.
Partee *v.* Mathews, 53 Miss. 140. § 295.
Partridge *v.* Davis, 20 Vt. 499. §§ 47, 183.
Exall *v.*, 8 Durn. & East, 308. § 208.
v. Jones, 38 Ohio St. 375. § 27.
Pasewalk, Bollman *v.*, 22 Neb. 761. § 152.
Pashby *v.* Mandigo, 42 Mich. 172. § 226.
Pasheller, Oakeley *v.*, 10 Bligh (N. S.), 548. § 36.
Pasley *v.* Freeman, 3 Term R. 51. § 73.

Passmore, Tyson *v.*, 2 Pa. St. 122. § 405.
Passumpsic Bank *v.* Goss, 31 Vt. 315. § 407.
Patchin *v.* Cromach, 13 Vt. 330. § 4.
v. Swift, 21 Vt. 292. § 82.
Paterson, City Council *v.*, 2 Bailey, Law (S. C.), 165. § 555.
Van Valkenbergh *v.*, 47 N. J. Law, 146. § 590.
Patillo *v.* Mayer, 70 Ga. 715. § 181.
Patrick, Jackson *v.*, 10 Rich. (S. C.) 197. § 431.
Pattani, Draper *v.*, 2 Spear (S. C.), 292. §§ 80, 89.
Pattee, Chute *v.*, 37 Me. 102. § 354.
Patten, Greening *v.*, 51 Wis. 146. § 332.
v. Gurney, 17 Mass. 182. § 73.
Huntress *v.*, 20 Me. 28. §§ 100, 235.
James *v.*, 8 Barb. (N. Y.) 344. § 89.
Patterson, Barney *v.*, 6 Harr. & Johns. (Md.) 182. § 80.
Bragg *v.*, 85 Ala. 233. §§ 254, 311.
v. Cave, 61 Mo. 439. § 153.
Conant *v.*, 7 Vt. 163. § 515.
v. Gibson, 81 Ga. 802. § 12.
Gwyn *v.*, 72 N. C. 189. § 408.
ads. Inhabitants of Township of Freehold, 38 N. J. Law, 255. § 547.
Johnston *v.*, 114 Pa. St. 398. §§ 45, 624.
v. Martin, 7 Ohio, 225. § 218.
v. Pope, 5 Dana (Ky.), 241. § 308.
v. Reed, 7 Watts & Serg. (Pa.) 144. § 189.
Sawyer's Adm'r *v.*, 11 Ala. 523. § 438.
Sutherland *v.*, 4 Ont. (Can.) 565. §§ 165, 191.
Swan *v.*, 7 Md. 164. §§ 306, 308.
Pattison, Belfield Union *v.*, 2 Hurl. & Gor. 623. § 554.
Patton, Clark *v.*, 4 J. J. Marsh. (Ky.) 33. § 358.
Patton *v.* Shanklin, 14 B. Mon. (Ky.) 13. § 381.
Paul *v.* Berry, 78 Ill. 158. § 33.
v. Jones, 1 Durn. & East, 599. § 220.
Mattingly *v.*, 88 Ind. 95. § 219.
v. Stackhouse, 38 Pa. St. 302. § 15.
Paulin, Bampton *v.*, 4 Bing. 264. §§ 63, 66, 68.
v. Kaighn, 3 Dutcher (N. J.), 503. §§ 261, 271.
Pawle *v.* Gunn, 4 Bing. N. C. 445. § 52.
Paw Paw *v.* Eggleston, 25 Mich. 36. § 547.
Pawling *v.* United States, 4 Cranch, 219. § 411.
Paxton, Burgett *v.*, 15 Bradw. (Ill. App.) 379. § 93.
Burgett *v.*, 99 Ill. 288. § 329.
Corporation of Ontario *v.*, 27 Up. Can. (C. P.) 104. § 553.
Janson *v.*, 22 Up. Can. (C. P.) 505. § 260.
Paxton's Ex'r, Womack *v.*, 84 Va. 9. §§ 140, 383.
Payne *v.* Able, 7 Bush (Ky.), 344. § 472.
v. Baldwin, 14 Barb. (N. Y.) 570. § 77.
Grider *v.*, 9 Dana (Ky.), 188. § 313.
v. Hook, 7 Wall. 425. § 587.
v. Ives, 3 Dow. & Ryl. 664. § 191.
Lucas *v.*, 7 Cal. 92. § 63.
McCoy *v.*, 68 Ind. 327. § 140.
v. Powell, 14 Tex. 600. § 356.
Royal Canadian Bank *v.*, 19 Grant's Ch. (Can.) 180. §§ 34, 117.
v. Webster, 19 Ill. 103. § 604.
v. Wilson, 7 Barn. & Cres. 423. § 17.
Peabody *v.* Chapman, 20 N. H. 418. § 209.
Frink *v.*, 26 Ill. App. 390. § 271.
v. Harvey, 4 Conn. 119. § 75.
v. Ohio, 4 Ohio St. 387. § 564.

Peacock *v.* State, 44 Tex. 11. § 500.
Peake, Blalock *v.*, 3 Jones' Eq. (N. C.) 323. § 317.
v. Estate of Dorwin, 25 Vt. 28. § 358.
Pearce, Bancroft *v.*, 27 Vt. 668. § 228.
Wren *v.*, 4 Smedes & Marsh. (Miss.) 91. §§ 15, 82, 102.
Pearl *v.* Deacon, 24 Beav. 186. § 335.
v. Wellmans, 11 Ill. 352. § 457.
Pearl Street Congregational Society *v.* Imlay, 23 Conn. 10. § 430.
Pearson, Anderson *v.*, 2 Bailey, Law (S. C.), 107. § 261.
v. Dailey, 7 Lea (Tenn.), 674. § 586.
v. Gayle, 11 Ala. 278. § 448.
Mahurin *v.*, 8 N. H. 539. § 245.
v. Parker, 3 N. H. 366. §§ 209, 211.
Pearsons, People's Bank *v.*, 30 Vt. 711. §§ 41, 352.
Pease *v.* Hirst, 10 B. & C. 122. §§ 121, 143.
Peay, Aikin *v.*, 5 Strob. Law (S. C.), 15. § 284.
v. Poston, 10 Yerg. (Tenn.) 111. § 361.
Pebbles, Shepard *v.*, 38 Wis. 373. § 639.
Peck *v.* Barney, 13 Vt. 93. §§ 187, 199, 204.
Cowles *v.*, 55 Conn. 251. §§ 13, 97, 100.
v. Druett's Adm'r, 9 Dana (Ky.), 486. § 420.
v. Frink, 10 Iowa, 193. §§ 98, 199.
v. Hozier, 14 Johns. 346. § 500.
Michigan State Bank *v.*, 28 Vt. 200. §§ 94, 117.
Whitehead *v.*, 1 Kelly (Ga.), 140. §§ 215, 235.
State *v.*, 53 Me. 284. § 408.
Pecke *v.* Julius, 2 Browne (Pa.), 31. §§ 94, 139.
Peckham *v.* Faria, 3 Doug. 13. § 75.
v. Lindell Glass Co., 9 Mo. App. 459. § 599.
Peebles, Calvert *v.*, 82 N. C. 334. §§ 303, 329.
Casey *v.*, 13 Neb. 7. § 517.
Peel *v.* Tatlock, 1 Bos. & Pul. 419. § 423.
Peer *v.* Kean, 14 Mich. 354. § 332.
Peers *v.* Oxford, 17 Grant's Ch. 472. § 419.
Peiper, Brady *v.*, 1 Hilton (N. Y.), 61. § 405.
Peirce *v.* Higgins, 101 Ind. 178. § 329.
Pell, Stephens *v.*, 2 Cromp. & Mees. 710. § 63.
Pelton *v.* Prescott, 13 Iowa, 567. § 384.
Pelzer *v.* Campbell, 15 S. C. 581. § 7.
Pelzer, Rodgers & Co. *v.* Steadman, 22 S. C. 279. § 330.
Pemberton *v.* Oakes, 4 Russ. 154. §§ 118, 330, 331.
Pence *v.* Gale, 20 Minn. 257. § 426.
Pendell, Bresler *v.*, 12 Mich. 224. § 76.
Pendlebury *v.* Walker, 4 Younge & Coll. (Exch.) 424. §§ 259, 403.
Pendleton *v.* Bank of Kentucky, 1 T. B. Mon. (Ky.) 171. §§ 366, 560, 627.
Miller *v.*, 4 Hen. & Munf. (Va.) 436. § 315.
Pendexter *v.* Vernon, 9 Humph. (Tenn.) 84. § 367.
Penfield *v.* Goodrich, 10 Hun (N. Y.), 41. § 37.
Pengelly, Fair *v.*, 34 Up. Can. (Q. B.) 611. § 342.
Penick, Bank of Limestone *v.*, 2 T. B. Mon. (Ky.) 98. § 380.
Penman, Moodie *v.*, 3 Dessaus. Eq. (S. C.) 482. § 129.
Penn *v.* Collins, 5 Rob. (La.) 213. § 389.
Crawford *v.*, 1 Swan (Tenn.), 388. § 575.
Turney *v.*, 16 Ill. 485. § 137.
Penn. Coal Co. *v.* Blake, 85 N. Y. 226. § 7.
Pennell, Inhabitants Cumberland Co. *v.*, 69 Me. 357. § 558.

Pennell *v.* Pentz, 4 E. D. Smith (N. Y.), 639. § 78.
Penniman *v.* Hartshorn, 13 Mass. 87. § 89.
v. Hudson, 14 Barb. (N. Y.) 579. § 101.
People *v.*, 37 Cal. 271. § 506.
Pennington *v.* Woodall, 17 Ala. 685. § 218.
Penuock, People *v.*, 60 N. Y. 421. § 528.
Penny *v.* Crane Bros. Manuf. Co., 80 Ill. 244. § 97.
Endicott *v.*, 14 Sm. & Mar. (Miss.) 144. § 90.
Penoyer *v.* Watson, 16 Johns. 100. § 117.
Penrice *v.* Crothwaite, 11 Martin (La.), O. S. 537. § 515.
Penton, Simpsou *v.*, 2 Cromp. & Mees. 430. § 77.
Pentz, Pennell *v.*, 4 E. D. Smith (N. Y.), 639. § 78.
People *v.* Abrahams, 6 Daly (N. Y. Com. Pl.), 120. § 511.
Adams *v.*, 12 Bradw. (Ill. App.) 380. § 503.
v. Admire, 39 Ill. 251. § 579.
Affeld *v.*, 12 Bradw. (Ill. App.) 502. § 27.
v. Aikenhead, 5 Cal. 106. § 543.
Albee *v.*, 22 Ill. 533. § 43.
v. Alleu, 86 Ill. 166. § 585.
Ammons *v.*, 11 Ill. 6. § 541.
v. Backus, 117 N. Y. 196. §§ 396, 549.
Bell *v.*, 94 Ill. 230. § 585.
v. Benfield, 80 Mich. 265. § 596.
v. Blackford, 16 Ill. 166. § 548.
v. Breyfogle, 17 Cal. 504. § 151.
Brooks *v.*, 15 Bradw. (Ill. App.) 570. § 632.
v. Brown, 2 Doug. (Mich.) 9. § 385.
Brown *v.*, 24 Ill. App. 72. § 509.
v. Budd, 57 Cal. 349. § 515.
v. Burkhart, 76 Cal. 607. §§ 588, 589.
v. Buster, 11 Cal. 215. § 540.
People *v.* Butler, 74 Mich. 643. §§ 569, 594.
v. Byron, 3 Johns. Cas. 531, 574. § 573.
v. Carey, 5 Daly (N. Y. Com. Pl.), 533. § 511.
v. Cary & Masters, 6 Daly (N. Y. Com. Pl.), 406. § 511.
v. Carpenter, 7 Cal. 402. § 512.
Cash *v.*, 32 Ill. App. 250. § 571.
Casper *v.*, 6 Bradw. (Ill. App.) 28. § 566.
Cawley *v.*, 95 Ill. 249. §§ 410, 422, 517, 546, 603, 628.
v. Chalmers, 60 N. Y. 154. §§ 93, 128.
v. Chisholm, 8 Cal. 29. § 434.
v. Coman, 5 Daly (N. Y. Com. Pl.), 527. § 511.
Combs *v.*, 39 Ill. 183. § 151.
Compher *v.*, 12 Ill. 290. § 548.
Coons *v.*, 76 Ill. 383. § 545.
Cooper *v.*, 85 Ill. 417. § 591.
v. Curry, 59 Ill. 35. § 540.
v. Cushing, 36 Hun (N. Y.), 483. § 598.
Davis *v.*, 1 Gilm. (Ill.) 409. § 371.
v. Dickeman, 3 Abb. Rep. Om. Cas. 520. § 567.
v. De Pelanconi, 63 Cal. 409. § 509.
v. Deery, 6 Daly (N. Y. Com. Pl.), 493. § 511.
v. Dunlap, 13 Johns. 437. § 586.
v. Edwards, 9 Cal. 286. § 517.
Elkin *v.*, 3 Scam. (Ill.) 207. § 537.
v. Evaus, 29 Cal. 429. § 540.
v. Faulkner, 31 Hun (N. Y.), 317. § 558.
v. Faulkner, 107 N. Y. 477. § 558.
v. Fields, 6 Daly (N. Y. Com. Pl.), 410. § 511.
v. Gardner, 55 Cal. 304. § 591.
v. Gillman, 58 Hun (N. Y.), 368. § 508.
Gingrich *v.*, 34 Ill. 448. § 499.
Green *v.*, 14 Bradw. (Ill. App.) 364. §§ 526, 564.

People v. Greene, 5 Hill (N. Y.), 647. § 502.
v. Haggerty, 5 Daly (N. Y. Com. Pl.), 532. § 511.
Haney v., 12 Col. 345. §§ 501, 508.
v. Harper, 91 Ill. 357. §§ 578, 608.
v. Hartley, 21 Cal. 585. § 151.
v. Herr, 81 Ill. 125. § 562.
v. Hilton, 36 Fed. Rep. 172 (Cir. Ct. E. D. Mich.). §§ 529, 565.
v. Hoover, 92 Ill. 575. § 591.
Huggins v., 39 Ill. 241. §§ 499, 504.
v. Huson, 78 Cal. 154. §§ 43, 518, 627.
Jack v., 19 Ill. 57. § 8.
v. Jansen, 7 Johns. 332. §§ 243, 555.
v. Jenkins, 17 Cal. 500. § 42.
v. Kennedy, 58 Mich. 372. § 503.
Kepley v., 123 Ill. 367. §§ 509, 510.
v. Kneeland, 31 Cal. 288. § 385.
v. Lee, 104 N. Y. 441. § 159.
v. Lucas, 93 N. Y. 585. § 566.
McClure v., 19 Bradw. (Ill. App.) 105. § 638.
v. McFarland, 9 Bradw. (Ill. App.) 275. §§ 495, 509.
v. McHatton, 2 Gilm. (Ill.) 638, 731. §§ 371, 548.
McLain v., 85 Ill. 205. § 543.
v. Meehan, 14 Daly (N. Y. Com. Pl.), 333. § 511.
v. Millham, 29 Hun (N. Y.), 151. § 502.
v. Missig, 7 Daly (N. Y. Com. Pl.), 23. § 511.
v. Moon, 3 Scam. (Ill.) 123. § 554.
v. Morrison, 75 Mich. 30. § 502.
Mussulman v., 15 Ill. 51. § 516.
v. Norton, 9 N. Y. 176. § 521.
v. Ogden, 10 Bradw. (Ill. App.) 226. § 503.
v. Organ, 27 Ill. 27. § 385.
v. Otto, 77 Cal. 45. § 617.
Pape v., 19 Bradw. (Ill. App.) 24. § 546.
People v. Penniman, 37 Cal. 271. § 506.
v. Pennock, 60 N. Y. 421. § 528.
Piercy v., 10 Bradw. (Ill. App.) 219. § 497.
Pinkstaff v., 59 Ill. 148. §§ 540, 545.
Plummer v., 16 Ill. 358. § 504.
Prickett v., 88 Ill. 115. § 548.
Pritchett v., 1 Gilman (Ill.), 525. § 24.
v. Race, 2 Bradw. (Ill. App.) 563. § 510.
Reitz v., 72 Ill. 435. § 576.
v. Russell, 4 Wend. 570. § 555.
v. Russell, 25 Hun (N. Y.), 524. § 630.
Sans v., 3 Gil. (Ill.) 327. § 515.
Satterfield v., 104 Ill. 448. § 532.
v. Schuyler, 4 N. Y. 173. § 566.
Seely v., 27 Ill. 173. § 412.
v. Shirley, 18 Cal. 121. § 512.
Shook v., 39 Ill. 443. § 499.
v. Skidmore, 17 Cal. 260. § 322.
v. Slocum, 1 Idaho, 62. § 175.
v. Sloper, 1 Idaho, 158. § 505.
Spillman v., 16 Bradw. (Ill. App.) 224. § 503.
v. Stacy, 74 Cal. 373. § 603.
Stern v., 96 Ill. 475. § 545.
Stern v., 102 Ill. 540. §§ 412, 555, 628.
Tappan v., 67 Ill. 339. § 535.
v. Tompkins, 74 Ill. 482. § 548.
v. Tormey, 122 Ill. 308. §§ 93, 532, 551.
v. Treadway, 17 Mich. 480. § 530.
v. Van Ness, 79 Cal. 84. §§ 25, 527, 588.
v. Vilas, 36 N. Y. 459. § 548.
Walsh v., 6 Bradw. (Ill. App.) 204. § 566.
Wann v., 57 Ill. 202. §§ 554, 574.
v. White, 11 Ill. 341. § 448.
v. White, 28 Hun (N. Y.), 289. §§ 238, 631.
v. Williams, 6 Daly (N. Y. Com. Pl.), 409. § 511.
Wilson v., 10 Bradw. (Ill. App.) 357. § 503.

People *v.* Wolf, 16 Cal. 385. § 643.
People's Bank *v.* National Bank, 101 U. S. 181. § 6.
v. Pearsons, 30 Vt. 711. §§ 41, 352.
People's Building Ass'n *v.* Wroth, 43 N. J. Law, 70. §§ 172, 425, 555.
People's Fire Ins. Co., Engler *v.*, 46 Md. 322. § 560.
People's Savings Bank, Russell *v.*, 39 Mich. 671. § 7.
Peoria Co., Smith *v.*, 59 Ill. 412. § 548.
Peoria, Second Nat. Bank of, *v.* Diefendorf, 90 Ill. 396. § 117.
Pepper, State *v.*, 31 Ind. 76. §§ 386, 408, 412.
Peppin *v.* Cooper, 2 Barn. & Ald. 431. § 168.
Percifull, Anthony *v.*, 8 Ark. (3 Eng.) 494. §§ 274, 286.
Percival *v.* McCoy (Cir. Ct. D. Iowa, N. D.), 13 Fed. Rep. 375. § 141.
Perdue, Montgomery Branch Bank *v.*, 3 Ala. 409. § 239.
Perfect *v.* Musgrave, 6 Price, 111. § 342.
Perham, Haddock *v.*, 70 Ga. 572. § 640.
v. Raynall, 9 Moore, 566. § 143.
Perigo, G. M. & T. Co. *v.* Grimes, 2 Col. 651. § 482.
Perkins *v.* Ament, 2 Head (Tenn.), 110. § 114.
v. Barstow, 6 R. I. 505. § 143.
Bockenstedt *v.*, 73 Iowa, 23. § 546.
v. Catlin, 11 Conn. 213. §§ 177, 182.
v. Elliott, 8 C. E. Green (N. J.), 526. § 7.
v. Goodman, 21 Barb. (N. Y.) 218. § 26.
Governor *v.*, 2 Bibb (Ky.), 395. § 569.
v. Kershaw, 1 Hill, Eq. (S. C.) 344. § 310.
Perkins *v.* Mayfield, 5 Port. (Ala.) 182. § 218.
v. Rudolph, 36 Ill. 306. § 482.
v. Stimmel, 114 N. Y. 359. § 574.
Thompson *v.*, 3 Mason, 232. § 71.
Watkins *v.*, 1 Ld. Raym. 224. § 77.
Williams *v.*, 21 Ark. 18. § 15.
Perley *v.* Loney, 17 Up. Can. (Q. B.) 279. § 29.
Ramsey *v.*, 34 Ill. 504. § 243.
Perpetual Ins. Co., Blair *v.*, 10 Mo. 559. §§ 395, 627.
Perrin, Chrisman *v.*, 67 Ind. 586. § 377.
Langford's Ex'r *v.*, 5 Leigh (Va.), 552. § 263.
Perrine *v.* Firemen's Ins. Co., 22 Ala. 575. § 430.
v. Hotchkiss, 58 Barb. (N. Y.) 77. § 213.
Perrins *v.* Ragland, 5 Leigh (Va.), 552. § 256.
Perry *v.* Armstrong, 39 N. H. 583. §§ 114, 360.
v. Barret, 18 Mo. 140. §§ 607, 613.
Horn *v.*, 14 Hun (N. Y.), 409. § 624.
v. Horn, 22 W. Va. 381. § 112.
Leech *v.*, 77 Ind. 422. § 487.
Robb *v.*, 35 Fed. Rep. 102. § 574.
v. Saunders, 36 Iowa, 427. § 431.
Todd *v.*, 20 Up. Can. (Q. B.) 649. § 523.
Wood *v.*, 9 Iowa, 479. § 293.
v. Yarborough, 3 Jones' Eq. (N. C.) 66. § 226.
Perryman *v.* McCall, 66 Ala. 402. § 165.
Perth, Cashin *v.*, 7 Grant's Ch. & App. Rep. 340. § 422.
Petefish, Skiles & Co. *v.* Watkins, 124 Ill. 384. § 330.
Peters *v.* Barnhill, 1 Hill, Law (S. C.), 237. §§ 211, 214.
Council of Middlesex *v.*, 9 Up. Can. (C. P.) 205. § 404.

Peters, Dougherty v., 2 Rob. (La.) 534. § 570.
Municipal Council of Middlesex v., 9 Up. Can. (C. P.) 205. § 401.
Purdy v., 35 Barb. (N. Y.) 239. § 107.
Roman v., 2 Rob. (La.) 479. § 553.
v. State, 10 Tex. App. 302. § 519.
Peters-Calhoun Co., Smokey v., 66 Miss. 471. § 570.
Peterson, Moore v., 64 Iowa, 425. § 605.
Ringleberg v., 76 Mich. 107. § 464.
Petit, Diamond v., 3 La. Ann. 37. § 464.
Petition of Griswold, 13 R. I. 125. §§ 495, 503.
Pettengill, Moss v., 3 Minn. 217. §§ 40, 434, 436.
Pettit, Watts v., 1 Bush (Ky.), 154. § 540.
Pettway, Dawson v., 4 Dev. & Bat. Law (N. C.), 396. § 260.
Petty v. Douglass, 76 Mo. 70. §§ 241, 353.
Haley v., 42 Ark. 392. § 526.
Petway, Eason v., 1 Dev. & Bat. Law (N. C.), 144. § 97.
Pevito v. Rodgers, 52 Tex. 581. § 27.
Peyton, State v., 32 Mo. App. 522. § 152.
Peyton's Adm'r, Morrow's Adm'r v., 8 Leigh (Va.), 54. § 38.
Pfeiffer v. Kingsland, 25 Mo. 66. § 13.
v. Knapp, 17 Fla. 144. §§ 342, 574.
Phares v. Barbour, 49 Ill. 370. § 428.
Pharr & McHugh v. Vinson, 32 La. Ann. 1280. §§ 45, 238.
Phears, Shepard v., 35 Tex. 763. § 98.
Phelan v. Johnson, 80 Iowa, 727. § 462.
Phelps, Boynton v., 52 Ill. 210. § 477.
City National Bank v., 86 N. Y. 484. §§ 160, 396.
Phelps v. Garrow, 8 Paige, Ch. 322. § 76.
Mathews v., 61 Mich. 327. §§ 156, 161.
National Bank v., 97 N. Y. 44. § 396.
Phenix Insurance Co. v. Findley, 59 Iowa, 591. §§ 42, 420.
v. Louisville & Nashville R. Co. (Cir. Ct. E. D. N. Y.), 8 Fed. Rep. 142. § 106.
Philadelphia & R. R. Co. v. Knight, 124 Pa. St. 58. §§ 18, 99.
v. Little, 41 N. J. Eq. 519. §§ 223, 435.
Philbrooks v. McEwen, 29 Ind. 347. § 445.
Philips, Trousdale v., 2 Swan (Tenn.), 384. § 627.
Phillips v. Astling, 2 Taunt. 206. §§ 201, 397.
Bateman v., 15 East, 272. § 81.
v. Bossard, 35 Fed. Rep. (Dist. Ct. D. S. C.) 99. § 425.
Bridges v., 17 Tex. 128. § 154.
Brinagar's Adm'r v., 1 B. Mon. (Ky.) 283. § 342.
v. Cooper, 59 Miss. 17. § 486.
v. Cox, 61 Ind. 345. § 183.
v. Foxall, Law Rep. 7 Q. 666. § 423.
Gold v., 10 Johns. 412. § 67.
Harrison v., 46 Mo. 520. § 273.
v. Plato, 42 Hun (N. Y.), 189. § 260.
v. Riley, 27 Mo. 386. § 607.
v. Rounds, 33 Me. 357. §§ 355, 369, 370.
v. Shackford, Cro. Eliz. 455. § 16.
v. Singer Sewing Machine Co., 88 Ill. 305. § 602.
v. Wade, 66 Ala. 52. § 145.
v. Wells, 2 Sneed, 154. § 449.
Phillipps v. Bateman, 16 East, 356. § 82.
v. Solomon, 42 Ga. 192. § 150.
Phipps, Brown v., 6 Sm. & Mar. (Miss.) 51. § 533.

Phipps, Craig *v.*, 23 Miss. 240. § 100.
Hampton *v.*, 108 U. S. 260. § 327.
v. Mansfield, 62 Ga. 209. § 219.
v. State, 25 Tex. App. 660. § 515.
Phœnix Fire Ins. Co. *v.* Mowatt, 6 Conn. 599. § 500.
Phœnix Ins. Co., Estate of Rapp *v.*, 113 Ill. 390. §§ 133, 424.
Phœnix Mut. Life Ins. Co. *v.* Holloway, 51 Conn. 310. § 419.
Phyfe *v.* Waddle, 2 Edwards' Ch. 47. § 405.
Physic, Geary *v.*, 5 Barn. & Cres. 234. § 80.
Pickens *v.* Finney, 12 Sm. & Mar. (Miss.) 468. § 444.
Kennedy *v.*, 3 Ired. Eq. (N. C.) 147. § 318.
v. Miller, 83 N. C. 543. § 256.
v. Yearborough's Adm'r, 26 Ala. 417. § 440.
Young *v.*, 45 Miss. 553. § 485.
Pickering *v.* Day, 2 Del. Ch. 333. §§ 338. 423, 536, 559.
v. Leiberman (Dist. Ct. Dist. Del.), 41 Fed. Rep. 376. §§ 4, 307.
Pickersgill *v.* Lahens, 15 Wall. 140. §§ 94, 139.
Pickett *v.* Bates, 3 La. Ann. 627. §§ 207, 212.
v. Boyd, 11 Lea (Tenn.), 498. § 480.
v. Gilmer, 32 La. Ann. 991. § 578.
v. Land, 2 Bailey, Law (S. C.), 608. § 242.
v. State, 16 Tex. App. 648. § 620.
Picksley, Reuss *v.*, 1 Exch. 342. § 89.
Pico *v.* Webster, 14 Cal. 202. § 636.
Picot *v.* Sigmago, 22 Mo. 587. § 41.
Pidcock *v.* Bishop, 3 Barn. & Cress. 605. § 420.
Pierce, Boynton *v.*, 79 Ill. 145. §§ 176, 182.
First National Bank *v.*, 99 Ill. 272. § 342.
v. Goldsberry, 31 Ind. 52. § 354.
v. Goldsberry, 35 Ind. 317. § 625.
Harris *v.*, 6 Ind. 162. § 182.
v. Holzer, 65 Mich. 263. § 318.
Pierce *v.* Kennedy, 5 Cal. 138. § 177.
Swift *v.*, 13 Allen, 136. § 78.
Walker *v.*, 21 Gratt. (Va.) 722. § 624.
Watriss *v.*, 32 N. H. 560. §§ 38, 243, 387.
v. Whiting, 63 Cal. 538. §§ 467, 473.
Piercy *v.* People, 10 Bradw. (Ill. App.) 219. § 497.
v. Piercy, 1 Ired. Eq. (N. C.) 214. § 458.
Pierron, Mason *v.*, 63 Wis. 239. § 297.
Mason *v.*, 69 Wis. 585. §§ 226, 293.
Pierse *v.* Irvine, 1 Minn. 369. § 182.
v. Miles, 5 Mont. 549. § 152.
Pierson *v.* Ells, 46 Hun (N. Y.), 336. § 480.
Piggott, Clancy *v.*, 4 Nev. & Mann. 496. §§ 77, 82.
Pigon *v.* French, 1 Wash. (N. S.) 278. § 205.
Pike, Allen *v.*, 3 Cush. 238. §§ 186, 188.
v. Brown, 7 Cush. 133. §§ 53, 72.
v. Irwin, 1 Sand. (N. Y.) 14. §§ 67, 74.
Lang *v.*, 27 Ohio St. 498. §§ 93, 449.
Marsh *v.*, 1 Sandf. Ch. 210. § 37.
Marsh *v.*, 10 Paige's Ch. 595. § 302.
v. Neal, 73 Me. 513. § 508.
State *v.*, 74 N. C. 531. § 632.
Pike's Adm'r *v.* Clark, 3 B. Mon. 262. § 356.
Pilgrim *v.* Dykes, 24 Tex. 383. § 371.
Pillans *v.* Van Mierop, 3 Burr. 1663. §§ 17, 67, 82.
Pillsbury, Concord *v.*, 33 N. H. 310. § 236.
Pinard *v.* George, 30 La. Ann. 384. § 460.
Pinckney *v.* Hagadorn, 1 Duer (N. Y.), 89. § 90.
Loundes *v.*, 1 Rich. Eq. (S. C.) 155. § 267.
Lowndes *v.*, 2 Strob. Eq. (S. C.) 44. § 249.

Ping, Walla Walla Co. *v.*, 1 Wash. Terr. (N. S.) 339. § 603.
Pinkstaff *v.* People, 59 Ill. 148. §§ 540, 545.
Pinkston *v.* Taliaferro, 9 Ala. 547. § 285.
Pinnell, Burke *v.*, 93 Ind. 540. § 645.
Pinney *v.* Hershfield, 1 Mont. 367. § 473.
Huey *v.*, 5 Minn. 310. §§ 238, 242, 405.
Pintard *v.* Davis, 1 Spencer (N. J.), 205. §§ 30, 242.
Piper, Dennis *v.*, 21 Ill. App. 169. § 353.
v. Newcomer, 25 Iowa, 221. § 29.
Pipkin *v.* Bond, 5 Ired. Eq. (N. C.) 91. § 342.
Vann *v.*, 77 N. C. 408. § 570.
Pitcher, Chickasaw County *v.*, 36 Iowa, 593. § 363.
Pitt *v.* Purssord, 8 Mees. & Wels. 538. § 293.
Pittman *v.* Chisolm, 43 Ga. 442. § 100.
Pitts *v.* Beckett, 13 Mees. & Wels. 743. §§ 80, 89.
v. Congdon, 2 N. Y. 352. § 67.
v. Fugate, Adm'x, 41 Mo. 405. § 633.
Parker *v.*, 73 Ind. 597. § 25.
Pittsburg, Ft. Wayne & C. R. R. Co. *v.* Shaeffer, 59 Pa. St. 350. § 425.
Pitzer *v.* Harmon, 8 Blackf. (Ind.) 112. § 211.
Place *v.* McIvain, 38 N. Y. 96. § 364.
Nat. Bank *v.*, 15 Hun, 564. § 356.
v. Taylor, 22 Ohio St. 317. § 562.
Placer Co. *v.* Dickerson, 45 Cal. 12. §§ 538, 627.
Plant, Woolfolk *v.*, 46 Ga. 422. §§ 235, 344.
Planters' Bank, Johnson *v.*, 4 Sm. & Mar. (Miss.) 165. § 448.
v. Lamkin, R. M. Charlton (Ga.), 29. § 423.
Planters' and Merchants' Bank *v.* Blair, 4 Ala. 613. § 114.
Plato, Phillips *v.*, 42 Hun (N. Y.), 189. § 260.
Platter *v.* Green, 26 Kan. 252. §§ 160, 161.
Plaxton, Yates *v.*, 3 Levinz, 235. § 505.
Plazentia, State *v.*, 6 Rob. (La.) 417. § 502.
Pleasanton's Appeal, 75 Pa. St. 344. § 134.
Pledge *v.* Buss, Johnson (Eng. Ch.), 663. §§ 401, 426.
Pleeker *v.* Hyde, 3 McLean, 279. § 117.
Plimpton, Robinson *v.*, 25 N. Y. 484. § 457.
Plumer, Eastman *v.*, 32 N. H. 238. § 333.
Plummer, Champion *v.*, 1 Bos. & Pul. (N. R.) 252. § 81.
Inhabitants of Alma *v.*, 4 Greenl. (Me.) 258. § 90.
v. People, 16 Ill. 358. § 504.
Plymouth Gold Mining Co., Tufts *v.*, 14 Allen, 407. § 80.
Poague, Wasson *v.*, 42 Iowa, 582. § 334.
Pocock, Fentum *v.*, 5 Taunt. 192. § 185.
Poe, Rhett *v.*, 2 How. 457. § 201.
Poillon *v.* Volkenning, 11 Hun (N. Y.), 385. § 630.
Polak *v.* Everett, Law Rep. 1 Q. B. Div. 669. §§ 426, 429.
Police Jury *v.* Haw, 2 La. (Miller), 41. §§ 402, 642.
Slattery *v.*, 2 La. Ann. 444. § 444.
Police Jury of Vermilion Parish *v.* Brookshier, 31 La. Ann. 736. §§ 175, 523.
Polk, Farmers' & Mechanics' Bank *v.*, 1 Del. Ch. 167. § 520.
v. Gallant, 2 Dev. & Bat. Eq. (N. C.) 395. § 237.
State *v.*, 14 Lea (Tenn.), 1. § 597.
v. State, 77 Tex. 289. § 524.
v. Wisener, 2 Humph. (Tenn.) 520. § 586.
Polkinghorne *v.* Hendricks, 61 Miss. 366. § 356.

Pollard v. Louisville, C. & L. R. R. Co., 7 Bush (Ky.), 597. § 624.
Norris v., 75 Ga. 358. § 145.
v. Stanton, 5 Ala. 451. § 643.
Poller v. United States, 107 U. S. 126. § 595.
Polleys, St. Maries v., 47 Wis. 67. §§ 357, 375.
Pomeroy, Abrams v., 13 Ill. 133. § 127.
Dwight v., 17 Mass. 308. § 405.
v. Tanner, 70 N. Y. 547. § 359.
Pond v. Clarke, 14 Conn. 334. § 218.
Pope v. Davidson, 5 J. J. Marsh. (Ky.) 400. § 222.
Martin v., 6 Ala. 532. § 330.
Patterson v., 5 Dana (Ky.), 241. § 308.
Pope's Adm'r, Lytle's Ex'rs v., 11 B. Mon. (Ky.) 297. § 287.
Poppenhousen v. Seeley, 3 Abb. Rep. Om. Cas. 615. § 459.
Pool v. Doster, 59 Miss. 258, 263. § 326.
v. Ellison, 56 Hun (N. Y.), 108. § 250.
Price v., 3 Hurl. & Colt. 437. § 425.
v. Roberts, 19 Bradw. (Ill. App.) 438. § 102.
v. Williams, 8 Ired. Law (N. C.), 286. § 272.
Poole v. Dyer, 123 Mass. 363. §§ 470, 516.
Holliday v., 77 Ga. 159. § 416.
Pooley v. Harradine, 7 Ell. & Bl. 431. §§ 29, 32, 375.
Poor Directors, Nason v., 126 Pa. St. 445. § 558.
Poorman v. Goswiler, 2 Watts (Pa.), 69. § 236.
Port v. Robbins, 35 Iowa, 208. §§ 405, 427.
Portage Co. Branch Bank v. Lane, 8 Ohio St. 405. § 381.
Porter, Arrington v., 47 Ala. 714. § 630.
City of Harrisonville v., 76 Mo. 358. § 591.
Porter v. Drennan, 11 Bradw. (Ill. App.) 362. § 91.
v. Hodenpuyl, 9 Mich. 11. § 347.
Lanahan v., 148 Mass. 596. § 469.
Miller v., 5 Humph. (Tenn.) 294. § 372.
v. Stanley, 47 Me. 515. § 543.
Posey, State v., 79 Ala. 45. § 515.
Post, Flanagan v., 45 Vt. 246. § 419.
v. Geoghehan, 5 Daly (N. Y. Com. Pleas), 216. § 77.
Jones v., 6 Cal. 102. §§ 80, 87.
v. Shafer, 63 Mich. 85. § 459.
v. Township Board of Sparta, 63 Mich. 323. § 10.
Post, Adm'r, v. Losey, 111 Ind. 74. §§ 35, 150.
Postell, Lipscomb v., 38 Miss. 476. § 580.
Posten, Moulton v., 52 Wis. 169. § 344.
Postlewait, Hunt v., 28 Iowa, 427. § 356.
Postmaster-General, Dox v., 1 Pet. 318. § 555.
v. McCall, 31 U. C. (C. P.) 364. § 595.
v. Munger, 2 Paine, 189. §§ 542, 548.
Poston, Peay v., 10 Yerg. (Tenn.) 111. § 361.
Potius, Bank of Pennsylvania v., 10 Watts (Pa.), 148. §§ 306, 367, 568.
Pott, Marberger v., 16 Pa. St. 9. § 183.
v. Nathans, 1 Watts & Serg. (Pa.) 155. § 262.
Potter, Besore v., 12 Serg. & Rawle (Pa.), 154. § 141.
v. Board of Trustees, 11 Bradw. (Ill. App.) 280. § 543.
v. Gronbeck, 117 Ill. 404. §§ 48, 50, 109, 135.
Moore v., 9 Bush (Ky.), 357. § 540.
Ridgeway v., 114 Ill. 457. § 223.
v. State, 23 Ind. 550. §§ 26, 520.
State v., 63 Mo. 212. § 408.
Wetherbee v., 99 Mass. 354. § 52.
Potter County, Clark v., 1 Pa. St. 159. § 556.

Pottle, Comins v., 22 Hun (N. Y.), 287. § 139.
Poulson, United States v. (Dist. Ct. E. Dist. Pa.), 30 Fed. Rep. 231. § 112.
Pow, Slagle v., 41 Ohio St. 603. § 360.
Powder Works, Child v., 44 N. H. 354. § 222.
Powell v. Allen, 11 Bradw. (Ill. App.) 129. §§ 308, 311.
v. Chicago Carpet Co., 22 Ill. App. 409. § 204.
Enicks v., 2 Strobh. (S. C.) 196. §§ 541, 586.
v. Kettle, 1 Gilm. (Ill.) 491. § 141.
v. Matthis, 4 Ired. Law (N. C.), 83. §§ 288, 291.
McLemore v., 12 Wheat. 554. § 342.
Payne v., 14 Tex. 600. § 356.
v. Powell, 48 Cal. 234. § 540.
v. Smith, 8 Johns. 249. §§ 213, 221.
State v., 40 La. Ann. 241. §§ 166, 168, 555.
State v., 67 Mo. 395. § 558.
Powell's Ex'rs v. White, 11 Leigh (Va.), 309. § 313.
Powers, State v., 52 Miss. 198. § 540.
Wilson v., 130 Mass. 127. § 355.
Wilson v., 131 Mass. 539. § 646.
Poyne v. Joyner, 6 Ark. (1 Eng.) 241. § 220.
Poyntz, Morrison v., 7 Dana (Ky.), 307. §§ 288, 290.
Praed v. Gardiner, 2 Cox, 86. § 321.
Praeger, Marcy v., 34 La. Ann. 54. § 175.
Prairie v. North, 78 N. C. 169. §§ 371, 591.
Prather, Dobson v., 6 Ired. Eq. (N. C.) 31. § 435.
Fensler v., 43 Ind. 119. § 605.
v. Johnson, 3 Harr. & Johns. (Md.) 487. § 209.
v. Vineyard, 4 Gilman (Ill.), 40. § 63.
v. Young, 67 Ind. 480. § 377.
Pratt, Benton v., 2 Wend. 385. § 73.
Pratt v. Hedden, 121 Mass. 116. § 17.
v. Humphrey, 22 Conn. 317. § 72.
v. Matthews, 24 Hun (N. Y.), 386. §§ 161, 387.
Milliken v.. 125 Pa. St. 374. § 144.
Taylor v., 3 Wis. 674. § 82.
v. Thornton, 28 Me. 355. § 252.
Trust & Deposit Co. v., 25 Hun (N. Y.), 23. § 579.
Pray, Commonwealth v., 125 Pa. St. 542. § 583.
Preble v. Baldwin, 6 Cush. 549. § 72.
Prendergrass, Davey v., 5 Barn. & Ald. 187. § 374.
Prentiss, Fellows v., 3 Denio, 512. §§ 162, 190, 363.
v. Garland, 64 Me. 155. § 102.
Thurston v., 1 Manning (Mich.), 193. § 221.
Prescott v. Brinsley, 6 Cush. 233. § 115.
Cornell v., 2 Barb. (N. Y.) 16. § 37.
v. Newell, 39 Vt. 82. § 291.
Pelton v., 13 Iowa, 567. § 384.
United States v., 3 How. 578. § 558.
Preslar, Stallworth v., 34 Ala. 505. §§ 287, 293, 295.
v. Stallworth, 37 Ala. 402. §§ 295, 312, 635.
Prestman, Drummond v., 12 Wheaton, 515. §§ 116, 117, 626.
Preston, Baker v., 1 Gil. (Va.) 235. § 628.
Commonwealth v., 5 T. B. Mon. (Ky.) 584. § 555.
v. Davis, 8 Ark. (3 Eng.) 167. § 137.
v. Gould, 64 Iowa, 44. § 295.
v. Henning, 6 Bush (Ky.), 556. § 352.
v. Hood, 64 Cal. 405. § 468.
v. Huntington, 67 Mich. 139. § 390.
v. Preston, 4 Gratt. (Va.) 88. §§ 262, 263.
Rhea v., 75 Va. 757. § 39.

Prettyman, Wagenseller *v.*, 7 Bradw. (Ill. App.) 192. § 283.
Price, Alsop *v.*, 1 Doug. (Eng.) 160. § 150.
v. Barker, 4 Ellis & Black. 760. § 376.
v. Cloud, 6 Ala. 248. §§ 616, 628.
v. Dime Savings Bank, 124 Ill. 317. §§ 34, 342.
v. Edmunds, 10 Barn. & Cress. 578. § 368.
v. Farrar, 5 Bradw. (Ill. App.) 536. § 564.
v. Kennedy, 16 La. Ann. 78. § 642.
Mutual Loan & Building Ass'n *v.*, 16 Fla. 204. § 168.
Mutual Loan & B'ld'g Ass'n *v.*, 19 Fla. 127. §§ 526, 555.
Parnell *v.*, 3 Rich. Law (S. C.), 121. § 344.
v. Pool, 3 Hurl. & Colt. 437. § 425.
v. Richardson, 15 Mees. & Wels. 539. § 85.
v. State, 42 Ark. 178. § 510.
Thigpen *v.*, Phillips' Eq. (N. C.) 146. § 223.
v. Truesdell, 28 N. J. Eq. (1 Stew.) 200. § 69.
Warner *v.*, 3 Wend. 397. § 258.
Price's Ex'rs, Harrison's Ex'rs *v.*, 25 Gratt. (Va.) 553. §§ 608, 614.
Prichard, Mason *v.*, 12 East, 227. § 92.
Prickett *v.* People, 88 Ill. 115. § 548.
Pride, Beckham *v.*, 6 Rich. Eq. (S. C.) 78. § 280.
v. Boyce, Rice's Eq. (S. C.) 275. § 141.
Priestner, Wood *v.*, Law Rep. 2 Ex. 66. §§ 92, 157.
Prigmore, White *v.*, 29 Ark. 208. § 454.
Prince *v.* Britt, 8 Heisk. (Tenn.) 290. § 524.
v. Clark, 127 Mass. 599. § 469.
Smith *v.*, 14 Conn. 472. § 218.
Tenney *v.*, 4 Pick. 385. §§ 13, 82, 182.
v. Towns (Cir. Ct. D. S. C.), 33 Fed. Rep. 161. § 578.
Prindle *v.* Page, 21 Vt. 94. § 281.
Pringle, Regina *v.*, 32 Up. Can. (Q. B.) 308. § 555.
v. Lezir, 1 Rich. N. S. (S. C.) 59. § 247.
Prior *v.* Kiso, 82 Mo. 241. § 390.
v. Williams, 3 Abb. Rep. Om. Cas. 624. § 141.
Pritchard *v.* Hitchcock, 6 Man. & Gr. 151. § 334.
Mason *v.*, 12 East, 227. § 160.
Pritchett *v.* People, 1 Gilman (Ill.), 525. § 24.
v. Wilson, 39 Pa. St. 421. § 415.
Probate Court *v.* St. Clair, 52 Vt. 24. § 408.
Probate Judge *v.* Abbott, 50 Mich. 479. § 586.
Brown *v.*, 42 Mich. 501. § 410.
Proctor, Commonwealth *v.*, 98 Ill. 558. § 432.
Kyle *v.*, 7 Bush (Ky.), 493. § 389.
White *v.*, 4 Tauut. 209. § 90.
Proffet, Ray *v.*, 15 Lea (Tenn.), 517. § 324.
Propert *v.* Parker, 1 Russ. & My. 625. § 89.
Prophit, Brown *v.*, 53 Miss. 649. §§ 356, 397.
Proseck *v.* State, 38 Ohio St. 606. § 517.
Prosser, Collins *v.*, 1 Barn. & Cress. 682. § 439.
v. Laqueer, 4 Hill (N. Y.), 420. § 137.
Luqueer *v.*, 1 Hill, 256. § 179.
Protection Ins. Co. *v.* Davis, 5 Allen, 54. §§ 195, 202.
Proudfoot *v.* Clevenger, 33 W. Va. 267. § 129.
Prout, Lenox *v.*, 3 Wheat. 520. § 438.
Prouty, Hamilton *v.*, 50 Wis. 592. §§ 344, 357.
Provincial Bank *v.* Cussen, Law Rep. Irish (18 Q. B., C. P. & Ex. Div.), 382. § 431.
Prusia *v.* Brown, 45 Hun (N. Y.), 80. § 464.

Pryor, Allen *v.*, 3 A. K. Marsh. (Ky.) 305. §§ 53, 67.
v. Leonard, 57 Ga. 136. § 129.
Puckett *v.* Bates, 4 Ala. 390. § 75.
Pueblo, Orman *v.*, 8 Col. 292. § 590.
Pugh *v.* Cameron's Adm'r, 11 W. Va. 523. § 235.
Weik *v.*, 92 Ind. 382. §§ 1, 426.
Pullen, Berry *v.*, 69 Me. 101. § 342.
Pulliam *v.* Withers, 8 Dana (Ky.), 98. §§ 16, 380.
Pulver, Armitage *v.*, 37 N. Y. 494. § 288.
Van Slyck *v.*, Hill & Denio (Lalor's Sup.), 47. § 64.
Purcell, State *v.*, 31 W. Va. 44. § 519.
Purdy, Hunt *v.*, 82 N. Y. 486. § 241.
Palmer *v.*, 83 N. Y. 144. § 36.
v. Peters, 35 Barb. (N. Y.) 239. § 107.
State *v.*, 67 Mo. 89. § 585.
Purefoy *v.* Jones, Freeman's Ch. 44. § 431.
Purmont, McCrea *v.*, 16 Wend. 460. § 89.
Purssord, Pitt *v.*, 8 Mees. & Wels. 538. § 293.
Purviance *v.* Sutherland, 2 Ohio St. 478. § 216.
Purvis *v.* Cartsaphan, 73 N. C. 575. § 35.
Ramey *v.*, 38 Miss. 499. § 613.
Putnam *v.* Schuyler, 4 Hun (N. Y.), 166. §§ 12, 416.
Putney, March *v.*, 56 N. H. 34. §§ 199, 202.
Pybus *v.* Gibb, 6 Ell. & Black. 902. § 548.
Pyke *v.* Searcy, 4 Porter (Ala.), 52. §§ 359, 585.
Quackenbush, Gadsen *v.*, 9 Rich. Law (S. C.), 222. § 108.
Henry *v.*, 48 Mich. 415. § 466.
Queen *v.* Fay, Irish Law (4 Q. B., C. P. & Ex.), 606. § 555.
v. Hall, 1 Up. Can. (C. P.) 406. § 170.
v. O'Callaghan, 1 Irish Eq. 439. § 305.
Quick, Board of Education of Auburn *v.*, 99 N. Y. 138. § 554.
Sikes *v.*, 7 Jones' Law (N. C.), 19. § 210.
Quigley, Quillen *v.*, 14 Nev. 215. §§ 242, 464.
Quillen *v.* Arnold, 12 Nev. 234. § 470.
Tracy *v.*, 65 Ind. 249. §§ 344, 377.
v. Quigley, 14 Nev. 215. §§ 242, 464.
Quin *v.* Hanford, 1 Hill (N. Y.), 82. §§ 63, 74.
Quine *v.* Mayers, 2 Rob. (La.) 510. § 471.
Quinichett, Choate *v.*, 12 Heisk. (Tenn.) 427. § 150.
Quinn *v.* Hard, 43 Vt. 375. § 406.
Milroy *v.*, 69 Ind. 406. §§ 1, 186, 193.
Quinnipaick, Jones *v.*, 29 Conn. 25. § 324.
Quintard *v.* D'Wolf, 34 Barb. (N. Y.) 97. § 62.
Quynn *v.* State, 1 Harr. & Johns. (Md.) 36. § 523.
Rabaud, D'Wolf *v.*, 1 Pet. 476. §§ 60, 74, 86.
Race, People *v.*, 2 Bradw. (Ill. App.) 563. § 510.
Rachel, Gillett *v.*, 9 Rob. (La.) 276. §§ 359, 397.
Radakissen Mitter, Bengal *v.*, 4 Moore's Privy Council Cas. 140. § 330.
Radcliff, Abeel *v.*, 13 Johns. 297. § 30.
Berg *v.*, 6 Johns. Ch. 302. § 141.
McCaffil *v.*, 3 Rob. (N. Y.) 445. § 77.
Rader *v.* Davis, 5 Lea (Tenn.), 436. §§ 152, 565.
Maddox *v.*, 9 Mont. 126. §§ 112, 571.
v. Yeargin, 85 Tenn. (1 Pickle), 486. § 586.
Radford, Booth *v.*, 57 Mich. 357. § 616.
Loosemore *v.*, 9 Mees. & Wels. 657. § 221.

Radway, Gottsberger *v.*, 2 Hilton (N. Y.), 342. § 84.
Rae *v.* Rae, 6 Irish Ch. 490. § 261.
Ragan *v.* Chenault, 78 Ky. 545. § 90.
Ragland *v.* Milam, 10 Ala. 618. § 266.
Perrins *v.*, 5 Leigh (Va.), 552. § 256.
Ragsdale, McLane *v.*, 31 Miss. 701. § 230.
Raiford, Austin *v.*, 67 Ga. 201. § 586.
Raikes *v.* Todd, 1 Perry & Dav. 138. § 85.
v. Todd, 8 Adol. & Ell. 846. § 82.
Railroad, Mumford *v.*, 2 Lea (Tenn.), 393. § 394.
v. Murrell, 11 Heisk. (Tenn.) 715. §§ 167, 600.
Rice *v.*, 32 Ohio St. 380. § 7.
v. Howard, 7 Wall. 392. § 5.
Taylor *v.*, 11 Lea (Tenn.), 186. § 5.
Railsback *v.* Greve, 58 Ind. 72. § 460.
Railton *v.* Mathews, 10 Cl. & Finn. 934. § 419.
Railway Co. *v.* Goodwin. 3 Wels., Hurl. & Gor. 320. § 395.
Rainbow *v.* Juggins, Law Rep. (5 Q. B. Div.) 422. § 447.
Rainey *v.* Yarborough, 2 Ired. Eq. (N. C.) 249. § 290.
Rains *v.* Story, 3 Car. & Payne, 130. § 78.
Ralph *v.* Eldredge, 58 Hun (N. Y.), 203. § 98.
v. United States, 9 Fed. Rep. 693 (Cir. Ct. N. D. Ill.). § 10.
Ralston *v.* Wood, 15 Ill. 159. §§ 285, 638.
Ramey, Allen *v.*, 4 Strob. Law (S. C.), 30. § 533.
v. Commonwealth, 83 Ky. 534. § 502.
v. Purvis, 38 Miss. 499. § 613.
Ramsay, Allshouse *v.*, 6 Whart. (Pa.), 311. § 62.
Commonwealth *v.*, 2 Duvall (Ky.), 386. § 8.
Ramsey *v.* Colbaugh, 13 Iowa, 164. § 473.
Ramsey *v.* Lewis, 30 Barb. (N. Y.) 403. § 271.
v. Perley, 34 Ill. 504. § 243.
v. Westmoreland Bank, 2 Pen. & Watts (Pa.), 203. § 443.
Ramskill *v.* Edwards, Law Rep. (31 Ch. Div.) 100. § 284.
Rand, Baker *v.*, 13 Barb. (N. Y.) 152. § 164.
Hall *v.*, 8 Conn. 560. §§ 163, 643.
v. Mather, 11 Cush. 1. § 52.
Randall, Cadwell *v.*, 36 Mich. 251. § 492.
Mobile Life Ins. Co. *v.*, 71 Ala. 220. §§ 360, 366.
Rochester *v.*, 105 Mass. 295. § 545.
v. Sackett, 77 N. Y. 480. § 139.
Watson *v.*, 20 Wend. 201. § 12.
Randolph *v.* Randolph, 3 Rand. (Va.) 490. § 227.
v. Simon, 29 Kan. 406. § 515.
Ranelaugh *v.* Hayes, 1 Vernon, 189. §§ 97, 238.
Raney *v.* Baron, Adm'r, 1 Fla. 327. § 464.
Brush *v.*, 34 Ind. 416. § 405.
McCabe *v.*, 32 Ind. 309. § 413.
Rankin *v.* Childs, 9 Mo. 665. §§ 186, 188, 204.
v. Collins, 50 Ind. 158. § 290.
Creighton *v.*, 7 Clark & Finnelly, 325. § 555.
v. Wilsey, 17 Iowa, 463. § 328.
Ransom, Berry *v.*, 12 N. Y. 462. §§ 60, 261.
Weller *v.*, 34 Mo. 362. § 361.
Ranson *v.* Sherwood, 26 Conn. 437. §§ 177, 641, 643.
Rany *v.* Governor, 4 Blackf. (Ind.) 2. § 169.
Rapelye *v.* Bailey, 3 Conn. 438. § 190.
v. Bailey, 5 Conn. 149. § 161.
Rapp *v.* Ducker, 9 Jones & Spencer (N. Y.), 235. § 201.
Ducker *v.*, 67 N. Y. 464. §§ 351, 355, 369, 431.
Rastall, Straton *v.*, 2 Durn. & East, 366. § 445.
Ratcliff *v.* Lennig, 30 Ind. 289. § 143.

Ratcliffe v. Graves, 1 Vern. 196. § 139.
v. Smith, 13 Bush (Ky.), 172. § 513.
Rathbone v. Boyd, 30 Kan. 485. § 487.
Douglass v., 5 Hill, 143. § 197.
v. Warren, 10 Johns. 587. § 493.
Rathburn, Brown & Co. v., 10 Oreg. 158. § 427.
Ratliff v. Trout, 6 J. J. Marsh. 606. § 82.
Ratliff & Williams, Garrott v., 83 Ky. 384. § 90.
Rausch, Trustees United Brethren v., 122 Ind. 167. § 601.
Ravenscroft, Tarr v., 12 Gratt. (Va.) 642. § 287.
Rawlings, Field v., 1 Gilm. (Ill.) 581. § 131.
Rawlinson, Williams v., Ryan & Moody, 233. § 160.
Rawson, Bell v., 30 Ga. 712. § 500.
Butler v., 1 Denio, 105. § 138.
Elam v., 21 Ga. 139. § 312.
v. Gregory, 59 Ga. 733. § 434.
v. Taylor, 30 Ohio St. 389. § 36.
Rawstone v. Parr, 3 Russ. 539. § 139.
Ray, Bond v., 5 Humph. (Tenn.) 492. § 576.
v. Brenner, 12 Kan. 105. § 448.
Brown v., 18 N. H. 102. § 268.
Commonwealth v., 3 Gray, 441. § 89.
v. Proffett, 15 Lea (Tenn.), 517. § 324.
Sizer v., 87 N. Y. 220. § 36.
v. State, 16 Tex. App. 268. § 620.
Wise v., 3 Greene (Iowa), 430. § 89.
Raymond, Kline v., 70 Ind. 271. § 383.
Hill v., 3 Allen, 540. § 76.
Lininger v., 9 Neb. 40. § 481.
Stowell v., 83 Ill. 120. §§ 102, 176.
Raynall, Perham v., 9 Moore, 566. § 143.
Rayner v. Bell, 15 Mass. 377. § 516.
Jackson v., 12 Johns. 291. §§ 63, 66.
v. Linthorne, 2 Car. & P. 124. § 90.
Rayner, Mussey v., 22 Pick. 223. §§ 157, 186, 203.
Raynolds, Farmers' Bank of Canton v., 13 Ohio, 85. § 446.
Rea, Benedict v., 35 Hun (N. Y.), 34. § 439.
Read, Congdon v., 7 R. I. 406. § 163.
v. Cutts, 7 Greenl. (Me.) 186. §§ 1, 201.
Furness v., 63 Md. 1. § 470.
Gourdin v., 8 Rich. Law (S. C.), 230. § 410.
Jones v., 1 Humph. (Tenn.) 335. § 616.
v. McLemore, 34 Miss. 110. § 402.
v. Nash, 1 Wils. 305. § 57.
Watson v., 1 Cooper's Ch. (Tenn.) 196. § 434.
Reade v. Lowndes, 23 Beav. 361. § 39.
Reader v. Kingham, 13 Com. B. (J. Scott), N. S. 344. § 72.
Readfield v. Shaver, 50 Me. 36. § 408.
Ream, Fogarty v., 100 Ill. 366. §§ 320, 526, 632.
Reams, Howell v., 73 N. C. 391. § 309.
Reaney, State v., 13 Md. 230. § 499.
Reardon, Cranor v., 39 Mo. App. 306. § 449.
Johns v., 11 Md. 465. §§ 35, 229.
Reasner, Brown v., 5 Bradw. (Ill. App.) 45. § 176.
Receivers of N. J. Midland R. R. Co. v. Wortendyke, 27 N. J. Eq. 658. § 306.
Redd v. Jones, 30 Gratt. (Va.) 123. § 577.
Reddick, Outlaw v., 11 Ga. 669. § 224.
Redfield v. Haight, 27 Conn. 31. §§ 43, 97, 217.
Redhead v. Caton, 1 Starkie, 12. § 57.
Redington, Waterville Bank v., 52 Me. 466. § 41.
Redman v. Deputy, 26 Irish, 338. § 356.
Hartman v., 21 Mo. App. 124. §§ 91, 376.
v. Marvil, 73 Ind. 593. § 140.
Swive v., Law Rep. 1 Q. B. Div. 536. § 362.

Redmond, Mayor and City Council of Natchitoches *v.*, 28 La. Ann. 274. §§ 112, 555.
Redwood City *v.* Grimmenstein, 68 Cal. 512. § 591.
Redwyn, Morrice *v.*, 2 Barnardiston, 26. § 208.
Reed *v.* Board of Education, 39 Ohio St. 635. § 597.
v. Cramb, 22 Ill. App. 34. § 34.
Dewey *v.*, 40 Barb. (N. Y.) 16. § 379.
v. Evans, 17 Ohio, 128. § 82.
v. Fish, 59 Me. 358. § 164.
Franklin Saving Inst. *v.*, 125 Mass. 365. § 403.
v. Holcomb, 31 Conn. 360. § 67.
v. Lane, 61 Vt. 481. § 4.
May *v.*, 125 Ind. 199. § 242.
McNeale *v.*, 7 Irish Ch. Rep. 251. § 315.
v. Nash, 1 Wils. 305. § 54.
v. Norris, 2 Mylne & Craig, 361. § 212.
v. Northrup, 50 Mich. 442. § 616.
Patterson *v.*, 7 Watts & Serg. (Pa.) 144. § 189.
Robinson *v.*, 46 Iowa, 219. § 382.
v. Sidener, 32 Ind. 373. § 414.
Sotheren *v.*, 4 Harr. & Johns. (Md.) 307. § 310.
Worcester Bank *v.*, 9 Mass. 267. § 174.
White *v.*, 15 Conn. 457. §§ 92, 103.
Reeder, Ohio Life Ins. & Trust Co. *v.*, 18 Ohio, 35. § 326.
Rees *v.* Berrington, 2 Ves. Jr. 540. §§ 238, 364.
Rees' Adm'r, Williamson's Adm'r *v.*, 15 Ohio, 572. § 295.
Reese, Bick *v.*, 52 Hun, 125. § 9.
Steele *v.*, 6 Yerg. (Tenn.) 263. § 541.
Reeve *v.* State, 34 Ark. 610. § 509.
Reeves *v.* Steele, 2 Head (Tenn.), 647. § 584.
Conner *v.*, 103 N. Y. 527. §§ 110, 630, 637.
Regina *v.* Miller, 20 Up. Can. (Q. B.) 485. § 172.
v. Pringle, 32 Up. Can. (Q. B.) 308. § 555.
v. Richardson, 17 Ont. (Can.) 729. § 10.
Reherd *v.* Long, 77 Va. 839. § 583.
Reichard, Ind. Dist. *v.*, 50 Iowa, 98. § 93.
Reid, Brink *v.*, 122 Ind. 257. § 377.
v. Cox, 5 Blackf. (Ind.) 312. § 612.
v. Flippen, 47 Ga. 273. §§ 230, 342.
v. Jackson, 1 Ala. 207. § 569.
Lindsey *v.*, 101 Pa. St. 438. § 632.
Lock *v.*, 6 Up. Can. Q. B. (O. S.) 295. § 88.
Norton *v.*, 11 S. C. 593. § 238.
v. Watts, 4 J. J. Marsh. (Ky.) 440. § 342.
Reigart *v.* White, 52 Pa. St. 438. § 1.
Reilly *v.* Dodge, 42 Hun (N. Y.), 646. §§ 25, 526, 527.
Reiner, Barnsback *v.*, 8 Minn. 59. § 230.
Reinhart *v.* Johnson, 62 Iowa, 155. § 268.
Reisnner *v.* Dessar, 80 Ind. 307. § 486.
Reitz *v.* People, 72 Ill. 435. § 576.
Rembert, Griffin *v.*, 2 Rich. N. S. (S. C.) 410. §§ 116, 204.
Remington, Clark *v.*, 11 Met. (Mass.) 361. § 192.
Wright *v.*, 41 N. J. Law, 48. § 12.
Remington Sewing Machine Co. *v.* Kezertee, 49 Wis. 409. §§ 421, 647.
Remmers, Lafayette Fire Ins. Co. *v.*, 30 La. Ann. 1347. § 460.
Remsen *v.* Beekman, 25 N. Y. 252. § 239.
v. Graves, 41 N. Y. 471. §§ 44, 366.
Rendell, Bowser *v.*, 31 Ind. 128. §§ 266, 380.
Renfroe *v.* Colquitt, 74 Ga. 618. § 534.

Renfroe, Gates *v.*, 7 La. Ann. 569. § 228.
Renfroe & Wilson, Mayo *v.*, 66 Ga. 408. § 517.
Reno *v.* Tyson, 24 Ind. 56. § 581.
Reno Real Estate Co., Culver *v.*, 91 Pa. St. 367. § 18.
Rensens. Mexican Construction Co. *v.*, 118 U. S. 49. § 461.
Respess, Farrow *v.*, 11 Ired. Law (N. C.), 170. § 100.
Respublica *v.* Gaoler of Philadelphia, 2 Yeates (Pa.), 263. § 496.
Reusch *v.* Demass, 34 Mich. 95. § 484.
Reuss *v.* Picksley, 1 Exch. 342. § 89.
Rey *v.* Simpson, 22 How. 341. §§ 181, 182.
Reynes *v.* Zacharies, Succession, 10 La. (Curry), 127. § 626.
Reynolds, Brady *v.*, 13 Cal. 31. §§ 177, 391.
  Brainard *v.*, 36 Vt. 614. § 98.
  v. Dechaums, 24 Tex. 174. § 8.
  Douglass *v.*, 7 Pet. 113. §§ 92, 94, 161, 186, 192, 201, 202, 204, 440.
  v. Edney, 8 Jones' Law (N. C.), 406. § 202.
  Griffith *v.*, 4 Gratt. (Va.) 46. § 406.
  v. Harrol, 2 Strobh. Law (S. C.), 87. § 513.
  Hershler *v.*, 22 Iowa, 152. § 372.
  Jenkins *v.*, 6 Moore, 86. § 82.
  Jenkins *v.*, 3 Brod. & Bing. 14. § 85.
  v. Magness, 2 Ired. Law (N. C.), 26. § 513.
  Sheldon *v.*, 14 La. Ann. 703. § 403.
  v. Skelton, 2 Tex. 516. § 211.
  State *v.*, 3 Mo. 70. § 568.
  v. Timmons, 7 Rich. (S. C.) 486. § 585.
  v. Ward, 5 Wend. 501. § 354.
  v. Wheeler, 10 J. Scott (N. R.), 561. § 260.
  Williams *v.*, 11 La. (6 Curry), 230. §§ 133, 339.
Rhea *v.* Gibson's Ex'r, 10 Gratt. (Va.) 215. § 385.
  v. Preston, 75 Va. 757. § 39.
  Riley *v.*, 5 Lea (Tenn.), 115. § 288.
Rhett *v.* Poe, 2 How. 457. § 201.
Rhinelander *v.* Barrow, 17 Johns. 538. § 339.
Rhoades, State *v.*, 6 Nev. 352. §§ 519, 521, 554, 628.
Rhodes, Cooper *v.*, 30 La. Ann. 533. § 460.
  v. Hart, 51 Ga. 320. § 381.
  Sherrod *v.*, 5 Ala. 683. § 260.
Rhoads *v.* Frederick, 8 Watts (Pa.), 448. § 386.
  Keller *v.*, 39 Pa. St. 513. § 230.
Rhodius, State *v.*, 37 Tex. 165. § 512.
Rhomberg, Trent *v.*, 66 Tex. 249. § 464.
Rice, Baird *v.*, 1 Call (Va.), 18. § 434.
  v. Barry, 2 Cranch (C. C.), 447. § 68.
  v. Carter, 11 Ired. (N. C.) 298. § 66.
  Clapp *v.*, 15 Gray, 557. §§ 261, 277, 291.
  v. Cook, 71 Me. 559. § 31.
  v. Downing, 12 B. Mon. (Ky.) 44. § 238.
  Everly *v.*, 20 Pa. St. 297. § 428.
  v. Filene, 6 Allen, 230. § 123.
  Hayden *v.*, 18 Vt. 353. § 261.
  Henderson *v.*, 1 Cold. (Tenn.) 223. § 15.
  v. Kirkman, 3 Humph. (Tenn.) 415. § 616.
  v. Loomis, 139 Mass. 302. § 108.
  v. Morris, 82 Ind. 204. § 329.
  v. Morton, 19 Mo. 263. §§ 40, 439.
  Munford *v.*, 6 Munf. (Va.) 81. § 169.
  v. Railroad, 32 Ohio St. 380. § 7.
  v. Rice, 108 Ill. 199. §§ 319, 329.
  v. Rice, 14 B. Mon. (Ky.) 335. § 214.
  v. Simpson, 9 Heisk. (Tenn.) 809. § 605.
  Smith *v.*, 27 Mo. 505. §§ 40, 127, 373.

Rice v. Southgate, 16 Gray, 142. § 207.
Veach v., 131 U. S. 293. § 573.
Whitaker v., 9 Minn. 13. § 143.
Rice's Appeal. 79 Pa. St. 169. § 324.
Rich, Brackett v., 23 Minn. 485. §§ 93, 198.
Chafoin v., 77 Cal. 476. §§ 177, 589.
Milk v., 15 Hun (N. Y.), 178. § 67.
Richard, Stoppani v., 1 Hilton (N. Y.), 509. § 13.
Richards, Bank of Newbury v., 35 Vt. 281. § 114.
v. Commonwealth, 40 Pa. St. 146. § 448.
Davis Sewing Machine Co. v., 115 U. S. 524. § 186.
v. Simms, 1 Dev. & Bat. Law (N. C.), 48. § 260.
v. Storer, 114 Mass. 101. § 470.
Walker v., 39 N. H. 259. § 76.
Walker v., 41 N. H. 388. §§ 78, 91.
v. Warring, 4 Abbott's Rep. Om. Cas. 47. § 179.
Whitaker v., 134 Penn. St. 191. §§ 19, 411.
v. Yoder, 10 Neb. 429. § 322.
Richardson, Austin v., 1 Gratt. (Va.) 310. § 26.
Bradley v. 23 Vt. 720. § 71.
Cross v., 30 Vt. 647. §§ 64, 69.
Cutter v., 125 Mass. 72. § 469.
Dougherty v., 20 Ind. 412. § 40.
v. Draper, 87 N. Y. 337. §§ 94, 140.
Emery v., 61 Me. 99. § 350.
Florence v., 2 La. Ann. 663. § 539.
Hunter v., 1 Duvall (Ky.), 247. § 315.
McIver v., 1 Maule & Sel. 557. § 191.
Mitchum v., 3 Strob. Law (S. C.), 254. § 413.
Nelson v., 4 Sneed, 307. § 185.
Packard v., 17 Mass. 122. § 82.
Price v., 15 Mees. & Wels. 539. § 85.
Richardson, Regina v., 17 Ont. (Can.) 729. § 10.
Roberts v., 39 Iowa, 290. § 342.
Sinclair v., 12 Vt. 33. § 77.
Vinal v., 13 Allen, 521. §§ 17, 201.
Richardson School Fund v. Dean, 130 Mass. 242. § 165.
Richeson, Crawford v., 101 Ill. 351. §§ 301, 320, 329.
Hook v., 115 Ill. 431. §§ 299, 320.
Richmond v. Marston, 15 Ind. 134. § 298.
v. Standclift, 14 Vt. 258. § 417.
Richmond & Petersburg R. R. Co. v. Kasey, 30 Gratt. (Va.) 218. §§ 424, 425.
Richter v. Cummings, 60 Pa. St. 441. § 310.
Richwine v. Scovill, 54 Ind. 150. § 102.
Ricker, Strong v., 16 Vt. 554. § 182.
Ricketson v. Giles, 91 Ill. 154. § 210.
Ricketts v. Harvey, 78 Ind. 152. § 648.
Rickley, Castle v., 44 Ohio St. 490. § 176.
Ricks, Bunting v., 2 Dev. & Bat. Eq. (N. C.) 130. § 237.
v. Gantt, 35 La. Ann. 920. § 101.
Grice v., 3 Dev. Law (N. C.), 62. § 197.
Riddell v. School District, 15 Kan. 168. § 168.
Riddle v. Baker, 13 Cal. 295. § 110.
v. Bowman, 27 N. H. 236. § 208.
Moss v., 5 Cranch, 351. § 402.
Parker v., 11 Ohio, 102. § 176.
Roberts v., 79 Pa. St. 468. § 102.
v. Thompson, 104 Pa. St. 330. § 373.
Tourns v., 2 Ala. 694. § 439.
Ridenhour, Hawkins v., 13 Mo. 125. § 249.
Rider, Ex'rs of Dennis v., 2 McLean, 451. § 242.
Ridgely, Miller v. (Cir. Ct. W. D. Tenn.), 22 Fed. Rep. 889. § 181.
Ridgeway v. Potter, 114 Ill. 457. § 223.

Ridgway, Governor *v.*, 12 Ill. 14. § 548.
Ridley, Nichol *v.*, 5 Yerg. (Tenn.) 63. § 80.
Ridsdale, Grant *v.*, 2 Harr. & Johns. (Md.) 186. § 158.
Riegel, Neberroth *v.*, 71 Pa. St. 280. § 77.
Riemer *v.* Schlitz, 49 Wis. 273. § 329.
Riggan *v.* Crain, 86 Ky. 249. § 90.
Riggans *v.* Brown, 12 Ga. 271. § 345.
Riggs, Lewis *v.*, 9 Tex. 164. § 604.
Moakley *v.*, 19 Johns. 69. § 100.
v. Waldo, 2 Cal. 485. § 177.
Righton, State *v.*, 36 La. Ann. 711. § 10.
Riker, Strong *v.*, 16 Vt., 554. § 180.
Riley, City of Fall R. *v.*, 140 Mass. 488. § 521.
v. Gerrish, 9 Cush. 104. § 182.
v. Gregg, 16 Wis. 666. §§ 29, 356.
v. Johnson, 8 Ohio, 526. § 406.
McMullen *v.*, 6 Gray, 500. § 52.
Phillips *v.*, 27 Mo. 386. § 607.
v. Rhea, 5 Lea (Tenn.), 115. § 288.
v. Stallworth, 56 Ala. 481. §§ 206, 208, 214.
Waters *v.*, 2 Harris & Gill (Md.), 305. § 284.
Rindge *v.* Judson, 24 N. Y. 64. § 160.
Rindskopf *v.* Doman, 28 Ohio St. 516. §§ 142, 347.
Rinehart, Miller *v.*, 119 N. Y. 368. § 105.
Rines, Smith *v.*, 32 Me. 177. § 228.
Ring, County of Scott *v.*, 29 Minn. 398, 401. §§ 537, 542, 543, 551.
v. Devlin, 68 Wis. 384. § 14.
v. Kelly, 10 Mo. App. 411. § 601.
Ringleberg *v.* Peterson, 76 Mich. 107. § 464.
Ringgold *v.* Newkirk, 3 Ark. (Pike), 96. § 197.
Ringo, Graham *v.*, 67 Mo. 324. § 137.
Ripley *v.* Gear, 58 Iowa, 460. § 468.
Risdon, Commonwealth *v.*, 8 Phila. (Pa.) 23. § 540.
Risley *v.* Brown, 67 N. Y. 160. § 139.
Ritchey, Hollinsbee *v.*, 49 Ind. 261. § 225.
Ritchie, Clark *v.*, 11 Grant's Ch. 499. § 403.
Ritenour *v.* Mathews, 42 Ind. 7. § 225.
Ritter *v.* Hamilton, 4 Tex. 325. § 604.
Territory *v.*, 1 Wyom. 318. § 591.
Ritter's Adm'r, Jones *v.*, 56 Ala. 270. §§ 540, 638.
Rittenhouse *v.* Kemp, 37 Ind. 258. § 349.
v. Levering, 6 Watts & Serg. (Pa.) 190. §§ 307, 316.
Rivers *v.* Thomas, 1 B. J. Lea (Tenn.), 649. § 181.
Willis *v.*, 80 Ga. 556. § 45.
Rives *v.* McLosk, 5 Stew. & Port. (Ala.) 330. § 248.
Winston *v.*, 4 Stew. & Port. (Ala.) 269. § 450.
Rix *v.* Adams, 9 Vt. 233. § 247.
Rizer *v.* Callen, 27 Kan. 339. § 211.
Roane, Adams *v.*, 7 Ark. (2 Eng.) 360. § 606.
Robb, Boynton *v.*, 22 Ill. 525. § 477.
v. Perry, 35 Fed. Rep. 102. § 574.
Robbins *v.* Ayres, 10 Mo. 538. § 66.
Chambers *v.*, 28 Conn. 544. § 68.
Chilton *v.*, 4 Ala. 223. § 349.
Glover *v.*, 49 Ala. 219. § 379.
Governor *v.*, 7 Ala. 79. § 541.
Port *v.*, 35 Iowa, 208. §§ 405, 427.
Roberson, Graham *v.*, 79 Ga. 73. § 2.
Robeson *v.* Roberts, 20 Ind. 155. §§ 435, 438.
Roberts *v.* Adam, 6 Port. (Ala.) 361. § 290.
v. Bane, 32 Tex. 385. § 375.
Brown *v.*, 9 La. Ann. 256. § 359.
Caldwell *v.*, 1 Dana (Ky.), 355. § 290.
Clark *v.*, 26 Mich. 506. § 28.
v. Colvin, 3 Gratt. (Va.) 358. § 342.
Cutter *v.*, 7 Neb. 4. §§ 408, 411, 517.

Roberts, Donohue *v.* (Cir. Ct. E. D. Mo.), 1 Fed. Rep. 449. § 587.
v. Donovan, 70 Cal. 108. §§ 399, 423.
Dunning *v.*, 35 Barb. (N. Y.) 463. § 89.
Eddy *v.*, 17 Ill. 505. § 62.
v. Green, 31 Ga. 421. § 494.
v. Griswold, 35 Vt. 496. §§ 17, 120.
v. Hawkins, 70 Mich. 566. § 102.
Hunt *v.*, 45 N. Y. 691. § 134.
Lilly *v.*, 58 Ga. 363. §§ 431, 436.
Lucas Co. *v.*, 49 Iowa, 159. § 426.
v. Miles, 12 Mich. 297. § 245.
Moor *v.*, 3 J. Scott (N. S.), 830. § 132.
Morton *v.*, 4 T. B. Mon. (Ky.) 491. § 363.
Pool *v.*, 19 Bradw. 438. § 102.
v. Richardson, 39 Iowa, 290. § 342.
v. Riddle, 79 Pa. St. 468. § 102.
Robeson *v.*, 20 Ind. 155. §§ 435, 438.
v. Sayre, 6 T. B. Mon. (Ky.) 188. § 315.
Simpson *v.*, 35 Ga. 180. § 513.
Slocumb *v.*, 16 La. (Curry), 173. § 504.
v. State, 22 Tex. App. 64. § 500.
v. State, 34 Kan. 151. §§ 508, 519.
State *v.*, 68 Mo. 234. § 371.
v. Stewart, 31 Miss. 664. §§ 342, 344, 353, 356.
Thompson *v.*, 17 Irish Com. Law, 490. § 174.
Wiley *v.*, 28 Mo. 388. § 80.
v. Woven Wire Mattress Co., 46 Md. 374. § 87.
Robertson, Burnap *v.*, 75 Ga. 689. § 416.
v. Coker, 11 Ala. 466. § 417.
v. Deatherage, 82 Ind. 511. § 259.
v. Findley, 31 Mo. 384. § 15.
Jenkins *v.*, 3 Drewry, 351. § 40.
Marchman *v.*, 77 Ga. 41. § 401.
v. Maxcey, 6 Dana (Ky.), 101. § 286.
Robertson, May *v.*, 13 Ala. 86. § 417.
v. Town, 76 Tex. 535. § 577.
v. Trigg's Adm'r, 32 Gratt. (Va.) 76. §§ 595, 628.
Robinson, Ashford *v.*, 8 Ired. Law (N. C.), 114. §§ 67, 82, 100, 142.
v. Berryman, 22 Mo. App. 509. § 382.
Boulware *v.*, 8 Tex., 327. § 211.
Broughton *v.*, 11 Ala. 922. § 295.
Campbell *v.*, 27 Grant's Ch. (Can.) 634. § 37.
Cassitys *v.*, 8 B. Mon. (Ky.) 279. § 624.
Cathcart *v.*, 5 Pet. 264. § 405.
v. Dale, 38 Wis. 330. § 365.
v. Epping, 24 Fla. 237. § 93.
v. Garth, 6 Ala. 204. § 90.
v. Gee, 1 Vesey, Sr. 251. §§ 34, 125.
Gray *v.*, 90 Ind. 527. § 141.
Hall *v.*, 8 Ired. Law (N. C.), 56. § 268.
Hendricks *v.*, 56 Miss. 694. § 94.
v. Hodge, 117 Mass. 222. § 580.
v. Lane, 14 Sm. & Mar. (Miss.) 161. § 62.
v. Larabee, 58 Vt. 652. § 94.
Lidderdale *v.*, 2 Brock. 159. § 309.
v. Lyle, 10 Barb. (N. Y.) 512. § 261.
v. Miller, 2 Bush (Ky.), 129. § 354.
v. Millard, 133 Mass. 236. § 554.
North *v.*, 1 Duvall (Ky.), 71. § 72.
v. Offnutt, 7 T. B. Mon. (Ky.) 540. §§ 142, 363.
v. Plimpton, 25 N. Y. 484. § 457.
v. Reed, 46 Iowa, 219. § 382.
v. Robinson, 20 S. C. 567. § 648.
v. Rogers, 84 Ind. 539. § 226.
Rucker *v.*, 38 Mo. 154. § 376.
v. Sherman, 2 Gratt. (Va.) 178. § 468.
v. Snyder, 97 Ind. 56. § 648.
v. Soule, 56 Miss. 549. § 150.
State Bank *v.*, 13 Ark. (8 Eng.) 214. § 149.
Thompson *v.*, 34 Ark. 44. §§ 239, 344, 353.

Robinson, Wyman *v.*, 73 Mo. 384. § 112.
Roche *v.* Chaplin, 1 Bailey (S. C.), 419. § 58.
Moffitt *v.*, 77 Ind. 48. §§ 35, 97.
Rochester *v.* Randall, 105 Mass. 295. § 545.
Rochester City Bank *v.* Elmwood, 21 N. Y. 88. § 561.
Talman *v.*, 18 Barb. 123. § 5.
Rochester Savings Bank *v.* Chick, 64 N. H. 410. §§ 346, 347.
Rock, Thayer *v.*, 13 Wend. 53. § 52.
Rockefeller, Stone *v.*, 29 Ohio St. 625. § 98.
Rockingham Bank *v.* Claggett, 29 N. H. 292. § 313.
Rockville Nat. Bank *v.* Holt, 58 Conn. 526. §§ 347, 376.
Rockwood, Merriam *v.*, 44 N. H. 81. § 407.
Sharpe's Ex'r *v.*, 78 Va. 24. § 587.
Roddie, Sevier *v.*, 51 Mo. 580. §§ 209, 634.
Rodenburger *v.* Bramblett, 78 Ind. 213. § 329.
Rodes *v.* Crockett, 2 Yerg. (Tenn.) 346. § 247.
Rodgers, Hall *v.*, 7 Humph. (Tenn.) 536. § 67.
v. M'Cluers' Adm'r, 4 Gratt. (Va.) 81. § 308.
Pevito *v.*, 52 Tex. 581. § 27.
Roe *v.* Hough, 3 Salk. 14. § 66.
Ingersoll *v.*, 65 Barb. (N. Y.) 346. § 12.
Rogers, Bailey *v.*, 1 Greenl. (Me.) 186. § 574.
Commonwealth *v.*, 53 Pa. St. 470. § 585.
Dickey *v.*, 19 Martin (La.), 7 N. S. 588. §§ 208, 229.
East River Bank *v.*, 7 Bosw. (N. Y.) 493. § 199.
Exeter Bank *v.*, 7 N. H. 21. § 396.
Hanford *v.*, 11 Barb. (N. Y.) 18. § 87.
Holliman *v.*, 6 Tex. 1. § 208.
Hyde *v.*, 59 Wis. 154. § 434.
Rogers, Musket *v.*, 5 Bing. N. C. 728. § 239.
v. Odom, 86 N. C. 432. § 531.
Robinson *v.*, 84 Ind. 539. § 226.
v. School Trustees, 46 Ill. 428. §§ 30, 243, 426.
Smith *v.*, 14 Ind. 224. § 97.
v. State, 99 Ind. 218. § 546.
Tobias *v.*, 13 N. Y. 59. § 276.
United States *v.* (Dist. Ct. S. D. N. Y.), 28 Fed. Rep. 607. § 520.
v. Waters, 2 Gill & Johns. (Md.) 64. § 68.
Wyke *v.*, 1 De Gex, Macn. & Gor. 408. §§ 365, 376.
Rohan, Skrainka *v.*, 18 Mo. App. 340. § 267.
Roler, Ballew *v.*, 124 Ind. 557. § 316.
Rolfe *v.* Lamb, 16 Vt. 514. § 130.
Rolleston, Carstairs *v.*, 1 Marsh. 207. § 148.
Rollins, Freeman's Bank *v.*, 13 Me. 202. § 352.
Lacy *v.*, 74 Tex. 566. § 270.
v. Love, 97 N. C. 210. § 460.
Rollstone National Bank *v.* Carleton, 136 Mass. 226. § 394.
Rolston *v.* Chick, 1 Stew. (Ala.) 526. § 18.
Rolt, General Steam Navigation Co. *v.*, 6 J. Scott (N. R.), 550. § 397.
Roman *v.* Peters, 2 Rob. (La.) 479. § 553.
Romero *v.* Desmarais, 4 N. M. 367. § 209.
Wagner *v.*, 3 N. M. 131. § 617.
Romeyn, Draper *v.*, 18 Barb. 166. § 342.
Romine *v.* Romine, 59 Ind. 346. § 211.
Rook, Lee *v.*, Moseley, 318. § 238.
Rooker *v.* Benson, 83 Ind. 250. § 298.
Rooksby *v.* State, 92 Ind. 71. § 516.
Roosevelt, Shannon *v.*, 17 Ga. 88. § 515.
Root, Amherst Bank *v.*, 2 Met. (Mass.) 522. §§ 172, 425, 555, 560, 625.

Root, Colt *v.*, 17 Mass. 229. § 72.
v. Dill, 38 Ind. 169. § 608.
Root & Sons' Music Co. *v.* Caldwell, 54 Iowa, 432. § 647.
Roots, McCarty *v.*, 21 How. 432. § 260.
Roper *v.* Cox, Law Rep. Irish (10 Q. B., C. P. & Ex. Div.), 200. § 421.
Garnett *v.*, 10 Ala. 842. § 150.
v. Sangamon Lodge No. 6, 91 Ill. 518. §§ 419, 422, 546.
Rorke, Rowland *v.*, 4 Jones (N. C.), 337. § 67.
Rosborough *v.* McAleley, 10 Rich. (S. C.) 235. § 429.
Rose, Hilary *v.*, 9 Phila. (Pa.) 139. § 100.
Jendervine *v.*, 36 Mich. 54. § 134.
v. Madden, 1 Kan. 445. §§ 31, 618.
Tillotson *v.*, 11 Met. (Mass.) 299. § 205.
v. Williams, 5 Kan. 483. §§ 29, 352.
Rose's Ex'rs, Watson *v.*, 51 Ala. 292. § 326.
Rosenbaum *v.* Goodman, 78 Va. 121. § 255.
v. Gunter, 2 E. D. Smith (N. Y.), 415. § 82.
Rosenberger, Lisk *v.*, 82 Mo. 46. § 608.
Rosendorf *v.* Mandel, 18 Nev. 129. § 589.
Rosenfield, Lindeman *v.*, 67 Ind. 246. §§ 342, 354.
Rosenthal, Bailey *v.*, 56 Mo. 385. § 456.
v. Sutton, 31 Ohio St. 406. § 292.
Ross *v.* Burton, 4 Up. Can. (Q. B.) 357. § 157.
Chapman *v.*, 12 Leigh (Va.), 565. § 60.
v. Clore, 3 Daua (Ky.), 189. § 233.
Comm'rs Berks Co. *v.*, 3 Binney (Pa.), 520. § 433.
Devers *v.*, 10 Gratt. (Va.) 252. § 374.
Ross *v.* Ferris, 18 Hun (N. Y.), 210. § 372.
v. Jones, 22 Wall. 576. § 604.
v. Menefee, 125 Ind. 432. § 205.
Salyers *v.*, 15 Ind. 130. § 259.
Taylor *v.*, 3 Yerg. (Tenn.) 330. §§ 82, 199.
Teaff *v.*, 1 Ohio St. 469. § 445.
v. Williams, 11 Heisk. (Tenn.) 410. § 254.
Wills *v.*, 77 Ind. 1. §§ 13, 16, 92, 191, 193, 644.
v. Wilson, 7 Smedes & Mar. (Miss.) 753. § 324.
v. Woodville, 4 Munf. (Va.) 324. § 413.
Rosswaag, State *v.*, 3 Mo. App. 11. § 639.
Roth, Beard *v.* (Cir. Ct. E. D. Ark.), 35 Fed. Rep. 397. § 587.
v. Miller, 15 Serg. & Rawle, 100. § 62.
Rothermal *v.* Hughes, 134 Pa. St. 510. § 406.
Rounds, Phillips *v.*, 33 Me. 357. §§ 355, 369, 370.
Rounsavell *v.* Wolf, 47 Wis. 353. § 648.
Rountree *v.* Rutherford, 65 Ga. 444. § 150.
Rouse *v.* Glissman, 29 Ill. App. 321. §§ 3, 14.
Routon, Lembe *v.*, 33 La. Ann. 1005. § 468.
Routon's Adm'r *v.* Lucy, 17 Mo. 399. §§ 605, 613.
Rowan *v.* Sharp's Rifle Co., 33 Conn. 1. §§ 34, 388.
Rowe, Besshears *v.*, 46 Mo. 501. § 17.
v. Buchtel, 13 Ind. 381. § 607.
Cross *v.*, 22 N. H. 77. § 114.
Ogden *v.*, 3 E. D. Smith (N. Y.), 312. § 389.
State *v.*, 103 Ind. 118. § 495.
v. Whittier, 21 Me. 54. § 66.
Rowell, Avery *v.*, 59 Wis. 82. § 19.
Rowland *v.* Rorke, 4 Jones (N. C.), 337. § 67.
Rowlett *v.* Ewbank, 1 Bush (Ky.), 477. § 16.

Rowley, Hosea v., 57 Mo. 357. § 352.
v. Jewett, 50 Iowa, 492. §§ 245, 383.
Laval v., 17 Ind. 36. § 312.
Rowney, Ardern v., 5 Esp. 254. § 67.
Royal Canadian Bank v. Payne, 19 Grant's Ch. (Can.) 180. §§ 34, 117.
Royal Ins. Co. v. Davies, 40 Iowa, 469. § 133.
Royce, McVickar v., 17 Up. Can. (Q. B.) 529. § 211.
Roye, Kimball v., 9 Rich. 295. § 113.
Royston v. Howie, 15 Ala. 309. § 438.
Ruan, Mahaska County v., 45 Iowa, 328. § 559.
Rubey v. Watson, 22 Mo. App. 428. § 329.
Ruble v. Norman, 7 Bush (Ky.), 582. § 333.
Ruhush v. State, 112 Ind. 107. §§ 503, 510.
Ruby, Smith v., 6 Heisk. (Tenn.) 546. § 484.
Rucker v. Cammeyer, 1 Esp. 105. § 90.
Frost v., 4 Humph. (Tenn.) 57. § 616.
v. Robinson, 38 Mo. 154. § 376.
State v., 59 Mo. 17. § 582.
Rucks v. Taylor, 49 Miss. 552. §§ 221, 230.
Rudd, Laub v., 37 Iowa, 617. § 114.
Schoolfield's Adm'r v., 9 B. Mon. (Ky.) 291. § 318.
Ruddell v. Childress, 31 Ark. 511. § 605.
Rudhall, Smith v., 3 Foster & Fin. 143. § 77.
Rudolf, Merchants' Bank v., 5 Neb. 527. § 252.
Rudolph, Perkins v., 36 Ill. 306. § 482.
Rudowskey, State v., 65 Ind. 389. § 509.
Rudy, Bank of Hopkinsville v., 2 Bush (Ky.), 326. § 308.
v. Wolf, 16 Serg. & R. (Pa.) 79. §§ 100, 101.
Rue, Hibbs v., 4 Pa. St. 348. §§ 129, 378.
Ruffner v. Love, 9 Rich. Law (S. C.), 335. § 204.
Ruggles v. Berry, 76 Me. 262. § 505.
Carroll Co. v., 69 Iowa, 269. § 408.
Coggeshall v., 62 Ill. 401. §§ 129, 212.
v. Holden, 3 Wend. 216. § 239.
Rumey & Co., Day v., 40 Ohio St. 446. § 434.
Rumsey, Smith v., 33 Mich. 183. §§ 291, 309.
Runde v. Runde, 59 Ill. 98. §§ 63, 67.
Rundle, Allen v., 50 Conn. 9, 588. §§ 100, 644.
Runner v. Commonwealth, 78 Ky. 556. § 502.
Rupert v. Grant, 6 Sm. & Mar. (Miss.) 433. § 344.
Rupp v. Over, 3 Brewster (Pa.), 133. § 233.
Rush v. Bishop, 60 Tex. 177. § 296.
Graham v., 73 Iowa, 451. § 380.
v. State, 20 Ind. 432. §§ 97, 323.
Rushing, State v., 17 Fla. 227. §§ 422, 524.
Russ, Hale v., 1 Greenl. (Me.) 334. § 516.
Russell v. Annable, 109 Mass. 72. § 151.
v. Ballard, 16 B. Mon. (Ky.) 201. § 115.
v. Brown, 21 Mo. App. 51. §§ 351, 376.
v. Clark, 7 Cranch, 69. §§ 73, 92.
Dillon v., 5 Neb. 484. § 342.
v. Failor, 1 Ohio St. 327. § 267.
v. La Roque, 11 Ala. 352. §§ 143, 222.
v. La Roque, 13 Ala. 149. § 328.
Montgomery v., 10 La. (Curry), 330. § 214.
v. Moseley, 3 Brod. & Bing. 211. §§ 17, 84.
People v., 25 Hun (N. Y.), 524. § 630.
People v., 4 Wend. 570. § 555.

Russell *v.* People's Savings Bank, 39 Mich. 671. § 7.
Shubrick's Ex'rs *v.*, 1 Des. (S. C.) 315. § 366.
v. State, 45 Ga. 9. § 511.
Taylor *v.*, 75 Ind. 386. § 486.
Teague *v.*, 2 Stew. (Ala.) 420. § 245.
Western *v.*, 3 Ves. & Bea. 187. §§ 80, 89.
v. Wiggins, 2 Story, 214. § 81.
Wright *v.*, 2 W. Black. 934. § 119.
Russell & Co. *v.* Klink, 53 Mich. 161. § 50.
Rutledge, Allison *v.*, 5 Yerg. (Tenn.) 193. § 117.
Rutherford *v.* Brachman, 40 Ohio St. 604. §§ 346, 377.
Rountree *v.*, 65 Ga. 444. § 150.
Rutherford, Adm'r, Burton *v.*, 49 Mo. 255. § 230.
Rutter *v.* Hall, 31 Ill. App. 647. §§ 580, 586.
Ryan *v.* Bradley, Taylor, Law & Eq. (N. C.) 77. § 505.
Kerns, Adm'r, *v.*, 26 Ill. App. 177. § 355.
Mayor, etc. *v.*, 9 Daly (N. Y. Com. Pl.), 316. §§ 113, 175.
v. Morton, 65 Tex. 258. §§ 122, 397, 427.
v. Shawneetown, 14 Ill. 20. §§ 34, 387.
v. State Bank, 10 Neb. 524. § 590.
Warden *v.*, 37 Mo. App. 466. § 388.
v. Williams' Adm'r, 29 Kan. 487. §§ 92, 93, 489.
Rydé *v.* Curtis, 8 Dow. & Ry. 62. § 84.
Jones *v.*, 5 Taunt. 488. § 28.
Ryder, Carhart *v.*, 11 Daly (N. Y. Com. Pl.), 101. § 109.
United States *v.*, 110 U. S. 729. §§ 320, 513, 621.
Sabin *v.* Harris, 12 Iowa, 87. § 201.
Sackett, Randall *v.*, 77 N. Y. 480. § 139.
Sackrider, Brady *v.*, 1 Sandf. (N. Y.) 514. § 76.
Sacramento *v.* Kirk, 7 Cal. 419. § 386.
Sacramento Co. *v.* Bird, 31 Cal. 66. § 553.
Sadler *v.* Hawkes, 1 Roll. Abr. 27, pl. 49. § 16.
Saffold *v.* Wade's Ex'r, 61 Ala. 214. § 324.
v. Scott, 37 Ga. 384. § 352.
Sage, Stocking *v.*, 1 Conn. 519. § 60.
v. Strong, 40 Wis. 575. § 398.
v. Wilcox, 6 Conn. 81. §§ 16, 58, 82, 197.
Sailly *v.* Elmore, 2 Paige, Ch. 497. §§ 243, 342.
Sailor, Daviess Co. Saving Ass'n *v.*, 63 Mo. 24. § 252.
Saint *v.* Ledyard, 14 Ala. 244. § 317.
Sale *v.* Darragh, 2 Hilton (N. Y.), 184. § 81.
Salem Manuf. Co. *v.* Brower, 4 Jones' Law (N. C.), 429. § 202.
Saleski, Callahan *v.*, 29 Ark. 216. § 454.
Salisbury *v.* Hale, 12 Pick. 416. § 202.
v. Van Hoesen, 3 Hill (N. Y.), 77. § 574.
Salkeld *v.* Abbott, Hayes (Irish), 576. § 313.
Saline Co. *v.* Bine, 65 Mo. 63. § 428.
Salmon *v.* Clagett, 3 Bland's Ch. (Md.) 125. § 376.
Claget *v.*, 5 Gill & John. (Md.) 314. §§ 376, 387.
Salmon Falls Manufacturing Co. *v.* Goddard, 14 How. 446. §§ 80, 89, 90.
Salmond, Sargent *v.*, 27 Me. 539. § 294.
Saltenberry *v.* Loucks, 8 La. Ann. 95. § 528.
Salter *v.* Salter's Creditors, 6 Bush (Ky.), 624. § 310.
Worden *v.*, 90 Ill. 160. § 14.
Salt Springs Nat. Bank *v.* Sloan, 57 Hun (N. Y.), 265. § 100.
Salts, Maxwell *v.*, 4 Cold. (Tenn.) 233. § 489.
Salyers *v.* Ross, 15 Ind. 130. § 259.

Sample v. Cochran, 82 Ind. 260. § 426.
v. Davis, 4 Greene (Iowa), 117. § 565.
Leaman v., 91 Ind. 236. § 297.
v. Martin, 46 Ind. 226. § 183.
Underwood v., 70 Ind. 446. § 648.
Sampson v. Barnard, 98 Mass. 359. § 386.
v. Hobart, 28 Vt. 697. § 64.
v. Solinsky, 75 Tex. 663. § 461.
Samuel v. Howarth, 3 Meriv. 272. §§ 243, 343.
v. Withers, 16 Mo. 532. § 417.
v. Zachery, 4 Ired. Law (N. C.), 377. § 288.
Sanborn v. Flagler, 9 Allen, 474. § 89.
Gookin v., 3 N. H. 491. § 580.
Neelson v., 2 N. H. 413. § 82.
Sanders, Allen v., 34 N. J. Eq. 203. § 589.
v. Bean, Busb. Law (N. C.), 318. § 570.
Buck v., 1 Dana (Ky.), 187. § 237.
v. Clason, 13 Minn. 379. § 66.
v. Edwards' Adm'x, 29 La. Ann. 696. § 587.
v. Etcherson, 36 Ga. 404. § 194.
Irwin v., 5 Yerg. (Tenn.) 287. § 453.
v. Sanders, 30 S. C. 229. § 492.
v. State, 62 Ind. 562. § 581.
Thompson v., 4 Dev. & Bat. Law (N. C.), 404. § 265.
v. Watson, 14 Ala. 198. § 322.
v. Weelburg, 107 Ind. 266. §§ 268, 284.
Sanderson v. Aston, Law Rep. 8 Exch. 73. §§ 399, 423.
v. Stevens, 116 Mass. 133. § 516.
Sandilands v. Marsh, 2 Barn. & Ald. 673. § 18.
Sands, Wayne v., Freeman, 351. § 12.
Sanford v. Allen, 1 Cush. 473. § 98.
McNeil v., 3 B. Mon. (Ky.) 11. § 258.
v. Norton, 14 Vt. 228. §§ 180, 182.
Sanford, Winn v., 145 Mass. 302. § 153.
Sangamon Lodge No. 6, Roper v., 91 Ill. 5, 18. §§ 419, 422, 546.
San Roman v. Watson, 54 Tex. 254. § 27.
Sans v. People, 3 Gil. (Ill.) 327. § 515.
Sapp v. Aiken, 68 Iowa, 699. § 211.
Sappington, State v., 67 Mo. 529. § 540.
Sarchett, Jones v., 61 Iowa, 520. §§ 365, 376.
Sargent v. Salmond, 27 Me. 539. § 294.
v. Wallis, 67 Tex. 483. § 526.
Sasscer v. Young, 6 Gill & Johns. (Md.) 243. § 436.
Sasser v. McDaniel, 73 Ga. 547. § 509.
Satterfield v. People, 104 Ill. 448. § 532.
Satterwhite, State v., 20 S. C. 536. § 4.
Sauer v. Griffin, 67 Mo. 654. § 460.
Saulet v. Trepagnier, 2 La. Ann. 427. § 443.
Saulsbury v. Weaver, 59 Ga. 254. § 7.
Saum, Flickinger v., 40 Ohio St. 591. § 583.
Saunders, Beeker v., 6 Ired. Law (N. C.), 380. § 101.
O'Bannon v., 24 Gratt. (Va.) 138. § 567.
Perry v., 36 Iowa, 427. § 431.
v. Wakefield, 4 Barn. & Ald. 595. §§ 13, 82.
Saunderson v. Jackson, 2 Bos. & Pul. 238. §§ 80, 89.
v. Jackson, 3 Esp. 189. §§ 80, 89.
Savage, Benneson v., 130 Ill. 352. § 367.
v. Burns, 3 Mont. 527. § 601.
Doughty v., 28 Conn. 146. §§ 403, 420.
v. Fox, 60 N. H. 17. §§ 15, 235.
Leavitt v., 16 Me. 72. § 374.
Taylor v., 12 Mass. 98. §§ 60, 266.
Wildes v., 1 Story, 22. § 192.
Savage's Adm'r v. Carleton, 33 Ala. 443. § 605.
Savery, McLott v., 11 Iowa, 323. § 137.
Savings Bank, Homer v., 7 Conn. 478. § 326.

Savings Bank *v.* Hunt, 72 Mo. 597. § 168.
v. Scott, 10 Neb. 83. § 7.
v. Strother, 28 S. C. 504. § 199.
Savory, Carkin *v.*, 14 Gray, 528. §§ 122, 359.
Sawtel, Harrison *v.*, 10 Johns. 242. § 60.
Sawyer *v.* Bradford, 6 Ala. 572. § 438.
Dearborn *v.*, 59 N. H. 95. § 202.
v. Fernald, 59 Me. 500. § 17.
Miller *v.*, 30 Vt. 412. § 268.
v. Seen, 27 S. C. 251. § 165.
Weare *v.*, 44 N. H. 198. §§ 148, 405.
Sawyers *v.* Baker, 72 Ala. 49. § 329.
v. Hicks, 6 Watts (Pa.), 76. §§ 373, 550.
Sawyer's Adm'r *v.* Patterson, 11 Ala. 523. § 438.
Saxton, Bissell *v.*, 66 N. Y. 55. §§ 545, 628.
Bissell *v.*, 77 N. Y. 191. § 526.
Sayer, Evers *v.*, 28 Mich. 47. § 453.
Sayles *v.* Sims, 73 N. Y. 551. §§ 31, 259.
Saylor, United States *v.* (Cir. Ct. E. D. Mich.), 31 Fed. Rep. 543. § 595.
Saylors *v.* Saylors, 3 Heisk. (Tenn.) 525. §§ 223, 324.
Sayre *v.* King, 17 W. Va. 562. §§ 364, 374.
Roberts *v.*, 6 T. B. Mon. (Ky.) 188. § 315.
Supplee *v.*, 51 Hun (N. Y.), 30. §§ 284, 293.
Sayward, Smith *v.*, 5 Greenl. 504. §§ 60, 64.
Scales *v.* Cox, 106 Ind. 261. § 605.
Scanlan *v.* Settle, Meigs (Tenn.), 169. §§ 301, 367.
Scanland, Jones *v.*, 6 Humph. (Tenn.) 195. § 521.
Scarff, Allen *v.*, 1 Hilton (N. Y.), 209. § 76.
Schaacht *v.* Odell, 52 Cal. 449. § 461.
Schaales, Gruenewald *v.*, 17 Mo. App. 324. § 462.
Schaeffer *v.* Bernero, 11 Mo. App. 562. § 588.
Wolff *v.*, 4 Mo. App. 367. § 580.
Wolff *v.*, 74 Mo. 154. §§ 408, 540.
Schaffer, Silmeyer *v.*, 60 Ill. 479. § 356.
Scheffler, Victor Sewing Machine Co. *v.*, 61 Cal. 530. § 399.
Scheid *v.* Leibshultz, 51 Ind. 38. § 26.
Scheifferly, Oaks *v.*, 74 Cal. 478. § 599.
Schenck, Macready & Burke *v.*, 41 La. Ann. 456. § 631.
Hewlett *v.*, 82 N. C. 234. § 588.
Schermerhorn *v.* Conner, 41 Mich. 374. §§ 98, 100.
Schindel *v.* Gates, 46 Md. 604. § 333.
Schlitz, Riemer *v.*, 49 Wis. 273. § 329.
Schloss *v.* White, 16 Cal. 65. § 565.
Schmaetter, Schmidt *v.*, 45 Mo. 502. § 180.
Schmidt, Auchampaugh, Adm'r, *v.*, 70 Iowa, 642. § 148.
Auchampaugh *v.*, 77 Iowa, 13. §§ 3, 245.
v. City of New Orleans, 33 La. Ann. 17. § 571.
v. Coulter, 6 Minn. 492. § 272.
v. Schmaetter, 45 Mo. 502. § 180.
Wright *v.*, 47 Iowa, 233. § 8.
Schmucker *v.* Steidemann, 18 Mo. App. 302. § 23.
Schnecko, Benne *v.*, 100 Mo. 250. §§ 310, 311.
Schneider *v.* Norris, 2 Maule & Sel. 286. §§ 80, 89.
Schnell *v.* North Side Planing Mill Co., 89 Ill. 581. § 178.
Wilson Sewing Machine Co. *v.*, 20 Minn. 40. § 87.
Schnitter, Smarr *v.*, 28 Mo. 478. § 364.
Schnitzell, Clay *v.*, 5 Phila. (Pa.) 441. § 262.
Schnitzell's Appeal, 49 Pa. St. 23. § 262.
Schofield, Dillon *v.*, 11 Neb. 419. § 487.
v. Hustis, 9 Hun (N. Y.), 157. § 581.

Schofield, Kenworthy v., 2 Barn. & Cress. 945. § 90.
Scholefield, Lawrie v., 4 Com. Pl. 622. § 160.
v. Templer, 4 De Gex & Jones, 429. § 148.
Schoolfield's Adm'r v. Rudd, 9 B. Mon. (Ky.) 291. § 318.
Schoonmaker, Stockbridge v., 45 Barb. (N. Y.) 100. § 131.
Schoonover v. Allen, 40 Ark. 132. § 306.
School Directors, Grim v., 51 Pa. St. 219. § 411.
v. Judice, 39 La. Ann. 896. §§ 517, 521, 642.
School District, Gargan v., 4 Col. 53. § 119.
Riddel v., 15 Kan. 168. § 168.
School Trustees, Rogers v., 46 Ill. 428. §§ 30, 243, 426.
Schreyer, Vanderbilt v., 91 N. Y. 392. §§ 88, 99.
Schroeppell v. Shaw, 3 N. Y. 446. §§ 243, 446.
Schuler, Breese v., 48 Ill. 329. § 236.
Schuster v. Weissman, 63 Mo. 552. § 553.
Schuyler, People v., 4 N. Y. 173. § 566.
Putnam v., 4 Hun (N. Y.), 166. §§ 12, 416.
Schwaebe, Hoffman v., 33 Barb. (N. Y.) 194. § 251.
Schwartz v. Hyman, 107 N. Y. 562. § 165.
Schwessler v. Dudley, 80 Ala. 547. § 320.
Scott v. Bailey, 23 Mo. 140. § 30.
v. Bradford, 5 Port. (Ala.) 443. § 607.
v. Calkin, 139 Mass. 529. § 182.
Connecticut Mutual Life Ins. Co. v., 81 Ky. 540. §§ 118, 422, 423.
v. Dewees, 2 Tex. 153. § 611.
v. Dickson, Adm'r, 108 Pa. St. 6. § 603.
Janes v., 59 Pa. St. 178. §§ 97, 100.
Scott v. Featherstone, 5 La. Ann. 306. § 301.
Fuller v., 8 Kan. 25. §§ 16, 18, 88, 176, 202.
v. Hall, 6 B. Mon. 285. § 356.
v. Harris, 76 N. C. 205. § 356.
Kleiser v., 6 Dana (Ky.), 137. § 322.
Leckie v., 10 La. (5 Curry), 412. § 21.
Mackenzie v., 6 Bro. Parl. Cas. 280. § 71.
Macrory v., 5 Wels., Hurl. & Gor. 907. §§ 68, 70.
McConnell v., 15 Ohio, 401. § 237.
McGehee v., 15 Ga. 74. § 575.
Mullen v., 9 La. Ann. 173. § 636.
v. Nichols, 27 Miss. 94. § 230.
v. Saffold, 37 Ga. 384. §§ 352, 356.
Savings Bank v., 10 Neb. 83. § 7.
v. Scott, 50 Mich. 372. § 487.
State v., 20 Iowa, 63. §§ 497, 499.
v. State, 46 Ind. 203. § 531.
Storr v., 6 Car. & Payne, 241. § 78.
v. Thomas, 1 Scam. (Ill.) 58. § 64.
v. Timberlake, 83 N. C. 382. § 253.
Williams v., 83 Ind. 405. §§ 377, 648.
Woodbridge v., 3 Brevard (S. C.), 193. § 222.
Scott & Culver, Lane & Saylor v., 57 Tex. 367. § 378.
Scofield v. Gaskill, 60 Ga. 277. § 259.
Healey v., 60 Ga. 450. § 259.
Scovill, Richwine v., 54 Ind. 150. § 102.
Scoville, Alger v., 1 Gray, 391. §§ 64, 72.
Screwmen's Benevolent Ass'n, Barry v., 67 Tex. 250. §§ 526, 628.
v. Smith, 70 Tex. 168. §§ 421, 590, 624.
Screws v. Watson, 48 Ala. 628. § 490.
Scroggin v. Holland, 16 Mo. 419. § 413.
Scudder, Barker v., 56 Mo. 272. §§ 67, 198.

Scudder, Menard *v.*, 7 La. Ann. 385. §§ 133, 157, 186, 187, 204.
Scully, Hiltz *v.*, 1 Cinc. 554. § 77.
v. Kirkpatrick, 79 Pa. St. 324. § 497.
Scultborpe, Mines *v.*, 2 Camp. 215. § 91.
Seabury *v.* Hungerford, 2 Hill, 80. § 179.
Seacord *v.* Morgan, 3 Keyes (N. Y.), 636. § 449.
Seals, Bailey *v.*, 1 Har. (Del.) 367. 498.
Seaman, Bartholomew *v.*, 25 Hun (N. Y.), 619. § 199.
v. Drake, 1 Caines' Rep. 9. § 150.
Searcy, Johnson *v.*, 4 Yerg. (Tenn.) 182. § 342.
Pyke *v.*, 4 Porter (Ala.), 52. §§ 359, 585.
Thompson *v.*, 6 Port. (Ala.) 393. § 578.
Searing *v.* Berry, 58 Iowa, 20. §§ 311, 645.
Searles, Wolleshlare *v.*, 45 Pa. St. 45. § 240.
Sears, Agawam Bank *v.*, 4 Gray, 95. § 381.
v. Bearsh, 7 La. Ann. 539. § 464.
v. Brink, 3 Johns. 210. § 82.
Habersham *v.*, 11 Oreg. 431. § 569.
v. Van Dusen, 25 Mich. 351. §§ 339, 340.
Seaver *v.* Bradley, 6 Greenl. (Me.) 60. § 203.
Hayes *v.*, 7 Greenl. (Me.) 237. § 580.
v. Young, 16 Vt. 658. § 247.
Seawell *v.* Cohn, 2 Nev. 308. § 370.
Seawell, Adm'r, *v.* Buckley's Distributees, 54 Ala. 592. § 580.
Seay, Long *v.*, 72 Mo. 648. §§ 168, 537.
Sebastian *v.* Bryan, 21 Ark. 447. § 574.
v. Johnson, 2 Duvall (Ky.), 101. § 24.
Second Nat. Bank *v.* Diefendorf, 90 Ill. 396. § 93.
Second Nat. Bank *v.* Gaylord, 34 Iowa, 246. § 202.
v. Hill, 76 Ind. 223. § 432.
Sedalia, W. & S. R'y Co. *v.* Smith, 27 Mo. App. 371. § 93.
Sedgwick, Amicable Mutual Life Ins. Co. *v.*, 110 Mass. 163. §§ 392, 396.
v. Bliss, 23 Met. 617. § 106.
Seeley *v.* Brown, 14 Pick. 177. § 505.
Campau *v.*, 30 Mich. 57. § 493.
Martin *v.*, 15 Neb. 136. § 570.
Poppenhousen *v.*, 3 Abb. Rep. Om. Cas. 615. § 459.
Seely, Bonney *v.*, 2 Wend. 481. §§ 211, 212, 217.
v. People, 27 Ill. 173. § 412.
Seen, Sawyer *v.*, 27 S. C. 251. § 165.
Sefton *v.* Hargett, 113 Ind. 592. § 29.
Seibert *v.* Thompson, 8 Kan. 65. §§ 268, 324.
v. True, 8 Kan. 52. § 324.
Seibrecht, Clapp *v.*, 11 La. Ann. 528. § 467.
Seiple *v.* Borough of Elizabeth, 3 Dutcher (N. J.), 407. § 42.
Seitz, Fulmer *v.*, 68 Pa. St. 237. § 379.
Selby *v.* Selby, 3 Meriv. 2. § 89.
Seligman *v.* Gray, 66 Mich. 341. § 439.
Sellers, Batturs *v.*, 5 Harr. & Johns. (Md.) 117. § 90.
v. Jones, 22 Pa. St. 423. § 440.
Selman, Justices *v.*, 6 Ga. 432. §§ 450, 576.
Selser *v.* Brock, 3 Ohio St. 302. §§ 379, 412.
Semmes, Burns *v.*, 4 Cranch, Cir. Ct. 702. § 186.
Semple *v.* Atkinson, 64 Mo. 504. § 364.
Danforth *v.*, 7 Leg. News, 203. § 356.
Uhler *v.*, 5 C. E. Green (N. J.), 288. § 218.
Serra 'E Hejo *v.* Hoffman & Co., 30 La. Ann. 67. § 150.
Seton *v.* Slade, 7 Vesey, 265. § 89.
Settle, Scanlan *v.*, Meigs (Tenn.), 169. §§ 301, 367.
Severance, Clay *v.*, 55 Vt. 300. § 208.

Sevier, Howell *v.*, 1 B. J. Lea, 360. § 356.
v. Roddie, 51 Mo. 580. §§ 209, 634.
Sewall *v.* Fitch, 8 Cowen, 215. § 90.
Lee *v.*, 2 La. Ann. 940. § 364.
Wright *v.*, 9 Rob. (La.) 128. § 126.
Sewell, Hill *v.*, 27 Ark. 15. §§ 444, 568.
Seymour, Harrison *v.*, Law Rep. 1 Com. Pl. 518. § 398.
v. Mickey, 15 Ohio St. 515. §§ 176, 182.
Morgan *v.*, 1 Reports in Chancery, 120. § 303.
Stone *v.*, 15 Wend. 19. § 338.
Welch *v.*, 28 Conn. 387. §§ 142, 167.
Shaeffer *v.* Clendenin, 100 Pa. St. 565. § 270.
Pittsburg, Ft. Wayne & C. R. R. Co. *v.*, 59 Pa. St. 350. § 425.
Shackford, Phillips *v.*, Cro. Eliz. 455. § 16.
Shackleford, State *v.*, 56 Miss. 648. § 526.
Weatherby *v.*, 37 Miss. 557. § 475.
Shafer, Post *v.*, 63 Mich. 85. § 459.
Stephens *v.*, 48 Wis. 54. § 636.
Shain, Bragg *v.*, 49 Cal. 131. § 397.
Shamburg *v.* Abbott, 112 Pa. St. 6. § 36.
Shane *v.* Francis, 30 Ind. 92. § 570.
Shanklin, Patton *v.*, 14 B. Mon. (Ky.) 13. § 381.
Shanks, Jasper Co. *v.*, 61 Mo. 332. § 614.
Shannon, Beers *v.*, 73 N. Y. 292. § 112.
v. McMullin, 25 Gratt. (Va.) 211. § 434.
v. Roosevelt, 17 Ga. 88. § 515.
Stelle *v.*, 62 Tex. 198. § 471.
Sharkey, Kiggin *v.*, 3 Lea (Tenn.), 707. § 565.
Sharman *v.* Brandt, 40 Law Jour. (N. S.) 312. § 90.
Sharon *v.* Sharon, 84 Cal. 433. § 492.
Sharp, Ashby *v.*, 1 Littell (Ky.), 156. § 450.
v. Bedell, 5 Gil. 88. § 449.
v. Fagan, 3 Sneed (Tenn.), 541. § 353.
v. Gage, 24 Iowa, 15. § 407.
Gerber *v.*, 72 Ind. 553. §§ 314, 329.
v. Miller, 57 Cal. 415. § 339.
Spring Hill Mining Co. *v.*, 3 Pugsley (N. B.), 603. § 557.
v. United States, 4 Watts (Pa.), 21. §§ 411, 517.
Sharp's Rifle Manuf'g Co., Rowan *v.*, 33 Conn. 1. §§ 34, 388.
Sharpe *v.* Smith, 59 Ga. 707. § 510.
v. Speckenugle, 3 Serg. & Rawle (Pa.), 463. § 150.
Sharpe, Adm'r, *v.* Connely, 105 N. C. 87. § 603.
Sharpe's Ex'r *v.* Rockwood, 78 Va. 24. § 587.
Shattuck, Eagle Mowing & Reaping Machine Co. *v.*, 53 Wis. 455. § 67.
Shaver *v.* Allison, 11 Grant's Ch. 355. § 397.
Cooper *v.*, 101 Pa. St. 547. § 99.
Readfield *v.*, 50 Me. 36. § 408.
Shaw, Bashford *v.*, 4 Ohio St. 264. §§ 101, 202.
v. Binkard, 10 Ind. 227. § 357.
Caton *v.*, 2 Harris & Gill (Md.), 13. § 194.
v. First Associated Reformed Presbyterian Church, 39 Pa. St. 226. § 363.
Grant *v.*, 16 Mass. 341. § 67.
Hodgson *v.*, 3 Mylne & Keen, 183. §§ 313, 321.
Kerr *v.*, 13 Johns. 236. § 82.
v. Lond, 12 Mass. 447. § 214.
v. McFarlane, 1 Ired. Law (N. C.), 216. § 426.
Schroeppell *v.*, 3 N. Y. 446. §§ 243, 446.
Sherburne *v.*, 1 N. H. 157. § 81.
v. Vandusen, 5 Up. Can. (Q. B.) 353. § 118.

Shaw v. Woodcock, 7 Barn. & Cres. 73. § 52.
Shawneetown, Ryan v., 14 Ill. 20. §§ 34, 387.
Sheahan, Edmonds v., 47 Tex. 443. § 212.
Sheehan, County of Waseca v., 42 Minn. 57. § 555.
Sheffield, Bothwell v., 8 Ga. 569. § 569.
Shehan v. Hampton, 8 Ala. 942. §§ 605, 618.
Sheid v. Stamps, 2 Sneed (Tenn.), 172. § 81.
Sheik, Trustees of Schools v., 119 Ill. 579. §§ 152, 206, 517.
Shekan, Martin v., 2 Col. 614. § 239.
Shelby, Crowdus v., 6 J. J. Marsh. (Ky.) 61. § 208.
v. Governor, 2 Blackf. (Ind.) 289. §§ 624, 636, 638.
Shelden, Smith v., 35 Mich. 42. §§ 1, 32, 36.
Sheldon v. Butler, 24 Minn. 513. § 67.
Cady v., 38 Barb. (N. Y.) 103. § 98.
v. Reynolds, 14 La. Ann. 703. § 403.
Stoll v., 13 Neb. 207. § 252.
v. Williams, 11 Neb. 272. § 446.
Shelton v. Farmer, 9 Bush (Ky.), 314. § 277.
Gower v., 16 Lea (Tenn.), 652. § 587.
v. Hurd, 7 R. I. 403. §§ 40, 243.
Weimer v., 7 Mo. 237. § 235.
Shepard, Johnson v., 35 Mich. 115. § 98.
Loveland v., 2 Hill (N. Y.), 139. § 100.
v. Ogden, 2 Scam. (Ill.) 257. § 230.
v. Pebbles, 38 Wis. 373. § 639.
v. Phears, 35 Tex. 763. § 98.
v. Taylor, 35 Tex. 774. § 128.
Shepherd, Brooks v., 4 Bibb (Ky.), 572. § 488.
v. Brown, 30 W. Va. 13. § 569.
v. May, 115 U. S. 505. § 37.
Wise v., 13 Ill. 41. § 316.
Sheppard, Forbes v., 98 N. C. 111. §§ 30, 376.
Sherbert, Mt. Olivet Cemetery Co. v., 2 Head (Tenn.), 116. § 66.
Sherburne v. Shaw, 1 N. H. 157. § 81.
Sherill, Benedict v., Lalor's Sup. to Hill & Denio, 219. § 116.
Sherley, Farmers' & Drovers' Bank v., 12 Bush (Ky.), 304. § 305.
Sherman v. Black, 49 Vt. 198. § 265.
Grimes v., 25 Neb. 843. § 219.
Hill v., 15 Iowa, 365. § 605.
Robinson v., 2 Gratt. (Va.) 178. § 468.
v. State, 4 Kan. 570. §§ 8, 506.
Walker v., 11 Met. (Mass.) 170. § 16.
Woods v., 71 Pa. St. 100. § 101.
Sherraden v. Parker, 24 Iowa, 28. § 442.
Sherrell v. Goodrum, 3 Humph. (Tenn.) 419. § 545.
Sherrod v. Rhodes, 5 Ala. 683. § 260.
v. Woodard, 4 Dev. Law (N. C.), 360. § 295.
Sherry v. State Bank, 6 Ind. 397. § 449.
Sherwood v. Collier, 3 Dev. Law (N. C.), 380. § 310.
Dart v., 7 Wis. 523. §§ 31, 137.
Hull v., 59 Mo. 172. § 279.
Lyman v., 20 Vt. 42. § 114.
Ranson v., 26 Conn. 437. §§ 177, 641, 643.
v. Stone, 14 N. Y. 267. § 71.
Shetler, Lambert v., 71 Iowa, 463. § 345.
Shewell v. Knox, 1 Dev. Law (N. C.), 404. § 186.
Shields, Barrow v., 13 La. Ann. 57. § 426.
Davis v., 24 Wend. 322. § 89.
Davis v., 26 Wend. 34. § 89.
Dignan v., 51 Tex. 322. §§ 22, 648.
v. Middleton, 2 Cranch, C. C. 205. § 67.
Miller v., 124 Ind. 166. § 7.
v. Smith, 8 Bush (Ky.), 601. § 584.
v. Smith, 78 Ind. 425. §§ 495, 515.

Shimer *v.* Hightshue, 7 Black. (Ind.) 238. § 449.
v. Jones, 47 Pa. St. 268. § 240.
Shine, Central Savings Bank *v.*, 48 Mo. 456. § 189.
Shine's Adm'r *v.* Central Savings Bank, 70 Mo. 524. § 93.
Shinn *v.* Budd, 1 McC. (N. J.) 234. § 298.
Shipherd, Backus *v.*, 11 Wend. 629. § 101.
Shippen's Adm'r *v.* Clapp, 36 Pa. St. 89. § 440.
Shirley, People *v.*, 18 Cal. 121. § 512.
v. Shirley, 7 Blackf. (Ind.) 452. § 89.
Shirreff *v.* Wilks, 1 East, 53. § 18.
Shitler, Lambert *v.*, 62 Iowa, 72. § 351.
Shock *v.* Miller, 10 Pa. St. 401. § 439.
Shoffner *v.* Fogleman, Winston, Law & Eq. (N. C.) 12. § 316.
Shook *v.* People, 39 Ill. 443. § 499.
v. Vanmater, 22 Wis. 507. §§ 60, 64.
Shores, Forest *v.*, 11 La. (Curry), 416. § 205.
Shorter, Jones *v.*, 1 Kelley (Ga.), 294. § 60.
Shortrede *v.* Cheek, 1 Adol. & Ell. 57. §§ 84, 86.
Shoup, United States *v.*, 21 Pac. Rep. 656. § 23.
Shouse, Taylor *v.*, 73 Mo. 361. § 189.
Showles, Coldham *v.*, 3 Man., Gr. & Scott, 312. § 87.
v. Freeman, 81 Mo. 540. § 112.
Shrempp, Heath *v.*, 22 La. Ann. 167. § 570.
Shriver *v.* Lovejoy, 32 Cal. 574. § 29.
Shropshire *v.* Kennedy, 84 Ind. 111. §§ 414, 416.
Shrout, Hutchcraft *v.*, 1 T. B. Mon. (Ky.) 206. §§ 540, 574.
Shryer, Bobbitt *v.*, 70 Ind. 513. §§ 258, 261, 265, 405.
Shryock, Weaver *v.*, 6 Serg. & Rawle (Pa.), 262. § 139.
Shubrick's Ex'rs *v.* Russell, 1 Des. (S. C.) 315. § 366.
Shultz *v.* Carter, Speer's Eq. (S. C.) 533. § 313.
Shumway, Brookins *v.*, 18 Wis. 98. § 359.
Shunk, Young *v.*, 30 Minn. 503. § 255.
Shupe *v.* Galbraith, 32 Pa. St. 10. § 16.
Shurts *v.* Howell, 30 N. J. Eq. 418. § 576.
Shuttleworth *v.* Levi, 13 Bush (Ky.), 195. §§ 22, 508.
Watts *v.*, 7 Hurl. & Nor. 353. §§ 405, 429, 443.
Shwarz, Grigsby *v.*, 82 Cal. 278. § 14.
Sibberns, Mayor of N. Y. *v.*, 3 Abb. Rep. Om. Cas. 266. § 548.
Sibley *v.* McAllister, 8 N. H. 389. § 448.
Sickler, Clark *v.*, 64 N. Y. 231. § 339.
Sickles, City of St. Louis *v.*, 52 Mo. 122. § 565.
Sidener, Reed *v.*, 32 Ind. 373. § 414.
Sidner *v.* Alexander, 31 Ohio St. 378. § 571.
Sidney, Maples *v.*, Cro. Jac. 683. § 16.
Sidney Road Co. *v.* Holmes, 16 Up. Can. (Q. B.) 268. § 411.
Sievewright *v.* Archibalds, 17 Ad. & Ell. (N. S.) 103. § 80.
Signiago, Picot *v.*, 22 Mo. 587. § 41.
Sigourney, Caldwell *v.*, 19 Conn. 37. § 143.
Clark *v.*, 17 Conn. 511. § 143.
v. Wetherell, 6 Met. (Mass.) 553. §§ 142, 367.
Sikes *v.* Quick, 7 Jones' Law (N. C.), 19. § 210.
Silence, Brewster *v.*, 8 N. Y. 207. §§ 84, 88.
Silk *v.* Eyre, Irish Rep. 9 Eq. 393. § 322.
Sill *v.* Leslie, 16 Ind. 236. §§ 178, 182.
Silliman, Exchange Bank *v.*, 65 N. Y. 475. §§ 315, 323.
Silly, Dartmouth *v.*, 7 Ell. & Black. 97. § 552.
Silmeyer *v.* Schaffer, 60 Ill. 479. § 356.
Silvey *v.* Dowell, 53 Ill. 260. § 269.

Simeon *v.* Cramm, 121 Mass. 492. § 470.
Simington, McLain *v.*, 37 Ohio St. 484. § 27.
Simmons *v.* Barefoots' Ex'rs, 2 Haywood (N. C.), 606. § 12.
Camp *v.*, 62 Ga. 73. §§ 176, 261.
v. Cates, 56 Ga. 609. § 330.
Church *v.*, 83 N. Y. 261. § 452.
Farebrother *v.*, 5 Barn. & Ald. 333. § 90.
v. Goodrich, 67 Ga. 750. § 341.
v. Gense, 46 Ga. 473. § 363.
v. Keating, 2 Starkie, 375. § 15.
O'Donohue *v.*, 31 Hun (N. Y.), 267. § 599.
Watertown Fire Ins. Co. *v.*, 131 Mass. 85. §§ 423, 424, 425.
Simms, Richards *v.*, 1 Dev. & Bat. Law (N. C.), 48. § 260.
Simpson, Bank *v.*, 90 N. C. 467. § 150.
v. Blunt, 42 Mo. 542. § 609.
Catton *v.*, 8 Adol. & Ell. 136. § 229.
Christie *v.*, 1 Rich. Law (S. C.), 401. § 90.
Colquitt *v.*, 72 Ga. 501. § 412.
Harris *v.*, 4 Litt. (Ky.) 165. § 504.
v. Mauley, 2 Cro. & Jer. 12. §§ 161, 418.
v. McPhail, 17 Bradw. (Ill. App.) 499. § 307.
v. Nance, 1 Spear (S. C.), 4. §§ 61, 63.
v. Penton, 2 Cromp. & Mees. 430. § 77.
Rey *v.*, 22 How. 341. §§ 181, 182.
Rice *v.*, 9 Heisk. (Tenn.) 809. § 605.
v. Roberts, 35 Ga. 180. § 513.
v. Simpson, 80 N. C. 332. § 577.
Tomlinson *v.*, 33 Minn. 443. § 93.
United States *v.*, 3 Pen. & Watts (Pa.), 437. § 342.
Waters *v.*, 2 Gilm. (Ill.) 570. § 371.
Simpson's Ex'rs *v.* Bovard, 74 Pa. St. 351. §§ 381, 411.
Simon, Randolph *v.*, 29 Kan. 400. § 515.
Simon *v.* Aldine Publishing Co., 14 Daly (N. Y. Com. Pl.), 279. § 461.
v. Motivos, 1 W. Black. 599. § 90.
v. Steele, 36 N. H. 73. §§ 80, 87, 124, 200.
Simond, Ludlow *v.*, 2 Caines' Cases in Error, 1. §§ 93, 397.
Simons *v.* County of Jackson, 63 Tex. 428. § 597.
Simonsen, Clay County *v.*, 1 Dak. 403. § 591.
v. Grant, 36 Minn. 439. § 397.
Sims, Creath's Adm'r *v.*, 5 How. 192. § 342.
Gaff *v.*, 45 Ind. 262. §§ 1, 197.
Gordon *v.*, 2 McCord, Ch. (S. C.) 151. § 90.
Sayles *v.*, 73 N. Y. 551. §§ 31, 259.
Simson *v.* Cooke, 8 Moore, 588. § 118.
Sinclair, Bank of Newbury *v.*, 60 N. H. 100. § 200.
v. Richardson, 12 Vt. 33. § 77.
Singer, Mundorff *v.*, 5 Watts (Pa.), 172. § 447.
v. Troutman, 49 Barb. (N. Y.) 182. 240.
Singer Mfg. Co. *v.* Bennett, 28 W. Va. 16. §§ 45, 259.
v. Drummond, 40 Hun (N. Y.), 260. § 408.
v. Forsyth, 108 Ind. 334. § 86.
v. Hester, 71 Mo. 91. § 199.
v. Hester (Cir. Ct. W. D. Mo. W. D.), 6 Fed. Rep. 804. § 602.
v. Hibbs, 21 Mo. App. 574. § 394.
v. Littler, 56 Iowa, 601. §§ 106, 202.
Singer Sewing Machine Co., Phillips *v.*, 88 Ill. 305. § 602.
Singleton, Mix *v.*, 86 Ill. 194. § 93.
v. Townsend, 45 Mo. 379. § 295.
Singley *v.* Cutter, 7 Conn. 291. § 86.
Singstack *v.* Harding, 4 Harr. & Johns. 186. § 90.
Sisson *v.* Barrett, 2 N. Y. 406. § 31.
Turner *v.*, 137 Mass. 191. § 566.

Sizer, Pringle *v.*, 2 Rich. N. S. (S. C.) 59. § 247.
v. Ray, 87 N. Y. 220. § 36.
Skaggs, Hecht *v.*. 53 Ark. 291. § 586.
Skeen, City of Indianapolis *v.*, 17 Ind. 628. § 124.
Skelton, Reynolds *v.*, 2 Tex. 516. § 211.
Skidmore, People *v.*, 17 Cal. 260. § 322.
v. Taylor, 29 Cal. 619. § 271.
Skiff *v.* Cross, 21 Iowa, 459. § 317.
Skillen, Brobst *v.*, 16 Ohio St. 382. § 537.
Skillern, Jenkins *v.*, 5 Yerg. (Tenn.) 288. § 464.
Skillett *v.* Fletcher, Law Rep. 1 Com. Pl. 217. § 398.
Skillin *v.* Merrill, 16 Mass. 40. § 278.
Skinner, Cleveland *v.*, 56 Ill. 500. § 516.
v. Conant, 2 Vt. 453. § 77.
Whittle *v.*, 23 Vt. 531. § 353.
Skip *v.* Edwards, 9 Mod. 438. § 398.
Skipwith, Williams *v.*, 34 Ark. 529. § 22.
Skofield *v.* Haley, 22 Me. 164. § 202.
Skrainka *v.* Rohan, 18 Mo. App. 340. § 267.
Slade, Seton *v.*, 7 Vesey, 265. § 89.
Slagee, Jefferson County *v.*, 66 Pa. St. 202. § 77.
Slagle *v.* Pow, 41 Ohio St. 603. § 366.
Slater, Emerson *v.*, 22 How. 28. §§ 60, 70.
Caballero *v.*, 14 Com. B. (5 J. Scott), 300. § 84.
Slattery *v.* Police Jury, 2 La. Ann. 444. § 444.
Slauker, Adm'r, Beaver *v.*, 94 Ill. 175. §§ 298, 315.
Slawson *v.* Ker, 29 La. Ann. 295. §§ 520, 570.
Sledge, Jennings *v.*, 3 Kelly (Ga.), 128. § 507.
Slee, Dunn *v.*, 1 Moore, 2. § 380.
Sleeper, Lane *v.*, 18 N. H. 209. § 218.
Slevin *v.* Morrow, 4 Ind. (2 Port.) 425. § 440.
State *v.*, 93 Mo. 253. § 574.
Slife, Huff *v.*, 25 Neb. 448. §§ 102, 242.
Slingerland *v.* Morse, 7 Johns. 463. § 64.
Sloan, Anderson *v.*, 1 Col. 484. § 464.
v. Creasor, 22 Up. Can. (Q. B.) 127. § 391.
Justices *v.*, 7 Ga. 31. § 578.
Salt Springs Nat. Bank *v.*, 57 Hun (N. Y.), 265. § 100.
v. Wilson, 4 Harr. & Johns. 322. § 82.
Sloane, State *v.*, 20 Ohio, 327. § 531.
Slocomb *v.* Roberts, 16 La. (Curry), 173. § 501.
Slocum, People *v.*, 1 Idaho, 62. § 175.
Sloo, Bank of Illinois *v.*, 16 La. (Curry), 539. §§ 186, 189.
Sloper, People *v.*, 1 Idaho, 158. § 505.
Sloteman, Mack *v.* (Cir. Ct. E. D. Wis.), 21 Fed. Rep. 109. § 601.
Sluby *v.* Champlain, 4 Johns. 461. § 228.
Small, Clark *v.*, 6 Yerg. (Tenn.) 418. §§ 13, 82.
v. Commonwealth, 8 Pa. St. 101. § 586.
v. Currie, 2 Drewry, 102. §§ 12, 419.
v. Currie, 5 De G., M. & G. 141. § 397.
Globe Bank *v.*, 25 Me. 366. § 197.
v. Older, 57 Iowa, 326. § 38.
Smalling *v.* King, 5 Lea (Tenn.), 585. § 532.
Smarr *v.* McMaster, 35 Mo. 349. § 370.
v. Schmitter, 38 Mo. 478. § 364.
Smart, Low *v.*, 5 N. H. 353. § 268.
Smee *v.* Hargreave, 6 Bing. 244. §§ 92, 158.
Smeidel *v.* Lewellyn, 3 Phila. 70. § 102.
Smiley, Buck *v.*, 64 Ind. 431. § 377.
Smith *v.* Allen, Saxton (N. J.), 43. § 141.
Andrews *v.*, Tyrwh. & Gr. 173. § 63.
v. Anthony, 5 Mo. 504. § 191.

Smith *v.* Arnold, 5 Mason (C. C.), 414. § 90.
v. Bainbridge, 6 Blackf. (Ind.) 12. § 198.
Bank of Brighton *v.*, 5 Allen, 413. § 24.
Bank of Brighton *v.*, 12 Allen, 243. §§ 559, 627.
Bank of St. Albans *v.*, 30 Vt. 148. §§ 29, 107.
v. Bank of Scotland, 1 Dow. 272. § 422.
v. Barker, 6 Watts (Pa.), 508. § 500.
Barnett *v.*, 17 Ill. 565. § 119.
Belcher *v.*, 7 Cush. 482. § 183.
v. Bing, 3 Ohio, 33. § 278.
Bizzell *v.*, 2 Dev. Eq. (N. C.) 27. § 242.
v. Bland, 7 B. Mon. (Ky.) 21. § 583.
Bleakley *v.*, 11 Simons, 150. § 89.
Brien *v.*, 9 Watts & Serg. (Pa.) 78. § 315.
Buckalew *v.*, 44 Ala. 638. § 239.
Buffington *v.*, 58 Ga. 341. § 514.
v. Carder, 33 Ark. 709. § 410.
v. Chicago & N. W. R. R. Co., 18 Wis. 17. § 126.
v. Clopton, 48 Miss. 66. §§ 30, 243, 364, 609.
v. Collins, 42 Kan. 259. § 50[illegible].
Colquitt *v.*, 65 Ga. 341. § 502.
Colquitt *v.*, 76 Ga. 709. § 598.
v. Commonwealth, 25 Gratt. (Va.) 780. § 371.
v. Commonwealth, 59 Pa. St. 320. § 569.
v. Compton, 6 Cal. 24. § 415.
v. Conrad, 15 La. Ann. 579. § 268.
Cowper *v.*, 4 Mees. & Wels. 519. § 150.
v. Crease's Ex'r, 2 Cranch, C. C. 481. §§ 243, 364.
v. Crooker, 5 Mass. 538. § 386.
Culbertson *v.*, 52 Md. 628. § 82.
v. Dann, 6 Hill (N. Y.), 543. § 123.
Davis *v.*, 5 Ga. 274. § 313.
Dennie *v.*, 129 Mass. 143. § 636.
Smith *v.* Dickinson, 6 Humph. (Tenn.) 261. § 49.
Dillon *v.*, 10 Heisk. 595. § 103.
v. Doak, 3 Tex. 215. §§ 30, 402.
v. Dunn, 6 Hill, 543. § 196.
Dunn *v.*, 12 Sm. & Mar. (Miss.) 602. § 402.
v. Evans, 1 Wils. 313. § 89.
v. Falconer, 11 Hun (N. Y.), 481. § 464.
Felton *v.*, 84 Ind. 485. § 316.
v. Finch, 2 Scam. (Ill.) 321. §§ 17, 67, 182.
First National Bank *v.*, 25 Iowa, 210. § 614.
v. Gillam, 80 Ala. 296. §§ 150, 324, 326.
v. Gorton, 10 La. (Curry), 374. § 178.
v. Governor, 2 Rob. (Va.) 229. § 625.
Grant *v.*, 46 N. Y. 93. § 118.
Grieve *v.*, 23 Up. Can. (Q. B.) 23. § 397.
Hall *v.*, 5 How. 96. § 210.
Hall *v.*, 14 Bush (Ky.), 604. §§ 408, 411, 412.
v. Harrison, 33 Ala. 706. § 298.
v. Hawkins, 6 Conn. 444. § 345.
v. Henesman, 30 Ohio St. 662. § 449.
v. Hodson, 50 Wis. 279. § 276.
Hoffman *v.*, 34 Hun (N. Y.), 485. § 486.
Hunt *v.*, 17 Wend. 179. § 343.
v. Hurltin, 124 Ind. 434. § 329.
v. Hyde, 19 Vt. 54. §§ 77, 138.
v. Hyde, 36 Vt. 303. § 356.
v. Ide, 3 Vt. 290. §§ 82, 86.
v. James, 1 Miles (Pa.), 162. § 221.
v. Jones, 5 Leigh (Va.), 165. § 90.
Johnston *v.*, 25 Hun (N. Y.), 171. §§ 43, 580.
Joslyn *v.*, 13 Vt. 353. §§ 143, 342.
v. Josselyn, 40 Ohio St. 409. § 424.

Smith, King *v.*, 2 Leigh (Va.), 157. § 402.
v. Kinney, 6 Neb. 447. § 220.
v. Kirkland, 81 Ala. 345. § 402.
v. Kitchens, 51 Ga. 158. § 501.
Lamp *v.*, 56 Ga. 589. § 506.
Leeming *v.*, 25 Grant's Ch. (Can.) 256. § 37.
v. Lovell, 2 Mont. 332. § 562.
Lowry *v.*, 97 Ind. 466. § 594.
v. Martin, 4 Des. Eq. (S. C.) 148. § 139.
McClure *v.*, 56 Ga. 439. § 512.
McCue *v.*, 9 Minn. 252. § 52.
v. McLain, 11 W. Va. 654. § 243.
v. McLeod, 3 Ired. Eq. (N. C.) 390. § 301.
v. Moberly, 10 B. Mon. (Ky.) 266. §§ 114, 407.
v. Montgomery, 3 Tex. 199. § 117.
Morgan *v.*, 7 Hun (N. Y.), 244. § 419.
v. Morrill, 54 Me. 48. § 261.
Nisbet *v.*, 2 Brown's Ch. Ca. 579. §§ 238, 373.
O'Donnell *v.*, 2 E. D. Smith (N. Y.), 124. § 67.
Osborne *v.* (Cir. Ct. D. Minn.), 18 Fed. Rep. 126. §§ 101, 106, 329.
v. Osborne, 31 Hun (N. Y.), 390. § 140.
Ovington *v.*, 78 Ill. 250. § 479.
v. Peoria Co., 59 Ill. 412. § 548.
Powell *v.*, 8 Johns. 249. §§ 213, 221.
v. Prince, 14 Conn. 472. § 218.
Ratcliffe *v.*, 13 Bush (Ky.), 172. § 513.
v. Rice, 27 Mo. 505. §§ 40, 127, 373.
v. Rines, 32 Me. 177. § 228.
v. Rogers, 14 Ind. 224. § 97.
v. Ruby, 6 Heisk. (Tenn.) 546. § 484.
v. Rudhall, 3 Foster & Fin. 143. § 77.
v. Rumsey, 33 Mich. 183. §§ 291, 309.
Smith *v.* Sayward, 5 Greenl. (Me.) 504. §§ 60, 64.
Screwmen's Benevolent Ass'n *v.*, 70 Tex. 168. §§ 421, 590, 624.
Sedalia, W. & S. R'y Co. *v.*, 27 Mo. App. 371. § 93.
Sharpe *v.*, 59 Ga. 707. § 510.
v. Shelden, 35 Mich. 42. §§ 1, 32, 36.
Shields *v.*, 8 Bush (Ky.), 601. § 584.
Shields *v.*, 78 Ind. 425. §§ 495, 515.
v. Smith, 1 Dev. Eq. (N. C.) 173. § 260.
v. Smith, 5 Ired. Eq. (N. C.) 34. § 224.
v. Smithson, 48 Ark. 261. §§ 448, 574.
v. Staples, 53 Ga. 300. § 528.
v. Starr, 4 Hun (N. Y.), 123. §§ 48, 50.
State *v.*, 16 Fla. 175. §§ 551, 555.
v. State, 12 Neb. 309. §§ 501, 516.
v. State, 46 Md. 617. § 287.
v. Steele, 25 Vt. 427. § 349.
v. Strout, 63 Me. 205. § 248.
v. Swain, 7 Rich. Eq. (S. C.) 112. § 313.
Terrell *v.*, 8 Conn. 426. § 433.
v. Townsend, 25 N. Y. 479. § 35.
Township Union *v.*, 39 Iowa, 9. §§ 558, 559.
Treat *v.*, 54 Me. 112. § 345.
Troy *v.*, 33 Ala. 469. § 324.
Trustees of Schools *v.*, 88 Ill. 181. § 546.
v. United States, 2 Wall. (U. S.) 219. § 385.
v. Van Wyck, 40 Mo. App. 522. § 165.
Williams *v.*, 48 Me. 135. § 352.
v. Winter, 4 M. & W. 454. § 347.
White *v.*, 33 Pa. St. 186. § 391.
White *v.*, 2 Jones' Law (N. C.), 4. § 545.
Yeary *v.*, 45 Tex. 56. § 342.
Smith's Ex'rs *v.* Anderson, 18 Md. 520. § 262.

Smith's Ex'rs, Ashby's Adm'x *v.*, 9 Leigh (Va.), 164. § 437.
Cope *v.*, 8 Serg. & Rawle (Pa.), 110. §§ 239, 342.
Smith Am. Organ Co., Morgan *v.*, 73 Ind. 179. § 599.
Smitha, Spurgeon *v.*, 114 Ind. 453. § 339.
Smithson, Smith *v.*, 48 Ark. 261. §§ 448, 574.
Smokey *v.* Peters-Calhoun Co., 66 Miss. 471. § 570.
Smyley *v.* Head, 2 Rich. Law (S. C.), 590. § 153.
Smyth *v.* Barbee, 9 Lea (Tenn.), 173. § 487.
Smythe, Drake *v.*, 44 Iowa, 410. § 372.
Snead, Davis, Adm'r, *v.*, 33 Gratt. (Va.) 705. § 592.
Sneed, Brown *v.*, 77 Tex. 471. §§ 548, 555.
Henry *v.*, 99 Mo. 407. §§ 46, 234.
Sneed's Ex'rs *v.* White, 3 J. J. Marsh. (Ky.) 525. § 62.
Snell *v.* Allen, 1 Swan (Tenn.) 208. § 627.
v. State, 43 Ind. 359. § 565.
v. Warner, 63 Ill. 176. § 210.
Wilson Sewing Machine Co. *v.*, 20 Minn. 40. § 80.
Snevily *v.* Ekel, 1 W. & S. 203. § 183.
v. Johnston, 1 Watts & Serg. 307. § 15.
Snider *v.* Greathouse, 16 Ark. 72. §§ 209, 633.
Snodgrass, Blair *v.*, 1 Sneed (Tenn.), 1. § 80.
Snow, Draper *v.*, 20 N. Y. 331. § 87.
First Congregational Society *v.*, 1 Cush. 510. § 324.
Snyder, Boyd *v.*, 49 Md. 325. §§ 81, 193, 194.
v. Click, 112 Ind. 293. §§ 3, 45, 193, 203.
v. Klose, 19 Pa. St. 235. § 405.
Robinson *v.*, 97 Ind. 56. § 648.
Vredenburgh *v.*, 6 Iowa (Clarke), 39. § 448.
Sohier *v.* Loring, 6 Cush. 537. § 376.
Sohre, Wendlandt *v.*, 37 Minn. 162. § 1.
Solary *v.* Stultz, 22 Fla. 263. §§ 194, 355.
Solinsky, Sampson *v.*, 75 Tex. 663. § 461.
Sollee *v.* Menzy, 1 Bailey, 620. §§ 117, 143, 163, 186.
Solomon, Lochrane *v.*, 38 Ga. 286. § 441.
Phillipps *v.*, 42 Ga. 192. § 150.
Somers *v.* Johnson, 57 Vt. 274. § 268.
Somersworth Savings Bank *v.* Worcester, 76 Me. 327. §§ 246, 437.
Somerville *v.* Marbury, 7 Gill & Johns. (Md.) 275. § 437.
McBroom *v.*, 2 Stew. (Ala.) 515. § 480.
Sommers, Commonwealth *v.*, 3 Bush (Ky.), 555. § 565.
Sooy *ads.* State, 38 N. J. Law, 324. §§ 22, 414.
State *v.*, 39 N. J. Law (10 Vroom), 539. §§ 338, 419, 422, 546.
v. State, 41 N. J. Law, 394. § 628.
Soper, Dennison *v.*, 33 Iowa, 183. § 205.
Taylor *v.*, 53 Mich. 96. § 102.
Sornberger, Thomas *v.*, 24 Wend. 275. § 504.
Sotheren *v.* Reed, 4 Harr. & Johns. (Md.) 307. § 310.
Soule *v.* Albee, 31 Vt. 142. § 72.
Hall *v.*, 11 Mich. 494. § 81.
Michigan State Ins. Co. *v.*, 51 Mich. 312. §§ 245, 246.
v. Norwood, Adm'r, 30 La. Ann. 486. § 588.
Norton *v.*, 2 Greenl. (Me.) 341. § 315.
Robinson *v.*, 56 Miss. 549. § 150.
v. United States, 100 U. S. 8. §§ 12, 595.
Soullard, Hulett *v.*, 26 Vt. 295. §§ 208, 217.
Southard, Trustees *v.*, 31 Ill. App. 359. §§ 29, 242.

South Carolina Mfg. Co. v. Bank, 6 Rich. Eq. (S. C.) 227. § 251.
South Carolina Society v. Johnson, 1 McCord, Law (S. C.), 41. § 167.
Southern Express Co., Frink v., 82 Ga. 33. § 112.
Southgate, Rice v., 16 Gray, 142. § 207.
Southwick, Cook v., 9 Tex. 615. §§ 176, 182.
Southworth, Lothrop v., 5 Mich. 436. § 640.
Spain, Miller v., 41 Ohio St. 773. § 346.
Spalding v. Bank, 9 Pa. St. 28. § 248.
Sparks, Dunn v., 1 Ind. 397. § 276.
Dunn v., 7 Ind. 490. § 260.
v. Farmers' Bank, 3 Del. Ch. 274. §§ 167, 555.
v. Hall, 4 J. J. Marsh. (Ky.) 35. § 342.
Todd v., 10 La. Ann. 668. § 585.
Spaulding v. Andrews, 48 Pa. St. 411. § 67.
v. Austin, 2 Vt. 555. § 215.
Spear, State v., 54 Vt. 503. § 516.
v. Ward, 20 Cal. 659. § 35.
Spears, Douglas v., 2 Nott & McC. (S. C.) 207. § 89.
Speckenugle, Sharpe v., 3 Serg. & Rawle (Pa.), 463. § 150.
Speed, Miller v., 9 Heisk. (Tenn.) 196. § 223.
Speidel, Leonard v., 104 Mass. 356. § 470.
Speis, Barton v., 5 Hun, 60. § 137.
Spence, Anderson v., 72 Ind. 315. § 57.
Spencer v. Almoney, 56 Md. 551, 562. § 236.
Bradwell v., 16 Ga. 578. § 639.
v. Carter, 4 Jones' Law (N. C.), 287. § 204.
v. Handley, 5 Scott (N. R.), 546. § 406.
v. Houghton, 68 Cal. 82. § 540.
Hurd v., 40 Vt. 581. § 426.
Okie v., 1 Miles (Pa.), 299. § 364.
v. Spencer, 95 N. Y. 353. § 37.
v. Thompson, 6 Irish Com. Law, 537. § 434.
Spencer, United States v., 2 McLean, 405. § 526.
Spencer, McKay & Co., Dixon v., 59 Md. 246. §§ 363, 364.
Sperb, McCoun v., 53 Hun (N. Y.), 165. §§ 226, 582.
Spicer, McMurray v., Law Rep. 5 Eq. 527. § 81.
v. Norton, 13 Barb. (N. Y.) 542. § 85.
Spier, Mizner v., 96 Pa. St. 533. § 100.
Spiers v. Houston, 4 Bligh (N. R.), 515. § 118.
Spies v. Gilmore, 1 N. Y. 321. § 179.
Spikes, Parry v., 49 Wis. 384. § 82.
Spillman v. People, 16 Bradw. (Ill. App.) 224. § 503.
Spinhorst, Kupfer v., 1 Kan. 75. § 618.
Spinney, Fourth Nat. Bank v., 120 N. Y. 560. § 561.
Splivalo, Lacoste v., 64 Cal. 35. § 541.
Sponsler, Wetzel v., 18 Pa. St. 460. §§ 239, 240.
Spooner, Boardman v., 13 Allen, 353. §§ 80, 90.
v. Dunn, 7 Ind. 81. § 64.
Sportsman, Kirk v., 48 Mo. 383. § 588.
Spotts, Guyer v., 85 Pa. St. 51. § 452.
Spottswood v. Dandridge, 4 Munf. (Va.) 289. § 579.
Sprague, Dugan v., 2 Ind. 600. § 366.
Town of Weston v., 54 Vt. 395. § 521.
Sprathin v. Hudspeth, Dudley (Ga.), 155. § 110.
Spratt, Clopton v., 52 Miss. 251. § 444.
Hughart v., 78 Ky. 313. § 577.
Sprigg, Cross v., 2 Macn. & Gor. 113. § 369.
v. Bank of Mount Pleasant, 10 Pet. (U. S.) 257. § 41.
Spring v. George, 50 Hun (N. Y.), 227. § 437.
Spring Hill Mining Co. v. Sharp, 3 Pugsley (N. B.), 603. § 557.
Springer, Bank v., 7 Ont. (Can.) 309. § 555.

Springer, Exchange Bank *v.*, 29 Grant's Ch. (Can.) 270. § 137.
v. Hutchinson, 19 Me. 359. § 49.
v. Toothaker, 43 Me. 381. §§ 243, 434.
Springer's Adm'r *v.* Springer, 43 Pa. St. 518. § 303.
Springfield, Nall *v.*, 9 Bush (Ky.), 673. § 361.
Springfield Manufacturing Co. *v.* West, 1 Cush. 388. § 504.
Sproson, Westhead *v.*, 6 Hurl. & Nor. 728. § 17.
Spurgeon *v.* Smitha, 114 Ind. 453. § 339.
Spurlock, Hopkins *v.*, 2 Heisk. (Tenn.) 152. § 239.
St. Albans Bank *v.* Dillon, 30 Vt. 122. § 153.
St. Clair, Probate Court *v.*, 52 Vt. 24. § 408.
St. John, Boyle *v.*, 28 Hun (N. Y.), 454. § 573.
Dodge *v.*, 96 N. Y. 260. § 576.
St. Johnsbury & L. C. R. Co., Eastern Township Bank *v.* (Cir. Ct. D. Vt.), 40 Fed. Rep. 423. §§ 6, 50.
St. Joseph F. & M. Ins. Co. *v.* Hauck, 71 Mo. 465. § 352.
St. Louis Building & Savings Ass'n *v.* Clark, 36 Mo. 601. § 323.
St. Louis, I. M. & S. R'y Co., Humphreys *v.* (Cir. Ct. S. D. N. Y.), 37 Fed. Rep. 307. § 104.
St. Maries *v.* Polleys, 47 Wis. 67. §§ 357, 375.
St. Paul, Brodie *v.*, 1 Vesey, Jr. 326. § 80.
Staats *v.* Howlett, 4 Denio, 559. § 84.
Stackhouse, Paul *v.*, 38 Pa. St. 302. § 15.
Stacy, People *v.*, 74 Cal. 373. § 603.
Stadt *v.* Hill, 9 East, 348. § 84.
Stafford *v.* Low, 16 Johns. 67. § 191.
v. Low, 20 Ill. 152. § 504.
v. State, 10 Tex. App. 46. § 500.
Stage *v.* Olds, 12 Ohio, 158. § 137.
Stagg *v.* Linnenfelser, 59 Mo. 336. § 176.
Stahl, Ward *v.*, 81 N. Y. 406. § 524.
Stainbank, Davies *v.*, 6 De Gex, Macn. & Gor. 679. §§ 244, 359, 369.
Staley *v.* Howard, 7 Mo. App. 377. § 460.
Stallings *v.* Johnson, 27 Ga. 564. § 354.
Stallworth, Preslar *v.*, 37 Ala. 402. §§ 287, 293, 295, 312, 635.
Riley *v.*, 56 Ala. 481. §§ 206, 208.
Stamford Bank *v.* Benedict, 15 Conn. 437. §§ 305, 330.
Stamford Banking Co. *v.* Ball, 4 De Gex, F. & J. 310. § 35.
Stamps, Bush *v.*, 26 Miss. 463. § 326.
Sheid *v.*, 2 Sneed (Tenn.), 172. § 81.
Standclift, Richmond *v.*, 14 Vt. 258. § 417.
Standley *v.* Miles, 36 Miss. 434. § 15.
Stanley, Belfast Banking Co. *v.*, Irish, 1 Com. Law, 693. § 342.
Inhabitants of Farmington *v.*, 60 Me. 472. §§ 555, 557.
Lemayne *v.*, 3 Levinz, 1. § 89.
Lobb *v.*, 5 Q. B. 574. § 89.
Mecorney *v.*, 8 Cush. (Mass.) 85. § 16.
Porter *v.*, 47 Me. 515. § 543.
v. Stanley, 112 Ind. 143. § 203.
Stanly *v.* Hendricks, 13 Ired. (N. C.) 86. § 63.
Stanton *v.* Commonwealth, 2 Dana (Ky.), 397. § 568.
Deakin *v.*, 3 Fed. Rep. 435. § 476.
Ide *v.*, 15 Vt. 685. § 80.
Pollard *v.*, 5 Ala. 451. § 643.
Stantons, Eddy *v.*, 21 Wend. 255. § 100.
Stansbury, United States *v.*, 1 Pet. 573. § 433.
Stansfield *v.* Johnson, 1 Esp. 101. § 90.
Stapler, Smith *v.*, 53 Ga. 300. § 528.

Staples, Consolidated Presbyterian Society *v.*, 23 Conn. 544. § 63.
v. Gokey, 34 Hun (N. Y.), 289. § 277.
Lord *v.*, 23 N. H. 448. § 211.
Stapleton's Adm'r, Hurley *v.*, 24 Mo. 248. § 215.
Star Wagon Co. *v.* Swezy, 59 Iowa, 609. § 204.
Stark *v.* Fuller, 42 Pa. St. 320. § 250.
Goodwin *v.*, 15 N. H. 218. § 516.
Starling *v.* Buttles, 2 Ohio, 303. § 607.
Starnes, Greene *v.*, 1 Heisk. (Tenn.) 582. § 223.
Starr, Bates *v.*, 6 Ala. 697. § 77.
v. Blatner, 76 Iowa, 356. § 383.
Smith *v.*, 4 Hun (N. Y.), 123. §§ 48, 50.
Starret *v.* Burkhalter, 86 Ind. 439. § 352.
Starrett *v.* Barber, 20 Me. 457. § 114.
Starrs, Cosgrove Brewing & Malting Co. *v.*, 5 Ont. (Can.) 189. §§ 118, 161.
Starry *v.* Johnson, 32 Ind. 438. § 439.
State, Adler *v.*, 35 Ark. 517. § 500.
Albertson *v.*, 9 Neb. 429. § 628.
Alcorn *v.*, 57 Miss. 273. § 531.
v. Alden, 12 Ohio, 59. § 339.
Allan *v.*, 61 Ind. 268. § 542.
Allason *v.*, 8 Heisk. (Tenn.) 312. § 173.
v. Allen, 2 Humph. (Tenn.) 258. § 500.
v. Alsup, 91 Mo. 172. § 545.
Armington *v.*, 45 Ind. 10. § 530.
Armstrong *v.*, 7 Blackf. (Ind.) 81. § 541.
v. Anderson, 16 Lea (Tenn.), 321. § 642.
v. Anthony, 30 Mo. App. 608. § 528.
Appleby *v.*, 45 N. J. Law, 161. § 531.
v. Atherton, 40 Mo. 209. §§ 422, 425.
v. Atkins, 53 Ark. 303. § 577.
v. Austin, 35 Minn. 51. § 151.
State, Bagot *v.*, 33 Ind. 262. § 628.
v. Baker, 64 Mo. 167. § 412.
Bales *v.*, 15 Ind. 321. § 545.
v. Barefoot, 104 N. C. 224. § 566.
v. Barrett, 121 Ind. 92. § 581.
v. Bartlett, 30 Miss. 624. § 520.
v. Bates, 36 Vt. 387. §§ 521, 557.
Bates *v.*, 75 Ind. 463. § 520.
v. Beard, 11 Rob. (La.) 243. § 370.
Beasley *v.*, 53 Ark. 67. § 502.
Belding *v.*, 25 Ark. 315. § 500.
Bennett *v.*, 58 Miss. 556. § 521.
v. Benton, 48 N. H. 551. § 516.
v. Benzion, 79 Iowa, 467. § 509.
Bergstrom *v.*, 58 Tex. 92. § 139.
v. Berning, 6 Mo. App. 105. § 540.
v. Berry, 34 Ga. 546. § 498.
v. Birchim, 9 Nev. 95. § 512.
v. Bird, 2 Rich. Law (S. C.), 99. § 538.
v. Blackmore, 7 Heisk. (Tenn.) 638. § 112.
v. Blair, 32 Ind. 313. § 385.
v. Blake, 2 Ohio St. 147. § 148.
Blalack *v.*, 3 Tex. App. 376. § 497.
v. Bobb & Alexander, 39 Mo. App. 543. § 503.
Bocard *v.*, 79 Ind. 270. § 624.
Boggs *v.*, 46 Tex. 10. §§ 558, 611.
v. Bond, 121 Ind. 187. § 529.
v. Boon, 44 Mo. 254. § 118.
v. Bowman, 10 Ohio, 445. § 151.
v. Bright, 14 S. C. 7. §§ 508, 510.
v. Britton, 102 Ind. 214. § 113.
Britton *v.*, 115 Ind. 55. § 113.
Brown *v.*, 6 Tex. App. 188. § 510.
v. Brown, 11 Ired. Law (N. C.), 141. § 566.
v. Brown, 16 Iowa, 314. §§ 502, 505.
Brown *v.*, 18 Tex. App. 326. §§ 408, 493.
Brown *v.*, 23 Kan. 235. §§ 540, 546.
v. Brown, 80 Ind. 425. § 585.
v. Bugg, 6 Rob. 63. § 145.

State v. Burnham, 44 Me. 278. § 500.
Butler v., 20 Ind. 169. § 551.
Carey v., 34 Ind. 105. § 531.
Carker v., 43 Ark. 132. § 495.
v. Carleton, 1 Gill (Md.), 249. § 371.
Carmody v., 105 Ind. 546. § 504.
v. Cason, 11 S. C. 392. §§ 569, 636.
v. Cayce, 85 Mo. 456. § 571.
v. Chadwick, 10 Oreg. 465. § 560.
v. Chandler, 79 Me. 172. § 509.
Chaudler v., 1 Lea (Tenn.), 296. §§ 523, 524.
v. Chandler, 79 Me. 172. § 493.
Childers v., 25 Tex. App. 658. § 575.
v. Churchill, 48 Ark. 426. §§ 93, 378, 385, 408, 411, 426.
v. Cobb, 71 Me. 198. § 508.
v. Cocke, 37 Tex. 155. § 512.
Cogswell v., 65 Ind. 1. § 577.
v. Cole, 13 Lea (Tenn.), 67. § 532.
Coman v., 4 Blackf. (Ind.) 241. § 371.
v. Cone, 32 Ga. 663. § 497.
v. Conover, 4 Dutcher (N. J.), 224. § 566.
v. Cook, 31 Mo. App. 57. § 463.
v. Cooper, 53 Miss. 615. §§ 520, 521, 642.
Cooper v., 5 Tex. App. 215. § 500.
v. Coppock, 79 Iowa, 482. § 509.
Cordray v., 55 Tex. 140. § 175.
v. Coste, 36 Mo. 437. § 638.
Cotton v., 64 Ind. 573. § 576.
Cowen v., 3 Tex. App. 380. § 509.
v. Craig, 58 Iowa, 238. § 381.
v. Crensbauer, 68 Mo. 254. §§ 22, 632.
Crisfield v., 55 Md. 192. § 208.
Cunningham v., 116 Ind. 433. § 510.
v. Cunningham, 10 La. Ann. 393. §§ 496, 505.
v. Dailey, 4 Mo. App. 172. §§ 539, 588.
v. Darby, 11 Mo. App. 528. § 617.
Darter v., 5 Blackf. (Ind.) 61. § 625.
State, Davis v., 5 Tex. App. 48. § 385.
v. Davis, 12 S. C. 528. § 503.
v. Davis, 88 Mo. 585. § 571.
v. Davis, 96 Ind. 539. § 594.
Dawson v., 38 Ohio St. 1. § 551.
Denio v., 61 Miss. 949. § 548.
Dennard v., 2 Kelly (Ga.), 137. § 501.
Dickenson v., 20 Neb. 72. §§ 43, 504.
v. Doane, 30 La. Ann. 1194. § 505.
Doepner v., 36 Ind. 111. § 562.
v. Donegan, 12 Mo. App. 190. § 580.
v. Donegan, 83 Mo. 374. § 632.
Douglass v., 44 Ind. 67. § 352.
v. Douglass, 69 Ind. 544. § 509.
v. Doyal, 12 La. Ann. 653. § 494.
v. Drake, 52 Ark. 350. § 587.
v. Druly, 3 Ind. 431. § 566.
v. Drury, 36 Mo. 281. § 540.
v. Dunn, 11 La. Ann. 549. §§ 386, 422.
Duncan v., 7 La. Ann. 377. § 555.
Durein v., 38 Kan. 485. § 508.
v. Egbert, 123 Ind. 448. § 600.
v. Engelke, 6 Mo. App. 356. § 639.
v. Estes, 101 N. C. 541. § 112.
v. Farmer, 21 Mo. 160. § 566.
v. Farrar, 77 Mo. 175. § 486.
Faurote v., 110 Ind. 463. § 601.
Fee v., 74 Ind. 66. § 577.
Feigert v., 31 Ohio St. 432. § 597.
v. Felton, 59 Miss. 402. § 542.
Finch v., 71 Tex. 52. § 524.
v. Findlay, 10 Ohio, 51. §§ 519, 521.
v. Findlay, 101 Mo. 368. §§ 8, 385.
v. Finn, 23 Mo. App. 290. § 588.
v. Finn, 98 Mo. 532. § 526.
Fleece v., 25 Ind. 384. § 512.
Fleenor v., 58 Ind. 166. § 514.
v. Fleming, 124 Ind. 97. § 532.
v. Fleming, 46 Ind. 206. § 575.
Flynn v., 42 Ark. 315. § 510.
Forrester v., 46 Md. 154. § 587.
v. Fortenberry, 54 Miss. 316. § 148.

State v. Fredericks, 8 Iowa, 553. § 24.
French v., 53 Miss. 651. § 617.
Fridge v., 3 Gill & Johns. (Md.) 103. § 42.
Friedline v., 93 Ind. 366. § 509.
v. Frith, 14 La. (Curry), 191. §§ 500, 505.
Frownfelter v., 66 Md. 80. §§ 422, 547, 642.
Fulton v., 14 Tex. App. 32. § 175.
Furlong v., 58 Miss. 717. § 570.
v. Garton, 32 Ind. 1. § 408.
Gary v., 11 Tex. App. 527. § 410.
v. Gilmore, 81 Me. 405. § 508.
v. Givan, 45 Ind. 267. § 531.
Glasgow v., 41 Kan. 333. § 503.
v. Glenn, 40 Ark. 332. § 514.
Goodin v., 18 Ohio, 6. § 536.
Goodwine v., 81 Ind. 109. § 596.
Gott v., 44 Md. 319. § 374.
Graham v., 66 Ind. 386. § 519.
Gray v., 78 Ind. 68. § 43.
v. Gregory, 88 Ind. 110. § 581.
v. Gregory, 119 Ind. 503. § 402.
v. Griffith, 63 Mo. 545. § 571.
v. Hampton, 14 La. Ann. 690. §§ 175, 517, 530.
v. Hammond, 6 Gill & Johns. (Md.) 157. § 372.
v. Hams, 89 Ind. 363. § 597.
v. Harbridge, 43 Mo. App. 16. §§ 554, 583.
Harmon v., 82 Ind. 197. § 571.
v. Harney, 57 Miss. 863. §§ 121, 520, 383, 384.
v. Harper, 6 Ohio St. 607. § 558.
Harris v., 54 Ind. 2. § 510.
Harris v., 55 Miss. 50. § 521.
v. Harrison, Harper, Law (S. C.), 88. § 535.
Harvey v., 94 Ind. 159. § 646.
v. Hathorn, 36 Miss. 491. § 554.
v. Hayes, 7 La. Ann. 118. § 556.
Heath v., 14 Tex. App. 213. § 385.
v. Hewitt, 72 Mo. 603. § 412.
v. Hicks, 2 Blackf. (Ind.) 336. § 525.
Higgins v., 87 Ind. 282. §§ 577, 589.
State v. Hill, 17 W. Va. 452. § 554.
v. Hindsdale-Doyle Granite Co., 117 Ind. 476. § 601.
Holmes v., 17 Neb. 73. §§ 27, 517.
v. Hood, 7 Blackf. (Ind.) 127. § 541.
v. Horn, 70 Mo. 466. § 500.
v. Horn, 94 Mo. 162. § 571.
Hortsell v., 45 Ark. 59. §§ 505, 510.
v. Hoshaw, 86 Mo. 193. § 632.
v. Howarth, 48 Conn. 207. §§ 587, 628.
v. Howley, 73 Me. 552. § 508.
Hughes v., 28 Tex. App. 499. § 495.
v. Hull, 53 Miss. 626, 645. §§ 540, 541, 580.
v. Humbird, 54 Md. 327. § 517.
v. Humphreys, 7 Ohio, 224. § 574.
Hunt v., 53 Ind. 321. § 408.
Hunt v., 124 Ind. 306. § 534.
Hutchings v., 24 Tex. App. 242. § 509.
Iglehart v., 2 Gill & Johns. (Md.) 235. § 638.
Irwin v., 10 Neb 325. §§ 152, 508.
Jackson v., 30 Kan. 88. § 503.
James v., 55 Miss. 57. § 521.
v. James, 82 Mo. 509. § 632.
v. Jean Defesse & C. Benoit, 18 La. Ann. 104. § 494.
v. Jennings, 14 Ohio St. 73. § 631.
v. Jones, 3 La. Ann. 9. § 504.
Jones v., 11 Tex. App. 412. § 505.
v. Jones, 82 Mo. 509. § 587.
v. Jones, 89 Mo. 470. § 526.
v. Judge, 28 La. Ann. 884. § 10.
v. Judge, 35 La. Ann. 737. § 462.
v. Keller, 11 Lea (Tenn.), 399. § 600.
Kelly v., 25 Ohio St. 567. §§ 521, 546.
v. Kelly, 32 Ohio St. 421. § 597.
King v., 18 Neb. 375. §§ 500, 509.
King v., 81 Ala. 92. § 402.
Kiser v., 13 Tex. App. 201. §§ 495, 509.

State *v.* Kurtzeborn, 78 Mo. 98. §§ 168, 537.
Lakin *v.*, 89 Ind. 68. § 571.
Lane *v.*, 27 Ind. 108. §§ 540, 626, 628.
v. Laughton, 19 Nev. 202. § 603.
Laurenson *v.*, 7 Harr. & Johns. (Md.) 339. § 521.
v. Le Cerf, 1 Bailey, Law (S. C.), 410. § 494.
Lee *v.*, 51 Miss. 665. §§ 495, 501, 510.
Lewis *v.*, 41 Miss. 686. § 498.
v. Lewis, 73 N. C. 138. §§ 42, 559.
v. Lidwell, 11 Mo. App. 567. §§ 537, 546, 588.
Lindley *v.*, 17 Tex. App. 120. § 500.
v. Littlefield, 4 Blackf. (Ind.) 129. § 562.
Littleton *v.*, 46 Ark. 413. §§ 504, 509.
v. Lockhart, 24 Ga. 420. § 509.
v. Long, 8 Ired. Law (N. C.), 415. § 565.
Lowry *v.*, 64 Ind. 421. § 526.
Madden *v.*, 35 Kan. 146. §§ 516, 644.
v. Mahon, 3 Harr. (Del.) 568. § 496.
v. Mann, 21 Wis. 684. § 566.
Marlar *v.*, 62 Miss. 77. § 555.
v. Martel, 3 Rob. (La.) 22. § 501.
Marx *v.*, 61 Miss. 478. § 509.
Mathena *v.*, 15 Tex. App. 460. § 175.
v. Matthews, 57 Miss. 1. § 591.
v. Matson, Adm'r, 44 Mo. 305. § 439.
v. Mayes, 54 Miss. 417. § 542.
v. McCormack, 50 Mo. 568. § 543.
McDonald *v.*, 77 Ind. 26. § 577.
v. McDonough, 9 Mo. App. 63. § 566.
v. McElhaney, 20 Mo. App. 584. § 509.
McGarry *v.*, 37 Kan. 9. § 503.
v. McGonigle, 101 Mo. 353. § 385.
McGovney *v.*, 20 Ohio, 93. § 132.
State *v.* McKee, 98 N. C. 500. § 628.
McLean *v.*, 8 Heisk. 22. §§ 523, 524, 548, 628.
Meadows *v.*, 114 Ind. 537. § 112.
v. Merrihew, 47 Iowa, 112. §§ 500, 502.
Merryman *v.*, 5 Har. & Johns. (Md.) 423. § 310.
Middleton *v.*, 120 Ind. 166. § 44.
v. Middleton's Sureties, 51 Tex. 185. § 338.
v. Miller, 5 Blackf. (Ind.) 381. § 312.
Miller *v.*, 63 Ind. 219. § 590.
v. Mills, 82 Ind. 126. § 42.
v. Millsaps, 69 Mo. 359. § 505.
v. Modrel, 69 Mo. 152. § 585.
Moody *v.*, 84 Ind. 433. §§ 541, 581.
Moore *v.*, 28 Ark. 480. § 126.
Moore *v.*, 49 Ind. 558. § 573.
v. Moore, 74 Mo. 413. § 558.
Morehead *v.*, 38 Kan. 489. §§ 501, 509.
v. Morgan, 59 Miss. 349. § 521.
v. Moses, 18 S. C. 366. § 541.
v. Moses, 20 S. C. 465. § 540.
Moss *v.*, 10 Mo. 338. § 169.
Mowbray *v.*, 88 Ind. 324. §§ 517, 590.
v. Muir, 20 Mo. 303. § 537.
Naugle *v.*, 101 Ind. 284. § 543.
v. Nevin, 19 Nev. 162. § 558.
Newcomer *v.*, 77 Tex. 286. § 524.
v. Newton, 33 Ark. 276. § 627.
v. Niçol, 30 La. Ann. 628. §§ 508, 509, 510.
Nichols, Adm'r, *v.*, 65 Ind. 512. § 628.
v. Norment, 12 La. (Curry), 511. § 501.
Nutzenholster *v.*, 37 Ind. 457. § 525.
v. O'Gorman, 75 Mo. 370. § 517.
v. Odom, 1 Spear's Law (S. C.), § 245. § 523.
Oglesby's Sureties *v.*, 73 Tex. 658. § 590.
v. Orr, 12 Lea (Tenn.), 725. § 543.
v. Orsler, 48 Iowa, 343. § 501.

State, Owen *v.*, 25 Ind. 371. § 581.
Paddleford *v.*, 57 Miss. 118. § 276.
v. Page, 63 Ind. 209. § 375.
Park *v.*, 4 Ga. 329. §§ 504, 515.
Park *v.*, 7 Mo. 194. § 448.
Parker *v.*, 8 Blackf. (Ind.) 292. § 627.
v. Parker, 72 Ala. 181. § 146.
Parr & Cockey *v.*, 71 Md. 220. §§ 577, 631.
v. Parsons, 89 N. C. 230. § 27.
Peacock *v.*, 44 Tex. 11. § 500.
v. Peck, 53 Me. 284. § 408.
v. Pepper, 31 Ind. 76. §§ 386, 408, 412.
Pepper *v.*, 22 Ind. 399. § 408.
Peters *v.*, 10 Tex. App. 302. § 519.
v. Peyton, 32 Mo. App. 522. § 152.
Phipps *v.*, 25 Tex. App. 660. § 515.
Pickett *v.*, 16 Tex. App. 648. § 620.
v. Pike, 74 N. C. 531. § 632.
v. Plazentia, 6 Rob. (La.) 417. § 502.
v. Polk, 14 Lea (Tenn.), 1. § 597.
Polk *v.*, 77 Tex. 289. § 524.
v. Posey, 79 Ala. 45. § 515.
Potter *v.*, 23 Ind. 550. §§ 26, 520.
v. Potter, 63 Mo. 212. § 408.
v. Powell, 40 La. Ann. 234. §§ 166, 168, 555.
v. Powell, 67 Mo. 395. § 558.
v. Powers, 52 Miss. 198. § 540.
Price *v.*, 43 Ark. 178. § 510.
Proseck *v.*, 38 Ohio St. 606. § 517.
v. Purcell, 31 W. Va. 44. § 519.
v. Purdy, 67 Mo. 89. § 585.
Quynn *v.*, 1 Harr. & Johns. (Md.) 36. § 523.
Ray *v.*, 16 Tex. App. 268. § 620.
v. Reaney, 13 Md. 230. § 499.
Reeve *v.*, 34 Ark. 610. § 509.
v. Reynolds, 3 Mo. 70. § 568.
v. Rhoades, 6 Nev. 352. §§ 519, 521, 554, 628.
v. Rhodius, 37 Tex. 165. § 512.
v. Righton, 36 La. Ann. 711. § 10.
State, Roberts *v.*, 22 Tex. App. 64. § 500.
Roberts *v.*, 34 Kan. 151. §§ 508, 519.
v. Roberts, 68 Mo. 234. § 371.
Rogers *v.*, 99 Ind. 218. § 546.
v. Rosswaag, 3 Mo. App. 11. § 639.
v. Rowe, 103 Ind. 118. § 495.
Rooksby *v.*, 92 Ind. 71. § 516.
Rubush *v.*, 112 Ind. 107. §§ 503, 510.
v. Rucker, 59 Mo. 17. § 582.
v. Rudowskey, 65 Ind. 389. § 509.
Rush *v.*, 20 Ind. 432. §§ 97, 323.
v. Rushing, 17 Fla. 226. §§ 422, 524.
Russell *v.*, 45 Ga. 9. § 511.
v. Sanders. 62 Ind. 562. § 581.
v. Sappington, 67 Mo. 529. § 540.
v. Satterwhite, 20 S. C. 536. § 4.
v. Scott, 20 Iowa, 63. §§ 497, 499.
Scott *v.*, 46 Ind. 203. § 531.
v. Shackleford, 56 Miss. 548. § 526.
Sherman *v.*, 4 Kan. 570. §§ 8, 506.
v. Slevin, 93 Mo. 253. § 514.
v. Sloane, 20 Ohio, 327. § 531.
Smith *v.*, 12 Neb. 309. §§ 501, 516.
v. Smith, 16 Fla. 175. §§ 551, 555.
Smith *v.*, 46 Md. 617. § 287.
Snell *v.*, 43 Ind. 359. § 565.
Sooy *ads.*, 38 N. J. Law, 324. §§ 12, 22, 414.
v. Sooy, 39 N. J. Law (10 Vroom), 539. §§ 338, 419, 422, 546.
Sooy, Jr., *v.*, 41 N. J. Law, 394. § 628.
v. Spear, 54 Vt. 503. § 516.
Stafford *v.*, 10 Tex. App. 46. § 500.
Steinbach *v.*, 38 Ind. 483. § 539.
Stephenson *v.*, 9 Tex. App. 459. § 509.
Sternberg *v.*, 42 Ark. 127. § 495.
v. Stevens, 103 Ind. 55. § 548.
v. Stewart, 74 Iowa, 336. § 516.
v. Stewart, 36 Miss. 652. §§ 172, 639.

State, Sugarman v., 28 Ark. 142. § 512.
Swan v., 48 Tex. 120. § 548.
Swerdsfeger v., 21 Kan. 475. § 509.
v. Swinney, 60 Miss. 39, 44. §§ 371, 548.
v. Swope, 72 Mo. 399. § 509.
v. Taylor, 6 Mo. App. 277. § 571.
v. Teague, 9 Rich. (S. C.) 149. § 628.
Tedford v., 67 Miss. 363. § 500.
v. Tennant, 30 La. Ann. 852. §§ 505, 508.
v. Thim, 77 Ala. 100. § 11.
Thomas v., 13 Tex. App. 496. § 175.
v. Thomas, 38 Tenn. (4 Pickle), 491. § 521.
v. Thompson, 62 Ind. 367. §§ 503, 509.
v. Thompson, 49 Mo. 188. § 517.
v. Thornton, 8 Mo. App. 27. §§ 551, 630.
v. Tiederman, 10 Fed. Rep. 20. § 630.
v. Tieman, 39 Iowa, 474. § 501.
Tillson v., 29 Kan. 452. §§ 151, 508.
v. Tomer, 7 Rich. Law (S. C.), 216. § 521.
Townsend v., 7 Tex. App. 74. § 515.
v. Traphagen, 45 N. J. 134. § 497.
Tucker v., 11 Md. 322. § 46.
Tucker v., 72 Ind. 242. §§ 12, 520.
v. Turner, 49 Ark. 311. § 590.
Urmston v., 73 Ind. 175. §§ 169, 528.
v. Vananda, 7 Blackf. (Ind.) 214. § 570.
Voris v., 47 Ind. 346. § 576.
Warren v., 11 Mo. 583. § 537.
Warwick v., 5 Ind. 350. § 576.
v. Watson, 38 Ark. 96. § 531.
v. Wayman, 2 Gill & Johns. 112. § 169.
Waymire v., 80 Ind. 67. § 569.
v. Weaver, 18 Ala. 293. § 508.
State v. Weaver, 92 Mo. 673. § 577.
Wegner v., 14 Tex. App. 213. § 385.
v. Weideman, 30 Mo. App. 647. § 508.
v. Wells, 8 Nev. 105. § 521.
v. Wells, 61 Tex. 562. § 524.
Wheeler v., 9 Heisk. (Tenn.) 393. §§ 559, 624.
Wheeler v., 39 Kan. 163. § 503.
v. White, 88 Ind. 587. § 566.
White v., 1 Blackf. (Ind.) 557. § 636.
v. White, 10 Rich. Law (S. C.), 442. § 528.
Widener v., 45 Ind. 244. § 503.
Williams v., 89 Ind. 570. §§ 541, 574, 581.
v. Williams, 19 S. C. 62. §§ 569, 589, 636.
Williams v., 25 Fla. 734. § 517.
Wilson v., 1 Lea (Tenn.), 316. § 535.
v. Windley, 99 N. C. 4. § 532.
v. Wolff, 10 Mo. App. 95. § 540.
v. Woods, 84 Mo. 163. § 380.
v. Wright, 37 Iowa, 522. § 506.
Wycough v., 50 Ark. 102. § 551.
v. Wyant, 67 Ind. 25. § 573.
v. Wylie, 86 Ind. 396. § 226.
Yost v., 80 Ind. 350. § 540.
Young v., 7 Gill & Johns. (Md.) 253. § 517.
v. Young, 23 Minn. 551. §§ 25, 542, 559.
State Bank, Bates v., 7 Ark. (2 Eng.) 394. § 605.
Comegys v., 6 Ind. 357. § 271.
v. Edwards, 20 Ala. 512. § 434.
v. Evans, 3 J. S. Green (N. J. Law), 155. § 411.
Ferguson v., 8 Ark. (3 Eng.) 416. § 342.
Findley v., 6 Ala. 244. § 407.
King v., 9 Ark. (4 Eng.) 185. § 342.
v. Mettler, 2 Bosw. (N. Y.) 392. § 63.
v. Robinson, 13 Ark. (8 Eng.) 214. § 149.

State Bank, Ryan *v.*, 10 Neb. 524. § 590.
Sherry *v.*, 6 Ind. 397. § 449.
Stone *v.*, 8 Ark. (3 Eng.) 141. § 362.
v. Watkins, 6 Ark. (1 Eng.) 123. § 243.
State Nat. Bank *v.* Haylen, 14 Neb. 480. § 50.
Statler, Glenn *v.*, 42 Iowa, 107. § 127.
Statts, Davis *v.*, 43 Ind. 103. § 153.
Staunton, Wade *v.*, 5 How. (Miss.) 631. § 366.
Stayner *v.* Joice, 82 Ind. 35. § 379.
Stead *v.* Liddard, 1 Bing. 196. § 87.
v. Liddard, 8 Moore, 2. § 84.
Steadman *v.* Guthrie, 4 Met. (Ky.) 147. § 187.
Pelzer, Rodgers & Co. *v.*, 22 S. C. 279. § 330.
Steamboat Stacy, Griff *v.*, 12 La. Ann. 8. § 446.
Steamer Belle Air, Holmes *v.*, 5 La. Ann. 523. § 464.
Stearns *v.* Bates, 46 Conn. 306. § 324.
v. Irwin, 62 Ind. 558. § 205.
v. Hall, 9 Cush. 31. § 81.
Whitney *v.*, 16 Me. 394. § 84.
Steckel, Koening *v.*, 58 N. Y. 475. § 332.
Stedman, Arnold *v.*, 45 Pa. St. 186. § 64.
v. Freeman, 15 Ind. 86. § 301.
Steel *v.* Dixon, Law Rep. (17 Ch. Div.) 825. § 268.
Steele, Agee *v.*, 8 Ala. 948. § 362.
v. Boyd, 6 Leigh (Va.), 547. § 359.
v. Faber, 37 Mo. 71. § 271.
v. Graves, 68 Ala. 17, 21. §§ 150, 581, 586.
v. Hoe, 14 Adol. & Ell. (N. S.) 431. § 86.
v. Mealing, 24 Ala. 285. §§ 268, 269, 272, 444.
v. Reese, 6 Yerg. (Tenn.) 263. § 541.
Reeves *v.*, 2 Head (Tenn.), 647. § 584.
Steele, Simons *v.*, 36 N. H. 73. §§ 80, 87, 124, 200.
Smith *v.*, 25 Vt. 427. § 349.
v. Towne, 28 Vt. 771. § 76.
v. Tutwiler, 57 Ala. 113. § 45.
Steer, Large *v.*, 121 Pa. St. 30, 33, 34. § 477.
Steere, Lackey *v.*, 121 Ill. 598. § 150.
Steger, Evarts *v.*, 6 Oreg. 55. § 586.
Steidemann, Schmucker *v.*, 8 Mo. App. 302. § 23.
Stein *v.* Jones, 18 Bradw. (Ill. App.) 543. § 390.
Miller *v.*, 2 Pa. St. 286. § 344.
Steinan, Hoffman *v.*, 34 Hun (N. Y.), 239. § 250.
Steinbach *v.* State, 38 Ind. 483. § 539.
Steiner, Huber *v.*, 2 Scott, 304. § 52.
Stelle *v.* Shannon, 62 Tex. 198. § 471.
Stelle's Case, 34 N. J. Eq. 199. § 593.
Stem, Miller *v.*, 12 Pa. St. 383. § 402.
Stemmons, Henley *v.*, 4 B. Mon. (Ky.) 131. §§ 305, 316.
Stephens *v.* Meek, 6 Lea (Tenn.), 226. § 284.
v. Monongahela Nat. Bank, 88 Pa. St. 157, 163. § 2.
Palmer *v.*, 1 Denio, 471. § 89.
v. Pell, 2 Cromp. & Mees. 710. § 63.
v. Shafer, 48 Wis. 54. § 636.
v. Squire, 5 Modern, 205. §§ 67, 68.
v. Winn, 2 Nott & McC. 372. § 82.
Stephenson, Hillegas *v.*, 75 Mo. 118. § 260.
v. State, 9 Tex. App. 459. § 509.
v. Taverners, 9 Gratt. (Va.) 398. § 223.
Ware *v.*, 10 Leigh (Va.), 155. § 75.
Steptoe's Adm'r *v.* Harvey's Ex'r, 7 Leigh (Va.), 501. § 374.
Sterling, Dundas *v.*, 4 Pa. St. 73. § 415.
Jester *v.*, 25 Hun (N. Y.), 344. § 37.
Parker *v.*, 10 Ohio, 357. § 498.

Sterling *v.* Stewart, 74 Pa. St. 445. § 332.
Stern *v.* Drinker, 2 E. D. Smith (N. Y.), 401. § 64.
v. People, 96 Ill. 475. § 545.
v. People, 102 Ill. 540. §§ 412, 555, 628.
Sternberg *v.* State, 42 Ark. 127. § 495.
Sterne *v.* Bank of Vincennes, 79 Ind. 549. § 438.
v. McKinney, 79 Ind. 578. § 438.
Sterns *v.* Marks, 35 Barb. (N. Y.) 565. § 118.
Sterrett, Lutt *v.*, 26 Kan. 561. § 449.
Stetson *v.* City Bank, 2 Ohio St. 167. § 627.
v. City Bank of N. O., 12 Ohio St. 577. § 175.
Thomas *v.*, 59 Me. 229. § 342.
Stevens *v.* Allmen, 19 Ohio St. 485. § 540.
Bank of Wooster *v.*, 6 Ohio St. 262. § 235.
v. Campbell, 6 Iowa (Clarke), 538. § 605.
Franklin Bank *v.*, 39 Me. 532. §§ 412, 419.
Gard *v.*, 12 Mich. 292. § 164.
v. Hurlburt, 25 Ill. App. 124. § 226.
v. Oaks, 58 Mich. 343. §§ 29, 375.
Sanderson *v.*, 116 Mass. 133. § 516.
State *v.*, 103 Ind. 55. § 548.
v. Tucker, 73 Ind. 73. § 284.
v. Tucker, 87 Ind. 109. § 256.
United States *v.*, 16 Fed. Rep. 101. § 621.
Stevenson *v.* Bay City, 26 Mich. 44. § 530.
v. Hoy, 43 Pa. St. 191. § 20.
v. McLean, 11 Up. Can. (C. P.) 208. § 117.
v. Palmer, 14 Col. 565. § 466.
Stewart, Atkinson *v.*, 2 B. Mon. (Ky.) 348. § 291.
Bank of United States *v.*, 4 Dana (Ky.), 27. § 325.
v. Barrow, 55 Ga. 664. § 233.
Stewart *v.* Behm, 2 Watts (Pa.), 356. § 151.
Blutcher *v.*, 11 Mees. & Wels. 857. §§ 62, 86.
Buckner's Adm'r *v.*, 34 Ala. 529. § 290.
v. Carter, 4 Neb. 564. § 27.
Central Mills Co. *v.*, 133 Mass. 461. § 517.
v. Davis' Ex'r, 18 Ind. 74. § 405.
Farmer *v.*, 2 N. H. 97. § 248.
Forest *v.*, 14 Ohio St. 246. §§ 101, 199.
v. Glenn, 5 Wis. 14. § 138.
v. Hinkle, 1 Bond, 506. §§ 17, 62.
Kurtz *v.*, 54 Ind. 178. § 82.
v. Lacoume, 30 La. Ann. 157. § 468.
v. Malone, 5 Phila. 440. § 67.
Miller *v.*, 4 Wash. (C. C.) 26. § 393.
Miller *v.*, 9 Wheat. 680. §§ 93, 393.
Mitchell *v.*, 10 Heisk. 18. § 103.
v. Parker, 55 Ga. 656. §§ 29, 345.
Roberts *v.*, 31 Miss. 664. §§ 342, 344, 353, 356.
State *v.*, 36 Miss. 652. §§ 172, 639.
State *v.*, 74 Iowa, 336. § 516.
Sterling *v.*, 74 Pa. St. 445. § 332.
Thomas *v.*, 117 Ind. 50. § 40.
Stickler *v.* Burkholder, 47 Pa. St. 476. § 240.
Stickney *v.* Mohler, 19 Md. 490. § 39.
Stillinger, Culbertson *v.*, Taney's Decisions (Campbell), 75. § 226.
Stillman *v.* Northrup, 109 N. Y. 473. §§ 48, 50.
Stillwater *v.* Aaron, 69 Mo. 539. §§ 342, 353, 356, 357.
Stillwell *v.* How, 46 Mo. 589. § 260.
v. Mills, 10 Johns. 304. § 574.
Stilwell, Hernandez *v.*, 7 Daly (N. Y. Com. Pl.), 360. § 197.
Wilson *v.*, 9 Ohio St. 467. § 97.
Stimmel, Perkins *v.*, 114 N. Y. 359. § 574.

Stimson, Begole v., 39 Mich. 288. § 494.
Stinson v. Brennan, Cheves' Law (S. C.), 15. § 214.
Gass v., 2 Sumner, 453. § 393.
Stirling, Crawford v., 4 Esp. 207. § 18.
v. Forrester, 3 Bligh, 575. § 439.
Stix, Wolf v., 99 U. S. 1. § 150.
Stobridge, Ford v., Nels. 24. § 205.
Stockbridge v. Schoonmaker, 45 Barb. (N. Y.) 100. § 131.
Stockebrand, Fisher v., 26 Kan. 565. § 339.
Stocker, Loew v., 68 Pa. St. 226. § 151.
Stocking v. Sage, 1 Conn. 519. § 60.
Stockmeyer v. Oertling, 35 La. Ann. 467. §§ 254, 267.
Stockton v. Coleman, 39 Ind. 106. § 235.
Kellogg v., 29 Pa. St. 460. §§ 131, 186, 187.
v. Stockton, 40 Ind. 225. § 439.
Wright's Adm'r v., 5 Leigh (Va.). 153. § 613.
Stoddard v. Kimball, 4 Cush. 604. § 407.
Stoker, Dick v., 1 Dev. Law (N. C.), 91. § 494.
Stokes v. Hodges, 11 Rich. Eq. (S. C.) 135. § 38.
Stoll v. Sheldon, 13 Neb. 207. § 252.
Stone v. Compton, 5 Bing. N. C. 142. § 419.
v. Dennison, 13 Pick. 1. § 52.
Gammon v., 1 Vesey, Sr. 339. § 303.
v. Hammell, 83 Cal. 547. § 211.
Osborne v., 30 Minn. 25. § 18.
v. Rockefeller, 29 Ohio St. 625. § 98.
Sherwood v., 14 N. Y. 267. § 71.
v. State Bank, 8 Ark. (3 Eng.) 141. § 362.
v. Seymour, 15 Wend. 19. § 338.
v. Symmes, 18 Pick. 467. § 62.
United States v., 106 U. S. 525. § 395.
v. White, 8 Gray, 589. § 380.
Stonebraker v. Ford, 81 Mo. 532. § 219.
Stoner v. Millikin, 85 Ill. 218. § 412.
Stoney, Beaubien v., Speer's Eq. (S. C.) 508. § 430.
Stonum, Governor v., 11 Ala. 679. § 143.
Stookey, Adm'r, Stratman v., 3 Bradw. (Ill. App.) 336. § 236.
Stoops v. Whittler, 1 Mo. App. 420. § 630.
Stoppani v. Richard, 1 Hilton (N. Y.), 509. § 13.
Storer, Richards v., 114 Mass. 101. § 470.
Storm v. Thorn, 3 Barb. (N. Y.) 314. § 40.
Storr v. Scott, 6 Car. & Payne, 241. § 78.
Storrs, Booth v., 75 Ill. 438. § 407.
Wright v., 6 Bosw. (N. Y.) 600. § 345.
Story, Rains v., 1 Car. & Payne, 130. § 78.
Stothoff v. Dunham's Ex'rs, 4 Harr. (N. J.) 181. §§ 284, 288.
Stoudt v. Hine, 45 Pa. St. 30. §§ 63, 64.
Stout v. Ashton, 5 T. B. Mon. (Ky.) 251. § 242.
v. Dilts, 1 Southard (N. J.), 218. § 317.
Happe v., 2 Cal. 460. § 84.
Mendelson v., 5 J. & S. (N. Y. Super. Ct.) 408. § 401.
Miller v., 5 Del. Ch. 259. §§ 207, 223, 298.
Ward v., 32 Ill. 399. §§ 29, 33.
Stovall v. Banks, 10 Wall. 583. § 580.
v. Border Grange Bank, 78 Va. 188. §§ 237, 260.
Stover, Oxley v., 54 Ill. 159. § 367.
Wolf v., 107 Pa. St. 206. § 262.
Stow, Best v., 2 Sandf. Ch. 298. § 405.
Stowe, Lee & Co. v., 57 Tex. 444. § 227.
Stowell v. Goodenow, 31 Me. 538. § 359.
v. Raymond, 83 Ill. 120. §§ 102, 176.

Strader *v.* Houghton, 9 Port. (Ala.) 334. § 239.
Strafford Bank, Mathewson *v.*, 45 N. H. 104. § 353.
Strait, Brown *v.*, 19 Ill. 88. § 66.
Strange *v.* Fooks, 4 Giff. 408. § 442.
Stratman *v.* Stookey, Adm'r, 3 Bradw. (Ill. App.) 336. § 236.
Straton *v.* Rastall, 2 Durn. & East, 366. § 445.
Stratton, Finn *v.*, 5 J. J. Marsh. (Ky.) 364. § 438.
Straw, Wainwright *v.*, 15 Vt. 215. § 76.
Strawbridge *v.* Baltimore & Ohio R. R. Co., 14 Md. 360. § 395.
Street *v.* Laurens, 5 Rich. Eq. (S. C.) 227. § 543.
v. Old Town Bank, 67 Md. 421. § 39.
Streeter Coal Co., Newman *v.*, 19 Bradw. (Ill. App.) 594. § 191.
Strever, Agawam Bank *v.*, 16 Barb. (N. Y.) 82. § 171.
Stribling, Hart *v.*, 25 Fla. 435. § 576.
Strickland, Masser *v.*, 17 Serg. & Rawle (Pa.), 354. § 636.
Stringer *v.* Montgomery, 111 Ind. 489. § 7.
Stringfellow *v.* Williams, 6 Dana (Ky.), 236. § 436.
Strohecker *v.* Cohen, 1 Spear (S. C.), 349. § 67.
Strong *v.* Baker, 25 Minn. 442. § 628.
Bangs *v.*, 4 N. Y. 315. § 40.
Bangs *v.*, 7 Hill (N. Y.), 250. §§ 40, 360.
Bangs *v.*, 10 Paige, Ch. 11. § 345.
v. Foster, 17 C. B. (8 J. Scott), 201. §§ 336, 342.
v. Giltinan, 7 Phila. (Pa.) 176. § 631.
Hedges *v.*, 3 Oreg. 18. § 62.
Lemmon *v.*, 55 Conn. 443. §§ 98, 100, 101.
Lemmon *v.*, 59 Conn. 448. § 48.
v. Lyon, 63 N. Y. 172. § 397.
v. Riker, 16 Vt. 554. §§ 180, 182.
Strong, Sage *v.*, 40 Wis. 575. § 398.
Trotter *v.*, 63 Ill. 272. §§ 40, 146.
v. Wooster, 6 Vt. 536. § 426.
Stroop *v.* McKenzie, 38 Tex. 132. § 29.
Strother, Savings Bank *v.*, 28 S. C. 504. § 199.
Strout, Smith *v.*, 63 Me. 205. § 248.
Strunk *v.* Ocheltree, 11 Iowa, 158. § 566.
Struthers *v.* Clark, 30 Pa. St. 210. § 130.
Stuart *v.* Lancaster, 84 Va. 772. § 363.
Stub, Commonwealth *v.*, 11 Pa. St. 150. § 578.
Stubbins *v.* Mitchell, 82 Ky. 535. § 291.
Stubbs, Boultbee *v.*, 18 Vesey, 20. § 376.
Studebaker *v.* Cody, 54 Ind. 586. §§ 47, 193.
v. Johnson, 41 Kan. 326. § 545.
Kirby *v.*, 15 Ind. 45. §§ 195, 399.
Studley *v.* Barth, 54 Mich. 6. § 76.
Stukely, Terry *v.*, 3 Yerg. (Tenn.) 506. § 452.
Stultz *v.* Ingles, 84 Va. 844. § 572.
Solary *v.*, 22 Fla. 263. §§ 194, 355.
Stunden, Corporation Village Ganandque *v.*, 1 Ont. (Can.) 1. § 419.
Sturgeon, Eddy *v.*, 15 Mo. 198. § 337.
Sturges, Fullerton *v.*, 4 Ohio St. 529. § 410.
United States *v.*, 1 Paine, 525. § 433.
Sublett *v.* McKinney, 19 Tex. 438. § 230.
Succession of Boutte, 32 La. Ann. 556. § 587.
Succession of Daigle, 15 La. Ann. 594. § 37.
Succession of Diggs, Gordon *v.*, 9 La. Ann. 422. § 467.
Succession of Dinkgrave, 31 La. Ann. 703. § 212.
Succession of Montgomery, 2 La. Ann. 469. § 224.

Succession of Pratt, 16 La. Ann. 357. § 444.
Sugarloaf, Butter *v.*, 6 Pa. St. 262. § 131.
Sugarman *v.* State, 28 Ark. 142. § 512.
Sugg, Briley *v.*, 1 Dev. & Bat. Eq. (N. C.) 366. § 312.
Sullivan *v.* Hugely, 48 Ga. 486. § 342.
v. Murphy, 23 Minn. 6. § 63.
v. State, 121 Ind. 342. § 587.
Summerhill *v.* Trapp, 48 Ala. 363. § 434.
v. Tapp, 52 Ala. 227. §§ 33, 438.
Summers, Fessenden *v.*, 62 Cal. 485. § 175.
Loop *v.*, 3 Rand. (Va.) 511. § 426.
Summit, King *v.*, 73 Ind. 312. §§ 91, 227.
Sumrall, Townsley *v.*, 2 Pet. 170. §§ 60, 67.
Supervisors of Albany *v.* Dow, 7 Hill (N. Y.), 583. § 558.
Supervisors of Kewaunee *v.* Knipfer, 37 Wis. 496. § 557.
Supervisors of Omro *v.* Kaime, 39 Wis. 468. § 558.
Supervisors of Rensellaer *v.* Bates, 17 N. Y. 242. § 522.
Supervisors of Richmond Co. *v.* Wandel, 6 Lans. (N. Y.) 33. §§ 534, 557.
Supervisors of St. Joseph *v.* Coffenbury, 1 Manning (Mich.), 355. § 22.
Supervisors of Washington Co. *v.* Dunn, 27 Gratt. (Va.) 608. §§ 520, 628.
Suppiger *v.* Garrels, 20 Bradw. (Ill. App.) 625. § 298.
Supplee *v.* Sayre, 51 Hun (N. Y.), 30. §§ 284, 293.
Sureties of Oswald *v.* Treasurers, 2 Bailey, Law (S. C.), 214. § 569.
Susong *v.* Vaiden, 10 Rich. (S. C.) 247. § 139.
Sutherland *v.* Carr, 85 N. Y. 105. § 524.
Sutherland *v.* Patterson, 4 Ont. (Can.) 565. §§ 165, 191.
Purviance *v.*, 2 Ohio St., 478. § 216.
Watson *v.*, 1 Cooper, Ch. (Tenn.) 208. § 237.
v. Woodruff, 26 Hun (N. Y.), 411. § 99.
Sutherlin, Allison *v.*, 50 Mo. 274. § 306.
Sutliff, Ingels *v.*, 36 Kan. 444. §§ 242, 353.
Sutton, Blore *v.*, 3 Meriv. 237. § 89.
Chapman *v.*, 2 Com. B. 634. § 17.
v. Irvine, 12 Serg. & Rawle, 13. § 18.
Mattingly *v.*, 19 W. Va. 19. § 227.
McCabe *v.*, 7 Lea (Tenn.), 248. § 479.
Rosenthal *v.*, 31 Ohio St. 406. § 292.
Wakeman *v.*, 2 Adol. & Ell. 78. § 91.
v. Williams, 77 Ga. 570. § 577.
Suydam *v.* Vance, 2 McLean, 99. §§ 368, 372.
v. Westfall, 2 Denio, 205. § 185.
Swain *v.* Barber, 29 Vt. 292. § 276.
Smith *v.*, 7 Rich. Eq. (S. C.) 112. § 313.
v. Wall, 1 Rep. Ch. 149. § 288.
Swallow, Walters *v.*, 6 Whart. (Pa.) 446. §§ 347, 352.
Swan, Goldshede *v.*, 1 Wels., Hurl. & Gor. 154. §§ 77, 86.
Messer *v.*, 4 N. H. 481. § 273.
v. Nesmith, 7 Pick. 220. § 71.
v. Patterson, 7 Md. 163. §§ 306, 308.
v. State, 48 Tex. 120. § 548.
Trammell *v.*, 25 Tex. 473. § 416.
Swaney, Knapp *v.*, 56 Mich. 345. § 601.
Swann, Day *v.*, 13 Me. 165. § 209.
Swearingen, Toland *v.*, 39 Tex. 447. § 483.
Swearinger, Gum *v.*, 69 Mo. 553. § 526.

Sweazy v. Kammer, 51 Iowa, 642. § 7.
Sweeney, Lomme v., 1 Mont. 584. § 486.
Harlan v., 1 Lea (Tenn.), 682. § 301.
Sweet v. Lee, 3 Man. & Gr. 452. §§ 82, 89.
Marston v., 66 N. Y. 207. § 91.
Sweet, Adm'r, v. Jeffries, 48 Mo. 279. § 317.
Sweeting, Manchester Iron Manuf. Co. v., 10 Wend. 163. § 239.
Sweetser v. French, 2 Cush. 309. §§ 18, 407.
Hill v., 5 N. H. 168. § 402.
Sweetzer, Leonard v., 16 Ohio, 1. § 137.
Swenson, Teberg v., 32 Kan. 224. § 210.
Swerdsfeger v. State, 21 Kan. 475. § 509.
Swezy, Star Wagon Co. v., 59 Iowa, 609. § 204.
Swift, Jones v., 94 Ind. 516. § 406.
Patchin v., 21 Vt. 292. § 82.
v. Pierce, 13 Allen, 136. § 78.
Swinburne, Craythorne v., 14 Ves. 160. §§ 261, 265.
Swindle, Coats v., 55 Mo. 31. §§ 29, 618.
Swing, Boyd v., 38 Miss. 182. § 521.
Swinney, State v., 60 Miss. 39, 44. §§ 371, 548.
Switzler, Matthews v., 46 Mo. 301. § 330.
Swive v. Redman, Law Rep. 1 Q. B. Div. 536. § 362.
Swope, Commonwealth v., 45 Pa. St. 535. § 533.
v. Forney, 17 Ind. 385. §§ 43, 403.
State v., 72 Mo. 399. § 504.
Sykes v. Dixon, 9 Adol. & Ell. 693. § 85.
Sylvester v. Downer, 18 Vt. 32. §§ 131, 198.
v. Downer, 20 Vt. 355. § 182.
Syme v. Bunting, 91 N. C. 48. § 531.
v. Montague, 4 Hen. & Munf. (Va.) 180. 467.
Symmes, Stone v., 18 Pick. 467. § 62.
Taber, Brown v., 5 Wend. 566. § 115.
Tabor v. Merchants' Nat. Bank, 48 Ark. 454. § 409.
Taggart, Fleenor v., 116 Ind. 189. § 570.
Taintor v. Taylor, 36 Conn. 242. § 500.
Talbot v. Gay, 18 Pick. 534. § 197.
v. Wilkins, 31 Ark. 411. § 298.
Talbott, McPherson v., 10 Gill & Johns. (Md.) 499. § 266.
Tucker v., 15 Ind. 114. § 405.
Taliaferro, Chaffe v., 58 Miss. 544. § 95.
Pinkerton v., 9 Ala. 547. § 285.
Tallmadge, Bay v., 5 Johns. Ch. 305. § 40.
Hart v., 2 Day (Conn.), 381. § 73.
Talmage v. Burlingame, 9 Pa. St. 21. § 358.
Tallman, Colgrove v., 2 Lans. (N. Y.) 97. §§ 32, 36.
Colgrove v., 67 N. Y. 95. §§ 36, 239.
v. Franklin, 14 N. Y. 584. § 80.
v. Rochester City Bank, 18 Barb. 123. § 5.
Tally, Martin v., 72 Ala. 23. §§ 588, 632.
Tandy, Medley v., 85 Ky. 566. § 606.
Tankersley v. Anderson, 4 Des. Eq. (S. C.) 44. § 221.
Tanner, Callihan v., 3 Rob. (La.) 299. §§ 342, 371.
Holden v., 6 La. Ann. 74. § 26.
Hollingsworth v., 44 Ga. 11. § 430.
v. Moore, 9 Q. B. 1. § 161.
Pomeroy v., 70 N. Y. 547. § 359.
Tapley v. Martin, 116 Mass. 275. § 422.
Tapp, Summerhill v., 52 Ala. 227. §§ 33, 438.
v. Lee, 3 Bos. & Pul. 367. § 73.
Tappan v. People, 67 Ill. 339. § 535.
Tappen, Elmendorph v., 5 Johns. 176. § 129.
v. Van Wagenen, 3 Johns. 465. § 506.
Tapscott, Weaver v., 9 Leigh (Va.), 424. § 216.

Tarr *v.* Ravenscroft, 12 Gratt. (Va.) 642. § 287.
Tarrant, Becket *v.*, 61 Tex. 402. § 295.
Tate, Campbell *v.*, 7 Lans. (N. Y.) 370. § 20.
v. Wymond, 7 Blackf. (Ind.) 240. § 374.
Tatem, Morphew *v.*, 89 N. C. 183. § 10.
Tatlock, Peel *v.*, 1 Bos. & Pul. 419. § 423.
Tator, Adams *v.*, 57 Hun (N. Y.), 302. § 247.
Tatton *v.* Wade, 18 Com. B. 370. § 73.
Tatum *v.* Bonner, 27 Miss. 760. § 105.
v. Holliday, 59 Mo. 422. § 571.
v. Tatum, 1 Ired. Eq. (N. C.) 113. § 322.
Taul *v.* Epperson, 38 Tex. 492. § 308.
Tavel, Lecat *v.*, 3 McCord, 158. §§ 82, 87.
Taverners, Stephenson *v.*, 9 Gratt. (Va.) 398. § 223.
Tayleur *v.* Wildin, Law Rep. 3 Exch. 303. §§ 108, 165.
Taylor *v.* Bank of New South Wales, Law Rep. (11 App. Cas.) 596. § 431.
v. Beck, 13 Ill. 376. § 242.
Breckenridge *v.*, 5 Dana (Ky.), 110. §§ 255, 283, 288, 635.
Bullock *v.*, 39 Mich. 137. § 383.
v. Burgess, 5 Hurl. & Nor. 1. § 342.
Bushong *v.*, 82 Mo. 660. §§ 212, 230, 329.
v. Davis, 38 Miss. 493. § 609.
v. Deming, 3 Nev. & Per. 228. § 87.
v. Drake, 4 Strobh. (S. C.) 431. §§ 74, 75.
v. Ex'r of Heriot, 4 Dev. Eq. (S. C.) 227. § 226.
v. Farmers' Bank of Kentucky, 87 Ky. 398. § 327.
v. Gilman, 25 Vt. 411. § 405.
v. Hillyer, 3 Blackf. (Ind.) 433. § 68.
v. Hortop, 22 Up. Can. (C. P.) 542. § 389.
Taylor *v.* Hunt's Ex'r, 34 Mo. 205. § 580.
v. Jeter, 23 Mo. 244. § 427.
v. Johnson, 17 Ga. 521. §§ 415, 567, 637.
Lawrence *v.*, 5 Hill, 107. § 90.
Leigh *v.*, 7 Barn. & Cress. 491. § 528.
Levy *v.*, 24 Md. 282. § 480.
v. Life Ass'n of America (Cir. Ct. W. D. Tenn.), 3 Fed. Rep. 465. §§ 11, 592.
v. Lohman, 74 Ind. 418. §§ 245, 332, 419.
Longan *v.*, 130 Ill. 412. § 628.
Loveman *v.*, 85 Tenn. (1 Pickle), 1. §§ 586, 642.
Martin *v.*, 8 Bush (Ky.), 384. § 434.
v. Means, 73 Ala. 468. § 287.
v. McClung's Ex'rs, 2 Houston (Del.), 24. §§ 117, 186.
v. Miller, Phillips' Eq. (N. C.) 365. § 223.
v. Mills, Cowper, 525. § 220.
Morrison *v.*, 21 Ala. 779. § 274.
v. Morrison, 26 Ala. 728. § 271.
Mosely *v.*, 4 Dana (Ky.), 542. § 62.
Pahlman *v.*, 75 Ill. 629. §§ 176, 381.
v. Parker, 43 Wis. 78. § 563.
Place *v.*, 22 Ohio St. 317. § 562.
v. Pratt, 3 Wis. 674. § 82.
v. Railroad Company, 11 Lea (Tenn.), 186. § 5.
Rawson *v.*, 30 Ohio St. 389. § 36.
v. Ross, 3 Yerg. (Tenn.) 330. §§ 82, 199.
Rucks *v.*, 49 Miss. 552. §§ 221, 230.
v. Russell, 75 Ind. 386. § 486.
v. Savage, 12 Mass. 98. §§ 60, 266.
Shepard *v.*, 35 Tex. 774. § 128.
v. Shouse, 73 Mo. 361. § 189.
Skidmore *v.*, 29 Cal. 619. § 271.
v. Soper, 53 Mich. 96. § 102.
State *v.*, 6 Mo. App. 277. § 571.

Taylor, Taintor *v.*, 36 Conn. 242. § 500.
v. Taylor, 64 Ind. 271. § 199.
v. Taylor, 8 B. Mon. (Ky.) 419. § 318.
Thompson *v.*, 11 Hun (N. Y.), 274. § 217.
Thompson *v.*, 12 R. I. 109. §§ 182, 208, 261.
Treasurers *v.*, 2 Bailey, Law (S. C.), 524. § 541.
v. Van Dusen, 3 Gray, 498. § 97.
Walker *v.*, 6 Car. & P. 752. § 65.
v. Wetmore, 10 Ohio, 490. §§ 117, 196.
Whitelaw *v.*, 45 Up. Can. (Q. B.) 446. § 77.
v. Wightman, 51 Iowa, 411. § 13.
v. Wilkinson, 1 Nevile & Perry, 629. § 505.
Taylor Co. *v.* King, 73 Iowa, 153. § 408.
Teaff *v.* Ross, 1 Ohio St. 469. § 445.
Teague *v.* Fowler, 56 Ind. 569. § 63.
v. Russell, 2 Stew. (Ala.) 420. § 245.
State *v.*, 9 Rich. (S. C.) 149. § 628.
Turner *v.*, 73 Ala. 554. §§ 310, 320.
Tebbetts, Wilson *v.*, 29 Ark. 579. § 613.
Teberg *v.* Swenson, 32 Kan. 224. § 210.
Tedford *v.* State, 67 Miss. 363. § 500.
Teed, Holland *v.*, 7 Hare, 50. § 118.
Teeters, Farmers' Bank *v.*, 31 Ohio St. 36. § 270.
Teevens, Commonwealth *v.*, 143 Mass. 210. § 505.
Telegraph Co., Doane *v.*, 11 La. Ann. 504. § 128.
Telford *v.* Telford, 31 Ill. App. 415. § 618.
Teller *v.* Bernheim, 3 Phila. (Pa.) 299. § 100.
Temple, Chollan *v.*, 39 Ark. 238. § 289.
Keate *v.*, 1 Bos. & Pul. 158. § 78.
Templeman, Long *v.*, 24 La. Ann. 564. § 144.
Templer, Scholefield *v.*, 4 De Gex & Jones, 429. § 148.
Temples, Treasurers *v.*, 2 Spear's Law (S. C.), 48. § 636.
Ten Eyck *v.* Brown, 3 Pinney (Wis.), 452. §§ 49, 138, 199.
v. Holmes, 3 Sandf. Ch. 428. § 325.
Tennant *v.* Orr, 15 Irish Com. Law, 397. § 126.
State *v.*, 30 La. Ann. 852. §§ 505, 508.
v. Tennant, 110 Pa. St. 478. § 144.
Tennell *v.* Jefferson, 5 Harr. (Del.) 206. § 247.
Tennessee Hospital *v.* Fuqua, 1 Lea (Tenn.), 608. § 577.
Tenney *v.* Prince, 4 Pick. 385. §§ 13, 82, 182.
Tennison *v.* Tennison, 114 Ind. 424. § 35.
Tenth National Bank *v.* Darragh, 1 Hun (N. Y.), 111. § 624.
Terrell *v.* Smith, 8 Conn. 426. § 433.
Territory, Ainsworth *v.*, 3 Wash. Terr. 270. §§ 509, 519.
Beall *v.*, 1 N. M. 507. § 578.
v. Carson, 7 Mont. 417. § 548.
v. Ritter, 1 Wyom. 318. § 591.
Terry, Annett *v.*, 35 N. Y. 256. § 638.
Callaway County Savings Bank *v.*, 13 Mo. App. 99. §§ 97, 329.
Couch *v.*, 12 Ala. 225. § 289.
London & County Banking Co. *v.*, Law Rep. (25 Ch. Div.) 692. § 118.
v. Stukely, 3 Yerg. (Tenn.) 506. § 452.
Wing *v.*, 5 Hill, 160. § 185.
Tessier *v.* Crowley, 17 Neb. 207. §§ 8, 19.
Teutonia Nat. Bank *v.* Wagner, 33 La. Ann. 732. §§ 45, 561.
Tewksbury, Evoy *v.*, 5 Cal. 285. § 82.
Thalheimer *v.* Crow, 13 Col. 397. §§ 236, 464.
Tharp *v.* Parker, 86 Ind. 102. § 375.
Thatcher, Ordinary *v.*, 41 N. J. Law, 403. § 409.

Thayer *v.* Daniels, 110 Mass. 345. § 230.
Cates *v.*, 93 Ind. 156. § 344.
v. Hurlburt, 5 Iowa (Clarke), 521. § 491.
Jones *v.*, 12 Gray, 443. § 145.
v. King, 31 Hun (N. Y.), 437. §§ 240, 355.
v. Rock, 13 Wend. 53. § 52.
Therasson *v.* McSpedon, 2 Hilton (N. Y.), 1. § 65.
Thigpen *v.* Price, Phillips' Eq. (N. C.) 146. § 223.
Thim, State *v.*, 77 Ala. 100. § 11.
Third National Bank *v.* Owen, 101 Mo. 558. § 422.
Thomas, Allison *v.*, 29 La. Ann. 732. §§ 40, 342, 371.
Armstead *v.*, 9 Ala. 586. § 350.
Bank of Upper Canada *v.*, 11 Up. Can. (C. P.) 515. § 32.
v. Beckman, 1 B. Mon. (Ky.) 29. §§ 214, 631.
v. Blake, 126 Mass. 320. § 526.
v. Blake, 136 Mass. 568. § 527.
Brinson *v.*, 2 Jones' Eq. (N. C.) 414. § 317.
v. Browder, 33 Tex. 783. § 565.
v. Burrus, 23 Miss. 550. § 46.
Chappee *v.*, 5 Mich. 53. § 615.
v. Cole, 10 Heisk. (Tenn.) 411. § 449.
v. Connelly, 104 N. C. 342. §§ 531, 566.
v. Cook, 8 Barn. & Cress. 728. §§ 60, 72.
v. Croft, 2 Rich. Law (S. C.), 113. § 16.
v. Davis, 14 Pick. 353. §§ 190, 192.
v. Dodge, 8 Mich. 51. §§ 81, 98.
v. Dow, 33 Me. 390. § 342.
Fish *v.*, 5 Gray, 45. § 64.
Guild *v.*, 54 Ala. 414. §§ 402, 408, 642.
v. Hinkley, 19 Neb. 324. §§ 23, 517.
Hoggatt *v.*, 35 La. Ann. 298. § 60.
v. Hubbell, 15 N. Y. 405. § 630.
Thomas *v.* Irwin, 90 Ind. 557. § 486.
v. Jennings, 5 S. & M. (Miss.) 627. § 176.
v. Liebke, 81 Mo. 675. § 206.
v. Mann, 28 Pa. St. 520. § 240.
Martin *v.*, 24 How. 315. § 385.
Owen *v.*, 3 Myl. & Keen, 353. § 80.
Rivers *v.*, 1 B. J. Lea (Tenn.), 649. § 181.
Scott *v.*, 1 Scam. (Ill.) 58. § 64.
v. Sornberger, 24 Wend. 275. § 504.
v. State, 13 Tex. App. 496. § 175.
State *v.*, 38 Tenn. (4 Pickle), 491. § 591.
v. Stetson, 59 Me. 229. § 342.
v. Stewart, 117 Ind. 50. § 40.
v. Turscott, 53 Barb. (N. Y.) 200. § 405.
v. Welles, 1 Root (Conn.), 57. § 74.
v. Williams, 10 Barn. & Cres. 664. §§ 17, 52, 68.
v. Wright, 98 N. C. 272. § 104.
Thomas' Adm'x, Cox *v.*, 9 Gratt. (Va.) 312. §§ 38, 42.
Thomas' Ex'r *v.* Cleveland, 33 Mo. 126. § 436.
Thompson *v.* Adams, 1 Freeman's Ch. (Miss.) 225. §§ 268, 439.
Allen *v.*, 10 N. H. 32. § 65.
Bank of Gettysburg *v.*, 3 Grant's Cases (Pa.), 114. § 442.
Board of Education *v.*, 33 Ohio St. 321. §§ 3, 14.
v. Bond, 1 Camp. 4. § 73.
v. Bowne, 39 N. J. Law (10 Vroom), 2. §§ 242, 342.
v. Buckhannon, 2 J. J. Marsh. 416. §§ 12, 22.
Chouteau *v.*, 3 Ohio St. 424. § 218.
v. Coffman, 15 Oreg. 631. § 29.
Cordier *v.*, 8 Daly (N. Y. Com. Pl.), 172. § 200.
v. Dickerson, 22 Iowa, 360. § 546.
Glass *v.*, 9 B. Mon. (Ky.) 235. § 436.
Guardian F. & L. Ass. Co. *v.*, 68 Cal. 208. § 422.

Thompson, Hall *v.*, 9 Up. Can. (C. P.) 257. § 147.
v. Hall, 16 Ala. 204. § 82.
v. Hall, 45 Barb. (N. Y.) 214. § 405.
Johnson *v.*, 4 Watts (Pa.), 446. § 353.
Ketler *v.*, 13 Bush (Ky.), 287. § 256.
Lichtenthaler *v.*, 13 Serg. & Rawle (Pa.), 157. § 239.
v. Linscott, 2 Greenl. (Me.) 186. § 229.
Lobaugh *v.*, 74 Mo. 600. § 153.
v. Lockwood, 15 Johns. 256. § 504.
v. Luck, 3 Man., Gr. & Scott, 540. § 439.
v. Massie, 41 Ohio St. 307. § 378.
McCormick *v.*, 10 Neb. 484. § 563.
McCruner *v.*, 21 Iowa, 244. § 381.
Morgan *v.*, 60 Iowa, 280. § 344.
Osborne *v.*, 35 Minn. 229. § 18.
v. Perkins, 3 Mason, 232. § 71.
Riddle *v.*, 104 Pa. St. 330. § 373.
v. Roberts, 17 Irish Com. Law, 490. § 174.
v. Robinson, 34 Ark. 44. §§ 239, 344, 353.
v. Sanders, 4 Dev. & Bat. Law (N. C.), 404. § 265.
Seibert *v.*, 8 Kan. 65. §§ 268, 324.
Spencer *v.*, 6 Irish Com. Law, 537. § 434.
State *v.*, 49 Mo. 188. § 517.
State *v.*, 62 Ind. 367. §§ 503, 509.
v. Taylor, 11 Hun (N. Y.), 274. § 217.
v. Taylor, 12 R. I. 109. §§ 182, 208, 261.
Trench *v.*, 6 Vt. 54. § 65.
Union Bank *v.*, 8 Rob. (La.) 227. §§ 559, 560.
Walrath *v.*, 4 Hill, 200. § 86.
Walrath *v.*, 6 Hill, 540. § 397.
v. Watson, 10 Yerg. (Tenn.) 362. § 239.
Thompson, Welfare *v.*, 83 N. C. 276. § 29.
Willey *v.*, 9 Met. (Mass.) 329. § 365.
v. Wilson's Ex'r, 13 La. (Curry), 138. § 210.
v. Young, 2 Ohio, 335. § 171.
Thompson National Bank, Marsh *v.*, 2 Bradw. (Ill. App.) 217. § 19.
Thomson, De Beil *v.*, 3 Beav. 469. § 80.
v. MacGregor, 81 N. Y. 592. § 526.
v. Palmer, 3 Rich. Eq. (S. C.) 139. § 311.
v. Searcy, 6 Port. (Ala.) 393. § 578.
Thorn, Gasquet *v.*, 14 La. (Curry), 506. § 201.
Storm *v.*, 3 Barb. (N. Y.) 314. § 40.
Thornburgh *v.* Marden, 33 Iowa, 380. § 245.
Thorndike, Choate *v.*, 138 Mass. 371. § 586.
Thorne, Dunlap *v.*, 1 Rich. (S. C.) 213. § 64.
v. Travelers' Ins. Co., 80 Pa. St. 15. § 21.
Trimble *v.*, 16 Johns. 152. § 239.
Thorner *v.* Field, 1 Bulstr. 120. § 17.
Thornhill *v.* Christmas, 10 Rob. (La.) 543. § 504.
Thornton *v.* Dabney, 23 Miss. 559. § 344.
Hankins *v.*, 1 Yerg. (Tenn.) 146. § 452.
v. Jenyns, 1 Man. & Gr. 166. § 86.
Pratt *v.*, 28 Me. 355. § 252.
v. National Exchange Bank, 71 Mo. 221. § 324.
State *v.*, 8 Mo. App. 27. §§ 551, 630.
v. Thornton, 63 N. C. 211. §§ 233, 438.
Tutt *v.*, 57 Tex. 35. § 208.
Weaver *v.*, 63 Ga. 655. § 631.
Thrall *v.* Benedict, 13 Vt. 248. § 114.

Thrasher v. Ely, 2 Smedes & Marsh. (Miss.) 139. § 199.
Hayden v., 18 Fla. 795. §§ 264, 275.
Thurber v. Corbin, 51 Barb. (N. Y.) 215. § 36.
Thurman v. Morgan, 79 Va. 367. § 592.
Thurston v. James, 6 R. I. 103. § 367.
v. Prentiss, 1 Manning (Mich.), 193. § 221.
Thwaits v. Curl, 6 B. Mon. (Ky.) 472. § 77.
Tickridge, Duncombe v., Aleyn, 94. § 58.
Tidball, Dinsmore v., 34 Ohio St. 411. § 424.
Tiddy v. Harris, 101 N. C. 589. § 312.
Tiederman, State v., 10 Fed. Rep. 20. § 630.
Tieman v. Haw, 49 Iowa, 312. §§ 566, 591.
State v., 39 Iowa, 474. § 501.
Tiffany v. Crawford, 1 McCarter (N. J.), 278. § 405.
v. Willis, 30 Hun (N. Y.), 266. § 101.
Tifft, Harding v., 75 N. Y. 461. § 330.
Tighee v. Morrison, 116 N. Y. 263. § 60.
Tilleston v. Nettleton, 6 Pick. 509. §§ 75, 78.
Tillman v. Wheeler, 17 Johns. 326. § 179.
Tillotson v. Rose, 11 Met. (Mass.) 299. § 205.
United States v., 1 Paine, 305. § 378.
Tillson v. State, 29 Kan. 452. §§ 151, 508.
Tilman, Whitworth v., 40 Miss. 76. § 217.
Timberlake, Furman v., 93 N. C. 66. § 589.
Scott v., 83 N. C. 382. § 253.
Timmier v. Trail, 2 Bailey Law (S. C.), 480. § 586.
Timmons, Reynolds v., 7 Rich. (S. C.) 486. § 585.
Tincher, Jones v., 15 Ind. 308. § 97.
Tinkler, Mozley v., 1 Cromp., Mees. & Ros. 692. § 189.
v. McCauley, 3 Mich. 188. § 49.
Tinkum v. Duncan, 1 Grant's Cas. (Pa.) 228. § 100.
Tinley, Molsom Bank v., 8 Ont. (Can.) 293. § 401.
Tinsley v. Kirby, 17 S. C. 1. §§ 21, 22, 42, 46.
v. Oliver's Adm'r, 5 Munf. (Va.) 419. § 313.
Tipton v. Carrigan, 10 Bradw. (Ill. App.) 318. § 448.
Delaney v., 3 Hayw. (Tenn.) 14. § 223.
Williams v., 5 Humph. (Tenn.) 66. §§ 226, 306.
Tischler v. Hofheimer, 83 Va. 35. § 161.
Tisinger, Garver v., 46 Ohio St. 56. § 593.
Titcomb v. McAllister, 77 Me. 353. § 274.
Tittle, Cramer v., 72 Cal. 12. § 9.
Titus v. Durkee, 12 Up. Can. (C. P.) 367. § 399.
v. Fairchild, 17 J. & S. (N. Y. Super. Ct.) 211. § 592.
Titzer, Boyd v., 6 Cold. (Tenn.) 568. § 606.
Tjader, Van Doren v., 1 Nev. 380. § 88.
Tobey, Todd v., 29 Me. 219. § 63.
Tobias v. Rogers, 13 N. Y. 59. § 276.
Todd, Bourne v., 63 Me. 427. § 580.
Chapman v., 60 Me. 282. § 439.
v. Greenwood School Dist., 40 Mich. 294. § 342.
McCracken v., 1 Kan. 148. §§ 517, 520.
v. Perry, 20 Up. Can. (Q. B.) 649. § 523.
Raikes v., 1 Perry & Dav. 138. § 85.
Raikes v., 8 Adol. & Ell. 846. § 82.
v. Sparks, 10 La. Ann. 668. § 585.
v. Tobey, 29 Me. 219. § 63.
Wilcox v., 64 Mo. 388. § 35.

Toland *v.* Swearingen, 39 Tex. 447. § 483.
Tompkins *v.*, 46 Tex. 584. § 468.
Toles *v.* Adee, 84 N. Y. 222. § 493.
v. Adee, 91 N. Y. 562. §§ 99, 519.
Tolhurst *v.* Brickinden, Cro. Jac. 250. § 16.
Tolle, Ex'x, *v.* Boeckeler, 12 Mo. App. 54. §§ 268, 324.
Tolleson, Foster *v.*, 13 Rich. 31. § 201.
Tombeckbee Bank, McGrew *v.*, 5 Port. (Ala.) 547. § 243.
Tomer, State *v.*, 7 Rich. Law (S. C.), 216. § 521.
Tomlins, Lord Bolton *v.*, 5 Adol. & Ell. 856. § 52.
Tomlinson, Gansen *v.*, 8 C. E. Green (N. J.), 405. § 125.
v. Gill, Amb. 330. § 57.
v. Gell, 6 Ad. & Ell. 564. §§ 17, 64.
v. Simpson, 33 Minn. 443. § 93.
Tomlinson Bros., Adams & French Harvesting Co. *v.*, 58 Iowa, 129. § 102.
Fuller *v.*, 58 Iowa, 111. § 446.
Tompkins, People *v.*, 74 Ill. 482. § 548.
v. Toland, 46 Tex. 584. § 468.
Toms, Commonwealth *v.*, 45 Pa. St. 408. § 170.
Toomer *v.* Dawson, Cheves (S. C.), 68. § 80.
v. Dickerson, 37 Ga. 428. § 445.
Toomey, People *v.*, 122 Ill. 308. §§ 93, 532, 551.
Tooth, Dutchman *v.*, 5 Bing. N. C. 211. § 84.
Toothaker, Springer *v.*, 43 Me. 381. §§ 243, 434.
Tootle *v.* Elgutter, 14 Neb. 158. § 160.
Topliff, Moore *v.*, 107 Ill. 241. §§ 36, 223, 329.
Toplis *v.* Grane, 5 Bing. N. C. 636. § 60.
Torney, Ledbetter *v.*, 11 Ired. Law (N. C.), 294. § 208.
Torp *v.* Gulseth, 37 Minn. 135. § 329.
Torrance, Gillespie *v.*, 25 N. Y. 306. § 236.
Torrence *v.* Alexander, 85 N. C. 143. § 33.
Torrey, Bone *v.*, 16 Ark. 83. §§ 211, 633.
Toulmin, Davis *v.*, 77 N. Y. 280. §§ 236, 281.
Tourns *v.* Riddle, 2 Ala. 694. § 439.
Tousey *v.* Bishop, 22 Iowa, 178. § 362.
Toussaint *v.* Martinnant, 2 Durn. & East, 100. § 205.
Tower, County of Redwood *v.*, 28 Minn. 45. §§ 542, 589.
Fay *v.*, 58 Wis. 286. §§ 347, 349, 356.
Towle, McLean *v.*, 3 Sandf. Ch. 117. § 315.
v. National Guardian Assurance Society, 3 Giff. 42. § 404.
v. Towle, 46 N. H. 431. § 640.
Towles, Atwell's Adm'r *v.*, 1 Munf. (Va.) 175. § 137.
Town, Robertson *v.*, 76 Tex. 535. § 577.
Town of Askum *v.* Lake, 12 Bradw. (Ill. App.) 25. §§ 409, 517.
Town of Barnet *v.* Abbott, 53 Vt. 120. §§ 596, 644.
Town of Metamora, Morley *v.*, 78 Ill. 394. §§ 546, 628.
Town of Monticello, Wilson *v.*, 85 Ind. 10. § 124.
Town of Union *v.* Bermes, 44 N. J. Law, 269. § 628.
Town of Weston *v.* Sprague, 54 Vt. 395. § 521.
Towne *v.* Ammidown, 20 Pick. 535. § 139.
v. Grover, 9 Pick. 306. § 74.
Steele *v.*, 28 Vt. 771. § 76.
Towns, Brayton *v.*, 12 Iowa, 346. § 570.
v. Farrar, 2 Hawks (N. C.), 163. § 101.
Prince *v.* (Cir. Ct. D. S. C.), 33 Fed. Rep. 161. § 578.
Townsend, Dykers *v.*, 24 N. Y. 57. § 90.
v. Everett, 4 Ala. 607. §§ 545, 628.

Townsend, Singleton v., 45 Mo. 379. § 295.
Smith v., 25 N. Y. 479. § 35.
v. State, 7 Tex. App. 74. § 515.
v. Whitney, 75 N. Y. 425. § 311.
Williams v., 1 Bosw. (N. Y.) 411. § 367.
Townsend National Bank v. Jones, 151 Mass. 454. § 465.
Township Board of Sparta, Post v., 63 Mich. 323. § 10.
Townsley v. Sumrall, 2 Pet. 170, 182. §§ 60, 67.
Trabue, Crutcher v., 5 Dana (Ky.), 80. §§ 235, 347.
Tracey, Overton v., 14 Serg. & Rawle (Pa.), 311. § 202.
Tracy v. Goodwin, 5 Allen, 409. § 636.
v. Quillen, 65 Ind. 249. §§ 344, 377.
Traders' National Bank v. Clare, 76 Tex. 47. § 38.
Trail, Timmier v., 2 Bailey, Law (S. C.), 480. § 586.
Trammel v. Trammel, 15 Tex. 291. § 461.
Trammell v. Swan, 25 Tex. 473. § 416.
Traphagen, State v., 45 N. J. 134. § 497.
Trapp, Summerhill v., 48 Ala. 363. § 434.
Trask, Duvall v., 12 Mass. 154. § 81.
v. Mills, 7 Cush. 552. § 131.
Tratt, Darnell v., 2 Car. & P. 82. § 58.
Traube, Home Savings Bank v., 6 Mo. App. 221. § 421.
Home Savings Bank v., 75 Mo. 199. §§ 174, 394.
Travelers' Ins. Co., Thorne v., 80 I a. St. 15. § 20.
Traver, Eddy v., 6 Paige's Ch. 521. §§ 302, 310.
Travis v. Travis, 48 Hun, 343. § 9.
Trayer & Noble, Fusz & Backner v., 39 La. Ann. 292. § 471.
Treadway, People v., 17 Mich. 480. § 530.
Treasurers v. Bates, 2 Bailey, Law (S. C.), 362. §§ 519, 624.
v. Hilliard, 8 Rich. Law (S. C.), 412. §§ 535, 567.
v. Johnson, 4 McCord, Law (S. C.), 458. § 433.
v. Lang, 2 Bailey, (Law (S. C.), 430. § 172.
v. Sureties of Oswald, 2 Bailey, Law (S. C.), 224. § 569.
v. Taylor, 2 Bailey, Law (S. C.), 524. § 541.
v. Temples, 2 Spear's Law (S. C.), 48. § 636.
Treasurers of Franklin Co. v. McElvain, 5 Ohio, 200. § 578.
Treasurers of Pickaway v. Hall, 3 Ohio, 225. § 578.
Treat v. Smith, 54 Me. 112. § 345.
Trecothick, Coles v., 9 Vesey, 234. §§ 80, 89, 90.
Trefethen v. Locke, 16 La. Ann. 19. § 204.
Treleavan, Kennaway v., 5 Mees. & Wels. 498. § 84.
Tremper v. Hemphill, 8 Leigh (Va.), 623. § 417.
Trenholm, Sourdin v., 25 S. C. 362. §§ 254, 259.
Trent v. Rhomberg, 66 Tex. 249. § 464.
Trent Navigation Co. v. Harley, 10 East, 34. § 447.
Trentman v. Eldridge, 98 Ind. 525. § 35.
v. Fletcher, 100 Ind. 105. § 405.
Trepagnier, Saulet v., 2 La. Ann. 427. § 443.
Trice v. Tunentine, 5 Ired. Law (N. C.), 236. § 515.
Tricket v. Mandlee, Sid. 45. § 16.
Trigg's Adm'r, Findlay v., 83 Va. 539. § 583.
Robertson v., 32 Gratt. (Va.) 76. §§ 595, 628.
Trimble v. Thorne, 16 Johns. 152. § 239.
Triplett v. Goff's Adm'r, 83 Va. 784. § 644.

Trippet, Jerauld *v.*, 62 Ind. 122. §§ 242, 434.
Trotter *v.* Crockett, 2 Port. (Ala.) 401. § 440.
v. Strong, 63 Ill. 272. §§ 40, 146.
Trousdale *v.* Philips, 2 Swan (Tenn.), 384. § 627.
Trout, Ratliff *v.*, 6 J. J. Marsh. 606. § 82.
Troutman, Singer *v.*, 49 Barb. (N. Y.) 182. § 240.
Trowbridge *v.* Wetherbee, 11 Allen, 361. § 52.
Troy *v.* Smith, 33 Ala. 469. § 324.
Truckee Lodge *v.* Wood, 14 Nev. 293. § 397.
True, Jenness *v.*, 30 Me. 438. § 138.
Seibert *v.*, 8 Kan. 52. § 324.
Truesdell *v.* Hunter, 28 Ill. App. 292. §§ 355, 400.
Price *v.*, 28 N. J. Eq. (1 Stew.) 200. § 69.
United States *v.*, 2 Bond, 78. § 173.
Wakefield Bank *v.*, 55 Barb. (N. Y.) 602. § 352.
Trumbo, Jordan *v.*, 6 Gill & Johns. (Md.) 103. § 342.
Trussell, Berrell *v.*, 4 Taunt. 117. §§ 13, 65, 82.
Trust & Deposit Co. *v.* Pratt, 25 Hun (N. Y.), 23. § 579.
Trust Co. *v.* National Bank, 101 N. J. 68. § 179.
Trustees, Coffin *v.*, 92 Ind. 337. § 16.
v. Southard, 31 Ill. App. 359. §§ 29, 242.
Tyler *v.*, 14 Oreg. 485. § 137.
Trustees, etc., Kagy *v.*, 68 Ill. 75. § 546.
Trustees of Athenæum, Foster *v.*, 3 Ala. 302. § 313.
Trustees of Free Schools *v.* Flint, 13 Met. (Mass.) 539. § 68.
Trustees of Schools *v.* Otis, 85 Ill. 179. § 141.
Baird *v.*, 106 Ill. 657. § 597.
Cassady *v.*, 105 Ill. 561. §§ 112, 589, 597, 628.
Trustees of Schools, House *v.*, 83 Ill. 368. § 448.
McIntyre *v.*, 3 Bradw. (Ill. App.) 77. § 526.
v. Sheik, 119 Ill. 579. §§ 152, 206, 517.
v. Smith, 88 Ill. 181. § 546.
Trustees Section Sixteen *v.* Miller, 3 Ohio, 261. § 250.
Trustees United Brethren *v.* Rausch, 122 Ind. 167. § 601.
Tucker *v.* Blandin, 48 Hun (N. Y.), 439. § 116.
v. Davis, 15 Ga. 573. § 504.
Graves *v.*, 10 Sm. & Mar. (Miss.) 9. §§ 406, 408.
v. Laing, 2 Kay & Johns. 745. §§ 246, 342.
v. State, 11 Md. 322. § 46.
v. State, 72 Ind. 242. §§ 12, 520.
Stevens *v.*, 73 Ind. 73. § 284.
Stevens *v.*, 87 Ind. 109. 256.
v. Talbott, 15 Ind. 114. § 405.
Wayland *v.*, 4 Gratt. (Va.) 267. §§ 243, 281, 294.
v. White, 5 Allen, 322. § 470.
Tuckerman *v.* French, 7 Greenl. (Me.) 115. § 186.
Kennebec Bank *v.*, 5 Greenl. (Me.) 130. §§ 342, 352.
Tudor *v.* Goodloe, 1 B. Mon. 322. § 356.
Tufts, Bunker *v.*, 55 Me. 180. § 209.
v. Plymouth Gold Mining Co., 14 Allen, 407. § 80.
Tunentine, Trice *v.*, 5 Ired. Law (N. C.), 236. § 515.
Tunis, Miller *v.*, 10 Up. Can. (C. P.) 423. § 151.
Tunnell *v.* Burton, 4 Del. Ch. 382. § 580.
Tunnicliff, Wood *v.*, 74 N. Y. 38. § 15.
Tunstead *v.* Nixdorf, 80 Cal. 647. § 599.
Turbeville, Harrison *v.*, 2 Humph. (Tenn.) 242. § 386.
Tureman, Ashby *v.*, 3 Littell (Ky.), 6. § 475.
Turk, Crawford *v.*, 24 Gratt. (Va.) 176. § 637.

Turley v. Hodge, 3 Humph. (Tenn.) 73. §§ 49, 183.
Molson's Bank v., 8 Ont. (Can.) 293. § 249.
Turman v. Looper, 42 Ark. 500. § 215.
Turnbull v. Brock, 31 Ohio St. 649. § 353.
Turner, Aldridge v., 1 Gill & Johns. (Md.) 427. §§ 13, 82.
Bovill v., 2 Chitty, 205. § 165.
v. Davies, 2 Esp. 478. § 264.
Dickerson v., 15 Ind. 4. § 185.
Ferguson v., 7 Mo. 497. § 438.
Griffith v., 4 Gill (Md.), 111. § 626.
Hubert v., 4 Scott (N. R.), 486. § 89.
v. Hubbell, 2 Day (Conn.), 457. § 54.
Jones v., 5 Litt. (Ky.) 147. § 145.
Kennebec Bank v., 2 Greenleaf (Me.), 42. § 30.
Kirby v., 6 Johns. Ch. 242. §§ 147, 573.
McCarter v., 49 Ga. 309. §§ 29, 608.
v. Miller, 28 Kan. 44. § 618.
Mitchell v., 37 Ala. 660. § 281.
v. Sisson, 137 Mass. 191. § 566.
State v., 49 Ark. 311. § 490.
v. Teague, 73 Ala. 554. §§ 310, 320.
v. Williams, 73 Me. 466. § 342.
Turner, Frazer & Co. v. Killian, 12 Neb. 580. § 566.
Turney v. Penn, 16 Ill. 485. § 137.
Turnour, Morrison v., 18 Vesey, 175. § 89.
Turnure v. Hohenthal, 4 Jones & Spencer (N. Y.), 79. § 201.
Turrell v. Boynton, 23 Vt. 142. §§ 356, 359.
Carpenter v., 100 Mass. 450. § 472.
Turscott, Thomas v., 53 Barb. (N. Y.) 200. § 405.
Turton v. Burke, 4 Wis. 119. § 77.
Tuska v. Eisner, 21 J. & S. (N. Y. Super. Ct.) 442. § 377.
Tuthill, Hoyt v., 33 Hun (N. Y.), 196. § 439.
Tutt v. Thornton, 57 Tex. 35. § 208.
Tuttle, Chrisman v., 59 Ind. 155. §§ 241, 354, 609.
v. Northrop, 44 Ohio St. 178. § 577.
Tutwiler, Steele v., 57 Ala. 113. § 45.
Tuxbury's Appeal, 67 Me. 267. § 577.
Twigg v. Augusta Savings Bank, 26 S. C. 612. § 437.
Twitty v. Houser, 17 S. C. 1. § 558.
v. Houser, 7 Rich. (S. C.) 153. § 585.
Twopenny v. Young, 3 Barn. & Cress. 208. § 367.
Twynam, Coope v., 1 Turner & Russ. 426. § 259.
Tyler, Bing v., 79 Ill. 249. § 126.
Curtis v., 9 Paige's Ch. 432. § 324.
v. Davis, 63 Miss. 345. § 487.
v. Trustees, 14 Oreg. 485. § 137.
v. Waddingham, 58 Conn. 375. §§ 25, 193.
Tynt v. Tynt, 2 Peere Wms. 542. § 97.
Tyree v. Parham's Ex'r, 66 Ala. 424. § 226.
v. Wilson, 9 Gratt. (Va.) 59. § 537.
Tyson v. Passmore, 2 Pa. St. 122. § 405.
Reno v., 24 Ind. 56. § 581.
Tyus v. De Jarnette, 26 Ala. 280. §§ 269, 301.
Uhler v. Applegate, 26 Pa. St. 140. §§ 353, 355.
v. Farmers' National Bank, 64 Pa. St. 406. § 17.
v. Semple, 5 C. E. Green (N. J.), 288. § 218.
Ulen v. Kittridge, 7 Mass. 233. § 90.
Underhill v. Palmer, 10 Daly (N. Y. Com. Pl.), 478. § 426.
Underwood v. Campbell, 14 N. H. 393. § 82.
v. Hossack, 38 Ill. 208. §§ 15, 16, 176.

Underwood *v.* Sample, 70 Ind. 446. § 648.
Vartie *v.*, 18 Barb. (N. Y.) 561. § 35.
Unger, Wofford *v.*, 55 Tex. 480. § 143.
Union Bank *v.* Beatty, 10 La. Ann. 378. § 413.
v. Beech, 3 Hurl. & Colt. 672. § 147.
v. Clossey, 10 Johns. 271. § 560.
v. Coster's Ex'r, 3 N. Y. 203. §§ 81, 87, 196, 202.
v. Forstall, 6 La. (Curry), 211. § 423.
v. Goran, 10 Sm. & Mar. (Miss.) 333. §§ 34, 370, 434.
Gustine *v.*, 10 Rob. (La.) 412. §§ 372, 376.
v. McClung, 9 Humph. (Tenn.) 98. §§ 351, 352.
Oberndorff *v.*, 31 Md. 126. § 332.
v. Thompson, 8 Rob. (La.) 227. §§ 559, 560.
Union & Am. Pub. Co., Beard *v.*, 71 Ala. 69. § 236.
Union City Bank, Garton *v.*, 34 Mich. 279. § 351.
Union Mutual Life Ins. Co. *v.* Hanford, 27 Fed. Rep. 588. § 37.
Union Nat. Bank *v.* First Nat. Bank, 45 Ohio St. 236. § 106.
Union Pacific R'y Co., Harrison *v.* (Cir. Ct. E. D. Mo.), 13 Fed. Rep. 522. § 18.
Union Society *v.* Mitchell, 26 Mo. App. 206. §§ 168, 537.
Union Steamboat Co., Green Bay & Minn. R. R. Co. *v.*, 107 U. S. 98. § 6.
United States *v.* Adams (Cir. Ct. D. Oreg.), 24 Fed. Rep. 348. § 558.
v. Allsburg, 4 Wall. 186. § 127.
v. Ambrose, 2 Fed. Rep. 552. § 519.
v. Ambrose, 7 Fed. Rep. 554. § 510.
v. Archer's Ex'r, 1 Wall. Jr. 173. § 139.
United States, Armstrong *v.*, Peters' Cir. Ct. 46. § 519.
v. Boeckner, 21 Wall. 652. § 396.
Boody *v.*, 1 Woodb. & M. 150. § 548.
v. Boyd, 5 How. 29. § 628.
v. Boyd, 15 Pet. 187. § 526.
Boyden *v.*, 13 Wall. 17. § 558.
v. Broadhead, 127 U. S. 212. § 112.
Broome *v.*, 15 How. 143. § 527.
Bruce *v.*, 17 How. 437. §§ 43, 546.
v. Buckland (Cir. Ct. D. S. C.), 33 Fed. Rep. 156. § 502.
Burroughs *v.*, 2 Paine, 569. § 324.
Butler *v.*, 21 Wall. 274. § 408.
Chadwick *v.* (Cir. Ct. D. Mass.), 3 Fed. Rep. 750. §§ 548, 595.
v. Cheeseman, 3 Saw. 424. § 170.
v. Cochran, 2 Brock. 274. § 337.
v. Corwine, 1 Bond, 339. § 399.
v. Cranston, 3 Cranch, 289. § 565.
v. Curtis, 100 U. S. 119. § 112.
v. Cushman, 2 Sumn. 426. § 139.
v. Cutter, 2 Curtis, 617. §§ 556, 627.
Dair *v.*, 16 Wall. 1. § 408.
v. Dashiel, 4 Wall. 182. § 558.
Dumont *v.*, 98 U. S. 142. § 623.
v. Eckford's Ex'rs, 1 How. 250. § 338.
v. Eldredge, 5 Utah, 161. §§ 508, 510, 516.
v. Evans, 2 Fed. Rep. 147. § 509.
Farrar *v.*, 5 Pet. 373. § 526.
Findlay's Ex'rs *v.*, 2 McL. 44. § 40.
v. Gaussen, Ex'r, 2 Woods, 92. § 548.
v. Goldstein's Sureties, 1 Dillon, 413. § 508.
v. Hammond, 4 Biss. 283. § 402.
Hart *v.*, 95 U. S. 316. §§ 555, 556.
v. Hough, 103 U. S. 71. § 595.
v. Howell, 4 Wash. 620. § 360.
Hunt *v.*, 1 Gall. 32. §§ 433, 555.
Hunter *v.*, 5 Pet. 173. § 433.
v. Jameson (Cir. Ct. D. Neb.), 16 Fed. Rep. 331. § 595.

United States v. Jones, 8 Pet. 399. § 416.
v. Jones (Cir. Ct. W. D. La.), 36 Fed. Rep. 759. § 558.
v. Keehler, 9 Wall. 83. § 558.
v. Kershner, 1 Bond, 432. § 338.
King v., 99 U. S. 229. § 595.
v. Kirkpatrick, 9 Wheat. 720. § 555.
v. Le Baron, 19 How. 73. § 527.
v. Linn, 2 McLean, 501. § 338.
v. Marks' Sureties, 3 Wall. Jr. 358. § 617.
v. Mason, 2 Bond, 183. § 520.
v. Maurice, 2 Brock. 96. § 521.
Minturn v., 106 U. S. 437. § 555.
v. Morgan, 11 How. 154. § 558.
v. Morgan (Dist. Ct. S. D. N. Y.), 28 Fed. Rep. 48. § 529.
Myers v., 1 McLean, 493. §§ 338, 526.
v. Mynderse, 11 Blatchf. 1. § 519.
v. Nicholl, 12 Wheat. 505. § 556.
v. O'Neill, 19 Fed. Rep. 567. § 385.
Osborne v., 19 Wall. 577. § 556.
Pawling v., 4 Cranch, 219. § 411.
Potter v., 107 U. S. 126. § 595.
v. Poulson (Dist. Ct. E. Dist. Pa.), 30 Fed. Rep. 231. § 112.
v. Prescott, 3 How. 578. § 558.
Ralph v., 9 Fed. Rep. 693 (Cir. Ct. N. D. Ill.). § 10.
v. Rogers (Dist. Ct. S. D. N. Y.), 28 Fed. Rep. 607. § 520.
v. Ryder, 110 U. S. 729. §§ 320, 513, 621.
v. Saylor (Cir. Ct. E. D. Mich.), 31 Fed. Rep. 543. § 595.
Sharp v., 4 Watts (Pa.), 21. §§ 411, 517.
v. Shoup, 21 Pac. Rep. 656. § 23.
v. Simpson, 3 Pen. & Watts (Pa.), 437. § 342.
Smith v., 2 Wall. (U. S.) 219. § 385.
Soule v., 100 U. S. 8. §§ 12, 597.
v. Spencer, 2 McLean, 405. § 526.
v. Stansbury, 1 Pet. 573. § 433.
v. Stevens, 16 Fed. Rep. 101. § 621.
United States v. Stone, 106 U. S. 525 § 595.
v. Sturges, 1 Paine, 525. § 433.
v. Tillotson, 1 Paine, 305. § 378.
v. Truesdell, 2 Bond, 78. § 173.
v. Wardell, 5 Mason, 82. § 540.
v. Watts, 1 New Mex. 553. § 558.
v. White, 4 Wash. 414. § 528.
Williams v., 1 How. 290. § 628.
v. Winstead, 12 Fed. Rep. 50. § 516.
v. Woodman, 1 Utah, 265. § 396.
v. Wright, 1 McLean, 509. § 539.
v. Vanzandt, 11 Wheat. 184. § 556.
United States Bank, Long v., 1 Freeman, Ch. 375. § 467.
University of Cambridge v. Baldwin, 5 Mees. & Wels. 580. § 119.
Unselt, Wilson v., 12 Bush (Ky.), 215. § 583.
Upton, Lockridge v., 24 Mo. 184. § 605.
v. Vail, 6 Johns. 181. § 73.
Urmston v. State, 73 Ind. 175. §§ 169, 528.
Williams v., 35 Ohio St. 296. § 7.
Vachon, Gilbert v., 69 Ind. 372. § 25.
Vahle, German Ins. & Savings Inst. v., 28 Ill. App. 557. § 367.
Vaiden, Bobo v., 20 S. C. 271. § 581.
Susong v., 10 Rich. (S. C.) 247. § 139.
Vail v. Foster, 4 N. Y. 312. § 324.
Mix v., 86 Ill. 40. § 476.
Upton v., 6 Johns. 181. § 73.
Valentine v. Christie, 1 Rob. (La.) 298. § 26.
Fullam v., 11 Pick. 156. § 493.
Vallandingham, Knox v., 13 Smedes & Mar. (Miss.) 526. § 265.
Valle, Bean v., 2 Mo. 103. § 82.
Valloton v. Gardner, R. M. Charlt. (Ga.) 86. § 190.
Van Allen v. Atch., Col. & Pac. R. R. Co., 3 Fed. Rep. 545 (Cir. Ct. D. Kan.). § 10.
Van Arman, Goles' Adm'r v., 18 Ohio, 336. § 137.

Van Buren, Davis *v.*, 6 Daly (N. Y. Com. Pl.), 391. § 139.
Davis *v.*, 72 N. Y. 587. § 139.
Van Campen, Abbey *v.*, 1 Freem. Ch. (Miss.) 273. § 227.
Van Cortland, Parkhurst *v.*, 14 Johns. 15. § 80.
Van Derveer *v.* Wright, 6 Barb. (N. Y.) 547. §§ 94, 142.
Van Doren *v.* Jjader, 1 Nev. 380. §§ 88, 176.
Van Dusen, Jackson *v.*, 5 Johns. 144. § 89.
Sears *v.*, 25 Mich. 351. §§ 339, 340.
Taylor *v.*, 3 Gray, 498. § 97.
Van Epps *v.* Walsh, 1 Woods, 598. § 550.
Van Hoesen, Salisbury *v.*, 3 Hill (N. Y.), 77. § 574.
Van Hook, McCreary *v.*, 35 Tex. 631. § 17.
Van Houten, Osborne *v.*, 45 Mich. 444. § 399.
Van Lear, Dodge *v.*, 5 Cranch, C. C. 278. § 80.
Van Mierop, Pillans *v.*, 3 Burr. 1663. §§ 17, 67, 82.
Van Ness, People *v.*, 79 Cal. 84. §§ 25, 527, 588.
Van Nopper, Oakley *v.*, 100 N. C. 287. § 462.
Van Norden, Washburn *v.*, 28 La. Ann. 768. § 129.
Van Nostrand, Gardner *v.*, 13 Wis. 543. § 368.
Van Orden *v.* Durham, 35 Cal. 136. § 326.
Van Patton & Marks *v.* Beals & Hammer, 46 Iowa, 62. § 4.
Van Reimsdyck *v.* Kane, 1 Gall. C. C. 633. § 67.
Van Rensselaer, Hamilton *v.*, 43 Barb. (N. Y.) 117. § 111.
Hamilton *v.*, 43 N. Y. 244. § 130.
v. Kirkpatrick, 46 Barb. 194. § 355.
Livingstone *v.*, 6 Wend. 63. § 268.
Van Sickel *v.* Buffalo Co., 13 Neb. 103. §§ 546, 547, 628.
Van Slyck *v.* Bush, 123 N. Y. 47. § 593.
v. Pulver, Hill & Denio (Lalor's Sup.), 47. § 64.
Van Slyke, Farmers' Nat. Bank *v.*, 49 Hun (N. Y.), 7. § 419.
Van Valkenbergh *v.* Paterson, 47 N. J. Law, 146. § 590.
Van Volkenburgh, Woolley *v.*, 16 Kan. 20. § 126.
Van Voorhis, Bostwick *v.*, 91 N. Y. 353, 363, 364. §§ 136, 422.
Van Vorst's Adm'x, Morris Canal & Banking Co. *v.*, 1 Zab. (N. J.) 100. §§ 395, 425, 560.
Van Wagenen, Tappen *v.*, 3 Johns. 465. § 506.
Van Wart *v.* Carpenter, 24 Up. Can. (Q. B.) 320. §§ 116, 117.
Van Winkle *v.* Johnson, 11 Oreg. 469. §§ 254, 283.
Van Wyck, Smith *v.*, 40 Mo. App. 522. § 165.
Vananda, State *v.*, 7 Blackf. (Ind.) 214. § 570.
Vance *v.* English, 78 Ind. 80. §§ 442, 445, 446.
v. Lancaster, 3 Haywood (Tenn.), 130. § 213.
Suydam *v.*, 2 McLean, 99. §§ 368, 372.
Vancil *v.* Hagler, 27 Kan. 407. § 605.
Vanderberg, Dixon *v.*, 35 N. J. Eq. 47. § 139.
Vanderbergh *v.* Vanderbergh, Law Rep. 1 Exch. 316. § 81.
Vanderbilt *v.* Schreyer, 91 N. Y. 392. §§ 88, 99.
Vanderlyn, Elting *v.*, 4 Johns. 237. § 16.
Vanderverr *v.* Ware, 65 Ala. 606. §§ 311, 312.
Vandusen, Shaw *v.*, 5 Up. Can. (Q. B.) 353. § 118.
Vankoughnet *v.* Mills, 5 Grant's Ch. 653. § 371.
Vanmater, Shook *v.*, 22 Wis. 507. §§ 60, 64.
Vann, May *v.*, 15 Fla. 553. § 295.
v. Pipkin, 77 N. C. 408. § 570.

Vanpelt, Craig v., 3 J. J. Marsh. (Ky.) 489. § 52.
Vanzandt, United States v., 11 Wheat. 184. § 556.
Varnam v. Harris, 1 Hun (N. Y.), 451. § 36.
Varrell, Andrews v., 46 N. H. 17. § 236.
Vartie v. Underwood, 18 Barb. (N. Y.) 561. § 35.
Vary v. Norton, 6 Fed. Rep. (Cir. Ct. W. D. Mich. S. D.) 808. §§ 29, 344, 356.
Vason, Forrester v., 71 Ga. 50. § 574.
Vaughan v. Evans, 1 Hill's Eq. (S. C.) 414. § 546.
Vaughn, Higdon v., 58 Miss. 572. §§ 467, 632.
Johnson's Adm'rs v., 65 Ill. 425. § 274.
Veach v. Rice, 131 U. S. 293. § 573.
Veazie v. Carr, 3 Allen, 14. § 359.
v. Willis, 6 Gray, 90. § 412.
Vedder, Albany Dutch Church v., 14 Wend. 165. § 425.
Venables, Harris v., Law Rep. 7 Exch. 235. § 16.
Vernon, Pendexter v., 9 Humph. (Tenn.) 84. § 367.
Verratt v. McAulay, 50 Ont. (Can.) 313. § 572.
Verret v. Belanger, 6 La. Ann. 109. § 638.
v. Bonvillam, 32 La. Ann. 29. § 480.
Vert v. Voss, 74 Ind. 565. § 329.
Vicksburg Bank v. Little, 67 Miss. 159. § 599.
Victor Sewing Machine Co. v. Crockwell, 2 Utah Terr. 557. § 602.
v. Crockwell, 3 Utah Terr. 152. § 92.
Murphy v., 112 U. S. 688. § 204.
v. Scheffler, 61 Cal. 530. § 399.
Victoria Mutual Fire Ins. Co. v. Davidson, 3 Ont. (Can.) 378. § 629.
Viele v. Hoag, 24 Vt. 46. §§ 243, 244.
Vielie v. Osgood, 8 Barb. (N. Y.) 130. §§ 80, 89.
Vilas v. Jones, 10 Paige, Ch. 76. § 356.
v. Jones, 1 N. Y. 274. §§ 243, 357.
People v., 36 N. Y. 459. § 548.
Village of Gibson, Leonard v., 6 Bradw. (Ill. App.) 503. § 373.
Villars v. Palmer, 67 Ill. 204. § 448.
Vinal v. Richardson, 13 Allen, 521. §§ 17, 201.
Vineyard, Prather v., 4 Gilman (Ill.) 40. § 63.
Vinyard v. Barnes, 124 Ill. 346. § 93.
Virden v. Ellsworth, 15 Ind. 144. §§ 137, 201.
Vivian v. Otis, 24 Wis. 518. § 545.
Vogel v. Leichner, 102 Ind. 55. §§ 29, 35.
Voiles v. Green, 43 Ind. 374. § 380.
Volkenning, Jordan v., 72 N. Y. 300. § 476.
Poillon v., 11 Hun (N. Y.), 385. § 630.
Voltz v. Harris, 40 Ill. 155. §§ 201, 202.
Von Storch, Otis v., 15 R. I. 41. § 29.
Voorhees, Paine v., 26 Wis. 522. § 365.
Voorhies v. Atlee, 29 Iowa, 49. § 101.
Voris v. State, 47 Ind. 345. § 576.
Vose v. Florida R. R. Co., 50 N. Y. 369. § 415.
v. Whitney, 7 Mont. 393. § 571.
Voss v. German-American Bank, 83 Ill. 599. § 432.
Vert v., 74 Ind. 565. § 329.
Vredenbergh, Waddington v., 2 Johns. Cas. 227. § 36.
Vredenburgh, Leonard v., 8 Johns. 29. §§ 13, 15, 17, 69, 82.
v. Snyder, 6 Iowa (Clarke), 39. § 448.
Waddell, Phyfe v., 2 Edwards' Ch. 47. § 405.
Waddington, Tyler v., 58 Conn. 375. §§ 25, 193.
v. Vredenbergh, 2 Johns. Cas. 227. § 36.

Wade, Bainbridge *v.*, 16 Ad. & Ell. (N. S.) 89. §§ 82, 84, 86.
v. Coope, 2 Simons, 155. § 321.
Dunn *v.*, 23 Mo. 207. § 260.
v. Green, 3 Humph. (Tenn.) 547. § 215.
Phillips *v.*, 66 Ala. 53. § 145.
v. Staunton, 5 How. (Miss.) 631. § 366.
Tatton *v.*, 18 Com. B. 370. § 73.
Wade's Ex'r, Saffold *v.*, 61 Ala. 214. § 324.
Wadlington *v.* Gary, 7 Sm. & Mar. (Miss.) 522. §§ 342, 355.
Miller *v.*, 5 Rich. N. S. (S. C.) 342. § 431.
Wadsworth *v.* Allen, 8 Gratt. (Va.) 174. §§ 117, 194, 203.
v. Lyon, 93 N. Y. 201. § 34.
Morris *v.*, 17 Wend. 103. § 198.
Waful, Mosier *v.*, 56 Barb. (N. Y.) 80. § 100.
Wagenseller *v.* Prettyman, 7 Bradw. (Ill. App.) 192. § 283.
Waggaman, City of New Orleans *v.*, 31 La. Ann. 299. § 175.
Waggoner, Billington *v.*, 33 N. Y. 31. § 356.
Wagner, Mease *v.*, 1 McCord (S. C.), 395. § 58.
v. Romero, 3 N. M. 131. § 617.
Teutonia Nat. Bank *v.*, 33 La. Ann. 732. §§ 45, 561.
Wagnon *v.* Clay, 1 A. K. Marsh. (Ky.) 257. § 68.
Wain *v.* Warlters, 5 East, 10. §§ 82, 85.
Wainwright *v.* Straw, 15 Vt. 215. § 76.
Wait, Burtis, Adm'r, *v.*, 33 Kan. 478. § 150.
v. Wait, 28 Vt. 350. § 67.
Wakefield *v.* Greenhood, 29 Cal. 597. § 74.
v. McKinnell, 9 La. (Curry), 449. § 497.
Saunders *v.*, 4 Barn. & Ald. 595. §§ 13, 82.
Wright *v.*, 17 Vesey, 454. § 89.
Wakefield Bank *v.* Truesdell, 55 Barb. (N. Y.) 602. § 352.
Wakeman *v.* Gowdy, 10 Bosw. (N. Y.) 208. § 440.
v. Sutton, 2 Adol. & Ell. 78. § 91.
Walden, Carney *v.*, 16 B. Mon. (Ky.) 388. § 131.
Waldo, Riggs *v.*, 2 Cal. 485. § 177.
Waldrip *v.* Black, 74 Cal. 409. §§ 212, 310, 645.
Waldron *v.* Harrison, 2 Oreg. 87. § 502.
v. Young, 9 Heisk. (Tenn.) 777. § 381.
Walker *v.* Constable, 1 Bos. & Pul. 306. § 90.
v. Dicks, 80 N. C. 263. § 227.
v. Drew, 20 Fla. 908. § 603.
v. Goldsmith, 7 Oreg. 161. §§ 34, 415.
v. Hardman, 4 Clark & Fin. 258. § 127.
v. Lathrop, 6 Iowa (Clarke), 516. § 230.
Lysaght *v.*, 5 Bligh (N. R.), 84, 86. §§ 331, 627.
Martin *v.*, 12 Hun (N. Y.), 46. §§ 226, 322.
v. McKay, 2 Met. (Ky.) 294. § 226.
Ontario Bank *v.*, 1 Hill (N. Y.), 652. § 312.
Pendlebury *v.*, 4 Young & Coll. (Exch.) 424. §§ 259, 403.
v. Pierce, 21 Gratt. (Va.) 722. § 624.
v. Richards, 39 N. H. 259. §§ 76, 78, 91.
v. Sherman, 11 Met. (Mass.) 170. § 16.
v. Taylor, 6 Car. & P. 752. § 65.
Wharton *v.*, 6 Dow. & Ry. 288. § 66.
White *v.*, 31 Ill. 422. §§ 201, 243, 374, 386.
v. Williams, 88 N. C. 7. § 460.
Walker & Hubbard *v.* Commonwealth, 79 Ky. 292. § 505.
Walker's Ex'rs, Cochran *v.*, 82 Ky. 220. § 277.

Wall, Carpenter *v.*, 4 Dev. & Batt. (N. C.) 144. § 67.
v. Covington, 83 N. C. 144. § 590.
Swain *v.*, 1 Rep. Ch. 149. § 288.
Wallace, Bellume *v.*, 2 Rich. Law (S. C.), 80. § 247.
Glenn *v.*, 4 Strob. Eq. (S. C.) 149. § 542.
v. Goold, 91 Ill. 15. § 176.
Grier *v.*, 7 Rich. (S. C.) 182. § 45.
Griffin *v.*, 66 Ind. 410. § 27.
v. Holly, 13 Ga. 389. § 572.
v. Hudson, 37 Tex. 456. § 35.
v. Jewell, 21 Ohio St. 163. § 380.
v. Lark, 12 S. C. 576. § 176.
Ordinary *v.*, 2 Rich. Law (S. C.), 460. § 638.
v. Wilder, 13 Fed. Rep. 707. § 406.
Walla Walla Co. *v.* Ping, 1 Wash. Terr. (N. S.) 339. § 603.
Waller *v.* Campbell, 25 Ala. 544. § 282.
Coleman *v.*, 3 Younge & Jer. 212. § 416.
Doud *v.*, 48 Iowa, 634. § 175.
Ennis *v.*, 3 Blackf. (Ind.) 472. § 90.
McKenny's Ex'rs *v.*, 1 Leigh (Va.), 434. § 438.
Waller's Heirs, Moore *v.*, 1 A. K. Marsh. (Ky.) 488. § 150.
Wallis, Sargent *v.*, 67 Tex. 483. § 526.
Walmsley, Lawrence *v.*, 12 J. Scott (N. R.), 799. §§ 362, 403.
Weir Plow Co. *v.*, 110 Ind. 242. §§ 93, 95, 388.
Walrath *v.* Thompson, 4 Hill, 200. § 86.
v. Thompson, 6 Hill, 540. § 397.
Walsh *v.* Bailie, 10 Johns. 180. § 117.
Gardner *v.*, 5 Ellis & Black. 83. § 380.
Garvin *v.*, 54 Vt. 367. § 495.
Jeffree, Adm'r, *v.*, 14 Nev. 143. § 585.
v. People, 6 Bradw. (Ill. App.) 240. § 566.
Van Epps *v.*, 1 Woods, 598. § 550.
Walter *v.* Middleton, 68 N. Y. 605. § 572.
Walters *v.* Kraft, 23 S. C. 578. § 143.
v. Swallow, 6 Whart. (Pa.) 446. §§ 347, 352.
Walton, Anderson *v.*, 35 Ga. 202. § 224.
Clay *v.*, 9 Cal. 328. § 70.
v. Mascall, 13 Mees. & Wels. 452. §§ 199, 201.
Wandel, Supervisors of Richmond Co. *v.*, 6 Lans. (N. Y.) 33. §§ 534, 557.
Wangler, Mundorff *v.*, 12 J. & S. (N. Y. Super. Ct.) 495. § 140.
Wann *v.* People, 57 Ill. 202. §§ 554, 574.
Wannemacher, Lerned *v.*, 9 Allen, 412. §§ 80, 89.
Waples *v.* Derrickson, 1 Harr. (Del.) 134. § 505.
Ward, Armistead *v.*, 2 P. & H. (Va.) 504. §§ 356, 364.
Bramble *v.*, 40 Ohio St. 267. §§ 347, 377.
Cavender *v.*, 28 S. C. 470. § 23.
v. Churn, 18 Gratt. (Va.) 801. § 411.
v. Ely, 1 Dev. Law (N. C.), 372. § 105.
Fearn *v.*, 80 Ala. 344. § 311.
v. Hackett, 30 Minn. 150. §§ 380, 407.
Hayes *v.*, 4 Johns. Ch. 123. §§ 97, 237, 238.
v. Henry, 5 Conn. 595. § 210.
v. Johnson, 6 Munf. (Va.) 6. § 372.
Jones *v.*, 71 Wis. 152. § 349.
Lamonte *v.*, 36 Wis. 558. § 491.
McKecknie *v.*, 58 N. Y. 541. § 369.
v. Northern Bank of Kentucky, 14 B. Mon. (Ky.) 283. § 114.
Reynolds *v.*, 5 Wend. 501. § 354.
v. Stahl, 81 N. Y. 406. § 524.
Spear *v.*, 20 Cal. 659. § 35.
v. Stout, 32 Ill. 399. §§ 29, 33.
v. Wick Bros., 17 Ohio St. 159. § 344.
v. Wilson, 100 Ind. 52. § 197.

Ward's Appeal, 100 Pa. St. 289. § 318.
Wardell v. McConnell, 23 Neb. 152. § 623.
United States v., 5 Mason, 82. § 540.
Warden, Barringer v., 12 Cal. 311. § 66.
v. Ryan, 37 Mo. App. 466. § 388.
Wardens of St. Saviors Southwark v. Bostock, 5 Bos. & Pul. 175. § 168.
Warder, Bloom & Co. v., 13 Neb. 476. § 199.
Wardlaw v. Harrison, 11 Rich. Law (S. C.), 626. § 188.
Wardwell, Green v., 17 Ill. 278. § 521.
Ware v. Adams, 24 Me. 177. § 17.
Allis v., 28 Minn. 166. § 359.
Gresham v., 79 Ala. 192. § 237.
v. Stephenson, 10 Leigh (Va.), 155. § 75.
Vanderveer v., 65 Ala. 606. §§ 311, 312.
Warfel v. Frantz, 76 Pa. St. 88. § 411.
Warfield v. Brand's Adm'r, 13 Bush (Ky.), 77. 586.
Elder v., 7 Harr. & Johns. (Md.) 391. §§ 76, 77.
v. Ludewig, 9 Rob. (La.) 240. § 342.
Waring, Couch v., 9 Conn. 261. § 148.
Warlters, Wain v., 5 East, 10. §§ 82, 85.
Warner, Adm'rs of Pond v., 2 Vt. 532. §§ 221, 222.
v. Beardsley, 8 Wend. 104. § 239.
v. Campbell, 26 Ill. 283. § 352.
Harris v., 13 Wend. 400. § 259.
v. Morrison, 3 Allen, 566. §§ 258, 267.
v. Price, 3 Wend. 397. § 258.
Snell v., 63 Ill. 176. § 210.
Warnock, Lightbound v., 4 Ont. Rep. 187. § 81.
Warre v. Calvert, 2 Nev. & Per. 126. § 122.
Warren v. Barker, 2 Duvall (Ky.), 155. § 73.
v. Branch, 15 W. Va. 21, 26. § 419.
Warren v. Fant's Trustees, 79 Ky. 1. §§ 347, 382.
v. Gilmore, 11 Cush. 15. § 500.
Grand Rapids Savings Bank v., 52 Mich. 557. § 39.
v. Lord, 131 Mass. 560. § 469.
Rathbone v., 10 Johns. 587. § 493.
v. State, 11 Mo. 583. § 537.
Warring, Richards v., 4 Abb. Rep. Om. Cas. 47. § 179.
Warrington v. Furbor, 8 East, 242. §§ 208, 210.
Warwick v. State, 5 Ind. 350. § 576.
Washburn v. Van Norden, 28 La. Ann. 768. § 129.
Wheeler v., 24 Vt. 293. § 370.
Wood v., 2 Pick. 24. § 151.
Washer, Kohn Bros. v., 69 Tex. 67. § 8.
Washington, Champomier v., 2 La. Ann. 1013. § 464.
Washington Ice Co. v. Webster, 125 U. S. 426. §§ 45, 481.
Wasson v. Hodshire, 108 Ind. 26. § 426.
Waterbury v. Andrews, 67 Mich. 281. § 234.
Waterhouse, Fielding v., 8 J. & S. (N. Y. Super. Ct.) 424. §§ 271, 298, 426.
Waterman v. Clark, 76 Ill. 428. § 236.
Home National Bank v., 30 Ill. App. 535. §§ 34, 135.
v. Meigs, 4 Cush. 497. § 81.
Water-Power Co. v. Brown, 23 Kan. 676. § 205.
Waters v. Carroll, 9 Yerg. (Tenn.) 102. § 531.
Chambers v., 7 Cal. 390. § 486.
v. Creagh, 4 Stew. & Port. (Ala.) 410. § 245.
v. Riley, 2 Harris & Gill (Md.), 305. § 284.
Rogers v., 2 Gill & Johns. (Md.) 64. § 68.
v. Simpson, 2 Gilm. (Ill.) 570. § 371.
Watertown Fire Ins. Co. v. Simmons, 131 Mass. 85. §§ 423, 424, 425.

Waterville Bank v. Redington, 52 Me. 466. § 41.
Wathen v. Glass, 54 Miss. 382. § 526.
Watkins, Hempstead v., 6 Ark. (1 Eng.) 317. § 239.
Petefish, Skiles & Co. v., 124 Ill. 384. § 330.
v. Perkins, 1 Ld. Raym. 224. § 77.
State Bank v., 6 Ark. (1 Eng.) 123. § 243.
v. Worthington, 2 Bland's Ch. (Md.) 509. § 233.
Watlington, Goss v., 6 Moore, 355. § 629.
Watriss v. Pierce, 32 N. H. 560. §§ 38, 243, 387.
Watrous v. Chalker, 7 Conn. 224. § 52.
Watson v. Alcock, 4 De Gex, Macn. & Gor. 242. § 444.
v. Beabout, 18 Ind. 281. § 137.
Gardner v., 76 Tex. 25. §§ 156, 159.
Goodyear v., 14 Barb. (N. Y.) 481. § 311.
Hamilton v., 12 Cl. & Finn. 109. § 419.
v. Hurt, 6 Gratt. (Va.) 633. § 176.
v. Jacobs, 29 Vt. 169. § 62.
Luding v., 3 Oreg. 256. § 17.
Mills v., 1 Sweeney (N. Y.), 374. § 37.
Penoyer v., 16 Johns. 100. § 117.
v. Poague, 42 Iowa, 582. § 334.
v. Randall, 20 Wend. 201. § 62.
v. Read, 1 Cooper's Ch. (Tenn.) 196. § 434.
v. Rose's Ex'rs, 51 Ala. 292. § 326.
Rubey v., 22 Mo. App. 428. § 329.
San Roman v., 54 Tex. 254. § 27.
Sanders v., 14 Ala. 198. § 322.
Screws v., 48 Ala. 628. § 490.
State v., 38 Ark. 96. § 531.
v. Sutherland, 1 Cooper, Ch. (Tenn.) 208. § 237.
Thompson v., 10 Yerg. (Tenn.) 362. § 239.
v. Whitten, 3 Rich. Law (S. C.), 224. § 585.
Watson, York Co. v., 15 S. C. 1. § 558.
Watson's Ex'rs, McLaren v., 26 Wend. 425. § 47.
Watt, Canada Agricultural Ins. Co. v., 30 Up. Can. (C. P.) 350. § 392.
Wright v., 52 Miss. 634. § 434.
Watts, Burch v., 37 Tex. 135. § 473.
v. Colquitt, 66 Ga. 492. § 637.
v. Eufaula Nat. Bank, 76 Ala. 474. §§ 298, 299, 301.
v. Pettit, 1 Bush (Ky.), 154. § 540.
Reid v., 4 J. J. Marsh. (Ky.) 440. § 342.
v. Shuttleworth, 5 Hurl. & Nor. 235. § 405.
v. Shuttleworth, 7 Hurl. & Nor. 353. §§ 429, 443.
United States v., 1 New Mex. 553. § 558.
Way v. Lewis, 115 Mass. 26. § 632.
v. Hearn, 11 J. Scott (N. S.), 774. § 350.
v. Wright, 5 Met. (Mass.) 380. § 499.
Wayland v. Tucker, 4 Gratt. (Va.) 267. §§ 243, 281, 294.
Wayman, Dorsey v., 6 Gill (Md.), 59. § 448.
State v., 2 Gill & Johns. (Md.) 254. §§ 112, 169.
Waymire v. State, 80 Ind. 67. § 569.
Wayne v. Commercial Nat. Bank, 52 Pa. St. 343. §§ 124, 422.
v. Kirby, 2 Bailey, Law (S. C.), 551. §§ 243, 372.
v. Sands, Freeman, 351. § 12.
Wayne Agricultural Co. v. Cardwell, 73 Ind. 555. § 412.
Helms v., 73 Ind. 325. § 412.
Wayne Circuit Judge, Lob v., 26 Mich. 186. § 615.
Weare v. Sawyer, 44 N. H. 198. §§ 148, 405.
Weatherbee, White v., 126 Mass. 450. § 43.
Weatherby, Brown v., 71 Mo. 152. § 385.
v. Shackleford, 37 Miss. 559. § 475.

Weatherly, Connelly *v.*, 33 Ark. 658. § 574.
Weathersbee, Frost & Co. *v.*, 23 S. C. 354. § 165.
Weatherwax, Johnson *v.*, 9 Kan. 75. §§ 411, 467, 468.
Weaver, Fishback *v.*, 34 Ark. 569. § 319.
Hall *v.* (Cir. Ct. D. Oreg.), 34 Fed. Rep. 104. § 383.
Hecht *v.* (Cir. Ct. D. Oreg.), 34 Fed. Rep. 111. § 133.
Saulsbury *v.*, 59 Ga. 254. § 7.
v. Shryock, 6 Serg. & Rawle (Pa.), 262. § 139.
State *v.*, 18 Ala. 293. § 508.
State *v.*, 92 Mo. 673. § 577.
v. Tapscott, 9 Leigh (Va.), 424. § 216.
v. Thornton, 63 Ga. 655. § 631.
White *v.*, 41 Ill. 409. § 176.
Webb *v.* Anspach, 3 Ohio St. 522. § 536.
v. Baird, 27 Ind. 368. § 408.
Bank of California *v.*, 94 N. Y. 467. § 330.
v. Hewitt, 3 Kay & Johns. 438. §§ 147, 376.
Weber, Detroit *v.*, 26 Mich. 284. §§ 547, 555, 557.
v. North, 51 Iowa, 375. § 580.
Webster *v.* Cobb, 17 Ill. 459. §§ 47, 176.
Commonwealth *v.*, 1 Bush (Ky.), 616. § 499.
Domestic Sewing Machine Co. *v.*, 47 Iowa, 357. §§ 392, 644.
v. Ela, 5 N. H. 540. § 81.
Kinnaird *v.*, Law Rep. 10 Ch. Div. 139. § 335.
Payne *v.*, 19 Ill. 103. § 604.
Pico *v.*, 14 Cal. 202. § 636.
Washington Ice Co. *v.*, 125 U. S. 426. §§ 45, 481.
Weddington *v.* Commonwealth, 79 Ky. 582. § 514.
Wedgewood, Inhabitants of Orono *v.*, 44 Me. 49. § 523.
Weed *v.* Bentley, 6 Hill (N. Y.), 58. § 234.
Weed *v.* Chambers, 40 Up. Can. (Q. B.) 1. § 95.
v. Clark, 4 Sandf. (N. Y. Sup. Ct.) 31. § 85.
Holmes *v.*, 24 Barb. (N. Y.) 546. § 217.
Weed Sewing Machine Co., Cox *v.*, 57 Miss. 350. § 195.
v. Oberreich, 38 Wis. 325. § 364.
v. Maxwell, 63 Mo. 486. § 153.
v. Winchel, 107 Ind. 260. §§ 106, 364, 382.
Weeks *v.* Burton, 7 Vt. 67. § 73.
Weelburg, Sanders *v.*, 107 Ind. 266. §§ 268, 284.
Wegner *v.* State, 14 Tex. App. 213. § 385.
Wehr *v.* German Evan. Luth. St. Matt. Cong., 47 Md. 177. §§ 394, 601.
Weideman, State *v.*, 30 Mo. App. 647. § 508.
Weik *v.* Pugh, 92 Ind. 382. §§ 1, 426.
Weiler *v.* Henarie, 15 Oreg. 28. § 92.
v. Hoch, 25 Pa. St. 525. § 239.
Weimer *v.* Shelton, 7 Mo. 237. § 235.
Weiner *v.* Bunbury, 30 Mich. 201. § 615.
Weir Plow Co. *v.* Walmsley, 110 Ind. 242. §§ 93, 95, 388.
Weissman, Schuster *v.*, 63 Mo. 552. § 553.
Welch, Bell *v.*, 9 Man., Gr. & Scott, 154. § 85.
City of San Jose *v.*, 65 Cal. 358. § 529.
Louisville Mfg. Co. *v.*, 10 How. 461. §§ 123, 202, 203.
v. Seymour, 28 Conn. 387. §§ 142, 167.
Welchman, Howard Banking Company *v.*, 6 Bosw. (N. Y.) 280. § 148.
Weld, Carroll *v.*, 13 Ill. 682. §§ 176, 182.
Draper *v.*, 13 Gray, 580. § 350.
v. Nichols, 17 Pick. 538. §§ 60, 72.
Welden, Hayden *v.*, 43 N. J. Law, 128. § 49.

Weldon *v.* Colquitt, 62 Ga. 449. § 510.
Welfare *v.* Thompson, 83 N. C. 276. § 29.
Welford *v.* Beezeley, 1 Ves. Sr. 6. § 89.
Wellmans, Pearl *v.*, 11 Ill. 352. § 457.
Wellington, Huntington *v.*, 12 Mich. 10, 11. §§ 67, 73.
Weller, Oaks *v.*, 13 Vt. 106. §§ 187, 203, 204.
v. Ransom, 34 Mo. 362. § 361.
Welles, Myers *v.*, 5 Hill (N. Y.), 463. § 364.
Thomas *v.*, 1 Root (Conn.), 57. § 74.
Wells, Davis *v.*, 104 U. S. 159. §§ 13, 186, 204.
v. Girling, 1 Brod. & Bing. 447. § 21.
v. Girling, 8 Taunt. 737. § 138.
v. Grant, 4 Yerg. (Tenn.) 491. § 536.
Hayes *v.*, 34 Md. 512. §§ 344, 360.
v. Kavanagh, 70 Iowa, 519. § 647.
Mace *v.*, 7 How. 272. § 220.
v. Mann, 45 N. Y. 327. § 17.
Merle *v.*, 2 Camp. 413. § 161.
v. Miller, 66 N. Y. 255. § 263.
v. Moore, 3 Rob. (La.) 156. § 128.
National Bank of Gloversville *v.*, 79 N. Y. 498. § 6.
Phillips *v.*, 2 Sneed, 154. § 449.
State *v.*, 8 Nev. 105. § 521.
State *v.*, 61 Tex. 562. § 524.
Wells Fargo & Co. *v.* Davis, 2 Utah Terr. 411. § 193.
Welsh *v.* Barrow, 9 Rob. (La.) 535. § 519.
v. Welsh, 4 Maule & Sel. 333. § 220.
Welsing, Lee Co. *v.*, 70 Iowa, 198. § 385.
Welty, Chase *v.*, 57 Iowa, 230. § 262.
Wendheim, Hubert *v.*, 64 Cal. 213. § 572.
Wendlandt *v.* Sohre, 37 Minn. 162. § 1.
Wennerhold, Humboldt Savings & Loan Society *v.*, 81 Cal. 528. §§ 174, 425, 561.
Wenrick, Commonwealth *v.*, 8 Watts (Pa.), 159. § 579.
Wentworth, Brigham *v.*, 11 Cush. 123. § 398.
Goodall *v.*, 20 Me. 322. § 266.
Werges, Mersman *v.*, 112 U. S. 139. §§ 229, 380.
Wernecke *v.* Kenyon's Adm'r, 66 Mo. 275. § 318.
Wertz, Mullindore *v.*, 75 Ind. 431. §§ 38, 645.
Wesley Church *v.* Moore, 10 Pa. St. 273. §§ 205, 230.
West *v.* Ashdom, 1 Bing. 164. § 493.
v. Bank of Rutland, 19 Vt. 403. § 208.
v. Belches, 5 Munf. (Va.) 187. § 269.
v. Brison, 99 Mo. 684. §§ 40, 245, 370.
v. Chasten, 12 Fla. 315. §§ 36, 223.
v. Colquitt, 71 Ga. 559. § 500.
Dunn *v.*, 5 B. Mon. (Ky.) 376. § 60.
v. Hayes, 117 Ind. 290. § 219.
v. Laraway, 28 Mich. 464. § 7.
Springfield Manufacturing Co. *v.*, 1 Cush. 388. § 504.
Westbrook *v.* Moore, 59 Ga. 204. § 175.
Western *v.* Russell, 3 Ves. & Bea. 187. §§ 80, 89.
Western B'ld'g Ass'n *v.* Fitzmaurice, 7 Mo. App. 283. §§ 383, 394, 601.
Western N. Y. Life Ins. Co. *v.* Clinton, 66 N. Y. 326. § 406.
Western Reserve Bank, Baldwin *v.*, 5 Ohio, 273. § 345.
Commercial Bank *v.*, 11 Ohio, 444. §§ 40, 436.
Western Stage Co., Whiting *v.*, 20 Iowa, 554. § 350.
Western Union Tel. Co., Widner *v.*, 47 Mich. 612. § 137.
Westhead *v.* Sproson, 6 Hurl. & Nor. 728. § 17.
Westfal, Kingsbury *v.*, 61 N. Y. 356. §§ 93, 108, 389.

Westfall, Chandler v., 30 Tex. 475. §§ 176, 182.
Suydam v., 2 Denio, 105. § 185.
Westmoreland, Lane v., 79 Ala. 372. § 205.
Westmoreland Bank, Ramsey v., 2 Pen. & Watts (Pa.), 203. § 443.
Weston, McCutcheon v., 65 Cal. 37. § 468.
Westphal v. Moulton, 45 Iowa, 163. § 105.
Wetherbee v. Kusterer, 41 Mich. 359. § 98.
v. Potter, 99 Mass. 354. § 52.
Trowbridge v., 11 Allen, 361. § 52.
Wetherell, Sigourney v., 6 Met. (Mass.) 553. §§ 142, 367.
Wetmore, Taylor v., 10 Ohio, 490, 491. §§ 117, 196.
Wetzel v. Sponsler, 18 Pa. St. 460. §§ 239, 240.
Weymouth, Bordelon v., 14 La. Ann. 93. § 364.
Iliff v., 40 Ohio St. 101. § 241.
Wharam, Matson v., 2 Term R. 80. §§ 70, 75, 76, 78.
Wharton v. Duncan, 83 Pa. St. 40. § 426.
v. Walker, 6 Dow. & Ry. 288. § 66.
Wheat v. Kendall, 6 N. H. 504. §§ 32, 354.
Wheatley's Heirs v. Calhoun, 12 Leigh (Va.), 264. § 302.
Wheaton v. Wheeler, 27 Minn. 464. § 359.
Whelan, Brand v., 18 Bradw. (Ill. App.) 186. § 59.
v. Keegan, 7 Irish Com. Law, 544. § 160.
Wheeler v. Benedict, 36 Hun (N. Y.), 478. § 239.
v. Collier, Moo. & Mal. 123. § 81.
v. Lewis, 11 Vt. 265. §§ 100, 101.
v. Mayfield, 31 Tex. 395. § 116.
Mayfield v., 37 Tex. 256. §§ 186, 190.
Wheeler v. Newton, 2 Eq. Cas. 44, ch. 5. § 89.
Reynolds v., 10 J. Scott (N. R.), 561. § 260.
v. State, 9 Heisk. (Tenn.) 393. §§ 559, 624.
v. State, 39 Kan. 163. § 503.
Tillman v., 17 Johns. 326. § 179.
v. Washburn, 24 Vt. 293. § 370.
Wheaton v., 27 Minn. 464. § 359.
v. Wheeler, 7 Mass. 169. § 494.
Wilson v., 29 Vt. 484. § 349.
Wheeler & Wilson Mfg. Co. v. Brown, 65 Wis. 99. § 394.
Wheeling v. Black, 25 W. Va. 266. §§ 534, 538.
Wheelock, Coburn v., 34 N. Y. 440. § 288.
Wood v., 25 Barb. (N. Y.) 625. § 67.
Yale v., 109 Mass. 502. § 153.
Wheelwright v. De Peyster, 4 Edwards' Ch. 232. § 35.
Loomer v., 3 Sandf. Ch. 135. § 35.
v. Moore, 2 Hall (N. Y.), 162. § 15.
Whinray, Northwestern R. R. Co. v., 1 Hurl. & Gor. (10 Exch.) 77. § 392.
Whipple v. Briggs, 28 Vt. 65. § 209.
v. Briggs, 30 Vt. 111. § 228.
Dunphy v., 25 Mich. 10. § 537.
Whitaker, Barnes v., 45 Wis. 204. § 563.
v. Crutcher, 5 Bush (Ky.), 621. § 408.
v. Kirby, 54 Ga. 277. § 245.
v. Rice, 9 Minn. 13. § 143.
v. Richards, 134 Penn. St. 191. §§ 19, 411.
Willison v., 7 Taunt. 53. § 493.
Whitby v. Harrison, 18 Up. Can. (Q. B.) 606. § 521.
Whitcomb v. Kephart, 50 Pa. St. 85. § 57.
Lees v., 5 Bing. 34. § 85.
v. Miller, 90 Ind. 384. § 407.
White v. Ault, 19 Ga. 551. § 34.
v. Banks, 21 Ala. 705. § 269.

White, Blake *v.*, 1 Younge & Coll. (Exch.) 420. § 352.
v. Blake, 22 Wend. 612. § 498.
v. Carlton, 52 Ind. 371. §§ 272, 286.
Carter *v.*, L. R. 25 Ch. D. 666. § 201.
v. Case, 13 Wend. 543. §§ 98, 101.
v. Cuyler, 1 Esp. 200. § 58.
v. Cuyler, 6 Durn. & East, 176. § 249.
v. Ditson, 140 Mass. 351. §§ 629, 645.
Doyle *v.*, 26 Me. 341. § 76.
v. Duggan, 140 Mass. 18. § 410.
v. East Saginaw, 43 Mich. 567. § 548.
Easter *v.*, 12 Ohio St. 213. § 61.
Ex'rs of White *v.*, 30 Vt. 338. § 210.
Gallagher *v.*, 31 Barb. (N. Y.) 92. §§ 101, 132.
v. German Nat. Bank Memphis, 9 Heisk. (Tenn.) 475. § 624.
Hall *v.*, 27 Conn. 488. §§ 515, 631.
Hunt *v.*, 1 Ind. (Carter), 105. § 574.
Langpre *v.*, 6 La. (Curry), 388. § 586.
Maryotts *v.*, 2 Starkie, 101. § 331.
v. Miller, 47 Ind. 385. §§ 205, 411.
v. Moore, 23 S. C. 456. § 94.
People *v.*, 11 Ill. 341. § 448.
People *v.*, 28 Hun (N. Y.), 289. §§ 238, 631.
Powell's Ex'rs *v.*, 11 Leigh (Va.), 309. § 313.
v. Prigmore, 29 Ark. 208. § 454.
v. Proctor, 4 Taunt. 209. § 90.
v. Reed, 15 Conn. 457. §§ 92, 163.
Reigart *v.*, 52 Pa. St. 438. § 1.
Schloss *v.*, 16 Cal. 65. § 565.
v. Smith, 2 Jones' Law (N. C.), 4. § 545.
v. Smith, 33 Pa. St. 186. § 391.
Sneed's Ex'rs *v.*, 3 J. J. Marsh. (Ky.) 525. § 62.
State *v.*, 10 Rich. Law (S. C.), 442. § 528.
White *v.* State, 1 Blackf. (Ind.) 557. § 636.
State *v.*, 88 Ind. 587. § 566.
Stone *v.*, 8 Gray, 589. § 380.
Tucker *v.*, 5 Allen, 322. § 470.
United States *v.*, 4 Wash. 414. § 528.
v. Woodward, 5 Man., Gr. & Scott, 810. §§ 17, 84.
v. Walker, 31 Ill. 422. §§ 201, 245, 374, 386.
v. Weatherbee, 126 Mass. 450. § 43.
v. Weaver, 41 Ill. 409. § 176.
v. Whitney, 51 Ind. 124. § 356.
White's Adm'r *v.* Life Association of America, 63 Ala. 419, 426. §§ 1, 339, 340, 342, 425.
White's Bank *v.* Myles, 73 N. Y. 335. §§ 156, 159.
White's Ex'rs *v.* Commonwealth, 39 Pa. St. 167. § 133.
White Lead Works, Whiting Co. *v.*, 58 Mich. 29. § 644.
White Line Transfer Co., Lucas *v.*, 70 Iowa, 541. §§ 44, 259.
White Sewing Machine Co. *v.* Hines, 61 Mich. 423. § 118.
v. Mullins, 41 Mich. 339. § 394.
Whiteford, Bewley *v.*, Hayes (Irish Rep.), 356. § 85.
Whitehead *v.* Peck, 1 Kelly (Ga.), 140. § 235.
Simmons *v.*, 81 Miss. 99. § 456.
Jones *v.*, 4 Ga. 397. §§ 1, 613.
Knight *v.*, 26 Miss. 245. § 35.
v. Peck, 1 Kelly (Ga.), 140. § 215.
v. Woolfolk, 3 La. Ann. 42. § 631.
Whitehouse *v.* Hanson, 42 N. H. 9. §§ 60, 258.
Hinde *v.*, 7 East, 558. § 90.
Whitehurst *v.* Coleen, 53 Ill. 247. § 615.
Whitelaw *v.* Taylor, 45 Up. Can. (Q. B.) 446. § 77.
Whitely, Nixon *v.*, 102 Ind. 360. § 7.
Whitfield *v.* Evans, 56 Miss. 488. § 579.
v. Hodges, 1 Mees. & Wels. 679. § 493.

Whiting v. Burke, Law Rep. 6 Ch. App. Cas. 342. § 256.
v. Clark, 17 Cal. 407. § 342.
Pierce v., 63 Cal. 538. §§ 467, 473.
v. Western Stage Co., 20 Iowa, 554. § 350.
Whiting Co. v. White Lead Works, 58 Mich. 29. § 644.
Whitman v. Bryant, 49 Vt. 512. § 75.
First National Bank Monmouth v., 66 Ill. 331. §§ 347, 405.
v. Gaddie, 7 B. Mon. (Ky.) 591. § 259.
Hartwell v., 36 Ala. 712. § 268.
Lemmon v., 75 Ind. 318. § 356.
Whitmarsh, Gillett v., 8 Adol. & Ell. (N. S.) 966. § 415.
Whitmore, Brooks v., 139 Mass. 356. § 540.
Brooks v., 142 Mass. 399. § 585.
Whitnash v. Genge, 3 Man. & Ryl. 42. § 629.
v. George, 8 Barn. & Cress. 556. § 629.
Whitney v. Allen, 21 Cal. 233. § 459.
Campion v., 30 Minn. 177. § 34.
v. Groot, 24 Wend. 82. §§ 164, 196.
McKinney v., 8 Allen, 207. § 73.
v. Stearns, 16 Me. 394. § 84.
Townsend v., 75 N. Y. 425. § 311.
Vose v., 7 Mont. 393. § 571.
White v., 51 Ind. 124. § 356.
Whiton v. Mears, 11 Met. (Mass.) 563. §§ 177, 197.
Whitridge v. Durkee, 2 Md. Ch. 442. § 238.
Whittemore, Hendricks v., 105 Mass. 23. §§ 60, 264.
v. Obear, 58 Mo. 280. § 403.
Whitten, Watson v., 3 Rich. Law (S. C.), 224. § 585.
Whittier v. Dana, 10 Allen, 326. § 81.
Helt v., 31 Ohio St. 475. § 449.
Rowe v., 21 Me. 545. § 66.
Whittle v. Skinner, 23 Vt. 531. § 353.
Whittler, Stoops v., 1 Mo. App. 420. § 630.
Whitworth v. Tilman, 40 Miss. 76. § 217.
Whyle, Evans v., 5 Bing. 485. § 122.
Whyte, Goddard v., 2 Giff. 449. § 303.
Wibaux v. Grinnell Live Stock Co., 9 Mont. 154. § 137.
Wichita Co., Wilson v., 67 Tex. 647. § 558.
Wick Bros., Ward v., 17 Ohio St. 159. § 344.
Wickens v. McMeekin, 15 Ont. (Can.) 408. § 169.
Wickham v. Wickham, 2 Kay & Johns. 478. § 71.
Widener v. State, 45 Ind. 244. § 563.
Widner v. Western Union Tel. Co., 47 Mich. 612. § 137.
Wieland v. Oberne, 20 Bradw. (Ill. App.) 118. § 236.
Wiggins, Bates v., 37 Kan. 44. § 231.
Calvin v., 27 Ind. 489. § 356.
Donley v., 52 Tex. 301. § 569.
Russell v., 2 Story, 214. § 81.
Wiggins' Appeal, 100 Pa. St. 155. § 153.
Wightman, Maples v., 4 Conn. 376. § 4.
Taylor v., 51 Iowa, 411. § 13.
Wilbern, Culver v., 48 Iowa, 26. § 235.
Wilbourn, Apperson v., 58 Miss. 439. § 287.
Wilbur & Son v. Hutte, 25 S. C. 246. § 578.
Wilcox, Cooper v., 2 Dev. & Bat. Eq. (N. C.) 90. § 434.
v. Campbell, 106 N. Y. 325. § 37.
v. Draper, 12 Neb. 138. § 193.
v. Fairhaven Bank, 7 Allen, 270. § 306.
McNutt v., 1 Freeman's Ch. (Miss.) 116. § 40.
McNutt v., 3 How. (Miss.) 417. § 468.
Sage v., 6 Conn. 81. §§ 16, 53, 82, 197.
v. Todd, 64 Mo. 388. § 35.
Wise v., 1 Day (Conn.), 22. § 73.
Woodward v., 27 Ind. 207. § 64.
Wild v. Howe, 74 Mo. 551. § 357.
Wild Cat Branch v. Ball, 45 Ind. 213. § 411.

Wilde v. Haycraft, 2 Duvall (Ky.), 309. § 162.
v. Jenkins, 4 Paige, 481. § 36.
Wilder, Lyon v., 24 J. & S. (N. Y. Super. Ct.) 67. § 10.
Wallace v., 13 Fed. Rep. 707. § 406.
Wildes v. Savage, 1 Story, 22. §§ 192, 197, 202.
Wildin, Tayleur v., Law Rep. 3 Exch. 303. §§ 108, 165.
Wilds v. Attix, 4 Del. Ch. 253. § 242.
Bramley v., 9 Lea (Tenn.), 674. § 532.
Wile v. Wright, 32 Iowa, 451. § 250.
Wiley, Booth v., 102 Ill. 84. § 237.
Gillett v., 126 Ill. 310. § 577.
v. Hight, 39 Mo. 130. § 357.
McKenzie v., 27 W. Va. 658. § 373.
v. Roberts, 28 Mo. 388. § 80.
Wilke, Hassey v., 55 Cal. 528. § 35.
Wilkin, Cornes v., 14 Hun (N. Y.), 428. § 284.
Wilkins, Bittick v., 7 Heisk. (Tenn.) 307. § 317.
Holbrow v., 1 Barn. & Cress. 10. § 201.
Jarvis v., 7 Mees. & Wels. 410. § 84.
Lucy v., 33 Minn. 21. § 1.
Talbot v., 31 Ark. 411. § 298.
Wilkins' Adm'r, Carlisle v., 51 Ala. 371. § 325.
Wilkinson, Clark v., 59 Wis. 543. §§ 112, 546.
v. Evans, 1 C. P. 407. § 80.
Fireman's Ins. Co. v., 35 N. J. Eq. 160. §§ 366, 367.
Taylor v., 1 Nevile & Perry, 629. § 505.
Wilks, Shirreff v., 1 East, 53. § 18.
Will, Brown v., 103 Ind. 71. § 7.
Willard, County of Pine v., 39 Minn. 125. §§ 518, 546, 547.
v. Fralick, 31 Mich. 431. § 616.
Robinson v., 133 Mass. 236. § 554.
Willett v. Kipp, 12 Hun (N. Y.), 474. § 572.
Willey, City of Maquoketa v., 35 Iowa, 323. § 437.
v. Thompson, 9 Met. (Mass.) 329. § 365.
Williams v. Bacon, 2 Gray, 387. §§ 80, 90.
v. Bosson, 11 Ohio, 62. § 185.
v. Boyd, 75 Ind. 286. §§ 36, 347.
Brettel v., 4 Wels., Hurl. & Gor. 623. §§ 18, 80, 87.
Cain v., 16 Nev. 426. § 439.
v. Cheney, 3 Gray, 215. § 222.
Connor v., 2 Rob. (N. Y.) 46. § 66.
v. Covilland, 10 Cal. 419. § 365.
Dineen v., 138 Mass. 367. § 502.
Dwight v., 4 McLean, 581. § 100.
v. Ewing, 31 Ark. 229. § 284.
Frierson v., 57 Miss. 451. § 144.
v. Gilchrist, 11 N. H. 535. § 334.
v. Glenn, 92 N. C. 253. § 261.
v. Golden, 10 Neb. 432. § 571.
v. Granger, 4 Day (Conn.), 444. § 199.
v. Greer, 4 Haywood (Tenn.), 235. § 214.
Gregory v., 3 Meriv. 582. § 72.
v. Harrison, 11 S. C. 412. § 4.
v. Helme, 1 Dev. Eq. (N. C.) 151. § 227.
Hogshead v., 55 Ind. 145. §§ 242, 434.
Hutton v., 35 Ala. 503. § 90.
James v., 3 Nev. & Man. 196. §§ 82, 85.
James v., 5 Barn. & Adol. 1109. § 85.
v. Jensen, 75 Mo. 681. § 342.
Kellar v., 10 Bush (Ky.), 216. §§ 262, 451.
v. Ketchum, 19 Wis. 231. § 84.
v. Kiernan, 25 Hun (N. Y.), 355. § 583.
Kingsbury v., 53 Barb. (N. Y.) 142. §§ 389.
v. Lake, 2 Ell. & Ell. 349. § 81.
v. Leper, 2 Wils. 308. §§ 64, 66, 68.
v. Leper, 3 Burr. 1886. § 63.

Williams, Lossee *v.*, 6 Lans. 228. § 17.
v. Marshall, 42 Barb. (N. Y.) 524. §§ 17, 151.
v. Martin, 2 Duvall (Ky.), 491. § 365.
v. McDaniel, 77 Ga. 4. § 503.
McKim *v.*, 134 Mass. 136. § 576.
v. McNair, 98 N. C. 332. § 574.
Mills *v.*, 16 S. C. 593. § 410.
Neilson *v.*, 42 N. J. Eq. 291. § 577.
Nelson *v.*, 2 Dev. & Bat. Eq. (N. C.) 118. § 435.
v. Owen, 13 Simons, 597. § 315.
Parmelee *v.*, 71 Mo. 410. § 137.
Parsons *v.*, 9 Conn. 236. § 489.
People *v.*, 6 Daly (N. Y. Com. Pl.), 409. § 511.
v. Perkins, 21 Ark. 18. § 15.
Pool *v.*, 8 Ired. Law (N. C.), 286. § 272.
Prior *v.*, 3 Abb. Rep. Om. Cas. 624. § 141.
v. Rawlinson, Ryan & Moody, 233. § 160.
v. Reynolds, 11 La. (6 Curry), 230. §§ 133, 339.
Rose *v.*, 5 Kan. 480. §§ 29, 352.
Ross *v.*, 11 Heisk. (Tenn.) 410. § 254.
Ryan *v.*, 29 Kan. 487. §§ 92, 93.
v. Scott, 83 Ind. 405. §§ 377, 648.
Sheldon *v.*, 11 Neb. 272. § 446.
v. Skipwith, 34 Ark. 529. § 22.
v. Smith, 48 Me. 135. § 352.
State *v.*, 19 S. C. 62. §§ 569, 589, 636.
v. State, 25 Fla. 734. § 517.
v. State, 89 Ind. 570. §§ 541, 574, 581.
Stringfellow *v.*, 6 Dana (Ky.), 236. § 436.
Sutton *v.*, 77 Ga. 570. § 577.
Thomas *v.*, 10 Barn. & Cres. 664. §§ 17, 52, 68.
v. Tipton, 5 Humph. (Tenn.) 66. §§ 226, 306.
v. Townsend, 1 Bosw. (N. Y.) 411. § 367.
Turner *v.*, 73 Me. 466. § 342.
Williams *v.* United States, 1 How. 290. § 628.
v. Urmston, 35 Ohio St. 296. § 7.
Walker *v.*, 88 N. C. 7. § 460.
v. Wood, 16 Md. 220. §§ 89, 90.
Wood *v.*, 61 Mo. 63. § 540.
Wornell *v.*, 19 Tex. 180. § 447.
v. Wright, 9 Humph. (Tenn.) 493. § 372.
Williams' Adm'r, Ryan *v.*, 29 Kan. 487. § 489.
v. Williams' Adm'r, 5 Ohio, 444. §§ 207, 230.
Williamson, Dumont *v.*, 18 Ohio St. 515. § 28.
Giddens *v.*, 65 Ala. 439. § 311.
Lasher *v.*, 55 N. Y. 619. § 236.
Mitchell *v.*, 6 Md. 210. §§ 97, 448.
v. Woodman, 73 Me. 163. § 43.
Williamson's Adm'r, Hall *v.*, 9 Ohio St. 17. § 474.
v. Rees' Adm'r, 15 Ohio, 572. § 295.
Williamston *v.* Howell, 4 Ala. 693. § 638.
Willis, Bartlett *v.*, 3 Mass. 86. § 22.
v. Bivins, 76 Ga. 745. § 492.
v. Commonwealth, 85 Ky. 68. § 515.
v. Davis, 3 Minn. 17. § 426.
Grabfelder *v.*, 10 Bradw. (Ill. App.) 330. § 342.
Havens *v.*, 100 N. Y. 482. § 361.
v. Ives, 1 Sm. & Mar. (Miss.) 307. § 30.
McKinney *v.*, 64 Miss. 82. § 481.
v. Rivers, 80 Ga. 556. § 45.
Tiffany *v.*, 30 Hun (N. Y.), 266. § 101.
Veazie *v.*, 6 Gray, 90. § 412.
v. Willis, 17 Simons, 218. § 401.
Willison *v.* Whitaker, 7 Taunt. 53. § 493.
Wills *v.* Ross, 77 Ind. 1. §§ 13, 16, 92, 191, 193, 644.
Wilmarth, Johnson *v.*, 13 Met. (Mass.) 416. § 202.

Wilmington, Columbia & Augusta R. R. Co. *v.* Ling, 18 S. C. 116. § 422.
Wilmot, Bank of Toronto *v.*, 19 Up. Can. (Q. B.) 73. § 392.
Wilsey, Rankin *v.*, 17 Iowa, 463. § 328.
Wilson *v.* Bank of Orleans, 9 Ala. 847. § 350.
v. Beavans, 58 Ill. 232. §§ 63, 67.
Blackwell *v.*, 2 Rich. Law, 322. § 497.
Bomar *v.*, 1 Bailey, Law (S. C.), 461. § 519.
v. Brown, 2 Beasley (N. J.), 277. § 298.
v. Burfoot, 2 Gratt. (Va.) 134. § 523.
v. Burney, 8 Neb. 39. § 329.
v. Campbell, 1 Scam. (Ill.) 493. § 97.
Cherry *v.*, 78 N. C. 164, 166. § 257.
Coffman *v.*, 2 Met. (Ky.) 542. § 402.
v. Coupland, 5 Barn. & Ald. 228. § 66.
v. Crawford, 47 Iowa, 469. § 205.
Crum *v.*, 61 Miss. 233. §§ 43, 145, 521.
v. Dawson, 52 Ind. 513. § 432.
De Greiff *v.*, 30 N. J. Eq. 435. § 630.
Donally *v.*, 5 Leigh (Va.), 329. § 335.
Dodd *v.*, 4 Del. Ch. 399. § 329.
v. Edwards, 6 Lans. (N. Y.) 134. § 122.
v. Field, 27 Hun (N. Y.), 46. § 150.
v. Foot, 11 Met. 285. §§ 29, 33.
Freeholders of Warren *v.*, 1 Harr. (N. J.) 110. § 545.
Gerould *v.*, 81 N. Y. 573. §§ 580, 585.
v. Glover, 3 Pa. St. 404. § 557.
Gregg *v.*, 50 Ind. 490. § 97.
Hancock *v.*, 46 Iowa, 352. § 638.
v. Hart, 7 Taunt. 295. § 90.
v. Hentges, 29 Minn. 102. § 67.
Wilson, Kaufman *v.*, 29 Ind. 504. § 605.
Kemmerer *v.*, 31 Pa. St. 110. § 440.
v. Langford, 5 Humph. 320. § 356.
v. Lloyd, Law Rep. 16 Eq. Cas. 60. §§ 36, 376.
v. Marshall, 15 Irish Com. Law Rep. 466. § 79.
v. Martin, 74 Pa. St. 159. § 88.
v. McVey, 83 Ind. 108. § 339.
Ogburn *v.*, 93 N. C. 115. § 319.
Payne *v.*, 7 Barn. & Cres. 423. § 17.
v. People, 10 Bradw. (Ill. App.) 357. § 503.
v. Powers, 130 Mass. 127. § 355.
v. Powers, 131 Mass. 539. § 646.
Pritchett *v.*, 39 Pa. St. 421. § 415.
Ross *v.*, 7 Smedes. & Mar. (Miss.) 753. § 324.
Sloan *v.*, 4 Harr. & Johns. 322. § 82.
v. State, 1 Lea (Tenn.), 316. § 535.
v. Stilwell, 9 Ohio St. 467. § 97.
v. Tebbetts, 29 Ark. 579. § 613.
v. Town of Monticello, 85 Ind. 10. § 124.
Tyree *v.*, 9 Gratt. (Va.) 59. § 537.
v. Unselt, 12 Bush (Ky.), 215. § 583.
Ward *v.*, 100 Ind. 52. § 197.
v. Wheeler, 29 Vt. 484. § 349.
v. Wichita Co., 67 Tex. 647. § 558.
Wingate *v.*, 53 Ind. 78. § 372.
v. Wright, 83 Ga. 38. § 543.
Wilson's Case, 38 N. J. Eq. 205. § 112.
Wilson's Ex'r, Thompson *v.*, 13 La. (Curry), 138. § 210.
Wilson & Co. *v.* Dean, 21 S. C. 327. § 104.
Wilson Sewing Machine Co. *v.* Schnell, 20 Minn. 40. §§ 80, 87.
Wimberly, Broughton *v.*, 65 Ala. 549. § 290.

Winchel, Weed Sewing Machine Co. *v.*, 107 Ind. 260. §§ 106, 364, 382.
Winchell *v.* Doty, 15 Hun (N. Y.), 1. § 107.
Winckworth *v.* Mills, 2 Esp. 484. § 60.
Winder *v.* Diffenderfer, 2 Bland's Ch. (Md.) 166. § 298.
Windley, State *v.*, 99 N. C. 4. § 532.
Windom, Lamberton *v.*, 18 Minn. 506. § 440.
Wing *v.* Terry, 5 Hill, 160. § 185.
Wingate, Harlan *v.*, 2 J. J. Marsh. (Ky.) 138. § 243.
v. Wilson, 53 Ind. 78. § 372.
Wingfield, McCloskey *v.*, 32 La. Ann. 38. §§ 466, 471.
Wingfield & Bridges, McClosky, Bigley & Co. *v.*, 29 La. Ann. 141. § 118.
Winham *v.* Crutcher, 2 Tenn. Ch. (Cooper), 535. § 97.
Winn, Dodd *v.*, 27 Mo. 501. § 439.
v. Sanford, 145 Mass. 302. § 153.
Stephens *v.*, 2 Nott & McC. 372. § 82.
Winne *v.* Col. Springs Co., 3 Col. 155, 159, 160. §§ 340, 344, 377.
Winneshiek Co. *v.* Maynard, 44 Iowa, 15. § 559.
Winstanley, Kastner *v.*, 20 Up. Can. 101. §§ 92, 191.
Winstead, United States *v.*, 12 Fed. Rep. 50. § 516.
Winston, Bullitt's Ex'rs *v.*, 1 Munf. (Va.) 269. § 373.
v. Fenwick, 4 Stew. & Port. (Ala.) 269. § 94.
v. Rives, 4 Stew. & Port. (Ala.) 269. § 450.
v. Yeargin, 50 Ala. 340. § 434.
Winter, Smith *v.*, 4 Mees. & Wels. 454. § 347.
Wintersmith, Greer *v.*, 95 Ky. 516. § 226.
Winterrowd, Hamilton *v.*, 43 Ind. 393. § 352.
Wintersoll *v.* Commonwealth, 1 Duvall (Ky.), 177. § 502.
Wire *v.* Miller, 45 Ohio St. 388. § 193.
Wise, Coffelt *v.*, 62 Ind. 451. § 12.
Foster *v.*, 46 Ohio St. 20. §§ 581, 585.
Levy *v.*, 15 La. Ann. 38. §§ 21, 642.
Parker *v.*, 6 Maule & Sel. 239. § 123.
v. Ray, 3 Greene (Iowa), 430. § 89.
v. Shepherd, 13 Ill. 41. § 316.
v. Wilcox, 1 Day (Conn.), 22. § 73.
Wiseman, Fetrow *v.*, 40 Ind. 148. §§ 4, 448.
Wisener, Polk *v.*, 2 Humph. (Tenn.) 520. § 586.
Wisner, Lee *v.*, 38 Mich. 82. §§ 16, 205, 646.
Wiswall, Jarman *v.*, 9 C. E. Green (N. J.), 267. § 138.
Wiswell, Liddell *v.*, 59 Vt. 365. §§ 276, 288.
Witchcott, Johnson *v.*, 1 Roll. Abr. 24, pl. 33. § 16.
Witherly *v.* Mann, 11 Johns. 578. § 511.
Withers *v.* Berry, 25 Kan. 373. §§ 176, 202.
Pulliam *v.*, 8 Dana (Ky.), 98. §§ 16, 380.
Samuel *v.*, 16 Mo. 532. § 417.
Withrow, Feamster *v.*, 12 W. Va. 611. § 212.
Witmer, Hill *v.*, 2 Phila. (Pa.) 72. § 34.
Wittmer *v.* Ellison, 72 Ill. 301. §§ 356, 374.
Wittrum *v.* Crommelin, 72 Cal. 89. § 461.
Witty, Ellis *v.*, 63 Miss. 117. § 10.
Wodenhouse, Farebrother *v.*, 23 Beav. 18. § 321.
Wofford *v.* Unger, 55 Tex. 480. § 143.
Wolbert, Commonwealth *v.*, 6 Binney (Pa.), 292. § 555.
Wolcott *v.* Hagerman, 50 N. J. Law, 289. § 270.
Woldridge *v.* Norris, Law Rep. 6 Eq. Cas. 410. § 223.

Wolf *v.* Banning, 3 Minn. 202. § 35.
Cotton's Guardian *v.*, 14 Bush (Ky.), 238. §§ 22, 576.
v. Finks, 1 Pa. St. 435. § 345.
Grant *v.*, 34 Minn. 32. § 77.
Kaufman *v.*, 77 Tex. 250. § 579.
People *v.*, 16 Cal. 385. § 643.
Rounsavell *v.*, 47 Wis. 353. § 648.
Rudy *v.*, 16 Serg. & R. (Pa.) 79. §§ 100, 101.
v. Stix, 99 U. S. 1. § 150.
Wolfe *v.* Browne, 5 Ohio St. 304. § 202.
Nugent *v.*, 111 Pa. St. 471. § 61.
Wolff *v.* Koppel, 5 Hill, 458. § 71.
v. Koppel, 2 Denio, 368. § 71.
v. Schaeffer, 74 Mo. 154. §§ 408, 540.
v. Schaeffer, 4 Mo. App. 367. § 580.
State *v.*, 10 Mo. App. 95. § 540.
v. Stover, 107 Pa. St. 206. § 262.
Wolleshlare *v.* Searles, 45 Pa. St. 45. § 240.
Womack *v.* Paxton's Ex'r, 84 Va. 9. §§ 140, 383.
Wonterline, Burks *v.*, 6 Bush (Ky.), 20. § 417.
Wood, Allen *v.*, 3 Ired. Eq. (N. C.) 386. § 290.
Balser *v.*, 69 Ind. 122. § 226.
v. Barstow, 10 Pick. 368. § 97.
v. Beach, 7 Vt. 522. § 86.
v. Benson, 2 Cromp. & Jer. 94. §§ 17, 52.
Binsse *v.*, 37 N. Y. 526. § 110.
v. Brett, 9 Grant's Ch. 452. § 147.
Claremont Bank *v.*, 10 Vt. 582. § 41.
v. Cook, 31 Ill. 271. § 572.
v. Corcoran, 1 Allen (Mass.), 405. § 62.
Crawford *v.*, 7 Ga. 445. §§ 566, 567.
Cross *v.*, 30 Ind. 378. § 356.
v. Dwarris, 11 Exch. 493. § 405.
Eberhardt *v.*, 2 Tenn. Ch. (Cooper), 488. § 276.
Eberhardt *v.*, 6 Lea (Tenn.), 467. § 267.
Wood *v.* Fisk, 63 N. Y. 245. § 139.
Lansing *v.*, 57 Mich. 201. § 597.
v. Leland, 1 Met. (Mass.) 387. § 295.
v. Mann, 125 Mass. 319. § 469.
v. Morgan, 5 Sneed (Tenn.), 79. § 440.
Morrow *v.*, 56 Ala. 1. § 548.
v. Newkirk, 15 Ohio St. 295. § 354.
v. Orford, 56 Cal. 157. § 464.
v. Perry, 9 Iowa, 479. § 293.
v. Priestner, Law Rep. 2 Ex. 66. §§ 92, 157.
Ralston *v.*, 15 Ill. 159. §§ 285, 638.
v. Tunnicliff, 74 N. Y. 38. § 15.
Truckee Lodge *v.*, 14 Nev. 293. § 397.
v. Washburn, 2 Pick. 24. § 151.
v. Wheelock, 25 Barb. (N. Y.) 625. § 67.
Williams *v.*, 16 Md. 220. § 89.
v. Williams, 61 Mo. 63. § 540.
v. Wood, 124 Ind. 545. § 232.
Woods' Adm'r, Denton *v.*, 11 Lea (Tenn.), 505. § 452.
Woods' Ex'r, Hacker *v.*, 33 Pa. St. 466. § 148.
Woodall, Pennington *v.*, 17 Ala. 685. § 218.
Woodard, Allen *v.*, 125 Mass. 400. § 237.
Sherrod *v.*, 4 Dev. Law (N. C.), 360. § 295.
Woodburn *v.* Carter, 50 Ind. 376. § 352.
v. Friend, 10 La. (Curry), 496. § 438.
Woodbury *v.* Bowman, 14 Me. 154. § 221.
v. Hammond, 54 Me. 332. § 577.
Woodbridge, McGuire *v.*, 6 Rob. (La.) 47. § 359.
v. Scott, 3 Brevard (S. C.), 193. § 222.
Woodcock *v.* Oxford & Worcester R. R. Co., 1 Drewry, 521. § 384.
Shaw *v.*, 7 Barn. & Cres. 73. § 52.

Wooddell v. Bruff, 25 W. Va. 465. § 537.
Woodin v. Durfee, 46 Mich. 424. § 411.
Woodgate, Devlin v., 34 Barb. (N. Y.) 252. § 67.
Woodley, Gorrie v., 17 Irish Com. Law Rep. 221. §§ 84, 89.
Woodman v. Mooring, 3 Dev. Law (N. C.), 237. § 333.
United States v., 1 Utah, 265. § 396.
Williamson v., 73 Me. 163. § 43.
Woodruff, Sutherland v., 56 Hun (N. Y.), 411. § 99.
Woods, Hart v., 7 Blackf. (Ind.) 568. § 90.
Justices v., 1 Kelly (Ga.), 84. §§ 546, 575.
Palmer v., 75 Iowa, 402. § 596.
v. Sherman, 71 Pa. St. 100. § 101.
State v., 84 Mo. 163. § 380.
v. Woods, 7 Ga. 587. § 544.
Williams v., 16 Md. 220. § 90.
Woodson v. Johns, 3 Munf. (Va.) 230. § 475.
v. Moody, 4 Humph. (Tenn.) 303. § 202.
Overton v., 17 Mo. 453. § 582.
Woodstock Bank v. Downer, 27 Vt. 539. §§ 126, 199, 204.
Woodville, Ross v., 4 Munf. (Va.) 324. § 413.
Woodward v. Clegge, 8 Ala. 317. § 427.
Grafton Bank v., 5 N. H. 99. §§ 356, 359.
Halderman v., 22 Kan. 734. §§ 353, 448.
v. Moore, 13 Ohio St. 136. § 632.
White v., 5 Man., Gr. & Scott, 810. §§ 17, 84.
v. Wilcox, 27 Ind. 207. § 64.
Woodwell, Hutchinson v., 107 Pa. St. 509. §§ 93, 429, 645.
Woodworth v. Bowes, 5 Ind. (3 Port.) 276. § 256.
Wooldridge v. Griffith, 59 Tex. 290. § 462.
Wooldridge, McGuire v., 6 Rob. (La.) 47. § 342.
Woolf, Combe v., 8 Bing. 156. §§ 342, 344.
Woolfolk v. Plant, 46 Ga. 422. §§ 235, 344.
Whitehead v., 3 La. Ann. 42. § 631.
Woolford v. Dow, 34 Ill. 424. § 354.
Wooley v. Louisville Banking Co., 81 Ky. 527. §§ 401, 440.
Woolley v. Jennings, 5 Barn. & Cres. 165. § 161.
v. Van Volkenburgh, 16 Kan. 20. § 126.
Woolsey v. Brown, 74 N. Y. 82. § 7.
Woolworth v. Brinker, 11 Ohio St. 593. §§ 361, 372.
Wooster, Strong v., 6 Vt. 536. § 426.
Wooten, Buie v., 7 Jones' Law (N. C.), 441. § 491.
Wootten, Odell v., 38 Ga. 224. § 472.
Worcester, Somersworth Savings Bank v., 76 Me. 327. §§ 246, 437.
Worcester Bank v. Reed, 9 Mass. 267. § 174.
Worcester Co. Institution v. Davis, 13 Gray, 531. § 204.
Worcester Mech. Sav. Bank v. Hill, 113 Mass. 25. § 418.
Worcester Savings Bank v. Hill, 113 Mass. 25. § 16.
Word, Crawford v., 7 Ga. 445. § 637.
Worden v. Salter, 90 Ill. 160. § 14.
Worneford v. Worneford, Strange, 764. § 89.
Wornell v. Williams, 19 Tex. 180. § 447.
Worrall v. Munn, 5 N. Y. 229. § 89.
Worsham, Moore v., 5 Ala. 645. § 337.
Worster, Manufacturing Co. v., 45 N. H. 110. § 632.
Wortendyke, Receivers of N. J. Midland R. R. Co. v., 27 N. J. Eq. 658. § 306.
Worth v. Cox, 89 N. C. 44. § 371.
Prairie v., 78 N. C. 169. § 371.

Wortham *v.* Brewster, 30 Ga. 112. § 355.
Worthington, Watkins *v.*, 2 Bland's Ch. (Md.) 509. § 233.
Woven Wire Mattress Co., Roberts *v.*, 46 Md. 374. § 87.
Wren, Bensinger *v.*, 100 Pa. St. 500. § 396.
v. Pearce, 4 Smedes & Mar. 91. §§ 15, 82, 102.
Wrenn, Cunningham *v.*, 23 Ill. 64. § 403.
Wright *v.* Andrews, 70 Me. 86. § 247.
v. Austin, 56 Barb. (N. Y.) 13. § 336.
v. Bartlett, 43 N. H. 548. §§ 352, 376.
v. Blunt, 74 Me. 92. § 505.
Brooks *v.*, 13 Allen, 72. § 351.
Brown *v.*, 7 T. B. Mon. (Ky.) 396. § 234.
Cohn *v.*, 66 Ga. 119. § 524.
Curry *v.*, 86 Tenn. 636. § 571.
v. Dannah, 2 Camp. 203. § 90.
Dufau *v.*, 25 Wend. 636. § 108.
Dugger *v.*, 51 Ark. 232. § 586.
v. Dyer, 48 Mo. 525. § 201.
v. Flinn, 33 Iowa, 159. § 114.
Fuller *v.*, 59 Ind. 333. § 486.
v. Garlinghouse, 36 N. Y. 539. § 185.
v. Griffith, 121 Ind. 478. §§ 156, 159, 193, 196.
v. Grover & Baker S. M. Co., 82 Pa. St. 80. § 309.
Guardians of Mansfield Union *v.*, 8 Heisk. (Tenn.) 22. § 524.
v. Hake, 38 Mich. 525. § 481.
Hardwick *v.*, 35 Beavan, 133. § 431.
v. Harris, 31 Iowa, 272. §§ 385, 563.
Hill *v.*, 23 Ark. 530. § 210.
Hutchinson *v.*, 61 N. H. 108. § 345.
v. Johnson, 8 Wend. 512. § 397.
v. Lang, 66 Ala. 389. §§ 588, 642.
Lawson *v.*, 1 Cox, 275. § 290.
Wright, Martin *v.*, 6 Adol. & Ell. (N. S.) 917. 157.
Mayor of Birmingham *v.*, 16 Ad. & Ell. (N. S.) 623. § 173.
McComb *v.*, 4 Johns. Ch. 659. § 90.
M'Whorter *v.*, 5 Ga. 555. § 247.
Mechanics' Bank *v.*, 53 Mo. 153. § 29.
v. Morley, 11 Ves. 12. § 322.
Northern Ins. Co. *v.*, 76 N. Y. 445. § 101.
v. Remington, 41 N. J. Law, 48. § 12.
v. Russell, 2 W. Black. 934. § 119.
v. Schmidt, 47 Iowa, 233. § 8.
v. Sewall, 9 Rob. (La.) 128. § 126.
State *v.*, 37 Iowa, 522. § 506.
v. Storrs, 6 Bosw. (N. Y.) 600. § 345.
Thomas *v.*, 98 N. C. 272. § 104.
United States *v.*, 1 McLean, 509. § 539.
Van Derveer *v.*, 6 Barb. (N. Y.) 547. §§ 94, 142.
v. Wakefield, 17 Vesey, 454. § 89.
v. Watt, 52 Miss. 634. § 434.
Way *v.*, 5 Met. (Mass.) 380. § 499.
Wile *v.*, 32 Iowa, 451. § 250.
Williams *v.*, 9 Humph. (Tenn.) 493. § 372.
Wilson *v.*, 83 Ga. 38. § 543.
Wright's Adm'r *v.* Stockton, 5 Leigh (Va.), 153. § 613.
Wroth, People's Building Ass'n *v.*, 43 N. J. Law, 70. §§ 172, 425, 555.
Wulff *v.* Jay, Law Rep. 7 Q. B. 756. §§ 442, 445.
Wyandotte, Bernhard *v.*, 33 Kan. 465. § 644.
Wyant, State *v.*, 67 Ind. 25. § 573.
Wyatt, Crosby *v.*, 10 N. H. 318. §§ 261, 295, 345.
Crosby *v.*, 26 Me. 156. §§ 261, 295, 345.
McGlothlin *v.*, 1 Lea (Tenn.), 717. § 575.
Wybrants *v.* Lutch, 24 Tex. 309. § 369.

Wyche *v.* Myrick, 14 Ga. 584. § 627.
Wycough *v.* State, 50 Ark. 102. § 551.
Wyke *v.* Rogers, 1 De Gex, M. & G. 408. §§ 365, 376.
Wylie, Brevard *v.*, 1 Rich. Law (S. C.), 38. § 632.
v. Gallagher, 46 Pa. St. 205. § 522.
v. Hightower, 74 Tex. 306. § 378.
Northampton Nat. Bank *v.*, 52 Hun (N. Y.), 146. § 473.
State *v.*, 86 Ind. 396. § 226.
Wyman *v.* Gray, 7 Harris & Johns. (Md.) 409. § 68.
Henniker *v.*, 58 N. H. 528. § 596.
Larson *v.*, 14 Wend. 246. §§ 76, 78.
v. Robinson, 73 Me. 384. § 112.
v. Yeomans, 84 Ill. 403. § 379.
Wymond, Tate *v.*, 7 Blackf. (Ind.) 240. § 374.
Wynn *v.* Brooke, 5 Rawle (Pa.), 106. § 217.
Green *v.*, Law Rep. 4 Ch. App. Cas. 204. § 147.
Wysors, Grubb *v.*, 32 Gratt. (Va.) 127. § 321.
Wythes *v.* Labouchere, 3 De Gex & Jones, 593. §§ 32, 419.
Xander *v.* Commonwealth, 102 Pa. St. 434. §§ 406, 574.
Yager, Drummond *v.*, 10 Bradw. (Ill. App.) 380. §§ 254, 260.
Yale *v.* Dederer, 18 N. Y. 265. § 7.
v. Edgerton, 14 Minn. 194. § 17.
v. Wheelock, 109 Mass. 502. § 153.
Yancey *v.* Brown, 3 Sneed (Tenn.), 89. § 196.
Harnsberger *v.*, 33 Gratt. (Va.) 527. §§ 152, 206, 268, 298.
Morrison *v.*, 23 Mo. App. 670. § 487.
Yandell, Lee *v.*, 69 Tex. 34. § 153.
Yantis, Letcher's Adm'r *v.*, 3 Dana (Ky.), 160. § 613.
Yarborough, Perry *v.*, 3 Jones' Eq. (N. C.) 66. § 226.
Rainey *v.*, 2 Ired. Eq. (N. C.) 249. § 290.
Yates, Bartley *v.*, 2 Hen. & Mun. (Va.) 398. § 26.
v. Donaldson, 5 Md. 389. § 29.
Kincaid *v.*, 63 Mo. 45. § 381.
v. Plaxton, 3 Levinz, 235. § 505.
Yazoo City, Mann *v.*, 31 Miss. 574. § 628.
Yearborough's Adm'r, Pickens *v.*, 26 Ala. 417. § 440.
Yeargain, Jones *v.*, 1 Dev. Law (N. C.), 420. § 28.
Yeargin, Rader *v.*, 85 Tenn. (1 Pickle), 486. § 586.
Winston *v.*, 50 Ala. 340. § 434.
Yeary *v.* Smith, 45 Tex. 56. § 342.
Yeates, Greenfield *v.*, 2 Rawle (Pa.), 158. § 121.
Yeomans, M'Doal *v.*, 8 Watts (Pa.), 361. § 98.
Wyman *v.*, 84 Ill. 403. § 379.
Yerby *v.* Grigsby, 9 Leigh (Va.), 387. §§ 89, 90.
Yingling, Freauer *v.*, 37 Md. 491. § 442.
Yoakley *v.* King, 10 Lea (Tenn.), 67. § 589.
Yoder, Richards *v.*, 10 Neb. 429. § 322.
Yongue *v.* Linton, 6 Rich. Law (S. C.), 275. § 253.
York *v.* Landis, 65 N. C. 535. § 226.
York Co. M. F. Ins. Co. *v.* Brooks, 51 Me. 506. §§ 408, 412.
v. Watson, 15 S. C. 1. § 558.
Yorkshire Railway Wagon Co. *v.* Maclure, Law Rep. (19 Ch. Div.) 478. § 6.
Yost *v.* State, 80 Ind. 350. § 540.
Young, Boling *v.*, 38 Ohio St. 135. § 342.
Bonner *v.*, 68 Ala. 35. § 588.
v. Brown, 53 Wis. 333. §§ 84, 159.
Chapeze *v.*, 87 Ky. 476. §§ 29, 259.
City Bank *v.*, 43 N. Y. 457. § 442.
v. Clark, 2 Ala. 264. § 288.
Dole *v.*, 24 Pick. 250. § 204.
Green *v.*, 8 Greenl. (Me.) 14. § 133.
Haslcham *v.*, 5 Ad. & Ell. (N. S.) 833. § 18.

Young, Harris *v.*, 40 Ga. 65. § 17.
Helm's Adm'r *v.*, 9 B. Mon. (Ky.) 394. § 325.
Johnson *v.*, 20 W. Va. 614. § 36.
Kims' Ex'r *v.*, 34 Pa. St. 60. § 153.
Kivett *v.*, 106 N. C. 567. § 594.
v. Lyons, 8 Gill (Md.), 162. §§ 288, 291, 292.
Oxley *v.*, 2 H. Black. 613. § 246.
v. Pickens, 45 Miss. 353. § 485.
Prather *v.*, 67 Ind. 480. § 377.
Sasscer *v.*, 6 Gill & Johns. (Md.) 243. § 436.
Seaver *v.*, 16 Vt. 658. § 247.
v. Shunk, 30 Minn. 503. § 255.
v. State, 7 Gill & Johns. (Md.) 253. § 517.
State *v.*, 23 Minn. 551. §§ 25, 542, 559.
Thompson *v.*, 2 Ohio, 335. § 171.
Twopenny *v.*, 3 Barn. & Cress. 208. § 367.
Waldron *v.*, 9 Heisk. (Tenn.) 777. § 381.
Young & Co., Carter Bros. *v.*, 9 Lea (Tenn.), 210. § 586.
Zacharies' Succession, Reynes *v.*, 10 La. (Curry), 127. § 626.
Zachery, Samuel *v.*, 4 Ired. Law (N. C.), 377. § 288.
Zahm *v.* First Nat. Bank, 103 Pa. St. 576. §§ 100, 644.
Zane *v.* Kennedy, 73 Pa. St. 182. § 312.
Zeilsdorff, Ketchum *v.*, 26 Wis. 514. § 486.
Zent's Ex'rs *v.* Heart, 8 Pa. St. 337. § 143.
Ziegler, Detroit Savings Bank *v.*, 49 Mich. 157. § 561.
Zimmermann *v.* Judah, 13 Ind. 286. § 399.
Judah *v.*, 22 Ind. 388. § 399.
Beach *v.*, 106 Ind. 495. § 344.
Zink, Johnson *v.*, 51 N. Y. 333. § 37.
Zollar *v.* Janvrin, 49 N. H. 114. § 472.
Zollickoffer *v.* Feth, 44 Md. 359. § 207.
Zschwetzke, Knobloch *v.*, 21 J. & S. (N. Y. Sup. Ct.) 391. § 37.
Zurcher *v.* Krohne, Feiss & Co., 63 Tex. 118. § 45.

THE LAW

OF

SURETYSHIP AND GUARANTY.

CHAPTER I.

OF THE CONTRACT.

What is surety or guarantor — Difference between them . . § 1
Contract of surety and indorser — Difference between stated 2
Origin and requisites of the contract 3
Liability of surety or guarantor who is an infant — Unsoundness of mind of surety . . 4
When guaranty by railroad company and bank valid, and by city void 5
Guaranty by railroad company and bank continued . . . 6
Liability of married woman who becomes surety 7
When statute says party shall not be received as surety he is nevertheless bound if he is received as such 8
Surety companies 9
Sufficiency of sureties — Pecuniary responsibility 10
Same continued — Residence of sureties 11
When duress a defense to surety or guarantor 12
There must be a consideration to support the contract . . . 13
Same continued . . . . . . § 14
Executory consideration to principal alone sufficient . . . 15
Agreement by creditor to forbear towards principal sufficient 16
Executed consideration to principal not sufficient — Damages to creditor sufficient 17
How far partner can bind firm as surety or guarantor . . . 18
Same continued 19
How far agent can bind principal as surety or guarantor . 20
Where act of principal is prohibited by law or is fraudulent, surety not bound 21
Voluntary bond not required by law, or different from bond required, valid 22
Same continued 23
Voluntary bond binds surety 24
Obligation of surety must be delivered, and takes effect from time of delivery 25
Surety bound when his name not mentioned in body of instrument — Not bound when penalty of bond blank 26
Same continued 27

When party liable on implied guaranty . . . . § 28
Joint maker of note may be shown by parol to be surety . 29
Joint maker of sealed instrument may be shown by parol to be surety 30
Liability of surety who adds the words "surety" or "security" to his name 31
If creditor knew of suretyship when he did the act complained of, this is sufficient to secure surety his rights . . 32
Surety must show that creditor knew of suretyship — What is sufficient evidence of the fact 33
Property pledged by one for debt of another occupies position of surety 34
Property of wife pledged for debt of husband occupies position of surety 35
When retiring member of firm becomes surety of other partners for firm debts 36
Vendor of land who sells it subject to mortgage is surety for mortgage debt 37
Joint obligors are sureties for each other — When sole maker of note or bond is surety, etc. 38
Stockholders of a corporation, liable for its debts, are not its sureties — When surety becomes principal, etc. . . . § 39
Surety entitled to same rights after judgment against him as before 40
Surety, who in terms binds himself as principal, not entitled to rights of surety 41
Surety estopped to deny recitals of his obligation 42
Same continued 43
Same continued — Reason . . 44
Same continued 45
When surety not estopped by recitals of obligations signed by him 46
Cases holding guaranty of note negotiable 47
Cases holding that guaranty of debt passes to assignee of debt 48
Cases holding guaranty of note not negotiable 49
Whether guaranty of bond negotiable, or lease assignable — When guaranty on back of note transfers title to note — Obligation of surety cannot be sold alone 50

§ 1. What is a surety or guarantor — Difference between them.— A surety or guarantor is one who becomes responsible for the debt, default or miscarriage of another person.[1] The words surety and guarantor are ofter used indiscrimi-

[1] In Jones *v.* Whitehead, 4 Ga. 397, Lumpkin, J., said: "Suretyship has been defined to be a lame substitute for a thorough knowledge of human nature." For a careful and excellent statement of what a surety is, see Smith *v.* Shelden, 35 Mich. 42, per Cooley, C. J. See, also, Wendlandt *v.* Sohre, 37 Minn. 162, where it is said: "A surety is any person who, being liable to pay a debt, is entitled, if it is enforced against him, to be indemnified by some other person who ought himself to have paid it before the surety was compelled to do so." And see further Carsan *v.* Maxwell, 39 Minn. 391, 393. Under the Louisiana Civil Code, the contract of suretyship is accessory, and presupposes the existence of a principal obligation. See Gay & Co. *v.* Blanchard, 32 La. Ann. 497.

nately as synonymous terms; but while a surety and a guarantor have this in common, that they are both bound for another person, yet there are points of difference between them which should be carefully noted. A surety is usually bound with his principal by the the same instrument, executed at the same time and on the same consideration. He is an original promisor and debtor from the beginning, and is held ordinarily to know every default of his principal. Usually he will not be discharged, either by the mere indulgence of the creditor to the principal, or by want of notice of the default of the principal, no matter how much he may be injured thereby. On the other hand, the contract of the guarantor is his own separate undertaking, in which the principal does not join. It is usually entered into before or after that of the principal, and is often founded on a separate consideration from that supporting the contract of the principal. The original contract of the principal is not his contract, and he is not bound to take notice of its non-performance. He is often discharged by the mere indulgence of the creditor to the principal, and is usually not liable unless notified of the default of the principal.[1] "The rules of the common law as to sureties are not strictly applied to guarantors, but rather the rules of the law merchant, and the true distinction seems to be this: That a surety is in the first instance answerable for the debt for which he makes himself responsible, and his contracts are often specialties, while a guarantor is only liable when default is made by the party whose undertaking is guarantied, and his agreement is one of simple contract."[2] The principal and

[1] McMillan *v.* Bull's Head Bank, 32 Ind. 11; Reigart *v.* White, 52 Pa. St. 438; Gaff *v.* Sims, 45 Ind. 262; Kramph's Ex'x *v.* Hatz's Ex'rs, 52 Pa. St. 525; Allen *v.* Hubert, 49 Pa. St. 259; Harris *v.* Newell, 42 Wis. 687. For a similar statement of the differences between the contract of suretyship and guaranty, see The Markland Mining & Mfg. Co. *v.* Kimmel *et al.*, 87 Ind. 560, 566; White's Adm'r *v.* Life Association of America, 63 Ala. 419, 423; Weik *et al. v.* Pugh *et al.*, 92 Ind. 382; La Rose *et al. v.* The Logansport Nat. Bank *et al.*, 102 Ind. 332, 335.

[2] Hubbard, J., in Curtis *v.* Dennis, 7 Metc. 510. In Kearnes *v.* Montgomery, 4 W. Va. 29, Maxwell, J. said: "The contract of a guarantor is collateral and secondary. It differs in that respect from the contract of a surety which is direct; and in general the guarantor contracts to pay if by the use of due diligence the debt cannot be made out of the principal debtor, while the surety undertakes directly for the payment, and

surety, being directly and equally bound, may be sued jointly in the same suit, while the guarantor, being bound by a separate contract and only collaterally liable, cannot usually be joined in the same suit with the principal.[1]

§ 2. Contract of surety and indorser — Difference between stated.— The rights, duties and liabilities of ordinary indorsers and sureties are so nearly alike that most acts which will discharge the one will also discharge the other. But there are points of distinction between them that are important to observe, "lest a principle exclusively applicable to one be perverted. For instance, without due demand and notice, at the maturity of a note, an indorser will be discharged — a surety continues liable upon his contract, though the creditor sleeps. A surety may spur the creditor into activity by notice to pursue the principal debtor, on pain, for neglect, that the surety will be no longer bound — not so an indorser. The latter cannot call upon the holder of a protested note to sue the drawer, and, if he refuses, thereby relieve himself; for, if he wishes instant recourse to the principal, it is his duty to pay the note and sue for himself."[2] Again it is said: "The liability of an ordinary indorser is greater than that of a surety. A surety becomes bound simply for the accommodation of his principal, and receives no consideration for the favor he bestows. He is bound only to the same extent as his principal, and whatever defense the principal succeeds in making inures to the benefit of the surety, whose undertaking is identical with that of the principal. By signing the paper he enters into no new or different contract to the payee from that into which his prin-

so is responsible at once if the principal debtor makes default." See a very excellent statement of the difference between direct and collateral guaranties in Milroy *v.* Quinn *et al.*, 69 Ind. 406, 410, 411, per Biddle, J.

[1] Read *v.* Cutts, 7 Greenleaf, 186. To similar effect see Clark *et al. v.* Morgan, 13 Bradwell (Ill. App.), 597; Abbott *v.* Brown, 30 Ill. App. 376. But under statute in Minnesota, an absolute guarantor, upon the same instrument with the maker of a promissory note, may be joined as defendant in the same action with the maker. Hammel *v.* Beardsley, 31 Minn. 314. So, also, a guarantor of the payment of rent accruing on a written lease, whose undertaking is indorsed thereon, may be sued jointly with the principal debtor. Lucy *v.* Wilkins, 33 Minn. 21.

[2] Trunkey, J., in Stephens *v.* Monongahela Nat. Bank, 88 Pa. St. 157, 163.

cipal has entered. Their obligation is generally contemporaneous, and is joint, or it may be both joint and several. But with an indorser it is different; he usually receives a consideration for his promise. If the note he indorsed is for any cause invalid, he is nevertheless bound; as, for instance, if it is without consideration, or is founded upon a gaming or usurious consideration, or was forged, he would be liable on his indorsement, notwithstanding the principal might on that account be released from its payment; or if, when he indorsed the paper, it had been barred by the statute of limitations, and no action could have been maintained on it against the maker, he would nevertheless have been bound by his contract to pay the money it was made to secure, according to its terms and stipulations."[1]

§ 3. **Origin and requisites of the contract.**— The party to whom the surety or guarantor becomes bound is called the creditor or obligee. The party for whom he becomes bound is called the principal or principal debtor. The surety or guarantor becomes such by means of contract. Some of the earliest contracts mentioned in history were those of suretyship, and the origin of the contract is shrouded in the mists of antiquity. Some at least of the incidents of suretyship were well understood in the remotest times. In the Bible it is written, "He that is surety for a stranger shall smart for it, and he that hateth suretyship is sure."[2] To constitute the contract of suretyship or guaranty, the same things are necessary as to constitute any other contract, viz.: That the parties be competent to contract; that they actually do contract; and that the contract, if not under seal, be supported by a sufficient consideration.[3] Any one competent to contract generally may enter into the contract of suretyship or guaranty.[4] Such

[1] Graham *v.* Roberson, 79 Ga. 72, 73, per Hall, J.

[2] Proverbs XI, 15. The supreme court of Iowa say: "It is doubtless a hardship on him [the surety] that he should be required to pay the debt, but he assumed liability for it when he signed the note. He is but paying the penalty which all men incur when they assume the relation of suretyship for others." Auchampaugh *v.* Schmidt, 77 Iowa, 13, 17.

[3] Where the guarantee accepts the guaranty, and, acting upon the faith of it, performs the consideration upon which it is given, the contract of guaranty is complete. Snyder *v.* Click, 112 Ind. 293.

[4] A sister-in-law may become bound as surety for a brother to whom she

contract must be in writing,[1] and not opposed to public policy.[2]

§ 4. **Liability of surety or guarantor who is an infant — Unsoundness of mind of surety.**— The contract of suretyship or guaranty made by an infant is not void, but may be ratified by him upon arriving at majority. But in order to charge one who was an infant when he made such a contract, it is necessary to show that subsequent to the time he became of age he had full knowledge that he was not bound, and afterwards distinctly ratified the contract.[3] The undertaking of an infant as surety for another on a note,[4] or on a recognizance for the appearance of a defendant named therein,[5] or for a stay of execution,[6] is not void, but only voidable, and if ratified and confirmed by him upon attaining his majority becomes a valid contract and enforceable against him. A person of unsound mind who becomes surety on a note cannot be held liable thereon, even though the person taking the note had no knowledge of the surety's unsoundness of mind.[7]

§ 5. **When guaranty by railroad company and bank valid, and by city void.**— Where, under the laws of Iowa, a railroad company had power to issue its own bonds to pay for the construction of its road, it was held it might guaranty the bonds of cities and counties which had been lawfully issued and were the means of accomplishing the same end.[8] A bank may guar-

looks for protection. Campbell & Jones *v.* Murray *et al.*, 62 Ga. 86.

[1] Ingersoll *v.* Baker, 41 Mich. 48; Bonine *v.* Denniston, 41 Mich. 292.

[2] As where sureties to an administrator's bond became such in consideration that the administrator deposit with them the proceeds of the estate during the pendency of proceedings in administration, they paying interest thereon and using the proceeds in their business. Deobold *v.* Oppermann, 111 N. Y. 531. For other cases involving the same principle, see Board of Education *v.* Thompson, 33 Ohio St. 321; Rouse *v.* Glissman, 29 Ill. App. 321.

[3] Owen *v.* Long, 112 Mass. 403; Hinely *v.* Margaritz, 3 Pa. St. 428; Fetrow *v.* Wiseman, 40 Ind. 148.

[4] Williams *v.* Hanison, 11 S. C. 412; Maples *v.* Wightman, 4 Conn. 376.

[5] Patchin *v.* Cromach, 13 Vt. 330; Reed *v.* Lane, 61 Vt. 481; State *v.* Satterwhite, 20 S. C. 536.

[6] Harner *v.* Dipple, 31 Ohio St. 72.

[7] Van Patton & Marks *v.* Beals & Hammer, 46 Ia. 62. The insanity of a surety whose share of the principal's debt has been paid by a co-surety, held not to excuse delay on the latter's part to demand contribution. Pickering *v.* Leiberman, 41 Fed. Rep. 376 (Dist. Ct. D. Del.).

[8] Railroad Company *v.* Howard, 7 Wall. 392. In Arnot *v.* Erie R. R.

anty the payment of bonds pledged by its debtor to a third person as collateral security for money with which the debtor pays the bank, even though the bonds have never been assigned to the bank.[1] In the last two cases the guarantor accomplished a legitimate object by means of its guaranty, and did not assume any more onerous obligation than if it had issued its own bonds in the one case or guarantied bonds assigned to it in the other. But where the municipal government of New Orleans guarantied certain notes of a corporation whose purpose it was to open up navigation through a portion of the city, it was held the guaranty was void, because the city had no authority to make it, although the city might lawfully have opened up the navigation. The court said: "It can hardly be maintained as a legal proposition that for every act for which an agent may expend money for his principal, he can bind his principal in a contract of suretyship. . . . The open and direct appropriation and expenditure of money by officers of a municipal corporation has nothing in it in common with the contingent and long-enduring contract of suretyship."[2]

§ 6. **Guaranty by railroad company and bank continued.**— A railroad company has no authority, in the absence of an explicit grant of such power, to guaranty a specified dividend on its stock as an inducement to purchasers.[3] And it is likewise beyond its power to guaranty the payment of the expenses of a musical festival.[4] In selling and disposing of bonds and other negotiable paper received by a railroad company in the transaction of its legitimate business, it may properly

Co., 5 Hun, 608, one railroad company guarantied the interest coupons on certain bonds of another railroad company. The bonds afterwards came into possession of the guarantor, and it transferred them for value. *Held*, it was estopped to deny its liability upon the guaranty of the coupons. And see Taylor *v.* Railroad Company, 11 Lea (Tenn.), 186, where the Memphis & Charleston Railroad Company guarantied the prompt payment and interest of bonds issued by the city of Memphis.

[1] Talman *v.* Rochester City Bank, 18 Barb. 123.

[2] Louisiana State Bank *v.* Orleans Navigation Company, 3 La. Ann. 294, per Eustis, C. J. This on the principle that, the principal contract being void, the guaranty falls with it. Joslyn *v.* Dow, 19 Hun (N. Y.), 494.

[3] Elevator Company *v.* Memphis & Charleston R. R. Co., 85 Tenn. (1 Pickle) 703.

[4] Davis *v.* Old Colony R. R. Co., 131 Mass. 258.

guaranty that they are genuine; and a guaranty of the payment of the same would be valid and binding on the company.[1] So a railroad company may, in consideration that a steamboat company carry passengers and freight for it, guaranty that the gross earnings of such steamboat company shall amount to a certain sum within a certain time.[2] Under statute authorizing railroad companies to lease and operate the roads of other companies, a contract of lease wherein a railroad company guaranties the payment of interest on bonds given in payment for the construction of a road is valid.[3] A guaranty by the directors of a railway company of the payment of rent of rolling stock is valid.[4] A bank may lawfully guaranty the payment of a note.[5] And it is held that the directors of a joint-stock bank may, where there are extensive powers conferred upon them, guaranty the payment of interest on the bonds of another company, when the company organized is of importance to the bank.[6]

§ 7. Liability of married woman who becomes surety.— A married woman cannot, unless enabled by statute, become surety for her husband or a stranger.[7] She cannot bind herself nor her separate property either at law or in equity by such a contract. The contract is absolutely void at law, and equity will not charge her separate estate where she has received no benefit.[8] In many states, by statute, a married

[1] Atchison, Topeka & Santa Fe R. R. Co. *v.* Fletcher, 35 Kan. 236.

[2] Green Bay & Minn. R. R. Co. *v.* Union Steamboat Co., 107 U. S. 98.

[3] Eastern Township Bank *v.* St. Johnsbury & L. C. R. Co. (U. S. Cir. Ct. D. Vt.), 40 Fed. Rep. 423.

[4] Yorkshire Railway Wagon Co. *v.* Maclure, Law Rep. (19 Ch. Div.) 478.

[5] People's Bank *v.* National Bank, 101 U. S. 181. Though it is held in New York that a national bank cannot become an accommodation indorser of a promissory note. National Bank of Gloversville *v.* Wells, 79 N. Y. 498, reversing 15 Hun, 51.

[6] *In re* West of England Bank and *Ex parte* Boaker, Law Rep. (14 Ch. Div.) 317. See further on this subject, Dobell *et al.* *v.* The Ontario Bank *et al.*, 3 Ont. (Can.) 299.

[7] Firemen's Ins. Co. *v.* Cross, 4 Rob. (La.) 508; Gosman *v.* Cruger, 7 Hun, 60, affirmed in 69 N. Y. 87, wherein it was held that she was not liable even though she became surety in compliance with an order of court. Married woman cannot in Arkansas become surety on an official bond. Hyner *v.* Dickinson, 32 Ark. 776.

[8] Yale *v.* Dederer, 18 N. Y. 265; same case again, 22 N. Y. 450; Perkins *v.* Elliott, 8 C. E. Green (N. J.), 526. It is the generally established doctrine that in order for a married woman to create a charge upon her separate estate the intention to charge the same must be clearly expressed,

woman may hold, manage and contract with reference to her separate property the same as if she were unmarried. She cannot, however, by virtue of such a statute become a surety. The intention was, by such statutes, to remove her disabilities for her interest, and not to enable her to contract onerous obligations from which she derived no benefit.[1] But where a statute provided that a married woman might contract the same as a *feme sole*, it was held that she might lawfully mortgage her homestead for an existing debt of her son.[2] So where a statute provided that the "contract of any married woman made for any lawful purpose . . . (should) be valid and binding and . . . (might) be enforced in the same manner as if she were sole," it was held that a married woman might become a surety, the contract of suretyship being a lawful contract, and in that case, for a lawful purpose.[3] But where a statute empowered a married woman "to contract, sell, transfer, mortgage, convey, devise and bequeath her own property and in the same manner and with the like effect as if she were unmarried," it was held that she could not enter into a contract of suretyship.[4] In many states a married woman is positively

or the contract must be one going to the direct benefit of the estate. Curtan *v.* David *et al.*, 18 Nev. 310; Savings Bank *v.* Scott, 10 Neb. 83.

[1] Athol Machine Co. *v.* Fuller, 107 Mass. 437. In West *v.* Laraway, 28 Mich. 464, where a married woman had signed a note with her husband as his surety, it was contended that although she was not personally bound, the note operated as a charge on her separate estate. But the court held otherwise, and said that if such were the case she would be in a worse position than a man or a *feme sole*, because a note by either of them would not be a lien on their property. In De Vries *v.* Conklin, 22 Mich. 255, the court in speaking of the married woman's statute said: "The disabilities are removed only so far as they operated unjustly and oppressively; beyond that they are suffered to remain. Having been removed with the beneficent design to protect the wife in the enjoyment and disposal of her property for the benefit of herself and her family, the statute cannot be extended by construction to cases not embraced by its language nor within its design." In South Carolina, after the amendment of the law limiting the right of a married woman to contract as to her separate estate, it is held that she cannot enter into or be bound by any contract of suretyship. Harris *v.* McCaslan, 31 S. C. 420; Gwynn *v.* Gwynn, 31 S. C. 482.

[2] Low *v.* Anderson, 41 Iowa, 476; and to similar effect see Hart *v.* Grigsby, 14 Bush (Ky.), 542.

[3] Mayo *v.* Hutchinson, 57 Me. 546.

[4] Russell *v.* People's Savings Bank, 39 Mich. 671.

forbidden to enter into or bind her estate by any contract of suretyship.[1] Under such a statute she cannot execute a mortgage upon her separate estate to secure her husband's debt,[2] though a conveyance by her of property held in trust for her husband to secure his debt is not invalidated by such statute.[3] Where a married woman, having a separate estate, executes a note as surety, it is presumed that she intends to bind her estate.[4] But where she is sued upon her individual note, which is secured by a mortgage on her separate estate, her husband joining, there is no presumption that she occupies the relation of surety or guarantor, and the burden is on her to show her suretyship.[5] A married woman may become surety for a partnership of which her son is a member,[6] and may mortgage her separate estate for the liabilities of a partnership of which her husband is a member.[7] Under a statute providing that a married woman may, when she is a party to an action, enter into any bond or undertaking, she is not disqualified from executing as surety an undertaking upon appeal.[8]

§ 8. **When statute says party shall not be received as surety, he is nevertheless bound if he is received as such.** A statute providing that attorneys shall not be received as bail in a criminal case is constitutional,[9] but such a statute is only directory; and if an attorney signs a bail bond, and is received as bail, he is bound, notwithstanding the prohibition of the statute.[10] So also, where a statute prohibited an attor-

[1] Such is the case in Georgia: Saulsbury *v.* Weaver, 59 Ga. 254; Beatie *v.* Calhoun, 73 Ga. 269. Iowa: Sweazy *v.* Kammer, 51 Iowa, 642. Indiana: Dodge *v.* Kinzy *et al.*, 101 Ind. 102; Nixon *v.* Whitely *et al.*, 102 Ind. 360.

[2] Brown *v.* Will, 103 Ind. 71; Cupp *et al.* *v.* Campbell, 103 Ind. 213.

[3] Stringer *v.* Montgomery *et al.*, 111 Ind. 489.

[4] Williams *v.* Urmston, 35 Ohio St. 296, overruling in so far as they conflict, Levi *v.* Earl, 30 Ohio St. 147, and Rice *v.* Railroad, 32 Ohio St. 380.

[5] Miller *v.* Shields, 124 Ind. 166.

[6] Pelzer *v.* Campbell, 15 S. C. 581. The court said: "None of the considerations of bad policy as to the wife's being allowed to sign as surety for her husband apply here."

[7] Penn. Coal Co. *v.* Blake, 85 N. Y. 226.

[8] Woolsey *v.* Brown, 74 N. Y. 82, affirming 11 Hun, 52.

[9] Johnson *v.* Commonwealth, 2 Duvall (Ky.), 410.

[10] Sherman *v.* The State, 4 Kan. 570; Jack *v.* The People, 19 Ill. 57; Holandsworth *v.* Commonwealth, 11 Bush, 617. In the case last cited the court said: "If those of the exempted or privileged classes persist in tender-

ney from becoming a surety upon an attachment bond, he is bound thereon if he becomes surety and the bond is approved.[1] Rules of court prohibiting attorneys from becoming sureties on appeal bonds,[2] or other causes pending therein, except under special leave, are directory merely, and attorneys who become sureties in violation thereof are liable on their obligations, and, at most, are guilty of contempt.[3] Where, however, a city charter prohibits an alderman from becoming surety on a bond to the city, a different rule seems to prevail, and it is held that if he executes such a bond he cannot be held liable thereon.[4] Where a statute provided that bail should be a resident of the state, a non-resident who was accepted as bail was held bound.[5] A statute provided that administrators should take notes with two sureties for certain debts due estates. A note in such case was taken with only one surety, and he was held liable, it not appearing that any fraud or imposition had been practiced upon him.[6]

§ 9. **Surety companies.**— Statutes authorizing the organization of corporations for the purpose of guarantying bonds and undertakings, as well as the fidelity of persons holding positions of public or private trust, are held valid, and such companies may lawfully become liable as sureties or guarantors.[7] The amount paid to such surety companies for becoming surety in an undertaking is not a taxable disbursement.[8] A statute requiring two sureties to all undertakings may be dispensed with where an appeal bond is signed by a guaranty

ing themselves as bail, and by becoming such procure the discharge of persons accused of crime, they will not be heard to say that they are not bound because they violated the law." See, also, Wright *v.* Schmidt *et al.*, 47 Iowa, 233, and Evans *v.* Harris, 15 J. & S. (N. Y. Superior Ct.) 366; Cook *v.* Caraway *et al.*, 29 Kan. 41. Statutes forbidding county courts from accepting an official bond with the name of a judge of the court as a surety thereon, *held* directory merely, and the bond is not void if the statute has been disregarded. State *v.* Findly, 101 Mo. 368.

[1] Tessier *v.* Crowley, 17 Neb. 207.

[2] The Ohio & Mississippi R'y Co. *v.* Hardy, 64 Ind. 454.

[3] Kohn Bros. *v.* Washer, 69 Tex. 67.

[4] City of Fond du Lac *v.* Moore, 58 Wis. 170.

[5] Commonwealth *v.* Ramsay, 2 Duvall (Ky.), 386.

[6] Reynolds *v.* Dechaums, 24 Tex. 174.

[7] Hurd *v.* Hannibal & St. Joseph R. R. Co., 33 Hun, 109; Cramer *v.* Tittle, 72 Cal. 12.

[8] Bick *v.* Reese, 52 Hun, 125.

company regularly organized for the purpose of guarantying bonds and undertakings.[1] It is not essential that surety and guaranty companies possess the qualifications required of sureties by statute, though the manner of justifying is the same; but the officer whose duty it is to approve the bond or undertaking may exercise his discretion as to whether the statement of the company's business justifies an approval.[2]

§ 10. **Sufficiency of sureties—Pecuniary responsibility.** Where a statute requires the pecuniary responsibility of sureties to be inquired into and determined by the officer approving the obligation of any surety, the surety's personal property as well as realty must be considered.[3] But where by statute a surety must not only be good and solvent and reside within the jurisdiction of the court, but must also have property susceptible of being legally reached by the sheriff and subjected by him to the payment of the pressing creditors' claims, it is held that a surety who carries all his property in his pocket, as, for example, negotiable securities, is not such a surety as the law requires.[4] The sufficiency of sureties to a contract is not shown by the mere production of the contract. The court must have some evidence upon which it can say that they were sufficient sureties.[5] "In estimating the sufficiency of sureties to bonds, it is the daily practice of the courts to take into account the obligatious entered into already by the party whose sufficiency is disputed, and we know of no good reason why it should not be so. If a score of attachments were taken out successively, and the same surety were given to each bond, who was proved to be worth the amount of the first and largest, and no more, it would be small safety to the bonds subsequently given to pronounce the same party sufficient as the sole surety to them."[6] Where sureties in justifying as to their pecuniary responsibility make statements

[1] Hurd *v.* Hannibal & St. Joseph R. R. Co., 33 Hun, 109; Travis *v.* Travis, 48 Hun, 343.

[2] Earle *v.* Earle, 17 J. & S. (N. Y. Superior Ct.) 57.

[3] Post *v.* Township Board of Sparta, 63 Mich. 323.

[4] State *ex rel.* Menge *v.* Righton, Judge, 36 La. Ann. 711, overruling so far as is inconsistent, State *ex rel.* Fabre *v.* Judge Fifth Dist. Ct., 28 La. Ann. 884.

[5] Regina *v.* Richardson, 17 Ont. (Can.) 729.

[6] Durham & Co. *v.* Lisso & Scheen, 32 La. Ann. 415, per Manning, J.

which they know to be false, they are guilty of perjury,[1] and may be committed for contempt of court.[2] A surety may, in order to avoid justification, deposit in court the amount for which he is bound, and in such case the deposit becomes the principal's and the surety the principal's creditor.[3] The substitution of a sufficient for an insufficient surety will not be made by the supreme court when the case is there on appeal;[4] neither will a federal court enter upon the sufficiency of the sureties on a bond, conditioned as required by the removal act and approved by the state court.[5] Legatees under a will, having no other property except that to be derived through the will, are insufficient sureties on the bond of the executor of the will.[6]

§ 11. Same continued — Residence of sureties.— A surety on an official bond cannot be heard to say that he is not liable thereon because the statute requires such sureties to be residents of the state,[7] or of the county,[8] and he is not. But where, however, a surety is so habitually absent from the state as to leave his domicile in doubt, he may properly be declared an insufficient surety.[9] In the federal court it is held

[1] Ralph *v.* United States, 9 Fed. Rep. 693 (Cir. Ct. N. D. Ill.). An affidavit of the qualification of a surety on an appeal bond, which leaves the name of the surety blank at the beginning of the affidavit, thus: "——, being first duly sworn," etc., but contains no other defect, held sufficient. Brown *v.* Jessup, 19 Oreg. 288.

[2] Egan *v.* Lynch, 17 J. & S. (N. Y. Superior Ct.) 454. A surety in justifying need not give, however, a description of his property, but only its amount and value. Hodgkin *v.* Holland, 34 Ark. 200.

[3] Lyon *v.* Wilder, 24 J. & S. (N. Y. Superior Ct.) 67.

[4] Durham & Co. *v.* Lisso & Scheen, 32 La. Ann. 415.

[5] Van Allen *v.* Atch., Col. & Pac. R. R. Co., 3 Fed. Rep. 545 (Cir. Ct. D. Kan.).

[6] Ellis *v.* Witty *et al.*, Ex'rs, 63 Miss. 117. Where a statute provided that all undertakings upon appeal should be accompanied by an affidavit of one of the sureties thereto that he is worth double the amount specified therein, held that the affidavit of another, as to the pecuniary reputation of a surety, was insufficient. Morphew *v.* Tatem, 89 N. C. 183.

[7] Board School Directors *v.* Brown *et al.*, 33 La. Ann. 383. In Arkansas the constitution prohibits non-residents from becoming sureties on the official bonds of county officers. Hyner *v.* Dickinson, 32 Ark. 776.

[8] State *v.* Thim, 77 Ala. 100. And even in the absence of a statutory provision requiring it, such a defense would be of no avail. The sureties on an attachment bond need not necessarily be residents of the county wherein the attachment was levied. Mobile Mut. Ins. Co. *v.* Cleveland, 76 Ala. 321.

[9] *Ex parte* Buckley, 53 Ala. 42.

that the sureties on a receiver's bond need not be citizens of the same state in which the action is pending.[1]

§ 12. **When duress a defense to surety or guarantor.**— If the surety or guarantor acts under duress in entering into the contract, he will not be bound.[2] And this for the same reason that a person sought to be charged on a contract of any other kind would not be bound, viz., because he never consented to it. But when the duress is exercised on the principal alone, a different question arises. It has been held that the duress of the principal, who is a stranger to the surety, will be no defense to the surety.[3] It has also been held, and it seems with the better reason, that the duress of the principal alone is a complete defense to the surety.[4] Where a statutory bond for the liberties of a prison was executed by the principal under duress, if the principal with the knowledge and consent of the surety claims and exercises the right of being on the liberties by virtue of such bond, they are both estopped to allege its invalidity.[5] Where a creditor caused the arrest of a debtor, and under a threat of sending him to state's prison forced him to sign a note, and his wife, who was then in a delicate condition, was induced by the same threats to indorse the note, it was held she might avail herself of the duress.[6] A state treasurer gave bond with sureties as required

[1] Taylor *v.* The Life Ass'n of America (Cir. Ct. W. D. Tenn.), 3 Fed. Rep. 465.

[2] Small *v.* Currie, 2 Drewry, 102.

[3] Wayne *v.* Sands, Freeman, 351; Simmons *v.* Barefoots' Ex'rs, 2 Haywood (N. C.), 606; Thompson *v.* Buckhannon, 2 J. J. Marsh. 416; Tucker *et al. v.* State, 72 Ind. 242. Duress of the principal will not avail the surety as a defense, unless the surety, at the time of executing the obligation, was ignorant of the circumstances which made it voidable by the principal. Hazard *v.* Griswold (Cir. Ct. D. R. I.), 21 Fed. Rep. 178.

[4] Hawes *v.* Marchant, 1 Curtis, 136; Owens *v.* Mynatt, 1 Heisk. (Tenn.) 675. The reason given in the last case is that if it were otherwise, the surety, being compelled to pay, could recover from his principal and thus the principal be deprived of his defense. See, also, Putnam *v.* Schuyler, 4 Hun, 166; Coffelt *et al. v.* Wise *et al.*, 62 Ind. 451. And see, also, Patterson *v.* Gibson, 81 Ga. 802.

[5] Hawes *v.* Marchant, 1 Curtis, 136.

[6] Ingersoll *v.* Roe, 65 Barb. (N. Y.) 346. But where a wife was induced to sign a note for her husband under threats that unless she did so he would poison himself, it was held no duress, and therefore such defense was not available to her in an action upon such note. Wright *et al. v.* Remington, 41 N. J. Law, 48. In Thompson *v.* Buckhannon, 2 J. J. Marsh. 416, Robertson, J., said: "If

by law, and afterwards held over under a constitutional provision, no successor being appointed. While holding over, he was "required and demanded" by the legislature to give a new bond in a much larger amount, and gave such bond with sureties. The sureties on the last bond claimed to be discharged on account of duress of their principal, but it was held there was no duress and that they were bound.[1] So when a board of supervisors threaten to declare an office vacant unless the incumbent executes the required bond, and the bond is accordingly executed, the sureties thereon cannot evade their liability on the ground of duress.[2] Where an officer executes a several, and not a joint and several, bond as required, a direction to execute a new bond which is done in compliance therewith cannot be considered as executed under duress.[3]

§ 13. **There must be a consideration to support the contract — Instances.**— As already stated, the contract of suretyship or guaranty, when not under seal, must, in order to render it valid, be supported by a sufficient consideration.[4] A consideration of one dollar is sufficient to support a contract of suretyship or guaranty for any amount, for the law cannot take account of the prudence or imprudence of the bargain the surety or guarantor has made.[5] But there must be some consideration,

an officer *colore officii* exacts a bond to himself which he has no authority to require, the security may avoid it as well as the principal, because being not only unauthorized but positively prohibited, it is totally void."

[1] Sooy *ads.* State, 38 N. J. Law, 324, adhered to in Sooy, Jr. *et al. v.* State, 41 N. J. Law, 394.

[2] State *v.* Harney *et al.*, 57 Miss. 863.

[3] Soule *v.* United States, 100 U. S. 8.

[4] Pfeiffer *v.* Kingsland, 25 Mo. 66; Barrell *v.* Trussell, 4 Taunt. 117–20; Saunders *v.* Wakefield, 4 Barn. & Ald. 595; Bailey *v.* Freeman, 4 Johns. 280; Leonard *v.* Vredenburgh, 8 Johns. 29; Cobb *v.* Page, 17 Pa. St. 469; French *v.* French, 2 Man. & Gr. 644; Aldridge *v.* Turner, 1 Gill & Johns. (Md.) 427; Tenney *v.* Prince, 4 Pick. 385; Clark *v.* Small, 6 Yerg. (Tenn.) 418; Cowles, Exr, *v.* Peck, 55 Conn. 251; Briggs *v.* Latham, 36 Kan. 205. See, on this subject, Barney *v.* Forbes, 118 N. Y. 580, affirming 44 Hun, 446.

[5] Lawrence *v.* McCalmont, 2 Howard (U. S.), 426; Jackson's Adm'r *v.* Jackson, 7 Ala. 791; Davis *v.* Wells, 104 U. S. 159. But where the consideration is one dollar, it may be shown by parol evidence what the real consideration was in fact — as that it was an extension of time. Taylor *v.* Wightman *et al.*, 51 Iowa, 411. In fact the entire transaction will be looked into in ascertaining the consideration. Wills *v.* Ross *et al.*, 77 Ind. 1.

usually either of benefit to the principal or surety, or detriment to the creditor, to support the contract. Leaving a claim in the hands of an attorney to control and collect is a sufficient consideration for a contemporaneous guaranty of the claim by him.[1] The liability of a surety on a note is a sufficient consideration for his subsequent written guaranty of its payment, whether at the date of the guaranty the right of action on the note is or is not barred by the statute of limitations.[2] A married woman without consideration became surety on the note of her husband. After the death of the husband she gave a new note for the amount of the former note and another note signed by her husband alone. Afterwards she gave another note and a mortgage to secure it, the only consideration for the last note being the note signed by her after her husband's death. It was held that all the papers executed by her were void for want of consideration.[3] One B., the assignee of a lease, assigned the lease to W., taking from W. and from R., his surety, an agreement to pay the rent. Held, this agreement was void for want of consideration. B. was liable for rent only so long as he held as assignee of the lease, and W. by accepting the assignment of the lease became liable for rent to the owner of the premises and not to B.[4]

§ 14. **Same continued.**— An essential requisite of the consideration upon which the contract of suretyship is based is that it must not be opposed to public policy. A note signed by a surety in consideration that the maker thereof shall not be prosecuted for embezzlement is void as opposed to public policy.[5] So a surety to a note made to a public officer for the private and illegal use or loan of public funds cannot be held liable thereon, for the reason that it is in contravention of public policy.[6] Commissions allowed to an agent for the sale of property are a sufficient consideration for his guaranty of

[1] Gregory *v.* Gleed, 33 Vt. 405.

[2] Miles *v.* Linnell, 97 Mass. 298. See on same subject, Buckner *v.* Clark's Ex'r, 6 Bush, 168.

[3] Hetherington *v.* Hixon, 46 Ala. 297.

[4] Stoppani *v.* Richard, 1 Hilton (N. Y.), 509.

[5] Rouse *v.* Glissman, 29 Ill. App. 321.

[6] Board of Education *v.* Thompson, 33 Ohio St. 321. See, also, an illustrative case involving the same principle, Deobold *v.* Oppermann, 111 N. Y. 531. And see, also, Ring *v.* Devlin, 68 Wis. 384.

notes taken by him in payment.[1] The surrender of an old note[2] or bond[3] is a sufficient consideration to support a guaranty of a new one.

§ 15. Executory consideration to principal alone sufficient.— It is not necessary to the validity of the consideration that any portion of it should move from the creditor to the surety or guarantor, provided the circumstances are such that a previous request on the part of the surety or guarantor is held to exist. A consideration moving to the principal alone contemporaneous with or subsequent to the promise of the surety or guarantor is sufficient.[4] If, after the original consideration has moved between the creditor and principal, the surety or guarantor signs upon a new consideration, moving from the creditor to the principal, this is sufficient.[5] When a guaranty on a note is without date, a jury may infer without further proof that it was made at the same time and on the same consideration as the note.[6] Where a promise that a surety or guarantor will become liable is part of the inducement on which the creditor acts in creating the original debt, this is a sufficient consideration to support the contract of the surety or guarantor who subsequently signs. A. told B. that if C. would lend B. money, he, A., would be surety for it. B. communicated this to C., and on the strength of it C. loaned B. money and took his note for it, due in one year. Three days after the note became due A. signed it, and he was held bound.[7] A principal executed and delivered a note to a cred-

[1] Newton Wagon Co. *v.* Diers, 10 Neb. 284. See further, cases on the sufficiency of the consideration, Lamb *v.* Briggs, 22 Neb. 138; Munson *v.* Adams, 89 Ill. 450; Worden *v.* Salter, 90 Ill. 160; Grigsby *v.* Shwarz, 82 Cal. 278; Barney *v.* Forbes, 118 N. Y. 580, affirming 44 Hun, 446.

[2] Churchill *v.* Bradley, 58 Vt. 403; Brewster *v.* Baker, 97 Ind. 260.

[3] Erie Co. Savings Bank *v.* Coit, 104 N. Y. 532.

[4] Wren *v.* Pearce, 4 Smedes & Marsh. (Miss.) 91; Freeman *v.* Freeman, 2 Bulst. 269; Bailey *v.* Croft, 4 Taunt. 611; Henderson *v.* Rice, 1 Cold. (Tenn.) 223; Robertson *v.* Findley, 31 Mo. 384; Leonard *v.* Vredenburgh, 8 Johns. 29; Morley *v.* Boothly, 10 Moore, 395; Bicksford *v.* Gibbs, 8 Cush. 154; McNaught *v.* McClaughry, 42 N. Y. 22; Savage *v.* Fox, 60 N. H. 17.

[5] Gay *v.* Mott, 43 Ga. 252.

[6] Bicksford *v* Gibbs, 8 Cush. 154; Underwood *v.* Hossack, 38 Ill. 208. On the same subject, see Snevily *v.* Johnston, 1 Watts & Serg. 307.

[7] Paul *v.* Stackhouse, 38 Pa. St. 302. The same principle was held in the case of a sale of goods by C. to B. under similar circumstances. Standley *v.* Miles, 36 Miss. 434.

itor which specified no time of payment, and at the same time agreed that he would procure B. to sign as surety if at any time the creditor should deem himself insecure. Afterwards the creditor returned the note to the principal, with the request that he would get B. to sign it, which he did, and B. was held liable.[1] The same principle was applied in a case where A. sold B. goods on the promise by B. that C. would guaranty the payment, and C. guarantied the payment of the note given by B. for the price of the goods about three hours after the note was given.[2] So a guaranty is binding when goods are contracted for one day by the principal, and the guaranty is executed the next day and delivered to the seller before the goods are delivered by him, because the sale was not complete till the goods were delivered.[3] A principal signed an undertaking, and at that time it was agreed between the principal and creditor that certain other parties should sign it as sureties. The writing was delivered by the principal to the creditor when it was signed, and the creditor afterwards and at another time presented it to the sureties, who signed it, and it was held they were bound.[4] A guaranty to "pay or cause to be paid the amount" awarded against one of the parties to an arbitration proceeding, executed concurrently with the agreement to submit to arbitration, is binding and valid.[5]

[1] McNaught *v.* McClaughry, 42 N. Y. 22.

[2] Wheelwright *v.* Moore, 2 Hall (N. Y.), 162. With reference to what is sufficient consideration for guaranty of promissory note by payee, who also indorses it, see Gillighan *v.* Boardman, 29 Me. 79.

[3] Simmons *v.* Keating, 2 Starkie, 375.

[4] Williams *v.* Perkins, 21 Ark. 18. Compton, J., said: "If the debt or obligation of the principal debtor is already incurred previous to the undertaking of the surety, then there must be a new and distinct consideration to sustain the promise of the surety. But if the obligation of the principal debtor be founded upon a good consideration, and at the time it is incurred or before that time the promise of the surety is made and enters into the inducement for giving the credit, then the consideration for which the principal debt is created is considered as a valid consideration also for the undertaking of the surety. . . . Although the signatures of the principal obligors were procured at one time and those of the sureties afterwards, nevertheless in contemplation of law their promises were contemporaneous and formed a part of one and the same general transaction, and the same consideration which supports the promise of the one also supports that of the other."

[5] Wood *v.* Tunnicliff, 74 N. Y. 38.

§ 16. Agreement by creditor to forbear towards principal sufficient.— An agreement on the part of the creditor to extend the time of payment to the principal for a definite time is a sufficient consideration for the contract of suretyship or guaranty, the one agreement being a consideration for the other, and the delay usually operating both as a benefit to the principal and a detriment to the creditor.[1] An agreement for forbearance for one year,[2] for a convenient time,[3] on an overdue note, for four years,[4] for a considerable time,[5] or for a reasonable time,[6] are any of them a sufficient consideration. An agreement on the part of the creditor for general indulgence toward the principal, without any definite time being specified, with proof of actual forbearance for a reasonable time, is sufficient.[7] An agreement for delay in consideration of further forbearance means forbearance for a convenient or reasonable time.[8] But in order that forbearance by the creditor towards the principal may be a sufficient consideration, there must be an agreement on the part of the creditor that he will forbear. Mere forbearance or omission on the part of the creditor to exercise his legal right without any agreement to that effect is not sufficient, because he may at any moment, and at his own pleasure, proceed. There must be promise for promise.[9] An agreement to withdraw, and the withdrawal of,

[1] Fuller *v.* Scott, 8 Kan. 25; Underwood *v.* Hossack, 38 Ill. 208; Pulliam *v.* Withers, 8 Dana (Ky.), 98; Dahlman *v.* Hammel, 45 Wis. 466; Coffin *v.* Trustees, 92 Ind. 337; Lee *v.* Wisner, 38 Mich. 82.

[2] Sage *v.* Wilcox, 6 Conn. 81.

[3] Sadler *v.* Hawkes, 1 Roll. Abr. 27, pl. 49; Tricket *v.* Mandlee, Sid. 45.

[4] Breed *v.* Hillhouse, 7 Conn. 523.

[5] Maples *v.* Sidney, Cro. Jac. 683.

[6] Johnson *v.* Whitchcott, 1 Roll. Abr. 24, pl. 33; Lonsdale *v.* Brown, 4 Wash. 148.

[7] Thomas *v.* Croft, 2 Richardson Law (S. C.) 113; Elting *v.* Vanderlyn, 4 Johns. 237; Oldershaw *v.* King, 2 Hurl. & Nor. 520; Rowlett *v.* Ewbank, 1 Bush (Ky.), 477; Wills *v.* Ross, 77 Ind. 1; Crears *v.* Hunter, Law Rep. (19 Q. B. Div.) 341; Davies *v.* Funston, 45 Up. Can. (Q. B.) 369.

[8] Caldwell *v.* Heitshur, 9 Watts & Serg. 51; Oldershaw *v.* King, 2 Hurl. & Nor. 520.

[9] Shupe *v.* Galbraith, 32 Pa. St. 10; Walker *v.* Sherman, 11 Met. (Mass.) 170; Mecorney *v.* Stanley, 8 Cush. (Mass.) 85; Breed *v.* Hillhouse, 7 Conn. 523; Crofts *v.* Beale, 11 Com. B. 172; Sage *v.* Wilcox, 6 Conn. 81. It was held in some old cases which have not been generally followed in later times, that an agreement to forbear for an indefinite period (Phillips *v.* Shackford, Cro. Eliz. 455), or for a short (Tolhurst *v.* Brickinden, Cro. Jac. 250), or some (Tricket *v.* Mandlee, Sid. 45), or a little time (1 Roll. Abr.

a suit or other proceeding against a principal is also a sufficient consideration.[1]

§ 17. Executed consideration to principal not sufficient — Damage to creditor sufficient.— Where the consideration between the principal and creditor has passed and become executed before the contract of the surety or guarantor is made, and such contract was no part of the inducement to the creation of the original debt, such consideration is not sufficient to sustain such contract.[2] One person entered into a contract with another by which he was to receive such other's promissory note without surety and the note was made and received. Afterwards the payee requested the maker to get a surety, and the maker took the note and had it subscribed by a third person, and returned it to the payee. There was no new consideration, and it was held the surety was not bound.[3] But where a bond was executed by the obligors and

23), would not be a sufficient consideration.

[1] Worcester Savings Bank *v.* Hill, 113 Mass. 25; Harris *v.* Venables, Law Rep. 7 Exch. 235.

[2] Tomlinson *v.* Gell, 6 Ad. & Ell. 564; Yale *v.* Edgerton, 14 Minn. 194; Williams *v.* Marshall, 42 Barb. 524; Thomas *v.* Williams, 10 Barn. & Cres. 664; Pratt *v.* Hedden, 121 Mass. 116; Farnsworth *v.* Clark, 44 Barb. 601; Eastwood *v.* Kenyon, 11 Ad. & Ell. 438; Ludwick *v.* Watson, 3 Oreg. 256; Parker *v.* Bradley, 2 Hill, 584; Hunt *v.* Bate, 3 Dyer, 272 (a); Stewart *v.* Hinkle, 1 Bond, 506; Leonard *v.* Vredenburgh, 8 Johns. 29; French *v.* French, 2 Man. & Gr. 644; McCreary *v.* Van Hook, 35 Tex. 631; Wood *v.* Benson, 2 Cr. & Jer. 94; 1 Roll. Abr. 27, pl. 49; Ashton *v.* Bayard. 71 Pa. St. 139; Payne *v.* Wilson, 7 Barn. & Cres. 423; Ellenwood *v.* Fults, 63 Barb. 321; Besshears *v.* Rowe, 46 Mo. 501; Lossee *v.* Williams, 6 Lans. 228; Harris *v.* Young, 40 Ga. 65; Sawyer *v.* Fernald, 59 Me. 500; Uhler *v.* Farmers' National Bank, 64 Pa. St. 406; Davis *v.* Banks, 45 Ga. 138; Badger *v.* Barnabee, 17 N. H. 120; Brown *v.* Brown, 47 Mo. 130; Ware *v.* Adams, 24 Me. 177; Clompton's Ex'rs *v.* Hall, 51 Miss. 482. But it is held that a guaranty for the payment of the hotel expenses of third persons to the extent of a stated sum is supported by a sufficient consideration as to the whole amount named, even though part of the expenses are already in great part incurred. Clune *v.* Ford & Eagan, 55 Hun, 479.

[3] Jackson *v.* Jackson, 7 Ala. 791. The court, Collier, C. J., among other things, said: "Any act in the nature of a benefit to the person who promises, or to any other person upon his request, or any act which is a trouble or detriment to him to whom the promise is made, is sufficient, and the amount of benefit or of trouble or detriment or its comparative value in relation to the promise is indifferent." See, also, Thorner *v.* Field, 1 Bulstr. 120; Hunt *v.* Bate, 3 Dyer, 272 (a).

the obligee refused to receive it unless it was guarantied, and A. thereupon guarantied it without any request from the obligors, and the obligee thereupon accepted the bond, it was held that the acceptance of the bond was a sufficient consideration for the guaranty.[1] A party sold a horse to another, being misled by false statements and representations of the purchaser, and took a note for the price. Discovering the fraud, the seller was about to rescind the contract and reclaim the horse. Upon being informed of these facts two days after the note was made, a surety put his name to the note and in consequence the property was not reclaimed. It was held that not reclaiming the horse was a good consideration for the agreement of the surety.[2] A guaranty of past and future advances made and to be made to a third person is good for the whole and the consideration sufficient.[3] But there must be an agreement on the part of the creditor to make the future advances, or he must actually make them, or there will be no consideration for the agreement to pay for the past advances, and it will be void.[4] It is not necessary that the consideration should consist of a benefit to the principal or surety. Any trouble, detriment or inconvenience to the creditor is sufficient.[5] When the consideration moves directly between the surety or guarantor and the creditor, the same rules apply which prevail with reference to the consideration for any other contract.[6]

[1] Gardner *v.* King, 2 Ired. Law (N. C.), 297.

[2] Harwood *v.* Kiersted, 20 Ill. 367. So also where a creditor claimed that he had been defrauded in the sale of goods to the debtor, and that unless further security was given he would reclaim them, and the debtor gives note with surety, and the creditor relinquishes his remedy, *held* the consideration was sufficient to bind the surety. Jaffray *v.* Brown, 74 N. Y. 393.

[3] Hargroves *v.* Cook, 15 Ga. 321; White *v.* Woodward, 5 Com. B. 810; Chapman *v.* Sutton, 2 Com. B. 634; Russell *v.* Moseley, 3 Bro. & Bing. 211. To the same effect with reference to attorneys' fees, see Roberts *v.* Griswold, 35 Vt. 496; also with reference to rent, see Vinal *v.* Richardson, 13 Allen, 521. To same effect as above, see Boyd *v.* Moyle, 2 Man. Gr. & S. 644. *Contra*, Wood *v.* Benson, 2 Cromp. & Jer. 94.

[4] Westhead *v.* Sproson, 6 Hurl. & Nor. 728; Boyd *v.* Moyle, 2 Com. B. 644. But see Morrell *v.* Cowan, Law Rep. (7 Ch. Div.) 151, reversing same case, Law Rep., 6 Eq. Div. 166.

[5] Wells *v.* Mann, 45 N. Y. 327; Colgin *v.* Henley, 6 Leigh (Va.), 85; Morley *v.* Boothly, 10 Moore, 395; Pillans *v.* Van Mierop, 3 Burr. 1663.

[6] Leonard *v.* Vredenburgh, 8 Johns. 29; Smith *v.* Finch, 2 Scam. (Ill.) 321.

§ 18. How far partner can bind firm as surety or guarantor.— One partner cannot usually bind the firm as sureties or guarantors for another.[1] The reason is that the business of a partnership is not commonly that of making contracts as sureties or guarantors; and the partner who makes such a contract acts outside the scope of his implied authority as agent of the firm. One member of a firm of attorneys has no right, in consideration of the discharge of their client from custody, to bind the firm to pay the debt of such client and the costs of suit.[2] So where certain partners were railroad contractors, and sublet a portion of their work to A., and it was necessary for A. to have brick to carry on the work, and he could not get them without coal, and one of the partners, without the knowledge of the others, gave a guaranty in the firm name for coal bought by A. for that purpose, it was held the guaranty did not bind the partnership.[3] Where, however, the partner who attempts to bind the firm has special authority for that purpose from the other members, he may bind the firm the same as any other agent having authority. So where the making of such a contract is within the usual scope of the business of the firm, it may be bound by the act of one partner in that regard. When the contract is made by a partner without authority, if the other members of the firm afterwards adopt it and act on it, the firm will be bound.[4]

[1] McQuewans *v.* Hamlin, 35 Pa. St. 517; Sutton *v.* Irwine, 12 Serg. & Rawle, 13; Rolston *v.* Chick, 1 Stew. (Ala.) 526; Sweetser *v.* French, 2 Cush. 309; Mayberry *v.* Bainton, 2 Harrington (Del.), 24; Duncan *v.* Lowndes, 3 Camp. 478; Crawford *v.* Stirling, 4 Esp. 207; Osborne *v.* Stone, 30 Minn. 25; Osborne *v.* Thompson, 35 Minn. 229. Where a partnership name is used by a member of the firm as surety, the presumption is that such use of the firm name is outside the firm business. Fore *et al. v.* Hitson *et al.*, 70 Tex. 517. An officer of a corporation cannot bind it as surety or guarantor. Culver *v.* Reno Real Estate Co., 91 Pa. St. 367.

[2] Hasleham *v.* Young, 5 Ad. & Ell. (N. S.) 833; Id., Dav. & Mer. 700. In Mauldin *v.* Branch Bank at Mobile, 2 Ala. 502, the court said, if an unauthorized indorsement by one member of a firm was on commercial paper, an innocent indorsee might recover against the firm. In Fuller *v.* Scott, 8 Kan. 25, when it was proved that a firm indorsed a note in blank in the firm name, the court said: "It would then be presumed that such indorsement was made in the firm business."

[3] Brettel *v.* Williams, 4 Wels., Hurl. & G. 623.

[4] Crawford *v.* Stirling, 4 Esp. 207; *Ex parte* Gardom, 15 Vesey, 286. See, also, on same subject, Sandilands *v.*

A firm sold a steamboat to A., and he gave a note for the purchase money to B., who was a creditor of the firm, in payment of the firm debt, and one of the firm signed the name of the firm to the note as sureties. It was held that the firm was bound, because it was in fact their own debt, and not the debt of another, that the note paid; and the substance, and not the form of the transaction, should be looked to.[1] One firm may become the surety of another firm, the same as one individual may become the surety of another.[2]

§ **19. Same continued.**— A partner cannot, by virtue of his partnership relation, sign the firm name as surety or guarantor of commercial paper not given in the course of the firm business.[3] And a note executed as the individual note of one partner, with a guaranty of the firm indorsed thereon, is *prima facie* an individual debt, and the burden of proof is upon the holder to show that it is in fact a firm transaction.[4] A partnership cannot become surety on a writ of error bond unless it appear therefrom the names of the members composing the firm as well as the authority for their becoming such security.[5] Where a bond containing the names of the members of a partnership as sureties thereto is signed by one partner, with the expectation, but not condition, that the other partners will likewise sign the same, the partner so signing will be individually liable thereon, but not the firm.[6] Where a partner signed the firm name to a guaranty that an employee of the firm would pay rent for his home so "long as said 'H.' remains in our employ," it was held that the partner alone and not the firm was bound.[7] Where, after the failure of a firm, one partner guaranties the payment of a firm obli-

Marsh, 2 Barn. & Ald. 673; Hope *v.* Cust, cited in Shirreff *v.* Wilks, 1 East, 53.

[1] Langan *v.* Hewett, 3 Smedes & Marsh. 122.

[2] Allen *v.* Morgan, 5 Humph. (Tenn.) 624. And it is held that one corporation may guaranty the bonds of another corporation. Phila. & R. R. Co. *v.* Knight *et al.*, 124 Pa. St. 58; Harrison *v.* Union Pacific R'y Co. (Cir. Ct. E. D. Mo.), 13 Fed. Rep. 522.

[3] Marsh *v.* Thompson National Bank, 2 Bradwell (Ill. App.), 217.

[4] Davis *v.* Blackwell, 5 Bradwell (Ill. App.), 32.

[5] Buchard *v.* Cavins, 77 Tex. 365, adhering to Donnelly *v.* Elser, 69 Tex. 287.

[6] Whitaker *v.* Richards, 134 Pa. St. 191.

[7] Avery *v.* Rowell, 59 Wis. 82.

gation, it is held that such guaranty is without any legal effect, and does not even entitle the holder to prove the same against the separate estate of the guarantor upon a subsequent adjudication in bankruptcy.[1] A guaranty signed in a firm name and also by each partner is held to be the contract of the firm and of each partner separately.[2] An undertaking in attachment signed by the principal and a partnership as surety has been held *prima facie* good.[3]

§ 20. **How far agent can bind principal as surety or guarantor.**— A party authorized to sign another's name as surety must pursue his authority strictly in order to bind the principal. Thus where a party was authorized to sign the name of A. as surety to a note and he signed the name of A. to the note as a principal, it was held A. was not bound.[4] One who is acting as agent of another, and as such, writing letters in his name, collecting money and giving receipts for the same in his name, indorsing bank checks, etc., has no power, without special authority, to bind his principal by the guaranty of the debt of a third person.[5] So an agent having a general power of attorney to transact business for his principal and sign his name to bonds, notes, etc., in connection with the business of the principal, cannot by virtue of such authority bind his principal as surety on a sequestration bond in a matter not connected with the business of the principal.[6]

§ 21. **Where act of principal is prohibited by law, or is fraudulent, surety not bound.**— When the act of the principal for which the surety undertakes to become responsible is prohibited by law, the surety will not be bound. Thus a statute provided that express companies should not do business in the state without recording in every county in which they did business a statement, showing the stockholders' names, residences, etc. An express company, without complying with the law, appointed an agent who gave bond with surety for the faithful performance of his duties. The agent collected

[1] *In re* Blumer & Co. (Dist. Ct. E. D. Pa.), 13 Fed. Rep. 622.

[2] *Ex parte* Harding, Law Rep. (12 Ch. Div.) 557.

[3] Tessier *v.* Crowley, 17 Neb. 207.

[4] Bryan *v.* Berry, 6 Cal. 394. And the doctrine of estoppel does not prohibit such want of authority being shown. Farmington Savings Bank *v.* Buzzell, 61 N. H. 612.

[5] Stevenson *v.* Hoy, 43 Pa. St. 191.

[6] Gates *v.* Bell, 3 La. Ann. 62.

money for packages sent and failed to pay it over, and it was held the surety was not bound. The bond being given for the performance of an illegal act, viz., sending packages by express, was void.[1] The same thing was held in a case where a statute prescribed the terms on which a foreign insurance company could do business in a state, appoint agents, etc. The court said: "It has often been held that an action founded on a transaction prohibited by statute cannot be maintained, although a penalty be imposed for violating the law, and it be not expressly declared that the contract be void."[2] So where a statute prohibited the making of a lease to a slave, the surety on a lease made to a slave was held not bound.[3] The court said: "The defense set up, that the contract under consideration is null and void because it contravenes public policy, is not a personal exception. If slaves were merely incapacitated from making a contract of lease, the case might be different; but there is no affinity between a prohibitory law, laying down rules of public policy, and one merely incapacitating a party for his own protection or interest." The distinction is here drawn between a prohibition to the principal on the grounds of public policy, and a mere personal exemption to the principal. As will be hereafter seen, a mere personal exemption to the principal, as infancy or coverture, will furnish no defense to the surety. On the same principle the surety on a note may show as a defense that it was given by the principal to pay a gambling debt.[4] So where the transaction which induces the giving of a note by the principal is fraudulent, the surety is not bound. Thus, A., being a trader in embarrassed circumstances, was indebted to B. for money lent and goods, and B. promised to induce A.'s creditors to agree to a composition on condition that A. would give him a note for the money lent, signed by A. and a surety; and it was agreed between A. and B. that the matter should be keep secret. The note was

[1] Daniels *v.* Barney, 22 Ind. 207. And where the legislature failed to direct the manner in which a constable might be chosen, and as a result there could not be a regularly commissioned constable in the state, it was held that the sureties on the bond of a constable appointed by a trial justice were not liable. Tinsley *v.* Kirby, 17 S. C. 1.

[2] Thorne *v.* Travelers' Ins. Co., 80 Pa. St. 15.

[3] Levy *v.* Wise, 15 La. Ann. 38.

[4] Leckie *v.* Scott, 10 La. (5 Curry), 412.

given, signed by a surety as agreed; B. endeavored to effect a composition and failed. *Held*, the surety was not liable. The fraud was that B., by undertaking to procure the composition, obtained a secret preference, and the note being void in its creation, could not be rendered valid by the subsequent fact that B. failed to effect a composition.[1]

§ 22. Voluntary bond not required by law, or different from bond required, valid.— The general rule is that a bond, whether required by statute or not, is good at common law if entered into voluntarily, for a valid consideration, and if it is not repugnant to the letter or policy of the law; and the surety on such bond is bound thereby.[2] The voluntary bond of a state treasurer which is not demandable by law,[3] of a county treasurer where there is no law requiring a bond to be given,[4] of a deputy collector of customs where there is no law prescribing a bond to be given,[5] of a plaintiff in an attachment suit when no bond is required by law,[6] are all valid and bind the sureties who sign them. But where a district judge, having no authority to do so, requires a father or natural tutor of a child to give bond for the faithful performance of his trust, and such a bond is given, the surety thereon is not liable. The maxim, that as a man consents to bind himself so shall he be bound, is not applicable to such a case, for the bond is not purely voluntary, but is required by the judge from the parties as the condition for the exercise of a function.[7] Where a bond is required by law to be given, the voluntary bond of an

[1] Wells *v.* Girling, 1 Brod. & Bing. 447; Id., 4 Moore, 78.

[2] Thompson *v.* Buckhannon, 2 J. J. Marsh. (Ky.) 416; Hoboken *v.* Harrison, 1 Vroom (N. J.), 73; Cotton's Guardian *v.* Wolf, 14 Bush (Ky.), 238. But it is held that in case of official bonds this principle is applicable only where the office "was authorized by law, and no obstacle existed in the way of its being filled." Tinsley *v.* Kirby, 17 S. C. 1. See *contra* to the rule as stated in the text, Williams *v.* Skipwith, 34 Ark. 529.

[3] Sooy *ads.* The State, 38 N. J. Law, 324.

[4] Supervisors of St. Joseph *v.* Coffenbury, 1 Manning (Mich.), 355. To the same effect see Missoula County *v.* Edwards, 3 Mont. 60; Comm'rs Jefferson County *v.* Lineberger *et al.*, 3 Mont. 231.

[5] Dignan *v.* Shields, 51 Tex. 322.

[6] Lartigue *v.* Baldwin, 5 Martin, O. S. (La.) 193.

[7] Ancion *v.* Guillot, 10 La. Ann. 124. So, a bond, unauthorized by law, taken by a sheriff from a person in his custody, is void, and the surety therein is not liable. Shuttleworth *v.* Levi, 13 Bush (Ky.), 195.

executor or administrator to the ordinary, which varies from the form prescribed by the statute,[1] of a cashier containing nothing contrary to law but varying from the statutory form,[2] of a plaintiff in replevin, in which the condition does not conform to the statute,[3] are all valid and binding on the sureties. Where a statute provided that the bond of a prisoner given for the liberty of the jail yard should be approved by two justices of the peace, and a bond was given but not approved by the justices, the sureties were held liable. The statutory requirement that the bond should be approved by two justices was intended to prevent oppression by the creditor in refusing sufficient sureties, and the creditor having accepted the bond, the intention of the statute was complied with.[4] A statute required that a bank cashier should give a bond conditioned for the faithful performance of his duties. The cashier gave a bond which provided for past as well as future delinquencies. *Held*, the bond was not void because it contained more than provided by statute. Being a voluntary bond and for a lawful purpose, it was good at common law.[5] A statute provided that in all cases where an execution should issue illegally, if affidavit of the fact was filed and a bond given, the execution should be suspended until the matter was determined, but the statute did not prescribe what the condition of the bond should be. An execution was issued to which no seal of the court was attached. An affidavit of its illegality was filed, and a bond given, the condition of which was:

[1] Ordinary *v.* Cooley, 1 Vroom (N. J.), 179.

[2] Grocers' Bank *v.* Kingman, 16 Gray, 473.

[3] Morse *v.* Hodson, 5 Mass. 314. See, also, Carlon *v.* Dixon, 12 Oreg. 144, where it was held the sureties on a replevin bond could not escape liability because the affidavit upon which the writ was founded was signed by the plaintiff instead of the justice, as required by statute.

[4] Bartlett *v.* Willis, 3 Mass. 86; Boone Co. *v.* Jones *et al.*, 54 Iowa, 699. And see, also, State *v.* Creusbauer *et al.*, 68 Mo. 254.

[5] Franklin Bank *v.* Cooper, 36 Me. 179. In Baker *v.* Morrison, 4 La. Ann. 372, a sequestration bond provided that the defendant should not send the property out of the jurisdiction of the court, etc., and should satisfy such judgment as should be rendered by the court. The last provision as to the payment of the judgment was not required by law, but was inserted by the sheriff. It was held not binding on the surety. The bond, under the circumstances, could not be said to be a voluntary one.

"Now if it shall appear that the said writ has not been properly issued in this, that there is no seal to said writ, then the above obligation to be void." The sureties were not liable by the terms of the bond, but the court held them for the amount of the execution suspended, on the ground that as the statute did not prescribe the condition of the bond, its condition must be found in the object of the statute; that it was undoubtedly the intention of the sureties to become bound according to the liabilities imposed by the statute; and that as the object intended by them had been accomplished, they were liable.[1] This case is of very questionable character, running counter, as it does, to the current of authority, which is, that a surety is not bound beyond the strict terms of his engagement. If it can be sustained at all, it can only be upon its own peculiar circumstances.

§ 23. **Same continued.**—In construing a voluntary common-law bond the intention of the statute becomes wholly immaterial, and the liability of the surety will not be extended by implication beyond the precise terms of his undertaking, which is to be strictly construed.[2] A bond voluntarily given by a principal and surety to secure the payment of a judgment in an issue then pending before a trial justice under an agricultural lien is not illegal and void, although there was no statute authorizing such bond.[3] An appeal bond given by an executor, though not required, is binding on the sureties thereon if the judgment appealed from be affirmed.[4] An official bond of a sheriff or county treasurer, voluntarily given, in no wise affects the liability of the sureties thereon because the bond is erroneously executed to the state instead of the proper county, or the territory instead of the county commissioners. Such a bond is valid as a common-law obligation.[5]

1 Mitchell *v.* Duncan, 7 Fla. 13.

2 Abrahams *v.* Jones, 20 Bradwell (Ill. App.), 83.

3 Cavender *v.* Ward, 28 S. C. 470.

4 Schmucker *v.* Steidemann, 8 Mo. App. 302.

5 Huffman *v.* Kopplekom, 8 Neb. 344; Kopplekom *v.* Huffman, 12 Neb. 95; Thomas *et al.* *v.* Hinkley, 19 Neb. 324; Comm'rs Jefferson Co. *v.* Lineberger, 3 Mont. 231. But see, *contra*, United States *v.* Shoup (Idaho), 21 Pac. Rep. 656, where it was held that the sureties on a recognizance, regular in form, though executed by mistake "to the people of the United States," instead of "to the people of the United States of the territory of Idaho," were held not liable thereon on the ground that the bond should have been reformed.

§ **24. Voluntary bond binds surety.**— The principle that the surety in a voluntary bond, made upon good consideration, and which does not contravene the policy of the law or the prohibition of a statute, is liable at common law on such bond, has been applied to a great variety of circumstances. Such a bond is valid, even though another bond be required by statute. Thus, where a statute required a bank cashier to give a bond with two or more sureties, and he gave a bond with only one surety, such surety was held liable. The statute did not say no other bond but the one required should be taken, and was only directory.[1] On the same principle the sureties on an administrator's bond, entered into before a probate judge *de facto* but not *de jure*, were held liable.[2] The sureties on a guardian's bond having become insolvent, the uncle of the minors demanded of the guardian that he give another bond, which he did, with a new surety. No new bond was required by the court, but, on a proper showing, one would have been required. *Held*, the surety on the last bond was bound.[3] So, where a testator by will directed that his executor need give no bond, but the executor falsely represented to A. that the court required a surety of him, and thereby induced A. to become surety on an executor's bond, which was approved by the court, A. was held liable. The fraud which the executor practiced on A. would not avoid the bond unless the obligee participated in it.[4] A statute required that tobacco inspectors should give a bond with certain conditions, in the sum of $2,000, and such a bond was given. Two days before the giving of the boud, an amendment to the statute had been passed, requiring a bond of $5,000, and changing the condition somewhat. The bond already given was held to bind the sureties as a common-law obligation.[5] Where a statute provided that injunction bonds should be given in the office of the clerk of the court, the judgment of which was enjoined, an injunction bond not thus given was held valid, although the injunction would have been dissolved for want of a proper bond, if ob-

[1] Bank of Brighton *v.* Smith, 5 Allen, 413.

[2] Pritchett *v.* The People, 1 Gilman (Ill.), 525.

[3] Elam *v.* Heirs of Barr, 14 La. Ann. 682. To similar effect see McWilliams *v.* Norfleet, 60 Miss. 987.

[4] Sebastian *v.* Johnson, 2 Duvall (Ky.), 101.

[5] Lane *v.* Kasey, 1 Met. (Ky.) 410.

jection had been made.[1] The sureties on the bond of a school fund commissioner, whose bond has not been approved by the proper authorities, but who has entered upon and exercised the duties of the office, and appropriated money, are liable on the bond at common law. The bond not being good as a statutory, but as a common-law bond, perhaps the common-law remedy on it would have to be pursued, and not the statutory remedy on statutory bonds.[2]

§ 25. Obligation of surety must be delivered, and takes effect from time of delivery.— In order to bind a surety or guarantor his contract must be delivered, and it takes effect from the time of its delivery. A. made a promissory note and delivered it to the payee, and the payee then gave the note to A. in order that he might get a surety to it and return it. A. got C. to sign the note as surety, but then refused to deliver it to the payee. The payee then sued A. and C. on the note, and it was held that C. was not liable.[3] The note had never been delivered after C. signed it, as A. was in no sense the agent of the payee to receive a delivery of the note. Moreover, if C. had been compelled to pay the note he could not have recovered indemnity from A., because A. by refusing to deliver the note had refused to consent to C. being his surety. Where a bond is signed by the principal on Saturday and by the surety on Sunday, but is not delivered till Monday, it takes effect from its delivery, and the surety is bound.[4] A law provided that in no case should a bank cashier's bond be signed by a director of the bank as surety. A bank director signed such bond as surety, but it was not approved till his term as director had expired. *Held*, the bond took effect from the time of its approval, and the surety was bound.[5]

[1] Cobb *v.* Curts, 4 Littell (Ky.), 235.

[2] The State *v.* Fredericks, 8 Iowa, 553.

[3] Chamberlain *v.* Hopps, 8 Vt. 94.

[4] Commonwealth *v.* Kendig, 2 Pa. St. 448. To similar effect, see State *v.* Young, 23 Minn. 551. Under precisely the same state of facts it was held in Indiana that the obligation of the surety was void because executed on Sunday. Parker *v.* Pitts, 73 Ind. 597. And see Gilbert *v.* Vachon *et al.*, 69 Ind. 372. The fact, however, that the negotiations which resulted in the contract of surety or guaranty took place on Sunday would not invalidate the contract where it was executed on a secular day. Tyler *v.* Waddington, 58 Conn. 375.

[5] Franklin Bank *v.* Cooper, 36 Me. 179.

An official bond, in order to bind a surety thereon, must, like any other contract, be delivered or accepted before it becomes operative; and it is held there can be no delivery of such a bond until it is approved by the proper authority.[1] The delivery of an official bond is presumptively at its date, but proof of the actual time of delivery may be shown.[2]

§ 26. Surety bound when his name not mentioned in body of instrument — Not bound when penalty of bond blank.— Although the name of a surety is not mentioned in any part of the body of a bond, but a blank intended for it is left unfilled, yet if he sign, seal and deliver it as his bond, he is bound.[3] So where the name of the surety is not mentioned in the obligatory part of a bond, but is mentioned in the recital of the condition, if he sign, seal and deliver it he is bound.[4] Where one signs a lease between the signature of the lessor and lessee, in which lease it is said that the lessee "binds himself and his security," but no name of a surety is mentioned in the lease, and the lease is signed in the presence of others who sign it as witnesses, the party who signs between the signature of the lessor and lessee will be held as surety on the lease.[5] So where a lease had been signed by the lessor and lessees, and D., whose name was not mentioned in the lease, signed his name to it after the names of the lessees, adding to his name the word "surety," it was held that it sufficiently appeared that D. was the surety of the lessees, and that he was originally and not collaterally liable.[6] A promissory note commenced as follows: "For value received, the Fishkill Iron Company promise to pay," etc. This note was signed by the president and agent of the company, their designations following their names. It was also signed by four other persons. *Held*, the last four signers were liable as sureties on the note, although they were not mentioned nor referred to in it. The court said it was suf-

[1] People *v.* Van Ness, 79 Cal. 84; City of Evansville *v.* Morris *et al.*, 87 Ind. 269.

[2] Reilly *v.* Dodge, 42 Hun (N. Y.), 646.

[3] Joyner *v.* Cooper, 2 Bailey, Law (S. C.), 199; Valentine *v.* Christie, 1 Rob. (La.) 298; Potter *v.* The State, 23 Ind. 550; Scheid *v.* Leibshultz, 51 Ind. 38; Neil *v.* Morgan. 28 Ill. 524; Danker *v.* Atwood, 119 Mass. 146.

[4] Bartley *v.* Yates, 2 Hen. & Mun. (Va.) 398.

[5] Holden *v.* Tanner, 6 La. Ann. 74.

[6] Perkins *v.* Goodman, 21 Barb. (N. Y.) 218.

ficient that the instrument expressed an obligation on the part of the principal. A blank indorsement would have been sufficient to hold the surety, and this was quite as effectual as a blank indorsement.[1] Where, however, the penalty of a bond is blank, it is void as to the sureties, and it cannot be held to be a covenant and thus bind them.[2]

§ 27. **Same continued.**— As has already been stated, it is immaterial in order to charge a surety that his name should appear in the body of the instrument, provided the intention that he shall be so charged appears clearly therefrom.[3] This principle is applicable to every variety of bonds. Thus, the sureties to a recognizance, who have signed the same, are liable thereon, whether their names are entered in the body of the bond or not.[4] And this is true of the sureties to an appeal bond,[5] injunction bond,[6] undertaking for attachment,[7] replevin bond,[8] official bond of a sheriff,[9] and clerk of court.[10] While it is unnecessary, then, that the name of the surety be recited in the body of the obligation, yet, if it does so appear, he must sign the same, or he will not be bound.[11] Where there is a greater number of signatures than seals to a bond, two or more of the signers may adopt one seal, and be charged as sureties, although all the signers do not appear in the body of the bond.[12]

§ 28. **When party liable on implied guaranty.**— Although a surety or guarantor generally becomes bound by express contract, yet persons are sometimes held as sureties or guarantors

[1] Parks *v.* Brinkerhoff, 2 Hill (N. Y.), 663. But see Blackener *v.* Davis, 128 Mass. 538, wherein it was held that a stranger to a contract who signed in such a manner as not to indicate the capacity in which he intended to become bound could not be held, and parol evidence was inadmissible to show him to be a surety.

[2] Austin *v.* Richardson, 1 Gratt. (Va.) 310.

[3] Partridge *v.* Jones, 38 Ohio St. 375; Hodgkin *v.* Holland, 34 Ark. 203.

[4] Holmes *v.* State, 17 Neb. 73. And see, to same effect, Stewart *v.* Carter, 4 Neb. 564.

[5] San Roman *v.* Watson, 54 Tex. 254.

[6] Griffin *et al.* *v.* Wallace *et al.*, 66 Ind. 410.

[7] McLain *v.* Simington, 37 Ohio St. 484.

[8] Affeld *et al.* *v.* People, 12 Bradwell (Ill. App.), 502.

[9] Hodgkin *v.* Holland, 34 Ark. 203.

[10] State *ex rel.* Howell *v.* Parsons, 89 N. C. 230.

[11] Pevito *v.* Rodgers, 52 Tex. 581.

[12] Building Association *v.* Cummings, 45 Ohio St. 664.

who do not so become bound. The law will, under certain circumstances, imply such contract. Thus, where two married women made a promissory note, and the payee indorsed it to A. before maturity, A. at that time knowing that the makers were married women, it was held that the indorsement of the note to A. was an implied guaranty that the makers were competent to contract in the character in which, by the terms of the note, they purported to contract; and the fact that A., when he took the note, knew the makers were married women, did not change the rule.[1] So the vendor of a promissory note, who transfers it by indorsement expressed to be without recourse, impliedly guaranties the genuineness of the signatures of the prior parties whose names appear on the note.[2] A person not a party to a promissory note, and who does not indorse it, but who sells it and receives the money, by implication guaranties the genuineness of the signatures; and this whether he receives the money paid for the note for himself or for another. The only way he can avoid such responsibility is by an agreement to the contrary.[3] So the purchaser of goods who transfers, without indorsement, the promissory note of a third party, impliedly guaranties that the sum expressed in the note is due.[4] A person who procures notes to be discounted at a bank impliedly guaranties the genuineness of the signatures of the makers and indorsers; and such implied contract is not a representation concerning the character, credit or ability of another, within the statute of frauds; and such person may be sued as a guarantor of the notes, if the signatures are forged.[5] The reason on which the last preceding cases are grounded is thus well expressed by the court in the case last cited: "It seems to fall under a general rule of law, that in every sale of personal property the vendor impliedly warrants that the article is, in fact, what it is described and purports to be, and that the vendor has a good title or right to transfer it." The agent of another for the sale of property,

[1] Erwin *v.* Downs, 15 N. Y. 575. To similar effect, see Ogden *v.* Blydenburgh, 1 Hilton (N. Y.), 182.

[2] Dumont *v.* Williamson, 18 Ohio St. 515.

[3] Lyons *v.* Miller, 6 Gratt. (Va.) 427.

[4] Jones *v.* Yeargain, 1 Dev. Law (N. C.), 420.

[5] Cabot Bank *v.* Morton, 4 Gray, 156, per Shaw, C. J. See, also, Jones *v.* Ryde, 5 Taunt. 488.

who has agreed not to sell for credit except to good and responsible parties, and to take no paper but good collectible paper, and such as he is willing to guaranty, and who takes paper he knows to be worthless, and turns it over to his employer, who is ignorant of its character, is liable as guarantor of such paper. He can be sued and judgment had against him without the paper being returned to him. He is not entitled to the paper till he pays the debt.[1]

§ 29. Joint maker of note may be shown by parol to be surety.— In view of the fact that a surety is entitled to certain rights and privileges to which the principal is not, it often becomes highly important to determine whether a party to an instrument is principal or surety, and if in fact a surety, when and where that fact may be shown.[2] When several parties execute a joint, or joint and several, promissory note not under seal, and there is nothing in the note to indicate that any of them are sureties, if some of them are in fact sureties and this is known to the creditor, such sureties may both at law and in equity show by parol that they were sureties and that they were known to be such by the creditor, and they will be entitled to all the rights, privileges and immunities of sureties, and will be discharged by any act of the creditor, after he had knowledge of the fact of suretyship, which would discharge any other surety.[3] But it must appear that the

[1] Clark *v.* Roberts, 26 Mich. 506.

[2] The supreme court of Indiana, in fixing and determining the question of suretyship, say: "It depends upon the relations existing between the makers of the note, and is determined by inquiring who received the consideration of the contract, or who, according to the arrangements actually made and existing among themselves, ought to pay the debt." Sefton *v.* Hargett *et al.*, 113 Ind. 592. And to secure such a determination it is essential that the parties be before the court on that issue. Knopf *v.* Morel, 111 Ind. 570. And see further, Gipson *et al.* *v.* Ogden, 100 Ind. 20. The rule for determining the suretyship of married women is also laid down by the same court in Vogel *v.* Leichner, 102 Ind. 55.

[3] Higdon *v.* Bailey, 26 Ga. 426; Lime Rock Bank *v.* Mallett, 34 Me. 547; Id., 42 Me. 349; Grafton Bank *v.* Kent, 4 N. H. 221; Matheson *v.* Jones, 30 Ga. 306; Piper *v.* Newcomer, 25 Iowa, 221; Cummings *v.* Little, 45 Me. 183; Kelley *v.* Gillespie, 12 Iowa, 55; Bank of St. Albans *v.* Smith, 30 Vt. 148; Davis *v.* Mikell, 1 Freeman. Ch. (Miss.) 548; Fraser *v.* McConnell, 23 Ga. 368; Corielle *v.* Allen, 13 Iowa, 289; Roberts *v.* Jenkins, 19 La. (Curry) 453; Brown *v.* Haggerty, 26 Ill. 469; Bradner *v.* Garrett, 19 La. (Curry) 455; Bruce *v.* Edwards, 1 Stew. (Ala.) 11; Jones *v.* Fleming, 15 La. Ann. 522; Flynn *v.* Mudd, 27 Ill. 323;

creditor at the time the act complained of was done knew of the fact of suretyship.[1] The great weight of authority and of reason is in favor of the law as above stated. The cause alleged against showing the fact of suretyship by parol is, that it contradicts or varies the terms of the instrument signed by the surety. The answer to this is, that such proof does not controvert the terms of the contract, but is simply proving a fact outside of and beyond such terms.[2] "It is a fact collateral to the contract, and no part of it."[3] "It is not to affect the terms of the contract, but to prove a collateral fact, and rebut a presumption."[4] The parties still remain bound by the same instrument and in the same manner. "Can you not prove the defendant an infant, a *feme covert*, or a bankrupt, in order to discharge him or her, and that, too, while others remain bound? Why not also prove him a surety?"[5] "The general rules of evidence are the same at law as in equity; and it is no more competent to vary the terms of a written instrument by parol evidence in equitable actions than in those strictly legal, unless in exceptional cases, for the purpose of maintaining an

Branch Bank at Mobile *v.* James, 9 Ala. 949; Kennedy *v.* Evans, 31 Ill. 258; Stewart *v.* Parker, 55 Ga. 656; Riley *v.* Gregg, 16 Wis. 666; Mechanics' Bank *v.* Wright, 53 Mo. 153; McCarter *v.* Turner, 49 Ga. 309; Coats *v.* Swindle, 55 Mo. 31; Mariners' Bank *v.* Abbott, 28 Me. 280; Harmon *v.* Hale, 1 Wash. Terr. (N. S.) 422; Welfare *v.* Thompson, 83 N. C. 276; Otis *v.* Von Storch, 15 R. I. 41; Irvine *v.* Adams, 48 Wis. 468; Trustees of Schools *v.* Southard *et al.*, 31 Ill. App. 359; Thompson *et al. v.* Coffman *et al.*, 15 Oreg. 631; Stevens *v.* Oaks, 58 Mich. 343; Chapeze *v.* Young, 87 Ky. 476. In Manley *v.* Boycot, decided by the Queen's Bench in 1853, it was held that the defense could not be set up, unless the holder when he took the note knew of the suretyship and agreed to treat the surety as such. But in Pooley *v.* Harradine, 7 Ell. & Bl. 431, decided in 1857, and in Greenough *v.* McClelland, 2 Ell. & Bl. 424, decided in 1860 by the same court, it was held that under the statute, allowing equitable defenses to be made at law, the defense might be made at law, where the creditor knew of the fact of suretyship, but did not agree to hold the surety as such. The court also held that but for the statute the defense could not have been made at law, but must have been made in equity. See, to same effect, Perley *v.* Loney, 17 Up. Can. Q. B. 279.

[1] Neel *v.* Harding, 2 Met. (Ky.) 247; Orvis *v.* Newell, 17 Conn. 97; Wilson *v.* Foot, 11 Met. 285; Murray *v.* Graham, 29 Iowa, 520.

[2] Valentine, J., in Rose *v.* Williams, 5 Kan. 483.

[3] Shaw, C. J., in Carpenter *v.* King, 9 Met. 511.

[4] Shaw, C. J., in Harris *v.* Brooks, 21 Pick. 195. Also, Breese, J., in Ward *v.* Stout, 32 Ill. 399.

[5] Lumpkin, J., in The Bank *v.* Mumford, 6 Ga. 44.

action or defense under some recognized head of equitable jurisdiction. The confusion and apparent conflict in the authorities must, I think, have originated in the idea that defenses of this character were equitable in their nature, and could only be available in a court of equity. When it was conceded that they were equally available in a court of law, it is difficult to find a reason for excluding the same evidence at law that is admissible in equity. However this may be, and without invoking any equitable rule, a conclusive answer to the objection to this evidence in any court, in my opinion, is that it does not tend to alter or vary either the terms or legal effect of the written instrument. The contract was in all respects the same, whether the defendant was principal or surety. In either case it was an absolute promise to pay $1,000 one day after date, nothing more and nothing less. There is neither condition nor contingency. It would have been precisely the same contract if the defendant had added the word 'surety' to his name. The addition of that word would not have varied it in the slightest degree. The only service it would have performed would have been to give notice to the other party of the fact. If this is shown *aliunde*, it is equally effective."[1] The equity of the surety to be discharged when he is prejudiced by the act of the creditor "does not depend upon any contract with the creditor, but upon its being inequitable in him to knowingly prejudice the rights of the surety against the principal;"[2] and it is as inequitable in the creditor to prejudice those rights when he is informed of the fact of suretyship by parol as when he is informed of it by the instrument itself. It has, however, been held by courts of high respectability, that the fact of suretyship could not, under the foregoing circumstances, be shown by parol.[3] It may be shown by parol that the maker of a

[1] See the elaborate opinion of Church, C. J., in Hubbard *v.* Gurney, 64 N. Y. 457. That the relation of suretyship may be shown *aliunde*, or by the instrument itself, see O'Howell *v.* Kirk, 41 Mo. App. 523.

[2] Coleridge, J., in Pooley *v.* Harradine, 7 Ell. & Bl. 431.

[3] Shriver *v.* Lovejoy, 32 Cal. 574; Bull *v.* Allen, 19 Conn. 101; Campbell *v.* Tate, 7 Lans. (N. Y.) 370; Hendrickson *v.* Hutchinson, 5 Dutcher (N. J.), 180. In Kerr *v.* Baker, Walker (Miss.), 140, and Farrington *v.* Gallaway, 10 Ohio, 543, it was held it could not be shown at law. In Stroop *v.* McKenzie, 38 Tex. 132, and in Ball *v.* Gilson, 7 Up. Can. C. P. 531, it

promissory note was in fact an accommodation drawer for a firm who were second indorsers, and he will be entitled to the same rights as any surety.[1] Parol evidence is admissible to show that one of three joint and several makers of a promissory note agreed with the others after its execution to pay the same.[2]

§ 30. Joint maker of sealed instrument may be shown by parol to be surety.— Where the instrument is under seal the fact of suretyship may be shown by parol at law, the same as if it was not under seal, although there is not, perhaps, quite the same unanimity in the decisions on this point as there is with reference to unsealed instruments. The same reasons which allow the fact of suretyship to be shown by parol in the case of unsealed instruments apply with equal force to the case of sealed instruments, and the uniform tendency of the later decisions is to allow a surety to make the same defenses at law as in equity. It has accordingly been held that one of the makers of a joint note under seal may, at law, show by parol that he is only a surety.[3] One of the makers of a joint and several sealed note may, at law, show by parol that he is a surety only.[4] The same thing was held with reference to a sealed note, where a statute had placed sealed and unsealed instruments on the same footing.[5] One of two or more obligors in a joint and several bond may prove

was held it could not be shown unless it was also shown that the creditor agreed to hold the surety as such. The same thing was held in Yates *v.* Donaldson, 5 Md. 389. In Hartman *v.* Burlingame, 9 Cal. 557, it was held that a joint maker of a promissory note, although known by the holder to be a surety, was not entitled to notice of demand and non-payment. The same thing was held substantially in Kritzer *v.* Mills, 9 Cal. 21. See, also, on this subject, Aud *v.* Magruder, 10 Cal. 282. In Coots *v.* Farnsworth, 61 Mich. 497, it is held, in a vigorous opinion by Morse, J., that parol evidence is inadmissible in any case to change the character of parties to a bond, as where it was sought to be shown that the principals named therein really signed as sureties.

[1] Marsh *v.* Consolidation Bank, 48 Pa. St. 510.

[2] Vary *v.* Norton (Cir. Ct. W. D. Mich. S. D.), 6 Fed. Rep. 808.

[3] Rogers *v.* School Trustees, 46 Ill. 428; Smith *v.* Doak, 3 Tex. 215.

[4] Fowler *v.* Alexander, 1 Heisk. (Tenn.) 425. And see a similar case in Cole *v.* Fox, 83 N. C. 463. The case of Fowler *v.* Alexander was decided in 1870. The same court, in 1836, in Deberry *v.* Adams, 9 Yerg. (Tenn.) 52, and in 1847, in Dozier *v.* Lee, 7 Humph. (Tenn.) 520, in similar cases, held that the fact could not, at law, be shown by parol.

[5] Smith *v.* Clopton, 48 Miss. 66.

by parol that he is a surety only where nothing to indicate the fact appears on the bond, and he will be entitled to give the creditor statutory notice to sue, the same as any other surety,[1] and will be discharged at law by time given the principal.[2] A. gave his individual bond and a mortgage to secure the same for a sum of money borrowed by him, one-half of which was for the use of, and was used by, B. Afterwards, A. paid all the money and sued B. at law for his share, and it was held that A. might show the fact of his suretyship, although it did not appear from the bond or mortgage.[3] A lease was made to two, one of whom was sole occupant of the premises, which he held over the term, and debt for the rent of the whole period of actual occupancy was brought against both. *Held*, that the lessee who did not occupy might show by parol tha the was only a surety, and consequently not liable for the holding over.[4] On the contrary, it has been held that when the instrument is under seal, the fact of suretyship cannot, at law, be shown by parol,[5] but it may in all cases be shown in equity.[6]

§ **31. Liability of surety who adds the words "surety" or "security" to his name.**— A party signed a promissory note, and added the word "security" after his name. It was held that it might be shown by parol that he was the principal. The court said the addition of the word "security" is "at most the statement of a fact forming no part of the contract; and if untrue may be shown to be so by parol as well as any other fact."[7] While the addition of such words as

[1] Creigh *v.* Hedrick, 5 West Va. 140. See, to same effect, Scott *v.* Bailey, 23 Mo. 140.

[2] Dickerson *v.* Comm'rs Ripley Co., 6 Ind. 128.

[3] Metzner *v.* Baldwin, 11 Minn. 150; Forbes *v.* Sheppard, 98 N. C. 111.

[4] Kennebec Bank *v.* Turner, 2 Greenleaf (Me.), 42. So the surety may show by parol that he was only liable for the rent accruing during the term given in the original lease, and not for that which might fall due under any renewal thereof which the lessee might elect to take. Knowles *v.* Cuddeback, 19 Hun (N. Y.), 590.

[5] Levy *v.* Hampton, 1 McCord, Law (S. C.), 145; Pintard *v.* Davis, 1 Spencer (N. J.), 205; Willis *v.* Ives, 1 Sm. & Mar. (Miss.) 307.

[6] See cases last cited and Burke *v.* Cruger, 8 Tex. 66.

[7] Rose *v.* Madden, 1 Kan. 445. In Sisson *v.* Barrett, 2 N. Y. 406, a promissory note was executed by A., B. and C., the principal debtor being A. The last signer of the note, C., added the word "surety" to his signature. *Held*, that without extrinsic

"surety" or "security" to the name of a signer of an instrument is *prima facie* evidence of his suretyship, yet parol evidence may be admitted to prove the contrary.[1] Where a note is executed by two persons, and one of them adds to his signature the word "surety," it is held that both are to be treated as makers of the note and may be joined as defendants in an action thereon.[2] A surety who signs a note made out in the singular number, "I promise," and adds to his name the word "surety," is liable thereon in a joint suit with the maker, who has also signed the note.[3] In another case such person was regarded as a joint promisor, and if he signed on the back of the note, as an original promisor.[4]

§ 32. **If creditor knew of suretyship when he did the act complained of, this is sufficient to secure surety his rights.** The fact that the holder of a negotiable instrument did not know of the suretyship of some of the parties when he took it will make no difference in the rule before stated. If he had no knowledge of the fact when he took the instrument, but was informed of it before doing the act complained of, this will be sufficient to entitle the surety to all the rights of any surety.[5] A promissory note was signed by several parties, two of them being in fact sureties, but that not appearing from the note, the payee assigned the note to a party who did not know of the suretyship at the time of the assignment, but was afterwards informed of it, and afterwards gave time to the principal. *Held*, the sureties were discharged.[6] The court said: "The principle obtains for the protection of the sureties, and the holder of such notes, knowing their relation, should avoid any act to endanger their rights; and we are unable to perceive the distinction as to when the knowledge was obtained — whether before or after the purchase, so that it was known

proof, C. was not to be presumed to be a surety for both A. and B. But in Sayles *v.* Sims, 73 N. Y. 551, it was held that the presumption was that he was surety for the other two, though it was not conclusive.

[1] Boulware *v.* Hartsook's Adm'r, 83 Va. 679.

[2] Hoyt *v.* Mead, 13 Hun (N. Y.), 327.

[3] Dart *v.* Sherwood, 7 Wis. 523.

[4] Rice *v.* Cook, 71 Me. 559.

[5] Bank of Missouri *v.* Matson, 26 Mo. 243; Colgrove *v.* Tallman, 2 Lans. (N. Y.) 97; Pooley *v.* Harradine, 7 Ell. & Black. 431. *Contra*, Bank of Upper Canada *v.* Thomas, 11 Up. Can. C. P. 515.

[6] Lauman *v.* Nichols, 15 Iowa, 161.

before the extension was made." In another case, depending on the same state of facts, the same thing was held. The court said: "The injury to the surety is the same as if the creditor had possessed the knowledge at the time the note was taken."[1] A financial company, by agreement with an agent, accepted bills of exchange which were discounted for the agent by a discount company, the agent guarantying payment of the bills. The discount company was not, at the time, aware of the relations between the acceptors and the agent, but was informed, before the bills matured, that the agent was principal and the acceptors were sureties, and afterwards gave time to the agent. *Held*, the acceptors were discharged, and might come into equity and have the bills canceled.[2] This rule is the logical and necessary result of holding that parol evidence of the creditor's knowledge of the fact of suretyship can be given at all. It is the fact of knowledge on the part of the creditor, coupled with certain equitable principles, and not any contract between him and the surety, which raises the equity on behalf of the surety; and it necessarily follows that the equity exists from the time the creditor has the knowledge.

§ 33. **Surety must show that creditor knew of suretyship — What is sufficient evidence of the fact.**— When a surety sets up claims depending on that relation and the fact of suretyship does not appear from the instrument signed by him, he must, in order to sustain such claims, prove that the creditor knew of the suretyship.[3] Where a promissory note was held by the payee and the note did not show the fact of suretyship, but it was proved that one of the makers was only a surety, the court held that it would be presumed that the creditor knew of the suretyship.[4] Where several persons ex-

[1] Wheat *v.* Kendall, 6 N. H. 504. To a similar effect, see Smith *v.* Shelden, 35 Mich. 42; Wythes *v.* Labouchere, 3 De Gex & Jones, 593.

[2] Oriental Financial Corporation *v.* Overend, Law Rep. 7 Ch. App. Cas. 142. This decision was affirmed by the House of Lords on appeal in 1874, and is the settled law of England. Liquidators of Overend, Gurney & Co. *v.* Liquidators of Oriental Financial Corporation, Law Rep. 7 Eng. & Irish App. Cas. 348.

[3] Wilson *v.* Foot, 11 Met. 285; Goodman *v.* Litaker, 84 N. C. 8; Torrence *v.* Alexander, 85 N. C. 143.

[4] Ward *v.* Stout, 32 Ill. 399. In Cummings *v.* Little, 45 Me. 183, it was held that whenever one having no interest in a note becomes a party to it at the request and for the accommodation of another, the rela-

ecute a promissory note and there is nothing on its face to show their relations to each other, there is no presumption from the order in which they sign that any, or which, of the signers are sureties.[1] Where three parties signed a bond and it did not appear from the face of the bond, who, if any one, was surety, the circumstances of one obligor making payments, and being resorted to by the creditor, raises a strong presumption that he was the principal; while the circumstances of another obligor not making payments, and not being called upon for them, raises a presumption that he was only surety.[2] A promissory note, some of the makers of which were in fact sureties, though nothing to indicate the suretyship appeared on the note, was transferred to A. after it was overdue and discredited. A., without any actual notice of the suretyship, gave time to the principal. *Held*, the fact that the note was overdue was not notice to A. of the fact of suretyship, and that the sureties were not discharged.[3] The court said: "He who takes a discredited note is presumed to be acquainted with every defense to which it is subject. But whether some of those whose names are upon a note are sureties is a matter wholly immaterial to the person who purchased the note, and he cannot be presumed to have inquired or to have learned in what character they signed, because that was a circumstance with which he had no concern."

§ 34. Property pledged by one for debt of another occupies position of surety.— When property of any kind is mortgaged or pledged by the owner to answer for the debt, default or miscarriage of another person, such property occupies the position of a surety or guarantor, and anything which would discharge an individual surety or guarantor who was personally liable, will, under similar circumstances, discharge such property.[4] This rule is applicable to every variety of circum-

tion of principal and surety exists, and the original holder, between whom and the principal the consideration passed, is presumed to have knowledge of the fact.

[1] Paul *v.* Berry, 78 Ill. 158; Summerhill *v.* Tapp, 52 Ala. 227.

[2] Doughty *v.* Bacot, 2 Desaus. Eq. (S. C.) 546.

[3] Nichols *v.* Parsons, 6 N. H. 30.

[4] Robinson *v.* Gee, 1 Vesey Sr. 251; Royal Canadian Bank *v.* Payne, 19 Grant's Ch. 180; Christiner *v.* Brown, 16 Iowa, 130; Denison *v.* Gibson, 24 Mich. 187; Joseph *v.* Heaton, 5 Grant's Ch. 636; Ryan *v.* Shawneetown, 14 Ill. 20; Lord Harberton *v.* Bennett, Beatty (Ir. Ch.), 386;

stances. A. being indebted to B., and C. being indebted to A., they get together and agree that B. shall surrender up A.'s note and take C.'s in its place, A. at the same time canceling his claim against C. for the same amount, and it is done accordingly. C. gives B. a mortgage to secure his note thus given on a piece of his property; A. also gives B. a mortgage on some of his property to secure the same note of C. *Held*, that by this transaction A.'s property became the surety of C., and was discharged by the giving of time to C.[1] A materialman took the note of the contractor for the materials furnished for a building, and extended the time of payment. The owner, having no notice of the claim, paid the contractor in full, before the note fell due. *Held*, the building occupied the position of surety for the contractor, and that the agreement to give time discharged the building from the lien.[2] When a wife mortgages her real estate for the debt of a firm of which her husband is a member, such real estate occupies the position of a surety, and if it becomes released at law, equity will not charge it.[3] A. held a judgment against B., which was a lien upon two tracts of B.'s land. B. sold one tract to C., the other tract being sufficient to pay the debt. D., with a knowledge of the sale of the one tract to C., procured a release from A. of the other tract, and then bought it of B.; and also bought A.'s judgment against B. *Held*, C.'s land was discharged from the lien of the judgment. After the sale of the tract to C., the creditors of B. were bound to resort to B.'s other land before coming on that sold to C. It occupied the position of a surety, and the surety's right to subrogation being destroyed, it was discharged.[4] On the same principle, where a mortgagor sells a portion of the mortgaged premises, and in the deed of conveyance expresses that the same is "subject to the payment by the said grantee of all existing liens upon said

Rowan *v.* Sharp's Rifle Co., 33 Conn. 1; Union Bank *v.* Govan, 10 Smedes & Mar. (Miss.) 333; Bowker *v.* Bull, 1 Simons (N. S.), 29; White *v.* Ault, 19 Ga. 551; Price *et al.* *v.* Dime Savings Bank, 124 Ill. 317, affirming Reed *v.* Cramb, 22 Ill. App. 34; Home National Bank *v.* Waterman, 30 Ill. App. 535; Burnap *v.* Nat. Bank of Potsdam, 96 N. Y. 125; Allen *v.* O'Donald (Cir. Ct. D. Oreg.), 28 Fed. Rep. 346; Campion *v.* Whitney, 30 Minn. 177; Walker *v.* Goldsmith, 7 Oreg. 161.

[1] White *v.* Ault, 19 Ga. 551.

[2] Hill *v.* Witmer, 2 Phila. (Pa.), 72.

[3] Leffingwell *v.* Freyer, 21 Wis. 392.

[4] Lowry *v.* McKinney, 68 Pa. St. 294.

premises," the effect of this charge is to make the part of the premises so conveyed the principal debtor for a proportionate part of the mortgage debt, and the mortgagor a surety only.[1] So where land subject to a judgment was sold for its full value by the judgment debtor to a third person, it was held that the land occupied the position of a surety, and was discharged by the creditor releasing subsequently acquired securities for the debt.[2] Where a mortgagor sells, for a consideration, mortgaged land, and conveys the same, the conveyance being silent as to the payment of the mortgage, and there is no covenant of title, the mortgagor remains the principal debtor, and the land security for the debt.[3] Where property standing in the relation of surety is alleged to have been discharged by an extension of time, the burden of proving the same is upon the person contending it.[4]

§ 35. Property of wife pledged for debt of husband occupies position of surety.— While a married woman cannot usually become personally bound for the debt of her husband, she may ordinarily pledge or mortgage her separate property for his debt, and if she does so, such property occupies the position of a surety or guarantor, and will be discharged by anything that would discharge a surety or guarantor who was personally liable.[5] Where a married woman mortgages her

[1] Hoy *v.* Bramhall, 4 C. E. Green (N. J.), 563.

[2] Barnes *v.* Mott, 64 N. Y. 397, affirming 6 Daly (Com. Pleas), 150.

[3] Wadsworth *v.* Lyon *et al.*, 93 N. Y. 201.

[4] Brokam *et al. v.* Field *et al.*, 33 Ill. App. 138.

[5] Johns *v.* Reardon, 11 Md. 465; Denison *v.* Gibson, 24 Mich. 187; Agnew *v.* Merritt, 10 Minn. 308; Wallace *v.* Hudson, 37 Tex. 456; Wolf *v.* Banning, 3 Minn. 202; Spear *v.* Ward, 20 Cal. 659; Niemcewicz *v.* Gahn, 3 Paige, 614; Stamford, etc. Banking Co. *v.* Ball, 4 De Gex, F. & J. 310; Gahn *v.* Niemcewicz, 11 Wend. 312; Knight *v.* Whitehead, 26 Miss. 245; Vartie *v.* Underwood, 18 Barb. (N. Y.) 561; Smith *v.* Townsend, 25 N. Y. 479; Bank of Albion *v.* Burns, 46 N. Y. 170; Coats *v.* McKee, 26 Ind. 223; Wilcox *v.* Todd, 64 Mo. 388; Purvis *v.* Cartsaphan, 73 N. C. 575; Hood *et al. v.* Jones, 5 Del. Ch. 77; Hassey *v.* Wilke, 55 Cal. 528; Bull *v.* Coe, 77 Cal. 54; Gray *v.* Holland, 9 Oreg. 512; Christian *v.* Keen, 80 Va. 369. Wife's property occupying the position of surety is released by an extension of the time of payment made without her consent. Eisenberg *v.* Albert, 40 Ohio St. 631; Post, Adm'r, *v.* Losey *et al.*, 111 Ind. 74. Contrary to the weight of authority, it is held in Alexander *v.* Bouton *et al.*, 55 Cal. 15, that the wife's property mortgaged for the debt of her husband occupies the position, not of surety, but of principal.

separate real estate for the debt of her husband, she will, after his death, be entitled to have her estate exonerated out of his assets. "In such case the wife is regarded as a surety."[1] Where a married woman pledged her property to indemnify the surety of her husband, the property thus pledged was treated in all respects as a surety.[2] Where a husband mortgages his property for his debt, and in the same mortgage the wife conveys her own separate property as security for the same debt, her property so conveyed will be treated in all respects as a surety.[3] Where the fact of suretyship does not appear from the mortgage, the wife must show that the creditor knew of the suretyship in order to entitle the property to stand in the position of a surety. But the fact of suretyship may be proved by parol.[4] Where a mortgage made by husband and wife, of the wife's property for the husband's debt, recited that it was made in consideration of $6,000 to the mortgagors and "each of them" paid, it was held the wife might show by parol that the debt was that of the husband, and thus avail herself of the rights of a surety with reference

The court base their decision upon the principle that, when a married woman makes a contract which she is authorized by law to make, the legal presumption is that she contracts as a principal; and in an action or suit with reference to it, if she contracted otherwise than as a principal, it is incumbent upon her to prove it; for as she possesses by law all the rights, she is subject to all the duties, of a contracting party. Alexander *v.* Bouton, 55 Cal. 15, 18, 19.

[1] Knight *v.* Whitehead, 26 Miss. 245. The rule for determining the suretyship of married women is thus stated in Vogel *v.* Leichner, 102 Ind. 55: "Whether a contract executed by a married woman is one of suretyship or not will be determined by a consideration of whether or not it was made by her or on her behalf, and upon a consideration moving to her or for the benefit of her separate estate. To the extent that the consideration was received by her, or inured to the benefit of her estate, she will be held to have contracted as principal. To the extent that the consideration was received by her husband, or any other person, or that it went to pay a debt or liability for which neither she nor her property was bound, it will be held a contract of suretyship." . . . And "whether she was principal or surety will be determined, not from the form of the contract, nor from the basis upon which the transaction was had, but from the inquiry, was the wife to receive, either in person or in benefit to her estate, or did she so receive, the consideration upon which the contract rests?"

[2] Hodgson *v.* Hodgson, 2 Keen, 704.

[3] Wheelwright *v.* De Peyster, 4 Edwards' Ch. 232; Loomer *v.* Wheelwright, 3 Sandf. Ch. 135.

[4] Gahn *v.* Niemcewicz, 11 Wend.

to the property.[1] Where the title to the wife's property mortgaged for her husband's debt is recorded, such record will be sufficient notice to the creditor of the fact of suretyship.[2] When a husband borrows money and secures it by mortgage on his wife's lands which she executes with him, and he lays out the money in permanent buildings and improvements on such lands, the lands do not occupy the position of a surety. The debt is, in reality, that of the wife.[3] A wife who joins with her husband in a mortgage of his real estate for the payment of his debt does not, as to such estate, occupy the position of a surety.[4] A husband mortgaged his real estate to secure his debt, and his wife joined in the mortgage, and waived her homestead rights. It was held she did not, with reference to such homestead rights, occupy the position of a surety, and could not take advantage of time given the husband.[5] The court admitted that if the separate estate had been mortgaged she would have been entitled to the rights of a surety, but said of a homestead, "if it is an estate, it is such an estate as has never been defined by law, an estate unknown to the common law, technically, no estate at all." Where a husband and wife execute a mortgage on two separate pieces of real estate, one of which belongs to the husband and the other to the wife, and the mortgage is executed for the purpose of securing the individual debt of the husband, the wife is surety for the husband to the extent of her mortgaged separate estate.[6] Where husband and wife execute a mortgage on her separate estate to secure the payment of notes of a partnership of which the husband was a member, such notes having already been secured by a mortgage of partnership property,

312; Niemcewicz *v.* Gahn, 3 Paige, 614.

[1] Spear *v.* Ward, 20 Cal. 659.

[2] Bank of Albion *v.* Burns, 46 N. Y, 170; Smith *v.* Townsend, 25 N. Y. 479; Trentman *v.* Eldridge, 98 Ind. 525.

[3] Dickinson *v.* Codwise, 1 Sandf. Ch. 214. To similar effect, see McFillen *v.* Hoffman, 35 N. J. Eq. 364.

[4] Hawley *v.* Bradford, 9 Paige, 200; Tennison *v.* Tennison, 114 Ind. 424. But see Dawson *v.* Bank of Whitehaven, Law Rep. 4 Ch. Div. 639.

[5] Jenness *v.* Cutler, 12 Kan. 500. In Iowa a homestead cannot be given as security for a debt. Bockholt *v.* Kraft *et al.*, 78 Iowa, 661. While in Georgia the homestead is, by the express terms of the constitution and laws, made liable therefor. McWatty *v.* Jefferson Co., 76 Ga. 352.

[6] Hubbard *v.* Ogden, 22 Kan. 363.

the wife is entitled to have the property mortgaged by the firm exhausted, before her separate estate can be subjected to the payment of the firm debts.[1]

§ 36. When retiring member of firm becomes surety of other partners for firm debts.— When one member of a partnership retires from the firm, and the remaining members agree with him to pay the firm debts, and these facts are known to the creditor, the member so retiring will be considered in law a surety.[2] And if he is compelled to pay a debt of the firm which the latter were bound to pay, he may recover the amount so paid in an action of *indebitatus assumpsit* against the remaining partners.[3] A. and B., being partners and indebted, A. died. B. then formed a partnership with D., and B. and D. agreed to pay the debts of the old firm. The creditor knew of this, and gave time of payment to B. and D. for three years for the debt of the old firm. *Held*, the estate of A. occupied the position of a surety and was discharged.[4]

[1] Moffitt *v.* Roche, 77 Ind. 48.

[2] Thurber *v.* Corbin, 51 Barb. (N. Y.) 215; Colgrove *v.* Tallman, 2 Lans. (N. Y.) 97; Williams *et al.* *v.* Boyd, 75 Ind. 286; Johnson *v.* Young, 20 W. Va. 614; Moore *v.* Topliff *et al.*, 107 Ind. 241. But where under such circumstances the creditor took from the remaining member his note for the firm debt, upon the agreement that if paid it should cancel the debt. but if not he should hold the firm for it, and the note was not paid, it was held the retiring member was not discharged. Varnam *v.* Harris, 1 Hun (N. Y.), 451. In Ohio it is held that the retiring partner remains liable as principal to the same extent as if he had not retired. Rawson *v.* Taylor *et al.*, 30 Ohio St. 389. And see Palmer *v.* Purdy, 83 N. Y. 144. Where, after two partners left the firm and leased premises, the remaining partners agreed to pay the rent thereafter accruing, though the lessor was not aware of this agreement, it was held in an action against the retiring member of the firm to recover such rent that they were not to be treated as sureties. Palmer *v.* Purdy, 83 N. Y. 144. Where upon the dissolution of a copartnership one partner agrees with the others to assume and pay the firm debts, such partner will be considered as a principal and the others as his sureties. Barber *v.* Gillson, 18 Nev. 89; Chandler *v.* Higgins, 109 Ill. 602; Bryan *v.* Henderson, 88 Tenn. (4 Pickle), 23; Bays *v.* Conner, 105 Ind. 415.

[3] Shamburg *v.* Abbott, 112 Pa. St. 6. And see Sizer *v.* Ray, 87 N. Y. 220.

[4] This was decided by the House of Lords in Oakeley *v.* Pasheller, 10 Bligh (N. S.), 548. To same effect see Smith *v.* Shelden, 35 Mich. 42. See, also, Colgrove *v.* Tallman. 67 N. Y. 95. This on the principle that where time is given to the continuing partnership, the retiring partner becomes discharged the same as any other surety if given without his

If a retiring member of a firm agrees to bear a portion of the loss upon a note taken by the other partners towards their distributive share of the partnership effects, provided the note cannot be collected from the maker, he occupies the position of surety for the maker *pro tanto*, and will be discharged if the holders of the note give time to the maker.[1] A. and B. were partners and indebted to C.; A. sold his interest in the partnership to B., who covenanted to pay all the partnership debts, and this was known to C. Afterwards B. made an arrangement under the bankruptcy act with his creditors, including C., by which C. agreed to take a less amount for the partnership debt and to extend the time. *Held*, A. occupied the position of a surety, and was discharged both by the giving of time and by the novation of the debt.[2] Where a member of a firm transferred his interest therein to a third person, who was received into the firm and assumed all the liabilities of the retiring member, it was held that such retiring member occupied the position of a surety for the firm debts to the extent that the assets of the firm were sufficient for their payment.[3] A. and B. were partners and dissolved their partnership, B. taking the business and agreeing to pay the firm debts. Afterwards, judgment for a firm debt was recovered against A. and B., which A. was obliged to pay, and, by agreement with the creditor, A. sued out execution on the judgment against the land of B. *Held* that, as between themselves, A. was the surety of B., and had a right to make the agreement with the creditor, and could hold the land against subsequent creditors of B.[4] Three persons were in partnership in mercantile business. Two sold out to the third, who agreed to pay the partnership debts. The partner thus assuming the

consent. Birkett *v.* McGuire, 31 Up. Can. (C. P. R.), 430. And see *quære*, Gates *v.* Hughes, 44 Wis. 332. See, also, Dodd *v.* Dreyfus, 17Hun, 600.

[1] Wilde *v.* Jenkins, 4 Paige, 481.

[2] Wilson *v.* Lloyd, Law Rep. 16 Eq. Cas. 60.

[3] Morss *v.* Gleason, 64 N. Y. 204. So where a partnership takes in a new partner, and subsequently one of the original partners retires, the new firm covenanting to pay the debts of the old firm, and the retiring partner pays a judgment recovered against the old firm, he is entitled to reimbursement from the new firm under their covenant, because as to them he is a surety. Sizer *v.* Ray, 87 N. Y. 220.

[4] Waddington *v.* Vredenbergh, 2 Johns. Cas. 227.

firm debts remained in possession of the former property of the firm, and was from time to time, for eight months, selling out the goods, when the firm debts having become due and not being paid, one of the retiring partners was sued for such firm debts, and thereupon filed a bill to compel the partner who assumed the debts to pay them from the property which had belonged to the partnership. *Held*, he occupied the position of a surety, and was entitled to the relief; a surety having a right to come into equity to compel the principal to pay the debt.[1]

§ 37. **Vendor of land who sells it subject to mortgage is surety for mortgage debt.**—If a party owning land, incumbered by mortgage to secure his debt, sells it, and the vendee, as part of the purchase price, agrees to pay the mortgage debt, the vendor, as between themselves at least, becomes the surety of the vendee for the mortgage debt, and the vendee becomes the principal, and the vendor will, as to such debt, be entitled to the same rights and remedies against the vendee that any surety has against his principal.[2] Whether the vendor in such case would be entitled to all the rights of a surety as against the creditor, who had knowledge of the facts, is not quite so clear upon authority. A. and B. purchased land jointly, and gave back a joint bond and mortgage for the purchase money; A. afterwards conveyed his half interest to B., and B. agreed to pay the mortgage and gave A. a bond of indemnity against the mortgage. *Held*, A. occupied the position of a surety, and was entitled to the same rights of subrogation to which any surety would have been entitled, notwithstanding the bond of indemnity.[3] Under a similar state of facts of

[1] West *v.* Chasten, 12 Fla. 315.

[2] Mills *v.* Watson, 1 Sweeney (N. Y.), 374; Cornell *v.* Prescott, 2 Barb. (N. Y.) 16; Marsh *v.* Pike, 1 Sandf. Ch. 210; Ayers *v.* Dixon, 78 N. Y. 318; Jester *v.* Sterling, 25 Hun, 344; Fish *v.* Hayward, 28 Hun, 456; Curry *v.* Hale *et al.*, 15 W. Va. 867. But see, *contra*, Chilton *v.* Brooks (Md. 1890), 20 Atl. Rep. 125. An express promise made to a vendor by the vendee of real estate, conveyed to him subject to a deed of trust executed to secure a debt, does not, without the assent of the creditor, make the vendee the principal debtor, and the vendor the surety. Shepherd *v.* May, 115 U. S. 505. A subsequent purchaser of mortgaged land does not stand as a surety, and cannot complain of an extension of the mortgage where he has a right to redeem. Case *v.* O'Brien, 66 Mich. 289.

[3] Cherry *v.* Monro, 2 Barb. Ch. 618. The same principle was held in Succession of Daigle, 15 La. Ann. 594.

which the creditor had notice (except that no bond of indemnity was given the vendor), it was held that the vendor was not discharged because the creditor released the mortgage on a portion of the land. This was placed upon the ground that while as between themselves the vendor was the surety of the vendee, yet the vendor did not occupy that relation as to the creditor, and was not entitled to the rights of a surety as against the creditor, unless the creditor, for a valuable consideration, agreed to accept him as a surety.[1] Where the owner of land incumbered by mortgage executed by him sold it subject to the incumbrance, it was held that in equity the land became the primary fund for the payment of the debt, that the vendor occupied the position of a surety, and upon payment of the mortgage debt was entitled to be subrogated to the rights of the creditor the same as any other surety.[2] Under a similar state of facts it was held that the vendor was a surety, and was discharged by time given the vendee by the creditor, even though it was expressly agreed between the vendee and creditor that the mortgage and the debt should remain in all other respects unaffected by the giving of time.[3] As the rights of the surety against the creditor do not depend upon contract between them, but are founded upon equitable principles; and as it is settled that if the creditor does not know of the suretyship when he takes the obligation of the

[1] James *v.* Day, 37 Iowa, 164. The same principle was held in Marsh *v.* Pike, 1 Sandf. Ch. 210, and the court, on a bill filed by the vendor, refused to compel the creditor to collect the money from the mortgaged premises, but granted relief against the vendee as a principal.

[2] Johnson *v.* Zink, 51 N. Y. 333; Mutual Life Ins. Co. *v.* Davies, 12 J. & S. (N. Y. Sup. Ct.) 172; Knobloch *v.* Zschwetzke, 21 J. & S. (N. Y. Sup. Ct.) 391, and 23 J. & S. (N. Y. Sup. Ct.) 556; Brown *et al.* *v.* Kirk, 20 Mo. App. 524; Wilcox *v.* Campbell, 106 N. Y. 325, affirming 35 Hun, 254.

[3] Calvo *v.* Davies, 8 Hun (N. Y.), 222, affirmed 73 N. Y. 211; Fish *v.* Hayward, 28 Hun, 456; George *v.* Andrews, 60 Md. 26; Paine *v.* Jones, 76 N. Y. 274, affirming 14 Hun, 577; Murray *v.* Marshall, 94 N. Y. 611; Spencer *v.* Spencer, 95 N. Y. 353; Union Mutual Life Ins. Co. *v.* Hanford, 27 Fed. Rep. 588. In Penfield *v.* Goodrich, 10 Hun (N. Y.), 41, and Meyer *v.* Lathrop, 10 Hun (N. Y.), 66, it was held that the vendor of land which he conveyed subject to a mortgage was not discharged by the creditor giving time to the vendee for payment of the mortgage debt. But it was admitted that the land was the primary fund for the payment of the debt, and that as between themselves the vendor was the surety of the vendee.

surety, but is informed of it afterwards, the rights of the surety then arise,— these principles seem to apply with full force to the point under consideration, and it seems clear, on principle, that the vendor in such cases as the foregoing is entitled, as against the creditor, to all the rights of any surety. Where a vendor sold land subject to a mortgage, and gave to the purchaser thereof a bond with surety conditioned to save harmless the purchaser from said mortgage, and agreeing to pay the same himself, the purchaser cannot, upon the maturity of the mortgage, ask a court of equity to order the vendor to pay the same; and a demurrer by the surety is good when it did not appear from the bill that the purchaser had been disturbed in possession and that no demand for payment by the mortgagee had been made.[1] Where a mortgagor, who has covenanted for the payment of the mortgage debt, sells his equity of redemption, he becomes surety of the purchaser for the amount of such debt.[2]

§ 38. **Joint obligors are sureties for each other — When sole maker of note or bond is surety, etc.**— Where several persons purchase land, it being understood between them that each shall have an equal share of it, and they all join in a bond for the purchase money, they are sureties for each other; and if one fails to pay any portion of his share, and the others pay it, the one failing to pay will have no interest in the land, which he or his creditors can reach, till his share is paid up.[3] In a similar case, where one of two joint purchasers paid more than his share, it was held that he was surety for the excess, and entitled to set up the bond as a specialty debt against the estate of his co-purchaser.[4] Each principal obligor in a joint bond is, as between them, a surety for his co-obligor.[5] Where two administrators and two sureties executed a joint and several administration bond, it was held that each of the administrators was surety for the other, and if one committed a *devastavit* the other was chargeable *pari passu* with the other

[1] Leeming *v.* Smith, 25 Grant's Ch. (Can.) 256.

[2] Campbell *v.* Robinson, 27 Grant's Ch. (Can.) 634.

[3] Deitzler *v.* Mishler, 37 Pa. St. 82.

[4] Stokes *v.* Hodges, 11 Rich. Eq. (S. C.) 135. To same effect, see Crafts *v.* Mott, 4 N. Y. 604.

[5] Hatch *v.* Morris, 36 Me. 419. For special case on same subject, see Cox *v.* Thomas' Adm'x, 9 Gratt. (Va.) 312.

sureties, but was not liable as principal.[1] When a promissory note is executed by two persons, the consideration going one-half to each of them, as between themselves, they are each principal for one-half the debt, and surety of the other for the other half.[2] The sole maker of a promissory note is sometimes entitled to stand in the position of a surety. Thus W., who was absent, wrote to N., requesting him to borrow of M. a sum of money to pay a debt of W., promising in the letter to repay the money on his return. This letter was shown to M., and the money was obtained, for which N. gave his individual note. W., on his return, went to M. with the money, and offered to pay N.'s note, but M. permitted W. to retain the money and agreed to wait for it. *Held*, N. was a surety and was discharged.[3] A. agreed to take B.'s notes for a certain debt about to be created, and also certain railroad shares as collateral security for the notes, provided B. would furnish him the bond of responsible parties conditioned that they would take the shares and notes at the end of two years and pay what should remain due on the notes. *Held* that, although such parties did not sign the notes, they were in fact sureties of B., and not original promisors, and that they were entitled to all the rights of sureties.[4] If a purchaser of goods, subsequent to the sale, gives a portion of them to A., and A. unites with the purchaser in a joint note for the purchase money, with the understanding that A. signs as surety only, the fact that A. received a part of the goods from the purchaser as a gift does not make him a principal in the note.[5] Where two persons give their joint note for money borrowed and received by them in equal shares, they will be held liable jointly as principals, each for the whole, and not as sureties for one another.[6]

[1] Morrow's Adm'r *v.* Peyton's Adm'r, 8 Leigh (Va.), 54. And see Nanz *v.* Oakley, 120 N. Y. 84, reversing 37 Hun, 495.

[2] Hall *v.* Hall, 34 Ind. 314, distinguished in Mullendore *et al.* *v.* Wertz, 75 Ind. 431; holding that a court of equity will look at all the circumstances of a case to determine whether or not a party is a surety. See Eyre *v.* Hollier, Lloyd & Goold (Temp. Plunket), 250.

[3] McQuesten *v.* Noyes, 6 N. H. 19.

[4] Watriss *v.* Pierce, 32 N. H. 560.

[5] Fraser *v.* McConnell, 23 Ga. 368.

[6] Small *v.* Older, 57 Iowa, 326. In Traders' National Bank *v.* Clare, 76 Tex. 47, it is held that under such circumstances the parties, as between themselves, are principals for the

§ 39. Stockholders of a corporation, liable for its debts, are not its sureties — When surety becomes principal, etc. Where the charter of a corporation made the stockholders "jointly and severally, personally liable for the payment of all debts or demands contracted by the said corporation," it was held the stockholders were principal debtors in their individual as well as their corporate capacity, and were not sureties of the corporation, nor discharged by time given to it.[1] Where the directors of a railroad company, in order to secure a loan for the company from a bank, each give their individual promissory note to the bank as collateral security, the relation of principal and surety is created between the company and the bank.[2] When two parties, for mutual accommodation, loan their notes to each other, neither thereby becomes a surety for the other. A. loaned two of his individual notes to B., which B. discounted, and A. had to pay. At the same time as the former loan, B. loaned two of his individual notes for the same amount, and due at the same time, to A. After paying the notes, A. claimed certain rights of subrogation as the surety of B. in the two notes which he had paid. *Held*, he was not a surety, and was not entitled to the subrogation.[3] A surety may, by subsequent dealings between himself and the creditor, become a principal. A surety on a note given for the price of a negro gave his note for a balance remaining due on the original note, in discharge of such balance. *Held*, that by this transaction the surety ceased to be the surety of his principal, and became his creditor, and that he could not make the defense to the last note that the negro was unsound, and the consideration of the first note had failed.[4] Judgment having been obtained against a surety, he entered into a new ar-

amount each received, and sureties as to the balance, and one of the sureties may assume the debt of one or more for whom he is surety and take a conveyance from such principal to protect himself.

[1] Harger *v.* McCullough, 2 Denio, 119. To same effect, see Moss *v.* McCullough, 7 Barb. (N. Y.) 279. In Michigan, it is held, under the individual liability statute, that a shareholder in a bank occupies, as regards the creditor, the position of surety for the bank; and he is deemed to undertake for the debts which the bank contracts. Grand Rapids Savings Bank *v.* Warren, 52 Mich. 557.

[2] Street *v.* Old Town Bank, 67 Md. 421.

[3] Stickney *v.* Mohler, 19 Md. 490.

[4] Fluker *v.* Henry's Adm'r, 27 Ala. 403.

rangement with the creditor, irrespective of the principal, by which execution was not to issue while he kept up certain policies on his life for securing the debt, and the creditor was to take a less amount than the judgment. It was held that by this arrangement the surety became a principal, and was no longer entitled to any of the rights of a surety.[1] Where a surety, for valuable consideration, agrees with the principal to pay the indebtedness, he thereby becomes the principal, and the principal becomes his surety.[2] Where a surety on a note against whom judgment has been obtained purchases real estate from the principal, who retains a lien for the purchase money, and it is agreed between them that the surety shall pay the judgment, the surety becomes the principal and the principal the surety.[3]

§ 40. Surety entitled to same rights after judgment against him as before.— The relation of principal and surety continues after judgment against the surety, and a surety is, both at law and in equity, entitled to the same rights, and will be discharged by the same act of the creditor after, as before, judgment.[4] It has in a few cases been held that the character of the surety as such became merged in the judgment, and that thenceforth he became a principal and was not entitled to the rights of a surety.[5] There is, however, very

[1] Reade *v.* Lowndes, 23 Beav. 361. To the effect that a surety does not become a principal by joining in a new obligation after his liability is fixed, see Merriken *v.* Godwin, 2 Del. Ch. 236.

[2] Chaplin *et al. v.* Baker, 124 Ind. 385.

[3] Rhea *v.* Preston, 75 Va. 757.

[4] Commercial Bank *v.* Western Reserve Bank, 11 Ohio, 444; Brown *v.* Ayer, 24 Ga. 288; Commonwealth *v.* Miller's Adm'rs, 8 Serg. & Rawle, 452; Moss *v.* Pettengill, 3 Minn. 217; Chambers *v.* Cochran, 18 Iowa. 159; Rice *v.* Morton, 19 Mo. 263; Bangs *v.* Strong. 7 Hill (N. Y.), 250; Smith *v.* Rice, 27 Mo. 505; Davis *v.* Mikell, 1 Freeman's Ch. (Miss.) 548; Newell *v.* Hamer, 4 How. (Miss.) 684; Curan *v.* Colbert, 3 Kelly (Ga.), 239; Brown *v.* Ex'rs of Riggins, 3 Kelly (Ga.), 405; Delaplaine *v.* Hitchcock, 4 Edwards' Ch. 321; Allison *v.* Thomas, 29 La. Ann. 732. A judgment against principal and sureties on a bond does not extinguish that relation; their rights *inter sese* remain after as before judgment. West *v.* Brison, 99 Mo. 684.

[5] McNutt *v.* Wilcox, 1 Freeman's Ch. (Miss.) 116. In Bay *v.* Tallmadge, 5 Johns. Ch. 305, Chancellor Kent held that, after judgment against bail in a civil case, the relation of principal and surety ceased, and the bail was not discharged by time given. The same principle was held in La Farge *v.* Herter, 3 Denio, 157, but the decided weight of New York authority is the other way. In

little conflict of authority on this subject. There is no good reason why a surety should not be entitled to the same rights after, as before, judgment. "The recovery of a judgment against the surety does not merge or destroy his character as such, or the relation which he sustains to his principal. Its only effect is to change the form of the security as between him and the debtor. Merging the contract between the creditor and the principal debtor or surety cannot affect the relation between the principal and surety. This relation is not necessarily created by the contract to which the creditor is a party, but may be created even without his knowledge."[1] "The judgment is technically a security of a higher nature, but it is a security for the same debt or duty as the contract on which it is founded."[2] "To give time, or to discharge the principal after judgment, would be as injurious to the surety as before judgment. In either case the injury is the same, and why not have the same protection?"[3] In another case the court said: "Had the facts now proved occurred before this judgment was rendered they would have opposed a good defense to the recovery of it; and if not availed of in defense, the judgment would have concluded them; occurring after the judgment, they are no more concluded by it than payment, or a release, or any other matter going to discharge it."[4] After joint judgment against principal and surety, the surety

Findlay's Ex'rs *v.* United States, 2 McLean, 44, it was held that judgment against the accommodation drawer of a bill of exchange merged the relation of principal and surety, and that thereafter the only right of the surety was to pay and have subrogation. In Marshall *v.* Aiken, 25 Vt. 328; McDowell *v.* Bank, 1 Harr. (Del.) 369, and Dunham *v.* Downer, 31 Vt. 249, it was held that the judgment merged the relation of principal and surety, so that at law the surety no longer had any rights as such, but that in equity all his rights remained. In Jenkins *v.* Robertson, 2 Drewry, 351, A. as principal, and B. as surety, were indebted to C. B. died, and C., in a creditor's suit, obtained a decree against his estate. Afterwards C. sued A. and took judgment, thereby giving time. *Held*, the estate of B. was not discharged. Its character as surety was merged in the decree, and all that followed was simply an execution of the decree. See, also, on this subject, Dougherty *v.* Richardson, 20 Ind. 412; Thomas *et al. v.* Stewart *et al.*, 117 Ind. 50.

[1] Bangs *v.* Strong, 4 N. Y. 315, per Pratt, J.

[2] Carpenter *v.* King, 9 Met. 511, per Shaw, C. J.

[3] Trotter *v.* Strong, 63 Ill. 272, per Walker, J.

[4] Shelton *v.* Hurd, 7 R. I. 403, per Ames, C. J.

will be discharged by time given the principal,[1] by creditor releasing levy on property of principal, and taking from principal bond and mortgage in payment for the debt,[2] by creditor releasing principal, who is taken in execution, and taking from him a fresh security for the debt.[3] The same rule prevails where separate judgments are recovered against the principal and surety.[4]

§ 41. Surety, who in terms binds himself as principal, not entitled to rights of surety.— Where a surety binds himself in terms as a principal in the obligation which he signs, he will be held as a principal, and will be entitled to none of the rights of a surety. "There is no rule of law which prohibits a surety from waving the right which belongs to him as such. Such a waiver has nothing in itself offensive to the policy of the law." The express terms of the obligation in such case exclude the idea of suretyship, and the creditor has a right to avail himself of the contract his vigilance has obtained.[5] Where three parties signed a joint and several note, the first one adding to his name the word "principal," the other two adding the word "sureties," it was held the one to whose name the word "principal" was attached could not show by parol that he was in fact a surety, and known to be such by the creditor. The court said that if the note had been silent as to who was principal and who surety, the suretyship might have been shown without contradicting the note; but in the present case, to allow the proof would be to contradict the terms of the note.[6] Several parties signed a note to a bank commencing as follows: "We, severally and jointly, all as principals, promise to pay," and it was held none of them could show they were sureties.[7] The court said: "Here is an

[1] Storms *v.* Thorn, 3 Barb. (N. Y.) 314; Blazer *v.* Bundy, 15 Ohio St. 57; McCrary *v.* Coley, Ga. Dec. 104; Carpenter *v.* Devon, 6 Ala. 718; Crawford *v.* Gaulden, 33 Ga. 173.

[2] La Farge *v.* Herter, 11 Barb. (N. Y.) 159.

[3] Eales *v.* Fraser, 6 Man. & Gr. 755.

[4] Manufacturers' & Mechanics' Bank *v.* Bank of Pennsylvania, 7 Watts & Serg. 335.

[5] Picot *v.* Signiago, 22 Mo. 587; McMillan *v.* Parkell, 64 Mo. 286.

[6] Waterville Bank *v.* Redington, 52 Me. 466.

[7] Derry Bank *v.* Baldwin, 41 N. H. 434. This decision was made at law, and one of the parties filed a bill in equity, claiming relief as a surety there, but it was denied him, and the court held that both at law and in equity he was concluded by the

express contract that each signer is a principal. Each contracts for himself with the holder that he is a principal; that he will so stand upon the note. This constitutes a part of the contract with the bank, as much as the sum to be paid or the time of payment or the promise to pay anything at any time does, and this fact as to the capacity in which the signer of the note binds himself, may often be as important a part of the contract as any other." A principal and several sureties signed a bond reciting that they all signed "as principals," and nothing appeared on the face of the bond to indicate that any of them were sureties. *Held*, the sureties were estopped by the bond to show they were sureties, and that they were not discharged by time given.[1] Where a note commenced, "We, each as principal, jointly and severally promise to pay," but one of the signers was a surety, and known to the creditor to be such, and time was given to the principal, which would ordinarily have discharged a surety, it was held the surety was not discharged.[2] But where in such a case the surety added to his signature the word "surety," it was held that he had all the rights of a surety and was discharged by time given.[3] A surety may also be estopped by his conduct from claiming the rights of a surety. A. appeared on a note as principal and B. as surety, and in various litigations concerning it for eight years A. professed to be the principal. In the meantime judgments had been recovered against B. by certain of his creditors. In a contest between A. and such creditors it was held that A. could not show, to the prejudice of the creditors, that he was in fact surety and B. principal on such note.[4]

§ 42. **Surety estopped to deny recitals of his obligation.** The general rule is that sureties are estopped to deny the facts recited in the obligations signed by them, and this whether the recitals are true or false in fact. Having once solemnly alleged the existence of the facts they cannot afterwards be

terms of his obligation. Heath *v.* Derry Bank, 44 N. H. 174.

[1] Sprigg *v.* Bank of Mount Pleasant, 10 Pet. (U. S.) 257; Menaugh *et al. v.* Chandler *et al.*, 89 Ind. 94.

[2] Claremont Bank *v.* Wood, 10 Vt. 582.

[3] People's Bank *v.* Pearsons, 30 Vt. 711.

[4] Goswiller's Estate, 3 Penr. & Watts, 200.

heard to deny it.[1] The plaintiff in a replevin suit, as a condition for a continuance granted him, was required to give an additional bond, and, in pursuance of such requirement, A., long after it had been taken in the case, signed the original replevin bond to the sheriff, which had been signed by other sureties. In a suit against A. on the bond, he set up the defense that the sheriff had no right to take a replevin bond in the suit at the time he, A., signed it, and that the bond was void. The bond on its face imported that it was executed when the suit was instituted, and when the sheriff had a right to take it, and it was held that the surety was estopped to deny that it was taken at that time.[2] In an action against the sureties in an undertaking purporting to have been given to procure the discharge of an attachment, they will not be allowed to show as a defense that no attachment was in fact issued. It is not essential to the validity of such an undertaking that an attachment shall actually be issued. Giving an undertaking which recites the issuance of an attachment when none has been issued is conclusive evidence of a waiver of the issuance of the attachment.[3] The surety on a receiver's recognizance, which recites that it has been duly acknowledged before a commissioner of the court is estopped to deny that fact.[4] When the bond of a city treasurer recited the fact that he had been elected to that office, and the sureties on the bond were sued for money received by him while acting in that capacity, it was held that they could not deny that he had been elected. The court said that by signing the bond they had enabled him to get the money of the city, and it was too late for them to deny his election.[5] When the bond of a bor-

[1] Monteith *v.* Commonwealth, 15 Gratt. (Va.) 172; Duhamp *v.* Nicholson, 14 Martin (La.), 2 N. S. 672; Cordle *v.* Burch, 10 Gratt. (Va.) 480; Borden *v.* Houston, 2 Tex. 594; Cecil *v.* Early, 10 Gratt. (Va.) 198; Cox *v.* Thomas' Adm'x, 9 Gratt. (Va.) 312; Lee *v.* Clark, 1 Hill (N. Y.), 56; State *v.* Lewis, 73 N. C. 138; May *v.* May, 19 Fla. 373. With respect to the liability of sureties on bonds, the doctrine as laid down in the text is held to apply only "to facts in connection with bonds possible and legal in themselves." Tinsley *v.* Kirby, 17 S. C. 1.

[2] Decker *v.* Judson, 16 N. Y. 439.

[3] Coleman *v.* Bean, 1 Abbott's Rep. Omitted Cas. (N. Y.) 394. To similar effect, see Higgins *v.* Healy, 15 J. & S. (N. Y. Sup. Ct.) 207.

[4] Driscoll *v.* Blake, 9 Irish Ch. Rep. 356.

[5] City of Paducah *v.* Cully, 9 Bush

ough collector recited that he was duly elected, it was held that the sureties therein could not show that the office had been abolished before his election.[1] Where the condition of a bond recited that A. was guardian, etc., it was held that neither A. nor the sureties on his bond could deny that he was guardian, nor set up as a defense any supposed irregularity in obtaining the appointment.[2]

§ 43. **Same continued.**— In an action against C. as surety for S., in a replevin bond conditioned for the redelivery of property attached to abide the final order of the court, he pleaded that at the time of, and prior to the institution of the original suit by attachment, S., the defendant therein, and the principal in the replevin bond, was dead. It was held that by signing the bond which purported to be signed by S. as a co-obligor, C. was estopped to deny that S. had signed it.[3] The official bond of an executor was made payable to four justices, one of whom was not a member of the court at the time. *Held*, that the surety, having executed the bond, was estopped to deny that any of those named in the bond as justices were such.[4] So where the bond of a guardian recites that the principal has been appointed guardian, the sureties therein are estopped to deny the jurisdiction of the court making the appointment.[5] The sureties on the bond of an Indian agent, which recites his appointment as such, are estopped to deny that fact.[6] The bond given by a coroner upon

(Ky.), 323. To same effect, see People *v.* Jenkins, 17 Cal. 500; Phenix Ins. Co. *v.* Findley *et al.*, 59 Ia. 591.

[1] Seiple *v.* Borough of Elizabeth, 3 Dutcher (N. J.), 407.

[2] Fridge *v.* The State, 3 Gill & Johns. (Md.) 103; State *ex rel.* Metsker *v.* Mills *et al.*, 82 Ind. 126. So the sureties on a trustee's bond are estopped from impeaching the validity of the appointment. Bassett *v.* Crafts, 129 Mass. 513.

[3] Collins *v.* Mitchell, 5 Fla. 364.

[4] Franklin's Adm'r *v.* Depriest, 13 Gratt. (Va.) 257.

[5] Norton *v.* Miller, 25 Ark. 108. Surety on replevin bond is estopped from denying jurisdiction of justice. Harbaugh *v.* Albertson, 102 Ind. 69. So sureties of a "committee" appointed for a lunatic are estopped from denying jurisdiction of court. Pannill's Adm'r *v.* Calloway, 78 Va. 387. But it is held that the sureties on a recognizance may show that the officer before whom the recognizance was taken had no authority to take it. Dickenson *et al.* *v.* State, 20 Neb. 72. And see Crum *v.* Wilson, 61 Miss. 233, where it was held that sureties on a guardian's bond were not estopped from showing that the court appointing him had no jurisdiction.

[6] Bruce *v.* United States, 17 How. (U. S.) 437. So the sureties on the

assuming the duties of sheriff recited that the sheriff was dead, and that thereby the coroner had become sheriff, and it was held that the sureties on the bond were estopped to deny those facts.[1] A guaranty purported to have been made in consideration of one dollar, but the actual consideration was that moving between principal and creditor. The guarantor attempted to prove that the one dollar had not been paid. *Held*, the parties in such a case are taken to have agreed that the actual consideration shall be estimated in money, at the sum expressed as a consideration in the contract, and where the parties have agreed that a legal consideration shall assume such a form, for the purposes of the contract, they are estopped from denying, in an action on the contract, that it was such in fact.[2] But where a contract for the delivery of sheep recited that $1,000 had been paid by the purchaser, and it was signed by the seller and certain sureties for him, in a suit on the contract it was held that the fact of the payment of the money might be contradicted. The court said: "We are of opinion, as it was stated to be a part of the consideration for the execution of said writing, that the writing is not conclusive upon the subject. The truth may be inquired into."[3]

§ 44. **Same continued — Reason.**— The holder of the bond of a corporation guarantied it as as follows: "I hereby guaranty the due payment of the money secured thereby." In a suit against him on the guaranty, the guarantor offered to show that the bond was invalid, and the corporation had no authority to make it; but it was held that he was estopped to show those facts. The court said: "The guaranty of the payment of the bond by the defendant imports an agreement or undertaking that the makers of the bond were competent to contract in the manner they have, and that the instrument is a binding obligation upon the makers."[4] In an action of covenant on a sealed guaranty of a lease, it was objected that there

bond of an administrator (Johnston *v.* Smith, 25 Hun, 171; White *v.* Weatherbee, 126 Mass. 450), or guardian (Gray *v.* State, 78 Ind. 68; Williamson *v.* Woodman, 73 Maine, 163), or wharfinger (People *v.* Huson, 78 Cal. 154), are estopped from denying the appointment respectively of such officers.

[1] Albee *v.* The People, 22 Ill. 533.

[2] Redfield *v.* Haight, 27 Conn. 31.

[3] Swope *v.* Forney, 17 Ind. 385.

[4] Remsen *v.* Graves, 41 N. Y. 471, per Mason, J. But the corporation

was no proof that one of the lessors executed the lease, but it was held that the guarantors were estopped from denying the execution of the lease by the lessees. The court said: "Entering into this guaranty was an acknowledgment by the guarantors that the lease was duly executed by both lessees."[1] In the cases already referred to on this subject, the question came up in a suit against the surety, on the obligation signed by him. The facts recited were, in most instances, within the knowledge of the surety, and the principal had usually acted in the capacity which the obligation recited he occupied, and derived a benefit therefrom, and became a defaulter therein. In such cases the issue is not the right of the principal to fill the position, but his right to retain money received by him while filling the same, and which belongs to others. To such cases the principles of equitable estoppel, as well as the rule that a man cannot aver against his own deed, apply. When the issue is as to the right of the principal to fill the position, different principles will apply. A person was appointed to fill an office created by a city, and gave an official bond with sureties, which recited that he had been appointed collector of assessments for street improvements, and was conditioned that he should pay the city treasurer all moneys which he might receive as such collector. The city had, in fact, no authority to create the office, but the court held the sureties were estopped to deny that the collector was an officer *de facto*.[2] The distinction above referred to was noticed by the court as follows: "The action is not to enforce upon him the execution of the duties of his office, or to recover damages for his failure to perform them. In such a case both he and his sureties might answer and say, perhaps successfully, there was no such office, and he was without legal power. But here the suit is founded upon an actual, complete execution of the duties of the office he claims to fill. He is *functus officio* as collector of taxes.

itself would not be estopped from setting up that the contract of suretyship entered into by it was *ultra vires*. Lucas *v.* White Line Transfer Co., 70 Iowa, 541.

1 Otto *v.* Jackson, 35 Ill. 349.

2 Hoboken *v.* Harrison, 1 Vroom (N. J.), 73. See, also, Middleton *et al.* *v.* State, 120 Ind. 166, where it was held that the sureties on the bond of a city clerk were estopped to deny the validity of an ordinance under which their principal received moneys and which ordinance was in existence when the bond was executed.

The money he has is the money of the city, which he has no right to retain, and which his sureties on the whole case, just as it is, have stipulated that he shall pay over to the city treasury."

§ 45. **Same continued.**— Sureties on a note or bond executed to a corporation or partnership are estopped from denying the legal existence of such corporation or partnership.[1] A guarantor of promissory notes is estopped from setting up as a defense, illegality of dealings between the original parties.[2] A surety on a bond is estopped from avoiding liability thereon, because the bond is other than he thought it to be, when he was not prevented from reading the same by any fraud of the obligee.[3] A surety for the payment of alimony is estopped from denying that the woman for whose benefit the money was directed to be paid is not the wife of the principal.[4] A surety for the purchase of slaves was held estopped from setting up that they were unsound.[5] Sureties on purchase-money notes, who have notice of all defects in title to the land sold, are estopped from setting up clouds upon the title.[6] Where sureties agreed with their principal to pay certain judgments rendered against them, they are estopped from denying the validity of such judgments.[7] Sureties to a replevin bond are estopped from showing that the property replevied was of less value than the amount stated in the replevin writ and bond.[8] A surety on the bond of an insolvent defaulting trustee, who, in ignorance of his right to proceed against a sound surety on

[1] Singer Mfg. Co. *v.* Bennett, 28 W. Va. 16; The Father Matthew Society *v.* Fitzwilliams, 84 Mo. 406, affirming 12 Mo. App. 445; Teutonia Nat. Bank *v.* Wagner *et al.*, 33 La. Ann. 732; Pharr *v.* McHugh & Vinson *et al.*, 32 La. Ann. 1280. See Ahrend *v.* Odiorne, 125 Mass. 50; Jefferson *v.* M'Carthy, 44 Minn. 26.

[2] Jackson *v.* Foote (Cir. Ct. N. D. Ill.), 12 Fed. Rep. 37.

[3] Johnston *et al.* *v.* Patterson, 114 Pa. St. 398. A surety is estopped from questioning the validity of a bond which he signed in blank, with the understanding that it was to be of a different character from the bond that was actually written and delivered. Willis *v.* Rivers, 80 Ga. 556; Craig *v.* Herring & Turner, 80 Ga. 709.

[4] Comm'rs of Charities *v.* O'Rourk, 34 Hun, 349.

[5] Grier *v.* Wallace, 7 Rich. (S. C.) 182.

[6] Ellis, Adm'r, *v.* Adderton, 88 N. C. 482.

[7] Apperson *v.* Gogin *et al.*, 3 Bradwell (Ill. App.), 48.

[8] Washington Ice Co. *v.* Webster, 125 U. S. 426.

an indemnifying bond executed in his favor, accepts notes of his principal in payment of the loss incurred by him in virtue of his suretyship on the bond, is estopped from proceeding against the surety on the indemnifying bond.[1] Where a wife transferred her separate real estate to her husband, for the purpose of enabling him to mortgage it as his property to secure a loan for his benefit, she will be estopped, as against a mortgagee who is not shown to have had knowledge that the conveyances were a contrivance to evade the statute prohibiting her from entering into contracts of suretyship, from asserting that such transfer was not *bona fide*.[2]

§ 46. **When surety not estopped by recitals of obligation signed by him.**— A surety is not in all cases estopped to deny the facts recited in the obligation signed by him. Thus, where the bond of a township recited that the township officers executing the same had been authorized, as the law required, to issue such bond, in a suit on the bond it was held the township might show that no such authority had been given. The court said that the doctrine that a party is estopped from contradicting the recitals of his own deed is applicable only where the deed is admitted to be the act of such party.[3] A court had appointed a guardian for a minor, and, while such appointment was unrevoked, appointed another, who gave a bond with surety, reciting that he had been appointed guardian. In a suit on this bond against the surety, it was held that the appointment of the last guardian was absolutely void, and that the surety might show the fact.[4] The court said: "It is certainly true that where a party makes a distinct and clear recital of any fact in a deed or other valid obligation, he will be estopped from denying the truth of such recital. But this doctrine presupposes a valid legal obligation, and we do not know any authority, and reason is certainly against the

[1] Bowers *v.* Cobb, Ex'r (Cir. Ct. D. Mass.), 31 Fed. Rep. 678.

[2] Long *v.* Crosson, 119 Ind. 3. For other cases, generally, on the doctrine of estoppel as governing sureties, see Steele *v.* Tutwiler, 57 Ala. 113; Nevin *v.* Fouch, 77 Ga. 47; Snyder *v.* Chick, 112 Ind. 293; Zurcher *v.* Krohne, Feiss & Co., 63 Tex. 118.

[3] Hudson *v.* Inhabitants of Winslow, 6 Vroom (N. J.), 437.

[4] Thomas *v.* Burrus, 23 Miss. 550, per Yerger, J. And it is likewise held that a surety on a constable's bond is not estopped from showing that the appointment of his principal was illegal and therefore a nullity. Tinsley *v.* Kirby, 17 S. C. 1.

proposition, that a party is estopped, by any recital contained in an instrument, from showing that the instrument containing it is absolutely null and void." An appeal bond was conditioned for the prosecution of an appeal from the judgment of a justice of the peace to the Anne Arundel county court. There was, in fact, no such court. *Held*, the sureties were not estopped to deny the existence of the court by the recital in the bond.[1] The court said: "Whether a court exists or not is something more than a mere question of fact, as to which parties may agree or be concluded by admissions. It must depend on the constitution or laws; and when the court can see that the supposed tribunal is not known to these, it must so decide, no matter what the parties may have admitted by estoppel or agreement." A defendant was taken under a bail writ, and the sheriff by mistake took a bond for the prison bounds, which recited the defendant's imprisonment to have been under a *ca. sa.* *Held*, the bond was void, and that the surety was not estopped to show there was no *ca. sa.* The grounds of the decision are set forth as follows: "It is a general rule of law, and a correct one too, that a man cannot aver against his own deed; but that is where he has alleged some particular fact within his own knowledge and which forms a part of the consideration for his undertaking; and that is the whole extent to which the cases relied on go. But the principle cannot be extended to an allegation coming from the other party, and which can be necessarily known only to him, although contained in the recital of a deed made by the defendant. . . . The person supposed to be estopped is the very person imposed upon. . . . It is to be observed that this is an allegation coming from the sheriff and not from the defendant. He could not find under what authority the sheriff acted but by his own representation; a person is only estopped from denying his own acts, but not the acts of another."[2] A surety on a note who was induced to become such by fraudulent representations is not estopped from setting up such fraud as a ground for setting aside a judgment confessed by him upon the note, it being shown that he had no knowledge of

[1] Tucker *v.* The State, 11 Md. 322, per Tucker, J.

[2] Miller *v.* Bagwell, 3 McCord, Law (S. C.), 429, per Nott, J.

such fraud.[1] And a married woman who has executed a mortgage on her lands to secure her husband's notes is not estopped from setting up fraud in the procurement of the mortgage.[2]

§ 47. **Cases holding guaranty of note negotiable.**— There is an irreconcilable conflict of authority as to whether or not a guaranty is negotiable, and when, if at all, it passes by an assignment of the original obligation, and there is no decided preponderance of authority either way. A stranger to a negotiable promissory note indorsed it in blank when it was made. The payee transferred the note, and the holder wrote a guaranty above the stranger's indorsement and brought suit upon it. *Held*, he was entitled to recover.[3] The court said: "The guaranty is general, specifying no person to whom the guarantor undertakes to be liable, and is upon the back of a negotiable instrument. In such case the guaranty runs with the instrument on which it is written and to which it refers, and partakes of its quality of negotiability, and any person having the legal interest in the principal instrument takes in like manner the incident and may sue upon the guaranty." A guaranty on the back of a negotiable promissory note, signed by the payee, was as follows: "I guaranty the payment of the within note." *Held*, the guaranty passed with the note, so that any subsequent *bona fide* holder, as well as the first holder after the guaranty was made, might sue on the guaranty.[4] These cases hold that where the guaranty is general, specifying no particular person to whom it runs, it is negotiable and passes with the note, and may be sued on at law, in his own name, by any subsequent holder of the note. It has been held that where the guaranty of a promissory note is a separate instrument from the note, the title to it will pass by delivery

[1] Melick *v.* First Nat. Bank of Tama City, 52 Iowa, 94.

[2] Henry *et al.* *v.* Sneed *et al.*, 99 Mo. 407.

[3] Webster *v.* Cobb, 17 Ill. 459. See, also, on same point, Heaton *v.* Hulburt, 3 Scam. (Ill.) 489. Guaranty of note is, in general, negotiable, even though an assignment of the same is made after the maturity of the note. Ellsworth *v.* Harmon, 101 Ill. 274.

[4] Partridge *v.* Davis, 20 Vt. 499. To the same effect, see Killian *v.* Ashley, 24 Ark. 511. See, also, Studebaker *v.* Cody, 54 Ind. 586; Cole *et al.* *v.* Merchants' Bank, 60 Ind. 350; Harbord *v.* Cooper, 43 Minn. 466. It is held that a guaranty may be transferred before a note to which it is attached, and which it was given to secure, becomes due. Everson *v.* Gere, 40 Hun, 248; affirmed, 122 N. Y. 290.

with the note for a good consideration, and this without any written assignment of the guaranty.[1] It has likewise been held that when a guaranty is written on a promissory note, and the note is transferred, the sale and delivery of the note with the guaranty upon it furnishes *prima facie* evidence of a sale of the contract of guaranty and that the holder of the note is the owner of the guaranty.[2] A general guaranty of payment of a promissory note, which named no person as the party guarantied, was not written on or attached to the note, and it was held that it might be enforced at law by any one who advanced money upon it declaring on it as a promise to himself. But it was further held that the guaranty, not being attached to or a part of the note, was not negotiable, and an action could only be brought upon it in the name of the person in whose hands it first became available. The court said that if it had been attached to the note, it might have been treated as an indorsement and would have been negotiable.[3] Where a guaranty written on a promissory note named the person guarantied, and proceeded, "I hereby guaranty the payment and collection of the within note to him or bearer," it was held that any subsequent holder of the note might sue on it in his own name.[4] The court said it was a new note for the payment of money, and, by its terms, negotiable. A note was drawn and signed by H., payable to N., and indorsed by N., the latter being an accommodation indorser for H., who was the principal. E. guarantied the note generally on its back, and the bank sued E. on his guaranty. *Held*, the bank need not prove affirmatively that the contract of guaranty was made with it. As N. in-

[1] Gould *v.* Ellery, 39 Barb. (N. Y.) 163.

[2] Cooper *v.* Dedrick, 22 Barb. (N. Y.) 516.

[3] McLaren *v.* Watson's Ex'rs, 26 Wend. 425, per Walworth, C. Senator Verplanck, in an able and exhaustive opinion, contended that the guaranty in this case was negotiable, but the majority of the court of errors held otherwise. Where a negotiable promissory note was indorsed by the payee for the accommodation of the maker, and on the back thereof was the following guaranty, viz.: "We hereby guaranty the payment of the within note," it was held that the contract of the guarantors was not with the payee, but with the first holder for value who took the note with the guaranty upon it. Baldwin *v.* Dow, 130 Mass. 416; Jones *v.* Dow, 142 Mass. 130.

[4] Ketchell *v.* Burns, 24 Wend. 456, per Nelson, C. J.

dorsed for the accommodation of H., and the bank was the first holder for value, the law implied that the guaranty was made to it. The court said that the guaranty was not distinguishable from a general letter of credit, on which an action might be maintained in the name of the person who gave the credit on the faith of it.[1]

§ 48. Cases holding that guaranty of debt passes to assignee of debt.— When the guaranty is not of the payment of a note, it has also been held that it passes by a transfer of the debt as an incident thereto. Thus, where a party by a separate covenant guarantied the payment of rent and the performance of the covenants of a lease, it was held that the guaranty ran with the land and passed to the grantee of the reversion, who might sue the guarantor in his own name for a breach of the covenant. The court said: "When the thing to be done or omitted concerns the lands or estate, that is the medium which creates the privity between the plaintiff and defendant."[2] A. being the owner of a bond, and mortgage securing the same, by writing on the back of the mortgage assigned the bond and mortgage to B., and the assignment then proceeded, "and hereby guaranty the collection of the within amount as it becomes due." B. assigned the bond and mortgage to C., the assignment to C. saying nothing about the guaranty. C. sued A. on the guaranty in his own name at law, and it was held he had a right to maintain the suit, even though the guaranty was not in terms assigned to him. "The transfer of the debt to him carried with it as an incident all the securities for its payment."[3] It has been held that parol evidence is competent to rebut the presumption that a judg-

[1] Northumberland Bank *v.* Eyer, 58 Pa. St. 97, per Sharswood, J. See to like effect, Baldwin *v.* Dow, 130 Mass. 416; Jones *v.* Dow, 142 Mass. 130.

[2] Allen *v.* Culver, 3 Denio, 284, per Jewett, J. The assignment of a lease by the lessee does not release a guarantor of the lessee from liability for a default of the lessee in the payment of the rent subsequent to such assignment. Oswald *v.* Fratenburgh, 36 Minn. 270. In Potter *v.* Gronbeck *et al.*, 117 Ill. 404, it is held that a guaranty of rent is not assignable. Holding that an assignment of a note carries with it a guaranty of its collectibility, see Lemmon *v.* Strong, 59 Conn. 448.

[3] Craig *v.* Parkis, 40 N. Y. 181, per Lott, J. And to similar effect where defendants assigned a bond and mortgage, it was held that the assignment carried with it a guaranty of the payment of the mortgage. Stillman *v.* Northrup, 109 N. Y. 473, overruling Smith *v.* Starr, 4 Hun, 123.

ment against an indorser passes by an assignment of a judgment against the principal when nothing is said in the assignment about the judgment against the indorser.[1] The state of Virginia guarantied the payment of interest on coupon bonds issued by the city of Wheeling, the guaranty being that the state guarantied the "punctual payment of the interest." It was held that if the guaranty was not transferable at law, it was in equity, and an interest passed in equity to each successive holder of the bond or coupon. The guaranty is an accessory of the bond or coupon, and follows and adheres to it in equity, and the right to enforce the guaranty must be determined by the right to demand payment of the bond or coupon.[2] H. and O. being partners, H. sold out his interest in the firm property to O., who agreed to pay the firm debts, among them a debt to the plaintiff. The defendant guarantied the performance of this agreement. The plaintiff's debt not having been paid, H. assigned to him his interest and claim under the agreement and the guaranty. *Held*, the plaintiff was entitled to recover against the defendant on the guaranty, which, having been made for his benefit, he could adopt and enforce.[3] Under a similar state of facts, except that H. did not assign the agreement and guaranty to the plaintiff, it was held that there was no privity between the plaintiff and the defendant, and the plaintiff could not recover against the defendant.[4]

§ 49. Cases holding guaranty of note not negotiable.— The payee of a negotiable promissory note indorsed it as follows: "I guaranty the payment of the within note without demand or notice," and sold it to A., who sold it to B., and B. sued the guarantor on the guaranty. *Held*, the guaranty was not negotiable, and the action could not be maintained.[5] Where a stranger to a note indorsed it in blank and added to his name the word "holden," it was held that this constituted him a guarantor, but that the guaranty was not negotiable, and could be enforced by no one except the person with whom it

[1] Bank *v.* Fordyce, 9 Pa. St. 275.

[2] Arents *v.* The Commonwealth, 18 Gratt. (Va.) 750.

[3] Claflin *v.* Ostrom, 54 N. Y. 581.

[4] Campbell *v.* Lacock, 40 Pa. St. 448.

[5] Springer *v.* Hutchinson, 19 Me. 359. To the same effect, see Ten Eyck *v.* Brown, 3 Pinney (Wis.), 452, and Turley *v.* Hodge, 3 Humph. (Tenn.) 73.

was made.[1] A negotiable promissory note and a guaranty of its payment by a stranger indorsed thereon were made at the same time. *Held*, the guaranty was not negotiable, and did not pass by a transfer of the note.[2] Where a guaranty was made on the back of a promissory note after the note was delivered, it was held that it did not pass by an assignment of the note.[3] A negotiable promissory note was signed by A. as maker. Underneath the note was written the following guaranty: "We will guaranty the payment of the above note given to (A.) for forty-two hundred and eighty dollars." *Held*, the guaranty was not negotiable, not being so by its terms, and that it could not be sued on by any one except the person to whom it was originally given.[4] A guaranty is not negotiable, nor does it become so by being indorsed upon negotiable paper, the payment of which it is designed to secure.[5]

§ 50. Whether guaranty of bond negotiable, or lease assignable — When guaranty on back of note transfers title to note — Obligation of surety cannot be sold alone.— A guaranty of the payment of a certain bond and mortgage "to Arthur Childs, the present owner and holder of said bond and mortgage, his executors and administrators," is not a personal guaranty, confined to Childs, his executors and administrators, and an assignee of said bond and mortgage may maintain an action on the guaranty for the payment of the same.[6] On the other hand, it has been held that a covenant of guaranty, written on the back of a bond, is no part of the bond, and does not pass by an assignment of it.[7] A guaranty of the interest on bonds, given in payment for the construction of a railroad, is not negotiable.[8] A guaranty for the payment of rent, and the performance of other covenants on the part of a lessee in

[1] Irish *v.* Cutter, 31 Me. 536; Bray *v.* Marsh, 75 Me. 452.

[2] Tinker *v.* McCauley, 3 Mich. 188.

[3] How *v.* Kemball, 2 McLean, 103. In Levi *v.* Mendell, 1 Duvall (Ky.), 77, it was held that only the equitable title to a guaranty on the back of a note passed by an assignment of the note.

[4] Smith *v.* Dickinson, 6 Humph. (Tenn.) 261.

[5] Hayden *v.* Welden, 43 N. J. Law, 128.

[6] Stillman *v.* Northrup, 109 N. Y. 473, overruling Smith *v.* Starr, 4 Hun, 123. To similar effect, see Craig *v.* Parkis, 40 N. Y. 181.

[7] Beckley *v.* Eckert, 3 Pa. St. 292.

[8] Eastern Township Bank *v.* St. Johnsbury & L. C. R. Co. (Cir. Ct. D. Vt.), 40 Fed. Rep. 423.

a lease, is not assignable, so as to pass legal title to the assignee.[1] A guaranty on the back of a negotiable promissory note signed by the payee, although it may not in itself be negotiable, is a sufficient indorsement of the note to transfer the title to it.[2] A warehouseman is not a guarantor of the title of property placed in his custody, although warehouse receipts are, by statute, negotiable.[3] Principal and surety signed an obligation; judgment was recovered against the holder of the obligation, and at an execution sale the debt due by the surety was sold, the principal being insolvent. It was held that the sale was invalid, and that the obligation of a surety could not be sold separate from that of the principal. The court said the obligation of the surety was accessory to that of the principal, and could not be separated from it.[4]

[1] Potter *v.* Gronbeck *et al.*, 117 Ill. 404.

[2] Myrick *v.* Hasey, 27 Me. 9. To same effect, see Heaton *v.* Hulbert, 3 Scam. (Ill.) 489; Russell & Co. *v.* Klink, 53 Mich. 161; Heard *et al.* *v.* Dubuque County Bank, 8 Neb. 10; adhered to in State Nat. Bank *v.* Haylen *et al.*, 14 Neb. 480.

[3] Insurance Co. *v.* Kiger, 103 U. S. 352. As to whether the sale and transfer of a shipbuilder's interest in a schooner transfers a guaranty that the earnings shall amount to a certain per cent. of her cost, see Bishop *v.* Alcott, 86 N. Y. 503, affirming 21 Hun, 253.

[4] Andrus *v.* Chretien, 7 La. O. S. (4 Curry), 318.

CHAPTER II.

OF THE STATUTE OF FRAUDS.

Text of the Statute of Frauds — *
General observations . . . § 51
Effect of the words "no action shall be brought" 52
Meaning of the words "any special promise" 53
What included in the words "debt, default or miscarriage." 54
The words "of another" contemplated the present or future primary liability of a principal 55
If there is no remedy against a third party, the promise need not be in writing — Leading case 56
When no liability incurred by third person, promise need not be in writing — Liability of principal need not be express. 57
When party for whom promise is made cannot become liable, promise need not be in writing. 58
When promise to indemnify within the statute — Principles involved 59
When promise to indemnify need not be in writing — Instances . 60
When promise to indemnify must be in writing — Instances. 61
If original debt extinguished or novated, promise not within the statute 62
When promise to pay out of proceeds of debtor's property not within statute 63
Creditor relinquishing lien which does not inure to benefit of promisor does not take promise out of statute 64
When the transaction amounts to a purchase of debt or lien by promisor, promise not within statute . . . . . § 65
When promisor, who is debtor to third person, agrees to pay his debt to creditor of such third person, promise not within statute 66
When promise is in effect to pay promisor's own debt, it is not within statute, although it incidentally guaranty debt of another 67
When promisor previously liable, promise not within statute . 68
New consideration passing between promisee and promisor will not alone take promise out of statute 69
Promise not within statute when main object is to benefit promisor himself — Observations . 70
Promise of *del credere* agent not within statute 71
Promise not within statute unless made to party to whom principal is liable 72
False representations of another's credit not within statute . . 73
Promise in substance to pay debt of another, no matter what its form, is within statute . . . 74
Promise to answer for future liability of third party is within statute 75
Promise within statute if any credit given to third person . 76
When promise is original or collateral, case holding it original 77

Whether promise is original or collateral is question of fact — Evidence — Case holding promise collateral . . . . § 78
If original promise in writing, verbal subsequent promise takes case out of statute of limitations — Verbal guaranty sufficient to support verbal account stated 79
The form of the writing 80
The whole promise must appear from the writing 81
Whether the consideration must appear from the writing . . 82
Reasons why the consideration should appear from the writing — Observations 83
When the consideration sufficiently appears from the writing . . . . § 84
When consideration does not sufficiently appear, or, consideration appearing, is insufficient — Instances 85
When writing ambiguous, it may be explained by parol evidence 86
When several papers may be read together to express consideration for promise . . . 87
Whether guaranty of note, judgment, certificate of deposit, or assigned mortgage must express consideration 88
Signature by party to be charged 89
Signature by agent 90
Pleading 91

§ 51. Text of the Statute of Frauds — General observations.— It was not necessary at common law that the contract of a surety or guarantor should be in writing in order to charge him. This being so, the Statute 29 Charles II., chapter 3, commonly called the Statute of Frauds, was passed. The fourth section of that statute, so far as pertinent to the subject under consideration, was as follows, viz.: "No action shall be brought whereby to charge the defendant upon any special promise to answer for the debt, default or miscarriages of another person, unless the agreement upon which such action shall be brought, or some memorandum or note thereof, shall be in writing and signed by the party to be charged therewith, or by some person thereunto by him lawfully authorized." The object of this statute was the "prevention of many fraudulent practices which are commonly endeavored to be upheld by perjury and subornation of perjury," and in certain cases, which from their nature particularly demanded it, the substitution of the certainty of written, for the uncertainty of unwritten, evidence. It was a wise and salutary enactment, and has been in terms, or with more or less modifications, generally re-enacted in the United States. Many decisions have been rendered on every portion of the Statute of Frauds, and among them will be found great conflict of authority. Perhaps the clearest method of presenting this subject will be to commence with the first words of the statute as above given, and proceed *seriatim* to the last, and this course will be pursued.

§ 52. **Effect of the words "no action shall be brought."** The Statute of Frauds does not provide that the contract to answer for another shall be illegal or void if not in writing. It says "no action shall be brought." The contract is just as legal since the enactment of the statute as it was before, but no action can be brought to enforce it. In most cases this amounts to the same thing as if the contract had been declared illegal, but in other cases it does not. When the contract has been entirely executed on both sides, the statute will not in any manner affect the relations of the parties.[1] Money paid by a surety or guarantor in pursuance of an unwritten promise cannot be recovered by him, although he could not have been compelled by law to pay it, and in such case the principal will be obliged to reimburse the surety or guarantor for the money thus paid.[2] By virtue of the authority of courts over their own officers, they will sometimes enforce an unwritten agreement by their officers which could not otherwise be enforced, because of the Statute of Frauds. Thus, the attorney for the defendant in a case, in consideration of the plaintiff staying proceedings therein, agreed to compromise the action and give his two promissory notes in payment. This he afterward refused to do, and the court entered a rule upon him compelling him to carry out his agreement. The court said: "Even supposing the undertaking to be void by the Statute of Frauds, this court may nevertheless exercise a summary jurisdiction over one of its own officers, an attorney of the court. The undertaking was given by the party in his character of attorney, and in that character the court may compel him to perform it. An attorney is conusant of the law, and if he give an undertaking which he knows to be void, he shall not be allowed to take advantage of his own wrong, and say that the

[1] Stone *v.* Dennison, 13 Pick. 1; Lord Bolton *v.* Tomlin, 5 Adol. & Ell. 856; Mushat *v.* Brevard, 4 Dev. (N. C.) 73.

[2] Shaw *v.* Woodcock, 7 Barn. & Cres. 73; McCue *v.* Smith, 9 Minn. 252; Crane *v.* Gough, 4 Md. 316; Pawle *v.* Gunn, 4 Bing. N. C. 445; Andrews *v.* Jones, 10 Ala. 400; Watrous *v.* Chalker, 7 Conn. 224; Craig *v.* Vanpelt, 3 J. J. Marsh. (Ky.) 489.

undertaking cannot be enforced."[1] As the prohibition is against the remedy, the courts of a country in which the statute prevails will not enforce an unwritten contract of suretyship or guaranty made in another country, which was perfectly valid and enforceable in the country where the contract was made.[2] This is upon the principle that while the validity and binding force of a contract depends upon the law of the country in which it is made, the remedy is always governed by the law of the country in which the action is brought. When a promise is, as to the thing promised, partly within and partly not within the Statute of Frauds, if the parts are so connected that the contracting parties must reasonably be considered to have contracted with reference to the performance of the whole, or a distinct promise cannot reasonably be made out as to the portion not within the statute, no action can be brought on any portion of the contract;[3] but where the portion of the promise which is not within the statute can be separated from that which is, an action may be sustained upon the portion not within the statute.[4]

§ 53. Meaning of the words "any special promise."—With reference to the kind of promise which the statute provides shall be in writing, the words are "any special promise." The intention was by these words to confine the statute to actual promises or promises in fact made, and so it has been interpreted.[5] Promises implied by law are not within the operation of the statute.

§ 54. What included in the words "debt, default or miscarriage."—The liability which the statute contemplated was for the "debt, default or miscarriage of another." These words, "debt, default or miscarriage," include torts of the

[1] *In re* Greaves, 1 Cromp. & Jer. 374, n. See, also, Evans *v.* Duncan, 1 Tyrw. 283.

[2] Leroux *v.* Brown, 12 Com. B. 801. See, also, Huber *v.* Steiner, 2 Scott, 304.

[3] Chater *v.* Becket, 7 Term R. 201; Thomas *v.* Williams, 10 Barn. & Cres. 664; Thayer *v.* Rock, 13 Wend. 53; McMullen *v.* Riley, 6 Gray, 500; Dyer *v.* Graves, 37 Vt. 369.

[4] Wood *v.* Benson, 2 Cromp. & Jer. 94; Id., 2 Tyrwh. 93; Rand *v.* Mather, 11 Cush. 1. Sèe, also, Hess *v.* Fox, 10 Wend. 436; Trowbridge *v.* Wetherbee, 11 Allen, 361; Wetherbee *v.* Potter, 99 Mass. 354; Dock *v.* Hart, 7 Watts & Serg. 172.

[5] Pike *v.* Brown, 7 Cush. 133; Sage *v.* Wilçox, 6 Conn. 81; Goodwin *v.* Gilbert, 9 Mass. 510; Allen *v.* Pryor, 3 A. K. Marsh. (Ky.) 305.

principal as well as breaches of contract by him, and apply to every case in which one person can become responsible for another. It seems at one time to have been considered that, if the principal was not chargeable on a contract, but was only liable in tort, the promise to answer for him would not be within the statute;[1] but all doubts on this subject have been set at rest, and it is settled that a promise to answer for the tort of another is within the statute. Thus, where one person, without the license of another, had ridden such other's horse and thereby caused its death, it was held that a promise by a third person to answer the damage caused thereby, in consideration that the owner of the horse would not bring an action against the person causing its death, was within the statute, and no action could be brought upon it unless it was in writing. The court said: "The wrongful riding the horse of another without his leave and license, and thereby causing his death, is clearly an act for which the party is responsible in damages, and therefore, in my judgment, falls within the meaning of the word 'miscarriage.'"[2] These words have been variously commented upon by different courts. It has been said by some that the words "debt" and "default" both referred to a liability accruing upon a contract; the word "debt" to such as is already incurred, and the word "default" to such as may be incurred in the future.[3] Of the word "miscarriage" it has been said: "Now the word 'miscarriage' has not the same meaning as the word 'debt' or 'default;' it seems to me to comprehend that species of wrongful act for the consequences of which the law would make the party civilly responsible."[4] Whatever meaning may be attached to any one of these words, the three together cover every case in which a surety or guarantor can become responsible in a civil action for another.

§ 55. The words "of another" contemplate the present or future primary liability of a principal.— The words "of

[1] Birkmyr *v.* Darnell, 2 Lord Raymond, 1085. See, also, Reed *v.* Nash. 1 Wils. 305.

[2] Kirkham *v.* Marter, 2 Barn. & Ald. 613, per Abbott, C. J. See, also, to same effect, Turner *v.* Hubbell, 2 Day (Conn.), 457.

[3] Castling *v.* Aubert, 2 East, 325, per Lord Ellenborough. See, also, Mountstephen *v.* Lakeman, Law Rep. 7 Q. B. 196, per Willes, J.

[4] Kirkham *v.* Marter, 2 Barn. & Ald. 613, per Abbott, C. J.

another person" have given rise to a vast number of decisions. As said by an able court: "The cases on this branch of the Statute of Frauds are so numerous that it would be a difficult task to review them; and the distinctions as to cases which are or are not within the statute are so nice, and often so shadowy, that it would be still more difficult to reconcile them."[1] The result of the authorities is that in order to bring the promise within the prohibition of the statute, it must be "collateral" to a liability on the part of a principal. In other words, there must, at the time the promise is made, be an actual primary liability of a principal to the promisee which continues after the making of the promise, or there must be contemplated, as the basis of such promise, the future primary liability of a principal. The foundation of the contract of suretyship and guaranty is the primary liability of another. In order to a clear and full understanding of the above general statement of the result of the authorities on this subject, a more detailed examination of such authorities will be necessary.

§ 56. **If there is no remedy against a third party the promise need not be in writing — Leading case.**— A leading and celebrated case on this subject is reported as follows: "Declaration — that in consideration the plaintiff would deliver his gelding to A., the defendant promised that A. should redeliver him safe, and evidence was given that the defendant undertook that A. should redeliver him safe; and this was held a collateral undertaking for another; for where the undertaking comes in aid only to procure a credit to the party, in that case there is a remedy against both, and both are answerable according to their distinct engagements; but where the whole credit is given to the undertaker, so that the other party is but his servant, and there is no remedy against him, this is not a collateral undertaking. But it is otherwise in the principal case, for the plaintiff may maintain detinue upon the bailment against the original hirer, as well as *assumpsit* upon the promise against the defendant. *Et per cur;* if two come to a shop, and one buys, and the other, to gain him credit, promises the seller, 'if he does not pay you, I will,' this is a

[1] Shaw, C. J., in Chapin *v.* Lapham, 20 Pick. 467.

collateral undertaking, and void without writing, by the Statute of Frauds. But if he says, 'let him have the goods, I will be your paymaster,' or 'I will see you paid,' this is an undertaking as for himself, and he shall be intended to be the very buyer, and the other to act but as his servant."[1] The principle here announced, that if there is "no remedy" against the third person, the promise is original and need not be in writing, has been applied to a great variety of circumstances.

§ 57. **When no liability incurred by third person, promise need not be in writing — Liability of principal need not be express.**— When no liability, present or prospective, is incurred by a third person, that is, when there is no principal, the Statute of Frauds does not apply. Thus, where A. brought an action for assault and battery against B., and the case was about to be tried, and C., in consideration that A. would withdraw his record, verbally promised to pay him £50 and costs, *held*, the promise of C. was not within the statute.[2] The ground upon which the decision was put is thus stated by the court: "Johnson [B.] was not a debtor; the cause was not tried; he did not appear to be guilty of any debt, default or miscarriage; there might have been a verdict for him, if the cause had been tried, for anything we can tell; he never was liable to the particular debt, damages or costs." So where a party promised, in consideration of the widow of an intestate permitting him to be joined with her in the letters of administration, that he would make good any deficiency of assets to pay debts, it was held the statute did not apply.[3] On the same principle, where goods are furnished to a person gratuitously, a verbal promise of a third person to pay for them is binding.[4] While there must be a liability on the part of some one to which the liability of the promisor is collateral, such liability need not be express; it is sufficient if it is implied

[1] Birkmyr *v.* Darnell, 1 Salk. 27; same case reported, 6 Mod. 248; and 2 Lord Raymond, 1085. For a review of this case, and generally on this subject, see opinion of Willes, J., in Mountstephen *v.* Lakeman, Law Rep. 7 Q. B. 196. And see the principle announced in the text illustrated in Baldwin *v.* Hiers, 73 Ga. 739; also, Cruse *v.* Foster & Estes, 76 Ga. 723.

[2] Read *v.* Nash, 1 Wils. 305, per Lee, C. J. The rule is that, if a third party is not liable, the undertaking is not within the statute. Anderson *v.* Spence, 72 Ind. 315.

[3] Tomlinson *v.* Gill, Amb. 330.

[4] Loomis *v.* Newhall, 15 Pick. 159.

by law.[1] In all cases where the promise is to answer for the tort of the principal, it is manifest that the liability of the principal is implied by law.

§ 58. **When party for whom promise is made cannot become liable, promise need not be in writing.**— A promise to answer for a party not legally competent to contract, or not answerable for his wrongful acts, is not within the Statute of Frauds as to any matter within such disability. There is in such case no liability on behalf of any one to which the promise is collateral. It is therefore an original promise, and need not be in writing.[2] Thus A. procured B. to advance money to pay for work in the garden of an infant. B. sued A. for the money, and the question was as to whether the evidence was sufficient to sustain the verdict. Although not strictly necessary to the decision of the case, one judge said: "The infant was not liable, and therefore it could not be a collateral undertaking. It was an original undertaking of the defendant to pay the money."[3] A father requested a merchant to assist his minor son in business, and promised verbally to indemnify him against any loss he might incur in so doing, and it was held the promise need not be in writing. The court, after saying that the son was a minor and not liable for the debt, proceeded: "The undertaking and promise of the defendant, therefore, was not collateral to any promise of the son, but was separate, independent and original."[4] A tailor furnished an infant ward with a frock coat, without the order of the guardian, but the guardian afterwards, in consideration of indulgence, verbally promised the tailor to pay for the coat. *Held*, the guardian was liable. The court, after saying that the ward was not liable for the price of the coat said: "the promise of the defendant [the guardian] was original, and

[1] Redhead *v.* Caton, 1 Starkie, 12; Whitcomb *v.* Kephart, 50 Pa. St. 85.

[2] As bearing on the question whether a promise to answer for a married woman need or need not be in writing, see Connerat *v.* Goldsmith, 6 Ga. 14; White *v.* Cuyler, 1 Esp. 200; Id., 6 Term R. 176; Darnell *v.* Tratt, 2 Car. & P. 82; Kimball *v.* Newell, 7 Hill, 116.

[3] Foster, J., in Harris *v.* Huntbach, 1 Burrows, 373.

[4] Shaw, C. J., in Chapin *v.* Lapham, 20 Pick. 467. The same principle was applied where a father promised to pay for a substitute in the army for his minor son, who had been drafted. See Downey *v.* Hinchman, 25 Ind. 453. See, also, Duncombe *v.* Tickridge, Aleyn, 94.

binding on him."[1] A wife, whose husband had died, leaving her his estate for life, remainder to his nephew, herself died, leaving particular directions as to her funeral. These directions a friend of the family undertook to see carried out, and bought certain articles for that purpose, telling the merchant verbally that the estate of the husband would pay for them, and if it did not, she would. *Held*, the estate of the husband was not liable for the articles thus purchased, and such friend was liable on her verbal promise. The court said: "When no action will lie against the party undertaken for, it is an original promise."[2]

§ 59. **When promise to indemnify within the statute — Principles involved.**— With reference to whether a promise to indemnify a person from loss in consequence of such person doing an act or assuming an obligation is within the statute, no general rule which will reconcile all the cases can be laid down. A mere promise of indemnity which is not collateral to any liability on the part of another, either express or implied, is not within the statute, and such a case illustrates the rule that when there is no principal the promise need not be in writing. On the other hand, when the promise to indemnify is in fact a promise to pay the debt of another, then clearly such promise is within the statute, and the fact that it is in form a promise to indemnify will make no difference.[3]

[1] Roche *v.* Chaplin, 1 Bailey (S. C.), 419, per Johnson, J. In Dexter *v.* Blanchard, 11 Allen, 365, the supreme court of Massachusetts decided expressly that the verbal promise of a father to pay the debt of a minor son was within the Statute of Frauds, and must be in writing, even though it was a debt which the son could not be coerced to pay. The decision was placed upon the ground that the contract of the minor was not void, but voidable, and was valid till avoided, etc. Neither the preceding case of Chapin *v.* Lapham, 20 Pick. 467, in the same court, nor any of the cases herein cited on this subject, were referred to or noticed. The cases referred to in the text seem to be founded on much the better reason, and are more in harmony with the cases on other phases of this subject.

[2] Mease *v.* Wagner, 1 McCord (S. C.), 395, per Huyer, J. See, also, Drake *v.* Flewellen, 33 Ala. 106.

[3] Carville *v.* Crane, 5 Hill, 483. See generally, on this subject, the exhaustive opinion of Comstock, C. J., in Mallory *v.* Gillett, 21 N. Y. 412. The weight of American authority is in favor of applying the Statute of Frauds to a contract of indemnity against the liability of a surety or guarantor for a third person, though an exception is generally recognized where the indemnitor is himself primarily liable for the debt guarantied.

These propositions are correct in principle and are fully sustained by authority. Many cases do not fall plainly under either head, and the confusion in the authorities has chiefly arisen from not keeping the distinction between the two cases clearly in mind, or from the application of these recognized principles to different states of fact. Great stress has often been laid upon the word "indemnify," when in fact none should be given to it, and the actual transaction should be carefully scanned to ascertain the true nature and bearings of the promise. The law on this subject has been thus stated by a celebrated judge: "Now it has been laid down that a mere promise of indemnity is not within the Statute of Frauds, and there are many cases which would exemplify the correctness of that decision. On the other hand, an undertaking to answer for the debt or default of another is within the Statute of Frauds, and no doubt some cases might be put where it is both the one and the other; that is to say, where the promise to answer for the debt or default of another would involve what might very properly and legally be called an indemnity. Where that is the case, in all probability the undertaking would be considered as within the Statute of Frauds if it were to answer for the debt or default of another, notwithstanding it might also be an indemnity."[1]

§ 60. When promise to indemnify need not be in writing — Instances.— A promise to indemnify a party against loss if he will commence or defend a suit has been held not to be within the Statute of Frauds. As where the indorser of a dishonored bill of exchange verbally promised to indemnify a subsequent indorsee against costs if he would bring an action against the acceptor, it was held the promise was not within the statute.[2] A promise to indemnify a party, if he will commit a trespass in order to raise a question of title, has been held not to be within the statute. The court said: "The promise was not to indemnify for the default of another; but was made to the plaintiff himself for an act to be done by him as the servant of the defendant below. It was an original

Brand *v.* Whelan, 18 Bradwell (Ill. App.), 186.

[1] Per Pollock, C. B., in Cripps *v.* Hartnoll, 4 Best & Smith, 414.

[2] Bullock *v.* Lloyd, 2 Car. & P. 119. See, also, to same effect, Howes *v.* Martin, 1 Esp. 162. *Contra,* Winckworth *v.* Mills, 2 Esp. 484.

understanding, and not a collateral promise."[1] So, also, a verbal promise to indemnify an occupier of land if he will resist a suit of the vicar for tithes has been held not to be within the statute.[2] An attorney authorized a distress for rent due his client, and verbally promised to indemnify the party executing the distress warrant from damage by reason of the goods being privileged from distress. *Held*, the promise to indemnify was not within the statute.[3] A party agreed to pay a certain sum annually to certain trustees of a church toward the support of a minister. The minister, for a consideration, promised to indemnify the party against loss by reason of such agreement. *Held*, the promise was not within the statute.[4] Where A., being bound to indemnify B. in a certain civil suit in which he was arrested, requested C. to become special bail for B., and promised to indemnify him, the promise was held to be an original undertaking and not within the statute. This decision was put upon the ground that, as A. was himself bound for B., the promise to C. was for A.'s own benefit.[5] A promise to indemnify one if he will become bail for another in a criminal case has been held not to be within the statute.[6] The reason given for this holding in one case is that the person bailed is under no obligation to indemnify the bail, and in another is that if the person bailed is under an implied obligation to indemnify the bail, the party requesting the bail to become such should be held to be the original promisor, and the party bailed only collaterally liable. Where a party who

[1] Per Redcliff, J., in Allaire *v.* Ouland, 2 Johns. Cas. 52. See, also, to same effect, Marcy *v.* Crawford, 16 Conn. 549; and see Weld *v.* Nichols, 17 Pick. 538; Chapman *v.* Ross, 12 Leigh (Va.), 565.

[2] Adams *v.* Dansey, 6 Bing. 506. See comments on this case by Lord Denman in Green *v.* Creswell, 10 Adol. & Ell. 453. And see Goodspeed *v.* Fuller, 46 Me. 141.

[3] Toplis *v.* Grane, 5 Bing. N. C. 636.

[4] Conkey *v.* Hopkins, 17 Johns. 113.

[5] Harrison *v.* Sawtel, 10 Johns. 242. See, also, Ferrell *v.* Maxwell, 28 Ohio St. 383. In a celebrated case which differed from the above only in the fact that A. was not bound to indemnify B., it was held that the promise must be in writing. Green *v.* Creswell, 10 Adol. & Ell. 453; Id., 2 Perry & Dav. 430.

[6] Cripps *v.* Hartnoll, 4 Best & Smith, 414; Holmes *v.* Knights, 10 N. H. 175. And to precisely similar effect, see Anderson *v.* Spence, 72 Ind. 315, and Keeshug *v.* Frazier, 119 Ind. 185; the former case, Anderson *v.* Spence, overruling Brush *v.* Carpenter, 6 Ind. 78.

was surety for the maker of a note procured others to sign as sureties, by promising to indemnify them, and save them harmless, it was held that such promise was an original undertaking, and not within the statute.[1] An oral guaranty to save harmless a person in consideration of his becoming surety on an administrator's bond is an original promise and not within the statute.[2]

§ 61. When promise to indemnify must be in writing — Instances.— Where an attorney requested a party to execute to the sheriff a bail bond in a civil case for his client, and promised to indemnify such party for so doing, it was held the promise was within the statute. The court said the test was that "the original party remained liable, and the defendant incurred no liability except from the promise."[3] A promise by one person to indemnify another against loss or damage in becoming the surety for a third in an undertaking of replevin has been held to be within the statute.[4] The court said: "If, therefore, the third person against whose debt, default or miscarriage the promise of indemnity is made, would himself be legally liable to pay the promisee such debt or damage, the promise of indemnity is to be regarded as col-

[1] Horn *v.* Bray, 51 Ind. 555. To same effect, see Thomas *v.* Cook, 8 Barn. & Cress. 728; Id., 3 Man. & Ry. 444. For cases holding or tending to establish that under various circumstances a promise to indemnify need not be in writing, see Chapin *v.* Merrill, 4 Wend. 657; Barry *v.* Ransom, 12 N. Y. 462; Taylor *v.* Savage, 12 Mass. 98; Smith *v.* Sayward, 5 Greenl. 504; Aldrich *v.* Ames, 9 Gray, 76; Cutter *v.* Emery, 37 N. H. 567; Harris *v.* Brooks, 21 Pick. 195; Whitehouse *v.* Hanson, 42 N. H. 9; Blake *v.* Cole, 22 Pick. 97; Hodges *v.* Hall, 29 Vt. 209; Hendrick *v.* Whittemore, 105 Mass. 23; Keith *v.* Goodwin, 31 Vt. 268; Byers *v.* McClanahan, 6 Gill & Johns. 250; Dunn *v.* West, 5 B. Mon. (Ky.) 376; Apgar's Adm'r *v.* Hiler, 4 Zab. (N. J.) 812; Lucas *v.* Chamberlain, 8 B. Mon. (Ky.) 276; Marsh *v.* Consolidation Bank, 48 Pa. St. 510; D'Wolf *v.* Raband, 1 Pet. 476; Stocking *v.* Sage, 1 Conn. 519; Jones *v.* Shorter, 1 Kelley (Ga.), 294; Townsley *v.* Sumrall, 2 Pet. 170; Emerson *v.* Slater, 22 How. (U. S.) 28; Shook *v.* Vanmater, 22 Wis. 507; Hoggatt *v.* Thomas *et al.*, 35 La. Ann. 298.

[2] Tighee *v.* Morrison, 116 N. Y. 263.

[3] Per Lord Denman in Green *v.* Cresswell, 2 Perry & Dav. 430; Id., 10 Adol. & Ell. 453.

[4] Easter *v.* White, 12 Ohio St. 219, per Sutliff, J. See to same effect, Kingsley *v.* Balcombe, 4 Barb. (N. Y.) 131. So a promise by one person to indemnify another against loss or liability in becoming security for stay of execution for a third person is within the statute. Nugent *v.* Wolfe, 111 Pa. St. 471.

ateral to his liability as principal, and within the statute." A promise by one person to another that he will indemnify such other from loss which he may sustain by reason of signing a sheriff's bond, has been held to be within the statute.[1] The same thing was held when one who was himself indemnified by property of the principal promised to indemnify a third person if he would sign a note of the principal as surety.[2] From the examples given, the confusion in the authorities on this subject will be apparent, as well as the necessity of carefully analyzing the facts of each case as it arises, and applying to it the principles which have already been shown to be established.

§ 62. **If original debt extinguished or novated, promise not within the statute.**— When the new promise has the effect of extinguishing the old debt, it amounts to an original undertaking, and is not within the statute.[3] In such case there is no third person liable as principal; there is no liability to which the promise is collateral; nor is there any obligation with which the promise concurs or runs together. A son did work for his father, for which the father was indebted, and the defendant, in consideration of the son releasing the father from such debt, verbally promised to pay it. *Held*, the promise was not within the statute and the defendant was bound.[4] The court said: "The plaintiff discharged the debt due to him from his father, in consideration of the defendant's promise to pay him the amount due him. This promise was not a promise to pay the debt of another within the

[1] Brown *v.* Adams, 1 Stew. (Ala.) 51.

[2] Draughan *v.* Bunting, 9 Ired. Law (N. C.), 10. For cases holding or tending to show that certain promises to indemnify must be in writing, see Simpson *v.* Nance, 1 Spears (S. C.), 4; Martin *v.* Black's Ex'rs, 20 Ala. 309; Macey *v.* Childress, 2 Tenn. Ch. (Cooper) 438.

[3] Curtis *v.* Brown, 5 Cush. (Mass.) 488; Allshouse *v.* Ramsay, 6 Whart. (Pa.) 311; Stone *v.* Symmes, 18 Pick. 467; Bird *v.* Gammon, 3 Bing. N. C. 883. As further illustrating this subject, see Gull *v.* Lindsay, 4 Wels. Hurl. & Gor. 45; Eddy *v.* Roberts, 17 Ill. 505; Watson *v.* Randall, 20 Wend. 201; Click *v.* McAfee, 7 Port. (Ala.) 62; Mead *v.* Keyes, 4 E. D. Smith (N. Y.), 510; Gleason *v.* Briggs, 28 Vt. 135; Andre *v.* Bodman, 13 Md. 241; Watson *v.* Jacobs, 29 Vt. 169; Robinson *v.* Lane, 14 Sm. & Mar. (Miss.) 161; Quintard *v.* D'Wolf, 34 Barb. (N. Y.) 97; Mosely *v.* Taylor, 4 Dana, (Ky.) 542; Stewart *v.* Hinkle, 1 Bond, 506; Hedges *v.* Strong, 3 Oreg. 18.

[4] Wood *v.* Corcoran, 1 Allen (Mass.), 405, per Hoar, J.

Statute of Frauds, but an original undertaking. The defendant promised to pay the money, not as surety or guarantor, but as the sole debtor; not as a collateral promise, but as a substituted promise. There was no debt of another as soon as the defendant's promise was made." Where a party was taken on a *ca. sa.*, and in consideration of the creditor discharging him from custody, a third person verbally promised to pay the debt, it was held that by such discharge the debt was extinguished and the promise was not within the statute. The court said: "By the discharge of Chase with the plaintiff's consent, the debt as between those persons was satisfied. . . . Then, if so, the promise by the defendant here is not a collateral but an original promise, for which the consideration is the discharge of the debt as between the plaintiff and Chase."[1] For the same reasons, where there is an entire novation of the debt, and the third party becomes verbally bound for the new debt along with the original debtor, the new agreement is not within the statute. Thus, where one person was indebted, and entered into partnership with another, and the two said to the creditor of the one that they wished the debt to be their joint debt and they would pay it, and the creditor consented, it was held the agreement was binding upon both, and need not be in writing, the effect of the agreement being to extinguish the first debt and substitute another for it.[2] Where a debtor asked his creditor to purchase certain railroad bonds, he guarantying that no loss would result therefrom, and the creditor relying upon this guaranty purchased the same and canceled the indebtedness, it was held that the guaranty was an original promise and not within the statute.[3]

§ 63. When promise to pay out of proceeds of debtor's property not within statute.— A promise to pay the debt of another out of the proceeds of the property of such other,

[1] Goodman *v.* Chase, 1 Barn. & Ald. 297, per Lord Ellenborough, C. J. To same effect, see Lane *v.* Burghart, 1 Adol. & Ell. (N. S.) 933; Cooper *v.* Chambers, 4 Dev. (N. C.) 261; Butcher *v.* Stewart, 11 Mees. & Wels. 857; Maggs *v.* Ames, 4 Bing. 470.

[2] *Ex parte* Lane, 1 De Gex, 300. See, also, on this subject, Baker *v.* Briggs, 8 Pick. 122; Choppin *v.* Gobbold, 13 La. Ann. 238; Roth *v.* Miller, 15 Serg. & Rawle, 100; Sneed's Ex'rs *v.* White, 3 J. J. Marsh. (Ky.) 525; Musgrave *v.* Glasgow, 3 Ind. 31.

[3] Allen *v.* Eighmie, 14 Hun (N. Y.), 559.

placed in the hands of the promisor for that purpose, is not within the statute.[1] In such case the promisor is simply an agent to distribute the property. The promise is an original one for the promisor alone. The party owing the debt is not liable on the promise, nor is any other person liable thereon except the promisor himself. In a leading case, one Taylor being in arrears for rent, and insolvent, conveyed all his effects for the benefit of his creditors, who employed Leper to sell them. On the day advertised for the sale, the landlord came to distrain the goods in the house, whereupon Leper promised to pay the rent if he would desist. *Held*, this promise was not within the statute.[2] Here the landlord relinquished his prior lien on the property, or, in other words, left the property in the hands of Leper, and Leper in effect agreed to apply the proceeds of the sale of the property to the payment of the debt of its owner. One of the judges said that "Leper became the bailiff of the landlord, and when he had sold the goods the money was the landlord's in his own bailiff's hands." Another judge said that Leper was not bound to pay the landlord more than the goods sold for. The property must be within the control of the promisor, in order to take the promise out of the statute; it is not sufficient that he is the agent of those who do control it.[3] A debtor left certain notes of third persons with another for collection, and he promised the debtor to collect the notes and pay the creditor a debt due him from the debtor. *Held*, the promise was not within the

[1] Meyer *v.* Hartman, 72 Ill. 442; Runde *v.* Runde, 59 Ill. 98; Corbin *v.* McChesney, 26 Ill. 231; Stephens *v.* Pell, 2 Cromp. & Mees. 710; Id., 4 Tyrwh. 6; Hitchcock *v.* Lukens, 8 Port. (Ala.) 333; Loomis *v.* Newhall, 15 Pick. 159; Andrews *v.* Smith, Tyrwh. & Gr. 173; Id., 2 Cromp. Mees. & Ros. 627; Todd *v.* Tobey, 29 Me. 219; Nelson *v.* Hardy, 7 Ind. 364; Lucas *v.* Payne, 7 Cal. 92; Stoudt *v.* Hine, 45 Pa. St. 30; Consolidated Presbyterian Society *v.* Staples, 23 Conn. 544; Wilson *v.* Bevans, 58 Ill. 232; McLaren *v.* Hutchinson, 22 Cal. 187; Clymer *v.* De Young, 54 Pa. St. 118; Cameron *v.* Clark, 11 Ala. 259; Hilton *v.* Dinsmore, 21 Me. 410; Goddard *v.* Mockbee, 5 Cranch (C. C.), 666; Laing *v.* Lee, Spencer (N. J.), 337; Lee *v.* Fontaine, 10 Ala. 755; Stanly *v.* Hendricks, 13 Ired. (N. C.) 86; McKenzie *v.* Jackson, 4 Ala. 230. *Contra*, Jackson *v.* Rayner, 12 Johns. 291.

[2] Williams *v.* Leper, 3 Burr. 1886; Id., 2 Wils. 308. To same effect, see Edwards *v.* Kelly, 6 Maule & S. 204; Bampton *v.* Paulin, 4 Bing. 264; Crawford *v.* King, 54 Ind. 6.

[3] Quin *v.* Hanford, 1 Hill (N. Y.), 82.

statute.[1] The court said: "This is no undertaking to pay the debt of a third party, within the Statute of Frauds; but it is an agreement by two persons for the use and benefit of a third, upon which such third person may maintain an action against the person promising, without proof of any written memorandum or consideration moving between the promisor and the party for whose benefit the contract has been made. It is a trust which, having once undertaken to execute, and entered upon the performance of the same, although voluntarily and without consideration other than such as the law implies, he is bound in law and equity to complete." The mere fact, however, that the promisor has in his possession property of the original debtor, which was not deposited with him for the purpose of paying the debt, will not of itself alone take the promise out of the statute.[2] It is also clearly established that when the creditor has a lien on property of the principal for the payment of his debt, which he relinquishes in consideration of the promise, and such lien inures to the benefit of the promisor, the promise is not within the statute.[3]

§ 64. Creditor relinquishing lien which does not inure to benefit of promisor does not take promise out of statute.— Whether the relinquishment of a lien which the creditor holds upon property of the principal for the payment of the debt, when the lien does not inure to the benefit of the promisor, is sufficient to take the promise out of the statute, seems to be clear upon principle, but is a very vexed question upon authority. In a leading case usually referred to as establishing that the relinquishment of a lien under such circumstances does take the promise out of the statute,[4] the promisor had sent certain

[1] Prather *v.* Vineyard, 4 Gilman (Ill.), 40, per Purple, J. To same effect, see Drakeley *v.* Deforest, 3 Conn. 272; Sullivan *v.* Murphy, 23 Minn. 6.

[2] Dilts *v.* Parke, 1 South. (N. J.) 219; State Bank at New Brunswick *v.* Mettler, 2 Bosw. (N. Y.) 392; Simpson *v.* Nance, 1 Spears (S. C.), 4; Hughes *v.* Lawson, 31 Ark. 613.

[3] See cases cited in this section. See, also, Teague *v.* Fowler, 56 Ind. 569.

[4] Houlditch *v.* Milne, 3 Esp. 86. It seems, however, that this case can be sustained upon other grounds. The case of Williams *v.* Leper, 2 Wils. 308; Id., 3 Burr. 1886, has also by several courts been thought to establish the same proposition, and decisions to that effect have been founded upon its authority. But from a careful examination of that case, it will appear that it is more properly referable to other grounds, and that it is an authority showing that a promise

carriages belonging to one Copey to the plaintiff to be repaired, and the promisor gave the orders concerning them. The bill for repairs was made out to Copey, but the promisor ordered the carriages packed and shipped, and verbally promised to pay for the repairs. The court[1] held the promise not within the statute, on the ground that the plaintiff had parted with his lien. A landlord, who had a lien for board upon the baggage of his guest, released the lien and allowed the guest to take the baggage upon the verbal promise of a third person to pay the debt. It was squarely held that the promise was not within the statute. The court said: "Where one has a complete and enforceable lien on the property of his debtor, a promise of a third person to pay the debt on condition that the property under the lien is given up will be held binding, and not within the Statute of Frauds. This upon the ground that the release of the lien is the surrender of a security operating in the nature of a payment, and therefore, if not a benefit to the promisor, is a prejudice to the creditor to the extent of his loss."[2] If, as here suggested, the surrender of the lien discharged the original debt, then, as already shown, the promise for that reason would not be within the statute. But the surrender of the lien does not usually extinguish the original debt. The surrender of the lien, being a detriment to the creditor, is undoubtedly a sufficient consideration for the promise; but why it should take the promise out of the statute, any more than any consideration which is a detriment to the creditor, or in fact any other sufficient consideration, it is difficult to perceive. What seems to be the true view of this subject, and the one which is sustained by the weight of authority, is

to apply the debtor's property in the hands of the promisor for that purpose, to the payment of his debt, is not within the statute.

[1] Lord Eldon.

[2] Per Butler, J., in Dunlap *v.* Thorne, 1 Rich. (S. C.) 213. To same effect, or sustaining same view, see Shook *v.* Vanmater, 22 Wis. 507; Love's Case, 1 Salk. 28; Slingerland *v.* Morse, 7 Johns. 463; Adkinson *v.* Barfield, 1 McCord (S. C.), 575; Mercien *v.* Andrus, 10 Wend. 461; Bushell *v.* Beavan, 1 Bing. N. C. 103. Nearly all of the authority holding to this effect is founded upon what is believed to be an erroneous view of the grounds upon which Williams *v.* Leper, 2 Wils. 308, rested. Mr. Browne, in his able work on the Statute of Frauds, pp. 195–204, holds that the mere relinquishment of a lien by the creditor does not take the promise out of the statute.

thus well expressed: "Where the plaintiff, in consideration of the promise, has relinquished some lien, benefit or advantage for securing or recovering his debt, and where by means of such relinquishment the same interest or advantage has inured to the benefit of the defendant, there his promise is binding without writing. In such case, though the result is that the payment of the debt of a third person is effected, it is so incidentally and indirectly, and the substance of the contract is the purchase by the defendant from the plaintiff of the lien, right or benefit in question. . . . It is not enough that the plaintiff has relinquished an advantage or given up a lien in consequence of the defendant's promise, if that advantage has not directly inured to the benefit of the defendant, so as to make it a purchase by the defendant from the plaintiff."[1]

§ 65. When the transaction amounts to a purchase of debt or lien by promisor, promise not within statute.— When the promise to pay the debt of another is made in consideration of the delivery by the creditor to the promisor of a security for such debt, or of an assignment of the debt itself to the promisor — that is, when the transaction amounts to a sale by the creditor to the promisor of the lien or the debt — the promise is not within the statute. The fact that the payment of the price by the purchaser is to take the form of discharging the debt of another is an incident in the transaction which does not deprive the purchase of its essential character as such. Thus an agent who had a lien on certain policies of insurance effected for his principal, for whom he had given his acceptances, was induced by the defendant to give him the policies and waive the lien; and the defendant, in consideration thereof, promised to pay one of the acceptances, and to deposit

[1] Per Shaw, C. J., in Curtis *v.* Brown, 5 Cush. 488. Supporting this view, see Chater *v.* Becket, 7 Term R. 201; Nelson *v.* Boynton, 3 Met. (Mass.) 396; Tomlinson *v.* Gell, 6 Adol. & Ell. 564; Cross *v.* Richardson, 30 Vt. 641; Alger *v.* Scoville, 1 Gray, 391; Sampson *v.* Hobart, 28 Vt. 697; Mallory *v.* Gillett, 23 Barb. (N. Y.) 610; Smith *v.* Sayward, 5 Greenl. (Me.) 504; Spooner *v.* Dunn, 7 Ind. 81; Fish *v.* Thomas, 5 Gray, 45; Stern *v.* Drinker, 2 E. D. Smith (N. Y.), 401; Scott *v.* Thomas, 1 Scam. (Ill.) 58; Van Slyck *v.* Pulver, Hill & Denio (Lalor's Sup.), 47; Corkins *v.* Collins, 16 Mich. 478; Arnold *v.* Stedman, 45 Pa. St. 186; Bird *v.* Gammon, 5 Scott, 213; Woodward *v.* Wilcox, 27 Ind. 207; Stoudt *v.* Hine, 45 Pa. St. 30; Fullam *v.* Adams, 37 Vt. 391.

money for the payment of the others as they became due. *Held*, the promise was not within the statute.[1] The chief justice said that the defendant "had in contemplation, not principally the discharge of Grayson [original debtor], but the discharge of himself. This was his moving consideration, though the discharge of Grayson would eventually follow. It is therefore rather a purchase of the securities which the plaintiff held in his hands. This is quite beside the mischief provided against by the statute, which was that persons should not, by their own unavouched undertaking, without writing, charge themselves for the debt, default or miscarriage of another." Another judge said: "This is to be considered as a purchase by the defendant of the plaintiff's interest in the policies. It is not a bare promise to the creditor to pay the debt of another due to him, but a promise by the defendant to pay what the plaintiff would be liable to pay if the plaintiff would furnish him the means of doing so." In another case, one Marden, being insolvent, a verbal agreement was entered into between several of his creditors and one Weston, whereby Weston agreed to pay the creditors ten shillings in the pound in satisfaction of their debts, which they agreed to accept and to assign their debts to Weston. *Held*, the promise of Weston was not within the statute. The court said: "It is perfectly clear that this was a contract to purchase the debts of the several creditors, instead of being a contract to pay or discharge the debts owing by Marden. . . . Instead of being a contract to discharge Marden from his debts, it was a contract to keep them on foot. . . . We all agree fully upon the point that it is a contract for the purchase of the debts of Marden, which is not prohibited by the Statute of Frauds.[2]

1 Castling *v.* Aubert, 2 East, 325, per Lord Ellenborough, C. J., and Lawrence, J. See, also, Walker *v.* Taylor, 6 Car. & P. 752; Fitzgerald *v.* Dresler, 7 Com. B. (N. S.) 374.

2 Anstey *v.* Marden, 1 Bos. & Pul. N. R. 124, per Chambre, J. See, also, as bearing upon this subject, Love's Case, 1 Salk. 28; Allen *v.* Thompson, 10 N. H. 32; Doolittle *v.* Naylor, 2 Bosw. (N. Y.) 206; French *v.* Thompson, 6 Vt. 54; Therasson *v.* McSpedon, 2 Hilton (N. Y.), 1; Hindman *v.* Langford, 3 Strobh. (S. C.) 207; Gardiner *v.* Hopkins, 5 Wend. 23; Olmstead *v.* Greenly, 18 Johns. 12. Mr. De Colyar, in his valuable work on the Law of Guaranties, pp. 171–174, holds to the view that the following cases may be supported by the rule here under consideration: Houlditch *v.* Milne, 3 Esp. 86; Barrell *v.* Trussel, 4 Taunt. 117;

§ 66. When promisor who is debtor to third person agrees to pay his debt to creditor of such third person, promise not within statute.— If A. be indebted to B., and B. be indebted to C., and they get together and agree that B.'s debt to C. shall be canceled, and A. shall pay the debt which he owed B. to C., such agreement is valid and binding without writing.[1] In such case A. pays his own debt with his own money to a substituted creditor, and the fact that by the transaction of the debt another is paid makes no difference. So where the defendant's brother was indebted to the plaintiff, and, being pressed for payment, sold the defendant a pair of horses at a price less than the debt due the plaintiff, and the defendant promised his brother that he would pay the purchase price to the plaintiff, the court said the promise was not within the statute: "It was not a promise to answer for the debt of another person, but merely to pay the debt of the person making the promise to a particular person designated by him to whom the debt belonged, and who had a right to make such payment a part of the contract of sale. Such promise was no more within the Statute of Frauds than it would have been if the defendant had promised to pay the price of the horses directly to his brother, of whom he purchased them."[2]

Williams *v.* Leper, 3 Burr. 1886; Id., 2 Wils. 308; Edwards *v.* Kelly, 6 Maule & S. 204; Bampton *v.* Paulin, 4 Bing. 264.

[1] Dearborn *v.* Parks, 5 Greenl. (Me.) 81; Wilson *v.* Coupland, 5 Barn. & Ald. 228; Hodgson *v.* Anderson, 5 Dow. & Ry. 735; Id., 3 Barn. & Cress. 842; Lacy *v.* McNeile, 4 Dow. & Ry. 7. It seems that the debt of B. must be extinguished by the transaction, in order to take the case out of the statute. Jackson *v.* Rayner, 12 Johns. 291; Wharton *v.* Walker, 6 Dow. & Ry. 288; Cuxon *v.* Chadley, 3 Barn. & Cress. 591; Liversidge *v.* Broadbent, 4 Hurl. & Nor. 603.

[2] Per Jewett, J., in Barker *v.* Bucklin, 2 Denio, 45. For cases deciding and tending to establish these views, see Roe *v.* Hough, 3 Salk. 14; Rice *v.* Carter, 11 Ired. (N. C.) 298; Barringer *v.* Warden, 12 Cal. 311; Israel *v.* Douglas, 1 H. Black. 239; Brown *v.* Strait, 19 Ill. 88; Fairlie *v.* Denton, 2 Man. & Ry. 353; Id., 8 Barn. & Cress. 395; Ford *v.* Finney, 35 Ga. 258; Cailleux *v.* Hall, 1 E. D. Smith (N. Y.), 5; Wharton *v.* Walker, 6 Dow. & Ry. 288; Id., 4 Barn. & Cress. 163; Rowe *v.* Whittier, 21 Me. 545; Cuxon *v.* Chadley, 3 Barn. & Cress. 591; McLaren *v.* Hutchinson, 22 Cal. 187; Meyer *v.* Hartman, 72 Ill. 442; Haydon *v.* Christopher, 1 J. J. Marsh. (Ky.) 382; Connor *v.* Williams, 2 Rob. (N. Y.) 46; Robbins *v.* Ayres, 10 Mo. 538; Clymer *v.* De Young, 54 Pa. St. 118; Mt. Olivet Cemetery Co. *v.* Sherbert, 2 Head (Tenn.), 116; Sanders

§ 67. When promise is in effect to pay promisor's own debt, it is not within statute, although it incidentally guaranty debt of another.— Whenever the promise is in effect to pay the debt of the promisor, even though the performance of the promise may extinguish the debt of a third person, the promise is not within the statute. A debtor gave to his creditor the note of a third person for the same amount as the debt, and guarantied the payment of the note. *Held*, the guaranty need not be in writing.[1] The same thing was decided where the payee and holder of a note transferred it in payment of his debt, and guarantied its payment by an instrument which did not sufficiently express the consideration. The court said: "Although this is in form a promise to answer for the debt or default of another in substance, it is an engagement to pay the guarantor's own debt in a particular way. He does not undertake as a mere surety for the maker, but on his own account, and for a consideration which has its root in a transaction entirely distinct from the liability of the maker."[2] A plaintiff advanced money for a defendant, and in payment of the debt thus created the defendant transferred to the plaintiff the note of a third person, payable in chattels, and guarantied its payment. *Held*, the guaranty need not be in writing.[3] The court said: "This was not an undertaking by the defendant to pay the debt of Eastman [maker of the note], but an agreement to pay his own debt in a particular way. The plaintiff had upon request paid a debt of $25 which the defendant owed to Sherwood, and had thus made himself a creditor of the defendant to that amount. If the

v. Clason, 13 Minn. 379; Maxwell *v.* Haynes, 41 Me. 559.

[1] Dyer *v.* Gibson, 16 Wis. 508. To same effect, see Barker *v.* Scudder, 56 Mo. 272; Hall *v.* Rodgers, 7 Humph. (Tenn.) 536; Fowler *v.* Clearwater, 35 Barb. (N. Y.) 143; Durham *v.* Manrow, 2 N. Y. 533; Adcock *v.* Fleming, 2 Dev. & Batt. Law (N. C.), 225; Eagle Mowing & Reaping Machine Co. *v.* Shattuck, 53 Wis. 455. Where, upon the sale of a promissory note, the vendor guaranties that it is good and will be paid at maturity, such guaranty is not within the Statute of Frauds and is valid though not in writing. Milk *v.* Rich, 15 Hun, 178.

[2] Brown *v.* Curtiss, 2 N. Y. 225, per Bronson, J. To same effect, see Dauber *v.* Blackney, 38 Barb. (N. Y.) 432; Pitts *v.* Congdon, 2 N. Y. 352; Sheldon *v.* Butler, 24 Minn. 513; Wilson *v.* Hentges, 29 Minn. 102.

[3] Johnson *v.* Gilbert, 4 Hill, 178, per Bronson, J.; Mobile & G. R. R. Co. *v.* Jones, 57 Ga. 198; Nichols *v.* Allen, 22 Minn. 283.

matter had not been otherwise arranged, the plaintiff might have sued the defendant and recovered as for so much money paid for him upon request. But the plaintiff agreed to accept payment in a different way, to wit: by the transfer of Eastman's note for the wood-work of a wagon, with the defendant's undertaking that the note should be paid. The defendant, instead of promising that he would pay himself, agreed that Eastman should pay. He might do that, whether Eastman was his debtor or not; and the fact that Eastman was a debtor does not change the character of the defendant's undertaking and make it a case of suretyship within the statute of frauds." The purchaser of personal property agreed by parol, in consideration thereof, to pay certain debts of his vendor due to a third person. *Held*, the promise was not within the statute. The court said: the promisor "received the property contracted for, and it is wholly immaterial to him what direction was given to the purchase money. The vendor contracted to have it paid to his creditors instead of himself, and it imposes no hardship upon the purchaser. It was his contract so to pay the purchase money, and such a contract is valid and binding in law, although it is not evidenced by any writing."[1] On the same general principles a verbal acceptance or promise to accept a bill of exchange is not within the statute when the promisor has funds of the drawer in his hands to pay it.[2] It amounts to a payment of his own debt, and it makes no difference whether he pay it to the drawer himself or to a creditor of the drawer who is designated by the bill of exchange.

[1] Per Scott, J., in Wilson *v.* Beavans, 58 Ill. 232. To the same effect, and illustrating this subject, see Ashford *v.* Robinson, 8 Ired. (N. C.) 114; Stewart *v.* Malone, 5 Phila. 440; Carpenter *v.* Wall, 4 Dev. & Batt. (N. C.) 144; Huntington *v.* Wellington, 12 Mich. 10; Ardern *v.* Rowney, 5 Esp. 254; Smith *v.* Finch, 2 Scam. (Ill.) 321; Reed *v.* Holcomb, 31 Conn. 360; Runde *v.* Runde, 59 Ill. 98; Allen *v.* Pryor, 3 A. K. Marsh. (Ky.) 305; Wait *v.* Wait, 28 Vt. 350; Hackleman *v.* Miller, 4 Blackf. (Ind.) 322; Rowland *v.* Rorke, 4 Jones (N. C.), 337; Devlin *v.* Woodgate, 34 Barb. (N. Y.) 252; Jones *v.* Palmer, 1 Doug. (Mich.) 379; Cardell *v.* McNeil, 21 N. Y. 336; Gold *v.* Phillips, 10 Johns. 412; Hodgson *v.* Anderson, 5 Dow. & Ry. 735; Id., 3 Barn. & Cres. 842; Stephens *v.* Squire, 5 Modern, 205; Orrell *v.* Coppock, 26 Law Jour. Ch. 269; Aiken *v.* Cheeseborough, 1 Hill, Law (S. C.), 172. *Contra*, Wood *v.* Wheelock, 25 Barb. (N. Y.) 625.

[2] Pillans *v.* Van Mierop, 3 Burr. 1663; Townsley *v.* Sumrall, 2 Pet.

§ 68. When promisor previously liable, promise not within statute.— If the promisor is already liable for the payment of the debt, his promise to pay it if a third person does not is not within the statute. This is but another application of the principle that a promise to pay the promisor's own debt is not within the statute, even though its performance may discharge the debt of another. Thus A., through the agency of a broker, sold a parcel of linseed to B., who, through the same broker, sold it at an increased price to C. The time for C. to pay the price was to arrive before that fixed for the payment by B. C. sent his clerk to the broker for the delivery order for the seed, and the broker took him to A., from whom the clerk obtained the order, upon the faith of a promise that C. would pay A. for the seed. It was held that the promise was not within the statute. The court said: "We are all agreed that the case is not within the Statute of Frauds. The law upon this subject is, I think, correctly stated in the notes to Forth *v.* Stanton, 1 Wms. Saund. 211*e*, where the learned editor thus sums up the result of the authorities: 'There is considerable difficulty on the subject, occasioned perhaps by unguarded expressions in the reports of the different cases, but the fair result seems to be that the question whether each particular case comes within this clause of the statute (sec. 4), or not, depends not on the consideration for the promise, but on the fact of the original party remaining liable, coupled with the absence of any liability on the part of the defendant or his property, except such as arises from his express promise.' I quite concur in that view of the doctrine, provided the proposition is considered as embracing the qualification at the conclusion of the passage; for though I agree that the consideration alone is not the test, but that the party taking upon himself the obligation upon which the action is brought makes himself responsible for the debt or default of another, still it must be taken with the qualification stated in the note above

182; Spaulding *v.* Andrews, 48 Pa. St. 411; Jones *v.* Council Bluffs Bank, 34 Ill. 313; O'Donnell *v.* Smith, 2 E. D. Smith (N. Y.), 124; Mason *v.* Dousay, 35 Ill. 424; Van Reimsdyck *v.* Kane, 1 Gall. C. C. 633; Leonard *v.* Mason, 1 Wend. 522; Grant *v.* Shaw, 16 Mass. 341; Strohecker *v.* Cohen, 1 Spears (S. C.), 349; Nelson *v.* First Nat. Bank of Chicago, 48 Ill. 36; Shields *v.* Middleton, 2 Cranch, C. C. 205; Pike *v.* Irwin, 1 Sand. (N. Y.) 14.

cited, viz.: an absence of prior liability on the part of the defendant or his property."[1] The doctrine here announced in terms, that, in order to bring the promise within the statute, there must be an absence of liability on the part of the promisor, except such as arises from his express promise, is based upon the soundest reason, and affords an explanation for many cases which could not otherwise be sustained upon principle. This doctrine is also applicable where the promise is to pay what the promisor was previously liable for jointly with others only; as in the case of a partnership, where the verbal promise of one partner to pay the partnership debt is valid.[2] But a promise by a firm to pay the individual debt of one partner;[3] or by a stockholder of a corporation to pay its debts,[4] must be in writing; because in neither case is there any pre-existing liability on the part of the promisor to pay.

§ 69. New consideration passing between promisee and promisor will not alone take promise out of statute.—In many of the cases which have held a verbal promise to answer for another binding when the original debtor also remained bound, great stress has been laid upon the fact that the promise was founded upon a new consideration moving between the creditor and the promisor, and the promise has been decided to be not within the statute for that reason alone. In a celebrated case, often cited to sustain this position, a most learned judge[5] said that "when the promise to pay the debt of another" arose "out of some new and original consideration of benefit or harm moving between the newly contracting

[1] Fitzgerald *v.* Dressler, 7 Com. B. (J. Scott) N. S. 374, per Cockburn, C. J. To this principle may be referred Williams *v.* Leper, 2 Wils. 308; Id., 3 Burr. 1886; Bampton *v.* Paulin, 4 Bing. 264; Thomas *v.* Williams, 10 Barn. & Cress. 664; Houlditch *v.* Milne, 3 Esp. 86. See, also, as further illustrating this point, Macrory *v.* Scott, 5 Wels., Hurl. & Gor. 907; Nelson *v.* Boynton, 3 Met. (Mass.) 396; Chambers *v.* Robbins, 28 Conn. 544; Hoover *v.* Morris, 3 Ohio, 56, and also cases heretofore cited on other branches of this subject.

[2] Stephens *v.* Squire, 5 Modern, 205; Aikin *v.* Duren, 2 Nott & McCord (S. C.), 370; Files *v.* McLeod, 14 Ala. 611; Howes *v.* Martin, 1 Esp. 162; Rice *v.* Barry, 2 Cranch, C. C. 447.

[3] Taylor *v.* Hillyer, 3 Blackf. (Ind.) 433; Wagnon *v.* Clay, 1 A. K. Marsh. (Ky.) 257.

[4] Trustees of Free Schools *v.* Flint, 13 Met. (Mass.) 539; Wyman *v.* Gray, 7 Harris & Johns. (Md.) 409; Rogers *v.* Waters, 2 Gill & Johns. (Md.) 64.

[5] Kent, C. J. (afterwards Chancellor), in Leonard *v.* Vredenburgh, 8 Johns. 29.

parties," the promise was not within the statute. Numerous cases have been decided upon the authority of this statement of the law; and it has been given as a reason for the decision of many cases which may well rest upon other grounds. The proposition of the learned judge was not necessary to a decision of the case in which it was laid down, and, as stated by him, cannot be supported on principle, nor by the later and best-considered authorities. There must be a consideration for every contract of suretyship or guaranty; and to hold that in every case where the consideration moves from the creditor to the surety or guarantor, the promise is not within the statute, would be to repeal the statute altogether in a very large class of cases. If such were the law, the verbal promise of a surety or guarantor, made in consideration of the payment to him of $1 by the creditor, would be valid if the promise was to pay a still subsisting debt of the principal, amounting to $1,000, or any greater sum. When the consideration passes between the surety or guarantor and the creditor, the promise will be within the statute or not, according to circumstances; but there must be some other circumstance besides the mere passage of the consideration to take the case out of the statute. In determining whether any particular case is within or without the statute, the true question is, "What is the promise?" not "What is the consideration?" An able court has said: "We believe it will be found that in all the cases now regarded as sound, where it has been held that a parol promise to pay the debt of another is binding, the promisor held in his hands funds, securities or property of the debtor devoted to the payment of the debt, and his promise to pay attaches upon his obligation or duty growing out of the receipt of such fund."[1] In another case in which this question was involved, the court said: "It must be admitted that the cases respecting the application of the Statute of Frauds are greatly confused and irreconcilable with each other. Upon no subject perhaps has there been more diversity of judicial decision. The value of the statute is everywhere admitted, and its language is plain, but in the supposed justice of a particular case a court has often lost sight of the exact rule prescribed by the legislature.

[1] See elaborate opinion of Poland, C. J., in which he sustains the views expressed in the text, Fullam v. Adams, 37 Vt. 391.

As much ingenuity has been expended in efforts to take individual cases out of the statute, as was formerly devoted to avoiding the Statute of Limitations, and in these ingenious efforts principles have been asserted, which, if sound, practically deny all effect to the expressed will of the legislature. Happily, there are glimmerings of late of a tendency to return to a plainer reading of the act, and to give to it a construction more consonant to the apparent mind of the legislature. . . . Without attempting any extended review of them [the authorities], we think certain principles may be safely considered as settled, or, if not settled, sustained by reason and the authority of the best-considered adjudications. It is not true, as a general rule, that a promise to pay the debt of another is not within the statute, if it rests upon a new consideration passing from the promisee to the promisor. A new consideration for a new promise is indispensable without the statute; and if a new consideration is all that is needed to give validity to a promise to pay the debt of another, the statute amounts to nothing, nor can it make any difference that the new consideration moves from the promisee to the promisor. The object of the statute is protection against 'fraudulent practices commonly endeavored to be upheld by perjury,' and to these all suits upon verbal contracts to answer for another's debt or default are equally exposed, no matter whence the consideration of the contract proceeded, or to whom it passed."[1]

§ 70. Promise not within statute when main object is to benefit promisor himself — Observations.— Another rule upon which many decisions have been founded is that where the main or immediate object of the promisor is not the payment of the debt of another, but to subserve some purpose of his own, the promise is not within the statute, although its performance may have the effect of discharging the debt of another. A contractor had been employed by a railroad company to build certain bridges on its line, and the company

[1] Per Strong, J., in Maule *v.* Bucknell, 50 Pa. St. 39; Kingsley *v.* Balcome, 4 Barb. (N. Y.) 131; Cross *v.* Richardson, 30 Vt. 647; Floyd *v.* Harrison, 4 Bibb (Ky.), 76; Lampson *v.* Hobart, 28 Vt. 700; Noyes *v.* Humphreys, 11 Gratt. (Va.) 636; Barber *v.* Bucklin, 2 Denio, 45; De Colyar on Guaranties, p. 141; Kelsey *v.* Hibbs, 13 Ohio St. 340. See, also, on this subject, Price *v.* Truesdell, 28 N. J. Eq. (1 Stew.) 200.

failing to make its payments as agreed, the contractor refused to go on. The defendant, who was a large stockholder in the road, had leased the company railroad iron to the value of $68,400, and, as security for payment, held an assignment of the proceeds of the road for that amount, which was to be paid in monthly instalments. If the bridges were not completed there would be no proceeds, and the company could not pay for the iron. The defendant verbally promised the contractor to pay him if he would go on and complete the bridges, and, to secure himself from loss by reason of such promise, the defendant took from the company securities, consisting of real estate, and the company's bonds, secured by mortgage on the road, to an amount deemed by the company and himself sufficient to indemnify him. The company was insolvent. *Held*, the defendant's promise was not within the statute.[1] The court said: "Whenever the main purpose and object of the promisor is not to answer for another, but to subserve some pecuniary or business purpose of his own, involving either a benefit to himself or damage to the other contracting party, his promise is not within the statute, although it may be in form a promise to pay the debt of another, and although the performance of it may incidentally have the effect of extinguishing that liability." This rule is but another application of the principle that a verbal promise to pay the promisor's own debt is valid even though its performance incidentally extinguishes the debt of a third person. The words of the statute themselves, taken in their ordinary meaning, afford the means of threading the labyrinth of authority on this subject, and in every new case, as it arises, of arriving at a proper result. The object of the statute was to require written evidence when the promise was merely to answer for another, and not to afford a pretext by which the promisor might avoid performing his own obligations, because in so doing he incidentally discharged the obligation of another. The mere fact

[1] Emerson *v.* Slater, 22 How. (U. S.), 28, per Clifford, J. To this principle may be referred the cases of Castling *v.* Aubert, 2 East, 325; Elkins *v.* Heart, Fitzg. 202; Macrory *v.* Scott, 5 Wels., Hurl. & Gor. 907; Jarmain *v.* Algar, 2 Car. & P. 249, and many of the cases already recited herein under other divisions of this subject. See, also, Lemmon *v.* Box, 20 Tex. 329; Clay *v.* Walton, 9 Cal. 328.

alone, that the leading object of the promisor is a benefit to himself, affords a very unsatisfactory test for determining whether, or not, the statute applies to any case, because it is often difficult to distinguish the leading object from other objects, and the object a person has in entering into a contract is usually immaterial, as he is bound by his contract as made. Neither is the nature of the consideration a sufficient test. The true test is, what is the substance of the transaction between the promisor and promisee? If it is a mere promise to answer for another, it is within the statute. If it is a promise to pay the promisor's own debt in a particular way, it is not within the statute.

§ 71. Promise of del credere agent not within statute.— The agreement of a *del credere* agent to pay for the goods sold through his agency is not within the Statute of Frauds. Such an agent agrees to be responsible for the goods so sold. By some courts he has been said to be a surety or guarantor, and by others an original and principal debtor. Whatever may be the technical position he occupies, it is settled that his promise is not within the statute.[1] The reason given by one court[2] was as follows: "The other and only remaining point is, whether the defendants are responsible by reason of their charging a *del credere* commission, though they have not guarantied by writing, signed by themselves. We think they are. Doubtless if they had for a percentage guarantied the debt owing, or performance of the contract by the vendee, being totally unconnected with the sale, they would not be liable without a note in writing signed by them, but being the agents to negotiate the sale, the commission is paid in respect of that employment; a higher reward is paid in consideration of their taking greater care in sales to their customers, and precluding

[1] Swan *v.* Nesmith, 7 Pick. 220; Bradley *v.* Richardson, 23 Vt. 720; Grove *v.* Dubois, 1 Term R. 112; Sherwood *v.* Stone, 14 N. Y. 267; Mackenzie *v.* Scott, 6 Bro. Parl. Cas. 280; Muller *v.* Bohlens, 2 Wash. C. C. 378; Thompson *v.* Perkins, 3 Mason, 232; Houghton *v.* Matthews, 3 Bos. & Pul. 485. See, also, on this subject, Wickham *v.* Wickham, 2 Kay & Johns. 478, remarks of Wood, V. C.; and Morris *v.* Cleasby, 4 Maule & Sel. 566.

[2] *Per* Parke, B., in Couturier *v.* Hastie, 8 Wels., Hurl. & Gor. 40, reversed on appeal to Exch. Ch., Hastie *v.* Couturier, 9 Wels., Hurl. & Gor. 102; but affirmed by the House of Lords, Couturier *v.* Hastie, 5 H. of L. Cas. 673.

all question whether the loss arose from negligence or not, and also for assuming a greater share of responsibility than other agents, namely, responsibility for the solvency and performance of their contracts by their vendees. This is the main object of the reward being given to them, and though it may terminate in a liability to pay the debt of another, that is not the immediate object for which the consideration is given." In determining this same question another court[1] said: "A guaranty, though by parol, is not always within the statute. Perhaps, after all, it may not be strictly correct to call the contract of the factor a guaranty in the ordinary sense of that word. The implied promise of the factor is merely that he will sell to persons in good credit at the time; and in order to charge him the negligence must be shown. He takes an additional commission, however, and adds to his obligation that he will make no sales unless to persons absolutely solvent; in legal effect, that he will be liable for the loss which his conduct may bring upon the plaintiff, without the *onus* of proving negligence. The merchant holds the goods, and will not part with them to the factor without this extraordinary stipulation, and a commission is paid to him for entering into it. What is this, after all, but another form of selling the goods? Its consequences are the same in substance. Instead of paying cash, the factor prefers to contract a debt, or duty, which obliges him to see the money paid. This debt or duty is his own, and arises from an adequate consideration. . . . Suppose a factor agrees by parol to sell for cash, but gives a credit. His promise is virtually that he will pay the amount of the debt he thus makes. Yet who would say his promise is within the statute? The amount of the argument for the defendant would seem to be that an agent for making sales, or, indeed, a collecting agent, cannot by parol undertake for extraordinary diligence, because he may thus have the debt of another thrown upon him. But the answer is, that all such contracts have an immediate respect to his own duty or obligation. The debt of another comes in incidentally as a measure of damages."

[1] Wolff *v.* Koppel, 5 Hill, 458, per Cowen, J., affirmed by court of errors, and same doctrine enunciated, Wolff *v.* Koppel, 2 Denio, 368.

§ 72. Promise not within statute unless made to party to whom principal is liable.— In order to bring the promise to answer for another within the Statute of Frauds, the promise must be made to the person to whom the other is already, or is thereafter to become, liable. A verbal promise to a debtor himself to pay or furnish him the means of paying his debt is not within the statute.[1] In a leading case on this subject the plaintiff was liable to one Blackburn on a note, and the defendant, upon sufficient consideration, promised the plaintiff to pay the note to Blackburn. *Held*, the promise was not within the statute.[2] The court said: "If the promise had been made to Blackburn, doubtless the statute would have applied. It would then have been strictly a promise to answer for the debt of another; and the argument on the part of the defendant is, that it is not less the debt of another because the promise is made to that other, viz.: the debtor, and not to the creditor, the statute not having, in terms, stated to whom the promise contemplated by it is to be made. But upon consideration, we are of opinion that the statute applies only to promises made to the person to whom another is answerable." A. owned a threshing machine, upon which he owed a balance to B. One C. purchased the machine of A., and paid him a certain sum, and verbally promised A. to pay B. the amount A. owed him on the machine, as part of the purchase money to be paid by C. to A. *Held*, the promise was not within the statute.[3] A., having a judgment against B., placed a warrant for his arrest in the hands of a bailiff, with instructions that he might take half the amount in satisfaction of the judgment. The bailiff being about to arrest B., one C. verbally promised the bailiff to pay him half the judgment, or surrender B. by the next

[1] Colt *v.* Root, 17 Mass. 229; Thomas *v.* Cook, 8 Barn. & Cress. 728; Morin *v.* Martz, 13 Minn. 191; Love's Case, 1 Salk. 28; Mersereau *v.* Lewis, 25 Wend. 243; Howard *v.* Coshow, 33 Mo. 118; Weld *v.* Nichols, 17 Pick. 538; Pratt *v.* Humphrey, 22 Conn. 317; Barber *v.* Bucklin, 2 Denio, 45; North *v.* Robinson, 1 Duvall (Ky.), 71; Jones *v.* Hardesty, 10 Gill & Johns. 404; Aldrich *v.* Ames, 9 Gray, 76; Preble *v.* Baldwin, 6 Cush. 549; Fiske *v.* McGregory, 34 N. H. 414; Pike *v.* Brown, 7 Cush. 133; Soule *v.* Albee, 31 Vt. 142; Alger *v.* Scoville, 1 Gray, 391; Gregory *v.* Williams, 3 Meriv. 582.

[2] Per Lord Denman, in Eastwood *v.* Kenyon, 11 Adol. & Ell. 438; Id., 3 Perry & Dav. 276.

[3] Crim *v.* Fitch, 53 Ind. 214.

Saturday, but did neither. *Held*, the promise was not within the statute. The court said: "It has been distinctly settled, that, to bring the promise within the statute, the promisee must be the original creditor. . . . The debts are totally distinct debts, as well as the debtors."[1] In another case, deciding the same thing as those already stated, the court said: "The statute applies only to promises made to the persons to whom another is already, or is to become, answerable. It must be a promise to be answerable for a debt of, or a default in, some duty by that other person towards the promisee."[2]

§ 73. False representations of another's credit not within statute.— False and deceitful verbal representations as to the standing and responsibility of a third person are not within the Statute of Frauds.[3] Such representations cannot, with any regard for the ordinary meaning of language, be held a "special promise" to answer for another. However much they may be within the mischief of the statute, they are clearly not within its language. In the leading case on this subject, one Freeman "falsely, deceitfully and fraudulently" asserted and affirmed, orally, that one Falch "was a person safely to be trusted and given credit to." The court held, upon great consideration, that Freeman was liable to an action in consequence of these representations.[4] In discussing and approving this case another court said:[5] "The case went not upon any new ground, but upon the application of a principle of natural justice long recognized in the law, that fraud or deceit, accompanied with damage, is a good cause of action. This is as just and permanent a principle as any in our whole jurisprudence. The only plausible objection to it is, that in its application to

[1] Reader *v.* Kingham, 13 Com. B. (J. Scott) N. S. 344, per Earle, C. J.

[2] Parke, B., in Hargreaves *v.* Parsons, 13 Mees. & Wels. 561.

[3] Eyre *v.* Duusford, 1 East, 318; Allen *v.* Adington, 7 Wend. 9; Haycraft *v.* Creasy, 2 East, 92; Warren *v.* Barker, 2 Duvall (Ky.), 155; Benton *v.* Pratt, 2 Wend. 385; Tapp *v.* Lee, 3 Bos. & Pul. 367; Wise *v.* Wilcox, 1 Day (Conn.), 22; Foster *v.* Charles, 6 Bing. 396; Hart *v.* Tallmadge, 2 Day (Conn.), 381; Patten *v.* Gurney, 17 Mass. 182; Russell *v.* Clark, 7 Cranch, 69; Gallagher *v.* Brunel, 6 Cowen, 347; Ewins *v.* Calhoun, 7 Vt. 79; Weeks *v.* Burton, 7 Vt. 67. Lord Eldon was strongly opposed to this doctrine, and thought it not good law. See Evans *v.* Bicknell, 6 Vesey, Jr. 174.

[4] Pasley *v.* Freeman, 3 Term R. 51.

[5] Upton *v.* Vail, 6 Johns. 181, per Kent, C. J.

this case it comes within the mischiefs which gave rise to the Statute of Frauds, and that therefore the representation ought to be in writing. But this, I apprehend, is an objection arising from policy and expediency, for it is certain that the Statute of Frauds, as it now stands, has nothing to do with the case." A statute has been passed in England, providing that no action shall be brought to charge any person by reason of any representations concerning the credit, ability, etc., of another, unless the representations are in writing,[1] and a similar statute has been enacted in several of the United States. When the verbal representation was also accompanied by a verbal promise to pay the debt of the third party, concerning whom the representation was made, the party making the representation has still been held liable. Thus, the representation and promise were "that one Leo was a good man and might be trusted to any amount; that the defendant durst be bound to pay for the said Leo; and that if Leo did not pay for the goods he would." It was objected that the injury might have arisen from a violation of the promise to pay, and that the action could not be maintained because of the Statute of Frauds, but the defendant was held liable.[2] The court said: "There never was a time in the English law when an action might not have been maintained against the defendant for this gross fraud. . . . There is no proof that the plaintiff ever considered the defendant as his debtor, or ever called upon him for the money, or relied upon his promise in the least degree. In the next place we must suppose every man to know the law, and if the plaintiff was acquainted with the law, he must have known that the defendant's promise was worth nothing, and could have given no credit to him upon it. He cannot have considered it in any other light than as a mode of expression by which the defendant intended more strongly to express his opinion of Leo's circumstances."

[1] 9 Geo. IV., ch. 14, § 6. For decisions on this subject, see Lyde *v.* Barnard, Tyrwh. & Gr. 250; Tatton *v.* Wade, 18 Com. B. 370; Haslock *v.* Fergusson, 7 Ad. & Ell. 86; Norton *v.* Huxley, 13 Gray, 285; Kimball *v.* Comstock, 14 Gray, 508; Mann *v.* Blanchard, 2 Allen, 386; McKinney *v.* Whitney, 8 Allen, 207; Huntington *v.* Wellington, 12 Mich. 11. See, also, on this subject, Browne on Frauds, pp. 169–177.

[2] Hamar *v.* Alexander, 5 Bos. & Pul. 241, per Sir James Mansfield. See, also, Thompson *v.* Bond, 1 Camp. 4.

§ 74. Promise in substance to pay debt of another, no matter what its form, is within statute.— When the promise is not in form, but is in substance, to pay the debt of another, it is within the statute. Thus, the defendant requested the plaintiff to sell a third person goods, and promised to indorse his note at six months for the price. *Held*, the promise was within the statute and could not be enforced.[1] The court, after saying that the promise was to become the third person's surety, proceeded: "To say, then, that this is not in effect to answer for their debt would be a sacrifice of substance to sound. It would be devising a formulary by which, through the aid of a perjured witness, a creditor might get round and defraud the statute. He may say, 'You did not promise to answer the debt due to me from A., but only to put yourself in such a position that I could compel you to pay it.' Pray where is the difference except in words? According to such reasoning, unless you recite the words of the statute in your undertaking, it will not reach the case. No legislative provision would be worth anything upon such a construction." In another case the plaintiff had contracted to supply goods to A., to be paid for in cash on each delivery. A. being desirous of obtaining the goods on credit, the defendant, who had an interest in the performance of the work upon which the goods were to be used, promised the plaintiff that if he would supply the goods to A. upon a month's credit, and allow him, the defendant, a certain per cent. upon the amount of the invoice, he would pay him, the plaintiff, cash, and take A.'s bill without recourse. *Held*, the promise was within the statute.[2] The court said: "A contract to give a guaranty is re-

[1] Per Cowen, J., in Carville *v.* Crane, 5 Hill, 483. See, also, Gallagher *v.* Brunel, 6 Cowen, 346; Taylor *v.* Drake, 4 Strobh. (S. C.) 431; Pike *v.* Irwin, 1 Sandf. (N. Y.) 14; Quin *v.* Hanford, 1 Hill, 82; Wakefield *v.* Greenhood, 29 Cal. 597. But see D'Wolf *v.* Rabaud, 1 Pet. 476.

[2] Per Pollock, C. B., in Mallet *v.* Bateman, Law Rep. 1 C. P. 163; S. C. 16 J. Scott (N. S.), 530. To similar effect, see Martin *v.* England, 5 Yerg. (Tenn.) 313; Thomas *v.* Welles, 1 Root (Conn.), 57. In Fitch *v.* Gardenier, 2 Abbott's Rep. Omitted Cas. 153, a suit was pending, which one of the parties wished to compromise, but his attorney promised, if he would go on, to make no charges for his services unless he was successful. *Held*, this was not a collateral undertaking or guaranty of collection, and need not be in writing to bind the attorney making it.

quired to be in writing as much as a guaranty itself. . . . This is in substance an engagement by which the buyers of goods are not to be exonerated, but the defendant is to indemnify the seller against their default." A verbal promise to procure some one else to sign a guaranty for a certain freight has been held not to be within the statute.[1] There the promise was that the creditor should have, not the promisor's, but a third person's guaranty for the debt. It has also been held that a promise by one who owes a party about to be sued by another that he will not pay without giving notice to the party about to sue, so that he may have an opportunity to attach the debt, is not within the statute.[2] The same thing has been held where one who receipted for attached property promised that it should be returned upon demand.[3] In these two last cases the promise was in effect to turn over to the creditor the debtor's own property, and not that of the promisor; and in none of the three last-mentioned cases was the promise to pay the debt, and in case of a breach the debt would not have been the measure of damages.

§ 75. **Promise to answer for future liability of third party is within the statute.**— If the future primary liability of a third person to the promisee is contemplated as the foundation of the promise, then the promise is within the statute, precisely the same as if the liability had existed when the promise was made. The distinction was at one time made, that, if there was no existing liability on the part of the third person when the promise was made, it was not within the statute, because there was nothing to which it was collateral.[4] This distinction has, however, long been overruled, and the law settled as above stated.[5] Thus, the defendant and A. came to the plaintiff's warehouse and agreed upon a parcel of goods for A., and the defendant said he would guaranty the payment. A. afterwards came alone and ordered other goods, when the plaintiff sent to the defendant and asked him whether

[1] Bushnell *v.* Beavan, 1 Bing. N. C. 103; Id., 4 Moore & Scott, 622.

[2] Towne *v.* Grover, 9 Pick. 306.

[3] Marion *v.* Faxon, 20 Conn. 486.

[4] Per Lord Mansfield, in Mowbray *v.* Cunningham, Hilary Term, 1773, cited in Jones *v.* Cooper, 227.

[5] Jones *v.* Cooper, 1 Cowp. 227; Matson *v.* Wharam, 2 Term R. 80; Mallet *v.* Bateman, Law Rep. 1 C. P. 163.

he would engage for A. The defendant replied: "You may not only ship that parcel, but one, two or three thousand pounds more, and I will pay you if he does not." The plaintiff, relying on this promise, afterwards delivered the goods to A. *Held*, the promise was within the statute.[1] The court said: "Before the case of Jones *v.* Cooper, I thought there was a solid distinction between an undertaking after credit given and an original undertaking to pay, and that in the latter case, the surety, being the object of the confidence, was not within the statute; but in Jones *v.* Cooper the court was of opinion that, wherever a man is to be called upon only in the second instance, he is within the statute; otherwise, where he is to be called upon in the first instance." In another case the defendant verbally authorized the plaintiffs, who were merchants, to let a third person have a certain amount of goods, and promised that he would guaranty the payment. The plaintiffs afterwards delivered the goods to the third person, and charged them on their books to the defendant for the third person. *Held*, the promise was to answer for the debt of another, and that it could not be enforced for want of writing.[2]

§ 76. Promise within statute if any credit given to third person.— If the party to whom goods are delivered, or for whose benefit a service is performed, incur thereby a debt, so that he is liable at all, then the undertaking of another, in aid of his liability and collateral to it, must be in writing to be binding, although the collateral undertaking may have been the principal inducement to the delivery of the goods or the performance of the service.[3] A landlord to whom rent was

[1] Peckham *v.* Faria, 3 Doug. 13, per Lord Mansfield. But see Whitman *v.* Bryant, 49 Vt. 512.

[2] Kinloch *v.* Brown, 2 Spear's Law (S. C.), 284. See, to same effect as text, Cahill *v.* Bigelow, 18 Pick. 369; Caperton *v.* Gray, 4 Yerg. (Tenn.) 563; Ware *v.* Stephenson, 10 Leigh (Va.), 155; *Ex parte* Williams, 4 Yerg. (Tenn.) 579; Noyes *v.* Humphreys, 11 Gratt. (Va.) 636; Tilleston *v.* Nettleton, 6 Pick. 509; Taylor *v.* Drake, 4 Strobh. (S. C.) 431; Newell *v.* Ingraham, 15 Vt. 422; Huntington *v.* Harvey, 4 Conn. 124; Leland *v.* Creyon, 1 McCord (S. C.), 100; Puckett *v.* Bates, 4 Ala. 390; Peabody *v.* Harvey, 4 Conn. 119.

[3] Walker *v.* Richards, 39 N. H. 259; Matson *v.* Wharam, 2 Term R. 80; Cahill *v.* Bigelow, 18 Pick. 369; Anderson *v.* Hayman, 1 H. Black. 120; Chase *v.* Day, 17 Johns. 114; Brunton *v.* Dullens, 1 Foster & Fin. 45 ; Bres-

due gave a warant to A. to distrain upon the tenant. The defendant, who was a creditor of the landlord, paid the broker that valued the goods, and put the plaintiff on the premises to keep possession of the goods, and promised to pay him his charges, and also to repay him certain sums to be advanced to another. *Held*, the promise was within the statute, on the ground that the landlord was responsible as principal for the necessary expenses of the distress, and consequently the promise was to pay the debt of another.[1] It makes no difference that the promisee relied principally upon the promisor; if the third party is at all liable to him, to do the same thing, the promise is within the statute. A contractor who was building a house for the defendant employed the plaintiff to furnish the stone, but failed to pay him. The defendant promised the plaintiff that, if he would go on and finish the work, he would pay him; but the contractor was not discharged from his liability to the plaintiff. *Held*, the promise was within the statute.[2] So where the plaintiff had contracted to deliver a quantity of rock to a third person at an agreed price, and before the delivery of the same the plaintiff made known to the defendant his determination not to deliver the rock upon the credit of such third person, and the defendant thereupon said to the plaintiff: "You bring the rock, and I will see you paid for it," the court held the promise was within the statute.[3] In these cases, and indeed in most of the cases on this subject,

ler *v.* Pendell, 12 Mich. 224; Brady *v.* Sackrider, 1 Sandf. (N. Y.) 514; Hill *v.* Raymond, 3 Allen, 540; Larson *v.* Wyman, 14 Wend. 246; Elder *v.* Warfield, 7 Harr. & Johns. (Md.) 391; Darlington *v.* McCunn, 2 E. D. Smith, (N. Y.), 411; Conolly *v.* Kettlewell, 1 Gill (Md.), 260; Hanford *v.* Higgins, 1 Bosw. (N. Y.) 441; Bushee *v.* Allen, 31 Vt. 631; Allen *v.* Scarff, 1 Hilton (N. Y.), 209; Steele *v.* Towne, 28 Vt. 771; Dixon *v.* Frazee, 1 E. D. Smith (N. Y.), 32; Boykin *v.* Dohlonde, 1 Sel. Cas. Ala. 502; Studley *v.* Barth, 54 Mich. 6. See, also, as to collateral promise, Glidden *v.* Child, 122 Mass. 433.

1 Colman *v.* Eyles, 2 Stark. 62.

2 Gill *v.* Herrick, 111 Mass. 501.

3 Doyle *v.* White, 26 Me. 341. But where a father whose son desired to purchase certain goods agreed with the owner that if he would let the son have such goods, he (the father) would see the debt paid or would pay it, this was held to be an original and not a collateral undertaking; though had the father promised to pay the debt if the son did not, then such undertaking would have been to answer for the debt, default or miscarriage of another, and should have been in writing. Baldwin *v.* Hiers, 73 Ga. 739; and see Cruse *v.* Foster, 76 Ga. 723.

the promise of the proposed surety or guarantor was principally relied upon by the promisee, and formed the inducement upon which he acted. When, by reason of the statute, the promisor does not become liable, no relief can be granted against him in equity, although he is proceeding against the promisee at law, in direct violation of his promise.[1] When credit is given to two jointly, and they are both principals, the statute does not apply to their engagement.[2]

§ 77. **When promise is original or collateral, cases holding it original.**— It is apparent that the question "To whom was the credit given?" often becomes highly important. If the credit is given to the promisor alone, his promise need not be in writing. But if credit is given to a third person, to any extent, and the promise is collateral to the liability of such third person, it must be in writing. The solution of this question is frequently a matter of great difficulty, and no general rule which will serve as a test can be given. In each case, the "expression used, the situation of the parties, and all the circumstances of the case, should be taken into consideration."[3] It has been held that a promise "to be the paymaster" of one who should render services to another was an original promise, and not within the statute, but that if the words were, "to see him paid," it was collateral, and within the statute.[4] Where the defendant inquired of the plaintiff the terms on which he would let C., his nephew, have newspapers to sell, and, on being told the terms, said: "If my nephew calls for the papers, I will be responsible for the papers he shall take," it was held that this was an original and absolute contract on the part of the defendant, and not within the statute.[5] An order was:

[1] Phelps *v.* Garrow, 8 Paige, Ch. 322.

[2] Gibbs *v.* Blanchard, 15 Mich. 292; Wainwright *v.* Straw, 15 Vt. 215; Hetfield *v.* Dow, 3 Dutch. (N. J.) 440; *Ex parte* Williams, 4 Yerg. (Tenn.) 579; Boyce *et al.* *v.* Murphy *et al.*, 94 Ind. 1.

[3] Elder *v.* Warfield, 7 Harr. & Johns. (Md.) 391.

[4] Watkins *v.* Perkins, 1 Ld. Raym. 224. See, also, Skinner *v.* Conant, 2 Vt. 453; Thwaits *v.* Curl, 6 B. Mon. (Ky.) 472; Briggs *v.* Evans, 1 E. D. Smith (N. Y.), 192; Jones *v.* Cooper, 1 Cowp. 227; Bates *v.* Starr, 6 Ala. 697; Matson *v.* Wharam, 2 Term R. 80. A promise to boarding-house keepers, for boarding hands in the employ of promisor's subcontractors, "to see them paid," is an original and not collateral agreement, and not within the statute. Grant *v.* Wolf, 34 Minn. 32.

[5] Chase *v.* Day, 17 Johns. 114.

"Please give the bearer, Henry Fink, the goods which he will select, not exceeding over five hundred and fifty dollars, on my account." Goods having been delivered to Fink on the order, it was held that the writer of the order was liable as principal, and not as guarantor.[1] If goods are sold on the credit of the promisor alone, his promise to pay for them need not be in writing, even though they are delivered to a third person.[2] In an important case on this subject, the plaintiff had been employed by a local board of health to construct a main sewer. Notice had been given to the owners of certain private houses to connect their house drains with this sewer within a certain time. The plaintiff, having been requested by the overseer to make these connections, asked who would pay him for it, when the defendant, who was chairman of the board, said: "Go on, Mountstephen, and do the work, and I will see you paid." It was held that, taking all the circumstances into consideration, the defendant was liable as principal, and his promise was not within the statute.[3] The court said: "In this case, seeing that the parties knew that the board was not liable, and that the plaintiff would not go on unless he had the board or the defendant liable, and did not care to have the defendant liable if the board was liable, the facts seem to exclude, and the jury might well find that they excluded, the notion of the defendant becoming surety for a liability, either past, present or future, upon the part of the board; and they might look upon the defendant's contract as a contract to pay, whether the board have been, or shall be, liable or not. Do that work now, and you shall be paid for that work; so that it is a case of principal liability." In another case, the promisor introduced a third person to an upholsterer, and asked

Where defendant requested a firm "to sell him (Connolly) any goods he wanted, and he (defendant) would be responsible," it was held, though not without doubt, that the promise of defendant was an original one. Post *v.* Geoghegan, 5 Daly (N. Y. Com. Pleas), 216.

[1] Neberroth *v.* Riegel, 71 Pa. St. 280.

[2] McCaffil *v.* Radcliff, 3 Rob. (N. Y.) 445.

[3] Mountstephen *v.* Lakeman, Law Rep. 7 Q. B. 196, per Willes, J. See, also, Smith *v.* Rudhall, 3 Foster & Fin. 143; Jefferson County *v.* Slagee, 66 Pa. St. 202; Edge *v.* Frost, 4 Dow. & Ry. 243; Hiltz *v.* Scully, 1 Cinc. 554; Whitelaw *v.* Taylor, 45 Up. Can. (Q. B.) 446; Black *v.* Doherty, 22 New Brunswick Rep. (Pugsley & Trueman), 215.

him if he had any objection to supplying such third person with some furniture, and that if he would, he, the promisor, "would be answerable," and that "he would see it paid at the end of six months." *Held*, this was an original undertaking, as principal, on the part of the promisor. The court said: "Whether the contract was original or collateral, viz.: whether it was binding on the parties to pay in the first instance and at all events, or only binding in case the other does not, will depend on the contract between the parties. I think that the expressions, 'I'll be answerable,' and 'I'll see you paid,' are equivocal expressions. And then we ought to look to the circumstances to see what the contract between the parties was. . . . It was left to the jury to say whether he was the original debtor, and they found that he was. I think the jury warranted in that finding. My opinion is founded substantially on the facts of the case, and not on the equivocal expressions, as I consider the words capable of being explained by other circumstances."[1]

§ 78. Whether promise original or collateral is question of fact — Evidence — Cases holding promise collateral.— The manner in which the transaction is entered in the creditor's books often has a controlling influence in determining the question, "To whom was the credit given?" The fact that the charge on the creditor's books was to a third party has been held to control an absolute promise to pay, and to show that the liability of the promisor was only collateral.[2] If the creditor makes out a bill to the third party, and presents

[1] Simpson *v.* Penton, 2 Cromp. & Mees. 430, per Bayley, B. See further, on this subject, Payne *v.* Baldwin, 14 Barb. (N. Y.) 570; Dixon *v.* Hatfield, 2 Bing. 439; Smith *v.* Hyde, 19 Vt. 54; Clancy *v.* Piggott, 4 Nev. & Mann. 496; Sinclair *v.* Richardson, 12 Vt. 33; Birkmyr *v.* Darnell, 1 Salk. 27; Id., 2 Ld. Raym. 1085; Turton *v.* Burke, 4 Wis. 119; Austen *v.* Baker, 12 Modern, 250; Hazen *v.* Bearden, 4 Sneed (Tenn.), 48; Hetfield *v.* Dow, 3 Dutch. (N. J.) 440; Gordon *v.* Martin, Fitzgibbon, 302; Baldwin *v.* Hiers, 73 Ga. 739; Cruse *v.* Foster & Estes, 76 Ga. 723. As to when guaranty is sufficiently ambiguous to admit of parol evidence to explain it, see Goldshede *v.* Swan, 1 Wels., Hurl. & Gor. 154.

[2] Anderson *v.* Hyman, 1 H. Black. 120; Matson *v.* Wharam, 2 Term, 80. On same subject, see Conolly *v.* Kettlewell, 1 Gill (Md.), 260; Leland *v.* Creyon, 1 McCord (S. C.), 100; Dixon *v.* Frazee, 1 E. D. Smith (N. Y.), 32. The fact that a certain person is charged on the plaintiff's book with goods is not conclusive evidence that the credit was given to him. Swift *v.* Pierce, 13 Allen, 136.

it to him in the first instance, this is strong evidence to show that the credit was given to him, and that the promisor was only collaterally liable.[1] But it is not conclusive evidence of that fact, and may be controlled by other circumstances.[2] These various facts are matters of evidence, tending more or less to show to whom the credit was given, and will be received against the plaintiff to establish that the credit was given to a third person; but they are not evidence in favor of the plaintiff to charge the defendant, for that would be to permit the plaintiff to manufacture evidence for himself.[3] An instance where the promisor was held only collaterally liable, and not bound without writing, was as follows: A first lieutenant in the navy, serving on board a ship, requested the plaintiff, a tailor and slopseller, to supply the crew of the ship with clothing, and at the same time said: "I will see you paid at the pay-table; are you satisfied?" The plaintiff replied, "Perfectly so." The clothing was delivered on board the ship, and the lieutenant compelled several of the sailors who did not want clothes to take them. The court thought the slopseller relied upon the power of the lieutenant to stop the money out of the sailors' pay, and not upon his personal liability, and viewed as a controlling circumstance that the amount due for the clothing was so large that it could not have been expected that the lieutenant would be able to liquidate it out of his pay.[4] So where the promisor, upon being asked to become responsible for goods to be furnished a third person, replied: "You may send them, and I'll take care that they are paid for at the time," it was held that under the circumstances he was only collaterally liable, and not bound unless his promise was in writing.[5] In another case, the plaintiff, an innkeeper, had furnished a dinner for a public celebration, under the direction of a committee of which the defendant was a member. It was the understanding that every person should pay for his

[1] Storr *v.* Scott, 6 Car. & Payne, 241; Pennell *v.* Pentz, 4 E. D. Smith (N. Y.), 639; Larson *v.* Wyman, 14 Wend. 246.

[2] Mountstephen *v.* Lakeman, Law Rep. 7 Q. B. 196.

[3] Cutler *v.* Hinton, 6 Rand. (Va.) 509; Walker *v.* Richards, 41 N. H. 388; Noyes *v.* Humphreys, 11 Gratt. (Va.) 636; Kinloch *v.* Brown, 1 Rich. (S. C.) 223.

[4] Keate *v.* Temple, 1 Bos. & Pul. 158.

[5] Rains *v.* Story, 3 Car. & Payne, 130.

own dinner. The defendant was captain of a military company which took dinner upon that occasion. While the servants of the plaintiff were collecting the pay, the defendant told them they need not call upon the members of the military company, as he would be responsible for them. *Held*, the promise was collateral, and within the Statute of Frauds.[1] From the examples which have been given, it is clear that the words made use of by the parties cannot alone be relied upon to show to whom the credit was given. It is a question of fact to be found by the jury in each particular case, and in its determination, not only the language made use of, but also the situation and surroundings of the parties, and every other fact and circumstance bearing upon the question, should be taken into consideration.

§ 79. **If original promise in writing, verbal subsequent promise takes case out of Statute of Limitations — Verbal guaranty sufficient to support verbal account stated.**— If the Statute of Frauds has once been satisfied by writing, a new verbal promise will be sufficient to take the case out of the Statute of Limitations. Thus the defendant, having entered into a guaranty in writing, and become liable upon it more than six years before the commencement of the suit, verbally promised, within six years, that the matter should be arranged. *Held*, he was liable. The Statute of Frauds was satisfied by the guaranty having been originally in writing. In order to take a case out of the Statute of Limitations, the new promise need not be in writing. The two statutes, the one requiring a writing, and the other not, should not be confounded.[2] It has been held that if a person who has verbally guarantied the price of goods sold, afterwards verbally promise to pay for them, he is liable on an account stated. Thus the defendant verbally undertook to see the plaintiff paid for goods supplied by him to A. at the defendant's request. After the goods had been supplied, and A. had made default in payment, the defendant verbally acknowledged his liability under the guaranty, and promised to pay the plaintiff the price of the goods. The court said, that while the statement of an ac-

[1] Tileston *v.* Nettleton, 6 Pick. 509.

[2] Gibbons *v.* McCasland, 1 Barn. & Ald. 690.

count and promise to pay could give no cause of action if the obligation on which it was founded never could have been enforced at law, yet here there was a clear legal liability under the guaranty which the Statute of Frauds did not vacate or annul, but rendered incapable of being enforced for want of legal evidence, and it was sufficient, under the authorities, to support a statement of account.[1]

§ 80. **The form of the writing.**— The statute proceeds, "unless the agreement or some memorandum or note thereof shall be in writing." From the use of the words "some memorandum or note thereof," the design seems to have been to dispense with formalities in the writing required. The agreement, memorandum or note must substantially express the real transaction, but the form in which it is expressed is wholly immaterial. It may be in the form of a letter,[2] of a receipt,[3] of an order,[4] of the return of a sheriff upon an execution,[5] of a vote of a corporation entered on its books,[6] or in any other form, provided it expresses the substance of the transaction. It is not necessary that it should consist of a single paper. Several letters or papers which on their face refer to each other may be taken together to make a complete agreement, note or memorandum.[7] But it is well settled that, in order that the several papers may be read together, they must on their face refer to each other, and that their mutual relation

[1] Wilson *v.* Marshall, 15 Irish Com. Law Rep. 466.

[2] Sanderson *v.* Jackson, 2 Bos. & Pul. 238; Foster *v.* Hale, 3 Vesey, Jr. 696; Western *v.* Russell, 3 Vesey & Bea. 187; Allen *v.* Bennet, 3 Taunt. 169; Brettel *v.* Williams, 4 Wels., Hurl. & Gor. 623.

[3] Barickman *v.* Kuykendall, 6 Blackf. (Ind.) 21; Ellis *v.* Deadman, 4 Bibb (Ky.), 466.

[4] Lerned *v.* Wannemacher, 9 Allen, 412.

[5] Nichol *v.* Ridley, 5 Yerg. (Tenn.) 63; Barney *v.* Patterson, 6 Harr. & Johns. (Md.) 182; Elfe *v.* Gadsden, 2 Rich. (S. C.) 373; Hanson *v.* Barnes, 3 Gill & Johns. (Md.) 359.

[6] Tufts *v.* Plymouth Gold Mining Co., 14 Allen, 407; Chase *v.* Lowell, 7 Gray, 33.

[7] Jackson *v.* Lowe, 1 Bing. 9; Allen *v.* Bennet, 3 Taunt. 169; Jones *v.* Post, 6 Cal. 102; Owen *v.* Thomas, 3 Myl. & Keen, 353; Simons *v.* Steele, 36 N. H. 73; Huddleston *v.* Briscoe, 11 Vesey, 583; Salmon Falls Manuf. Co. *v.* Goddard, 14 How. (U. S.) 446; Wilson Sewing Machine Co. *v.* Schnell, 20 Minn. 40; Learned *v.* Wannemacher, 9 Allen, 412; Tallman *v.* Franklin, 14 N. Y. 584; Chapman *v.* Bluck, 5 Scott, 515; Parkhurst *v.* Van Cortland, 14 Johns. 15.

cannot be shown by parol evidence.[1] There are, however, a few cases which seem to countenance a contrary doctrine.[2] A writing which is signed by the party to be charged may be read together with one which is not signed.[3] If, when all the papers which refer to each other are read together, the terms of the contract are doubtful, they are not sufficient to satisfy the statute.[4] The agreement, note or memorandum may be written with ink or pencil, or may be printed or stamped,[5] and it may be executed at the time the contract is made, or at any subsequent time before the suit is brought.[6]

§ 81. **The whole promise must appear from the writing.**— Whatever the form of the writing may be, and whether it consist of one or more parts, all the essential terms of the contract (unless, perhaps, the consideration) must appear from it, and parol evidence cannot be introduced to aid it.[7] Thus, in a letter written by the defendant to the plaintiff, relating to a proposed mortgage, but which did not itself say anything

[1] Jacob *v.* Kirk, 2 Moody & Rob. 221; Clinan *v.* Cooke, 1 Schoales & Lefroy, 22; Moale *v.* Buchanan, 11 Gill & Johns. (Md.) 314; Wiley *v.* Roberts, 27 Mo. 388; Morton *v.* Dean, 13 Met. (Mass.) 385; Boardman *v.* Spooner, 13 Allen, 353; Freeport *v.* Bartol, 3 Greenl. (Me.) 340; Nichols *v.* Johnson, 10 Conn. 192; Abeel *v.* Radcliff, 13 Johns. 297; Ide *v.* Stanton, 15 Vt. 685; O'Donnell *v.* Leeman, 43 Me. 158; Adams *v.* McMillan, 7 Port. (Ala.) 73; Blair *v.* Snodgrass, 1 Sneed (Tenn.), 1; Boydell *v.* Drummond, 11 East, 142; Wilkinson *v.* Evans, Law Rep. 1 C. P. 407.

[2] Allen *v.* Bennet, 3 Taunt. 169; Salmon Falls Manuf. Co. *v.* Goddard, 14 How. (U. S.) 446. See, also, Bird *v.* Blossee, 2 Vent. 361; Johnson *v.* Dodgson, 2 Mees. & Wels. 653.

[3] De Beil *v.* Thomson, 3 Beav. 469; Gale *v.* Nixon, 6 Cow. (N. Y.) 445; Coles *v.* Trecothick, 9 Vesey, 234; Dodge *v.* Van Lear, 5 Cranch, C. C. 278; Western *v.* Russell, 3 Vesey & Bea. 187; Toomer *v.* Dawson, Cheves (S. C.), 68; Saunderson *v.* Jackson, 3 Esp. 180.

[4] Brodie *v.* St. Paul, 1 Vesey, Jr. 326; Boydell *v.* Drummond, 11 East, 142.

[5] Draper *v.* Pattani, 2 Spears (S. C.), 292; Schneider *v.* Norris, 2 Maule & Sel. 286; Vielie *v.* Osgood, 8 Barb. (N. Y.) 130; Saunderson *v.* Jackson, 2 Bos. & Pul. 238; Jacob *v.* Kirk, 2 Moody & Rob. 221; M'Dowell *v.* Chambers, 1 Strobh. Eq. (S. C.) 347; Geary *v.* Physic, 5 Barn. & Cres. 234; Clason *v.* Bailey, 14 Johns. 484; Pitts *v.* Beckett, 13 Mees. & Wels. 743.

[6] Williams *v.* Bacon, 2 Gray, 387; Sievewright *v.* Archibald, 17 Ad. & Ell. (N. S.) 103. As to the matters treated of in this section, see, at greater length, Browne on Frauds, ch. 17.

[7] Stearns *v.* Hall, 9 Cush. 31; Hall *v.* Soule, 11 Mich. 494; Bryan *v.* Hunt, 4 Sneed, 543; Whittier *v.* Dana, 10 Allen, 326; Cummings *v.* Arnold, 3 Met. (Mass.) 486.

about the mortgage, the following words were used: "I will take any responsibility myself respecting it, should there be any." *Held*, the defendant was not bound.[1] The court said the whole promise must appear from the writing, and proceeded: "The letter, if read by itself, without reference to any previous conversations, would be a promise to be responsible for any sum of money, however large, at any rate of interest, secured by any kind of mortgage, on any land, with any title. That, however, would be an unreasonable construction, and is not its true meaning; it evidently refers to previous conversations in which these particulars are supplied. The whole promise, therefore, is not in writing, as the statute requires that it should be." So where, under certain shipping articles of two seamen, and under the word "sureties," a party signed his name, it was held he was not liable; because, while it appeared that he was a surety, it did not appear what his agreement was, nor for what he became surety.[2] The court said: "The memorandum ought to state substantially what the undertaking of the surety is." The writing must identify, with reasonable certainty, both the contracting parties, but only the party sought to be charged need sign it.[3] Thus the defendant signed, and handed to T. the following document: "Sir, I beg to inform you that I shall see you paid the sum of 800*l*. for the ensuing building which you undertake to build for T." He intended it to be handed by T. as a guaranty to J., who was then negotiating with T. to erect for him the building referred to. T. having agreed with the plaintiff instead of J. that the plaintiff should erect the building, delivered the document to him without the defendant's knowledge or authority. The defendant afterward heard of and ratified

[1] Holmes *v.* Mitchell, 7 J. Scott (N. S.), 361, per Williams, J. Neither was defendant held liable where he signed the following document: "I will guaranty that the security offered by Mr. John Fleming for the balance of your account will be executed and forwarded within ten days." Lightbound *v.* Warnock, 4 Ont. Rep. 187.

[2] Dodge *v.* Lean, 13 Johns. 508.

[3] Champion *v.* Plummer, 1 Bos. & Pul. (N. R.) 252; Waterman *v.* Meigs, 4 Cush. 497; Jacob *v.* Kirk, 2 Moody & Rob. 221; Sherburne *v.* Shaw, 1 N. H. 157; Farwell *v.* Lowther, 18 Ill. 252; Nichols *v.* Johnson, 10 Conn. 192; Wheeler *v.* Collier, Moo. & Mal. 123; Webster *v.* Ela, 5 N. H. 540; Allen *v.* Bennet, 3 Taunt. 169; Sheid *v.* Stamps, 2 Sneed (Tenn.), 172.

this delivery. *Held*, the defendant was not liable, because the writing did not contain the name of the person for whom it was intended. The court said: "It is essential to the validity of any such agreement, or memorandum thereof, that it should contain the names of both parties to the agreement. It is true that there is no necessity that both parties should sign it. . . . But it must still contain all the essentials of an agreement, and therefore *inter alia* the names of both parties. . . . In this very case, supposing the guaranty to be valid, it might have been put into the hands of some person for whom the defendant never intended it, and an attempt might have been made on the one hand to enforce, and on the other to resist, it by parol evidence as to who was the person really intended."[1] If it appears from the writing with reasonable certainty for whom it is intended, it is sufficient. The payee of a promissory note, payable to bearer, signed the following guaranty on its back: "In consideration of . . . I hereby guaranty the payment of the within note." The court said a guaranty must indicate the person for whom it was intended, either by name, or as one of a class, and as the guaranty referred to the note, it should be read with it, and it was therefore payable to the bearer, whoever he might be, and was valid.[2] With reference to a general letter of credit, it has been said that it "is addressed to any and every person, and therefore gives to any person to whom it may be shown, authority to advance upon its credit. A privity of contract springs up between him and the drawer of the letter, and it becomes, in legal effect, the same as if addressed to him by name."[3] In such case the

[1] Williams *v.* Lake, 2 Ell. & Ell. 349, per Cockburn, C. J. As to the matters treated of in this section, see more fully, Browne on Frauds, ch. 18.

[2] Palmer *v.* Baker, 23 Up. Can. C. P. 302. To the same general effect, see Thomas *v.* Dodge, 8 Mich. 51; Nevius *v.* Bank of Lansingburgh, 10 Mich. 547.

[3] Union Bank *v.* Coster's Ex'rs, 3 N. Y. 203, per Pratt, J. And so where certain persons guarantied that they would become individually responsible for the malt and hops which their manager should purchase for the use of their brewery during the year, not to exceed $2,500, it was held that "this contract of guaranty . . . is analogous to a general letter of credit which authorizes any person to whom it is presented to act upon the proposition therein contained," and that "any person, being a dealer in malt, was authorized to act on the faith of it, and being general, addressed to no particular person, several persons in succession could well

writer of the letter is liable to the party making the advances. It has also been held that the mere fact that the name of the plaintiff appears in the writing is not sufficient, unless such name also appears from the writing to be that of the promisee, or party to whom the defendant is liable.[1] The subject-matter of the contract must appear from the writing, but it may be expressed in general terms, and parol evidence is admissible to identify it.[2]

§ 82. **Whether the consideration must appear from the writing.**— The common law required, as necessary to the validity of every contract not under seal, that it be supported by a sufficient consideration. It was just as necessary that there should be a consideration for the contract to pay the debt of another, after, as before, the passage of the Statute of Frauds.[3] The statute did not dispense with anything which was before essential to the validity of a contract; on the contrary, it added something in the case of a promise to pay the debt of another, by requiring it to be in writing, when before no writing was necessary. Under the portion of the statute now under consideration, an important question has arisen, which has been the occasion of great contrariety of decision; the question being, whether or not it is necessary that the agreement, or memorandum, or note thereof, need express the consideration for the promise as well as the promise itself. It was firmly settled by the English courts that the writing

contract in reference to it, and all be entitled to recover, provided no more be recovered in the aggregate than the amount specified in the contract." Boyd *v.* Snyder, 49 Md. 325. Holding to same effect, see Laurason *v.* Mason, 3 Cranch, 492; Russell *v.* Wiggins, 2 Story, 214; Adams *v.* Jones, 12 Pet. 207; Duval *v.* Trask, 12 Mass. 154; Birckhead *v.* Brown, 5 Hill, 634; Carnegie *v.* Morrison, 2 Met. (Mass.) 381; Lafargue *v.* Harrison, 70 Cal. 380.

[1] Bailey *v.* Ogden, 3 Johns. 399; Vanderbergh *v.* Vanderbergh, Law Rep. 1 Exch. 316.

[2] Bateman *v.* Phillips, 15 East, 272; Sale *v.* Darragh, 2 Hilton (N. Y.), 184; Hall *v.* Soule, 11 Mich. 494; Nichols *v.* Johnson, 10 Conn. 198; Atwood *v.* Cobb, 16 Pick. 227; Hurley *v.* Brown, 98 Mass. 545; McMurray *v.* Spicer, Law Rep. 5 Eq. 527; Baumann *v.* James, Law Rep. 3 Ch. App. 508; Horsey *v.* Graham, Law Rep. 5 Com. P. 9.

[3] Barrell *v.* Trussell, 4 Taunt. 117; Leonard *v.* Vredenburgh, 8 Johns. 29; Saunders *v.* Wakefield, 4 Barn. & Ald. 595; Aldridge *v.* Turner, 1 Gill & Johns. (Md.) 427; Tenny *v.* Prince, 4 Pick. 385; Pillan *v.* Van Mierop, 3 Burr. 1663; Clark *v.* Small, 6 Yerg. (Tenn.) 418. See on this subject, Kurtz *v.* Stewart, 54 Ind. 178.

must express the consideration for the promise,[1] when the Mercantile Law Amendment Act was passed.[2] Among other things this act provides that "no special promise to be made by any person after the passing of this act, to be answerable for the debt, default or miscarriage of another person, being in writing and signed by the party to be charged therewith, or by some other person by him thereunto lawfully authorized, shall be deemed invalid to support an action, suit or other proceeding to charge the person by whom such promise shall have been made, by reason only that the consideration for such promise does not appear in writing or by necessary inference from a written instrument." While the Statute of Frauds has been generally re-enacted in the United States, it has not, in all cases, been done in the words of the original statute. In those states where the original wording is retained, some have decided that the consideration must, and others that it need not, be expressed in the writing. In the states where the word "promise" has been coupled with the word "agreement," it is generally held that the writing need not express the consideration.[3] In several of the states the

1 The leading case holding this doctrine is Wain *v.* Warlters, 5 East, 10, decided in 1804. The correctness of this decision was denied by Lord Eldon in *Ex parte* Minet, 14 Vesey, 189, and *Ex parte* Gordon, 15 Vesey, 286, and was doubted in other cases. See Phillipps *v.* Bateman, 16 East, 356; Goodman *v.* Chase, 1 Barn. & Ald. 297. The question was again directly presented in Saunders *v.* Wakefield, 4 Barn. & Ald. 595, and the court unanimously held that the consideration must appear from the writing. After that decision the question was considered settled. See Jenkins *v.* Reynolds, 6 Moore, 86; Id., 3 Brod. & Bing. 14; Raikes *v.* Todd, 8 Adol. & Ell. 846; Sweet *v.* Lee, 3 Man. & Gr. 452; Morley *v.* Boothly, 3 Bing. 107; Bainbridge *v.* Wade, 16 Ad. & Ell. (N. S.) 89; Hawes *v.* Armstrong, 1 Bing. N. C. 761; James *v.* Williams, 3 Nev. & Man. 196; Cole *v.* Dyer, 1 Cro. & Jer. 461; Clancy *v.* Piggott, 4 Nev. & Man. 496.

2 19 and 20 Vict., ch. 97, sec. 3.

3 Of the states where the word "agreement" is retained, as in the original statute, it has been held that the consideration must appear from the writing. In Georgia: Henderson *v.* Johnson, 6 Ga. 390; Hargroves *v.* Cooke, 15 Ga. 321. In Indiana: Gregory *v.* Logan, 7 Blackf. 112 (since changed by statute). In Maryland: Sloan *v.* Wilson, 4 Harr. & Johns. 322; Hutton *v.* Padgett, 26 Md. 228; Elliott *v.* Giese, 7 Harr. & Johns. 457; Edelen *v.* Gough, 5 Gill, 103; Ordeman *v.* Lawson & Bro., 49 Md. 135; Culbertson *v.* Smith, 52 Md. 628; Emerson *v.* Aultman & Co., 69 Md. 125. In Michigan: Jones *v.* Palmer, 1 Doug. 379. In New Hampshire: Underwood *v.* Campbell, 14 N. H. 393; Neelson *v.* Sanborn, 2 N. H. 413. In New Jersey: Buckley

statute provides in terms whether or not the consideration shall be expressed in the writing. It would probably subserve no useful purpose to attempt a review of the American cases, with reference to ascertaining on which side of this question the preponderance of authority lies. It may be here remarked that when the writing is under seal, no consideration need be expressed in it. The seal itself imports a consideration, and is sufficient to satisfy the statute.[1]

§ 83. **Reasons why the consideration should appear from the writing — Observations.**— One of the reasons given for holding that the consideration must appear from the writing is that, according to its strict legal meaning, the word "agreement" includes the whole contract between the parties, and, among other things, the consideration as well as the promise; and that the words "memorandum or note thereof" relate to the word "agreement," and were intended to, and do, dispense with nothing, unless, perhaps, matters of form. This seems to be a solid ground upon which to rest this interpretation of the statute. As already seen, it is generally held by the courts,

v. Beardslee, 2 South. 572; Laing *v.* Lee, Spencer, 337. In New York: Sears *v.* Brink, 3 Johns. 210; Kerr *v.* Shaw, 13 Johns. 236; Castle *v.* Beardsley, 10 Hun, 343. In South Carolina: Stephens *v.* Winn, 2 Nott & McC. 372. But see Lecat *v.* Tavel, 3 McCord, 158. And in Wisconsin: Taylor *v.* Pratt, 3 Wis. 674; Parry *v.* Spikes, 49 Wis. 384. On the other hand, it has been held that the consideration need not appear from the writing. In Connecticut: Sage *v.* Wilcox, 6 Conn. 81. In Maine: Levy *v.* Merrill, 4 Greenl. 180; Gilligan *v.* Boardman, 29 Me. 81. In Massachusetts: Packard *v.* Richardson, 17 Mass. 122 (since changed by statute). In Missouri: Bean *v.* Valle, 2 Mo. 103; Halsa *v.* Halsa, 8 Mo. 303; Little *v.* Nabb, 10 Mo. 3. In North Carolina: Miller *v.* Irvine, 1 Dev. & Bat. 103; Ashford *v.* Robinson, 8 Ired. 114. In Ohio: Reed *v.* Evans, 17 Ohio, 128. And in Vermont: Smith *v.* Ide, 3 Vt. 290; Patchin *v.* Swift, 21 Vt. 292; Gregory *v.* Gleed, 33 Vt. 405. Where the word "promise" is coupled with the word "agreement," it has been held that the consideration need not be expressed. In Alabama: Thompson *v.* Hall, 16 Ala. 204. In California: Baker *v.* Cornwall, 4 Cal. 15; Evoy *v.* Tewksbury, 5 Cal. 285; Ellison *v.* Jackson, 12 Cal. 542. In Florida: Dorman *v.* Executor of Richard, 1 Fla. 281. In Kentucky: Ratliff *v.* Trout, 6 J. J. Marsh. 606. In Mississippi: Wren *v.* Pearce, 4 Smedes & Mar. 91. In Tennessee: Taylor *v.* Ross, 3 Yerg. 330; Campbell *v.* Findley, 3 Humph. 330; Gilman *v.* Kibler, 5 Humph. 19. In Texas: Ellett *v.* Britton, 10 Tex. 208. And in Virginia: Colgin *v.* Henley, 6 Leigh, 85.

[1] Douglass *v.* Howland, 24 Wend. 35; Rosenbaum *v.* Gunter, 2 E. D. Smith (N. Y.), 415; McKensie *v.* Farrell, 4 Bosw. (N. Y.) 192.

even those which hold that the consideration need not be expressed, that all the other essential terms of the contract must appear from the writing. The consideration is not strictly a part of the promise of the party to be charged, but is something which moves from others, and is the inducement to him for making the promise. The consideration is, however, a part of the contract, and if the word "agreement" means the same as the word "contract," then the original Statute of Frauds required that it should appear from the writing. Another reason, much relied upon, is that if the consideration was allowed to be proved by parol, it would open the door to all the evils which the Statute of Frauds was designed to remedy. This is not true in point of fact. The agreement is in words; the consideration is usually something material, which is more susceptible of proof, and less liable to mistake, than the words of the contract. There seems to be no more danger of perjury in allowing the consideration for the promise to pay the debt of another to be proved by parol, than allowing the consideration for any other contract to be proved in the same way. The same objection would exclude oral evidence from every case. The rule that the consideration must appear from the writing was a great hardship on the commercial world, and produced much more fraud than it prevented. Recognizing this fact, the English parliament, and the legislatures of several of the United States, have expressly provided by statute that the written promise to pay the debt of another need not express the consideration, and the results, so far from being disastrous, have proved highly satisfactory.

§ 84. **When the consideration sufficiently appears from the writing.**— In the courts holding that the consideration must appear from the writing, it is not necessary that such consideration be formally and precisely expressed. It is sufficient if it appear by necessary implication from the terms of the written instrument. The rule is thus well expressed: "It would undoubtedly be sufficient, in any case, if the memorandum is so framed that any person of ordinary capacity must infer from the perusal of it that such, and no other, was the consideration upon which the undertaking was given. Not that a mere conjecture, however plausible, that the consideration stated in the declaration was that intended by the memorandum, would be sufficient to satisfy the statute; but there must be a well-grounded inference, to be necessarily collected from the terms of the memorandum, that the consideration stated in the declaration, and no other consideration, was intended by the parties as the ground of the promise.[1] A guaranty was as follows: "I guaranty the payment of any goods which J. Stadt delivers to J. Nichols." *Held*, it sufficiently appeared that the delivery of the goods was the consideration for the promise.[2] The same thing was held when the words were as follows: "Sir, I will be accountable to you for the payment, within six months, of the seed order forwarded by my son" (naming him).[3] The same thing was held when the guaranty was in these words: "Mr. Clark, of this place, will purchase a small stock of cloths and clothing of you, which I hope you will sell to him cheap, and I have no doubt he will make you a valuable customer. I hereby guaranty the collection of any amount which you may credit him with not exceeding $2,000."[4] In another case the writing was as follows: "I do hereby agree to become surety for R. G., now your traveler, in the sum of £500 for all money he may receive on your account." *Held*, it sufficiently appeared that the consideration for the undertaking was the continuation of the traveler in the service of

[1] Hawes *v.* Armstrong, 1 Bing. N. C. 761, per Tindal, C. J. For cases in which it was held that the consideration sufficiently appeared from the writing, and which illustrate this subject, see Grant *v.* Hotchkiss, 26 Barb. (N. Y.) 63; Boehm *v.* Campbell, 8 Taunt. 679; Shortrede *v.* Cheek, 1 Adol. & Ell. 57; Gorrie *v.* Woodley, 17 Irish Com. Law Rep. 221; Bainbridge *v.* Wade, 16 Adol. & Ell. (N. S.) 89; Hoad *v.* Grace, 7 Hurl. & Nor. 494; Lysaght *v.* Walker, 5 Bligh (N. R.), 1; Id., 2 Dow & Clark, 211; Broom *v.* Batchelor, 1 Hurl. & Nor. 255; Oldershaw *v.* King, 2 Hurl. & Nor. 517; Staats *v.* Howlett, 4 Denio, 559; Boehm *v.* Campbell, 3 Moore, 15; Jarvis *v.* Wilkins, 7 Mees. & Wels. 410; White *v.* Woodward, 5 Man., Gr. & Scott, 810; Caballero *v.* Slater, 14 Com. B. (5 J. Scott) 300; Edwards *v.* Jevons, 8 Man., Gr. & Scott, 436; Pace *v.* Marsh, 1 Bing. 216; Id., 8 Moore, 59; Johnston *v.* Nicholls, 1 Man., Gr. & Scott, 251; Church *v.* Brown, 21 N. Y. 315; Williams *v.* Ketchum, 19 Wis. 231; Stead *v.* Liddard, 8 Moore, 2; Russell *v.* Moseley, 3 Brod. & Bing. 211; Dutchman *v.* Tooth, 5 Bing. N. C. 577; Id., 7 Scott, 710; Emmott *v.* Kearns, 5 Bing. N. C. 559; Gottsberger *v.* Radway, 2 Hilton (N. Y.), 342.

[2] Stadt *v.* Lill, 9 East, 348.

[3] Nash *v.* Hartland, 2 Irish Law Rep. 190.

[4] Eastman *v.* Bennett, 6 Wis. 232, followed and approved in Young *v.* Brown, 53 Wis. 333.

his employers.[1] The same thing was held for the same reason when the words were: "I hereby guaranty to you the sum of £250 in case Mr. P. should make default in the capacity of agent and traveler to you."[2] Where the writing was: "I hold myself responsible to . . . (plaintiffs) to the amount of $2,000, for any drafts they have accepted or may hereafter accept for John Latouche," it was held that it sufficiently appeared that, in consideration that the plaintiffs would accept for Latouche, the defendant agreed to be responsible.[3] In another case the words were: "I agree to be security to you for J. C., late in the employ of J. P., for whatever you may intrust him with while in your employ, to the amount of £50." *Held*, the consideration sufficiently appeared. It might fairly be implied that J. C. had left one service, and that the guaranty was given in consideration of his being taken into another.[4] The insertion of the words "for value received," in the writing, are a sufficient expression of the consideration to satisfy the statute.[5] When a guaranty under seal expressed a consideration of one dollar in hand paid to the guarantor, it was held that the guaranty was valid and binding, even though the dollar had never been paid. The court said that, in order to invalidate the guaranty, it must be shown, not only that the dollar had not been paid, but also that there was no agreement to pay it.[6]

§ 85. **When consideration does not sufficiently appear, or, consideration appearing, is insufficient — Instances.**— In a case where the writing was as follows: "Inclosed I forward you the bills drawn per J. A. upon and accepted by L. D., which I

[1] Ryde *v.* Curtis, 8 Dow. & Ry. 62.

[2] Kennaway *v.* Treleavan, 5 Mees. & Wels. 498.

[3] Hutton *v.* Padgett, 26 Md. 228.

[4] Newbury *v.* Armstrong, 6 Bing. 201; Id., 3 Moore & Payne, 509; Id., Moody & Malkin, 389.

[5] Day *v.* Elmore, 4 Wis. 190; Mosher *v.* Hotchkiss, 3 Abb. Rep. Omitted Cas. (N. Y.) 326; Id., 2 Keyes, 589; Cheeney *v.* Cook, 7 Wis. 413; Miller *v.* Cook, 23 N. Y. 495; Douglass *v.* Howland, 24 Wend. 35; Whitney *v.* Stearns, 16 Me. 394; Cooper *v.* Dedrick, 22 Barb. (N. Y.) 516; Howard *v.* Holbrook, 9 Bosw. (N. Y.) 237; Lapham *v.* Barrett, 1 Vt. 247; Connecticut, etc. Ins. Co. *v.* Cleveland R. R. Co., 41 Barb. (N. Y.) 9; Brewster *v.* Silence, 8 N. Y. 207; Martin *v.* Hazard Powder Co., 2 Col. 596; Osborne & Co. *v.* Baker, 34 Minn. 307; Dahlman *v.* Hammel, 45 Wis. 466.

[6] Childs *v.* Barnum, 11 Barb. (N. Y.) 14. It has been held that if the consideration expressed was a fictitious one, it was sufficient. Happe *v.* Stout, 2 Cal. 460.

doubt not will meet due honor, but in default thereof, I will see the same paid," it was held the consideration did not sufficiently appear.[1] The same thing was held when the words were: "I hereby guaranty to pay W. H., etc., $10 per month until the sum of $300, due by Messrs. B. & H., etc., shall be paid."[2] When the undertaking was: "I hereby undertake to secure to you the payment of any sums of money you have advanced or may hereafter advance to . . . or on their account with you, commencing the 1st November, 1831, not exceeding 2,000*l*.," it was held that the consideration for the guaranty of the past advances did not sufficiently appear. The court said: "The consideration must either appear on the face of them (guaranties) or by necessary inference from them, for unless this is the case parol evidence is not excluded. The terms of the instrument do not lead to any clear inference that the future advances were, as the declaration alleges, the consideration for guarantying the bygone advances."[3] A guaranty was: "Bill Oct. 2d, 1844, $1,306.29. I hereby agree to guaranty the payment of U. & Co.'s note for the above amount, in favor of . . . payable nine mos. after date thereof." *Held*, it plainly expressed a past consideration, and was void for that reason.[4]

[1] Hawes *v.* Armstrong, 1 Bing. N. C. 761; Id., 1 Scott, 661.

[2] Palsgrave *v.* Murphy, 14 Up. Can. C. P. 153. So a guaranty upon a separate piece of paper from a note to which is said to refer, in the following language, to wit: "We guaranty the payment of a note indorsed by . . . the amount being five hundred dollars, date of note April 19th, 1875," was held void for want of a sufficient consideration appearing on its face. Ordeman *v.* Lawson & Bro., 49 Md. 135.

[3] Raikes *v.* Todd, 1 Perry & Dav. 138; Id., 8 Adol. & Ell. 846.

[4] Weed *v.* Clark, 4 Sandf. (N. Y. Sup. Ct.) 31. For cases holding that the consideration is not sufficiently expressed, or that an insufficient consideration is expressed, and illustrating this point, see Morley *v.* Boothby, 3 Bing. 107; Id., 10 Moore, 395; James *v.* Williams, 5 Barn. & Adol. 1109; Church *v.* Brown, 29 Barb. (N. Y.) 486; Bushell *v.* Beavan, 1 Bing. N. C. 103; Allnutt *v.* Ashenden, 5 Man. & Gr. 392; Id., 6 Scott (N. R.), 127; Spicer *v.* Norton, 13 Barb. (N. Y.) 542; Bell *v.* Welch, 9 Man., Gr. & Scott, 154; Bewley *v.* Whiteford, Hayes (Irish Rep.), 356; Wain *v.* Warlters, 5 East, 10; Lees *v.* Whitcomb, 5 Bing. 34; James *v.* Williams, 3 Nev. & Man. 196; Sykes *v.* Dixon, 9 Adol. & Ell. 693; Bentham *v.* Cooper, 5 Mees. & Wels. 621; Price *v.* Richardson, 15 Mees. & Wels. 539; Cole *v.* Dyer, 1 Cromp. & Jer. 461; Jenkins *v.* Reynolds, 3 Brod. & Bing. 14.

§ 86. When writing ambiguous, it may be explained by parol evidence.—When the words of the writing are ambiguous, and may be construed to express a past or a future consideration, parol evidence of the situation and surroundings of the parties at the time the contract was made may be given, in order to arrive at a true interpretation of the language employed by them. Thus a writing was: "As there was no time set for the payment of your account, and Mr. J. thought it would be an accommodation to him to have you wait until . . . if that will answer your purpose, I will be surety for the payment," etc. *Held*, the words "your account" were ambiguous, and might as well mean your "account to be made," as "your account already made;" that parol evidence was admissible to show it was for an account to be made, and that the writing sufficiently expressed the consideration.[1] So, where the words were: "In consideration of E. R. & Co. giving credit to D. G., I hereby engage to be responsible to, and pay any sum not exceeding 120*l.* due to E. R. & Co. by D. J.," parol evidence of extrinsic circumstances was admitted to show that the words, "giving credit," were intended to apply to a certain credit which had been agreed upon, and it was held that the writing disclosed a sufficient consideration.[2] When the words were: "In consideration of your being in advance" to the third party, parol evidence was admitted to show that at the time the writing was executed, no advance had been made.[3] The same thing was held when the words were: "In consideration of your having advanced,"[4] and in both cases the consideration was held to be sufficiently expressed. Where the words were: "I hereby guaranty B.'s account with A.," and it was shown by parol that there was a pre-existing account to which the words could apply, it was held that the guaranty was void for want of a sufficient consideration.[5]

[1] Walrath *v.* Thompson, 4 Hill, 200.

[2] Edwards *v.* Jevons, 8 Man., Gr. & Scott, 436.

[3] Haigh *v.* Brooks, 10 Adol. & Ell. 309.

[4] Goldshede *v.* Swan, 1 Wels., Hurl. & Gor. 154.

[5] Allnut *v.* Ashenden, 5 Man. & G. 392. For cases further illustrating this subject, see Butcher *v.* Steuart, 11 Mees. & Wels. 857; Lysaght *v.* Walker, 5 Bligh (N. R.), 1; Singley *v.* Cutter, 7 Conn. 291; Shortrede *v.* Cheek, 1 Adol. & Ell. 57; Arms *v.*

§ 87. When several papers may be read together to express consideration for promise.— It is not necessary that the consideration should be expressed in the writing which contains the promise. If it appears from any other writing which is so referred to in that which contains the promise as to become a part of it, this is sufficient. Thus, the plaintiff having pressed W. for payment of a debt, the defendant, who was W.'s attorney, sent to the plaintiff a bill accepted by W., at two months, inclosed in a letter in which the defendant said: "W., being disappointed in receiving remittances, and you expressing yourself inconvenienced for money, I send you his acceptance at two months." The plaintiffs refused to take the bill unless the defendant put his name to it. Whereupon the defendant wrote upon the back of the letter: "I will see this bill paid for W." The court said that, reading all the papers together, the promise was that, "in consideration of your forbearing to sue W. for two months, I will pay the bill if he fails to do so," and the defendant was held liable.[1] Certain parties executed a contract as agents for another, and at the same time executed a guaranty of the contract, but the guaranty did not express a consideration. *Held*, that the guaranty and contract, being contemporaneous, were all one transaction, and should be read together; and a sufficient consideration was expressed in the contract to sustain the guaranty.[2] A., by letter, in which the consideration sufficiently appeared, entered into an agreement with B., and B. became a party to the engagement by writing a few lines at the bottom of a copy of A.'s letter. C. became guarantor for B. to A. by an indorsement on the back of this copy of A.'s letter, in which indorsement reference was made to the terms of the agreement on the other side. In an action on the guaranty it was held that the reference in the indorsement to the terms of the agreement was a sufficient memorandum of the consideration to satisfy the Statute of Frauds.[3] But where a valid written

Ashley, 4 Pick. 71; Thornton *v.* Jenyns, 1 Man. & Gr. 166; Wood *v.* Beach, 7 Vt. 522; Steele *v.* Hoe, 14 Adol. & Ell. (N. S.) 431; Smith *v.* Ide, 3 Vt. 290; Bainbridge *v.* Wade, 16 Adol. & Ell. (N. S.) 89; D'Wolf *v.* Raband, 1 Pet. 476; Singer Mfg. Co., *v.* Forsyth *et al.*, 108 Ind. 334.

[1] Emmott *v.* Kearns, 5 Bing. N. C. 559; Id., 7 Scott, 687.

[2] Jones *v.* Post. 6 Cal. 102.

[3] Stead *v.* Liddard, 1 Bing. 196. So

contract to pay for stock deliverable at a future day was signed by the buyer, and at the same time, and as an express condition of the seller's making the bargain, the defendant indorsed on the same paper: "I guaranty the within contract," the guaranty was held void because it did not express a consideration. The court said the contracts could not be read together because they were not executed by the same parties. The one was a promise to pay absolutely, the other only in case of the default of the principal, etc.[1]

§ 88. **Whether guaranty of note, judgment, certificate of deposit, or assigned mortgage must express consideration.**— Whether the guaranty of a promissory note must, in order to be valid, express a consideration, has been differently decided by different courts, and sometimes by the same court. Thus, at the time a note was made, and on the same piece of paper, a guarantor wrote under the note: "I hereby guaranty the payment of the above note." *Held*, the guaranty was void, because it expressed no consideration.[2] The court said the two contracts were entirely different in their nature, and between dif-

where a contract of guaranty is entered into contemporaneously with the principal contract which is a written lease, and is either incorporated in the latter, or so distinctly refers to it as to show that both agreements are parts of an entire transaction, the statute does not require a consideration to be expressed in the guaranty distinct from that expressed in the principal contract. Highland *v.* Dresser, 35 Minn. 345. For further cases to similar effect, see Simons *v.* Steele, 36 N. H. 73; Wilson Sewing Machine Co. *v.* Schnell, 20 Minn. 40; Coldham *v.* Showler, 3 Man., Gr. & Scott, 312; Hanford *v.* Rogers, 11 Barb. (N. Y.) 18; Adams *v.* Bean, 12 Mass. 139; Brettel *v.* Williams, 4 Wels., Hurl. & Gor. 623; Bailey *v.* Freeman, 11 Johns. 221; Coe *v.* Duffield, 7 Moore, 252; Lecat *v.* Tavel, 3 McCord (S. C.), 158; Union Bank *v.* Coster's Ex'r, 3 N. Y. 203; Dorman *v.* Bigelow, 1 Fla. 281; Colbourn *v.* Dawson, 10 Com. B. (1 J. Scott) 765; Roberts *et al. v.* Woven Wire Mattress Co., 46 Md. 374.

[1] Draper *v.* Snow, 20 N. Y. 331. To similar effect, see Hutson *v.* Field, 6 Wis. 407; Otis *v.* Haseltine, 27 Cal. 80.

[2] Brewster *v.* Silence, 8 N. Y. 207. This case overruled Manrow *v.* Durham, 3 Hill, 584, which held to the contrary. Brewster *v.* Silence was followed and approved in Glen Cove Mut. Ins. Co. *v.* Harrold, 20 Barb. (N. Y.) 298. To similar effect, see Hunt *v.* Brown, 5 Hill, 145; Hall *v.* Farmer, 5 Denio, 484. In Anderson *v.* Norvill, 10 Brad. (Ill. App.) 240, and Osborne & Co. *v.* Lawson *et al.*, 26 Mo. App. 549, it is held that a guaranty of the payment of a note is an independent contract and therefore must be supported by an independent consideration. As to the sufficiency of the consideration, see Anderson *v.* Norvill, and Osborne *v.* Lawson, *supra*.

ferent parties, and could not be read together. A party agreed to become surety on an overdue promissory note, under seal, and because there was no room at the bottom of the note for his signature, indorsed his name in blank on its back. He was held not liable.[1] The court said: "The indorsement in blank of a note not negotiable is not such written evidence of a promise to pay as the Statute [of Frauds] requires." A guaranty indorsed on a promissory note at the time of its execution, as follows: "We guaranty the payment of the within note," was held void, because it did not express a consideration.[2] Where a stranger to a note before its delivery indorsed it in blank, it was held that he was a guarantor, and his guaranty was void, because it did not express a consideration.[3] On the other hand, when a party was paid a money consideration for guarantying a note already executed by the principals, and in execution of his contract to guaranty indorsed his name in blank on the back of the note, it was held that it sufficiently expressed the consideration.[4] The court said that under the circumstances a guaranty of a note might have properly been written over the indorsement, and further: "It is in the nature of a note or bill, and equally so of an indorsement, even in blank, that it imports a consideration the same as a specialty." Where a party indorsed a promissory note as follows: "I agree to stand security for the payment of the within amount," it was held that the note and indorsement should be taken together as one instrument, and that they sufficiently expressed the consideration.[5] A married woman executed a promissory note, which contained the words "for value received," and at the same time a stranger wrote below the note, "I hereby guaranty the payment of the above note on maturity." The court said that both instruments, having been executed at the same time, should be considered together, and showed a sufficient consideration; but it would have been otherwise if they had been executed at different times.[6] Where a guaranty is made contemporaneously with a

[1] Wilson *v.* Martin, 74 Pa. St. 159.

[2] Lock *v.* Reid, 6 Up. Can. Q. B. (O. S.) 295.

[3] Van Doren *v.* Tjader, 1 Nev. 380.

[4] Oakley *v.* Boorman, 21 Wend. 588. This case was subsequently disapproved by the same court. See Brewster *v.* Silence, 8 N. Y. 207. To same effect as Oakley *v.* Boorman, see Fuller *v.* Scott, 8 Kan. 25.

[5] Dorman *v.* Bigelow, 1 Fla. 281.

[6] Nabb *v.* Koontz, 17 Md. 283.

certificate of deposit, on which it is indorsed, it is unnecessary that there should be a separate and distinct consideration to uphold the guaranty. The consideration upon which the certificate of deposit is executed is sufficient to sustain the guaranty.[1] Where a mortgagee assigned a bond and mortgage, and into the assignment was incorporated a guaranty of the mortgage "by due foreclosure and sale," it was held that inasmuch as the guaranty was not essential to the assignment, and was, so far as its legal effect was concerned, a separate instrument, it was not supported by a sufficient consideration, and was void.[2] Where a person assigned a judgment for the purpose of raising money thereon, and guarantied its payment, *held*, the object of the guarantor being to subserve a purpose of his own and not to answer for the default of another, was not within the statute and need not express a consideration.[3]

§ 89. **Signature by party to be charged.**— The statute requires that the writing shall be "signed by the party to be charged therewith, or some other person thereunto by him lawfully authorized." Even though the document is all written by the party to be charged, it must still be signed by him,[4] but need not be sealed.[5] Whether sealing alone is sufficient is an open question, but the better opinion seems to be that it is.[6] A mark by a marksman is a sufficient signature.[7] A printed signature is sufficient, especially when it is subsequently recognized by the party, or where part of the instru-

[1] Jones & Bro. *v.* Kuhn, 34 Kan. 414.

[2] Vanderbilt *v.* Schreyer, 91 N. Y. 392, reversing 21 Hun, 537.

[3] Little *v.* Edwards, 69 Md. 499.

[4] Hawkins *v.* Holmes, 1 P. Wms. 770; Barry *v.* Law, 1 Cranch (C. C.), 77; Selby *v.* Selby, 3 Meriv. 2; Bailey *v.* Ogden, 3 Johns. 399; Hubert *v.* Turner, 4 Scott (N. R.), 486; Anderson *v.* Harold, 10 Ohio, 399.

[5] Worrall *v.* Munn, 5 N. Y. 229; Farris *v.* Martin, 10 Humph. (Tenn.) 495; Wheeler *v.* Newton, 2 Eq. Cas. 44, ch. 5.

[6] Lemayne *v.* Stanley, 3 Levinz, 1; Worneford *v.* Worneford, Strange, 764; Gryle *v.* Gryle, 2 Atkyns, 177; Grayson *v.* Atkinson, 2 Ves. Sr. 454; Smith *v.* Evans, 1 Wils. 313; Wright *v.* Wakeford, 17 Vesey, 454; Cherry *v.* Heming, 4 Wels., Hurl. & Gor. 631.

[7] Selby *v.* Selby, 3 Meriv. 2; Jackson *v.* Van Dusen, 5 Johns. 144; Hubert *v.* Moreau, 12 Moore, 216; Schneider *v.* Norris, 2 Maule & Sel. 286; Baker *v.* Dering, 8 Adol. & Ell. 94; Taylor *v.* Dening, 3 Nev. & Per. 228; Morris *v.* Kniffin, 37 Barb. (N. Y.) 336; Barnard *v.* Heydrick, 49 Barb. (N. Y.) 62.

ment is in his handwriting.[1] A signature by initials is sufficient,[2] and the christian name may be denoted by an initial or left out altogether.[3] It is doubtful whether the signature of a person mentioned in the writing as a contracting party, but who on the paper professes to sign as a witness, is sufficient.[4] The signature of a party to instructions for a telegraphic message accepting a written offer is sufficient.[5] The signature may be at the top, in the body or at the foot of the writing. There is no restriction in this regard, except that the signature must be so placed as to authenticate the instrument as the act of the person executing it.[6] The rule has been thus well stated: "Although the signature be in the beginning or middle of the instrument, it is as binding as if at the foot of it; the question being always open to the jury, whether the party, not having signed it regularly at the foot, meant to be bound by it as it then stood, or whether he left it so unsigned because he refused to complete it."[7] The statute provides that the writing shall be signed by the "party to be charged therewith." If it

[1] Saunderson *v.* Jackson, 3 Esp. 180; Lerned *v.* Wannemacher, 9 Allen, 412; Schneider *v.* Norris, 2 Maule & Sel. 286; Merritt *v.* Clason, 12 Johns. 102; Commonwealth *v.* Ray, 3 Gray, 441; Vielie *v.* Osgood, 8 Barb. (N. Y.) 130; Davis *v.* Shields, 26 Wend. 341; Pitts *v.* Beckett, 13 Mees. & Wels. 743.

[2] Salmon Falls Man. Co. *v.* Goddard, 14 How. (U. S.) 447; Gorrie *v.* Woodley, 17 Irish Com. Law R. 221; Palmer *v.* Stephens, 1 Denio, 471; Jacob *v.* Kirk, 2 Moody & Rob. 221; Sanborn *v.* Flagler, 9 Allen, 474; Sweet *v.* Lee, 3 Man. & Gr. 452.

[3] Lobb *v.* Stanley, 5 Q. B. 574.

[4] Welford *v.* Beezeley, 1 Ves. Sr. 6; Gosbell *v.* Archer, 2 Adol. & Ell. 500; Blore *v.* Sutton, 3 Meriv. 237; Coles *v.* Trecothick, 9 Vesey, 234; Hill *v.* Johnston, 3 Ired. Eq. (N. C.) 432.

[5] Godwin *v.* Francis, Law Rep. 5 Com. P. 295; Dunning *v.* Roberts, 35 Barb. (N. Y.) 463. As to whether the name of the party must actually appear, or whether a designation by which he may be identified is sufficient, see Selby *v.* Selby, 3 Meriv. 2; Hubert *v.* Moreau, 12 Moore, 216; Baker *v.* Dering. 8 Adol. & Ell. 94.

[6] Lemayne *v.* Stanley, 3 Levinz, 1; Id., Freeman, 538; Fessenden *v.* Mussey, 11 Cush. 127; Holmes *v.* Mackrell, 3 Com. B. (N. S.) 789; Wise *v.* Ray, 3 Greene (Iowa), 430; Knight *v.* Crockford, 1 Esp. 190; McConnell *v.* Brillhart, 17 Ill. 354; Ogilvie *v.* Foljambe, 3 Meriv. 53; James *v.* Patten, 8 Barb. (N. Y.) 344; Morrison *v.* Turnour, 18 Vesey, 175; Yerby *v.* Grigsby, 9 Leigh (Va.), 387; Bleakley *v.* Smith, 11 Simons, 150; Davis *v.* Shields, 24 Wend. 322; Propert *v.* Parker, 1 Russ. & My. 625; Draper *v.* Pattani, 2 Spear (S. C.), 292; Western *v.* Russell, 3 Ves. & Bea. 187; Merritt *v.* Clason, 12 Johns. 102; Penniman *v.* Hartshorn, 13 Mass. 87; Williams *v.* Wood, 16 Md. 220; Hawkins *v.* Chace, 19 Pick. 502; 2 Smith's Lead. Cas. 249.

[7] Johnson *v.* Dodgson, 2 Mees. &

is signed by the party to be charged, it is not necessary that it be signed by the other party to the contract, although, as already shown, such other party must be designated by it.[1]

§ 90. **Signature by agent.**— The writing may be signed by the party to be charged, or by "some other person thereunto by him lawfully authorized." Generally, any one who may be an agent for any other purpose may be an agent for signing the writing required by the statute, but neither party can be the agent of the other for this purpose.[2] The same person may act as the agent of both parties. This is illustrated by the familiar case of an auctioneer, who, being the agent of the owner of property, sells it to the highest bidder. He thereupon becomes the agent of such bidder to complete the contract, and, by entering his name in the usual place as purchaser, binds him as such.[3] The same is true of public officers, who sell property at auction, such as sheriffs and deputy-sheriffs,[4]

Wels. 653, per Lord Abinger, C. B.; Saunderson *v.* Jackson, 2 Bos. & Pul. 238.

[1] Reuss *v.* Picksley, Law Rep. 1 Exch. 342; Clason *v.* Bailey, 14 Johns. 484; Laythoarp *v.* Bryant, 2 Bing. N. C. 755; Morin *v.* Martz, 13 Minn. 191; Huddleston *v.* Briscoe, 11 Vesey, 583; McCrea *v.* Purmont, 16 Wend. 460; Martin *v.* Mitchell, 2 Jacob & Walk. 413; Douglass *v.* Spears, 2 Nott & McC. (S. C.) 207; Hatton *v.* Gray, 2 Ch. Cas. 164; Barstow *v.* Gay, 3 Greenl. (Me.) 409; Seton *v.* Slade, 7 Vesey, 265; Shirley *v.* Shirley, 7 Blackf. (Ind.) 452; Fowle *v.* Freeman, 9 Vesey, 351; Allen *v.* Bennett, 3 Taunt. 169; Penniman *v.* Hartshorn, 13 Mass. 87.

[2] Wright *v.* Dannah, 2 Camp. 203; Rayner *v.* Linthorne, 2 Car. & P. 124; Sharman *v.* Brandt, 40 Law Jour. (N. S.) 312; Farebrother *v.* Simmons, 5 Barn. & Ald. 333; Boardman *v.* Spooner, 13 Allen, 353; Robinson *v.* Garth, 6 Ala. 204; Bent *v.* Cobb, 9 Gray, 397. See, also, on this subject, Bird *v.* Boulter, 4 Barn. & Adol. 443; Ennis *v.* Waller, 3 Blackf. (Ind.) 472; Brant *v.* Green, 6 Leigh (Va.), 16.

[3] Morton *v.* Dean, 13 Met. (Mass.) 385; Kenworthy *v.* Schofield, 2 Barn. & Cress. 945; McComb *v.* Wright, 4 Johns. Ch. 659; White *v.* Proctor, 4 Taunt. 209; Gill *v.* Bicknell, 2 Cush. 355; Simon *v.* Motivos, 1 W. Black. 599; Id., 3 Burr. 1921; Cleaves *v.* Foss, 4 Greenl. (Me.) 1; Hinde *v.* Whitehouse, 7 East, 558; Anderson *v.* Chick, Bailey, Ch. (S. C.) 118; Emmerson *v.* Heelis, 2 Taunt. 38; Endicott *v.* Penny, 14 Sm. & Mar. (Miss.) 144; Walker *v.* Constable, 1 Bos. & Pul. 306; Gordon *v.* Sims, 2 McCord, Ch. (S. C.) 151; Coles *v.* Trecothick, 9 Vesey, 234; Singstack *v.* Harding, 4 Harr. & Johns. 186; Buckmaster *v.* Harrop, 7 Vesey, 341; Smith *v.* Jones, 5 Leigh (Va.), 165; Stansfield *v.* Johnson, 1 Esp. 101; Adams *v.* McMillan, 7 Port. (Ala.) 73; Blagden *v.* Bradbear, 12 Vesey, 466; Browne on Frauds, p. 386.

[4] Robinson *v.* Garth, 6 Ala. 204; Christie *v.* Simpson, 1 Rich. Law (S. C.), 401; Ennis *v.* Waller, 3 Blackf.

administrators,[1] commissioners of court,[2] etc. The authority of the agent may be conferred in the same manner as the authority of any other agent, and even if he have no authority when he sign, his act may be afterwards ratified by the principal by parol.[3] It is not necessary that the agent who signs should be appointed by writing,[4] unless the writing he executes is under seal, when his authority must also be under seal.[5] It is not necessary that the agent should sign the name of the principal to the writing. If he signs his own name, parol evidence will be admitted to prove the agency and charge the principal.[6] Where a person's name has been signed to a note as surety without authority, a subsequent promise to pay the note is not binding.[7]

§ **91. Pleading.**— In a declaration in a suit against a surety or guarantor, it is not necessary to state that the promise was in writing.[8] This is founded on the general principle that

(Ind.) 472; Carrington *v.* Anderson, 5 Munf. (Va.) 32; Brant *v.* Green, 6 Leigh (Va.), 16.

1 Smith *v.* Arnold, 5 Mason (C. C.), 414.

2 Gordon *v.* Sims, 2 McCord, Ch. (S. C.) 151; Hutton *v.* Williams, 35 Ala. 503; Hart *v.* Woods, 7 Blackf. (Ind.) 568. But the power of an auctioneer, in this regard, is confined to those who act in that capacity. See Anderson *v.* Chick, Bailey, Eq. (S. C.) 118; Batturs *v.* Sellers, 5 Harr. & Johns. (Md.) 117; Sewall *v.* Fitch, 8 Cowen, 215.

3 Gosbell *v.* Archer, 2 Adol. & Ell. 500; Holland *v.* Hoyt, 14 Mich. 238; Maclean *v.* Dunn, 4 Bing. 722. *Contra*, Ragan *v.* Chenault, 78 Ky. 545. But a subsequent ratification in writing is valid. Riggan *v.* Crain, 86 Ky. 249.

4 Mortlock *v.* Buller, 10 Vesey, 292; Inhabitants of Alna *v.* Plummer, 4 Greenl. (Me.) 258; Rucker *v.* Cammeyer, 1 Esp. 105; McWhorter *v.* McMahan, 10 Paige, 386; Wright *v.* Dannah, 2 Camp. 203; Lawrence *v.* Taylor, 5 Hill, 107; Greene *v.* Cramer, 2 Connor & Law. 54; Hawkins *v.* Chace, 19 Pick. 502; Clinan *v.* Cook, 1 Schoales & Lef. 22; Ulen *v.* Kittredge, 7 Mass. 233; Graham *v.* Musson, 7 Scott, 769; Yerby *v.* Grigsby, 9 Leigh (Va.), 387; Coleman *v.* Bailey, 4 Bibb (Ky.), 297; Johnson *v.* McGruder, 15 Mo. 365; Johnson *v.* Dodge, 17 Ill. 433.

5 Blood *v.* Hardy, 15 Me. 61.

6 Wilson *v.* Hart, 7 Taunt. 295; Dykers *v.* Townsend, 24 N. Y. 57; Salmon Falls Ins. Co. *v.* Goddard, 14 How. (U. S.) 447; Curtis *v.* Blair, 26 Miss. 309; Yerby *v.* Grigsby, 9 Leigh (Va.), 387; Williams *v.* Woods, 16 Md. 220; Merritt *v.* Clason, 12 Johns. 102: McConnell *v.* Brillhart, 17 Ill. 354; Williams *v.* Bacon, 2 Gray, 387; Pinckney *v.* Hagadorn, 1 Duer (N. Y.), 89.

7 Garrott *v.* Ratliff & Williams, 83 Ky. 384.

8 Walker *v.* Richards, 39 N. H. 259; Lilley *v.* Hewitt, 11 Price, 494; Ecker *v.* McAllister, 45 Md. 290; Macey *v.* Childress, 2 Tenn. Ch. (Cooper), 438; Marston *v.* Sweet, 66 N. Y. 207; Porter *v.* Drennan, 13 Brad. (Ill. App.) 362.

where a statute makes a writing necessary to a common-law matter where it was not so before, in declaring on that matter it is not necessary to state that it is in writing, although it must be proved in evidence; but when the matter is created by statute, and a writing is required, then the pleading must allege the existence of the writing. When it is pleaded that there was no writing, it may be replied generally that there was a writing, without setting it out.[1] The fact that there was no writing need not be specially pleaded, but may be taken advantage of under the general issue.[2] In case of an ordinary guaranty, the contract of guaranty must be declared on specially, and it cannot be given in evidence under the common counts in *assumpsit*.[3] But where the guarantor of the payment of a note has, by the form of his guaranty indorsed thereon, waived compliance with every condition, the non-observance of which by the payee would ordinarily release a guarantor or surety, the guaranty will be admissible against him under the common counts in *assumpsit* brought by the payee.[4] If a guaranty contains a promise to pay the debt of A., an averment that A. was a minor when he contracted the debt will take the case out of the Statute of Frauds.[5] In an action on a guaranty, a plea by defendant of "never was indebted as alleged" puts the consideration as well as the promise in issue, and a further plea denying the consideration is bad on demurrer.[6] An answer by a surety that he became such without consideration moving either to the principal or himself has been held to set up a good defense.[7]

1 Wakeman *v.* Sutton, 2 Adol. & Ell. 78.

2 Mines *v.* Sculthorpe, 2 Camp. 215; Eastwood *v.* Kenyon, 3 Perry & Dav. 276.

3 Emerson *v.* Aultman & Co., 69 Md. 125.

4 Emerson *v.* Aultman & Co., 69 Md. 125.

5 King *v.* Summit, 73 Ind. 312.

6 Little *v.* Edwards, 69 Md. 499.

7 Hartman *v.* Redman, 21 Mo. App. 124.

CHAPTER III.

OF THE LIABILITY OF THE SURETY OR GUARANTOR GENERALLY.

Construction of the contract . § 92
Surety and guarantor favorites in law, and are not chargeable beyond strict terms of their engagement 93
Rule that surety is favorite in law, and rules for construing contract must not be confounded — Parties may practically construe contract . . 94
Contract of suretyship and guaranty prospective in its operation 95
When consideration paid to guarantor not usurious — Measure of damages on guaranty of note 96
When surety may be sued before principal — Property of surety may be first taken on execution against principal and surety 97
When guarantor of collection liable — When mortgage on property of principal must be foreclosed before guarantor liable 98
Same continued 99
When guarantor secondarily liable — When creditor must use diligence against principal, and what will excuse its use 100
What is due diligence . . . 101
When neither previous proceedings against principal nor his insolvency necessary to charge guarantor 102
When a writing does not amount to a guaranty — Instances . . . . § 103
Same continued 104
When a writing does amount to a guaranty — Instances . . 105
Same continued 106
Guaranty of payment "when due" of overdue notes and of void certificate of deposit, valid 107
When surety for rent liable if tenant holds over — Burning of house and landlord getting insurance does not discharge surety for rent 108
Liability of surety for rent continued 109
When surety concluded by result of litigation between other parties 110
When surety for debt liable for additional damages . . . 111
Whether surety liable beyond penalty of his bond . . . 112
Same continued 113
When surety on note liable if it is not discounted by party to whom it is payable . . 114
When surety on note not liable if it is discounted by party other than payee 115
When guarantor on general guaranty, or on guaranty addressed to another, liable to person acting on it . . . 116
When guarantor not liable to any one except party to whom guaranty is addressed . . 117

Surety for several not liable for one — Surety for one not liable for several . . . . . . § 118
Surety to or for firm not liable if partners changed — Surety for performance of award not liable if arbitrators changed . 119
When surety for the acts of one person liable if such acts performed by him and a partner 120
When obligation given by surety to firm binds him after change in firm 121
Surety not liable beyond scope of his obligation — Instances 122
Liability of surety or guarantor — Special cases 123
When surety cannot set up illegal acts of creditor or principal as a defense 124
When surety not liable for specific performance — Surety not charged to exonerate estate of principal — Other cases 125
What payment by person indemnified will charge surety — When surety liable for costs — Other cases 126
Surety not liable for greater sum than principal — Other cases 127
Sureties on assignee's bond not liable to those who defeat the assignment — Principal cannot allege for error that surety is discharged — Other cases 128
When surety released if creditor and principal intermarry — Surety not liable to party who pays debt at principal's request — Other cases 129
When agreement to pay in good notes not guaranty that notes in which payment is made are good — Other cases . . . § 130
Surety for return of slave liable, if death of slave caused by principal — Other cases . 131
Surety for balance which may remain due after sale of property not liable till completed sale made — Other cases . . 132
When guaranty not revoked by death of guarantor — When surety cannot relieve himself from future liability by notice 133
When death of guarantor revokes guaranty — When surety may terminate his liability by notice 134
Same continued 135
When notice revoking guaranty takes effect 136
When surety may be sued jointly with principal . . . 137
When recovery on common money counts cannot be had against surety — Surety for alimony cannot be compelled by motion to pay it — Other cases 138
When surety who is not liable at law will not be charged in equity 139
When surety's estate held liable 140
When equity will charge surety who is not liable at law . . 141
When new promise revives liability of surety or guarantor 142
Statute of Limitations — When new promise or partial payment by principal takes case out of statute as to surety . 143
Contract of suretyship, by what law governed 144

§ 92. Construction of the contract.— The first step towards ascertaining the liability of a surety or guarantor is to determine the meaning of his contract. The rules which should govern in the construction of such contracts are therefore of great importance. It has been said by several courts that a strict construction in favor of the surety or guarantor should be adopted and all doubts resolved in his favor.[1] The better and generally received opinion, however, is that this contract should be construed the same as any other contract, and that the same rules should be applied to ascertain the true intention of the parties.[2] It has been said that letters of credit and commercial guaranties should not be construed the same as bonds, which are usually entered into with deliberation,[3] but that they "ought to receive a liberal interpretation. By a liberal interpretation we do not mean that the words should be forced out of their natural meaning, but simply that the words should receive a fair and liberal interpretation, so as to attain the object for which the instrument is designed and the purposes to which it is applied. We should never forget that letters of guaranty are commercial instruments generally drawn up by merchants in brief language; sometimes inartificial, and often loose in their structure and form; and to construe the words of such instruments with a nice and technical care would not only defeat the intentions of the parties, but render them too unsafe a basis to rely on for extensive credits, so often sought in the present active business of commerce throughout the world."[4] This whole subject has been thus ably summarized: "In guaranties, letters of credit and other obligations of sureties, the terms used and language employed are to have a reasonable interpretation, according to the intent of the parties, as disclosed by the instrument read in the light of the surrounding circumstances and the purposes for which it was made. If the terms are ambiguous, the ambiguity may be explained by reference to the circumstances surrounding the parties, and by such aids as are allowable in other cases, and if an ambiguity still remains, I know of no reason

[1] Nicholson *v.* Paget, 1 Cromp. & Mees. 48; Id., 3 Tyr. 164.

[2] Kastner *v.* Winstanley, 20 Up. Can. Com. P. 101; White *v.* Reed, 15 Conn. 457; Locke *v.* McVean, 33 Mich. 473; Crist *v.* Burlingame, 62 Barb. (N. Y.) 351; First Nat. Bank of Baltimore *v.* Gerke, 68 Md. 449; Weiler *v.* Henarie, 15 Oreg. 28.

[3] Bell *v.* Bruen, 1 How. (U. S.) 169, per Catron, J.

[4] Lawrence *v.* McCalmont, 2 How. (U. S.) 426, per Story, J. "No far-fetched equities nor overstrained constructions are allowable as against sureties." Ryan *v.* Williams, Adm'r, 29 Kan. 487, 497.

why the same rule which holds in regard to other instruments should not apply; and if the surety has left anything ambiguous in his expressions, the ambiguity be taken most strongly against him.[1] This certainly should be the rule to the extent that the creditor has in good faith acted upon and given credit to the supposed intent of the surety. He is not liable on an implied engagement, and his obligation cannot be extended by construction or implication beyond the precise terms of the instrument by which he has become surety. But in such instruments the meaning of written language is to be ascertained in the same manner and by the same rules as in other instruments, and, when the meaning is ascertained, effect is to be given to it."[2]

§ 93. Surety and guarantor favorites in law, and are not chargeable beyond strict terms of their engagement.— A rule never to be lost sight of in determining the liability of a surety or guarantor is, that he is a favorite of the law and has a right to stand upon the strict terms of his obligation, when such terms are ascertained.[3] This is a rule universally recognized by the courts, and is applicable to every variety of circumstances. Its existence has no doubt given rise to many of the expressions used by courts, when they have said that in construing the contract every intendment should be made in favor of the surety or guarantor, when in fact it should have no controlling influence at all on the construction of the contract. As illustrating the view of this rule held by the courts, it has been said: "Where any act has been done by the obligee that may injure the surety, the court is very glad

[1] To this effect see, also, Bailey *v.* Larehar, 5 R. I. 530; Mayer *v.* Isaac, 6 Mees. & Wels. 605; Mason *v.* Pritchard, 12 East, 227; Hargreave *v.* Smee, 6 Bing. 244; Wood *v.* Priestner, Law Rep. 2 Exch. 66; Hoey *v.* Jarman, 39 N. J. Law (10 Vroom), 523.

[2] Belloni *v.* Freeborn, 63 N. Y. 383, per Allen, J. On same subject, and to same effect, see Douglass *v.* Reynolds, 7 Pet. (U. S.) 113; Russell *v.* Clark's Ex'r, 7 Cranch, 69; Wills *v.* Ross *et al.*, 77 Ind. 1; Victor Sewing Machine Co. *v.* Crockwell, 3 Utah Ter. 152; Allen *v.* Central Savings Bank, 4 Mo. App. 66.

[3] People *v.* Chalmers, 60 N. Y. 154; Chase *v.* McDonald, 7 Harr. & Johns. (Md.) 160. "A surety is everywhere in law a favored debtor. He is, moreover, a necessity in many of the most important business transactions of life, both public and private, and the policy of the law is, that he should be favored more than other debtors, since he is, or may be,

to lay hold of it in favor of the surety."[1] Again: "No principle is more firmly settled in this state than this: that sureties may stand on the very terms of a statutory bond or undertaking. So clearly has this doctrine been announced and acted upon, that it may be regarded as entering into the condition of such an undertaking that it will not be extended by the courts beyond the necessary import of the words used. It will not be implied that the surety has undertaken to do more or other than that which is expressed in such obligation."[2] Again: "It is now too well settled to admit of doubt that a guarantor, like a surety, is bound only by the strict letter or precise terms of the contract of his principal, whose performance of it he has guarantied; that he is in this respect a favorite of the law, and that a claim against him is *strictissimi juris*."[3] Again: "Nothing can be clearer, both upon principle and authority, than the doctrine that the liability of a surety is not to be extended by implication beyond the terms of his contract. To the extent and in the manner and under the circumstances pointed out in his obligation, he is bound, and no further. It is not sufficient that he may sustain no injury by a change in the contract, or that it may be even for his benefit. He has a right to stand upon the very terms of his contract, and if he does not assent to any variation of it, and a variation is made, it is fatal."[4] The principle is clearly stated and one of the reasons for it given as follows: "It is a well-settled rule, both at law and in equity, that a surety is not to be held beyond the precise terms of his contract; and except in certain cases of accident, mistake, or fraud, a court of equity will never lend its aid to fix a surety beyond what he is fairly bound to at law. . . . This rule is founded

to a certain extent, powerless to protect himself." State *v.* Churchill *et al.*, 48 Ark. 426, 442.

[1] Law *v.* The East India Company, 4 Vesey, 824.

[2] Lang *v.* Pike, 27 Ohio St. 498, per Ashburn, J. No covenants that do not appear on the face of a bond can be implied as against the sureties thereon. Bishop *v.* Freeman, 42 Mich. 533.

[3] Kingsbury *v.* Westfall, 61 N. Y. 356, per Gray, C. To similar effect, see The Markland Mining & Mfg. Co. *v.* Kimmel *et al.*, 87 Ind. 560, 566.

[4] Miller *v.* Stewart, 9 Wheat. 680, per Story, J.; The Independent District of Mason City *v.* Reichard *et al.*, 50 Iowa, 98; Tomlinson *v.* Simpson, 33 Minn. 443.

upon the most cogent and salutary principles of public policy and justice. In the complicated transactions of civil life the aid of one friend to another in the character of surety or bail becomes requisite at every step. Without these constant acts of mutual kindness and assistance the course of business and commerce would be prodigiously impeded and disturbed. It becomes, then, excessively important to have the rule established that a surety is never to be implicated beyond his specific agreement."[1]

§ 94. Rule that surety is favorite in law, and rules for construing contract must not be confounded — Parties may practically construe contract.— The rules for construing the contract of a surety or a guarantor should by no means be confounded with the rule that sureties and guarantors are favorites of the law, and have a right to stand upon the strict terms of their obligations. There is no legal prohibition against entering into a contract of suretyship or guaranty. For any contract which it is legal to make, it is legal that a surety or guarantor shall become responsible. In the construction of the contract of a surety or guarantor, as well as of every other contract, the true question is: What was the intention of the parties, as disclosed by the instrument read in the light of the sur-

[1] Per Kent, C. J. (afterwards Chancellor), in Ludlow *v.* Simond, 2 Caines' Cas. in Error, 1. See, also, remarks of Mr. Justice Swayne in Magee *et al.* *v.* Manhattan Life Ins. Co., 92 U. S. 93, 98; and see to like effect, State *v.* Churchill, 48 Ark. 426, 442; opinions of Brickell, C. J., in City Council of Montgomery *v.* Hughes, 65 Ala. 201, 204, and Blakewell, J., in Fisse *v.* Einstein, 5 Mo. App. 78, 86, 87. For miscellaneous cases illustrating the doctrine that the liability of sureties or guarantors cannot be extended by implication or construction beyond the precise terms of their contract, see the following: Vinyard *v.* Barnes, 124 Ill. 346; People *v.* Toomey, 122 Ill. 308; Burlington Ins. Co. *v.* Johnson, 120 Ill. 622; Dodgson *v.* Henderson, 113 Ill. 360; Second Nat. Bank of Peoria *v.* Diefendorf, 90 Ill. 396; Mix *v.* Singleton, 86 Ill. 194; Burgett *v.* Paxton, 15 Brad. (Ill. App.) 379; Weir Plow Co. *v.* Walmsley, 110 Ind. 242; Irwin *v.* Kilburn, 104 Ind. 113; Noyes *v.* Granger, 51 Iowa, 227; Henrie *v.* Buck, 39 Kan. 381; Ryan *v.* Williams, 29 Kan. 487; Edwards *v.* Ellis, 27 Kan. 344; Hays *v.* Closon, 20 Kan. 120; Nat. Bank of Baltimore *v.* Gerke, 68 Md. 449; Shine's Adm'r *v.* Central Savings Bank, 70 Mo. 524; Sedalia, W. & S. R'y Co. *v.* Smith, 27 Mo. App. 371; Lee *v.* Hastings, 13 Neb. 508; Gunn *v.* Geary, 44 Mich. 615; Robinson *v.* Epping, 24 Fla. 237; Hutchinson *v.* Woodwell, 107 Pa. St. 509; Burson *v.* Andes, 83 Va. 445; Packard *v.* Herrington, 41 Kan. 469.

rounding circumstances? The contract of the surety or guarantor being just as legal as that of the principal, there is no good reason for holding that in arriving at the intention of the parties, one set of rules shall govern when the principal, and another when the surety or guarantor, is concerned. To say that a certain set of words in a contract mean one thing when the principal is defendant, and that the same words in the same contract mean another thing simply because the defendant is a surety or guarantor, is absurd. The meaning of the words is not affected by the fact that the party sought to be charged is principal, surety or guarantor. On the other hand, a surety or guarantor usually derives no benefit from his contract. His object generally is to befriend the principal. In most cases the consideration moves to the principal, and he would be liable upon an implied contract, while the surety or guarantor is only liable because he has agreed to become so. He is bound by his agreement, and nothing else. No implied liability exists to charge him. It has been repeatedly decided that he is under no moral obligation to pay the debt of his principal.[1] Being then bound by his agreement alone, and deriving no benefit from the transaction, it is eminently just and proper that he should be a favorite of the law, and have a right to stand upon the strict terms of his obligation. To charge him beyond its terms, or to permit it to be altered without his consent, would be, not to enforce the contract made by him, but to make another for him. The parties themselves may give a practical construction to a guaranty, and that construction will be enforced. Where a guaranty was such that standing alone it would not have been held to be continuing, but the parties had for some time acted upon it as a continuing guaranty, it was held that it should be so construed. The court said: "We have found no case where the parties have been allowed to repudiate any such long standing

[1] Winston *v.* Fenwick, 4 Stew. & Port. (Ala.) 269; Harrison *v.* Field, 2 Wash. (Va.), 136; Pickersgill *v.* Lahens, 15 Wall. 140; Pecke *v.* Julius, 2 Browne (Pa.), 31; Van Derveer *v.* Wright, 6 Barb. (N. Y.) 547; Hendricks *v.* Robinson, 56 Miss. 694; White *v.* Moore, 23 S. C. 456. But in Vermont it is held that the moral obligation resting upon one whose debts have been discharged in bankruptcy is a sufficient consideration for a guaranty of their payment. Robinson *v.* Larabee, 58 Vt. 652. And see, on this subject, Richardson *v.* Draper *et al.*, 87 N. Y. 337.

and unequivocal practical construction of their contract."[1] Evidence by the clerks of a party to whom a letter of credit was addressed, showing that he understood it to be a continuing guaranty, and acted upon it as such, has been held competent in a suit against the writer of such letter. The court said the evidence was competent to show that advances had been made on the faith of the guaranty, if for no other purpose.[2]

§ 95. **Contract of suretyship and guaranty prospective in its operation.**— In conformity to the well-established rule that the liability of sureties on official bonds cannot cover delinquencies prior to the execution of the bond, unless the bond itself states that it shall have retroactive effect, it is held that the ordinary contract of guaranty shall be construed likewise. Thus, where a married woman, to obtain credit for her husband from a wholesale merchant, gave the latter the following guaranty, viz.: "In consideration of your having at my request agreed to supply and furnish goods to (my husband) C., I do hereby guaranty to you the sum of £500. This guaranty is to continue in force for the period of six years and no longer,"— *held*, the guaranty was limited to goods supplied to the husband *after it was given*[3] and not before. So a guaranty in the following language, viz.: "In consideration of your supplying my son with what goods he may from time to time require of you this season, on your usual terms of credit, I do hereby guaranty the payment of the same." *Held*, the guaranty applied only to the goods purchased after it was given, and not to those previously furnished.[4] Defendant executed a contract of guaranty that "F." would pay for all coal which might be delivered to him by plaintiff within a certain time, and at such price as may be agreed on between "F." and plaintiff. *Held*, the guaranty had reference to future contracts fixing terms of payment.[5] A surety for the performance of a contract to sell goods on commission is not liable for a default

[1] Per Redfield, C. J., in Michigan State Bank *v.* Pecks, 28 Vt. 200.

[2] Douglass *v.* Reynolds, 7 Pet. (U. S.) 113.

[3] Morrell *v.* Cowan, Law Rep. 7 Ch. Div. 151, reversing Law Rep. 6 Ch. Div. 166.

[4] Weed *et al.* *v.* Chambers, 40 Up. Can. (Q. B.) 1.

[5] Delaware, L. & W. R. R. Co. *v.* Burkard *et al.*, 114 N. Y. 197.

respecting goods purchased by the principal and in his possession prior to the execution of the contract.[1] Where a promissory note has been given by a principal and surety, secured by a deed of trust on the surety's property, showing that the surety's purpose was to obtain further advances for the principal, and the payee discounts the work and applies a part of the proceeds to the payment of a past indebtedness, *held*, not binding on the surety.[2] A guaranty of the payment of rent under a lease, given during the term created by the lease, and at a time when rent, which has become due, is in arrear, by which the guarantor "agrees to become security for an agreement of lease," . . . "whereby, *should* any default be made in the payment of said rent," the guarantor binds himself "to pay any deficiency which may be due," is a guaranty for the payment of any rent that may thereafter become due and payable under the lease, and not for the payment of rent already due.[3]

§ 96. When consideration paid to guarantor not usurious — Measure of damages on guaranty of note.— The *bona fide* sale of one's credit by way of guaranty, or by making a note for another's accommodation, though for a consideration exceeding the legal rate of interest, is not usurious if the transaction is not connected with a loan between the parties. "As the law now stands, a man has as good a right to sell his credit as he has to sell his goods or his lands, and if he deal fairly he may take as large a price as he can get for either of them."[4] However small the consideration may be which the guarantor receives, he is liable for the full amount of the debt guarantied, however large, if such be the scope of his contract. Thus, after a note for $7,868.80 had been executed and delivered by the principals, one Oakley, in consideration of $190, agreed to guaranty the payment of the note, and in execution of the agreement indorsed it in blank. *Held*, he was liable for the full amount of the note. The court said: "It is not for us to hamper Mr. Oakley or any other citizen in such a way as to

[1] Weir Plow Co. *v.* Walmsley *et al.*, 110 Ind. 242.

[2] Chaffe *v.* Taliaferro, 58 Miss. 544.

[3] Brooks *v.* Baker, 9 Daly (N. Y. Com. Pleas), 398. See, to the general effect, also, where a guaranty was held to be not of a past indebtedness, Johnson *v.* Fisher, 4 Col. 242.

[4] Moore *v.* Howland, 4 Denio, 264, per Bronson, C. J.

preclude his making money by insuring the debts of his neighbors. It is enough that he has not been imposed upon."[1] When the guaranty is that there is a certain sum due on a note, the measure of damages is the value of a judgment for that amount, if one had been obtained against the makers. And in such case, when the makers are solvent but the note has been paid, the measure of damages is the full amount guarantied to be due.[2]

§ 97. When surety may be sued before principal — Property of surety may be first taken on execution against principal and surety.— Whether a surety or a guarantor becomes liable to suit immediately upon the default of, and before any steps are taken against, the principal, depends in every case upon the terms of his contract. When, by the terms of the contract, the obligation of the surety or guarantor is the same as that of the principal, then, as soon as the principal is in default, the surety or guarantor is likewise in default, and may be sued immediately and before any proceedings are had against the principal.[3] This results from the fact that he had a right to contract such a liability, and, having done so, he is bound by his engagement. In such case no demand on the principal is necessary.[4] Nor is any demand on the surety or guarantor necessary. The bringing of the suit is a sufficient demand.[5] Nor need unliquidated damages be liquidated by a previous suit against the principal.[6] Where the bond of a deputy treasurer to a treasurer provided that the treasurer should be "kept free from all incumbrances, blame, damage and loss" from any acts of the deputy, the deputy having made default, it was held that the treasurer had a right to re-

[1] Oakley v. Boorman, 21 Wend. 588, per Cowen, J. To same effect, see Cooper v. Page, 24 Me. 73.

[2] Head v. Green, 5 Bissell, 311.

[3] Penny v. Crane Bros. Manuf. Co., 80 Ill. 244; Wilson v. Campbell, 1 Scam. (Ill.) 493; Redfield v. Haight, 27 Conn. 31; Smith v. Rogers, 14 Ind. 224; Ranelaugh v. Hayes, 1 Vernon, 189; Abercrombie v. Knox, 3 Ala. 728; Garey v. Hignutt, 32 Md. 552; Geddis v. Hawk, 1 Watts (Pa.), 280, overruling Hawk v. Geddis, 16 Serg. & Rawle, 23; Hoey v. Jarman, 39 N. J. Law (10 Vroom), 523.

[4] Carr v. Card, 34 Mo. 513; Mitchell v. Williamson, 6 Md. 210.

[5] Byrne v. Ætna Ins. Co., 56 Ill. 321; Hough v. Ætna Life Ins. Co., 57 Ill. 318, which were cases of sureties on bonds of insurance agents; Wood v. Barstow, 10 Pick. 368, which was a case of a surety on an executor's bond.

[6] Janes v. Scott, 59 Pa. St. 178.

cover on the bond against the sureties for such default, although he had not himself paid anything on account thereof.[1] When the surety or guarantor is in default, the creditor is not, before proceeding against him, obliged to exhaust a mortgage which he holds on the property of the principal for the payment of the same debt.[2] "It is clearly competent for a creditor to secure himself both by a lien on property and the engagement of a third person undertaking for the payment by the debtor. And the creditor is not obliged to proceed in equity upon his mortgage, but has the election either to seek a foreclosure or prosecute an action at law upon the promise of the debtor and his surety."[3] A suit against a surety on a note will not be delayed because the principal has been adjudged a bankrupt and the note has been filed by the payee in the bankruptcy proceedings, and a judgment rendered for his distributive share of the assets. The surety can himself pay the note, and prove his claim against the estate of the principal.[4] Upon an appropriation by the sheriff of the proceeds of a sale of A.'s real estate, a judgment against A. as the surety of B. must be paid in preference to subsequent judgments against A., although it appear that the same judgment is a lien upon the real estate of B., which is a sufficient security for its payment. The remedy of the subsequent creditors of A. is by subrogation. The holder of the older judgment has a legal right to his money at once, and will not be delayed to benefit other creditors.[5] The state sold certain land to a party, who gave bond with surety for the purchase money. The certificate of purchase provided that in case of default in payment the premises should be "im-

[1] Baby *v.* Baby, 8 Up. Can. (Q. B.) 76. To same effect, see Wilson *v.* Stilwell, 9 Ohio St. 467; Grant *v.* Hotchkiss, 26 Barb. (N. Y.) 63.

[2] Jones *v.* Tincher, 15 Ind. 308; New Orleans Canal & Banking Co. *v.* Escoffie, 2 La. Ann. 830; Day *v.* Elmore, 4 Wis. 190; Jones *v.* Ashford, 79 N. C. 172; Callaway County Savings Bank *v.* Terry, 13 Mo. App. 99; Ranelaugh *v.* Hayes, 1 Vernon, 189. But where a husband and wife mortgaged her separate estate to secure certain notes given by a partnership of which her husband was a member, and which were already secured by a mortgage of partnership property, it was held the wife was entitled to have the partnership mortgage exhausted before subjecting her separate estate to the payment of the firm debts. Moffitt *v.* Roche, 77 Ind. 48.

[3] Cullum *v.* Gaines, 1 Ala. 23, per Collier, C. J.

[4] Gregg *v.* Wilson, 50 Ind. 490.

[5] Neff's Appeal, 9 Watts & Serg. (Pa.) 36. See, also, on this subject, Tynt *v.* Tynt, 2 Peere Wms. 542.

mediately forfeit and revert to the state." *Held*, the surety might be sued for the whole purchase money remaining unpaid. The state had an option to enforce the payment of the whole of the purchase money, or to resell the land and hold the surety for the balance, if any, which might remain unpaid after such resale.[1] After a joint judgment is rendered against principal and surety, the sheriff may collect all the money from the surety.[2] The holder of an execution issued on a judgment against a principal and two sureties may cause it to be levied on land of one of the sureties, and, there being no fraud or collusion, it is no objection to the validity of such levy that it was made at the request of the principal and the other surety and of the holder, who purchased the rights of the judgment creditor with money furnished by the principal and such other surety.[3] One of the "novels" of Justinian allowed sureties the right to require that before they were sued the principal debtor should, at their expense, be prosecuted to judgment and execution. This rule prevails in most of the countries which have adopted the civil law. According to the Roman law before the time of Justinian, the creditor could, as he can by the common law when the surety is in default, apply to the surety first.[4] The common-law rule, as above stated, prevails in England, in the United States where not changed by statute, and in other countries which have adopted the common law.

[1] Rush *v.* The State, 20 Ind. 432.

[2] Keaton *v.* Cox, 26 Ga. 162; Eason *v.* Petway, 1 Dev. & Bat. Law (N. C.), 44. To similar effect, see Northwestern Mut. Life Ins. Co. *v.* Allis, 23 Minn. 337; Winham *v.* Crutcher, 2 Tenn. Ch. (Cooper), 535.

[3] Taylor *v.* Van Dusen, 3 Gray, 498.

[4] See opinion of Kent, C., in Hayes *v.* Ward, 4 Johns. Ch. 123, and authorities there cited. For the fundamental distinction between guaranties of payment and of collection, see McMurray *et al.* *v.* Noyes, 72 N. Y. 523; Cowles *v.* Peck, 55 Conn. 251; Jones *v.* Ashford, 79 N. C. 172; Osborne & Co. *v.* Lawson, 26 Mo. App. 549. In McMurray *et al.* *v.* Noyes, *supra*, at pp. 524, 525, Rapallo, J. thus states the distinction: "The fundamental distinction between a guaranty of payment and of collection is, that in the first case the guarantor undertakes unconditionally that the debtor will pay, and the creditor may, upon default, proceed directly against the guarantor, without taking any steps to collect of the principal debtor, and the omission or neglect to proceed against him is not (except under special circumstances) any defense to the guarantor; while in the second case the undertaking is that if the demand cannot be collected by legal proceedings, the guarantor will pay,

§ 98. When guarantor of collection liable — When mortgage on property of principal must be foreclosed before guarantor liable.— While it is established that a surety or guarantor may be sued as soon as he is in default, it is often difficult to determine when such default has occurred. It has been held that a guaranty of the collection of the debt of another, or that such debt is collectible, means that it is "collectible by due course of law," the same as if those words had been written in the guaranty, and that legal proceedings must be had and exhausted against the parties liable when the guaranty was executed before a cause of action arises against the guarantor. These cases hold that the prosecution of such legal proceedings are a condition precedent to any liability on the part of the guarantor, and that it makes no difference if the previous parties liable for the debt are, and have all the time been, insolvent.[1] The guarantor of collection is in such case liable for the costs incurred in the endeavor to collect the debt from the previous parties.[2] It is generally held that a guarantor that a debt is collectible is only liable in case it is not collectible, because otherwise he is not in default.[3] But it

and consequently legal proceedings against the principal debtor, and a failure to collect by those means are conditions precedent to the liability of the guarantor; and to these the law, as established by numerous decisions, attaches the further condition that due diligence be exercised by the creditor in enforcing his legal remedies against the debtor."

[1] Craig *v.* Parkis, 40 N. Y. 181 (three judges dissenting); Mains *v.* Haight, 14 Barb. (N. Y.) 76; Cumpston *v.* McNair, 1 Wend. 457; French *v.* Marsh, 29 Wis. 649; Newell *v.* Fowler, 23 Barb. (N. Y.) 628; Cady *v.* Sheldon, 38 Barb. (N. Y.) 103; Burt *v.* Horner, 5 Barb. (N. Y.) 501; Shepard *v.* Phears, 35 Tex. 763; Lemmon *v.* Strong, 55 Conn. 443. And a declaration on a guaranty of the collection of a note is demurrable if it does not state that legal proceedings have been taken to enforce collection without effect. Bosman *v.* Akeley, 39 Mich. 710. A guaranty to pay all notes which should "prove to be uncollectible" is unenforceable until judgment and execution are returned unsatisfied. Ralph *v.* Eldredge, 58 Hun (N. Y.), 203.

[2] Mosher *v.* Hotchkiss, 2 Keyes (N. Y.), 589; Id., 3 Abb. Rep. Omitted Cas. 326. But it is held that a guaranty of collection will not render the guarantor liable for expenses incurred in the collection, when by the terms of the guaranty it is so stipulated. National Bank *v.* Marbourg, 22 Kan. 535. A guaranty of "all costs and expenses paid or incurred in collecting" a note has reference to definite legal costs, and not to uncertain allowances for the creditor's trouble in dunning the maker of the note. Wetherbee *v.* Kusterer, 41 Mich. 359.

[3] Foster *v.* Barney Vt. 60.

is the doctrine of a majority of the courts, and seems the better opinion, that the fact that it is not collectible may be shown by any other competent evidence as well as the fruitless prosecution of a suit against the previous parties liable for the debt, and if such parties are actually insolvent, no suit against them is necessary to charge the guarantor.[1] Where the payee of a note, by an indorsement on its back, guaranties its collection, and the note is secured by a collateral mortgage, which is referred to in it, and which is assigned at the same time as the note, he is not liable upon the guaranty until resort has been had to the mortgage as well as to the note, for the collection of the money secured.[2] So where the defendants transferred to the plaintiffs two notes, with a lien on a canal-boat given to secure their payment, and also executed a guaranty of the notes, conditioned that the plaintiffs should use all proper and reasonable means to collect them of the maker before resorting to the defendants on the guaranty, it was held that the lien on the boat must be exhausted before the defendants could be sued on their guaranty.[3] In these two cases, according to the fair construction of the terms of the guaranties, the guarantors were not in default until the liens on the property of the principals were exhausted. They do not at all conflict with the cases which hold that, where the surety or guarantor, by the terms of his contract, is in default, he may be sued at once without the creditor being obliged to foreclose a mortgage for the same debt on the property of the principal.

§ 99. **Same continued.**— Where, upon assignment of bonds and mortgage, there was a guaranty that if, in case of foreclosure and sale of the mortgaged premises, there should arise a deficiency, the guarantor would pay the same on demand, it

[1] White *v.* Case, 13 Wend. 543; Peck *v.* Frink, 10 Iowa, 193; Brackett *v.* Rich. 23 Minn. 485; Stone *v.* Rockefeller, 29 Ohio St. 625; M'Doal *v.* Yeomans, 8 Watts (Pa.), 361; Thomas *v.* Dodge, 8 Mich. 51; Sanford *v.* Allen, 1 Cush. 473; Dana *v.* Conant, 30 Vt. 246; Cooke *v.* Nathan, 16 Barb. (N. Y.) 342; Jones *v.* Greenlaw, 6 Cold. (Tenn.) 342; Cady *v.* Sheldon, 38 Barb. (N. Y.) 103; Lemmon *v.* Strong, 55 Conn. 443. But see Schermerhorn *v.* Conner, 41 Mich. 374.

[2] Barman *v.* Carhartt, 10 Mich. 338; Johnson *v.* Shepard, 35 Mich. 115. No proceedings need be had under the mortgage, however, if it is wholly valueless. Cady *v.* Sheldon, 38 Barb. (N. Y.) 103.

[3] Brainard *v.* Reynolds, 36 Vt. 614.

was held that the guaranty was not one of payment; but the foreclosure and sale were conditions precedent, to be performed with due diligence in order to establish the liability of the guarantor.[1] An undertaking by a surety in a penal sum, that, if the principal is discharged from arrest, he shall at all times hold himself amenable to the processes of the court, is an undertaking of such a nature that proceedings must be taken against the principal before the obligation of the surety to pay arises, and therefore the issuing of process and entry of judgment are conditions precedent to the liability of the surety.[2] Judgment may be entered against the guarantor of a judgment in favor of an assignee of the same without first showing unsuccessful efforts to collect from the principal debtor, where the guarantor guarantied the collection of the same and confessed judgment on the guaranty.[3] In an action on a guaranty of collection of a debt, where the defense is that the debtor was not prosecuted with due diligence, evidence of acquiescence of the guarantor in the delay is admissible as showing a waiver by the guarantor of his right to take advantage of the creditor's indulgence.[4]

§ 100. When guarantor secondarily liable — When creditor must use diligence against principal, and what will excuse its use.— A guaranty on the back of a note was: "I hereby guaranty the payment of the within note." *Held*, the guarantor was not primarily liable, and in order to charge him it was necessary that the creditor should be diligent in endeavoring to collect the note from the principal, unless diligence would have been unavailing.[5] The same thing was held

1 McMurray *et al.* *v.* Noyes, 72 N. Y. 523; Vanderbilt *v.* Schreyer, 91 N. Y. 392, reversing 21 Hun, 537; Briggs *v.* Norris, 67 Mich. 325.

2 Toles *v.* Adee *et al.*, 91 N. Y. 562. See same case on former appeal, 84 N. Y. 222.

3 Cooper *v.* Shaver, 101 Pa. St. 547.

4 Mead *v.* Parker, 111 N. Y. 259, affirming 41 Hun, 577. That a guarantor of the payment of principal and interest of certain bonds and coupons as they mature may be sued before the maturity of the same, see Sutherland *v.* Woodruff, 26 Hun (N. Y.), 411. That he is liable for interest on overdue coupons, see Philadelphia, etc. R. R. Co. *v.* Knight, 124 Pa. St. 58.

5 Farrow *v.* Respess, 11 Ired. Law (N. C.), 170. The same was held on an indorsement guarantying "the within note good till paid." Cowles *v.* Peck, 55 Conn. 251. And see to similar effect, Lemmon *v.* Strong, 55 Conn. 443; Allen *v.* Rundle, 50 Conn. 588.

where the assignor of a non-negotiable note and a judgment guarantied the "payment" of the same;[1] where the assignor of a bond covenanted to "stand security for the payment of it;"[2] where the guaranty was, "I do hereby assign and guaranty the payment of the within bond;"[3] where two receipts of an officer for the collection of certain bills were assigned, as follows: "I trade the above to . . . for value received, and guaranty the payment of the same;"[4] and where under a note was written: "I do hereby guaranty the payment of the above note."[5] The payee of a note indorsed it as follows: "I hereby guaranty this note good until January 1, 1850." *Held*, the effect of the guaranty was that the makers of the note should be in a condition that payment of the note could be enforced against them till January 1, 1850, if legal diligence was used.[6] Due diligence on the part of the creditor against the prior parties liable for the debt, or an excuse that they were insolvent, have been held necessary to charge the guarantor, when the assignment of certain notes stated: "We hereby agree to hold ourselves ultimately responsible with the above parties;"[7] when the indorsement on a note was, "to be liable only in the second instance;"[8] and when in the assignment of a bond the words were: "I . . . hold myself liable for the ultimate payment."[9] In the foregoing cases the fair import of the guarantor's contract was considered to be that he did not become liable to suit unless due diligence was used to collect the money from the prior parties, if they were solvent. If the

[1] Benton *v.* Gibson, 1 Hill, Law (S. C.), 56.

[2] Rudy *v.* Wolf, 16 Serg. & R. (Pa.) 79.

[3] Johnston *v.* Chapman, 3 Pen. & Watts (Pa.), 18.

[4] Craig *v.* Phipps, 23 Miss. 240.

[5] Isett *v.* Hoge, 2 Watts (Pa.), 128. To similar effect, see Mizner *v.* Spier, 96 Pa. St. 533. Where a note was executed to a bank containing an indorsement guarantying the payment of the same without protest, it was held that the words "without protest" simply qualified the contract so as to exclude the specific defense on the part of the guarantor, that, by not protesting the note, prior indorsers were released, and did not require the bank to forbear making demand of the makers of the note. Zahm *v.* First Nat. Bank, 103 Pa. St. 576.

[6] Hammond *v.* Chamberlin, 26 Vt. 406. As to what is a guaranty of collection necessitating diligence against the principal, see Evans *v.* Bell, 45 Tex. 553.

[7] Johnston *v.* Mills, 25 Tex. 704.

[8] Pittman *v.* Chisolm, 43 Ga. 442.

[9] Lewis *v.* Hoblitzell, 6 Gill & Johns. (Md.) 259.

prior parties were wholly insolvent, then the fair import of the contract was held to be that no such diligence was necessary. When, however, the contract expressly provides that the guarantor shall not be liable until after "due course of law" has been exhausted against the prior parties, there is no room for construction, and the exact diligence stipulated for, no matter how vain it may be, nor how insolvent the parties, must be used to charge the guarantor.[1] The reason is, that the parties have so agreed, and the court cannot make a contract for them, which it would do if it dispensed with anything required by the contract. On the same principle, where a surety for the payment of rent stipulated that he should be notified of the tenant's default, it was held that he must be so notified, or he would not be bound, even though he was not in any manner injured by want of the notice.[2] In cases where the guarantor is not liable unless diligence is used by the creditor against the previous parties, the guarantor may, by parol, waive the use of such diligence.[3] When a note is guarantied to be collectible, all prior solvent parties, such as an indorser,[4] and the estate of a deceased indorser,[5] must be ex-

[1] Dwight *v.* Williams, 4 McLean, 581; Moakley *v.* Riggs, 19 Johns. 69; Eddy *v.* Stantons, 21 Wend. 255; Salt Springs Nat. Bank *v.* Sloan, 57 Hun (N. Y.), 265. The precise opposite of this has been held in Heralson *v.* Mason, 53 Mo. 211, upon the ground that, the principal being insolvent, the law would dispense with a fruitless prosecution. This is nothing more nor less than to make a contract for the guarantor without his consent, and enforce it against him. In an action against the guarantor of the collectibility of a note, the burden of proof is on the plaintiff to show that he has exhausted all legal remedies against the maker, or that the latter is insolvent, or that the guarantor had waived legal proceedings, if the latter be the case. Allen *et al. v.* Rundle *et al.*, 50 Conn. 9. And the plaintiff, if he claims to have exhausted his remedy at law, must show this fact by recovery of judgment, issue and return of execution unsatisfied at return day. Schermerhorn *v.* Conner, 41 Mich. 374. If the case was instituted in a justice court, a transcript of the judgment must have been filed in the circuit court and an issue and return of execution thereon. Schermerhorn *v.* Conner, 41 Mich. 374.

[2] Corporation of Chatham *v.* McCrea, 12 Up. Can. C. P. 352; Hilary *v.* Rose, 9 Phila. (Pa.) 139.

[3] Day *v.* Elmore, 4 Wis. 190; Ege *v.* Barnitz, 8 Pa. St. 304; Goodwin *v.* Buckman, 11 Ia. 308. *Contra,* Mosier *v.* Waful, 56 Barb. (N. Y.) 80.

[4] Loveland *v.* Shepard, 2 Hill (N. Y.),

[5] Benton *v.* Fletcher, 31 Vt. 418. If there are several principals, all must be exhausted. Aldrich *v.* Chubb, 35 Mich. 350.

hausted before the guarantor is in default. When the effect of the undertaking is to guaranty the solvency of the prior parties, and no particular kind of diligence is stipulated for in the contract, the fact that such prior parties are actually insolvent, constitutes a breach of the guaranty. In such case, no suit need be brought against such prior parties; and such insolvency may be shown by any other competent evidence, as well as by fruitless legal proceedings against such prior parties.[1] If an execution, by virtue of which a levy upon all property of the prior parties might have been made, is returned by the proper officer *nulla bona*, this is *prima facie* evidence of the insolvency of such parties; but it is otherwise if the execution is issued by a justice of the peace, and real estate cannot, by virtue of it, be levied upon.[2] If the execution is thus returned within four days after it is issued, it is sufficient; for while a sale could not have been made in that time, property could have been found to levy upon if there had been any available for that purpose.[3] A promise by the guarantor to pay the debt, or giving his note for it, after the principal has failed to pay, is an admission that there has been no failure to use due diligence on the part of the creditor against the principal, and such diligence need not be otherwise proved in a suit against the guarantor.[4]

§ **101. What is due diligence.**— When the terms of the guaranty and the circumstances of the parties are such that

139; Dana *v.* Conant, 30 Vt. 246. Thus, where A. indorsed on a promissory note a guaranty of payment, and afterwards B. indorsed thereon a guaranty of collection, it was held that no recovery could be had against B. until it was shown that reasonable diligence had been used to collect the note from both the maker and the first guarantor, or legal excuse for the neglect of such diligence. Summers *v.* Barrett *et al.*, 65 Iowa, 292.

[1] Pittman *v.* Chisolm, 43 Ga. 442; Johnston *v.* Mills, 25 Tex. 704; Benton *v.* Gibson, 1 Hill, Law (S. C.), 56; Cates *v.* Kittrell, 7 Heisk. (Tenn.) 606; Lewis *v.* Hoblitzell, 6 Gill & Johns. (Md.) 259; McClurg *v.* Fryer, 15 Pa. St. 293; Ashford *v.* Robinson, 8 Ired. Law (N. C.), 114; Janes *v.* Scott, 59 Pa. St. 178; Farrow *v.* Respess, 11 Ired. Law (N. C.), 170; Huntress *v.* Patten, 20 Me. 28; Bull *v.* Bliss, 30 Vt. 127; Wheeler *v.* Lewis, 11 Vt. 265.

[2] Gilbert *v.* Henck, 30 Pa. St. 205.

[3] Day *v.* Elmore, 4 Wis. 190.

[4] Tinkum *v.* Duncan, 1 Grant's Cas. (Pa.) 228; Teller *v.* Bernheim, 3 Phila. (Pa.) 299. A surety cannot charge the creditor with laches until he has in vain prompted him to sue the principal. See Coles' Adm'r *v.* Ballard, 78 Va. 139.

the creditor, in order to charge the guarantor, is bound to use due diligence against the parties previously liable for the debt, the question then arises: "What is due diligence?" "Due diligence generally, and in the absence of any special facts, would require suit to be instituted at the first regular term of the court after maturity, and the obtaining judgment and execution thereon as soon as practicable by the ordinary rules and practice of the court."[1] By another court due diligence has been said to be that which a vigilant creditor employs when he has no other security than the obligation of the principal debtor. If the creditor employs legal process against the principal debtor without delay, the *prima facie* presumption is that he has been duly diligent, but suing out process simply, and letting it run its course, may not be due diligence. If the creditor has special knowledge of how he can collect the money, he must collect it, even if more than the regular process of suit is necessary.[2] What is due diligence in each particular case will depend upon the circumstances of that case. A judgment against the prior parties liable for the debt, promptly obtained, and execution issued thereon, are *prima facie* evidence of due diligence. If, in such case, other facts exist which show that due diligence has not been used, the burden of proving them is on the guarantor.[3] If the prior parties are without the state, but have property in the state, known to the creditor, which can be reached by attachment, the creditor must, in the exercise of due diligence, attach such property.[4] But if the creditor did not know, and by the use of reasonable diligence could not have ascertained, the facts which would have authorized an attachment, then he is not chargeable with negligence, if he does not cause an attachment to be issued.[5] If the prior parties are solvent, but live in another state, and have no property in the state where the creditor resides, it has been held that the creditor need not, in

[1] Voorhies *v.* Atlee, 29 Iowa, 49, per Cole, C. J. And a return of *nulla bona* to the execution. Jones *v.* Ashford, 79 N. C. 172; Osborne *v.* Smith (Cir. Ct. D. Minn.), 18 Fed. Rep. 126; Ricks *et al.* *v.* Gantt, 35 La. Ann. 920; Durand *et al.* *v.* Bowen, 73 Iowa, 573.

[2] Hoffman *v.* Bechtel, 52 Pa. St. 190; National Loan & Building Association *v.* Lichtenwalner, 100 Pa. St. 100.

[3] Backus *v.* Shipherd, 11 Wend. 629; Aldrich *v.* Chubb, 35 Mich. 350. See, also, on this subject, Nichols *v.* Allen, 22 Minn. 283.

[4] White *v.* Case, 13 Wend. 543.

[5] Forest *v.* Stewart, 14 Ohio St. 246.

the exercise of due diligence, pursue such prior parties in such other state.[1] If the creditor causes an attachment to be levied on the property of the principal, but fails to collect the money because the attachment is defectively served, he does not use due diligence, and the guarantor is discharged.[2] A delay on the part of the creditor in bringing suit against the previous parties for upwards of six months;[3] for seven months;[4] for fourteen months;[5] for seventeen months;[6] and for five years and six months,[7] have been held to be unreasonable, and not the exercise of due diligence. Where a guaranty that certain notes then due were good was made April 21, 1841, and no demand was made on the parties primarily liable till July 29, 1842, and no notice of default was given the guarantor till February 29, 1844, it was held that due diligence had not been used, and the guarantor was not bound.[8] A guaranty made April 10th was as follows: "I warrant the within note good and collectible until the 1st day of July." Suit was commenced by the holder April 12th, and he could have obtained judgment in April, and the money could have been made, but in consequence of his negligence he did not get judgment until September, when the money could not be made. *Held*, the guarantor was not bound.[9] The institution of a suit against the principal six days after the maturity of a note, and prosecuting it diligently to judgment, has been held to be due dili-

1 Towns *v.* Farrar, 2 Hawks (N. C.), 163.

2 Beach *v.* Bates, 12 Vt. 68.

3 Craig *v.* Parkis, 40 N. Y. 181.

4 Penniman *v.* Hudson, 14 Barb. (N. Y.) 579. A delay of nine months in foreclosing a mortgage discharges a guarantor of the collection of the mortgage. Northern Ins. Co. *v.* Wright. 76 N. Y. 445, affirming 13 Hun, 166.

5 McMurray *v.* Noyes, 72 N. Y. 523. In this case the holder of a bond and mortgage delayed foreclosure for fourteen months after they were due. For ten months of this time the mortgaged property was a sufficient security; but afterwards the buildings thereon were destroyed by fire, and the value thereof reduced below the amount of the mortgage debt. *Held*, the delay was sufficient to constitute laches discharging a guarantor. McMurray *v.* Noyes, 72 N. Y. 523.

6 Burt *v.* Horner, 5 Barb. (N. Y.) 501.

7 Tiffany *v.* Willis, 30 Hun (N. Y.), 266. But see Lemmon *v.* Strong, 55 Conn. 443, where it was held that an action against the maker of a note on demand, brought seven years after the guaranty thereof was executed, was not unreasonably brought.

8 Beeker *v.* Saunders, 6 Ired. Law (N. C.), 380. See, also, Mains *v.* Haight, 14 Barb. (N. Y.) 76.

9 Wheeler *v.* Lewis, 11 Vt. 265.

gence.[1] The same thing was held where judgment had been obtained against the principal, and an execution -against his property had been returned *nulla bona* two days after the suit against the guarantor was commenced.[2] In the spring of 1860, a guaranty of a note due the 1st of the following September was made. From the time the note became due, till 1865, the state was engaged in war, and no debts could be collected, and upon the ending of the war the principal became insolvent. No suit was brought upon the guaranty till 1867. *Held*, due diligence had been used, and the guarantor was bound.[3] So where suit was not brought against the principal for ten months, but he was all the time insolvent, it was held that the guarantor was chargeable, although the guaranty was such that suit within a reasonable time must have been commenced against the principal. The insolvency of the principal in such case has a bearing upon the question as to what is a reasonable time.[4] The question of due diligence, when the facts are not disputed, has been held to be one of law for the court.[5] It has also been held to be a question of fact for the jury.[6] And again, it has been held to be a mixed question of law and fact, which must be passed upon by the jury under the instructions of the court.[7] This latter seems the most reasonable view, and the one best supported by legal analogy. Where a debtor gave his check on funds in a bank for the payment of a debt, and the creditor waited seven days before presenting the same for payment, when it was dishonored, the debtor's funds in the meantime having been appropriated, it was held that the creditor had not exercised reasonable diligence in getting his money, and the surety for the debt was discharged.[8]

§ 102. When neither previous proceedings against principal nor his insolvency necessary to charge guarantor.— When the terms of a guaranty of payment fix the time within which the payment shall be made, if the payment is not made

[1] Foster *v.* Barney, 3 Vt. 60.

[2] Woods *v.* Sherman, 71 Pa. St. 100.

[3] Kinyon *v.* Brock, 72 N. C. 554.

[4] Bashford *v.* Shaw, 4 Ohio St. 264; Gallagher *v.* White, 31 Barb. (N. Y.) 92.

[5] Burt *v.* Horner, 5 Barb. (N. Y.) 501; Battle *v.* Blake, 1 Dev. Law (N. C.), 381; Neal *v.* Freeman, 85 N. C. 441.

[6] Rudy *v.* Wolf, 16 Serg. & Rawle (Pa.), 79; Johnston *v.* Chapman, 3 Pen. & Watts (Pa.), 18; Woods *v.* Sherman, 71 Pa. St. 100.

[7] Backus *v.* Shipherd, 11 Wend. 629.

[8] Fegley *v.* McDonald, 89 Pa. St. 128.

within the time prescribed there is a breach of the guaranty, and no steps need be taken against the principal, nor need his insolvency be shown in order to charge the guarantor. This was held where the defendant gave an order for lumber, to be delivered to a third person, which specified: "I will see you paid between this and the closing of the year;"[1] where a bond due on a certain day was guarantied as follows: "For value received, we, the undersigned, guaranty the payment of the within bond according to its terms;"[2] where the guaranty was for the payment of a note "when due;"[3] and where the promisee, in a negotiable note, payable in six months, sold it, having made and signed the following indorsement: "I guaranty the payment of the within note in six months."[4] Where a state guarantied the "punctual payment of the interest" on certain bonds of a city, it was held that the state was liable immediately upon the default of the city, without any proceedings being had against it. The court said that while a guarantor was usually only liable after due diligence had been used to collect from the principal, yet the intention in each particular case must prevail, and in this case it was evidently the intention that the state should become liable immediately upon the default of the city.[5] A guaranty commenced as follows: "For a valuable consideration I hereby guaranty the prompt payment of . . . " (certain notes — describing them), and concluded: "And I hereby obligate myself as firmly for the prompt payment thereof as if I had signed the same." *Held*, the guarantor was liable immediately upon default by the principals.[6] Where the payee of a negotiable note, after it was due, indorsed it as follows: "I guaranty the payment of this note, and costs, if any are made on it," it was held that the guarantor might be sued at once, and

[1] Cochran *v.* Dawson, 1 Miles (Pa.), 276. An absolute guarantor of the payment of a certificate of deposit or note, *held* not released by delay of creditor in enforcing payment from the principal (Hooker *v.* Gooding, 86 Ill. 60), or delay to enforce a lien until it became lost. Adams & French Harvester Co. *v.* Tomlinson Bros., 58 Iowa, 129.

[2] Roberts *v.* Riddle, 79 Pa. St. 468.

[3] Campbell *v.* Baker, 46 Pa. St. 243.

[4] Cobb *v.* Little, 2 Greenl. (Me.) 261.

[5] Arents *v.* Commonwealth, 18 Gratt. (Va.) 750.

[6] Blackburne *v.* Boker, 1 Pa. Law Jour. Rep. 15. For a case holding that, if a party was liable at all, he was only secondarily liable, see Richwine *v.* Scovill, 54 Ind. 150.

it was not necessary to proceed against the principal or show his insolvency.[1] Where the indorsement of a note by the payee thereof was, "I guaranty the payment of the within," it was held that no demand on the principal or notice of his default was necessary to charge the guarantor. The court said: "A guaranty of payment like the one in question is not conditional, but an absolute undertaking that the maker will pay the note when due."[2] It has also been held that the guaranty of "payment" of the debt of another is broken as soon as the principal is in default, without more, the distinction drawn being between a guaranty that the principal will pay and a guaranty that he is solvent. He may not pay and yet be solvent.[3] In all cases of guaranty of the payment of the debt of another, whether the guarantor is immediately liable upon the default of the principal, without more, depends upon the terms of his contract as construed by the court.[4] Where a note is transferred by a debtor to a creditor in payment of a debt, with a guaranty that it is good as gold and will be paid when due, and the note is in fact worthless for want of consideration, the guaranty is broken as soon as made, and may be sued upon immediately.[5] A guaranty of a lease was: "I

[1] Burnham *v.* Gallentine, 11 Ind. 295.

[2] Brown *v.* Curtis, 2 N. Y. 225, per Bronson, J. See, also, on this subject, Heaton *v.* Hulbert, 3 Scam. (Ill.) 489. And see, as supporting the doctrine of the text, Huff *v.* Slife, 25 Neb. 448; Hungerford *v.* O'Brien, 37 Minn. 306; Pool *v.* Roberts, 19 Brad. (Ill. App.) 438; Stowell *v.* Raymond, 83 Ill. 120; Roberts *v.* Hawkins, 70 Mich. 566.

[3] Wren *v.* Pearce, 4 Smedes & Mar. (Miss.) 91. See, also, Bank of New York *v.* Livingston, 2 Johns. Cas. 409.

[4] In Pennsylvania it is held that a contract of guaranty creates only a contingent liability, which becomes absolute by due and unsuccessful diligence to obtain satisfaction from the principal, or by circumstances that excuse diligence. Gilbert *v.* Henck, 30 Pa. St. 205. In Illinois a guarantor is held to be liable immediately upon default of his principal. Heaton *v.* Hulbert, 3 Scam. 489. Close attention should in every case be paid to the terms of the contract of the person who becomes responsible for the debt of another, by whatever name he may be called. Cases have sometimes been improperly decided from the fact that a person to whom a certain designation, such as "guarantor," applied, has been held to the same liability as his class generally, the special terms of his agreement being overlooked.

[5] Koch *v.* Melhorn, 25 Pa. St. 89. See, to exactly similar effect, Taylor *v.* Soper, 53 Mich. 96.

hereby guaranty and become security for the faithful performance of . . . the party of the second part in the above indenture." *Held*, the guarantor was liable immediately upon the default of his principal.[1] The same thing was held where, upon the back of a paper providing for the delivery on demand of certain shares of stock, the following was written: "I hereby become security of . . . for the fulfillment of the within obligation."[2]

§ **103. When a writing does not amount to a guaranty — Instances.**— A party wrote to others as follows: "I have the pleasure of recommending to you my friend . . . as a person in whom confidence can be placed. I am due him $400, but it is inconvenient for me to raise the money just now; should you give him time on the machine till . . . it will confer a favor on me, and you may rest assured that the money will be forthcoming at the proper time." A machine was sold on the strength of this letter. *Held*, the writer was not liable for the price of the machine. There was no promise to pay and no fraud.[3] Plaintiffs had given credit to McC. for goods, but had not delivered them, whereupon the defendant wrote to the plaintiffs: "McC. wishes you to send down his stove, for he wants to put it up to-morrow morning. He is good for the amount he got from you." *Held*, the defendant was not liable for the goods sold. His letter contained no promise to pay, and was a mere declaration that one who had obtained credit was good.[4] The defendant delivered the following letter to the plaintiff: "Let . . . have what goods he may want on four months, and he will pay as usual." *Held*, this was not a guaranty, but at most an expression of confidence that the party purchasing would pay for the goods bought, and there being no ambiguity about it, there was no occasion to resort to the surrounding circumstances or the relations of the parties.[5] Certain soldiers purchased goods of a merchant which were charged to the persons purchasing

[1] Smeidel *v.* Lewellyn, 3 Phila. (Pa.) 70.

[2] Ashton *v.* Bayard, 71 Pa. St. 139. To similar effect, see Prentiss *v.* Garland, 64 Me. 155.

[3] Case *v.* Luse, 28 Iowa, 527.

[4] Kimball *v.* Roye, 9 Rich. Law (S. C.), 295.

[5] Eaton *v.* Mayo, 118 Mass. 141.

them, and bills were made out to them. Across the face of each bill was written the word "accepted," and the name of the brigade quartermaster was signed thereto. *Held*, the quartermaster was not liable for the bills; the word "accepted" did not import a guaranty. If a guaranty had been intended, it would have been as easy to have written the word "guarantied" as the word "accepted."[1] A letter to this effect, viz.: "Any assistance you may render him will be duly appreciated," and vouching for his "industry, correct moral habits and attention to business," held not a guaranty for money to be advanced.[2]

§ **104. Same continued.**— An instrument in the ordinary form of a promissory note, except that it contains the words, "this note given to secure the payment of the Universalist Church debt," is a promissory note and not a contract of guaranty, the words quoted being merely a recital of the consideration.[3] The following letter in reply to an inquiry as to the solvency of an applicant for credit, viz.: "I have no fear in becoming responsible for the goods, but dislike to be troubled with the settlement of other merchants' bills. . . . I see no reason [why] you should doubt him and ask for security. I recommend him as being a safe man to sell to, and I think you ought to allow him credit. . . . His credit is good here, as I furnish him with all his groceries and supplies. I hope you will ship his goods at once. . . . I will look to your interests in the matter." *Held* not to be a guaranty, and the facts stated therein did not constitute a cause of action against the writer as a guarantor.[4] But if the writer thereof knew the statements contained in the letter to be false, he would be liable in damages to an action for deceit.

[1] Hatch *v.* Antrim, 51 Ill. 106.

[2] Mitchell *v.* Stewart & Bro., 10 Heisk. (Tenn.) 18. And see, also, further illustration as to what was held not a guaranty, Dillon *v.* Smith, 10 Heisk. (Tenn.) 595.

[3] Clanin *v.* Esterly Harvesting Machine Co., 118 Ind. 372.

[4] Thomas *v.* Wright, 98 N. C. 272. For further cases illustrating when a writing does not amount to a guaranty, see the following: Bank of Montreal *v.* Munster Bank, 11 Irish Law Rep. 417; Eckman & Vetsburg *v.* Brash & Son, 20 Fla. 763; Meinhardt Bros. & Co. *v.* Mode, 22 Fla. 279; Beadle Co. Nat. Bank *v.* Hyman, 33 Ill. App. 618; Humphreys *v.* St. Louis, I. M. & S. R'y Co. (Cir. Ct. S. D. N. Y.), 37 Fed. Rep. 307; Wilson & Co. *v.* Dean, 21 S. C. 327.

§ 105. When a writing does amount to a guaranty — Instances.— A party wrote on the back of a promissory note as follows: "I assign this note to . . . and indorse the prompt payment of it." *Held*, that the word "indorse" meant "guaranty," and that the party was bound as guarantor. The special indorsement was made either to restrict or enlarge the liability of the indorser. It was not used to restrict it. "The word [indorse] must be construed with reference to the words 'prompt payment' in the same clause of the sentence, and when thus interpreted it is obvious that the word 'indorse' was used in its broadest popular sense, which is sometimes synonymous with the word 'guaranty.'"[1] In articles for the purchase of land the purchaser covenanted to pay for the same in notes "such as he would be responsible for." *Held*, this agreement amounted to a guaranty of such notes as he transferred in payment for the land.[2] A letter written by a party to merchants with whom he had been in the habit of dealing, introducing to them his brother, who was a stranger, stating that the brother was going to their city to purchase goods, and requesting them to introduce him to some of the houses with which the writer dealt, "with assurance that any contract of his will and shall be promptly paid," is a guaranty, and binds the writer to payment for the goods sold. The court said: "As a guaranty is regarded as a mercantile instrument, it is not to be interpreted by any strict technical rules of construction, but by what may fairly be presumed to have been the intention and understanding of the parties."[3] H. held a mortgage on G.'s land to secure a debt presently due, and C. held a mortgage of the equity of redemption of the same land. C. wrote to H. that he was "willing to agree to see him paid" $500 for G. on account of G.'s mortgage to H., within sixteen months. *Held*, this was not a mere proposal for an arrangement, but, under the circumstances, a promise to pay. The

[1] Tatum *v.* Bonner, 27 Miss. 760.

[2] Ward *v.* Ely, 1 Dev. Law (N. C.) 372. As to what amounts to a guaranty, see, also, Westphal *v.* Moulton, 45 Iowa, 163, and Miller *v.* Rinehart, 119 N. Y. 368. As to whether an agreement is a guaranty or original contract, held to be determined from the circumstances of the case. Harris *v.* Frank, 81 Cal. 280.

[3] Moore *v.* Holt, 10 Gratt. (Va.) 284, per Lee, J.

court said the intention was plain, and "the courts never catch at words where the meaning is clear." [1]

§ 106. **Same continued.**— The following indorsement on the back of a promissory note, viz.: "For a valuable consideration to me paid by S. B., and for value received, I promise to pay S. B. the within note," signed and witnessed, is a guaranty.[2] A promise to "see you paid for your trouble" is not an absolute promise, but a guaranty that payment shall be made.[3] A statement upon the back of a promissory note, to the effect that "we know them to be good," is a guaranty that the note is good and collectible at maturity.[4] A promise "that if the plaintiff would endeavor to collect the amount of the loss described from the Grand Trunk Railway Company, they, the defendants, would pay the said claim if the (said) railway did not do so," is a guaranty of the collection of the debt.[5] Where a sewing-machine agent agreed with the company that for all unpaid machines sold by him the purchaser should give his note to the company for the unpaid balance, he (the agent) to indorse and guaranty the collection of such notes, it was held that the agent, by indorsing such notes in compliance with the agreement, became a guarantor.[6] The contract of bondsmen, on the bond of a bank cashier, conditioned for the faithful discharge of their principal's duties, is a contract of guaranty.[7]

§ 107. **Guaranty of payment "when due" of overdue note and of void certificate of deposit, valid.**— A note was made payable in three years from date, and after the expiration of that time a party covenanted that it should be paid "according to its tenor." It was contended that the contract was impossible of fulfillment, and not binding. But the court said:

[1] Colgin *v.* Henley, 6 Leigh (Va.), 85, per Cabell, J.

[2] Bunker *v.* Ireland, 81 Me. 519.

[3] Sedgwick *v.* Bliss, 23 Neb. 617.

[4] Union Nat. Bank *v.* First Nat. Bank, 45 Ohio St. 236.

[5] Phenix Ins. Co. *v.* Louisville & Nashville R. Co. (Cir. Ct. E. D. N. Y.), 8 Fed. Rep. 142.

[6] Osborne *v.* Smith (Cir. Ct. D. Minn.), 18 Fed. Rep. 126.

[7] La Rose *et al. v.* The Logansport Nat. Bank *et al.*, 102 Ind. 332, Elliott and Zollars, JJ., dissenting; The Weed Sewing Machine Co. *v.* Winchel *et al.*, 107 Ind. 260; Singer Mfg. Co. *v.* Littler, 56 Iowa, 601. See further on this subject, Cole *et al. v.* Merchants' Bank, 60 Ind. 350; Jones *v.* Ashford, 79 N. C. 172.

"The contract is to be construed with reference to the state of things then known to the parties as existing, and it being thus known to them that the day of payment of the note had already passed, the parties must be understood to be contracting with reference to a note overdue, and the guaranty was equivalent to a stipulation for the payment of a note payable on demand." [1] The same thing was held when, on the back of an overdue note, a guaranty was indorsed for the payment of the note "when due." [2] A guaranty of payment upon a negotiable note, over the signature of the indorser, is, in the absence of proof, presumed to have been written at the same time as the signature.[3] Principal and surety signed a note payable to a bank ten days after date. The principal, without the knowledge of the surety, left the note with the bank as collateral for what he then owed or might thereafter owe it. Suit was brought on the note by the bank against the surety, and the only claim of the bank was for money advanced the principal after the note was due. *Held*, the surety was not liable. He was by the face of the note only liable for its amount at the end of ten days, and this was a very different thing from standing as a continuing guarantor.[4] The party to whom a certificate of deposit was issued transferred it to another, who had no connection with and was ignorant of the circumstances attending its origin, with a guaranty of the payment thereof. The certificate was void for matters *dehors* its face. *Held*, the guarantor was liable for the amount of the certificate. The court said the guaranty was in effect a representation that the instrument or claim was perfectly valid, as well as a promise to pay it.[5]

§ 108. **When surety for rent liable if tenant holds over — Burning of house, and landlord getting insurance, does not discharge surety for rent.**— A lessor, by a lease commencing "I agree to and with the said J. to lease to him," demised to

[1] Crocker *v.* Gilbert, 9 Cush. 131. No demand on the maker of an overdue note is necessary before charging a guarantor thereof. Winchell *v.* Doty, 15 Hun (N. Y.), 1.

[2] Gunn *v.* Madigan, 28 Wis. 158.

[3] Gilman *v.* Lewis, 15 Me. 452.

[4] Bank of St. Albans *v.* Smith, 30 Vt. 148.

[5] Purdy *v.* Peters, 35 Barb. (N. Y.) 239. For a case holding that if a guaranty is made *ultra vires*, and the paper guarantied afterwards comes to the guarantor's possession, and is issued by it with the guaranty uncanceled, the guaranty is binding, see Arnot *v.* Erie R. R. Co., 67 N. Y. 315.

J. certain premises, and by the same phrase agreed, in the same instrument, at the option of J., to lease him the premises for another year upon the same terms and conditions. The defendant, by a covenant next following in the same instrument the stipulation for another year, agreed "that in case the said J. shall neglect or refuse to pay the aforesaid rent in the manner aforesaid, I will pay the same within ten days thereafter." *Held*, that the defendant was liable for the second year's rent as well as the first.[1] The same thing was held where a lease was for one year, but contained this provision: "This contract is to be renewed for three consecutive years, if it is fulfilled to the satisfaction of both parties," and the defendant, whose name was not mentioned in the lease, wrote at the bottom of it, "security for Frederick S. Gaylord," the lessee.[2] The plaintiff, by a lease which contained no stipulation for a renewal, demised to J. a house for one year, at a certain rent, payable quarterly, and it was provided that J., before the expiration of the term, should give one quarter's notice of his intention to quit. The defendant, by a separate instrument, guarantied the faithful performance of the covenants of the lease; "also the punctual payment" of the rent. J. did not give the notice, and held over. *Held*, the guarantor was not liable for any rent after the expiration of the first year.[3] A. rented a house and lot to B., and C. became surety on the lease. The house was destroyed by fire, and A. had insurance on it to its full value, which he got, and refused to rebuild. *Held*, that neither B. nor C. were discharged from the payment of rent by these facts. Having agreed to pay the rent, they were obliged to do so, even though the house was destroyed, and A. was under no obligation to insure for their benefit.[4]

[1] Deblois *v.* Earle, 7 R. I. 26. So a guarantor for "the payment of rent" on a lease "for the term of one year" . . . "and such further time as the lessee may hold the same," is liable if the lessee holds over after the expiration of the year and fails to pay rent for such further time. Rice *v.* Loomis, 139 Mass. 302.

[2] Decker *v.* Gaylord, 8 Hun (N. Y.), 110. To same effect, see Dufau *v.* Wright, 25 Wend. 636. Holding guarantor of rent, reserved by defective lease, liable for rent reserved if lessee occupies the premises, see Clark *v.* Gordon, 121 Mass. 330.

[3] Gadsen *v.* Quackenbush, 9 Rich. Law (S. C.), 222. See, also, on this subject, Brewer *v.* Knapp, 1 Pick. 332.

[4] Kingsbury *v.* Westfall, 61 N. Y.

§ 109. **Liability of surety for rent continued.**— Where a person guarantied the payment of another's rent "so long as said M. shall occupy said premises," it was held that the word "occupy" denoted the whole period of tenancy.[1] A surety for rent is exonerated from liability if the lessor has, by breach of a covenant in the lease, caused damages to the lessee equal to the amount of the rent.[2] In an action against a surety for rent, alleged fraud on the part of the landlord in failing to disclose the bad reputation of the house, is no defense where the tenant has entered and remained in possession without repudiating the contract of letting.[3] A surety for rent has an interest in personal property mortgaged to the landlord to secure the rent, and he may call upon him for an accounting; but the landlord has a right to a reasonable time in which to sell the property, and, so long as the delay is not unreasonable or unjustifiable, the surety cannot complain.[4] A surety for rent is not released as to rents subsequently accruing because of a release or an extension of the time of payment of rent due.[5] In an action against a guarantor of rent, recovery must be had on the guaranty, and not under the common counts in *assumpsit*.[6]

§ 110. **When surety concluded by result of litigation between other parties.**— If the effect of the obligation of the surety is that he shall be bound by the result of litigation between other parties, he is, in the absence of fraud and collusion, concluded by such result. Thus, a party gave bond with sureties in a chancery suit to abide the decree of the superior court. A decree was finally entered in said court, which the principal endeavored to have set aside, alleging fraud in obtain-

356. Holding guarantor for rent, on tenancy from year to year, discharged if the landlord gives notice terminating the tenancy, even though the tenancy is afterwards continued, see Tayleur *v.* Wildin, Law Rep. 3 Exch. 303. A surety for rent is also discharged if the tenant surrenders part of the demised premises and the rent is thereby reduced. Holme *v.* Brunskill, Law Rep. 3 Q. B. Div. 495.

[1] Morrow *v.* Brady, 12 R. I. 130. Payment of a note either by surety or principal extinguishes it as to the surety. Neylan *v.* Green, 82 Cal. 128.

[2] McAlester *v.* Landers, 70 Cal. 79.

[3] Carhart *v.* Ryder, 11 Daly (N. Y. Com. Pleas), 101.

[4] Coe *v.* Cassidy, 72 N. Y. 133, affirming 6 Daly (N. Y. Com. Pleas), 242.

[5] Coe *v.* Cassidy, 72 N. Y. 133, affirming 6 Daly (N. Y. Com. Pleas), 242.

[6] Potter *v.* Gronbeck *et al.*, 117 Ill. 404.

ing the same. Under the circumstances of the case it was held that the principal could have no relief, and that the sureties stood in no better position. The court said that they had undertaken to abide the event of the suit and must do so. The sureties stood in no better position than the principal, subject to the single exception that, if a judgment or decree had been procured by collusion between the principal and the creditor, the sureties would not be bound thereby.[1] A party arrested for a debt fraudulently contracted gave bond with surety, which provided "that if the fraud complained of shall be established the said . . . security shall be liable for the debt of the complaining creditor." The fraud was established by verdict and judgment, by which the amount of the debt was also established. *Held*, the surety was concluded by the judgment, even as to the amount of the debt.[2] A lease provided that the time when the rent commenced should be determined by arbitrators, which was done, and a certain amount was thus ascertained to be due. There was a surety on the lease who became responsible for the rent for one year, according to the terms of the lease. The surety being sued for the amount found due by the award, it was held that, in the absence of collusion or fraud, the surety was concluded by the award and could not show there was in fact no rent due.[3] A surety signed a bond with the claimant of some property. Another party gave the surety a bond, conditioned to save him harmless from loss or damage on account of the bond he had executed. In a suit on the last bond against the maker thereof the plaintiff offered in evidence a writ and judgment by which he had been adjudged to pay $100 on account of signing the first bond. *Held*, this was sufficient to authorize a recovery, and he was not obliged to show the evidence by which the judgment had been obtained.[4]

[1] Riddle v. Baker, 13 Cal. 295. So, the sureties on an indemnifying bond given to protect a sheriff against any judgment that might be recovered against him for making a levy are, in the absence of any charge of fraud or collusion, concluded by a judgment recovered against him by the owner of the property seized. Connor v. Reeves, 103 N. Y. 527, affirming 35 Hun, 507.

[2] Keane v. Fisher, 10 La. Ann. 261.

[3] Binsse v. Wood, 37 N. Y. 526.

[4] Sprathin v. Hudspeth, Dudley (Ga.), 155.

§ 111. When surety for debt liable for additional damages. When such is the effect of his obligation the surety for a debt is also bound for stipulated damages. Thus, a note provided for the payment of twenty per cent. per annum on its amount, as liquidated and agreed damages, if it was not paid at maturity. The following guaranty was written on the back of the note: "For value received, we guaranty the payment of the within note when due." *Held*, the guarantors were liable for the damages, for they were as much a part of the note as any other.[1] So sureties on a promissory note, which stipulates "that a reasonable sum, to be fixed by the court, for attorney's fees, shall be allowed and taxed as costs against the parties making the notes," are liable for such attorney's fees.[2] A statute provided that interest at the rate of ten per cent. might be contracted for; but if usury was contracted for, the creditor should only recover the principal sum, and judgment for ten per cent. against the debtor and in favor of the state should be entered for the benefit of the school fund. Suit was brought against a principal and surety on a note, and the surety set up and established usury. *Held*, judgment should be entered against both principal and surety and in favor of the state for the ten per cent. The statute did not except sureties and the court would not.[3] A surety who guaranties the punctual payment of "the interest" on a money bond in which there is no stipulation for interest is liable for interest accruing after the bond becomes due. As there was no interest on the bond when the guaranty was made, the guarantor must have intended to become liable for the interest to accrue after the bond was due.[4]

§ 112. Whether surety liable beyond penalty of his bond. The surety on a bond cannot generally be held liable for any sum greater than the penalty thereof.[5] A surety in a stipula-

[1] Gridley *v.* Capen, 72 Ill. 11.

[2] First Nat. Bank of Fort Dodge *v.* Breese, 39 Iowa, 640. Where a guarantor of the payment of a note also agreed to "pay all costs and expenses paid or incurred in collecting the same, including attorney's fees," it was held that the guarantor was only liable for such costs, expenses and attorney's fees as were incurred in suing the maker, and not when they were incurred in suing him on his guaranty. Abbott *v.* Brown, 131 Ill. 108, affirming 30 Ill. App. 376.

[3] McIntosh *v.* Likens, 25 Iowa, 555.

[4] Hamilton *v.* Van Rensselaer, 43 Barb. (N. Y.) 117.

[5] Clark *v.* Bush, 3 Cow. 151; Fairlie

tion given on the release from attachment of the property of a respondent in a suit in admiralty cannot, where the stipulation is in a sum certain, be compelled to pay more than that sum, although the stipulation is conditioned to pay such sum as shall be awarded to the libelant by the final decree in the suit.[1] Where the surety on a sheriff's official bond has paid under judgments rendered on it the amount of the penalty, he can be held responsible for no more. "The principle which limits the liability of the surety by the penalty of his bond inheres intrinsically in the character of his engagement. He does not undertake to perform the acts or duties stipulated by his principal, and would not be permitted to control their performance, and could not where his principal was a public officer."[2] When, however, the surety is bound to the same extent as the principal, and is himself in default, a sum in excess of the penalty of the bond, but not exceeding the legal rate of interest on the amount for the payment of which he is in default, may be recovered against him as damages for the detention.[3] "It may be a reasonable doctrine that a surety, who has bound himself under a fixed penalty for the payment of money, or some other act to be done by a third person, has marked the utmost limit of his own liability. But when the time has come for him to discharge that liability, and he neglects or refuses to do so, it is equally reasonable, and altogether just, that he should compensate the creditor for the delay which he has interposed. . . . The question, in short, is not what is the measure of a surety's liability under a penal bond, but what does the law exact of him for an unjust delay in payment, after his liability is ascertained and the debt is actually due from him."[4] The surety's liability for interest

v. Lawson, 5 Cow. 424; Oshiel *v.* De Graw, 6 Cow. 63; State *v.* Estes, 101 N. C. 541; Showles *v.* Freeman, 81 Mo. 540; Wilson's Case, 38 N. J. Eq. 205; Graeter *v.* De Wolf, 112 Ind. 1; Meadows *v.* The State, 114 Ind. 537; Fraser *v.* Little, 13 Mich. 195; Johnson *v.* McMillan, 13 Col. 423.

[1] Brown *v.* Burrows, 2 Blatch. 340.

[2] Leggett *v.* Humphreys, 21 How. (U. S.) 66, per Daniel, J.

[3] Lewis *v.* Dwight, 10 Conn. 95; State *v.* Wayman, 2 Gill & Johns. (Md.) 254; Harris *v.* Clap, 1 Mass. 308; Judge of Probate *v.* Heydock, 8 N. H. 491; Mayor and City Council of Natchitoches *v.* Redmond, 28 La. Ann. 274; Perry *v.* Horn, 22 W. Va. 381.

[4] Brainard *v.* Jones, 18 N. Y. 35, per Comstock, J. To precisely similar effect, see Frink *et al.* *v.* Southern

accrues either after proper demand on the principal and his refusal to pay, or from the commencement of the suit, in which latter case interest accrues from the day of service.[1]

§ **113. Same continued.**— The sureties on a bond given to secure the performance of work undertaken by their principal are liable for the actual damages sustained by the obligee, but not for a penalty which the principal separately agrees to forfeit in case of his failure to perform as stipulated.[2] A finding in an action on a bond that the sureties thereon are liable for a sum greater than the penalty of the bond is not invalid because of the excess. "The greater includes the less, and it will hardly be claimed that because the debt exceeds the security the creditor must not only bear the loss of the excess but of the other also."[3] Where a statute provides that a surety on a constable's bond may limit the amount of his liability thereon, this does not limit the recovery of costs against the surety; and execution thereon may issue although the amount directed to be levied upon exceeds the penalty of the bond.[4] "Such provision has reference only to the amount the sureties are chargeable with on the penalty of the bond. It has no reference to the costs of the action upon the bond."[5]

§ **114. When surety on note liable if it is not discounted by party to whom it is payable.**— When a surety becomes a party to a negotiable promissory note, payable to a particular person, with the design of raising money to be used by the

Express Co., 82 Ga. 33; Wyman *v.* Robinson *et al.*, 73 Me. 384; Clark *v.* Wilkinson, 59 Wis. 543; Maddox *v.* Rader, 9 Mont. 126. But it is held that this doctrine does not control in the case of a bond conditioned for the performance of a covenant other than for the payment of money. In such a case, *quantum damnificatus* is the issue. Beers *v.* Shannon, 73 N. Y. 292, reversing 12 Hun, 161.

[1] Cassady *et al.* *v.* Trustees of Schools, 105 Ill. 561; United States *v.* Curtis, 100 U. S. 119; United States *v.* Poulson (Dist. Ct. E. Dist. Pa.), 30 Fed. Rep. 231. But see, *contra*, State *v.* Blakemore, 7 Heisk. (Tenn.) 638, and United States *v.* Broadhead, 127 U. S. 212.

[2] Dill *et al.* *v.* Lawrence, 109 Ind. 564.

[3] Odd Fellows *v.* Morrison, 42 Mich. 521.

[4] Mayor, etc. *v.* Ryan, 9 Daly (N. Y. Com. Pleas), 316. But see Gay *v.* Hults *et al.*, 56 Mich. 153.

[5] Daly, J., in Mayor *v.* Ryan, 9 Daly (N. Y. Com. Pleas), 316, 320. For the liability of sureties on guardian's bond where there is no penalty named therein, see State *v.* Britton, 102 Ind. 214; Britton *v.* State, 115 Ind. 55.

principal for a certain purpose, and the note is not discounted by the payee, but is discounted by another, and the money is applied to the purpose intended, it is generally held that the surety is liable for the note.[1] To the objection that the surety has a right to choose his creditor, it is answered that, if the payee had discounted the note, he might the next moment have transferred it to another, and so the surety cannot in such case choose his creditor, and as the object which the surety had in view has been accomplished, he is in nowise prejudiced, and is bound. A., being principal, and B., surety, executed a note payable to a bank, for the purpose of enabling A. to raise money on it for his benefit. The bank refused to discount the note for A., and C. being told by A. that the bank would discount the note, himself advanced the money on it to A. and took it to the bank, which again refused to discount it. C. then got the bank to discount the note for him, and afterwards B. gave the bank notice not to discount it. *Held*, the bank must be considered as having adopted the payment of the note made by C., and could sue on the note for C.'s use.[2] In another case, J., being indebted to P., gave him a note signed by himself and sureties, payable to a bank, with the agreement between J. and P. that P. should get it discounted and apply the proceeds, and if it could not be discounted it should be returned; but this agreement was not known to the sureties. P. could not get the note discounted, but left it with the bank as collateral security for a debt he owed it, and so informed J., who made no objection; after the note came due it was by agreement between J. and P., and without the sureties' knowledge, applied on J.'s indebtedness to P., and P. thereafter prosecuted a suit which the bank had commenced for his benefit. *Held*, that as the note had accomplished the purpose intended the sureties were bound.[3] A. as principal, and B. as surety, signed a note payable in six months to C.,

[1] Keith *v.* Goodwin, 31 Vt. 268; Starrett *v.* Barber, 20 Me. 457; Bank of Middlebury *v.* Bingham, 33 Vt. 621; Planters' and Merchants' Bank *v.* Blair, 4 Ala. 613; Bank of Newbury *v.* Richards, 35 Vt. 281; Browning *v.* Fountain, 1 Duvall (Ky.), 13; Ward *v.* Northern Bank of Kentucky, 14 B. Mon. (Ky.) 283; Thrall *v.* Benedict, 13 Vt. 248.

[2] Bank of Burlington *v.* Beach, 1 Aiken (Vt.), 62.

[3] Bank of Montpelier *v.* Joyner, 33 Vt. 481. To similar effect, see Smith *v.* Moberly, 10 B. Mon. (Ky.) 266; Perry *v.* Armstrong, 39 N. H. 583.

for the purpose of enabling A. to get cloth to the amount of the note from C. A. got cloth from C. amounting to more than half the note, and C. not having enough of the cloth, D. furnished the rest on an understanding between A., C. and D. that a *pro rata* share of the note should inure to the benefit of D. Afterwards C. transferred the entire note to D., and he sued on it. *Held*, B. was liable.[1] Principal and surety executed a note with the expectation that with it the principal would buy a yoke of oxen of A., and give the surety a mortgage on them for his indemnity. The principal did not buy the oxen of A., but bought a yoke of oxen of B., he knowing that the note had been given to buy the oxen of A., but not knowing of the agreement about the mortgage. The oxen purchased from B. did not come to the face of the note, and $6.25 was credited on the back of the note when it was delivered to B. *Held*, both the principal and surety were liable on the note. It was used for the purpose intended, and the credit on its back was not an alteration of it any more than a credit at any other time would have been.[2] A. bought a horse of B., and in payment for it gave his note, with two sureties, payable to a bank or order. It was intended to raise money on the note to pay for the horse, but there was no evidence that the sureties knew the purpose for which the note was given. The bank refused to discount the note, and before it became due the sureties notified the bank not to discount it. After the note became due the bank indorsed it to B., who had always held it, and he sued upon it. *Held*, the sureties were liable. The court said: "It [the note] has not followed, perhaps, the precise channel that was anticipated, but it has not been turned from a strictly legal channel."[3] Principal and surety executed a note to a married woman for some land, and she alone made a deed for it, which was void. Afterwards she died, leaving her property, by will, to her husband. The principal became insolvent, and after the note became due, discovering that his title was bad, applied to the husband, who made him a deed for the land. *Held*, the surety was liable on the note. The principal could not repudiate it, hav-

1 Lyman *v.* Sherwood, 20 Vt. 42.

2 Laub *v.* Rudd, 37 Iowa, 617.

3 Cross *v.* Rowe, 22 N. H. 77, per Eastman, J.

ing received the consideration, and as the surety had executed the note for the purpose of purchasing the land, and it had been used for that purpose, he was bound.[1] The condition of a bond that the principal shall pay "all notes, acceptances and other obligations whatever," given by him for his indebtedness, is applicable not alone to his several notes, but also to notes, if given for his contemplated indebtedness, in which other parties are joint promisors with him.[2] A. made a note payable to B., and C. executed the note with A. as joint maker, the object being to raise money for A.'s use. B. did not discount the note, nor indorse it, but D. did advance money on it to A., and sued A. and C. on it in the name of B. The court held C. liable, and said the law was that if C. signed the note with the understanding that it was to be passed to B. and no one else, then he was not liable. But if C. signed as surety with the general purpose of enabling A. to raise the money on the note, without limiting him as to the person to whom he was to pass it, he would be liable to any one to whom it was passed.[3]

§ 115. When surety on note not liable if it is discounted by party other than payee.— When a surety signs a negotiable note with the principal for a particular purpose, and it is diverted from that purpose by the principal, and the party taking it has then knowledge of facts sufficient to charge him with notice of such diversion, the surety is not bound.[4] But if the party taking the note has no such notice, express or implied, and takes the note in good faith and for value, the surety will be bound to him notwithstanding such diversion.[5] A party became surety on a note for $100, payable to a bank, for the purpose of purchasing lumber for the principal with $75 of the money, and paying $25 of it to the surety and his

[1] Campbell *v.* Moulton, 30 Vt. 667.

[2] Parham Sewing Machine Co. *v.* Brock, 113 Mass. 194.

[3] Perkins *v.* Ament, 2 Head (Tenn.), 110. The fact that a person was induced to sign his name as surety to a negotiable note without reading it, under representations of the maker that it was payable to a bank, when it was in fact payable to an individual, constitutes no defense to the note in an action thereon by the payee, when it does not appear that he had any knowledge of the alleged fraud. Wright *v.* Flinn, 33 Iowa, 159.

[4] Brown *v.* Taber, 5 Wend. 566.

[5] McWilliams *v.* Mason, 31 N. Y. 294.

partner for a debt due them from the principal. The bank never discounted the note, but another creditor of the principal, to whom he owed $22, took out that sum and gave the principal the balance in money. Suit was brought against the surety in the name of the bank, for the use of the party discounting the note, and it was held he was not liable. "From the fact that the defendant was willing to become surety to a particular party to raise money for particular objects, it would be unreasonable to infer that he consented to assume a general liability to any party and for any purpose." The note had been diverted from the purpose intended, and the party who took it had notice thereof, from the fact that on its face it was payable to the bank.[1] So where principal and surety, for the purpose of raising money for the principal's family, signed a note payable to the order of a bank, which the bank refused to discount, and the principal gave it to a creditor of his to pay a pre-existing debt, it was held the surety was not liable. The fact that the note was payable to the bank was sufficient notice to the creditor that the note was made for the purpose of raising money, and, if he had inquired, he would have found that his taking the note would defeat the very purpose for which the surety signed.[2] Principal and sureties signed a note payable to a bank, with the understanding that it should be discounted at the bank. The note never was discounted by the bank, but was sold by the principal to one Cook, who sued it in the name of the bank. *Held*, the sureties were not liable. The court said the sureties might have been willing to be bound to the bank, but to no one else. "The reason for such a preference may be perfectly satisfactory and prudential. Then, as the sureties . . . agreed to be bound to the bank only, and signed the note with the understanding that it was to be delivered to and discounted by the bank, and that they were not to be bound unless it should be so delivered and discounted, the sale and delivery of the note to Cook, without their knowledge or assent, had no binding operation as to them."[3] The same thing was held

[1] Manufacturers' Bank *v.* Cole, 39 Me. 188.

[2] Russell *v.* Ballard, 16 B. Mon. (Ky.) 201.

[3] Conway *v.* Bank of U. S., 6 J. J. Marsh. (Ky.) 128, per Robertson, C. J. The precise opposite of this was held in Farmers' and Mechanics' Bank *v.*

where the note was payable to a bank or order, and it was discounted by a third person, the fact that the note was payable to the bank being held sufficient notice to such third person.[1] It has been held that an accommodation drawer of a bill of exchange, made payable to a particular bank for the purpose of being discounted by the bank named, cannot be held liable on the bill to a third person who, after discount by the bank had been refused, took the bill from the principal for value, and also that such drawer cannot be held liable to the bank where it subsequently discounts the bill for such third person, with notice of the suretyship of the drawer.[2] In holding that a note by principal and surety, made payable to a bank, but discounted by a third person, did not bind the surety, the court said: "He might be willing to lend his name to procure a loan from a party who would indulge him — who would advance to his principal the full face of the note — when he would be utterly unwilling to go security to one who was his personal enemy, or who would exact harsh terms or heavy interest of his principal."[3] Again, it has been held, that if a note payable to a particular person is signed by a surety and sold to another person, the surety is not liable thereon, without his express or implied consent, but such consent may be inferred from the course of business between the parties. This was held, "not upon the ground that there has been a change of contract prejudicial to him, but that there has been no completed contract at all; that there was no delivery to the only party to whom the note, by its very terms, was to be delivered, and therefore that the contract, which was merely undertaken to be made, never took effect."[4] From the cases referred to it appears there is some conflict of authority on this subject. Unless the party suing on the note is the *bona fide* holder thereof for value, without notice, and has the right to sue thereon in his own name, there seems to be much force in the

Humphrey, 36 Vt. 554; Briggs *v.* Boyd, 37 Vt. 534. It seems that in these two last cases the surety was held liable on a contract he never consented to make, and which the taker of the note should have known he never consented to make.

[1] Prescott *v.* Brinsley, 6 Cush. 233. To same effect, see Allen *v.* Ayers, 3 Pick. 298.

[2] Knox Co. Bank *v.* Loyd's Adm'r, 18 Ohio St. 353.

[3] Clinton Bank *v.* Ayres, 16 Ohio, 283, per Birchard, C. J.

[4] Chase *v.* Hathorn, 61 Me. 505, per Peters, J.

objection that the surety has a right to choose his creditor. A reason not already suggested is, that while the payee, if he had discounted the note, would have had the power to sell it to another, yet he might not have done so. In every instance much will depend upon the form of the paper and the special circumstances of the case.

§ 116. When guarantor on general guaranty, or on guaranty addressed to another, liable to person acting on it.—Where a letter of credit is general, addressed to all persons, any one to whom it is presented may act upon and enforce it.[1] A letter of credit addressed to one with the design that it be shown to others to induce them to act upon it, may be sued on by such others in their own names, if acted upon by them.[2] An action may be maintained by the several partners of a firm, upon a guaranty given to one of them, if there be evidence that it was given for the benefit of all.[3] D., who was a merchant in the country, dealing in all sorts of merchandise, being about to purchase a stock of goods in New York, received from A., who had been his partner, a guaranty addressed to no person named, by which A. agreed to be responsible for what goods D. might purchase in New York. *Held*, A. was liable to every person from whom D. purchased goods in pursuance of the guaranty; that the guaranty was not limited to the first person who sold goods on its credit; and that A. was liable for goods sold on the credit usual in such cases.[4] Defendant signed a letter of credit addressed to F., as follows: "As you request, we are willing to help you in the purchase of a stock of goods. We will, therefore, guaranty the payment of any bills which you may make under this letter of credit in Baltimore, not exceeding fifteen hundred dollars." *Held*, that any person advancing goods to F. upon the faith of the guaranty could maintain an action thereon against the

[1] Birckhead *v.* Brown, 5 Hill (N. Y.), 634; affirmed on error, 2 Denio, 375. See, on this subject, Wheeler *v.* Mayfield, 31 Tex. 395; Mayfield *v.* Wheeler, 37 Tex. 256.

[2] Lonsdale *v.* Lafayette Bank, 18 Ohio, 126.

[3] Garrett *v.* Handley, 4 Barn. & Cress. 664. A. and D. were real estate partners. M. wrote to A. that he would guaranty a certain payment if A. would rent him a certain plantation. *Held*, M. was liable on the guaranty whether the renting was done by A. or by A. and D. Anderson *v.* May, 10 Heisk. (Tenn.) 84.

[4] Lowry *v.* Adams, 22 Vt. 160.

defendant as guarantor.[1] A letter of credit was as follows: "James McElroy — Dear Sir: Mr. John Tichenor is going to the city to purchase goods. . . . I will guaranty the payment of such debts as he may contract for the purchase of goods on credit." McElroy was at that time a clerk in a store, but had no store of his own. Tichenor bought goods from four different houses on the strength of the guaranty, the whole amounting to a less sum than that mentioned in the guaranty. *Held*, the guarantor was liable for all the bills. The court said it was apparent from the face of the guaranty that McElroy was not expected to furnish the goods. "It is a general letter of credit addressed through McElroy, a common friend, to the merchants in the city."[2] Defendant addressed to J. V. & Co. the following guaranty: "In consideration of your filling the orders for goods from your Birmingham house of J. C. & Co., say the spring importations, I hereby hold myself responsible for and guaranty the payment of the same to you." J. V. & Co. were the agents in New York for the Birmingham house referred to. The goods having been furnished to J. C. & Co., it was held that the Birmingham house could sue on the guaranty, if intended for their benefit, and whether so intended might be proved by parol.[3] A guaranty was as follows: "Captain Charles Drummond — Dear Sir: My son William, having mentioned to me that, in consequence of your esteem and friendship for him, you had caused and placed property of your and your brother's in his hands for sale, and that it is probable from time to time you may have considerable transactions together; on my part I think proper to guaranty to you the conduct of my son, and shall hold myself liable, and do hold myself liable, for the faithful discharge of all his engagements to you, both now and in future. George Prestman." *Held*, this guaranty extended to and covered a debt incurred by William Prestman to Charles Durand and his brother Richard Durand, as partners, it being proved that the transactions to which the letter related were with them as partners, and that no other brother of Charles

[1] Griffin *v.* Rembert, 2 Rich. N. S. (S. C.) 410. To the same effect, see Manning *v.* Mills, 12 Up. Can. (Q. B.) 515.

[2] Benedict *v.* Sherill, Lalor's Sup. to Hill & Denio, 219.

[3] Van Wart *v.* Carpenter, 21 Up. Can. (Q. B.) 320.

Durand was interested therein. The court said that, according to the ordinary construction of the words of the guaranty, they were intended to apply to a partnership liability.[1] One who guaranties a bond and mortgage to enable the mortgagee to sell the same to a contemplated purchaser is liable on his guaranty to a different purchaser who relied upon the guaranty.[2] In all these cases the guaranty, although addressed to no one, or to the purchaser, or to a third person, or to one of several, was held to be intended for the party advancing upon it, and the guarantor was for that reason held liable.

§ 117. **When guarantor not liable to any one except party to whom guaranty is addressed.**— Usually a guaranty, when addressed to a particular party, can only be acted upon and enforced by such party.[3] A guaranty was on its face addressed to "Col. Smith & Pilgrim," but on its back it was addressed to Smith only. The day previous to the date of the letter the partnership of Smith & Pilgrim was dissolved, and Smith alone sold the goods. *Held*, the guarantor was not liable. The face of the guaranty only could be considered, and not the address on the back. As there was no ambiguity about the guaranty, parol evidence could not be received to vary it.[4] A letter of credit was addressed to A. After the date of the letter A. entered into partnership with B., and A. & B. furnished the goods. *Held*, the writer of the letter was not liable for the goods so furnished. A.'s manner of doing business may have been different from that of the firm, or the writer of the letter may have expected favors from A. which the firm would not grant him.[5] In another case in which the same thing was decided the court said: "It is a case of pure guaranty, a contract which is said to be *strictissimi juris*, and one in which the guarantor is entitled to a full disclosure of every point which would be likely to bear upon his disposition to enter into it. . . . He has a right to prescribe the exact terms upon which he will enter into the obligation, and

[1] Drummond *v.* Prestman, 12 Wheat. 515.

[2] Tucker *v.* Blandin, 48 Hun (N. Y.), 439.

[3] Taylor *v.* Wetmore, 10 Ohio, 490; Pleeker *v.* Hyde, 3 McLean, 279; Second Nat. Bank of Peoria *v.* Diefendorf, 90 Ill. 396.

[4] Smith *v.* Montgomery, 3 Tex. 199.

[5] Sollee *v.* Mengy, 1 Bailey, Law (S. C.), 620.

to insist on his discharge in case those terms are not observed. It is not a question whether he is harmed by a deviation to which he has not assented. He may plant himself upon the technical objection, this is not my contract, *non hæc in fœdera veni*."[1] A., of New York, gave a letter of credit to B., addressed to C., in Albany, requesting him to deliver goods to B. on the best terms, to a certain amount. C., instead of delivering the goods himself, gave B. a letter to D., in Geneva, requesting him to deliver goods to B. to the same amount, and engaging to be responsible. D. delivered the goods to B. In an action by C. against A. for the amount it was held he was not liable. A. had the right to stand on the terms of his contract, and, moreover, D. may not have given B. as good terms or sold the goods as cheap as C. would have done.[2] Two firms, composed of the same members, were doing business in the same city, but in different parts thereof, the name of one firm being Taylor, Gillespie & Co., and that of the other David B. Taylor & Co. A party knowing these facts gave a letter of credit addressed to "Messrs. Taylor & Gillespie," and the firm of David B. Taylor & Co. gave credit on it. *Held*, the guarantor was not liable. The guaranty was intended for Taylor, Gillespie & Co., and the other firm could not recover on it. A partnership consists of something besides its individual members. It has its stock in trade, place of business, books, bills, papers, accounts, etc.[3] A letter of credit purported to bind the guarantors to "any person in Macon, Georgia, who may feel disposed" to advance goods. Without the writer's consent this was changed by inserting Griffin in place of Macon, and the goods were bought in Griffin. *Held*, the guarantors were not bound.[4] A mortgage was given to secure the debt of a third party to the extent of $800, so long as the creditor should continue to sell goods to such third party. Subsequently, the creditor transferred his

[1] Barns *v.* Barrow, 61 N. Y. 39, per Dwight, C. To same effect, see Stevenson *v.* McLean, 11 Up. Can. (C. P.) 208; Allison *v.* Rutledge, 5 Yerg. (Tenn.) 193; Bussier *v.* Chew, 5 Phil. (Pa.) 70. A letter of credit addressed to P. & Co. will not authorize advances by P. alone after the firm is dissolved. Penoyer *v.* Watson, 16 Johns. 100.

[2] Walsh *v.* Bailie, 10 Johns. 180.

[3] Taylor *v.* McClung's Ex'r, 2 Houston (Del.), 24.

[4] Johnson *v.* Brown, 51 Ga. 498.

business to other persons, with whom the debtor continued to deal for some time. During the course of such dealing the debtor paid in more than sufficient to cover the amount of the mortgage. *Held*, the payments must be applied to the oldest items of account, and that the mortgage was discharged.[1] A guaranty commenced: "C. C. Trowbridge, Esq., President, Detroit, Mich.," and there was no further designation of the party addressed; money was advanced on the guaranty by the Michigan State Bank, of which Trowbridge was president. *Held*, it might be shown by parol that the guaranty was intended for the bank. The court said that a guaranty follows the general rule of law with reference to simple contracts, "which is that they may be sued either in the name of the nominal or of the real party, . . . and in the present case, the letter of credit being addressed to the person as president, and the showing him president of the plaintiffs' bank, and of no other institution, renders it certain that it was intended for the plaintiffs' benefit."[2] The following letter of credit, viz.: "Messrs. Bingham Bros., Evansville, Ind., Dear Sirs — Any drafts that you draw on Mr. A. Feigelstock, of our city, we guaranty to be paid at maturity. Kaufman Bros.," was held to be a special guaranty, and that where plaintiff, an Indiana bank, discounted certain drafts drawn by Bingham Bros. on Feigelstock, it acquired no right of action on the guaranty.[3]

§ 118. Surety for several not liable for one — Surety for one not liable for several.— The sureties on a bond conditioned that the principal shall pay for all purchases made by him from the obligee are not liable for purchases made from the obligee by a partnership of which the principal has subsequently become a member.[4] A. wrote to B. as follows: "Any-

[1] Royal Canadian Bank *v.* Payne, 19 Grant's Ch. (Can.) 180.

[2] Michigan State Bank *v.* Pecks, 28 Vt. 200, per Redfield, C. J. For other cases where parol evidence was held admissible, see Wadsworth *v.* Allen, 8 Gratt. (Va.) 174; Garrett *v.* Handley, 4 Barn. & Cres. 664; Van Wart *v.* Carpenter, 21 Up. Can. (Q. B.) 320; Drummond *v.* Prestman, 12 Wheat. 515. If there is no ambiguity, parol evidence is not admissible. Smith *v.* Montgomery, 3 Tex. 199.

[3] Evansville Nat. Bank *v.* Kaufman *et al.*, 93 N. Y. 273, reversing 24 Hun, 612.

[4] Parham Sew. Mach. Co. *v.* Brock, 113 Mass. 194. To same effect, see Shaw *v.* Vandusen, 5 Up. Can. (Q. B.) 353. And to similar effect, see Con-

thing you can do for the bearer, Major S. M. Neill, whom I introduce as my friend, will be done for me, he being a merchant in Clinton. P. S. If you should accept for Mr. Neill for $1,000, I will be bound by this note." On the strength of this B. guarantied two drafts of Hardesty & Neill. *Held,* A. was not liable for such guaranty. A. "might have been willing to become the surety of Neill, and not of Hardesty & Neill. The engagement was personal as to Neill."[1] The defendant executed a bond as surety to an insurance company for the fidelity of A., who was appointed an agent of the company at Adelaide, and who was about to, and afterwards did, enter into partnership (as merchants) with B., also an agent of the company at that place. The condition of the bond was that A. should well and truly account for all money received by him. *Held,* the defendant was not, under this bond, responsible for money received by the firm A. & B., notwithstanding he was aware at the time he signed the bond that A. was about to become B.'s partner.[2] A bond given by the defendant to the plaintiff recited that A. had been appointed agent for the plaintiff, and was conditioned for A.'s good behavior. At the time the bond was given the defendant knew that A. was to be employed only as a partner with B. Afterwards A. & B. received money, as partners, for which they did not account. *Held,* the defendant was not liable for the money so received by A. & B. "When a party makes himself surety for the conduct, not of A. & B., but of A., the stronger proof you give that he knew the relation in which A. and B. stood to each other the stronger you make the inference arising from his mentioning only A."[3] A guaranty for goods to be sold to a firm will not cover advances made to one member of the partnership after its dissolution.[4] If a guaranty is given to a partnership and one of the members dies,[5] or there is a change

necticut Mutual Life Ins. Co. *v.* Scott, 81 Ky. 540; White Sewing Machine Co. *v.* Hines, 61 Mich. 423.

[1] Bell *v.* Norwood, 7 La. (4 Curry), 95, per Bullard, J.

[2] Montefiore *v.* Lloyd, 15 J. Scott (N. S.), 203.

[3] London Assurance Co. *v.* Bold, 6 Adol. & Ell. (N. S.) 514, per Lord Denman, C. J. See, also, where the sureties on precisely such a bond in legal effect, and on the same plea, were released. Connecticut Mutual Life Ins. Co. *v.* Scott, 81 Ky. 540.

[4] Cremer *v.* Higginson, 1 Mason, 323.

[5] Holland *v.* Teed, 7 Hare, 50. To same effect, that the death of part-

in the membership of the firm in any other way,[1] the guaranty will not cover any advances which are afterwards made. A., B. and C. were partners as bankers, and their partnership articles provided that if any one of them died the legal representatives of such one might take his place in the business. D. agreed to become responsible "for all sums of money, not exceeding £20,000, which were then or should afterwards become due (from E.) to A., B. and C., and the survivors, or survivor, of them, or the executors or administrators of such survivor." A. died, and his legal representative became a member of the firm. *Held*, D. was not liable for any advances made to E. after the death of A.[2] A bond recited that A. and B. were bankers at Sunderland, and was conditioned that they would remit to plaintiff all such sums as they, "or either of them," should draw on plaintiff. A. died, and B. afterwards drew bills. *Held*, the surety on the bond was not liable for such bills. From the whole instrument, the intention appeared to be to become responsible for bills which the two partners, or one of them, during the existence of the partnership, should draw.[3] But where a party agreed to guaranty such notes as should be indorsed by a firm, and the firm was dissolved, and one of the partners was, by power of attorney, authorized by the others to transact any remaining partnership business, it was held the guarantor was liable for indorsements made by such partner in the firm name in closing up the partnership business.[4] A party agreed to guaranty the payment for such goods as should be sold to two partners. A bill of goods was so sold, and immediately afterwards the seller arranged with one of the partners that

ner releases a guarantor to the firm, The Cosgrave Brewing & Malting Co. *v.* Starrs, 5 Ont. (Can.) 189. And see London & County Banking Co. *v.* Terry, Law Rep. (25 Ch. Div.) 692. A surety cannot be held on a judgment against a partnership, which has ceased to exist by the death of one of the partners before the date of the judgment. McClosky, Bigley & Co. *v.* Wingfield & Bridges, 29 La. Ann. 141.

[1] Spiers *v.* Houston, 4 Bligh (N. R.), 515; Dry *v.* Davy, 2 Perry & Dav. 249.

[2] Pemberton *v.* Oakes, 4 Russell, 154.

[3] Simson *v.* Cooke, 8 Moore, 588. To similar effect, see Hawkins *v.* New Orleans Print. & Pub. Co., 29 La. Ann. 134.

[4] New Haven Co. Bank *v.* Mitchell, 15 Conn. 206.

the other should go out of the firm, and took the note of the remaining partner alone for the goods, the note being payable to a third person. *Held*, these transactions discharged the guarantor, as the whole course of dealing was changed.[1] The guarantor for goods to be sold to a partnership is not liable for goods sold to the partnership after a change in the members composing it.[2] Sureties became bound for the performance of a particular act (the sale of property) by two persons, one of whom died, and the other sold the property and failed to account for it. *Held*, the sureties were not liable for such failure. They became sureties for both parties, and might not have been willing to become bound for the acts of one alone.[3] A. gave B. a guaranty for goods to be purchased by C., to the extent of 200*l*., the guaranty not being a continuing one. C. took D. as a partner, and B. sold C. and D. goods on the credit of the guaranty to the extent of more than 200*l*., and C. and D. failed. Afterwards, B. sold C. alone goods on the credit of the guaranty. *Held*, B. could not recover on the guaranty for the goods sold C. and D., because they were not within its terms. Nor could he recover for the goods sold to C. alone, because then, by his own act, the circumstances of C. were changed, and he was jointly with D. saddled with a debt of more than 200*l*.[4] A surety for gas, to be supplied to a person on certain premises, is not liable for gas supplied to another person on the same premises, even if the person for whom he became responsible did not notify the gas company of the change in the proprietorship of the premises.[5] The defendant guarantied that certain parties would receive and pay a certain price for a steam-engine and two boilers of a given capacity, particularly described. By agreement of the principals, without the consent of the defendant, an engine with three boilers, and of greater capacity and power, at an additional price, was substituted, and it was held that the defendant was not liable therefor. The court said that the defendants may be supposed to have known the circumstances of his principals, their ability to pay, the power of an engine which

[1] Bill *v.* Barker, 16 Gray, 62.

[2] Backhouse *v.* Hall, 6 Best & Smith, 507.

[3] State *v.* Boon, 44 Mo. 254.

[4] Shaw *v.* Vandusen, 5 Up. Can. (Q. B.) 353.

[5] Manhattan Gas Light Co. *v.* Ely, 39 Barb. (N. Y.) 174.

could be profitably employed, and may have been willing to guaranty the contract first made, and totally unwilling to guaranty the substituted one.[1] All these cases are illustrations of the rule that the surety will only be bound to the extent, and in the manner, and under the circumstances that he consented to become liable. A party who guaranties a note signed by two may, however, under certain circumstances, be liable for the default of one. Thus, A. and B. signed a note, B. signing upon the express condition that he should not be bound unless C. also signed the note as maker. C., knowing these facts, did not sign the note as maker, but guarantied its collection. B., by suit in chancery, had his name stricken from the note, because the terms upon which he signed had not been complied with, and C. claimed that he was thereby discharged from his guaranty. *Held*, that as C. knew B. was not bound when he signed the guaranty, it was the same as if he had guarantied the note of A. alone, and he was liable. "Where the surety knows that the undertaking of the principal is liable to be defeated, he must be considered as entering into his obligation with reference to such a contingency."[2]

§ 119. Surety to or for firm not liable if partners changed — Surety for performance of award not liable if arbitrators changed.— A surety for the good behavior of the clerk of a sole trader is not liable for his acts or defaults after the sole trader takes in a partner.[3] George Smith was doing business under the name of George Smith & Co., as banker, and employed Noble as teller in the bank, Noble giving bond with sureties for his conduct. Afterwards Smith entered into a contract with Willard such as the court held constituted them partners. The firm name continued the same, and Noble continued teller the same, and, after the arrangement with

[1] Grant *v.* Smith, 46 N. Y. 93.

[2] Sterns *v.* Marks, 35 Barb. (N. Y.) 565, per Morgan, J.

[3] Wright *v.* Russell, 2 W. Black. 934. If a surety becomes bound to or for several persons, the engagement must be understood to be in behalf of those persons collectively and jointly, and in case of the death of any of them it will not continue on behalf of the survivors, unless the obligation so states, or the persons to or for whom the surety is bound are described as a class, body or the like, so as to plainly imply that the security is given to or for a class or body. Gargan *et al.* *v.* School Dist. No. 15, 4 Col. 53.

Willard, became a defaulter. *Held*, the sureties were not liable for such default. The court said: "The money then which Noble abstracted was not Smith's, but it belonged to Smith and Willard. Smith alone is the obligor in the bond, and the sureties only undertook for the principal that he should act with fidelity to Smith when in his employ alone. They never undertook to answer for him when in the employ of Smith and Willard, or of any other person than Smith."[1] B., C. and J., who were partners, being appointed agents for the sale of certain books, gave bond with sureties, conditioned that they and the survivors, and survivors of them, and such other person and persons as should, or might at any time thereafter, in partnership with them, or any or either of them, act as agents for selling books, would duly account. J. retired from the partnership, and it was held that the sureties were not liable for any subsequent acts of B. and C.[2] The condition of a bond recited that the obligor had "taken and employed . . . (A.) as a servant, and in the nature of a clerk to him . . . (obligee), and likewise as his book-keeper;" and provided that A. should serve faithfully and account for all money, etc., to the obligee and his executors. *Held*, the surety in the bond was not liable for money received by A. after the death of the obligee, although he was continued in the same employment by the obligee's executor. No service, except to the obligee, was contemplated, although it might have become necessary to account to his executors.[3] Two parties agreed to leave a matter in dispute between them to certain arbitrators named, or a majority of them, and one of the parties gave bond with sureties that he would perform the award. Afterwards, without the knowledge of the sureties, two new arbitrators were substituted, and an award was rendered, a majority of the original arbitrators concurring therein. *Held*, the sureties were not liable for the award.[4]

§ 120. When surety for the acts of one person liable if such acts performed by him and a partner.— Under certain circumstances a surety for the acts of one person will be held

[1] Barnett *v.* Smith, 17 Ill. 565, per Caton, J.

[2] University of Cambridge *v.* Baldwin, 5 Mees. & Wels. 580.

[3] Barker *v.* Parker, 1 Durn. & East, 287.

[4] Mackey *v.* Dodge, 5 Ala. 388.

liable for such acts, even though they are performed by such person as the partner of another. Thus, the defendant executed a bond of indemnity, conditioned that one F., who had been appointed by the plaintiffs their general agent to sell sewing machines, should pay over the proceeds of the sales. F., after his appointment, took in a partner. The plaintiffs knew of this, and the machines were afterwards delivered at the firm's place of business, but they were all delivered on the order of F., and charged to his individual account. In an action on the bond, it was held that while the surety would not have been bound for the acts of any firm, as such, of which F. might be a member, yet the agencies employed by F. in disposing of the machines did not change his relations with his principals so long as they confined their dealings to him; and the delivery of the goods at the place of business of the firm was not sufficient to establish that they changed, or intended to change, such relations, as they could not have based a refusal to deliver upon the ground that F. had taken a partner.[1] A. agreed with B., an attorney, to pay him for all such services as he had rendered or should render C. Afterwards B. took in a partner and rendered services for C., in the pay for which his partner was entitled to share, but the services were rendered by B. *Held*, A. was liable for the services. The fact that B.'s partner was entitled to receive part of the money for the latter services rendered by B. made no difference.[2] By law, no one but persons licensed for that purpose had authority to sell goods at auction, and a licensed auctioneer had to give bonds. A., being a licensed auctioneer, gave bonds with surety, but was conducting the business in the name of A. & B. as partners, B. not being licensed *Held*, the sureties of A. were liable for goods thus sold by him. As no one but a licensed auctioneer could legally sell goods at auction, if they were properly sold, it must be considered the act of A., "and the obligation which he and his sureties contracted in consequence of the privilege granted to him by the government ought not to be impaired by the circumstance of his

[1] Palmer *v.* Bagg, 56 N. Y. 523. To similar effect, see Hayden *v.* Hill, 52 Vt. 259. See, generally, as to liability of guarantor of sewing-machine contract, Davis Sewing Machine Co. *v.* McGinnis, 45 Iowa, 538.

[2] Roberts *v.* Griswold, 35 Vt. 496.

having conducted the affairs of his office with the aid of a partner in the profits, any more than they would be if he had acted by the assistance of a hired clerk. His situation in relation to his partner did not concern the public who applied to him as an auctioneer."[1] These decisions do not controvert the rule that the surety for a single individual is not liable for a partnership of which such individual is a member, but each case, from its peculiar circumstances, was held not to come within the rule.

§ 121. **When obligation given by surety to firm binds him after change in firm.**— An obligation given to a firm, securing it against loss from the acts or default of another, is sometimes held to bind the obligor for matters occurring subsequent to a change in the members of the firm. Thus a principal and three sureties signed a promissory note, payable on demand to a firm "or order," for 300*l*. The note was made for the purpose of enabling the principal to obtain credit with the firm. *Held*, that the note being payable to the members of the firm, or order, and being evidently intended to be a continuing security, the makers were liable upon it, notwithstanding a change in the members of the firm.[2] A bond recited that the plaintiff "had agreed to take one Philip Jones into their service and employ, as a clerk in their shop and counting-house," and was conditioned that he should account "for and pay the plaintiffs all sums of money," etc. Subsequently a new partner was taken into the firm of the plaintiffs, and Jones afterwards made default. *Held*, the sureties were liable for such default. The court said the security was intended to be given to the house as a house, and "the circumstance of taking in a new partner makes no difference, either as to the quantity of business or the extent of the engagement. He continues to carry on the business of the plaintiffs, and this contract is co-extensive with his continuance in the house. This is a security to the house of the plaintiffs, and no change of partners will discharge the obligor."[3] This decision can only be sustained upon the ground

[1] Kuhn *v.* Abat, 14 Martin (La.), 2 N. S. 168, per Mathews, J.

[2] Pease *v.* Hirst, 10 Barn. & Cress. 122. See, also, to like effect, Greer *v.* Bush *et al.*, 57 Miss. 575.

[3] Per Mansfield, C. J., in Barclay *v.* Lucas, 1 Durn. & East, 291, note; Id., 3 Doug. 321.

that it was the intention of the parties, and the effect of the obligation, to give the security to the house as a house, the same as if it had been a corporation, and regardless of who might compose it. A surety executed a bond conditioned for the faithful service of a clerk to a railway company. While the service continued, that company and another railway company were dissolved and united into one company by a statute which provided that all bonds, etc., made in favor of or by the dissolved companies should inure to the benefit of and bind the new company. *Held*, the surety was liable for a default of the clerk after the union of the two companies. The court placed its decision entirely on the words of the statute, and said it made the bond the same as if the name of the amalgamated companies had been mentioned therein.[1] Where a bond is directed by statute to be taken by a corporate body, but no form is prescribed, it is good though taken in the names of the individual members thereof as obligees.[2]

§ 122. Surety not liable beyond scope of his obligation — Instances.— A written guaranty of "the payments of all powder consigned" to a certain person for sale does not render the guarantor liable for a sale to the consignee of the powder remaining unsold upon closing the account between the consignor and the consignee.[3] A guaranty of the payment of a certain sum of money in consideration of the building of a bridge by a county at a place then fixed by a report of viewers is not binding if the bridge is built at another place.[4] A guaranty that O. would consign the plaintiffs sugar to the value of $30,000 does not, in case of the failure of O. therein, bind the guarantors for more than the $30,000, as for commissions on the advances made to O. on the faith of the guarantied consignment and for exchange, etc. If O. had consigned the sugar, the guarantor would not have been liable at all, and his liability cannot exceed the stipulated value of the sugar.[5] A party guarantied the payment for gold with which the plaintiff should supply a goldsmith for the purposes of his

[1] Eastern Union Railway Co. *v.* Cochrane, 9 Wels, Hurl. & Gor. 197.

[2] Greenfield *v.* Yeates, 2 Rawle (Pa.), 158.

[3] Carkin *v.* Savory, 14 Gray, 528. To same effect, see Wilson *v.* Edwards, 6 Lans. (N. Y.) 134.

[4] Mercer County *v.* Coovert, 6 Watts & Serg. (Pa.) 70.

[5] Dunlop *v.* Gordon, 10 La. Ann. 243.

trade. The plaintiff discounted bills for the goldsmith, and gave him for them part gold and part money. The gold was applied to the goldsmith's trade, but he did not indorse the bills. *Held*, the guarantor was not liable for the gold so furnished. He meant only to pay for gold sold the goldsmith, and this was not sold, but paid on the purchase of bills of exchange.[1] A guarantor of payment of any loss which may arise by reason of the sale of goods which, by stipulation between the principal parties, are to be sold within ninety days, is not liable if, by agreement between such parties, the goods are not sold within that time, and the time for sale is extended to one hundred and eighty days.[2] A guaranty provided that the guarantor would be answerable to the plaintiffs to the extent of 5,000*l*. for the use of the house of S. & Co. When the guaranty was given S. & Co. were indebted to the plaintiffs, for which the plaintiffs held their notes and bills. Upon receiving the guaranty, the plaintiffs canceled the notes and delivered up the bills to S. & Co., and S. & Co. thereupon delivered the bills and a new note back to the plaintiffs, but no money passed. *Held*, the guaranty only contemplated future loans to S. & Co., and the transaction did not amount to a loan which would charge the guarantor.[3] The defendant was surety by a bond to the plaintiff for the performance of a contract by S., according to an agreement which provided that S. was to be paid by instalments and one-fourth retained till after the work was done. The plaintiffs made advances to S. not called for by the contract, and in excess of the work done by him. S. failed to complete the work, and the plaintiffs got others to complete it. The amount paid to S. and the last contractor exceeded the contract price, but the value of the work done by S. and the price paid the last contractor did not together equal the contract price. *Held*, the plaintiff could recover nothing on the guaranty. The advances made by him to S. were made in his own wrong, and he must lose them.[4] Sureties for the faithful performance of his duties, by

[1] Evans *v.* Whyle, 5 Bing. 485; Id., 3 Moore & Payne, 130.

[2] Fisher *v.* Cutter, 20 Mo. 206.

[3] Glyn *v.* Hertel, 8 Taunt. 208.

[4] Warre *v.* Calvert, 2 Nev. & Per. 126; Id., 7 Adol. & Ell. 143. Approved and followed in a case similar in principle in Texas. Ryan *v.* Morton, 65 Tex. 258.

the freight agent of a railroad company, are not responsible for money received by another person appointed by the railroad company and in its employ at the same station, but who is under the orders of such freight agent.[1]

§ 123. Liability of surety or guarantor — Special cases.— A guaranty was as follows: "I will be accountable to you for payment within six months of the seed order forwarded by my son, R. A. H., and also for payment within three months of six hundred barrels of vetches, to be forwarded by the first steamer." The seeds were furnished and the vetches were not. *Held*, the seeds might be recovered for, as the contract was not entire. That portion concerning the vetches was distinct from the other, to be paid for in a different time, etc.[2] The condition of a bond executed by E. to the F. & M. Bank, was that A. shall and will from time to time ask for and receive from said bank certain sums of money, at no time exceeding $5,000. Now if said A. shall well and truly pay, or cause to be paid, to said bank, all such sums as he may as aforesaid receive, then the obligation to be void, etc. *Held*, taking the whole instrument together, it was the intention of E. to restrict the whole amount of the indebtedness of A. to the bank, at any one time, to $5,000, and the bank having allowed him to become indebted in a larger amount, E. was not liable at all. E. may have thought that A. could not successfully handle more than $5,000; and such may have been the fact. Having restricted his liability, he could only be held to his contract as he had made it.[3] In a case very similar to this, it was held that the surety was liable for the amount specified in the bond, notwithstanding a greater sum had been advanced. The court said if it was intended that a greater advance than the sum mentioned in the bond should avoid it, then the bond should have said so.[4] These cases do not differ in principle. The court, in one case, held that the intention of the surety appeared, from the instrument, to be that he should not be bound at all if a greater sum than that stipulated was advanced. In the other case, the court held that no such inten-

[1] C. & A. R. R. Co. *v.* Higgins, 58 Ill. 128.

[2] Nash *v.* Hartland, 2 Irish Law Rep. 190.

[3] Farmers' & Mechanics' Bank *v.* Evans, 4 Barb. (N. Y.) 487.

[4] Parker *v.* Wise, 6 Maule & Sel. 239.

tion appeared. A guarantor for the price of goods ordered, but not yet sent, is not discharged by the fact that the purchaser, upon receiving the goods, was dissatisfied with them, but finally agreed to keep them upon the seller deducting ten per cent. from the original price.[1] A guaranty of the payment of different kinds of goods, to be sold on a credit of six months, does not render the guarantor liable for anything, if one kind of the goods is sold on a credit of four, and another on a credit of six months. The guaranty offered was entire, and if not accepted as offered, it could not be accepted at all, and there was no contract.[2] Where the contract, the performance of which is guarantied, provides for notes at four months, to be renewed, if desired, for sixty days, at eight per cent. interest, the guarantor is not holden for notes running six months, with interest for four months at seven per cent., and thereafter at eight per cent.; nor for six months' notes with interest at eight per cent., commencing four months after date.[3] So a guarantor for the price of goods to be sold on a credit of six months, is not liable if the goods are so sold, but afterwards the term of credit is, by agreement between the purchaser and seller, lengthened as to a part and shortened as to another part.[4] A surety who agrees to indemnify A. if he will give his drafts at three months to B., in order to enable B. to raise money to pay C., is not liable, if A. give B. the money, instead of the drafts, to pay C., and B. with the money pays C.[5] The reason is that B. became immediately liable to A. for the money so advanced, when, if the original agreement had been carried out, such liability would not have arisen for three months, and this time may have been of great value to B. It made no difference that three months' time was actually given B., for there was no certainty that it would be given. A guaranty as follows: "I hereby guaranty the payment of any purchases of bagging and rope which . . . may have occasion to make between this and the first of December next," extends the liability of the guarantor to purchases upon a reasonable credit made before the first of December, although

[1] Rice *v.* Filene, 6 Allen, 230.

[2] Leeds *v.* Dunn, 10 N. Y. 469.

[3] Locke *v.* McVean, 33 Mich. 473.

[4] Henderson *v.* Marvin, 31 Barb. (N. Y.) 297.

[5] Bonser *v.* Cox, 6 Beav. 110. See, also, 4 Beav. 379.

the time of payment was not to arrive till after that day.[1] When a guarantor agrees to be responsible for a bill of goods to be sold on three months' credit, he is liable, if the seller take the note of the purchaser, at three months, for the goods. It was a credit of three months, as usually understood in the commercial world, and the fact that the note had three days of grace after the expiration of the three months made no difference, as no business man would have thought of cutting off the days of grace.[2] A. gave B. the following guaranty: "I have given C. an order to purchase cotton, and . . . I have, in such case, to request that you will honor his drafts to the amount of those he may send to you for sale on my account, and I engage that his bills on me so transmitted shall be regularly accepted and paid." *Held*, the guarantor was liable for drafts drawn by C. on A., and honored by B., on the representation of C. that they were for A.'s benefit, when they were not so in fact. The fair construction of the guaranty was, that A. would be liable for such bills as C. should represent he had drawn on A.'s account.[3]

§ 124. When surety cannot set up illegal acts of creditor or principal as a defense.— A contract providing for the return to the owner, who had loaned them, of certain shares of railroad stock, and for the payment of interest for their use, was signed, in the name of the railroad company which borrowed them, by its president, and guarantied by certain parties. *Held*, the guarantors were estopped to deny that the president of the company had authority to sign the contract. By guarantying the contract, they had in substance asserted its validity, and to permit them to deny it would be to allow them to take advantage of their own wrong.[4] The teller of a bank had authority to issue due bills for the bank, for a special purpose, and issued such bills, not for such purpose, but to raise money for himself. *Held*, that neither he nor his surety could set up a want of power in the bank to issue them. The teller and his sureties were "not as parties to the instrument entitled to contest them, although they were issued for the bank in the name of the teller. As well might the teller

[1] Louisville Mfg. Co. *v.* Welch, 10 How. (U. S.) 461.

[2] Smith *v.* Dann, 6 Hill (N. Y.), 543.

[3] Ogden *v.* Aspinwall, 7 Dow. & Ryland, 637.

[4] Simons *v.* Steele, 36 N. H. 73.

contend that, as he committed a fraud, the bank was not bound by his act. This he could not be heard to do."[1] A party was, by resolution of a city council, appointed the city's agent to negotiate certain bonds of the city on specified terms. The agent accepted the trust and gave bond with sureties for the faithful performance of his duties. He afterwards borrowed $5,000 for thirty days, for which he gave the city's note, and put up as collateral thereto, $21,000 of city bonds. This money he did not pay over. The city paid the note for $5,000, and took up the bonds, and sued the surety of the agent for the $5,000. *Held*, he was liable, and it made no difference, under the circumstances, whether the bonds were legally or illegally issued by the city, nor whether or not it was bound by the note, signed by the agent. The city adopted the act of the agent, and paid the note to save its credit, and he and his sureties were liable for the money received by him.[2] But where the seller and purchaser of a national bank had both been guilty of acts in the purchase and sale which were prohibited by the banking act, and impaired the value of the bank, it was held that the surety of the purchaser was not liable, and this although the purchaser did not seek to rescind the contract. Both the creditor and principal had been guilty of an act prohibited by law which was injurious to the surety, and the equity of the surety to a discharge did not depend upon the fact that the principal should desire to rescind the contract.[3]

§ 125. When surety not liable for specific performance — Surety not charged to exonerate estate of principal — Other cases.— A second tenant in tail joined in a mortgage and bond with the first tenant in tail, who received the money lent thereon. The first tenant in tail died, and it was held that his creditors could not, by bill in equity, have the money secured by the mortgage made out of the mortgaged premises, so as to exonerate the personal estate of the first tenant in tail.[4] A. held two mortgages on the same property, each of them to secure a separate note. He sold the second

[1] Wayne *v.* Com. Nat'l Bank, 52 Pa. St. 343, per Thompson, J.

[2] City of Indianapolis *v.* Skeen, 17 Ind. 628; Wilson *et al.* *v.* Town of Monticello, 85 Ind. 10.

[3] Denison *v.* Gibson, 24 Mich. 187.

[4] Robinson *v.* Gee, 1 Vesey Sr. 251.

mortgage, and the note secured by it, to B., and guarantied the payment of the note; and transferred the other note and mortgage to C., as collateral security. *Held*, the guaranty of the note which A. sold to B. did not give such note, and the mortgage securing it, a preference over the other. The only effect of the guaranty was to render A. personally liable.[1] A. owed B. two notes, each for 1,000*l*., on one of which C. was surety. A. had a security up with B. for both debts, and became bankrupt. B. proved both claims against his estate, and received a dividend, and also received a certain sum from the security. *Held*, C. was only liable for one-half the sum proved by B. against A.'s estate, after deducting therefrom one-half of both sums received by B.[2] A. purchased land from C., and gave his note with B. as surety for the purchase money, C. also retaining a lien on the land to secure the purchase money. A. became insolvent, and the land was sold under execution, and purchased by D. Afterwards, C. obtained judgment on the note against A. and B., and levied his execution on the land. *Held*, D. could not compel C. to exhaust the property of B. before selling the land. If B. had paid the debt, he would immediately have been subrogated to C.'s lien, and D. would have been in no better position.[3] A party gave bond, with surety, to convey two hundred acres of land, situated within a certain district. Upon default of the principal, it was held that the surety could not be compelled to specifically perform the contract by conveying land of his own, although he owned more than the required amount and kind within the prescribed district. The surety covenanted that the principal, not himself, would convey. He could only be held liable in damages, and not for a specific performance.[4] Three parties purchased, jointly, separate lots of ground, and each gave his notes for one-third of the amount. The act of sale declared that each had a one-third interest in the property, and provided "that, to secure the payment of the aforesaid notes, the purchasers hereby mortgage the herein described property." Two of the purchasers paid their notes,

[1] Gansen *v.* Tomlinson, 8 C. E. Green (N. Y.), 405.

[2] Coates *v.* Coates, 33 Beav. 249.

[3] Cole County *v.* Anguey, 12 Mo. 132.

[4] Johnson *v.* Hobson, 1 Litt. (Ky.) 314.

and it was held that their land could not be sold to pay the note of the third. The court said it was the same as if each had given a separate mortgage on his portion of the land, and when any one paid, it operated the release of his land.[1] But where two joint owners of a piece of land jointly mortgaged it to secure the several notes of each of them, it was held that the interest of both might be sold to pay the note of one.[2]

§ 126. What payment by person indemnified will charge surety — When surety liable for costs — Other cases.— When a party indemnified by bond with surety, against the payment of money, is obliged to pay it, and does pay it by giving his negotiable note, which is accepted as payment, he may sue the surety, and recover the same as if he had paid in money.[3] The guarantor of a note is not liable for protest fees, because protest is not necessary in order to fix his liability.[4] Nor is the guarantor of a note, who is absolutely liable, without any suit against the maker, chargeable with the costs of such a suit.[5] But where one partner, by bond with surety, agreed to pay all the firm debts, and failed to do so, and the retiring partner was arrested in another state for one of the debts, and paid the debt and costs, it was held that the surety was liable for such costs.[6] A guaranty was as follows: "Gentlemen, you will please to credit Mr. A. to the extent of 30*l.*, monthly, from time to time, and in default of his not paying, I will be accountable for the above amount." *Held*, the guaranty was not limited to 30*l.* in all, but authorized an advance of 30*l.* every month, even though the aggregate indebtedness might amount to much more than 30*l.*[7] Where a lease provided for the payment of rent in monthly instalments, and a party guarantied the prompt performance of all the covenants thereof by the lessee, the guarantor is liable, and may be sued for the rent each month as it becomes due.[8] Where one who has contracted with A. to indemnify and keep him harmless

[1] Erwin *v.* Greene, 5 Rob. (La.) 70.

[2] Hunt *v.* McConnell, 1 T. B. Mon. (Ky.) 219.

[3] Lee *v.* Clark, 1 Hill (N. Y.), 56; Gage *v.* Lewis, 68 Ill. 604.

[4] Woolley *v.* Van Volkenburgh, 16 Kan. 20.

[5] Woodstock Bank *v.* Downer, 27 Vt. 539.

[6] Wright *v.* Sewall, 9 Rob. (La.) 128.

[7] Tennant *v.* Orr, 15 Irish Com. Law, 397.

[8] Bing *v.* Tyler, 79 Ill. 248.

as to "liabilities" incurred by him as indorser for B. permits a judgment to be taken against A. on such indorsement, it is not necessary that the judgment should have been collected to enable A. to maintain an action for breach of the contract.[1] A note was guarantied to be "good and collectible two years." *Held*, the guaranty covered the period of two years after the maturity of the note, as the note was not collectible till it was due.[2] Where a bond of $1,000 is required of an accused person, and he gives such a bond, in which each of the two sureties becomes bound for $500, the bond is valid.[3]

§ 127. **Surety not liable for greater sum than principal — Other cases.**— A surety who signs in the absence, and without the knowledge, of the principal is bound.[4] A guaranty may have a retrospective operation, where it appears from the instrument that such was the intention of the parties; and an instrument may be ante-dated so as to embrace a particular transaction; and the date of the instrument is evidence of the time when the parties intended it to take effect.[5] Suit was commenced against the principal and one surety, on a paymaster's official bond, and judgment for $10,000 recovered. Afterwards suit was brought against another surety on the bond, and a greater recovery than $10,000 claimed. *Held*, that as the liability of the principal was fixed at $10,000 by the first judgment, the surety in the last suit could not be held liable for more. Otherwise the surety would be held to a greater liability than the principal.[6] If the consideration upon which a surety signs fails, he is discharged, and may come into equity and have his obligation canceled.[7] A common money bond, payable on demand, given by a principal and surety, to a person then the creditor of the principal, is presumed to be given for the existing debt, and not to cover future advances by the creditor to the principal.[8] When a surety, who had an opportunity to read it, but did not,

[1] Smith *v.* Chicago & N. W. R. R. Co., 18 Wis. 17.

[2] Marsh *v.* Day, 18 Pick. 321. As to liability of the surety on a bond "to be binding only one year from date," see Davis *v.* Copeland, 67 N. Y. 127.

[3] Moore *v.* The State, 28 Ark. 480.

[4] Hughes *v.* Littlefield, 18 Me. 400.

[5] Abrams *v.* Pomeroy, 13 Ill. 133.

[6] United States *v.* Allsburg, 4 Wall. 186.

[7] Cooper *v.* Joel, 1 De Gex, Fish. & Jo. 240.

[8] Walker *v.* Hardman, 4 Clark & Fin. 258.

signed a bond for the payment of a debt, believing it, from the representations of the principal, to be a bond for the delivery of attached property, he is guilty of such gross negligence as will prevent him from having relief in equity against the bond.[1] A guarantor that a party shall not become bankrupt is not liable unless a commission of bankruptcy is sued out against such party.[2] The same causes which will discharge a surety on a promissory note will ordinarily discharge an indorser of the same.[3] If a note is void for usury, a guaranty thereof, which has no other consideration than the note, is also void for the usury.[4]

§ 128. Sureties on assignee's bond not liable to those who defeat the assignment — Principal cannot allege for error that surety is discharged — Other cases.— The sureties on the bond of an assignee, given pursuant to a statute with reference to voluntary assignments for the benefit of creditors, are not liable for the failure of their principal to account for the assets in his hands, as required by a judgment in favor of creditors declaring the assignment void as to them, and directing the assignee to pay over the assets and avails thereof in his hands, to be applied in satisfaction of their claims. The bond was not intended for the benefit of persons who attacked and defeated the assignment, and thereby defeated the trust, but was for the good behavior of the assignee as trustee under the assignment.[5] When the surety is discharged on the trial of a case against principal and surety, in the court below, the principal cannot allege for error in the court above such discharge of the surety. "The release of the surety, whether erroneous or not, could in nowise prejudice the defendant or

[1] Glenn *v.* Statler, 42 Iowa, 107.

[2] Bulkeley *v.* Lord, 2 Stark. 406.

[3] Smith *v.* Rice, 27 Mo. 505.

[4] Heidenheimer *v.* Mayer, 10 Jones & Spen. (N. Y.) 506. But the demand and receipt by a national bank of usurious interest from indorsers upon notes discounted by it, the payment of which notes was guartied to the bank, does not avoid the contract of guaranty between the guarantor and the bank, unless the law regulating the rate of interest provides that the taking of illegal interest shall render void the contract. Lazear *v.* Nat'l Union Bank of Md., 52 Md. 78, 121.

[5] People *v.* Chalmers, 60 N. Y. 154. But they are liable if the principal refuses to obey an order made to subvert the assignment. Adams *v.* Hyams (Cir. Ct. D. Conn.), 8 Fed. Rep. 417.

affect his liability as principal, and he will not, therefore, be heard to complain of it."[1] The surety on a note given for the price of a horse, and which is void because it is payable in Confederate money, is not liable on the note, because it is void; nor is he liable for the price of the horse, because his only liability existed by virtue of the note.[2] A surety is bound to ascertain his principal, and where, by mistake, he signs a bond for the lessee of a telegraph company instead of for the company, to release property from attachment, he will be bound.[3] If it is agreed that a certain party shall be surety on a bond to a sheriff, and a blank bond is taken to him and he signs it, and dies, and afterwards the bond is filled up according to the agreement and delivered to the sheriff, the estate of the surety is liable on the bond. As the surety had been previously agreed upon, the contract was complete as soon as the surety signed.[4] The sureties on the bond of an assignee for the benefit of creditors, which provides that the assignee shall "faithfully execute the trusts confided to him," are concluded by the final decree of a court upon the account of the assignee, by which he is directed to pay the claim of a specific creditor.[5] It has been held that the fact that a voluntary bond is not stamped is no defense to the sureties therein. They or their principal should have stamped it.[6]

§ 129. **When surety released if creditor and principal intermarry — Surety not liable to party who pays debt at principal's request — Other cases.**— A party who, at the request of the principal alone, pays the debt for which a principal and surety are bound, cannot usually collect the amount so paid from the surety. Thus, where an executor, supposing the estate of his testator to be solvent, paid in full a debt due by the testator on which there was a surety, it was held that the executor could not, upon the estate proving insolvent, recover any portion of the sum so paid from the surety.[7] A. as

[1] Fewlass *v.* Abbott, 28 Mich. 270.

[2] Shepard *v.* Taylor, 35 Tex. 774.

[3] Doane *v.* Telegraph Co., 11 La. Ann. 504.

[4] Wells *v.* Moore, 3 Rob. (La.) 156.

[5] Little *v.* The Commonwealth, 48 Pa. St. 337.

[6] McGovern *v.* Hoesback, 53 Pa. St. 176.

[7] Paine *v.* Drury, 19 Pick. 400. Holding the same principle with reference to the surety on a distiller's bond, see Elmendorph *v.* Tappen, 5 Johns. 176. And so where an ad-

principal, with others as his sureties, executed a note to B., a *feme sole*, and afterwards A. and B. intermarried; under the provisions of an ante-nuptial contract between them, the note did not pass to A. upon the marriage, but remained the separate property of B. *Held*, that upon the marriage the wife lost her remedy by action against the husband, and the sureties were thereby discharged.[1] A creditor authorized his agent, B., to administer on the estates of any of his debtors who might die intestate. B. administered on one of those estates, and gave bond with C. as surety for the faithful performance of his duty as administrator. B. used the funds of the estate and became bankrupt. *Held*, C. was not liable to the creditor for B.'s default. B. was the agent of the creditor, and represented him in that regard. C. was therefore the surety of the creditor, and the creditor had no cause of action against his own surety.[2]

§ **130. When agreement to pay in good notes not guaranty that notes in which payment is made are good — Other cases.**— Where, in an agreement for the sale of goods, it was stipulated that a part of the purchase money should be paid in "good obligations," and certain notes were tendered to the seller, and received and receipted for by him "on payment of goods," there is no guaranty of the solvency of the makers of such notes. The insertion of the word "good" implied no

ministrator, with money of his decedent, pays on a note executed by his decedent as principal, with sureties, an amount in excess of the sum applicable out of the assets of that debt, under the mistaken belief that he was surety on such note, he cannot recover against a surety on said note the amount so paid in excess of the ratable share of the assets applicable to such debt. Proudfoot *v.* Clevenger, 33 W. Va. 267.

[1] Govan *v.* Moore, 30 Ark. 667.

[2] Moodie *v.* Penman, 3 Dessaus. Eq. (S. C.) 482. Holding that a surety for a suit to be commenced at the next term of court is not liable for a suit commenced at the third term, see Hibbs *v.* Rue, 4 Pa. St. 348. To the effect that a surety cannot prevent a judgment against the principal from being amended, see Pryor *v.* Leonard, 57 Ga. 136. As to when a guaranty, which by its terms is not to be produced till the death of the parties, is valid if produced before, see Washburn *v.* Van Norden, 28 La. Ann. 768. Holding that where a surety is paid by the principal the amount of a debt for which he is liable, and thereupon agrees to pay the creditor, he becomes the principal, and the principal becomes the surety, as between them, see Coggeshall *v.* Ruggles, 62 Ill. 401. See further, as to when surety may become principal, Hurlun *v.* Ely, 55 Cal. 340.

guaranty, but gave the seller a right to refuse notes which did not answer that description; and having received the notes as good, and receipted for them, he has not, in the absence of fraud, any claim upon the purchaser."[1] A guaranty was as follows: "This may certify that we, being acquainted with Frank Stevens, and reposing great confidence in his honesty, and the goods you may see fit to intrust him with, we will hold ourselves good for, provided he should sell them and abscond with the money or squander them away; and this shall be your note against us." *Held*, this was a mere guaranty of the honesty of Stevens. The guarantors were not liable unless Stevens sold the goods and absconded, or squandered them; and a failure to pay for the goods was not evidence that they had been squandered.[2] A guaranty that the owner of stock in a corporation shall receive dividends thereon of a specified amount, for a certain number of years, by paying to the guarantor all he receives above that amount, is valid. It is not a wager, but "not only in words, but also in its plain design, a guaranty to the plaintiffs of a certain yearly profit on railroad stock owned by them.[3] On a transfer of certain shares of railroad stock, the assignor guarantied "that said stock shall yield annually six per cent. dividends for the space of three years." *Held*, this was a guaranty that the stock was equal in value to stock yielding annual dividends of six per cent., and not merely a guaranty that the assignee should receive six per cent. annually for three years on the par value of the stock. The measure of damages was the difference between the actual value of the stock assigned and stock which would have yielded dividends of six per cent. for the three years.[4] A guaranty on a bond was as follows: "For value received, I guaranty the punctual payment of the interest on the within bond, and will pay the interest on demand in default of its payment by . . . " [the principal]. The bond was due in six and a half years, and the interest was payable semi-annually. *Held*, the guaranty only extended to the payment of interest falling due before the time of payment of the principal sum. If it was otherwise, and the bond

[1] Corbet *v.* Evans, 25 Pa. St. 310.

[2] McDougal *v.* Calef, 34 N. H. 534.

[3] Elliot *v.* Hayes, 8 Gray, 164, per Metcalf, J.

[4] Struthers *v.* Clark, 30 Pa. St. 210.

was never paid, the guarantor would be liable for interest forever.[1] If the principal borrow money to pay a note, the law will not imply an authority in him from those who signed the note as sureties only, to borrow the money on the joint credit of the principal and sureties, nor a promise from the sureties to the lender to repay the money so borrowed.[2]

§ 131. Surety for return of slave liable, if death of slave caused by principal — Other cases.— A surety who executes a bond for the hire of a slave, which contains a covenant for the return of the slave at the end of a year, is not discharged from his obligation to return the slave by the fact that before the end of the year such slave dies in consequence of the inhuman treatment which he receives at the hands of the principal. The death of the slave was not the act of God or the owner. The principal and surety "are joint covenantors, equally bound for the performance of the covenant, and neither can exonerate himself from liability on the ground that the wrongful act of the other has rendered a performance by him impossible."[3] A party wrote a letter introducing another, stating that he wanted to purchase a certain amount of goods, and concluding, "I consider him perfectly good, and, if required, will indorse for him to that amount." *Held*, he was not liable for goods sold on the strength of this letter, unless he had been requested to indorse, and had refused. The guaranty was conditional, to be created by indorsement, if required, and the protection of the party writing the letter may have depended upon the form of the security.[4] A bond provided that a secretary of state should return certain fees, if it should be decided by the legislature or supreme court that they were not chargeable to a fund commissioner. *Held*, the sureties were not liable unless the legislature or supreme court decided as provided in the bond. A decision by one house of the legislature was not sufficient, and neither the sureties nor their principal were bound to procure the decision.[5] A covenant to indemnify A. against all damages and

[1] Hamilton *v.* Van Rensselaer, 43 N. Y. 244; Melick *v.* Knox, 44 N. Y. 676.

[2] Rolfe *v.* Lamb, 16 Vt. 514.

[3] Carney *v.* Walden, 16 B. Mon. (Ky.) 388, per Simpson, J.

[4] Stockbridge *v.* Schoonmaker, 45 Barb. (N. Y.) 100.

[5] Field *v.* Rawlings, 1 Gilm. (Ill.) 581.

costs which he may incur in consequence of indorsing any notes of B., past or prospective, relates only to indorsements made by A. for the accommodation and at the request of B., and does not extend to indorsements by A. of notes given him by B. for debts of B. due to A.[1] A statute concerning paupers provided that a settlement might be gained "by any person who shall *bona fide* take a lease of any real estate of the yearly value of ten dollars, and shall dwell upon the same one whole year, and pay the said rent." A. took a lease of ground for a year at a rent of $1 a month, and paid $1.50 rent himself, and his surety, B., paid the balance. *Held*, this was sufficient to entitle A. to a settlement. It was the same as if A. had borrowed the money from B. and paid the rent.[2] Upon a bond conditioned that one J. should pay to plaintiffs monthly, "and every month during the time for which he should act as their agent, all moneys which he then had received or which he should receive for premiums, etc., and should repay to the applicants all moneys which he had then received or should receive for insurances not accepted by the plaintiffs, and should in all things well and faithfully conduct himself as their agent," it was held the sureties were only liable for moneys received after the bond was executed.[3]

§ 132. Surety for balance which may remain due after sale of property not liable till completed sale made — Other cases.— An executor's bond, describing the testator as James L. Findley, cannot by parol evidence be made applicable to the estate of Joseph L. Findley, although it was the intention to give the bond in the estate of the latter, and the mistake was a clerical error.[4] In consideration that the plaintiff would advance 1,200*l*. to a third person, upon mortgage of certain leasehold premises, the defendant promised that if, after any

[1] Trask *v.* Mills, 7 Cush. 552.

[2] Butler *v.* Sugarloaf, 6 Pa. St. 262.

[3] Canada West, etc. Ins. Co. *v.* Merritt, 20 Up. Can. (Q. B.) 444. As to what is guaranty and not an original undertaking, see Kellogg *v.* Stockton, 29 Pa. St. 460. As to when sureties of life insurance agent are not liable for renewal premiums received by him, see Crapo *v.* Brown, 40 Iowa, 487. As to what must be stated in declaration against guarantor that a note is collectible, see Sylvester *v.* Downer, 18 Vt. 32.

[4] McGovney *v.* The State, 20 Ohio, 93. The guaranty must be strictly complied with or the guarantor is not liable. Bigelow *v.* Benton, 14 Barb. (N. Y.) 123.

"sale" of said premises duly made, the premises did not pay the debt, the defendant would immediately make good the difference. The premises were put up for sale and knocked down to W. for 650*l.*, who paid a deposit of 100*l.* and signed the usual contract, but afterwards refused to complete the purchase, and the plaintiff sued him on the contract, which suit was pending. The plaintiff then sued the defendant on the guaranty. *Held*, the suit was premature and could not be sustained. The word "sale" meant a completed sale. Otherwise there was no means of ascertaining the damage.[1] A guaranty on the back of a bond was as follows: "I . . . do hereby guaranty and bind myself and heirs to . . . for the payment of the amount of the within bond." The condition of the bond was that the obligors should at a certain time pay a sum of money, "on receiving from the obligee a title" to certain land. *Held*, the covenants were mutual and dependent, and the plaintiff could not recover without showing a tender of a deed for the land to the obligor.[2] A. covenanted with B. that C. should sell and account for all merchandise which B. might put into his hands. B. settled with C., and a balance was found due from C., for which B. took his note due one day after date. *Held*, if the note was not paid A. was liable on his covenants, for taking the note was nothing more than was reasonably within the contemplation of the parties.[3] If the payee of a note guaranties its collection and transfers it, and afterwards takes it up and then transfers it to another person, who agrees to take it at his own risk, but the guaranty is not erased, the payee is not liable to the holder on the guaranty. When the payee took up the note the guaranty became *functus officio*, and there was no contract of guaranty between the payee and the holder.[4]

§ 133. **When guaranty not revoked by death of guarantor — When surety cannot relieve himself from future liability by notice.**— When the engagement of a surety is a contract, and not a bare authority, it is not usually revoked by his death, and his estate remains liable, the same as he would

[1] Moor *v.* Roberts, 3 J. Scott (N. S.), 830.

[2] Gardner *v.* King, 2 Ired. Law (N. C.), 297.

[3] Bush *v.* Critchfield, 5 Ohio, 109.

[4] Gallagher *v.* White, 31 Barb. (N. Y.) 92.

have been if he had lived.[1] Thus, where a party became surety for a deputy-sheriff, his estate was held liable for a breach committed three years after his death. The court said: "The efficacy of contracts does not cease upon the death of one of the contracting parties. . . . Whether a man undertakes for himself or others in regard to future transactions, the contingency that death may remove him before the obligation can be fulfilled must be in the contemplation of all parties, but it remains unaffected by that event."[2] A written continuing guaranty was given by A. and B., which, by its terms, was to continue in force till revoked by written notice. A. died, leaving a solvent estate, and four years after his death, no notice having been given, a liability was created, covered by the guaranty, which B. had to pay, and he sued the estate of A. for contribution. *Held*, he was entitled to recover. The court said: "What obstructs one from indemnifying against the consequences of an event which may not happen for more than four years after his death, more than giving his promissory note, which may not reach maturity for more than four years from his death? It is asked how long such a guaranty shall continue in force, and the answer is, until it be ended according to its terms."[3] When a guaranty was as follows: "I request you will give credit in the usual way of your business, to L., and in consideration of your doing so, I hereby engage to guaranty the regular payment of the running balance of his account with you till I give you notice to the contrary, to the extent of 100*l.* sterling," it was held that the estate of the guarantor was liable for goods supplied after his death.[4] A party who has entered into a contract as surety cannot ordinarily, by notice, relieve himself from future liability for his

[1] Hightower *v.* Moore, 46 Ala. 387; White's Ex'rs *v.* The Commonwealth, 39 Pa. St. 167; Royal Ins. Co. *v.* Davies, 40 Iowa, 469. And to same effect, see Hecht *v.* Weaver (Cir. Ct. D. Oregon), 34 Fed. Rep. 111; Estate of Rapp *v.* The Phœnix Ins. Co., 113 Ill. 390; Lloyds *v.* Harper, Law Rep. (16 Ch. Div.) 290. But see National Eagle Bank *v.* Hunt, 16 R. I. 148. See, on this subject, Carter *v.* Hampton's Adm'x, 77 Va. 631.

[2] Green *v.* Young, 8 Greenl. (Me.) 14, per Weston, J.

[3] Knotts *v.* Butler, 10 Rich. Eq. (S. C.) 143, per Wardlaw, C. J. To same effect, see Fennell *v.* McGuire, 21 Up. Can. (C. P.) 134.

[4] Bradbury *v.* Morgan, 1 Hurl. & Colt. 249. To similar effect, see Menard *v.* Scudder, 7 La. Ann. 385.

principal, in the absence of a stipulation to that effect; thus, a party on taking in a clerk, took from him a bond with surety for his good behavior. The time of service was not fixed, but it was to be determinable at the option of either the clerk or the employer. The surety died, and his executrix gave notice to the employer that she should no longer consider herself liable on the bond. The employer read the notice to the clerk, and required him to execute a new bond with another surety, which was done. *Held*, the estate of the first surety was liable for defaults of the clerk occurring after the notice was given. The employer did not agree to release the estate, and his acts upon receiving the notice did not operate as such a release.[1] Upon a bond by a surety, conditioned for a collecting clerk's paying over money received by him from time to time, and at all times during his continuance in the service, it has been held that the surety cannot discharge himself from further liability by giving notice on a particular day that from thenceforward he will not remain surety. The court said if he desired to have the right to terminate his suretyship by notice, he should have so specified in his contract.[2] Where a guaranty was revocable, it was held it could not be revoked so as to prejudice the party who had already acted upon it, nor prevent him from renewing obligations which he had taken on the faith of it.[3] It has been held that a general guaranty continues in force till it is shown by the guarantor to have been rescinded.[4] If a wife mortgages her real estate for the debt of her husband, the land remains liable after her death.[5]

§ 134. When death of guarantor revokes guaranty — When surety may terminate his liability by notice.— One who guaranties the performance of a contract by another has the right, after the default of his principal, which would justify its termination, to require that the contract be terminated and the claim against himself as surety be confined to the damages then recoverable.[6] A surety upon an ordinary lease

[1] Gordon *v.* Culvert, 2 Simons, 253; affirmed, 4 Russell, 581; Exchange Bank *v.* Barnes, 7 Ont. (Can.) 309, 320.

[2] Calvert *v.* Gordon, 3 Man. & Ryl. 124.

[3] Williams *v.* Reynolds, 11 La. (6 Curry), 230.

[4] Knight *v.* Fox, Morris (Iowa), 305.

[5] Miner *v.* Graham, 24 Pa. St. 491.

[6] Hunt *v.* Roberts, 45 N. Y. 691.

for one year (with provision that if there was a holding over it should run for another year, unless the landlord sooner determined it, and upon which there had been such a holding that the tenancy was one from year to year) gave three months' notice in writing to the landlord that, at the expiration of the then current year, he would no longer be responsible for rent, and it was held that at the expiration of that year he was released from further liability.[1] It has been held that the death of a person who has given a letter of credit authorizing another to draw on him to a certain amount for a limited period, and agreeing to accept the drafts drawn and pay them if not paid by the drawer at maturity, will operate as a revocation of all authority to thereafter draw on his credit so as to bind his estate, though the person to whom and for whose security the letter was given has no notice of his death, and the period for which the authority was given has not expired.[2] The court treated it as a question of agency, and said that the death of the principal revoked the authority of the agent, while admitting that if there had been a contract the death of the guarantor would not have affected it. It has also been held that a guaranty to secure money to be advanced to a third party on discount, to a certain extent for the space of twelve months, may be revoked within that time.[3] The court said the promise, by itself, created no obligation unless advances were made, and the fact that twelve months was mentioned in the guaranty limited the time beyond which it should not extend, instead of making a binding contract for that time. Both these cases may well be sustained by the fact that the writings in each were simply offers to guaranty, which were only binding so far as they were acted on, and

And where sureties guarantied the fidelity and honesty of their principal as agent of an insurance company, it was held that, upon discovering a conversion of funds by their principal, they had a right to give notice to the company terminating their liability. Emery *v.* Baltz *et al.*, 94 N. Y. 408. While a surety may terminate his liability by notice, yet he can only be discharged subject to rights which a creditor may have acquired on the faith of a continuance of the suretyship. Jendervine *v.* Rose, 36 Mich. 54.

[1] Estate of Desilver, 9 Phila. (Pa.) 302. To similar effect, see Pleasanton's Appeal, 75 Pa. St. 344.

[2] Michigan State Bank *v.* Estate of Leavenworth, 28 Vt. 209.

[3] Offord *v.* Davies, 12 J. Scott (N. S.), 748.

might at any time be revoked, the same as any other offer before it is accepted.[1] A guaranty was determinable by six months' notice, and the guarantor died, leaving as his executor the debtor, on whose behalf the guaranty was given. The creditors, knowing these facts, and also that there was no personal estate to answer the guaranty, continued to make advances to the debtor for two or three years. *Held*, the creditors could not recover against the guarantor's estate for any advances made after his death. This was not put upon the ground that the guarantor's death terminated the guaranty, for the court said it did not think that alone would terminate it, but upon the ground that when the creditor knew there was no personal estate, it would be presumed that the advances were not made on the guaranty, and that it would be grossly inequitable to allow the creditor to charge the real estate under the circumstances.[2] It has been held that doubtful expressions in a subsequent correspondence should not be construed as revoking an explicit guaranty.[3]

§ 135. **Same continued.**— Where one of several joint guarantors revokes his guaranty at any time before acceptance, and the person to whom the revocation is made accepts the guaranty without informing the others of such revocation, they will be released from liability as joint guarantors.[4] A continuing guaranty, in the absence of express provision, is revoked as to subsequent advances by notice of the death of the guarantor.[5] But a guaranty by a partnership is not terminated by the death of the sole surviving member of the partnership.[6]

§ 136. **When notice revoking guaranty takes effect.**— Where a surety on the bond of a bank cashier notified one of the directors and vice-president that he wished no longer to be the cashier's surety, and that he had so notified the cashier,

[1] To this effect, see, also, Jordan *v.* Dobbins, 122 Mass. 168.

[2] Harriss *v.* Fawcett, Law Rep. 8 Ch. App. Cas. 866. See, also, same case in court below, Law Rep. 15 Eq. Cas. 311.

[3] Lanusse *v.* Barker, 3 Wheat. 101.

[4] Potter *v.* Gronbeck *et al.*, 117 Ill. 404, affirming 17 Brad. (Ill. App.) 251.

[5] Coulthart *v.* Clementson, Law Rep. (5 Q. B. Div.) 42. For other cases holding that the death of the guarantor revokes his guaranty, see Hyland *v.* Habich, 150 Mass. 112; Home Nat. Bank *v.* Waterman, 30 Ill. App. 535.

[6] Kernochan *v.* Murray, 111 N. Y. 306.

it was held that, whatever might be the effect of such notice, it could not operate instantaneously, for the directors must have a reasonable time to give notice to the cashier and the other sureties, and to procure a new bond. The court say: "If the effect of the notice is to be such as is now claimed on the part of the appellant, that is, if it discharged Haight [the surety], and, in consequence thereof, discharged all the other sureties, the instant it was communicated to the bank, it might be quite embarrassing and damaging to the bank. The cashier might be so situated that the directors could not immediately arrest his discharge of duty or his ability to bind the bank, and hence reasonable time at least must be given to the bank in such a case to act after receiving the notice."[1]

§ 137. When surety may be sued jointly with principal.— When principal and surety are jointly liable on the same contract, they may be sued jointly for its enforcement, and this whether or not the fact of suretyship appears from the instrument.[2] A surety who signs a note made out in the singular number, "I promise," and adds to his name the word "surety," is liable in a joint suit with the maker, who has also signed the note.[3] But where sureties on a joint and several note had been released *pro tanto* by the creditor surrendering a security for the debt of less value than the debt, it was held that the principal and sureties could not be sued at law together, because, as the principal was liable for the full amount, and the sureties for only a portion, no judgment could be entered according to the liability of the parties.[4] A principal bound himself by bond for the payment of a certain sum of money.

[1] Bostwick *v.* Van Voorhis, 91 N. Y. 353, 363, 364, per Earl, J. That the revocation of a guaranty must be exercised reasonably, see La Rose *v.* Logansport Nat. Bank, 102 Ind. 332.

[2] Kleckner *v.* Klapp, 2 Watts & Serg. (Pa.) 44; Craddock *v.* Armor, 10 Watts (Pa.), 258. But the weight of authority is probably to the effect that a guarantor and his principal, or a guarantor and the maker of a note, cannot be sued jointly. See Abbott *v.* Brown, 131 Ill. 108, affirming 30 Ill. App. 376; Clark *v.* Morgan, 13 Bradwell (Ill. App.) 597; Graham *v.* Ringo, 67 Mo 324; Parmerlee *v.* Williams, 71 Mo. 410; Tyler *v.* Trustees, 14 Oreg. 485; Barton *v.* Speis, 5 Hun, 60. See same case on appeal, 73 N. Y. 133; and see on this subject, Neil *v.* Board of Trustees, 31 Ohio St. 15, 41; Widner *v.* Western Union Tel. Co., 47 Mich. 612.

[3] Dart *v.* Sherwood, 7 Wis. 523; Fond du Lac Harrow Co. *v.* Haskins, 51 Wis. 135.

[4] Cummings *v.* Little, 45 Me. 183.

Immediately under the signature of the principal, on the same paper, certain sureties wrote: "We hereby bind ourselves as security for said Olds (principal) for the full and faithful performance of the above agreement," and signed and sealed under these words. The bond was executed and delivered by principal and sureties at the same time and on the same consideration. *Held*, they were all liable together in one suit. The court said: "Where several persons execute an instrument in parol, or under seal, upon the same consideration, at the same time and for the same purpose, and taking effect from a single delivery, they are in legal effect joint contractors or obligors. . . . The particular form or manner in which the parties have affixed their signatures to a contract or bond is immaterial. It matters not whether those who execute as sureties sign their names directly under that of the principal, and then append to each name the fact of signing merely as surety, or whether, as in this instance, the sureties write between their names and that of the principal that they sign as securities, and then affix their signatures."[1] The same thing was held, when at the foot of a money bond a surety had written: "I . . . join in the above obligation with . . . (principal) and am his security for the above sum of . . .;"[2] and where, under a contract for the payment of wages, a surety wrote: "I . . . agree to stand as surety for . . . (principal) in the above agreement."[3] A. and B., being partners, dissolved their partnership, and B. executed an agreement to A. that he would pay the firm debts. C. signed this agreement with B., writing before his name the word "security." The firm was at the date of the agreement indebted to D., who sued A., B. and C. in a joint action for his debt, and it was held they were liable, on the ground that C. was a surety, and primarily liable, and, the contract having been made for the benefit of the creditors of the firm, any of the creditors might sue on it.[4] Where a third party guarantied a lease, as follows: "For value received, I guaranty the pay-

[1] Stage *v.* Olds, 12 Ohio, 158, per Read, J. To same effect, see Leonard *v.* Sweetzer, 16 Ohio, 1. And, also, Neil *v.* Board of Trustees, 31 Ohio St. 15.

[2] Atwell's Adm'r *v.* Towles, 1 Munf. (Va.) 175.

[3] Watson *v.* Beabout, 18 Ind. 281.

[4] Dunlap *v.* McNeil, 35 Ind. 316.

ment of the rent, as stipulated by said . . . (principal), in case of non-payment by him," it was held that the guarantor and lessee could not be sued jointly for rent. The court said: "The undertaking or contract of the guarantor was distinct from that of the principal and collateral thereto, and his liability dependent upon a contingency, namely, the non-payment of rent by the lessee."[1] The same thing was held where, under a lease, sureties wrote: "For the payment of said contract being fulfilled on the part of said . . . (principal), we, the undersigned, will become responsible;"[2] and where, on alease under seal, a guaranty not under seal was as follows: "I hereby become security for . . . (principal) for the rent specified in the within lease."[3] But where a party, not the lessee, joined in the execution of a lease, and guarantied on his part that the payments of rent should be made as they became due, it was held that he might be jointly sued with the lessee.[4] Where a stranger to a note payable in clocks, at the time of its execution wrote on its back, "I guaranty the fulfillment of the within contract,"[5] and where, under similar circumstances, a stranger to a note payable to bearer indorsed it, "for value received, I guaranty the payment of the within note and waive notice of non-payment,'[6] it was held that the maker and indorser might be sued jointly. But where a third party wrote on the back of a bond, "I do join with . . . (principal) as his security for the performance of the agreement mentioned in the present note," it was held that he could not be sued jointly with the maker, on the ground that their undertakings were distinct and different.[7] Where a bond is executed by sureties for the fulfillment of a contract entered into by their principals in a separate instrument, both principals and sureties may be sued jointly in an action for a breach of the contract.[8] In an action against the

[1] Virden *v.* Ellsworth, 15 Ind. 144, per Hanna, J. See a similar ruling on the guaranty of the payment of a note, Mowery *v.* Mast & Co., 9 Neb. 445.

[2] Cross *v.* Ballard, 46 Vt. 415.

[3] Turney *v.* Penn, 16 Ill. 485.

[4] McLott *v.* Savery, 11 Iowa, 323.

[5] Goles' Adm'r *v.* Van Arman, 18 Ohio, 336. See, *contra*, Mowery *v.* Mast & Co., 9 Neb. 445.

[6] Prosser *v.* Laqueer, 4 Hill (N. Y.), 420. See, *contra*, Mowery *v.* Mast & Co., 9 Neb. 445.

[7] Preston *v.* Davis, 8 Ark. (3 Eng.) 167.

[8] Wibaux *v.* Grinnell Live Stock Co., 9 Mont. 154.

sureties on the bond of a clerk in a banking house, conditioned for his good behavior, and where he defaulted and absconded, it was held that the principal was a necessary party defendant.[1]

§ 138. When recovery on common money counts cannot be had against surety — Surety for alimony cannot be compelled by motion to pay it — Other cases.— A joint and several promissory note was signed by two, one adding to his name the word "surety." They were sued on the common money counts. *Held*, no recovery could be had on those counts against the surety. The court said: "The rule is nearly or quite universal that there can be no recovery against a surety where his character appears on the face of the instrument, without declaring specially on the contract. . . . In the common case of a suit against the makers of a promissory note, the instrument may be given in evidence under the money counts, for the reason that the note is evidence of money lent to or had and received by the makers to the plaintiff's use. But when one of them signs as a surety for the other, and that fact appears on the face of the instrument, the note furnishes no evidence that he received the whole or any part of the consideration. Indeed, it proves the contrary."[2] Where a statute provided that the maker, drawer, indorser or acceptor of a bill of exchange or promissory note might be joined in one suit, it was held that this did not authorize a joint suit against the maker and guarantor of a promissory note,[3] it having been previously decided by the same court, that in the absence of a statute the maker and guarantor of a note could not be sued together.[4] A statute provided that in case of a foreclosure of a mortgage, a decree for any balance due after sale of the mortgaged premises might be made against any of the parties to the suit who were liable. *Held*, that a mortgagee who assigned the mortgage and guarantied the debt was a proper but not a necessary party to a suit to

[1] Exchange Bank *v.* Springer, 29 Grant's Ch. (Can.) 270.

[2] Butler *v.* Rawson, 1 Denio, 105, per Bronson, C. J. To same effect, see Wells *v.* Girling, 8 Taunt. 737.

[3] Stewart *v.* Glenn, 5 Wis. 14.

[4] Ten Eyck *v.* Brown, 3 Pinney (Wis.), 452. As to who may sue on a guaranty, see Jenness *v.* True, 30 Me. 438. As to when an agreement is collateral and not original, see Smith *v.* Hyde, 19 Vt. 54.

foreclose the mortgage, and a personal decree might be rendered against him for any deficiency.[1] Under nearly the same circumstances, it has been held that the guarantor was not a proper party to the foreclosure suit, and that no personal decree could be rendered against him.[2] The surety for alimony in a divorce suit cannot be compelled to pay the alimony by motion, but must be sued on his bond.[3]

§ 139. When surety who is not liable at law will not be charged in equity.— When the surety in a joint obligation dies, there is no remedy at law on the obligation against his estate, and, in the absence of fraud or mistake, equity will not charge his estate with the payment of such obligation. Where an obligation is joint, and all the obligors participated in the consideration, or there is any previous equity which imposes a moral obligation to pay on all the obligors, there a court of equity will enforce the obligation against the estate of the deceased obligor, because the reasonable presumption is that the parties intended the obligation to be joint and several, but through fraud or mistake it was made joint only. But "this presumption is never indulged in the case of a mere surety, whose duty is measured alone by the legal force of the bond, and who is under no moral obligation whatever to pay the obligee, independent of his covenant, and consequently there is nothing on which to found an equity for the interposition of a court of chancery." The surety may have had the obligation made joint, with express reference to the contingency of his death.[4] Where a joint appeal bond is signed by two sureties, and one of them dies, his estate is discharged from

1 Jarman *v.* Wiswall, 9 C. E. Green (N. J.), 267.

2 Borden *v.* Gilbert, 13 Wis. 670.

3 Appeal of Guenther, 40 Wis. 115.

4 Pickersgill *v.* Lahens, 15 Wall. 140, per Davis, J.; Harrison *v.* Field, 2 Wash. (Va.) 136; Risley *v.* Brown, 67 N. Y. 160; distinguished in First Nat. Bank *v.* Morgan, 73 N. Y. 593, affirming 6 Hun, 346; Pecke *v.* Julius, 2 Browne (Pa.), 31; Weaver *v.* Shryock, 6 Serg. & Rawle (Pa.), 262; Rawstone *v.* Parr, 3 Russ. 539; Kennedy *v.* Carpenter, 2 Whart. (Pa.) 344; Other *v.* Iveson, 3 Drew. 177; Towne *v.* Ammidown, 20 Pick. 535; Dixon *v.* Vandenberg *et al.*, 35 N. J. Eq. 47; Davis *v.* Van Buren, 6 Daly (N. Y. Com. Pleas), 391. *Contra*, Smith *v.* Martin, 4 Des. Eq. (S. C.) 148; following Smith *v.* Martin, see Susong *v.* Vaiden, 10 Rich. (S. C.) 247; and the following Texas cases: Mays *v.* Cockrum, 57 Tex. 352; Bergstroem *v.* State, 58 Tex. 92; Glascock *v.* Hamilton, 62 Tex. 143; Boyd *et al.* *v.* Bell *et al.*, 69 Tex. 735.

liability, both at law and in equity, and the fact that the bond was given in pursuance of a statute does not affect the liability thereunder. In cases of suretyship, the contract is the measure of liability, and a statute under which it is made will not be so construed as to enlarge the obligation of the surety beyond the terms of his contract.[1] Principal and surety signed a joint and several bond, by which they bound themselves as "principals" for the conduct of the principal. Suit was brought on the bond jointly against the principal and surety, and a joint judgment was recovered against them. Afterwards the principal became insolvent and the surety died. *Held*, that the remedy at law being gone against the estate of the surety, equity would not charge it. The bond was merged in the judgment, and after judgment the obligee could not have sued the principal and surety separately.[2] A mortgage to secure the debt of F. & Bro. to the complainant was executed by F. and his wife on premises which were the separate property of the wife; afterwards the complainant executed a satisfaction of the mortgage, upon F.'s promise to give a new mortgage and obtain the wife's signature thereto, which signature, however, the wife refused to give. *Held*, the satisfaction would not be annulled, and the mortgage enforced against Mrs. F., she being only liable as surety, and there being no accident or mistake in the execution of the satisfaction, and no fraud on her part. The court said: "The obligation of the surety is *stricti juris*, and if his contract is not binding at law, there is no liability in equity founded on the consideration between the principal parties. A court of equity will not enforce a liability upon a surety where he is not held at law."[3]

§ **140. When surety's estate held liable.**— When the surety or guarantor in a joint obligation is directly benefited from the contract, his estate will not be discharged from liability.

[1] Wood *v.* Fisk, 63 N. Y. 245. To similar effect, see Chard *v.* Hamilton, 56 Hun (N. Y.), 259; Davis *v.* Van Buren, 72 N. Y. 587, affirming 6 Daly (Com. Pleas), 391; Randall *v.* Sackett, 77 N. Y. 480. Upon an affirmance of the judgment appealed from, the surviving surety will be held liable for the amount secured by the appeal bond. Comins *v.* Pottle, 22 Hun (N. Y.), 287.

[2] United States *v.* Archer's Ex'r, 1 Wall. Jr. 173; disapproving United States *v.* Cushman, 2 Sumn. 426.

[3] Leffingwell *v.* Freyer, 21 Wis. 392, per Dixon, C. J. To similar effect, see Ratcliffe *v.* Graves, 1 Vern. 196.

Thus where a stockholder in a corporation executed a joint guaranty of the payment of its bonds and died before the bonds fell due, it was held that the liability upon the guaranty was not extinguished by his death. The joint guarantors owned nearly the entire stock of the corporation, and whatever would benefit the company would of course benefit them.[1] Where, in some states, all causes of action founded on contract survive, the estate of a deceased surety on a joint, but not several, promissory note will not be discharged from liability.[2] If a surety in terms binds his estate it will be held liable.[3] Judgment against all the makers of a promissory note does not relieve a surety's estate from the lien of the judgment.[4] Where it is proved that a principal has no estate it has been held not error to charge the estate of the surety.[5] But proper efforts must have been made to subject the principal's land to satisfaction.[6]

§ 141. **When equity will charge surety who is not liable at law.**— Equity will, in many instances, afford relief against a surety where there is no remedy at law. Thus, equity will set up a lost bond against a surety. "The reason is, that the surety is not discharged by the loss of the bond, and the court only relieves against the accident by setting up the evidence of the debt."[7] Equity will reform a joint guardian's bond so as to hold it joint and several, where it appears clearly to have been the intention of the parties to give a joint and several bond, and relief will, insuch case, be granted against the estate of a deceased surety. The court said: "When the contract does not express the agreement or intention of the parties to the injury of the obligee, and this is clearly made to appear, equity will reform the instrument, as well against sureties as principals."[8] Where, by mistake, property mortgaged by a

[1] Richardson *v.* Draper *et al.*, 87 N. Y. 337, affirming 23 Hun, 188.

[2] McCoy *v.* Payne, 68 Ind. 327; Hudelson *v.* Armstrong, 70 Ind. 99; Redman *v.* Marvil, 73 Ind. 593.

[3] Mundorff *v.* Wangler, 12 J. & S. (N. Y. Superior Ct.) 495.

[4] Baskin *v.* Andrews, 53 Hun, 95; and see, also, Smith *v.* Osborne, 31 Hun, 390.

[5] Jones *v.* Degge, 84 Va. 685.

[6] Womack *v.* Paxton's Ex'r, 84 Va. 9.

[7] Kerney's Adm'r *v.* Kerney's Heirs, 6 Leigh (Va.), 478, per Carr, J. To same effect, see East India Company *v.* Boddam, 9 Ves. 464.

[8] Olmsted *v.* Olmsted, 38 Conn. 309, per Butler, C. J. For case holding bond joint and several, and estate of

surety is misdescribed, equity will reform the mortgage. In this case the court said: "Where the surety is aware of, and consents to, the purpose to which his obligation is to be applied, and it is so used, though without consideration, except that advanced to the principal, equity will reform any mistake of fact, so that the obligation shall fulfill its purpose."[1] Where principal and sureties signed a prison-bounds bond, and which, by mistake, misrecited the judgment on which the principal was imprisoned, it was held that equity would reform the bond.[2] Where principal and surety signed a joint bond by mistake, the intention being to sign a joint and several bond, and the principal died, it was held the surety could, by bill in equity, compel the payment of the bond by the estate of the principal as a specialty debt.[3] A. agrees to be bound in a bond as surety to B., and signs and seals it accordingly, but by the neglect of the clerk A.'s name is not inserted. The obligee shows A. the condition, and his name and seal, and demands payment, and threatens to sue him unless he gives fresh security, which A. agrees to do, but, after finding the mistake, refuses, not being bound at law, yet equity will compel him.[4] In cases such as the preceding, equity affords relief on the ground of accident or mistake; but where it is sought to reform an instrument against a surety on the ground of mistake, evidence of the necessary facts must be so clear as to leave no doubt. It has been said that "although an instrument may undoubtedly be reformed on parol proof, yet where, as here, the relief sought is adverse to the pre-existent equity of a surety, the evidence should be so clear as to leave the fact without a shadow of a doubt."[5] A devise to executors with

surety chargeable, see Besore *v.* Potter, 12 Serg. & Rawle (Pa.), 154. See Gray *v.* Robinson, 90 Ind. 527, where a judgment against principal and sureties was satisfied by the sureties, without any knowledge of a mistake therein, and it was held equity would not correct the judgment as against them.

[1] Prior *v.* Williams, 3 Abb. Rep. Om. Cas. 624, per Peckham, J.

[2] Smith *v.* Allen, Saxton (N. J.), 43.

[3] Pride *v.* Boyce, Rice's Eq. (S. C.) 275. Equity will reform an indemnity bond so as to conform to the mutual intention of all parties. Percival *v.* McCoy (Cir. C. D. Ia. W. D.), 13 Fed. Rep. 379. In Trustees of Schools *v.* Otis, 85 Ill. 179, it is held that equity will not reform an official bond as against the sureties therein.

[4] Crosby *v.* Middleton, Finch's Precedents, 309.

[5] Moser *v.* Libenguth, 2 Rawle (Pa.),

authority to sell the real estate of the testator for the payment of his debts applies as well to a joint and several bond, executed by him as surety for his co-obligor, as to any other debts, and a court of chancery will compel a sale of the real estate, so as to pay such bond.[1] A law concerning the sale of school lands prescribed the form of the notes to be given for the purchase of such lands, made them joint and several obligations, and specially declared that the surety should, in all respects, be liable as principal. A principal and surety signed a joint note for the purchase of such lands, and the surety died. *Held*, the estate of the surety was chargeable in equity for the amount of the note; the decision being placed on the ground alone that the statute made the surety liable as principal, and, being a public law, must be presumed to have been known to all the parties.[2] A trustee having in his hands funds arising out of property sold under a decree of court, became delinquent, and, having wasted the fund, died intestate, having before committed breaches of his bond, for which both he and his sureties would have been liable at law if he had lived. A claimant of the fund in the hands of the trustee could not place himself in a position to proceed at law on the bond, because of the death of the trustee. *Held*, equity would afford him relief on the bond against the sureties. There was a clear right against the sureties, which could not be enforced at law because of the accident of the death of the principal, and the fact that there was a right, and no remedy at law, was sufficient alone to give equity jurisdiction. The law on the subject was well and concisely stated by the court, as follows: "A court of equity will do nothing to extend the liability of securities beyond the clear intent and import of their contract. But if to such an extent they cannot at law be held liable by reason of fraud, accident or mistake, a court of equity, to prevent a failure of justice, will interfere and enforce the execution of their contract, according to its obvious meaning and design."[3]

428, per Gibson, C. J.; Smith *v.* Allen, Saxton (N. J.), 43.

[1] Berg *v.* Radcliff, 6 Johns. Ch. 302.

[2] Powell *v.* Kettle, 1 Gilm. (Ill.) 491.

[3] Brooks *v.* Brooke, 12 Gill & Johns. (Md.) 306, per Dorsey, J. But see Edes *et al.* *v.* Garey & Lanahan, 46 Md. 24, where an appeal from an order sustaining a demurrer to a bill by residuary legatees, to enforce the personal liability of sureties on a

§ 142. When new promise revives liability of surety or guarantor.— If facts exist which are sufficient to discharge a surety or guarantor, and he, with full knowledge of the existence and effect of such facts, promises to pay the debt, the weight of authority is that he will be bound.[1] Where time had been given which would have discharged the surety on a note, and he, knowing this, paid part of the note, and promised to pay the balance, it was held he had waived any defense he might have had by reason of such giving of time.[2] Where the holder of a note had been guilty of such laches as would have discharged the guarantor, but the guarantor, on demand of the holder, paid him the interest due on the note, knowing and protesting he was not liable on his guaranty, it was held he had waived the laches, and continued liable on the guaranty; and this, notwithstanding the fact that he paid the interest, because of the threat of the holder that, unless he paid the interest, he would sue him for other large debts which he owed the holder.[3] But the surety or guarantor will not be bound by such new promise, unless he made the same with a full knowledge of the facts which would entitle him to a discharge,[4] and of their legal effect.[5] After time has been given by the creditor, which would discharge the surety on a note, his liability is not revived by a payment made on the note by him with money of principal, although at the time of such payment he gave no intimation that the money was not his own.[6] It has been held that after the guarantor of a note is discharged by the laches of the holder, a new promise on his part will not bind him, unless there is also a new consideration.[7] Where the sureties on an official bond were, in fact, not liable for the default of their principal, and without seeing the bond acknowledged they were liable and promised to pay the defalcation, but afterwards, upon inspection of the bond, were advised they were not liable, and then

testamentary bond for a *devastavit*, alleged to have been committed by an executor, was affirmed.

[1] Ashford *v.* Robinson, 8 Ired. Law (N. C.), 114.

[2] Hinds *v.* Ingham, 31 Ill. 400.

[3] Sigourney *v.* Wetherell, 6 Met. (Mass.) 553.

[4] Gamage *v.* Hutchins, 23 Me. 565.

[5] Robinson *v.* Offutt, 7 T. B. Mon. (Ky.) 540. *Contra*, Rindskopf *v.* Doman, 28 Ohio St. 516.

[6] Lime Rock Bank *v.* Mallett, 42 Me. 349.

[7] Van Derveer *v.* Wright, 6 Barb. (N. Y.) 547.

refused to pay, it was held that as they promised under a mistake of law they were not liable.[1]

§ 143. Statute of limitations — When new promise or partial payment by principal takes case out of statute as to surety.— If a principal and surety execute a joint, or joint and several note, bond or other obligation, a new promise or a partial payment by the principal will avoid the bar of the statute of limitations as to the surety as well as to the principal.[2] This is placed upon the ground that, as they are jointly liable, the admission or act of one is the admission or act of both. A written acknowledgment of the debt by the principal, within the period prescribed by the statute of limitations, will not take the case out of the statute against a guarantor for the price of goods sold the principal, because in such case the principal and guarantor are not joint debtors.[3] If a claim against a deceased surety, as surety, is not presented till his estate is settled, it is barred the same as any other claim, and it makes no difference that the claim had been proved against the estate of the principal, and it could not be known till that estate was settled how much of the claim it would pay.[4] Where a surety is about to be sued, and before the statute of limitations has barred the debt he hands to the creditor for suit a note which had been executed to him by the principal as an indemnity, it is such an admission of indebtedness on his part as will start the statute running from that time as to him.[5] It has been held that the sureties in a judgment at law, which has been enjoined by the unconscionable litigation of

[1] Welch *v.* Seymour, 28 Conn. 387. As to liability of surety who becomes such under mistake of fact, see Miller *v.* Gardner, 49 Iowa, 234.

[2] Hunt *v.* Bridgam, 2 Pick. 581; Perham *v.* Raynall, 9 Moore, 566; Craig *v.* Calloway County Court, 12 Mo. 94; Frye *v.* Barker, 4 Pick. 382; Joslyn *v.* Smith, 13 Vt. 353; Pease *v.* Hirst, 10 Barn. & Cress. 122; Clark *v.* Sigourney, 17 Ct. 511; Whitaker *v.* Rice, 9 Minn. 13; Caldwell *v.* Sigourney, 19 Ct. 37; Perkins *v.* Barstow, 6 R. I. 505; Zent's Ex'rs *v.* Heart, 8 Pa. St. 337. *Contra,* Coleman *v.* Forbes, 22 Pa. St. 156. In South Carolina the liability of sureties on a joint and several promissory note, where the principal has from time to time made payments thereon, is not continued by such payments, but they are discharged at the expiration of the statutory period of limitation from the maturity of the note. Walters *v.* Kraft, 23 S. C. 578.

[3] Meade *v.* McDowell, 5 Binney (Pa.), 195.

[4] Ratcliff *v.* Leunig, 30 Ind. 289.

[5] Russell *v.* La Roque, 11 Ala. 352.

the principal until it has become barred by the statute of limitations, are in privity with the principal and bound to all the legal consequences of his acts, and will not, therefore, be allowed to avail themselves of the advantage of the statute thus obtained, and they will be enjoined in equity from setting it up at law.[1] The statute of limitations commences running in favor of a surety or guarantor from the time he is liable to suit, and this, as already seen, may or may not be the same time the principal becomes so liable.[2]

§ 144. Contract of suretyship, by what law governed.— As a general rule the liability of sureties and guarantors depends upon and is governed by the law of the place of their contract.[3] Thus, in an action against a surety on a note in New Hampshire, the note having been executed and made payable in Vermont, the law relating to sureties in the latter state is to be applied and by that law they are governed.[4] But if the contract was entered into with the intention that it shall operate and be acted on in a state other than the one in which it was executed, the surety or guarantor will be held to have contracted with reference to the laws of such state, and he will be liable accordingly.[5]

[1] Davis *v.* Hoopes, 33 Miss. 173.

[2] On this subject, see The Governor *v.* Stonum, 11 Ala. 679; Bank *v.* Knotts, 10 Rich. Law (S. C.), 543; Sollee *v.* Mengy, 1 Bailey, Law (S. C), 620; Wofford *v.* Unger, 55 Tex. 480.

[3] Long *v.* Templeman, 24 La. Ann. 564. And a subsequent change of the principal's domicile does not alter the rule. Long *v.* Templeman, *infra.*

[4] Howard *v.* Fletcher, 59 N. H. 151. The right of a surety to discharge his liability by notice to the creditor to sue the principal, held determined by the law of the place of the contract. Tenant *v.* Tenant, 110 Penn. St. 478.

[5] Frierson *v.* Williams *et al.*, 57 Miss. 451; Milliken *v.* Pratt, 125 Mass. 374.

CHAPTER IV.

OF THE LIABILITY OF THE SURETY WHEN THE PRINCIPAL IS DISCHARGED, OR NOT ORIGINALLY BOUND.

When surety not liable if principal not bound — General principles . . . . . . § 145
Discharge of principal generally releases surety 146
Surety not discharged by release of principal, when remedies against surety reserved, when he is fully indemnified, etc. . 147
Miscellaneous cases on discharge of surety when principal is not bound, etc. 148
When discharge of principal, after judgment against surety, releases surety 149
Surety not discharged if principal released by act of law . § 150
Whether surety bound when principal does not sign the obligation 151
Same continued 152
When surety bound for contract of infant or married woman which is not binding on them 153
Discharge of surety does not release principal 154
When surety discharged by mental or physical incapacity of principal 155

§ 145. **When surety not liable if principal not bound — General principles.**— The obligation of a surety or guarantor is usually accessory to that of the principal, and, as a general rule, wherever there is no principal there can be no surety; and whatever discharges the principal releases the surety. This is not, however, universally true. With reference to this it has been well said that "A surety is not entitled to every exception which the principal debtor may urge. He has a right to oppose all which are inherent to the debt; not those which are personal to the debtor. Pothier distinguishes them into exceptions *in personam* and exceptions *in rem*. The latter, which go to the contract itself, such as fraud, violence, or whatever entirely avoids the obligation, may be pleaded by the surety; but the former, which are grounded on the insolvency or partial solvency of the debtor, or which result from a cession of his property, or are the consequence of his minority, cannot be opposed to the creditor." [1] Where a statute pro-

[1] Baldwin *v.* Gordon, 12 Martin (La.), O. S. 378, per Porter, J. See, also, State *v.* Bugg, 6 Rob. (La.) 63; Jarrett *v.* Martin, 70 N. C. 459; Phillips *v.*

hibited the making of a particular kind of note by a bank, it was held that such a note was void, and a guaranty of the note was likewise void.[1] Where property of the principal sufficient to satisfy the debt was levied on, it was held that such levy satisfied the debt as to the principal, and consequently as to the surety. The court said: "It would be as difficult for me to conceive of a surety's liability continuing after the principal obligation was discharged as of a shadow remaining after the substance was removed."[2] A justice of the peace required two parties who were before him for examination to enter into a joint recognizance with surety when he had no right to require a joint obligation from both, but only had power to require a several recognizance from each. Such a joint recognizance was given, and it was held that it was void as to the principals and consequently as to the surety. The court said: "It is a corollary, from the very definition of the contract of suretyship, that the obligation of the surety being accessory to the obligation of the principal debtor or obligor, it is of its essence that there should be a valid obligation of such principal, and that the nullity of the principal obligation necessarily induces the nullity of the accessory. Without a principal there can be no accessory. Nor can the obligation of the surety, as such, exceed that of the principal."[3] But a guaranty of a note, described therein by the name of its maker, its date, amount and day of payment, and which is shown to the guarantor, and a commission paid to him at the time of signing the guaranty, binds him to pay the note upon non-payment thereof by the maker, after the usual demand and notice, although the note is made payable to the maker's own order, and never indorsed by him, and the want of such indorsement is not known to either party till after the day of payment. He had agreed to guaranty that particular instru-

Wade, 66 Ala. 53; Bean *v.* Chapman, 62 Ala. 58; Norris *v.* Pollard, and Morgan *v.* Pollard, 75 Ga. 358.

[1] Swift *v.* Beers, 3 Denio, 70.

[2] Farmers' and Mechanics' Bank *v.* Kingsley, 2 Doug. (Mich.) 379. See, also, Stull *v.* Davison, 12 Bush (Ky.), 167; Evans *v.* Raper, 74 N. C. 639.

[3] Ferry *v.* Burchard, 21 Conn. 597, per Storrs, J. Holding that because bond is void as to principal because of duress, it is not void as to surety, who was under no duress, see Jones *v.* Turner) 5 Litt. (Ky.) 147. The sureties on a guardian's bond are not liable thereon if the court appointing the guardian had no jurisdiction.

ment, and was bound by his obligation.[1] It was agreed between the agent of a railroad company and the plaintiff that no appeal should be taken from an award to be made in a pending arbitration between the company and the plaintiff, but both parties should abide the award. Thereupon the president of the company, together with the agent, personally guarantied to the plaintiff the performance by the company of said agreement. *Held*, the guarantors were liable in case of a breach of the agreement, even if the latter was not binding on the company, and the guarantors were estopped from denying the existence of the company.[2]

§ 146. **Discharge of principal generally releases surety.**— As a general rule, if the principal is released by the creditor, without reservation, the surety is also thereby discharged. Thus, a joint judgment was obtained against the principals and sureties on a note. The creditor agreed with one of the principals to discharge him from the judgment if he would give security for the payment of about one-fourth of the amount thereof, and the security was accordingly given. *Held*, the sureties were thereby discharged. The court said that if in such a case the surety was held liable, "he could not recover over against the principal, because he is discharged from the debt, and owes the creditor nothing, and the surety could not recover for money paid to the use of the principal, as he owes nothing; and when the surety makes the payment, it cannot be for the use of the principal debtor."[3] A creditor agreed to accept from the principal 5*s*. in the pound in full of his demand, upon having a collateral security for that sum from a third person. He was induced to agree to this by the representation of the agent of the principal that a surety would continue liable for the residue of the debt. *Held*, the surety was discharged. The representations, being as to the legal effect of the instrument, were immaterial, and did not avoid it.[4] A. was indebted to B. and others, and C. was surety for the debt due B. Afterwards A. became bankrupt, and all his

Crum *v.* Wilson, Adm'r, *et al.*, 61 Miss. 233.

[1] Jones *v.* Thayer, 12 Gray, 443.

[2] Mason *v.* Nichols, 22 Wis. 376.

[3] Trotter *v.* Strong, 63 Ill. 272; Brown *v.* Ayer, 24 Ga. 288. See, also, Anthony *v.* Capel, 53 Miss. 350; State *v.* Parker, 72 Ala. 181.

[4] Lewis *v.* Jones, 4 Barn. & Cress. 506.

creditors signed a composition deed, agreeing to accept 7*s.* in the pound, in full payment of their claims, in drafts accepted by C. as surety. B. added before his name to the composition deed the words, "Without prejudice to any additional security we may hold." *Held*, notwithstanding the reservation, B. could not enforce C.'s original liability. If all the creditors had held securities from C. for the full amount due them, then such a reservation would have made the composition nugatory. Moreover, to allow B. to enforce this liability might operate to the prejudice of the other creditors.[1]

§ 147. Surety not discharged by release of principal when remedies against surety reserved, when he is fully indemnified, etc.— If the creditor, at the time he releases the principal, reserves his remedies against the surety, such release amounts to a covenant not to sue only, and does not discharge the surety.[2] This has been held where the creditor by mistake executed an absolute release to the principal, but the agreement verbally was that the creditor's rights against the surety should be reserved.[3] By a mortgage deed the debtor covenanted to pay the principal and interest of a debt, and a surety covenanted to pay the interest. The principal afterwards by deed assigned his property to a trustee on trust, to sell and divide the proceeds among his creditors. The creditors released the debtor from the debts due them respectively, but there was a proviso in the deed of release that nothing therein should affect any right or remedy which any creditor might have against any other person in respect of any debt due by the principal. *Held*, the surety was not discharged. The court said: "The release cannot be construed to be absolute, because then no rights could be reserved in any case, and the courts have therefore held that such a release is not to be construed as absolute, but only as a covenant not to sue. That being so, the remedy is

[1] Grundy *v.* Meighan, 7 Irish Law Rep. 519.

[2] Bateson *v.* Gosling, Law Rep. 7 Com. Pl. 9; Hall *v.* Thompson, 9 Up. Can. (C. P.) 257. See, also, Wood *v.* Brett, 9 Grant's Ch. 452; Bell *v.* Manning, 11 Grant's Ch. 142; Boatmen's Savings Bank *v.* Johnson, 24 Mo. App. 316; Union Bank *v.* Beech, 3 Hurl. & Colt. 672. To contrary effect, see Webb *v.* Hewitt, 3 Kay & Johns. 438. The consent of the surety to the release of the principal prevents such release operating as a discharge of the surety. Osgood *v.* Miller, 67 Me. 174.

[3] Bank of Montreal *v.* McFaul, 17 Grant's Ch. 234.

gone as between the debtor and creditor, inasmuch as the creditor cannot sue the debtor, but as against all other persons the rights of the creditor are reserved."[1] Judgment was recovered against a surety, and a separate judgment was recovered against the principal, which included also other claims. The creditor afterwards offered to give the control of the judgment against the principal to the surety, but the surety refused it. Afterwards the creditor agreed with the principal that he never would enforce the judgment against him, and assigned the judgment against the principal to a third person for the principal's benefit, but he reserved the right to proceed on the judgment against the surety. *Held*, the surety was not discharged.[2] A., B. and C. executed a joint and several bond as guardians, with T. as surety. The ward, after coming of age, executed a release to A., adding: "But this release is not to apply to or affect my claims against B., my active guardian, and whose account remains unsettled." *Held*, in equity, that the release as to A. was good, and that it was also a good defense to T., so far as he was surety for A., but that T. remained bound for B. and C.[3] If, before the release of the principal, the surety has paid a part of the debt and secured the remainder, such release will not discharge such surety.[4] A surety who is fully indemnified is not discharged by the release of the principal. In such case the surety himself occupies the position of a principal.[5]

§ 148. **Miscellaneous cases on discharge of surety when principal is not bound, etc.**— Certain parties, professing to be the representatives of a school district, made a note with sureties, and raised money on it to build a school-house. The district had no power to borrow money for such a purpose, and it was held that it was not liable on the note, but that the sureties were liable thereon.[6] It has been held that the discharge of one of two joint guardians by the orphans' court

[1] Green *v.* Wynn, Law Rep. 4 Ch. App. Cas. 204, per Lord Hatherly, C.; affirming Green *v.* Wynn, Law Rep. 7 Eq. Cas. 28.

[2] Hubbell *v.* Carpenter, 5 N. Y. 171.

[3] Kirby *v.* Turner, 6 Johns. Ch. 242; Kirby *v.* Turner, Hopkins' Ch. 309.

[4] Hall *v.* Hutchons, 3 Mylne & Keen, 426.

[5] Moore *v.* Paine, 12 Wend. 123. He holds the money for the benefit of the creditor, to whom he occupies the position of a debtor. Crim *et al.* *v.* Fleming, 101 Ind. 154.

[6] Weare *v.* Sawyer, 44 N. H. 198.

does not discharge the surety on their official bond. This was put on the ground that the court had the power to do this when the surety became bound, and he must be presumed to have consented that it might be done.[1] A surety concurs with the principal in suggesting to the creditor, who is pressing for his money, to accept a transfer of a mortgage, which the principal knows to be fictitious, but the surety believes to be genuine. The creditor, believing the mortgage to be genuine, accepted it, released the surety, and erased his name from the securities. Upon the faith of this release, the friends of the surety advanced him money for the purpose of relieving him from all other liabilities. Upon discovery of the fraud, it was held that the creditor was entitled to be restored to all his rights against the surety, in the same manner as if he had never been released, nor his name erased from the securities.[2] The period of limitation to actions on bonds was fifteen years, and against officers for breaches of official duty, one year. Suit was brought on the official bond of an auditor against his sureties, for dereliction of duty on the part of the auditor, more than a year after he went out of office. *Held*, the statute was a bar in favor of the sureties.[3] If the creditor sues the principal and takes judgment for less than the amount due, and such judgment is satisfied, he cannot maintain a suit against the surety for the remainder of the debt.[4] A testator appointed, as his executors, two persons who were indebted to him on a bond — one as principal, the other as surety. *Held*, the bond was discharged by the appointment of the principal

So the sureties on an attachment bond given by a county will be liable thereon, even though the bond be not binding on the county. State *v.* Fortinberry, 54 Miss. 316.

[1] Hocker *v.* Wood's Ex'r, 33 Pa. St. 466.

[2] Scholefield *v.* Templer, 4 De Gex & Jones, 429, affirming Scholefield *v.* Templer, Johns. (Eng. Ch.) 155.

[3] State *v.* Blake, 2 Ohio St. 147. If the debt of the principal is barred, a mortgage given by his surety to secure it is unenforceable. Bridge's Adm'r *v.* Blake, 106 Ind. 332. See Auchampaugh, Adm'r, *v.* Schmidt, 70 Iowa, 642, where it was held that in an action against a surety on a promissory note made in Illinois, where the principal resided, and where action against him was barred. but where the surety removed to Iowa before action was barred in Illinois, and the action was begun against him in Iowa before it would have otherwise been barred by the statute of Iowa, the bar of the statute against the principal was by reason thereof barred also as against the surety.

[4] Couch *v.* Waring, 9 Conn. 261.

as executor, and thereby became *functus officio* as to the surety.[1]

§ 149. When discharge of principal, after judgment against surety, releases surety.— If the principal is discharged because of matters inherent in the transaction, even after judgment against the surety, the latter will be exonerated thereby. Thus, a sheriff and his sureties were sued on his official bond for his non-feasance, and severed in their defenses. Judgment was rendered against the sureties on demurrer, and the next day the issue was tried against the sheriff and he was found not guilty. *Held*, the sureties might therefore maintain a bill to perpetually enjoin the judgment against them. The court said the rights of the surety were the same after as before judgment. When the liability of the principal ceases, that of the surety should cease also. This principle was controlling even though the sureties knew all the facts before the judgment against them, except the discharge of the principal. That was a fact which occurred after the judgment, and was the fact which discharged them.[2] In a suit against a sheriff and the sureties on his official bond, judgment was recovered against all of them. The sheriff alone appealed, and on a final trial was acquitted. *Held*, the judgment against the sureties could not afterwards be enforced.[3] G. sold B. and W. negroes introduced into the state in violation of law. B. and W. executed a note in part payment for the slaves, which M. indorsed. G. sued B. and W. at law on the note, and they set up the illegality of the consideration thereof and were discharged. G. at the same time sued M., the indorser, who, being ignorant of the facts concerning the consideration, made no defense,

[1] Eichelberger *v.* Morris, 6 Watts (Pa.), 42. Where an instrument guarantied certain notes, the amount of which was carried out and footed up, it was held the guarantor was liable for the full amount, although the principal was entitled to a reduction as against the creditor. James *v.* Long, 68 N. C. 218. Holding that the accommodation drawer of a note is not released by the release of the payee, where the holder did not know of the suretyship, see Carstairs *v.* Rolleston, 1 Marsh. 207. Holding that the accommodation acceptor of a bill of exchange is not discharged if the holder, who did not know of the suretyship when he took the draft, after learning that fact releases the drawer, see Howard Banking Company *v.* Welchman, 6 Bosw. (N. Y.) 280.

[2] Ames *v.* Maclay, 14 Iowa, 281.

[3] Beall *v.* Cochran, 18 Ga. 38.

and judgment was had against him. *Held*, M. could sustain a bill for perpetual injunction as to the judgment against him, on the ground that his principal had been discharged, and this although he might have ascertained the facts as to the consideration by inquiry.[1] A. bought slaves and gave his notes with B. as surety for the price. Having cause to rescind the sale, A. brought suit to procure a rescission thereof. Pending such suit the vendor brought suit against A. and B. on the note, and recovered judgment against B. by default. A. afterwards, in his rescission suit, obtained a decree canceling the notes. *Held*, the effect of that decree was to discharge B.[2] The principal in a bond for the payment of money was sued alone for a breach thereof, and upon pleas of payment and accord and satisfaction there was a verdict and judgment in his favor. *Held*, this was not a defense to a surety who was afterwards sued on the same bond. The court said the judgment would not have been conclusive against the surety if it had been against the principal, and should not be conclusive in his favor when in favor of the principal.[3] The fact that the discharge of the principal should in such case of itself release the surety seems to have been overlooked.

§ 150. Surety not discharged if principal released by act of law.— The discharge of the principal by the act of the law, in which the creditor does not participate, will not release the surety. A familiar illustration of this rule is that of the discharge of the principal in bankruptcy or under insolvent laws, in which case the surety is generally held not to be discharged thereby.[4] A creditor pending an action against a surety who

[1] Miller *v.* Gaskins, 1 Smedes & Mar. Ch. (Miss.) 524.

[2] Dickason *v.* Bell, 13 La. Ann. 249.

[3] State Bank *v.* Robinson, 13 Ark. (8 Eng.) 214.

[4] Alsop *v.* Price, 1 Doug. (Eng.) 160; Garnett *v.* Roper, 10 Ala. 842; Cowper *v.* Smith, 4 Mees. & Wels. 519; Kane *v.* Ingraham, 2 Johns. Cas. 403; Seaman *v.* Drake, 1 Caines' Rep. 9, Inglis *v.* Macdougal, 1 Moore, 196; Claflin *v.* Cogan, 48 N. H. 411; Moore *v.* Wallers' Heirs, 1 A. K. Marsh. (Ky.) 183; Jones *v.* Hagler, 6 Jones' Law (N. C.), 542; Bank *v.* Simpson, 90 N. C. 467; Wolf *v.* Stix, 99 U. S. 1; Wilson *v.* Field, 27 Hun (N. Y.), 46; Lackey *v.* Steere, 121 Ill. 598; Steele *v.* Graves, 68 Ala. 21, overruling Jones *v.* Knox, 46 Ala. 53; Smith *v.* Gillam, 80 Ala. 296; McCombs *v.* Allen, 18 Hun (N. Y.), 190; Serra 'E Hijo *v.* Hoffman & Co., 30 La. Ann. 67; Robinson *v.* Soule, 56 Miss. 549; Jones *v.* Hawkins, 60 Ga. 52; Cochrane *v.* Cushing, 124 Mass. 219. But see, *contra*, Choate *v.* Quinichett, 12 Heisk. (Tenn.) 427; Rountree *v.* Rutherford,

contested his liability proved the debt under a commission of bankruptcy against the principal, and by his signature enabled the bankrupt to obtain his certificate, though the surety had given him notice not to sign it. *Held*, the surety was not discharged.[1] A state statute provided that "The obligation of the surety is accessory to that of his principal, and if the latter from any cause becomes extinct, the former ceases of course." A principal having been discharged in bankruptcy, it was held that the statute was only an affirmation of the common law, and the words "from any cause" meant any cause dependent on the act or negligence of the creditor, and that the surety was not discharged. The court said: "The discharge of the principal which discharges a surety must be a discharge by some act or neglect of the creditor, and a discharge by operation of law being, as it is, against the consent and beyond the power of the creditor, does not discharge the surety."[2] Judgment having been recovered against a debtor, he gave bond with surety that the judgment should be paid within nine months. The debtor was afterwards arrested by virtue of the judgment, and discharged under the insolvent law. *Held*, the surety was not thereby released. The court said: "That the arrest on *a capias ad satisfaciendum* is in itself a satisfaction of the debt is a position not to be maintained unless the plaintiff consented to the discharge; then, indeed, the debt is gone. . . . Here the plaintiff gave no consent to the discharge of . . . (the principal). It was effected by act of law, which, like the act of God, injures no man."[3] The lien of a mortgage given by a surety to secure a debt of the principal is not released by the latter's discharge in bankruptcy.[4] And this is true where the mortgage is given by a wife on her separate property to secure the husband's debts. The discharge of the husband in bankruptcy does not release the wife.[5]

65 Ga. 444; Rutherford *v.* Rountree, 67 Ga. 725.

[1] Browne *v.* Carr, 2 Russ. 600.

[2] Phillipps *v.* Solomon, 42 Ga. 192, per McKay, J. A composition with creditors under the bankrupt act does not discharge the sureties, and the remedy against them remains. Fisse *v.* Einstein, 5 Mo. App. 78.

[3] Sharpe *v.* Speckenugle, 3 Serg. & Rawle (Pa.), 463, per Tilghman, C. J.

[4] Post, Adm'r, *v.* Losey, 111 Ind. 74.

[5] Burtis, Adm'r, *v.* Wait, 33 Kan. 478.

§ 151. Whether surety bound when principal does not sign the obligation.—As to whether the surety is bound when the principal, who is named in the instrument, does not sign it, there is great conflict of authority. It has been held that in such case the surety is not liable, and in holding this with reference to the bail bond in a civil suit, the court said: "Now we think it essential to a bail bond that the party arrested should be principal. It is recited that he is, and the instrument is incomplete and void without his signature. The remedy of the sureties against the principal would wholly fail, or be much embarrassed, if such an instrument as this should be held binding. Suppose they wish to arrest the principal in some distant place, or in some other state, what evidence would they carry with them that they were his bail? There is nothing to estop him from denying the fact, nor any proof that it was true."[1] Where in the body of a county treasurer's official bond his name was recited, but he neither signed nor sealed it, the sureties who signed it were held liable. The court said the treasurer was liable to the county without any bond, and also liable to his sureties for any amount paid by them, even though he did not sign the bond. They might not be able to produce the bond as evidence, but this was no greater inconvenience than if the bond had been lost. The words of the statute which provided for giving bond with surety might well be construed to mean giving bond by surety.[2] One who has by an instrument indorsed on a lease

[1] Bean *v.* Parker, 17 Mass. 591, per Parker, C. J.; Bunn *v.* Jetmore, 70 Mo. 228. To same effect, with reference to surety on prison-bounds bond, Curtis *v.* Moss, 2 Rob. (La.), 367; with reference to surety on bond of a county treasurer, People *v.* Hartley, 21 Cal. 585; with reference to surety on bond of town treasurer, Johnston *v.* Kimball Township, 39 Mich. 187; with reference to surety on an appeal bond, State *v.* Austin, 35 Minn. 51; with reference to surety on bond of a treasurer of a corporation, Goodyear Dental Vulcanite Co. *v.* Bacon, 151 Mass. 460; and with reference to the surety on an administrator's bond, Wood *v.* Wasbburn, 2 Pick. 24. *Contra*, Parker *v.* Bradley, 2 Hill (N. Y.), 584; Miller *v.* Tunis, 10 Up. Can. (C. P.) 423. And a recognizance unsigned by the principal held not void as to the surety. Tillson *v.* State, 29 Kan. 452.

[2] State *v.* Bowman, 10 Ohio, 445. To same effect, where a bond was conditioned that the principal should pay for such goods as he should purchase, see Williams *v.* Marshall, 42 Barb. (N. Y.) 524. Where a bond

guarantied the fulfillment of the covenants of the lease by the lessees, naming them, is bound by his guaranty, although the lease is executed by only one of the lessees, where it appears that both lessees occupied the demised premises, and had possession of all the property mentioned in the lease for the whole term.[1] It has been held that a bond given for the purpose of obtaining a dissolution of an attachment of partnership property, and executed in the name of the firm by only one of two partners named as principals therein, cannot be enforced against the surety without evidence of the assent of the other partner to its execution.[2] But where one member of a firm signed the firm name to a note under seal, which consequently did not bind the other member, it was held that a surety on the note was not, for that reason, discharged.[3] Where a surety signed a bond which purported to have been signed by the principal, but had not in fact been signed by him nor by his authority, it was held the surety was not discharged, unless he delivered the bond as an escrow.[4] Principal and surety entered into a recognizance for the appearance of the principal at the March term of the court to answer an indictment. The principal did not appear, and the surety alone, at the March term, entered into a recognizance for the appearance of the principal at the May term. No default was entered on the first recognizance. The principal did not appear at the May term. *Held*, the surety was liable on the last recognizance. He would not have been liable but for the previous recognizance; because, otherwise, the surety might control the person of the principal without his consent. But in this case, the principal, having entered into the first recognizance, could not

provided for the payment by each of several sureties of $1,000, it was held that the bond showed an obligation on behalf of each surety to pay the sum of $1,000, and on behalf of the principal to pay the aggregate of all the sums. People *v.* Breyfogle, 17 Cal. 504.

[1] McLaughlin *v.* McGovern, 34 Barb. (N. Y.) 208. A bond executed to a municipal corporation by sureties to secure the performance of a lease by the lessee is valid though not executed by the lessee. Mayor *v.* Kent, 25 J. & S. (N. Y. Sup. Ct.) 109.

[2] Russell *v.* Annable, 109 Mass. 72.

[3] Stewart *v.* Behm, 2 Watts (Pa.), 356.

[4] Loew *v.* Stocker, 68 Pa. St. 226. To similar effect, with reference to a promissory note, see Chase *v.* Hathorn, 61 Me. 505.

make this objection, and the surety could not complain because, by entering into the last recognizance, he saved a forfeiture of the first.[1]

§ 152. Same continued.— The liability of sureties on a recognizance,[2] replevin bond,[3] school treasurer's bond,[4] bond of indemnity,[5] attachment bond,[6] bond to prevent attachment,[7] appeal bond,[8] constable's bond [9] and bond to secure the performance of a lease [10] is not affected because of the principal's failure to sign the obligation or have his name inserted therein. And if a surety in snch cases pays the obligation, his right to indemnity from the principal remains the same as though the principal had signed.[11] There is no presumption that sureties have waived their principal's signature when he has not signed with them.[12]

§ 153. When surety bound for contract of infant or married woman which is not binding on them.— Where a party becomes the surety of a married woman, an infant, or other person incapable of contracting, he is bound, although the principal is not. With reference to this it has been said that: "Fraud, illegality, or mistake, which may rescind the contract of the principal, induces the discharge of the sureties; but if the invalidity of the contract rests upon reasons personal to the principal, in the nature of a privilege or protection, the

[1] Combs *v.* The People, 39 Ill. 183. Holding that several persons who execute a bond may show by parol that they are all sureties for a person who did not sign the bond, see Artcher *v.* Douglass, 5 Denio, 509.

[2] State *v.* Peyton *et al.*, 32 Mo. App. 522; Irwin *v.* State, 10 Neb. 325.

[3] Cahill's Appeal, 48 Mich. 616.

[4] Trustees of Schools *v.* Sheik, 119 Ill. 579, reversing 16 Brad. (Ill. App.) 49.

[5] Bollman *v.* Pasewalk, 22 Neb. 761.

[6] Adams *v.* Kellogg, 63 Mich. 105.

[7] McIntosh *v.* Hurst, 6 Mont. 287; Pierse *v.* Miles, 5 Mont. 549. This under statute.

[8] Johnson *v.* Johnson, 31 Ohio St. 131. This by statute.

[9] Rader *v.* Davis, 5 Lea (Tenn.), 436.

[10] Mayor *v.* Kent, 25 J. & S. (N. Y. Sup. Ct.) 109.

[11] Trustees of Schools *v.* Sheik *et al.*, 119 Ill. 579, reversing 16 Brad. (Ill. App.) 49; Harnsberger *v.* Yancey, 33 Gratt. (Va.) 527.

[12] Hall *v.* Parker, 39 Mich. 287. If a bond can be charged against sureties without their principal's signature, it can only be by positive proof that they had delivered it to become operative as against themselves alone. Hall *v.* Parker, 39 Mich. 287.

principal acquires a personal defense against the contract," but the contract subsists, and the sureties may be charged thereon. The disability of the principal may be the very reason why the surety was required.[1] An infant bought a tract of land and gave his note with sureties for the purchase money. On coming of age he disaffirmed the sale. *Held*, the sureties were discharged thereby. The court said: "As a general proposition, it is undoubtedly correct that infancy does not protect the indorsers or sureties of an infant, or those who have jointly entered into his voidable undertaking. But the cases in which this principle has been decided are clearly distinguishable from the present one. Here the undertaking of the sureties goes to the whole consideration. . . . By the disaffirmance of the contract the plaintiff gets back his land, and the consideration which upheld the contract is extinguished. It would be a strange doctrine which would give him back his land and allow him to recover from the sureties the purchase money also."[2]

§ 154. **Discharge of surety does not release principal.**— If the creditor release the surety he does not thereby discharge the principal. The reason why the discharge of one joint debtor discharges all is that the responsibility of the one not released is thereby increased. This reason does not apply to the case of the discharge of the surety, for the surety is not liable to the principal, but the principal is bound to indemnify the surety. The discharge of the surety is nothing beyond what the principal himself was bound to effect, and therefore no injustice is done him.[3]

[1] Smyley *v.* Head, 2 Rich. Law (S. C.), 590, per Frost, J.; St. Albans Bank *v.* Dillon, 30 Vt. 122; Kimball *v.* Newell, 7 Hill, 116; Nabb *v.* Koontz, 17 Md. 283; Davis *v.* Statts, 43 Ind. 103; Weed Sewing Machine Co. *v.* Maxwell, 63 Mo. 486; Yale *v.* Wheelock, 109 Mass. 502; Jones *v.* Crosthwaite, 17 Iowa, 393; Lee *v.* Yandell *et al.*, 69 Tex. 34; Winn *v.* Sanford, 145 Mass. 302; Wiggins' Appeal, 100 Pa. St. 155; Lobaugh *v.* Thompson, 74 Mo. 600.

[2] Baker *v.* Kennett, 54 Mo. 82, per Wagner, J.; Patterson *v.* Cave, 61 Mo. 439. See, also, on this subject, Kuns' Ex'r *v.* Young, 34 Pa. St. 60.

[3] Mortland *v.* Himes, 8 Pa. St. 265; Bridger *v.* Phillips, 17 Tex. 128; McIlhenny Co. *v.* Blum, 68 Tex. 197; Burson *v.* Kincaid, 3 Pen. & Watts (Pa.), 57; Carroll *et al.* *v.* Corbitt, 57 Ala. 579.

§ 155. When surety discharged by mental or physical incapacity of principal.— In an action against sureties on a joint and several bond conditioned for their principal's paying over public moneys, the sureties pleaded that they were discharged from liability because their principal became wholly incapacitated from performing his duties by reason of his lunacy. *Held*, a good defense.[1] On the other hand, it was held no defense to the sureties on such a bond, that their principal was rendered incapable of performing his duties by reason of his complete paralysis.[2]

[1] Grove *v.* Johnston, Law Rep. (Irish, 24 Q. B. & Ex. Div.) 352.

[2] The Belfast Banking Co. *v.* Hamilton, 12 Law Rep. (Irish) 105.

CHAPTER V.

OF CONTINUING GUARANTIES.

When guaranty ambiguous it may be explained by parol — No general rule for determining whether guaranty continuing or not . . . . § 156
Continuing guaranties — Instances 157
Continuing guaranties — Instances 158
Continuing guaranties — Instances 159
When guaranty not exhausted by the advance of the amount mentioned therein 160
When guaranty exhausted and when not exhausted by the advance of the amount mentioned therein . . . . . § 161
What not continuing guaranty — Instances 162
What not continuing guaranty — Instances 163
What not continuing guaranty — Instances 164
What not continuing guaranty — Instances 165

§ 156. When guaranty ambiguous it may be explained by parol — No general rule for determining whether guaranty continuing or not.— A question often arising upon guaranties is whether the guaranty is confined to a single credit or transaction, or whether it is continuing and covers several credits or transactions. As already shown, the true rule for construing guaranties is to give effect to the intention of the parties as expressed in the instrument, read in the light of the surrounding circumstances. Numerous instances of the views on this subject entertained by the courts will be found upon an examination of the cases cited in this chapter. When the words of a guaranty will equally well bear the construction that it is or is not continuing, an ambiguity arises which may be explained by parol evidence of the situation and surroundings of the parties and the construction which they have put upon it.[1] This subject is well illustrated by the following remarks of a learned judge, made in deciding whether a guar-

[1] Hotchkiss *v.* Barnes, 34 Conn. 27; Grahame *v.* Grahame, Law Rep. Irish (19 Ch. Div.), 249; The Columbia Sewer Pipe Co. *v.* Ganser, 58 Mich. 385; Gardner *v.* Watson, 76 Tex. 25.

anty was continuing or not: "It is obvious that we cannot decide that question upon the mere construction of the document itself, without looking at the surrounding circumstances to see what was the subject-matter which the parties had in their contemplation when the guaranty was given. It is proper to ascertain that for the purpose of seeing what the parties were dealing about; not for the purpose of altering the terms of the guaranty by words of mouth passing at the time, but as part of the conduct of the parties, in order to determine what was the scope and object of the intended guaranty. Having done that, it will be proper to turn to the language of the guaranty to see if that language is capable of being construed so as to carry into effect that which appears to have been really the intention of both parties."[1] Where a guaranty is, from its terms, clearly not a continuing one, but is limited to one transaction, parol evidence of the previous dealings or of the dealings contemplated between the creditor and the principal, or that the guarantor had previously agreed to give the plaintiff a guaranty for future advances, and that the goods were sold relying on such guaranty, or that the relations of the principal parties were well known to the guarantor, is not admissible to show the guaranty to be a continuing one, for that would be to contradict the instrument and not explain an ambiguity.[2] As the terms of guaranties, and the circumstances under which they are given, differ in almost every case, no definite rules for determining whether a guaranty shall be considered a continuing one or not can be given. The only way to illustrate the subject is to refer to facts of decided cases, and this course will be pursued.

§ 157. Continuing guaranties — Instances.— A guaranty was as follows: "Mr. J. B. Maynard being about to commence the retailing of dry goods at Connelton, Ind., and desiring to open a credit with the firm of James Lowe & Co., of the city

[1] Per Willes, J., in Heffield *v.* Meadows, Law Rep. 4 Com. Pleas, 595; White's Bank *v.* Myles, 73 N. Y. 335. In Mathews *v.* Phelps, 61 Mich. 327, it is held that when the amount of the guarantor's liability is limited, and the *time* is not, it will be held to be a continuing guaranty. And in Wright *v.* Griffith, 121 Ind. 478, it is held that unless the words in which the guaranty is expressed fairly imply that the liability of the guarantor is limited, it is regarded as continuing until revoked.

[2] Boston & Sandwich Glass Co. *v.* Moore, 119 Mass. 435.

of Louisville, I hereby undertake and contract with said Lowe & Co. to become responsible to them for the amount of any bill or bills of merchandise sold by them to said Maynard, agreeably to the terms of sale agreed upon between the parties, without requiring said Lowe & Co. to prosecute suit against said Maynard therefor." *Held*, to be a continuing guaranty and not confined to the first few bills bought by Maynard upon commencing business.[1] When the writing was: "In consideration of your supplying Mr. John McGuire supplies of, etc., out of your store for his business, we agree to become responsible for the payment of $200 for such goods, and guaranty the payment of that amount, whether the same be due on note or book account to you for said" . . . it was held to be a continuing guaranty.[2] A writing was as follows: "To whom it may concern: The bearer, M. R., son of the subscriber, is about to establish a store in Portland, of books and stationery, and now goes on to Boston to obtain an assortment of stock for that purpose. He will commence on a limited scale, with the intention of enlarging the business next spring. He wishes to purchase school books, etc., upon a credit of four or six months, and miscellaneous books, paper, etc., on commission. For the faithful management of the business and punctual fulfillment of contracts relating to it, the subscriber will hold himself responsible." *Held*, a continuing guaranty for such purchases as the son might make.[3] The following was held to be a continuing guaranty: "In consideration of your agreeing to supply goods to K. at two months' credit, I agree to guaranty his present or any future debt with you to the amount of 60*l*. Should he fail to pay at the expiration of the above credit, I bind myself to pay you within seven days of receiving notice from you."[4] The defendant's son being indebted to the plaintiffs for coals supplied on credit, and the plaintiffs refusing to continue to supply coals unless a guaranty was given them, the defendant gave this guaranty: "In consideration of the credit given by the H. G. C. Co. to my son for coal supplied by them to him, I

[1] Lowe *v.* Beckwith, 14 B. Mon. (Ky.) 150.

[2] Fennell *v.* McGuire, 21 Up. Can. (C. P.) 134.

[3] Mussey *v.* Rayner, 22 Pick. 223.

[4] Martin *v.* Wright, 6 Adol. & Ell. (N. S.) 917.

hereby hold myself responsible as a guaranty to them for the sum of 100*l*., and in default of his payment of any accounts due, I bind myself by this note to pay to the H. G. C. Co. whatever may be owing to an amount not exceeding the amount of 100*l*." *Held*, a continuing guaranty. The court said: "The question in these cases depends not merely on the words; but, when the words are at all ambiguous, requires a consideration of the circumstances to aid the construction. . . . The words 'whatever may be owing' . . . seem not suitable to a specific and ascertained sum already due, but have a direct and proper application to what might afterwards become due."[1] A letter contained the following: "I do recommend my friend, Mr. J. B. Scudder, of the parish of East Baton Rouge, a planter, and any funds that he may raise, or acceptances, in case he does not pay, I feel bound to pay." *Held*, a continuing guaranty; the guarantor and Scudder being both planters, and the circumstances showing that a continuing guaranty was intended.[2] This is a continuing guaranty: "I hold myself accountable to you for any goods Mr. Francis Murphy may purchase of you to the amount of 250*l*. currency."[3] Also the following: "Sir, you can let J. L. Day have what goods he calls for, and I will see that the same are settled for."[4]

§ 158. Continuing guaranties — Instances.— A. bought from B. certain hides, but before they were delivered, B. having heard that A. had transferred his property, refused to deliver the hides until C. would become responsible therefor. C., learning this, telegraphed to B.: "We agree to be answerable for the skins," and afterwards wrote, vouching for A.'s honesty, and concluding: "What you have heard was done to protect him from a dishonorable tradesman, and will in no way, we hope, be to the injury of his creditors. Having every confidence in him, he has but to call upon us for a cheque, and have it with pleasure, for any account he may have with you, and when to the contrary we will write you." *Held*, the let-

[1] Wood *v.* Priestner, Law Rep. 2 Exch. 66, per Kelly, C. B.; affirmed, Wood *v.* Priestner, Law Rep. 2 Exch. 282.

[2] Menard *v.* Scudder, 7 La. Ann. 385.

[3] Ross *v.* Burton, 4 Up. Can. (Q. B.) 357.

[4] Hotchkiss *v.* Barnes, 34 Conn. 27.

ter was a continuing guaranty unlimited in amount. The court said: "It was calculated to induce the plaintiffs to give credit to a man to whom they would not otherwise have given it."[1] One Tully, being about to go into business, and desiring credit, a relative of his wrote to certain merchants as follows: "Please let Mr. P. Tully have the paints, oils, varnishes, etc., he wants. I will be security for the amount for what he will owe you." *Held*, a continuing guaranty.[2] The material part of the guaranty was: "I will guaranty their engagements, should you think it necessary, for any transaction they may have with your house." *Held*, the guaranty was a continuing one, and in force till countermanded by the guarantor.[3] "I do hereby agree to guaranty the payment of goods to be delivered, in umbrellas and parasols, to . . . according to the custom of their trading with you, in the sum of 200*l*.," is a continuing guaranty.[4] The following is a continuing guaranty: "I hereby agree to guaranty the payment to A. for any goods which may be purchased of him by B., not, however, binding myself to become responsible for a larger sum than $500, except by another special agreement, the above guaranty to remain in force until it is withdrawn by me."[5] The following is a continuing guaranty: "Whereas, W. C. is indebted to you, and may have occasion to make further purchases from you; as an inducement to you to continue your dealings with him, I undertake to guaranty you in the sum of 100*l*., payable to you in default on the part of the said W. C., for two months."[6] A. and B. executed a bond to C. in the penal sum of $1,500, conditioned "to pay or cause to be paid to C. all sums or sum of moneys, responsibilities, debts and dues which B. might owe C., equal to the sum of $1,500, either contracted or which might thereafter be contracted." *Held*, this was a continuing guaranty, and covered indebtedness of B. to the extent of $1,500, although part of the debts contracted by B. under the guaranty had been paid by him. *Held*, also, that notes of B. made to a third party, and by

[1] Nothingham Hide Co. *v.* Bottrill, L. R. 8 Com. Pl. 694, per Keating, J.

[2] Boehme *v.* Murphy, 46 Mo. 57.

[3] Grant *v.* Ridsdale, 2 Harr. & Johns. (Md.) 186.

[4] Hargreave *v.* Smee, 6 Bing. 244; Id., 3 Moore & Payne, 573.

[5] Melendy *v.* Capen, 120 Mass. 222.

[6] Allan *v.* Kenning, 9 Bing. 618; Id., 2 Moore & Scott, 768.

such third party indorsed to C., were within the terms of the guaranty. The court said: "Such a debt is a debt due to . . . (C.) as much as any other. This is the criterion the parties have chosen to adopt, and it is not for the court to restrict it."[1]

§ 159. **Continuing guaranties — Instances.**— Where guarantors of a bank, selected as a state depository for canal tolls, executed a bond to the state that the bank shall "well and faithfully account for and pay over all moneys deposited with it, or for which it shall in any way become liable," and also "account for and pay over all moneys now on deposit in said bank, or due or to become due therefrom to the people," it was held in an action on such guaranty that the guarantors were bound for the continuing security of the deposit existing at the time of the execution of said bond, as well as for subsequent deposits.[2] The following writing: "Messrs. G. Bros.— Please let my daughter, Mrs. W. E. H., have what goods she wants, and I will stand good for the money to settle the bills. You will find the pay part all right with her, I think," was held to be a continuing guaranty.[3] A written agreement signed by a guarantor, in terms guarantying payment "for all goods F. F., of N., and H. F., of M, may buy from B. Young & Son," was construed to be a continuing guaranty.[4] The following letter, viz.: "I have to-day seen Chas. E. Grayson, and upon consulting with him I am willing to become his security to the amount of $500 worth of goods, instead of $250 as heretofore, provided you extend to him a credit of $500 worth of goods additional, on his own individual account or responsibility," was held a continuing guaranty.[5] A letter of credit given to a bank in the following language, "Please discount for Mr. C. to the extent of $4,000. He will give you customers' paper as collateral. You can also consider me responsible to the bank for the same," was held to be a continuing guaranty, and that the writer's liability did not cease with the discount and payment of the sum stated.[6]

[1] Lewis *v.* Dwight, 10 Conn. 95, per Williams, J.

[2] People *v.* Lee *et al.*, 104 N. Y. 441. See, also, Merchants' Nat. Bank *v.* Hall, 18 Hun, 176.

[3] Wright *v.* Griffith *et al.*, 121 Ind. 478.

[4] Young *v.* Brown, 53 Wis. 333.

[5] Gardner, Adm'r, *v.* Watson, 76 Tex. 25.

[6] White's Bank *v.* Myles, 73 N. Y. 335.

§ 160. When guaranty not exhausted by the advance of the amount mentioned therein.— A bond was conditioned to indemnify and save harmless the obligee for "such sums as they in their banking business should within ten years advance or pay, or be liable to advance or pay, for or on account of their accepting, discounting, etc., any bill of exchange, etc., which A. B. should from time to time draw upon or make payable, etc., at their house; and also other sums which they, within the period aforesaid, should otherwise lay out, pay, etc., on the credit of A. B. or on his account, and also all such wages and allowances for advancing, paying, etc., such bills, etc., not exceeding 5,000*l.* in the whole, together with interest on such advances." *Held*, a continuing guaranty and not exhausted by the first advance of 5,000*l.*[1] Where the instrument was as follows: "Sir, I hereby guaranty the payment of any amount of goods you may give to B., not exceeding 40*l.* sterling," it was held to be a continuing guaranty, the first part being unlimited, and the second part only limiting it as to amount.[2] A guaranty was as follows: "I agree to be responsible for the price of goods purchased of you, either by note or account, by H., at any time hereafter, to the amount of $1,000." Goods were sold on the credit of the guaranty to the amount of more than $1,000, which were paid for, and more goods were sold, when H. became insolvent, owing more than $1,000 that had been sold on the credit of the guaranty. *Held*, the guaranty was continuing and not exhausted by the first sales amounting to $1,000, and that the guarantor was liable for $1,000. The court said: "When by the terms of the undertaking, by the recitals of the instrument, or by reference to the custom and course of dealing between the parties, it appears that the guaranty looked to a future course of dealing for an indefinite time, or a succession of credits to be given, it is to be deemed a continuing guaranty, and the amount expressed is to limit the amount for which the guarantor is to be responsible, and not the amount to which the dealing or whole credit given is to extend."[3] The same thing was held when the guaranty

[1] Williams *v.* Rawlinson, Ryan & Moody, 233.

[2] Whelan *v.* Keegan, 7 Irish Com. Law, 544.

[3] Bent *v.* Hartshorn, 1 Met. (Mass.) 24, per Shaw, C. J.

was: "I will be and am responsible for any amount for which . . . may draw on you, for any sum not exceeding $1,500, on condition of your acceptance of the same."[1] Also, when the material part of a guaranty was: "For any goods he hath or may supply W. P. with, to the amount of 100*l.*"[2] A guaranty to be "accountable that B. will pay you for glass, paints, etc., which he may require in his business, to the extent of $50," is a continuing guaranty, and not exhausted by the first $50 of credit given to B. "Had the guarantor desired or intended to limit his responsibility to a single transaction, or to several transactions not exceeding that sum in all, it was easy to have said it in plain and unmistakable terms; that if he has failed to do so, and by equivocal language induced the guarantee to part with the goods, he should be held to abide the consequences."[3] The same thing was held where the guaranty was: "I will be responsible for what stock . . . (A.) has had, or may want hereafter, to the amount of $500."[4] An obligation was as follows: "In consideration of the Union Bank agreeing to advance and advancing to R. & Co. any sum or sums of money they may require during the next eighteen months, not exceeding in the whole 1,000*l.*, we hereby jointly and severally guaranty the payment of any such sum as may be owing to the bank at the expiration of said period of eighteen months." *Held*, under the circumstances (which should be considered), this was a continuing guaranty. The words, "not exceeding in the whole 1,000*l.*, . . . were intended to express the limit of the defendants' liability, and not to prohibit the bank from making any further advances to R. & Co."[5] A guaranty of goods to be sold "from time to time,"

[1] Crist *v.* Burlingame, 62 Barb. (N. Y.) 351.

[2] Mason *v.* Pritchard, 12 East, 227.

[3] Rindge *v.* Judson, 24 N. Y. 64, per James, J. See, also, Platter *v.* Green, 26 Kan. 252. So an undertaking executed to a bank by a firm, viz.: "We hold ourselves responsible for the payment of any sum not to exceed $5,000, Mr. C. H. W. may require of your bank for legitimate purposes," was held to be a continuing guaranty. City National Bank *v.* Phelps, 86 N. Y. 484, affirming to this point, 16 Hun, 158.

[4] Gates *v.* McKee, 13 N. Y. 232. A guaranty in the following words, "Please let Mr. Jno. Newman have credit for goods to the amount of one hundred dollars, and for the payment of which I hold myself responsible," was held to be continuing. Tootle *v.* Elgutter, 14 Neb. 158.

[5] Lawrie *v.* Scholefield, Law Rep. 4 Com. Pl. 622, per Smith, J.

to an amount not exceeding a specified sum, is a continuing guaranty until the sums remaining unpaid reach the designated limit, even though the aggregate of the purchases far exceeds it.[1]

§ 161. When guaranty exhausted and when not exhausted by the advance of the amount mentioned therein.— A guaranty, not under seal, of "the sum of $500, to be drawn out in merchandise by W. from time to time as he may want; this guaranty to remain good until further order, or until April 1, 1857," is continuing, and renders the guarantor liable to the extent of $500 for goods sold within the prescribed period, even though more than that amount of goods have been sold on the credit of the guaranty and paid for by the principal within that time.[2] The same thing was held where the guaranty was as follows: "In consideration of your supplying my nephew, V., with china and earthenware, I guaranty the payment of any bills you may draw on him, on account thereof, to the amount of 200*l*."[3] An obligation was as follows: "Our friend . . . (A.), to assist him in business, may require, your aid from time to time, either by acceptance or indorsement of his paper or advances in cash; in order to save you from harm by so doing, we do hereby bind ourselves, severally and jointly, to be responsible to you at any time for a sum not exceeding $8,000, should the said . . . (A.) fail to do so." *Held*, a continuing guaranty and not exhausted by the first sale of eight thousand dollars' worth of goods.[4] The following has been held to be a continuing guaranty, and not exhausted by the first sales under it: "Gentlemen, my brother Roswell is wishing to go into business in New York, by retailing goods in a small way. Should you be disposed to furnish him with

[1] Crittenden *v.* Fiske *et al.*, 46 Mich. 70.

[2] Hatch *v.* Hobbs, 12 Gray, 447. See, also, Pratt *v.* Matthews, 24 Hun (N. Y.), 386, which was an instrument guarantying the payment of coal, provided the amount in default should not at any time exceed the sum of $1,000. *Held*, the guaranty was a continuing one, and that the proviso was a limitation upon the guarantor's liability, and not upon the amount of coal to be furnished; and the fact that the indebtedness at times exceeded that sum did not relieve the guarantors. And see, also, Delaware, Lack. & W. R. R. Co. *v.* Burkhard, 36 Hun (N. Y.), 57, and Conway *v.* Cunningham, 6 Rich. (S. C.) 351.

[3] Mayer *v.* Isaac, 6 Mees. & Wels. 605.

[4] Douglass *v.* Reynolds, 7 Pet. 113.

such goods as he may call for, from three hundred to five hundred dollars' worth, I will hold myself accountable for the payment, should he not pay, as you and he shall agree."[1] M. wrote to L. thus: "Mr. B. informs me that in conversation with Mr. S., of your firm, he stated to B., 'if he would get me to be responsible for him to you, or, in other words, to give B. a letter of credit to you, he would sell him on longer time, say nine months or a year.' This is therefore to inform you that I will be responsible for B. to the amount of $1,000." *Held*, to be a continuing guaranty until goods to the amount of $1,000 were purchased, but no longer.[2] Where a guaranty was, "Mr. Lyman Wilson wishes to buy stock for his shop and pay in six months or before, we will be surety for him for a sum not to exceed $100," it was held that the plaintiffs were authorized to deliver stock to Wilson to the amount of $100 on the credit of the guaranty, and that it need not all be sold at once, but might be sold and delivered from time to time, within a reasonable period.[3]

§ 162. **What not continuing guaranty — Instances.**— Twenty-seven persons signed a guaranty, by which they agreed to be each bound for $100 for the purchasers "for any goods" they might buy of the sellers, the goods to be paid for at such time as might be agreed upon between the purchasers and sellers, "and each of us to be bound for $100, and no more." *Held*, this was not a continuing guaranty, and only bound the guarantors for goods sold at any time or times, which in the whole amount to $2,700.[4] Where a guaranty was: "I, . . . agree

[1] Rapelye *v.* Bailey, 5 Conn. 149.

[2] Lawton *v.* Maner, 10 Rich. Law (S. C.), 323.

[3] Keith *v.* Dwinnell, 38 Vt. 286. For other examples of continuing guaranties, see Hitchcock *v.* Humfrey, 5 Man. & Gr. 559; Id., 6 Scott (N. R.), 540; Farmers' & Mechanics' Bank *v.* Kerchival, 2 Mich. 504; Heffield *v.* Meadows, Law Rep. 4 Com. Pl. 595; Coles *v.* Pack, Law Rep. 5 Com. Pl. 65; Burgess *v.* Eve, Law Rep. 13 Eq. 450; Simpson *v.* Mauley, 2 Cro. & Jer. 12; Bastow *v.* Bennett, 3 Camp. 220; Merle *v.* Wells, 2 Camp. 413; Tanner *v.* Moore, 9 Q. B. 1; Hoad *v.* Grace, 7 Hurl. & Nor. 494; Woolley *v.* Jennings, 5 Barn. & Cres. 165; Platter *v.* Green, 26 Kan. 252; Clark *v.* Hyman, 55 Iowa, 14; The Cosgrave Brewing & Malting Co. *v.* Starrs, 5 Ont. (Can.) 189; Cochran *v.* Kennedy, 10 Daly (N. Y. Com. Pl.), 347; Dover Stamping Co. *v.* Noyes, 151 Mass. 342; Crathern *v.* Bell, 45 Up. Can. (Q. B.) 473; Grahame *v.* Grahame, Law Rep. (Irish), 19 Ch. Div. 249; Tischler *v.* Hofheimer, 83 Va. 35; Mathews *v.* Phelps, 61 Mich. 327.

[4] Wilde *v.* Haycraft, 2 Duvall (Ky.), 309.

to become surety to . . . (A.) for any bills contracted by . . . (B.) from this date, said bills in the aggregate not to exceed $300," it was held not to be continuing, and that it was exhausted by the sale of the first $300 worth of goods.[1] A bond recited that Colburn (principal), having occasion for divers sums of money, not exceeding in the whole the sum of 3,000*l*., had applied to the plaintiffs to advance the same at such times and in such parts and proportions as he might require. *Held*, this was not a continuing guaranty, but was exhausted by the first advances to the extent of 3,000*l*.[2] The following guaranty was held to be not continuing, and to cover only one transaction: "I guaranty the sum of $500 value in glass shades, purchased by my son A. from B. Terms of purchase to be sixty days from date of invoice, and if not paid within ninety days, draft to be drawn on me for the amount."[3] The following obligation was held not to be a continuing guaranty: "I hereby agree to be answerable for the payment of 50*l*. for T. Lerigo, in case T. Lerigo does not pay for the gin, etc., which he receives from you, and I will pay the amount."[4] When a guaranty was: "I hereby agree to guaranty to you the payment of such an amount of goods, at a credit of one year, interest after six months, not exceeding $500, as you may credit to . . . (A.)," it was held to be not continuing. The court said: "Where by the terms of the guaranty it is evident the object is to give a standing credit to the principal, to be used from time to time, either indefinitely or until a certain period, there the liability is continuing; but where no time is fixed, and nothing in the instrument indicates a continuance of the undertaking, the presumption is in favor of a limited liability as to time, whether the amount is limited or not."[5] A guaranty was as follows: "I hereby

[1] Bussier *v.* Chew, 5 Phila. (Pa.) 70.

[2] Kirby *v.* The Duke of Marlborough, 2 Maule & Sel. 18.

[3] Boston & Sandwich Glass Co. *v.* Moore, 119 Mass. 435. The following instrument: "Please deliver to H., goods as he may want from time to time, not exceeding in amount $300, and if not paid for by him within thirty days, I will be responsible for the same," was held not a continuing guaranty, but was exhausted and satisfied by the first purchase by H. of goods to the amount of $300, followed by payment. Cutler *v.* Ballou, 136 Mass. 337.

[4] Nicholson *v.* Paget, 1 Cromp. & Mees. 48; Id., 3 Tyrwh. 164.

[5] Fellows *v.* Prentiss, 3 Denio, 512, per Hand, Senator.

agree to be answerable to K. for the amount of five sacks of flour, to be delivered to T., payable in one month." Five sacks of flour were delivered to T., and a few days after five more were delivered. Shortly afterwards three and a half of the first five were returned. *Held*, the guarantor was only liable for one and a half sacks, as the guaranty was exhausted by the delivery of the first five sacks.[1]

§ **163. What not continuing guaranty — Instances.**— A portion of a letter was as follows: "The object of the present letter is to request you, if convenient, to furnish them (principals) with any sum they may want, so far as $50,000, say $50,000. They will reimburse you the amount, together with interest, as soon as arrangements can be made to do it, and as our embargo cannot be continued much longer, we apprehend there will be no difficulty in this. We shall hold ourselves answerable to you for the amount." *Held*, this was not a continuing guaranty, but was exhausted by the advance of $50,000.[2] The following was held not to be a continuing guaranty: "Sir, for any sum that my son, George Reed, may become indebted to you, not exceeding $200, I will hold myself accountable."[3] A sealed promise to pay "whatever sum may be due for all articles of book account furnished to J. at his request and for his use, and for which he is now indebted, and for all other articles of book account furnished on this day or at any future day, provided said articles of book account do not exceed the sum of $250," applies only to the existing debt, and articles furnished in addition to make up the sum of $250, and when these are paid does not continue to secure any future balance of account.[4] The material portion of a writing was: "We here offer ourselves in security to any gentleman who may feel disposed to give him (purchaser) credit, not exceeding $700, to be bound and held firmly by this writing to pay the said sum of $700 or any less sum." *Held*, this was not a continuing guaranty, and only authorized the giving of credit one time.[5] R., doing business as a retail dealer in furniture, obtained from C. a writing addressed to the plaintiff, who was

[1] Kay *v.* Groves, 6 Bing. 276; Id., 3 Moore & Payne, 634.

[2] Cremer *v.* Higginson, 1 Mason, 323.

[3] White *v.* Reed, 15 Conn. 457.

[4] Congdon *v.* Read, 7 R. I. 406.

[5] Aldricks *v.* Higgins, 16 Serg. & Rawle, 212.

a wholesale furniture dealer, as follows: "There is a fair prospect that R. could sell a few chamber suits if he had them. If you let him have them, we will see that you receive pay for them as sold or soon thereafter." *Held*, the guaranty contemplated but a single sale of chamber suits only, accompanied or speedily followed by delivery.[1] A guaranty was in the following words: "Whereas, Joel Hall has agreed to indorse Samuel Cooper's notes at the Middletown Bank to the amount of $4,000, I hereby agree to be responsible to said Hall for one-half the amount of any loss he may sustain by said indorsement; and I agree to pay the one-half of any payments which said Hall may be obliged to pay in the same manner and at the same time, which I should be obliged to pay it, provided I was joint indorser with him on said notes." *Held*, not a continuing guaranty, and that the party signing it was only liable to contribute as to the first $4,000 of notes indorsed by Hall.[2] This guaranty was held not continuing: "Sir: . . . (A.) wishing to alter his present mode of doing business and make arrangements in Charleston, has requested me to continue my assistance by lending him my name. I have therefore consented that he shall use it for the amount of from $1,000 to $1,500. He will in future carry on business on his own account, and make his own remittances."[3]

§ 164. What not continuing guaranty — Instances.— The fact that a guaranty did not limit the amount for which the guarantor might become liable has sometimes had a controlling influence, and induced the court to hold it not to be continuing. Thus, a guaranty was: "If you will let the bearer have what leather he wants, and charge the same to himself, I will see that you have your pay in a reasonable length of time." *Held*, it was confined to a single transaction. The court said: "We think it is limited to a single purchase or transaction. We must hold this, or that it is unlimited, both as to time and amount. Every person is supposed to have some regard to his own interest, and it is not reasonable to presume any man of ordinary prudence would become surety for another without limitation as to time or amount, unless he has done so in

[1] Hayden *v.* Crane, 1 Lans. (N. Y.) 181.

[2] Hall *v.* Rand, 8 Conn. 560.

[3] Sollee *v.* Mengy, 1 Bailey, Law (S. C.), 620.

express terms or by clear implication."[1] The same thing was held where the guaranty was as follows: "We consider J. V. E. good for all he may want of you, and will indemnify the same." The court said: "Ordinarily, the instruments that have been held to be continuing guaranties limited the amount of the credit, which greatly diminished the responsibility."[2] "Please let the bearer . . . (A.) buy merchandise to the amount of two or three hundred dollars, on six months, and I will see that you have your pay," is not a continuing guaranty.[3] An instrument was as follows: "P. . . . having informed me that he is making some purchases from you, and not being acquainted with you, that you wish some reference. Though not personally acquainted, yet I would say from my knowledge of P. . . . that you might credit him with perfect safety, and that anything he might purchase from you I would see paid for." *Held*, not a continuing guaranty, and that it was limited to the purchases then being made.[4] The defendants addressed to the plaintiffs the following letter: "Whatever goods you sell to A. B. to be sold in our store, we will consent that he may take the money out of our concern to pay for the same, etc. The said A. B. shall have liberty of taking the pay out of our concern as fast as the goods are sold." *Held*, if this was a guaranty, it was not a continuing one. The court said: "If the plain terms of the contract may be fulfilled by being confined to one transaction, courts are not anxious to extend it to others."[5] A guaranty was as follows: "I engage to guaranty the payment of Mr. Amos Molden to the extent of 60*l*., at quarterly account bill two months for goods, to be purchased by him of William and David Melville." *Held*, the guaranty only covered advances made during one quarter.[6]

§ 165. **What not continuing guaranty — Instances.**— A request that plaintiff would send one P. "a full line of samples suitable for spring and summer at the lowest figure," add-

[1] Gard *v.* Stevens, 12 Mich. 292, per Manning, J.

[2] Whitney *v.* Groot, 24 Wend. 82, per Nelson, C. J.

[3] Reed *v.* Fish, 59 Me. 358.

[4] Anderson *v.* Blakely, 2 Watts & Serg. (Pa.) 237.

[5] Baker *v.* Rand, 13 Barb. (N. Y.) 152, per Hand, J.

[6] Melville *v.* Hayden, 3 Barn. & Ald. 593.

ing, "and I will guaranty the payment of any goods you may sell him," was held not a continuing guaranty, but referred to and covered one transaction, and not to a number of transactions that might run through a series of years.[1] One K. wrote the following letter to a grocer, viz.: "The bearer, . . . my son-in-law, wishes to place a stock of groceries in his provision and meat store. . . . To enable him to do this, I am willing to be responsible to you for the amount of groceries he may order of you." *Held*, not a continuing guaranty.[2] A letter addressed to a lumber merchant requesting him to "send my son-in-law the lumber he asks for, and it will be all right," is held not a continuing guaranty.[3] "In consideration of your agreeing to advance to W. & Co. not exceeding the sum of $7,000 and interest, I hereby guaranty to you the repayment of the sums advanced," was held not a continuing guaranty."[4] And the following guaranty, viz.: "Messrs. ——— ———: The bearer, Mr. ———, is visiting your city, buying a few goods in your line, and anything you may be able to sell him will be paid promptly as agreed on, which I herewith guaranty," was held not a continuing guaranty.[5] A guaranty executed to wholesale merchants to secure credit for a bill of goods in the following language, viz.: "I hereby guaranty the payment of bills as they mature, purchased by E. S. M. of R. P. S. & Son . . . to the amount of thirteen hundred dollars," was held not a continuing guaranty.[6]

[1] Schwartz *v.* Hyman, 107 N. Y. 562.

[2] Knowlton *v.* Hersey, 76 Me. 345.

[3] Birdsall *v.* Heacock, 32 Ohio St. 177.

[4] Frost & Co. *v.* Weathersbee, 23 S. C. 354.

[5] Morgan *v.* Boyer, 39 Ohio St. 324.

[6] Smith *et al.* *v.* Van Wyck, 40 Mo. App. 522. See, also, Gerson *v.* Hamilton, 30 La. Ann. 737. For other cases in which the guaranty has been held not to be continuing, see Tayleur *v.* Wildin, Law Rep. 3 Exch. 303; Allnutt *v.* Ashenden, 5 Man. & Gr. 392; Bovill *v.* Turner, 2 Chitty, 205; Kirby *v.* The Duke of Marlborough, 2 Maule & Sel. 18; Sutherland *v.* Patterson, 4 Ont. (Can.) 565; Sawyer *v.* Seen, 27 S. C. 251; Perryman *v.* McCall, 66 Ala. 402; Malone *v.* Crescent City M. & T. Co., 77 Cal. 38; Bloom & Co. *v.* Kern, 30 La. Ann. 1263; Richardson School Fund *v.* Dean, 130 Mass. 242.

CHAPTER VI.

OF CASES WHERE THE SURETY ON A GENERAL OBLIGATION IS LIABLE ONLY FOR A LIMITED TIME OR ACT OR AMOUNT.

When liability of surety on general bond limited by the recitals thereof . . . . . § 166
Surety on general bond of annual officer only liable for one year 167
Surety on general bond of annual officer only liable for one year 168
When surety on general bond only liable for one year . . 169
When liability of surety on general bond limited by circumstances — Instances . . . 170
When general obligation of surety limited by special circumstances . . . . . . § 171
When sureties on bond of annual officer bound for more than a year 172
When general words of obligation not limited by other words or circumstances . . 173
When general words of obligation not limited by other words or circumstances . . 174
Liability of sureties who obligate themselves each for a specific sum 175

§ 166. When liability of surety on general bond limited by the recitals thereof.— When the words of the condition of a bond are general and indefinite as to the time during which the surety shall remain liable, if there is a recital in the bond, specifying the time during which the prescribed duty is to be performed by the principal, the general words will be limited by the recital, and the surety will only be liable for the time therein specified. The reason is that, taking the whole instrument together, it is but fair to presume that the parties had in contemplation only a liability for the time specified. It is a rule of construction adopted for the purpose of effectuating the intention of the parties. In the leading case on this subject the bond recited that Thomas Jenkins had been appointed deputy postmaster, "to execute the said office from the 24th day of June next coming, for the term of six months," and was conditioned for his good behavior "during all the time that he, the said Thomas Jenkins, shall continue deputy postmaster." Jenkins held the office more than two years, and the surety was sued for a default of his happening two years after his appointment. *Held*, the surety was not liable for anything happening after the first six months. The general words of the bond were restrained by the special ones. "This time, which is indefinite in itself, ought to be construed only for the said six months for which the condition recites that Jenkins was appointed to be deputy postmaster, and to which the condition relates."[1] The condition of a bond reciting that the defendant had agreed with the plaintiffs to collect their revenues "from time to time for twelve months," and afterwards stipulating that "at all times thereafter, during the continuance of his employment, and for so long as he should continue to be employed," he should justly account and obey orders, etc., confines the obligation to the period of twelve months mentioned in the recital.[2] In construing an agreement in the form of a bond, in which a surety became liable for the due fulfillment of an agent's duties, therein particularly enumerated, a general clause in the obligatory part of the bond must be interpreted strictly, and controlled by reference to the prior clauses specifying the extent of the agency. *Held*, accordingly, that money received by an agent on account of his employers, during the time of his agency, but not in pursuance of the particular agency, disclosed to the surety by the specified conditions in the bond, were not covered by the surety's obligation, "that during the whole time the said . . . (agent) shall continue to act as agent as aforesaid, in consequence of the above-recited agreement, he shall well and truly account for and pay to us (the employers) all sums of money received by him on our account."[3]

§ 167. Surety on general bond of annual officer only liable for one year.—Sureties on the general bond of an annual officer are generally held to be liable only for one year. The sureties are presumed to have contracted with reference to the law. and the general words of the obligation are restrained

[1] Lord Arlington *v.* Merricke, 2 Saund. 403, per Hale, C. J. See, also, Keith *v.* Fenelon Falls Union School, 3 Ont. (Can.) 194. Sureties for the fidelity of an officer appointed for a limited term are not liable for his defaults beyond the term of the appointment or commission under which the bond was furnished. State *v.* Powell *et al.*, 40 La. Ann. 241.

[2] Company of Proprietors of the Liverpool Water-works *v.* Atkinson, 6 East, 507.

[3] Napier *v.* Bruce, 8 Clark & Fin. 470.

and limited thereby. Thus, the office of sheriff being annual, and he being appointed and commissioned for one year, gave bond with surety conditioned for his good behavior "during his continuance in office." He acted a second year without a new nomination or commission, and without having renewed his bond. *Held*, the sureties were not liable for taxes collected by the sheriff the second year. The court said: "The expression in the bond, 'during the continuance in office,' must clearly have reference to the actual duration of the office by virtue of the appointment under which the bond was taken."[1] A bond made by the defendant's testator as surety for E. recited that E. had been and still was collector of the land tax, etc., of a parish, and was conditioned for the due payment by him from time to time, and at all times thereafter, of all money which he should from time to time collect from the inhabitants of the parish on account of any tax then imposed, or which might thereafter be imposed. The office of collector was annual. *Held*, the surety was only liable for one year. The court said that, in order to make him liable for a longer time, the words of the bond must be clear and unmistakable. If he could be held for more than one year, he could, with equal propriety, be held for fifty years, or any length of time in the future.[2] Where, according to the by-laws of an insurance company, the office of secretary was annual, and a secretary was appointed for a year, and gave bond conditioned for his good behavior "during his continuance in office by virtue of his appointment," and at the end of the first year, and for several years thereafter, he was re-elected without any new bond being required or given, it was held the sureties were only liable for the first year. If it were otherwise, there would be no limit to their liability, and no means by which they could terminate it.[3] A constable entered into a general bond for the performance of his duties as such, "agreeably to

[1] Commonwealth *v.* Fairfax, 4 Hen. & Munf. (Va.) 208, per Roane, J. To similar effect, see Railroad *v.* Murrell, 11 Heisk. (Tenn.) 715; Fresno Enterprise Co. *v.* Allen, 67 Cal. 505. But see Sparks *et al.* *v.* Farmers' Bank, 3 Del. Ch. 274.

[2] Hassell *v.* Long, 2 Maule & Sel. 363, per Lord Ellenborough, C. J.

[3] Kingston Mut. Ins. Co. *v.* Clark, 33 Barb. (N. Y.) 196. To the same effect, see Welch *v.* Seymour, 28 Ct. 387; South Carolina Society *v.* Johnson, 1 McCord, Law (S. C.), 41.

his appointment, and in conformity with the existing laws of the state." The office of constable was by law limited to a year, but there was a provision that all officers should hold until their successors were elected. *Held*, the sureties were not liable for any defalcation of the constable happening more than a year after his appointment, although no successor had been appointed, and he still held the office. The court said: "If a person is surety for the fidelity of another in an office of limited duration, or the appointment to which is only for a limited period, he is not obliged beyond that period. . . . The condition here is for the faithful performance of the duties of high constable, agreeably to his appointment, and in conformity with existing laws. . . . The commission, and the law under which it was made, necessarily enter into the obligation in construing its extent, and must be considered by the court."[1]

§ 168. **Surety on general bond of annual officer only liable for a year.**— The sureties on the bond of the treasurer of a manufacturing corporation, who by statute is to be chosen annually, "and hold his office until another is chosen and qualified in his stead," where the bond is general for his good behavior and not restricted as to time, are bound only for the year for which he was chosen, and for such further time as is reasonably sufficient for the election and qualification of his successor, although the corporation fail to elect a successor at the next annual meeting. The court said that where the office is annual, the general words of the bond are restrained by that fact. The liability of the sureties is not limited to a year exactly, but may extend a few days longer, till the usual time for holding the meetings of the officers of the corporation. The words, "hold his office till another is chosen," may be applied to this fact, and should not change the general rule.[2] A

[1] Mayor, etc. of Wilmington *v.* Horn, 2 Har. (Del.) 190, per Harrington, J.

[2] Chelmsford Co. *v.* Demarest, 7 Gray, 1, per Shaw, C. J. See further, Long *v.* Seay, 72 Mo. 648; Lionberger *v.* Krieger, 13 Mo. App. 313; State *v.* Kurtzeborn, 78 Mo. 98, affirming 9 Mo. App. 245; Union Society *v.* Mitchell, 26 Mo. App. 206; State *v.* Powell, 40 La. Ann. 241; Mutual Loan & Building Ass'n *v.* Price, 16 Fla. 204. But in Inhabitants of Norridgewock *v.* Hale, 80 Me. 362, it is held that the sureties on the official bond of a town treasurer whose office is an annual one are not liable for a misappropriation of the town moneys after their

collector of church and poor rates gave bond with surety, conditioned that he would account to the church wardens "and their successors" for all money received by him. The office of the wardens was annual, and as a consequence that of the collector was annual also. *Held*, the sureties were only liable for the collector's acts during one year. The court said the words "and their successors" meant that he must account to the successors for acts done by him during the first year, to the successor of one if he died during the year, or to the successors of all at the end of the year.[1] Certain sureties became bound for the acts of a collector of church rates, the office being an annual one. The bond was conditioned for the collector accounting "unto the wardens of the grand account for the time being, or hereafter to be, of all such sum and sums of money so by him collected and received." *Held*, the sureties were not liable after the first year. The court remarked: 'Can we say that they intended to be bound for an indefinite, period?"[2] The office of county treasurer being annual, a treasurer was elected in 1790, and gave bond with surety, conditioned that he should "faithfully discharge the duties of the office of treasurer of said county, and account for all sums of money which he . . . (should) receive for the use of the said county." He was elected annually until 1806, but gave no new bond. *Held*, no recovery could be had on the bond for anything transpiring after the first year.[3] The office of tax collector being by act of parliament an annual one, a collector gave a bond with surety, which recited his appointment under the act, and was conditioned for the due collection by him of the rates and duties at all times thereafter. *Held*, the due collection of taxes for one year was a compliance with the bond. With reference to the general words of the bond,

principal's term expired and before his successor qualified, notwithstanding the bond stipulated that the principal should " well and truly perform his trust as treasurer during the time for which he was chosen, and until another should be chosen in his stead."

1 Leadley *v.* Evans, 9 Moore, 102, per Best, J.

2 The Wardens of St. Saviors Southwark *v.* Bostock, 5 Bos. & Pul. 175, per Mansfield, C. J.

3 Bigelow *v.* Bridge, 8 Mass. 275. To same effect, see Riddel *v.* School District, 15 Kan. 168. See the same holding on a similar state of facts with reference to sureties' liability on bond of bank cashier. Savings Bank *v.* Hunt, 72 Mo. 597.

the court said: "These words must be construed with reference to the recital and to the nature of the appointment there mentioned."[1]

§ 169. When surety on general bond only liable for one year.— The condition of a bond was that the principal should "from time to time, and at all times, so long as he . . . (should) continue to hold said office or employment," faithfully demean himself as clerk. To a suit on this bond against the surety he pleaded that the employment of the clerk was only for one year, and that no default had happened within the year. Replication that by consent of all parties the clerk was retained longer than a year. *Held*, the replication was bad.[2] A bond from the deputy to the high sheriff, conditioned for the faithful performance of his duty as deputy "during his continuance in office," without specifying the length of time, is binding on him and his sureties for the transactions of one year only, the term of the high sheriff being limited to that time.[3] Debt against a sheriff and his sureties on a bond dated March, 1820, conditioned for the faithful discharge of the sheriff's duties until the next August election and until his successor should be elected and qualified. The breach assigned was that the sheriff had failed to pay over, etc., the revenue of the county for 1822. *Held*, that although the sheriff may have been elected his own successor and may have neglected to qualify under the new appointment, still the sureties were not liable for his acts after he received his new commission.[4] The condition of a bond recited that S. had been appointed (under a statute making the office annual) treasurer of a borough, and it provided that he should duly perform the office according to the provisions of said statutes, and of "such statutes as should be thereafter passed relating to said office." He continued to hold the office for several years under successive appointments, and did not comply with certain statutes passed subsequent to the first year. *Held*, his sureties were not liable for such default. The words "such statutes as should

[1] Peppin *v.* Cooper, 2 Barn. & Ald. 431, per Abbott, C. J.

[2] Kiton *v.* Julian, 4 Ellis & Black. 854, followed in Wickens *v.* McMeekin *et al.*, 15 Ont. (Can.) 408.

[3] Munford *v.* Rice, 6 Munf. (Va.) 81.

[4] Rany *v.* The Governor, 4 Blackf. (Ind.) 2. To similar effect, see Moss *v.* The State, 10 Mo. 338; Urmston *et al.* *v.* The State *ex rel.*, 73 Ind. 175.

be thereafter passed" meant such as should be passed during the first year.[1] Where a statute provided that the period of administration on estates should be one year, but if the estate was not settled at that time the judge might extend it a year, and so on for five years, it was held that the sureties on a general bond of an administrator, given when the administration commenced, were only liable for one year.[2] The office of register in chancery being annual, a party was appointed to it, and gave bond conditioned for his good behavior "whilst he shall continue in the office," and also "during the time he hath officiated in the said register's office." He continued in office four years. *Held*, the sureties were not liable beyond the first year. The court said: "The provisions of the constitution (making the office annual) form the basis of the contract, and, like the recital in the condition of the bond, restrain the indefinite expressions used in it and adapt them to the intention of the parties."[3]

§ **170. When liability of surety on general bond limited by circumstances — Instances.**— A bond reciting that A. had been appointed assistant overseer of a parish was conditioned for the due performance of his duties "thenceforth from time to time, and at all times, so long as he should continue in such office." The office was not annual, but the overseer was appointed annually thereafter for several years, and at an increased salary. *Held*, the sureties on the bond were not liable for anything happening after his re-appointment at an increased salary. The re-appointment on different terms was a revocation of the first appointment.[4] A treasurer was appointed by the governor, and gave bond with surety conditioned for his good behavior "as such treasurer," the term of office of a treasurer then being during the pleasure of the governor. Afterwards a statute was passed providing that the treasurer should be elected by the people and hold office for three years. The same party was elected treasurer and gave a new bond. *Held*, the first set of sureties were not liable for the treasurer's default after his election. They may have been

[1] Mayor of Cambridge *v.* Dennis, Ell., Black. & Ell. 660.

[2] Flores *v.* Howth, 5 Tex. 329.

[3] State *v.* Wayman, 2 Gill & Johns. (Md.) 254.

[4] Bamford *v.* Iles, 3 Wels., Hurl. & Gor. 380.

willing to be bound for him if he held office during the pleasure of the governor, but not if the holding was for a fixed term.[1] Subsequent to the passage of the United States internal revenue act of 1864 the assistant treasurer of the United States and treasurer of the branch mint at San Francisco gave a bond conditioned as provided by the act of 1846. The bond provided that he should faithfully discharge the duties of his office and all "other duties as fiscal agents of the government which may be imposed by this or any other act." The act of 1864, which provided that stamps might be furnished to assistant treasurers, also provided that bond for the payment for the same might be required from them. Said assistant treasurer got stamps for which he gave no new bond, and did not pay for them. *Held*, the sureties on the general bond were not liable for the stamps. If congress had supposed the general bond covered the case, why was a new bond provided for? The general words in the bond should not cover the case. "We think these words only intended to include such duties as naturally and ordinarily belong to the particular officer giving the bond, or have some obvious relation to such duties, and such as the sureties, acquainted with the duties of the various public officers as usually devolved upon them by law, might reasonably be expected to contemplate at the time of executing the bond, as likely to be imposed upon their principal in case the exigencies of government should require it, and not those duties which are more usually imposed upon, and more appropriately belong to, an entirely different class of officers."[2] The sureties in a bond given by the register of wills for the performance of his duties generally, and the payment of all money received for the use of the state, are not responsible for collateral inheritance tax collected by him. The terms of his bond were broad enough to cover this tax, but the act establishing the tax provided for the giving of a special bond therefor. The court said: "It seems to us very plain, therefore, that the general bond is not intended to se-

[1] The Queen *v.* Hall, 1 Up. Can. (C. P.) 406.

[2] United States *v.* Cheeseman, 3 Sawyer, 424, per Sawyer, J., Field, J., concurring. See, also, on this subject, to same general effect, Holt *v.* McLean, 75 N. C. 347.

cure either payment of these collections or the giving of the special bond to secure them."[1]

§ 171. When general obligation of surety limited by special circumstances.— A bank cashier gave a bond with sureties for his good behavior in office. The charter of the bank would have expired in 1818, but before that time, and after the sureties signed the obligation, the charter was extended by act of the legislature. No new bond was given, but the cashier continued to act during the extended period. *Held*, the sureties were not liable for any of his defalcations after the time when the original charter expired.[2] M. required machinery for a cheese factory, and gave A. an order for it, which he refused to fill without security. B. thereupon wrote to A. as follows: "I recommend M. to you, and if he should fail in his promise to you for anything in your way, I consider myself jointly liable for the amount of $200, payable in six months to your firm." A. thereupon filled the order. *Held*, the meaning of the guaranty, when considered with reference to the surrounding circumstances, was that it applied to the specific order M. had given for machinery and to no other.[3] A. and B. executed a note for $4,000, payable on demand, the note being joint and several, and both appearing as principals, but B. was in fact the surety of A., and that was known by a bank, to the cashier of which the note was payable. The note was made to enable A. to raise money at the bank. The bank advanced A., from time to time, over $32,000, all of which was paid, and then advanced $2,000, which was not paid, and the bank thereupon sued A. and B. on the note. *Held*, B. was not liable. The note was no more than an express guaranty for $4,000, and was exhausted by the first advance of that amount.[4] The bond of the treasurer of a manufacturing corporation provided for the faithful discharge of his duties "during the time for which he had been elected, and for and during such further time as he . . . (might) continue therein by any re-election or otherwise." He was re-elected at the next annual election, and served five

[1] Commonwealth *v.* Toms, 45 Pa. St. 408.

[2] Thompson *v.* Young, 2 Ohio, 335.

[3] Boyle *v.* Bradley, 26 Up. Can. (C. P.) 378.

[4] Agawam Bank *v.* Strever, 16 Barb. (N. Y.) 82.

months of that term, and then resigned, and his successor was appointed and held seven months; at the next annual election the first treasurer was elected again, and served and committed defaults. *Held*, the sureties were not liable for such defaults. They were liable for more than one year by the express terms of the bond, but were only liable for a continuous holding. The fact that for awhile the principal did not hold the office ended the liability of the sureties. "The word 'continue' excludes all idea of intermission in the office."[1]

§ 172. **When sureties on bond of annual officer bound for more than a year.**— While sureties on the general bond of an annual officer are usually held to be liable only for one year, because such is presumed to have been the intention of the parties, yet there is nothing to prevent such sureties from becoming bound for a longer time, and, if an intention to that effect clearly and unequivocally appears, they will be so held. Thus, the office of treasurer of a borough being annual, A. was appointed thereto, and gave bond conditioned for the due accounting for all such moneys as he should or might recover or receive "in virtue of . . . said appointment as treasurer, as aforesaid, during the whole time of . . . continuing in said office, in consequence of the said election, or under any annual or other future election of the said council to said office." Afterwards, and during the year, the term of office was by statute changed to a holding during the pleasure of the council, and at the expiration of the year A. was again appointed treasurer, and continued in office a long time. *Held*, the sureties were liable for defaults of A. happening after the first year.[2] By statute, the commission of an auctioneer did not necessarily expire in one year, but might continue for three years without renewal of his bond. M., having applied

[1] Middlesex Mfg. Co. *v.* Lawrence, 1 Allen, 339, per Dewey, J. A bond executed by an official for the faithful performance of his duties during a particular term of office, and for any succeeding terms for which he might afterwards be elected, is presumptive evidence of a consideration for the undertaking of the sureties to be responsible after the expiration of the first term; and for a defalcation subsequently occurring, an action may be maintained against the sureties on the bond. Metropolitan Loan Ass'n *v.* Esche, 75 Cal. 513.

[2] Oswald *v.* Mayor of Berwick, 5 H. of L. Cas. 856. See, also, People's Bldg. Ass'n *v.* Wroth *et al.*, 43 N. J. Law, 70. See, on this subject, Hall *v.* Brackett, 62 N. H. 509.

for appointment as auctioneer, gave bond conditioned that he should perform all the duties of auctioneer, etc., "during the period he . . . (should) continue to act as auctioneer under the commission that . . . (might) be granted to him." He was afterwards commissioned for one year. *Held*, the liability of the sureties did not expire in one year, but continued while M. acted as auctioneer.[1] A bond given to secure the faithful performance of his duties by a collector of parochial rates (who was by statute to be appointed by trustees for a year and then to be capable of re-election) was conditioned that "from time to time, and at all times thereafter, during such time as he should continue in his said office, whether by virtue of his said appointment, or of any re-appointment thereto, or of any such retainer or employment by or under the authority of the said trustees or their successors, to be elected in the manner directed by the said act, he should use his best endeavor to collect the moneys received by means of the rates in the then present or any subsequent year." *Held*, the obligation of the bond was not confined to the year for which he was originally appointed, but extended also to all subsequent years in which he was continuously re-appointed.[2] A statute provided that the sureties of a clerk should be liable for the whole period he might continue in office, and his bond provided for his good behavior "during the whole period the said . . . shall or may continue in said office." The clerk was re-elected for a new term, but gave no new bond. *Held*, the sureties on his original bond were liable for his acts during his second term. The court based its decision upon the express provisions of the statute and the terms of the bond, and held that a recital in the beginning of the bond that the clerk had been elected for four years did not change the re-

[1] Daly *v.* Commonwealth, 75 Pa. St. 33. Holding the sureties on a guardian's second bond, given upon his removal to a new county, liable for a defalcation before committed by him, see State *v.* Stewart, 36 Miss. 652.

[2] Augero *v.* Keen, 1 Mees. & Wels. 390. To similar effect, see People's Building Association *v.* Wroth *et al.*, 43 N. J. Law, 70, where sureties for the treasurer of a corporation, whose office was annual, executed a bond conditioned for his good behavior during his continuance in office, "whether of the present term for which he has been elected, or of any succeeding terms to or for which he may be elected." Their liability was held to continue.

sult.[1] The commission of a collector of customs appointed him "a collector of her majesty's customs in the province of Canada," and the bond was conditioned for the performance of his duties generally. In a suit on the bond, the surety pleaded that the bond was executed in reference to the office of collector at B., and that he made no default while at B., but was transferred to another place, and there made default. *Held*, the plea was bad, as the bond was clearly general and could not be narrowed in its application by alleging that something less was meant.[2] In 1831, while a statute was in force which provided that a cashier should hold his office until removed therefrom or another was appointed in his stead, a cashier was appointed and gave bond for the faithful discharge of the duties of his office. In 1832 he was re-appointed, but gave no new bond. The record of his appointment both times stated that he was appointed "for the year ensuing." He held the office without any new appointment till 1836, when he committed a default. *Held*, the sureties on the bond given when he was first appointed were liable therefor. The law made the office a continuing one, and the parties had this fact in contemplation when the bond was made.[3]

§ 173. **When general words of obligation not limited by other words or circumstances.**— The liability of sureties on the general bond of a manufacturer of tobacco, given in pursuance of the United States revenue law, does not cease upon the expiration of his license as such manufacturer. The provision of the law making the neglect of a manufacturer of tobacco to procure a license a punishable offense was not designed for the benefit of sureties, but to protect the govern-

[1] Treasurers *v.* Lang, 2 Bailey, Law (S. C.), 430.

[2] Regina *v.* Miller, 20 Up. Can. (Q. B.) 485.

[3] Amherst Bank *v.* Root, 2 Met. (Mass.) 522. So where a town treasurer, who held his office until removed therefrom, gave bond with surety conditioned for the faithful performance of his duties "so long as he shall remain in the said office," and he was re-appointed annually for several years, when he defaulted, it was held that the re-appointments were not equivalent to removals and re-appointments, but were a retention in office of the same treasurer, and that his sureties were not in consequence thereof discharged. Corporation of Adjala *v.* McElroy, 9 Ont. (Can.) 580.

ment against the frauds of the manufacturer.[1] The office of tax collector continued two years, but the law required the collector to give a bond as to the state taxes every year. The bond given by a collector on going into office recited that he had been elected for two years, and provided that he should "well and truly collect all state taxes which, by law, he ought to collect, and well and truly account for and pay over all taxes by him collected, or which ought to be by him collected, according to law." *Held*, the sureties were liable for the state taxes received by the collector the second year.[2] A statute provided that a sheriff should hold office for one year, and might, "with his own consent and the approbation of the executive, be continued for two years." The first year a sheriff held office, a deputy gave bond conditioned for his good behavior "for and during the time said . . . (sheriff) may continue in office." The sheriff continued in office two years. *Held*, the sureties on the bond of the deputy were liable for his acts during the second year.[3] When the bond of an officer is general in its terms, and the office is not annual, the liability of the surety is not, in the absence of special circumstances, limited to a year.[4] A party was elected cashier of a bank in 1814, when it was first organized, and again in 1815 and 1817, by directors chosen annually, and he continued to act as cashier from his first election till 1823, when he committed a breach of duty. *Held*, a bond given by him with sureties upon his first election, for the faithful performance of his duties "so long as he should continue in said office," covered this breach of duty, it not appearing in the bond, or the charter, or regulations of the bank, that the office was annual. "There was nothing to make the sureties suppose it was limited to a year."[5] A deed of guaranty made in Lower Canada by C. recited that one M., who had been a member of the firm of C. & Sons, required pecuniary assistance to meet the engagements of that firm, which was agreed to be afforded by a bank, and by such guar-

[1] United States *v.* Truesdell, 2 Bond, 78.

[2] Allison *v.* The State, 8 Heisk. (Tenn.) 312.

[3] Jacob *v.* Hill, 2 Leigh (Va.), 393.

[4] Mayor of Birmingham *v.* Wright, 16 Ad. & Ell. (N. S.) 623.

[5] Dedham Bank *v.* Chickering, 3 Pick. 335, per Parker, C. J.

anty C. and others agreed to become sureties for all the then present and future liabilities of M. with the bank. M. contracted debts with the bank which had no reference to the firm of C. & Sons. *Held*, that although the recital in the instrument was special, yet it did not control the generality of the subsequent operative words, and that the guarantors were liable for such advances.[1]

§ 174. When general words of obligation not limited by other words or circumstances.— By statute the term of office of the chairman of the superintendents of schools continued for one year, and until his successor was appointed. *Held*, the sureties on his bond were liable for money received by him more than a year after he was appointed, he being then in office and no successor having been appointed; the decision being put upon the ground that his term of office continued until a successor was appointed.[2] A bond recited that A. had been taken into the service of a bank as a writing clerk, and was conditioned for his due performance of that service "and all and every other service of the . . . (bank), wherein he he is, or shall, or may be, employed." He was afterwards appointed cashier of a branch bank of the bank to which the bond ran, and afterwards made default. *Held*, his sureties were liable for such default.[3] A bond recited that the principal had been appointed accountant in a bank, and provided that he should well and faithfully perform all duties in the bank which from time to time might be required of him, and should faithfully account for all moneys which might be intrusted to his care, and should "also continue in said service for the term of two years unless sooner discharged." *Held*, the bond covered the acts of the accountant as long as he continued in the office, and was not limited to two years.[4]

[1] Bank of British North America *v.* Cuvillier, 14 Moore's Privy Council Cas. 187.

[2] Chairman of Schools *v.* Daniel, 6 Jones' Law (N. C.), 444.

[3] Thompson *v.* Roberts, 17 Irish Com. Law, 490, held by a divided court. The fact that the book-keeper of a bank performed the duties of teller was also held not to relieve the sureties on his bond given for the faithful performance of his duties as book-keeper for defaults committed while acting in the capacity of teller. Home Savings Bank *v.* Traube, 75 Mo. 199.

[4] Worcester Bank *v.* Reed, 9 Mass. 267.

The defendant, as surety, executed a bond, the condition of which recited an agreement between the directors of an East India railway company and P., whereby it was agreed that P. should forthwith proceed to such place in the East Indies, at such time and by such conveyance as the company should direct, and should there serve the company at a certain salary per month, to commence on the day of his embarkation at Southampton. The condition was in the terms of the recited agreement, but mentioned no place of embarkation. The company paid P.'s passage on a vessel about to leave Southampton, but the vessel left before he was ready, and the company directed him to go to Marseilles and meet the vessel. This he failed to do, nor did he go to the East Indies. *Held*, the surety was liable. The words in the recital, "his embarkation at Southampton," only referred to the time his salary was to commence. The surety agreed that he should go in the manner the company directed, and the general words were not restrained by anything in the recital.[1] The bond of a note clerk in a bank provided for the faithful performance of his duties, and recited that he "had been appointed note clerk, to continue in office during the will of the present or any future board of directors of said bank." The directors of the bank were annual officers, but there was no limitation as to the time a note clerk should continue in office. *Held*, the liability of the sureties on the clerk's bond was not limited to one year. The clerk was not clerk of the directors, but of the bank, and the term of office of the clerk was not limited by the official term of the directors.[2]

§ 175. Liability of sureties who obligate themselves each for a specific sum.— It is generally held that a surety to a note or bond may, at the time of his becoming such, fix his liability as between himself and others who sign with him, by

[1] Evans *v.* Earle, 1 Hurl. & Gor. 1.

[2] Louisiana State Bank *v.* Ledoux, 3 La. Ann. 674. Where the bond of an officer of a corporation is conditioned for the faithful performance of his duties so long as he shall continue in office, the fact that he is appointed by a board of directors which is elected for only one year will not limit the liability of the sureties to that year, but it is held to continue throughout the term of his actual holding if his appointment is general and unlimited. Humboldt Savings & Loan Society *v.* Wennerhold *et al.*, 81 Cal. 528.

limiting his liability to a specific sum, in which case he cannot be held beyond the amount set opposite his name.[1] Thus, the sureties on the official bond of a sheriff,[2] tax collector,[3] city treasurer,[4] and bank clerk,[5] who have limited their liability when signing the bond to certain specified sums, which sums were set opposite their respective signatures, cannot be held chargeable beyond such sums. So sureties to a joint and several recognizance, who have limited their respective liabilities to fractional parts of the penalty, cannot be held individually for the full amount of the bond.[6] When the sureties on a tax collector's bond obligate themselves each for a specific sum, the state is entitled, in case the collector becomes a defaulter, to a judgment against each surety for the whole amount for which he is bound, if the defalcation is for so much, although the judgments against the sureties may amount to much more than the defalcation. If judgment was rendered against the each surety for only his aliquot part of the defalcation, and one or more of the sureties proved insolvent, the state would lose so much. But no matter how much may be the aggregate of the judgments, no more than the amount of the defalcation can be collected from the sureties.[7] Where a statute provides that a surety on a constable's bond may limit the amount of his liability thereon, this does not limit the recovery of costs

1 City of New Orleans *v.* Waggaman, 31 La. Ann. 299; Westbrook *v.* Moore, 59 Ga. 204; People *v.* Slocum, 1 Idaho, 62; Houck *v.* Graham, 123 Ind. 277. But see, *contra*, Cordray *v.* State, 55 Tex. 140.

2 Marcy *v.* Praeger, 34 La. Ann. 54; Florat *v.* Handy, 35 La. Ann. 816.

3 Police Jury of Vermilion Parish *v.* Brookshier, 31 La. Ann. 736.

4 City of Butte *v.* Cohen, 9 Mont. 435.

5 Commercial Nat. Bank *v.* Gorham, 11 R. I. 162.

6 Thomas *v.* State, 13 Tex. App. 496. Where the liability of each surety is for the full penalty of the bond, the fact that they are bound "jointly and severally" does not bring it within the ruling of Thomas *v.* State, *supra.* Fulton *v.* State, 14 Tex. App. 32. Under late Texas Criminal Code, *held*, that surety to a recognizance cannot now limit his liability. Mathena *v.* State, 15 Tex. App. 460.

7 State *v.* Hampton, 14 La. Ann. 690; Stetson *v.* City Bank of N. O., 12 Ohio St. 577. Where one became surety for one-third of a debt, and another for two-thirds thereof, a part of which was subsequently discharged by a payment of a portion of a judgment recovered thereon, *held*, that neither surety could insist upon an application of the entire amount paid to the release of his liability. Doud *v.* Waller, 48 Iowa, 634.

against the surety, and execution may issue against him although the amount directed to be levied upon exceeds the penalty of the bond.[1] "Such provision has reference only to the amount the sureties are chargeable with on the penalty of the bond. It has no reference to the costs of the action upon the bond."[2]

[1] Mayor, etc. of N. Y. *v.* Ryan, 9 Daly (N. Y. Com. Pleas), 316. See Gay *v.* Hults *et al.*, 56 Mich. 153.

[2] Daly, J., in Mayor *v.* Ryan, 9 Daly (N. Y. Com. Pleas), 316, 320.

CHAPTER VII.

OF THE LIABILITY OF ACCOMMODATION PARTIES TO NEGOTIABLE INSTRUMENTS, AND OF THE BLANK INDORSER OF ANOTHER'S OBLIGATION.

When stranger to a note who indorses it in blank is guarantor . . . . § 176
When stranger to a note who indorses it in blank is guarantor 177
When the blank indorser of a note is not a guarantor . . 178
Cases holding blank indorser of note liable as indorser, and express guarantor liable as maker 179
When blank indorser of note is liable as joint maker . . . 180
Liability of blank indorser — General observations . . . 181
Liability of blank indorser may be shown by parol — Writing authorized agreement above blank indorsement does not vitiate actual agreement . . § 182
When indorsement in terms expresses liability of indorser, he is held according to such terms 183
Liability of indorsers under special indorsements and circumstances 184
Liability of accommodation parties to bills of exchange — Special cases 185

§ 176. When stranger to a note who indorses it in blank is guarantor.— As to what is the precise liability of a stranger to an obligation who indorses it in blank, there is great conflict among the decided cases. The weight of authority is that a stranger to a promissory note, payable to a particular person, who at or before the time of its delivery to the payee indorses it in blank, is, in the absence of evidence as to the liability intended to be assumed, liable as guarantor. The reasoning upon which these decisions are based is that such indorser intended to assume some liability. If he had intended to become a joint maker, he would have signed the note on its face. Not being a party to the note, the title to it does not pass by his indorsement, and he is not liable as indorser. And being neither principal nor indorser, in order to effectuate the presumed intention of the parties, he will be held liable as guarantor.[1] The same thing has been held where a stranger to a note indorsed it in blank after it was delivered by the payee.[2] In such cases the holder of the note may, at the time of the trial or any time before, write a guaranty over the name of the indorser,[3] and this may be done after the death of the indorser.[4] A party gave a storage receipt for grain, and a stranger to it indorsed it in blank for the purpose of becoming a guarantor. The grain was not delivered, and the holder of the receipt filled the blank above the name of the indorser with a guaranty, and sued on it. *Held*, the blank might be so filled, and that this took the case out of the Statute of Frauds. The court said: "On such an instrument he [the indorser] cannot become liable as indorser; nor can he become liable as maker unless he places his name on the instrument at the time of its execution, and as in such case he manifestly intends to become liable in some capacity or other to the holder, it can only be as guarantor."[5] In the absence of evidence the presumption is that the blank indorsement of a note by a stranger was made at the time the note was exe-

[1] Firman *v.* Blood, 2 Kan. 496; Fuller *v.* Scott, 8 Kan. 25; Withers *v.* Berry, 25 Kan. 373; Jones *v.* Kuhn, 34 Kan. 414; Chandler *v.* Westfall, 30 Tex. 475; Horton *v.* Manning, 37 Tex. 23; Van Doren *v.* Tjader, 1 Nev. 380; Watson *v.* Hurt, 6 Gratt. (Va.) 633; Clark *v.* Merriam, 25 Conn. 576; Champion *v.* Griffith, 13 Ohio, 228; Castle *v.* Rickly, 44 Ohio St. 490; Cushman *v.* Dement, 3 Scam. (Ill.) 497; Camden *v.* McKoy, 3 Scam. (Ill.) 437; Klein *v.* Currier, 14 Ill. 237; Heintz *v.* Cahn, 29 Ill. 308; Pahlman *v.* Taylor, 75 Ill. 629; Hamilton *v.* Johnston, 82 Ill. 39; Stowell *v.* Raymond, 83 Ill. 120; Eberhart *v.* Page, 89 Ill. 550; Wallace *v.* Goold, 91 Ill. 15; Ives *v.* McHard, 103 Ill. 97, affirming 2 Bradw. (Ill. App.) 176; Brown *v.* Reasner, 5 Bradw. (Ill. App.) 45; De Witt Co. Nat. Bank *v.* Nixon, 125 Ill. 615. The Illinois cases cited *infra* hold that a stranger signing under such circumstances is presumed to do so as guarantor, but that this presumption may be rebutted to show what the real intention of the parties was. In California, under the code, a stranger who indorses before delivery is held not as a guarantor but as an indorser. Fessenden *v.* Summers, 62 Cal. 485. See *contra* to doctrine in the text, Levi *v.* Mendell, 1 Duv. (Ky.) 77.

[2] Thomas *v.* Jennings, 5 S. & M. (Miss.) 627; Killian *v.* Ashley, 24 Ark. 511; Stagg *v.* Linnenfelser, 59 Mo. 336.

[3] Boynton *v.* Pierce, 79 Ill. 145; Fear *v.* Dunlap, 1 Greene (Iowa), 331; Chandler *v.* Westfall, 30 Tex. 475; Gist *v.* Drakely, 2 Gill (Md.), 330; Leech *v.* Hill, 4 Watts (Pa.), 448. *Contra*, Needhams *v.* Page, 3 B. Mon. (Ky.) 465.

[4] Horton *v.* Manning, 37 Tex. 23.

[5] Underwood *v.* Hossack, 38 Ill. 208, per Walker, J.

cuted.[1] And the same presumption exists where the instrument upon which the indorsement is made is a receipt for the delivery of grain, and not negotiable.[2] It has been held that if the blank indorsement of a note by a stranger to it is made after it has been in circulation, the indorser will not, in the absence of proof, be held as guarantor, but will be held as indorser simply, the presumption being that the note was transferred from holder to holder by blank indorsement.[3] A stranger to a bond, who indorsed it in blank and transferred it to his creditor in payment of a debt, has been held liable as guarantor.[4] Where a promissory note was made by M. payable to E. or order, and indorsed by C., it was held that while at common law the liability of C. was that of second indorser, yet under a statute converting so-called second indorsers into sureties, the liability of C. was that of surety for M.[5] An allegation that defendant, by writing his name on the back of the note, guarantied its payment, and that upon the strength of such guaranty the said note was received for value, is a sufficient statement that defendant was a guarantor.[6]

§ 177. **When stranger to a note who indorses it in blank is guarantor.**— By the common law of Connecticut, the blank indorsement of a note (negotiable or not negotiable) by a stranger to it, in the absence of evidence, implies *prima facie* a contract on the part of the indorser that the note is due and payable according to its tenor; that the maker shall be of ability to pay it when it comes to maturity, and that it is collectible by due diligence on the part of the holder.[7] Another court has held that when a person not before a party to a note puts his name on its back, out of the course of regular negotiability, he is not an indorser according to the strict commercial sense of that term. "He is termed a guarantor,

[1] Carroll *v.* Weld, 13 Ill. 682; Webster *v.* Cobb, 17 Ill. 459; White *v.* Weaver, 41 Ill. 409; Boynton *v.* Pierce, 79 Ill. 145; Cook *v.* Southwick, 9 Tex. 615.

[2] Underwood *v.* Hossack, 38 Ill. 208.

[3] Webster *v.* Cobb, 17 Ill. 459; White *v.* Weaver, 41 Ill. 409.

[4] Kearnes *v.* Montgomery, 4 W. Va. 29.

[5] Collins *v.* Everett, 4 Ga. 266. See, also, Camp *v.* Simmons, 62 Ga. 73.

[6] Wallace *v.* Lark, 12 S. C. 576.

[7] Ranson *v.* Sherwood, 26 Conn. 437. For other decisions of the same court on this subject, see Clark *v.* Merriam, 25 Conn. 576; Castle *v.* Candee, 16 Conn. 223; Perkins *v.* Catlin, 11 Conn. 213.

and this is so whether his inscription is simply in blank, or preceded by the words 'I guaranty.' . . . A name written on the back of a note gave to the writer his title of indorser, and fixed the character of his liability. If the name was written without regular succession, according to commercial usage, a distinction in the description of the latter was instituted, and he was called 'guarantor.' This distinction, however, was only in name; the act performed by each is precisely the same; and it is a well settled and safe rule that the act discloses the intent. . . . Where one writes his name on the back of a promissory note, either in blank or accompanied by the use of general terms, his undertaking is attended with all the rights and all the liability of an indorser *stricti juris*."[1] In a later case in the same court, it is held that where a person not before a party to a note indorses it before its delivery, his liability is that of a surety, and demand and notice are necessary in order to fix his liability, and the doctrine of the case last referred to is fully approved. The court said: "In England he is held to be a guarantor, and his contract is that the maker of the note will pay at maturity, or, if he does not, the guarantor will. No demand or notice is considered necessary as a condition precedent to fix the liability of the guarantor." After saying there was great conflict of authority, the court, speaking of guarantor and indorser, proceeded: "Each undertakes that the maker will pay the note at maturity, and in case of being compelled to pay it for the principal, each has recourse upon his principal to recover the amount paid."[2] The law on this subject has been thus stated by another court: "The mere indorsement upon a note, of a stranger's name in blank, is *prima facie* evidence of guaranty.

[1] Riggs *v.* Waldo, 2 Cal. 485, per Heydenfeldt, J.

[2] Jones *v.* Goodwin, 39 Cal. 493. In Bryan *v.* Berry, 6 Cal. 394, the supreme court of California decided that it made no difference on what part of a note the name of a party who was secondarily liable appeared; he was liable as indorser. It did not profess to follow authority, which it said was full of refinements and contradictions, but professed to adopt a safe and certain rule, free from all obscurity. Bryan *v.* Berry was, however, overruled by Aud *v.* Magruder, 10 Cal. 282. The decisions on this subject in California are not harmonious. For other cases, see Pierce *v.* Kennedy, 5 Cal. 138; Brady *v.* Reynolds, 13 Cal. 31; and Chafoin *v.* Rich, 77 Cal. 476.

To charge such person as a maker, there must be proof that his indorsement was made at the time of execution by the other party, or if afterwards, that it was in pursuance of an agreement or intention that he should become responsible from the date of the execution. Such agreement or intention may be proved by parol. The rule is the same whether the instrument is negotiable or not."[1] A. made his note payable to B. It was afterwards transferred to C., who for a valuable consideration transferred it to D., and at the same time wrote his name in blank on its back. There was no other name on the back of the note. *Held*, C. was liable as guarantor. The court said: "The defendant cannot be charged as a surety, for he was no party to the original contract. . . . Nor can he be charged as indorser, for the note was not indorsed by the payee."[2] A party made a note payable to himself or order, and two parties, strangers to the note, indorsed it. The blanks above the names of the indorsers were filled with separate guaranties, and then the maker indorsed it and delivered it to the holder. *Held*, the indorsers were not liable as guarantors but as indorsers. "Where the note creates no valid obligation against the maker, and can create none until it is indorsed and transferred by the payee, the presumption is that the person writing his name in blank upon the back of the note assumes the obligation of an indorser. Inasmuch as the note can never have any validity until the name of the payee appears upon it as an indorser, the person writing his name in blank upon the note understands that, when the note takes effect, his name will appear upon it as a second indorser, and it is reasonable to conclude that such was the position which he intended to occupy." And all persons receiving such note are by its form notified of these facts.[3]

§ 178. **When the blank indorser of a note is not a guarantor.**— After a promissory note became due, the holder agreed to extend the time of payment about ten months, if the maker would get F. to indorse the note. Without know-

[1] Champion *v.* Griffith, 13 Ohio, 228. For other decisions of the same court on this subject, see Parker *v.* Riddle, 11 Ohio, 102; Seymour *v.* Mickey, 15 Ohio St. 515.

[2] Whiton *v.* Mears, 11 Met. (Mass.) 563.

[3] Blatchford *v.* Milliken, 35 Ill. 434, per Beckwith, J.

ing of this agreement, F. indorsed the note in blank, only writing over his signature the date of making it. In a suit against F. on the note, it was held he was not a maker nor indorser, and could not be held as guarantor, because a guaranty must be in writing, and if such a guaranty might have been written over the signature, it had not been done.[1] The payee of a note indorsed it in blank. A guaranty was written over his name in a different hand. *Held*, the presumption was that the indorser was an assignor, and only secondarily liable. The court said: "The fact that a contract of guaranty is found written above the name of the indorser, in a handwriting not his own, would not of itself be sufficient to raise a presumption that it was done by his authority, or that the contract was there when he wrote his name, because the presence of his name is to be accounted for by the fact that as payee of the note, it was necessary for him to indorse it in order to give it negotiability. To hold that any person through whose hands a note may pass can write a guaranty over a blank indorsement, and then require the indorser to disprove it, would be fruitful of fraud, and dangerous to every person who has occasion to receive and indorse a promissory note."[2] It has been held that where the name of a stranger to a note occupies the position of a second indorser, he cannot be held as guarantor, unless it is established by extraneous evidence that he agreed to become a guarantor.[3] Upon a note in this form: "We, A. and B., as principal, and C. and D. as surety, promise to pay to the order of ourselves," etc., and signed on its face only by A. and B., and indorsed successively by A., B., C. and D., the liability of D. is that of surety or joint promisor in a note payable to the order of the principals and by them indorsed. It was claimed that he was an indorser only as the note was indorsed by the promisee. The court said that would have been so if the note had been in the

[1] Moore *v.* Folsom, 14 Minn. 340.

[2] Dietrich *v.* Mitchell, 43 Ill. 40, per Lawrence, J. See, also, on similar point, Klein *v.* Currier, 14 Ill. 237. When the name of the payee appears in blank on the back of the note, it is presumed that he is indorser only and not a guarantor. Schnell *v.* North Side Planing Mill Co., 89 Ill. 581.

[3] Bogue *v.* Melick, 25 Ill. 91. To same effect, see Kayser *v.* Hall, Adm'r, 85 Ill. 511.

usual form: "But this note is peculiar, and the application of the rule is controlled by the express declaration in the contract itself of the nature of the liability assumed."[1] With reference to the liability of a stranger to it, who indorses a note in blank, the following has been held: "When a man puts his name on the back of negotiable paper before the payee has indorsed it, he means to pledge in some shape his responsibility for the payment of it. . . . In the absence of legal evidence of any different contract, he assumes the position of second indorser; and . . . to render his engagement binding as to any holder of the note, the implied condition that the payee shall indorse before him must be complied with, so as to give him recourse against such payee."[2] On the other hand, it has been held that where a person, not a party to a bill or note, indorses his name on it, he is presumed to have done so as a surety, and not as an indorser; and if such indorser signs his name, thus intending to become indorser and not surety, it will make no difference, as it is an error of law which will not avail him in the absence of fraud by the other party.[3]

§ 179. **Cases holding blank indorser of note liable as indorser, and express guarantor liable as maker.**— A stranger to a note before its delivery wrote upon its back the following: "For value received I guaranty the payment of the within note, and waive notice of non-payment." *Held*, this constituted him a joint maker of the note, and that he could be sued jointly with the other makers. The court said: "How is this distinguishable from a direct signature as surety?" In the latter case both promise to see the money paid at the day. A man writes thus: 'I promise that $100 shall be paid to A. or bearer;' who would doubt that such a promise would be a good note? The use of the word guaranty, or warrant, or stipulate, or covenant, or other word importing an obligation, does not vary the effect. Read the obligation of a man who signs a note with his principal 'A. B., surety;' both and each stipulate in the language of the note I have supposed. Both

[1] National Pemberton Bank *v.* Lougee, 108 Mass. 371, per Colt, J.

[2] Eilbert *v.* Finkbeiner, 68 Pa. St. 243, per Sharswood, J. To same effect, see Sill *v.* Leslie, 16 Ind. 236.

[3] Smith *v.* Gorton, 10 La. (Curry), 374.

promise that the payee shall receive."[1] The same court held that a party who in express terms guarantied the payment of a note was not an indorser, but was a guarantor, and that he did not come under the designation of an indorser, within the terms of a statute providing for the severing of actions in suits against makers and indorsers of notes.[2] A stranger to a negotiable note indorsed it in blank before it was delivered. No demand of payment had been made, nor had notice of dishonor been given the indorser. *Held*, he was not liable on his indorsement. He was an indorser and could not be held as a guarantor. The court said that an indorser, even though a stranger to a note and signing before its delivery, could not be held as a guarantor unless it was impossible to hold him in any other character. If the note was negotiable, he could not be held as guarantor. But if it was not negotiable, he might be held as guarantor, because in such case, as there is "no possibility of raising the ordinary obligation of indorser, there is then room to infer that a different obligation was intended." The question depends entirely on the fact of negotiability.[3] It was subsequently held by the same court that a stranger to a non-negotiable note, who before its delivery indorsed it in blank, was liable either as maker or guarantor, and not as indorser.[4]

§ 180. When blank indorser of note is liable as joint maker.— There is a class of cases peculiar to New England which hold that, in the absence of evidence, a stranger to a promissory note, who indorses it in blank before its delivery, is liable as a joint maker. The reasoning upon which these decisions rest is thus stated by the court: "He is not liable as

[1] Luqueer *v.* Prosser, 1 Hill (N. Y.), 256, per Cowen, J. See the precisely opposite held in an action on a similar guaranty. Mowery *v.* Mast & Co., 9 Neb. 445.

[2] Miller *v.* Gaston, 2 Hill (N. Y.), 188. A guaranty of the payment of a note is not an indorsement, although itself indorsed on the note. Trust Co. *v.* National Bank, 101 U. S. 68.

[3] Hall *v.* Newcomb, 3 Hill (N. Y.), 233; affirmed by the court of errors, Hall *v.* Newcomb, 7 Hill, 416. To same or similar effect, see Seabury *v.* Hungerford, 2 Hill, 80; Ellis *v.* Brown, 6 Barb. (N. Y.) 282; Tillman *v.* Wheeler, 17 Johns. 326; Spies *v.* Gilmore, 1 N. Y. 321.

[4] Richards *v.* Warring, 4 Abbott's Rep. Omitted Cas. 47. In New Brunswick it is held that indorsement by a stranger before delivery made the indorser liable as maker. Bell *v.* Moffat, 4 Pug. & Bur. (N. B.) 121.

indorser, for the note is not negotiated or title made to it through his indorsement; nor as guarantor, because there is no separate or distinct consideration; but he means to give security and validity to the note by his credit and promise to pay it, if the promisor does not, and that upon the original consideration, and therefore he is a promisor and surety, and it is immaterial to this purpose on what part of the note he places his name."[1] The same court held that strangers to a note, who before its delivery indorsed their names in blank upon it, were not liable as joint makers, if the payee afterwards and before its delivery indorsed his name upon it above theirs. The court said that the rule holding indorsers in any case to be joint makers was anomalous, and peculiar to Massachusetts, and should not be extended beyond what the court was bound to do by previous decisions.[2] Where a stranger to a non-negotiable note, at the time it was made, indorsed it in blank, it was held that in the absence of proof he was liable as an original promisor or surety, and might be sued jointly with the maker.[3] It has also been held that, where it is the intention of the parties that an indorser shall be a joint maker, it makes no difference if his signature appears on the back of the instrument, and he is liable to be sued jointly with the other maker.[4] A corporation made a promissory note under seal. A stranger indorsed it and was sued on such indorsement. *Held*, the right of action was not on the sealed instrument, but on the indorsement, which was a collateral and distinct contract, and the indorser, having become such on a valuable consideration, became absolutely liable to pay the money.[5]

[1] Per Shaw, C. J., in Chaffee *v.* Jones, 19 Pick. 260; Baker *v.* Briggs, 8 Pick. 122; Martin *v.* Boyd, 11 N. H. 385; Flint *v.* Day, 9 Vt. 345; Sanford *v.* Norton, 14 Vt. 228; Strong *v.* Riker, 16 Vt. 554. To same effect, see Chaffee *v.* The Memphis, C. & N. W. R. R. Co., 64 Mo. 193; Melton *v.* Brown, 25 Fla. 461. And it is held that, being a joint maker, he is not entitled to notice of dishonor, nor is he discharged by the payee's delay in making demand on him, though he may, through much delay, have lost all chance of indemnity from the original maker. Neither is this liability modified by the fact that the payee may have known the relation between the maker and indorser to have been one of suretyship. Carpenter *v.* McLaughlin, 12 R. I. 270.

[2] Clapp *v.* Rice, 13 Gray, 403.

[3] Cook *v.* Southwick, 9 Tex. 615. See, also, Good *v.* Martin, 95 U. S. 90.

[4] Schmidt *v.* Schmaetter, 45 Mo. 502.

[5] Gist *v.* Drakely, 2 Gill (Md.), 330.

§ 181. Liability of blank indorser — General observations. The law with reference to the liability of the blank indorser of a promissory note has been thus summarized by a court of high authority: "When a promissory note, made payable to a particular person or order, . . . is first indorsed by a third person, such third person is held to be an original promisor, guarantor or indorser, according to the nature of the transaction and the undertaking of the parties at the time the transaction took place. If he put his name on the back of the note at the time it was made, as surety for the maker, and for his accommodation, to give him credit with the payee, or if he participated in the consideration for which the note was given, he must be considered as a joint maker of the note. On the other hand, if his indorsement was subsequent to the making of the note, and he put his name there at the request of the maker, pursuant to a contract with the payee for further indulgence or forbearance, he can only be held as guarantor. But if the note was intended for discount, and he put his name on the back of it, with the understanding of all the parties that his indorsement would be inoperative until it was indorsed by the payee, he would then be liable only as a second indorser in the commercial sense, and as such would clearly be entitled to the privileges which belong to such indorsers."[1] It is apparent from the cases which have been cited that the question, "What is the liability which, in the absence of explanatory evidence, the law imposes upon the blank indorser of the obligation of another?" is one to which no answer can be given that will harmonize all the authorities. The decisions have been almost as various as the forms of the obligations indorsed. Some courts have held that the nature of the liability depended entirely on whether or not the indorsed instrument was negotiable, while other courts have held that the nature of the liability was not at all affected by the fact of the negotiability of the indorsed instrument. A

[1] Rey *v.* Simpson, 22 How. (U. S.) 341, per Clifford, J. See, also, Good *v.* Martin, 95 U. S. 90; Burton *v.* Hansford, 10 W. Va. 470; Rivers *v.* Thomas, 1 B. J. Lea (Tenn.), 649; Hoffman *v.* Moore, 82 N. C. 313; Heise *v.* Bumpass, 40 Ark. 545. In Noll *v.* Oberhellmann, 20 Mo. App. 336, and Patillo *v.* Mayer, 70 Ga. 715, accommodation indorsers are held as surety for the maker. See Moynahan *v.* Hanaford, 42 Mich. 329.

controlling influence has in numerous other respects been given to circumstances by some courts which have been wholly ignored by others. Nor is the conflict of authority confined to courts of different states, but there are several instances of the same court holding different views of the subject at different times. Other courts, while following their own former decisions, have admitted they were contrary to the weight of authority. It follows, of course, that no general rules can be laid down.[1]

§ 182. Liability of blank indorser may be shown by parol — Writing unauthorized agreement above blank indorsement does not vitiate actual agreement.— It is, however, well settled that the agreement upon which the blank indorser of another's obligation signed, and the liability which he intended to assume, may (at least between the original parties, or those parties and a holder with notice) be shown by parol evidence, and he will be held only according to such agreement and intention.[2] The fact that the indorser's name is on the back of the obligation is itself evidence that he intended to assume some liability, but what liability the writing does not in terms show. The parol evidence does not, therefore, contradict the terms of any writing. It merely establishes a contract which is consistent with the writing. It has been said that such instru-

[1] See the perplexities of the law on this subject considered by Hammond, J., in Miller *v.* Ridgely (Cir. Ct. W. D. Tenn.), 22 Fed. Rep. 889.

[2] Sanford *v.* Norton, 14 Vt. 228; Cook *v.* Southwick, 9 Tex. 615; Burton *v.* Hansford, 10 W. Va. 470; Strong *v.* Ricker, 16 Vt. 554; Baker *v.* Briggs, 8 Pick. 122; Sill *v.* Leslie, 16 Ind. 236; Good *v.* Martin, 17 Am. Law Reg. 111; Rey *v.* Simpson, 22 How. (U. S.) 341; Seymour *v.* Mickey, 15 Ohio St. 515; Perkins *v.* Catlin, 11 Ct. 213; Carroll *v.* Weld, 13 Ill. 682; Clark *v.* Merriam, 25 Ct. 576; Smith *v.* Finch, 2 Scam. (Ill.) 321; Harris *v.* Pierce, 6 Ind. 162; Boynton *v.* Pierce, 79 Ill. 145; Levi *v.* Mendell, 1 Duvall (Ky.), 77; Leech *v.* Hill, 4 Watts (Pa.), 448; Chandler *v.* Westfall, 30 Tex. 475; Lacy *v.* Lofton, 26 Ind. 324; Pierse *v.* Irvine, 1 Minn. 369; Browning *v.* Merritt, 61 Ind. 425; Thompson *v.* Taylor, 12 R. I. 109; Martin *v.* Marshall, 60 Vt. 321; Harrison *v.* McKim, 18 Iowa, 485. In Kellogg *v.* Dunn, 2 Met. (Ky.) 215, it was held that a blank indorser could not be shown by parol to be a joint maker, because that would be to contradict the instrument. And in Hall *v.* Newcomb, 7 Hill (N. Y.), 416, it was said, on the same ground, that parol evidence would not be received to show that the blank indorser of a note intended to become a guarantor. For cases at variance with the text, see Mason *v.* Burton, 54 Ill. 349; Beattie *v.* Browne, 64 Ill. 360. Though see Jones *v.* Albee, 70 Ill. 34.

ments are anomalous, and, the law not fixing the relation of the indorser, the intention of the parties controls. Again, it has been held that the introduction of parol evidence in such cases is a well-settled exception to the rule which forbids written instruments to be contradicted or varied by parol, and is a necessity for the convenience of commerce. In a suit against the indorser of a note, he offered to prove by parol that he indorsed it as surety, and that it was understood between him and the creditor, at the time the indorsement was made, that the note was to be paid by him out of money which he might collect from accounts of the principal then in his hands. The code provided that parol evidence should not be received beyond or against a written act. *Held*, the evidence was admissible. The court said: "The evidence offered was neither to contradict nor explain a written instrument, but to prove a collateral fact or agreement in relation to it."[1] With reference to the reception of parol evidence to explain a blank indorsement, another court has said: "Nor does this position impugn the doctrine that written contracts are not to be varied by parol, for here is no contract in writing. There is evidence of a contract of some kind, but its particular terms are not given on the paper, but are left to be ascertained by parol."[2] Where the payee of a bill of exchange brings suit against the two drawers, one of whom is served with process and the other not, the one who is served may at the trial introduce parol evidence to show that he and the plaintiff, by a prior arrangement between themselves, were, when they severally drew and indorsed the bill, joint sureties for the accommodation of the other drawer, and by such proof defeat the action, if he has paid upon the bill an amount equal to that paid by the plaintiff.[3] Where a note was indorsed in blank by a stranger to it, and the holder wrote over the indorsement a guaranty with waiver of notice, when such was not the agreement upon which the indorser signed, it was held that this did not, in the absence of fraud, vitiate the agreement actually made; and that such agreement might be recovered upon, notwithstanding the erroneous indorsement. The court said there

[1] Dwight *v.* Linton, 3 Rob. (La.) 57, per Murphy, J.

[2] Barrows *v.* Lane, 5 Vt. 161, per Phelps, J.

[3] Kelly *v.* Few, 18 Ohio, 441.

was no alteration of a written contract, because there was no written contract to be altered. There was only a blank indorsement, and the liability assumed by the indorser depended upon the agreement of the parties, and this was not affected by the erroneous indorsement.[1]

§ 183. When indorsement in terms expresses liability of indorser, he is held according to such terms.— Where the indorsement in terms expresses the liability intended to be assumed by the indorser, there is no room for extraneous evidence or presumptions of law, and he will be held to the expressed liability, and to that only. Thus, where the indorsement by a stranger to a note was, "I guaranty the payment of the within note," it was held he was a guarantor only and not a maker or surety.[2] The payee of a note who signs his name to these words written on the back thereof, "I hereby guaranty the within note," is not liable thereon as indorser, but as guarantor.[3] The legal holder of a note, but not the payee, indorsed upon it, "I warrant this note collectible when due." *Held*, he was a guarantor and not an indorser.[4] Two parties were bound to another as principal and surety. The note on which they were liable was due, and the creditor, who was pressing for payment, offered to take the notes of a third person, held by the principal, if the principal and surety would indorse such notes. This was done, the principal indorsing in blank, and the surety thus: "Sam'l K. Allen as security." *Held*, Allen was not liable as guarantor.[5] An engagement indorsed on a bill or promissory note, under seal, for $500, of the same date with the note, was as follows: "I hereby acknowledge to be security for the within amount of $500 until

[1] Seymour *v.* Mickey, 15 Ohio St. 515. See, also, Riley *v.* Gerrish, 9 Cush. 104; Josselyn *v.* Ames, 3 Mass. 274; Sylvester *v.* Downer, 20 Vt. 355; Tenney *v.* Prince, 4 Pick. 385. On the same principle it was held that where a note was indorsed by a stranger after its maturity in consideration of forbearance, such indorsement imported a guaranty of the payment of it. Scott *v.* Calkin, 139 Mass. 529.

[2] Oxford Bank *v.* Haynes, 8 Pick. 423. An indorsement upon a certificate of deposit, viz.: "I hereby guaranty the payment of the within certificate," is a contract of guaranty. Nat. Loan & Bldg. Society *v.* Lichtenwalner, 100 Pa. St. 100.

[3] Belcher *v.* Smith, 7 Cush. 482.

[4] Benton *v.* Fletcher, 31 Vt. 418. To a contrary effect when the express guarantor was the payee, see Partridge *v.* Davis, 20 Vt. 499.

[5] Allen *v.* Coffil, 42 Ill. 293.

satisfactorily paid by" W. A. *Held*, the indorser was liable as surety and not as guarantor. The court said: "The word security has an established and well-known meaning in the minds of most people, and indicates an obligation to stand for the sum absolutely, unless discharged by the supine negligence of the obligor after notice. It is in broad contrast with the word guaranty, which imports a conditional liability if due steps are taken against the principal."[1] Where the indorsement on the back of a note was, "I transfer the within note to . . . (A.) and guaranty the payment of the same," it was held that this, being a guaranty in terms, could not be recovered on as a blank indorsement. "There is no implication of a promise where one is expressed."[2] Where the payee of a note indorsed it as follows, "I assign the within note to . . . (A.) and warrant the solvency of the maker," it was held he was not liable as a general indorser, but that his liability was restricted by the special terms of his indorsement.[3] Where strangers to a note, at the time it was made, indorsed it as follows: "We guaranty payment," it was held they were guarantors and not sureties, and could not require the holder to sue the maker, as provided by statute in the case of sureties.[4] One who places his name on the back of a promissory note, at the time of its execution, designating himself as surety, is held liable as surety, originally and jointly with the maker, and not as an indorser.[5]

§ 184. Liability of indorsers under special indorsements and circumstances.— The owner of a negotiable note payable to another party, and not transferred by indorsement, sold and delivered it for value, indorsing upon it his name, and, in addition, the words "Holden thirty days." *Held*, he was liable to pay the note on condition that payment was demanded of the maker, and he was notified of the maker's default, within thirty days, and not otherwise.[6] A., B. and C. signed a note payable to D., and B. and C. added to their names the word

[1] Marberger *v.* Pott, 16 Pa. St. 9, per Coulter, J.

[2] Snevily *v.* Ekel, 1 Watts & Serg. (Pa.) 203.

[3] Turley *v.* Hodge, 3 Humph. (Tenn.) 73.

[4] Sample *v.* Martin, 46 Ind. 226.

[5] Phillips *v.* Cox, 61 Ind. 345.

[6] Knight *v.* Knight, 16 N. H. 107.

"surety." E. indorsed the note in blank, and it was discounted by D. and the money paid to E. In the absence of all evidence on the subject, it was held that E. was the surety of the other parties to the note, and that he was discharged by time given them.[1] A stranger to a note indorsed it as follows: "I assign the within note as security to Charles C. Jones." Jones was the payee of the note, and the indorsement was made subsequent to the making of the note. *Held*, the indorser was not a joint maker, and could not be sued jointly with the maker.[2] It has been held that one who purchases an unindorsed negotiable note, and afterwards writes his name with the word "holden" on its back and sells it for value, is chargeable as guarantor.[3] A. wrote on the back of a note, then two years past due, the following: "We waive time, notice and protest, and guaranty the payment of the within." *Held*, such guarantor did not assume payment of the debt at any particular time, and the circumstances of the guaranty might be alleged and proved to explain when payment was to be made.[4]

§ 185. Liability of accommodation parties to bills of exchange — Special cases.— It has been held that the indorsers of an accommodation bill of exchange are not joint sureties, but are liable to each other in the order of their becoming parties.[5] Where there were two drawers of a bill of exchange, and one of them was surety only, and the drawee, having no funds of the principal in his hands, accepted and paid the bill with knowledge of the fact of suretyship, and afterwards sued the drawers to recover the amount paid, it was held the law raised an implied promise to pay on the part of the principal, but there could be no recovery against the surety, even though he had signed as drawer, with the express intention of becoming bound as surety. A bill of exchange never imports an obligation on the drawer to pay the amount to the drawee.

[1] Bank of Orleans *v.* Barry, 1 Denio, 116.

[2] Goode *v.* Jones, 9 Mo. 866.

[3] Irish *v.* Cutter, 31 Me. 536. See, also, to similar effect, Bray *v.* Marsh, 75 Me. 452.

[4] Donley *v.* Bush, 44 Tex. 1.

[5] Williams *v.* Bosson, 11 Ohio, 62. Holding the accommodation acceptor of a draft to be a principal, see Marsh *v.* Low, 55 Ind. 271.

The contract was not sufficient to effectuate the intention and render the surety liable.[1] A. drew a bill of exchange on B., which B. refused to accept unless A. procured some responsible party to sign the bill with him. A. then procured C. to sign the bill with him as drawer, C. being merely a surety, and B. knowing that fact. When the bill became due B. paid it out of his own funds and sued A. and C. for indemnity. C. claimed that he was not liable, because the bill, having been paid by the party on whom it was drawn, was dead, and there could be no recovery on it, and there was no implied *assumpsit* against him. The court held C. was liable. "He must be taken to have put his name on the bill in view of the well-established principle of law that if the drawer has no funds in the hands of the drawee to meet the payment of the bill at maturity, in consequence of which the latter has it to pay with his own funds, a right of action instantly arises in his favor, not, indeed, upon the bill, but in *assumpsit*, to recover the money thus advanced, founded upon an implied promise. This is one of the known fixed legal consequences, resulting from the relation of drawer. . . . Upon general principles of law, the liability of a surety is co-extensive with that of the principal, and it is wholly unimportant whether the liability arises out of an express or implied understanding on the part of the principal. The surety is as much bound for the implied as for the express promises and undertakings of his principal; in this respect the law knows no distinction."[2] It has been held that the accommodation acceptor of a bill of exchange is not a surety, and is not discharged by time given the drawer. The court said: "He who accepts a bill, whether for value or to serve a friend, makes himself at all events liable as acceptor, and nothing can discharge him but payment or release."[3] A. drew a draft at two months, addressed to E., payable to the order of B., and concluding as follows: "Charge the same to the account of your obedient servant." It was signed first by

[1] Wing *v.* Terry, 5 Hill (N. Y.), 160.

[2] Nelson *v.* Richardson, 4 Sneed (Tenn.), 307, per McKinney, J. To same effect, see Dickerson *v.* Turner, 15 Ind. 4; Suydam *v.* Westfall, 2 Denio, 205, reversing Suydam *v.* Westfall, 4 Hill, 211.

[3] Fentum *v.* Pocock, 5 Taunt. 192; Id., 1 Marsh. 14, per Mansfield, C. J.

A., and then by C., the word "surety" being added to C.'s signature, and then as follows: D., "surety for the above surety." D. signed the draft without C.'s knowledge. B. discounted the draft and sent it to E., who paid it without funds, under an agreement to that effect with A.; afterwards D. paid the draft to E., and sued C. for indemnity. *Held*, he was not entitled to recover. C. was not liable by the terms of the draft to the acceptors, and was liable to nobody on the draft unless the acceptors failed to pay, being in effect their sureties. Neither was he liable for money paid to his use, because he never desired the acceptors to advance any money for him.[1]

[1] Wright *v.* Garlinghouse, 26 N. Y. 539.

CHAPTER VIII.

OF THE NOTICE AND DEMAND NECESSARY TO CHARGE A GUARANTOR.

When guarantor must be notified of acceptance of guaranty — Reasons therefor . . § 186
Writer of general letter of credit entitled to notice of its acceptance 187
When writer of guaranty, addressed to a particular person, must be notified of its acceptance 188
When guarantor entitled to notice of acceptance of guaranty — Special cases . . . 189
When guarantor entitled to notice of acceptance of guaranty — Special cases . . . 190
When guarantor entitled to notice of acceptance of guaranty — Special cases . . . 191
When guarantor must be notified of advances made under guaranty 192
When guarantor of definite liability of another not entitled to notice of acceptance of guaranty 193
When guarantor not entitled to notice of acceptance of guaranty — Special cases . . . 194
When guarantor not entitled to notice of advances made to principal 195
Cases holding guarantor for indefinite amount on credit to be given not entitled to notice of acceptance of guaranty § 196
When guarantor entitled to notice of default of principal . 197
When demand of payment on principal and notice of his default necessary to charge guarantor 198
When demand of payment on principal and notice of his default to guarantor not necessary to charge guarantor — Guaranty of promissory note, etc. 199
When guarantor bound without notice of default of principal — Other cases 200
When no notice of default in payment by principal need be given guarantor of overdue debt, of lease, and of negotiable instrument by separate contract 201
If principal be insolvent when debt becomes due, no demand on him nor notice of his default necessary to guarantor 202
What is the reasonable time within which notice must be given — Pleading 203
How notice may be proved — What amounts to waiver of it 204

§ 186. When guarantor must be notified of acceptance of guaranty — Reasons therefor.— A question often arising upon commercial guaranties is whether, in order to charge the guarantor, it is necessary that he be notified of the acceptance of the guaranty by the person acting upon it. When the guaranty is a letter of credit, or is an offer to become responsible for a credit which may or may not be given to another, at the option of the party to whom the application for credit is made, the great weight of authority is that the guarantor must within a reasonable time be notified of the acceptance of the guaranty.[1] The most satisfactory reasons exist for these decisions. It is of the highest importance to the person thus offering his credit that he should know he is to be looked to for payment. Knowing that fact he can regulate his dealings with his principal accordingly. He will have an opportunity to secure himself and guard against loss. Concerning this subject it has been said: "It would, indeed, be an extraordinary departure from that exactness and precision which peculiarly distinguish commercial transactions, which is an important principle in the law and usage of merchants, if a merchant should act on a letter of this character and hold the writer responsible without giving notice to him that he had acted on it."[2] Another reason much relied upon by the courts is that the transaction only amounts to an offer to guaranty until the party making the offer is notified of its acceptance, when the minds of the parties meet and the contract is completed. Where the transaction is admitted to amount only to an offer to guaranty, it is universally held that in order to charge the party making the offer he must within a reason-

[1] This is the firmly settled doctrine of the supreme court of the United States. Edmondston *v.* Drake, 5 Pet. 624; Douglass *v.* Reynolds, 7 Pet. 113; Lee *v.* Dick, 10 Pet. 482; Adams *v.* Jones, 12 Pet. 207; Davis *v.* Wells, 104 U. S. 159; Davis Sewing Machine Co. *v.* Richards, 115 U. S. 524. These decisions have been, with few exceptions, followed and approved in the United States. Lawton *v.* Maner, 9 Rich. Law (S. C.), 335; Sollee *v.* Meugy, 1 Bailey, Law (S. C.), 620; Claflin *v.* Briant, 58 Ga. 414; Burns *v.* Semmes, 4 Cranch Cir. Ct. 702; Shewell *v.* Knox, 1 Dev. Law (N. C.), 404; Taylor *v.* McClung's Ex'rs, 2 Houston (Del.), 24; Tuckerman *v.* French, 7 Greenl. (Me.) 115; Kellogg *v.* Stockton, 29 Pa. St. 460; Bank of Illinois *v.* Sloo, 16 La. (Curry), 539; Menard *v.* Scudder, 7 La. Ann. 385; Kinchelse *v.* Holmes, 7 B. Mon. (Ky.) 5; Allen *v.* Pike, 3 Cush. 238; Mussey *v.* Rayner, 22 Pick. 223; Rankin *v.* Childs, 9 Mo. 665; Mayfield *v.* Wheeler, 37 Tex. 256; McCollum *v.* Cushing, 22 Ark. 540; Howe *v.* Nickels, 22 Me. 175; Geiger *v.* Clark, 13 Cal. 579; Cook *v.* Orne, 37 Ill. 186; Milroy *v.* Quinn, 69 Ind. 406.

[2] Edmondston *v.* Drake, 5 Pet. 624, per Marshall, C. J.

able time be notified that his offer is accepted. The courts, however, differ more or less as to what is a guaranty and what is an offer to guaranty.

§ 187. Writer of general letter of credit entitled to notice of its acceptance.— The rule that a guarantor of future credits is entitled to notice applies with special force to general letters of credit: "For it might otherwise be impracticable for the guarantor to know to whom and under what circumstances the guaranty attached and to what period it might be protracted."[1] A party gave a letter of credit to another, agreeing to guaranty payment for purchases made by that other, to a certain amount. The party purchased goods on the strength of the guaranty, but no notice was given the guarantor. *Held*, he was not liable. The court said: "A party giving a letter of guaranty has a right to know whether it is accepted, and whether the person to whom it is addressed means to give credit on the footing of it or not. It may be most material, not only as to his responsibility, but as to his future rights and proceedings. It may regulate, in a great measure, his course of conduct and his exercise of vigilance in regard to the party in whose favor it is given."[2] A. wrote to B. that if he would assume the debt of C. and procure the discharge of C.'s bail, he, A., would execute his note for 50*l*. B. complied with the request, but did not notify A. of the fact. *Held*, A. was not liable. The court said: "When a proposition is made by a man for a thing to be done for himself, he must know, when done, that it is done on his proposition. But when he proposes his responsibility for a thing to be done for another, he may not know that it is done, or, even if he does, he will not know whether it was done on his proposition, or on the sole credit of the third person, or on some other security. . . . If he is to stand as surety, he must have the right to keep watch of his principal and his circumstances."[3] A. gave B. a letter of credit addressed to C. in a distant city, and agreeing to guaranty any purchases which might be made by B. of C., or any person to whom B. might be introduced

[1] Per Story, J., in Adams *v.* Jones, 12 Pet. 207.

[2] McCollum *v.* Cushing, 22 Ark. 540, per English, C. J.

[3] Oaks *v.* Weller, 13 Vt. 106, per Collamer, J. See, also, Peck *v.* Barney, 13 Vt. 93.

by C. Several parties sold goods on the strength of the guaranty, but no notice was given to A. *Held*, A. was not bound.[1] A writing was as follows: "The bearer, . . . wishing to travel with my son, please furnish with a suitable stock, and all will be right." *Held*, an offer to guaranty, and that the writer was not liable unless the proposition was accepted and he notified of such acceptance. The court said: "A mere offer, not accepted, is not a contract; and a mere mental acceptance of a proposition, not communicated to the party to be charged, is not an acceptance at all in the eye of the law. It is important to the interests of the business community that every one should know the extent of his liabilities, in order that he may take the proper measures to meet them."[2] A banker being in failing circumstances and anticipating a run on his bank, certain persons signed and published an instrument as follows: "We, the undersigned, agree to guaranty the depositors of Wm. E. Culver in the payment in full of their demands against said Culver, on account of money deposited with him. We have entire confidence in his ability to meet all demands on him." A depositor brought suit on this guaranty, alleging that he had a large amount of money in the bank when the guaranty was signed, and was about to withdraw it, but relying on the guaranty he permitted it to remain. *Held*, that under this state of facts such depositor must aver and prove notice to the guarantors of the acceptance of the guaranty, and a general averment of notice would not be sufficient. The court said: "Where the offer is to guaranty a debt for which another is primarily liable in consideration of some act to be performed by the creditor, mere performance of the act is not sufficient to fix the liability of the guarantor, but the creditor must notify the guarantor of his acceptance of the offer, or of his intention to act upon it. . . . The rule is that a person thus proposing to become surety for another is not bound to inquire as to the acceptance of his proposal, but the creditor must show reasonable notice."[3]

[1] Kinchelse *v.* Holmes, 7 B. Mon. (Ky.) 5. To the same effect, when the guaranty was a continuing one, addressed to no one in particular, see Menard *v.* Scudder, 7 La. Ann. 385.

[2] Kellogg *v.* Stockton, 29 Pa. St. 460, per Lewis, C. J.

[3] Steadman *v.* Guthrie, 4 Met. (Ky.) 147.

§ 188. When writer of guaranty, addressed to a particular person, must be notified of its acceptance.— The rule is generally held to be the same where the writing is addressed to a particular person and is acted on by him. Thus, where a guaranty was as follows: "Gentlemen: . . . (A. and B.) wish to draw on you at six and eight months; you will please accept their draft for $2,000 and I do hereby guaranty the punctual payment of it," it was held the guarantor must be notified within a reasonable time of the acceptance of the draft.[1] A guaranty was as follows: "I would recommend. . . (A.) and go security for him to any reasonable amount, so you can fill his orders and feel yourself secure as when I was doing business with you." *Held*, the guarantor was not liable unless notified of the acceptance of the guaranty. The court said it made no difference if the guarantor had before verbally requested the creditor to give the credit, and proceeded: "It is difficult to imagine how precedent request alone can supply the place of subsequent notice, since, after request made and proffer of guaranty, the merchant may refuse the credit or advance craved, and without notice the surety cannot know whether he has or not."[2] A. applied to R. to purchase lumber to build a ferry-boat, and R. refused to credit him without security. A. mentioned the name of C. as surety, and his name was acceptable. A few days afterwards A. presented an order for the lumber in C.'s handwriting, at the foot of which was written, "Messrs. Rankins (R.) will furnish the above bill as soon as possible, and I will order what more I may want for my boat in a short time. James McCurtney (A.). I hereby guaranty the payment of the above bill, January 29, 1842. Wm. Childs" (C.). The lumber was afterwards sold. *Held*, C. must be notified of the acceptance of the guaranty in order to charge him.[3] The same thing was held where the defendants wrote to the plaintiffs as follows: "We take pleasure in commending Mr. C. to you as a gentlemen worthy of your confidence, and if he should have any dealing with you we hereby bind ourselves to make good and pay any amount he may be indebted to you on settlement,

[1] Lee *v.* Dick, 10 Pet. 482.

[2] Kay *v.* Allen, 9 Pa. St. 320, per Bell, J.

[3] Rankin *v.* Childs, 9 Mo. 665.

not exceeding $1,500. This guaranty to remain in full force until revoked by us."[1] Where the writing was as follows: "For value received, I, Moses Dudley, of Chesterfield, New Hampshire, guaranty to pay James M. Beebe & Co., of Boston, for two thousand dollars' worth of goods delivered to Charles P. Dudley, of Lowell, when he may call for them," it was held that as the engagement related to goods to be delivered, and no time was fixed within which the delivery was to be made, it was a collateral agreement or guaranty, and not an absolute undertaking, and that the guarantor must, in order to charge him, be notified within a reasonable time of sales made under it.[2] Where the maker of a continuing guaranty had no notice of its acceptance for three years, he was held not liable. In an able opinion the court summarized the law on this subject as follows: "In cases of a written guaranty for a debt yet to be created, and uncertain in its amount, the guarantor should have notice in a reasonable time that the guaranty is accepted, and that credit has been given on the faith of it. . . . The distinction is between an offer to guaranty a debt about to be created, the amount of which the party making the offer does not know, and it is uncertain whether the offer will be accepted so that he may be ultimately liable, and the case of an absolute guaranty, the terms of which are definite as to its extent and amount. In the latter case no notice is necessary to the guarantor, whereas in the former case the contract is not completed until the offer is accepted."[3] In an action on the following guaranty, viz.: "H. R. Horton, Esq.: If Mr. J. G. Haley, contracts with you for lime and plaster, . . . promising to pay your bills from moneys received by him for work done," . . . I will guaranty the faithful performance of such contract with you, it was held that the guarantor was entitled to notice of the acceptance of the guaranty, and that without such notice the guaranty did not take effect; and it was also held that the guaranty was not negotiable.[4]

§ 189. When guarantor entitled to notice of acceptance of guaranty — Special cases.— If a promise be made to pay the debt of another, provided the creditor will take the debt-

[1] Wardlaw *v.* Harrison, 11 Rich. Law (S. C.), 626.

[2] Beebe *v.* Dudley, 26 N. H. 249.

[3] Allen *v.* Pike, 3 Cush. 238, per Wilde, J.

[4] King *v.* Batterson, 13 R. I. 117.

or's note, payable at a distant day, the promisor must have notice that the proposition is acceded to and the note accepted, or he will not be liable on his guaranty.[1] A guaranty was as follows: "F. informs me that you are about publishing an arithmetic for him. I have no objection to be answerable as far as 50*l.*; for my reference, apply to B." (Signed) G. T. The guaranty was written by B. and signed by G. T., and then B. wrote at the bottom, "Witness to G. T——. B." It was forwarded by B. to the plaintiffs, who never communicated their acceptance of it to G. T. *Held*, G. T. was not liable. The court said: "The transaction cannot be tortured into a consummate and perfect contract. The contract was not complete till notice; and with regard to the agency of Brooke (B.), there is nothing to show that the plaintiffs might not have been dissatisfied with his opinion of the defendant's solvency. . . . The subsequent words render the point quite clear that the defendant only intended to be bound by the instrument in case upon inquiry the plaintiffs should be satisfied with regard to his solvency."[2] A. wrote to B. that C. desired the loan of $15,000, and if B. would loan it to C. he would be responsible for that amount, and would leave, as collateral for the loan, a mortgage for $15,000, then in B.'s hands, and that if B. did not feel like loaning the amount he would assist C. to get it elsewhere. *Held*, this was a guaranty, or an offer to guaranty, on the part of A., and, in order to render him liable for any advances made, he must have notice of acceptance within a reasonable time. The court said: "There is a marked difference between an overture or proposition to guaranty, and a simple contract of suretyship. The one is a contingent liability. The other is an actual undertaking."[3] A. wrote a letter to the plaintiffs, promising to accept and pay bills to the extent of $50,000, drawn on them by B., of Illinois, and discounted by the plaintiffs. C., by an indorsement on the letter, guarantied the payment of such bills as might be drawn in pursuance thereof. Bills to the extent

[1] Patterson *v.* Reed, 7 Watts & Serg. (Pa.) 144.

[2] Per Lord Abinger, C. B., and Parke, B., in Mozley *v.* Tinkler, 1 Cromp., Mees. & Ros. 692; Id., 5 Tyrwh. 416; Id., 1 Gale, 11.

[3] Central Savings Bank *v.* Shine, 48 Mo. 456, per Wagner, J. See, also, Taylor *v.* Shouse, 73 Mo. 361.

of $37,000 were drawn, not paid, and protested. No notice was given to the guarantor of the acceptance of the guaranty, or the advances made thereon, until after the dishonor of the bills. *Held*, the guarantor was entitled to notice of the acceptance of the guaranty, and of the advances made under it, and that he was not liable, for want of such notice.[1] A party being about to purchase goods exhibited to the seller a letter from a third party, addressed to the purchaser, containing, among other things, the following: "For the amount of such goods as you wish to purchase on six months' credit, not exceeding one thousand dollars, I will guaranty at two and a half per cent." Upon the faith of this he obtained goods, giving therefor his promissory note, payable in six months, with grace. *Held*, this was not an authority to the purchaser to bind the writer at all events, nor was the purchaser thereby constituted his agent for the purpose of receiving notice of its acceptance, but that it was a case of collateral guaranty, in which seasonable notice of acceptance was necessary to charge the guarantor.[2] It has been held that in an action for breach of an agreement which is in the nature of a guaranty, if the circumstances alleged as the foundation of the defendant's liability are more properly within the knowledge of the plaintiff than the defendant, notice thereof should be averred in the declaration, and proved on the trial.[3]

§ 190. When guarantor entitled to notice of acceptance of guaranty — Special cases.— Where a party gave a letter of credit to another, addressed to certain merchants, stating: "Should you be disposed to furnish him with such goods as he may call for, from three hundred to five hundred dollars' worth, I will hold myself accountable for the payment, should he not pay as you and he shall agree," it was held to be a collateral undertaking, and that the guarantor was entitled to notice of the acceptance of the guaranty and the amount of credit given.[4] Where an offer of guaranty of rent for a year was made in writing, accompanied by a request in writing for an answer, it was held that the party making the offer must

[1] Bank of Illinois *v.* Sloo, 16 La. (Curry), 539.

[2] Bradley *v.* Cary, 8 Greenl. (Me.) 234.

[3] Lewis *v.* Bradley, 2 Ired. Law (N. C.), 303.

[4] Rapelye *v.* Bailey, 3 Conn. 438.

be notified of its acceptance, in order to charge him.[1] Part of a letter written by A. to B., concerning a debt already contracted by third parties, was as follows: "I wish you to show him (James Hale) some lenity, as much as you think proper for the collection of it from Mr. Lovejoy, and I will, if you please, stand responsible for the payment of it at the time you and James may agree on." *Held*, this was an offer to guaranty, and not a completed contract; that the writer of the letter was entitled to notice of the acceptance of his offer within a reasonable time, and not having received any such notice for over two years, he was not bound.[2] A party addressed to certain merchants a note, stating that he would be responsible at the end of three years, for goods sold to F., to the amount of $1,000. The merchants sold F. goods on the strength of the guaranty to the amount of about $1,000, but did not notify the writer of the note of the acceptance of the guaranty, nor of the amount sold, till two years and eight months after the transaction. *Held*, the writer of the note was not liable. The court said: "Not only is this notice essential to that exactness and precision, as well as to the good faith and confidence, which should characterize mercantile contracts, but it is equally demanded by a regard to the rights and interests of the defendant; and the most unjust results would follow were a contrary doctrine to prevail. He ought to have the notice to enable him to take such prudential measures as would guard him against eventual loss; to exercise a watchful supervision over the proceedings of him for whom he became responsible; to make payment, if necessary, and to secure himself by suit."[3] A letter, after introducing a party, proceeded as follows: "Any favor you may show in introducing him to the different houses, so that he may be able to fill his orders, will be highly appreciated by him, and will be indorsed by me, if necessary, for the amount of his purchases." Goods were sold on this letter, for which the purchaser gave his individual note, due in six months. No

[1] Valloton *v.* Gardner, R. M. Charlt. (Ga.) 86. To similar effect, see Thomas *v.* Davis, 14 Pick. 353.

[2] Beekman *v.* Hale, 17 Johns. 134. To the effect that, when the letter is an offer to guaranty, the writer must be notified of its acceptance, see Fellows *v.* Prentiss, 3 Denio, 512.

[3] Craft *v.* Isham, 13 Conn. 28, per Bissell, J.

notice was given the writer of the letter till after the note was due. *Held*, he was not liable, his agreement being to guaranty if necessary; and he should have been promptly notified of the sale, or requested to guaranty the note.[1]

§ 191. When guarantor entitled to notice of acceptance of guaranty — Special cases.— Where I. gave a writing to P. providing that he would indorse any bill or bills which S. might give to P. in part payment of an order for certain goods then executing for him, I. to allow 5*l*. per cent. on the amount of the bills for the guaranty; and in part payment for the goods S. gave P. a bill at eighteen months, which the latter kept for seventeen months and ten days, and then, finding that S. was insolvent, applied for the first time to I. for his indorsement, tendering the amount of commission, it was held I. was not liable. The writing was a simple offer to guaranty upon being paid a consideration. If P. intended to accept the offer he should have done so within a reasonable time, and paid the commission.[2] A. wrote to B. recommending certain parties and giving certain explanations, and added at the end of his letter: "If in addition to the foregoing explanation you shall require any individual guaranty, I shall have no objection to give you that pledge." *Held*, the letter was not a guaranty, but a statement that if an application was made a guaranty would be given, and no guaranty having been required for more than two years, the inference was that the credit was given solely to the principal, and that the offer to guaranty was not accepted.[3] One H., requiring some spirits for the purposes of his trade, received from the defendant, a friend of his, a letter of introduction to the plaintiff, a distiller, to whom the defendant was well known, but H. an entire stranger. There had not been any previous application by H. to the plaintiff for credit. The letter was as follows: "The bearer is Mr. Joseph Hugill, a friend of mine, who wishes to purchase some proof spirits, which he hears that you manufacture. If you can arrange matters to your mutual satisfaction I am sure that Mr. Hugill will prove a reliable person to deal with. I will myself, with pleasure, become security for anything he may be disposed to give an order for." *Held*, this was not a

[1] Mayfield *v.* Wheeler, 37 Tex. 256.

[2] Payne *v.* Ives, 3 Dow. & Ryl. 664.

[3] Stafford *v.* Low, 16 Johns. 67.

guaranty, but an offer to guaranty, and in order to charge the writer of the letter it was necessary to notify him of the acceptance of the offer.[1] A guaranty was as follows: "Wm. Mitchell, Jr., will probably call on you to purchase your horse, and should you conclude to sell you can do so. Take his note, and I will be responsible for the payment on his return." *Held*, that in order to hold the guarantor he must be notified of the sale. The court said: "In an action upon a guaranty, unless the instrument given in evidence as such purports to be an absolute and conclusive engagement, the plaintiff must show that he gave notice to the defendant that he accepted it as such."[2] The plaintiff having declined to furnish goods to A.'s house on his credit alone, a writing was given to A. by the defendant to this effect: "I understand A. & Co. have given you an order for rigging, etc. I can assure you, from what I know of A.'s honor and probity, you will be perfectly safe in crediting them to that amount; indeed, I have no objection to guaranty you against any loss from giving them this credit." This writing was handed over by A. to the plaintiffs, together with a guaranty from another house, which they required in addition, and the goods were thereupon furnished, but the defendant was not notified that they were furnished nor that he was relied upon for payment. *Held*, the defendant was not liable. The writing was not a perfect and conclusive guaranty, but only a proposition tending to a guaranty,[3] A person who promises that, if the creditors of an embarrassed debtor will grant an extension of time he will guaranty the punctual payments of the debts pursuant to the extension, must be given notice by the creditors of their acceptance of the guaranty, otherwise he will not be liable thereon; and the fact that there were over twelve hundred creditors was held not to defeat the rule on the ground of inconvenience in getting notice from all.[4]

[1] Kastner *v.* Winstanley, 20 Up. Can. (C. P.) 101.

[2] Smith *v.* Anthony, 5 Mo. 504.

[3] McIver *v.* Richardson, 1 Maule & Sel. 557. And to similar effect, see Sutherland *v.* Patterson, 4 Ont. (Can.) 565. For further cases holding a guarantor entitled to notice of the acceptance of the guaranty, see the following: Wills *v.* Ross, 77 Ind. 1; Furst & Bradley Mfg. Co. *v.* Black, 111 Ind. 308; Duncan *v.* Heller, 13 S. C. 94; Coe *v.* Buehler, 110 Pa. St. 366; Newman *v.* Streator Coal Co., 19 Brad. (Ill. App.) 594.

[4] Gardner *v.* Lloyd, 110 Pa. St. 278.

§ 192. When guarantor must be notified of advances made under guaranty.— When the guaranty relates only to a single transaction, notice of its acceptance usually conveys to the guarantor knowledge of the extent of his liability; and in such case no other notice is necessary. Where, however, the guaranty is a continuing one, notice of its acceptance does not have this effect. In such case the same reasons which require notice of the acceptance of the guaranty also require notice of the advances made under it. It has accordingly been held, and is well established, that in the case of a continuing guaranty, not only must notice of acceptance be given, but also, within a reasonable time after all the transactions are closed, the guarantor must be notified of the amount due under the guaranty.[1] As to this matter, the following has been said by an eminent judge: "All such cases must stand upon their own circumstances, and do not seem to furnish just grounds for a general rule."[2] A notice of the amount due after all the transactions are closed is sufficient, and it is not necessary to give notice of each successive sale as it is made.[3] The maker of a continuing guaranty was duly notified of its acceptance. Goods were sold under it, but no notice of the amount so sold nor of default in payment by the principal was given till two years after the close of the transaction, when the principal had become insolvent. *Held*, the guarantor was not liable. The court said: "Good faith, we think, requires that, when a party gives credit to another on the responsibility or undertaking of a third person, he should give immediate notice to the latter of the extent of the credit, especially when, as in the case under consideration, a continuing guaranty is given without limitation of the time of its continuance, or of the amount of credit for which the guarantor might be held responsible."[4] A., B. and C. were in partnership. D. gave A. and B. a guaranty to be responsible for one-half of any loss

[1] Douglass *v.* Reynolds, 7 Pet. 113; Montgomery *v.* Kellogg, 43 Miss. 486; Howe *v.* Nickels, 22 Me. 175; Wildes *v.* Savage, 1 Story, 22; Cremer *v.* Higginson, 1 Mason, 323; Norton *v.* Eastman, 4 Greenl. (Me.) 521; Killian *v.* Ashley, 24 Ark. 511; Babcock *v.* Bryant, 12 Pick. 133; Thomas *v.* Davis, 14 Pick. 353.

[2] Wildes *v.* Savage, 1 Story, 22, per Story, J.

[3] Lowe *v.* Beckwith, 14 B. Mon. (Ky.) 150.

[4] Clark *v.* Remington, 11 Met. (Mass.) 361, per Wilde, J.

which they might suffer in the business with C. The partnership having been dissolved, it was held that D. was not liable on his guaranty, unless he had been notified within a reasonable time after the dissolution of the partnership of any loss within the scope of his undertaking. The guaranty was for an uncertain sum, and its duration was not fixed, and therefore the amount to be paid, and when it was due, could only be ascertained by winding up the concern, which was a matter over which the guarantor had no control, and he was consequently entitled to notice.[1]

§ **193. When guarantor of definite liability of another not entitled to notice of acceptance of guaranty.**— When one directly binds himself to be responsible for another's contract already made, and of which he has knowledge when he signs, no notice of the acceptance of the guaranty is necessary.[2] This principle has been applied to a case where a party guarantied the payment for sewing machines to be furnished another under an existing contract of which he knew, and it was held that no notice of acceptance was necessary to charge the guarantor.[3] The same thing was held where the guaranty of a lease was made at the same time the lease was executed, and was a part of the consideration for the execution of the lease.[4] Where a party guarantied the payment of a particular sum at a given time, the court held that no notice to him was nec-

[1] Courtis *v.* Dennis, 7 Met. (Mass.) 510.

[2] Wills *v.* Ross, 77 Ind. 1; Snyder *v.* Click, 112 Ind. 293; Nading *v.* McGregor, 121 Ind. 465; Furst & Bradley Manuf. Co. *v.* Black, 111 Ind. 308; Wilcox *v.* Draper, 12 Neb. 138; Klosterman *v.* Olcott, 25 Neb. 382; Milroy *v.* Quinn, 69 Ind. 406; Wells, Fargo & Co. *v.* Davis, 2 Utah Terr. 411; Wire *v.* Miller, 45 Ohio St. 388. Neither is notice of acceptance necessary when the guaranty is executed contemporaneously with the contract guarantied. Wright *v.* Griffith, 121 Ind. 478. When the guaranty, however, is collateral and the debt guarantied yet to be created, the amount of which is uncertain, notice of acceptance must be given within a reasonable time to the guarantor. Milroy *v.* Quinn, 69 Ind. 406.

[3] Davis Sewing Machine Co. *v.* Jones, 61 Mo. 409.

[4] Mitchell *v.* McCleary, 42 Md. 374. Where guarantors, who were directors of a brewing, malting and distilling company, guarantied the payment of malt and hops which their manager should purchase for the use of the brewery, it was held not a mere offer to guaranty but an absolute undertaking to those furnishing malt or hops on the faith of it, and no notice of the extent of the credit given on the faith of the guaranty was necessary. Boyd *v.* Snyder, 49 Md. 325.

essary, and said: "It is not an indefinite promise either as to amount or time of performance. The party knew what he had contracted to pay, and when it was to be paid, and it was his business to see that the amount was paid."[1] A party executed a guaranty on the back of a note in the following words: "I hereby guaranty the payment of this note within four years from this date." *Held*, the guaranty was absolute that the note should be paid within four years, "and demand and notice were not necessary in this any more than in all other cases of absolute and unconditional engagements."[2] A. having bought a cow at an administrator's sale, and the administrator having refused to deliver her on A.'s credit alone, A. gave his note for the price, and B. wrote to the administrator as follows: "I, the undersigned, will sign the note with . . . (A.) for the cow bought of the Wilkerson estate." *Held*, a completed guaranty, and that no notice of acceptance was necessary to charge B. The court said: "There is a well-recognized distinction between an offer or proposition to guaranty and a direct promise of guaranty. The former requires notice of acceptance and acting upon it, while the latter does not."[3] A., who was digging ore for B. under a parol contract to dig it as fast as B. wanted it, refused to proceed with the work unless B. would give him a guaranty for the fulfillment of the contract on his part. The contract was thereupon reduced to writing and signed by B., who procured C. to put on it his guaranty of the same date as follows: "We agree to warrant the performance of the within and above contract on the part of said B." *Held*, no notice of the acceptance of this guaranty was necessary in order to charge C. The contract and guaranty, having both been signed at the same time, were part of the same transaction. The delivery of the guaranty was not an incipient step in the making of the contract, but was the completion of the contract, and no notice could make it more complete.[4] A party desiring to purchase carpets pro-

[1] Mathews *v.* Chrisman, 12 Smedes & Mar. (Miss.) 595, per Sharkey, C. J.

[2] Breed *v.* Hillhouse, 7 Conn. 523, per Hosmer, C. J. See, also, to similar effect, City Savings Bank *v.* Hopson, 53 Conn. 453; Tyler *v.* Waddingham, 58 Conn. 375; Studebaker *v.* Cody, 54 Ind. 586.

[3] Carman *v.* Elledge, 40 Iowa, 490, per Cole, J.

[4] Bushnell *v.* Church, 15 Conn. 406.

posed to the seller that he would get a certain person to guaranty notes for the purchase money, which proposition was satisfactory to the seller. The person referred to wrote in a postscript to a letter of the purchaser that he would guaranty the payment of the notes. The seller then shipped the carpets and the purchaser signed the notes, but when they were presented to the party who agreed to guaranty them, he evaded doing so. It was held that, having agreed to guaranty a specific bill, no notice to him of the acceptance of the guaranty was necessary. "The moment he wrote that acceptance of Orne's offer the bargain was complete. He then knew the goods were to be furnished upon his credit. He knew his guaranty was already accepted, and that he would be responsible for the goods if furnished before the guaranty was withdrawn, and within a reasonable time; any further notice of the acceptance of the guaranty would have been superfluous."[1]

§ **194. When guarantor not entitled to notice of acceptance of guaranty — Special cases.**— Certain stockholders of a company, by an instrument under their hands and seals, guarantied the payment of all the debts of the company then outstanding, and bound themselves to pay all of said debts to the "creditors of the company who will not sue, but indulge the company upon their claims for ten months from this time." *Held*, that a creditor of the company at that time, who indulged it ten months, was entitled to recover the amount of his debt against the company from said stockholders without having notified them that he would so indulge it. The instrument signed by the stockholders was an absolute present guaranty, and not an offer to guaranty.[2] The following instrument, viz., "Mr. J. C., I will guaranty the payment to you of $625 in treasury warrants, to be paid on or before the 20th of August, on and for account of Mr. J. W., July 13, 1844," was held not to be a guaranty in the legal sense of the term, but an original undertaking to pay J. C. the money specified at the appointed time, and no notice of any kind was necessary to charge the maker of the instrument.[3] A guar-

[1] Cooke *v.* Orne, 37 Ill. 186, per Lawrence, J.

[2] Sanders *v.* Etcherson, 36 Ga. 404.

[3] Mathews *v.* Chrisman, 12 Smed. & Mar. (Miss.) 595. An instrument appended to a bill for merchandise

anty was as follows: "If D. A. Wills purchases a case of tobacco on credit, I agree to see the same paid for in four months." When Wills returned from market, he showed the guarantor a bill for a case of tobacco, saying he had bought it and paid for it with his note. The court held the guaranty was absolute, and notice of acceptance was not necessary to charge the guarantor. The only condition was that the goods should be furnished, and that was done. When Wills told the guarantor he had bought a case of tobacco, he should have inquired and ascertained the facts.[1] A. agreed to furnish B. with books for sale, at a certain price, upon condition that B. should get a good guarantor to the contract. Upon the back of the contract was written as follows: "We guaranty to . . . (A.) that the above-named . . . (B.) will well and truly perform all his above and foregoing undertakings, pursuant to the tenor and effect of said contract." C. signed this guaranty, and B. delivered it to A. Books were delivered according to the contract, but C. was not notified of the acceptance of the guaranty. *Held*, he was liable for the price of the books. The court said: "An absolute present guaranty, complete in its terms and fixing the liability of the guarantor, takes effect as soon as acted upon."[2] A guaranty was as follows: "Mr. A. Ferm tells me that he is about to loan from you $500, and wishes me to state that I will become his eventual security for the payment; this I am willing to do, as I have found him punctual on similar occasions." Three hundred dollars were loaned on the faith of the guaranty. *Held*, no notice of the acceptance of the guaranty was necessary to charge the guarantor. "The substance of the letter is this: 'I will become his eventual security for payment.' Here is, then, no conditional agreement, but a conclusive undertaking."[3] A guaranty requested the delivery of goods to a purchaser, and promised to pay for them if the purchaser made

in the following language, viz.: "In consideration of seven and one-half per cent. I guaranty the above bill to the amount of $200," is a guaranty and not an offer to guaranty, which would require acceptance by the beneficiary and notice thereof to the guarantor. Solary *v.* Stultz, 22 Fla. 263.

[1] Case *v.* Howard, 41 Iowa, 479.

[2] Bright *v.* McKnight, 1 Sneed (Tenn.), 158.

[3] Caton *v.* Shaw, 2 Harris & Gill (Md.), 13. See Boyd *v.* Snyder, 49 Md. 325.

default, and concluded as follows: "Of which default you are required to give us reasonable and proper notice." *Held*, no notice of the acceptance of the guaranty need be given the guarantor to charge him. He had stipulated for a certain kind of notice, viz.: notice of the default of his principal, and, therefore, no other notice was required.[1] In the greater portion of the foregoing cases, holding notice of acceptance not necessary to charge the guarantor, as in many of the cases holding such notice necessary, the distinction is drawn between an absolute guaranty and an offer to guaranty. There is no conflict in principle between those cases, but in the application of the principle to special circumstances there is not entire harmony in the decisions.

§ 195. **When guarantor not entitled to notice of advances made to principal.**— Upon the same general principles, where the guaranty is a completed undertaking to be responsible for the existing contract of another, of which the guarantor has knowledge, it has been held that no notice of advances to the principal is necessary to charge the guarantor.[2] A. and B. agreed to buy of C. his crop of strawberries for the year, and to pay therefor on delivery. D. added to the agreement this clause: "On the part of the said Dillons (A. and B.), I hold myself with them responsible for their part of the above contract." C. delivered the berries to A. and B. as they ripened, without being paid for them on delivery or afterwards. D. had no notice of the failure of A. and B. to pay till suit was brought against him three months after the delivery of the berries. It was held that D. by signing the contract became directly, and not collaterally, liable, and it was his duty without notice to see that the contract was performed. Delivering the berries without getting pay for them as delivered did not change the contract.[3] A., who was cultivating a large number of trees on his land, agreed in writing with B. to cultivate them there till September 13th, and at that time to deliver to B. at the place of their growth fifteen thousand trees, to be designated and counted by the parties. It was stipulated that if either party failed to perform his contract he

[1] Wadsworth *v.* Allen, 8 Gratt. (Va.) 174.

[2] Bushnell *v.* Church, 15 Conn. 406.

[3] Kirby *v.* Studebaker, 15 Ind. 45.

should forfeit $3,000. Underneath was written as follows: "In case B., one of the parties named in the foregoing instrument, should incur the forfeiture mentioned therein, we hereby guaranty the payment of the same;" which was signed by C. as guarantor. A. cultivated the trees as agreed, and was always ready to perform, but B. failed of performance on his part. *Held*, that C. was liable, and no notice of B.'s default need be given to fix his liability. The court said: "None is bound to give notice to another of that which that other person may otherwise inform himself of. Nor is notice necessary where the thing lies as much in the cognizance of the one as of the other. . . . In the present case . . . (C.) was privy to the contract made by . . . (B.); he, as well as . . . (A.), knew its terms and its time of performance, and by an inquiry could have ascertained whether a forfeiture against which he had himself stipulated had occurred."[1] A party gave an agreement to pay his instalments on shares in an insurance company, and another party guarantied the performance of the agreement. *Held* that, although the amount which was to become due on the agreement was uncertain when it was made, yet notice of that amount was not necessary to be given the guarantor, as he himself should have taken notice of the amount. The court said that, where the unascertained liability existed on the face of the original contract, it was the duty of the guarantor to see that the principal performed his contract.[2] A bond signed by a principal and two sureties stated that the principal required money to carry on his business, and required advances from the bank, and "in case of his failure to pay any such loans and advances as aforesaid," the same might be collected from the signers. The bank advanced money to the principal, but did not notify the sureties of the same. *Held*, no such notice was necessary to charge the sureties. They were joint original promisors who were directly liable, and not guarantors who were collaterally liable.[3] A. executed a writing, whereby he agreed with B.

[1] Hammond *v.* Gilmore's Adm'r, 14 Conn. 479, per Church, J.

[2] Protection Ins. Co. *v.* Davis, 5 Allen, 54.

[3] McMillan *v.* Bull's Head Bank, 32 Ind. 11. For a similar conclusion respecting a bond conditioned to answer for the debts and defaults of a sewing machine agent, who was the principal obligor therein, see Cox *v.* Weed Sewing Machine Co., 57 Miss. 350.

that he would at all times hold himself responsible to B. to the amount of $20,000, without notice to be given to him by B. This writing was simultaneously delivered by A. and accepted by B., and B., on the credit thereof, discounted paper indorsed by C. *Held*, that no notice of the acceptance of the guaranty or the amount advanced under it was necessary to charge A. The court said this was not such a case as that of a letter of credit. A letter of credit is a mere proposition, and, until it is accepted and notice of that fact given, the minds of the parties have not met, and there is no contract. "Its reception is unavoidable; its acceptance as a promise optional; its delivery is with a view to its acceptance, and must therefore necessarily precede it. Until such acceptance it is not consummated into a contract, but remains a mere proposition, and there has been no meeting of the minds of the parties." But in this case the delivery of the instrument "was not an incipient step in the formation of the contract, but the result of previous negotiation and agreement, and constituted the very consummation of the contract."[1]

§ 196. Cases holding guarantor for indefinite amount on credit to be given, not entitled to notice of acceptance of guaranty.— There is a class of cases which hold that where the guaranty relates to advances to be made, and the party to make them, as well as the amount to be advanced, are not ascertained, the guarantor is liable without notice of the acceptance of the guaranty, or of the amount advanced. These decisions, while they are the law where they were rendered, are opposed to the great weight of authority, and seem to be founded on much less satisfactory reasons than the cases holding the opposite view. But even here the conflict is more in the application of principles to special facts than in principles themselves. All courts recognize the principle that it is necessary to the completion of a contract that the minds of both contracting parties shall meet; the conflict is as to when they have met. They all hold that a mere offer to guaranty, the same as any other offer, is not binding unless accepted; the conflict is as to whether the guarantor must be notified of the acceptance of the guaranty, and whether the writing

[1] New Haven Co. Bank *v.* Mitchell, 15 Conn. 206, per Storrs, J.

amounts to an offer to guaranty or to a completed guaranty. A guaranty addressed to a mercantile firm in these words, "We consider Mr. J. good for all he may want of you, and will indemnify the same," was held to be a completed guaranty, of the acceptance of which it was not necessary to notify the guarantor. The court said: "Unless there is something in the nature of the contract or terms of the writing creating or implying the necessity of acceptance or notice as a condition of liability, neither are deemed requisite. . . . The party entering into an absolute engagement for the responsibility of his friend should see to the performance of it. The relation in which the parties afterwards stand to each other presupposes privity and knowledge of the credit obtained."[1] A letter of guaranty was as follows: "If you will let A. have one hundred dollars' worth of goods on a credit of three months, you may regard me as guarantying the same." *Held*, the guarantor was liable without any notice of the acceptance of the guaranty. "Here the undertaking was absolute. The defendant said to the plaintiff, in substance: 'If you will deliver the goods I will guaranty the payment.' We cannot add a condition that the defendant shall have notice. He should have provided for that himself in the proposal made to the plaintiff. I know there are cases which require notice, but we think they are not based on the common law, and for that reason they have not been followed in this state."[2] Where A., by a general letter of credit, undertook to accept and pay drafts to be drawn by B. to a given amount, and C., at the foot of the letter, at the same time, wrote and signed these words: "I hereby agree to guaranty the due acceptance and payment of any draft or drafts issued in virtue of the above credit," it was held that C. was liable to the party advancing money on the guaranty, without any notice of its acceptance.[3] A guaranty addressed to a merchant, after explaining

[1] Whitney *v.* Groot, 24 Wend. 82, per Nelson, C. J.

[2] Smith *v.* Dunn, 6 Hill, 543, per Bronson, J. To similar effect, see Wright *v.* Griffith *et al.*, 121 Ind. 478.

[3] Union Bank *v.* Coster's Ex'r, 3 N. Y. 203. Following and approving these cases, see Lonsdale *v.* Lafayette Bank, 18 Ohio, 126; Powers *v.* Bumcratz, 12 Ohio St. 273, overruling Taylor *v.* Wetmore, 10 Ohio, 491. In Clark *v.* Burdett, 2 Hall (N. Y.), 217, this principle was applied to the case of a continuing guaranty.

who the bearer was, went on, "I want you to sell him a bill of goods on the best terms you can afford; I will guaranty the payment of every dollar." *Held*, no notice of the acceptance of the guaranty or the default of the principal was necessary to charge the guarantor.[1] Where the agreement to accept a letter of credit on the part of the person to whom it is addressed is contemporaneous with the writing of the letter, and is known to the writer, there no other notice of acceptance of guaranty is necessary to charge him.[2]

§ 197. When guarantor entitled to notice of default of principal.— Whether demand of payment must be made of the principal, and notice of his default be given, in order to charge the guarantor, is a question depending very much upon the nature of the particular guaranty. Where the liability of the guarantor is not direct, but is collateral and dependent upon the default of another, notice of such default to such guarantor, within a reasonable time, has been held necessary where a guaranty of a note was as follows: "I guaranty the payment of the within note to . . . (A.), for value received;"[3] where a debtor transferred to his creditor certain notes of third persons in payment of his own debt, and promised, if the creditor could not collect the notes, he would pay them;[4] and where an instrument was as follows: "I have this day sold to Kannon a note on Wortham for $412, which I guaranty to said Kannon, waiving all exception of my not assigning said claim, and holding myself bound for the same for value."[5] So, where the holder of a promissory note failed to give the guarantor of the same notice of its non-payment for nine months after its dishonor, and the maker was solvent when the note became due, but afterwards became insolvent, it was held the guarantor was discharged. The court said: "It is clearly conformable to the general principles of right and justice that the creditor, who knows of the delinquency

[1] Yancey *v.* Brown, 3 Sneed (Tenn.), 89.

[2] Wildes *v.* Savage, 1 Story, 22. To similar effect, see Paige *v.* Parker, 8 Gray, 211.

[3] Cox *v.* Brown, 6 Jones' Law (N. C.), 100. To same effect, see Grice *v.* Ricks, 3 Dev. Law (N. C.), 62; Ringgold *v.* Newkirk, 3 Ark. (Pike), 96; Foote *v.* Brown, 2 McLean, 396; Gamage *v.* Hutchins, 23 Me. 565.

[4] Adock *v.* Fleming, 2 Dev. & Bat. Law (N. C.), 225.

[5] Kannon *v.* Neely, 10 Humph. (Tenn.) 288. To similar effect, see Sage *v.* Wilcox, 6 Conn. 81.

of his debtor, and withholds information of it from the guarantee, by reason of which the debt is actually lost when it might have been saved by either, should not throw the loss upon the guarantee."[1] The payee of a note sold it and indorsed a guaranty of its payment upon it. No demand was made on the maker of the note, and he remained solvent for six months after it became due, and afterwards became insolvent. Two years after the note became due, notice of non-payment was given the guarantor, and demand of payment made on him. *Held*, he was not liable. The court said: "The undertaking of the guarantor of a promissory note is conditional, and he will be discharged by the neglect of the holder to demand payment of the maker, and give the guarantor notice of the non-payment, provided the maker was solvent when the note fell due, and afterwards became insolvent."[2] A party guarantied the punctual payment of two accepted bills. When the bills became due the acceptors were solvent, and so continued for four months, and then became insolvent. No notice was given to the guarantor within the next four years. *Held*, he was discharged. The court said: "In the case before us, the guaranty was that the acceptances should be promptly met by the acceptors. An agreement in such case to pay at all events, without reference to or reliance upon the acceptors, could not be inferred. His warranty was that the acceptors would pay as they were bound to do, and not that he himself would pay without regard to whether they did so or not."[3] Where certain parties guarantied the performance of a contract for the purchase of a lot of cattle, and the payment therefor, and for eighteen months after the maturity of the

[1] Oxford Bank *v.* Haynes, 8 Pick. 423, per Parker, C. J. And if it appear that the principal was solvent at the maturity of the obligation, but became insolvent before demand of payment or notice given, except under special and peculiar circumstances, damages will be presumed. Newton Wagon Co. *v.* Diers, 10 Neb. 284.

[2] Talbot *v.* Gay, 18 Pick. 534, per Wilde, J. Generally, as to when guarantor is entitled to notice of principal's default, see Lowe *v.* Beckwith, 14 B. Mon. (Ky.) 150; Ward *v.* Wilson, 100 Ind. 52; Furst & Bradley Mfg. Co. *v.* Black, 111 Ind. 308; Hernandez *v.* Stilwell, 7 Daly (N. Y. Com. Pleas, 360). Failure to give such notice is of course a matter of defense, but damages must be shown as a result of such failure. La Rose *v.* Logansport Nat. Bank, 102 Ind. 332.

[3] Globe Bank *v.* Small, 25 Me. 366, per Whitman, C. J.

contract the principal was solvent, but afterwards became insolvent, and no notice of his default was given the guarantors, it was held they were discharged.[1] A guarantor of a promissory note payable on demand is discharged from his contract of guaranty by the omission of the holder to give him notice within a reasonable time of demand on the maker and non-payment by him, provided the maker was solvent when the guaranty was made, and became insolvent before notice of non-payment was given.[2] In cases where notice of the principal's default is necessary to charge the guarantor, the same strictness is not required as in the case of indorsers. The notice need not be given immediately upon the principal's default. If it is given within a reasonable time, that is sufficient.[3]

§ 198. **When demand of payment on principal and notice of his default necessary to change guarantor.**—When the advances are made to the principal on a letter of credit signed by the guarantor, the weight of authority is that demand of payment must be made on the principal, and notice of his default be given the guarantor within a reasonable time, in order to charge him, unless the principal be insolvent when the debt becomes due. The law upon this subject and the reasons upon which it is founded have been thus stated: "A demand upon him (the principal), and the failure on his part to perform his engagements, are indispensable to constitute a *casus fœderis.* The creditors are not indeed bound to institute any legal proceedings against the debtor, but they are required to use reasonable diligence to make demand, and to give notice of the non-payment. The guarantors are not to be held to any length of indulgence of credit which the creditors may choose, but have a right to insist that the risk of their responsibility shall be fixed and terminated within a reasonable time after the debt has become due."[4] Where O., by an instrument under seal, assigned certain contracts for

[1] Gaff *v.* Sims, 45 Ind. 262.

[2] Whiton *v.* Mears, 11 Met. (Mass.) 563. To similar effect, see Nelson *v.* Bostwick, 5 Hill, 37; Douglass *v.* Rathbone, 5 Hill, 143.

[3] Bull *v.* Bliss, 30 Vt. 127; Dunbar *v.* Brown, 4 McLean, 166; Talbot *v.* Gay, 18 Pick. 534, and many of the cases cited in this chapter to other points.

[4] Per Story, J., in Douglass *v.* Reynolds, 7 Pet. 113. See, also, M'Collum *v.* Cushing, 22 Ark. 540. In Smith *v.* Bainbridge, 6 Blackf. (Ind.)

the payment of money, and covenanted that the sum set opposite each contract, in a schedule annexed to the assignment, was due and would be paid, it was held that O. being a guarantor of the amount due on the contracts, in order to maintain a suit against him, it was necessary to aver a previous demand of payment from the persons bound by the contracts. The contracts having been assigned to the plaintiff, they alone could demand and receive payment, and they must make such demand before coming upon the guarantor.[1] Certain parties entered into a guaranty, in part as follows: "We hereby engage to see you paid, in due course, for the bill of goods bought by Mr. Ross from you on the 27th inst." A particular bill of goods which had been previously bargained for were delivered on the strength of the guaranty. *Held*, that this was not an original undertaking, but an undertaking to pay if Ross did not, and that the guarantors were entitled to prompt notice of his default unless he was insolvent.[2] Where a guaranty provided that when a note became due it should be good and collectible, it was held that it did not bind the guarantor unless diligence was used to collect the note, and the guarantor was notified that it could not be collected. The court said that, if a party stipulates to do a thing himself, or that another shall do it, he must take notice whether or not it is done. But when he stipulates that the party he contracts with can, by his diligence, do a certain thing, the case is different. "He is not then supposed to know, nor does he assume to know, the means taken, or the result. Notice is, therefore, required, for the reason assigned by Judge Swift, that it would be against principle to admit a man to be sued when he has no knowledge of the existence of the demand." [3] A. and B. each owned an interest in the same land. A. transferred his interest to B., and guarantied that if the title proved defective the grantor of the two would recompense B. for the loss of the

12, a delay of eighteen months in notifying the guarantor was held to be unreasonable, and to discharge the guarantor.

[1] Mechanics' Fire Ins. Co. *v.* Ogden, 1 Wend. 137. *Contra*, Barker *v.* Scudder, 56 Mo. 272.

[2] Mayberry *v.* Bainton, 2 Harr. (Del.) 24.

[3] Sylvester *v.* Downer, 18 Vt. 32, per Royce, J. As to the notice necessary to charge a guarantor of collection, see Brackett *v.* Rich, 28 Minn. 485.

title. *Held*, that demand on the grantor by B., and notice of his default to A., were necessary before bringing suit against A. on the guaranty. Whether A. had to pay at all depended upon a contingency, and in order to put him in default it was necessary to demand payment from the grantor, and notify A. of his default.[1]

§ 199. **When demand of payment on principal and notice of his default to guarantor not necessary to charge guarantor — Guaranty of promissory note, etc.**— Where the contract of guaranty absolutely and unconditionally provides that the debtor shall pay a given sum at a stated time, no demand of payment on the principal or notice of his default is necessary before suing the guarantor.[2] This principle has been very generally applied to guaranties of promissory notes.[3] Where a party guarantied the payment of a note if it should not be "duly honored and paid" by the maker, according to its tenor and effect, it was held he was liable on his guaranty if the note was not paid by the maker, even though no demand of payment was made on the maker before suit was brought against him. The court said: "Now it is clear that a request for the payment of a debt is quite immaterial unless the parties to the contract have stipulated that it shall be made; if they have not, the law requires no notice or request, but the debtor is bound to find out the creditor and pay him the debt when due."[4] The payees of a note indorsed it as follows: "For value received we guaranty the payment of the

[1] Morris *v.* Wadsworth, 17 Wend. 103.

[2] Mann *v.* Eckford's Ex'rs, 15 Wend. 502; Peck *v.* Barney, 13 Vt. 93; East River Bank *v.* Rogers, 7 Bosw. (N. Y.) 493; March *v.* Putney, 56 N. H. 34; Bank *v.* Hammond, 1 Rich. Law (S. C.), 281; Eneas *v.* Hoops, 10 Jones & Spen. (N. Y. Superior Ct.) 517; Taylor *v.* Taylor, 64 Ind. 356; Kline *v.* Raymond, 70 Ind. 271; Furst & Bradley Manuf. Co. *v.* Black, 111 Ind. 308; Fitch *v.* Citizens' Nat. Bank, 97 Ind. 211; Coburn *v.* Brooks, 78 Cal. 443; Bloom & Co. *v.* Warder, 13 Neb. 476; Koenig *v.* Bramlett, 20 Mo. App. 636; Hofheimer *v.* Losen, 24 Mo. App. 652; Osborne *v.* Lawson, 26 Mo. App. 549.

[3] Forest *v.* Stewart, 14 Ohio St. 246; Williams *v.* Granger, 4 Day (Conn.), 444; Mallory *v.* Lyman, 3 Pinney (Wis.), 443; Ten Eyck *v.* Brown, 3 Pinney (Wis.), 452; Clark *v.* Merriam, 25 Ct. 576; Levi *v.* Mendell, 1 Duvall (Ky.), 77. See, also, Gammell *v.* Parramore, 58 Ga. 54; Kenney *v.* Masemam, 14 Daly (N. Y. Com. Pleas), 379; Bartholomew *v.* Seaman, 25 Hun (N. Y.), 619.

[4] Walton *v.* Mascall, 13 Mees. & Wels. 452, per Parke, B.

within note at maturity." *Held*, "as between them (the guarantors) and the maker of the note, the holder was under no obligation to demand payment of the maker, and on his default to notify the guarantors, for they undertook to pay at all hazards at maturity, the one being as much bound as the other. . . . Their duty was, and of each of them, on its maturity, to go to the holder and take it up. The holder was under no legal or moral obligation to hunt them and make a demand."[1] The same thing was held where the guaranty of a note was as follows: "I guaranty the said note is good, and the payment of the same;"[2] where the payee of a note indorsed it as follows: "I do assign the within note to . . . (A.) for value received, and guaranty the punctual payment of the same at maturity;"[3] where the payee of a non-negotiable note indorsed it as follows: "I guaranty the within at maturity;"[4] when a guaranty was in these words: "On the 25th December, 1824, we bind ourselves to see the within note paid;"[5] where a party wrote on the back of a note: "I hereby guaranty the payment of balance due on note . . . within sixty days from the 2d day of May, 1843, balance due this day, $292.22;"[6] and where a guaranty on the back of a note was as follows: "I guaranty the payment of the within note to C. Edgerton or order."[7] In the case last referred to, the court said: "Where the guaranty of payment is absolute and unconditional, we are of opinion that it is not necessary, in order to make out a *prima facie* case for recovery, to aver or prove either demand or notice." Moss obligated himself to deliver on a given day, and at a specified place, seventy bushels of salt to Hunter. Hunter transferred this obligation by assignment, and guarantied the payment of the salt as follows: "For value received I assign the within note to . . . (A.) and

[1] Gage *v.* Mechanics' Nat. Bank of Chicago, 79 Ill. 62, per Breese, J. To same effect, see Singer Manuf. Co. *v.* Hester, 71 Mo. 91.

[2] Woodstock Bank *v.* Downer, 27 Vt. 539.

[3] Thrasher *v.* Ely, 2 Smedes & Marsh. (Miss.) 139.

[4] Peck *v.* Frink, 10 Iowa, 193. To precisely like effect, see Savings Bank *v.* Strother, 28 S. C. 504. In the latter case the court raised the *quære* whether the above rule would apply to the guaranty of a *negotiable* instrument.

[5] Taylor *v.* Ross, 3 Yerg. (Tenn.) 330.

[6] Cooper *v.* Page, 24 Me. 73.

[7] Clay *v.* Edgerton, 19 Ohio St. 549, per Brinkerhoff, C. J. See, also, Neil *v.* Board of Trustees, 31 Ohio St. 15, 22.

guaranty the payment of the same." *Held*, this was an absolute engagement to deliver the salt at the time and place specified, if the maker did not, and demand on the maker and notice to the guarantor were not necessary to charge the guarantor.[1] A memorandum at the foot of a promissory note in these words: "I hereby obligate myself that the above note shall be paid in three years from this 4th day of June, 1838," made in consideration that the payee should delay payment until two years after the maturity of the note, was held to be an original undertaking, which did not require that demand of payment should be made of the maker and notice of his default be given in order to charge the guarantor.[2]

§ 200. **When guarantor bound without notice of default of principal — Other cases.**— The same principle has been applied and notice to the guarantor of the principal's default held not to be necessary in a variety of other cases. Thus where A. agreed to account with B. and pay over to him such sum as he should be found to be indebted, and C. covenanted that A. should perform the agreement, it was held that an action lay against C. by B., for the default of A., without previously giving C. notice of such default.[3] A contract provided for the return of certain shares of railroad stock which were loaned, and for the payment of interest for their use. At the same time the contract was executed certain parties guarantied it as follows: "We, the undersigned, guaranty the fulfillment of the above obligation, and hereby promise said Hiram Simons that said stock shall be returned at the time specified, agreeable to the above contract." *Held*, no demand on the principal or notice of default on his part was necessary to charge the guarantors.[4] A. and B., being partners, dissolved their partnership, and A. agreed to pay the partnership debts, and gave B. bond, with C. as surety, that he would do so. *Held*, that no notice of A.'s default in paying the partnership debts was necessary to be given C. before B. could sue him. The court said: "It is a general rule that where one guaran-

[1] Hunter *v.* Dickinson, 10 Humph. (Tenn.) 37.

[2] Reed *v.* Evans, 17 Ohio, 128.

[3] Douglas *v.* Howland, 24 Wend. 35, in which Mr. Justice Cowen delivered an elaborate opinion repudiating the entire doctrine that notice of acceptance of a guaranty is necessary to charge the guarantor.

[4] Simon *v.* Steele, 36 N. H. 73.

ties the act of another his liability is commensurate with that of his principal, and he is no more entitled to notice of the default than the latter. Both must take notice of the whole at their peril."[1] Where a guaranty stated that if the principal did not pay the creditor a certain sum "in three months from this time," the guarantor agreed "to guaranty to said Dickerson the payment of said sum of money." It was held that no notice of the non-payment by the principal was necessary to charge the guarantor.[2] A guaranty stated that if certain merchants would furnish a purchaser goods, the guarantor would "be accountable to you for all his contracts or engagements, as you and he may agree, and in case he does not fulfill them as agreed, I will guaranty the payment thereof." Goods were sold and the guarantor notified thereof. *Held*, it was not necessary, in order to charge him, that payment should first be demanded of the principal and notice of his default be given.[3] In April, 1825, the defendant guarantied the payment of money due from his son to the plaintiff upon a sale of timber. The plaintiff received part payment from the son, and made repeated unsuccessful applications to him for the residue till December, 1827, when he became bankrupt. The plaintiff never disclosed to the defendant the result of these applications, but on December 27, 1827, sued him on his guaranty. *Held*, the guarantor was liable, on the ground that mere passive delay on the part of the creditor will not discharge the surety.[4] A guaranty that the principal will "return" a certain sum of borrowed money by a particular date has been held to render the guarantor liable without any demand on the principal or notice of his default having been given.[5] Where the guaranty is for a certain indebtedness that may be incurred by the principal before a certain day, notice of the acceptance of the guaranty is held to be implied, and notice of the principal's default is unnecessary, therefore, to charge the guarantor.[6]

[1] Gage *v.* Lewis, 68 Ill. 604, per Sheldon, J.

[2] Dickerson *v.* Derrickson, 39 Ill. 574.

[3] Noyes *v.* Nichols 28 Vt. 159.

[4] Goring *v.* Edmonds, 6 Bing. 94; Id., 3 Moore & Payne, 259.

[5] Cordier *v.* Thompson, 8 Daly (N. Y. Com. Pleas), 172.

[6] Bank of Newbury *v.* Sinclair, 60 N. H. 100.

§ 201. When no notice of default in payment by principal need be given guarantor of overdue debt, of lease, and of negotiable instrument by separate contract.— The rule that no notice of the principal's default need be given in order to charge the unconditional guarantor of an existing demand is specially applicable to a guaranty of a debt made after the debt is due. In such case the principal is in default when the guaranty is made, and the reasons requiring notice do not apply. Thus H. was indebted to R. in a certain sum then due and payable, and C., in consideration of an indemnity given by H., and of R.'s engagement not to sue H. for twelve months, promised to pay R. the debt at that time, unless the same should have been paid by H. *Held*, this was an original and absolute undertaking, and no demand on H., or notice of his default, was necessary in order to charge C.[1] The same thing has been held in the case of a guaranty of an overdue promissory note, when the guaranty on the back of the note was: "I assign the within note to . . . (A.), and guaranty the payment thereof, for value received;"[2] when a stranger to a note wrote on it, after it was due, "I hereby guaranty the payment of the within note, ninety days from the date of this guaranty;"[3] and when the payee of an overdue note indorsed it as follows: "I assign the within note to . . (A.), for value received, and guaranty its prompt and full payment."[4] It is not usually necessary, in order to charge the guarantor of rent to come due under a lease, that demand should be made on the principal, and the guarantor be notified of his default. Thus a party, by a writing on the back of a lease running five years, bound himself to pay the lessors "all rents, and damages of every kind they may sustain by reason of the non-compliance or fulfillment of the stipulations of the within lease by said" lessee. The lessee occupied the premises about half the term, and then left them. About three years after he left, the lessors demanded the rent of the guar-

[1] Read *v.* Cutts, 7 Greenl. (Me.) 186.

[2] Foster *v.* Tolleson, 13 Rich. Law & Eq. (S. C.) 31. And see a case precisely similar, Munro *v.* Hill, 25 S. C. 476. See, though, *contra*, Benton *v.* Gibson, 1 Hill (S. C.), 56.

[3] Sabin *v.* Harris, 12 Iowa, 87.

[4] Wright *v.* Dyer, 48 Mo. 525. To same effect, see Lane *v.* Levillian, 4 Ark. (Pike), 76.

antor, and brought suit on the guaranty, but they had before given the guarantor no notice of the default of the lessee. *Held*, the guaranty was an absolute undertaking, and the guarantor was liable.[1] In an action against the guarantor of rent already due, and to become due for a certain time, from a tenant at will, it has been held that it is not necessary to prove a demand of payment on the tenant, and notice of the non-payment to the guarantor, unless the terms of the guaranty, or the nature and circumstances of the particular case, require it. The court in an able opinion, which presents a clear view of the law on this point, said: "The subject of the guaranty was the payment of certain sums at certain times, both absolute, and fixed by the terms of the guaranty itself. It required no act of the plaintiff to precede the performance by Bailey (principal), except the permission for Bailey to remain, which the defendant knew had been given. If Bailey made a corresponding agreement to do what the defendant agreed he should do, it was broken by the mere fact of non-payment, without demand upon him. The same fact was of itself a breach of the defendant's contract of guaranty. A formal demand upon Bailey is not necessary to make his failure to pay the rent a breach of his obligation, and the defendant's contract is simply that Bailey shall perform his agreement. But whether Bailey made such a corresponding agreement or not, the defendant, by his guaranty, undertook that Bailey should perform certain specific acts, and he is liable on his agreement for Bailey's failure to do those acts. . . . In a suit against a guarantor it is undoubtedly necessary to allege and prove a breach of the contract of guaranty, but it is only necessary to show such acts as would constitute a breach of the particular contract in suit. If the guaranty be for the performance of a specific act of another, and be absolute in terms, whatever is sufficient to show default in that other person will ordinarily show a breach of the contract of guaranty, and a right of action upon it."[2] One who is not a party to a

[1] Voltz *v.* Harris, 40 Ill. 155, explaining and modifying White *v.* Walker, 31 Ill. 422. To same effect, see Ducker *v.* Rapp, 9 Jones & Spencer (N. Y.), 235; Turnure *v.* Hohenthal, 4 Jones & Spencer (N. Y.), 79. *Contra*, Virden *v.* Ellsworth, 15 Ind. 144.

[2] Vinal *v.* Richardson, 13 Allen, 521, disapproving Ilsley *v.* Jones, 12 Gray, 260.

negotiable instrument, but guaranties its payment by a separate contract, is not discharged by want of demand on the principal and notice of dishonor to the grantor, unless the guarantor is injured thereby.[1]

§ 202. If principal be insolvent when debt becomes due, no demand on him, nor notice of his default, necessary to guarantor.—If the principal debtor be insolvent when the debt becomes due, and afterwards so remain, no demand need be made on him, or notice of his default be given the guarantor, in most cases where it would otherwise be necessary, unless some loss or damage can be shown to have occurred to the guarantor in consequence; and he will only be discharged to the extent that he is injured.[2] Delay and damage must both concur to discharge the guarantor.[3] In this respect a guarantor differs from an indorser of a negotiable instrument, for while an indorser must be at once notified, independent of all considerations, it is otherwise with a guarantor.[4] With reference to this subject, it has been said that guarantors "insure, as it were, the solvency of their principals, and therefore, if the latter become bankrupt and notoriously insolvent, it is the same thing as if they were dead, and it is nugatory to go through the ceremony of making a demand upon them."[5] Another court has clearly and correctly expressed

[1] Hitchcock *v.* Humfrey, 5 Man. & Gr. 559; Id., 6 Scott (N. R.), 540; Lewis *v.* Brewster, 2 McLean, 21; Hank *v.* Crittenden, 2 McLean, 557; Holbrow *v.* Wilkins, 1 Barn. & Cress. 10; Id., 2 Dow. & Ry. 59; Reynolds *v.* Douglass, 12 Pet. 497; Carter *v.* White, L. R. 25 Ch. D. 666; Rhett *v.* Poe, 2 How. (U. S.) 457; Walton *v.* Mascall, 13 Mees. & Wels. 72; Gasquet *v.* Thorn, 14 La. (Curry), 506. *Contra*, Philips *v.* Astling, 2 Taunt. 206.

[2] Louisville Manuf. Co. *v.* Welch, 10 How. (U. S.) 461; Johnson *v.* Wilmarth, 13 Met. (Mass.) 416; Bank *v.* Knotts, 10 Rich. Law (S. C.), 513; Leech *v.* Hill, 4 Watts (Pa.), 448; Skofield *v.* Haley, 22 Me. 164; Beebe *v.* Dudley, 26 N. H. 249; Farmers' & Mechanics' Bank *v.* Kercheval, 2 Mich. 504; Union Bank *v.* Coster's Ex'r, 3 N. Y. 203; Wolfe *v.* Browne, 5 Ohio St. 304; Reynolds *v.* Douglass, 12 Pet. 497; Gillighan *v.* Boardman, 29 Me. 79; Bashford *v.* Shaw, 4 Ohio St. 264; Voltz *v.* Harris, 40 Ill. 155; Fear *v.* Dunlap, 1 Greene (Iowa), 331; Fuller *v.* Scott, 8 Kan. 25; Withers *v.* Berry, 25 Kan. 373; Wildes *v.* Savage, 1 Story, 22. To the same effect, see many other cases cited in this chapter to other points.

[3] Woodson *v.* Moody, 4 Humph. (Tenn.) 303.

[4] Gibbs *v.* Cannon, 9 Serg. & Rawle (Pa.), 198; Overton *v.* Tracey, 14 Serg. & Rawle (Pa.), 311.

[5] March *v.* Putney, 56 N. H. 34, per

the law on this subject, as follows: "The guarantor is entitled to notice, but cannot defend himself for want of it, unless the notice has been so long delayed as to raise a presumption of payment, or waiver, or, unless he can show that he has lost, by the delay, opportunities for obtaining securities, which a notice, or an earlier notice, would have secured him. . . . If the notice be delayed for a very short time, but by reason of the delay the guarantor loses the opportunity of obtaining indemnity, and is irreparably damaged, he would be discharged from his obligation. But if the delay were for a long period, and it was nevertheless clear that the guarantor would have derived no benefit from an earlier notice, the delay would not impair his obligation."[1] When the guaranty is such from its terms, or otherwise, that notice is necessary to put the guarantor in default, such notice may, if the principal be insolvent when the debt becomes due, and so remain, be given at any time before suit brought, and the same diligence is not required as in cases where the principal is solvent when the debt becomes due. The insolvency of the principal has a controlling influence on the question of the reasonable time in which notice should be given.[2]

§ 203. **What is the reasonable time within which notice must be given — Pleading.**— No general rule can be laid down as to the time within which notice of the acceptance of the guaranty, or of the default of the principal, must be given the guarantor when such notice is necessary. All that can be said is, that the notice must be given within a reasonable time, the circumstances of each particular case being considered.[3] What is such reasonable time has been held to be a question of law,[4] especially where there is no dispute about

Stanley, J. See, also, Dearborn *v.* Sawyer, 59 N. H. 95.

[1] Second Nat. Bank *v.* Gaylord, 34 Iowa, 246, per Day, J. To same effect, see Davis Sewing Machine Co. *v.* Mills, 55 Iowa, 543; Singer Manuf. Co. *v.* Littler, 56 Iowa, 601.

[2] Salem Manuf. Co. *v.* Brower, 4 Jones' Law (N. C.), 429; Protection Ins. Co. *v.* Davis, 5 Allen, 54; Paige *v.* Parker, 8 Gray, 211; Salisbury *v.* Hale, 12 Pick. 416. See, also, on this subject, Reynolds *v.* Edney, 8 Jones' Law (N. C.), 406.

[3] Montgomery *v.* Kellogg, 43 Miss. 486; Howe *v.* Nickels, 22 Me. 175.

[4] Salem Mfg. Co. *v.* Brower, 4 Jones' Law (N. C.), 429; Craft *v.* Isham, 13 Conn. 28.

the facts.[1] This question can very seldom, however, be resolved into a mere question of law, to be decided by the court, but must generally be a mixed question of law and fact, to be determined by the jury under proper instructions by the court.[2] It has been held that in determining whether notice of the acceptance of a continuing guaranty has been given within a reasonable time, reference must be had to the time of the acceptance of the guaranty, and not to the last sale under it.[3] Where a guaranty was a continuing one for certain drafts to be accepted, it was held that if the course of dealing between the parties was sufficient to justify a finding that the guarantor had notice of acceptance, it might be inferred that notice accompanied each transaction. The guaranty being continuous, the notice would be continuous also.[4] When notice of default in payment on the part of the principal is necessary to charge the guarantor, the declaration should aver the notice; but a general statement of notice, as "of which premises the defendant had due notice," is sufficient.[5] If notice is alleged in the declaration when it is not necessary, in order to charge the guarantor, the allegation may be treated as surplusage, and need not be proved.[6]

§ 204. How notice may be proved — What amounts to waiver of it.— When notice to the guarantor is necessary in order to charge him, such notice need not be proved by direct evidence, but may be inferred from circumstances.[7] The no-

[1] Seaver *v.* Bradley, 6 Greenl. (Me.) 60.

[2] Lowry *v.* Adams, 22 Vt. 160; Louisville Manuf. Co. *v.* Welch, 10 How. (U. S.) 461; Wadsworth *v.* Allen, 8 Gratt. (Va.) 174; Seaver *v.* Bradley, 6 Greenl. (Me.) 60.

[3] Mussey *v.* Rayner, 22 Pick. 223.

[4] First Nat. Bank of Dubuque *v.* Carpenter, 41 Iowa, 518.

[5] Lewis *v.* Brewster, 2 McLean, 121; Oaks *v.* Weller, 16 Vt. 63. That failure to give notice of the non-performance of a guarantied contract, where loss results to the guarantor, is matter of defense, see Furst & Bradley Mfg. Co. *v.* Black, 111 Ind. 308; Stanley *v.* Stanley, 112 Ind. 143; Snyder *v.* Click, 112 Ind. 293; Wells, Fargo & Co. *v.* Davis, 2 Utah Terr. 411.

[6] Gibbs *v.* Cannon, 9 Serg. & Rawle (Pa.), 198.

[7] Rankin *v.* Childs, 9 Mo. 665; Lawton *v.* Mauer, 9 Rich. Law (S. C.), 335; Ruffner *v.* Love, 33 Ill. App. 601. Written notice to a guarantor of the default of a lessee, with a certificate of the sheriff that he had served the same upon the guarantor, is competent evidence of service of the notice. Taylor *v.* Taylor, 64 Ind. 356.

tice need not be in writing nor in any particular form.[1] It may be given by letter.[2] It need not be given by the creditor. If knowledge is brought to the guarantor in any manner he can protect himself.[3] It may be inferred from what took place at the time of giving the guaranty, subsequent casual conversations of the guarantor with third persons, and his conduct and remarks in reference to the collection of the demand of the person for whose benefit the guaranty was given.[4] It is sufficient if the notice is given by the person for whom the guarantor became holden.[5] Notice of "about the amount" of goods furnished under a guaranty is sufficient.[6] It has been held that notice was sufficiently shown by the fact that the guarantor and the principal were close neighbors and relatives, and that the guarantor took other steps to further the credit of the principal with the creditor, and knew of advances made by the creditor to the principal.[7] Where a father-in-law lived just across the street from his son-in-law, and frequently passed his store, and dealt with him occasionally, it was held these facts did not constitute notice to the father-in-law of the acceptance of a guaranty for goods to be sold the son-in-law.[8] The fact that the principal and guarantor were relatives and had been partners has been given weight, and, with other circumstances, held to be sufficient evidence of notice to the guarantor.[9] An acknowledgment by the guarantor of his liability and a promise to pay supersedes the necessity of any further evidence of notice of the acceptance of the guaranty,[10] and of default of the principal.[11] Where the guaranty expressly waives demand and notice, the guarantor is liable to an action thereon without previous demand or notice;[12] and in such case the

[1] Reynolds *v.* Douglass, 12 Pet. 497. It need not be in writing unless so stipulated. Lee *v.* Briggs, 39 Mich. 592. See, also, Ruffner *v.* Love, 33 Ill. App. 601.

[2] Dole *v.* Young, 24 Pick. 250.

[3] Griffin *v.* Rembert, 2 Rich. Law, N. S. (S. C.) 410; Oaks *v.* Weller, 16 Vt. 63.

[4] Woodstock Bank *v.* Downer, 27 Vt. 539.

[5] Oaks *v.* Weller, 16 Vt. 63; Noyes *v.* Nichols, 28 Vt. 159; Powell *v.* Chicago Carpet Co., 22 Ill. App. 409.

[6] Noyes *v.* Nichols, 28 Vt. 159. But see Spencer *v.* Carter, 4 Jones' Law (N. C.), 287.

[7] Menard *v.* Scudder, 7 La. Ann. 385.

[8] Craft *v.* Isham, 13 Conn. 28.

[9] Lowry *v.* Adams, 22 Vt. 160.

[10] Peck *v.* Barney, 13 Vt. 93.

[11] Breed *v.* Hillhouse, 7 Conn. 523.

[12] Bickford *v.* Gibbs, 8 Cush. 154. See, also, Bray *v.* Marsh, 75 Me. 452.

guaranty cannot be contradicted by oral evidence of a contemporaneous agreement to collect the note from the principal and of laches in pursuing him.[1] The guarantor cannot complain of want of notice of acceptance of the guaranty when his acts and declarations amount to a waiver of such notice.[2] Where partners have, before dissolution of the firm, waived demand and notice in an indorsement, it will be binding on them after dissolution.[3]

So, in a suit on a bond it is not necessary to allege or show any notice to the surety of a default by the principal, where the bond expressly waives "presentment for payment, notice of non-payment, protest or notice of protest, and diligence." Murphy *v.* Victor Sew. Mach. Co., 112 U. S. 688. And see, to same effect, Crittenden *v.* Fiske, 46 Mich. 70.

[1] Worcester Co. Institution *v.* Davis, 13 Gray, 531.

[2] Trefethen *v.* Locke, 16 La. Ann. 19. As where he guaranties a note "unconditionally at all times," — in such event he thereby waives demand and notice of acceptance. Davis *v.* Wells, 104 U. S. 159.

[3] Star Wagon Co. *v.* Swezy, 59 Iowa, 609.

CHAPTER IX.

OF THE RIGHTS OF THE SURETY OR GUARANTOR AGAINST THE PRINCIPAL.

Promise by principal to indemnify surety implied — When cause of action accrues to surety . . . . § 205
General principles respecting surety's right to indemnity . 206
Surety may pay by instalments, and sue principal for every instalment—Implied contract of indemnity arises when surety becomes bound . . 207
Surety who pays the debt may sue principal in *assumpsit*, and is entitled to full indemnity from all or any one of the principals 208
When joint sureties can, and when they cannot, maintain joint suit for indemnity . . 209
Surety who has not been requested to become such cannot recover indemnity — Surety who pays may immediately sue principal without demand or notice 210
Snrety who pays the debt with his own note or property may at once sue the principal for indemnity 211
Surety who extinguishes the debt for less than the full amount can only recover from principal the value of what he paid 212
Surety can only recover from principal the amount paid, and not consequential or indirect damages 213
Effect of judgment against surety on liability of principal for indemnity — Notice — Statute of limitations, etc. . § 214
How claim of surety against principal affected by usury — Wager 215
When surety of one partner entitled to recover indemnity from the firm 216
When principal liable to surety for costs paid by surety . . 217
Mortgage for indemnity of surety valid — What it covers 218
Rights of surety who has been indemnified 219
Effect of the bankruptcy of the principal on the surety's claim for indemnity 220
When surety may by express contract recover indemnity from principal before paying the debt — Mortgage of indemnity, etc. 221
When special contract of indemnity will not authorize surety to recover before paying the debt, etc. 222
Surety may, before paying the debt, bring suit in chancery to compel principal to pay it 223
Cases in which a surety may have relief in equity before paying the debt 224
Cases in which a surety cannot recover indemnity from the principal 225

Set-off — Surety may bid at execution sale of principal's property — Surety may assign his claim against the principal, etc. . . . . . § 226
When insolvent principal cannot collect debt due him by surety — Verbal guarantor who pays debt may recover indemnity — Other cases . . 227
Surety on note who pays without notice of failure of consideration may recover indemnity — When surety, who has joined in fraudulent scheme with principal, may recover indemnity — Other cases . . . . § 228
Other cases as to rights of surety against principal 229
Statute of limitations as between surety and principal . . . 230
When surety may replevy property of principal 231
When surety has lien on property of principal 232

§ 205. Promise by principal to indemnify surety implied — When cause of action accrues to surety.— Upon payment by the surety or guarantor of the debt for which he is bound, the same being then due, a right of action for reimbursement immediately arises in his favor and against the principal.[1] In the absence of an express agreement the law implies a promise of indemnity on the part of the principal.[2] If the debt is due, the right of action on this implied promise accrues to the surety or guarantor at the time he pays the debt or a part of it, and not before.[3] Consequently a surety cannot commence an attachment suit against his principal before the note he has signed is due, and before he has paid it, under the provision of a statute allowing an attachment to be brought in certain cases where "nothing but time is wanting to fix an absolute indebtedness." Here something besides time is wanting, for the principal may pay the debt when due

[1] And it is no objection to a recovery in such action that such payment was made upon a judgment recovered by the creditor against them both. The surety by reason of such payment is entitled to the benefit of the judgment against the principal and may enforce it against him by execution. Kimmel *v.* Lowe, 28 Minn. 265. And see, also, Wilson *v.* Crawford, 47 Iowa, 469.

[2] Martin *v.* Ellerbe's Adm'r, 70 Ala. 326.

[3] Pigon *v.* French, 1 Wash. (U. S.) 278; Ford *v.* Stobridge, Nels. 24; Forest *v.* Shores, 11 La. (Curry), 416; Cotton *v.* Alexander, 32 Kan. 339; Harper *v.* McVeigh, 82 Va. 751; Lee *v.* Wisner, 38 Mich. 82; Lane *v.* Westmoreland, 79 Ala. 372; Stearns *v.* Irwin, 62 Ind. 558; Covey *v.* Neff, 63 Ind. 391. And this is true with respect to the estate of the principal. Surety cannot seek to charge his principal's estate until he has first paid the debt. *In re* Estate of Hill, 67 Cal. 238.

and the surety never be damnified.[1] Judgment was obtained against a surety on a note which he paid. The amount of the note was within the jurisdiction of a justice of the peace, but the amount of the judgment, and which was paid, was not. *Held*, the surety could not sue for indemnity before a justice, as his cause of action arose upon payment of the judgment and was for the amount paid.[2] A surety who had not paid the debt for which he had become bound had effects of the principal in his hands which had not been left with him for his indemnity. He was summoned as garnishee of the principal, and it was held that he was liable even though he was afterwards sued for, and obliged to pay, the debt of the principal. He had no right of action against the principal when summoned as garnishee.[3] If the surety takes a bond of indemnity from the principal, it has been held that he cannot upon paying the debt sue the principal upon an implied promise, but is confined to his remedy on the bond upon the ground that "Promises in law only exist where there is no express stipulation."[4] But it has been held that where a surety takes security for his indemnity from a stranger, the presumption is that it is cumulative, and the implied obligation of the principal to indemnify the surety is not waived or merged.[5] The implied promise of indemnity arises in favor of the surety who pays the debt without suit against him.[6] The surety may, without the request of the principal, pay the debt before it is due, and after it is due sue the principal for indemnity. In such case the cause of action accrues to the surety at the time the debt becomes due.[7] With reference to this matter an eminent judge has said: "Why may not a surety take measures of precaution against loss from a change in the circumstances of his principal and accept terms of compromise before the day which may not be attainable after it? He may ultimately have to bear the burden of the debt, and may therefore provide for the contingency by reducing the weight of

[1] Dennison *v.* Soper, 33 Iowa, 183.

[2] Blake *v.* Downey, 51 Mo. 437.

[3] Ingalls *v.* Dennett, 6 Greenl. (Me.) 79.

[4] Toussaint *v.* Martinnant, 2 Durn. & East, 100, per Buller, J.

[5] Wesley Church *v.* Moore, 10 Pa. St. 273. See, to this point, Water Power Co. *v.* Brown, 23 Kan. 676.

[6] Mauri *v.* Heffernan, 13 Johns. 58.

[7] White *v.* Miller, 47 Ind. 385; Tillotson *v.* Rose, 11 Met. (Mass.) 299.

it. Nor is he bound to subject himself to the risk of an action by waiting till the creditor has a cause of action. He may, in short, consult his own safety, and resort to any measure calculated to assure him of it which does not involve a wanton sacrifice of the interests of his principal."[1]

§ 206. **General principles respecting surety's right to indemnity.**— A surety seeking indemnity from his principal must sue in his own name; he cannot sue in the name of his obligee.[2] A surety's right to indemnity cannot be defeated because the principal's name did not appear in the body of the obligation,[3] nor because he did not execute it.[4] To deprive a surety, who has been damnified, of recourse upon his principal for indemnity, it must appear in the obligation in distinct terms, and is then strictly construed.[5] Where a stranger pays the principal's debt and the surety reimburses him, the surety is entitled to be indemnified by the principal.[6] The fact that a surety suffered judgment to go against him by default, contrary to a statute prohibiting sureties from permitting judgments against them by default, has been held not to defeat his right of indemnity from the principal for money paid on such judgment.[7]

§ 207. **Surety may pay by instalments, and sue principal for every instalment — Implied contract of indemnity arises when surety becomes bound.**— When the debt becomes due the surety may pay a part of it and immediately sue the principal for the amount so paid. If he pays different parts at different times, he may sue the principal for each part when he pays it. This is not making several claims of one, because the debt due the creditor is not the surety's cause of action. His cause of action is the payment which he has made for the principal, and it is complete the instant he makes the payment.[8] "However convenient it might be to limit the number of ac-

But he cannot sue for indemnity before the debt is due. Ross *v.* Menefee, 125 Ind. 432.

[1] Gibson, C. J., in Craig *v.* Craig, 5 Rawle (Pa.), 91.

[2] Hardware Co. *v.* Deere, Mansur & Co., 53 Ark. 140.

[3] Harnsberger *v.* Yancey, 33 Gratt. (Va.) 527.

[4] Trustees of Schools *v.* Sheik *et al.*, 119 Ill. 579.

[5] Thomas *v.* Liebke, 81 Mo. 675, affirming 9 Mo. App. 424.

[6] Harper's Adm'r *v.* McVeigh's Adm'r, 82 Va. 751.

[7] Riley *v.* Stallworth, 56 Ala. 481.

[8] Bullock *v.* Campbell, 9 Gill (Md.), 182; Williams, Adm'r, *v.* Williams,

tions in respect of one suretyship, there is no rule of law which requires the surety to pay the whole debt before he can call for reimbursement."[1] A surety paid the creditor part of the amount due on a note with a view of reducing it within the jurisdiction of a justice of the peace, and sued the principal for the sum so paid. *Held*, that as he was bound for the debt he had a right to make a partial payment and recover the amount paid without regard to the intent with which the payment was made.[2] Although the surety cannot, in the absence of express contract, sue the principal for indemnity before he actually pays the debt, yet the implied contract for indemnity arises immediately upon the surety becoming bound. The law upon this point has been thus stated: "It is clear that the contract of a principal with his surety to indemnify him for any payment which the latter may make to the creditor, in consequence of the liability assumed, takes effect from the time when the surety becomes responsible for the debt of the principal. It is then that the law raises the implied contract or promise of indemnity. No new contract is made when the money is paid by the surety, but the payment relates back to the time when the contract was entered into by which the liability to pay was incurred. The payment only fixes the amount of damages for which the principal is liable under his original agreement to indemnify the surety."[3] This was held in a case where the question was whether the principal was entitled to a homestead. The same principle was held where a voluntary conveyance was made by the principal after the surety became bound, but before he paid the debt, and the conveyance was set aside at the suit of the surety.[4] A. was indebted to B. in $100, but he was surety for B. for $500. B. conveyed all his accounts to an assignee before A. paid anything on account of his suretyship; afterwards A. paid the amount for which he was liable as surety. *Held*, the assignee

Adm'r, 5 Ohio, 444; Pickett *v.* Bates, 3 La. Ann. 627.

[1] Davies *v.* Humphreys, 6 Mees. & Wels., per Parke, B.

[2] Hall *v.* Hall, 10 Humph. (Tenn.) 352.

[3] Per Bigelow, J., in Rice *v.* Southgate, 16 Gray, 142. See, further, as to when the implied contract for indemnity arises. Miller *v.* Stout, 5 Del. Ch. 259; Zollickoffer *v.* Feth, 44 Md. 359; Martin *v.* Ellerbe's Adm'r, 70 Ala. 326.

[4] Choteau *v.* Jones, 11 Ill. 300. To similar effect, see Hatfield *v.* Merod, 82 Ill. 113.

could recover nothing from A. The court said: "We think there exists in a surety an equity from the time of his assuming the relation, by virtue of the implied undertaking on the part of the principal to see him indemnified, and that although no perfect right of action accues until actual payment, still such payment has such reference to the original undertaking of suretyship, that it overrides any equities of a subsequent date."[1]

§ 208. **Surety who pays the debt may sue principal in assumpsit, and is entitled to full indemnity from all or any one of the principals.**— The surety or guarantor who has paid the debt of the principal may maintain an action of *assumpsit* against the principal for money paid at his request.[2] It has been held that if the surety in any way (as by his land being sold on execution) extinguishes or pays the debt of the principal, it is, so far as the principal is concerned, equivalent to paying money for his benefit and at his request, and the surety may maintain general *assumpsit* against the principal for money paid.[3] The surety cannot recover indemnity from the principal by an action in tort.[4] If one of several joint guarantors pays the debt for which all are bound, he has thereby a separate right of right of action against the prin-

[1] Barney *v.* Grover, 28 Vt. 391, per Redfield, C. J. See, also, Morrow *v.* Morrow, 2 Tenn. Ch. (Cooper), 549; Loughridge *v.* Bowland, 52 Miss. 546.

[2] Morrice *v.* Redwyn, 2 Barnardiston, 26; Davies *v.* Humphreys, 6 Mees. & Wels. 153; Ford *v.* Keith, 1 Mass. 139; Exall *v.* Partridge, 8 Durn. & East, 308; Warrington *v.* Furbor, 8 East, 242. See, also, Crisfield *v.* State, 55 Md. 192. But in equity the surety is subrogated to all the securities held by the creditor (Ferguson's Adm'r *v.* Carson's Adm'r, 86 Mo. 673; Crisfield *v.* State, 55 Md. 192), and the rule at common law does not apply. Where a surety pays the note of his principal and then has the note assigned to him, it is held he cannot sue his principal on the note, but may maintain an action of implied *assumpsit* against him for the sum paid. Frevert *v.* Henry, 14 Nev. 191. A statutory remedy given a surety against his principal for money paid is held to be cumulative merely, and does not preclude a common-law action. Riley *v.* Stallworth, 56 Ala. 481.

[3] Hulett *v.* Soullard, 26 Vt. 295. The payment of a note by a surety is not, as between himself and the principal, an extinguishment of the same, and his right of action against the principal is held to be upon the note, and not on an implied *assumpsit.* Tutt *v.* Thornton, 57 Tex. 35, overruling Holliman *v.* Rogers, 6 Tex. 1. But see directly the contrary in Frevert *v.* Henry, 14 Nev. 191.

[4] Ledbetter *v.* Torney, 11 Ired. Law (N. C.), 294.

cipal.[1] The law implies a several *assumpsit* by the principal to reimburse the surety who pays the debt; and, therefore, if the surety who pays the debt releases his co-surety from all claim for contribution, such release does not affect his claim for indemnity against the principal.[2] Unless there is an express agreement to the contrary, the surety is entitled to claim indemnity from all his principals. Thus certain parties, being appointed executors of a will, part of them made a joint bond as such, and a surety also signed the bond. Afterwards A., another of the executors, signed the bond. There was but the one surety, and, when he signed the bond, he stated that he signed it as surety for B., one of the executors, and wished the other executors to get different bondsmen. B. was guilty of a default and died, and afterwards judgment was recovered on the bond against the surviving executors, including A., and also against the surety. The surety paid the judgment, and sued all the surviving executors for indemnity. *Held*, that A., by signing the bond subsequent to the time the surety signed, recognized the surety as his surety, and this was equivalent to a previous request, and that A. and all the surviving executors were liable for the indemnity of the surety.[3] If the surety is bound for several principals, he is entitled to recover from any one of them the whole of what he has paid. Each of the principals is debtor for the whole of the debt to the creditor, and the surety, being liable for each of them, has, by paying the debt, freed each of them from the creditors' claim for the whole, and consequently has a right to recover the whole amount from any one of them.[4] He may recover the whole amount from the surviving one of two principals,[5] or from the estate of a deceased principal where there are several surviving principals.[6]

[1] Lowry *v.* Lumbermen's Bank, 2 Watts & Serg. (Pa.) 210.

[2] Crowdus *v.* Shelby, 6 J. J. Marsh. (Ky.) 61.

[3] Babcock *v.* Hubbard, 2 Conn. 536. Where H. made a note indorsed by W. and R. and sent to T., who was obliged to indorse it in order that it might be discounted, and he was subsequently compelled to pay it, *held*, that he was in equity entitled to full indemnity from H., W. and R. Thompson *v.* Taylor, 12 R. I. 109.

[4] Apgar's Adm'rs *v.* Hiler, 4 Zabr. (N. J.) 812; Dickey *v.* Rogers, 19 Martin (La.), 7 N. S. 588; Bunce *v.* Bunce, Kirby (Conn.), 137; Clay *v.* Severance, 55 Vt. 300.

[5] Riddle *v.* Bowman, 27 N. H. 236.

[6] West *v.* Bank of Rutland, 19 Vt. 403.

§ 209. When joint sureties can, and when they cannot, maintain joint suit for indemnity.— If there are several sureties for the same debt, and each pays a portion of it from his individual momey, they cannot join in a suit against the principal for the money so paid.[1] Where, however, the payment is made by several sureties from a joint fund, they may join in an action against the principal. Thus, two sureties who were jointly liable as such for a debt, borrowed money to pay a portion of it, for which they gave their joint note, and to pay the balance they gave their joint note to the creditor, who accepted it as payment. *Held*, they might properly bring a joint suit for indemnity against the principal.[2] Three parties having jointly guarantied a debt and received a mortgage of indemnity, two of them paid the debt, and they all joined in a bill to foreclose the mortgage. *Held*, they might properly do so.[3] A judgment was rendered against several persons as heirs of a surety, and they gave a surety for a stay of execution, but afterwards paid the judgment. *Held*, they might jointly sue the principal for indemnity. "Their liability arose upon the fact that we must presume that his (the ancestor's) estate came into their hands; otherwise they would not have been responsible. It was their joint debt, then, as heirs," and having made payment jointly they were entitled to join in a suit for indemnity.[4] Where several individuals, acting as partners, and in their partnership name, became sureties for another partnership, and after the dissolution of both partnerships were called upon to pay, and jointly paid, the amount for which they were so liable, it was held that they might maintain a joint action for indemnity.[5] B. and G. were joint sureties, and B. died. His executor was a

[1] Sevier *v.* Roddie, 51 Mo. 580; Parker *v.* Leek, 1 Stew. (Ala.) 523; Appleton *v.* Bascom, 3 Met. (Mass.) 169; Peabody *v.* Chapman, 20 N. H. 418; Bunker *v.* Tufts, 55 Me. 180.

[2] Pearson *v.* Parker, 3 N. H. 366. To same effect, see Whipple *v.* Briggs, 28 Vt. 65, and Enos *v.* Leach, 18 Hun (N. Y.), 139. As to the weight and sufficiency of evidence in such a case, see Romero *v.* Desmarais, 4 N. M. 367.

[3] Dye *v.* Mann, 10 Mich. 291. Holding that sureties who have paid for the default of a tax collector, and been authorized by statute to bring suits for their indemnity against persons owing taxes, may join in such suits, see Prather *v.* Johnson, 3 Harr. & Johns. (Md.) 487.

[4] Snider *v.* Greathouse, 16 Ark. 72.

[5] Dav *v.* Swann, 13 Me. 165.

partner in business with G., and the two partners paid the debt out of their joint funds as partners. *Held*, they could not join in a suit for indemnity. They were not joint sureties, nor was the money paid for a partnership debt. Having made the payment on a matter foreign to their partnership concerns, it operated as a severance of their joint interest in the money paid.[1]

§ 210. Surety who has not been requested to become such cannot recover indemnity — Surety who pays may immediately sue principal without demand or notice.— A surety cannot ordinarily recover indemnity from the principal, unless he became surety at the request of the principal, either express or implied.[2] After a bond had been executed by principal and surety, another person, at the instance of the holder, but without the knowledge or consent of the maker, guarantied the bond by indorsing on it as follows: "This is a good bond." He was compelled to pay the bond, and sued the original surety for indemnity. *Held*, he was not entitled to recover, because he was not an indorser in the usual sense of that term, and he had not been requested to become surety by the party he sought to charge.[3] A. and B. were principals and C. and D. sureties in a bond. Before signing, it was agreed that C. should be the surety of A., and D. the surety of B., but this did not appear from the instrument. C. and D. each paid

[1] Gould *v.* Gould, 8 Cowen, 168.

[2] Ex'rs of White *v.* White, 30 Vt. 338; McPherson *v.* Meek, 30 Mo. 345; King *v.* Hannah, 6 Brad. (Ill. App.) 495. When request to guaranty will be implied, see Ricketson *v.* Giles, 91 Ill. 154. In seeking indemnity from the principal, the surety, it is held, need not allege in his complaint a request from the principal to pay for him. Clanton *v.* Coward, 67 Cal. 373.

[3] Carter *v.* Black, 4 Dev. & Bat. Law (N. C.), 425. But where the principal maker in a promissory note, after others, who, in fact, are sureties for him, had signed the same, procured another person, in their absence and without their knowledge, to indorse the same as guarantor, who was afterwards compelled to pay the same, the fact that the guarantor became liable without the request of the sureties was held no defense in an action against them by the guarantor. They all being liable primarily, a request of any one of them to guaranty payment was the act of all. Hamilton *v.* Johnston, 82 Ill. 39. Where the guarantor pays his principal's obligation because he is legally bound to do so, he is held entitled to indemnity, notwithstanding the guaranty was given and debt paid without request of the principal. Teberg *v.* Swenson, 32 Kan. 224.

one-half of the debt, and A. indemnified C. Afterwards D. sued A. and B. for indemnity. *Held*, he could not recover anything from A. The court said: "The obligation of principals to reimburse to securities the money paid by them is not founded on the bonds which securities give for their principals, but on the express contracts of indemnity which the parties make, or upon the implied promise raised by the law upon the payment of money for another at his request."[1] Where the surety of a surety pays the debt of the principal under a legal obligation from which the principal was bound to relieve him, such payment is a sufficient consideration to raise an implied *assumpsit* on the part of the principal to repay the amount, although the payment was made without a request from the principal.[2] A request may be inferred from circumstances. Thus, a party signed an appeal bond from a judgment by a justice of the peace, as surety for appellants, who appeared in the appellate court and defended the suit, and were beaten, and the surety had to pay a portion of the judgment. *Held* that, from the fact that the principal appeared and defended in the appellate court, a request to the surety to become such would be inferred.[3] A surety who has paid the debt of the principal may at once, without notice to him or making any demand of indemnity, sue him for reimbursement. The contract of indemnity "is supposed to arise at the moment when the surety contracts his obligation, and it is broken the moment when the surety is damnified." It is the duty of the principal to take notice of the fact that the surety has been damnified.[4]

§ 211. **Surety who pays the debt with his own note or property may at once sue the principal for indemnity.**— The surety who, in satisfaction of the debt of the principal, gives his own note, which the creditor receives as payment of the debt, may immediately, and before paying the note given by

[1] Hill *v.* Wright, 23 Ark. 530, per Fairchild, J.

[2] Hall *v.* Smith, 5 How. (U. S.) 96.

[3] Snell *v.* Warner, 63 Ill. 176.

[4] Ward *v.* Henry, 5 Conn. 595, per Bristol, J.; Thompson *v.* Wilson's Ex'r, 13 La. (Curry), 138; Collins *v.* Boyd, 14 Ala. 505; Sikes *v.* Quick, 7 Jones, Law (N. C.), 19. On same subject, see Warrington *v.* Furbor, 8 East, 242.

him, sue the principal for indemnity.[1] A surety gave his note for the debt of the principal, which was accepted by the creditor as payment. The surety never paid the note, became insolvent, and afterwards sued the principal for money paid. *Held*, he was entitled to recover. The court clearly stated the law on this subject, and the reasons for it, thus: "Anything which the party paying and the party receiving think proper to regard as money must generally be so regarded in a court of justice. Property delivered and accepted as money may be so considered. . . . Bank bills, which are nothing but the promissory notes of a corporation, are in all the affairs of life, and in all the courts, regarded as money. A payment of the debt of a third person, at his request, in bank bills, would sustain an action for money paid, laid out and expended. . . . If a surety discharges the debt of his principal by his own note, which is accepted as payment, is it not as much money paid, laid out and expended, as if he had paid it in the notes of a bank?"[2] Where the land of the surety has been levied on to satisfy the debt of the principal, and has been applied to that purpose, the surety may recover indemnity in an action for money paid.[3] A judgment was rendered against principal and surety which was replevied (stayed) by the surety alone. The legal effect of the replevin was to extinguish the judgment. *Held*, the surety might at once sue the principal for indemnity without paying the amount due on the replevin bond.[4] A principal being indebted for rent, he and the cred-

[1] Doolittle *v.* Dwight, 2 Met. (Mass.) 561; Bone *v.* Torrey, 16 Ark. 83; Mims *v.* McDowell, 4 Ga. 182; Pearson *v.* Parker, 3 N. H. 366; Elwood *v.* Deifendorf, 5 Barb. (N. Y.) 398; Witherly *v.* Mann, 11 Johns. 518; White *v.* Miller, 47 Ind. 385; Hommell *v.* Gamewell, 5 Blackf. (Ind.) 5; Sapp *v.* Aiken, 68 Iowa, 699; Rizer *v.* Callen, 27 Kan. 339. *Contra*, where the note given by the surety was non-negotiable. Pitzer *v.* Harmon, 8 Blackf. (Ind.) 112; Bennett *v.* Buchanan, 3 Ind. 47; Romine *v.* Romine, 59 Ind. 346.

[2] Peters *v.* Barnhill, 1 Hill, Law (S. C.), 237, per O'Neall, J. And under the same state of facts it has been held that he was entitled to contribution. McGehee *v.* Owen, 61 Ala. 440. But in Lynch *v.* Hancock, 14 S. C. 66, it was held that where a surety gave his note in payment of a debt he was not entitled to recover the amount of the note from his principal, unless he could show that the note had been paid or that he had the means to pay it. And to same effect, see Stone *v.* Hammell, 83 Cal. 547.

[3] Lord *v.* Staples, 23 N. H. 448; Bonney *v.* Seely, 2 Wend. 481.

[4] Burns *v.* Parish, 3 B. Mon. (Ky.) 8.

itor and a surety met, and the surety gave the creditor a mortgage on his property for an extended time to secure the debt, and the creditor released the principal and received the mortgage in full payment of the debt. *Held*, the surety might sue the principal for money paid before paying the mortgage.[1] It has been held that the possession of a note by the surety, which was signed by him and the principal, was *prima facie* evidence that he had paid it.[2] But it seems that in order to have this effect it must also be shown that the note had been delivered to the payees and was at one time their property.[3]

§ 212. Surety who extinguishes the debt for less than the full amount can only recover from the principal the value of what he paid.— If the surety extinguishes the debt of the principal for any sum less than the full amount thereof, he can, in the absence of express contract, only recover from the principal the amount paid by him,[4] and interest thereon,[5] and costs.[6] The implied contract is that the surety shall be indemnified only, and he will not be allowed to speculate out of his principal. If he pays in depreciated bank notes, or other money which is below par, but is taken by the creditor at par, he can only recover from the principal the par value of such money.[7] If he pays in land he can only recover the value of

[1] McVicar *v.* Royce, 17 Up. Can. (Q. B.) 529. To the effect that the surety cannot sue the principal for money paid when he has made payment by his bond, see Boulware *v.* Robinson, 8 Tex. 327; Morrison *v.* Berkey, 7 Serg. & Rawle (Pa.), 238.

[2] Reynolds *v.* Skelton, 2 Tex. 516.

[3] Landrum *v.* Brookshire, 1 Stew. (Ala.), 252.

[4] Eaton *v.* Lambert, 1 Neb. 339; Pickett *v.* Bates, 3 La. Ann. 627; Coggeshall *v.* Ruggles, 62 Ill. 401; Crozier *v.* Grayson, 4 J. J. Marsh. (Ky.) 514; Blow *v.* Maynard, 2 Leigh (Va.), 29; Mathews *v.* Hall's Adm'r, 21 W. Va. 510; Succession of Dinkgrave, 31 La. Ann. 703; Delaware, Lackawanna & Western R. R. Co. *v.* Oxford Iron Co., 38 N. J. Eq. 151.

[5] Hicks *v.* Baily, 16 Tex. 229; Miles *v.* Bacon, 4 J J. Marsh. (Ky.) 457; Bushong *v.* Taylor, 82 Mo. 660; Waldrip *v.* Black, 74 Cal. 409.

[6] Feamster *v.* Withrow, 12 W. Va. 611. A surety cannot recover attorney's fees from his principal, for which the note provides, when he paid the note at maturity and was not required to incur such expenses. Gieseke, Adm'r, *v.* Johnson, 115 Ind. 308; Carpenter *v.* Minter, 72 Tex. 370.

[7] Kendrick *v.* Forney, 22 Gratt. (Va.) 748; Miles *v.* Bacon, 4 J. J. Marsh. (Ky.) 457; Hall's Adm'r *v.* Creswell, 12 Gill & Johns. (Md.) 36; Crozier *v.* Grayson, 4 J. J. Marsh. (Ky.) 514; Butler *v.* Butler's Adm'r, 8 W. Va. 674; Feamster *v.* Withrow, 9 W. Va. 296; 12 W. Va. 611; Matthews *v.* Hall's Adm'r, 21 W. Va. 510. See, also, on this subject, Edmonds *v.* Sheahan, 47 Tex. 443.

the land. "He is entitled to recover the amount paid, not the amount extinguished by that payment."[1] A surety paid the debt of his principal to a bank, a small portion in bills of the bank, and the balance by his note to the bank. During all that time the notes of the bank were worth only fifty cents on the dollar, but the bank received them at par for debts due it. *Held*, that as the bank had received the note of the surety as payment of the debt, he might, before paying the note, sue the principal for indemnity, but could only recover fifty per cent. of the amount of the note and the actual value of the money he had paid, that being the extent of his damage.[2] If the surety, who compounds a debt for which his principal and himself have become jointly liable, takes an assignment of the debt to a trustee for himself, he can only claim against his principal the amount which he has paid. He occupies in that regard the same position as an agent, and cannot speculate out of his principal. "It is on a contract for indemnity that the surety becomes liable for the debt. It is by virtue of that situation, and because he is under an obligation as between himself and the creditor of his principal, that he is enabled to make the arrangement with that creditor. It is his duty to make the best terms he can for the person in whose behalf he is acting."[3]

§ 213. **Surety can only recover from principal the amount paid, and not consequential or indirect damages.**— In the absence of an express agreement to the contrary, a surety who has paid the debt of his principal can only recover from the principal the amount paid by him. He cannot recover anything for what he has been obliged to sacrifice, by selling his property for less than its value, nor for any incidental loss. "To these disadvantages he voluntarily exposes himself when he becomes surety, and the law affords him no relief against his principal for these consequential damages. . . . To

[1] Bonney *v.* Seely, 2 Wend. 481, per Savage, C. J.

[2] Jordan, Adm'r, *v.* Adams, 7 Ark. (2 Eng.) 348.

[3] Reed *v.* Norris, 2 Mylne & Craig, 361, per Lord Cottenham, C. *Contra*, Blow *v.* Maynard, 2 Leigh (Va.), 29, where it is said that there is nothing in the relation of principal and surety which will prevent the surety from buying the claim against the principal, and taking an assignment of it and holding it for the full amount, the same as a stranger might.

establish a different rule would create endless confusion, collusion, combination and fraud."[1] He cannot, when he has not paid the debt, but has been discharged under an insolvent act, recover from the principal damages which he has suffered by being imprisoned on account of the debt.[2] He may agree with his principal upon a certain price for the use of his credit, but unless there is a special agreement he can recover nothing for it. It has been held that where there is an express agreement that something shall be paid, nothing can be recovered unless the sum to be paid is fixed by the agreement.[3] A party became surety in a duty bond to the United States, which was captured in time of war by the English, and by them a capias was issued against the obligors in the bond. The surety fled, to avoid being arrested, and thereby his business was broken up and he was put to great expense, and not having paid the bond, he sued certain parties for indemnity who had agreed to save him harmless. *Held*, he was not entitled to recover. The court said that if a surety is broken up by paying the debt of his principal, he cannot recover for such consequential damages. "Flight to avoid payment of the debt is an accident wholly unforeseen, and its consequences cannot be considered as provided for. The principal had a right to calculate upon his surety's ability to pay, and did not stipulate to save him harmless from anything but the payment of money."[4]

§ 214. Effect of judgment against surety on liability of principal for indemnity — Notice — Statute of limitations, etc.— The surety on a note, who, without knowing of a defense, has let judgment go against him by default, and has paid the judgment, may recover indemnity from the principal, notwithstanding the fact that the principal, who was sued at the same court in another suit, by defending the same obtained a judgment in his favor. "To the suggestion that the surety might have resisted and defeated the recovery, he may reply that he was a stranger to the consideration of the note, and

[1] Vance *v.* Lancaster, 3 Haywood (Tenn.), 130, per Roane, J. See, also, to effect that surety can only recover from the principal or his estate the amount actually expended, *In re* Estate of Hill, 67 Cal. 238.

[2] Powell *v.* Smith, 8 Johns. 249.

[3] Perrine *v.* Hotchkiss, 58 Barb. (N. Y.) 77.

[4] Hayden *v.* Cabot, 17 Mass. 169, per Parker, C. J.

was privy to nothing more than the terms of an absolute obligation, which he bound himself to make good, if not punctually fulfilled. But if he had been made privy to the principal's defense, then he might have lost his right to redress."[1] So, where principal and surety were sued on a note, and the signature of the principal not being proved on the trial, judgment was had against the surety alone, which he paid, it was held that he might recover indemnity from the principal.[2] If the principal has notice of the suit against his surety, he is bound by the result of the litigation, and a foreign judgment has the same effect in this regard as one of the courts in which the suit for indemnity is brought.[3] In such case, the principal cannot complain that the suit was unskilfully defended by the surety.[4] The fact that when a surety is sued he fails to notify his principal of such suit will not preclude him from recovering indemnity.[5] If the surety on a bond which ought probably to have been avoided on the ground of illegality in the consideration has made a reasonable defense in a suit brought on the bond, and has been defeated and paid the judgment, he may recover indemnity from the principal.[6] A surety sued in one state on a warranty of a slave there made may in another state recover against his principal, who had notice of the pendency of such suit, whatever is legally adjudged against the surety by the laws of the state in which the suit against him was brought.[7] The administratrix of a surety was sued for the debt of the principal after it was barred by the statute of limitations as to the estate of the surety, but before it was barred by the statute as against the principal. Instead of pleading the statute, she submitted the matter to referees, who

[1] Stinson *v.* Brennan, Cheves' Law (S. C.), 15, per Butler, J. The fact, also, that he suffered judgment against him by default, contrary to a statute prohibiting sureties from allowing judgments to go against them by confession on default, is held to make no difference in their right to indemnity for money paid on such judgment. Riley *v.* Stallworth, 56 Ala. 481.

[2] Peters *v.* Barnhill, 1 Hill's Law (S. C.), 234.

[3] Konitzky *v.* Meyer, 49 N. Y. 571. See, also, on this subject, Hare *v.* Grant, 77 N. C. 203.

[4] Rice *v.* Rice, 14 B. Mon. (Ky.) 335.

[5] Williams *v.* Greer, 4 Haywood (Tenn.), 235.

[6] Montgomery *v.* Russell, 10 La. (Curry), 330.

[7] Thomas *v.* Beckman, 1 B. Mon. (Ky.) 29.

awarded that she should pay the debt, which she did. *Held*, the principal was liable to reimburse the money so paid. The principal was liable to pay the debt, and it made no difference to him that the surety had done so, without insisting on the bar of the statute.[1] But where a party was surety for another in a bond replevying an execution, and by statute in such case, if an execution was not issued by the creditor within one year after he had a right to issue it, the surety was discharged, and execution was not so issued, and the surety, after he was discharged by the terms of the law, paid the debt, without having it assigned to him, it was held he could not recover indemnity from the principal. As he was under no obligation to pay the debt, the law would not imply a contract of indemnity.[2]

§ 215. **How claim of surety against principal affected by usury — Wager.**— If the surety to a contract tainted with usury of which he has knowledge pays the usury, it has been held that he cannot recover such usury from the principal, but can only recover what the creditor could have recovered.[3] But where the surety on an usurious note, who did not know of the usury when he signed it, but had knowledge of the fact when he paid it, sued the principal for indemnity, it was held he was entitled to recover unless he had been notified by the principal not to pay the note before he paid it. The principal might avail himself of the statute against usury, but was not obliged to do so, and the surety could not know his intention in that regard, unless notified thereof.[4] So, where the creditor had recovered a judgment against principal and surety, and the surety had paid the judgment, it was held that the principal could not set up against the claim of the surety for

[1] Shaw *v.* Loud, 12 Mass. 447.

[2] Kimble *v.* Cummins, 3 Met. (Ky.) 327. Neither does he occupy any better attitude than a mere stranger or volunteer, and he cannot therefore be substituted to the creditor's rights against the principal or the principal's vendee. Dawson *v.* Lee, 83 Ky. 49; Lee *v.* Hill, 83 Ky. 49.

[3] Jones *v.* Joyner, 8 Ga. 562; Mims *v.* McDowell, 4 Ga. 182; Whitehead *v.* Peck, 1 Kelly (Ga.), 140. But see, however, Jackson *v.* Jackson, 51 Vt. 253.

[4] Ford *v.* Keith, 1 Mass. 139. For a case holding (under peculiar circumstances) that a surety can recover indemnity from the principal for usury which he has been compelled to pay, see Kock *v.* Block, 29 Ohio St. 565.

indemnity the fact that part of the judgment was for usury.[1] A surety having become liable on a note, the principal executed to him a bill of sale of chattels for his indemnity. *Held*, the bill of sale was executed upon sufficient consideration, even though the original note was usurious, unless the surety was privy to the usury.[2] Where a note was given to secure money bet in the state of Missouri, on the election of a president of the United States (such bet being prohibited by law), and a surety on the note, who knew when he signed it the consideration for which it was given, was compelled by legal process in a foreign jurisdiction to pay the same, it was held he could not recover indemnity from the principal. He was privy to an illegal transaction, and could ground no claim to relief upon it. If the principal could be in this manner compelled to pay, the policy of the law in making the note void would be defeated.[3]

§ 216. When surety of one partner entitled to recover indemnity from the firm.— When a partner gives his individual note, with surety, for a debt of the firm, and the surety pays it, he may recover indemnity at law from all the members of the firm.[4] The same thing was held where the note was under seal.[5] A. and B. were partners, and A. hired help for which the firm would on general principles of law have been liable, but gave his individual bond with C. as his surety for the hire. C. had the debt to pay, and brought a suit in equity to recover indemnity from A. and B. *Held*, he was entitled to recover from both.[6] One of several partners executed a bond in his individual name to the United States, for duties on goods imported on account of the partnership, and the plaintiffs executed the bond as sureties. The plaintiffs paid the debt and brought an action for money paid against

[1] Wade *v.* Green, 3 Humph. (Tenn.) 547. Or that the original contract between himself and the creditors was tainted with usury. Maples *v.* Cox, 74 Ga. 701; Turman *v.* Looper, 42 Ark. 500. But see Lucking's Adm'r *v.* Gegg, 12 Bush (Ky.), 298.

[2] Spaulding *v.* Austin, 2 Vt. 555.

[3] Hurley *v.* Stapleton's Adm'r, 24 Mo. 248.

[4] Burns *v.* Parish, 3 B. Mon. (Ky.) 8; Hikes *v.* Crawford, 4 Bush (Ky.), 19; McKee *v.* Hamilton, 33 Ohio St. 7.

[5] Purviance *v.* Sutherland, 2 Ohio St. 478.

[6] Weaver *v.* Tapscott, 9 Leigh (Va.), 424.

all the partners. *Held*, they were not entitled to recover, as there was no privity between them and the partners, who did not sign the bond. The bond being under seal discharged the claim of the United States for the duties, and its remedy was thereafter on the bond, and against the parties alone who signed it. The remedy of the sureties was against the partner who signed the bond, although the court in one case said it might be, if such partner was insolvent and the firm owed him, the sureties could have relief in equity.[1]

§ 217. When principal liable to surety for costs paid by surety.— Whether the surety, who has paid costs on account of the debt of the principal, can recover such costs from the principal, depends upon the circumstances of each case. It has been held that he may recover from the principal costs which he has in good faith incurred and paid, litigating the claim upon which he is surety.[2] An eminent judge, in discussing this subject, said: "If, when a surety was sued upon the debt of his principal, and was unable to pay it, and the same went into judgment and was levied upon his land, he must lose all costs recovered, and the expenses of the levy, because he did not pay the principal's debt more promptly than the debtor himself, whose duty it was to do it, and save the surety all trouble, it would certainly afford a remarkable instance of absurd refinement, not to say refined absurdity; and if the debt may be recovered (by the surety of the principal) as money paid, so equally may the costs."[3] Where a joint judg-

[1] Embree *v.* Ellis, 2 Johns. 119; Krafts *v.* Creighton, 3 Rich. Law (S. C.), 273.

[2] Downer *v.* Baxter, 30 Vt. 467; Bennett *v.* Dowling, 22 Tex. 660; Borlaud *v.* Curry, Irish Law Rep. (4 Q. B., C. P. & Ex.) 273; Feamster *v.* Withrow, 12 W. Va. 611. See, also, on this subject, Whitworth *v.* Tilman, 40 Miss. 76; Thompson *v.* Taylor, 11 Hun (N. Y.) 274; affirmed in 72 N. Y. 32.

[3] Per Redfield, C. J., in Hulett *v.* Soullard, 26 Vt. 295. To same effect, see Wynn *v.* Brooke, 5 Rawle (Pa.), 106; McKee *v.* Campbell, 27 Mich. 497. "But the principal is not liable for costs and expenses unnecessarily incurred by the surety in litigation carried on by him in order to get rid of his liability or defeat the efforts of a party seeking to enforce it." . . . "It is incumbent on the surety, seeking to recover from his principal costs and expenses incurred in litigation, to show that the litigation was entered into in good faith and upon reasonable grounds, and was a measure of defense, necessary to the interest of both parties, and was calculated so to result. Cranmer *v.* McSwords, 26 W. Va. 412.

ment is recovered against principal and surety, and the surety pays the judgment and costs, he may recover such costs from the principal. The principal has a right to defend the suit, and the surety is justified in letting the claim proceed to judgment, in the hope that the money may be made from the principal.[1] If the principal has agreed, in writing, to save the surety harmless, the surety may, on such agreement, recover costs which he has paid on account of the principal's debt.[2] If the surety on a note, who is indemnified from loss on account of his suretyship, incurs expenses in defending a suit on the note, contrary to the expressed wishes of the principal, and after he is notified by the principal that there is no defense, he cannot hold the principal liable for such expenses.[3] It has been held that where a surety knows there is no defense to the suit against him, he can recover no costs except those of a judgment by default.[4] A. undertook to pay certain debts of B., and C. guarantied A.'s undertaking. A. failed to pay one of the debts, and B. was sued for it, and a judgment was had against him for the amount due and costs of suit. *Held*, B. could not recover such costs from C. He should have paid the debt without suit, and prevented the making of costs.[5]

§ 218. Mortgage for indemnity of surety valid — What it covers.— The liability of a surety or guarantor for the debt of his principal before he has made any payment on account thereof is a sufficient consideration for the execution of a mortgage or trust deed for his indemnity, and such mortgage or trust deed will take precedence of any subsequent lien on the property incumbered thereby.[6] A promissory note for the payment of a certain sum of money executed for the purpose of indemnifying the payee against his liability as a surety for

[1] Apgar's Adm'r *v.* Hiler, 4 Zab. (N. J.) 812.

[2] Bonney *v.* Seely, 2 Wend. 481.

[3] Beckley *v.* Munson, 22 Conn. 299.

[4] Holmes *v.* Weed, 24 Barb. (N. Y.) 546. On this subject, see Whitworth *v.* Tilman, 40 Miss. 76. And in May *v.* May, 19 Fla. 373, it was held that under such circumstances the sureties should bear the costs themselves when interposing improper defenses.

[5] Redfield *v.* Haight, 27 Conn. 31. And see to similar effect, Cranmer *v.* McSwords, 26 W. Va. 412.

[6] Kramer *v.* Farmers' & Mechanics' Bank, 15 Ohio, 253; Uhler *v.* Semple, 5 C. E. Green (N. J.), 288; Perkins *v.* Mayfield, 5 Port. (Ala.) 182; Hawkins *v.* May, 12 Ala. 673; Lane *v.* Sleeper, 18 N. H. 209; Bank of Alabama *v.* M'Dade, 4 Port. (Ala.) 252; Pennington *v.* Woodall, 17 Ala. 685.

the maker of an administration bond, and to enable him to secure himself by an attachment of the property of the maker, is valid, notwithstanding the payee at the time of its execution has not been damnified. The existing liability with an implied promise to pay that amount upon the principal indebtedness, forming a sufficient consideration for the note, the note will be enforced against the objections of other creditors.[1] Where principal and surety have signed notes, and before the maturity thereof the principal deposits money with the surety upon the agreement that the surety shall apply the money so received to the payment of the notes, the principal cannot afterwards repudiate the agreement, the suretyship being a sufficient consideration to support it.[2] Where a mortgage is given for the indemnity of a surety, it remains valid for that purpose, notwithstanding the evidences of the debt or the instruments by which the surety is bound may be changed. This was held where a mortgage was given conditioned to save the mortgagee harmless from his indorsement of certain specified notes, and such notes, as they became due, were renewed by the substitution of other notes or drafts having different names upon them, but the obligation of the mortgagee was preserved through the whole series of renewals.[3] So a mortgage to secure accommodation indorsers on a note payable to a particular bank, and so described in the mortgage, is valid to secure the same indorsers, though that bank did not discount the note, and another bank discounted a similar note for the same purpose and with the same indorsers.[4]

§ 219. **Rights of surety who has been indemnified.**— That a principal may lawfully indemnify his surety against loss in consequence of his suretyship is settled.[5] A chattel mortgage given to secure a surety is good, therefore, as against creditors of the mortgagor (the principal).[6] Where a county officer, having the legal title to land, conveys the same to the sureties

[1] Haseltine *v.* Guild, 11 N. H. 390. To the same effect, where the surety expressly promised the principal to pay the debt, see Gladwin *v.* Garrison, 13 Cal. 330.

[2] Mandigo *v.* Mandigo, 26 Mich. 349.

[3] Pond *v.* Clarke, 14 Conn. 334; Smith *v.* Prince, 14 Conn. 472. To same effect, see Markell *v.* Eichelberger, 12 Md. 78; Chouteau *v.* Thompson, 3 Ohio St. 424.

[4] Patterson *v.* Martin, 7 Ohio, 225.

[5] Essex Freeholders *v.* Lindsley, 41 N. J. Eq. 189.

[6] Grimes *v.* Sherman, 25 Neb. 843.

on his bond for indemnity, equity will not interfere at the instance of a holder of a secret equity.[1] Where a person executes a mortgage to indemnify a surety on an appeal bond, the surety, although he suffers no loss, is entitled to enforce the lien of the mortgage to the extent of the taxes paid by him on the real estate pending the appeal.[2] Where a mortgage is given to indemnify the mortgagees against loss as sureties of the mortgagor, the sureties, in the absence of a provision in the mortgage authorizing it, are not entitled to possession of the mortgaged property until they have paid the mortgage debt or some part of it.[3] Money deposited by a principal with his surety to indemnify him against probable loss, cannot, it is held, be recovered by the principal even though he committed no default and the surety was not injured because of the liability assumed.[4]

§ 220. Effect of the bankruptcy of the principal on the surety's claim for indemnity.— A surety who, after the bankruptcy of the principal, pays the debt, may generally recover indemnity from the principal for the money so paid. The reason is that until he has paid the debt he usually has no cause of action against the principal and no claim which he can prove against the principal's estate.[5] Upon this principle it has been held that a person discharged under an insolvent act is liable to his surety for the arrears of an annuity due since his discharge, which the surety has been obliged to pay.[6] If, however, the bankrupt or insolvent act expressly provides for the adjustment of the claim for indemnity which a surety,

[1] Phipps *v.* Mansfield, 62 Ga. 209.

[2] West *v.* Hayes, 117 Ind. 290.

[3] Stonebraker *v.* Ford, 81 Mo. 532. But where a chattel mortgage given to indemnify a surety is conditioned that the surety shall be entitled to the possession of the property if the debt be not paid at maturity, payment by the surety is held not necessary to give him the right to possession. Mattingly *v.* Paul, 88 Ind. 95.

[4] Herman *v.* Jeuchner, Law Rep. (15 Q. B. Div.) 561. For surety's rights under deed of trust given to indemnify him, see Kassing *v.* International Bank, 74 Ill. 16.

[5] Paul *v.* Jones, 1 Durn. & East, 599; McMullin *v.* Bank of Penn Township, 2 Pa. St. 343; Taylor *v.* Mills, Cowper, 525; Cake *v.* Lewis, 8 Pa. St. 493; Buel *v.* Gordon, 6 Johns. 126; Emery *v.* Clarke, 2 J. Scott (N. S.), 582; Comfort *v.* Eisenbeis, 11 Pa. St. 13; Haddens *v.* Chambers, 2 Dall. (Pa.), 236. But see Mace *v.* Wells, 7 How. (U. S.) 272, reversing Wells *v.* Mace, 17 Vt. 503.

[6] Page *v.* Bussell, 2 Maule & Sel. 551; Welsh *v.* Welsh, 4 Maule & Sel. 333.

who is liable at the time of the bankruptcy, may have, by reason of afterwards paying the debt, the terms of the statute will of course prevail. It has been held that such claim may be proved under the United States bankrupt law of 1867, and it will be barred unless it is proved.[1] A guardian made default and was afterwards discharged in bankruptcy. His surety was afterwards compelled to pay the defalcation and sued him for indemnity. *Held*, the surety was entitled to recover, as debts created by embezzlement were expressly excepted from the operations of the bankrupt act, and this debt was so created.[2] If, after the surety has paid the debt, the principal becomes a bankrupt and is discharged as such, the discharge will bar the claim of the surety against the principal.[3] Thus, where the surety on a guardian's bond paid the ward an indebtedness due him by the guardian, and the surety subsequently died and his administrators sued the guardian in *assumpsit* for the amount so paid, it was held that the guardian's discharge in bankruptcy was a good defense and barred the surety's right to recover.[4]

§ 221. When surety may by express contract recover indemnity from principal before paying the debt — Mortgage of indemnity, etc.—While the surety or guarantor has usually, in the absence of express contract, no right of action against the principal for indemnity until he has actually paid the debt, yet he may by express contract be given such right of action before payment of the debt. Thus, where a bond of indemnity given to a surety on a lease was conditioned for the payment of the rent, and to save him harmless from liability, it was held the surety could recover from the obligor the amount of the rent in arrear, even though he had not himself paid it. The court said: "When a bond is, as in this case, conditioned as well to pay the debt or sum specified as to indemnify and save harmless the obligee against his liability to pay the same, the obligee may recover the entire debt or demand upon default in the payment without having paid anything."[5] The

[1] Lipscomb *v.* Grace, 26 Ark. 231, disapproving Poyne *v.* Joyner, 6 Ark. (1 Eng.) 241.

[2] Halliburton *v.* Carter, 55 Mo. 435.

[3] Smith *v.* Kinney, 6 Neb. 447.

[4] Cromer *v.* Cromer's Adm'r, 29 Gratt. (Va.) 280.

[5] Belloni *v.* Freeborn, 63 N. Y. 383, per Allen, J.

same thing was held where a bond to a sheriff was conditioned to save him harmless from all "loss and liabilities" which he might sustain by selling certain property levied on by him, and a judgment was recovered against him for selling the property, which judgment he had not paid.[1] So, where a mortgage was given to indemnify a surety, it was held he might foreclose the mortgage as soon as he was sued for the debt, and before he had paid it.[2] Where A., being the principal in a bond, gave a deed of trust, one of the provisions of which was that the trustee should "save harmless" B., who was his surety in the bond, and another provision was that the trustee, "whenever required by the creditors of A., or by any surety who may be threatened with loss by reason of his suretyship, shall proceed to sell sufficient property to answer the ends of" the deed of trust, it was held that the trustee was not bound to wait till the surety was actually damnified by having been compelled to pay the money, but that it was the duty of the trustee to relieve him, whenever he had funds for the purpose. The court said that, in equity, the money might be applied directly to the relief of the surety without passing into his hands and thus endangering the creditor.[3] Where the principal placed in the hands of his surety a horse for his indemnity, "upon condition that if (he) had the money to pay," etc., it was held that, upon the debt becoming due and remaining unpaid, the surety might sell the horse and pay the debt with the proceeds.[4] Principal and surety being joint makers of a promissory note, the principal covenanted with the surety to pay the amount specified in the note to the payees thereof on a given day, but made default. In an action

[1] Jones *v.* Childs, 8 Nev. 121. To similar effect, see Carman *v.* Noble, 9 Pa. St. 366.

[2] Tankersley *v.* Anderson, 4 Des. Eq. (S. C.) 44. To similar effect, see Thurston *v.* Prentiss, 1 Manning (Mich.), 193. See, also, on this point, Darst *v.* Bates, 51 Ill. 439. So, also, the surety may, before paying the debt, file his bill in equity against the creditors and his principal, to be substituted to a mortgage security given by the principal to the creditors. Moore *v.* Topliff, 107 Ill. 241.

[3] Daniel *v.* Joyner, 3 Ired. Eq. (N. C.) 513.

[4] Bird *v.* Benton, 2 Dev. Law (N. C.), 179. A surety who has been compelled to pay the debt within the period of the statute of limitations may enforce a mortgage of indemnity against the principal after the remedy of the creditor against the principal has been barred by that statute. Rucks *v.* Taylor, 49 Miss. 552.

on this covenant it was held that the surety was entitled to recover the full amount of the note, although he had not paid any of it.[1] A surety being liable upon two promissory notes due at different times, took from the principal a bond and warrant of attorney, the penalty being in double the amount of the two notes, and the condition being for the payment of a sum equal to the amount of the two notes, at a time previous to the maturity of either. The first note became due and the surety was obliged to pay it, and before the last note was due, and while it was unpaid, he entered up judgment on the bond for the amount of both notes. *Held*, the judgment was properly entered and might be enforced even though the principal offered to pay the surety the amount he had paid on the first note.[2] Where a party, in contemplation of suicide, tied up in a bundle and left cash and notes indorsed to a surety, and addressed the bundle to the surety with directions that as soon as his death should be known the surety should, from the proceeds, indemnify himself, and if anything remained give it to the principal's children, and the surety received and claimed the property, it was held he might retain so much thereof as was necessary for his indemnity, and this upon the ground that, where a trust is created for a person without his knowledge, he may afterwards affirm it.[3] If the principal expressly agree to save the surety harmless from all loss and damage on account of the suretyship, the surety may, without paying the debt, recover damages for imprisonment which he has suffered on account of the debt.[4] The allowance by commissioners of a debt of the principal against the estate of a surety, when duly reported to the probate court and registered among the claims against the estate, is a damnification, and will entitle the administrator to sue the principal upon his special promise to "indemnify and save harmless" the surety.[5] A promise by a principal to pay into the hands of a surety for his indemnity the amount for which he is bound, "whenever the surety shall be called upon by the creditor for payment, or shall have reason to doubt the ultimate ability of the prin-

[1] Loosemore *v.* Radford, 9 Mees. & Wels. 657. To similar effect, see Dorrington *v.* Minnick, 15 Neb. 397.

[2] Smith *v.* James, 1 Miles (Pa.), 162.

[3] Woodbury *v.* Bowman, 14 Me. 154.

[4] Powell *v.* Smith, 8 Johns. 249.

[5] Adm'rs of Pond *v.* Warner, 2 Vt. 532.

cipal to save him harmless," is a valid promise as against the creditors of the principal, and an action may be sustained on it by the surety against the principal, without paying any of the debt.[1]

§ 222. **When special contract of indemnity will not authorize surety to recover before paying the debt, etc.**— The right of the surety or guarantor to recover indemnity from the principal before himself paying the debt manifestly depends upon the terms or legal effect of the express contract for indemnity. The liability of the surety for the debt of the principal is a sufficient consideration to support such a contract as against the principal or any of his creditors, and the terms or legal effect of the contract for indemnity will prevail, each particular case being governed by its own circumstances. After a note signed by principal and surety was due, the principal gave the surety a contract of indemnity, engaging to pay the note to the creditor "so as wholly to indemnify and save harmless the . . . (surety) from his liability on said note by reason of signing the same as surety." *Held*, this was but a common contract of indemnity, and the surety must have sustained actual damage to entitle him to sue on it, as it could not be presumed that the contract was made to entitle the surety to sue on it at once. If the note had not been due when the contract of indemnity was made, its construction would have been different.[2] Where a surety receives from the principal, as indemnity, the principal's note payable at a particular time, it has been held that he might sue upon it, although he had not been compelled to pay the debt, the fair presumption being that, by making the note payable at a day certain, the parties intended to provide an indemnity against suit rather than against ultimate loss. Where the note given by the principal to the surety for his indemnity is in the nature of a collateral security only, it has been held that the surety may, on such note, recover whatever sum he has actually paid out, up to the time of trial, and no more.[4] If an

[1] Fletcher *v.* Edson, 8 Vt. 294.

[2] Adm'rs of Pond *v.* Warner, 2 Vt. 532. See, also, Jeffers *v.* Johnson, 1 Zab. (N. J.) 73.

[3] Russell *v.* La Roque, 11 Ala. 352.

[4] Little *v.* Little, 13 Pick. 426; Osgood *v.* Osgood, 39 N. H. 209; Child *v.* Powder Works, 44 N. H. 354. *Contra*, Woodbridge *v.* Scott, 3 Brevard (S. C.), 193. See on this subject, Williams *v.* Cheney, 3 Gray, 215.

indemnified surety, by his own act, causes property of the principal levied on for the payment of the debt to be released, the indemnitor is thereby discharged. Thus, C. as p incipal, and A. as surety, executed a note, and B. at the same time gave A. an agreement to save him harmless from all loss on account of such suretyship. The creditor obtained a judgment against A. and C., and levied on property of C. sufficient to satisfy the debt. A. then replevied (stayed) the judgment for two years, the effect of which was to release the property of C. from the levy. Before the two years expired, C. became insolvent, and A. had the debt to pay. *Held*, he could recover nothing from B., as he had by his own act prevented the payment of the debt by C.'s property.[1] A mortgage given by a principal to a surety for his indemnity can only be held by him for the very purpose for which it was given, and where it is given to indemnify him against payment of half a debt it will not cover a payment of the other half.[2] Nor will such a mortgage cover a loan made by the surety to the principal.[3]

§ 223. Surety may, before paying the debt, bring suit in chancery to compel principal to pay it.— After the debt for which a surety or guarantor is liable has become due, he may, without paying the debt and without being called upon by the creditor, file a bill in equity to compel the principal to pay the debt, it being unreasonable that a surety or guarantor should always have a cloud hanging over him, even though not molested for the debt.[4] This principle is universally recognized, and has been applied to a great variety of circumstances. Thus, a surety on a bond to secure a money debt was secured by another bond of indemnity, entered into by the principal debtor's father, who had died, having by will

[1] Pope *v.* Davidson, 5 J. J. Marsh. (Ky.) 400.

[2] Newell *v.* Hurlburt, 2 Vt. 351. On same point, see McDowell *v.* Crook, 10 La. Ann. 31.

[3] Clark *v.* Oman, 15 Gray, 521.

[4] West *v.* Chasten, 12 Fla. 315; Antrobus *v.* Davidson, 3 Merivale, 569; Irick *v.* Black, 2 C. E. Green (N. J.), 189; Bishop *v.* Day, 13 Vt. 81; Thigpen *v.* Price, Phillips' Eq. (N. C.) 146; Taylor *v.* Miller, Phillips' Eq. (N. C.) 365; Saylors *v.* Saylors, 3 Heisk. (Tenn.) 525; Greene *v.* Starnes, 1 Heisk. (Tenn.) 582; Howell *v.* Cobb, 2 Cold. (Tenn.) 104; Philadelphia & Reading R. R. Co. *v.* Little, 41 N. J. Eq. 519; Delaware, Lackawanna & Western R. R. Co. *v.* Oxford Iron Co., 38 N. J. Eq. 151; Miller *v.* Stout, 5 Del. Ch. 259; Moore *v.* Topliff, 107 Ill. 241.

devised certain property specifically upon trust to pay the debt. The creditor having applied to the surety, the surety had recourse to the executors, who said they had no funds in hand, and that they were unable under the will to raise the money by sale of any portion of the testator's estate, except under a decree of the court. *Held*, that the surety, although he had not paid anything, was entitled to maintain a bill against the executors for administration, payment of the debt and indemnity, and that it was not necessary that the bill should be filed on behalf of all the creditors. The court said the following was the rule: "A court of equity will also prevent injury in some cases by interposing before any actual injury has been suffered by a bill which has been sometimes called a bill *quia timet*, in analogy to proceedings at the common law, where in some cases a writ may be maintained before any molestation, distress or impleading. Thus a surety may file a bill to compel the debtor on a bond in which he has joined to pay the debt when due, whether the surety has been actually sued for it or not; and upon a covenant to save harmless, a bill may be filed to relieve the covenantee under similar circumstances."[1] A surety whose principal is dead may, before paying the debt, file a bill against the creditor and the executor of the debtor, to compel the executor to pay the debt, so as to exonerate the surety from liability. He may enforce, for his exoneration, any lien of the creditor on the estate of the principal, and may bring any suit in equity which the creditor could bring for settlement of accounts and administration of the assets, whether legal or equitable, but the creditor must be a party, that he may receive the money when it is recovered.[2] The fact that an administrator had become insolvent and wasted the assets, it has been held, will not, before the time for settling the estate has come, entitle the surety of such administrator to file a bill to prevent persons who owed the estate from paying the administrator, and to compel the administrator to give the surety security. The court said payment by the debtors ought not to be enjoined, as they

[1] Woldridge *v.* Norris (Law Rep.), 6 Eq. Cas. 410, per Giffard, V. C. See, also, Miller *v.* Speed, 9 Heisk. (Tenn.) 196.

[2] Stephenson *v.* Taverners, 9 Gratt. (Va.) 398.

might become insolvent, and the surety, not having originally demanded indemnity, could not demand it subsequently, but after the time for settling the estate arrived, a bill might be filed by the surety to compel the distribution of the assets.[1] A mortgagee who is also surety for the debt secured by the mortgage has no right to have the mortgaged premises sold before the debt becomes due, even though the same are in a state of ruin and decay, in consequence of storms, and are daily getting worse. The court said: "The security was taken with knowledge of the situation and character of the property, and of the risks to which it was exposed. It does not belong to the court to give a party better security than he elected to take, where there has been no fraud or mistake, nor any abuse or waste of the subject. I am not informed that there exists any precedent for a bill *quia timet* adapted to such a case. All the cases in the English law, in which even a surety may file a bill *quia timet*, are those in which the debt was due from the principal debtor; and I do not know of any principle of equity that will justify us in giving aid to the surety before the debt is due, when the parties have not provided in their contract for such a case."[2] A surety on the bond of an executor or trustee cannot maintain a bill in equity against his principal for an accounting and the appointment of a receiver.[3]

§ 224. Cases in which a surety may have relief in equity before paying the debt.— A surety or guarantor who holds a mortgage on the property of his principal may, after the maturity of the debt, and before paying it, have the mortgage foreclosed, and the proceeds thereof applied to the payment of the debt.[4] It has been held that for any sum which a surety for the price of land purchased by another has paid, or is liable to pay, on that account, he has an equity to be reimbursed

[1] Delaney *v.* Tipton, 3 Hayw. (Tenn.) 14.

[2] Campbell *v.* Macomb, 4 Johns. Ch. 534, per Kent, C.

[3] McElroy *v.* Hatheway, 44 Mich. 399; Ridgeway *v.* Potter, 114 Ill. 457. Neither can a surety by bill in equity require his principal to give other and additional security, and on his failure to do so have him removed. Ridgeway *v.* Potter, 114 Ill. 457.

[4] Kramer *v.* Farmers' & Mechanics' Bank, 15 Ohio, 253; De Cottes *v.* Jeffers, 7 Fla. 284; Maskell *v.* Eichelberger, 12 Md. 78; Succession of Montgomery, 2 La. Ann. 469; Hellams *v.* Abercrombie, 15 S. C. 110.

or exonerated by a sale of the land, and to that end he has a right to file his bill to prevent a conveyance to the purchaser by the vendor, who has kept the title as a security for the purchase money.[1] Where the surety of an insolvent principal obtains, without fraud, the legal title to a fund belonging to his principal, equity will not compel him to surrender the legal title to his principal, so that the principal may dispose of the fund as he pleases; but, if the surety has not paid the debt, will authorize and compel him to apply the fund to its satisfaction.[2] Where a joint judgment was recovered against a principal and surety, and the principal had property subject to execution, on which the judgment was a lien, and sold such property to a person who was about to remove the same without the jurisdiction of the court, it was held the surety might by suit in chancery prevent the removal of the property.[3] Where a party was surety on a bond given by a deputy-sheriff to the sheriff, and had taken a mortgage on personal property for his indemnity, and the sheriff and the deputy had collected money for which the sheriff was sued, and the deputy had departed the jurisdiction, and the mortgaged property had come into the possession of a third party upon a pretended claim of right, which party was charged with an intention of removing it beyond the jurisdiction of the court, it was held that the court would restrain such third party from removing the property, and require bond and security for its forthcoming to answer the claim of the surety.[4]

§ 225. Cases in which a surety cannot recover indemnity from the principal.— The surety who pays a debt for which the principal is not liable cannot generally recover the money so paid from the principal. Thus, where the surety in a bond against incumbrances paid the costs of defending two suits which the bond did not cover, under the mistaken belief that he was liable therefor, it was held he could not recover the same from his principal.[5] So where, in an action of replevin,

[1] Smith *v.* Smith, 5 Ired. Eq. (N. C.) 34.

[2] McKnight *v.* Bradley, 10 Rich. Eq. (S. C.) 557.

[3] Anderson *v.* Walton, 35 Ga. 202.

[4] Ontlaw *v.* Reddick, 11 Ga. 669.

[5] Bancroft *v.* Abbott, 3 Allen, 524. If surety pays principal's debt with knowledge of facts which would discharge himself or his principal, he cannot recover indemnity. Noole *v.* Blount, 77 Mo. 235.

a bond with surety is filed by the plaintiff, and possession of the property is obtained by him, and afterwards the suit is dismissed by agreement of the parties, the plaintiff agreeing to pay the defendant a certain sum, but no judgment is rendered, if the surety afterwards, without the request of the plaintiff, pays the amount agreed to be paid to the defendant, he cannot recover the same from his principal, as the payment is, in such case, a voluntary one on the part of the surety.[1] Where a county court borrowed money without any legal authority so to do, and the plaintiff became the county's surety on the bond for the borrowed money, a part of which he had since been compelled to pay, it was held that such plaintiff had no right to call upon the county to reimburse him for the amount already paid, or to exonerate him from the payment of the balance remaining unpaid. The county was not in any manner bound to the creditor, and could not be to the surety.[2] Where a surety paid a debt after personal property of the principal sufficient to satisfy the debt had been levied upon, it was held he could not recover indemnity from the principal. The levy was *prima facie* a satisfaction of the debt, and the surety had paid a debt which the principal had already paid.[3] A surety being imprisoned on account of the debt of two principals, agreed with one of them that he would pay one-half the debt if such principal would pay the other half, and this was done. The surety then sued both principals for indemnity. *Held*, he could not recover from the one with whom he had made the agreement. The implied presence of indemnity which the law would have raised was superseded by the express contract.[4] But it has beeu held that an agreement by a surety that he will surrender a note of the principal, if the principal will procure his release from his obligation as surety, is void for want of consideration, the ground of the decision being that the principal was bound to indemnify the surety, and, in procuring his release, he had only done what he was under a legal obligation to do.[5] The master of a vessel,

[1] Hollinsbee *v.* Ritchey, 49 Ind. 261.

[2] Davis *v.* Board of Comm'rs, 72 N. C. 441; Davis *v.* Comm'rs Stokes Co., 74 N. C. 374.

[3] Brown *v.* Kidd, 34 Miss. 291. To a contrary effect, see Clark *v.* Bell, 8 Humph. (Tenn.) 26.

[4] Duncan *v.* Keiffer, 3 Bin. (Pa.) 126.

[5] Ritenour *v.* Mathews, 42 Ind. 7.

as principal, together with a surety, entered into a bond that the vessel should not take any slave from one of the Bahama Islands. A slave concealed himself in the vessel and was taken to New York, where the surety filed a bill against the principal for a *ne exeat* and indemnity. *Held*, the bill could not be sustained, as it was not certain that either principal or surety was liable, and the court would never lend its aid to enforce a forfeiture.[1] Where a surety buys a judgment against himself and his principal in the name of another person, he cannot recover indemnity from the principal without first satisfying the judgment. He may either proceed upon the judgment or satisfy the judgment and sue the principal for money paid, but he cannot do both.[2]

§ 226. Set-off — Surety may bid at execution sale of principal's property — Surety may assign his claim against the principal, etc.— In a suit by administrators of an insolvent estate against one who was surety in a note for the decedent, such surety is entitled to set off a payment by him of such note, although the payment was made after the institution of the suit by the administrators against him. It is not like a claim brought by a party after suit is brought against him, for, although the surety's right to indemnity from the principal was not perfect till he paid the debt, yet it was "founded upon a contract which existed before."[3] If the surety for a debt pay the same before it is due, the payment will, after the debt has become due, but not before, be a legal set-off against a note of the surety payable to the principal and held by him.[4] Where a surety who had not paid the debt filed a bill against his principal, alleging that the principal was about to remove from the state and carry with him all his property, and prayed for an injunction to prevent the removal, etc., it was held that, in the absence of any statutory provision on the

[1] Gibbs *v.* Mennard, 6 Paige, Ch. 258.

[2] Hodges *v.* Armstrong, 3 Dev. Law (N. C.), 253. And see, on this subject, Lewis *v.* Lewis, 92 Ill. 237.

[3] Beaver *v.* Beaver, 23 Pa. St. 167, per Lewis, J. *Contra*, Walker *v.* McKay, 2 Met. (Ky.) 294.

[4] Jackson *v.* Adamson, 7 Blackf. (Ind.) 597. For miscellaneous cases illustrating the doctrine of set-off as applied between principal and surety, see Tyree *v.* Parham's Ex'r, 66 Ala. 424; Lynch *v.* Hancock, 14 S. C. 66; Balser *v.* Wood, 69 Ind. 122; State *v.* Wylie, 86 Ind. 396; Convery *v.* Langdon, 66 Ind. 311.

subject, he was not entitled to relief.[1] It has been held that a surety, either before or after paying the debt, may file a bill to set aside fraudulent conveyances made by his principal or co-surety,[2] and the contrary has also been held.[3] A surety having property of his principal in his hands may surrender the same on an execution against his principal, and may purchase the same at the sale under the execution,[4] and he may so purchase although the judgment is rendered against him and his principal jointly.[5] But where a principal debtor, with money sufficient to pay the debt in his pocket, suffered the property of his surety to be sold on an execution against him, and the surety and himself became the purchaser, it was held to be doubtful whether, even at law, such sale, as against the surety, was not a mere nullity, and that in a court of equity such a purchaser would not be allowed to set up a title thus acquired against his surety.[6] A bond given by an executor (who had been appointed executor by the will but had not given bond) for the payment to his surety of one-half his commissions from time to time, as they may be allowed, in consideration of his consenting to become such surety, is a valid instrument. It is not an agreement to pay money in order to obtain an appointment, but a legitimate means of carrying out the wishes of the testator.[7] A principal executed a deed of trust to secure certain debts, among them one on which

[1] Buford *v.* Francisco, 3 Dana (Ky.), 68.

[2] Taylor *v.* Ex'r of Heriot, 4 Dev. Eq. (S. C.) 227; Martin *v.* Walker, 12 Hun (N. Y.), 46; Pashby *v.* Mandigo, 42 Mich. 172. In a bill by a surety of a guardian to set aside a fraudulent conveyance of his principal, the complaint is insufficient until there has first been an administration on the guardian's estate. Baugh *v.* Boles, 66 Ind. 376.

[3] Williams *v.* Tipton, 5 Humph. (Tenn.) 66. The bill must not fail to show to whom the surety was indebted at the time he made the conveyance, nor that the principal had not, up to the date of the conveyance, faithfully discharged his duties. Robinson *v.* Rogers, 84 Ind. 539. As to what facts are evidence of a fraudulent conveyance, see Mason *v.* Pierron, 69 Wis. 585.

[4] Horsefield *v.* Cost, Addison (Pa.), 152.

[5] Carlos *v.* Ansley, 8 Ala. 900. But if the principal purchased lands of the surety on execution against them jointly he acquires no title thereto. Madgett *v.* Fleenor, 90 Ind. 517. Such purchase inures to the surety's benefit. Greer *v.* Wintersmith, 85 Ky. 516.

[6] Perry *v.* Yarborough, 3 Jones' Eq. (N. C.) 66.

[7] Culbertson *v.* Stillinger, Taney's Decisions (Campbell), 75.

there was a surety. The surety had to pay the debt, and assigned all his interest in the deed of trust to a third person. *Held*, such third person might enforce and have the benefit of the deed of trust.[1] A surety who has two indemnities may usually resort to either, at his option.[2]

§ 227. **When insolvent principal cannot collect debt due him by surety — Verbal guarantor who pays debt may recover indemnity — Other cases.**— A principal who is insolvent cannot collect a debt which the surety owes him without first indemnifying the surety. "A surety has in respect to his liability the rights of a creditor as against his principal; and upon the insolvency of the principal debtor he may retain any funds belonging to such debtor, by way of indemnity against his liability; otherwise a surety in such a case would be wholly without remedy when the plainest principles of justice are in his favor."[3] And the assignee of a judgment obtained by the principal against the surety will in such case stand in no better position than the principal.[4] An executor, being surety for his testator, paid the debt after the testator's death. *Held*, he had a right to retain this debt, the same as he would have a right to retain any other debt of equal degree due by the testator to him.[5] One who has verbally guarantied the debt of another at his request may pay the same and recover indemnity from his principal, and the Statute of Frauds will be no defense in such case, although it would be a defense to an action on the guaranty. The contract of guaranty was not void, and the guarantor had a right to perform his parol agree-

[1] York *v.* Landis, 65 N. C. 535. Where a surety holds a note and chattel mortgage for indemnity and assigns the same, his assignee cannot enforce the mortgage until the mortgagee has paid the debt for which he was surety, or in some way has been damnified. Stevens *v.* Hurlburt, 25 Ill. App. 124.

[2] Muller *v.* Down, 94 U. S. 444. See, also, McCoun *v.* Sperb, 53 Hun, 165.

[3] Abbey *v.* Van Campen, 1 Freem. Ch. (Miss.) 273. See, also, Mattingly *v.* Sutton, 19 W. Va. 19. And to like effect, Walker *v.* Dicks, 80 N. C. 263, wherein is also established the proposition that the surety before suffering loss may use his liabilities as such, as an equitable counterclaim or set-off against a debt he owes his insolvent principal. And see Merwin *v.* Austin, 58 Conn. 22.

[4] Williams *v.* Helme, 1 Dev. Eq. (N. C.) 151. See, also, directly in point, Walker *v.* Dicks, 80 N. C. 263, and Scott *v.* Timberlake, 83 N. C. 382.

[5] Boyd *v.* Brooks, 34 Beav. 7. *Contra*, Anonymous, Godbolt, 149.

ment.[1] If the surety, on a note given by an infant for necessaries, pay it, he may recover indemnity from the infant. "If the infant is not liable on the note, as he would not be if he elected to avoid such liability, an *assumpsit* upon the delivery of the goods must be considered as subsisting against him, and the note of the surety be regarded as collateral security for the payment.[2] As long as a judgment against the principal can be enforced in any way, either by *scire facias* or action of debt, the payment of such judgment by a surety is not voluntary, and he may recover indemnity from the principal.[3]

§ 228. Surety on note who pays without notice of failure of consideration may recover indemnity — When surety, who has joined in fraudulent scheme with principal, may recover indemnity — Other cases.— A payment made by a surety in compromise of his supposed liability upon a disputed claim against him and his principal may be recovered by the surety from the principal if it turns out that there was an actual liability, and the principal has or is entitled to the benefit of the payment in discharge of so much of the original claim against him.[4] A surety who, without notice of the failure of consideration of a note, pays it after it is due, may, notwithstanding such failure of consideration, recover indemnity from the principal.[5] After judgment against the surety in a replevin bond, he paid the judgment and sued his principal for indemnity. The principal set up that he had no title to the property replevied, and the surety knew it at the time, and the replevin was sued out by collusion between him and the surety to get the property, and that they were joint tort-feasors and neither could recover from the other. *Held*, no defense. The court said: "If the giving of the bond was a fraud it was one of a singular character, for it indemnified the in-

[1] Beal *v.* Brown, 13 Allen, 114. To similar effect, see Lee & Co. *v.* Stowe, 57 Tex. 444; Board of Comm'rs *v.* Jameson, 86 Ind. 154. A verbal guaranty that a note is genuine, made by the assignor at the time of its assignment upon a sufficient consideration, is valid. King *v.* Summitt, 73 Ind. 312.

[2] Conn *v.* Coburn, 7 N. H. 368. But see Ayers *v.* Burns' Adm'r, 87 Ind. 245. In Fagin *v.* Goggin, 12 R. I. 398, it is held that where a surety pays a judgment on a recognizance given by an infant, the latter is bound to reimburse the surety.

[3] Randolph *v.* Randolph, 3 Rand. (Va.) 490.

[4] Bancroft *v.* Pearce, 27 Vt. 668.

[5] Gasquet *v.* Oakey, 19 La. (Curry), 76. See on this subject, Gates *v.* Renfroe, 7 La. Ann. 569.

tended victim. This suit is not brought upon any illegal contract."[1] Where a bond with A. as surety is given to the United States, and B. is mentioned in the bond as the importer, and A. pays the bond, he may maintain an action for indemnity against B., although in fact a third person was owner of the goods. The claim of the United States was extinguished by the bond, and the surety has a right to sue the principal in such bond.[2] A principal placed in the hands of his surety certain securities for his indemnity. The surety paid a portion of the debts for which he was liable, and collected from the securities in his hands an amount as great as he had paid out, but he still remained liable for other debts of the principal. *Held*, he must apply the money so collected to indemnifying himself for the money already paid by him for the principal, and that he could not then sue the principal for indemnity.[3]

§ 229. **Other cases as to rights of surety against principal.**— If several parties sign a note as principals and one of them pays it, he may sue the others for indemnity and show by parol that they were principals and he a surety.[4] So where two of three parties who signed a note added to their names the word "surety," and one of them paid it, he may, in a suit for indemnity against the other, show that he was a principal notwithstanding the addition to his name of the word "surety."[5] The same thing was held where a principal, during his minority, contracted a debt for which a surety gave his note; and after his majority, the principal, on the bottom of the note, acknowledged himself holden as co-surety.[6] It has been held that the fact that after a note becomes due a new surety signs it will not prevent the original surety, who afterwards pays the note, from recovering indemnity from the principal. The payment was not voluntary, the addition of the name of the new surety not annulling the original liability on the note.[7] A husband and wife owned real estate, each one-half in fee, and made a mortgage to secure the debt of the husband, which was not properly acknowledged, and did not

[1] Smith *v.* Rines, 32 Me. 177, per Howard, J.

[2] Sluby *v.* Champlain, 4 Johns. 461.

[3] Whipple *v.* Briggs, 30 Vt. 111.

[4] Dickey *v.* Rogers, 19 Mart. (La.) 7 N. S. 588.

[5] Apgar's Adm'r *v.* Hiler, 4 Zabr. (N. J.) 812.

[6] Thompson *v.* Linscott, 2 Greenl. (Me.) 186.

[7] Catton *v.* Simpson, 8 Adol. & Ell.

convey the wife's interest. Subsequently they made another mortgage to secure a debt of the husband to another party, which was duly acknowledged and the mortgaged property was sold. *Held*, the proceeds should be applied, first, to pay the last mortgage, and the overplus should be applied to reimburse the wife for her land so sold; she being as to it the surety of her husband, and her equity as such surety being to have all the property mortgaged by her husband applied to pay the debt for which she was surety before her property was touched.[1] If an official bond, given by a sheriff and his sureties, be so worded as not to be joint and several, but joint only, a court of chancery is the proper tribunal to give the sureties relief against the estate of the sheriff after his death, upon their being compelled to pay a sum of money on account of the delinquency of such sheriff in his life-time.[2] It is not necessary for the principal to make the surety a party to a suit in chancery which he may bring to assert any equity he may have against the demand for which he and the surety are bound at law.[3]

§ 230. Statute of limitations as between surety and principal.— Ordinarily, the statute of limitations begin to run in favor of the principal, and against the surety who pays the debt, from the time of such payment, and not from the time when the debt became due, because, until the surety has been compelled to make such payment, there is no breach of the implied promise of the principal to indemnify him.[4] When a surety has paid money for the principal, part inside and part outside the statute of limitations, on account of the same debt, all payments outside the statute are barred thereby.[5] On a con-

136. See, also, Mersman *v.* Werges, 112 U. S. 139.

[1] Johns *v.* Reardon, 11 Md. 465.

[2] Mountjoy *v.* Bank's Ex'rs, 6 Munf. (Va.) 387.

[3] Bently *v.* Gregory, 7 T. B. Mon. (Ky.) 368.

[4] Thayer *v.* Daniels, 110 Mass. 345; Burton *v.* Rutherford, Adm'r, 49 Mo. 255; Bauer *v.* Gray, Adm'r, 18 Mo. App. 164; Scott *v.* Nichols, 27 Miss. 94; Shepard *v.* Ogden, 2 Scam. (Ill.) 257; Wesley Church *v.* Moore, 10 Pa. St. 273; Bullock *v.* Campbell, 9 Gill (Md.), 182; Walker *v.* Lathrop, 6 Iowa (Clarke), 516; Barnsback *v.* Reiner, 8 Minn. 59; Reid *v.* Flippen, 47 Ga. 273; McLane *v.* Ragsdale, 31 Miss. 701; Rucks *v.* Taylor, 49 Miss. 552; Considine *v.* Considine, 9 Irish Law Rep. 400. See, also, on this subject, Keller *v.* Rhoads, 39 Pa. St. 513; Bushong *v.* Taylor, 82 Mo. 660; and Harrah *v.* Jacobs, 75 Iowa, 72.

[5] Davies *v.* Humphreys, 6 Mees. & Wels. 153. The contrary has been held

tract to indemnify a plaintiff against costs, which he is afterwards called on to pay, the cause of action arises when he pays, and not when the costs are incurred, or the attorney's bill delivered to such plaintiff, and the statute of limitations, therefore, begins to run from the time of such payment.[1] A. and B. were sureties of C., and shortly after the debt became due A. paid it. Four years afterwards B. paid A. one-half the sum A. had paid. All these payments were made without suit. After the statute of limitations had run from the time A. paid, and before it had run from the time B. paid, B. sued C. for indemnity. *Held*, B.'s claim for indemnity was not barred by the statute. The cause of action of B. against C. accrued at the time of the payment by B. to A.[2] Where a party upon whom a bill of exchange was drawn paid it for accommodation of the drawer, and after the statute of limitations would have barred an open account, and before it would have barred a suit on the bill of exchange, he sued the drawer for indemnity, it was held he could recover, because he was entitled to subrogation to the rights of the creditor against the principal, and his claim was therefore on the bill of exchange. The court said: "The rights to which he is entitled to be thus subrogated are those which the creditor had while the obligation of the contract subsisted, not such as he had after the debt has been paid. . . . The doctrine is that the payment entitles the surety to be subrogated to all the rights of the creditor. It was his right to sue upon the contract. The surety upon payment is subrogated to this right, and may in like manner maintain his action."[3] When a surety pays the creditor the amount of a judgment against him and the principal, and the creditor assigns the judgment to the surety, he may avail himself of the judgment, and the statute of limitations will not apply to the judgment as it would to the implied *assumpsit* that would accrue to him upon paying off the judgment.[4]

where the principal was not notified of the payment of the first instalments. See Williams, Adm'r, *v.* Williams, Adm'r, 5 Ohio, 444. Supporting the rule in the text, see Arbogast *v.* Hays, 98 Ind. 26.

[1] Collinge *v.* Heywood, 9 Adol. & Ell. 633.

[2] Odlin *v.* Greenleaf, 3 N. H. 270.

[3] Sublett *v.* McKinney, 19 Tex. 438, per Wheeler, J.

[4] Morrison *v.* Page, 9 Dana (Ky.), 428.

§ 231. **When surety may replevy property of principal.**— Where a surety signed the principal's notes, and in consideration therefor the principal orally agreed to convey personal property to him for the purpose of saving him harmless against any loss or damage by reason of his suretyship, and afterwards a receiver of the principal in another action took possession of such personal property, it was held that the surety, after the maturity of the notes, was entitled to replevy the property, and this, too, even though he had not actually been damnified.[1] A surety on a replevin bond, however, has not such a legal interest in his principal's property as will give him a right to replevy against one wrongfully dispossessing the principal of his property.[2]

§ 232. **When surety has lien on property of principal.**— Where a club by resolution authorized a committee to raise funds for the purpose of improving and adding to their buildings and furnishing them, and the committee, being unable to raise the money even by a mortgage of the club property, borrowed the same from a bank, several individual members of the committee becoming guarantors to the bank, who were afterwards compelled to pay the amount, it was held that the guarantors upon payment had a lien on the premises so added to and improved.[3] The master of the rolls said: "In the name of common sense could the club say, 'We will not allow you to be repaid it, for we did not authorize you to advance it; though it is true we authorized the improvements to be made, we only authorized them to be so made by borrowed money; we have availed ourselves of them, we have played in the new billiard-rooms and slept in the new bed-rooms built with your money; but we will not recoup you?' I think that the club could not be listened to for a moment in putting forward such an unconscionable proposition."[4]

[1] Bates *v.* Wiggin *et al.*, 37 Kan. 44.

[2] Jimmerson *v.* Green, 7 Neb. 26. Neither can a surety on a stay bond replevy his unexempt property levied on to collect a judgment, even where his principal had no property. McGlothlin *v.* Madden, 16 Kan. 466.

[3] Minnitt *v.* Lord Talbot, Law Rep. Irish (1 Ch. Div.), 143.

[4] Page 152. And see the same case, Law Rep. Irish (7 Ch. Div.), 407. In Wood *v.* Wood, 124 Ind. 545, it is held that a surety who pays his principal's debt has no lien on land purchased with the money for which it was contracted, though induced to become such by the principal's promise that he should have a lien.

CHAPTER X.

OF THE RIGHTS OF THE SURETY OR GUARANTOR AGAINST THE CREDITOR AND THIRD PERSONS.

Surety not discharged by lawful act of creditor — Instances § 233
How fraud of the creditor operates on liability of the surety 234
Surety may avail himself of defense of usury 235
Whether surety may avail himself of set-off in favor of principal and against creditor . 236
Creditor not bound to exhaust securities put up by principal before suing surety — When surety without paying may enforce securities for the debt 237
Surety may compel creditor to proceed against principal . 238
Cases holding that surety by request and without suit may compel creditor to proceed against principal 239
Requisites of the request to sue 240
Same continued — Sufficiency of notice 241
Cases holding that the surety cannot, by request alone, accelerate the movements of the creditor against the principal 242
Surety may make the same defense at law as in equity — Whether he must make his defense at law when sued at law 243
Whether surety, having failed to make defense at law, can have relief in equity 244
If creditor lead a surety to believe debt is paid and surety is injured, he is discharged . § 245
When surety not discharged although he believe debt is paid 246
Rights of surety against third persons — Indemnity of surety 247
Surety entitled to benefit of collaterals — Creditor not bound to notify surety, when . . 248
Surety not discharged because creditor tells him his signing is a mere matter of form — Other cases 249
Surety may defend suit against principal — How liability of surety affected by fraud — Other cases 250
When surety cannot recover money paid by him to creditor — Party who is indebted may become surety and secure suretyship debt to exclusion of other creditors — Other cases 251
Surety may enforce trust made for his benefit without his knowledge — Other cases . 252
When surety for a portion of a debt entitled to share in dividend of estate of insolvent principal — Other cases . . 253

§ 233. Surety not discharged by lawful act of creditor — Instances.— Under the general head rights of the surety against the creditor might properly be treated most of the grounds for the discharge of the surety, as it is an invasion of those rights which furnishes the grounds for such discharge. Separate chapters have, however, been devoted to an examination of the most important of those grounds, and it is proposed here to treat only of those rights of the surety against the creditor which do not properly fall under other subdivisions of this work. "A creditor discharges a surety by any dealing or arrangement with the principal debtor without the surety's assent, which at all varies the situation, rights or remedies of the surety."[1] But "the act of the creditor which injures the surety, or increases his risk, or exposes him to greater liability, which will operate as a discharge, must be some act which the law does not authorize or sanction, or the omission of some act specially enjoined by the law."[2] Thus, the fact that a creditor, after principal and surety are bound for a certain sum, lends the principal a much larger sum, and takes a bond from the principal for such larger sum, does not discharge the surety.[3] So where the proprietor of a newspaper sold it, together with its press, type, good-will, etc., and the purchaser gave notes with surety for the purchase money, and the vendor afterwards started in the same town another newspaper, which took so much patronage from the newspaper he had sold that the purchaser was unable to pay his notes, it was held the surety was not discharged, as the starting and carrying on of the new newspaper, there being no agreement to the contrary, was a legal and permissible act on the part of the vendor.[4] Where a creditor, who was an attorney, obtained, as attorney for other creditors, an adjudication in bankruptcy against the principal judgment debtor, and thus prevented a lien from attaching on part of his property, it was held the surety was not discharged thereby. The act of the creditor was lawful, and even if it worked an injury to the surety he could not complain.[5] A decedent directed by his will that all his real estate should be sold, and the proceeds

[1] Per Lord Truro, C., in Owen *v.* Homan, 3 Macn. & Gor. 378. See, also, Watkins *v.* Worthington, 2 Bland's Ch. (Md.) 509. If the surety consent to the injurious act he is not discharged. Burns *v.* Parks, 53 Ga. 61.

[2] Stewart *v.* Barrow, 55 Ga. 664, per Warner, C. J.

[3] Eyre *v.* Everett, 2 Russell, 381.

[4] Rupp *v.* Over, 3 Brewster (Pa.), 133.

[5] Thornton *v.* Thornton, 63 N. C. 211.

divided among certain of his children. One of his daughters married A., and he purchased a tract of the decedent's land at the executor's sale, and gave a note, with B. as surety, for the purchase money. The surety and all parties then expected that the note would be paid by the distributive share of A.'s wife. She afterwards commenced a suit for divorce against A., in which she was successful, and had most of her distributive share decreed to her. The note was not paid, and the surety claimed to be discharged, because the fund he had relied upon for payment had been diverted from its purpose. *Held*, he was not discharged, as the diversion of the fund was not the act of the creditor. but was the result of the wrongdoing of the principal.[1]

§ 234. **How fraud of the creditor operates on liability of the surety.**— If a surety is induced to become such by a fraud perpetrated on him by the creditor, as by false representations as to material facts, that will be a good defense; but "the representation to avoid the contract as to the surety must be a fraud on him as such, and in that character."[2] If the creditor intrusts the note of the principal and sureties to the principal for some fraudulent purpose, and consents that he shall make the sureties believe the debt is paid, and they are thus induced to forego any advantage they would otherwise have had, the sureties will be discharged. But it is otherwise if the note was intrusted to the principal for an honest purpose and the creditor did not know of or consent to the false representations.[3] On a composition between a debtor and creditor, they induced a third person to become surety for the payment of one-half the debt, by representing to him that this was to be in full of all demands; and the debtor, in pursuance of a previous arrangement, of which the surety was unapprised, gave his own note for an additional sum. *Held*, the note was void and could not be enforced against the maker, who was the principal debtor, on the ground that the taking of such note was a fraud on the surety, of which the principal might avail himself.[4] But where a party bought a team for $700, and re-

[1] Ross *v.* Clore, 3 Dana (Ky.), 189.

[2] Evans *v.* Keeland, 9 Ala. 42, per Ormond, J. To similar effect, see Waterbury *v.* Andrews, 67 Mich. 281.

[3] Adm'r of Wilson *v.* Green, 25 Vt. 450.

[4] Weed *v.* Bentley, 6 Hill (N. Y.), 56.

quested a surety to sign a note for $500 in payment for the same, and the seller, in answer to an inquiry by the surety, told him the price of the team was $500, and the surety thereupon signed the note, and the purchaser, without the knowledge of the surety, gave the seller a note for $200 in addition, it was held that this last note was binding on the purchaser. The court said: "The surety has no interest in the transaction between the principal and creditor beyond his own indemnity. He is not supposed to stipulate or assume that the principal shall receive any specific benefit from the transaction, analogous to that which parties to a creditor's composition arrange for their common debtor. The principal stands in no relation of tutelage or wardship to the surety that lays the foundation of any presumption that the latter, in assuming suretyship, is arranging an advancement or the like for the principal."[1] A surety for the price of property bought by the principal cannot usually set up as a defense that a fraud was perpetrated on the principal in making the sale, unless the principal himself repudiates the transaction. This is on the principle that the contract of the surety is accessory to the principal debt, and if the debtor himself admits the debt to be due, the surety cannot be permitted to deny it, for that would be to permit the principal to "retain the fruits of the contract, whilst the surety would avoid the performance of his obligation on the ground of its invalidity."[2] The president and chief stockholder of a national bank had caused it to be guilty of several acts prohibited by the banking law, and for which it might have been wound up. While the bank was in this condition he sold it, and was in such sale guilty of other violations of the banking law, for which the bank might have been wound up. A third party, without the knowledge of these facts, became the surety of the purchaser on certain notes for part of the purchase price, and gave a mortgage on her property to secure the purchase money. The bank soon after failed, and the surety upon learning the facts filed a bill to obtain relief from the notes and mortgage. *Held*, the relief should be granted. It was urged that the purchasers did not seek to rescind the sale,

[1] Mead *v.* Merrill, 30 N. H. 472, per Woods, C. J.; re-affirmed, 33 N. H. 437.

[2] Evans *v.* Keeland, 9 Ala. 42, per Ormond, J.; Brown *v.* Wright, 7 T. B. Mon. (Ky.) 396.

and that it would be inequitable to allow them to retain the property and discharge the surety. But the court said that through the violation of law by the bank president, who was the creditor, the bank was rendered substantially worthless, and proceeded: "Indeed, it may be deduced from settled principles in this country and in England, in accordance with what is distinctly affirmed in the civil law, that the agreement of the surety is not binding where the bargain between the primary parties out of which it springs is contaminated by positive irregularities. . . . Having been induced to become surety in the purchase of a bank, when her principals and the seller without her knowledge adopted terms and conditions which were illegal, greatly injurious to the bank, prejudicial to her interests and serving to impair her chance of protection and indemnification, she ought not, on applying for relief from her undertaking, to have the doors of the court closed against her, upon the objection that the seller and her principals have allowed the matter to stand. . . . Here we have positive illegality, a violation of public policy, and a fraud of a public nature, which was adapted to operate, and did operate, against complainant with all the severity and mischief of a direct fraud upon her."[1]

§ 235. Surety may avail himself of defense of usury.— The surety on a note may avail himself of the defense of usury to the same extent that the principal can. If it was otherwise, the principal would stand in a better position than his surety, and the surety could either not recover indemnity from the principal for the usury paid by him, or the statute against usury would be evaded.[2] Principal and surety signed a replevin (stay) bond, and the principal paid large amounts of usurious interest at various times for extensions. *Held*, the

[1] Denison *v.* Gibson, 24 Mich. 187, per Graves, J. A wife may invoke equitable intervention in her behalf where she has executed a mortgage on her lands to secure notes given by her husband, and where such mortgage was procured by fraud. Henry *et al. v.* Sneed *et al.*, 99 Mo. 407.

[2] Gray's Ex'rs *v.* Brown, 22 Ala. 262; Stockton *v.* Coleman, 39 Ind. 106; Huntress *v.* Patten, 20 Me. 28; Weimer *v.* Shelton, 7 Mo. 237; Conger *v.* Babbet, 67 Iowa, 13; Keim & Co. *v.* Avery, 7 Neb. 54. If the principal cannot plead usury the surety cannot. Pugh *v.* Cameron's Adm'r, 11 W. Va. 523. That surety cannot avail himself of defense of usury, see Savage *v.* Fox, 60 N. H. 17; Culver *v.* Wilbern, 48 Iowa, 26.

surety might, by a separate bill filed for that purpose, with or without the consent of the principal, be allowed as credits on his bond the usurious interest paid by the principal.[1] Where a judgment was entered on a bond tainted with usury, of which usury the surety had no knowledge when he became bound, and the creditor filed a bill to subject equities of the surety to the payment of the judgment, it was held that the surety could not by cross-bill allege the usury and have relief against it without a tender of the amount due in equity.[2] It has been held that, after a principal has been discharged in bankruptcy, a surety when sued for the debt cannot set off usury paid by the principal to the creditor on contracts other than the one sued on, and this upon the ground that by the terms of the bankrupt act all debts due the bankrupt pass to his assignee.[3] Where a surety, knowing a debt was usurious, paid it, and the principal paid him by a transfer of property, and then sued the creditor to recover the usury, which he might have done if he had himself paid the usury in money, it was held he was not entitled to recover.[4]

§ 236. Whether surety may avail himself of set-off in favor of principal and against creditor.— As to whether a surety, when sued for the debt of his principal, can at law avail himself of a set-off existing in favor of the principal against the creditor, the cases do not agree, but the weight of authority is that he may so avail himself of such set-off.[5] The reasoning upon which these decisions proceed has been thus expressed: "Although by our statute proper matters for set-

[1] Curtcher *v.* Trabue, 5 Dana (Ky.), 80. But in Lamoille Co. Nat. Bank *v.* Bingham, 50 Vt. 105, it was held that payment by the principal of usurious interest on a note did not enable the surety to insist that such excess above lawful interest be applied as a payment of the note *pro tanto*.

[2] Bank of Wooster *v.* Stevens, 6 Ohio St. 262.

[3] Woolfolk *v.* Plant, 46 Ga. 422.

[4] Whitehead *v.* Peck, 1 Kelly (Ga.), 140.

[5] Andrews *v.* Varrell, 46 N. H. 17; Hollister *v.* Davis, 54 Pa. St. 508; Cole *v.* Justice, 8 Ala. 793; Bronaugh *v.* Neal, 1 Rob. (La.) 23; Concord *v.* Pillsbury, 33 N. H. 310. See, to similar effect, Himrod *v.* Baugh, 85 Ill. 435; Hayes *v.* Cooper, 14 Bradw. (Ill. App.) 490; Becker *v.* Northway, 44 Minn. 61. And see Coffin *v.* McLean, 80 N. Y. 560, wherein it seems to be held that in an action against principal and surety the insolvency of the plaintiff is a sufficient ground in equity for the allowance of a set-off existing in favor of the principal against the plaintiff.

off are mutual demands only, . . . yet it is not considered as conflicting with this rule to offset a note signed by a principal and his surety against a note running to such principal alone; the debt in such case being considered as the debt of the principal."[1] In an action at law against a principal and surety on a note, it has been held competent to recoup the damages of the principal growing out of the contract to the same extent as if the note had been given by the principal and he alone were sued.[2] The same thing has been held to be a good equitable defense to an action at law under a statute allowing equitable defenses to be made at law.[3] In debt on the bond of a city marshal, against the principal and sureties, it was held that the claim of the marshal alone against the city for services was admissible as a set-off, notwithstanding the fact that the bond was under seal.[4] Judgment was recovered by a creditor against a principal and surety, and the principal recovered a judgment against the creditor, who was insolvent. *Held*, the surety might, by suit in chancery, have the one judgment set off against the other, as the debts were in reality mutual, and equity would look beyond the form of the debt to the actual facts.[5] A. held the note of B., on which C. and D. were sureties. A. sued B. and recovered a judgment, but for a less amount than he claimed, in consequence, as he alleged, of B.'s false swearing. A. then swore out a warrant for the arrest of B. on a charge of perjury, and B. fled the state. In consideration that A. would drop the prosecution, B. gave A. the note of one Mills for $500, which was all the property B. had. *Held*, that C. and D. might, by suit in chancery, have the note applied to the payment of the debt for which they were liable.[6] On the other hand, it has been held that a surety cannot at law avail of a set-off recoupment or counter-claim existing in favor of the principal against the creditor.[7] This is put upon the ground that the principal has

1 Per Sargent, J., in Andrews *v.* Varrell, 46 N. H. 17.

2 Waterman *v.* Clark, 76 Ill. 428. To same effect, see Stratman *v.* Stookey, Adm'r, 3 Bradw. (Ill. App.) 336.

3 Beehervaise *v.* Lewis, Law Rep. 7 Com. Pleas, 372.

4 Concord *v.* Pillsbury, 33 N. H. 310. See, also, to like effect, Spencer *v.* Almoney, 56 Md. 551, 562.

5 Downer *v.* Dana, 17 Vt. 518.

6 Breese *v.* Schuler, 48 Ill. 329.

7 Gillespie *v.* Torrance, 25 N. Y. 306; Lafarge *v.* Halsey, 1 Bosw. (N. Y.) 171; Emery *v.* Baltz, 22 Hun (N. Y.), 434; Lasher *v.* Williamson, 55

a right to bring a separate action for his claim against the creditor, and that he could not do this if the surety was allowed to set it up as a defense, and thus he might lose a much larger sum than that for which the surety was liable.[1] It was, however, admitted in those cases, that the surety might have relief in equity by a suit to which the principal was a party. It has also been held that the creditor cannot at law set off a debt which he claims to be due him from a guarantor against a debt which he owes such guarantor.[2]

§ 237. Creditor not bound to exhaust securities put up by principal before suing surety — When surety without paying may enforce securities for the debt.— According to the English law, the creditor cannot be compelled, before proceeding against the surety, to exhaust a mortgage or other security which he may hold from the principal for the payment of the debt, although it is otherwise by the civil law.[3] The remedy of the surety is to himself pay the debt, and he will then be subrogated to, and may enforce, all liens held by the creditor for the payment of the debt. A creditor in New Jersey, where the parties resided, took from B., the holder of a promissory note indorsed by the plaintiff, on a loan of money al-

N. Y. 619; Davis *v.* Toulmin, 77 N. Y. 280; Thalheimer *v.* Crow, 13 Col. 397. If the surety pleads as a set-off a demand due his principal, he must show that the demand has been assigned to him, or that he makes it with the principal's consent, and the consent must be such as to bind the principal. Graff *v.* Kahn, 18 Bradw. (Ill. App.) 485; Wieland *v.* Oberne, 20 Bradw. (Ill. App.) 118; Baltimore & Ohio R. R. Co. *v.* Bitner, 15 W. Va. 455; Beard *v.* The Union & Am. Pub. Co., 71 Ala. 69. On this subject, see Poorman *v.* Goswiler, 2 Watts (Pa.), 69; Osborne *v.* Bryce (Cir. Ct. E. D. Wis.), 23 Fed. Rep. 171; Aultman *v.* Hefner, 67 Tex. 54.

[1] And also upon the principle that a surety cannot set up defenses personal to the principal. Henry *v.* Daley, 17 Hun (N. Y.), 210.

[2] Morley *v.* Inglis, 4 Bing. N. C. 58; Id., 5 Scott, 314.

[3] Watson *v.* Sutherland, 1 Cooper, Ch. (Tenn.) 208; Hayes *v.* Ward, 4 Johns. Ch. 123; Buck *v.* Sanders, 1 Dana (Ky.), 187; Allen *v.* Woodard, 125 Mass. 400. See on same subject, Gary *v.* Cannon, 3 Ired. Eq. (N. C.) 64. See, also, Irick *v.* Black, 2 C. E. Green (N. J.), 189. See the civil law rule in Hill & Co. *v.* Bourcier & Pond, 29 La. Ann. 841. In Virginia it is held that the principal's lands must first be exhausted before subjecting that of the sureties. Moore *v.* Friedenwald, 77 Va. 57; Stovall *v.* Border Grange Bank, 78 Va. 188; Horton *v.* Bond, 28 Gratt. (Va.) 815. But if principal's lands are so incumbered that nothing can be realized, lands of surety may be held. Bell *v.* McConkey, 82 Va. 176. See

leged to be usurious, a bond and mortgage, which was, if valid, an ample security for the debt, and, instead of resorting to the bond and mortgage or to the principal, sued the plaintiff in New York on his indorsement. The plaintiff filed a bill to enjoin the suit at law till the bond and mortgage were exhausted in New Jersey, and it was held he was entitled to relief. The court held the law to be as above stated, and granted the relief solely on the ground that there was reason to believe that the bond and mortgage had been rendered frail and insecure by the illegal act of the holder of the note, and the court would not permit the surety to be forced to pay the money and then litigate this doubtful question with the maker of the bond and mortgage, as it was more equitable that the creditor should first litigate it.[1] Where principal and surety have both mortgaged property for the debt of the principal, the surety is entitled to have the property of the principal sold first to satisfy the debt.[2] When the principal is insolvent, the surety has, under certain circumstances, a right, before paying the debt, to file a bill to enforce a lien for its payment. This was held where a slave was sold under a decree of court and a lien retained for the purchase money, for which a surety also became bound, and the slave was levied on by other creditors;[3] where land belonging to an estate was sold and a lien retained on it for the purchase money;[4] and where certain persons had in their hands funds belonging to a clerk of a court in his representative capacity.[5] Where a judgment had been rendered against principal and surety, and the principal was insolvent, it was held that a court of chancery would entertain jurisdiction of a suit brought by the surety for the purpose of reach-

on this subject, also, Booth *v.* Wiley, 102 Ill. 84.

[1] Hayes *v.* Ward, 4 Johns. Ch. 123.

[2] Neimcewicz *v.* Gahn, 3 Paige Ch. 614; James *v.* Jacques, 26 Tex. 320. To precisely similar effect, see Keel *v.* Levy, 19 Oreg. 450; Pacific Guano Co. *v.* Anglin, 82 Ala. 492; Gresham *v.* Ware, 79 Ala. 192.

[3] Henry *v.* Compton, 2 Head (Tenn.), 549.

[4] Polk *v.* Gallant, 2 Dev. & Bat. Eq. (N. C.) 395. To same effect, see Green *v.* Crockett, 2 Dev. & Bat. Eq. 390; Arnold *v.* Hicks, 3 Ired. Eq. (N. C.) 17; Egerton *v.* Alley, 6 Ired. Eq. (N. C.) 188. A surety upon a note for the purchase money of land sold under a decree of court has the right, on default of his principal, to require a resale in exoneration of his liability. *Ex parte* Pettillo, 80 N. C. 50.

[5] Bunting *v.* Ricks, 2 Dev. & Bat. Eq. (N. C.) 130.

ing credits of the principal in the hands of third parties, and appropriating them in payment of the judgment, although the surety had not paid the debt.[1]

§ 238. Surety may compel creditor to proceed against principal.— It is settled by a long-continued and unvarying ing current of authorities that the surety may, by a suit in chancery, after the debt becomes due and before he pays it, compel the creditor to proceed to collect the debt from the principal, provided he indemnify the creditor against loss from a fruitless suit against the principal.[2] As the mere passive delay of the creditor in proceeding against the principal, however long continued and however injurious to the surety, will not ordinarily discharge him,[3] this right to accelerate the movements of the creditor is of great importance. Even if the surety should suffer no injury by the delay, it is unreasonable that he should always have such a cloud as the debt of the principal hanging over him. It is likewise settled that the surety may, upon the terms of bringing the amount due into court, compel the creditor to prove the debt in bankruptcy against the estate of the principal.[4]

§ 239. Cases holding that surety by request and without suit may compel creditor to proceed against principal.—As to whether the surety may without suit accelerate the movements of the creditor against the principal there is great conflict of authority. There is a numerous and well-considered class of authorities which hold that if, after the debt is due, the surety, verbally or in writing, request the creditor to sue the principal, who is then solvent, and the creditor fail to do

[1] McConnell *v.* Scott, 15 Ohio, 401.

[2] Ranelaugh *v.* Hays, 1 Vernon, 189; Hays *v.* Ward, 4 Johns. Ch. 123; Antrolus *v.* Davidson, 3 Merivale, 569–79; King *v.* Baldwin, 2 Johns. Ch. 554; Lee *v.* Rook, Moseley, 318; Whitridge *v.* Durkee, 2 Md. Ch. 442; Nisbet *v.* Smith, 2 Brown's Ch. Ca. 579; Hogaboom *v.* Herrick, 4 Vt. 131; Rees *v.* Berrington, 2 Ves. Jr. 540; Huey *v.* Pinney, 5 Minn. 310; Kent *v.* Matthews, 12 Leigh (Va.), 573; Rice *v.* Downing, 12 B. Mon. (Ky.) 44; *In re* Babcock, 3 Story, 393. And see, also, Norton *v.* Reid, 11 S. C. 593. The fact that a surety or guarantor had an interest in prosecuting the principal by the creditor does not render him guilty of maintenance. Board Comm'rs *v.* Jameson, 86 Ind. 154.

[3] Pharr *v.* McHugh & Union, 32 La. Ann. 1280; People *v.* White, 28 Hun (N. Y.), 289; Newton *v.* Hammond, 38 Ohio St. 430.

[4] Wright *v.* Simpson, 6 Vesey, 714; *Ex parte* Rushforth, 10 Vesey, 409; *In re* Babcock, 3 Story, 393.

so, and the principal afterwards becomes insolvent, the surety is thereby discharged. The reasoning upon which these decisions are founded is that equity will compel the creditor to sue the principal and make the money from him, because he is primarily liable for it, and it is the duty of the creditor to get payment from him if possible. If it is his duty to do this there is no reason why he should not be compelled to do it upon the request of the surety *in pais*, as well as by filing a bill in chancery against him. Where the creditor does any act injurious to the surety, or omits to do an act when required which equity and his duty to the surety enjoin it upon him to do, and the omission is injurious to the surety, in either case the surety will be discharged. To delay under such circumstances is against conscience, and in its effect is a fraud upon the surety.[1] The fact that there was a statute providing for the discharge of the surety, if the creditor failed to sue, upon being required in writing by the surety to do so, has been held to make no difference, the statute being held to be merely cumulative, and not to impair the right of a surety to be discharged upon a verbal request.[2] In order that the request may have this effect, the principal must, at the time

[1] Pain *v.* Packard, 13 Johns. 174; King *v.* Baldwin, 17 Johns. 384, reversing the decision of Chancellor Kent, in King *v.* Baldwin, 2 Johns. Ch. 554, by the casting vote of Lieut. Gov. Taylor, a layman. The two first named cases are the leading authorities on the view of the subject which they hold. They have been followed, or decisions to the same effect rendered, in Manchester Iron Manuf. Co. *v.* Sweeting, 10 Wend. 163; Hempstead *v.* Watkins, 6 Ark. (1 Eng.) 317; Thompson *v.* Robinson, 34 Ark. 44; Martin *v.* Shekan, 2 Col. 614; Hancock *v.* Bryant, 2 Yerg. (Tenn.) 476; Cope *v.* Smith, Ex'r, 8 Serg. & Rawle (Pa.), 110; Hopkins *v.* Spurlock, 2 Heisk. (Tenn.) 152; Thompson *v.* Watson, 10 Yerg. (Tenn.) 362; Colgrove *v.* Tallman, 67 N. Y. 95; Wheeler *v.* Benedict, 36 Hun (N. Y.), 478; Bruce *v.* Edwards, 1 Stew. (Ala.) 11. See Trimble *v.* Thorne, 16 Johns. 152, as to application of this principle to the indorser of a promissory note. And to this latter point, see, also, Converse *v.* Cook, 25 Hun, 44; same case again, 31 Hun, 417, wherein it was held that an accommodation indorser was not a surety in such a sense as to enable him to discharge himself from liability on a note by proving a request to the holder thereof to enforce payment by the maker, and the failure of the holder so to do.

[2] Thompson *v.* Watson, 10 Yerg. (Tenn.) 362; Strader *v.* Houghton, 9 Port. (Ala.) 334; Herbert *v.* Hobbs, 3 Stew. (Ala.) 9: Goodman *v.* Griffin, 3 Stew. (Ala.) 160.

thereof, be solvent and able to pay all his debts, according to the ordinary usage of trade.[1] The request need not be accompanied by an offer to pay the expenses of the suit, unless the creditor expressly puts his refusal to sue upon these grounds.[2] If the creditor have a mortgage on property of the principal for the security of the debt, which is ample for that purpose when the debt becomes due, and refuse after request by the surety to foreclose the mortgage till the property greatly depreciates in value, it has been held that the surety is thereby discharged.[3] It has also been held that if the creditor, after request by the surety, fail to present his claim against the estate of an insolvent principal, and the debt is thereby lost, the surety is released *pro tanto*.[4] A guaranty given by the

[1] Herrick *v.* Borst, 4 Hill (N. Y.), 650. To similar effect, see Huffman *v.* Hulbert, 13 Wend. 377; Merritt *v.* Lincoln, 21 Barb. 249; Field *v.* Cutler, 4 Lans. (N. Y.) 195. The liability of the surety to a note is not lessened or terminated by the failure of the holder to sue the maker, upon the surety's request, when it appears that the maker was at the time of the request, and at all times thereafter, insolvent. Marsh *v.* Dunckel, 25 Hun (N. Y.), 167.

[2] Wetzel *v.* Sponsler, 18 Pa. St. 460.

[3] Remsen *v.* Beekman, 25 N. Y. 552. where the doctrine of King *v.* Baldwin, although previously questioned by judges in the same state, was approved on principle and followed as authority. If the principle of King *v.* Baldwin is correct, it would seem clear that the above decision is also correct. The precise opposite has, however, been held in Branch Bank at Montgomery *v.* Perdue, 3 Ala. 409, and in Haden *v.* Brown, 18 Ala. 641, by a court which held the doctrine of King *v.* Baldwin. The same court held that, after judgment against principal and sureties, the sureties were not discharged by the failure of the creditor upon request to levy on the property of the principal, and the subsequent insolvency of the principal. Buckalew *v.* Smith, 44 Ala. 638. And also that a lessor was not bound to distrain property of the lessee upon the request of the surety; the distinction seeming to be made between forcing the creditor to proceed generally and forcing him to proceed in a particular way against particular property. Brooks *v.* Carter, 36 Ala. 682. To the same effect as the last case, see Ruggles *v.* Holden, 3 Wend. 216. It has also been held that a creditor is not bound upon request to arrest a principal who is insolvent, but had friends who would probably have paid the debt if he had been arrested. Warner *v.* Beardsley, 8 Wend. 194. It has been held by another court that a creditor was not bound at the request of the surety to levy on property of the principal. Newell *v.* Hamer, 4 How. (Miss.) 684. On this subject, see, also, Bank *v.* Klingensmith, 7 Watts (Pa.), 523; Weiler *v.* Hoch, 25 Pa. St. 525; Baldwin *v.* Gordon, 12 Martin (La.), O. S. 378.

[4] McCollum *v.* Hinkley, 9 Vt. 143. The general doctrine of King *v.* Baldwin is repudiated by the same

defendant was to be void if the plaintiff should omit to avail himself to the utmost of any security he held of R. He held a bill drawn by R. and accepted by an insolvent, still in prison. *Held*, he was not bound before suing on the guaranty to prosecute the insolvent.[1] A. was indebted to B. for one year's rent of certain premises, for which B. had lost his landlord's lien, by lapse of time. A. was also indebted to C. for rent for the current year, for which C. had a lien if he chose to enforce it, and for which last rent D. was surety. The property of A. was levied on by execution at the suit of third parties, and D. notified C. to file his claim for rent with the sheriff, by which the lien would have been preserved and the debt made. C. refused to do this, and the debt was lost. *Held*, the surety D. was discharged.[2] Upon the sale of a guarantied bond and mortgage, the guarantor was held not released from liability because of the failure of an assignee of the bond and mortgage to comply with a notice requiring him to proceed to collect the debt by legal proceedings, and the property after such notice depreciated in value and the obligor became insolvent. It was held the duty of the guarantor to pay the debt himself and make the money out of his principal.[3]

§ 240. **Requisites of the request to sue.**—The notice to the creditor to sue, which will discharge the surety if not complied with, should be so clear and distinct that the meaning of the surety can be at once apprehended without explanation or argument.[4] A request to "push (the surety) and keep pushing him," when it is understood by both parties to be a request to collect the debt by legal means, is sufficient. A request to collect the money by dunning, or in any other way than by legal proceedings, is not sufficient.[5] A notice by the surety in a note to the holder "to collect it, as he would not stand

court. Hogaboom *v.* Herrick, 4 Vt. 131; Hickok *v.* Farmers' & Mechanics' Bank, 35 Vt. 476.

1 Musket *v.* Rogers, 5 Bing. N. C. 728; Id., 8 Scott, 51.

2 Lichtenthaler *v.* Thompson, 13 Serg. & Rawle (Pa.), 157.

3 Newcomb *v.* Hale, 90 N. Y. 326.

4 Wolleshlare *v.* Searles, 45 Pa. St. 45; Shimer *v.* Jones, 47 Pa. St. 268; Conrad *v.* Foy, 68 Pa. St. 381; Fidler *v.* Hershey, 90 Pa. St. 363; Denick *v.* Hubbard, 27 Hun (N. Y.), 347; Thayer *v.* King, 31 Hun (N. Y.), 437; Goodwin *v.* Simonson, 74 N. Y. 133.

5 Singer *v.* Troutman, 49 Barb. (N. Y.) 182.

bail any longer," is sufficient.[1] It has been held that the request to sue must be accompanied by an explicit declaration that unless suit is brought the surety will no longer remain liable. Therefore, where a surety wrote to a creditor, as follows: "I therefore notify you that I will be no longer considered bail. Please take another bond for him or payment," it was held the request was not sufficient.[2] The request to sue a note when due avails nothing if made before the note is due. The request must be made at the time of, or after, the maturity of the obligation.[3] The surety may make the request by agent, and if he has a general agent who transacts all his business, it is the duty of such agent to make such request without any special directions. Where the creditor is not in the neighborhood, and has left the note in the hands of an agent for collection, the request may be made of such agent.[4] The request may be made of the counsel of an absent or non-resident plaintiff in a judgment.[5] Where a married woman is the owner of a note, a request made of her husband to put the note in suit will not avail the surety. The husband is not *ipso facto* the agent of the wife in that regard.[6] It has been held that the request to sue would not avail the surety if the principal lived in another county.[7] But it has also been held that the surety might avail himself of such request when the principal lived in another state, but had property in the state in which the creditor resided, which might have been subjected to the payment of the debt.[8] Where the creditor has failed to sue upon request, it has been held that the burden of proof is on him to show, in a suit against the surety, that the money could not have been collected if suit had been brought against the principal when the request was made.[9]

[1] Stickler *v.* Burkholder, 47 Pa. St. 476.

[2] Greenawalt *v.* Kreider, 3 Pa. St. 264. To similar effect, see Erie Bank *v.* Gibson, 1 Watts (Pa.), 143, and Fidler *v.* Hershey, 90 Pa. St. 363.

[3] Hellen *v.* Crawford, 44 Pa. St. 105. And see Fidler *v.* Hershey, 90 Pa. St. 363.

[4] Wetzel *v.* Sponslers' Ex'rs, 18 Pa. St. 460. See, also, on this point, Geddis *v.* Hawk, 10 Serg. & Rawle (Pa.), 33.

[5] Thomas *v.* Mann, 28 Pa. St. 520.

[6] Shimer *v.* Jones, 47 Pa. St. 268.

[7] Alcorn *v.* The Commonwealth, 66 Pa. St. 172.

[8] Hancock *v.* Bryant, 2 Yerg. (Tenn.) 476.

[9] Stickler *v.* Burkholder, 47 Pa. St. 476.

§ 241. Same continued — Sufficiency of notice.— A surety cannot, it is held, claim his release from an obligation on a verbal notice to the creditor to proceed against the principal. A notice under such circumstances must, to be available, be in writing.[1] And where the creditor fails to sue after notice to him to sue, the surety must show clearly the nature and terms of the notice before he can be discharged.[2] Judicial notice will be taken of the date of a notice, and, if given on Sunday, it will be held void.[3] In a suit to foreclose a mortgage it appeared that the surety sought to be charged told the plaintiff to collect the mortgage "and not to let it run over the time it is due." *Held*, the notice was insufficient, and delay in bringing foreclosure did not discharge him.[4] So, a notice by a surety to a note to the holder thereof that he "must make Daniel (the principal) come to time this fall" was held not such a notice as would constitute a defense upon failure of the holder to sue.[5] The following notice, however, to the payee and holder of a note by a surety thereon, "to at once proceed to collect the note you hold, upon which I am surety; I will stand no longer," was held sufficient.[6]

§ 242. Cases holding that the surety cannot, by request alone, accelerate the movements of the creditor against the principal.— The great majority of cases on the subject hold, in the absence of any statutory provision, that if after the debt is due the surety request the creditor to sue the principal, who is then solvent, and the creditor fails to do so, and the principal afterwards becomes insolvent, the surety is not thereby discharged. The ground upon which these decisions rest is, that the principal and surety are both equally bound to the creditor, who may have taken a surety in order that he might not have to sue the principal. If the surety desires a suit brought against the principal, he may himself pay the debt, and immediately sue the principal. The contrary doctrine is an innovation, and was unknown to the common law.[7]

[1] Petty *v.* Douglass, 76 Mo. 70.

[2] King *v.* Haynes *et al.*, 35 Ark. 463.

[3] Chrisman *v.* Tuttle, 59 Ind. 155.

[4] Hunt *v.* Purdy, 82 N. Y. 486.

[5] Lawson *v.* Buckley, 49 Hun (N. Y.), 329.

[6] Iliff *v.* Weymouth, 40 Ohio St. 101.

[7] Jenkins *v.* Clarkson, 7 Ohio, 72; Carr *v.* Howard, 8 Blackf. (Ind.) 190; Halstead *v.* Brown, 17 Ind. 202; Ex'rs of Dennis *v.* Rider, 2 McLean, 451; Davis *v.* Huggins, 3 N. H. 231;

The surety on the bond of a note clerk of a bank was informed by the bank of an embezzlement committed by the clerk, and, before paying any portion of the amount embezzled, requested the bank to cause the arrest of the clerk, which it refused to do. *Held*, the surety was not, in the absence of any indication of a fraudulent connivance at the escape of the clerk, discharged thereby.[1] Where the holder of two notes made by the same party commenced an action against him, declaring on the common counts for a greater sum than the aggregate of both notes, and attached property sufficient to satisfy both, but did not intend to include in the action one of the notes, which was signed by a surety, and there were subsequent attachments of the same property by other creditors, it was held that the plaintiff was not bound to comply with the request of the surety, to put into the action the note signed by him, even though he offered to indemnify the plaintiff for so doing.[2] Much may be said in favor of both views of this question concerning the right of the surety, by request and without suit, to accelerate the movements of the creditor against the principal. The objection that the rule permitting it is an innovation might, with equal propriety, be urged against most of

Pickett *v.* Land, 2 Bailey, Law (S. C.). 608: Nichols *v.* McDowell, 14 B. Mon. (Ky.) 5; Frye *v.* Barker, 4 Pick. 382; Stout *v.* Ashton, 5 T. B. Mon. (Ky.) 251; Gage *v.* Mechanics' Nat'l Bank of Chicago, 79 Ill. 62; Dillon *v.* Holmes, 5 Neb. 484; Huff *v.* Slife, 25 Neb. 448; Inkster *v.* First Nat'l Bank of Marshall, 30 Mich. 143; Langdon *v.* Markle, 48 Mo. 357; Hartman *v.* Burlingame, 9 Cal. 557; Dane *v.* Corduan, 24 Cal. 157; Hickok *v.* Farmers' & Mechanics' Bank, 35 Vt. 476; Hogaboom *v.* Herrick, 4 Vt. 131; Caston *v.* Dunlap, Rich. Eq. Cas. (S. C.) 77; Croughton *v.* Duval, 3 Call (Va.), 69; Boutte *v.* Martin, 16 La. (Curry), 133; Taylor *v.* Beck, 13 Ill. 376. On same subject, see Huey *v.* Pinney, 5 Minn. 310; Benedict *v.* Olson, 37 Minn. 431; Bizzell *v.* Smith, 2 Dev. Eq. (N. C.) 27; Thompson *v.* Bowne, 39 N. J. Law (10 Vroom), 2; Hogshead *v.* Williams, 55 Ind. 145; Jerauld *v.* Trippet, 62 Ind. 122; Harris *v.* Newell, 42 Wis. 687; Pintard *v.* Davis, 1 Spencer (N. J.), 205; affirmed, Pintard *v.* Davis, 1 Zab. (N. J.) 205; Findley *v.* Hill, 8 Oreg. 247; May *v.* Reed, 125 Ind. 199; Wilds *v.* Attix, 4 Del. Ch. 253. And see, generally, that mere delay of creditor to sue principal when requested to do so by surety will not discharge surety, Trustees *v.* Southard, 31 Ill. App. 359; Newton *v.* Hammond, 38 Ohio St. 430; Quillen *v.* Quigley, 14 Nev. 215; Ingels *v.* Sutliff, 36 Kan. 444; Miller *v.* Arnold, 65 Ind. 488.

[1] Louisiana State Bank *v.* Ledoux, 3 La. Ann. 674.

[2] Adams Bank *v.* Anthony, 18 Pick. 238.

the causes which are now recognized as entitling the surety to his discharge. These causes are the outgrowth of equitable principles inherent in the relation of principal and surety; and several of the most important of them, which are now nowhere disputed, have been established by decisions of the courts during the present century. The rule under consideration was first announced by the supreme court of New York, in the year 1816, and is a doctrine recognized only by some of the American courts, no decisions to a similar effect having been made by the courts of England. Although repudiated by a majority of the courts of the United States, the rule is supported by strong equities, and is in harmony with the general well-recognized rules governing the relation of principal and surety. Recognizing the justice and equity of this rule, the legislatures of many of the United States have, by statute, provided that the surety may, by notice, require the creditor to proceed against the principal.

§ 243. **Surety may make the same defense at law as in equity — Whether he must make his defense at law when sued at law.**— "The subject of equitable relief in behalf of sureties is one of original jurisdiction in a court of chancery. The peculiar rights of a surety originated in, and are exclusively the outgrowth of, equity. Formerly it was held in several instances that the remedy of the surety was only in equity and could not be made available in courts of common law. But it is now held, as a general rule, that the liability of sureties is governed by the same principles at law as in equity. And probably with few exceptions the same considerations which are sufficient in equity to discharge the surety will be available for the same purpose at law."[1] On the ground that the surety can make the same defense at law that he can in equity, it has been held that when sued at law the surety must avail himself of such defenses as he can there make, and if he

[1] Per Isham, J., in Viele *v.* Hoag, 24 Vt. 46. To same effect, see Heath *v.* Derry Bank, 44 N. H. 174; Samuell *v.* Howarth, 3 Meriv. 272; Baker *v.* Briggs, 8 Pick. 122; Rogers *v.* School Trustees, 46 Ill. 428; Watriss *v.* Pierce, 32 N. H. 560; State Bank *v.* Watkins, 6 Ark. (1 Eng.) 123; Smith *v.* Clopton, 48 Miss. 66; The People *v.* Jansen, 7 Johns. 332; Shelton *v.* Hurd, 7 R. I. 403; Maxwell *v.* Connor, 1 Hill, Eq. (S. C.) 14; Wayne *v.* Kirby, 2 Bailey, Law (S. C.), 551; Springer *v.* Toothaker, 43 Me. 381. *Contra*, Ex'r of McCall *v.* Adm'r of Evans, 2 Brev. (S. C.) 3.

does not, that he cannot afterwards avail himself of such defenses in equity, unless he was prevented from so doing by fraud, accident or the wrongful act of the other party, without any negligence or other fault on his part.[1] On the other hand it has been held that if a surety when sued at law does not there make his defense and judgment is recovered against him, he can afterwards come into equity and have relief. The reason is that the discharge of a surety was a matter of original equity jurisdiction, and the fact that courts of law now entertain jurisdiction of the matter does not oust equity of its original jurisdiction. "Where the jurisdiction of courts of chancery and courts of law is concurrent in consequence of courts of law having enlarged their jurisdiction by their own acts, or of its having been enlarged by act of the legislature without prohibitory words, the party may make his election as to the tribunal in which he will make his defense."[2]

§ 244. **Whether surety, having failed to make defense at law, can have relief in equity.**— It has been held that, where there is no question that the defense of a surety can be made at law, then it must be made there, and the decision of that tribunal is conclusive. "But if it be doubtful whether a court of law can take cognizance of the defense, and there exists no doubt of the jurisdiction of a court of equity, and if in such a case a defendant at law, under the influence of such doubt, omits to make his defense, or if he bring it forward and it be overruled under the idea that it is no defense at law, it is not granting a new trial for a court of equity to afford relief, notwithstanding the trial at law."[3] A surety being sued at law

[1] Vilas *v.* Jones, 1 N. Y. 274; Schroeppell *v.* Shaw, 3 N. Y. 446; Ramsey *v.* Perley, 34 Ill. 504; Kenner *v.* Caldwell, Bailey, Eq. Cas. (S. C.) 149; Maxwell *v.* Connor, 1 Hill, Eq. (S. C.) 14; M'Grew *v.* Tombeckbee Bank, 5 Port. (Ala.) 547; Herbert *v.* Hobbs, 3 Stew. (Ala.) 9; Dickerson *v.* Comm'rs Ripley Co., 6 Ind. 128; Smith *v.* McLain, 11 W. Va. 654.

[2] Hempstead *v.* Conway, 6 Ark. (1 Eng.) 317, per Oldham, J.; Wayland *v.* Tucker, 4 Gratt. (Va.) 267; Harlan *v.* Wingate, 2 J. J. Marsh. (Ky.) 138; Smith *v.* Crease's Ex'r, 2 Cranch, C. C. 481. On this subject, see, also, Sailly *v.* Elmore, 2 Paige Ch. 497.

[3] King *v.* Baldwin, 17 Johns. 384, per Spencer, C. J. To similar effect, see Rathbone *v.* Warren, 10 Johns. 587. It has, however, been held that a party who failed to make his defense at law because he was advised and believed that he could not do so, could not afterwards have relief in equity. Dickerson *v.* Commissioners of Ripley County, 6 Ind. 128. In an action upon a bond conditioned for

might have made his defense there, but did not, and pending such suit filed a bill in chancery for discovery, and setting up his defense as surety, and it was held he was entitled to the relief sought by his bill.[1] It has been held that, if a surety is sued at law and makes an unsuccessful defense there, he cannot afterwards set up the same defense in equity.[2] But it has also been held that, if he sets up one defense at law and is unsuccessful in that, he may afterwards set up another defense in equity.[3] Judgment was recovered against principal and surety, and the creditor afterwards gave time to the principal. The creditor afterwards sued the principal and the surety on the judgment, and the surety defended on the ground that the giving of time discharged him, but was unsuccessful in his defense, and judgment was rendered against him. He then filed a bill to restrain the second judgment at law, setting up the same matter of defense that he had urged at law, and it was held that he was entitled to relief. This was put upon the ground that, after the first judgment at law, the relation of principal and surety was so far merged that the surety could not make his defense at law.[4] Much of the confusion of the cases on this subject has arisen from the fact that originally most of the defenses of a surety had to be made in equity, and could not be set up as a defense to a suit at law, and the rule permitting the same defense to be made at law that would avail the surety in equity was adopted by various courts at different times, and is not even now fully recognized by all of them. Where the surety can and does make his defense at law, the great weight of authority is that the decision of the court of law is conclusive on him. The weight of authority also is that if he can make his defense at law, but does not, and judgment is rendered against him, he cannot afterwards have relief against such judgment on any ground which he might have relied on in the suit at law. Where the

the performance of a decree, a surety cannot, either in law or equity, avail himself of a defense which his principal might have, but did not, set up in the case in which such decree was rendered. Griswold *v.* Hazard, 28 Fed. Rep. 597, following Hazard *v.* Griswold, 21 Fed. Rep. 178.

[1] Viele *v.* Hoag, 24 Vt. 46.

[2] Cooper *v.* Evans, Law Rep. 4 Eq. Cas. 45.

[3] Davis *v.* Stainbank, 6 De Gex, M. & G. 679.

[4] Dunham *v.* Downer, 31 Vt. 249.

case is such that a court of law will not entertain his defense, then if he had a good equitable defense he will be relieved from the judgment by a court of chancery. A sheriff received certain claims for collection, and collected them and paid the proceeds over to the person entitled to them, but did not take up his receipt given for the claims. The sheriff died, and his receipt came into the hands of the successor of the person who gave the claims to him for collection, and he sued the sureties of the sheriff for the amount of the claims, and recovered, and they paid the judgment. Afterwards, learning the facts, they filed a bill to have the money they had paid returned to them, and it was held that they, having been guilty of no laches, and not knowing of their defense when the judgment was rendered, were entitled to relief.[1]

§ 245. If creditor lead a surety to believe debt is paid and surety is injured, he is discharged.— If the creditor tells the surety that the debt is paid when in fact it is not, and the surety in consequence thereof releases a security, or omits to secure himself, or is in any manner injured thereby, the surety is discharged.[2] And this is true even though the creditor is honestly mistaken in the statement which he makes.[3] The creditor having caused the injury should suffer it. The same thing was held where the surety on a sealed note was given by the payee a release not under seal, and induced to believe for several years, and until the principal became insolvent, that he was discharged.[4] So where, after joint judgment against principal and surety, the creditor, by his statements

[1] Hickman *v.* Hall, 5 Littell (Ky.), 338.

[2] Bank *v.* Haskell, 51 N. H. 116; High *v.* Cox, 55 Ga. 662; Waters *v.* Creagh, 4 Stew. & Port. (Ala.) 410; Thornburgh *v.* Marden, 33 Iowa, 380. And to same effect, see, also, Rowley *v.* Jewett, 56 Iowa, 492. If a surety is given to understand that the principal alone will be looked to for payment and is lulled into security to his loss, he will be discharged. West *v.* Brison, 99 Mo. 684. So fraudulent conduct that lulls the surety into groundless confidence to his loss discharges him. Harmon *v.* Hule, 1 Wash. Terr. (N. S.) 422.

[3] Baker *v.* Briggs, 8 Pick. 122; Carpenter *v.* King, 9 Met. (Mass.) 511. And involving the same principle, see Canadian Bank of Commerce *v.* Green, 45 Up. Can. (Q. B.) 81.

[4] Teague *v.* Russell, 2 Stew. (Ala.) 420. Sureties on a note having been induced to believe for nearly five years that the note had been satisfied, and thereby deprived of seeking indemnity, are released. Brooking *v.* Farmers' Bank, 83 Ky. 431.

to the surety, led him to believe the debt was paid and he would not be troubled about it, and these statements were made under such circumstances as to justify the surety in believing and acting on them, and he was thereby induced to abstain from securing himself, when he might easily have done so, until the principal became insolvent, it was held he was discharged.[1] The surety on a note applied to the holder, and told him that if he had to pay the note he wished to do it soon, as he could then secure himself; to which the holder replied that he would look to the principal for payment and he need give himself no trouble about it. The surety took no steps in the matter, but it did not appear that the principal became insolvent. *Held*, the surety was discharged.[2] The holder of a promissory note, believing it was paid in a trade he supposed he had made with the principal, so informed the surety, who knew nothing to the contrary for five years. It was not clear whether the circumstances of the principal had become better or worse. *Held*, the surety was discharged, and that it made no difference what the circumstances of the principal had become. The court said the language of the code was, not only "injures the security," but also "exposes him to greater liability or increases his risk." The surety had a right to notify the creditor, or to pay the debt himself and sue the principal; he might have obtained additional security, etc.. All these he was deprived of and lulled to sleep for five years. If the principal remained solvent the creditor was not injured, but the surety was discharged.[3] In an action against the surety on a sewing machine agent's bond it appeared that at the time the surety gave notice to the company to whom

[1] Roberts *v.* Miles, 12 Mich. 297. To similar effect, see White *v.* Walker, 31 Ill. 422.

[2] Harris *v.* Brooks, 21 Pick. 195. *Contra*, see Mahurin *v.* Pearson, 8 N. H. 539; Auchampaugh *v.* Schmidt, 77 Iowa, 13. See, also, Michigan State Ins. Co. *v.* Soule, 51 Mich. 312, wherein it was held that a creditor's mere statement to his debtor's surety that the debtor's responsibility was sufficient security for the debt, and that he would not be called upon, did not estop the creditor from resorting to the surety if the claim was not renounced and the surety was not misled by the assurance to his disadvantage.

[3] Whitaker *v.* Kirby, 54 Ga. 277. On this subject, see Hogaboom *v.* Herrick, 4 Vt. 131; Bullard *v.* Ledbetter, 59 Ga. 109; Taylor *v.* Lohman, 74 Ind. 418.

the bond was executed not to deliver any more machines to the agent on the credit of the bond; the company's general agent stated to the surety that he need give himself "no uneasiness on account of the bond," saying, "I have never sued a bondsman yet; I shall get it out of Davis (the principal) and you need not trouble yourself further about it." *Held*, these statements did not estop the company from recovering.[1]

§ 246. **When surety not discharged although he believe debt is paid.**— If a note be delivered up to be canceled by mistake, and the payee before its maturity notify the makers of the mistake, and that he still looks to them for payment, it has been held that he may recover upon the note as well against the surety as against the principal, provided the surety has not, prior to such notice, relying upon the surrender of the note, relinquished securities held by him for his indemnity, or been in some manner damnified.[2] Where a creditor told a surety that he considered the principal possessed of property sufficient to discharge the liability, that he had given or would give him time, that the principal would pay the debt, and that he did not want the surety any longer, it was held the surety was not discharged, there being no evidence that he relied on such representations or was injured thereby.[3] The same thing was held where the surety said to the creditor that he must make the debt out of the principal, and the creditor replied that he need put himself to no further trouble about the debt, as he had made a present of it to the principal, there being no evidence that the surety was injured thereby.[4] The holder of a note commenced suit on it, and levied an attachment on the property of the principal. The surety was informed thereof, and in consequence neglected to secure himself. Afterwards the creditor dismissed the attachment suit and sued the surety. *Held*, the surety was not discharged, as the creditor made no agreement with, nor representation to, him that he would rely solely on the attachment or prosecute the suit.[5]

[1] Howe Machine Co. *v.* Farrington, 82 N. Y. 121.

[2] Blodgett *v.* Bickford, 30 Vt. 731.

[3] Brubaker *v.* Okeson, 36 Pa. St. 519. See, also, Michigan State Ins. Co. *v.* Soule, 51 Mich. 312.

[4] Driskell *v.* Mateer, 31 Mo. 325. See, also, Michigan State Ins. Co. *v.* Soule, 51 Mich. 312.

[5] Barney *v.* Clark, 46 N. H. 514. And where a judgment creditor, in a judgment against principal and

Where the creditor knew that the surety was negotiating a loan for the principal, for the purpose of paying off therewith the debt for which the surety was liable, and the creditor promised the principal without consideration to give him further time, and the surety in consequence desisted from his attempt to raise the money, and the principal failed to pay the debt, it was held the surety was not discharged.[1] A. having sent an order to B. for certain goods, C. agreed to guaranty payment to B. upon an undertaking of D. to indemnify C. B. accordingly informed C. that the goods were preparing, and afterwards shipped them to A. without notifying C. that they were shipped. Afterwards D. desired to recall his indemnity, upon which C. wrote to B. to know whether he had executed the order, to which no answer was given by B. for a considerable time, he having gone abroad in the interim. Upon this, C., supposing from the silence of B. that the order was not executed, gave up his indemnity to D. *Held*, C. was not discharged from his guaranty.[2]

§ 247. **Rights of surety against third persons — Indemnity of surety.**— The principal may, before the debt has been paid by the surety, confess a judgment in favor of the surety for his indemnity, and the lien of such judgment will be valid as against the creditors of the principal.[3] So a conveyance made by the principal to the surety, in consideration of an agreement by the surety to pay the debt, is valid as against the creditors of the principal.[4] The surety to whom a chattel

surety, levied upon real estate of the principal and surety, subject to a prior attachment, and on account thereof and defects in the levy the creditor made nothing, *held*, on *scire facias* to revive the execution, that the proceedings under the prior execution did not discharge the surety. Somersworth Savings Bank *v.* Worcester, 76 Me. 327.

[1] Tucker *v.* Laing, 2 Kay & Johns. 745.

[2] Oxley *v.* Young, 2 H. Black. 613.

[3] Miller *v.* Howry, 3 Pen. & Watts (Pa.), 374; Pringle *v.* Sizer, 2 Rich. N. S. (S. C.) 59; Tennell *v.* Jefferson, 5 Harr. (Del.) 206. But a judgment by confession under such circumstances is invalid where the surety has simply signed his note for the amount of the debt and agreed to pay it, but had not paid it at the time of the entry of the confessed judgment. Adams *v.* Tator, 57 Hun, 302.

[4] M'Whorter *v.* Wright, 5 Ga. 555. And to similar effect, see Kendall *v.* Baltis, 26 Mo. App. 411, wherein it was held that such conveyance was good, even though the principal may have intended to hinder and delay creditors, provided the surety did not

has been mortgaged by the principal for his indemnity may, before paying the debt, maintain trover against creditors of the principal who have taken and converted the chattel.[1] And in such case one of three sureties has a right to recover damages, if the property is of sufficient value, to the full extent of the debt for which he is liable, notwithstanding the fact that the consideration mentioned in the mortgage is only one-third of the debt.[2] Where property is mortgaged by the principal to a creditor to secure his debt, and the mortgage is also conditioned that such creditor shall indemnify a surety for any money which he may be obliged to pay to another creditor of the principal to whom such surety is liable, such condition will be enforced.[3] Where a surety has become bound, but has a right to withdraw from his obligation, an agreement for his indemnity, afterwards given by a third person in consideration of his remaining bound, is a valid contract, and the consideration is sufficient.[4] But where, after a surety had become bound, a third person, in consideration that he would remain bound an indefinite time, agreed in writing to indemnify him from loss, it was held that the agreement for indemnity was void for want of consideration, as the surety had assumed no liability beyond that which existed when the agreement for indemnity was made.[5] A surety who holds the written agreement of a third person conditioned for his indemnity does not waive such agreement by afterwards taking security for his indemnity from the principal.[6] The principals in a note agreed with their surety that, if he would sign it, they would keep him indemnified by the use and application of a particular fund, as the surety might desire, or that they would secure him in any other way he might suggest. *Held*, this did not give the surety a lien on the particular fund, and

participate in his principal's intent. In such case the surety is not entitled to notice of non-payment because by his own act he has substituted himself in his principal's place. Wright *v.* Andrews, 70 Me. 86.

[1] Bellume *v.* Wallace, 2 Rich. Law (S. C.), 80.

[2] Barker *v.* Buel, 5 Cush. 519.

[3] Rodes *v.* Crockett, 2 Yerg. (Tenn.) 346.

[4] Carroll *v.* Nixon, 4 Watts & Serg. (Pa.) 517; Carman *v.* Noble, 9 Pa. St. 366.

[5] Rix *v.* Adams, 9 Vt. 233.

[6] Drury *v.* Fay, 14 Pick. 326. Generally, on the subject of indemnity, see Seaver *v.* Young, 16 Vt. 658.

it could not afterwards be assigned to him when the principal was in failing circumstances, so as to cut off other creditors. The surety having an option to take the particular fund or some other security, no lien was created.[1]

§ 248. Surety entitled to benefit of collaterals — Creditor not bound to notify surety, when.— Where bank bills have been received from the principal by the creditor as a collateral security for the debt, it lies on the creditor, in a suit against a surety for the same debt, to show what has been done with them.[2] A creditor who holds railroad bonds as collateral security does not lose his right to hold the bonds by suing the principal and imprisoning him upon getting judgment. Nor does he waive his lien on such bonds if he promise, without consideration, to give them up.[3] Where the note of a stranger is received by a creditor from his debtor as collateral security for a debt, the creditor is not bound to notify the debtor of a proposition of the maker of the note to discharge it in property, though by a failure of the creditor to receive such property the amount of the note is ultimately lost.[4] Where a submission to arbitration is made by a written agreement, a surety in the agreement need not be notified of the sitting of the arbitrators. "The reasons for such notice are no stronger than they would be for notice to bail of the progress of the cause against the principal."[5] The payee of a note is not bound to notify one of several makers of a note who is a surety of non-payment by the principal, and an agreement with the principal not to notify the surety will not be such a fraudulent concealment as will discharge him. "If the plaintiff's not giving notice could not be fraudulent, could his agreement not to do it be so? Could his agreeing not to do what he was under no moral or legal obligation to do be a fraudulent concealment? . . . An agreement not to inform and an agreement to conceal are two very different things."[6]

[1] Elliott v. Harris, 9 Bush (Ky.), 237.

[2] Spalding v. Bank, 9 Pa. St. 28.

[3] Smith v. Strout, 63 Me. 205. The surety has a right to insist that a collateral security shall be so applied as to relieve him. Kirkman v. Bank of America, 2 Cold. (Tenn.) 397.

[4] Rives v. McLosk, 5 Stew. & Port. (Ala.) 330.

[5] Farmer v. Stewart, 2 N. H. 97, per Woodbury, J.

[6] Grover v. Hoppock, 2 Dutcher (N. J.), 191, per Vredenburgh, J.

§ 249. Surety not discharged because creditor tells him his signing is a mere matter of form — Other cases.— Where the creditor has no security for his debt but the joint and several bond of sureties with their principal, he has a right to call upon any one of the sureties to pay it, and a court will not delay enforcing his claims until the several remedies against the other sureties may be exhausted.[1] Where the surety on a note given for property purchased at administrator's sale, when requested by the principal to sign it, was told by the payee that his signature was only wanted as a form to comply with the requirements of the ordinary, it was held that no fraud was thereby practiced on the surety which avoided the note as to him. The court said it was so common to say to a surety, when getting him to sign, that it was a mere matter of form, that it deceives no one.[2] Where the payee of a note merely advises the principal to carry his property to a better market out of the state, and sell it and pay his debts, and if unable to pay all to pay *pro rata*, it is not a fraud upon, and will not operate as a release of, the sureties on the note.[3] The deed or bond of a surety under seal for the simple contract debt of a principal, in which the principal does not join, does not, by operation of law, extinguish the simple contract debt of the principal.[4]

§ 250. Surety may defend suit against principal — How liability of surety affected by fraud — Other cases.— A surety has a right for his own protection to defend an action against his principal.[5] The holder of a mortgage assigned it with a guaranty that there was a certain amount due on it. The assignee in his own name sued the maker, and recovered

[1] Lowndes *v.* Pinckney, 2 Strob. Eq. (S. C.) 44.

[2] Singley *v.* Head, 2 Rich. Law (S. C.), 590. But see Molson's Bank *v.* Turley, 8 Ont. (Can.) 293.

[3] Hawkins *v.* Ridenhour, 13 Mo. 125.

[4] White *v.* Cuyler, 6 Durn. & East, 176.

[5] Jewett *v.* Crane, 35 Barb. (N. Y.) 208. And on the same principle it was held that where a person brought replevin, gave bond and received the property, and before trial became insolvent and did not appear, and judgment went against him, the surety on the replevin bond, in order to protect himself, should have been allowed to prosecute the action brought by his principal after the latter had abandoned it. Hoffman *v.* Steinau, 34 Hun (N. Y.), 239. In such cases the pleadings are sufficient without amendment. Pool *v.* Ellison, 56 Hun (N. Y.), 108.

a less amount than that guarantied to be due, and the guarantor made and desired to argue a motion for new trial, and told the assignee that, unless he was allowed to argue the motion, he should consider himself discharged. The assignee stated that he did not want a new trial in the case, and refused to allow the guarantor to argue the motion, and judgment was thereupon entered for the smaller sum. It did not appear whether there was sufficient ground for a new trial, but the court said the guarantor had a right to argue the motion, and it was a valuable right of which the assignee would not be permitted to deprive him, and it was held that he was discharged.[1] A bond with surety was conditioned that a lessee would complete certain improvements on premises therein described within four years. Before the expiration of that time the lessor lawfully ejected the lessee from the premises. *Held*, the surety was not bound for the completion of the improvements, as the lessor had, although lawfully, prevented them from being completed.[2] Although the release of the principal in a bond may have been obtained by a fraud practiced by him upon the obligee, yet if the surety was not a party to the fraud, and the obligee suffers several years to elapse without bringing suit or notifying the surety of the fraud, during which time the principal becomes insolvent, these circumstances will discharge the surety.[3] After a surety had in fact been discharged by time given the principal, the attorney of the principal represented to the surety that he was not discharged, and the surety, relying thereon, deposited certain title deeds as security for the debt, and afterwards, in order to regain possession of such deeds, gave certain notes. *Held*, the surety was not liable on such notes. The court said that money paid by mistake might be recovered back, and on the same principle the surety had a defense to the notes.[4] Where F. was induced through fraudulent representations of the vendor to purchase a patent-right, and W. was also induced thereby to deposit with the vendor a government bond as security that F. would pay the purchase price, and the patent

[1] Stark *v.* Fuller, 42 Pa. St. 320.

[2] Trustees of Section Sixteen *v.* Miller, 3 Ohio, 261.

[3] Gordon *v.* McCarty, 3 Wharton (Pa.), 407; McCarty *v.* Gordon, 4 Wharton (Pa.), 321.

[4] Bristow *v.* Brown, 13 Irish Com. Law Rep. 201.

was worthless, and F. repudiated the sale, it was held that W. might recover the amount of the bond in an action against the vendor, and that his remedy was not alone against F., his principal.[1] Joint judgment having been recovered against principal and surety, the surety pointed out property which he said belonged to the principal and told the sheriff to levy on it, which he did, and it was sold to the creditor for the amount of the debt. Two years afterwards the surety released a mortgage which he held for his indemnity. The principal had in fact no title to the property sold, and became insolvent. *Held*, the surety was not discharged. He had not been misled and injured by the creditor, but on the contrary had misled and injured the creditor.[2]

§ 251. When surety cannot recover money paid by him to creditor — Party who is indebted may become surety, and secure suretyship debt to exclusion of other creditors — Other cases.—If a surety, with full knowledge of facts which will discharge him, pays the debt, he cannot recover the amount so paid from the creditor. He had a right to waive his defense, and by paying does so.[3] A surety who pays a judgment rendered by a court below against the principal, which is afterwards reversed on error at the suit of the principal, cannot recover the amount so paid from the creditor. The payment, although in fact made by the surety, is in law a payment by the principal.[4] A surety who has paid the debt of the principal cannot recover indemnity from a party who has agreed with the principal to pay the debt, there being no privity between the surety and such party.[5] Money was loaned to a corporation on its bond and mortgage, and the stockholders became individually liable as sureties for the repayment of the loan. *Held*, that other creditors of the corporation had no equity to compel the lender to exhaust his remedy against the sureties before resorting to the corporation for payment.[6] In

[1] Wile *v.* Wright, 32 Iowa, 451.

[2] Chambers *v.* Cochran, 18 Iowa, 159.

[3] Geary *v.* Gore Bank, 5 Grant's Ch. 536.

[4] Garr *v.* Martin, 20 N. Y. 306. And see, also, involving this point, Hatch *v.* Hamlin, 12 Daly (N. Y. Com. Pl.), 272.

[5] Hoffman *v.* Schwaebe, 33 Barb. (N. Y.) 194.

[6] South Carolina Mfg. Co. *v.* Bank, 6 Rich. Eq. (S. C.) 227.

consideration of an extension of time given to one firm, another firm executed a mortgage on its property to secure the debt. At that time the firm which executed the mortgage had creditors who afterwards filed a bill to set aside the mortgage as fraudulent against them. *Held*, they were not entitled to relief. The court said the mortgage was not voluntary, but was founded on a good consideration, viz.: the extension of time to the principal debtor. A person or firm that is indebted may become surety for another, the same as if such person or firm was not indebted, and such suretyship debt will be as valid as any other debt, and may be secured by the surety the same as any other debt.[1]

§ 252. Surety may enforce trust made for his benefit without his knowledge — Other cases.— Where a conveyance of land is made by absolute deed, and the grantee gives back to the grantor a written contract, promising to sell the land at a certain time, and to pay two notes with the proceeds, and to pay the balance to the grantor, such grantee holds the land in trust, and it is his duty to sell the same at the time specified and apply the proceeds as provided by the contract; and if a third person be a surety on one of the notes, although he might not have known of the trust when it was undertaken, yet, after he is informed of it and can enforce its execution, the original parties to it cannot annul it, and he can enforce it in equity.[2] Real property was mortgaged by a debtor to his surety to indemnify him against his indorsements, and also to secure $3,000 due from the principal to the surety. *Held*, the creditors might, by suit in chancery, reach the property thus mortgaged, but the surety, as to the $3,000, should share with the creditors *pro rata*.[3] Where the principal assigns a fund to trustees to pay a creditor whom the surety afterwards pays, and the proceeds of the fund are then paid over in money by the trustees to the admininistrator of the principal, the surety is entitled to the benefit of the fund, and may recover it from the administrator in an action in his own name for money had

[1] Allen *v.* Morgan, 5 Humph. (Tenn.) 624. To contrary effect, when the firm became surety for one of its members, see Kidder *v.* Page, 48 N. H. 380.

[2] Pratt *v.* Thornton, 28 Me. 355.

[3] New London Bank *v.* Lee, 11 Conn. 112.

and received.[1] Where lands are conveyed to a trustee by the principal, to be sold for the benefit of his sureties, the sureties may bid and purchase at the trustees' sale the same as a stranger.[2] The creditors of a party resolved to accept a composition, payable in three instalments, there being a surety for the payment of the third instalment. Before the resolution accepting the composition was passed the debtor had agreed with the surety to indemnify him by depositing goods with him, and this agreement was not made known to the creditors. After the resolutions were registered the surety accepted bills of exchange for the amount of the third instalment of the composition, and certain goods were deposited with him by the principal. The principal paid the first instalment, but failed to pay the second, and thereupon filed a liquidation petition. Afterwards the surety paid the third instalment. *Held*, the agreement with the surety for indemnity was valid, and he was entitled to retain the goods as against the trustee, under the liquidation. The creditors had no specific lien on the property, and after the composition was accepted the principal might do as he pleased with it.[3] A. became surety for B., who agreed orally to give A. a mortgage on a house and lot for indemnity, and to insure the house for his benefit, which he did, the policy of insurance being payable to A. Afterwards B. sold the house and lot to C., who took it with a knowledge of the foregoing facts. C. canceled the policy of insurance on the house and took out a new one, payable to himself. The house was burned, and it was held that A. was entitled in equity to have the insurance money applied in exoneration of his liability for B.[4] It has been held that the principal, or, if he be dead, his personal representative, is a necessary party to suit in chancery against the surety on a lost note.[5] It has also been held that the cashier of a bank has no authority, by virtue of his office, to release a surety upon a negotiable instrument held by the bank, unless he is officially empowered so to do.[6]

[1] Miller *v.* Ord, 2 Binney (Pa.), 382.

[2] Landis *v.* Curd, 63 Mo. 104.

[3] *Ex parte* Burrell, *In re* Robinson, Law Rep. 1 Ch. Div. 537.

[4] Miller *v.* Aldrich, 31 Mich. 408.

[5] Greathouse *v.* Hord, 1 Dana (Ky.), 105.

[6] Daviess Co. Sav. Ass'n *v.* Sailor, 63 Mo. 24; Merchants' Bank *v.* Rudolf, 5 Neb. 527. These two cases do

§ 253. When surety for a portion of a debt entitled to share in dividend of estate of insolvent principal — Other cases.— If a party gives a guaranty in which his liability is limited to a specified sum, to secure to that extent any floating balance which may become due the creditor from the principal, and the principal becomes insolvent, owing the creditor more than the amount limited in the guaranty, such guarantor is entitled to share in the dividend, out of the estate of the principal, where there is not enough of such estate to pay the balance, above the amount of the guaranty due the creditor.[1] But if the intention is to guaranty the whole debt to the extent of the amount mentioned in the guaranty, then the guarantor is not entitled to a share in such dividend. Upon this subject the court said it was a mere question of construction of the guaranty, and proceeded: "The class of cases referred to do not lay down any general doctrine that where there is a surety with a limit on the amount of his liability for the whole debt exceeding that limit, he is entitled to the benefit of a ratable proportion of the dividends paid on the whole debt; but only that where the surety has given a continuing guaranty, limited in amount, to secure the floating balance which may from time to time be due from the principal to the creditor, the guaranty is, as between the surety and the creditor, to be construed both at law and in equity as applicable to a part only of the debt, co-extensive with the amount of his guaranty; and this upon the ground at first confined to equity, but afterwards extended to law, that it is inequitable in the creditor, who is at liberty to increase the balance, or not to increase it, at the expense of the surety."[2] It has been held that, upon the insolvency of the principal, a surety is considered in equity as a creditor, and may retain against an assignee for value, and without notice, any funds of the principal which

not agree as to whether the surety is discharged by representations made by the cashier to the surety that the debt is paid. An attorney at law, in virtue of his employment to make collections, has no authority to release a surety on a promissory note without payment; such authority must be proved. Stoll *v.* Sheldon, 13 Neb. 207. As to the power of an attorney at law, by virtue of his office, to do acts which will discharge a surety, see Givens *v.* Briscoe, 3 J. J. Marsh. (Ky.) 529.

[1] Hobson *v.* Bass, Law Rep. 6 Ch. App. Cas. 792.

[2] Ellis *v.* Emmanuel, Law Rep. 1 Exch. Div. 157, per Blackburn, J.

he has in his hands.[1] But where an attachment act provided that if the debtor was "truly indebted" to the person in whose hands the property was at the time of the service of the attachment writ, such person might retain it to pay his debt, and an attachment was levied on property of the principal, in the hands of a surety, which had not been pledged to the surety, for his indemnity, and the surety had not then paid the debt, it was held the surety could not retain the property.[2] Where a surety guaranties a limited part of a debt and not an unpaid balance thereof, with a limitation as to the amount of the liability in case of insolvency, whatever is paid as a dividend arising from that part of the debt must, it is held, be applied to discharge that portion; but when the guaranty contemplates the protection of the creditor against any ultimate balance that may arise upon the dealings between the debtor and creditor, this rule does not apply.[3]

1 Battle *v.* Hart, 2 Dev. Eq. (N. C.) 31. To similar effect, see Scott *v.* Timberlake, 83 N. C. 382.

2 Yongue *v.* Linton, 6 Rich. Law (S. C.), 275.

3 Dumont *v.* Fry (Cir. Ct. S. D. N. Y.), 14 Fed. Rep. 293.

CHAPTER XI.

OF THE RIGHTS OF SURETIES AND GUARANTORS BETWEEN EACH OTHER — CONTRIBUTION.

The right to contribution subsists between co-sureties — Reasons upon which it is founded . . . . § 254
Co-sureties bound by different instruments liable to contribution 255
Instances where sureties bound by different instruments held liable to contribution . . . 256
Same continued — When not liable to contribute 257
It makes no difference with the right to contribution that one surety does not know that another became bound as such 258
When sureties for the same debt not liable to contribution — Instances 259
When accommodation parties to negotiable instruments are co-sureties 260
The true relation between several sureties may be shown by parol evidence 261
Surety who becomes bound during course of remedy against principal not co-surety with original surety 262
Contribution cannot be recovered when it would be inequitable 263
When surety, who becomes liable at the request of another surety, not liable to contribution 264
Surety of surety not liable to contribution 265
Surety who becomes principal liable for whole amount paid by former co-surety — Other cases . . . . § 266
Surety who pays debt for which principal or another surety is not liable cannot have contribution 267
When one surety entitled to benefit of indemnity secured by another surety 268
Instances of indemnity taken by one surety inuring to the benefit of all the sureties . 269
Same continued — Cases where indemnity to one surety does not inure to benefit of co-sureties 270
If surety surrender lien for his indemnity on property of principal, he discharges co-surety from contribution . 271
If surety negligently lose indemnity, co-surety released from contribution . . . 272
Surety who obtains indemnity after all the sureties have paid an equal amount is not obliged to share it with the others 273
When suit for contribution can be brought by surety holding indemnity 274
Surety may, before paying debt, file bill to compel co-surety to contribute and to restrain him from transferring his property 275

Discharge of surety in bankruptcy does not release him from contribution to co-surety, who pays subsequently . . . . § 276
When surety who is discharged from liability to creditor liable to contribute to co-surety, who subsequently pays 277
Rights of bail, who pays the debt, against the principal and sureties for the debt . . 278
When surety who pays judgment may have execution thereon against co-surety . 279
How liability to contribution affected by giving of time to one of several co-sureties . . 280
Contribution as affected by release of principal or of co-surety — Failure of consideration — Set-off, etc. . . . 281
How far judgment against one surety evidence against co-surety in suit for contribution — Failure of consideration 282
When surety can recover contribution for costs paid by him 283
Estate of deceased co-surety liable for contribution . . 284
Surety who pays by his note may recover contribution from co-surety 285
What contribution surety who pays in land entitled to recover . . . . § 286
When surety who has paid less than his share of the debt cannot recover contribution . . 287
In what proportion co-sureties are liable to contribute . . 288
Surety may recover contribution either at law or in equity 289
Whether surety must show insolvency of the principal in order to recover contribution 290
When suit for contribution should be joint and when several 291
Who not necessary parties to a bill for contribution . . . 292
Surety may without compulsion pay debt when due and immediately sue co-surety for contribution without demand or notice 293
When liability to contribution attaches 294
When claim for contribution barred by the statute of limitations 295
Rights of sureties as against each other governed by what law — Residence of co-surety in suit for contribution . . 296
Pleading — Former adjudication — Co-surety as witness — Evidence 297

§ 254. The right to contribution subsists between co-sureties — Reasons upon which it is founded.— The principal question which arises between co-sureties is that of contribution. The right to contribution results from the maxim that equality is equity.[1] The creditor may collect all the debt from the principal or any one of several sureties, or he may collect from every surety his proper proportion. If, having this right, he collects it all from one surety, the law clothes such surety with the same power and enables him to

[1] Van Winkle *v.* Johnson, 11 Oreg. 469.

enforce contribution. "Natural justice says that one surety, having become so with other sureties, shall not have the whole debt thrown upon him by the choice of the creditor, in not resorting to remedies in his power, without having contribution from those who entered into the obligation equally with him. The obligation of co-sureties to contribute to each other is not founded in contract between them, but stood upon a principle of equity until that principle of equity had been so long and so generally acknowledged that courts of law in modern times have assumed jurisdiction. This jurisdiction of the courts of common law is based upon the idea that the equitable principle had been so long and so generally acknowledged and enforced, that persons in placing themselves under circumstances to which it applies may be supposed to act under the dominion of contract, implied from the universality of that principle. For a great length of time equity exercised its jurisdiction exclusively and individually; the jurisdiction assumed by courts of law is comparatively of very modern date."[1] It has also been said that "This right to contribution has been considered as depending rather upon a principle of equity than upon contract; but it may well be considered as resting alike on both for its foundation; for although generally there is no express agreement entered into between joint sureties, yet from the uniform and almost universal understanding which seems to pervade the whole community, that from the circumstance alone of their agreeing to be, and becoming accordingly, co-sureties of the principal, they mutually become bound to each other to divide and equalize any loss that may arise therefrom to each other, or any of them, it may with great propriety be said that there is at least an implied contract."[2] Until the surety has made a payment of the obligation, or assumed more than his share of the debt, he cannot

[1] Lansdale *v.* Cox, 7 T. B. Mon. (Ky.) 401, per Bibb, C. J. See, also, that courts of law have adopted the equitable doctrine of contribution, Jeffries *v.* Ferguson, Adm'r, 87 Mo. 244.

[2] Agnew *v.* Bell, 4 Watts (Pa.), 31, per Kennedy, J.; and see, to like purport, Drummond *v.* Yager, 10 Bradw. (Ill. App.) 380. The right to contribution does not necessarily arise from contract, but, rather, has its foundation in principles of natural justice. McGehee *v.* Owen, 61 Ala. 440; Bragg *v.* Patterson, 85 Ala. 233.

enforce contribution against a co-surety.[1] But it is not necessary that the amount paid by him should be fixed by a judgment.[2] The fact that the judgment paid by the surety was irregular or void, held no defense to a co-surety in a suit for contribution.[3]

§ 255. **Co-sureties bound by different instruments liable to contribution.**— Co-sureties are liable to contribution, but sureties for the same principal who are not co-sureties are not so liable. Much of the learning on this subject is devoted to who are and who are not co-sureties. Where all the sureties sign the same instrument and become equally bound thereby, they are of course co-sureties and liable to contribute to each other. So, also, when several sureties become bound for the debt, default or miscarriage of the same principal, with reference to the same transaction, even though they become bound by different instruments,[4] at different times and for different amounts, they are generally considered co-sureties and held liable to contribution. In the leading case on this subject the principal was receiver of the fines and forfeitures of the customs of the outports, and to secure the performance of his duties gave three separate bonds in the same penalty, but signed by different sureties. It was held that the sureties in the three bonds were liable to each other for contribution. The court said: "If a view is taken of the cases, it will appear that the bottom of contribution is a fixed principle of justice, and is not founded in contract. . . . In the particular case of sureties, it is admitted that one surety may compel another to contribute to the debt for which they are jointly

[1] Backus *v.* Coyne, 45 Mich. 584; and to the same effect, see Gourdin *v.* Trenholm, 25 S. C. 362.

[2] Bright *v.* Lennon, 83 N. C. 183. The rule determining the right to contribution is thus stated by the Louisiana supreme court: "The three necessary conditions are that the surety who is demanding contribution, and the surety from whom it is demanded, must each have been surety for the same debtor and for the same debt, and satisfaction of the debt must have been enforced against the surety demanding contribution by a law-suit." Manning, J., in Stockmeyer *v.* Oertling, 35 La. Ann. 467.

[3] Ross *v.* Williams, 11 Heisk. (Tenn.) 410.

[4] And there is no presumption, because a surety or guarantor bound himself by a different instrument, that he did not thereby intend to contribute if one of the others bound on another instrument paid, nor to call on them for contribution if he paid. Young *v.* Shunk, 30 Minn. 503.

bound. On what principle? Can it be because they are jointly bound? What if they are jointly and severally bound? What if severally bound by the same or different instruments? In every one of those cases sureties have a common interest and a common burthen. They are bound as effectually *quoad* contribution as if bound in one instrument, with this difference only, that the sums in each instrument ascertain the proportions, whereas if they are all joined in the same engagement, they must all contribute equally."[1]

§ 256. **Instances where sureties bound by different instruments held liable to contribution.**— Where an administrator upon assuming the duties of his office gave bond with sureties, and eight years afterwards, upon being required to do so, gave an additional bond with other sureties, it was held that the sureties on both bonds were liable to contribute to each other.[2] The same thing was held where an injunction was issued upon a bond given with one surety, which surety was held to be insufficient, and a new bond was given with two other sureties.[3] Where a sheriff had been required, under an act of the legislature, to procure additional security, and had at different times entered into new bonds with new sureties, it was held that all the sureties on all the bonds were liable to contribution.[4] Execution was taken out against D. as principal, and A. and B. as sureties, and levied on the goods of D., who gave a forthcoming bond in which A., B. and E. were bound as sureties for D. Execution was issued on the forthcoming bond, and E. was compelled to pay the debt. *Held*, E. was co-surety with A. and B., and not a surety for them, and could recover contribution from them as co-sureties,

[1] Deering *v.* The Earl of Winchelsea, 2 Bos. & Pul. 270, per Eyre, C. B.; Id., 1 Cox, 318. See, also, Mayhew *v.* Crickett, 2 Swanston, 193; Breckinridge *v.* Taylor, 5 Dana (Ky.), 110. It is immaterial that the sureties are bound by different instruments and without the knowledge of one another, provided they are bound for the same principal and by the same engagement. Rosenbaum *v.* Goodman, 78 Va. 121.

[2] Cobb *v.* Haynes, 8 B. Mon. (Ky.) 137. To precisely similar effect, see Pickens *v.* Miller, 83 N. C. 543. The same thing was held where a guardian under similar circumstances gave two bonds. Bell's Adm'r *v.* Jasper, 2 Ired. Eq. (N. C.) 597. And to the same point, Stevens *v.* Tucker, 87 Ind. 109.

[3] Bentley *v.* Harris' Adm'r, 2 Gratt. (Va.) 358.

[4] Harris *v.* Ferguson, 2 Bailey, Law (S. C.), 397. So where a sheriff was required by statute to give annually

but not full indemnity as if they were principals.[1] A bond was executed by A. as principal, and B. and C. as sureties, with the stipulation that the sureties should not be discharged by any new arrangement between the creditor and the principal. B. compounded with his creditors. The bond became due and payable, and the creditor threatening to sue unless A. got another surety in place of B., one D., by a separate writing, became liable for the whole amount of the bond, "according to the tenor thereof." D. was compelled to pay the bond, and it was held he was entitled to contribution from C. The court said that D. became surety for the same debt for which C. was surety, "and in that case, in whatever way he became surety, if the other surety is called on to pay, he must contribute."[2] In another case, A. and B. as principals gave a note to C., with D. as surety thereon. C. sold and indorsed the note to E. To obtain further time A. and B. proposed to give a new note with D. and F. as sureties. E. declined to give up the old note or receive the new one in its stead unless C. would become a party to the new note, and C. thereupon signed it, adding after his name the words "as security." *Held*, that C., D. and F. were co-sureties, and that D., who had paid the note, was entitled to contribution from C. and F. The court said that: "Whenever several persons are sureties bound for the same duty, they stand in the relation of co-sureties, and are liable to contribution. . . . Nor will their becoming sureties at different times, without the knowledge of each other, or even by different instruments, affect their obligation."[3]

§ 257. **Same continued — When not liable to contribute.**— In an action for contribution against sureties on different instruments it is held unnecessary that notice should be given before instituting proceedings.[4] Where a sheriff executed a bond for the collection of general taxes, and another bond for

a renewal bond, or oftener if ordered by the court, the sureties on the renewal bond are held to be co-sureties with those on the first bond and liable to contribution. Ketler *v.* Thompson, 13 Bush (Ky.), 287.

[1] Perrins *v.* Ragland, 5 Leigh (Va.), 552.

[2] Whiting *v.* Burke, Law Rep. 6 Ch. App. Cas. 342, per James, L. J.; affirming Law Rep. 10 Eq. Cas. 539.

[3] Woodworth *v.* Bowes, 5 Ind. (3 Port.) 276, per Stuart, J.

[4] Bright *v.* Lennon, 83 N. C. 183.

the collection of special taxes, the sureties on the first bond were held as liable for any defalcation on the bond given for the collection of special taxes as on the bond given for the collection of general taxes, and they were held entitled, therefore, to contribution from the sureties on the special tax bond.[1] So the right to contribution exists between the sureties on a sheriff's official bond and those on his bond as tax collector, where the duties of the latter office are by statute incumbent on the sheriff.[2] And where the treasurer of a loan and savings society gave two separate bonds with sureties conditioned for the faithful discharge of his duties, it was held the right to contribution existed between the sureties on the bonds, and the fact that the society was subsequently incorporated and the treasurer's name of office was changed constituted no defense.[3] In an action by a municipality against a surety company on its independent guaranty of the good conduct of a city chamberlain, the defense was that, as the municipality had discharged a co-surety, they (the surety company) were not liable, because in their contract of guaranty they stipulated that they should possess the same right of contribution as any other surety. *Held*, that even though the co-surety had been discharged, this operated only to relieve the surety company to the extent to which they would have had a right to contribution, and that they would have been discharged to this extent as a matter of equity, independently of their contract, and furthermore, the surety company and the other surety were in no sense joint sureties.[4] An officer holding over, executed a bond for the full term. but having been afterwards re-elected, executed a new bond for the unexpired portion of the term. *Held*, that the sureties on the first bond were not co-sureties with those on the last bond and could not be compelled to contribute.[5] Where a surety on all of several official bonds is compelled to pay damages on any one of them, he is entitled to contribution from his associates on that bond; but when his associates are different in the other bonds, this right is held to be defeated by a recovery in one action upon more than one bond.[6]

[1] Cherry *v.* Wilson, 78 N. C. 164, 166.

[2] Burnett *v.* Millsaps, 59 Miss. 333.

[3] Murray *v.* Gibson, 28 Grant's Ch. (Can.) 12.

[4] Corporation of the City of London *v.* Citizens' Ins. Co., 13 Ont. (Can.) 713.

[5] Boone Co. *v.* Jones, 58 Iowa, 373.

[6] Cassady *v.* Board of Trustees, 93 Ill. 394.

§ 258. **It makes no difference with the right to contribution that one surety does not know that another became bound as such.**— As the right to contribution results from equitable principles, and not from express contract, such right is not at all affected by the fact that the surety seeking contribution, or from whom it is sought, had no knowledge that the other had assumed the obligation of a surety for the same thing. Thus it has been held that a surety, who becomes such without the knowledge of one who is already bound, and pays the debt, may recover contribution from the first surety.[1] A. as principal, and B. and C. as sureties, signed a note, but the fact of suretyship did not appear therefrom. The holder afterwards became dissatisfied with the solvency of the signers of the note, and A. procured D. to sign the note under the names of the other signers thereof, upon a consideration moving from A. to D. Afterwards A. became insolvent, and C. was obliged to pay the note. *Held*, he was entitled to contribution from D. The court said that the right to contribution exists only among those sureties who are liable for the same thing. But equity looks at substance more than form, and if several persons enter into contracts of suretyship, which are the same in their legal character and operation, though by different instruments, at different times, and without the knowledge of each other, they will be bound to mutual contribution.[2] In another case, A., B. and C. signed a note, B. and C. being sureties; but that fact not appearing from the note, A., being in possession of the note, asked D. to sign it, telling him B. and C. were principals. D. thereupon signed it, adding after his name the word "surety." D. was obliged to pay the note, and it was held that he could recover contribution from B. and C. as co-sureties, but could not recover indemnity from them as principals.[3]

[1] Chaffee *v.* Jones, 19 Pick. 260. Holding that no agreement is necessary to entitle sureties who sign a note at different times to contribution from each other, see Warner *v.* Morrison, 3 Allen, 566.

[2] Monson *v.* Drakeley, 40 Conn. 552. But see Matthews *v.* Millsaps, 58 Miss. 564, where it was held that the sureties on a sheriff's bond, having paid a liability thereon, had no right to call upon a person for contribution who had never been in any manner legally liable thereon, although he may have intended to become a surety.

[3] Whitehouse *v.* Hanson, 42 N. H. 9. To similar effect, see Norton *v.*

§ 259. When sureties for the same debt not liable to contribution — Instances.— Where, after the principal and surety had signed a note, a third party also signed it, and added to his signature the words "surety for the above parties," it was held that such third party was not a co-surety with the first surety and was not liable to him for contribution. The court said: "The defendant had a right to qualify his contract as he pleased, consistent with the rules of law. He refused to sign as a co-surety with the other sureties, but did sign as surety for the whole, in which there was certainly nothing unlawful."[1] It has been held that, "where separate bonds are given with different sureties, and one is intended to be subsidiary to and a security for the other in case of default in the payment of the latter, the sureties in the second bond would not be compellable to aid those in the first bond by contribution."[2] Where several sureties became bound by separate bonds for the same amount on account of one principal to the same creditor, but the amount of all the bonds did not equal the sum due from the principal to the creditor, it was held that every surety being bound for an individual sum, they were not co-sureties, and there was no right to contribution between them.[3] A. being indebted to B. in 1,200*l.*, C., D. and E., each separately, agreed to become A.'s surety by a separate instrument for 400*l.* C. and D. each executed a separate instrument,

Coons, 3 Denio, 130. See, also, Warner *v.* Price, 3 Wend. 397; McNeil *v.* Sanford, 3 B. Mon. (Ky.) 11; Beaman *v.* Blanchard, 4 Wend. 432. *Contra*, Hunt *v.* Chambliss, 7 Smedes & Mar. (Miss.) 532; Keith *v.* Goodwin, 31 Vt. 268, and Bobbitt *v.* Shryer, 70 Ind. 513.

[1] Harris *v.* Warner, 13 Wend. 400, per Nelson, J. So where one of two sureties to a sewing machine agent's bond added to his signature the words "security for all prior parties," it was held there was no contribution between said sureties. Singer Mfg. Co. *v.* Bennett, 28 W. Va. 16. See to precisely similar effect, Sayles *v.* Sims, 73 N. Y. 551; Robertson *v.* Deatherage, 82 Ill. 511. Where, however, one signed a note under an agreement with the principal that he was to be liable, not as surety for the principal alone, but for both the principal and a prior surety, it was held that he could show such agreement by parol, and recover of the prior surety whatever he may have been compelled to pay on account of his suretyship. Chapeze *v.* Young, 87 Ky. 476. See, further, as to when contribution will not be allowed, Gourdin *v.* Trenholm, 25 S. C. 363.

[2] Salyers *v.* Ross, 15 Ind. 130, per Davison, J. To similar effect, see Whitman *v.* Gaddie, 7 B. Mon. (Ky.) 591.

[3] Pendlebury *v.* Walker, 4 Younge & Coll. (Exch.) 424.

with A., to B., in the sum of 400*l.*, but E. would not execute any instrument. C., being sued, claimed to be discharged, because E. had not executed an instrument as agreed. The lord chancellor thought the agreements of C., D. and E. to become sureties had no connection with each other, and if E. had executed the instrument as agreed he would not have been co-surety with C., and C. was therefore not discharged.[1] In another case A. borrowed money on a mortgage of his estates D. and S., to which B., a prior incumbrancer on estate D., and C., a prior incumbrancer on estate S., were parties, and consented to give the mortgage priority over their respective charges, but it was stated in the mortgage that they joined for no other purpose. The lands were subsequently sold and the mortgage paid out of their joint proceeds. The residue of the fund produced by the sale of estate S. was not sufficient to pay C.'s incumbrance. *Held*, C. was not entitled to contribution against B., there not having been any common liability to pay a common demand. The court said: "The foundation of the right (to contribution) is . . . a common liability for a demand upon the parties in common. Now, in the present case, there is no common liability for a common demand. Each party agreed upon his own behalf to postpone his own particular charge. It has so turned out that by reason of a deficient fund there is not sufficient to pay all the charges, and therefore the parties giving priority have lost their respective charges. But where is the common liability for the same demand? There being no common liability, there is no foundation for any equities among themselves."[2] Where a surety on an official bond aids his principal in a breach thereof he is not entitled to contribution for damages consequent to said breach.[3] Where a corporation's contract of suretyship is *ultra vires* it is not liable to contribution.[4] Where the surety of a bankrupt bought his principal's lands at an assignee's sale, he was held not entitled to contribution.[5]

[1] Coope *v.* Twynam, 1 Turner & Russ. 426, per Lord Eldon.

[2] *In re* Keily, 9 Irish Ch. 87, per Brady, C.

[3] Scofield *v.* Gaskill, 60 Ga. 277; Healey *v.* Scofield, 60 Ga. 450.

[4] Lucas *v.* White Line Transfer Co., 70 Iowa, 541.

[5] Boulware *v.* Hartsook's Adm'r, 83 Va. 679.

§ 260. When accommodation parties to negotiable instruments are co-sureties.— The weight of authority is, that successive accommodation indorsers of negotiable instruments are not, in the absence of an agreement to that effect, co-sureties, nor liable to contribution as between each other.[1] To constitute the relation of co-sureties between such indorsers there must be an agreement to that effect between them, or some fact or circumstance must exist from which such an agreement can be inferred. If a binding agreement to that effect is established, such indorsers will be held liable to contribution as co-sureties. But it has been held that such an agreement made between such indorsers after they have signed, and without any new consideration, is not binding. And where, after a note was due, the first and second indorsers wrote a letter to the creditor, stating they were jointly liable, and asking for time, it was held that this did not render them co-sureties.[2] It has been held that the accommodation indorser of a note is not, in the absence of an agreement to that effect, liable as co-surety with a surety who signed the note on its face, as maker.[3] So it has been held that a stranger who, in terms, guaranties a note on its back, is not, in the absence of an agreement to that effect, a co-surety with a surety who

[1] Sherrod *v.* Rhodes, 5 Ala. 683; McCarty *v.* Roots, 21 How. (U. S.) 432; McCune *v.* Belt, 45 Mo. 174; Stillwell *v.* How, 46 Mo. 589; Hillegas *v.* Stephenson, 75 Mo. 118; McGurk *v.* Huggett, 56 Mich. 187; Phillips *v.* Plato, 42 Hun (N. Y.), 189: Armstrong *v.* Harshman, 61 Ind. 52. *Contra*, see Daniel *v.* McRae, 2 Hawks (N. C.), 590; Richards *v.* Simms, 1 Dev. & Bat. Law (N. C.), 48; Stovall *v.* Border Grange Bank, 78 Va. 188; Janson *v.* Paxton, 22 Up. Can. (C. P.) 505. In Dillenbeck *v.* Dygert, 97 N. Y. 303, it was held that where one of several accommodation makers of a joint and several promissory note paid the same, and then subsequently transferred the note for value to a third person, he also transferred therewith the right to demand contribution from the other makers, and the transferee's possession of the note will be evidence of its payment. In Drummond *v.* Yager, 10 Brad. (Ill. App.) 380, it was held that a person might be so situated as not to be liable to the holder of a note, and yet retain to the sureties thereon such relation that in the event of payment by one he would be liable to contribution.

[2] Cathcart *v.* Gibson, 1 Rich. Law (S. C.), 10. See, also, on this point, Dunn *v.* Wade, 23 Mo. 207.

[3] Smith *v.* Smith, 1 Dev. Eq. (N. C.) 173; Dawson *v.* Pettway, 4 Dev. & Bat. Law (N. C.), 396; Briggs *v.* Boyd, 37 Vt. 534. But see Houck *v.* Graham, 106 Ind. 195.

had previously signed it on its face.[1] A., for the purpose of raising money for himself, drew a bill on B., which B. accepted for A.'s accommodation. Being unable to get the bill discounted without a third name, A. procured C. to indorse it. The bill being unpaid at maturity, the holder agreed to renew it, and accordingly a new bill was drawn by B. upon A., and indorsed by C. *Held*, that B., who had the bill to pay, was entitled to contribution from C.[2] It has been held that the mere fact that one party drew and another indorsed a bill of exchange for the sole accommodation of another did not establish the fact that they were co-sureties, but it might be shown by parol that they were co-sureties.[3] *Prima facie*, an indorser of a promissory note is not a co-surety with a surety who signs the note as maker, but it may be shown by parol evidence that they were, in fact, co-sureties.[4]

§ 261. The true relation between several sureties may be shown by parol evidence.— It is a general rule that the true relation subsisting between the several parties bound for the performance of a written obligation may be shown by parol evidence. An unwritten agreement made between such parties prior to, or contemporaneously with, their executing an instrument as sureties, by which one promises to indemnify the other from loss, may be proved by parol, and the surety who made the agreement cannot, in such case, recover contribution from the other.[5] In such a case the court said: "The legal effect of a written contract is as much within the protection of the rule which forbids the introduction of parol evidence as its language. . . . But we think it is limited to the stipulations between the parties actually contracting with each other by the written instrument." The liability to contribution does not arise from contract, but from equitable principles. There is no agreement between the sureties contained in the obligation signed by them. The agreement is between the obligors and the obligee. As between the various sureties there is no written agreement; there is only an equi-

[1] Longley *v.* Griggs, 10 Pick. 121.

[2] Reynolds *v.* Wheeler, 10 J. Scott (N. R.), 561.

[3] Dunn *v.* Sparks, 7 Ind. 490.

[4] Nurre *v.* Chittenden, 56 Ind. 462. And to like effect, see Houck *v.* Graham, 106 Ind. 195.

[5] Craythorne *v.* Swinburne, 14 Ves. 160; Hunt *v.* Chambliss, 7 Smedes & Mar. (Miss.) 532; Rae *v.* Rae, 6 Irish

table presumption, raised by the fact of payment, that the sureties ought to contribute equally for the default of the principal. This equity can be rebutted by parol.[1] Where several parties sign an obligation, and one of them adds after his name the word "surety," it may be shown by parol he is surety for, or co-surety with, the other. The word "surety" indicates that he is surety for somebody, but does not show for whom.[2] It is competent for one of two sureties on a promissory note to prove by parol that he signed as surety both of his principal and the other surety, and on an undertaking by the other surety to indemnify him. The court, in deciding such a case, said: "It is not offering parol evidence to vary or explain the written contract; it was a collateral contract, independent of and consistent with it. The law regards all joint signers of an obligation as principals. It is by assuming an equitable jurisdiction that evidence is admitted of some of the parties having signed as sureties, and there is nothing to forbid the further evidence of their having fixed and arranged their respective liabilities as between themselves by their own contract."[3] The surety on the face of a note and an accommodation indorser may, as between themselves, be shown by parol to be co-sureties by virtue of a verbal understanding to that effect.[4] So several successive accommodation indorsers of a negotiable instrument may be shown by parol to be co-sureties.[5] In an action by one surety against another for contribution, parol evidence of the payment made by the plaintiff is admissible and sufficient, notwithstanding it was made upon an execution, which is not produced, issued on a judgment against the principal and sureties.[6] Parol evidence is admis-

Ch. 490. To contrary effect, see Norton v. Coons, 6 N. Y. 33.

[1] Barry v. Ransom, 12 N. Y. 462, per Dennis and Dean. JJ. To same effect, see Paulin v. Kaighn, 3 Dutcher (N. J.), 503.

[2] Robinson v. Lyle, 10 Barb. (N. Y.) 512; Adams v. Flanagan, 36 Vt. 400; Bobbitt v. Shryer, 70 Ind. 513, 516. See, also, to this point, Fernald v. Dawley, 26 Me. 470; Crosby v. Wyatt, 23 Me. 156.

[3] Anderson v. Pearson, 2 Bailey, Law (S. C.), 107.

[4] Harshman v. Armstrong, 43 Ind. 126.

[5] Clapp v. Rice, 13 Gray, 403; Smith v. Morrill, 54 Me. 48. So, parol evidence is admissible in a contest between so-called indorsers, who are in reality sureties, to show their actual relation to one another. Camp v. Simmons, 62 Ga. 73.

[6] Hayden v. Rice, 18 Vt. 353.

sible to show the intention of the parties to a note, and they will be held liable according to their intention.[1] Thus, where it appeared on the face of a note that certain persons thereon were sureties, it was held in an action for contribution that parol evidence was admissible to show that they were really principals or joint makers.[2]

§ 262. **Surety who becomes bound during course of remedy against principal not co-surety with original surety.** A surety who becomes bound for a debt during the course of legal proceeedings against the principal for the collection of the same is not a co-surety with the original surety for the debt, nor entitled to contribution from him; and if such original surety afterwards has to pay the debt, he is entitled to subrogation to the creditor's rights against such subsequent surety, and may collect the whole amount that he has paid from such subsequent surety.[3] Where a judgment was recovered against principal and surety, and the principal alone appealed, giving a different surety on the appeal bond, and the judgment was affirmed, and was paid by the surety in the appeal bond, it was held that he could not recover contribution from the original surety.[4] Judgment was rendered against A. and B. in the county court, and they appealed to the circuit court, giving C. as surety on the appeal bond. Judgment was rendered against all three of them in the circuit court, and they all appealed to the supreme court, and gave an appeal bond as principals, with D. as their surety. The judgment was affirmed in the supreme court, and was paid by C. *Held*, C. could not recover contribution from D.[5] If, after

[1] Thompson *v.* Taylor, 12 R. I. 109. And where a note does not conclusively show the relation between the parties thereto, parol evidence is admissible to show it. Klepper *v.* Borchsenius, 13 Bradw. (Ill. App.) 318.

[2] Williams *v.* Glenn, 92 N. C. 253; Mansfield *v.* Edwards, 136 Mass. 15.

[3] Where a judgment against a principal and surety has been appealed by the principal alone, giving a different surety on the appeal bond, and the original surety pays the judgment, he is equitably entitled to be subrogated to the rights of the judgment creditor against the surety on the appeal bond. Friberg *v.* Donovan, 23 Ill. App. 58.

[4] Chaffin *v.* Campbell, 4 Sneed (Tenn.), 184. On the other hand, if the original surety paid the judgment he would be subrogated to the rights of the judgment creditor against the surety on the appeal bond. Friberg *v.* Donovan, 23 Ill. App. 58.

[5] Cowan *v.* Duncan, Meigs (Tenn.),

separate judgments are obtained against principal and surety, a third person interposes and gives his note for the debt to obtain a stay of execution, and judgment is obtained on the note, and then the first surety is obliged to pay the debt, he is entitled to have an assignment of the judgment on the note of such third person, to indemnify him for such payment. The surety is entitled to subrogation to every security which the creditor obtains for the payment of the debt. The second "surety stipulating at the instance of the principal to pay the debt suffers no absolute injustice in being obliged to do so, since he is compelled to perform no more than he undertook, and has no right to complain that he is not allowed to use as payment by himself the money which proceeds from another person whom his principal was previously bound to save harmless. . . . It is sufficient that it is settled that if the interposition of the second surety may have been the means of involving the first in the ultimate liability to pay, the equity of the first surety decidedly preponderates."[1] An execution was issued against a principal and sureties, and the principal alone obtained an injunction to stay the judgment, and gave an injunction bond with a different surety. The surety in the injunction bond having been compelled to pay the judgment, it was held that he could not recover contribution from the original sureties. Without their solicitation he had prolonged their liability, by preventing the money being made out of their principal, as it would have been but for his interference. To make them contribute would be grossly inequitable.[2]

470. To a similar effect, in the case of sureties on a *supersedeas* and stay bond, see Smith's Ex'rs *v.* Anderson, 18 Md. 520; Kellar *v.* Williams, 10 Bush (Ky.), 216. Where a surety, against whom judgment was rendered, failed to object to a stay of execution taken by the principal, it was presumed that he consented thereto; and in that case the surety on the stay bond, as between him and the original surety, was held not chargeable with primary liability to pay the judgment. Chase *v.* Welty, 57 Iowa, 230.

[1] Pott *v.* Nathans, 1 Watts & Serg. (Pa). 155, per Sargent, J.; Clay *v.* Schnitzell, 5 Phila. (Pa.) 441; Schnitzell's Appeal, 49 Pa. St. 23. And see Wolff *v.* Stover, 107 Pa. St. 206. Holding the same thing in the case of an original surety and a surety on an appeal bond, see Mitchell *v.* De Witt, 25 Tex. (Supplement), 180.

[2] Brandenburg *v.* Flynn's Ex'r, 12 B. Mon. (Ky.) 397; Bohannon *v.* Combs, 12 B. Mon. (Ky.) 563.

Judgment was recovered against a principal and sureties, and execution was levied on the property of one of the sureties, who executed a forthcoming bond with another of the sureties (whose property had not been levied on) as his surety in the forthcoming bond, and the bond was forfeited. The surety in the forthcoming bond paid the debt, and it was held that he was entitled to contribution from all the sureties for the debt.[1] It has been held that where a judgment is recovered against one surety, the suing out a writ of error to the supreme court by him, and giving bond for its prosecution, does not destroy his right to contribution from a co-surety bound within him for the debt on which the judgment was recovered.[2] Where successive securities for a debt have been given in judicial proceedings at the request of the debtor alone, to enable him to prolong litigation, it is held that, as between themselves, the sureties will be liable to exoneration in the inverse order of their undertaking.[3]

§ **263. Contribution cannot be recovered when it would be inequitable.**— As the right to contribution between co-sureties is founded on equitable principles, contribution will not be enforced between them when it would be inequitable. Thus, two parties, A. and B., were sureties of C. On one occasion, when some of C.'s land was being sold, he endeavored to stifle competition at the sale, and the land was sold to B. for more than as much less than it was worth as A. and B. were liable for as sureties. Afterwards B. had the debt to pay, and in a suit by him for contribution it was held that he either bought and held the land for C., or bought it for himself by C.'s efforts, at enough less than it was worth to indemnify him, and he was not entitled to contribution from A. The court said: "The right to contribution amongst sureties rests not in contract, but in natural equity. . . . If a party base his right to recover upon principles of natural equity, the defendant may appeal to the same principles in his defense."[4] A., B. and C. were sureties for D. in a bond, and judgment was

[1] Preston *v.* Preston, 4 Gratt. (Va.) 88.

[2] John *v.* Jones, 16 Ala. 454.

[3] Chrisman *v.* Jones, 34 Ark. 73.

[4] Dennis *v.* Gillespie, 24 Miss. 581, per Fisher, J. For special cases on this subject, see McGehee *v.* McGehee, 12 Ala. 83; Wells *v.* Miller, 66 N. Y. 255; Glasscock *v.* Hamilton, 62 Tex. 143.

recovered against A., B. and D., but not against C. Execution was sued out and levied on the property of D., who gave a forthcoming bond, in which A., B. and a third party joined as sureties. Execution was awarded on the forthcoming bond, and levied on the property of A. *Held*, he could not recover contribution from C. The money would have been made from the property of the principal if the last bond had not been given, and it was inequitable that C. should suffer by the giving of such bond.[1] So, where A., B. and C. were co-sureties, and judgment was recovered against them all, and execution was levied on property of A., who gave a forthcoming bond, with B. as surety, and this bond was forfeited and the property lost, and A. became insolvent, and B. paid the debt, it was held that B. could only recover from C., as contribution, one-third of the amount paid by him, instead of one-half, which he would otherwise have been entitled to recover.[2] Where property is conveyed to a trustee, to indemnify a surety for various indorsements, and by agreement between the principal and surety the property is sold in a certain way, and in consideration thereof the surety agrees to pay all the debts of the principal for which he is bound as surety, and does pay a debt contemplated by the agreement on which there is a co-surety, he cannot recover contribution from such co-surety.[3]

§ 264. **When surety, who becomes liable at the request of another surety, not liable to contribution.**— If one surety, in order to induce another to become bound as surety, agrees to indemnify him from all loss which he may suffer in consequence thereof, such an agreement is valid and will be enforced.[4] The weight of authority is, also, that if one surety becomes bound at and solely because of the request of another surety, even though there be no express agreement on the part of the latter to indemnify the former, yet the surety making the request, if he is compelled to pay the debt, cannot recover contribution from the surety who signed in consequence of such request. With reference to this it has been said: "Where one has been induced to become surety at the

[1] Langford's Ex'r *v.* Perrin, 5 Leigh (Va.), 552.

[2] Preston *v.* Preston, 4 Gratt. (Va.) 88.

[3] John *v.* Jones, 16 Ala. 454.

[4] Jones *v.* Letcher, 13 B. Mon. (Ky.) 363.

instance of the other, though he thereby renders himself liable to the person to whom the security is given, there is no pretense for saying that he shall be liable to be called upon by the person at whose request he entered into the security."[1] If, however, a surety becomes bound at the request of the principal, coupled with the request of another surety, it has been held that he is liable for contribution to the surety who joins with the principal in making the request.[2] It has also been held that the mere fact that one surety became such at the request of another did not release the former from liability to contribute to the latter. This was in one case put on the ground that there was an implied contract between co-sureties to contribute, and a simple request by one to the other to become surety was not sufficient to rebut the presumption of such implied contract.[3] As already seen, the right to contribution results from equitable principles, and contribution will not, in the absence of express contract, be enforced contrary to equity. It may well be said that it would be inequitable to compel the party who became bound at the request of another, to contribute to that other, if a loss is sustained in consequence of the assumption of such liability.

§ 265. **Surety of surety not liable to contribution.**— The surety of a surety is not generally liable to contribution at the suit of the party for whom he is surety. Thus, the plaintiff signed a note as surety, upon the erroneous supposition, springing from the deceit and falsehood of the principal, and in no way imputable to the defendants, that the defendants would sign as co-sureties with him. Afterwards the defendants, in good faith and without any knowledge of what the plaintiff supposed as to their signing, signed the note, upon

[1] Turner *v.* Davies, 2 Esp. 478, per Lord Kenyon; Cutter *v.* Emery, 37 N. H. 567; Byers *v.* McClanahan, 6 Gill & Johns. (Md.) 250; Danel *v.* Ballard, 2 Dana (Ky.), 296.

[2] Hendricks *v.* Whittemore, 105 Mass. 23.

[3] Bagott *v.* Mullen, 32 Ind. 332; McKee *v.* Campbell, 27 Mich. 497. To similar effect, see Burnett *v.* Millsapps, 59 Miss. 333. And where a surety became such at the request of a co-surety, who agreed to indemnify and save him harmless, it was held that he might, after the money became due, maintain a bill in equity to compel the co-surety to pay the debt not only as to money already paid, but whatever he might be liable to pay on account of his suretyship. Hayden *v.* Thrasher, 18 Fla. 795.

the distinct understanding with the principal and the payee that they signed as sureties for the plaintiff and other previous signers, and not as co-sureties with the plaintiff. *Held*, they did not thereby become co-sureties with the plaintiff, nor were they liable to him for contribution,[1] Where, after certain sureties had signed a note, another signed it, and added to his name the words "security to above," it was held that the first sureties could not recover contribution from the latter unless it was made satisfactorily to appear that he intended to become co-surety with them.[2] A. being indebted, and the creditor pressing for payment, an application was made by B. to a bank, which advanced the money on two bonds, one of which was signed by A. as principal and C. as surety. The other bond recited the first one, and the advance of the money to A. and C. at the request of B., and was conditioned to be void if A. and C., or either of them, paid the first bond. It was understood by parol between B. and the bank that he was not to be liable unless both A. and C. failed to pay, and that he was not a co-surety with either of them. *Held*, that C. upon paying the debt could not recover contribution from B. The court said that B. "might limit his engagement with reference to them as he thought proper, and the bond upon the face of it makes him surety only for the principal and the other surety."[3] Where A., the surety in an undertaking for the discharge of an attachment, became fixed by a judgment against his principal and united with him in an undertaking for a *supersedeas*, and an additional surety was required in the latter undertaking, which the principal with the assent of A. procured, and B. became such surety, it was held that no right of contribution arose in favor of A. against B. in case A. had to pay the debt.[4]

[1] Adams *v.* Flanagan, 36 Vt. 400. See, also, Baldwin *v.* Fleming, 90 Ind. 177.

[2] Thompson *v.* Sanders, 4 Dev. & Bat. Law (N. C.), 404. See, also, Sherman *v.* Black, 49 Vt. 198; Oldham *v.* Broom, 28 Ohio St. 41; Baldwin *v.* Fleming, 90 Ind. 177; Bobbitt *v.* Shryer, 70 Ind. 513.

[3] Craythorne *v.* Swinburne, 14 Vesey, 160, per Lord Eldon, C. To the effect that a surety of a surety is liable to contribution, see Cooke *v.* ——, Freeman's Ch. 97. And see Chapeze *v.* Young, 87 Ky. 476.

[4] Hartwell *v.* Smith, 15 Ohio St. 200. To similar effect, see Knox *v.* Vallandingham, 13 Smedes & Mar. (Miss.) 526.

§ 266. Surety who becomes principal liable for whole amount paid by former co-surety — Other cases.— When one of several sureties afterwards assumes the character of a principal he becomes liable to the other sureties as principal for the whole amount paid by them. Thus, R., having contracted to erect a building, assigned his contract to C., who then executed to him a bond with M., G. and others as sureties, conditioned to pay R. for stone already quarried for the building. Afterwards, with the knowledge and consent of the sureties, C. assigned the building contract to M., with a condition that M. should perform all the undertakings and assume all risks and liabilities imposed upon C. as assignce of the contract. M. accepted the assignment, performed the work and received the benefits of the building contract, but failed to pay for the stone. G. having been compelled to pay the sum due for the stone, it was held that he was entitled to recover from M., as principal, the full amount paid by him.[1] A., being desirous of borrowing $50 at a bank, applied to B. and C. to be his sureties, when it was agreed between A. and B., in the presence of C., that $100 should be borrowed, and that B. should have half the sum. A note for $100 was signed by the three and discounted at the bank. B. received one-half the money and gave A. his note for it. C. having paid the note, it was held that he had a right to recover from B., as principal, the whole sum so paid.[2] A promissory note, by its terms payable at a bank, was signed by principal and surety with the expectation that it would be discounted at the bank. The bank refused to discount the note unless the creditor signed the note on its face as a maker. He did this under an express understanding with the bank that he was not thereby to become a co-surety with the other parties, but the surety of all of them. He had to pay the note, and it was held that he could recover the whole amount from the surety.[3] A. became surety for B. and C., partners in trade, upon their note payable to D. for $2,000, and B. conveyed to A. certain of his property for indemnity. Shortly afterwards B. bought

[1] Gray v. McDonald, 19 Wis. 213. On this subject see, also, Ragland v. Milam, 10 Ala. 618.

[2] Jones v. Fitz, 5 N. H. 444. To similar effect, see McPherson v. Talbott, 10 Gill & Johns. (Md.) 499.

[3] Bowser v. Rendell, 31 Ind. 128.

out all C.'s interest in the business, and agreed to pay all the partnership debts. B. became insolvent and did not pay the note, and judgment on the same was obtained against C., who paid it, and A. conveyed to C. two thousand dollars' worth of the property conveyed by B. to him for his indemnity. *Held*, that this last conveyance might lawfully be made, and could not be impeached by a judgment creditor of B.[1] The owner of imported goods consigned them to a commission merchant for sale, who entered them at the custom-house, giving his bond for the import duties, upon which bond the owner and another became sureties, and the consignee immediately charged the owner with the amount of the duties, and afterwards failed before the bond became due. The owner paid the money due on the bond, and it was held he could recover contribution from the other surety in the bond. The court said that, on account of the nature of the transaction, the debt was that of the consignee, and the owner and the other surety were co-sureties.[2] Three parties contracted for the purchase of land, which was to be conveyed to them in three equal shares. They gave for the purchase money three joint notes for equal amounts, signed by them all. *Held*, each one was principal for one-third of each note, and co-surety of the others for two-thirds of each, and their rights and liabilities must be determined on that basis.[3]

§ 267. **Surety who pays debt for which principal or another surety is not liable cannot have contribution.**— As a general rule, one surety cannot recover contribution from another when the debt paid by the surety seeking contribution was either not binding on the principal or not binding on the other surety. Thus, a surety who, knowing all the facts, pays a note which is void for usury, cannot recover contribution from a co-surety on the note. A surety ordinarily has no greater rights against a co-surety than the creditor has against them both; and in such case the creditor has no lawful claim against any of them.[4] But if the surety paying a note tainted

[1] Butler *v.* Birkey, 13 Ohio St. 514.

[2] Taylor *v.* Savage, 12 Mass. 98.

[3] Goodall *v.* Wentworth, 20 Me. 322.

[4] Russell *v.* Failor, 1 Ohio St. 327; Briggs *v.* Hinton, 14 B. J. Lea (Tenn.), 233. There must have been a legal obligation on the surety to pay, against whom judgment and execution could have been obtained. Stockmeyer *v.* Oertling, 35 La. Ann. 467; Skrainka *v.* Rohan, 18 Mo. App. 340.

with usury had at the time of such payment no knowledge of the usury, he may recover contribution from a co-surety.[1] Where one surety on an official bond was sued at law, and a judgment recovered against him for a demand for which he was not liable as surety, it was held he could not call on his co-surety for contribution. The court said that the surety who pays "takes the place of the original creditor, and may be resisted on the same principles, and in the same way."[2] Two co-sureties were sued jointly, and judgment was rendered in favor of them both. The creditor appealed to the supreme court from the judgment in favor of one of them, and such judgment was as to such surety reversed, and judgment in the supreme court was rendered against such surety for a large amount, which he paid. *Held*, he could not recover contribution from the other surety. The judgment which as to him remained in force in the court below established the fact that he was not liable to the creditor, and consequently not liable for contribution.[3] It has been held that a surety who pays a debt, after he might have defeated it by pleading the statute of limitations, can recover contribution from a co-surety on the ground that the surety who paid was under no obligation, legal or equitable, to defeat a just claim by such a plea.[4] A surety paid the debt of a deceased principal after the claim against his estate had been barred by the statute of non-claim, and it was held he was entitled to contribution from a co-surety. The debt, although barred as against the estate of the principal, was not barred as against the surety who paid it, and he was liable for it when he made the payment.[5] Where a surety pays a note which he could have defeated because of an alteration therein made without his consent, it is held that he may compel contribution from co-sureties who subsequently sign.[6] But where a surety pays a balance due upon a bond with knowledge of the existence of a covenant on the part of

[1] Warner *v.* Morrison, 3 Allen, 566.

[2] Lowndes *v.* Pinckney, 1 Rich. Eq. (S. C.) 155, per Dunkin, C.

[3] Ledoux *v.* Durrive, 10 La. Ann. 7.

[4] Jones *v.* Blanton, 6 Ired. Eq. (N. C.) 115. And to same effect, see Bright *v.* Lennon, 83 N. C. 183. But see precisely the opposite, held in Cocke *v.* Hoffman, 5 B. J. Lea (Tenn.), 105, and Eberhardt *v.* Wood, 6 B. J. Lea (Tenn.), 467.

[5] Evans *v.* Evans, 16 Ala. 465.

[6] Houck *v.* Graham, 106 Ind. 195.

the obligee to a co-surety not to sue him, he will not be entitled to contribution.[1]

§ 268. When one surety entitled to benefit of indemnity secured by another surety.— If one of several sureties after all have signed, and before the debt has been paid, and without any agreement to that effect before he became liable, obtains from the principal anything for his indemnity, such indemnity inures to the benefit of all the sureties, and the surety obtaining it immediately becomes the trustee of it for the benefit of all the sureties, even though he obtained it by his own exertions and it was intended for his sole benefit.[2] In such case, as all the sureties are alike liable for a common principal, it will be presumed that the surety taking the indemnity takes it for the benefit of all the sureties, or if he does not, then his taking from the effects of the common principal for his sole benefit is a fraud on the other sureties, and he will not be permitted to have the benefit of the indemnity alone, but must share it with the others. Where, after two sureties became bound, one received indemnity from the principal, with which he paid more than one-half the debt, and the other surety paid the remainder, it was held the latter might recover from the former one-half the amount which he had paid.[3] It has also been held that the surety who has partial indemnity in his hands, and pays all the debt, can only recover from his

[1] Craven *v.* Freeman, 82 N. C. 361.

[2] Seibert *v.* Thompson, 8 Kan. 65; Steele *v.* Mealing, 24 Ala. 285; Miller *v.* Sawyer, 30 Vt. 412; McLewis *v.* Furgerson, 5 The Reporter, 330; McCune *v.* Belt, 45 Mo. 174; Hartwell *v.* Whitman, 36 Ala. 712; Smith *v.* Conrad, 15 La. Ann. 579; Hinsdill *v.* Murray, 6 Vt. 136; Leary *v.* Cheshire, 3 Jones' Eq. (N. C.) 170; Low *v.* Smart, 5 N. H. 353; Gregory *v.* Murrell, 2 Ired. Eq. (N. C.) 233; Hall *v.* Robinson, 8 Ired. Law (N. C.), 56; Fagan *v.* Jacocks, 4 Dev. Law (N. C.), 263; Steel *v.* Dixon, Law Rep. (17 Ch. Div.) 825; Reinhart *v.* Johnson, 62 Iowa, 155; Sanders *v.* Weelburg, 107 Ind. 266; McGhee *v.* Owen, 61 Ala. 440; Munden *v.* Bailey, 70 Ala. 63; Tolle, Ex'x, *v.* Boeckeler, 12 Mo. App. 54; Cannon *v.* Connaway, 5 Del. Ch. 559. To a contrary effect, see Thompson *v.* Adams, 1 Freeman's Ch. (Miss.) 225; Cooper *v.* Martin, 1 Dana (Ky.), 23; Hall *v.* Cushman, 16 N. H. 462. Sureties who become such after the liability of the original sureties is fixed, held not entitled to share in indemnity. Hornsberger *v.* Yancy, 33 Gratt. (Va.) 527. And it is held they are not entitled to share in such indemnity where they are liable on separate bonds for the same principal. Somers *v.* Johnson, 57 Vt. 274.

[3] Agnew *v.* Bell, 4 Watts (Pa.), 31.

co-surety one-half the sum which would remain after applying the amount of the indemnity on the sum paid.[1] A. and B. were co-sureties on a note for C., and B. was indebted to C. on a note of about the same amount. It was afterwards agreed between B. and C. that C. should deliver to B. his note, and that B. should pay that amount of the note on which he and A. were sureties, and B.'s note was delivered to him by C. Afterwards B. and C. made a different agreement with reference to the amount of B.'s note. B. had to pay the note on which he and A. were sureties, and sued A. for contribution. *Held*, that when B. received his own note from C., as above, he received it for the benefit of A. as well as himself, and could not divert it from the purpose for which he received it, and he could only recover from A. a *pro rata* share after deducting the amount of the note.[2] Where a surety, after he becomes bound and before he is damnified, takes a mortgage on property of the principal to indemnify himself, if there are several demands on which he is surety with different co-sureties, and the security is taken generally for his indemnity, it has been held that the indemnity shall be apportioned among all the demands *pro rata*.[3] Where a surety took from the principal a mortgage to secure a debt due from the principal to such surety and also to indemnify such surety against loss as such, and there was no provision in the mortgage as to which debt should be paid first, it was held that the proceeds of the mortgage should be applied *pro rata* to the payment of the debt due from the principal to the surety, and to the payment of the debts for which the surety was liable as such with a co-surety.[4] But in a similar case it was held that the surety who took the indemnity might first pay from the proceeds the debt due him individually.[5] One of two sureties paid the debt and took an assignment of a mortgage given by the principal to secure the debt. He then foreclosed the mortgage (after first requesting his co-surety to pay one-half the debt

[1] Currier *v.* Fellows, 27 N. H. 366.

[2] Hall *v.* Robinson, 8 Ired. Law (N. C.), 56. Holding that an indemnity placed in the hands of one surety for the benefit of all cannot be diverted from that purpose, Hinsdill *v.* Murray, 6 Vt. 136; Hayes *v.* Davis, 18 N. H. 600.

[3] Brown *v.* Ray, 18 N. H. 102.

[4] Moore *v.* Moberly, 7 B. Mon. (Ky.) 299.

[5] Brown *v.* Ray, 18 N. H. 102.

and take an assignment of the mortgage jointly with him), and bid in the property for a nominal sum. In a suit by him against his co-surety for contribution, it was held that he was a trustee of the mortgaged premises for his co-surety and bound to account for their value at the time they were sold, and not at a subsequent time, and was entitled to commissions for his trouble.[1]

§ 269. Instances of indemnity taken by one surety inuring to the benefit of all the sureties.— To prevent circuity of action and attain the ends of natural justice, equity will completely indemnify one of the sureties in a bond by means of a lien on the property of the principal existing in favor of another surety for the indemnity of such other surety, and for that purpose the court will compel the creditor (all the parties being before it) to resort to that property in the first place for the satisfaction of the debt.[2] Two sureties having become bound, the principal placed an indemnity in the hands of one of them, and he assumed to pay the debt, and, after having paid it in part, procured a third person to purchase the debt for his benefit. The assignee sued the debt in his own name and recovered a judgment against both sureties, and had an execution issued and levied on the property of the surety who had no indemnity. *Held*, equity would interfere and compel the payment of the debt by the indemnified surety, and restrain its collection from the other surety.[3] A principal gave a surety who was liable with a co-surety a mortgage for his indemnity, the mortgage stating the debts it was given to secure. The mortgagee afterwards had to pay as surety for his principal a certain sum for which he became liable after the making of the mortgage. *Held*, the mortgagee must account to his co-surety for the mortgaged property, and could not retain anything from the proceeds thereof to indemnify himself from loss on account of the debt for which he subsequently became surety.[4] In order to indemnify his several sureties, a principal assigned to a trustee a claim to be collected for their benefit. Before this claim was collected the

[1] Livingston *v.* Van Rensselaer, 6 Wend. 63.

[2] West *v.* Belches, 5 Munf. (Va.) 187.

[3] Silvey *v.* Dowell, 53 Ill. 260.

[4] Steele *v.* Mealing, 24 Ala. 285.

sureties were each compelled to pay an equal portion of the debt. One of the sureties (A.) obtained judgment against the principal for the sum paid by him, on which the principal was arrested, and gave a prison bounds bond with sureties, which he forfeited, and the sureties thereon became liable. The assignee afterwards collected the claim for the benefit of the sureties. *Held*, that neither A. nor the sureties in the prison bounds bond could come on the fund in the hands of the trustee till all the other sureties had been fully indemnified. A., having obtained another security, had two funds to look to, while the other sureties only had one; and he must first exhaust the one in which they were not interested. The sureties in the prison bounds bond were not in as good a position as A., because the effect of their act was to defeat the recovery of indemnity from the principal.[1] Complainants and defendants were bound as sureties for one S., to whom the defendant was indebted, and judgment was recovered against all the sureties, which they paid in equal proportions. S., as indemnity to the defendant for the sum paid by him, caused the notes which he held against the defendant to be surrendered to him. *Held*, the complainants were entitled to contribution from the defendant, and that the amount of the notes so surrendered to the defendant should be accounted for by him to his co-sureties.[2] Two co-sureties were offered security by their principal upon condition that they should execute a release to him, which offer was accepted by one and rejected by the other. The party accepting the security realized from it more than enough to pay half the common debt, and applied the proceeds to the payment thereof. The surety refusing to accept the security was forced to pay the portion of the debt still due, and sued his co-surety for contribution. *Held*, he was not entitled to recover. The court said contribution would not be enforced when it would be inequitable, and it would be inequitable to enforce it in this case.[3]

§ 270. Same continued — Cases where indemnity to one surety does not inure to benefit of co-sureties.— A mortgage executed to one or more of several sureties on an official bond

[1] Givens *v.* Nelson, 10 Leigh (Va.), 382.

[2] Tyus *v.* De Jarnette, 26 Ala. 280.

[3] White *v.* Banks, 21 Ala. 705.

is held to inure not only to the benefit of all who were sureties on such bond at the date of the mortgage, but to all who subsequently may become such; as, for example, under an order of court requiring additional sureties in pursuance of law.[1] It is held no defense to a surety when sued for his principal's debt that his co-surety had secured indemnity from his principal solely for himself, as such indemnity inures to the benefit of all, and the surety so holding it does so as trustee and for the joint benefit of his co-sureties.[2] In an action for contribution where the co-surety for his indemnity had received property which he turned into money and applied in part payment of the debt, it was held that the money so applied must be considered as a payment made by the principal, and the co-surety was liable for an aliquot portion of the balance.[3] Where accommodation indorsers of a promissory note each paid one-half the balance due the discounting bank on the same, and at the request of the maker his wife assigned part of a certain judgment which she held against him to one of the sureties for his individual indemnity, the maker joining in the assignment, it was held that the co-surety was entitled to share equally in the indemnity.[4] But where the principal's wife mortgaged her separate real estate for the exclusive use and benefit of one of her husband's sureties, it was held that such mortgage did not inure to the benefit of the co-sureties.[5] The court said that the rule entitling co-sureties to share in indemnity given to one surety from the principal did not apply where such indemnity was furnished by a stranger. And it is held, also, that such rule does not extend to the benefit of sureties upon another separate and distinct bond or obligation made by the principal. Thus, where a county treasurer executed two official bonds, one the general official bond, and the other to secure school funds, and he executed a mortgage to the sureties upon his general bond, it was held that such security did not inure to the benefit of the sureties upon the bond for the school funds.[6]

[1] Farmers' Bank *v.* Teeters, 31 Ohio St. 36.

[2] Glasscock *v.* Hamilton, 62 Tex. 143.

[3] Wolcott *v.* Hagerman, 50 N. J. Law, 289.

[4] Shaeffer *v.* Clendenin, 100 Pa. St. 565.

[5] Leggett *v.* McClelland, 39 Ohio St. 624.

[6] Lacy *v.* Rollins, 74 Tex. 566.

§ 271. If surety surrender lien for his indemnity on property of principal he discharges co-surety from contribution.— If after several sureties become liable, and before the debt is paid, one of the sureties, not having stipulated for the same before he became bound, obtains a mortgage or other lien on property of the principal for his indemnity, such lien inures to the benefit of his co-sureties, and if it is afterwards lost by his positive act, his co-sureties will be discharged from liability to contribute to him to the extent that they are injured; and a defense founded on such facts may be made both at law and in equity.[1] In a case in which it was held that a surety cannot recover contribution from a co-surety whose right to subrogation to a judgment against the principal he has rendered unavailable, the court said: "A co-surety has, of course, the same responsibility for keeping alive securities in favor of his co-surety, from whom he claims contribution, as a creditor has in behalf of sureties."[2] A. and B. were co-sureties on the bond of an administrator, and, being sued on the same by the next of kin, compromised the suit by each paying $1,100, under the advice of counsel, from an honest belief that both were liable in a larger amount on account of a *devastavit* and the insolvency of the principal. It was afterwards discovered that B., who had administered on the estate of the principal, had, by a misapprehension of law, but honestly and under advice of counsel, given up assets of their principal for the payment of another claim, which, if they had been held by him, would have saved them both from loss on account of their suretyship. *Held*, A. could not sustain a bill to throw the whole loss on B., it not appearing that B. had concealed the fact of having parted with the assets, or had been guilty of any fraud or imposition.[3] A surety does not release his co-surety from contribution by the fact that after he has paid the debt he surrenders to the principal certain notes which

[1] Paulin *v.* Kaighn, 5 Dutch. (N. J.) 480, overruling Paulin *v.* Kaighn, 3 Dutch. (N. J.) 503; Ramsey *v.* Lewis, 30 Barb. (N. Y.) 403; Taylor *v.* Morrison, 26 Ala. 728. Holding that where the debt is paid by one surety he does not thereby obtain any right to a collateral security for the same debt put up by another surety, see Bowditch *v.* Green, 3 Met. (Mass.) 360.

[2] Fielding *v.* Waterhouse, 8 Jones & Spencer (N. Y.), 424, per Sedgwick, J.

[3] Brandon *v.* Medley, 1 Jones' Eq. (N. C.) 313.

the principal had deposited with him to secure another debt, and which it was expressly agreed should be delivered up as soon as the latter debt was paid. In such case no lien in which the co-surety is interested is lost.[1] After A. and B. became co-sureties, the principal put into A.'s hands, for his indemnity, certain notes of a third person. A. inquired about the notes, and was informed that they would soon be paid, and they were soon after paid; but before that time A. returned them to the principal upon the principal giving him a satisfactory bond of indemnity. A., having paid the debt, sued B. for contribution. *Held*, that A. was the trustee of the notes for B. as well as himself; but as there was no evidence that the bond was not as good as the notes, nor that A. had failed to act with ordinary prudence, B. could not complain, and was not discharged from contribution.[2] Where a surety failed to enforce an indemnity held by him, it was held that he could not call upon his co-surety for contribution.[3]

§ 272. **If surety negligently lose indemnity, co-surety released from contribution.**— The surety who holds a lien on property of the principal for the payment of the debt, concerning which lien he is chargeable as trustee for his co-sureties as well as himself, must be active in preserving the lien to the same extent that any other trustee under similar circumstances would be obliged to be diligent, and if through his negligence the lien is rendered unavailable for the payment of the debt, his co-sureties will be released from contribution to him, to the extent that they are injured thereby. Negligence under such circumstances is equivalent to a positive act producing the same result.[4] Thus, where a surety held a chattel mortgage for his indemnity on slaves of the principal, and, after the mortgage might have been foreclosed, he suf-

[1] Higgins *v.* Morrison's Ex'r, 4 Dana (Ky.), 100.

[2] Carpenter *v.* Kelly, 9 Ohio, 106. Holding that the surety who obtains a mortgage for the benefit of the other sureties will be allowed for his trouble and expenses, see Comegys *v.* State Bank, 6 Ind. 357. Holding that a surety may give to his co-sureties a mortgage to secure them against his liability for contribution' see Steele *v.* Faber, 37 Mo. 71. Holding that if money is deposited with a trustee by one surety for the indemnity of his co-sureties, if such co-sureties consent thereto, the money must be returned to the owner, see Skidmore *v.* Taylor, 29 Cal. 619.

[3] Frink *v.* Peabody, 26 Ill. App. 390.

[4] Schmidt *v.* Coulter, 6 Minn. 492.

fered some of the slaves to be sold by the sheriff for another debt of the principal, and lost as a security, it was held that he must account to his co-surety, who had paid the debt for the slaves so lost by his negligence.[1] So where property was conveyed by the principal for the indemnity of one of two sureties, and it was sold for that purpose, but through the negligence of the surety for whose indemnity it was conveyed, the purchase money was not collected and was lost, it was held he could not recover contribution from his co-surety.[2] The surety who receives from his principal a chattel mortgage of slaves and other property must account to his co-surety for such of the property as is wasted in consequence of his laches and for the value of the hire of the slaves.[3] A surety is not, however, accountable to his co-surety for a loss arising by reason of his failure to record a chattel mortgage given by the principal for his indemnity, when he agreed with the principal at the time he took the mortgage that he would not record it. In such case he is bound by the agreement, and the co-surety has no greater rights than he has.[4]

§ 273. Surety who obtains indemnity after all the sureties have paid an equal amount is not obliged to share it with the others.— After the debt of the principal is paid by several sureties in equal proportions, the equities between them as co-sureties cease, and each becomes an independent creditor of the principal for the amount paid by him. In such case, if one afterwards receives indemnity from the principal, the others are entitled to no part thereof.[5] So where one of two sureties paid the entire debt, and the principal afterwards paid him for his sole benefit one-half the amount, it was held that he was afterwards entitled to recover from his co-surety the other half of the debt he had paid for the principal.[6] One of two sureties, with the consent of the other, gave up a security which he had taken for the benefit of both, on receiving a written promise of the principal that he would pay the debt or return the security. This promise was not performed,

[1] Steele *v.* Mealing, 24 Ala. 285.

[2] Chilton *v.* Chapman, 13 Mo. 470.

[3] Goodloe *v.* Clay, 6 B. Mon. (Ky.) 236.

[4] White *v.* Carlton, 52 Ind. 371. To similar effect, see Pool *v.* Williams, 8 Ired. Law (N. C.), 286.

[5] Messer *v.* Swan, 4 N. H. 481; Harrison *v.* Phillips, 46 Mo. 520.

[6] Gould *v.* Fuller, 18 Me. 364.

and the sureties paid the debt of $1,080, by giving them joint and several notes therefor, payable on time. Before the note was paid or payable, the surety to whom the promise was made sued the principal for breach thereof, and in consequence received from him $600. *Held*, he was liable for one-half of this amount to his co-surety.[1] In this case, although the money was received after the debt was paid, the promise was made before that time. A. was collector of state revenue, and gave a bond, with B. and C. as sureties. He collected certain money of the state which he deposited in his own name in a private bank instead of in the state bank, where it should have been deposited. A. became a defaulter for a much larger sum, and B. and C. each paid one-half of the defalcation. B. then sued A. for indemnity, and garnished the private bank, and by legal proceedings got the money there deposited. *Held*, C. was entitled to one-half the money thus obtained by B., on the ground that the money belonged to the state and not to A., and each surety, when he paid, was entitled to subrogation to the claim of the state against A., and consequently each was entitled to one-half the money.[2]

§ 274. When suit for contribution can be brought by surety holding indemnity.— Although there is a conflict of authority on the subject, the weight of authority seems to be that the fact that the surety who pays the debt has in his hands an indemnity other than money, and more or less valuable, will not prevent him from suing a co-surety for contribution, and recovering such amount as he is then entitled to, irrespective of the sum that may afterwards be realized from the indemnity; but he will be accountable to the co-surety for a proper proportion of whatever sum he may afterwards realize from the indemnity.[3] A surety who had some indemnity in his hands paid the debt and sued his co-surety for contribution. *Held*, the amount he had received from the indemnity should be deducted from the amount he had paid, and a judgment for one half the remainder should be rendered against the co-surety. If the party holding the indemnity afterwards realizes anything from it, he must account to his co-surety for

[1] Doolittle *v.* Dwight, 2 Met. (Mass.) 561.

[2] Harrison *v.* Phillips, 46 Mo. 520.

[3] Johnson's Adm'rs *v.* Vaughn, 65 Ill. 425.

one-half of it, but the fact that he had the indemnity would not prevent him from recovering.[1] A principal gave his sureties a mortgage on slaves for their indemnity, and judgment was afterwards recovered against the principal and sureties, which one of the sureties paid. The sureties filed a bill to foreclose the mortgage which was pending. The surety who paid the debt brought suit against the principal to recover the amount paid by him, and the suit was pending. The surety who paid the debt then sued a co-surety for contribution, and it was held that, notwithstanding the pendency of the other two suits, he was entitled to recover.[2] Where a surety held for his indemnity certain bonds of third persons, and judgment had been recovered against him, the principal, and a co-surety, of which he had obtained an equitable assignment, it was held that equity would not permit him to enforce the collection of one-half the judgment from the co-surety, unless he showed that he could not have collected the bonds by reasonable diligence.[3] It has been held that a surety who is fully indemnified cannot recover contribution from his co-surety.[4] It has also been held that the surety who has partial indemnity in his hands, in the shape of property of the principal, can only recover from a co-surety one-half the amount paid by him after deducting therefrom the value of the property.[5]

§ 275. Surety may, before paying debt, file bill to compel co-surety to contribute and to restrain him from transferring his property.— The remedy between co-sureties is usually sought after the debt has been paid by some of them, but a surety may, before he has paid the debt, file a bill against his co-surety to compel him to contribute to its payment.[6] So where judgment was recovered against a principal and two sureties, and the principal was insolvent, and one of the sureties, having some real estate in his wife's name, was about to sell it to an innocent purchaser, it was held that the

[1] Bachelder *v.* Fiske, 17 Mass. 464. See, also, Titcomb *v.* McAllister, 77 Me. 353.

[2] Anthony *v.* Percifull, 8 Ark. (3 Eng.) 494.

[3] Kerns *v.* Chambers, 3 Ired. Eq. (N. C.) 576.

[4] Morrison *v.* Taylor, 21 Ala. 779.

[5] Currier *v.* Fellows, 27 N. H. 366. But if the surety has in his hands sufficient money or property of the principal to indemnify him, and he fails to discharge the indebtedness, he cannot recover contribution. Neely *v.* Bee, 32 W. Va. 519.

other surety, before paying the debt, might by suit in chancery restrain him from selling the property till the debt for which they were liable as sureties was paid. The court said: "While at law the surety has no remedy until he has paid the debt, equity, with a view of placing the performance of the duty where it primarily belongs, will interpose at the instance of the surety, as soon as the debt becomes due, to compel its payment by the principal. . . . A court of equity, to prevent a multiplicity of suits, in order to do right and distribute justice, will, in the first instance, impose the discharge of the duty or performance of the obligation upon the party primarily and ultimately bound. Instead, therefore, of requiring the surety to pay, and then reimbursing him by decree against the principal, it permits the surety at once to resort to the court to compel the principal to discharge his obligation. Although the question is new and without precedent in the books so far as we have been able to see, this equity is quite as strong in favor of a surety (where the principal is insolvent) against his co-surety. It is well supported by authority, and thoroughly approved, for the reason that, if the principal has made or is about to make secret or fraudulent dispositions of his property, so as to throw the debt upon his surety, the latter may have ample remedy. If the principal is insolvent, and therefore the debt rests as a common and equal burden upon the sureties, do not the same considerations appeal with equal force to the chancellor that he may see to it that one of them shall not, by secret or fraudulent contrivances or conveyances of property, fasten the whole of it upon the other? We think that the principle may well have this extended application."[2] After a judgment creditor had filed a creditor's bill against the principal and others, to subject money or assets fraudulently assigned by the principal to such others, a surety for the debt paid it, upon the express condition that he should have the right to prosecute the creditor's bill. *Held*, that paying the judgment did not, under the circumstances, extinguish it, and the surety had a right to prosecute the creditor's bill.[3]

[1] McKenna *v.* George, 2 Rich. Eq. (S. C.) 15. And, in principle, see, to like effect, Hayden *v.* Thrasher, 18 Fla. 795.

[2] Bowen *v.* Hoskins, 45 Miss. 183, per Simrall, J.

[3] Harris *v.* Carlisle, 12 Ohio, 169.

§ 276. Discharge of surety in bankruptcy does not release him from contribution to co-surety, who pays subsequently.— The discharge of a surety in bankruptcy does not usually release him from a claim to contribution by a co-surety who afterwards pays the debt. In a case in which this was held the court said: "There was here no debt capable of estimation in order to its being proved, because two contingencies were to be taken into consideration; first, whether the original debtor would not himself pay the debt, and secondly, whether this defendant would ever be called upon to pay it. I do not see how it is possible to say that any such debt existed between these parties as could have been proved under the commission."[1] If a surety, after his discharge in bankruptcy, voluntarily pays a balance due upon a bond on which he is surety, he is held entitled to contribution from a co-surety.[2]

§ 277. When surety who is discharged from liability to creditors liable to contribute to co-surety, who subsequently pays.— It has been held that the release of one surety, without the consent of his co-surety, from liability to the creditor, will not discharge him from liability to contribute to the co-surety, who is subsequently compelled to pay the debt.[3] But where suit was brought against one of two sureties, and judgment recovered, which such surety paid, and before the judgment was rendered the other surety, who was not sued, became released by the statute of limitations, it was held that the latter was thereby released from liability to contribution. In this case the surety who was sued had a statutory right to have compelled a suit to be brought against the other surety.[4]

[1] Clements *v.* Langley, 2 Nev. & Man. 269, per Denman, C. J.; Goss *v.* Gibson, 8 Humph. (Tenn.) 197; Eberhardt *v.* Wood, 2 Tenn. Ch. (Cooper), 488; Dunn *v.* Sparks, 1 Ind. 397; Swain *v.* Barber, 29 Vt. 292; Keer *v.* Clark, 11 Humph. (Tenn.) 77; Smith *v.* Hodson, 50 Wis. 279; Liddell *v.* Wiswell, 59 Vt. 365; Byers *v.* Alcorn, 6 Bradw. (Ill. App.) 39; Paddleford *v.* State, 57 Miss. 118. To contrary effect, see Tobias *v.* Rogers, 13 N. Y. 59, distinguished in Johnson *v.* Harvey, 84 N. Y. 363; Miller *v.* Gillespie, 59 Mo. 220. See, also, on this subject, Hays *v.* Ford, 55 Ind. 52.

[2] Craven *v.* Freeman, 82 N. C. 361.

[3] Hill *v.* Morse, 61 Me. 541; Clapp *v.* Rice, 15 Gray, 557.

[4] Shelton *v.* Farmer, 9 Bush (Ky.), 314, followed and approved in Cochran *v.* Walker's Ex'rs, 82 Ky. 220. A surety to an undertaking upon appeal is not discharged because action against his co-surety, who is a non-resident, is barred by the statute of

§ 278. Rights of bail, who pays the debt, against the principal and sureties for the debt.— If one of two sureties in a bail bond in a civil action voluntarily pays the judgment against the principal before the bail are fixed, he cannot recover contribution from his co-surety in the bond. The latter had a right to relieve himself from liability by surrendering the body of the principal, and he could not be deprived of this right by a voluntary payment by the other surety.[1] An attachment of B.'s property was dissolved upon a bond being given by him with C. and D. as sureties. The creditor, A., recovered a judgment in the attachment suit against B., which was not paid, and then brought suit on the bond and recovered a judgment therein against B., C. and D., and arrested B. on the execution issued on this judgment. B. applied to take the oath for the relief of poor debtors, and entered into the statutory recognizance with E. as surety to deliver himself up for examination. . . . After a breach of the condition of the recognizance, C. and D. paid the amount of the judgment to which they were parties to A., and brought suit in his name for their benefit on the recognizance against E. *Held*, they could not recover. Payment of the judgment by them discharged it and released E. There was no privity between C. and D. and E. They were sureties for A. under different contracts. They were all principals as to E.; nor did the doctrine of subrogation apply.[2] Principal and surety executed a bond, but the fact of suretyship did not appear from it. Suit was commenced on the bond, and the principal was arrested and gave bail, who at that time had no knowledge of the suretyship. The surety was not served, and no judgment was rendered against him. The bail was obliged to pay the debt, and sued the surety for indemnity. *Held*, he was not entitled to recover.[3] A. and B. owed a note upon which suit was commenced, and A. was arrested and C. became his bail. Judgment was recovered against A. and B., which C., as the bail of A., was obliged to pay. *Held*, that C. was not entitled to recover indemnity from B., as there was no privity between

limitations, and he in consequence thereof lost his right to contribution. Staples *v.* Gokey, 34 Hun, 289.

[1] Skillin *v.* Merrill, 16 Mass. 40.

[2] Holmes *v.* Day, 108 Mass. 563.

[3] Smith *v.* Bing, 3 Ohio, 33.

them. It was the case of a person paying the debt of another without any request, express or implied.[1]

§ 279. When surety who pays judgment may have execution thereon against co-surety.— Judgment was recovered against A., B., C. and D., who were co-sureties. A., B. and C. paid the judgment, and had execution issued thereon and placed in the sheriff's hands, with directions to make one-fourth of it from the property of D. No property of D. was found, and A., B. and C. filed a creditor's bill against him to reach his effects. *Held*, the sureties who paid were entitled to subrogation to the creditor's rights in the judgment, so as to proceed against their co-surety D., and that a court of equity would prevent the extinction of a judgment, so as to afford a surety a remedy against a co-surety.[2] Although this is the approved doctrine, it has been held that a surety who pays a judgment thereby extinguishes it, and that he cannot afterwards have an execution thereon against his co-surety.[3]

§ 280. How liability to contribution affected by giving of time to one of several co-sureties.— If one of two co-sureties consents to the giving of time to the principal, and the other does not, and the one who so consents afterwards has the debt to pay, he cannot recover contribution from the surety who did not consent to the extension. The latter was discharged from his obligation to the creditor, and likewise from contribution, by the extension. There is no stronger obligation between co-sureties that they shall contribute than there is that they shall pay the creditor, and a giving of time releases them from the creditor, and will, under the foregoing circumstances, release them from each other.[4] A. was creditor, B. principal, and C., D. and E. sureties on a bond, which became due, and C. gave his obligation to A., payable by instalments, in payment of the debt. Subsequently, and after the payment of the first instalment, C. took from B. his bond for an extended time to secure the same debt. *Held* that, by the payment of

[1] Osborn *v.* Cunningham, 4 Dev. & Bat. Law (N. C.), 423.

[2] Cuyler *v.* Ensworth, 6 Paige's Ch. 32.

[3] McDaniel *v.* Lee, 37 Mo. 204; Hull *v.* Sherwood, 59 Mo. 172.

[4] Brown *v.* McDonald, 8 Yerg. (Tenn.) 158; Beckham *v.* Pride, 6 Rich. Eq. (S. C.) 78; Boughton *v.* Bank of Orleans, 2 Barb. Ch. 458.

3

the original debt as above, C. became subrogated to the place of A., the creditor, and that by giving time to B. the same results followed as if C. had been the original creditor. C. could not, therefore, recover contribution from D.[1] After judgment against a principal and two sureties the creditor gave time to one of the sureties. *Held*, he thereby discharged the other surety from liability to him for the portion of the debt which the surety to whom the time was given was liable to contribute.[2] Two sureties entered into an indemnity bond, and one of them, being pressed for payment, gave a warrant of attorney to confess judgment for the debt, due at a future time, and afterwards paid the debt. *Held*, that the giving of time to him by the creditor did not discharge his co-surety from liability to contribute.[3]

§ 281. **Contribution as affected by release of principal or of co-surety — Failure of consideration — Set-off, etc.**— If a surety releases the principal from liability to indemnify him, he thereby releases his co-surety from contribution.[4] If there are three sureties, and one of them pays the debt and releases one of the others upon payment of less than his share, he may recover from the third surety one-third of the debt which he has paid.[5] The right to contribution between co-sureties is not destroyed by the fact that they agree among themselves to pay and do pay the debt due a bank, in the notes of the bank.[6] Where a surety is released by the creditor, with the consent of his co-sureties, he thereupon ceases to be co-surety with them, and is not afterwards liable to them for contribution.[7] If one of several co-sureties agrees to pay the entire note on which they are liable, but the consideration for the agreement fails, and he afterwards pays the note, he will not be prevented by the agreement from recovering contribution from his co-sureties. The action for contribution being an equitable one, equitable principles should prevail.[8] It has

[1] Cameron *v.* Boulton, 9 Up. Can. (C. P.) 537.

[2] Ide *v.* Churchill, 14 Ohio St. 372.

[3] Dunn *v.* Slee, 1 Moore, 2.

[4] Draughan *v.* Bunting, 9 Ired. Law (N. C.), 10; Fletcher *v.* Jackson, 23 Vt. 581.

[5] Currier *v.* Baker, 51 N. H. 613.

[6] Derossett *v.* Bradley, 63 N. C. 17.

[7] Moore *v.* Isley, 2 Dev. & Batt. Eq. (N. C.) 372. See Lusby *v.* Carr, Ex'r, 60 Md. 192, which was an abandonment by agreement of the right to contribution that otherwise existed.

[8] Prindle *v.* Page, 21 Vt. 94.

been held that in an action by a surety against his co-surety for contribution, the latter cannot defend by setting up by way of counter-claim, recoupment or set-off a cause of action existing in favor of the principal against the plaintiff.[1] A. being principal, and B., C. and D. sureties, they all became insolvent except D., who paid the debt. Before such payment, but after C. and D. became sureties, D. executed his bond to C. for a sum less than half the amount of the debt for which they were liable as A.'s sureties, and C. assigned this bond to a trustee for the benefit of his creditors. *Held*, the trustee stood in no better position than C., and D. might by bill in equity set off C.'s liability to him as co-surety against his liability on the bond.[2] A. and B. were the payees and accommodation indorsers of a note made for the accommodation of C., and signed by him. Having been obliged to pay the note, A. sued C. for indemnity, after his remedy against C. on the note was barred by the statute of limitations, but within apt time after he paid the money. *Held*, he was not entitled to recover. The court said that his only remedy against C. was on the note, and that was barred by the statute. Until the time of Lord Mansfield, the surety had no remedy at law against his principal on an implied promise. His remedy for reimbursement was in equity, unless he took a bond to secure indemnity. Implied promises will not be raised where there is no necessity for it. "If the party choose to take a security, there is no occasion for the law to raise a promise. Promises in law only exist where there is no express stipulation between the parties."[3]

§ 282. How far judgment against one surety evidence against co-surety in suit for contribution — Failure of consideration.— Where a judgment was recovered against a principal and one surety, which was paid by the latter, it was held in a suit by such surety against a co-surety, for contribution, that the co-surety could not show as a defense that the con-

[1] O'Blenis *v.* Karing, 57 N. Y. 649. And see Davis *v.* Toulmin, 77 N. Y. 280.

[2] Wayland *v.* Tucker, 4 Gratt. (Va.) 267.

[3] Kennedy *v.* Carpenter, 2 Wharton (Pa.), 344. Holding that one surety on a sheriff's bond cannot recover at law on the bond against his co-sureties, see Mitchell *v.* Turner, 37 Ala. 660.

sideration of the note on which they were both sureties had failed. The court said: "No question of consideration is involved in the contest between co-sureties, for they enter into the undertaking without reference, as between themselves, to the consideration paid their principal. If his contract was entirely without consideration, the relative rights of these parties would be precisely the same, and on payment by one, the right to contribution is called into existence. Each has impliedly agreed with the other to protect him to the extent of the joint undertaking against the consequences arising out of the failure of the principal."[1] It has been held that a joint judgment against co-sureties is, in a suit between them for contribution, conclusive evidence that a cause of action existed against them.[2] Where a judgment is recovered against part of the sureties, in a bond which is satisfied by them, it has been held in a suit by them against their co-sureties, for contribution, that such judgment is competent evidence to show the amount of the payment made by the plaintiffs, and the circumstances under which it was made, but not for the purpose of proving the liability.[3]

§ 283. **When surety can recover contribution for costs paid by him.**—Whether a surety can recover from his co-surety contribution for the costs of a suit against him, for the collection of the debt, depends upon the circumstances of each case. Where a joint judgment is recovered against the principal and two sureties, or against two sureties alone, and one of them pays it, he can recover one-half of the costs of the suit from his co-surety. In holding this principle it has been said: "The failure to pay which occasioned the costs was imputable to the defendant as much as to the plaintiff. The plaintiff paid the execution, including the costs. . . . The costs cannot be distinguished from the debt. Every equitable principle which entitles the plaintiff to contribution for the one applies equally to the other."[4] So a surety may recover contribution from his co-surety for the costs and expenses of

[1] Cave *v.* Burns, 6 Ala. 780, per Goldthwaite, J.

[2] Waller *v.* Campbell, 25 Ala. 544.

[3] Fletcher *v.* Jackson, 23 Vt. 581.

[4] Davis *v.* Emerson, 17 Me. 64, per Weston, C. J. See, also, Briggs *v.* Boyd, 37 Vt. 534; Gross *v.* Davis' Adm'r, 87 Tenn. (3 Pickle), 226; Van Winkle *v.* Johnson, 11 Oreg. 469.

defending a suit against him for the debt, if the defense was made under such circumstances as to be regarded prudent.[1] Where the only surviving surety on a joint bond (he alone being subject to an action at law) is sued, and defends the action *bona fide*, and thereby reduces the amount of the creditor's demand, the representatives of a deceased co-surety are liable to contribute towards payment of the costs and other expenses incurred in defending the action at law.[2] Where two co-sureties executed a warrant of attorney on which judgment was entered up, it was held that the surety who paid the judgment and costs could recover one-half the costs from his co-surety.[3] It has, however, been held that a surety cannot recover from his co-surety any part of the costs of defending himself in a suit against him by the creditor, unless the co-surety authorized him to defend the action.[4] Attorney's fees incurred by a surety in making a prudent defense are held recoverable in an action for contribution.[5] "There can be no doubt but that a surety, or one standing in such a position, will be justified in employing counsel and incurring costs and expenses, to which his co-sureties must afterwards contribute, in defending against illegal demands. Nor will the right of the surety to recover in such cases be made dependent upon his success, as that would compel him to act at his peril. It is sufficient if he acted as a prudent man would, in the light of facts and circumstances showing a probability of success in whole or in part sufficient to justify the expense likely to be incurred."[6]

§ 284. Estate of deceased co-surety liable for contribution.— If two co-sureties become bound in a joint, or joint and several obligation, and one of them dies, and the other, before or after such death, pays the debt, he can recover contribution from the estate of such deceased co-surety, either at law or in

[1] Fletcher *v.* Jackson, 23 Vt. 581. See, also, Breckenridge *v.* Taylor, 5 Dana (Ky.), 110; Bright *v.* Lennon, 83 N. C. 183; Wagenseller *v.* Prettyman, 7 Bradw. (Ill. App.) 192.

[2] McKenna *v.* George, 2 Rich. Eq. (S. C.) 15.

[3] Kemp *v.* Finden, 12 Mees. & Wels. 421.

[4] John *v.* Jones, 16 Ala. 454; Knight *v.* Hughes, Moody & Mal. 247.

[5] Gross *v.* Davis' Adm'r, 87 Tenn. (3 Pickle), 226. But see, however, Acers *v.* Curtis, 68 Tex. 423.

[6] Marston, C. J., in Backus *v.* Coyne, 45 Mich. 584, 586.

equity, to the same extent as if such co-surety was alive. As between co-sureties there is an implied agreement for contribution at the time they sign, and this implied agreement is not joint, but several. It is like any other promise to pay money for which the personal representative of the deceased promisor is liable; and it makes no difference whether the default was committed before or after the death of the promisor.[1] The death of one of the co-sureties under a joint and several continuing guaranty does not of itself determine the future liability of the surviving co-surety.[2]

§ 285. **Surety who pays by his note may recover contribution from co-surety.**— If two co-sureties are bound for a debt, and one of them pays it by giving his own note for it, which is accepted by the creditor as payment, the surety thus paying may at once, and before paying the note so given as payment, sue his co-surety for contribution, the same as if he had paid the debt in money. In holding this, it has been said: "Where one person is obligated to pay money for the use of another, a payment made in any mode, either property or negotiable paper or securities, if such payment is received as full satisfaction of the demand, it is equivalent to, and will be treated as, a payment in cash. . . . Where the payment is received as a complete satisfaction, and the debt or obligation is extinguished, it is a matter of no moment to the person to whose use the payment is made whether it is made in money, property or obligations. The benefit to him is the same, and the obligation to refund should be the same."[3]

1 Bradley *v.* Burwell, 3 Denio. 61, followed in Cornes *v.* Wilkin, 14 Hun, 428; Supplee *v.* Sayre, 51 Hun, 30; Ramskill *v.* Edwards, Law Rep. (31 Ch. Div.) 100; Aikin *v.* Peay, 5 Strob. Law (S. C.), 15; Conover *v.* Hill, 76 Ill. 342; Bachelder *v.* Fiske, 17 Mass. 464; Stothoff *v.* Dunham's Ex'rs, 4 Har. (N. J.) 181; McKenna *v.* George, 2 Rich. Eq. (S. C.) 15; Stephens *v.* Meek, 6 B. J. Lea (Tenn.), 226; *In re* Blumen & Co., 13 Fed. Rep. 623. *Contra*, Waters *v.* Riley, 2 Harris & Gill (Md.), 305. See this case disapproved in Johnson *v.* Harvey, 84 N. Y. 363. As to when the estate of a deceased surety, which has been distributed to his heirs, is liable to contribute to a co-surety who has paid the debt, see Williams *v.* Ewing, 31 Ark. 229; Stevens *v.* Tucker, 73 Ind. 73. An action for contribution against the estate of a deceased co-surety is held to be triable by jury. Sanders *v.* Weelburg, 107 Ind. 266.

2 Beckett *v.* Addyman, Law Rep. (9 Q. B. Div.) 783.

3 Ralston *v.* Wood, 15 Ill. 159, per Caton, J.; Pinkston *v.* Taliaferro, 9

§ 286. **What contribution surety who pays in land entitled to recover.**—Where a surety paid the debt of the principal in lands, it was held, in a suit for contribution by him against a co-surety, that the price at which the lands were taken as payment by the creditor would ordinarily be the amount on which the damages should be founded; but if the lands were taken at a very high price, as a compromise of a doubtful claim, the actual value of the lands might, perhaps, be the basis of the damages, and in such case the actual value of the lands should be allowed, no matter what they cost the surety.[1] Where a principal was insolvent, and one of two co-sureties paid the debt in real estate, which was taken by the creditor at about twice its value, on account of the failing condition of the parties, it was held that the surety thus paying was entitled to recover from his co-surety, as contribution, one-half of what the real estate was worth, and no more.[2]

§ 287. **When surety who has paid less than his share of the debt cannot recover contribution.**— A surety who has paid a portion of the debt, leaving the remainder unpaid, cannot usually recover contribution from his co-surety, unless the amount so paid by him is more than his share of the common debt. The co-surety may, in such case, pay the remainder to the creditor. In holding this, it has been said that: "The right to contribution is founded, not on contract, but on the principle that equality of burden, as to a common right, is equity. . . . Where joint promisors or co-sureties have received equal benefits, or been relieved from common burthens, neither shall recover over against another, unless for the excess paid by him beyond his due proportion or equal share."[3] If, however, a surety discharges the entire debt by

Ala. 547; Anthony *v.* Percifull, 8 Ark. (3 Eng.) 494; Hutchins *v.* McCauley, 2 Dev. & Bat. Eq. (N. C.) 399; White *v.* Carlton, 52 Ind. 371; Robertson *v.* Maxcey, 6 Dana (Ky.), 101; Bell *v.* Boyd, 76 Tex. 133. *Contra*, Brisendine *v.* Martin, 1 Ired. Law (N. C.), 286; Nowland *v.* Martin, 1 Ired. Law (N. C.), 307.

[1] Jones *v.* Bradford, 25 Ind. 305.

[2] Hickman *v.* McCurdy, 7 J. J. Mar. (Ky.) 555.

[3] Fletcher *v.* Grover, 11 N. H. 368, per Woods, J. For a case identical in principle and strictly analogous to Fletcher *v.* Grover, see Apperson *v.* Wilbourn, 58 Miss. 439. See, also, Smith *v.* State, 46 Md. 617; *Ex parte* Snowdon, Law Rep. (17 Ch. Div.) 44; Gross *v.* Davis, 87 Tenn. (3 Pick.) 226; Davies *v.* Humphreys, 6 Mees. & Wels. 153; Lytle's Ex'rs *v.* Pope's Adm'r, 11 B. Mon. (Ky.) 297; Taylor *v.* Means, 73 Ala. 468. Of course if

payment of less than his share, he may recover contribution from his co-surety.[1] Where one of two co-sureties of an insolvent administrator purchased, at a discount, legacies for which the sureties were bound, it was held he could only charge his co-surety for one-half of what he paid for the legacies and one-half the expense of purchasing them.[2]

§ 288. **In what proportions co-sureties are liable to contribute.**— If one of several co-sureties who are equally bound for the debt pays it, he has a right in equity to recover, as contribution from his solvent co-sureties, a *pro rata* amount of the sum paid by him, based upon the number of solvent co-sureties, and excluding the insolvent ones.[3] The fact that one of several co-sureties has left the state has in this regard been considered equivalent to his insolvency.[4] As a general rule the surety who has paid the debt can at law only recover from his solvent co-sureties an aliquot part of the debt, based on the whole number of co-sureties, solvent and insolvent.[5] But in a state where there were no courts of equity, it was held that the surety who paid the debt might at law recover contribution based on the number of solvent co-sureties, and excluding the insolvent ones.[6] On a question of contribution,

the surety pays more than his share of the common debt, he is entitled to contribution from his co-sureties such as will meet the equity of the case. Bryan *v.* McDowell, 15 B. J. Lea (Tenn.), 581.

[1] Stallworth *v.* Preslar, 34 Ala. 505.

[2] Tarr *v.* Ravenscroft, 12 Gratt. (Va.) 642.

[3] Powell *v.* Matthis, 4 Ired. Law (N. C.), 83; Young *v.* Lyons, 8 Gill (Md.), 162; Samuel *v.* Zachery, 4 Ired. Law (N. C.), 377; Klein *v.* Mather, 2 Gilman (Ill.), 317; Burroughs *v.* Lott, 19 Cal. 125; Young *v.* Clark, 2 Ala. 264; Breckinridge *v.* Taylor, 5 Dana (Ky.), 110; Magruder *v.* Admire, 4 Mo. App. 133. In Moore *v.* Bruner, 31 Ill. App. 400, it is held to be the rule at law that where one of several sureties pays a judgment in full he may recover from each of his co-sureties, without regard to their solvency, a *pro rata* share of the sum so paid, with interest from date of payment. That a surety is entitled to judgment of contribution against all his co-sureties only *pro rata*, without regard to the insolvency of any one of them, see Riley *v.* Rhea, 5 B. J. Lea (Tenn.), 115; Gross *v.* Davis, 87 Tenn. (3 Pickle), 226. In *Re* MacDonaghs, Irish (10 Eq.), 269, it is held co-sureties contribute in proportion to the amounts for which they were originally respectively bound.

[4] McKenna *v.* George, 2 Rich. Eq. (S. C.) 15; Liddell *v.* Wiswell, 59 Vt. 365.

[5] Stothoff *v.* Dunham's Ex'rs, 4 Harr. (N. J.) 181; Morrison *v.* Poyntz, 7 Dana (Ky.), 307; Cowell *v.* Edwards, 2 Bos. & Pul. 268; Acers *v.* Curtis, 68 Tex. 423.

[6] Henderson *v.* Duffee, 5 N. H. 38.

partners who sign in the partnership name are to be regarded as but one surety.[1] Whatever the number of the principals may be, it cuts no figure with reference to the amount of contribution which will be enforced between co sureties.[2] If three co-sureties agree among themselves when they sign, that if the principal fails to pay they will each pay one-third, the surety who pays the whole debt can only recover from a solvent co-surety one-third of the amount so paid, even though the other co-surety is insolvent.[3] Where three persons give a note for their joint debt, each is to be considered with respect to the other as a surety with regard to two-thirds, and as a principal with regard to one-third of the debt; and if one be insolvent and another pays the whole debt, the third shall contribute one-half to the one who pays.[4] Where co-sureties are bound for the same thing, but in different amounts, they are liable to contribute in the proportion of the amounts of the obligations signed by them respectively. Thus, A. became bound for a deputy-sheriff in a bond of $2,000. B. became liable for the same deputy on a similar bond for $18,000. A. was obliged to pay the $2,000. *Held*, he was entitled to recover from B. eight-ninths of the amount so paid by him.[5] In another case A. was a guardian, and B. became his surety in a bond of $10,000. C. subsequently became A.'s surety in a bond of $5,000; both sureties being liable for the same thing but in these amounts. *Held*, that B. might recover from C. one-third of the amount which he had paid for the default of the common principal.[6] But where several stockholders of a corporation, each owning different amounts of stock, signed a note as surety for the corporation, and one of them paid such note, it was held he was entitled to recover contribution from his co-sureties, based on their number, and not on the amount of stock held by them respectively.[7]

§ 289. Surety may recover contribution either at law or in equity.— One of several co-sureties who has paid the debt may recover contribution from the others in a suit at law for

[1] Chaffee *v.* Jones, 19 Pick. 260.

[2] Kemp *v.* Frinden, 12 Mees. & Wels. 421.

[3] Swain *v.* Wall, 1 Rep. Ch. 149.

[4] Henderson *v.* Duffee, 5 N. H. 38.

[5] Armitage *v.* Pulver, 37 N. Y. 494.

[6] Bell *v.* Jasper, 2 Ired. Eq. (N. C.) 597. To same effect, see Jones *v.* Blanton, 6 Ired. Eq. (N. C.) 115.

[7] Coburn *v.* Wheelock, 34 N. Y. 440.

money paid for their use, or he may bring his suit for contribution in chancery. Originally the only remedy was in chancery, but courts of law afterwards assumed jurisdiction. The fact, however, that courts of law have assumed jurisdiction in this matter, or that it has been conferred upon them by statute, does not oust equity of its original jurisdiction. With reference to this it has been said: "The right to sue in chancery for contribution was an established head of chancery jurisdiction in the time of Queen Elizabeth on the plain principles of natural justice. . . . Ultimately courts of law entertained actions between sureties, but the court of chancery did not on that account renounce its jurisdiction. This tribunal still exercises a concurrent jurisdiction in all cases for contribution between sureties."[1]

§ 290. **Whether surety must show insolvency of the principal in order to recover contribution.**— In an action at law by a surety against his co-surety for contribution, the weight of authority seems to be that the insolvency of the principal need not be averred or proved.[2] It has, however, been repeatedly held that, in a suit in equity by one surety against another for contribution, no recovery can be had unless the principal is shown to be insolvent, on the ground that the right to contribution does not rest on contract, but on natural justice, and this element is wanting when the principal is solvent.[3] As the right to contribution is grounded upon the same reasons, both at law and in equity, it seems that the rule should be the same in both jurisdictions.

[1] Couch *v.* Terry, 12 Ala. 225, per Collier, C. J.; Kemp *v.* Finden, 12 Mees. & Wels. 421; Mansfield *v.* Edwards, 136 Mass. 15; Bachelder *v.* Fiske, 17 Mass. 464; Sloo *v.* Pool, 15 Ill. 47; Foster *v.* Johnson, 5 Vt. 60; Crowder *v.* Denny, 3 Head (Tenn.), 359. *Contra*, Carrington *v.* Carson, Conf. Rep. (N. C.) 216. See, on this subject, Chollan *v.* Temple, 39 Ark. 238; Broughton *v.* Wimberly, 65 Ala. 549.

[2] Judah *v.* Mieure, 5 Blackf. (Ind.) 171; Caldwell *v.* Roberts, 1 Dana (Ky.), 355; Buckner's Adm'r *v.* Stewart, 34 Ala. 529; Rankin *v.* Collins, 50 Ind. 158; Roberts *v.* Adams, 6 Port. (Ala.) 361. *Contra*, Morrison *v.* Poyntz, 7 Dana (Ky.), 307. To the effect that the surety seeking contribution may show the principal's general reputation for insolvency, such as unsatisfied executions against him, see Leak *v.* Covington, 99 N. C. 559.

[3] Daniel *v.* Ballard, 3 Dana (Ky.), 296; Rainey *v.* Yarborough, 2 Ired. Eq. (N. C.) 249; Bolling *v.* Donegby, 1 Duvall (Ky.), 220; Allen *v.* Wood, 3 Ired. Eq. (N. C.) 386; Lawson *v.*

§ 291. When suit for contribution should be joint and when several.— Where two or more co-sureties jointly pay the debt, they may join in a suit either at law or in equity against a co-surety for contribution,[1] but when each pays separately they cannot usually join in such a suit.[2] If one of several co-sureties pays the debt, he cannot usually maintain a joint action for contribution against his co-sureties.[3] A surety who has paid the debt cannot sue his principal and a co-surety jointly for reimbursement.[4] If two co-sureties pay the debt by their joint note, they may join in a suit for contribution against another co-surety, even though the latter became surety for them on the note with which they paid the debt.[5] Where three of four co-sureties paid part of the debt in money, each paying an equal amount, and for the remainder gave their note, which was accepted as payment, it was held that each might maintain a separate suit for contribution against the fourth surety.[6] Four parties were liable as co-sureties, and two of them each gave one-third the amount of the debt to a third surety, who put the remaining third necessary to pay the debt with the money thus given him, and therewith paid the debt. *Held*, the three sureties thus paying might join in a suit against the fourth for contribution. This was put upon the ground that each of the three sureties had paid the one-fourth which he ought to pay, and then each had contributed an equal sum to pay the amount for which the other surety was liable, and had paid it in one payment. The court said: "We are of opinion that when three persons, each of whom is responsible for an entire sum due from another, join in making the payment of that sum by a contribution agreed

Wright, 1 Cox, 275; McCormack's Adm'r *v.* Obannon's Ex'r, 3 Munf. (Va.) 484. To substantially similar effect, see Glasscock *v.* Hamilton, 62 Tex. 143; Jackson *v.* Murray, 77 Tex. 644.

[1] Dussol *v.* Brugniere, 50 Cal. 456; Fletcher *v.* Jackson, 23 Vt. 581.

[2] Lombard *v.* Cobb, 14 Me. 222; Prescott *v.* Newell, 39 Vt. 82.

[3] Powell *v.* Matthis, 4 Ired. Law (N. C.), 83.

[4] Burnham *v.* Choat, 5 Up. Can. K. B. (O. S.) 736.

[5] Prescott *v.* Newell, 39 Vt. 82.

[6] Atkinson *v.* Stewart, 2 B. Mon. (Ky.) 348. Upon the strength of this decision it was subsequently decided by the court that, as between sureties, a discharge of their obligation by the creditor's acceptance of a note of one of them was equivalent to a payment in money under the statute. Stubbins *v.* Mitchell, 82 Ky. 535.

on among themselves for that purpose, they may join in one action to recover it from the person for whose benefit the payment has been made."[1] Ten parties became sureties in a bond, and the principal and four of the sureties became insolvent. Five of the solvent sureties paid the debt, each paying an equal amount, and brought a joint bill in equity for contribution against the remaining solvent surety. *Held*, the bill could be maintained, although it was admitted that if the action had been at law several suits would have been necessary.[2] A., B. and C. being co-sureties, judgment was recovered against them, and execution was levied on separate property belonging to each. A. and B. paid the judgment and filed a joint bill against C. and others, to be subrogated to the lien of the levy on the land of C., and to set aside certain conveyances thereof by C., which were alleged to be fraudulent. *Held*, the bill might be maintained. The court said that the object sought by the suit was the benefit of the levy. The levy is an entire thing in the sense of giving a lien capable of being enforced by sale for complainant's benefit; and their rights and interests, however separate in regard to their payments to the creditor, and in regard to their claim against the pocket of their co-surety, come together and join in the pursuit and subjection of the lien.[3]

§ 292. Who not necessary parties to a bill for contribution, etc.— To a suit in equity by a surety who has paid the debt against a co-surety for contribution, neither an insolvent principal nor insolvent co-sureties or the personal representatives of insolvent deceased co-sureties are necessary parties.[4] It has also been held that a solvent co-surety who lives out of the state is not a necessary party to a suit in equity for contribution between the other sureties.[5] Where one of two partners is insolvent, and has absconded, and the other is dead,

[1] Clapp *v.* Rice, 15 Gray (Mass.), 557, per Hoar, J.

[2] Young *v.* Lyons, 8 Gill (Md.), 162.

[3] Smith *v.* Rumsey, 33 Mich. 183, per Graves, J.

[4] Byers *v.* McClanahan, 6 Gill & Johns. (Md.) 250; Johnson's Adm'rs *v.* Vaughn, 65 Ill. 425; Young *v.* Lyons, 8 Gill (Md.), 162; Bruce *v.* Bickerton, 18 W. Va. 342. Neither is the person to whom payment was made a necessary party. Rosenthal *v.* Sutton, 31 Ohio St. 406. But as to when the principal is a necessary party in a suit for contribution, see Chrisman *v.* Jones, 34 Ark. 73.

[5] Jones *v.* Blanton, 6 Ired. Eq. (N. C.) 115.

leaving a solvent estate, a surety for the firm, who has paid the debt, may proceed in equity against the estate of the deceased partner, without prosecuting a suit against the survivor.[1]

§ 293. Surety may without compulsion pay debt when due, and immediately sue co-surety for contribution without demand or notice.— As soon as the debt becomes due, any one of several co-sureties may, without suit or compulsion on him of any kind, at once pay the debt and recover contribution from his co-sureties. All the co-sureties are equally liable for the whole debt, and a payment of the debt by one of them after it is due and without compulsion is in no sense a voluntary payment.[2] And in such case the surety who pays the debt may immediately and without any demand on his co-surety, or notice to him, sue him for contribution. In holding this it has been said that, upon payment by the surety, "the law immediately raised an obligation from the defendant to the plaintiff to pay an aliquot part of this sum, according to the number of the sureties. It was a present debt. It was a payment for the use of the defendant upon his request, implied by law; no special demand and notice were therefore necessary." [3]

§ 294. When liability to contribution attaches.— The liability of one surety to another for contribution, and of the principal to a surety for indemnity, attaches or springs up at the time the obligation which they have signed is delivered, and whenever payment may be made by the surety, he is considered as a creditor of his principal or co-surety from the time the obligation was made and delivered. This principle is ap-

[1] Horsey *v.* Heath, 5 Ohio, 353.

[2] Judah *v.* Mieure, 5 Blackf. (Ind.) 171; Nixon *v.* Beard, 111 Ind. 137; Bradley *v.* Burwell, 3 Denio, 61, followed in Supple *v.* Sayre, 51 Hun, 30; Stallworth *v.* Preslar, 34 Ala. 505; Pitt *v.* Purssord, 8 Mees. & Wels. 538; Lucas *v.* Guy, 2 Bailey, Law (S. C.), 403; Linn *v.* McClelland, 4 Dev. & Batt. Law (N. C.), 458; Machardo *v.* Fernandez, 74 Cal. 362. But see Curtis *v.* Parks, 55 Cal. 106. See compulsory payment defined by Royce, C. J., in Aldrich *v.* Aldrich, 56 Vt. 324. The fact that a surety paid under an execution which could have been quashed on motion is held not to affect his right to contribution. Jenkins *v.* Lockard's Adm'r, 66 Ala. 377.

[3] Chaffee *v.* Jones, 19 Pick. 260, per Shaw, C. J.; Cage *v.* Foster, 5 Yerg. (Tenn.) 261; Wood *v.* Perry, 9 Iowa, 479; Parham *v.* Green, 64 N. C. 436; Mason *v.* Pierron, 69 Wis. 585. *Contra,* Carpenter *v.* Kelly, 9 Ohio, 106.

plicable to a case where, after the obligation is delivered, and before it is paid, the principal or co-surety makes a conveyance of his property which the surety who pays seeks to set aside as fraudulent.[1]

§ 295. When claim for contribution barred by the statute of limitations.— The statute of limitations begins to run between co-sureties at the time the debt is paid, irrespective of the time when the obligation was entered into or became due.[2] The surety who has paid more than his share of the debt may, for every separate payment he makes, sue his co-security for contribution, and the statute of limitations runs against each payment from the time it is made.[3] Where suit is commenced against one of two co-sureties before the debt is barred by the statute of limitations, and judgment is recovered against him, and the debt paid by him after the time when the statute would have been a bar if no suit had been previously brought, and after the debt is barred by the statute against the co-surety, the statute begins to run between the sureties from the time of payment, and the surety who pays may recover contribution from his co-surety at any time after such payment and within the statutory limitation.[4] Where a surety on

[1] Sargent *v.* Salmond, 27 Me. 539; Wayland *v.* Tucker, 4 Gratt. (Va.) 267. The liability to contribution as between co-sureties arises when the common obligation is assumed. Jenkins *v.* Lockard's Adm'r, 66 Ala. 377. Surety's mere passiveness in asserting his rights does not prejudice his right to contribution, where such delay has worked no injustice to his co-sureties. McGehee *v.* Owen, 61 Ala. 440.

[2] Wood *v.* Leland, 1 Met. (Mass.) 387; Singleton *v.* Townsend, 45 Mo. 379; Broughton *v.* Robinson, 11 Ala. 922; Knotts *v.* Butler, 10 Rich. Eq. (S. C.) 143; Camp *v.* Bostwick, 20 Ohio St. 337; Preslar *v.* Stallworth, 37 Ala. 402; Sherrod *v.* Woodard, 4 Dev. Law (N. C.), 360; Stallworth *v.* Preslar, 34 Ala. 505; May *v.* Vann, 15 Fla. 553; Becket *v.* Tarrant, 61 Tex. 402; Martin *v.* Frantz, 127 Pa. St. 389; Leak *v.* Covington, 99 N. C. 559. In Mississippi, where a surety pays a judgment, the statute runs from the date of the judgment and not from the time of its payment. Partee *v.* Mathews, 53 Miss. 140. In Magruder *v.* Admire, 4 Mo. App. 133, it is held that surety's right of action against co-surety does not accrue until he has paid in excess of his proportionate share of liability.

[3] Davies *v.* Humphreys, 6 Mees. & Wels. 153.

[4] Crosby *v.* Wyatt, 10 N. H. 318; Crosby *v.* Wyatt, 23 Me. 156. For case holding surety discharged from contribution by long delay under peculiar circumstances, see Williamson's Adm'r *v.* Rees' Adm'r, 15 Ohio, 572.

a joint note, whose liability thereon is barred by the statute, waives his privilege and pays the note, it is held he may sue the co-surety who has not been discharged.[1] A surety suing for contribution must do so within the statutory period or he will be barred.[2]

§ 296. Rights of sureties as against each other governed by what law — Residence of co-surety in suit for contribution.— The legal right of sureties as against each other is not governed by the *lex loci contractus;* neither is there any implied obligation that they shall reside or remain in any particular locality. Thus where a surety on a note made in Vermont, after the bar of the statute of limitations there, voluntarily and without the knowledge of his co-surety, but with no fraudulent intent, removed to New Hampshire, and was there sued by the payee and judgment rendered against him, which he paid, *held*, in a suit for contribution, that the payment was compulsory and not voluntary, and that his co-surety was liable.[3] A surety on a joint and several administrator's bond may sue his co-sureties thereon for contribution in any county in which either of them resided.[4]

§ 297. Pleading — Former adjudication — Co-surety as witness — Evidence.— A bill by a surety against a co-surety to compel contribution and set aside certain conveyances and subject them to liability is not a creditor's bill, and a court of equity may, upon suitable averments, grant the proper relief, without requiring the surety to first exhaust his remedy at law by judgment and execution.[5] In a suit for contribution against a co-surety, where the principal was also made a defendant, it was sought to obtain not only a judgment against the co-surety for the amount which he ought to contribute, but also to subject to the payment of such judgment, or to the lien of the original judgment, land which the co-surety had conveyed to the principal and which conveyance was alleged to be fraudulent. *Held*, that the bill to state a cause of action against the principal must show that the surety was insolvent or some necessity existed for resorting to such land in the event of judgment

[1] McClatchie *v.* Durham, 44 Mich. 435.

[2] Preston *v.* Gould, 64 Iowa, 44.

[3] Aldrich *v.* Aldrich, 56 Vt. 324.

[4] Rush *v.* Bishop, 60 Tex. 177.

[5] Moore *v.* Baker (Cir. Ct. E. D. Wis.), 34 Fed. Rep. 1.

against the co-surety, but that it was not necessary as against the principal that an execution against the co-surety should have been returned unsatisfied.[1] In a suit against sureties on a promissory note, an answer by one that he is liable only as surety, and judgment accordingly, and that the property of the others be first exhausted, is not an adjudication which binds the other surety so as to bar a suit by him against his co-surety for contribution.[2] In a suit by the administrator of a surety against his principal and co-surety for reimbursement, the co-surety is an incompetent witness, and a letter from him and certain extracts from private books are inadmissible.[3]

[1] Mason *v.* Pierron, 63 Wis. 239.
[2] Leaman *v.* Sample, 91 Ind. 236.
[3] Harper *v.* McVeigh, 82 Va. 751.